# The American
# Immigration Collection

# Historical Aspects
# of the
# Immigration Problem

### EDITH ABBOTT

*Arno* Press and *The New York Times*

NEW YORK 1969

# THE UNIVERSITY OF CHICAGO
## SOCIAL SERVICE SERIES

*Edited by*
THE FACULTY OF THE GRADUATE SCHOOL OF
SOCIAL SERVICE ADMINISTRATION

# HISTORICAL ASPECTS OF THE IMMIGRATION PROBLEM

## SELECT DOCUMENTS

THE UNIVERSITY OF CHICAGO PRESS
CHICAGO, ILLINOIS

—

THE BAKER & TAYLOR COMPANY
NEW YORK

THE MACMILLAN COMPANY OF CANADA, LIMITED
TORONTO

THE CAMBRIDGE UNIVERSITY PRESS
LONDON

THE MARUZEN-KABUSHIKI-KAISHA
TOKYO, OSAKA, KYOTO, FUKUOKA, SENDAI

THE COMMERCIAL PRESS, LIMITED
SHANGHAI

# HISTORICAL ASPECTS
## *of the*
# IMMIGRATION PROBLEM

## SELECT DOCUMENTS

*By*

### EDITH ABBOTT

*Dean of the Graduate School of Social Service Administration
and Professor of Social Economy in the
University of Chicago*

THE UNIVERSITY OF CHICAGO PRESS
CHICAGO ⸱ ILLINOIS

Composed and Printed By
The University of Chicago Press
Chicago, Illinois. U.S.A.

# THE UNIVERSITY OF CHICAGO SOCIAL SERVICE SERIES

## PREFATORY NOTE

The present volume is one of a series of source books in the social service field. The series has been planned primarily to provide adequate scientific material heretofore not available for the use of students in the Graduate School of Social Service Administration of the University of Chicago and other institutions of the same kind. In a report on the work of such schools (James H. Tufts, *Education and Training for Social Work*, 1923), attention was called to the "general complaint of the lack of sufficient source material in form which is most desirable for critical teaching and which can be placed in the hands of all students." The report went farther and expressed confidence that ultimately the schools themselves would meet this need, and added: "Publication of such material is an illustration of what has been previously referred to as one of the two great functions of the professional school, namely, raising the standard of the profession through research and publication."

This volume, with those that have preceded it and the others that are nearing completion and are to follow it, represent an attempt on the part of the members of the Faculty of one of these schools to help to meet this need. It is believed, however, that the different volumes in the series will be useful, not only to those interested in social service, but to those whose interests lie in other departments of the wide field of the social sciences.

# PREFACE

The documents in this volume have been selected to supplement an earlier source book in immigration published two years ago for the use of university and college students. The first source book was described in the preface as "a collection of published documents and hitherto unpublished case records that will throw light on some of the historical, legal, and social aspects of the subject." In the earlier volume some historical documents were included in the section dealing with the Passenger Acts and in the section devoted to the admission, exclusion, and expulsion of aliens. The original plan for Part III of that volume included a third series of documents, illustrating the history of our domestic immigration problems. This plan was altered for two reasons: first, because the first volume had reached the limit of what was practicable in the matter of length; second, the historical sources were so rich and varied, as well as so inaccessible to most students, that the preparation of a second volume entirely devoted to these historical documents seemed an undertaking that would be of great value not only to university students but to the wider public interested in the immigration problem.

A brief explanation of the scope of the present volume is needed. The collection covers only the period of the so-called "old immigration"; and while this period does not come to a sudden end, the year 1882, when the control of immigration was assumed by the federal government, is a date that may conveniently be regarded as the end of the old period and the beginning of the new. In general, therefore, the documents in this volume relate to the history of immigration before the period of federal control. Like the earlier volume, the present collection of documents is confined to European immigration because it is believed that immigration from Europe is a problem fundamentally different from Oriental immigration.

A further point has to do with the arrangement of the documents. Two methods were considered. The first was an arrangement by chronological periods, classifying the documents within each period according to the five general subjects in this volume; another and simpler plan was to classify all the documents under certain important subject heads with a chronological listing under each head, and this simpler plan was the one adopted. There are, however, some documents dealing with more than one subject; and, except in a few cases of exceptional length, the document has not been mutilated in order to distribute the matter under different subject heads. An effort has been made to present documents of sufficient length to state adequately the writer's point of view; and for the controversial periods an effort has been made to select documents reflecting the different points of view.

It is probably unnecessary to explain that the introductory notes to the different sections are brief, because it is the purpose of the volume to let the documents speak for themselves and to give the student an opportunity to interpret the material for himself.

Finally, if some explanation or justification of this volume is needed, it lies in the fact that immigration has been, throughout our history, one of the great outstanding facts of our national life. During the period of approximately one hundred years from the close of the Napoleonic wars to the opening of the Great War, more than thirty-five million immigrants came to the United States. It is to this unparalled migration of the masses from the Old World that we owe in large measure our position as the greatest and richest country in the world. The history of this great movement has been singularly neglected. The immigration problems of today had their counterparts in the problems of yesterday, and students of present-day problems cannot afford to overlook the experience of the past with similar problems. Social experimentation is costly. As the greatest of the immigrant-receiving countries our experience deserves more careful study than it usually receives.

Moreover, during the years since 1914 we have received relatively few immigrants, and there has been more opportunity for thoughtful consideration of questions of immigration policy. We had, for all practical purposes, a cessation of immigration at several earlier periods of our history—during the Revolutionary War, again during the Napoleonic Wars and the War of 1812, again during our Civil War, and finally during the Great War. During the earlier periods the cessation of immigration was only temporary. Whether the present restrictionist policy is to be permanent or temporary it is too soon to say, but it is a period when some time may well be given to a consideration of the long-time values involved in our immigration legislation.

It is significant that, in an editorial in the New York *Nation* published on August 20, 1874, Godkin said "[the immigration question] will not be settled by a comparison of certificates of national character given or refused to individual emigrants, nor will it be settled once for all at any time. The sudden changes in trade and commercial centers, the growing facility of locomotion, the growth and importance of the unions, all make the question much more complicated than formerly." It is interesting that, more than fifty years later, this statement is still true.

In conclusion, I wish to express my indebtedness to Miss Maud E. Lavery, research assistant in the Graduate School of Social Service Administration, for help in assembling this material and preparing it for publication, for proofreading, and preparation of the Index. I am also under obligation for clerical assistance to the Local Community Research Committee of the University of Chicago. Finally, it is a pleasure again to acknowledge the generous gift of Mr. Julius Rosenwald toward the publication of the Social Service Series, which has made possible the publication of the present volume.

EDITH ABBOTT

UNIVERSITY OF CHICAGO
April 12, 1926

# TABLE OF CONTENTS

## SECTION I

### CAUSES OF EMIGRATION: EMIGRATION CONDITIONS IN THE UNITED KINGDOM AND NORTHERN EUROPE

## SECTION II

## ECONOMIC ASPECTS OF THE IMMIGRATION PROBLEM

## SECTION III

### EARLY PROBLEMS OF ASSIMILATION

## SECTION IV

### PAUPERISM AND CRIME AND OTHER DOMESTIC IMMIGRATION PROBLEMS

## SECTION V

## PUBLIC OPINION AND THE IMMIGRANT

# SECTION I

## CAUSES OF EMIGRATION: EMIGRATION CONDITIONS IN THE UNITED KINGDOM AND NORTHERN EUROPE

# SECTION I

INTRODUCTORY NOTE

The causes of modern emigration have, in general, belonged in two groups: (1) adverse conditions in Europe—economic distress, political or religious oppression, and the kind of class distinctions that create an underprivileged class in respect to education and other opportunities for getting on in the world; and (2) the attractions of America— attractions that were sometimes painted in colors that were too rosy.

The peoples of Europe heard of the promise of American life from various sources. At an early day emigration agents were employed by shipowners or land speculators to stimulate emigration. Thus Document 1 describes the activities of the so-called "Newlanders" in Germany; and Document 2, the methods of stimulating emigration in eighteenth-century London. Later, other methods of promoting emigration were adopted. Throughout the emigration districts of Ireland, for example, "handbills placarded on every corner, tree, and pump, and public place" contrasted the American Eldorado with Irish poverty and distress (Document 23).

But greater numbers heard of America from books written by those who had tried the experiment of American life and who claimed to have succeeded. Famous examples of books of this kind were Crève-coeur's *Letters from an American Farmer* (Document 3), which led thousands of people to emigrate and undoubtedly caused some calamities like the ill-advised founding of Gallipolis (Document 7). Similarly, Morris Birkbeck's enthusiastic *Letters from Illinois* (Document 10) led many of his fellow-countrymen to seek a new and better England on the western frontier. Personal letters from the immigrants to relatives and friends were again an important cause of emigration. Sometimes they were passed from hand to hand, and of these no record remains. But some of them were published and had a wide circulation. A letter from Joseph Priestley (Document 4) was printed in the newspapers and widely circulated in the northern manufacturing towns of England, and an open letter from some Welsh immigrants in Pennsylvania describing their flourishing condition for the benefit of their old neighbors was distributed as a handbill in Wales (Document 6).

Some of the personal letters written by immigrants to their relatives and friends were collected and published in Manchester (Document 9) as early as 1818. Poulett Scrope, an active advocate of emigration both in and out of Parliament, also printed a collection of *Letters from Poor Persons* who had emigrated at parish expense (Document 20), in order to spread information about the inducements to emigrate among "the labouring poor and their friends." On the other hand, fear lest British subjects might be led to emigrate in too great numbers led those who were less sanguine of the opportunities offered to their fellow-countrymen to publish cautionary letters and books such as *Look before You Leap* (Document 5); and from time to time English travelers like Emanuel Howitt (Document 11) published discouraging reports of the situation and prospects of those who had emigrated.

Economic conditions in Europe in relation to emigration were widely discussed during the period from 1815 to 1860 in official investigations and reports, in parliamentary debates, and by the economists of that day. The parliamentary committee on emigration from the United Kingdom examined a large number of witnesses who were asked to describe the conditions that were driving people to emigrate from the various English counties (Document 16) or from Ireland (Document 18) or Scotland. Parliamentary discussions of the period are very illuminating. Emigration was constantly suggested as a remedy for the miseries of the people. Petitions presented to the House of Commons by the Scotch weavers, whose families "were crying to them for bread," implored the government to assist them to emigrate; and the statement made in Parliament that "thousands and tens of thousands" of Scotch weavers were "on the verge of starvation" went without contradiction (Document 17). Comments in the papers of the United Kingdom deploring the conditions which were driving the "productive population" into exile were eagerly copied in America (Documents 8 and 19). An account of the situation by a well-known statistician, John M'Gregor, is of especial interest (Document 21).

During the first two decades of the nineteenth century the large proportion of the immigrants were from England, Ireland, and Scotland. But shortly after the close of the Napoleonic wars the movement gained momentum not only in the United Kingdom (Document 8) but in Germany and Switzerland as well. Ludwig Gall (Document 12) and the petition of the German redemptioners (Document 15) indicate some of the reasons for emigration; and the movement received a great impetus from the famous letters of Gottfried Duden (Document 14). The chief sources of German emigration in the first half of the nineteenth century were the regions of the upper and middle Rhine—the Grand Duchy of Baden, Würtemberg, the two Hesses, and Bavaria (Document 25). German emigration differed in many respects from emigration from the United Kingdom; the attitude of the governments and the character of the immigrants were equally different. But on the whole, and stated in a large way (Document 26), the European emigrant was everywhere escaping from material discomforts and was going to a country where he believed material conditions would be more advantageous.

The literature of Irish emigration is so extensive, so varied, and so interesting that the difficulty is not to find adequate material describing the great exodus but to choose the most important documents from a wealth of sources. During the forty years preceding our Civil War more than two million Irish immigrants poured into the United States. The "state of Ireland" was a constant subject of discussion in Parliament and was the occasion of a score of Bluebooks. In the reports of Sir George Nicholls, the poor-law commissioner sent out by Lord John Russell (Document 22), emigration is discussed as a possible remedy for the destitution which was chronic in Ireland.

In selecting documents relating to Irish emigration no attempt is made to deal with the question, so largely political in its bearing, of the causes or responsibility for Irish distress. It was all very well for Nicholls to report that the people in Donegal were "too numerous, too thick upon the land," and that, as one of them declared, they "were eating each other's heads off"; but a long series of reports of other British officials and commissions had over and over again called attention to the fact that Ireland needed freedom to develop her resources; that she was suffering from English landlordism and English misrule.

But it is not possible in these documents to attempt to set forth the deep-seated causes of distress among the Irish people. We are concerned here with the fact that, from whatever cause, there were in Ireland nearly two and a half million people in distress for lack of employment during thirty weeks in the year, and that the Irish laborer was "frequently compelled to live, with his family, upon a diet of potatoes, without milk, unprovided with such clothing as decency required, and sheltered in a hovel wholly unfit for the residence of man" (Document 24). So also in the third report of the commission to inquire into the poor-laws of Ireland, which was quoted later in Parliament by Lord John Russell, it was said officially that a great portion of the Irish laborers were "insufficiently provided at any time with the commonest necessaries of life. Their habitations are wretched hovels, several of the family sleep together upon straw or upon the bare ground, sometimes with a blanket, sometimes without so much to cover them. Their food commonly consists of dry potatoes; and with these they are at times so scantily supplied as to be obliged to stint themselves to one spare meal in the day" (Document 27).

Long before the year of the "Great Famine" in Ireland it had been frequently prophesied that if and when a failure of the potato crop occurred there would be nothing but starvation for the Irish poor. The impending doom was discussed in Parliament by Lord John Russell, then prime minister, as early as January, 1847. At that time he spoke of the situation as "the visitation of a calamity which is, perhaps, almost without a parallel . . . . a famine of the thirteenth century acting upon the population of the nineteenth century."

Again, it is not within the scope of this volume to deal with the attitude of the British government and the "governing classes" to Irish distress, nor with the wisdom or lack of wisdom of the relief methods adopted. Our concern is with the effect of the famine on emigration. In a public letter to Lord John Russell the urgency of state aid for emigration was discussed, and it was argued that there was no way out except by "a great mortality or a great emigration." Emigration on a vast scale was accordingly urged by many friends of Ireland. The situation was carefully analyzed. Amongst the poorer classes in Ireland there was said to be a disposition to emigrate that had no assignable limit. On the other hand, emigration could not exceed "either the demand for immigrant labor in new countries or the means possessed by the Irish poor of paying for a passage." The proposal was therefore made for government expenditure in aid of Irish colonization in Canada (Document 28).

However, even without government assistance, it was clear that the starving and destitute were going to be able to find their way to Canada or the United States in large numbers. "Early in the year 1847 the roads to the Irish seaports were thronged with families hastening to escape the evils which impended over their native land." What the government failed to do, their relatives in America did, and in the twelve months ending April 1, 1847, the large sum of $5,000,000 had been sent from the United States and Canada to assist others to emigrate (Document 30). The vast emigrations of this period were disclosed later by the Irish census which was taken in 1851 and which showed a loss of population between 1841 and 1847 "computed at the enormous sum of 2,496,414 persons." When they were able, "people fled before the famine" (Document 30), and those who were left behind were buried in the famine pits, not by thousands but by hundreds of thousands. Some of the consequences of this vast migration of the sick, destitute, and starving in the countries to which they went are described in Part IV of this volume.[1]

Wholesale emigration in Ireland continued after the famine period, assisted in some districts by the poor-law authorities and by the Irish landlords who found it cheaper to send their destitute tenants to America than to support them in Irish poorhouses (Document 31). The continual outpouring of emigrants, not only from Ireland but from England and Scotland, was thoughtfully discussed in Great Britain (Document 32). It was pointed out that a generation of popular education had made the people better informed both as to conditions at home and opportunities abroad. The "repulsion of low wages and low profits at home" and the "new country attraction of high profits and high wages" were old conditions. What was new was the fact that the great mass of the people were no longer ignorant of the prosperity that existed in the new world. "It is little suspected," commented a writer in the conservative *Specator*, "what a large amount of printed matter relating to America circulates among those classes which supply the stream of British emigration; and this influence is probably trifling when compared with that of private letters from America addressed in countless numbers to a class which has only of late years learned to read."

A new factor in promoting emigration was the effort of the frontier states to attract immigrants who would help them to turn the prairie sod or subdue the wilderness. As early as 1852 Wisconsin had created the office of "Commissioner of Emigration." Public funds were used to subsidize a campaign of education through the distribution of pamphlets and the publication of newspaper articles that set forth the advantages and opportunities of the great West (Document 33).

The increase in German immigration during the period from 1830 to 1860 caused much discussion in Germany. Much of this emigration was organized, the people coming in groups and following a carefully made plan. Some of the plans were notorious failures, like the famous

[1] For an account of their sufferings at sea and the general subject of steerage conditions and attempted legislation in the United States, see the first volume of this series, E. Abbott, *Immigration: Select Documents and Case Records* (Chicago, 1924) Part I, Section I.

*Mainzer Adels Verein* (Document 34). German writers like Gottfried Menzel (Document 35) and Karl Büchele (Document 36) discussed the relative opportunities in America and at home in order to spread abroad more authentic information as to the types of persons who were likely to succeed, and to discourage those who were unfit for life in the New World from emigrating. Germany was warned, however, against attempting to regulate emigration in the interest of the State (Document 37).

An attempt has been made to include in Section I some contemporary accounts of economic conditions in England, Scotland, and Ireland, in Germany, and Switzerland, and Scandinavia, the countries of the so-called "old immigration," which furnished the great mass of emigrants in the period from 1820 to 1861. Whatever the situation may have been at an earlier day, in the nineteenth century emigration from Europe to the United States was in the main an economic movement. "People emigrate from Switzerland," said Huber-Saladin in a well known discourse of 1844, "neither for religious or political reasons, those two great and powerful causes of the emigrations of other centuries; an emigrant leaves the fatherland today in disgust because he cannot own there enough soil to live reasonably well, or at least in order not to die of hunger and to live after some fashion" (Document 39).

It must not be overlooked, however, that there were in Europe spiritual as well as material conditions which drove into exile some of the best of the subjects of the various European states. But the political and religious exiles in the nineteenth century were relatively few. They came in the large numbers from Germany—religious communities like the Rappists of Harmony and the Separatists of Zoar,[1] and the political fugitives and exiles like Francis Lieber (Document 13), who came over in larger numbers after the political disturbances of 1830 and 1848. But the "politicals," the "Zwei and dreiziger" and the "Acht und vierziger," although they made an important contribution to American life, were influential out of all proportion to their numbers.

On the eve of the Civil War, when emigration was suddenly

---

[1] There are many accounts of these religious communities; see e.g., Ernst Ludwig Brauns, *Amerika und die moderne Volkerwanderung* (Potsdam, 1833); Franz Löher, *Geschichte und Zustände der Deutschen in Amerika* (Leipzig, 1847). See also William A. Hinds, *American Communities* (Oneida, New York, 1878); Charles Nordhoff, *Communistic Societies in the United States* (New York, 1875), and G. B. Landis, "The Society of Separatists of Zoar," *Annual Report of the American Historical Association*, 1898, pp. 165–220.

brought to a standstill a French economist and statistician, Alfred Legoyt, wrote an interesting review of European emigration with the detachment of an observer from a country that lay outside of the emigration stream (Document 38). There is little, perhaps, that is new or original in Legoyt's survey, but it presents a convenient summary of emigration conditions in Europe as they appeared to an intelligent and unbiased traveler in the period before the war.

New conditions of emigration appear during and after the war (Document 40). The victories of the Union armies gave fresh "impulse and vigor" to the tide of emigration. Even before the end of hostilities the flood gates were reopened. "From the valley of the Mississippi to the Pacific coast," there were farm lands for all. Not only the "great, growing, thriving West," but a new South, in which slavery had been abolished, "beckoned to the working classes of the world." In some of these states the example of Wisconsin was followed, and a systematic effort was made to set forth the advantages of the new states to the prospective emigrating classes of Europe (Documents 42 and 43). The growth of manufactures in the North was attracting skilled mechanics from the "vast hives of industry in Lancashire" (Document 41).

The increase in the number of departures from Great Britain, the rise "in the emigration barometer," as a member of Parliament described it, was said to be "a signal of unparalleled distress" at home. So acute was this distress of the poor that for the first time in more than two decades the old discussion of state aid to promote emigration was raised again in the House of Commons. A new state-aided scheme of emigration was vigorously advocated in Parliament (Document 44), but Gladstone at this period, like Lord John Russell at an earlier day, refused to embark on "the great speculation of wholesale emigration."

Hard times in the United States were always a cause of falling off in immigration (Document 45). The statement, "Bad times in Europe regularly increase, and bad times in America invariably diminish, emigration" was confirmed again during the financial depression in America following the year 1873. Not only was there a marked and sudden decrease in immigrant arrivals, there was a very considerable increase in immigrant departures—"a strong current setting from the United States toward the shores of Europe."

The inevitable turn of the tide came again toward the close of the decade, and this time it was from Germany that the largest numbers of immigrants arrived. Compulsory military service, a growing burden of taxation, poor crops at home, and America "once more inviting them to share its reviving prosperity" were all factors in the new German exodus (Document 46), which by 1881 had assumed such proportions that German statesmen became alarmed and anxious consideration was given to the possibly serious effects of the loss of population in the Fatherland (Document 47). The economic consequences of emigration, however, will be dealt with in a separate section. The documents in the following section have been selected to illustrate the conditions, both in Europe and in America, that caused the great migrations of the period of the "old immigration."

# CAUSES OF EMIGRATION: EMIGRATION CONDITIONS IN THE UNITED KINGDOM AND NORTHERN EUROPE

## 1. Recruiting German Immigrants, 1749–50[1]

Last autumn about twenty-five ships arrived here with Germans. The number of those who arrived alive was 1,049, among whom there were also about twelve who were in part regular schoolmasters in the old country, but on account of small pay, and in the hope of improvement, moved into this, and in part they had been engaged in other pursuits. They would have better remained where they were. Some come who in part have public certificates, and in part letters to me from their parsons. I, however, can help them but little. In this month, ships again frequently arrive with Germans, so that about ten have already come. The province is crowded full of people, and living becomes continually more expensive. Those who come in free—who had something in the old country, but consumed that which they had on an expensive voyage—and see that it is otherwise than was represented to them, whine and cry. Woe on the emigrants, who induced them to this! One of these in Germantown had wished to shoot himself recently from desperation. The Newlanders,[2] as they are here called, are such as do not work,

[1] Extract taken by permission from a letter written by the German Lutheran pastor, Peter Brunnholtz, in Philadelphia, May 21, 1750, published in *Reports of the United German Evangelical Lutheran Congregations in North America* (Hallesche Nachrichten Series No. 2), pp. 412–14. Translated by Rev. Jonathan Oswald and reprinted by Lutheran Publication Society, Philadelphia, 1881.

[2] [For interesting contemporary accounts of the activities of the so-called "newlanders," see "Pastor Mühlenbergs Nachricht von merkwürdigen Exempeln aus seiner Amtsführung" (Sechstes Exempel) in *Hallesche Nachrichten* (neue Ausgabe), II, 459–61, and *Gottlieb Mittelberger's Reise nach Pennsylvanien im Jahre 1750 und Rückreise nach Teutschland im Jahre 1754: Enthaltend nicht nur eine Beschreibung des Landes nach seinem gegenwärtigen Zustande, sondern auch eine ausführliche Nachricht von den unglückseligen und betrübten Umständen der meisten Teutschen, die in dieses Land gezogen sind und dahin ziehen*, Frankfurt und Leipzig, 1756 (the latter conveniently available in a translation by Carl T. Eben, Philadelphia, 1898). And for later studies, Karl Frederick Geiser, *Redemptioners and Indentured Servants in the Colony and Commonwealth of Pennsylvania* (New Haven, 1901), pp. 18 ff., and Frank R. Diffenderffer, *The German Immigration into Pennsylvania through the Port of Philadelphia, 1700 to 1775*, Part II, "The Redemptioners," pp. 189–94, 199, 298. Mittelberger ascribed the large German emigration "to the deceptions and per-

and still wish to become rich speedily, and for this reason they go out into Würtemberg and vicinity, and persuade the people to come into this country, alleging that everything was here that they could wish for, that such a country like this there was none in the world, and that everyone could become as rich as a nobleman, etc. These deceivers have this profit in it, that they with their merchandise are brought in free, and in addition, for every head they bring to Amsterdam or to Rotterdam, they receive a certain sum from the merchants. The owners of these vessels derive much money herefrom in freightage. They pack them into the ships as if they were herring, and when they arrive, there are so many sick and dying among them that it is pitiful to behold them. Those, however, who have nothing, and are in debt also for their passage, are taken into small huts, where they lie upon straw, and are corrupted like cattle, and in part half deprived of their reason, so that they can scarcely perceive anything of the parson's consolations. The government and assembly have meanwhile made some ordinances and institutions, but whether the difficulty will be remedied thereby time will show. It would be just and right if a regular report of such things were put into the German newspapers here and there in Europe.

---

suasions practiced by the so-called 'newlanders.'" However, Friedrich Kapp, in his *Geschichte der deutschen Einwanderung in Amerika*, I, "Geschichte der Deutschen im Staate New York" (3 Aufl.; New York, 1869) makes some interesting comments on Mittelberger's narrative (pp. 302–7), from which the following is translated:

"It would certainly be a very false conclusion to infer from the statements of Mittelberger that the emigration of the last century was induced solely by trickery, deceit, and persuasion. To be sure, they played their part in it, but they appear particularly upon the surface; . . . . the real ground for the emigration fever lay in the unhealthy political and economic conditions, . . . . in the oppression caused by these conditions, and in the discontent of individuals with themselves and with the conditions surrounding them. Emigration was already in progress before commercial speculation took possession of it. . . . . A neighbor hears of the plans of the others, he joins in, one possibly on good grounds, another without thinking much, drawn by the love of change. Then come the first letters from the emigrants, which naturally sound more favorable and promising. Over there beyond the seas is a free land where each can do as he pleases, and although he must also work, yet he knows for whom, and why. That is the constant refrain, and naturally the news spreads through the whole village. Those formerly indifferent get the idea of emigrating. Not all can be false, half must be true, reasons the one left behind. If something goes wrong with him, then he thinks of America. Still he does not carry out his plan until with a new misfortune, an unexpected episode, the resolution to emigrate is finally made and the break with the fatherland is complete.

"The misery and oppression of the conditions of the little states promoted emigration much more dangerously and continuously than the worst 'newlander.' "]

Still what good would it do? The farmers don't get to read the papers, and many indeed would not believe it, as they moreover have a mind to come.

## 2. Methods of Stimulating Emigration in London in the Eighteenth Century[1]

In your frequent excursions about the great metropolis, you cannot but observe numerous advertisements, offering the most seducing encouragement to adventurers under every possible description; to those who are disgusted with the frowns of fortune in their native land, and to those of an enterprising disposition who are tempted to court her smiles in a distant region. These persons are referred to agents, or crimps, who represent the advantages to be obtained in America, in colours so alluring that it is almost impossible to resist their artifices. Unwary persons are accordingly induced to enter into articles by which they engage to become servants, agreeable to their respective qualifications, for the term of five years, every necessary accommodation being found them during the voyage, and every method taken that they may be treated with tenderness and humanity during the period of servitude, at the expiration of which they are taught to expect that opportunities will assuredly offer to secure to the honest and industrious a competent provision for the remainder of their days.

The generality of the inhabitants in this province are very little acquainted with those fallacious pretences, by which numbers are continually induced to embark for this continent. On the contrary, they too generally conceive an opinion that the difference is merely nominal between the indented servant and the convicted felon; nor will they readily believe that people who had the least experience in life, and whose characters were unexceptionable, would abandon their friends and families, and their ancient connections, for a servile situation in a remote appendage to the British Empire. From this persuasion they rather consider the convict as the more profitable servant, his term being for seven, the latter only for five years; and I am sorry to observe that there are but few instances wherein they experience different treatment. . . . .

The situation of the free-willer is, in almost every instance, more to be lamented than either that of the convict or the indented servant; the deception which is practiced on those of this description being at-

[1] Extract from William Eddis, *Letters from America, Historical and Descriptive; Comprising Occurrences from 1769 to 1777, Inclusive* (London, 1792), pp. 67–69, 71–78.

tended with circumstances of greater duplicity and cruelty. Persons under this denomination are received under express conditions that, on their arrival in America, they are to be allowed a stipulated number of days to dispose of themselves to the greatest advantage. They are told that their services will be eagerly solicited, in proportion to their abilities; that their reward will be adequate to the hazard they encounter by courting fortune in a distant region; and that the parties with whom they engage will readily advance the sum agreed on for their passage; which, being averaged at about nine pounds sterling, they will speedily be enabled to repay, and to enjoy, in a state of liberty, a comparative situation of ease and affluence.

With these pleasing ideas they support with cheerfulness the hardships to which they are subjected during the voyage; and, with the most anxious sensations of delight, approach the land which they consider as the scene of future prosperity. But scarce have they contemplated the diversified objects which naturally attract attention; scarce have they yielded to the pleasing reflection that every danger, every difficulty, is happily surmounted, before their fond hopes are cruelly blasted, and they find themselves involved in all the complicated miseries of a tedious, laborious, and unprofitable servitude.

Persons resident in America, being accustomed to procure servants for a very trifling consideration, under absolute terms, for a limited period, are not often disposed to hire adventurers, who expect to be gratified in full proportion to their acknowledged qualifications; but, as they support authority with a rigid hand, they little regard the former situation of their unhappy dependants.

This disposition, which is almost universally prevalent, is well known to the parties who on your side of the Atlantic engage in this iniquitous and cruel commerce. It is, therefore, an article of agreement with these deluded victims, that if they are not successful in obtaining situations on their own terms within a certain number of days after their arrival in the country, they are then to be sold, in order to defray the charges of passage, at the discretion of the master of the vessel, or the agent to whom he is consigned in the province.

You are also to observe, that servants imported, even under this favourable description, are rarely permitted to set their feet on shore until they have absolutely formed their respective engagements. As soon as the ship is stationed in her berth, planters, mechanics, and others repair on board; the adventurers of both sexes are exposed to view, and very few are happy enough to make their own stipulations, some very extraordinary qualifications being absolutely requisite to obtain this distinction; and even when this is obtained, the advantages are by no means equivalent to their sanguine expectations. The residue, stung with disappointment and vexation, meet with horror the moment which dooms them, under an appearance of equity, to a limited term of slavery. Character is of little importance; their abilities not being found of a superior nature, they are sold as soon as their term of election is expired, apparel and provision being their only compensation; till, on the expiration of five tedious, laborious years, they are restored to a dearly purchased freedom.

From this detail, I am persuaded, you will no longer imagine that the servants in this country are in a better situation than those in Britain. You have heard of convicts who rather chose to undergo the severest penalties of the law, than endure the hardships which are annexed to their situation, during a state of servitude on this side the Atlantic. Indolence, accompanied with a train of vicious habits, has, doubtless, great influence on the determination of such unhappy wretches; but it is surely to be lamented that men whose characters are unblemished, whose views are founded on honest and industrious principles, should fall a sacrifice to avarice and delusion, and indiscriminately be blended with the most profligate and abandoned of mankind.

It seems astonishing that a circumstance so well known, particularly in this province, should not have been generally circulated through every part of the British Empire. Were the particulars of this iniquitous traffic universally divulged, those who have established offices in London, and in the principal seaports, for the regular conduct of this business, would be pointed out to obloquy, and their punishment would serve as a beacon to deter the ignorant and unwary from becoming victims to the insidious practices of avarice and deceit.

I am ready to admit there is every appearance of candour on the part of the agents, and their accomplices. Previous to the embarcation of any person under the respective agreements, the parties regularly comply with the requisitions of a law wisely calculated to prevent clandestine transportation; they appear before a magistrate, and give their voluntary assent to the obligations they have mutually entered into. But are not such adventurers induced to this measure in consequence of ignorance and misrepresentation? Assuredly they are. They are industriously taught to expect advantages infinitely superior to their most sanguine view in Britain. Every lucrative incentive is delineated in the most flattering colours; and they fondly expect to acquire that independence in the revolution of a few years, which the longest life could not promise, with the exertion of their best abilities, in the bosom of their native country.

### 3.  What America Offered to the Poor of Europe[1]

Europe contains hardly any other distinctions but lords and tenants; this fair country alone is settled by freeholders, the possessors of the soil they cultivate, members of the government they obey, and the framers of their own laws, by means of their representatives. This is a thought which you have taught me to cherish; our distance from Europe, far from diminishing, rather adds to our usefulness and consequence as men and subjects. Had our forefathers remained there, they would only have crowded it, and perhaps prolonged those convulsions which had shook it so long. . . . . Colonists are entitled to the consideration due to the most useful subjects; a hundred families barely existing in some parts of Scotland will here, in six years, cause an annual exportation of 10,000 bushels of wheat: 100 bushels being but a common quantity for an industrious family to sell, if they cultivate good land. It is here, then, that the idle may be employed, the useless become useful, and the poor become rich; but by riches I do not mean gold and silver, we have but little of those metals; I mean a better sort of wealth, cleared lands, cattle, good houses, good clothes, and an increase of people to enjoy them.

There is no wonder that this country has so many charms, and

---

[1] Extract from J. Hector St. John de Crèvecoeur, *Letters from an American Farmer* (London, 1782), pp. 69–80, 84–87. The *Letters* were first published in London in 1782 and in the same year another edition was published in Dublin. The popularity of the *Letters* is indicated by the fact that within a year a second English edition and a second Irish edition had been published, and no fewer than nine reviews of it appeared in England and Ireland with lengthy extracts from the book. A French translation of the *Letters* appeared in Paris in 1784 and a second French edition in 1787. The first American edition appeared in 1793. The *Letters* were severely criticized by Samuel Ayscough, *Remarks on the Letters from an American Farmer* (London, 1783). Ayscough feared the effect of the *Letters* would be an overstimulation of emigration. That the alluring picture of American life painted by Crèvecoeur did cause large numbers of emigrants to leave their homes in the United Kingdom and in France cannot be questioned. The 500 French emigrants who founded the unfortunate colony of Gallipolis on the Scioto (see Document 7, p. 30) had probably been influenced in part by the writings of Crèvecoeur. A convenient reprint of the *Letters* with prefatory and introductory notes was published in 1904 by the Columbia University Press. For a recent life of Crèvecoeur, see J. P. Mitchell, *St. Jean de Crèvecoeur* (1916). For another Crèvecoeur document, see pp. 416–22.

presents to Europeans so many temptations to remain in it. A traveller in Europe becomes a stranger as soon as he quits his own kingdom; but it is otherwise here. We know, properly speaking, no strangers; this is every person's country; the variety of our soils, situations, climates, governments, and produce, hath something which must please every body. No sooner does an European arrive, no matter of what condition, than his eyes are opened upon the fair prospect; he hears his language spoke, he retraces many of his own country manners, he perpetually hears the names of families and towns with which he is acquainted; he sees happiness and prosperity in all places disseminated; he meets with hospitality, kindness, and plenty every where; he beholds hardly any poor, he seldom hears of punishments and executions, and he wonders at the elegance of our towns, those miracles of industry and freedom. He cannot admire enough our rural districts, our convenient roads, good taverns, and our many accommodations; he involuntarily loves a country where every thing is so lovely. When in England, he was a mere Englishman; here he stands on a larger portion of the globe, not less than its fourth part, and may see the productions of the north, in iron and naval stores; the provisions of Ireland, the grain of Egypt, the indigo, the rice of China. He does not find, as in Europe, a crowded society, where every place is overstocked; he does not feel that perpetual collision of parties, that difficulty of beginning, that contention which oversets so many. There is room for every body, in America. Has he any particular talent, or industry? he exerts it in order to procure a livelihood, and it succeeds. Is he a merchant? the avenues of trade are infinite. Is he eminent in any respect? he will be employed and respected. Does he love a country life? pleasant farms present themselves; he may purchase what he wants, and thereby become an American farmer. Is he a laborer, sober and industrious? he need not go many miles, nor receive many informations before he will be hired, well fed at the table of his employer, and paid four or five times more than he can get in Europe. Does he want uncultivated lands? thousands of acres present themselves, which he may purchase cheap. Whatever be his talents or inclinations, if they are moderate, he may satisfy them. I do not mean that every one who comes will grow rich in a little time; no, but he may procure an easy, decent maintenance, by his industry. Instead of starving, he will be fed; instead of being idle, he will have employment; and these are riches enough for such men as come over here. The rich stay in Europe, it is only the middling and the poor that emigrate. Would you wish to travel in independent idleness, from north to south, you will find easy access, and the most cheerful reception at every house; society without ostentation, good cheer without pride, and every decent diversion which the country affords, with little expence. It is no wonder that the European who has lived here a few years is desirous to remain; Europe with all its pomp is not to be compared to this continent, for men of middle stations, or labourers.

An European, when he first arrives, seems limited in his intentions, as well as in his views; but he very suddenly alters his scale; two hundred miles formerly appeared a very great distance, it is now but a trifle; he no sooner breathes our air than he forms schemes, and embarks in designs he never would have thought of in his own country. There the plentitude of society confines many useful ideas, and often extinguishes the most laudable schemes which here ripen into maturity. Thus Europeans become Americans.

But how is this accomplished in that crowd of low, indigent people, who flock here every year from all parts of Europe? I will tell you; they no sooner arrive than they immediately feel the good effects of that plenty of provisions we possess; they fare on our best food, and are kindly entertained; their talents, character, and peculiar industry are immediately inquired into; they find countrymen every where disseminated, let them come from whatever part of Europe. Let me select one as an epitome of the rest. He is hired, he goes to work, and works moderately; instead of being employed by a haughty person, he finds himself with his equal, placed at the substantial table of the farmer, or else at an inferior one as good; his wages are high, his bed is not like that bed of sorrow on which he used to lie; if he behaves with propriety, and is faithful, he is caressed, and becomes, as it were, a member of the family. He begins to feel the effects of a sort of resurrection; hitherto he had not lived, but simply vegetated; he now feels himself a man, because he is treated as such; the laws of his own country had overlooked him in his insignificancy; the laws of this cover him with their mantle. Judge what an alteration there must arise in the mind and thoughts of this man; he begins to forget his former servitude and dependence, his heart involuntarily swells and glows; this first swell inspires him with those new thoughts which constitute an American.

What love can he entertain for a country where his existence was a burthen to him; if he is a generous good man, the love of his new adoptive parent will sink deep into his heart. He looks around, and sees many a prosperous person, who but a few years before was as poor as himself. This encourages him much, he begins to form some little scheme, the first, alas, he ever formed in his life. If he is wise he thus spends two or three years, in which time he acquires knowledge, the use of tools, the modes of working the lands, felling trees, etc. This prepares the foundation of a good name, the most useful acquisition he can make. He is encouraged, he has gained friends; he is advised and directed, he feels bold, he purchases some land; he gives all the money he has brought over, as well as what he has earned, and trusts to the God of harvests for the discharge of the rest. His good name procures him credit. He is now possessed of the deed, conveying to him and his posterity the fee simple and absolute property of two hundred acres of land, situated on such a river. What an epoch in this man's life! He is become a freeholder, from perhaps a German boor—he is now an American, a Pennsylvanian, an English subject. He is naturalized, his name is enrolled with those of the other citizens of the province. Instead of being a vagrant, he has a place of residence; he is called the inhabitant of such a county, or of such a district, and for the first time in his life counts for something; for hitherto he has been a cypher. I only repeat what I have heard many say, and no wonder their hearts should glow, and be agitated with a multitude of feelings, not easy to describe. From nothing to start into being; from a servant to the rank of master; from being the slave of some despotic prince, to become a free man, invested with lands, to which every municipal blessing is annexed!

What a change indeed! It is in consequence of that change that he becomes an American. . . . . Ye poor Europeans, ye, who sweat, and work for the great—ye, who are obliged to give so many sheaves to the church, so many to your lords, so many to your government, and have hardly any left for yourselves—ye, who are held in less estimation than favourite hunters or useless lap-dogs—ye, who only breathe the air of nature, because it cannot be withheld from you; it is here that ye can conceive the possibility of those feelings I have been describing; it is here the laws of naturalization invite every one to partake of our great labours and felicity, to till unrented, untaxed lands! . . . . It is not every emigrant who succeeds; no, it is only the sober, the honest, and industrious: happy those to whom this transition has served as a powerful spur to labour, to prosperity, and to the good establishment of children, born in the days of their poverty, and who had no other portion to expect but the rags of their parents, had it not been for their happy emigration. Others again have been led astray by this enchanting scene; . . . . they have mouldered away their time in inactivity, misinformed husbandry, and ineffectual endeavours. How much wiser, in general, the honest Germans than almost all other Europeans; they hire themselves to some of their wealthy landsmen, and in that apprenticeship learn every thing that is necessary . . . . and by dint of sobriety, rigid parsimony, and the most persevering industry, they commonly succeed. Their astonishment at their first arrival from Germany is very great—it is to them a dream; the contrast must be powerful indeed; they observe their countrymen flourishing in every place; they travel through whole counties where not a word of English is spoken; and in the names and the language of the people, they retrace Germany. They have been an useful acquisition to this continent, and to Pennsylvania in particular; to them it owes some share of its prosperity: to their mechanical knowledge and patience, it owes the finest mills in all America, the best teams of horses, and many other advantages. The recollection of their former poverty and slavery never quits them as long as they live.

The Scotch and the Irish might have lived in their own country perhaps as poor, but enjoying more civil advantages, the effects of their new situation do not strike them so forcibly, nor has it so lasting an effect. From whence the difference arises I know not, but out of twelve families of emigrants of each country, generally seven Scotch will succeed, nine German, and four Irish. The Scotch are frugal and laborious, but their wives cannot work so hard as German women, who, on the contrary, vie with their husbands, and often share with them the most severe toils of the field, which they understand better. They have therefore nothing to struggle against but the common casualties of nature. The Irish do not prosper so well; they love to drink and to quarrel; they are litigious, and soon take to the gun, which is the ruin of every thing; they seem beside to labour under a greater degree of ignorance in husbandry than the others; perhaps it is that their industry had less scope, and was less exercised at home. . . . . There is no tracing observations of this kind, without making at the same time very great allowances, as there are every where to be found a great many exceptions. The Irish themselves, from different parts of that kingdom, are very different. It is difficult to account for this surprising locality; one would think on so small an island an Irishman must be an Irishman; yet it is not so, they are different in their aptitude to, and in their love of, labour.

The Scotch, on the contrary, are all industrious and saving; they want nothing more than a field to exert themselves in, and they are commonly sure of succeeding. The only difficulty they labour under is that technical American knowledge which requires some time to obtain; it is not easy for those who seldom saw a tree, to conceive how it is to be felled, cut up, and split into rails and posts. . . . .

Agreeable to the account which several Scotchmen have given me of the north of Britain, of the Orkneys, and the Hebride Islands, they seem, on many accounts, to be unfit for the habitation of men; they appear to be calculated only for great sheep pastures. Who then can blame the inhabitants of these countries for transporting themselves hither? This great continent must in time absorb the poorest part of Europe; and this will happen in proportion as it becomes better known, and as war, taxation, oppression, and misery increase there. The Hebrides appear to be fit only for the residence of malefactors, and it would be much better to send felons there than either to Virginia or Maryland. What a strange compliment has our mother country paid to two of the finest provinces in America! England has entertained in that respect very mistaken ideas; what was intended as a punishment is become the good fortune of several; many of those who have been transported as felons, are now rich, and strangers to the stings of those wants that urged them to violations of the law: they are become industrious, exemplary, and useful citizens. . . . . This is no place of punishment; were I a poor hopeless, breadless Englishman, and not restrained by the power of shame, I should be very thankful for the passage. It is of very little importance how and in what manner an indigent man arrives; for if he is but sober, honest, and industrious, he has nothing more to ask of heaven. Let him go to work, he will have opportunities enough to earn a comfortable support, and even the means of procuring some land; which ought to be the utmost wish of every person who has health and hands to work. . . . .

After a foreigner from any part of Europe is arrived, and become a citizen; let him devoutly listen to the voice of our great parent, which says to him, "Welcome to my shores, distressed European; bless the hour in which thou didst see my verdant fields, my fair navigable rivers, and my green mountains! If thou wilt work, I have bread for thee; if thou wilt be honest, sober, and industrious, I have greater rewards to confer on thee—ease and independence. I will give thee fields to feed and clothe thee; a comfortable fire-side to sit by, and tell thy children by what means thou hast prospered; and a decent bed to repose on. I shall endow thee beside with the immunities of a freeman. If thou wilt carefully educate thy children, teach them gratitude to God, and reverence to that government, that philanthropic government, which has collected here so many men and made them happy. . . . . Go thou and work and till; thou shalt prosper, provided thou be just, grateful, and industrious."

### 4. A Letter from America, 1796[1]

NORTHUMBERLAND, (PENNSYLVANIA) October 4, 1796

MY DEAR SIR:

Every account I have from England makes me think myself happy in this peaceful retirement, where I enjoy almost everything I can wish in this life, and where I hope to close it, though I find it is reported, both here and in England, that I am about to return. . . . .

The advantages we enjoy in this country are indeed very great. Here we have no poor; we never see a beggar, nor is there a family in want. We have no church establishment, and hardly any taxes. This particular state pays all its officers from a treasure in the public funds. There are very few crimes committed, and we travel without the least apprehension of danger. The press is perfectly free, and I hope we shall always keep out of war.

I do not think there ever was any country in a state of such rapid improvement as this at present; but we have not the same advantages for literary and philosophical pursuits that you have in Europe, though even in this respect we are every day getting better. Many books are now printing here, but what scholars chiefly want are old books, and these are not to be had. We hope, however, that the troubles of Europe will be the cause of sending us some libraries, and they say that it is an ill wind that blows no profit.

[1] This letter, written by Joseph Priestley to a friend in England, was dated October 4, 1796. It was first published in a newspaper in Leeds, England, and was reprinted by William Cobbett (see *Porcupine's Works*, IX, 312–13). Cobbett said it was published in England "in all the manufacturing towns, and was evidently intended to be so published, in order to induce people to emigrate." The letter was denounced by Cobbett as "an abominable falsehood," because it said that in America there were no poor. Cobbett thought the letter had been "the means of inveigling one thousand people to America." Discussing the subject at a later date, Cobbett said: "Of the mischiefs which American independence has produced in the world, that of seducing thousands upon thousands of ignorant Europeans from their homes, to die with hunger and sickness in the woods and swamps of the United States, is not the least. I could fill a volume with the names of the miserable wretches who have been thus ruined in the space of a very few months. I could relate facts that would astonish any European." (See *Porcupine's Works*, IX, 252–53, 389, 399.)

I sincerely wish, however, that your troubles were at an end, and from our last accounts we think there must be a peace, at least from the impossibility of carrying on the war.

With every good wish to my country and to yourself, I am, dear sir,

Yours sincerely

J. PRIESTLEY.

## 5. An Attempt to Discourage Emigration[1]

With infinite regret the publisher of the following letters has observed the careless and unthinking manner in which numbers of his fellow-countrymen desert their native soil, to seek their fortunes on the continent of America.

The reasons which induce most persons to transport themselves across the Atlantic Ocean may generally be reduced to the three following classes: First, either the embarrassed state of their finances, or the dread of passing the ordeal of criminal justice. Secondly, the desire of enjoying the blessings derived from living under a free government, uncorrupted by luxury, and unburthened by taxation; and thirdly, the prospect of enjoying the advantages of a plentiful and cheap country, where a greater recompense is obtained for the services they are able to render to society, in their several professions, than they can hope to receive in Great Britain.

On the first, which must be allowed to be a very cogent reason, it is not the intention of the publisher to digress, except to ask, "Where will not the debtor fly, to escape confinement for life, in the sepulchral gloom of a goal? Where will not the criminal seek refuge to evade the hand of justice, and elude the insulted laws of his country?" . . . .

On the third head, he wishes more to arrest the public attention, as he conceives it more interesting to those for whose use and benefit he has collected the following letters. Without troubling their heads about government, the industrious artizan, and labourious mechanic

[1] Extract from *Look before You Leap; or A Few Hints to Such Artizans, Mechanics, Labourers, Farmers, and Husbandmen, as Are Desirous of Emigrating to America, Being a Genuine Collection of Letters, from Persons Who Have Emigrated, Containing Remarks, Notes and Anecdotes, Political, Philosophical, Biographical and Literary, of the Present State, Situation, Population, Prospects, and Advantages of America, together with the Reception, Success, Mode of Life, Opinions and Situation, of Many Characters Who Have Emigrated, Particularly to the Federal City of Washington, Illustrative of the Prevailing Practice of Indenting and Demonstrative of the Nature, Effects, and Consequences of that Public Delusion* (London, 1796), pp. i–viii, xiii–iv, xxxi–v, 85–87, 95–96, 102–3, 119.

must live. It is the law of nature, paramount to every other consideration, that they should; and whatever becomes of systems of empire and
modes of legislation, the industrious and sober, the active and virtuous
tradesman has an indefeasible right and claim upon society for comfort
and security. Let us examine how far emigration to America will answer this end. That there are many most admirable theories, which,
from inseparable circumstances, can never be reduced to practice, is
generally acknowledged. The same may be remarked concerning the
glittering prospects so officiously obtruded upon public view, to induce
a frequent emigration to America. Many well-meaning persons are en-
raptured with the favourable accounts circulated with such unexampled industry of that extensive continent. The beautiful descriptions so luxuriantly picturesque of American scenery, and the exaggerated encomiums upon the state of American society, warm the
imagination; regardless of scrutinizing their veracity, the deluded adventurer hasily undertakes the project of realizing his sanguine expectations; he bustles among his friends; collects every atom of his
property; stretches every pinion of his hopes, and full of fervent enthusiasm and anxious expectancy, reaches the desired shore; when alas!
the material object and pleasing fruition of his wishes "vanishes into
thin air," and leaves him the desponding dupe of deception and
credulity.

Such was precisely the situation of the writers of some of the letters
contained in this publication. They formed part of a company consisting of near forty persons, who sailed the 19th March, 1795, in the
"Two Sisters," Isaac Hilton, Master, bound for Alexandria in Virginia.
Labouring under the delusive hopes of bettering their fortunes, they
had formed the project of visiting those bewitching shores, which were
to administer a felicity not to be attained in their native country. Accordingly an agreement was entered into with the captain of the "William Penn," bound for Philadelphia; and every necessary preparation
was made for the intended voyage.

It is a fact not generally known, but undoubtedly true, that there
are always plenty of agents hovering like birds of prey on the banks of
the Thames, eager in their search for such artizans, mechanics, husbandmen, and labourers, as are inclinable to direct their course for
America. These harpies improve their already unsettled dispositions,
and induce them to visit such parts of the continent as are most suitable to the interests of their employers. It happened in the present instance that one of these miscreants darted his piercing eye upon some

of our unwary adventurers, who, listening favourably to his delusions, quickly imparted to him their intentions, and making their new-found friend a confidant, as quickly introduced him to the rest of their companions, who unanimously craved his advice as to their future conduct in that country to which they were destined. . . . .

The artful sycophant proceeded next to extol their courage in having formed so laudable an idea as to emigrate from this intolerable country to such a happy, such a heavenly, land as America. When we speak of America, says he, we comprehend a most extensive continent, situated so as to experience a variety of different climates; and though the part from which you are fortunately rescued is attended with many unpleasing circumstances, still, (continued he) must be confessed there are other parts which, I will be bold to say, cannot be equalled on the face of the globe. To such persons as you appear to be, what a prospect does Virginia, that land of milk and honey, open to your view! There, the eye of humanity is never shocked at the sight of penury and want, there merit never languishes in neglect; there, every happiness capable of being enjoyed in these sublunary regions, is to be obtained: innumerable opportunities present themselves and press forward to persons of your description, who cannot fail of making rapid fortunes, in the several professions of which you are the masters; consider, my dear friends, the wide and extensive field of action for mechanics of every description in the famous federal city of Washington, now building by order of the United States, in which, over and above his extravagant wages, the certain recompense, for every mechanic, will be the free gift of a ground lot for his own use in the first city in the world.

If I were to advise you, I would point out this emporium of human felicity to your serious consideration; it offers you every advantage, and is replete with every comfort. Its very climate is grateful to Englishmen, and seems to invite them to partake of its salubrity, if we may judge of the uninterrupted state of health they enjoy after once feeling its invigorating influence.

The credulity of his audience readily led them to believe every iota which he uttered, and implicitly to adopt his recommendation. The previous engagements with the captain of the "William Penn," were immediately cancelled, and fresh entered into with the broker and the captain of the "Two Sisters," bound for Alexandria, the nearest port to Washington. . . . .

This anecdote is related to inform those persons who are inoculated with the desire of deserting their native country, and of transporting themselves to drain the unwholesome bogs, and cultivate the rank lands of America, that there are agents employed at a considerable expense, expressly for the purpose of inveigling them to quit their friends and connections, in order to seek an ideal romantic happiness in a solitary uncultivated waste, little calculated and still less capable of conferring the comforts and benefits of society. . . . . There is a legion of these harpies dispersed over this kingdom, successfully employed in taking advantage of the distress naturally accompanying the urgency of the times. There is another species of American agents, who are a kind of Jackalls, employed in providing prey for such ravenous animals as the character which I have already described. I mean the persons who are continually publishing the most delusive and flattering accounts of this land of promise.

These invaders of domestic happiness, and improvers of popular discontent, pompously inform the miserable inhabitants of this unhappy island of those hardships under which they are groaning. They then in flowing declamations point out the superior advantages enjoyed by all classes in America, with such glowing colors and intoxicating language, that it seldom fails to have the desired effect. Examine the descriptions given by Franklin, Morse, Jefferson, Brissot, Winterbotham, and though last, not least, the puffs of the agents for the sale of American lands. . . . .

One species of abject misery consequent upon emigration has been hitherto unnoticed—but to the *labouring poor* it is tremendously awful, and pregnant with horrors of the most unprecedented nature. I mean the custom of *indenting*, or, to speak perhaps more precisely, of buying a voluntary exile and a bitter slavery. Those voracious harpies of whom in this preface we have had already too much occasion to make mention are in the habits of stimulating the *labouring poor* to cross the Atlantic upon an indenture—by which they bind themselves for a certain term, from two to seven years, as the indented servants of an austere captain or imperious landholder, whose only object is to derive a profit from their misfortune, and to aggrandize himself at the expense of industry in distress. These contracts have been common on the coasts of Ireland and Scotland for some time, but lately, even the metropolis is invested with them, and the panders of American opulence walk unblushingly to practice their delusions through the streets of London.

The situations of the unfortunate labourers who fall into their hands may be in some degree conceived, but cannot be easily described. They are sometimes employed on the coasts, but more generally sent into the interior, where every species of brutal insolence and overbearing tyranny is exercised upon their feelings. . . . .

There is at the present juncture, a very large concern of this kind, going on by a wholesale agent in Bloomsbury Square. The bird's-eye prospect held forth by this recruiting cajoler to those credulous persons who are superficial observers, and only accustomed to view one side of a subject, is highly romantic. The trap is Kentucky, and the bait nothing short of an independency, after the time of apprenticeship is expired. A friend of the publisher's has been in company with several of the unfortunate men who have been worked upon to indent themselves as common labourers, though the greatest part of them were artizans and mechanics of very valuable descriptions.

The terms of agreement are such as to elude the wholesome provisions of the legislature against enticing artizans from this kingdom; and further to secure the efforts of the *indented* to be applied in such manner as their *owners* may be pleased to direct. . . . . The miscreant alluded to in this note has chartered no less than six ships to convey his miserable game to their land of bondage; the infatuated wretches enslaved by him in this manner, amount to upwards of one thousand, and the time fixed for their departure is the ensuing month. . . . .

(The following letters were written to a master carpenter, who was so far distempered with the American mania, as to quit a very genteel situation and respectable connection in order to accumulate a rapid fortune at the Federal City of Washington.)

NORFOLK
August 16, 1794

. . . . If you come to NORFOLK for that boasted encouragement our countrymen are taught to expect in England, you will be most *miserably disappointed*. I have seen upwards of three hundred poor persons, chiefly from Ireland, landed from one ship bemoaning with tears their own credulity, and lamenting most pathetically their departure from their native homes. These poor creatures are marched in small bodies by persons employed for that purpose to the different plantations where they are forced to indent themselves for *so many years* to the planters, who pay the captains what is called the *redemption money* for them. You will perhaps be surprised that such transactions are permitted in what is called the *land of liberty*, but I assure you this is thought nothing of here, and is actually the case. . . . .
There is one very unpleasant circumstance which attends us Englishmen here, which is, that most of the natives entertain the idea, *we quit our country for crimes*, and dare not return. I assure you I have been taunted with this already several times. . . . .

GEORGE-TOWN NEAR WASHINGTON
January 21, 1795

. . . . Doubtless you have heard much of Kentucky. To this country·
all the abandoned, the credulous, the unsettled, and the wretched in these
states, are flocking in numbers. Most of the poor distressed objects I meet
are indenting themselves to proprietors of land in Kentucky, in order to be
conveyed there, carriage free; although the probability of such persons ever
returning is scarcely possible. . . . . The substance of what I have been
able to collect is, that the poor creatures who have been induced to *indent
themselves* are in situations the most pitiable; they are treated by their *masters* in a similar manner *to the felons formerly transported from England to
Virginia.* Instead of being put in possession of portions of land, and quickly
discharging their engagements, they sink deeper into debt, and this by the
means of being obliged to purchase on credit at the most extravagant charges
from their masters the stores and necessaries of which they stand in need.
Thus situated they are never free from the landholder who is an absolute tyrant, while his miserable *indented servants are likely to remain slaves forever.*
Great numbers die from the change of climate, want of proper sustenance,
and the very unusual and laborious employ to which they are rigorously subjected by their vigilant overseers. Those situated upon the bordering territory are often scalped by the Indians, and their lives are in continual jeop-
ardy. If my paper would contain all the information I have received respecting this enticing country, and also if I had time to write, I assure you
it would form a striking contrast to a pamphlet, now laying beside me, and
which I received when in London, from *the Kentucky agents in Threadneedle-
street.* . . . .

### 6.  An Open Letter from Welsh Immigrants in Pennsylvania, 1800[1]

*The Welch People Residing in Cambria, in the State of Pennsylvania,
to Their Brethren in Wales, Greeting:*

We have received many letters from you of late, which have occasioned us much sorrow. It grieves us that we are not able to stretch
unto you an hand of relief across the ocean. In answer to your inquiries, we need not say that in the *United States* there are almost all

[1] This letter was printed in America in 1800 and reprinted in Wales in 1801 "upon a quarter-sheet" of paper for circulation in Wales. Cobbett reprinted the letter
in *Porcupine's Gazette* with an attack on the practices of the "landjobbers" who were,
he thought, artificially stimulating emigration. "The whole pamphlet," he said,
"is a base and infamous trick to decoy the poor Welch from their homes, to go and
augment the population and the value of land at *Cambria,* where *Theophilus Rees,*
and his relation *Morgan Rees,* have purchased great quantities of land, and where
they have already ruined hundreds of poor creatures whom they have deluded
thither" (*Porcupine's Works,* IX, 410–12).

sorts of soils and climates. In the more southern ones, the weather is hot, and the summer long. In the northern ones, though the summer is sufficiently warm, the winter is long and cold. The states of *New York* and *Pennsylvania* are esteemed the best for Europeans; the latter, on various accounts, should have the pre-eminence. In regard to our settlements, perhaps there may be many places easier to cultivate, and more convenient for a market; but it is not every where that the poor can have land before they pay for it. The soil here is rich enough to bear all kinds of grain, and very good for hay and pasture. Well adapted for rearing cattle, and the making of cheese and butter. Our springs are numerous, and as pure as in any part of the world. We have plenty of brooks to erect mills, and navigable rivers to the east within twenty or thirty miles, and to the west within twelve. No country abounds more with *sugar canes*, so that every family can make it for their own use. Hitherto we have a market for everything we have to dispose of at *Beula*, a town in the middle of our settlement. There is a sufficient quantity of land for some thousands of people, and it is certain that three-fourths of it is sufficiently good to cultivate. It may now be purchased from 9s. to 18s. per acre. If one-fourth or one-fifth part of the money be paid at the time of purchasing, credit may be had for the remainder for five or seven years. The poor may have a lease for seven or ten years for nothing more than to build a cottage on the land, and cultivate as many acres as will be sufficient to support them. Though there be some difficulties at first in every new settlement, yet we think such places answer better for the diligent than to purchase land at a high price near the great towns.

There are some among us that were worth but little, who have now corn and cattle to sell.

Our end in establishing this settlement was for the general good of the *Welch*, particularly that they may have the privilege of hearing the gospel in their own language. There are in *Cambria* preachers of different denominations, living together in peace and amity. We have three or four Welch sermons every first day in the week, and there are English preachers in *Beula*. There are 350 lots in (and some near) the town given to support a school; more than 1,000 books have been purchased for a general library, and 200 acres of land for the support of the preachers, not of any one particular sect or party, but such as are esteemed worthy, of every denomination, and profess *that Jesus is the Son of God, and Saviour of Men*. We do not mention the above privileges to allure you into this neighbourhood, if you can do better in any other. . . . .

Though having met with many difficulties, as it is natural to expect the first years, we now increase our stock every year. Within the last four years, upwards of 100 families have come to our neighbourhood, and 100 more may get a comfortable livelihood here. Should any of you be disposed to come over here, we would advise you to consult the captain of the vessel with respect to victuals that will be necessary for your voyage, with a sufficient quantity of bread, water, salt, meat, potatoes, oatmeal, and malt liquor.

After landing in *America*, many sorts of people will be met with; some will say this is the best place, and some another. All who are acquainted with our nation know it is easy to impose upon a *Welchman;* therefore, we would advise them to be upon their guard. They who have families would do well to get a waggon immediately after their landing, and remove all their goods out of the ship into it, and convey them to the place of their destination without delay. If they come hither (though they abide not), it will be cheaper for them to leave their families with us until they can find a place to their satisfaction, than in the cities, which in the summer are unhealthy to strangers, but the country round is as healthy as any part of *Wales*. Should any of the poor be disposed to come, and not able to bear the expense of their voyage, if their friends be able to assist them, and can depend on their faithfulness, they will not be long here before they are repaid with thankfulness. . . . .

(Signed)

THEOPHILUS REES<br>WILLIAM JENKINS<br>REES LLOYD<br>SIMON JAMES, etc.

### 7. French Immigrants in the Wilderness[1]

A certain association, called the Scioto Company, proposed at Paris in 1790, with much parade, the sale of some lands in the best part of the United States, at 120 cents an acre. They dealt out the most liberal promises and charming prospects, such as people are generally accustomed to offer on these occasions:

[1] "Gallipolis, or the French Colony at Scioto." Extract from C. F. Volney, *A View of the Soil and Climate of the United States of America*, translated by C. B. Brown (Philadelphia, 1804), pp. 322–30. For an interesting account of Volney's American adventure, see H. T. Tuckerman, *America and Her Commentators* (New York, 1864), pp. 97–107.

A climate wholesome and delightful, frost, even in winter, almost entirely unknown, and a river called, by way of eminence, the *beautiful*, and abounding in excellent fish, of a vast size. Noble forests, consisting of trees that spontaneously produce sugar (*the sugar maple*), and a plant that yields ready-made candles (*myrica cerifera*). Venison in plenty, the pursuit of which is uninterrupted by wolves, foxes, lions, or tigers. A couple of swine will multiply themselves a hundred fold in two or three years, without taking any care of them. No taxes to pay, no military services to be performed.

These munificent promisers forgot to say that these forests must be cut down before corn could be raised; that for a year at least they must bring their daily bread from a great distance; that hunting and fishing are agreeable amusements, when pursued for the sake of amusement, but are widely different when followed for the sake of subsistence; and they quite forgot to mention, that though there be no bears or tigers in the neighbourhood, there are wild beasts infinitely more cunning and ferocious, in the shape of men, who were at that time at open and cruel war with the whites.

In truth, the market value of these lands, at that time, in America, was no more than six or seven cents an acre. In France, in Paris, the imagination was too heated to admit of doubt or suspicion, and people were too ignorant and uninformed to perceive where the picture was defective, and its colours too glaring. The example, too, of the wealthy and reputedly wise confirmed the popular delusion. Nothing was talked of, in every social circle, but the paradise that was opened for Frenchmen in the western wilderness; the free and happy life to be led on the blissful banks of the Scioto. At length Brissot[1] published his travels, and completed the flattering delusion; buyers became numerous and importunate, chiefly among the better sort of the middle class; single persons and whole families disposed of their all, flattering themselves with having made excellent bargains at a crown an acre, because in France, near Paris, good ground was worth above eighty or a hundred crowns. Each one set off, in his own time, from some French port, in the course of 1791, and Paris heard no more of these adventurers.

On my arrival in America, in October, 1795, I made some enquiry after these people, but could only hear a vague story that they were

[1] [Jacques Pierre Brissot de Warville, 1754–1793, who visited the United States in 1788 and published an account of his travels in 1791, *Nouveau voyage dans les États Unis de l'Amérique Septentrionale, fait en 1788* (3 vols.) English translations were published in Dublin in 1792, London in 1794, and Boston in 1797. In 1919 it was reprinted in the "Great American Historical Classics Series."]

buried somewhere in the western wilds, and had not prospered. Next summer I shaped my course through Virginia, and after travelling three hundred miles to Staunton, two hundred more over a rugged desert to the Great Kenhawah, and sixty miles down that river, through a scene still more dreary and desolate, to the Ohio, I at last reached a village called Point Pleasant, four miles from Gallipolis; by this splendid appellation (which means *French city*) the emigrants denominated their settlement. My eagerness to see the face and hear the language of my countrymen, once more, made me hasten thither without delay.

Colonel Lewis, a kinsman of General Washington, facilitated my journey. I went on, but reflecting that I was going to visit Frenchmen disappointed in their dearest hopes, their vanity mortified, and their mortification likely to be aggravated by the sight of one, who had probably foretold their misfortunes to some of them, my impatience was greatly diminished. It was night-fall before I reached the village, and I could perceive nothing but a double row of small white houses, built on the flat top of a bank of the Ohio, which here laves the foot of a cliff fifty feet high. The water being low, I climbed the bank, by a slope formed in its side, and was conducted to a log house called an inn. It was kept by a Frenchman, who asked me but few questions, and his demeanour evinced the truth of all my prognostics.

Next day I took a view of the place, and was struck with its forlorn appearance; with the thin pale faces, sickly looks, and anxious air of its inhabitants. They were shy of conversing with me. Their dwellings, though made externally cheerful by whitewash, were only log huts, patched with clay, and roofed with shingles, consequently damp, unwholesome, and uncomfortable. The village forms an oblong quadrangle of two rows of contiguous buildings, which a spark would consume altogether. This, with many other faults, they owe to the negligence of the company. Adjoining these huts are gardens, fenced with thorn, destitute of trees, but well stocked with useful vegetables. Behind these gardens runs a creek, nearly parallel to the river, which makes the site of the town nearly a peninsula. This creek, at low water, shows a bottom of black mud, and the overflowings of the river run up this creek, and spread themselves over some pestiferous marshes. Southeast lies the broad expanse of the river, but in front and to the north there appear nothing but interminable forests. . . . . I collected from several persons the following history of their disastrous expedition.

About five hundred mechanics, artists, and tradesmen, in easy circumstances, and of good morals, arrived in 1791 and 1792 at New York, Philadelphia, and Baltimore, from France. Each paid twenty or twenty-four guineas passage money, and their journeys by land, in both hemispheres, cost them an equal sum. Thus dispersed, without any common plan of operations, they made, separately, their way towards Pittsburg and the Ohio, where their new home was situated. After many mistakes on the road, and a great waste of time and money, they reached a point, marked out upon a map, where the company had erected barracks for their accommodation. This company soon after became bankrupt, failing in its payments to the Ohio company, the original proprietors. These, of course, not deeming themselves bound by the engagements of their debtors, refused the land to the emigrants. A vexatious lawsuit was the consequence, the more distressing to them, as their money was now exhausted. The United States were at war with the Indians, who disputed the right of the former to this very district. After the defeat of St. Clair, the savages blockaded the poor Frenchmen in their settlement, made captives of four, and scalped a fifth, who survived this dreadful operation.

Despondency overwhelmed them: some of them forsook the fatal spot, and withdrew into the country better peopled, or passed into Louisiana. At last, after four years of dangers, hardships, and vexations, the poor remnant obtained a tract of 912 acres, for a new advance of 1,100 dollars. This *boon* they owed to a son of General Putnam, who benefited them in a still more signal and disinterested manner, by refusing 1,200 dollars offered by two Frenchmen, with a view of getting the whole into their own hands, and then extorting an exorbitant price from their companions.

They were again fortunate in receiving, from the Congress of 1795, a gratuitous present of 20,000 acres, opposite Sandy Creek. This bounty was the more remarkable, because the animosity against France, which broke out the next year, began already to prevail in that assembly. Of this land, 4,000 acres belonged to those whose activity had promoted the gift, and the rest was distributed among eighty-two or eighty-four persons who remained.

When I paid my visit, only a year had elapsed since this arrangement had been made, and the settlement had already begun to revive and prosper, in such a manner as showed what great things would have been effected, had not its progress been checked by such heavy misfortunes. Still the situation of the colonists was far from being agreeable. All the labours of clearing and tillage were imposed on the family itself of the proprietor, labourers not being to be hired but at enormous prices. It may easily be imagined how severe a hardship it was, on men brought up in the ease and indolence of Paris, to chop trees, to plough, to sow, to reap, to labour in the field or the barn, in a heat of 85 or 95 degrees. . . . .

Such is the condition of the Scioto colony, which does not altogether realize the pictures of the inland paradise given by American farmers, nor the glories of the future capital of the Ohio and its realms, predicted by a certain writer. . . . .

I wished to leave this settlement with a persuasion that they were doing well and would prosper; but, besides the original and incurable error in the choice of situation, I am afraid that their despondency will never be entirely removed, since there will always be some cause for it, and since the French nation are less qualified for settling a new country than the emigrants from England, Ireland, or Germany. Among fifteen instances of farms, cultivated or formed by Frenchmen, which were mentioned to me in America, only two or three were likely to thrive. As to collecting men in villages, such as Gallipolis, those that have been formed on the frontiers of Louisiana or Canada, and have been left to shift for themselves, have generally dwindled, and sooner or later disappeared; while plain men, from the British Isles or Germany, who have pierced the heart of the forest with their families only, and even ventured alone into the Indian territory, have generally made good their footing, and have prospered and multiplied.

### 8.   Emigration from England in 1816[1]

Great alarm seems to be felt in England, on account of the disposition to emigrate manifested by all ranks of the community. The middling orders, endeavoring to save something from the wreck of their fortunes, are collecting in various parts of the country with a view to *exportation;* nay, we have heard, that three villages, or what we in Ireland, perhaps, might call handsome country towns, have had meetings sufficiently open when the plan of emigration was regularly discussed, and the practicability of its accomplishment unanimously admitted. As they were principally small farmers, agricultural pursuits were those which occurred to them; but as they were aware of the extraordinary value of labor in America, they felt this circumstance as a serious impediment to their project. It was then proposed to article a certain

[1] Extract from the *Dublin Evening Post*, June 8, 1816, reprinted in *Niles' Weekly Register*, X (August 17, 1816), 408.

number of laborers out of employment for two years, with their passage free, at a reasonable salary. When it was known to the common people, the difficulty was not in the engagement but in the selection of objects. However, determined to do nothing unadvisedly, they chose two delegates, one of them being their curate, to go to the seat of the American government to make the proper inquiries, and to pave the way for the young colony. The deputies are now actually on their voyage.

It is no wonder that such an event as this should excite alarm. In itself, perhaps, it is of no great consequence whether 800 or 1,000 individuals remain or depart from the country; but it is its *example*. If it should become systematic, and while distress and taxes continue, there is every danger that it may become so—there is no conjecturing where it will terminate. The trading towns, or we should have said, the towns which were once the scenes of trade and business, will assemble next—and we feel persuaded that the only impediment presented to the tide of population in its westerly course, will be the difficulty of transportation, and want of adequate means to support the intermediate period of the voyage.

We shall here insert a letter from our correspondent, which we received yesterday. It is on this very extraordinary impulse which the times have communicated to the people of England:

LONDON<br>Monday Night

We are sorry to learn, that the emigration from this country to America rather increases than diminishes. The most of our ships in the West Indies, it is stated, have been deserted by the seamen, who have been tempted to try their fortunes in America, insomuch that all the ships that have recently sailed for the West Indies, have been almost doubly manned, in order to fill up the vacancies abroad, and to get to England the homeward-bound fleet.

We say nothing of the sailors, for they *are* blamable in deserting their allegiance; but can the people, as some shallow men pretend, be blamed for flying from misery and destruction? It is not denied that the most horrible distress prevails in England. We shall give a few paragraphs from the London papers of Monday, which, if proof were wanted, affords most melancholy evidence of the fact.

Several hundred persons have recently been discharged from the iron works and mines, in the neighborhood of Wellington, Ketly, Coalpit, Bank, Ironbridge, etc., in consequence of the depressed state of trade. At Wellington, in particular, the distress of the lower orders is very great. On Sunday sen'night the town was literally crowded with persons out of employ, many of whom in vain applied to the recruiting parties.

Who can blame these men if they wish to go to America, where they are sure of getting employment—of being well paid for their labor—of sleeping well, and of eating well? No one, surely, except the inconsiderate. But, unfortunately, people in the condition of these laborers often leave their families behind them, a burden to the parish. The following is an extract from a London journal on the subject:

Numbers of the laboring poor who have applied at the different sessions for certificates to enable them to go to America, have been wicked enough to leave behind them their wives and children to be supported by the parishes from which they have fled.

How hard this is upon the remaining occupants it is not necessary to say. They can scarcely support themselves. "It is incredible," says the *Globe*, "in the small provincial towns throughout England, what a number of decent and respectable families have sunk through the distresses of the times. and the enormous weight of taxation, into bankruptcy and obscurity."

Such is the state of the country, and such are the people whom the well-fed hirelings blame for a wish to change the glorious and expensive constitution of England, for the rude but plentiful democracy of America.

But it is not to America alone that emigrants betake themselves. By the following paragraph it should seem, that the Russian government are offering tempting baits to the wretched artisan.

There is a report, of the accuracy of which we do not pretend to judge, that measures have been taken to induce many of our artisans to go to Russia. Certainly the Russians have recently had extraordinary opportunities of obtaining information respecting everything particular, both in the machinery and management of British manufactures.

### 9. Letters from Emigrants to Friends and Relatives in England[1]

MANCHESTER, IN VIRGINIA
May 7th, 1818

DEAR FATHER AND MOTHER:

. . . . Since I engaged with Mr. Ball, I have been offered considerably more, to go to the West; but I'll not go till I know whether brother Thomas will come or not. My hope is that he will, for his own good. I wish you all were here. If a man be industrious and steady, he reaps the fruit of his own labour.

---

[1] Extract from J. Knight, *Important Extracts from Original and Recent Letters Written by Englishmen, in the United States of America, to Their Friends in England* (2d series, Manchester, 1818), pp. 7–8, 20–28, 41–44

The people here are the most hospitable I ever saw. Do not let want of money stop you, for I will furnish the sum you need, be it what it may; and I will find you work plenty. . . . .

From your affectionate son,

G. PLATT

CHARLESTON
8th March, 1818

DEAR FRIEND:

. . . . I hope you will come over as I did, and I dare say you will be able to send for your wife, in three months. Never mind landing here without money, as we all got work before we left the vessel. The sooner you come the better; you will never repent. Here are all the particulars I know.

I am yours, &c.,

JOHN REDFERN

GERMANTOWN
August 13th, 1818

DEAR MOTHER:

I write to say we are all in good health, and hope this will find you so. . . . . Tell my brother John I think he would do very well here; my husband can go out and catch a bucket of fish in a few minutes; and John brings as many apples as he can carry, when he comes from school; also cherries, grapes, and peaches. We get as much bread, as we can all eat in a day, for seven pence; altho' it is now called dear. Dear mother, I wish you were all as well off as we now are: there is no want of meat and drink here. We have a gallon of spirits every week; and I have a bottle of porter per day myself, in short, I have everything I could wish. . . . . Tell little Adam, if he was here, he would get puddings and pies every day. Tell my old friends I shall be looking for them next spring; and also tell my brother John and sister Ann, if they were here, they would know nothing of poverty. I live like an Indian Queen. . . . . Manufacturing is improved; weavers can get 31s. 6d. per week; children, nine or ten years old, get 6s. 9d., and from 12 to 13, 9s. in the factory where my husband works. Wm. Latham is the manager of a carpet manufactory and has £2 14s. a week. Respects to all enquiring friends.

Your affectionate daughter,

ALICE BARLOW

PATERSON, NEW JERSEY
4th May, 1818

DEAR SIR:

. . . . Here is abundance of fruit. Apples are about four-pence per peck. . . . . Now we get beef and pudding, tea and rum pretty regularly; to us, who have long been half-starved in England, it appears like a continual feast.

. . . . No fawning, cringing adulation here: the squire and the mechanic converse as familiarly as weavers do in England. We call no man master here.

It is very distressing to hear that my old neighbours are working for six or eight shillings a week, while we murmur at thirty or forty.

I hope this will find all my old friends in good health, though I know it will find many of them poor. Tell them I should like to see them all here. I remain yours, &c.,

DANIEL RIDGEWAY

PHILADELPHIA, 2nd November, 1817

DEAR BROTHERS AND SISTERS:

. . . . They say things are bad here, but I think they are good indeed. I have seen many from England; some have been here two and others three weeks, and got employ at from 10 to 14 dollars per month besides lodging and board.

. . . . The land is rich indeed, and every industrious farmer may become a freeholder of the United States, by paying eighty dollars, being the first instalment for a quarter of a section of land; and though he has not a shilling left, he may easily gain as much off the land, as will pay the other instalments, before they become due. The land being his own, there is no limit to his prosperity; no proud tyrant can lord it over him; he has no rent to pay; no game, timber, or fishing laws to dread; few and small taxes to pay; no excise laws to harrass him; no tythe nor poor's rate; so that the farmers are prosperous and happy. May the father of the human race pour down abundant blessings upon the authors and finishers of such a benevolent system. James has got rid of the English yoke, and is working at £2. a week, and paying 13s. 6d. for board and lodging. For breakfast he has coffee, beef, mutton, bacon, potatoes, butter, bread, pickles, &c., &c., and the rest of his living is as good. . . . .

Yours, &c.,

MATTHEW FARRAR

PHILADELPHIA, 4th June, 1818

MY DEAR FAMILY:

To answer all your doubts in as few words as possible, if you come hither, I can by my own labour (mind you) procure all the good that this world affords in eating, drinking, or clothing; and not work above ten hours a day. For heaven's sake father do come and end your days in a country, where the labouring bee enjoys the honey which he collects. Brother David you must come hither, if you ever mean to do good for your family. Brothers Peter and Thomas, do contrive to come, as soon as possible. Brothers William and Thomas, you never can do better than come hither: there are not many finishers who can do good work. My sister Betty and your Ann, would almost keep the family by trimming. Betty and Mary Ogden got work the second day after landing. My dear sister Susy, come and be happy in this land of plenty. If Sally Whitehead was here, she would easily get three dollars a week with winding. Give my love to your brothers and sister, and tell them, I believe if they came hither, they would never repent it. Tell Thomas McDonald, they dress much better here than with you; I never hear of clemming here. George Platt says to David Garlick, I deserve hanging for writing about this country as I have done; but ask him whether the drone, or the working bee, deserves hanging worse. When you come . . . . bring plenty of bedding, looking-glasses, copper kettles and bellows. . . . . Tell Dr. Wild, he might enjoy his rum and coffee, and never light a candle the year round if he was here. My love to every neighbour and friend.

JONATHAN JACKSON

CARMI, WHITE'S COUNTY, ILLINOIS STATE, NORTH AMERICA
25th September, 1818
DEAR MOTHER:

I now sit down in a country, where fortune is within my reach. I suffered a little for want of money, but I now look beyond all that. . . . . Lands such as you never saw, which you may use for three years, and then it wants no manure. I have purchased one hundred and sixty acres, on a fine level plain, where there is not a tree to be seen, they are always covered with grass. Coins are sometimes found in sinking wells, a proof it has been inhabited. There are a great many thousand of acres of these lands in these parts. I intend purchasing eighty acres of woodland, then I shall have two hundred and forty acres.

These two hundred and forty acres, sown with Indian corn, will produce from sixty to a hundred bushels per acre, suppose we take the average at seventy, that upon the whole will be sixteen thousand eight hundred, which sells at $\frac{3}{4}$ of a dollar per bushel, and very scarce at that price. Perhaps you may think this strange, but if you were here you would not think so, for the people will not work; they can live with the greatest ease and don't want to be rich; but they who come here and are industrious, make great fortunes in a short time. The inhabitants cultivate very little land, but live principally on hunting, and breeding cattle and hogs; this is done with the greatest ease, they being surrounded by land possessed by no one, where the cattle and hogs feed very fast without trouble or expense. . . . .

You will please to notice, that this letter has no reference to the Atlantic States, there, everything is quite reversed: people had better stay at home than go there. I have travelled two thousand miles into the interior of America, where every European must come to do himself good. The people here want me to take the Oath and become an American, but I will not, unless you will come, then I shall have no objection; the people here are very benevolent and obliging to Englishmen. Now my dear mother, I want you to send me word that you, my brothers and sister will come after me: this would be the most joyful news I could receive; a hundred pound would bring you all comfortably.

I never experienced such health before, I am getting quite fat.

If you cannot consent to come, let my brothers come, and we can, in about five years, get money enough to return and live comfortably.

Yours, &c.,

N. B. Although the Editor has been favoured with the original letter; yet he has been desired to suppress the writer's name.

WHEELING, VIRGINIA<br>April 10th, 1818

DEAR BROTHER:

. . . . This is the country for a man to enjoy himself: I do not mean Virginia, but Ohio, Indiana, and the Missouri Territory; where you may see prairies 60 miles long and ten broad, not a stick nor a stone in them, at two dollars an acre, that will produce from seventy to one hundred bushels of Indian corn per acre: too rich for wheat or any other kind of grain. I measured Indian corn in Ohio State, last September, more than fifteen feet high, and some of the ears had from four to seven hundred grains. I believe I saw more peaches and apples rotting on the ground, than would sink the British fleet. I was at many plantations in Ohio where they no more knew the number of their hogs than myself. . . . . And they have such flocks of turkies, geese, ducks, and hens, as would surprise you: they live principally upon fowls and eggs: and in summer upon apple and peach pies. The poorest family has a cow or two and some sheep: and in the fall can gather as many apples and peaches as serves the year round. Good rye whiskey; apple and peach brandy, at forty cents per gallon, which I think equal to rum. Excellent cyder at three dollars per barrel of thirty-three gallons, barrel included.

There is enough to spare of everything a person can desire; have not heard either man or woman speak a word against the government or the price of provisions.

The poorest families adorn the table three times a day like a wedding dinner—tea, coffee, beef, fowls, pies, eggs, pickles, good bread; and their favourite beverage is whiskey or peach brandy. Say, is it so in England?

If you knew the difference between this country and England you would need no persuading to leave it and come hither. It abounds with game and deer; I often see ten or fifteen together; turkies in abundance, weighing from eighteen to twenty-four pounds. The rivers abound with ducks and fish. There are some elks and bears. We have no hares, but swarms of rabbits: the woods are full of turtle doves, and eight or nine kinds of wood peckers. Robin red-breast about the size of your pigeon.

Your affectionate,

SAMUEL CRABTREE

FORKS OF WHEELING, February 10th, 1818
FALLS OF SCHUYLKILL, March 9th, 1818

DEAR BROTHER:

I wish all that are related to me, would try America: surely it becomes every father to have a tender regard for his offspring: and what poor man in England, can leave his family (without remorse), exposed to enormous rents and taxes, and every necessary of life at an enormous price: when ¾ of their earnings must go to support a lewd, luxurious, arbitrary race of tyrants who style themselves Governors: this country is infinitely preferable to such a place.

Here a man may get land for two dollars per acre, not burthened with taxes—his neighbours will raise him a house (good enough for the Prince Regent) in two or three days for a sup of whiskey—then they will let him have horses, cows, and hogs, at a very moderate price; and on credit if required. I allow people cannot run to the store or shop here, in a few minutes for every trifle: but they can grow their own wool, and manufacture it into comfortable raiment—In short the following stanza is very applicable to us.

> Let the wealthy and great,
> Roll in splendor and state,
> I envy them not, I declare it:
> I eat my own lamb,
> My own chickens and ham,
> I shear my own fleece and I wear it.

Siddalls cannot come too soon: 'tis pity Sunderland did not come with us: there is plenty of land such as he never saw at two dollars per acre. You pay eighty dollars on entering a quarter section (160 acres) eighty more at the end of two years—eighty more the third year—and at the end of the fourth year, the last eighty dollars; and during these four years the land is not subject to any kind of tax.

The Gentleman we board with bought a barrel of cyder (32 gallons) for three dollars, the empty barrel could not be worth less than one. A man has full scope for his industry and ingenuity here, without being checked by excise officers. He may make his own soap, candles, and sugar. Grow his own barley, wheat, oats, rye, Indian corn, apples, and peaches. He may brew good ale, or distil whiskey, or both, without being infested by those *birds of prey;* yea, he may powder his head as white as snow, without being annually taxed a guinea.

You may print as much of this as you please—my respects to my father, mother, wife, children and friends.

SAMUEL CRABTREE

WASHINGTON, July 24, 1818

DEAR BROTHER, &c.:

There is plenty of work for mechanics of all sorts here, and the general price for labour is a dollar per day, and some a little more. Farmers give so much, and meat and lodging—young women may have good places and good wages: our daughters could all have engaged almost as soon as they landed, with Quakers and people of rank—It was soon noised in the town, that there was a great family arrived, and the captain spoke so well of us, that they invited us to dinner. . . . .

Yours,

J. ROWLEY

ALEXANDRIA, 22nd July, 1818
DEAR PARENTS:

. . . . J. Rowley got work for himself and sons at Washington: and his daughters were wanted by great numbers: chiefly Quakers I believe. He has done much better in coming hither, than he would have done at New York or Philadelphia. There are so many emigrants arriving there, that it is impossible for all of them to get work. We spoke a vessel from Waterford, with more than 300 on board for New York. . . . .

Yours, &c.,

R. WILLIS

NEW YORK, 27th March, 1818
DEAR BROTHER:

Accept my thanks for helping my family out of the pinfold. We are in good health and doing well. Any industrious person may do well here. Money is scarce, but we get plenty of all the blessings of life. I have placed my family 40 miles W. of this city, in a pleasant and healthy situation, in a good, large brick house, with three acres of land—a number of good apple trees, and a garden. Rent £10 a year. . . . .

I keep a store or exchange house: my neighbours are wealthy farmers. What they want I bring from New York, and in exchange take their produce. . . . . I do not get much money, but it affords me a good living and will make a handsome property in a short time, as I make handsome profits and can live cheap.

I can pasture a cow for ten pence a week and rise in the morning when I please: no factory bells to call one up at half-past four o'clock.

In this country the rich don't call the industrious people the "Swinish multitude." The judge of the district, the justice of the peace, and the parson of our parish, are all pleased to pay, and receive visits from us.

Anyone may do well here, no matter what his trade be: if one does not do, another will. I never enjoyed the comforts of life so much as at present. I have a good stomach and plenty to eat. When children are born they are called blessings here, and not their deaths as in England.

There are poor people here, but no hungry children crying for bread in vain, they have all enough and to spare. This is the promised land, flowing with milk and honey.

If an honest man is set naked on the American shore, he may soon make an independence. 'Tis the duty of those who have a number of children to place them where they can get a living—this is that place.

I feel for all my acquaintance, inform them I will assist those of them who will come. Poor people live as well as the rich; they work when they please, and where they please. I wish my mother was here. Good fortune has attended me ever since I left England. My son James goes a hunting and shooting, and I can eat partridge as well as any knave in England. I remain, dear brother, your well-wisher,

LUKE BENTLEY

## 10. The Opportunities of a Farmer in Illinois[1]

November 22, 1817 . . . . Now that I am settled down, having reached the point I aimed at on starting, and which seemed continually to recede as we advanced, I again take up my pen. You and our other friends have probably wondered at our having proceeded so far west. . . . .

I am so well satisfied with the election we have made, that I have not for a moment felt a disposition to recede. . . . . Society we shall not want, I believe; and with the fear of that want every other fear has vanished. The comforts and luxuries of life we shall obtain with ease and in abundance: pomp and state will follow but too quickly. . . . .

I have built a temporary dwelling on my intended settlement, and have spent some time there. This has made me better acquainted with

[1] Extract from Morris Birkbeck, *Letters from Illinois* (Philadelphia, 1818), pp. 17–28, 34–37, 49, 85, 146–52.

Morris Birkbeck was born in England and died in Illinois in 1825. He was an English farmer, who emigrated to America in 1817 and first published, in 1817, *Notes on a Journey in America*. The publication of the *Letters* followed in 1818. With the help of his associate, George Flower, who, like Birkbeck, had been a well-to-do English farmer and had money to invest in western lands, an English settlement was founded in Edwards County, Illinois. For an interesting history of the colony, see George Flower's account in *Chicago Historical Society Collections*, Vol. I, an extract from which will be found in Section II of this volume, p. 230.

Birkbeck's *Notes* and *Letters* were widely read and were the subject of much controversy. Many English emigrants found their way to his settlement, although later "travelers" attempted to discourage emigration by publishing their less favorable accounts of life on the Illinois prairies.

One of Birkbeck's critics, W. Faux (*Memorable Days in America, 1818–20*, p. 298) said, "No man since Columbus has done so much toward peopling America as Mr. Birkbeck, whose publications, and the authority of whose name, had effects truly prodigious; and if all could have settled in Illinois whom he had tempted to cross the Atlantic and the mountains, it had now been the most populous state in the Union. America, and the western country generally, are benefited by and indebted to him."

our situation; and as farther knowledge confirms and increases my favourable view of it, my communication may have its use. I would not persuade or invite anyone to follow us, but I wish my friends to know that my undertaking proceeds to my entire content. . . . .

The power of capital here is great almost beyond calculation: the difficulty seems to be in the choice of objects, out of the various ways of doubling and redoubling it, which present themselves to the enterprizing. These I do not much attend to; my line is land and cultivation. My intended settlement is a square of a mile and a half each way, containing 1,440 acres. I made an estimate a few days ago for my own government merely, of the amount required for my establishment on this estate, on a liberal plan, which I shall copy faithfully, without altering an item. This will enable you to compare the situation and prospects of a farmer in England with those of a proprietor in Illinois, at the outset.

As to the annual profits here, I am not yet prepared with data for a very particular statement. The price of wheat may be reckoned at three shillings and fourpence sterling per bushel, and of beef and pork at two pence per pound. The land is fertile and easy of tillage; the wear of ploughshares almost nothing, as they require sharpening by the smith but once a year; and we shall have labourers in plenty, at a price not much exceeding that of England; putting horse labour and man's labour together, they will be quite as cheap. Then we have no rent, tithe, or poor's rate, and scarcely any taxes, perhaps one farthing per acre.

But omitting the annual income, about which I know enough to feel no anxiety, let us consider that at the end of fourteen years, when we may suppose the lease of the most favoured English farmers to terminate, a stock of various kinds, of great value, will be accumulated by the proprietor here; the worth of his estate, in the regular course of improvement, will be increased to the amount of 6 or 8,000£, and no *renewal* wanted; also, that the capital required by the English farmer of such an estate, is at least double to that required by the Illinois proprietor at the outset of the undertaking. . . . .

November 24, 1817. I have now been an inhabitant of this place more than four months; my plans of future life have acquired some consistency; I have chosen a situation, purchased an estate, determined on the position of my house, and have, in short, become so familiar with the circumstances in which I have thus deliberately placed myself and family, that I feel qualified to give you a cool account of my experiences, of the effect of this great change of condition on my mind, now that I may be supposed but little under the influence of the charm of novelty, or the stimulus of pursuit. . . . .

I have not for a moment felt despondency, scarcely discouragement, in this happy country, this land of hope! Life here is only *too* valuable, from the wonderful efficiency of every well-directed effort. Such is the field of delightful action lying before me, that I am ready to regret the years wasted in the support of taxes and pauperism, and to grieve that I am growing old now, that a really useful career seems just beginning. I am happier, much happier, in my prospects, I feel that I am doing well for my family: and the privations I anticipated seem to vanish before us.

We shall have some English friends next summer; and a welcome they shall experience. But if not one had the resolution to follow the track we have smoothed before them, we should never wish to retrace it, except perhaps as travellers. As to what are called the comforts of life, I feel that they are much more easily obtainable here than they have ever been to me; and for those who are to succeed me, I look forward with a pleasure which can only be understood by one who has felt the anxieties of an English father.

I expect to see around me in prosperity many of my old neighbors, whose hard fare has often embittered my own enjoyments. Three of them have already made the effort, and succeeded in getting out to us. This delights us, but we have by no means depended on it; joyful as we are at the prospect of giving them an asylum.

Two more are waiting at Philadelphia for an invitation which is now on its way. . . . .

I have just read a statement of five hundred emigrants per week passing through Albany westward, counting from the first of September. This occurred on *one* road.

I sat down to write to you under an impression that you would be deterred, and might be prevented from following us, by difficulties, some real and serious, others not so; and I thought it might be useful to you, as I knew it would be pleasant, to find that I am satisfied as to my own undertaking. It is for this reason that you are treated with so much about myself. I wish I could put you in possession of *all* my mind, my entire sentiments, my daily and hourly feeling of contentment: not that *you* would be warranted thereby to place yourself and family along side of mine. . . . .

November 30, 1817 . . . . I have secured a considerable tract of land, more than I have any intention of holding, that I may be able to accommodate some of our English friends. Our soil appears to be rich, a fine black mould, inclining to sand, from one to three or four feet deep, lying on sandstone or clayey loam; so easy of tillage as to reduce the expense of cultivation below that of the land I have been accustomed to in England, notwithstanding the high rates of human labour. The wear of plough-irons is so trifling, that it is a thing of course to sharpen them in the spring once for the whole year. Our main object will be live stock, cattle, and hogs, for which there is a sure market at a good profit. Twopence a pound you will think too low a price to include a profit; but remember, we are not called upon, after receiving our money for produce, to refund a portion of it for rent, another portion for tithe, a third for poor's rates, and a fourth for taxes; which latter are here so light, as scarcely to be brought into the nicest calculation. You will consider also, that money goes a great deal farther here, so that a less profit would suffice. The fact is, however, that the profits on capital employed any way in this country are marvellous; in the case of live stock the outgoings are so small, that the receipts are nearly all clear.

The idea of exhausting the soil by cropping, so as to render manure necessary, has not yet entered into the estimates of the western cultivator. Manure has been often known to accumulate until the farmers have removed their yards and buildings out of the way of the nuisance. They have no notion of making a return to the land, and as yet there seems no bounds to its fertility.

For about half the capital that is required for the mere cultivation of our worn-out soils in England, a man may establish as a proprietor here, with every comfort belonging to a plain and reasonable mode of living, and with a certainty of establishing his children as well or better than himself—such an approach to certainty at least as would render *anxiety* on that score unpardonable.

Land being obtained so easily, I had a fancy to occupy here just as many acres as I did at Wanborough; and I have added 160 of timbered land to the 1,440 I at first concluded to farm. I shall build and furnish as good a house as the one I left, with suitable outbuildings, garden, orchard, &c., make 5,000 rods of fence, chiefly bank and ditch, provide implements, build a mill, support the expenses of housekeeping, and labour until we obtain returns, and pay the entire purchase money of the estate, for less than half the capital employed on Wanborough farm. At the end of fourteen years, instead of an expiring lease, I or my heirs will probably see an increase in the value of the land, equal to fifteen or twenty times the original purchase.

In the interval my family will have lived handsomely on the produce, and have plenty to spare, should any of them require a separate establishment on farms of their own.

Thus I see no obstruction to my realising all I wished for on taking leave of Old England. To me, whose circumstances were comparatively easy, the change is highly advantageous; but to labouring people, to mechanics, to people in general who are in difficulties, this country affords so many sure roads to independence and comfort, that it is lamentable that any, who have the means of making their escape, should be prevented by the misrepresentations of others, or their own timidity. . . . .

January 7, 1818 . . . . I *own* here a far better estate than I *rented* in England, and am already more attached to the *soil*. Here, every citizen, whether by birthright or adoption, is part of the government, identified with it, not *virtually*, but in fact; and eligible to every office, with one exception, regarding the Presidency, for which a birthright is necessary. . . . .

February 2, 1818 . . . . We are waiting with some impatience for the season of commencing our farming operations. The horses are ready, and the ploughs and harness in a state of forwardness. We hope to begin work in March, and to be settled in May. Farming will be as good a business here, I think, as in England, with this difference, that instead of paying rent for our land, our land will pay rent to us, by its increasing value. There are a few other circumstances of difference with which you are acquainted, regarding tithes, taxes, and poor-rates. . . . .

March 24, 1818 . . . . We are in a good country, are in no danger of perishing for want of society, and have abundant means of supplying every other want.

But I am sorry to inform you that our plan of colonizing extensively, with a special view to the relief of our suffering countrymen of the lower orders, is not at present successful. A good number may be benefited by the arrangements we are making for their reception on a contracted scale; but the application to Congress, alluded to in my journal, which was calculated principally for the service of that class, has, I fear, proved abortive. I have transmitted to Congress, through the hands of our member for Illinois, the following memorial:

*To the Representatives of the United States in Congress assembled, the Memorial of Morris Birkbeck, an English farmer, lately settled in the territory of the Illinois, respectfully states:*

That a number of his countrymen, chiefly yeoman farmers, farming labourers, and rural mechanics, are desirous of removing with their families and their capital into this country, provided that, by having situations prepared for them, they might escape the weariness and expensive travel in quest of a settlement, which has broken the spirits and drained the purses of many of their emigrant brethren, terminating too frequently in disappointment.

Many estimable persons of the classes above mentioned have reposed such a degree of confidence in the experience of your memorialist, as would attract them to the spot which he has chosen for himself. Their attention has accordingly been directed with some anxiety to his movements; and when after a laborious journey through the states of Ohio and Indiana, he has at length fixed on a situation in the Illinois adapted to his private views, settlements are multiplying so rapidly around it, that it does not afford a scope of eligible unappropriated land, to which he could invite any considerable number of his friends.

There are, however, lands as yet unsurveyed lying about twenty miles north of this place, on which sufficient room might be obtained; and the object of this memorial is to solicit the grant by purchase of a tract of this land, for the purpose of introducing a colony of English farmers, labourers and mechanics.

Feeling, as does your memorialist, that the people of England and the people of America are of one family, notwithstanding the unhappy political disputes which have divided the two countries, he believes that this recollection will be sufficient to insure, from the representatives of a free people, a favourable issue to his application in behalf of their suffering brethren.

Morris Birkbeck

. . . . Other petitions for grants of land in favour of particular descriptions of emigrants have been rejected during this session, for reasons which my friends give me to understand will be fatal to mine.[1] The following I consider to be the tenor of these objections:

That no public lands can be granted or disposed of but according to the general law on that subject, without a special act of legislation.

That although in certain cases such special acts have been made in

---

[1] [The question of public policy involved in land grants or land sales to foreign "colonies" on special terms instead of under the general law is discussed in an interesting letter from Thomas Jefferson to George Flower, who was Birkbeck's associate in establishing the "English Colony" in Illinois (*Chicago Historical Society's Collections*, I, 77–79.)]

favour of bodies of foreign emigrants, it has always been on the ground, and in consideration of, a *general public* benefit accruing; such as the introduction of the culture of the vine by the Swiss colony at Vevay, Indiana, and the olive in Louisiana.

That it is not agreeable to the general policy of this government to encourage the settlement of foreigners in distinct masses, but rather to promote their speedy amalgamation with the community of American citizens.

And that all such grants are liable to be abused by speculators for private emolument.

. . . . It would be sufficient for our purpose that certain lands, which are not yet surveyed, and of course unproductive, might be opened to us as an asylum, in which English emigrants *with* capital might provide for English emigrants *without* it. The title of these lands might remain in the United States until the purchase should be completed by actual settlers, paying the price on entry.

The nationality in some particulars which might be retained by such a settlement, would not surely be found to weigh against its usefulness. When it is considered that the men with capital who emigrate as farmers are republicans to the core; that to such men, and the sons of such, the republic whose protection they now solicit, owes its existence—what is this nationality? is it not American in its essential qualities?

The poorer order of emigrants from England, what they have of politics is of the same cast; but the ignorance, the nullity, of a great proportion of the *rural* English population on these subjects, is wholly incomprehensible in this country.

Humanity, interest, necessity, will call for the interference of the general government on behalf of those unfortunate persons who are cast destitute on the eastern shores, and on behalf of those cities and states which are burthened by them. But their countrymen, themselves citizens of the United States, or becoming so, would anticipate this interference, and crave permission to provide for them on some unappropriated spot.

## 11. Words of Caution to Prospective Immigrants, 1819[1]

As for general emigration, I imagine, by the time I reach England, it will have begun to subside. The voice of disappointment will cer-

[1] Extract from E. Howitt, *Selections from Letters Written during a Tour through the United States, in the Summer and Autumn of 1819* (Nottingham, 1820), pp. 215-18.

tainly have risen above that of wild and romantic adventure, and made itself heard. At present, it is the height of folly. Such is the present state of things here, that neither farmers nor mechanics can succeed: the vast number of sheriffs' sales, are a sufficient proof of this. The country is inundated with the vast torrent of emigration, that has been flowing into it; and . . . . the new arriver must be content to penetrate far into the wilderness, and undergo fatigues, expense, and hardships, which he can badly estimate by his fireside.

The tide of emigration, like that of the ocean, must ebb as well as flow, and this is the ebbing period; but, if such be the distress of England, and so gloomy its prospects, that emigration is (to anyone) an object of desire, I would certainly advise them to remove hither rather than to a new colony. The pioneers of civilization, those who advance first into an untrodden desert, and begin the work of culture and population, ought to be schooled to the office by a suitable education; they must be inured from childhood to a rude and desultory life, to every inconvenience of poverty and irregularity of climate, to struggle against difficulties which would daunt, and amidst sufferings which would destroy all besides. The towns-man, the mechanic, and even the farmer, accustomed to regularity of life, must, in such a situation, become a wretched object, and, most probably, the victim of his change of habits. But here, at least, they may find some degree of civil security, and may fix themselves on a track which has felt the first efforts of civilization, and is still in the verge of society: but it must be *the distressed* alone, who can hope to find alleviation here. There may be some who may improve their situations. Farmers, of considerable capital, who, by purchasing a track that will supply their families with food, and reserve a portion of that capital, to procure clothes and other necessaries, may live comfortably, and look forward to an increasing value of their estates. Mechanics, whose superior skill or good fortune, may meet with profitable employ; but the state of trade and glut of emigration, both preclude the possibility of the majority securing to themselves situations which will counterbalance the difficulties and hardships they will certainly find: amongst these, the impositions of the older inhabitants are not the least. The old American (or Yankee) looks with the most sovereign contempt upon the emigrant: he considers him a wretch, driven out of a wretched country, and seeking a subsistence in his glorious land. His pride is swelled, and his scorn of the poor emigrant doubled, not merely by this consideration, but by the prevailing notion that but few come here who have not violated the laws of their native realm.

If a word is said of one returning, "Oh (says the Yankee), he'll none return: the stolen horse will keep him here."

With their insatiate thirst of gain, and these contemptuous notions of emigrants, they seem to consider them fair objects of plunder; and are prepared, in every transaction, to profit by their ignorance of the value of their goods, the custom and laws of the country, and the character of the people. Whoever comes here, should come with his eyes and ears open, and with the confirmed notion, that he is going to deal with sharpers. If he is not careful in purchasing necessaries for his inland journey, he will pay ten-fold for them; and when he is there, withou᷉ equal caution, he will be liable to purchase land of a squatter: that is, a man who has taken possession of it, cultivated it without any title, and is subject to be ejected every day by the legal owner. With this, the evils of the banking system are to be taken into the account. I have stated, in a former letter, the causes which tend to bind a purchaser to the soil, and make him a pauper and a slave upon it; add to this, the extremes of heat and cold, the tormenting and disgusting swarms of vermin.

## 12. Emigration Conditions in Germany and Switzerland, 1820[1]

After the re-establishment of peace in 1815 a vigorous revival of the emigration spirit was noticeable. This movement was a result of that discontent, that dissatisfaction among all classes, existing in various quarters.

Another factor in the emigration movement was that the people were obliged to adopt economies and unaccustomed savings of all kinds which in turn paralyzed industry and greatly increased the distress of the lower classes in the hard year of 1817. The result was

[1] Extract translated from Ludwig Gall, *Meine Auswanderung nach den Vereinigten Staaten im Frühjahr 1819 und meine Rückkehr nach der Heimath im Winter 1820* (Trier, 1822), Vol. I, pp. 11–24.

In addition to the references in the documents and accompanying footnotes in this volume, other references dealing with German emigration will be found in the excellent bibliography of Albert B. Faust, *The German Element in the United States* (Boston, 1909), Vol. II; Ernest Bruncken, "Germans in America," *Annual Report of the American Historical Association for the Year 1898*, pp. 347–53; Ernest Bruncken, "Political Refugees in the United States, 1815–16," in *Deutsch-Amerikanische Geschichstblätter*, III, 33–48 and IV, 33–59; T. S. Baker, in *Americana Germanica*, I, No. 2, pp. 97–102; Gustav Körner, *Das deutsche Element in den Vereingten Staaten von Nordamerika*, 1818–1848 (2d ed., New York, 1884); Anton Eickhoff, *In der neuen Heimath* (New York, 1884).

the general spread of the opinion that parts of Germany and Switzerland suffered from overpopulation.

Under these conditions it appeared to be clear that the unemployed poor would no longer be in a position to earn bread even at the lowest price, and that in such circumstances every year of crop failure must bring unusual sufferings to the poorer classes. A large number of people must therefore seek for relief either in creating quite new sources of employment or in emigration.

How very widespread was this anxiety concerning the means of subsistence is shown by the fact that according to the public press the stream of emigration which, in the course of the year 1818, had led nearly 30,000 persons down the Rhine past Mainz, did not appear to diminish during the following year. The scarcity of the year 1817 was not the sole cause of this emigration, for otherwise emigration activity would have ceased when the scarcity came to an end in September, 1817.

After all, discontent seems to have been the most active cause of emigration. By this I do not mean a discontent with the new order of things and with the measures of the gove.nment that have been so often supposed to exist among the people. For did not the stream of emigration flow most freely from Würtemberg and from Switzerland, the lands where everything either remained as of old or where changes generally recognized to be for the better had taken place. No, I mean that discontent with one's lot which was a consequence of the sudden deprivation of commodities which people had come to look upon as necessaries. . . . .[1]

As signs of a generally felt need and with the stamp of truth two

[1] [Gall's account of the emigration movement during this period is substantially that adopted by Wolfgang Menzel in his *Geschichte der Deutschen*, which was originally published in 1824–25. Thus Menzel wrote of the revival of emigration after 1815 as follows: "But it was not until after the wars, more particularly during the famine in 1816 and 1817, that emigration across the sea was again carried on to a considerable extent. In 1817, thirty thousand Swiss, Würtembergers, Hessians, and inhabitants of the Palatinate emigrated, and about an equal number were compelled to retrace their steps from the sea-coast in a state of extreme destitution on account of their inability to pay their passage and of the complete want of interest in their behalf displayed by the governments. Political discontent increased in 1818 and 1819, and each succeeding spring thirty thousand Germans sailed down the Rhine to the land of liberty in the far west." See translation, 4th German ed. (London, 1849), III, 447–48. See also the interesting account of the emigrations of this period in the later history of Franz Löher, *Geschichte und Zustände der Deutschen in Amerika* (2. ausg. Göttingen, 1855), pp. 253–58.]

publications appeared which painted with fresh colors the horrible picture of the sufferings of the unemployed poor and of the emigrants who were in need of guidance. . . . . One of these publications[1] contained a letter from J. J. Mayersohn in St. Gall to the royal Prussian consul in New York, Herr J. W. Schmidt, as follows: "In consequence of the complete unemployment and unexampled dearness of the necessaries of life, we have in Switzerland, especially in the cantons of Glarus, Appenzell, and St. Gall, such misery as I cannot describe to you. In spite of all means of help, people are dying by the thousand from hunger and want of every kind and a great number, both of those who have means and of those who are without means, wander to Russia and America. From various quarters I have been asked to give information as to how men, whether with or without property, who wished to go to the United States must set about it in order to maintain safely a shelter and means of subsistence for themselves by labor and industry. Therefore you would do a real service, especially to my countrymen who in such numbers have the desire to emigrate thither, to describe the ways and means of emigration. For example, what state offers the most advantages to the Swiss? To those who support themselves with agriculture and to those who have been engaged in cattle-raising or in the manufacture of muslin or cotton and linen? What can they expect in America? From whom can they get advice? And what should those who have property take with them?

"It is obvious that the working classes can no longer multiply on this soil according to the wishes of their nature, and the unemployed man will no longer be able to undertake the support of a family. Almost every week we read credible accounts of hundreds (Swiss and German) who through their inexperience have become the easy prey of deceitful enlisting officers and dishonest ship captains. Some languished in Holland. Many were destroyed on ship board through want and by infectious diseases. Others came back home in the most pitiable condition, and of those who lived to see the longed-for shores of America, the promised land of their anticipation, how many found there only new misery and greater loneliness. . . . ."

The second of the publications referred to appeared under the title *Der Deutsche in Nordamerika* and contained the elaborate reports of Herr von Fürstenwärther on the fate of the Germans emigrated to the United States and what the immigrant must expect.

---

[1] *Zuverlässige Nachrichten über die Vorbedingungen unter welchen Auswanderungen nach den Vereinigten Staaten von Nord Amerika ohne Vermessenheit versucht werden dürfen.*

Minister von Gagern,[1] who published this book with an introduction, added the following concluding words: "These migrations, in spite of the discouraging news and incidents of the past year, were not entirely discontinued this year. Emigration always will return as something natural in Germany, for we are suffering from overpopulation, while the millions of fertile acres and homesteads in North America which still await the plough and human hand are limitless. While we have this degree of overpopulation, the statesman must regard a gentle and continuous streaming off of the classes with too small properties as something undoubtedly desirable, as a movement likely to increase immensely domestic tranquility. Simultaneously and without attracting attention the value of man—his hand and work— also increases at home. In this way we improve and populate our earth more quickly than would otherwise be possible in the old world and also in the new."

### 13. Emigration for Political Reasons[2]

In the year 1815 I, the youngest of five brothers, at the age of fifteen, joined the army. We were all volunteers; two of us had been in the earlier campaign, four in the last, and all were wounded. I received at Namur two very dangerous wounds, from which I slowly recovered in the hospitals on the Rhine, long after the establishment of peace. With my mind very much excited, which my youth and soldierly life easily explains, I returned to Berlin and joined the Turners. In 1819 I was arrested, together with Doctor Jahn. Among my papers several foolish and absurd political essays were found, but nothing to convict me of participation in criminal acts or as a member of secret societies. After four months' imprisonment I was liberated and informed that I had not been found guilty of any punishable act, but that I could not be matriculated in any Prussian university and could never receive an appointment under government. In other German universities I was also prevented from entering, with the exception of Jena, where I remained some time and then went to Dresden to

---

[1] [For an interesting account of the mission undertaken by Moritz von Fürstenwärther for his kinsman Baron von Gagern, see an article by Max J. Kohler, in *Deutsch-Amerikanische Geschichtsblätter*, XVII (1917), 393–415.]

[2] Extract taken by permission from *The Life and Letters of Francis Lieber*, edited by Thomas Sergeant Perry (Boston: James R. Osgood and Company, 1882), pp. 156–60. The extract is taken from Lieber's petition to the Prussian king for a pardon.

study surveying. When the insurrection of the Greeks broke out I resolved to join the Philhellenes, having had sufficient opportunity to convince myself that in Prussia no career was open to me. I went to Greece, and returned in 1822, first going to Rome, where one of the best and most distinguished men of our time took an interest in me— Mr. Niebuhr. . . . . When Mr. Niebuhr returned to Germany I accompanied him as far as Innsbruck. How great was my grief when, on my arrival in Berlin, I found that I was still suspected by the police. Under these circumstances I thought it best to go at once and freely to his Excellency Mr. Von Kamptz, and to inquire whether or not I might remain peaceably in Prussia. Mr. Buttman, to whom I had brought a recommendation from Mr. Niebuhr, strengthened me in this purpose. His Excellency received me with great kindness, and he caused a ministerial order to be issued to the effect that I should no longer be molested unless I gave new occasion for investigation. Notwithstanding this promise I was once more arrested. No real accusation was made, but I was required to give evidence against a certain Major von Fahrentheil, whom I had visited at Erfurt before I went to Greece. Although the little I knew amounted to nothing but idle gossip, the idea was so abhorrent to me that I might destroy the happiness of a high-standing officer, a husband, and father of many children, that I stubbornly refused to give any information with regard to this visit. This was the only charge made against me since my return from Greece, nor had I held any unlawful communication, either by letter or deed, with anyone.

My benefactor, Niebuhr, received a call to Berlin as Councillor of State, and came to see me in Köpenick, where I was imprisoned, as may be seen in his published letters.

Soon after this I was released, and proceeded to Mecklenburg, where I passed the summer in the house of Count Bernstorff, as tutor and friend to his sons. On my return to Berlin dark clouds again gathered around me, examinations followed each other closely, and a third imprisonment seemed unavoidable. I felt my courage breaking under this endless condition of mistrust, which I seemed powerless to prevent, and thus, with the most profound regret and in bitter tears, I left Berlin to escape from Prussia and from the circle of her influence. I fled to England. In London I had hard and sad days. . . . . I remained a year in England, and went from there to the United States where I hope I have not dishonored the Prussian name.

## 14.  The Attractions of Pioneer Life in Missouri[1]

As soon as the emigrating family has reached the site of the new home [in the West], a halt is made and a fence is built where the buildings are to stand. . . . . The choice of a place for the house is determined especially by the neighborhood of a good spring or a brook. Over the spring a small building is at once erected partly to protect it from impurities and partly to preserve the milk, butter, and meat in a cool place.

The next labor is now the building of a dwelling-house. . . . . The trunks of the trees are felled in the vicinity and dragged thither by horses or oxen. The house is erected with the help of the neighbors if there are not hands enough in the family. But not more than four or five persons are needed for the erection of a dwelling of this sort. . . . .

When the building is completed, and this requires scarcely more than two or three weeks, the family already feels at home; and the next thing on the schedule is to prepare the arable land for agriculture. Usually a man begins by fencing the chosen tract of land in order to use it first as a closed pasture for horses and oxen which one wishes to keep for use nearby.

Nothing can be more erroneous than the European conception of

[1] Extract translated from Gottfried Duden, *Bericht über eine Reise nach den westlichen Staaten Nordamerika's und einen mehrjährigen Aufenthalt am Missouri (in den Jahren 1824, 1825, 1826, und 1827) in Bezug auf Auswanderung und Uebervölkerung* (2. ausg.; Bonn, 1834), pp. 75–109.

Duden's *Bericht* appeared first in 1829 and went through three editions in 1829, 1834, and 1853. His somewhat too favorable account of pioneer life is supposed to have given impetus to German emigration in the thirties of the last century, but the political disturbances served, of course, as an additional and important stimulus. T. S. Baker in the *Americana Germanica*, I, No. 2, p. 62, gives a very interesting account of this period under the title "America as the Political Utopia of Young Germany." Writing of Duden, he says, "It was Duden who, in a time of universal discontent and uncertainty, directed the attention of the German masses to the Western parts of the American Union, which were being settled just at that time." Mr. Baker thinks that the romantic and poetic side of the book "made it all the more attractive to the minds of the readers, and when it is remembered that Duden was supposed to be a thoroughly trustworthy man—a man who had enjoyed a university education, had served creditably in the army, and had occupied important positions in the Prussian civil service, the attention which his utterances attracted does not seem strange" (pp. 66–67). Later, when the immigrants who reached Missouri found that Duden's descripiton of pioneer life failed to give an adequate picture of its hardships and difficulties, he was called "Duden der Lügenhund."

The *Bericht* is written in the form of letters to a friend in Germany.

the hardships of converting the forest land into arable land. Even Volney speaks of four years being needed to clear a small field. In criticism of all the descriptions that have been written I merely mention that here, where day labor is paid at the rate of 62½ cents, the whole work on a single field (160 square perches) does not come to more than the small sum of $6, or 15 Dutch gulden. . . . .[1] The uprooting of the trees is not to be thought of. Such an undertaking would be laughed at here. Only shrubs and bushes are cleared away by the roots. . . . .

Large trees are never cut down. Only trees of one foot or less in diameter are felled, and they are cut so low that the stumps do not disturb the ploughshares. All large trees are merely killed, that is, girdled, cut around into the wood. As a result of the girdling most of them die in about fourteen days so that they draw nothing more from the soil and also no longer shade it. . . . .

The cold weather very seldom interrupts the outdoor work for more than two consecutive days. Even in January the weather is not always unfavorable for cutting out the underbrush. The winter cannot be very severe in a place where horses, cows, pigs, not to mention the youngest calves, winter without stables. . . . .

As long as the settler does not have sufficient meat from the domestic animals, the hunting grounds keep him in provisions. Flesh of the domestic animals is, to be sure, not dear here; a pound of ox flesh costs only 1½ cents, and pork, 2 cents (3 kreutzer). But there are so many deer, stag, turkeys, hens, pigeons, pheasants, snipes, and other game that a good hunter without much exertion provides for the needs of a large family. Throughout the whole United States, hunting and fishing are entirely free, and in the unenclosed spaces anyone can hunt when and how he pleases, small as well as large game, with dogs, nets, slings, and rifles.

There are two varieties of deer here in Missouri, and they are for the most part very fat. The meat is savory, but the hunter seldom takes the whole animal with him. He is satisfied with the hind quarters

[1] [Duden added a footnote to the 1834 edition of the *Bericht*, saying that this statement had been declared to be untrue and it had been claimed that the cost was two or three times the amount he had indicated. In reply he said he could do no more than pledge his honor and his name in support of the truth of this statement, and he refers to his reputation in the Rhine district, where he had served twelve years as a magistrate, in support of his veracity. This, he thought, should be accepted as a guaranty that no selfish motives would induce him to jeopardize the welfare of his fellow-countrymen.]

and the skin, and hangs the rest of the animal on a tree so that some one else can take home a roast if he wishes. Wild turkeys are found in droves of twenty to fifty. They are especially fat toward Christmas. I have my neighbor deliver some to me every week, especially for soups, for I am not a good hunter. These turkeys must weigh at least 15 pounds or the hunter would not even take them home with him. I pay 12½ cents a piece for them.[1] The bison is no longer to be seen. He has moved farther to the west and north. Bears are still seen occasionally, and I hear wolves howling almost every evening. Yet the sheep wander about here without a shepherd, and the farmer suffers as little from wild animals as from robbers and thieves. However, there are complaints that toward the end of April and the middle of May the young pigs are endangered by the she wolves who are rearing their young. . . . .

The garden is provided with the best European kitchen vegetables. Peas and beans flourish beyond all expectations, and only the finer kinds of beans are seen. In order to avoid either poles or a special bed, it is customary to sow them in the corn fields where the high cornstalks serve the rows of beans as a support. In the same fields are also sown pumpkins, lettuce, and many other things. All these things flourish simultaneously in the rich soil without the least manure after twenty years as well as in the first years. I protest that there is no exaggeration in this statement and that I have thoroughly convinced myself of its truth. . . . .

Every year there are, in abundance, cucumbers and melons—watermelons, which the French call *pasteques*—and also the melons which are known in Germany and which are here called muskmelons. And, let it be understood, these are raised without any cultivation. A good fruit for the household is also the potato—here called "sweet potato." The common potato is called the "Irish potato." Sweet potatoes demand a long summer, and in Germany would not develop properly. Cooked in steam with a little water they taste like the best chestnuts. I enjoy them greatly in the morning with my coffee. The plants run over the ground like cucumbers.

In the second year cotton will also be raised, although north of

[1] [Duden appended here the following footnote]: "Board and lodging is to be had here for one dollar a week. Usually this includes also the free maintenance of a horse. Such an abundance also explains the hospitality which prevails in most families. Where there is a house, one can always find shelter and entertainment and rarely will a farmer take payment from a fellow countryman—let alone ask for it. . . . ."

Missouri only for family needs. It is the special aim of the American farmer to provide food and drink and also clothing, except special finery, without paying out any money for such things. For this reason, also, flax and hemp are raised and a small flock of sheep maintained. These products are entirely worked up in the household. The spinning wheel is found everywhere; and if there is no loom in the house, the housewife or one of her daughters from time to time goes to a neighbor who has one of these implements. Just as most of the men understand shoemaking, so most women make not only their own but their husband's clothing—and pretty well according to the changing demands of fashion.

After the household is once organized in this fashion and the first necessaries supplied, then the whole family lives carefree and happily without a single piece of ready money. . . . . For taxes alone is ready money needed. But these taxes are so unimportant that one scarcely thinks of them. Land acquired from the government is entirely tax free for the first five years. . . . .

From this sketch, the average lot of the planters here may be judged, and you may decide for yourself what is still needed for the comfort and well-being of the settlers. . . . .

If the planter has two slaves, he can confine himself entirely to duties of inspection without laying his own hand to anything; and the housewife will have just as little to complain of in the work of the household. There is a superfluity of food at hand. Beer also can be easily brewed since hops enough are found in the woods. The apple and peach orchards, which no estate is without, give cider and brandy. Although a very good brandy is also made from corn, yet the brandy from apples and peaches is preferred. I have bought old corn brandy at 30 cents a gallon which came up to the best French brandy.[1] Meanwhile even without slaves the farmer lives in a situation which is infinitely superior to that of a German farmer of the same property. The soil is so productive that the corn crop demands nothing but a mere breaking of the soil, a single ploughing. . . . .

Preparation for the next sowing requires the removal of the corn-stalks of the previous harvest. These are either cut down, mostly by children, or broken down, then piled together with a harrow and

[1] In all American inns French brandy is found which is unadulterated but for the most part colored too dark. A drink of this with sugar and water costs usually about 12½ cents. Ice is added to it here in the summer, especially in the seacoast cities where it serves as an addition to beer. . . . .

burned. The man who has no harrow makes use very simply of a bunch of branches drawn by one of the horses.

For the sowing of the wheat, rye, and oats less work is likewise required than in Europe. These crops to be sure suffer much from weeds. But an ample supply of land, which does not need to be so carefully used, makes up for this, and European methods of care would here be wasteful of human strength. . . . .

Finally I must meet the erroneous opinion that the difficulty of social intercourse is a dark side of the boasted condition of the American settler; one must get rid of this idea that a complete separation from one's neighbors is involved and one must remember that a distance of two or three English miles here is negligible even for the women folk. No family is so poor that it does not have at least two horses. Everyone directs his first efforts to securing these animals which are maintained here at so little expense. The next thing is a good saddle, and it is nothing unusual to expend $24 to $30 for a lady's saddle (a sum that would indeed cover three of them on the Atlantic coast, for example, in Baltimore, where saddles are cheaper than in Germany). Women and girls, old and young, ride without any difficulty. . . . .

May 10, 1826

Last autumn I received the money sent me from Europe, and I decided . . . . in the spring to build upon my own plantation. And this is what I have done. Toward the end of March the plan had succeeded so far that the new estate appeared to be ready for occupancy. I had already become so familiar with the American mode of life that I did not hesitate a moment to move in with my two horses, dogs, and cows. . . . . Everything is well fenced, and the field has been prepared for cultivation in the usual way. . . . .

In the meadow is a beautiful spring, which has withstood the great dryness of the past year and over which I have had a protecting shelter built. The way from the dwelling to this spring is a shady walk formed by high oaks, ashes, walnuts, and sassafras trees. The branches and beautiful foliage of the white walnut trees droop like a weeping willow from its splendid height almost to the ground. In front of the dwelling house a shady roof is formed and in a garden, some steps away, melons, cucumbers, and other kitchen vegetables are sprouting. . . . .

My mode of life is as follows: At sunrise I go out in the open, usually with a gun. I roam about for perhaps an hour, shooting partridges, pigeons, or squirrels, and also turkeys—which I can do better with a rifle—and then turn to eat my breakfast. After breakfast I take my books in hand, and I added an unusually large number of books to my baggage, packed in small boxes with locks. I then busy myself as peacefully with the sciences as I ever did in Germany. Shortly before dinner I put them down and wander in the garden or to the spring and after dinner I go for a ride, either to visit the neighbors, or alone in the woods, on the heights, and in the valleys, delighting in the beauties of nature. How far this can be called life in the wilderness you may judge by the fact that I recently allowed the neighboring planters to build a schoolhouse on my land and also by the fact that the newspapers from St. Charles and St. Louis always arrive on the second day after they are printed.

### 15. German Immigrants Ask Assistance to Come as "Redemptioners," 1827[1]

It will be seen by the following extract of a letter from the American consul at Rotterdam to Gov. Troup, that the services of Germans of honesty, sobriety, and industry, can be had on good terms for any purposes of agriculture, manufactures, or internal improvement. Men of capital might make them useful and profitable in either of those departments of industry in different sections of our country; and, their manners, habits, and character qualifying them for free government, they and their posterity would become valuable members of our community, as they have proven themselves in other states of the union.

UNITED STATES CONSULATE, ROTTERDAM, 21st April, 1827

SIR: I had the honor of addressing your excellency on the 17th inst., inclosing therewith copies of letters received from a most respectable gentleman residing in the kingdom of Würtemberg, and expressive of the prevailing distress raging amongst its subjects, and that in order to maintain tranquillity, and the internal peace of the government, passports were readily granted them for their emigration to any foreign country, provided they make known their intention thereto in their respective districts.—And as the German character is well known for industry, sobriety, and honesty, thus I beg leave to recommend the subject to your excellency's notice and further support, inasmuch as those who wish to go to Georgia, will ultimately become settlers and an acquisition to our state—Many of them, unfortunately have not the means of paying their passage over to the United States. To any who would advance these they would engage their services and time, say for two years—

[1] Extract from the *Georgia Journal*, reprinted in *Niles' Weekly Register*, XXXIII (September 1, 1827), 5.

The expenses of the Germans bound from this for any port in the United States, are estimated at about $40 per person, including their sea-stores. This amount was paid for all those shipped last year for Baltimore.

I have the honor to remain, your excellency's most respectful and obedient servant,

E. WAMBERSIE.

## 16.  Emigration Conditions in Certain English Counties[1]

[From the testimony of E. J. Curteis regarding emigration from Sussex]:

*Are you of opinion that the labourers in Sussex, who find themselves permanently out of employ, would be disposed to emigrate to any part of the British colonies abroad, provided they were convinced that they would obtain a subsistence and acquire a degree of independence as the result of such emigration?*—I am satisfied they would, to a great extent; I cannot persuade them to enlist in the naval or military service, by any inducement, but they all have an inclination to go abroad; the parishes frequently encourage them to go by an advance of money, but they very often return; I should think about one fourth of those who have emigrated with the assistance of the parish, have returned again; and the parishes are now unwilling to contribute, lest they should not get entirely rid of the paupers in consequence of their returning.

*How much money have the parishes advanced in cases of that kind?*— I think they have gone as far as thirty and forty pounds, to get rid of families.

*For a family of what number?*—A man and a woman, and five or six children; they go to the United States of America. I should say about one person in four returns, after having gone, finding that he must work when he gets to America; the object is idleness, or rather an expectation of gaining a livelihood more easily than in this country.

*Are you of opinion that in the event of the labourers being disposed to emigrate, the parishes would be disposed to mortgage the poor-rates, in repayment of the whole or part of the sum advanced for the purpose of emigration?*—I think certainly.

*You have stated to the Committee, that a great proportion of the emigrants, who have gone to the United States, have returned and become again chargeable to the parishes?*—Yes.

*Are you of opinion that it would be desirable, in case of any extended assistance being granted to emigration, to pass an Act depriving those emi-*

[1] Extract from Great Britain, *Minutes of Evidence before Select Committee on Emigration from the United Kingdom, 1826,* pp. 114–16, 132–35.

*grants who partake of such facilities of the claims they legally have on the support of the parish?*—I think it would be a very salutary act, and the people who should emigrate would have no inducement to return; they must then exert themselves when they were once abroad, knowing it would not avail them to return. . . . .

[Communication from a farmer in East Sussex, read by E. J. Curteis]:

I conceive the subject of emigration to be deserving of the most serious attention of government, and likewise of a great many parishes, and particularly in this part of the country. Unless we can be relieved of the surplus labourers, the consequences in a short time must be dreadful; nearly every parish in this part of the country has a large surplus of labourers, with an immense increase following very close. The great cause of this has been by the over indulgence of the magistrates towards the poor.

I have about eighty labourers in my own employment, and I can safely say their earnings are as follows: sixty of them from 13s. to 14s. per week; the remaining twenty men inferior, from 10s. to 11s. per week,[1] as we have a considerable surplus doing little or nothing; but our wish is to keep every man from the poor-rate, not having more than three children not able to work. I must here too observe, that the difficulty of raising money to pay for labour and the support of the poor in this neighbourhood, is greater than ever I remember. . . . .

[From the testimony of T. L. Hodges regarding emigration from Kent]:

*Are you able to inform the Committee as to the state of pauperism in the district immediately adjoining your residence in Kent?*—In that district of the county where I live, called the Weald of Kent, there is in almost every parish, and has for several years past been, a considerably larger number of people than the agricultural demands require; the consequence of that has been, the parishes are in considerable distress, the poor-rates are enormously high, and these people are obliged to be employed on the roads; the bad effects of that I need not enlarge upon; in consequence of this, the only possible way by which at present these parishes can relieve themselves is by promoting emigration, and the tide of emigration from that county is now setting to New York. . . . .

*Is the Committee to understand that pecuniary facilities have been given to aid the parties in the emigration?*—They have.

*What sum has within your knowledge been advanced for the removal of any emigrant pauper?*—The expense of a recent emigration, only a

---

[1] Notwithstanding these wages are paid, I could easily reduce the whole to 10s. per week.

week since, has been at the rate of 13£ 10s. per head for grown persons, including all costs and charges.

*Can you describe the manner in which that 13£ is expended?*—Seven pounds the passage money, in American ships, the regular New York packets, from the London docks; 3£ 10s. provisions; two sovereigns in money given to each person, to be in his pocket on landing at New York; of the remaining sum, I think 4s. 6d. is for fees paid on landing at New York, and a few shillings expenses of carriage up from that part of Kent to London. . . . .

*Have you the means of informing the Committee what is the annual average expense of those paupers who have been sent from the parishes within your knowledge to the United States?*—No, I am not able to state that; I could state it if they were a whole year out of employ; but some of those persons might be out of employment for nine months perhaps and get employment for three at some lower rate of wages, which is the case probably with the greater part of them. I have got some parish returns, showing the number of persons out of employ in that country; I think they give men of this description from 7s. 6d. to 8s. a week, that would be about 20£ a year.

*The expense of a pauper supported by the parish rates during the whole year would be 20£?*—Yes, that sum at least.

*Would that be the expense of a man and woman?*—He would be expected to maintain his wife for that.

*Are you of opinion that the parishes would be disposed to avail themselves of any facilities for the purpose of effecting the emigration of those paupers to any British colony?*—I have no doubt whatever of that fact; in short I have made inquiry throughout several parishes lately, and I found them all most desirous of having the opportunity.

*Are you disposed to think the paupers themselves would be glad to avail themselves of those facilities?*—In the present mode of relieving that country by emigration to New York, the paupers are exceedingly thankful to be so removed from this country; I saw a letter yesterday from one man, thanking the parish for what they had done for him; and hoping that some day or other he should be able to make them a return; I mention it to show that it is not at all compulsory (of course there can be no compulsion); they are exceedingly desirous of being sent. If therefore they are so desirous of being sent in this direction, government must offer them inducements in another quarter, or they will not go. If a prospect of removal to Canada does not hold out advantages, such as they know they can secure to themselves immediately in the United States, I fear it would be very difficult to persuade any of them to go. I think if land was offered them, and assistance for a period till they could get their crops, that would be a temptation that would induce them to go at once. . . . .

*From the town of New York, or the part of that country in which they are settled?*—From the place in which they are settled. In one parish where I made inquiry last Tuesday, I was informed that the reports constantly arriving from the persons who went from that parish contain the most favourable accounts of their welfare; and almost all the labourers of the parish are constantly pressing the overseers to send them there.

*Do you know what part of the state of New York they are gone to?*— To the county around the city of New York, and particularly Albany. . . . . In the parish of Smarden, two or three years since, fifty-two men, women, and children emigrated to New York; of this number twenty-seven were sent at the expense of the parish, the other twenty-five went at their own charges. The reports constantly arriving from them contain the most favourable accounts of their welfare, so much so that almost all the labourers of that parish are desirous of going to America. The method adopted by the parish of providing the means of sending the above twenty-seven persons was by borrowing a sum of money from an individual residing in the parish and repaying it out of the rates by installments of 50£ every half year, until the whole was paid off, which is now the case.

## 17. Emigration Proposed for Scotch Weavers

### A. HOUSE OF COMMONS, DECEMBER 5, 1826[1]

Lord A. Hamilton presented a petition from the Weavers of Glasgow, and of the county of Lanark, representing their extreme distress, and praying for relief. . . . . Many of them, they said, were without any employment at all. . . . . They said that most of them had worked for fourteen or sixteen hours a day, and at the end of the week earned only six, five, and some as little as four shillings and sixpence. That he also knew to be the fact. It was further stated by the petitioners, that in consequence of their necessities they were destitute of decent clothing, and were thereby prevented from attending divine service. . . . . The families of weavers were crying to them for bread, which they were unable to give: how then was it possible that they

[1] Extract from *Hansard's Parliamentary Debates*, Vol. XVI (2d series, 1826–27), cols. 227–29.

could afford clothes? He knew many worthy and honest men among the weavers, who lamented this circumstance, with reference not only to the present calamity but to the evils which it would entail upon their offspring, whom they could not send either to schools for education, or to places of divine worship, and who would therefore lose every opportunity of becoming imbued with those right principles which alone could safely guide them in their progress through life. He declared that he had not overstated the case of by far the larger portion of the petitioners. The prayer of the petition . . . . did not ask for charity; but, feeling their utter helplessness and hopelessness, the petitioners asked for that which was the punishment of crime—exile: they asked for the means of emigrating from their native land. That of itself spoke volumes as to the actual sufferings which they were enduring. . . . . The Glasgow and Strathaven weavers had associated themselves, under the notion that they would be permitted to go out in a society. The bonds of affection and the ties of kindred would not then be severed, and the pain of separation from friends, from country, and from the early associations of life, would be mitigated. But he feared that such an arrangement, however, in some respects desirable, could not be made.

### B. HOUSE OF COMMONS, DECEMBER 7, 1826[1]

Sir James Graham said he was sorry to find that they [the ministers] were ready to see thousands of their fellow countrymen . . . . exiled from their native land. The system of emigration was contrary to the spirit of our laws, and opposed to many of our most ancient regulations. He admitted, that it was necessary to do something to relieve the distresses under which so many of our artisans were at present sinking. . . . . He could state to the House, that the hand-weavers did not at present receive more than 5s. a week; for which sum they laboured fourteen hours a day. They were most of them a year's rent in arrear, and were therefore liable not only to have that small portion of their property which remained unpledged, sold to defray the claims upon them but to be ejected from their tenements. Their diet was of the humblest description, oatmeal and potatoes, and their whole appearance showed that they were reduced to an extremity of want. In fact, there were thousands and tens of thousands of them on the verge of starvation at that moment. He was not going to examine

[1] Extract from Debate on Petitions from Glasgow and Calton in favor of emigration, *Hansard's Parliamentary Debates*, Vol. XVI (2d series, 1826–27), cols. 299–302.

into the causes which had led to this distress; but he believed that one, and perhaps the chief, was placed beyond the reach of parliamentary interposition: he alluded to the improvements which had been recently made in the power-looms. The hand weavers could not be converted into power-loom weavers, and they were thus compelled to continue a hopeless struggle with power-loom weavers, at a rate of wages which was regularly decreasing. Under these circumstances, some special remedy ought to be applied by the government to the distresses of the country. He thought they were so great as even to justify a grant of public money to relieve them. . . . .

Secretary Peel said . . . . when it was recollected, that an expense of 20£ was to be incurred for each emigrant, it could not be expected that the excess of the population could be sensibly relieved by emigration. One might, however, see an advantage in supplying the waste lands in the North American provinces with an active population, inasmuch as it would create an increased demand for British manufactures. There would also be, in his opinion, a great advantage to the colonies by encouraging emigration upon a large scale, even though it might not mitigate the distress of the mother country. . . . .

Mr. Benett contended, that it would be better to put the waste lands of England into cultivation, than to send our population abroad to engage in similar employment. The waste lands of England would long since have been cultivated, had it not been for the embargo of tithes and taxation which was laid upon them. He thought it extraordinary that, at a time when we had eleven millions of acres ready for cultivation, we should send our population at the expense of 20£ a man, to cultivate the woods and deserts of Canada. He believed that nothing was wanted in Ireland but the security of life and property, to rescue the waste lands of that country from their present uncultivated state. If life and property were rendered secure in that country, English and Scotch capital would soon flow in. . . . . If the prayer of the numerous petitions which the hon. member for Aberdeen had presented should be granted, the House would have a number not only of manufacturing but also of agricultural labourers, praying to be banished from their country. He trusted, however, that both classes of labourers would soon find employment in their native country, and would long remain in it, adding to its wealth, and increasing its resources.[1]

[1][A manufacturer of Carlisle testifying before the Select Committee on Emigration from the United Kingdom, 1827 (*Minutes of Evidence*, pp. 281–82), said that, although his weavers asked only to be sent to Canada, "My impression is, that if

## 18.  Emigration Conditions in Ireland, 1824–26

### A. FROM THE TESTIMONY OF THE REVEREND MICHAEL COLLINS[1]

*Has any plan occurred to you by which these occasional famines could be relieved; any general plan of providing for the poor?*—I conceive the great cause of scarcity and distress is, that there is nothing to draw off the surplus population from exclusive dependence on the soil for support; they must consequently look to the land alone for the means of employment. The land proprietors have taken up an opinion latterly, that the cause of their distress is the overstocking the land with people; and as the leases fall in, they get rid of the surplus population by turning them out entirely from their lands. Those poor people, not getting employment, either erect temporary habitations like sheds on the highway, or they come into towns, and crowd themselves into small apartments; perhaps four or five families will live in a garret or small hovel, huddled together there, without clothes or bedding, or food, living upon the chance of employment in the town as labourers. That employment they cannot procure. It is only three weeks or about a month ago, that I saw on an estate, to which I alluded before, a certain farm that had forty families residing on it, thinned in this manner.

*What was the extent of it?*—I suppose it might be 500 acres, including the bad land; a great deal of bad land upon it. Those forty families consisted of 200 individuals. When the lease fell in, in pursuance of the general system adopted amongst the landlords, twenty-eight or thirty of those families, consisting of 150 individuals, were dispossessed; they were allowed to take with them the old roofs of the cabins, that is, the rotten timber and rotten straw; and with those they contrived to erect sheds upon the highway. The men could get no employment, the women and children had no resource but to go to beg; and really it was a most affecting scene to behold them upon the highway, not knowing

---

they were sent to Canada, their object would be to go to the United States; they are generally the best and the steadiest workmen who wish to leave the country. . . . . If sent to Canada, some might settle there as agricultural labourers; but I think, with the majority of them, their object would be to go to the United States." One petition referred to had been signed by 65 heads of families, but the witness said: "I saw some of them, and they said if there had been time the numbers would have been doubled. They see no prospect of any termination to their sufferings, but on the contrary the last reduction makes them consider their case hopeless."]

[1] Extracts from the evidence taken before committees on the state of Ireland, 1824 and 1825. Reprinted in Great Britain, *Report from the Select Committee on Emigration from the United Kingdom*, 1826, Appendix 11, pp. 314–15.

where to go to. This system is becoming prevalent, and therefore I conceive the cause of distress to be the excess of population with want of employment; and there being no legal provision for securing subsistence for those poor people that are thrown as destitute vagrants upon the world. . . . .

The redundant population of this island is looked upon by them as a main cause of the decreasing value of land, and of the inability of tenants to pay rent; it has therefore become a favourite object with the owners of land to thin the population on their estates, under the idea that being too numerous they consume the whole produce of the land, and leave nothing for the owners; yet if this plan be acted upon, as it is beginning to be, extensively, what is to become of the people? They have not the means to emigrate, nor can they get land or employment at home. A poor man thus dismissed, with his family, from his dwelling and land, with perhaps one or two cows, a few sheep or a horse; the whole of which may not, at existing prices, be worth five pounds, seeks, in the first instance, to procure a lot of land from some middleman, who has cleared the farm of the pauper tenants whom he had previously ruined, and who is induced to take him as tenant, because he possessed a cow, a horse, or some sheep; the rent is such as the middleman chooses to impose, the tenant being willing to promise any thing rather than go into a town, where he knows he cannot find employment, and hoping to get subsistence for a year or two, on his new holding; but at the end of a year, all that he has is seized for his new master, and he is ultimately compelled to seek an asylum in some hovel or town, trusting for his support to the precarious chances of daily labor.

*Are there a great number of persons, throughout the country, circumstanced like those you have just described?*—The system is becoming more general; the system of turning off the surplus population is becoming quite prevalent.

*Are you of opinion, that any plan can be devised for giving relief to the poor in cases of emergency?*—I think that the tendency on the part of landlords to turn off, in that unmerciful way, their surplus stock, as they call it, of men, would be considerably checked, if there were some legal obligation imposed upon them to provide for those poor people, till they could provide for themselves, or to do as I heard was done in Scotland by the Marchioness of Stafford, when she lessened the population upon her estates. She procured temporary accommodation for the deprived tenants, shipped them at her own cost for America, and settled them there: I have heard that she did so; and those people are much better off than they would have been had they continued in the Highlands.

*Do you think that any plan of emigration, carried on at the expense of government, would prove effectual?*—I think that a plan of emigration might answer very well for the present, but unless some other plan was adopted to check the progressive disproportion between employment and population, the evil would be of constant recurrence; and then the system of emigration should be kept up perpetually.

### B. TESTIMONY OF THE LORD BISHOP OF LIMERICK[1]

The evil to be met is a redundant population; it is now in the process of curing itself, in the most painful way, by the ejectment, destitution, and starvation of those poor people whom I would call *surreptitious* tenantry. These are left upon the roads to raise miserable hovels in the ditches. The object should be, in some way, to provide for them; and, so far as practicable, in such a way as would not only check the evil, but prevent its recurrence. . . . .

The evil is *pressing*, is *immediate*. It calls, therefore, for an *immediate* remedy. Take *any* system of home relief, it must be *gradual* in its operation; before it can be brought to bear, the present sufferers will have died off, and others will have supplied their place, but not without a dreadful course of intermediate horrors. Now emigration is an instantaneous relief. . . . . The sufferers are *at once* taken away; and, be it observed, from a country where they are a nuisance and a pest, to a country where they will be a benefit and blessing. . . . .

The existing state of things is truly frightful; when tenantry (the under-tenants of under-tenants) are dispossessed, after a season of patient suffering, they go into some other district, perhaps a peaceable one; where they fail not to find friends, clansmen, and factionaries, whom they bring back with them by night, to avenge their cause; it is avenged in blood; and, where occasion offers, the service is repaid in kind. Thus, the whole country is set in flames. This will be quite intelligible to those who know the system of mutual understanding that pervades the districts, I may say, of each province. I will mention one instance that came within my own knowledge. I beg, however, not to mention the part of Ireland in which it occurred. It was a case of the dispossessed tenantry of an estate. They were certainly surreptitious;

[1] Extract from Great Britain, *Minutes of Evidence before the Select Committee on Emigration from the United Kingdom, 1826*, pp. 143–44.

they had, also, not paid their rental. They were, at length, suddenly and simultaneously dispossessed; they were in the most deplorable state, without house, without food, without money; starving, and almost dying, in the ditches. I saw an affecting memorial on their behalf praying that the proprietor on whose estate they had been, would procure for them the privilege and means of emigration. They had, to my knowledge, been exemplary in peaceableness, amidst surrounding disturbance. But, from want perhaps rather of power than of will, their petition was not granted. I ventured to predict that if they were not in some way relieved, the consequences in the winter would be dreadful. And so they were. They brought their friends, just in the way I have been describing, from other districts. Blood followed! afterwards, prosecutions, convictions, executions.

Now, though it be true, that emigration could not *at once* take away *all* that may be burthensome to the country, though it could not, even *finally* do so, it would give relief to *many*, and hope to *all*. At present they are in a state of hopelessness, despairing recklessness; therefore they scruple not the worst. Give them hope, and they will endure; particularly if it is known that good character will be a recommendation.

### C. TESTIMONY OF DR. WILLIAM MURPHY[1]

*You are aware that emigration has taken place from the neighbourhood of Cork?*—Yes; and it is going on now very briskly.

*To what part is that emigration chiefly directed?*—Chiefly to Canada, and to the States.

*Will you describe the circumstances under which that is taking place at this moment?*—The description of persons that go there from the south of Ireland through Cork, are generally small farmers that have saved a little, and some rich ones; but the great bulk are labourers. It is a very extraordinary circumstance that scarcely a tradesman in the city emigrates; I have had some correspondence with a person who is principally employed in forwarding the emigration there, a ship-broker, and he says, there is scarcely a tradesman, even among those that are well employed, that can ever save as much as will take him over; now the labourers do save sometimes, for the labourers are much more comfortable than the tradesmen are, although receiving much less wages; they are more temperate, and they are more managing than the tradesmen. The great bulk going now are small farmers and labourers.

[1] *Ibid., 1827*, pp. 385–86.

*What is the amount of money with which those small farmers emigrate?*
—The passage to Canada is about 2£ 10s., and they seldom charge
them for children; it costs them 4£ 10s. to go to the States.

*What are their views when they get there?*—They are better pleased to
be employed by the farmers as labourers than to get ground themselves,
for they know that they will eventually be able to become proprietors;
and all the accounts from those who have gone out have been very favourable, they have generally written to their friends to come out to
them; their accounts are so good from Canada, that emigration is likely to increase; one man told me that he had so many applications to
him, that he thinks that he expects to ship about seven thousand persons in this present spring. About two thousand have been shipped
already.

*Do they principally go to Canada?*—To Canada and New York; out
of that number, there are about eight hundred to New York.

*What is the description of those that went to New York?*—Farmers and
labourers, and a few weavers; they have had communications with the
States, and they say that weavers are wanted at Philadelphia.

*Do the agricultural population appear much inclined to go to New
York?*—Yes, they are more anxious to go to the States.

*If you state that they are more anxious to go to the United States than
to the Canadas, how do you account for so large a proportion as twelve hundred out of two thousand having gone to the Canadas?*—For cheapness;
numbers come to Cork who have nothing but their 2£ 10s. and a bag
of potatoes to take with them.

*Then in fact the better description of persons go to New York?*—Yes;
and some with a good deal of money have gone to Canada. There are a
great many of the men that go from the county of Limerick—very snug
farmers; I had some conversation with several of them about their
views; they were anxious, they said, to get rid of rents and tithes, and
to become proprietors themselves; and they were afraid there would be
another disturbance in Ireland, which they would never wish to witness
again.

*Have they lately renewed those expressions of apprehension?*—Yes,
it was very lately before I came over that I had conversation to this
effect.

## 19. Some Newspaper Comments on Emigration, 1828–30

### A. SEPTEMBER 13, 1828[1]

Scotland, and especially from the western parts and the islands, is pouring out people for North America, chiefly for Canada; and they are shipped off in a very distressing manner, for the want of accommodations and supplies, because of their poverty and wretchedness of means.

### B. JULY 11, 1829[2]

The *Irish Vindicator* relates the following as an evidence of the influence of Catholic emancipation on emigration from Ireland:

A vessel sailing from the port of Dublin, for America, with between two and three hundred passengers on board, was met in the bay, by the Holyhead steam packet, the captain of which threw on board some English papers, containing accounts of the passing of the Catholic relief bill. The greater number of emigrants hearing this news, and overjoyed with the prospect of living in their renovated country, obliged the captain to put them ashore, and, willingly forfeiting their passage money, returned to the scenes of their former life, and expected happiness to be derived from the liberation of their native land.

### C. JUNE 12, 1830[3]

The English papers have many paragraphs on the subject of emigration. Great numbers of persons, it seems, had arrived at Hull, Glasgow, &c., to embark for the United States, and Canada. A Glasgow paper says:

The manufacturing and commercial speculations which are fostered and encouraged by the tariff laws of America, have had the effect of draining our country of its improvements, and many of its productive population.

Another paper states, that many of the farmholders of Kent are likely to have their farms thrown on their hands, as the rage for emigration is very general among the small farmers. The *Sheffield Courant* remarks:

Never, we believe, was distress so great as it is at this time on the borders of Derbyshire and Staffordshire. Removals, sales, distraints for rent, and emigration to America, are without precedent.

[1] Extract from *Niles' Weekly Register*, XXXV, 40.

[2] *Ibid*, XXXVI, 317.

[3] *Ibid.*, XXXVIII, 296.

Cobbett, struck with the vast population that is moving away, has addressed a letter to a Mr. Horton,[1] the author of *Three Letters on Emigration*. We quote Cobbett's letter entire:

SIR: You need be in no anxiety about getting rid of the industrious people of England; you may withdraw your proposition for mortgaging the poor-rates, in order to raise money for transporting them to the banks of Nova Scotia and the wilds and swamps of Canada. They are going of their own accord, and at their own expense. From Kent and Sussex about 2,000; from Yarmouth 400; from Boston, by canal, to Liverpool, recently, about 200; from Yorkshire and Lancashire, by way of Liverpool, 1,500, or thereabouts, now recently; from Hull, gone this year, and going, about 7,000! From Scotland about 2,000. All, with the exception of the poor amongst the Scotch, bound for the United States; for, though some of the Hull and Yarmouth ships are bound for Quebec, the people are going to the United States. I have been on board one of the ships now going from this place. I have had great pleasure in finding that these spirited people have too much sense to think of remaining an hour longer than necessary [here]. . . . . Some of these people carry 2,000 pounds each with them. Three millions of gold will, this very year, go from England to the United States, by the means of emigration. No, no, . . . . the paupers do not go. The aged, the deformed, the decrepit, the orphans, the lazy the insane; these all remain to be kept. . . . .

### D. JUNE 19, 1830[2]

The pressure of emigration to America is without precedent—from England, Ireland, Scotland, and Wales. The British presses are filled with paragraphs on the subject. In some cases "unemployed laborers" and their families (i.e., paupers), were shipping off, by public contributions or private charities—but by far the greater part were farmers, mechanics, and manufacturers (with their families—aged men and children at the breast) who had a little money to begin business with in the "new world." A Scotch paper observes that the "American tariff laws have the effect of draining our country of its improvements, and many of its productive population." Another observes: "It is lamentable to witness the emigration of numbers of such a respectable and industrious class. As most of the families go to join friends who had preceded them, and thriven since the change; the whole party were in high spirits, and, so altered is the national character—seemed to leave their native land without a symptom of regret.

[1] [Sir Robert John Wilmot-Horton, 1784–1841, a leading advocate of state aid for emigration.]

[2] Extract from *Niles' Weekly Register*, XXXVIII, 305–6.

The quays at Greenock, Hull, Liverpool, Waterford, &c. were thronged with persons about to embark—it was supposed that 2,000 had left the last named place, only, in the present season—and the press was not relieved. A large proportion of them are females. It is stated that the whole emigration from Ireland, in the present year, will exceed 30,000—and that "a moity, at least, of these will be Protestants." The want of means to leave the country seems to afford the only reason why this amount should not be mightily increased.

### E. JULY 31, 1830[1]

*Ireland.* The *Newry Examiner* supposes that from 10 to 15,000 persons had left the province of Ulster, only, for America, during the late spring, saying:

We regret to say that it is the fate of the country which they leave that is most to be deplored. The honest, the industrious, the independent, are quitting us, and going to enrich another land and add strength to another state. This year the emigrants are almost entirely of the *agricultural* class. High rents and heavy taxation, exorbitant tithes and grinding leases, are driving the *small farmers* out of the country, and even a cursory glance at the passing emigrants will show that the persons who are going into voluntary exile are not those who could be best spared.

### 20. Emigration Stimulated by Letters from Successful Pauper Immigrants, 1830[2]

#### INTRODUCTION

In the beginning of last year (1830) a strong desire to emigrate to America, showed itself among the labouring population of the parish of Corsley, near Warminster, in Wilts. They, like their fellow labourers throughout the south of England, had been long suffering from want of work and low wages. It happened that a certain Joseph Silcox, the brother of a respectable farmer of that parish, had lately returned from Canada, after a residence there of two or three years; and being a dissenting preacher, he had frequent opportunities of holding forth to his neighbours on the vast difference between the condition of industrious labourers in this country and in America, and on the advantages they would derive from emigrating there. He declared his own inten-

---

[1] *Ibid.*, p. 402.

[2] Extract from G. Poulett Scrope, *Extracts of Letters from Poor Persons Who Emigrated Last Year to Canada and the United States.* Printed for the information of the labouring poor and their friends in this country (2d ed., London, 1832), 1–4, 9, 17, 19–21, 29–30.

tion of returning immediately; and a considerable number of his neighbors became desirous of following his example.

With this view some labourers who possessed property sold it in order to pay the expenses of their voyage. Others, who had not wherewithal to do this, resorted to the parish, and begged earnestly to be assisted to remove from a place where they could not obtain a living and were a burden to their neighbors, to one where they understood that by honest industry they might maintain themselves and their families in comfort and independence.

The parish officers, being thus importuned, and being also of opinion that the removal of several families who had long been, and would, most probably, long continue to be, a heavy and still increasing charge upon their rates, must prove as great a relief to the rate-payers as to the poor themselves, consented to give the aid that was asked of them: and for this purpose raised a sum of a few hundred pounds, partly by the sale of two houses belonging to the parish, and partly by subscription; the Marquis of Bath, the principal landed proprietor in the parish, contributing £50. The expenses of some families and single labourers were paid in full. To others partial assistance was given according to their circumstances. In the whole, sixty-five individuals left the place, and embarked for Canada, in a vessel which sailed from Newport, in Glamorganshire, the 7th of April, 1830.

Accounts have since been received from many of the emigrants, by letter to their friends in Corsley and the neighborhood. . . . . The tenor of all their communications has invariably been to the effect that, though those *who are foolishly home-sick*, may be dispirited for the first few weeks, and those *who will not work* are not likely to be better off in that country than in any other, *any labourer or mechanic, who is willing to exert himself, may be sure of obtaining full employment at high wages, and the very best of living;* employment, not for the men only, but for every member of his family likewise, down to children of six years old; with the prospect of purchasing land on exceedingly cheap terms, out of his savings, if he choose to set up as an independent farmer on his own property.

. . . . Encouraged by these favourable accounts, similar emigrations have taken place in the spring of *this* year, from the neighbouring parishes of Westbury, Frome, and Warminster; and the accounts that have arrived from the emigrants immediately upon their landing, are as favourable as could have been hoped for. . . . .

More than one of the following letters exhibit the *English pauper* turned into an independent farmer, cultivating his own land, *at the end of a short half-year* from his quitting his native parish in a state of des-. titution.

LETTERS

5. From Thomas Lister (weaver, of Westbury) Philadelphia, April 26, 1830:

I hope brother William and family will come all together, for they can get spinning here. I have just begun to work in a broad loom, and I think I shall get on with it. There is hundreds of factories here, both cotton and woollen, and some weavers wanted in the same shop with me. It is a very pleasant country as ever I saw. Clear days for weeks together, not a cloud to be seen. I hope brother James and wife will come, if he is married, for a shoemaker can do very well here. Meat is very cheap, about two-pence half-penny per pound, and flour. A pint of gin for three-pence, and there is no complaining in our streets. . . . .

7. From John Down (weaver, of Frome) New York, August 12, 1830.

My Dear Wife:

I have got a situation in a Factory, in a very pleasant vale about 7 miles from Hudson, and I am to have the whole management of the factory, and the master is going to board me till you come to his house. A farmer took me one day in his wagon into the country, from Hudson, to see a factory, and I dined with him, and he would not have a farthing, and told me I was welcome to come to his house at any time; they had on the table puddings, pyes, and fruit of all kind that was in season, and preserves, pickles, vegetables, meat, and everything that a person could wish, and the servants set down at the same table with their masters. They do not think of locking the doors in the country, and you can gather peaches, apples, and all kinds of fruit by the side of the roads. . . . . I can go into a store, and have as much brandy as I like to drink for three half-pence, and all other spirits in proportion. If a man like work he need not want victuals. It is a foolish idea that some people have, that there is too many people come here, it is quite the reverse; there was more than 1,000 emigrants came in the day after I landed, and there is four ships have arrived since with emigrants. But there is plenty of room yet, and will be for a thousand years to come. My dear, all that I want now is to see you, and the dear Children here, and then I shall be happy, and not before. You know very well that I should not have left you behind me, if I had money to have took you with me. It was sore against me to do it. But I do not repent of coming, for you know that there was nothing but poverty before me, and to see you and the dear children want was what I could not bear. *I would rather cross the Atlantic ten times than hear my children cry for victuals once.* Now, my dear, if you can get the parish to pay for your pas-

sage, come directly; for I have not a doubt in my mind I shall be able to keep you in credit. You will find a few inconveniences in crossing the Atlantic, but it will not be long, and when that is over, all is over, for I know that you will like America. . . . . Poverty is unknown here. You see no beggars.
. . . .

### 8. C. Henitage (day-labourer, of Corsley) October 4th, 1830.

I have a good place of service, and have a good master. I live 7 miles from New York. He keeps a tavern and takes in drivers. I have bargained with him against Christmas, at six dollars a month, and I get five dollars more, that runs to £2.2s., and I do have my board and washing and lodging in to it. I do sit down to table with my master every day, and now I can have a glass of wine or two every day, and not cost me nothing. It is a fine country and a free country. For the carpenters 10s. a day here, and the wheelers get about the same. But the people tell me that they get more farther up the country. Don't you be afraid to come, for you do better with £2. here than you will with £4. in England, for things are cheaper here. And poor men get good wages, for I could have five places if I was a mind, now I am got known by the people, but I have a good place and shall stay. This is the place for people to come if they do try, for here is plenty of work here, for people don't buy things here and not pay for it. I hope I shall have a little land myself soon as well as he, and I hope I shall pay for it. This is the place to live in if a man is steady. If people did but know how people do get on here, you would all come to America. . . . .

### 16. From John West (shoemaker, of Corsley) Germantown, near Philadelphia, May 20th, 1831.

I wish, and do often say that we wish you were all in this happy land. We have good food and raiment, and all the comforts of life, &c. I have not heard one person say it was *bad times* since I have been here. There is a Poor-house here. Twenty-five old men and women is the greatest number in the winter, the main of whom are now gone. There are none paid out of the house. There is a great many ill-conveniences, but no empty bellies. 'Tis no good for a man to come here without he work hard. Farmer's men work from sunrise to sunset, all the year round; they get from 10 to 12 dollars per month and their board, or three-fourths of a dollar per day. A carpenter's and a mason's trade is a very good trade here. But they must not toss and turn a brick so many times as James Singer do. A Brick-maker is a very good trade.   I was told that a brick-maker will earn two or three dollars a day at New York and Philadelphia. *A man can do better here with a family than with none. For children at 6 years old can work and get some money.* A man nor woman need not stay out of employment one hour here. *No war nor insurrection here. But all is plenty and peace.*

## 21. Various Causes of Emigration from the United Kingdom[1]

In British America, notwithstanding the difficulties which are incident to all new countries, it is a well-established fact, substantiated by the evidence of all who have marked the progress of new settlers, that all those who have with persevering industry and frugality applied their labour to the cultivation of forest lands, have, with few exceptions, succeeded in acquiring the means of comfortable independence, and all that is requisite to render rural life happy.

It frequently happens, however, that emigrants are disappointed in realising the prospects they entertained on leaving their native country. Lured by low, unprincipled, interested persons, into the belief that all they can possibly wish for is to be obtained with little difficulty on the shores and amidst the forests of America, they consequently embark with sanguine, unattainable expectations. No sooner, however, do they tread the lands of the western world, than the delusion vanishes; and they then discover that neither food, clothing, nor any article of necessity, use, or luxury, is to be obtained without labour, money, or some exchangeable value.

These disappointments, productive of no small degree of anxiety and discontent, are caused by emigrants not being told of the difficulties as well as the advantages of new countries: for, persons preparing to leave these kingdoms require not only to be informed of all that is necessary to govern them before deciding on leaving their abodes at home, but honest advice also to guide them afterwards, until they are enabled to secure a comfortable living in the land to which they go.

The Board of Emigration has, it is true, circulated useful information in a brief shape; but it was vain to expect that its members would attend to the detailed advice and intelligence necessary for emigrants to know. It would indeed be well, if adequate persons were appointed by government at the principal ports in the United Kingdom for the purpose of giving correct information to emigrants; in order to prevent as far as possible, the daily frauds practised on them at the seaports. . . . .

To those who are anxious to emigrate, but who have not the means, it is a matter of difficulty to advise how to proceed; various plans are often adopted. Unmarried men and women, who were unable to pay their passages, have frequently bound themselves for two or three years to serve those who paid for carrying them to America.

[1] Extract from John M'Gregor, *British America* (2d ed.; Edinburgh, 1833), II, 517–19, 538–41, 550–56.

Letters from persons who have been settled some years in America, to their friends in the mother countries, have long been a powerful cause of emigration. Money, also, is frequently sent by settlers in America, to enable their friends to follow; and by these means more have been induced to emigrate than by all others.

Associations have lately been formed in parishes for the purpose of assisting persons to emigrate. Those who may be aided in the expense of emigrating by their parishes, should carry with them a certificate of character as to sobriety, honesty, and industry; and it will likely be of importance for those who bear the expense of their removal, to send them under the protection of those who will undertake to guard them against going in ill-found, unsafe ships, and from imposition on landing in the colonies.

The following very prudent plan has long prevailed in Scotland, and, having been generally attended with success, can scarcely be recommended too much.

When a family, or a few families, determine on emigrating, some of the sons or relations that are grown up, are sent forward to prepare for the reception of the families who are to follow afterwards. It often occurs that the young men thus sent to America have, for two or three years, to earn money, which they remit to pay the passage of their friends.

Young Irishmen, also, who have at different times found their way to America, have not unfrequently, by working for three or four years in the towns, or among the settlements, or by employing themselves in the fisheries, accumulated considerable sums of money, which have been forwarded to Ireland, in order to bring after them their parents, brothers, or sisters, and often young women to whom they were previously affianced or attached. This I know to be a very common trait in the character of the Irish peasantry, and no circumstance can illustrate a more powerful force of affectionate attachment.

The leading fault of Irish emigrants is their apparent indifference about fixing at once on the permanent and certain employment which the cultivation of the soil alone can secure to them. Transient labour among the old settlers, employment at the public works, seems more congenial to their habits than working on a wood farm on their own account. Exceptions, however, there are to this general observation; and, in comparing the condition of the Irish settlers in America with that of the peasantry in Ireland, I may say, without the least fear of being incorrect, that I have beheld more apparent wretchedness, and, I would infer, real misery, in one day's travelling in Ireland, than I have witnessed during several years' residence in, and while travelling through the principal parts of, the British empire in North America. My observations, while travelling among new settlements, always led me to the conclusion, that many of the inconveniences and all the dreariness of emigration would soon disappear, if several families, say ten to twenty or more, from the same parish in the United Kingdom, were to remove to America and settle together in one place. Mutual ideas, habits, and wants would unite them, and they would soon find their social condition happy and prosperous. The practice of the Swiss and German emigrants is, in this respect, worthy of imitation. They embark at Havre in the American packet ships, and, on their arrival at New York, go immediately on board the *tow boats* for Albany, and thence like birds of passage to their destination in the Western States, where they settle together, and soon prosper. They form a most excellent class of inhabitants, quiet, honest, and industrious.

About one-third of the emigrants landing at New York are of this description. I saw many of them embarking last year (1832) at Havre, and the circumstance offered ample materials for reflection. They had forever left the country of their forefathers, passed through France, to cross what they never before beheld—the ocean—in order to fix their future destinies in the wilds of the Western World. . . . .

The causes of emigration are chiefly poverty, dissatisfaction in respect to public measures, or ambition.

The majority of those who emigrate to America are driven abroad by the goadings of poverty; another class is formed of adventurous men, who go to seek fortunes in other countries, with the hope of again returning to their own; a third class is composed of men of genius, whose schemes have been frustrated, or whose hopes have been blighted at home; and a fourth class includes individuals who are not only discontented with their condition in the land of their forefathers, but displeased also with all public measures: these men are not, probably, compelled to emigrate from necessity, but from a spirit of dissatisfaction natural to them. Of this unfortunate description, I have discovered numbers in all the provinces. They at first fix on a farm, and as they do not find that their ardent expectations are realised in a year or two, they attribute their bad fortune to the ill-fated spot they have chosen, which they leave for another, where no better success attend them. In this manner, roaming about from place to place, the chances inevitably are, that they wear out their constitutions, and waste their labour to no good purpose.

Immediately after the last war, a crisis in the affairs of men necessarily occurred. The peace threw thousands either altogether, or in a great measure, out of employment. The articles which labour produced were many of them not further required; and the demand for, and the price of, the remainder, were reduced by the death of the war monopoly, and the great reduction in the naval and military departments. Agriculture and commerce continued for some time to languish, while the spirits of the farmers began to droop, and those of the manufacturers to ferment. In the minds of some men, evils, under the impression of misfortunes, produced discontent; others, [after] the transition from their former artificial affluence to a condition which made them feel their real position, broke out into invectives against the measures of government, and into a declared indifference to their country.

The labouring classes, when out of employment, generally find relief if they emigrate to America; and there are others whose spirits have been soured by misfortunes, either brought upon them by their own imprudence, or by accidental circumstances, who blame their country, and, with an avowal of hatred to it, expatriate themselves. It is assuredly fit, and perhaps necessary, that such men should go abroad. Fresh activity may renew in them the energy of youth; and while they spend the remainder of their days in other countries, experience, fortunately, never fails to convince them that it is impossible for them to forget, or not to love, their own.

It is vain and inconsistent to expect that the government of any nation can relieve effectually the miseries of many hundreds of thousands of paupers, who have been principally born in poverty, and reared in the abodes of hunger, improvidence, and ignorance. The most that we can hope is that their sufferings may be ameliorated. It requires the gradual operation of an age, at least, to change the habits, and to direct to steady purposes the energies, of a vast population.

Many circumstances have combined to produce the present alarming extent of pauperism; the remote causes are not within my province to enquire into; but in Ireland, which we may consider the very empire of mendicity, superabundant population is certainly the immediate cause of beggary. That the Irish peasantry are improvident, cannot be denied. This, again, arises from ignorance and want of education, which reconcile them to exist in a state scarcely superior to that in which the brute tribes live. Therefore, in the absence of reflection, and the attendant disregard of future consequences as to the means of supporting a family, at about the same age that the young men of England and Scotland are leaving school, and their parents anxiously considering what occupation they are to follow, or what trade they are to learn by an apprenticeship of five or seven years, the Irish peasantry link into premature marriages, and thereby multiply the endless evils of poverty.

In countries like America, where labour is dear, and the population scanty in proportion to the vast extent of land, early marriages are not by any means attended with the same evils as in Ireland, where the population is superabundant, inasmuch as there is not sufficient employment for the inhabitants. A great proportion of the pauperism that exists in Great Britain is caused by the seemingly endless influx of Irish beggars. Were there no mendicants but those born within the parishes of England and Scotland, our feelings would not be harrowed by the famished, half-naked, unfortunate beings that assail us in every town, village, and along every road in both countries.[1]

The removal of a great portion of the redundant population of the United Kingdom to our colonies, which has for some time engaged the attention of the government, may be considered the best temporary expedient to relieve the mother countries from the burden of pauperism. That those who are sent to the colonies will be removed from the pressure of poverty, I have no doubt; and the consequent effect which this measure may have on the United Kingdom will doubtless depend on the extent to which emigration may be effected. It is also matter of no common consideration, in the political point of view, that each individual who leaves these kingdoms, and settles in British colonies, not only relieves this country to the amount of provisions he consumes, and the additional employment given to others by his absence, but he creates, by consuming British manufactures, an annual employment in the mother country of about 40s. for himself and each of his offspring: this, on a large scale of emigration, and the consequent in-

[1] We may every day, at the pier-heads of Liverpool, at Glasgow, and other places, witness the landing of hundreds of ragged, squalid objects (men, women, and children), from Ireland. These people come over under the pretence of looking for employment, and proceed begging on their way through the country. Before leaving Ireland, they are told it is physically impossible that they can be so miserable in England or in Scotland, as in their own country; that they can beg from one place to another; that if they are eventually sent back by the parishes, they will be provided for; and that they can, in spite of all the vigilance of overseers and police officers, return again to England. An Irish pauper, from having either learned the benefit of living on the industry of England by his own experience, or by acquiring previously the rudiments of ingenious begging, is wonderfully eloquent and *au fait*, in the way of amusing select vestries or police officers, while giving an account of himself.

crease, by the natural ratio, of the population of our colonies, and decrease in the offspring of paupers in the United Kingdom, will augment to an enormous amount. It appears, however, that other measures should be pursued at the same time, with respect to Ireland. Infusing, by means of education, such useful knowledge into the minds of the peasantry as will gradually introduce habits of thinking and of orderly industry, is a measure, assuredly, of primary necessity: providing, as far as possible, employment for the labouring classes within the kingdom, is also an object of paramount consideration.

Another plan of great magnitude, although the policy will be by many denounced, but which would, nevertheless, be of eminent benefit to the country, comprehends the removal, as speedily as may be consistent with humanity, of the mud cabins; the introduction of poor-rates; and the destruction of the whole system of sub-letting.

In carrying into effect a grand scheme of emigration, for the purpose of disburdening the United Kingdom of a poverty-smitten people, it becomes necessary to consider the probable consequence of introducing a great mass of that description to our colonies.

Our North American possessions will require for many years a vast accession of settlers; but, at the same time, it must be remembered, that the men whose labour and energy are wanted, with the present inhabitants, to cultivate and raise those great countries to the mighty importance of which they are susceptible, should, generally speaking, possess correct principles and industrious habits, as well as strong physical qualities.[1]

Apprehension of distress, and many other evils, being introduced with large bodies of paupers, are very generally entertained in the colonies; and unless adequate means be provided to carry such emigrants to the place of location, and to support them for a reasonable time afterwards, it would certainly be improper to inundate the colonies with a pauper population. . . . .

Whether emigration on the plan formerly recommended by the committee of the House of Commons, or as lately proposed in Parliament, be ever carried into effect or not, voluntary emigration, at the expense of the emigrants themselves, will still continue to go on in the usual way.

[1] It is notorious that, while the number of criminal offences have greatly increased during late years in America, few instances of guilt can be traced to the old settlers. A life of continued poverty is usually so lamentably at variance with virtue, that we must ascribe the more frequent occurrence of crime in our colonies chiefly to the previous indigence of many of the emigrants.

## 22. Emigration as a Possible Remedy for Irish Destitution, 1836–37[1]

### A. 1836

Emigration ought not, I think, under any circumstances, to be looked to as an ordinary resource. An excess of population is an evil; to relieve that excess by emigration is so far a good; but it may be doubted whether the parent stock is not enfeebled by the remedy thus applied. In general, the most active and enterprising emigrate, leaving the more feeble and less robust and resolute at home. Thus a continual drain of its best elements lowers the tone and reduces the general vigour of the community, at the same time that it imparts an additional stimulus to the tendency towards an undue increase of population, which was the immediate cause of disease.

In saying this, I do not contend against the resort to emigration as a relief from an existing evil, but merely wish to point out the inexpediency of encouraging it as an approved practice in our social system. The necessity for its adoption should be regarded as an indication of disease, which it would be better to prevent than thus to relieve. The means of prevention will be found in the education and improved moral and prudential habits of the community. In proportion as these prevail, will its general character be elevated; and individuals will feel a wholesome dread of entailing upon themselves burdens which will depress their position in the social scale. In Ireland, unhappily, these prudential considerations do not prevail at all, or prevail in a very imperfect degree; and the consequence is, that marriages are daily contracted with the most reckless improvidence. Boys and girls marry, literally without habitation or any means of support, trusting, as they say, to Providence, as others have done before them. It is quite lamentable to witness the effects of this ignorant recklessness, which, by occasioning an excessively rapid increase in their numbers, tends to depress the whole population, and to extend the sphere of wretchedness and want.

Emigration not only may, but I believe must, be had recourse to as a present means of relief, whenever the population becomes excessive in any district, and no opening for migration can be found. The actual

[1] Extract from *Poor Laws—Ireland. Three Reports* by George Nicholls (English Poor Law Commissioner) to Her Majesty's Principal Secretary of State for the Home Department (Lord John Russell) (London, 1838). The extracts given are from the first (1836) report, pp. 55–56, and from the second (1837) report, pp. 96–99. The third report is quoted in the extract from Lord John Russell's speech; see Document 27 in this section.

excess of population will be indicated by the pressure of able-bodied labourers upon the workhouse. If any considerable number of these enter the workhouse, and remain there subject to its discipline, it may be taken as a proof of their actual inability to provide for themselves, and of the consequent excess of labourers beyond the means of employ. Under such circumstances, emigration must be looked to as the best, if not the only present remedy; and express provision should, I think, be made in the Act, for defraying the expense which this would occasion, as well as for the regulations under which it should be carried into effect.

With reference to the expense, I propose that the charge of emigration should in every case be equally borne by the Government and the Union from which the emigrants proceed. This division of the charge appears to me to be equitable; for, although the Union only is immediately benefited, yet eventually the whole empire is relieved, excess in one portion of it tending to occasion an excess in the whole. The emigration should, I think, be limited to a British colony, where such arrangements might be made, through the intervention of the Colonial Office, as would serve to protect the emigrants on their first arrival, and also ensure their obtaining employment at the earliest period. This is important, alike for themselves and the community; at home they were a burden—in their new position they will increase the general productive powers of the empire, as well as enlarge the demand for British produce. In every case, however, the emigration should be conducted under the control of the central authority, and be subjected to such regulations as the Government may deem it right to establish.

I propose also, that, whenever it shall appear that any owners and occupiers of land, within a period of (say) three years antecedent to the passing of the Act, shall have actually incurred an expense in effecting the emigration of labourers and others, a moiety of the actual outlay so incurred may, at the discretion of the central authority, be repaid to such land-owners and occupiers—the charge to be borne jointly by the Government and the Union in which the property of such land-owner may be included: provided, however, that the moiety of such outlay so to be repaid shall in no case exceed (say) 5£. for each of such emigrants. This provision will enable the central authority to deal equitably with respect to certain individuals, who have recently, at great personal charge, effected the emigration from their estates and neighbourhoods of a portion of the surplus population; and as the Unions when established, and the whole community, will be benefited by what has thus been done, it seems right that they should bear a moiety of the charge.

B. 1837

I am very sensible of the difficulties which beset the question of emigration, in principle as well as in its details. Having stated these pretty fully in my former Report, I will not now enter into a general consideration of the subject, but confine my observations to the specific point—as to whether any and what provision should be made in the Irish Poor Law Bill for the purposes of emigration.

Without attempting to decide the question whether Ireland, as a whole, is over-populous—whether there are such means of employment as to afford, if properly developed, adequate support for all—it is yet, I think, quite apparent, that in certain parts of the country there is an actual excess of population beyond the existing means of employment; and, wherever this excess exists, it must operate to lower the price of labour, and to increase the competition for land; and thus to force down the mode of living to a lower level, and to depress the whole population in the moral and social scale.[1]

These are universally admitted to be the inevitable consequences of an excess of population in any district: and an examination of the country must, I think, convince any impartial observer that such excess does actually exist in certain districts in Ireland, producing there all the consequences above indicated. In parts of Donegal, for instance, the people are so crowded together, and so impoverished by competition in their struggles to obtain the common necessaries of life, that,

[1] [For example, Nicholls thought that, although in the northern counties of Ireland the extent of poverty was less than in the west and south, there was great destitution in the north, especially in Donegal, where small holdings and minute subdivisions of land prevailed to a greater extent than in any other part of Ireland.

"Nothing [he wrote] can exceed the miserable appearance of the cottages in Donegal, or the desolate aspect of a cluster of these hovels, always teeming with an excessive population. Yet if you enter their cabins, and converse with them frankly and kindly, you will find the people intelligent and communicative, quick to comprehend, and ready to impart what they know. They admitted that they were too numerous, too thick upon the land, and that, as one of them declared, they were eating each other's heads off, but what could they do? There was no employment for the young people, nor relief for the aged, nor means nor opportunity for removing their surplus numbers to some more eligible spot. They could only therefore live on, hoping, as they said, that times might mend, and that their landlords would sooner or later do something for them. Yet, with all this suffering, no disturbance or act of violence has occurred in Donegal. During the severe privations of the last summer, when numbers were actually in

unless some step be taken in the first instance for lessening this competition, either by removing the surplus hands, or by increasing the
amount of employment, or by both measures combined, it will, I fear,
be impossible to effect any very material change in their condition.

The means of employment may, no doubt, be very generally and
profitably increased, by the intervention of the landlords, the application of capital, and an extended cultivation of the soil; but this alone,
in the present condition of many districts in Ireland, will not be sufficient; the remedy from these sources, although good in itself, and absolutely essential to the final attainment of the object, will yet necessarily be slow in its general application. But the evil is present and
pressing, and emigration appears to be the only immediate remedy, or
rather palliative, of the state of things existing in Donegal, and which
exist likewise in other parts of the west and south of Ireland. It seems to
me, under such circumstances, that it is only by emigrating one part
of the surplus population, and providing employment for another part,
that the excessive competition adverted to, and its attendant evils,
can be remedied. Of the means for effecting an increase of employment, I need not here speak. Several measures have been submitted
to Parliament with this avowed object, and I understand it to be the
intention of Government to take the whole subject into its early consideration.

With respect to emigration, the opinion expressed in my last Report, that it should be provided for in the Bill, has been confirmed by
what has recently come under my notice; and I now recommend the
insertion of a clause essentially similar to that in the English Poor Law
Bill, authorising Boards of Guardians, under the direction of the Com-

---

want of sustenance, there was no dishonesty, no plundering—the people starved,
but they would not steal; and, although their little stock of cattle and moveables has
been notoriously lessening these last four years, and especially in the last year, which
seems to have swallowed up nearly all their visible means, they have yet paid their
rents—the occupier's share of the produce has been insufficient for his own support,
yet the landlord's share has generally been paid in full; and I was assured, by the
agent of one of the largest proprietors, that he had no arrears worth noticing.

"To improve the condition of such a people would immediately increase the
productive powers of the country, which is a point well deserving the attention of
the great landowners, with whom it will mainly rest. . . . .

"In the case of Donegal, a twofold remedy seems to be necessary—namely, emigration and extended cultivation. The former requires no explanation, and, as regards the latter, I will only remark, that capital can perhaps be in no way more
profitably employed in Ireland than in draining, reclaiming and improving the land"
(1837 Report, p. 77)].

missioners, to defray out of the poor-rates the expense of emigrating the surplus population of any Union. To ensure the proper application of the funds, and a judicious and impartial selection of the individuals, it will be necessary to place all the details of the measure under the immediate control of the Commissioners. With regard to the expense, I suggested last year that one-half should be borne by the Union whence the emigrants removed, and the other half by Government. Without urging this suggestion at present, it may be sufficient to point out that an agency by which emigration might be conducted already exists. There are emigration agents at the ports of Dublin, Belfast, Cork, Londonderry, Sligo, and Limerick, who might superintend the embarkation of the emigrants. There is an agent at Quebec who might afford them protection and assistance on landing; and agents with similar duties might be appointed in the other colonies to which emigrants proceed. The expense of the officers who would thus superintend the embarkation is now defrayed by the British Government, and the expense of the colonial agents might be borne by the colonies. A portion of the cost of conveying the emigrants to their destination might probably be defrayed out of the fund derived from the sale of waste lands in the colonies; and if, from this or any other source, a moiety of the cost of conveyance was obtained, the Unions from which the emigrants proceeded would be benefited, and the colonies would reap the advantage of an increased supply of labour.

It has been said, that if any such provision were made, the spontaneous emigration which now takes place would be immediately stopped. To a certain extent, perhaps, this would be the case: and I am disposed to think it would not be altogether an evil. The individuals who now spontaneously emigrate are, for the most part, possessed of more means, and more mental and physical energy, than their neighbours. They are, in fact, forced out by the growth of a lower class at home. The best go—the worst remain. An active, thrifty, provident individual, who by the exercise of these qualities has acquired some little capital, seeing no room for employing it at home, embarks with it for the United States or the Canadas, and thus the country sustains a double loss: but if means were adopted for emigrating the actual surplus population of a district, room would be made for such individuals and they would probably remain at home, at least a portion of them would; and thus, instead of the best of the people only leaving the country, as at present, the emigrants would consist of persons possessing the average qualifications of their class, and the mass of the people would be preserved from deterioration as far as it may be connected with this circumstance.

A legislative provision for the purposes of emigration does not therefore seem open to any serious objection, on the ground of its tendency to prevent spontaneous emigration; whilst in other respects it would, I think, in the present condition of Ireland, be productive of immediate and important benefits, and facilitate the introduction of those improvements in the condition and habits of the people, which are so greatly to be desired.

### 23.  Methods of Stimulating Emigration, 1837[1]

*State of New York. City and County of New York.* Michael Gaugan, at present in the city of New York, being duly sworn, doth depose and say, that he is a native of Ireland, and last resided in the city of Dublin in Ireland, previous to his coming to this country with his family, consisting of himself, wife, son, and daughter. That up to the time of his coming to this country, he was employed as assistant engineer on the grand canal Ballanhasloe, to Dublin, which situation he had held for the last thirteen years, at a salary of one pound one shilling sterling per week, besides a house and an acre of ground or more; in which situation he lived respectably and comfortably with his family; and should have continued to do so had he not been induced by the false representations held out to his countrymen generally, in an evil hour, to quit his employment, his home and his friends, to come to this country, under an expectation that with his acquirements in civil engineering, he should soon become a wealthy man.

And this deponent further says, that there were hand bills, placarded on every corner, tree, and pump and public place in the city of Dublin, and for forty or fifty miles in the surrounding country, stating, in substance, that the people were fools not to leave the country, where there was nothing but poverty staring them in the face. That laborers were so much wanted in America, that even women were employed to work at men's work—that work was plenty in America, and wages high, to wit, 9 or 10 shillings a day, British money, and his diet. And deponent further says that William Wiley of Dublin, the agent of

<hr />

[1] Taken from *N. Y. Mercantile Advertiser* and reprinted in *Niles' Weekly Register*, LII (August 26, 1837), 409. This deposition was published with some others apparently secured by members of the New York Common Council in an effort to prevent "impositions upon New York by the hucksterers of, and traders and speculators in, foreigners."

Rawson and McMurray of New York, told this deponent that he, deponent, could get ten pounds British money per month, and his diet as wages; that every one was on a perfect equality in America; that the common laboring man received high wages, and sat at the same table and ate with his master, and gave deponent such a glowing picture of the wealth of America, and that with ease, an independent fortune could be made; that he (deponent) determined to relinquish his situation on the grand canal and bring his family to America, expecting, and so stated to his employer, that he might expect to see him return again in three years a rich man.

And this deponent further states, that there is one or more agent in every principal town in Ireland, who receives a commission for collecting and forwarding emigrants to Liverpool, where they take ship for America.

And this deponent further says, that he arrived in this city in the ship "Troy," Captain Allen, on the 16th day of June last past, with 204 passengers, that a majority of them were men in good employment at home, and lived comfortably and contented, until these passenger agents appeared in the country, a great part of whom have already returned home to Ireland, disappointed and disgusted at the gross impositions that had been practised upon them. That deponent is now without means for the support of himself and his family, and has no employment, and has already suffered great deprivation since he arrived in this country; and is now soliciting means to enable him to return with his family home to Ireland.

[Signed] Mich'l Gaugan

## 24. Overpopulation and Emigration in the United Kingdom, 1840[1]

. . . . It cannot, with propriety, be said that there is, in England, any very considerable or universal excess of population surpassing the means of employment; but that such excess should rather be characterised as partial, local, and temporary. As an instance of undeniable surplus of labour, in particular employments, I need only refer to the case of the hand-loom weavers, whose destitution has so often attracted the notice and the sympathy of this House. As an example of low wages, occasioned by a redundance of the labouring population in particular districts, I would remind the House of the remuneration of labour in

[1] Extract from speech of William Smith O'Brien in *Hansard's Parliamentary Debates*, Vol. LIV (3d series, 1840), cols. 835–39. A further portion of this debate will be found in the following section, Doc. 16, p. 275.

the counties of Wiltshire and Devonshire, [where] in many instances, the labourer does not receive more than six or seven shillings a week as his hire. Of the sufferings occasioned to the working classes in England, by occasional want of employment during particular seasons, the manufacturing districts of England afford too frequent illustration. . . . .

The simplest mode, however, of viewing this question, in regard to England, is, perhaps, to look at the amount expended on the relief of the poor; and when we find that, even after all the reductions which have been effected under the operation of the Poor Law Amendment Act, the poor-rate amounted, in 1838, in England and Wales, to not less than 4,406,907£, we are compelled to conclude that the privations of the working classes must have been, in the aggregate, of fearful extent: since it has been found necessary to raise, by compulsory taxation, so large a sum for their relief. I may here also observe, that, as a considerable proportion of this amount was expended in the relief of the able-bodied poor, whatever portion was so employed, may be regarded as a fund which might have been employed to assist the persons so relieved to emigrate, without imposing upon the community any burden beyond that which it has actually sustained in maintaining them in a state of idleness at home.

As, however, I wish to avoid the appearance of exaggerating the distresses of the poor, in order to make out a case in favour of emigration, I am contented to rest my argument, with regard to England, upon the simple proposition, that the labouring classes will not voluntarily abandon their homes, unless, by doing so, they can materially improve their condition; and if, by emigration, they can escape the penury which creates the desire to leave their country, and can obtain comfort and independence in the colonies, we are bound, by every consideration of humanity, to enable them so to improve their condition.

With respect to Scotland, and particularly with respect to the Highland districts, there is, unhappily, no ground for, in any degree, qualifying the statement that the population of those districts greatly exceeds the number for whom profitable occupation can be provided. In 1837, the inhabitants of the Western Highlands appear to have been reduced almost to the extremities of famine, from which they were relieved only by the charitable interference of external aid; and from all the most recent accounts which have been brought under my notice, I am induced to believe that they are now exposed to a recurrence of the same calamity. So strong, indeed, are the apprehensions entertained upon this subject, both by the landed proprietors, and by the population at large, that there have been several recent meetings for the purpose of urging the Government to promote an extensive system of emigration from the Highlands, as the only resource which can save them from the most appalling destitution. Several petitions of a similar character have also been addressed to this House, from one of which I shall quote a short extract, as descriptive of the present condition of the Highlands, and of the feelings by which that condition is accompanied, in reference to the question of emigration. It proceeds from the town of Portree, in the island of Skye, was presented in April of the present year, and bears 688 signatures. It states:

That the appalling state of want to which many thousands of the inhabitants of the Highlands, and islands of Scotland were reduced in the year 1837, and the misery that has existed in some of the Highland districts since that period, now loudly demand the adoption of an extensive and systematic plan of emigration, as the only means of preventing a recurrence, year after year, of the same degree of frightful distress and suffering.

As it is unnecessary for me to accumulate further evidence upon a point which cannot be disputed, I now turn to Ireland, and am compelled to undertake the painful duty of presenting to the House a picture of the condition of the labouring classes in my own country. Here, at least, it is impossible to exaggerate. Ireland is, in truth, the country which is chiefly interested in your determination to-night. Now, in asking the representatives of Great Britain to apply their best endeavour to relieve, by emigration, the superabundant and destitute population of Ireland, I will not appeal to those feelings of humanity which induce the English people to seek out objects, in every quarter of the globe, to which they may direct their benevolent exertions for the improvement of mankind; nor will I claim anything from that sense of justice which ought to remind you that almost all the evils under which Ireland still suffers have been, either remotely or immediately, occasioned by English misgovernment; but I apply myself to the more ignoble motive of self-interest, and suggest the obvious reflection, that unless the condition of the labouring classes in Ireland be elevated to that standard of comfort which is the right of every human being, it will follow, as an unavoidable consequence, that the working population of England must be reduced to the same level of misery and indigence as theirs.

It is contrary to every law which regulates the social system to suppose that, in two countries so closely united, there can permanently exist two separate scales by which English and Irish labour shall be differently remunerated.

Evidence respecting the destitution of the working classes in Ireland is scarcely needed. It is to be found in every authentic document which describes the condition of that country. Three years have scarcely elapsed since a Parliamentary Commission of Inquiry reported to this House that it might be computed that about 2,385,000 persons, connected with the labouring population, are in distress for thirty weeks in the year, from the want of employment. In the same report, the Commissioners of Poor Inquiry estimate that, in England 1,055,982 agricultural labourers create agricultural produce to the value of 150,-000,000£. per annum, whilst, in Ireland, 1,131,715 produce to the value of only 36,000,000£. They also calculate that, as the cultivated land in England may be estimated at 34,250,000 acres, whilst the cultivated land of Ireland is 14,600,000 acres, there are five labourers in Ireland for every two labourers in England engaged in the cultivation of any given quantity of land. If, therefore, there were the same proportion of labourers to land in Ireland as in England, then about 450,-000 labourers would be required for its cultivation, whereas, in 1831, there were 1,131,715. These results are so startling, that, I own, I view them with some distrust. But the rate of wages affords an infallible test by which we may measure the redundancy of the population, as compared with the means of employment. Now I state with confidence to the House, as well from my own personal observation, as from innumerable sources which cannot be questioned, that the average wages of the Irish labourer, throughout the greater part of that kingdom, do not amount, throughout the year, to 3s. per week—I ought, perhaps, rather to say, to 2s. 6d.

My assertion cannot be contested, when I state that the industrious labourer, often as estimable in all the moral relations of life as any of his superiors, is frequently compelled to live, with his family, upon a diet of potatoes, without milk, unprovided with such clothing as decency requires, and sheltered in a hovel wholly unfit for the residence of man. If the crop of potatoes which he has sown upon his morsel of conacre ground should fail in any degree, he is reduced to that absolute extremity of want, which may be properly designated as starvation. I may state, also, that the unmarried farm servant, whose situation ought to present the most favourable condition of the labourer, living in a farmer's family, receives only one guinea a-quarter, besides his board and lodging. Out of this pittance, he has to provide his clothing.

Let me remark, here, that this is about one-seventh of the wages which the same individual would receive, with superior accommodation and maintenance, as a farm servant in Canada.

We know, also, that, of late years, a very extensive system of eject-ment has prevailed in Ireland—not for the purpose of securing the pay-ment of rent, which is, of course, an incident essential to the mainte-nance of the right of property, but—in order to effect the consolida-tion of farms, for the general improvement of the estates. In the great majority of cases, I fear that such ejectment has been wholly unac-companied by any concurrent provision for the ejected cottier. Noth-ing can be conceived more truly deplorable than the condition of a per-son so ejected. From having been the occupier of a few acres of land, for which he has often paid his rent with the utmost punctuality, he now becomes a forlorn outcast, unable even to procure employment, still less to regain the occupation of land.

Is it surprising that a population in such a state should occasion-ally be tempted to commit acts of violence? What sympathy can they feel with the possessors of property? What, to them, are the advan-tages of law and order? Accordingly, we find that they are too often stimulated to do wrong by despair. Hence we hear of land being turned up, in order to induce the farmers to let out a larger quantity of con-acre for the growth of provision for the labourer; and we find that an extensive ejectment rarely takes place without the accompaniment of outrage. Let it not be supposed that I plead any excuse in this, or jus-tification, for acts of violence; but whilst I cannot withhold my ad-miration from the patient resignation which renders crime and outrage the exception in Ireland, and restrains the Irish poor, under unparal-leled privations, within the limits of the law, I feel bound to assign the true cause to which occasional disturbances may be traced.

### 25. General Causes of German Emigration[1]

Few subjects are more interesting, and none more important, than the process by which the surplus population of Europe is every day being poured into the unpeopled districts of the old and new world, forming there the framework of future nations, which are doubtless destined to carry our knowledge and the traditions of our society to a period when we ourselves may no longer exist as nations. Hitherto the stream has flowed principally from the United Kingdom, particularly

[1] Extracts from *Chambers's Edinburgh Journal* (new series), V (June 13, 1846), 387–89.

Ireland, which the difficulty of obtaining subsistence must, for many years to come, make an emigrating country. An unexampled peace of thirty-one years' duration has likewise had its natural effect on the continent, by the immense increase of population, to stimulate emigration; but more slowly and partially than among us; and it is only within the last ten years that it has grown to an amount, and assumed a direction, which promises serious results.

France has not for the last century been an emigrating country, which may mainly be accounted for by the less independent and energetic character of the people; the greater comfort of the peasantry, who are almost all small proprietors, farming their own lands; and, above all, the enormous chasm in the population left by the revolutionary wars, which alone are computed to have swept away thirteen millions of Frenchmen. . . . .

Germany is the only other country, besides Great Britain, from which emigration takes place on a great scale, and is likely to lead to important results. Since the year 1840, she has sent out annually 60,000 settlers, about our own average. In the present year, the number is stated in the English papers at 80,000. It is very probable that this number will continue for the future, and even increase, as the predisposing causes are not occasional, but permanent, in the subsisting state of the country. The reasons which are all-powerful there, are not the same as actuate us. The results, too, are very different. . . . .

The chief emigration to America at present is from the Upper and Middle Rhine, the Grand Duchy of Baden, Würtemberg, the two Hesses, and Bavaria. In Bavaria especially, whole village communities sell their property for whatever they can get, and set out, with their clergyman at their head. "It is a lamentable sight," says a French writer, "when you are travelling in the spring or autumn on the Strasburg road, to see the long files of carts that meet you every mile, carrying the whole property of the poor wretches, who are about to cross the Atlantic on the faith of a lying prospectus. There they go slowly along; their miserable tumbrils—drawn by such starved, drooping beasts, that your only wonder is, how they can possibly hope to reach Havre alive—piled with the scanty boxes containing their few effects, and on the top of all, the women and children, the sick and bedridden, and all who are too exhausted with the journey to walk. One might take it for a convoy of wounded, the relics of a battlefield, but for the rows of little white heads peeping from beneath the ragged hood." These are the emigrants from Bavaria and the Upper Rhine, who have no sea-port nearer than Havre. Those from the north of Germany, who are comparatively few in number, sail mostly from Bremen. The number of these likewise is increasing. From 1832 to 1835 inclusive, 9,000 embarked every year from Bremen; from 1839 to 1842, the average number was 13,000; which increased to 19,000 in the year 1844.

Society in Germany is so much more rudimentary than in England, that it is remarkable to see this same tendency exhibiting itself in the two nations. In Germany population is comparatively sparse, in Great Britain it is dense; in the one there is great wealth and profound poverty, in the other the extremes of property rarely exist; the one has a large and dominant town population, the other has fewer towns in proportion than any country in Europe; the one teems with political activity, in the other political activity is not, or at least has not yet taken to itself a practical presence and a name.

The dread of destitution is a motive to emigrate in Germany, as in England; but not a principal motive. This is clear from the fact that the emigration does not take place in those districts where there is most want, but exists equally where population is dense, and where it is thinly distributed. In Westphalia, for instance, a great number of small proprietors have lately sold their lands, and sailed for America— each of whom, it is reckoned, has taken with him at least thirty pounds' worth of goods and money. The Bavarians emigrate alike from the Rhine country, where population is thickly clustered together, and from the upland districts, where there are not eighty inhabitants to the square mile.

The one great cause of this almost national movement is the desire for absolute political and religious freedom; the absence of all restrictions upon the development of society; and the publication of opinions which cannot be realized at home. The great agitation in society, caused first by the French domination, and then by the convulsive rise against it, has never passed away. In that gigantic struggle, when everything rested on the popular soul, the bonds of privilege and class were tacitly abandoned, and could never thenceforth be reunited as before. The promises of having constitutional governments, at that time made by the sovereigns to their subjects, have been but partially fulfilled. There is nothing that can be called oppression on the part of the governments; the mass of the people are well satisfied with their rulers and with reason, for the actual executive has been generally excellent; but there are many restrictions, and the young, the restless, and the imaginative thirst for their ideal freedom, and many of them seek for the realization of Utopia in America. Complete religious equality is a still more powerful want in a country where Catholics and Protestants are so nearly balanced, and where the state of parties is such, that the minority in faith, though nominally equal in law, must always live under the cold shade of an alien creed. This of itself has urged many across the Atlantic. It is probable that the present schism among the German Catholics will add to the number of the emigrants from religious causes.

Another motive has been the great success of some of the earlier settlers. The Moravians and Shakers, who have emigrated from Germany, have worked wonders in some parts. In 1815, the Separatists, another religious body, sometimes called Rappists, from their head, M. Rapp, sailed from Würtemberg with a capital only of £1,200, and formed a settlement on the Ohio. At the present time, the real property in land belonging to the society is reckoned at £340,000, exclusive of personal property, and a large sum of money in the funds. The success of the colony of Zoar has been equally striking. It was founded twenty years ago by a few families with a scanty capital, and now possesses 40,000 acres of land, a disposable capital of £100,000, and an immense quantity of machinery and stock, foundries, tan-pits, and mills in abundance. This extraordinary affluence is because these two colonies were founded on the principle of a community of property, and have been throughout under a strict religious government. But the present emigrants forget this; and looking only at the prosperity achieved, they think that as the Moravians and Rappists have succeeded, they must succeed to the same extent, without either the same capital or self-denial.

It is not to be expected that the German governments should look with indifference on this constant and increasing defalcation of their subjects. It is not, as we have said, the very poor that emigrate; they cannot, in fact; but it is those who have some little to spare. Every emigrant is reckoned to take with him equal to £25 of English money, which would give an annual subtraction of £1,500,000 pounds—a serious loss in a country which has little superfluous capital. And be it remembered that this is all loss. Lord Brougham said, in one of his speeches, with equal truth and force, of the English emigrants, that not an axe falls in America but sets in motion a shuttle at Manchester. But the Germans in America consume English, not German commodities, and remit nothing to Germany in the shape of produce. As it is hopeless to try to stop the tide, the German governments have exerted themselves of late to turn it in a direction nearer home—to Hungary and the countries along the Lower Danube, where there is an immensity of rich virgin soil untouched. Austria, in particular, is naturally very much interested in establishing a German population in Hungary, to balance the Slavonic element; and with this view a number of pamphlets have been drawn up and circulated, with a comparative view of the advantages of emigration to Hungary and the United States, but as yet with little effect.

### 26. Why the United States Attracts Emigrants, 1846[1]

From 1776 down to 1845 the Americans have always believed that it is their republican government that attracts emigrants to the United States. . . . . The influence of American institutions acts in a very indirect way upon European emigration. When the emigrants are established in the United States, they often eagerly take advantage of the privileges that are offered them; but they did not leave their native villages to seek political rights in another hemisphere. The time of the Puritans and of William Penn is past. Theories of social reform have given way to a practical desire for immediate well-being.

European emigration is the result of material discomforts; the remedy sought is an improvement in material conditions. For the emigrant it is not the political organization of the United States that is preferable to the institutions of Europe; it is the material condition of America that attracts him, for conditions in America are entirely different and almost always more advantageous to the emigrating classes.

Land, which is cheap, of an almost unlimited extent, fertile enough to make capital unnecessary for its exploitation, is a powerful attraction for the agricultural populations of Europe. During the nineteenth century this attraction has been more powerful than any institution made by men. If they wish to check the immigrant invasion, the Americans should modify the laws regulating the sale of their public lands. . . . . [2]

Such are the resources offered to every immigrant who arrives in the United States. The law of the federal domain insures his material interests. The day after landing he receives the title to an assured position in the agricultural organization of his adopted country, while the

[1] Extract translated from A. van der Straten-Ponthoz, *Recherches sur la situation des émigrants aux États-Unis de l'Amérique du Nord* (Bruxelles, 1846), pp. 19–20, 29–31.

[2] [A detailed description of the public-land policy of the United States has been omitted here.]

naturalization law provides for him the possession of the rights of citizenship.

In the political and social organization of the United States, the two laws, of public lands and of naturalization, have a combined influence upon the whole matter of emigration. If the law of naturalization places the alien in a probationary situation for five years, the law of the federal domain gives to him without delay abundant resources for using this period of probation to create an independent position for himself. . . . .

Those emigrants who stop in the seacoast cities . . . . instead of going to work on the federal domain are a disturbing element in the working of American institutions. These urban emigrants exercise the prerogatives of citizenship only as the followers of the political parties of which they become the blind instruments. They accept the passions of party politics without having an understanding of social interests involved.

Both American laws relating to naturalization and public domain have an equal influence as regards the situation in Europe. To the classes there who are seeking especially an opportunity for productive labor and a less laborious existence, the law regulating the sale of public lands promises assured resources. To those individuals who are restless and harassed by their eagerness for reform, the naturalization law offers the exercise of all the rights of a republican government in the midst of all the theories of democracy. . . . .

These then are the conditions presented by a vast region in North America to the pressing demands of European emigrants. These two laws . . . . are the advantages offered to emigrants by the American people.

### 27.  State Aid for Irish Emigration Condemned, 1847[1]

Lord John Russell [introducing the new government measures on the state of Ireland in the House of Commons, January 25, 1847], spoke as follows:

. . . . In proceeding to consider the condition of the country in which this calamity has occurred, I think it is the safest course to use

[1] Extract from *Hansard's Parliamentary Debates*, Vol. LXXXIX (3d series, 1847), cols. 427–49. In addition to the sources referred to in this volume further contemporary accounts of economic conditions in Ireland before 1865 may be found in other volumes of *Hansard's Debates* and in the reports of other investigating commissions. A convenient summary of the early reports, many of which are not available in American libraries, will be found in the *Report of the Royal Commis-*

the guarded language of the report made on the inquiry respecting provision made by the Poor Laws in Ireland, and to ask the House to infer from that report how great was likely to be the calamity if there should be a total failure of the potato crop in that country. In the First Report of that Poor Inquiry Commission—a commission including many persons of considerable authority, who were Irishmen, and well acquainted with their country—they give their reason for not making a report so soon as was expected. . . . .

In their Third Report, which was the foundation of the measure that was then adopted, they state:

It appears that in Great Britain the agricultural families constitute little more than a fourth, while in Ireland they constitute about two-thirds of the whole population; that there were in Great Britain, in 1831, 1,055,982 agricultural labourers; in Ireland 1,131,715, although the cultivated land of Great Britain amounts to about 34,250,000 acres, and that of Ireland only to about 14,600,000. . . . . It further appears that the agricultural produce of Great Britain is more than four times that of Ireland; that agricultural wages vary from 6d. to 1s. a day; that the average of the country in general is about 8½d.; and that the earnings of the labourers come, on an average of the whole class, to from 2s. to 2s. 6d. a week, or thereabouts, for the year round. Thus circumstanced, it is impossible for the able-bodied, in general, to provide against sickness or the temporary absence of employment, or against old age, or the destitution of their widows and children, in the contingent event of their own premature decease. A great portion of them are insufficiently provided at any time with the commonest necessaries of life. Their habitations are wretched hovels; several of a family sleep together upon straw or upon the bare ground, sometimes with a blanket, sometimes even without so much to cover them. Their food commonly consists of dry potatoes; and with these they are at times so scantily supplied as to be obliged to stint themselves to one spare meal in the day. There are instances of persons being driven by hunger to seek sustenance in wild herbs. They sometimes get a

sion on the Poor Law, 1909, Ireland (Cd. 4630). For other accounts see also the following: Elizabeth Fry and John Gurney, Report on a Late Visit to Ireland (London, 1827); J. R. Elmore, Letters on the State of Ireland (London, 1828); Michael Sadler, Ireland, Its Evils and Their Remedies (London, 1829); John Barrow, A Tour round Ireland (London, 1836); Gustave de Beaumont, Ireland, Social, Political and Religious (Eng. trans.; London, 1839); Sidney Godolphin Osborne, Gleanings in the West of Ireland (London, 1850); Transactions of the Central Relief Committee of the Society of Friends during the Famine in Ireland, 1846–47 (Dublin, 1852); George Nicholls, History of the Irish Poor Law (London, 1856); John Stuart Mill, England and Ireland (2d ed.; London, 1856); Adolphe Perraud, Études sur l'Irlande contemporaine, especially Vol. II (Paris, 1862); Nassau W. Senior, Journals, Conversations, and Essays Relating to Ireland (2d ed.; London, 1868).

herring, or a little milk; but they never get meat, except at Christmas, Easter, or Shrove-tide. Some go in search of employment to Great Britain during the harvest, others wander through Ireland with the same view. The wives and children of many are occasionally obliged to beg; they do so reluctantly and with shame, and in general go to a distance from home, that they may not be known. Mendicancy, too, is the sole resource of the aged and impotent of the poorer classes in general, when children or relatives are unable to support them. To it, therefore, crowds are driven for the means of existence; and the knowledge that such is the fact leads to an indiscriminate giving of alms, which encourages idleness, imposture, and general crime.

Such was the description, given upon the most undoubted authority, of the state of the labouring classes in Ireland, even amidst time of comparative plenty: it may be easily imagined that when those who are best off, in the most prosperous years, earn scarcely sufficient, those who had then been on the brink of famine, must have been unable to resist the flood of destitution and wretchedness which has overwhelmed them by the failure of the potato crop. Such has been unfortunately the case in the present year, during the visitation of a calamity which is, perhaps, almost without a parallel, because it acts upon a very large population, a population of nearly 8,000,000—for the Irish have gradually increased to that amount—while the famine is such as has not been known in modern times; indeed, I should say it is like a famine of the thirteenth century acting upon the population of the nineteenth.

Such being the general condition of the population, and the nature of the calamity that had befallen them, I will state what is the course which was adopted during the past year and down to the present time. When Parliament met last year, it was apprehended that, the potatoes having been much injured, there was danger of a very great scarcity in that country. That apprehension was not fully justified by the event. It was impossible, as I think, for anyone exactly to say, what the extent of the misfortune would be; but the fact, I believe, was there having been a very plentiful crop of potatoes in the previous year, that although there was a very great quantity of potatoes injured in 1845, yet the quantity of food in Ireland in the early part of last year was not very deficient. Parliament, however, took means very early in the Session to supply food to the destitute by means of giving employment upon the roads, and by public works. It was enacted, that upon presentment sessions being held in any barony, there should be a power to apply for money from the Treasury upon loan, and there should be a grant of money. Under this law, presentments were made to the extent of more than 1,000,000£, I think; the presentments to the 31st of

August, I believe, were 1,372,000£; what was recommended by the Board of Works amounted to 476,000£, and there was actually expended to that time 290,000£. . . . .

There is another subject, likewise, with respect to which I am not prepared to make any statement to the House, but upon which I know large expectations are entertained in Ireland—I allude to emigration. I confess I think that, although Parliament may assist emigration to a certain extent, the extravagant expectations which are entertained on this head can never possibly be fulfilled. It is stated by Sir Robert Kane, and truly, that when persons are removed from a locality by emigration, the number removed is never so large as to produce a sensible effect on the population. I do not believe that any emigration which may take place as the result of either private or public exertion can ever, according to the ordinary amount of emigration, produce such an effect as to enable the remaining population to earn a competent amount of wages. But before we make extraordinary efforts to increase emigration, it is necessary to consider an important point. If we attempt to go beyond that which is the ordinary annual emigration, and to convey a million of persons at once across the ocean, you must look not only to the advantage which you suppose would arise from not having those persons in Ireland competing with other labourers, but you must also inquire what funds, what means, there are in the country to which they must be carried, to secure them subsistence. If by the public means, and a large addition to the public burdens, you convey a hundred thousand persons to the United States, that country would have just cause to complain of our having cast our paupers on her shores, to be maintained by her, when their maintenance was a primary obligation upon ourselves. Then, again, if we should attempt to introduce a hundred thousand emigrants into Canada, the market would be glutted by the redundant supply; and the labourers there, instead of obtaining a fair amount of the means of subsistence, as they do now, would enter into a fierce competition with each other, and thus a state of things would be produced in Nova Scotia and Canada in some respects similar to that from which the emigrants had fled at home.

In considering the subject of emigration when I held the seals of the Colonial Department, I was, I confess, disposed to go further than I did; and the obstacle was of a financial nature rather than any unwillingness on my part. It appeared to me, however, that the best mode by which emigration could be promoted was by taking charge of

the emigrant, not at his present place of abode, not at the port of embarkation, but at the port where he disembarked, and then convey
him to some field where he would find a market for his labour. Accordingly, I proposed for that purpose a grant of money, which has
since been continued, being in some years more and in some years less,
by means of which many emigrants have been conveyed to Montreal,
to Kingston, and other places in the western part of Canada, and placed
in situations where they could earn a subsistence. Now, the emigration which has been going on in this way of late years has been very
large. In 1845 the number so emigrating to our North American colonies was 31,303, and to the United States, 58,538, making altogether
about 90,841. In the first three-quarters of the year 1846, which contains the great bulk of emigration, the number emigrating to the North
American colonies was 42,404, to the United States 67,792, making a
total number of 110,196. The character of the emigration in 1846 is
very similar to that of the two previous seasons. Mr. Hawke, an emigration agent, stated in his report that he was not aware that the number of indigent settlers in 1846 had been much greater, in proportion,
than usual; but there certainly was a larger number of the Irish emigrants in a state of destitution as to clothes and bedding, far exceeding
anything he had ever before witnessed. The agent at Quebec stated in
his report that " . . . . there is little, if any, distress among the emigrants of the last year, unless as the consequence of their own fatuity.
Employment is generally to be procured at remunerative wages, and
provisions and necessaries are plentiful." Seeing, then, that there had
been a large amount of emigration last year—seeing that it was observed by the emigration agents that there were still a large number
of pauper families from Ireland—I should be deterred from attempting
to give a stimulus to emigration, which might have one of two effects:
either of sending out a great number of paupers who would be unable
to find employment, or, what would perhaps be equally objectionable,
causing a waste of the public money by carrying at the expense of the
country those who were able to obtain the means of paying for their
passage, but who, instead of calling upon their friends and relatives in
Canada and other colonies for assistance, would come upon the public
funds. Such a system would be destructive of all habits of prudence
and foresight. Sir, there are some difficulties in the way of emigration,
occasioned by the provisions of the Passenger Act,[1] under the consider-

---

[1] [For material dealing with the "Passenger Acts," or as they are more commonly called in this country "steerage laws," see the first volume of this series
E. Abbott, *Immigration: Select Documents and Case Records*, Part I.]

ation of the Government, which we hope to remove; but whatever measures we may bring forward to facilitate emigration, we wish it to be understood that we do not mean to propose any scheme of a great or extended nature. I know not whether Sir R. Kane's estimate of the resources of Ireland is to be taken altogether as a sober one; but he maintains that so great are her agricultural, independent of her other resources—so great are her mineral resources and means of manufacturing employment by water power, that no less than 17,000,000 of people could be maintained in that country. I will not enter into that calculation; but this I will say, that I do think, if a good agricultural system was introduced into Ireland; if there was good security for the investment of money in land; if the proprietors themselves would undertake the task of improving the country, and if other classes would co-operate with them—I say I do not think the present population of Ireland is excessive.

## 28. Colonization Preferred to Emigration, 1847[1]

The actual excess of numbers in Ireland is so great as to be incurable without a diminution of numbers. It is idle to hope that the balance between employment and labour will be redressed by increase of employment alone; nay, the actual excess of numbers is an impediment fatal to the beneficial operation of measures intended to increase employment. There is a circle of evil which we believe cannot be broken through save by a great mortality or a great emigration. Supposing starvation to be prevented this year by maintaining millions of destitute people at the public cost, what, we must ask, is to happen in the year 1848 and in the year 1849? We do suppose that a great mortality will be prevented by this means, but this is not a remedy; it is only a palliative; and we cannot help believing, that without a positive diminution of numbers, the remedies which may be intended for permanent effect will at best only mitigate the evil; nay, that in the long run this may prove one of those cases in which palliatives have the effect of increasing the difficulty of a radical cure.

Let us pause for a moment, to consider more carefully the nature and extent of the crisis with which we have to deal. It is perfectly notorious and undeniable that the destruction of the potato crop in Ireland must produce, not only an immense amount of temporary misery,

[1] Extract from a letter to Lord John Russell, the Prime Minister, which was signed by W. H. Gregory, M.P.; M. J. O'Connell, M.P.; J. R. Godley, published in the London *Spectator*, XX, Supplement of April 3, 1847, pp. 1–5.

but a complete revolution in the agriculture and social economy of that country. Hitherto, the great mass of the Irish agricultural labourers and their families (who constitute nearly three-fourths of the whole population) have depended almost entirely for their support on potatoes; that is, on the lowest and cheapest kind of food. Henceforward they must cease to do so; and, consequently, means must be found for supplying them with cereal food, that is, with food *more than twice as expensive* as potatoes. This sudden and compulsory transition from a lower to a higher kind of food constitutes a phenomenon unparalleled in history; and we believe that public attention has not been sufficiently drawn to its inevitable consequences. . . . .

In order, then, to enable Ireland to feed her inhabitants, there are but two alternatives which can be suggested: first, the introduction of capital *ab extra* to such an amount, and its application in such a manner, as will immediately and greatly increase production; or, secondly, such a diminution of the numbers to be fed as will preserve them within the limits of the existing resources. Now, the first alternative requires only to be stated in order that all may see the impossibility of its application. The very nature of the disease precludes the use of the remedy. Capital will not flow into a country where the whole social system is in process of revolution, where millions are struggling for life, and where, consequently, there cannot be security or protection for person and property. . . . . Unless, then, the people of England are prepared to say that they will, for many years to come, supply the Irish people with imported food at an immense expense, or suffer them to starve by millions, they must turn to the second alternative with a deep and earnest desire that safe and salutary means may be found for insuring its immediate and extensive application. It is to diminish the redundant numbers of Ireland by means of well-regulated emigration.

. . . . Inasmuch as the object of emigration is to remove a pressure of excessive numbers, so heavy as to prevent the operation of measures otherwise calculated to produce a sound state of social economy in Ireland, so it is essential that the amount of emigration should be sufficient for the purpose in view. An emigration which might be termed great, and which might be very large in comparison with any that has yet taken place, would be of no avail at all unless it were large enough. However large it were, if it were short of the requisite amount, it would not be a remedy, but only a palliative. . . . .

In order to produce the results which we have in view, we are persuaded that emigration must be limited by nothing but the indisposition to emigrate; that it must be coextensive with the motives which lead to emigration. When it should be seen that emigration from Ireland was beginning to diminish, not in consequence of any decrease of demand for Irish labour in new countries, nor in consequence of any diminution of the means of paying for a passage, but in consequence of a general facility of obtaining employment in Ireland, whether that facility had been occasioned by increase of employment or decrease of numbers, or both; then—that is, when the motives to remaining at home were seen to be growing stronger than the motives to emigration —it would be obvious that the amount of emigration had been sufficient. There appears to be no other adequate test of the sufficiency of this remedy in aid. We must own, therefore, that we contemplate a very large increase of emigration.

Comparing the probable amount of a sufficient increase with any increase that is likely to take place in consequence of measures hitherto adopted by the Legislature, we must confess that those measures (such as the arrangements at present made for aiding poor Irish emigrants on their arrival in British North America) appear not only totally inadequate, but likewise really irrelevant to the present emergency. There is a good deal of vague remark about present emigration from Ireland, and assistance afforded by Government to the emigrants, as a probable means of beneficially affecting the social state of Ireland: the two subjects are mentioned together, as if there was really an important connexion between them. We object to this view of the matter, as claiming for present arrangements by the State, with regard to emigration from Ireland, a degree of importance which in nowise belongs to them. The arrangements, so far as they go, are useful and praiseworthy; the present emigration is good for the emigrants; good for the new countries where they settle; good for the manufacturers and commerce of the United Kingdom, whose field of employment for capital and labour is enlarged by it; often good for the particular localities relieved; but it has no closer relation to the cure of Irish distress considered nationally, than a spark has to fire as a means of giving warmth.
. . . .

Amongst the poorer classes in Ireland, there is a disposition to emigrate and settle in new countries, which has no assignable limit. If, at this time, the power to emigrate were coextensive with the inclination, millions would seek a home in countries where land is cheap, and the wages of labour and the profits of capital are both higher than anywhere in Europe. In that case, the entire process of an effectual social reform in Ireland might be commenced without delay. But the power to emigrate has obvious limits: it cannot exceed either the demand for immigrant labour in new countries, or the means possessed by the Irish poor of paying for a passage. The aim of our plan is to extend these limits—to cause such an increase of the new-country demand for labour, and of the means of removing, that the prevalent disposition to emigrate shall be unchecked.

But we must emphatically declare that it is not our object to increase mere emigration from Ireland. The going forth of the poorest and most helpless class of people in the world, to be hewers of wood and drawers of water in distant countries, is not to be deplored only because, on the whole, it is better than the existing alternative. But, though for that reason not to be regretted, still it is attended by circumstances which render it so unsatisfactory and displeasing as to produce comparatively little desire for its extension. Nor can there be a doubt that emigration from Ireland, in order to be much extended, must be altered in character. As well, therefore, from a feeling of repugnance to the present kind of emigration—which has been justly termed a shovelling out of our paupers—as from a conviction that the mode must be greatly changed in order to increase the quantity, we trust that her Majesty's Government and Parliament may see fit to treat emigration as but a part of something else—that is, as one of the elements of colonization. We are not the advocates of an augmented emigration from Ireland, but of an Irish colonization which would comprise increased emigration. . . . .

That part of the Irish nation to which a measure of colonization would be chiefly applicable, consists, for the most part, of the descendants of the ancient native population as distinguished from the Anglo-Irish, and presents a social aspect widely different from that of the latter—different in circumstances and position, as well as in religion, habits, and character. While they constitute the great majority in point of numbers, they possess, comparatively speaking, a very small amount of property, and especially of property in land. It is needless, and would be out of place, to advert to the causes of this disproportion; but there is one effect of it which we are satisfied must be deeply impressed on the minds of those who would frame a good plan of colonization for Ireland: the Irish Roman Catholic population comprises so small a proportion of the middle and highest classes that it may be said to consist mainly of an indigent and uneducated peasantry. The exceptions from this rule consist mainly of a very few landowners, a few lawyers and other professional men, and some merchants and tradesmen—but few in comparison with the proportion of the richer classes among the Protestants; and, lastly, the clergy. The Irish Roman Catholic people may be said to have, practically, almost no aristocracy—no natural leaders but their priesthood; while, from their peculiarities of character and circumstances, they stand more in need of leadership than any people on the face of the earth. . . . .

There is another influence, however, to which we attach a high degree of importance. It is that of nationality. Apart from religion, the Irish Roman Catholics are what may be termed a national people; that is, they are a people bound together and separated from the rest of the world by peculiarities and sympathies of historical recollections, of actual circumstances, of customs and sentiments, and perhaps of origin or blood. They mix but little with any other people, either in England, Scotland, the English part of Ireland, or even in the new countries to which vast numbers of them emigrate. This, like their religion and its potent influence on them, is a fact of which no human power can alter the complexion; and we believe it to be one on which a sound measure of Roman Catholic Irish colonization must of necessity be founded. We believe that, in order to plant any number of them happily in a new country, and in order to render that country attractive to great numbers of them, their national sympathies and associations, as well as their religion, must be carefully preserved and deliberately used for the furtherance of the best results which religion and nationality are capable of producing. It appears to us, therefore, most unadvisable to scatter Irish emigration over numerous distinct colonies. . . . .

But an Irish Roman Catholic emigration must chiefly consist of mere labourers seeking employment by the capital of the country to which they emigrate. Of capital for the employment of emigrants food is the main item. Of such capital the greatest abundance exists in North America; and there is no other country in which it exists in sufficient abundance for the objects in view.

But the great part of North America is a foreign country. We do not stop to ask whether it would be allowable or possible for the Government to make arrangements with that of the United States for the reception and absorption of a great Irish emigration in the latter country, because there are circumstances in the United States, independent of the point of foreign dominion, which unfit that country for the prosperity of a great Irish colonization. If ever two nationalities came into collision by meeting, it is the Irish and the American in the United States. Everywhere in the United States, the Irish-born part of the population is only tolerated by the native Americans as what has been termed "a serviceable nuisance"; it is a population of foreigners and outcasts, exceedingly valuable as a mass of labour which gives productiveness to capital in a country where the natives dislike working for hire, but socially despised, and in so many ways ill-treated, that practically it does not enjoy that equality of rights which is the boast of the American democracy. Your Lordship is doubtless aware of the recent organization of a party in the United States with the name of Native Americans. The object of this association is to give effect to the American sentiment of hostility to the Irish. The existence of that sentiment in the United States, founded as it is on antipathies of religion and race, and prevailing in a country whose Irish-born inhabitants must, under any circumstances, be a small minority, would be a fatal impediment to the employment of the religious and national peculiarities of the Irish as a means of prosperous colonization, even if the United States were in the British Empire. The American Union is only suitable for a mere immigration of the Irish as hewers of wood and drawers of water. We turn, therefore, to the part of North America in which no such impediments exist. In British North America, an Irish colonization, if it were so conducted as to be orderly and prosperous, would be cordially welcomed by the present inhabitants. A colonization directed to British North America might be regulated and fostered by the British Government. The field of colonization, therefore, which we propose, is the British provinces in the neighbourhood of the St. Lawrence. . . . .

The introduction of British capital into Canada, as a means of enriching the colony and increasing employment for Irish emigrants, would be brought about, we conceive, without any cost to the State; but the above-mentioned aids of settlement would not be provided by private enterprise; and therefore a direct outlay on the part of the State is required for them. Irish settlement, to use a common expression, does not "pay" in Canada. . . . . Wherefore, it may be said, neither ought the State to embark in it. But in reply to this objection, we must observe, that although commercial speculation is not a proper function of the State, the taking care of its people assuredly is. The question of cost to the State, therefore, is one of political expediency—we had almost said, necessity. Either in Ireland or somewhere else, the State must incur a heavy outlay in consequence of the state of Ireland. The question, then, is, Which of the two would be the less costly and the more effectual—expenditure in Ireland, or expenditure on Irish colonization in Canada? That expenditure in Canada would be the more effectual there cannot be the slightest doubt; for expenditure in Ireland will have no effect in diminishing numbers—none but a bad effect, perhaps, except the saving of lives; whereas expenditure on Irish settlement in Canada, in aid of Irish colonization, would be a cost once incurred, and, if its amount were sufficient, would put an end to the expenditure in Ireland. . . . .

We also think that it would be necessary for the Imperial Government to assist in defraying the cost of passage for poor emigrants. The source from which funds for this purpose are principally derived is remittance from America to Ireland by emigrants who have saved money, and who thus aid their friends and relatives at home in following their example. The discovery of the large amount of such remittances has only just been made by the British public and Government; so little, under ordinary circumstances, do the British Government and public know of the state of Irish emigrants in America, and of their sympathies and intercourse with the Irish at home. But large as the sum is—unusually great as it will be this year—its limits are sure to be too narrow for so great an emigration as would make a sensible impression on the population of Ireland. We look, therefore, to a further outlay by the Government in the shape of passage-money for emigrants.

## 29. The Irish Famine Exodus of 1847[1]

In the autumn and winter of 1846 efforts were made to induce the Government to take an active part in assisting emigration by an apportionment of the expense of passage and outfit between the public, the landlords, and the emigrants themselves; but, on a full consideration of the subject, it appeared that the emigration about to take place in the ensuing season to Canada and the United States, without any assistance from the public, was likely to be quite as large as those countries could properly absorb, and that the consequence of the interference of the Government would be that the movement would be carried beyond those limits which were consistent with safety, and that a burden would be transferred to the taxpayers of the United Kingdom,

[1] Extract from "The Irish Crisis," *Edinburgh Review*, LXXXVII (January, 1848), 289–97, 303.

which would otherwise be borne by those to whom it properly belonged, owing to their interests being more immediately concerned. It is also a point of primary importance, that those persons should emigrate, who, from age, health, character, and circumstances, are best able to contend with the hardships and difficulties of a settler's life, and it was considered that this object would be most fully attained if the emigration was entirely voluntary. The true test of fitness in this case is the possession, on the part of each individual concerned, of the will and ability to emigrate; and the probability of helpless multitudes being sent forth, who, both for their own sakes and for that of the colony, ought to have remained at home, is increased in proportion as other motives and other interests besides those of the emigrant himself influence his act of expatriation. For these reasons Her Majesty's ministers determined to confine themselves to taking increased securities for the safety of the emigrants during their voyage, and their early and satisfactory settlement after their arrival abroad. Several additional emigration agents were appointed to Liverpool and to different Irish ports; the annual vote in aid of colonial funds for the relief of sick and destitute emigrants from the United Kingdom was increased from 1000£ to 10,000£; provision was made for giving assistance in the case of emigrant ships driven back by stress of weather, and the Governor-General of Canada was informed that Her Majesty's Government would be prepared to defray its fair share of any further expense that might have to be incurred in giving the emigrants necessary relief, or in forwarding them to places where they might obtain employment.

Early in the year 1847 the roads to the Irish sea-ports were thronged with families hastening to escape the evils which impended over their native land. The complaint in Ireland, at the time, was that those who went belonged to the best and most substantial class of the agricultural population. The complaint afterwards in Canada was, that those who came were the helpless and destitute. The fact was, that the emigrants generally belonged to that class of small holders, who being somewhat above the level of the prevailing destitution, had sufficient resources left to enable them to make the effort required to effect their removal to a foreign land; and the steps taken by them to convert their property into an available form, had for months before been the subject of observation. Large remittances, estimated to amount to 200,000£ in the year ending on the 30th March,. 1847, were also made by the Irish emigrants settled in the United States, and the British North American provinces, to enable their relations in Ireland to follow them. The emigration of 1846 from the United Kingdom, which was the largest ever known up to that time, amounted to 129,851 persons; the emigration of the first three-quarters of 1847 was 240,461; and almost the whole of it was from Ireland to Canada and the United States.

Even this does not represent the full extent of the outpouring of the population of Ireland which took place in this eventful year. From the 13th January to the 1st November, 278,005 immigrants arrived at Liverpool from Ireland, of whom only 122,981 sailed from that port to foreign countries. The conflux of this mixed multitude was formidable both to the health and resources of the inhabitants of Liverpool. . . . .

There is no subject of which a merely one-sided view is more commonly taken than that of Emigration. The evils arising from the crowded state of the population, and the facility with which large numbers of persons may be transferred to other countries, are naturally uppermost in the minds of landlords and rate-payers; but Her Majesty's Government, to which the well-being of the British population in every quarter of the globe is confided, must have an equal regard to the interests of the emigrant and of the colonial community of which he may become a member. It is a great mistake to suppose that even Canada and the United States have an unlimited capacity of absorbing a new population. The labour market in the settled districts is always so nearly full, that a small addition to the persons in search of employment makes a sensible difference; while the clearing of new land requires the possession of resources,[1] and a power of sustained exertion not ordinarily belonging to the newly-arrived Irish emigrant.

In this, as well as in the other operations by which society is formed or sustained, there is a natural process which cannot with impunity be departed from. A movement is continually going on towards the back woods on the part of the young and enterprising portion of the settled population, and of such of the former emigrants as have acquired means and experience; and the room thus made is occupied by persons recently arrived from Europe, who have only their labour to depend upon. The conquest of the wilderness requires more than the ordinary share of energy and perseverance, and every attempt that has yet been

[1] Settlers in the backwoods must have the means of support from twelve to fifteen months after their arrival, and this cannot be accomplished for less than 60£, at the lowest estimate, for each family consisting of a man, his wife, and three children, or equal to 3½ adults on an average.

made to turn Paupers into Backwoodsmen by administrative measures, has ended in signal failure. As long as they were rationed, they held together in a feeble, helpless state; and when the issue of rations ceased, they generally returned to the settled parts of the country. Our recent experience of the effects of a similar state of dependence in Ireland, offers no encouragement to renew the experiment in a distant country, where the difficulties are so much greater, and a disastrous result would be so much less capable of being retrieved.

It must also be observed, that from an early period of the present distress, two modes of meeting the calamity presented themselves, which have since acquired greater distinctness in people's minds, and have been acted upon in a more and more systematic manner. The first of these was to stimulate the industry of the people, to augment the productive powers of the soil, and to promote the establishment of new industrial occupations, so as to cause the land once more to support its population, and to substitute a higher standard of subsistence, and a higher tone of popular character, for those which prevailed before. This plan aimed at accomplishing the object without the pain or risk of wholesale expatriation; and the result proposed by it was to increase the strength and prosperity of the country and the happiness of the people, by enabling the present population to maintain itself comfortably at home by the exercise of its industry. The Government adopted this plan from the first, and has since promoted its success by every means in its power. The other plan was to relieve the mother country by transferring large masses of people to the Colonies, and great efforts were made to obtain the command of public funds to assist in paying the expense of this emigration.

The main point, therefore, is, that by taking an active part in assisting emigration, the Government would throw their weight into the scale with the last of these two plans. They would assist it by their means; and, what is of far more consequence, they would countenance it by their authority: and in the same degree, they would discourage and relax the efforts of those who are exerting themselves to carry out the opposite plan. In order to appreciate the full ultimate effect of such an interposition, it must be remembered that the solution of the great difficulty by means of emigration carried out on the scale and in the manner proposed, offers to the promoters of it the attraction of accomplishing their object by a cheap and summary process; while the other remedy, of enabling the population to live comfortably at home, can be arrived at only by an expensive, laborious, and protracted course of exertion: and it therefore behoves the Government, which holds the balance between contending parties, to take care to which side it lends its influence on a social question of this description.

Those who have purchased or inherited estates in which a redundant population has been permitted or encouraged to grow up, may with propriety assist some of their people to emigrate, provided they take care to prevent their being left destitute on their arrival in their new country. The expense of assisting emigration under such circumstances properly falls on the proprietor. A surplus population, whether it be owing to the fault or to the misfortune of the proprietor or his predecessors, must, like barrenness, or the absence of improvements, be regarded as one of the disadvantages contingent on the possession of the estate; and he who enjoys the profits and advantages of the estate, must also submit to the less desirable conditions connected with it. So long as emigration is conducted only at the expense of the proprietor, it is not likely to be carried to an injurious or dangerous extent, and it will press so heavily on his resources, as to leave the motives to exertion of a different kind unimpaired. Emigration is open to objection only when the natural checks and correctives have been neutralised by the interposition of the Government, or other public bodies. It then becomes the interest and policy of the landed proprietor to make no exertion to maintain his people at home, to produce a general impression that no such exertion could be successfully made, and to increase by every possible means the pressure upon those parties, who, having the command of public funds, are expected to give their assistance; and the responsibility of the consequences, whatever they may be, becomes transferred from the individual proprietors to the Government or public body which countenances and promotes their proceedings. . . . .

The fearful problem to be solved in Ireland, stated in its simplest form, is this: A large population subsisting on potatoes which they raised for themselves, has been deprived of that resource, and how are they now to be supported? The obvious answer is, by growing something else. But that cannot be, because the small patches of land which maintained a family when laid down to potatoes, are insufficient for the purpose when laid down to corn or any other kind of produce; and corn cultivation requires capital and skill, and combined labour, which the cotter and conacre tenants do not possess.

### 30.  The Distressed Condition of Ireland, 1847: An Irish View[1]

. . . . The state of the country grew worse from day to day. It is difficult now to realise the condition of the western population in the autumn of 1847; but a witness of unexceptionable impartiality has painted it in permanent colours. A young Englishman[2] representing the Society of Friends, who in that tragic time did work worthy of the Good Samaritan, reported what he saw in Mayo and Galway in language which for plain vigour rivals the narratives of Defoe. This is what he saw in Westport:

The town of Westport was in itself a strange and fearful sight, like what we read of in beleaguered cities; its streets crowded with gaunt wanderers, sauntering to and fro with hopeless air and hunger-struck look—a mob of starved, almost naked, women around the poor-house clamouring for soup tickets—our inn, the head-quarters of the road engineer and pay clerks, beset by a crowd of beggars for work .

As he approached Galway, the rural population were found to be in a more miserable condition:

Some of the women and children that we saw on the road were abject cases of poverty and almost naked. The few rags they had on were with the greatest difficulty held together, and in a few weeks, as they are utterly unable to provide themselves with fresh clothes unless they be given them, they must become absolutely naked.

And in another district:

As we went along, our wonder was not that the people died, but that they lived; and I have no doubt whatever that in any other country the mortality would have been far greater; that many lives have been prolonged, perhaps saved, by the long apprenticeship to want in which the Irish peasant has been trained, and by that lovely, touching charity which prompts him to share his scanty meal with his starving neighbour.

The fishermen of the Cladagh, who were induced to send the Whig Attorney-General to Parliament a few months before, had to pledge the implements of their calling for a little daily bread:

Even the very nets and tackling of these poor fishermen, I heard, were pawned, and, unless they be assisted to redeem them, they will be unable to take advantage of the herring shoals, even when they approach their coast. . . . . In order to ascertain the truth of this statement, I went into two or

[1] Extract from Sir Charles Gavan Duffy, *Four Years of Irish History, 1845–1849* (London: Cassell, Petter, Galpin & Co., 1883), pp. 430–33, 527–32.

[2] W. E. Forster. These extracts are taken from the *Transactions of the Central Relief Committee of the Society of Friends.*

three of the largest pawnshops, the owners of which fully confirmed it and said they had in pledge at least a thousand pounds' worth of such property and saw no likelihood of its being redeemed.

In a rural district which he revisited after an interval he paints a scene which can scarcely be matched in the annals of a mediaeval plague:

One poor woman whose cabin I had visited said, "There will be nothing for us but to lie down and die." I tried to give her hope of English aid, but, alas! her prophecy has been too true. Out of a population of 240 I found thirteen already dead from want. The survivors were like walking skeletons —the men gaunt and haggard, stamped with the livid mark of hunger—the children crying with pain—the women in some of the cabins too weak to stand. When there before I had seen cows at almost every cabin, and there were besides many sheep and pigs owned in the village. But now all the sheep were gone—all the cows—all the poultry killed—only one pig left— the very dogs which had barked at me before had disappeared; no potatoes— no oats.

Speaking of Clifden, he says:

To get to their work many of the men have to walk five, even seven, Irish miles; the sergeant of a police station by the road-side told us that the custom of these men was to take a little meal gruel before starting in the morning, taking but one meal one day and treating themselves with two the next. He mentioned cases in which they had worked till they fell over their tools. Four- and- sixpence per week thus earned, the sole resource of a family of six, with Indian meal, their cheapest food, at 2/10 to 4/- per stone! What is this but slow death—a mere enabling the patient to endure for a little longer time the disease of hunger?

The young man pointed the moral which these horrible spectacles suggested with laudable courage:

I would not now discuss the causes of this condition, nor attempt to ap- portion blame to its authors; but of this one fact there can be no question: that the result of our social system is that vast numbers of our fellow-coun- trymen—of the peasantry of one of the richest nations the world ever knew— have not leave to live. . . . .

The weekly returns of the dead were like the bulletin of a fierce campaign. As the end of the year approached, villages and rural dis- tricts, which had been prosperous and populous a year before, were desolate. In some places the loss amounted to half the resident popu- lation. Even the paupers shut up in poor-houses did not escape. More than one in six perished of the unaccustomed food. The people did not everywhere consent to die patiently. In Armagh and Down groups of men went from house to house in the rural districts and insisted on being fed. In Tipperary and Waterford corn-stores and bakers' shops were sacked. In Donegal the people seized upon a flour-mill and pillaged it. In Limerick 5,000 men assembled on Tory Hill, and declared that they would not starve. A local clergyman restrained them by the promise of speedy relief. "If the Government did not act promptly, he himself would show them where food could be had." In a few cases crops were carried away from farms. The offences which spring from suffering and fear were heard of in many districts, but they were encountered with instant resistance. There were 30,000 men in red jackets, carefully fed, clothed, and lodged, ready to maintain the law. Four prisoners were convicted at the Galway assizes of stealing a filly, which they killed and ate to preserve their own lives. In Enniskillen two boys under twelve years of age were convicted of stealing one pint of Indian meal cooked into "stirabout," and Chief Justice Blackburn vindicated the outraged law by transporting them for seven years. Other children committed larcenies that they might be sent to gaol, where there was still daily bread to be had. In Mayo the people were eating carrion wherever it could be procured, and the coroner could not keep pace with the inquests; for the law sometimes spent more to ascertain the cause of a pauper's death than would have sufficed to preserve his life.

The social disorganisation was a spectacle as afflicting as the waste of life; it was the waste of whatever makes life worth possessing. All the institutions which civilise and elevate the people were disappearing one after another. The churches were half empty; the temperance reading-rooms were shut up; the mechanics' institute no longer got support; only the gaols and the poor-houses were crowded. A new generation, born in disease and reared in destitution, pithless and imbecile, threatened to drag down the nation to hopeless slavery. Trade was paralysed; no one bought anything which was not indispensable at the hour. The loss of the farmers in potatoes was estimated at more than twenty millions sterling, and with the potatoes the pigs which fed on them disappeared. The seed procured at a high price in spring again failed; time, money, and labour were lost, and another year of famine was certain. All who depended on the farmer had sunk with him; shopkeepers were beggared, tradesmen were starving, the priests living on voluntary offerings were sometimes in fearful distress when the people had no longer anything to offer. . . . .

When the increased mortality was pressed on the attention of the Government, Lord John Russell replied that the owners of property in Ireland ought to support the poor born on their estates. It was a perfectly just proposition if the ratepayers were empowered to determine the object and method of the expenditure; but prohibiting reproductive work, and forcing them to turn strong men into paupers, and keep them sweltering in workhouses instead of labouring to reclaim the waste lands—this was not justice. . . . .

The people fled before the famine to England, America, and the British colonies. They carried with them the seed of disease and death. In England a bishop and more than twenty priests died of typhus, caught in attendance on the sick and dying. The English people clamoured against such an infliction, which it cannot be denied would be altogether intolerable if these fugitives were not made exiles and paupers by English law. They were ordered home again, that they might be supported on the resources of their own country; for though we had no country for the purpose of self-government and self-protection, we were acknowledged to have a country when the necessity of bearing burdens arose.

More than a hundred thousand souls fled to the United States and Canada. The United States maintained sanitary regulations on shipboard which were effectual to a certain extent. But the emigration to Canada was left to the individual greed of ship-owners, and the emigrant ships rivalled the cabins of Mayo or the fever sheds of Skibbereen. Crowded and filthy, carrying double the legal number of passengers, who were ill-fed and imperfectly clothed, and having no doctor on board, the holds, says an eye-witness, were like the Black Hole of Calcutta, and deaths occurred in myriads. The survivors, on their arrival in the new country, continued to die and to scatter death around them. At Montreal, during nine weeks, eight hundred emigrants perished, and over nine hundred residents died of diseases caught from emigrants. During six months the deaths of the new arrivals exceeded three thousand. No preparations were made by the British Government for the reception, or the employment, of these helpless multitudes. The *Times* pronounced the neglect to be an eternal disgrace to the British name. Ships carrying German emigrants and English emigrants arrived in Canada at the same time in a perfectly healthy state. The Chief Secretary for Ireland was able to inform the House of Commons that of a hundred thousand Irishmen who fled to Canada in a year 6,100 perished on the voyage, 4,100 on their arrival, 5,200 in the hospitals, and 1,900 in the towns to which they repaired. The Emigrant Society of Montreal paints the result during the whole period of the famine, in language not easily to be forgotten:

From Grosse Island up to Port Sarnia, along the borders of our great river, on the shores of lakes Ontario and Erie, wherever the tide of emigration has extended, are to be found one unbroken chain of graves, where repose fathers and mothers, sisters and brothers, in a commingled heap, no stone marking the spot. Twenty thousand and upwards have gone down to their graves!

This was the fate which was befalling our race at home and abroad as the year '47 closed. There were not many of us who would not have given his life cheerfully to arrest this ruin, if only he could see a possible way; but there was no way visible.

On the other hand, ten vessels arrived at Montreal in one month carrying Irish emigrants, four thousand four hundred and thirty-seven in all. Of these, eight hundred and four had died on their passage, and eight hundred and forty-seven were seriously diseased. The "Larch," from Sligo, carried four hundred and forty passengers, of whom a hundred and eight died, and a hundred and fifty were seriously diseased. The "Virginia" sailed with five hundred and ninety-six passengers, of whom one hundred and fifty died at sea, and one hundred and eighty-six were disabled by disease (*Montreal Herald*).

### 31.   Irish Emigration Assisted by Irish Landlords (1849–50)[1]

When I first reached Kenmare[2] in the winter of 1849–50, the form of destitution had changed in some degree; but it was still very great. It was true that people no longer died of starvation; but they were dying nearly as fast of fever, dysentery, and scurvy within the walls of the workhouse. Food there was now in abundance; but to entitle the people to obtain it, they were compelled to go into the workhouse and "auxiliary sheds,"[3] until these were crowded almost to suffocation. And although out-door relief had also been resorted to in consequence of the impossibility of finding room for the paupers in the houses, yet

---

[1] Extract from W. Steuart Trench, *Realities of Irish Life* (2d ed.; London, 1869), pp. 115–36, 171–73.

[2] [The writer is describing his work as agent for Lord Lansdowne's Irish estates after the "Great Famine" in Ireland.]

[3] The workhouses being at this time quite unable to hold the numbers who crowded in, large auxiliary timber sheds were erected in convenient places, and in these were housed immense numbers of paupers, for whom room could not be found in the main building.

the quantity of food given was so small, and the *previous destitution through which they had passed was so severe*, that nearly as many died now under the hands of the guardians, as had perished before by actual starvation.

In illustration of this state of things, I may mention an event which occurred to myself, soon after my arrival in the district.

I was in the habit, at this time, of attending the meetings of the Poor Law Board of Guardians, of which I had not yet become a member.

The numbers at that time receiving relief in the whole union of Kenmare were somewhere about ten thousand. In June, 1849, six months previous to my coming, they had reached the highest point, about ten thousand four hundred persons being then in receipt of relief. They had diminished slightly at the time to which I allude. . . . .

My first step was to endeavor to relieve, in some degree, the plethora of the poorhouse; and for this purpose I offered employment outside, to all those who had entered it chargeable to Lord Lansdowne's estate. I promised them reasonable wages in draining, subsoiling, removing rocks and stones, and such like out-of-door labour. No sooner had I made this proposal, than about two hundred gaunt half-famished men, and nearly as many boys and women, appeared in my field next morning, all of them claiming my promise, but none of them having any tools wherewith to labour! Here was a new dilemma. The offer of employment had been accepted with only too great avidity; but the creatures had not a spade, nor a pick-axe, nor a working tool amongst them. Fortunately a large depôt of these articles had lain stored in a tool-house hard by—remnants of the public works. These I immediately appropriated, and before noon about one-half the people were employed. The remainder I sent again to the poorhouse, telling them, however, to return the next day and I would endeavour to procure implements to lend them. They did so. And partly by buying, partly by borrowing, and by making some of them work with their hands alone, I managed to keep most of them employed.

But although at first this system met with great approbation in the district, yet I found it quite impossible to continue it. In the first place, not much more than one-fourth of a reasonable value in labour could be obtained from those who proposed to work; and in the next, being now in employment, they had of course to leave the workhouse. Where then were they to lodge at night? Every lane, every alley, every cabin in the town was crowded to excess with these unhappy work people, and they slept by threes and fours together wherever they could get a pallet of straw to lie upon. But I plainly saw that this could not go on. The townspeople began to complain of the scenes in the town at night; and when a wet day came and the people could not work, nearly one-half of them were obliged to return for the day to the poor-house, creating immense confusion by the sudden influx of such a body of famished newcomers, and the remainder wandered about, objects of the utmost compassion.

Accordingly, after the most anxious deliberation, I arrived at the final conclusion that this system could not be carried on. I felt it would be madness in me to assume the responsibility of keeping three hundred paupers in employment, most of them removed only one step from the grave, as, if any accident should happen to prevent them from obtaining *daily pay*, whether they had work or not, which I had hitherto managed at great inconvenience to give them, many lives might be lost in a night; a result for which I—not in law, but perhaps in public opinion —might immediately be called to account.

I therefore resolved . . . . to go myself to Lord Lansdowne to state to him the whole circumstances of the case, and to recommend him to adopt an extensive system of voluntary emigration as the only practicable and effective means of relieving this frightful destitution.

This plan, accordingly, I carried into effect. And in the month of November, 1850, I went over to England. . . . . The broad sketch of the plan I laid before him was as follows: I showed him by the poor-house returns, that the number of paupers off his estate and receiving relief in the workhouse amounted to about three thousand. That I was wholly unable to undertake the employment of these people in their present condition, on reproductive works; and that if left in the workhouse, the smallest amount they could possibly cost would be 5£ per head per annum, and thus that the poor-rates must necessarily amount, for some years to come, to 15,000£ per annum, unless these people died or left—and the latter was not probable. . . . .

The remedy I proposed was as follows. That he should forthwith offer *free emigration* to every man, woman, and child now in the poor-house or receiving relief and *chargeable to his estate*. That I had been in communication with an Emigration Agent, who had offered to contract to take them to whatever port in America each pleased, at a reasonable rate per head. That even supposing they all accepted this offer, the total, together with a small sum per head for outfit and a few shillings on landing, would not exceed from 13,000£ to 14,000£, a sum less than it would cost to support them in the workhouse for a single year. That in the one case he would not only free his estate of this mass of pauperism which had been allowed to accumulate upon it, but would put the people themselves in a far better way of earning their bread hereafter; whereas by feeding and retaining them where they were, they must remain as a millstone around the neck of his estate, and prevent its rise for many years to come; and I plainly proved that it would be cheaper to him, and *better for them*, to pay for their emigration at once, than to continue to support them at home. . . . .

I shall not readily forget the scenes that occurred in Kenmare when I returned, and announced that I was prepared at Lord Lansdowne's expense to send to America every one now in the poor-house who was chargeable to his lordship's estate, and who desired to go; leaving each to select what port in America he pleased—whether Boston, New York, New Orleans, or Quebec.

The announcement at first was scarcely credited; it was considered by the paupers to be too good news to be true. But when it began to be believed and appreciated, a rush was made to get away at once.

The organisation of the system required, however, much care and thought.

The mode adopted was as follows: two hundred each week were selected of those apparently most suited for emigration; and having arranged their slender outfit, a steady man, on whom I could depend, Mr. Jeremiah O'Shea, was employed to take charge of them on their journey to Cork, and not to leave them or allow them to scatter, until he saw them safely on board the emigrant ship. This plan succeeded admirably; and week after week, to the astonishment of the good people of Cork, and sometimes not a little to their dismay, a batch of two hundred paupers appeared on the quays of Cork, bound for the Far West.

A cry was now raised that I was exterminating the people. But the people knew well that those who now cried loudest had given them no help when in the extremity of their distress, and they rushed from the country like a panic-stricken throng, each only fearing that the funds at my disposal might fail before he and his family could get their passage.

So great was the rush from the poor-house to emigrate and so great was the influx into the house to qualify (as I generally required the application of that sure test of abject poverty before I gave an order for emigration), that the guardians became uneasy, and said the poor-house would be filled with those seeking emigration, even faster than it could be emptied. But I told them not to be alarmed—that all demands should be met. And thus, two hundred after two hundred, week after week, departed for Cork, until the poor-house was nearly emptied of paupers chargeable to the Lansdowne estate; and in little more than a year 3,500 paupers had left Kenmare for America, all free emigrants, without any ejectments having been brought against them to enforce it, or the slightest pressure put upon them to go.

Matters now began to right themselves; only some fifty or sixty paupers remained in the house, chargeable to the property over which I had the care, and Lord Lansdowne's estate at length breathed freely.

It must be admitted that the paupers despatched to America on such a sudden pressure as this, were of a very motley type; and a strange figure these wild batches of two hundred each—most of them speaking only the Irish language—made in the streets of Cork, as well as on the quays of Liverpool and America. There was great difficulty in keeping them from breaking loose from the ship, not only in Cork but in Liverpool, where the ships touched before they left for the West. Their chief device was to escape out of the ships almost naked, to hide all their good clothes which had been furnished them as an outfit, and to appear only in their worst rags. In this costume they took delight in rushing through the streets of Cork and Liverpool in large bodies, to the real terror of the inhabitants. In short, I do believe that so strange, unmanageable, and wild a crew had never before left the shores of Ireland. But notwithstanding their apparent poverty, they were all in the most uproarious spirits; there was no crying nor lamentation, as is usual on such occasions; all was delight at having escaped the deadly workhouse.

I need hardly dilate upon the abuse and vituperation which the adoption of such an extensive system of emigration brought down upon me from many well-known quarters. The whole thing had been done so quickly, that no efforts of opponents could in the least prevail against it; but no sooner was it completed than I became the object of the vilest and most bitter abuse. I was accused of an extensive system of "clearing the land *by eviction*," though I had not evicted a single tenant for the purpose, nor sent one person away, except by the earnest entreaty of the emigrant himself. . . . .

I have gone through much laborious work during my life, but I never went through any which pressed so hard upon my powers of endurance as the arrangements for the emigration at Kenmare. The tide of emigrants was so enormous, each pressing his individual claim, and terrified lest all the money should be exhausted before his or her name could be entered upon the emigration list, that I was compelled to station several stout men at the door of my office to keep the place clear, or the pressure of the crowd outside would absolutely have burst it in. . . . . I carefully investigated the case of each; and having granted or declined the application, as the merits of the case deserved (and at that time I refused very few), they were passed on, their names having been entered for America. The joy depicted on the countenances of those who came out, and to whom immediate emigration was promised, contrasted with the anxiety of those who were still awaiting the decision of their fate at the entrance door, was one of the most striking incidents of the scene. . . . .

[Later, on undertaking the management of Lord Bath's estate] I made it one special condition that I should not be required to eject any tenant off the estate without being at liberty to provide for him by emigration or otherwise, at the landlord's expense: and thus that no one should be turned out in misery on the roadside or into the poorhouse, without at least the offer being made him of providing for himself and family by free emigration to America.

On Lord Bath's estate the tenants had been allowed to fall into heavy arrears, so that not less than 30,000£ was due upon the estate when I undertook its management. Many of the tenants had not paid any rent whatever for periods varying from two to six years.

My first step on coming to Carrickmacross—a locality with which my previous experience on Mr. Shirley's estate had made me well acquainted—was to offer free emigration, at the expense of the landlord, to any tenant who chose to accept it, and to his immediate family, provided he would surrender his land; giving him at the same time his stock and crop and all that he had or could make money of, and forgiving him all rent and arrears—no matter how much he owed. I was aware that in making this proposal it would not be accepted by any except those who could not pay; and from those, all I required on the landlord's part was the bare worn-out land.

A large number of the utterly insolvent availed themselves of this proposal—resigned their land, and took shipping forthwith for America; but liberal as the offer was, it provoked the bitter hostility of the most reckless and violent of the tenantry. These at last saw that they must now be forced to come to terms; they must settle their accounts or emigrate. Hitherto they had declined to do either. They had paid no rent, and yet they held possession of their land. This they plainly saw could now go on no longer.

The plan acted most advantageously over the property. Large sums were paid in by those who found themselves able to do so, and the paupers prepared for emigration. A few, however, stood out, and would neither emigrate nor pay; and one man, named Traynor, plainly told me "that he had held the land for six years without paying any rent, that it was worth fighting for, and 'by the powers,' he would never pay while he could still hold out against the law!" This man afterwards narrowly escaped being hanged for conspiracy to murder Patrick MacMahon, one of my bailiffs. He was arrested and put into gaol, climbed over a high prison wall, and ran for it, got himself packed amongst a hamper of eggs, slipped over thus to Liverpool, and was never heard of afterwards.

### 32.  The Continuing Causes of Emigration from the United Kingdom[1]

. . . . Irish emigration is the product of two causes, opposite in character, but concurring in tendency—repulsion from Ireland, and attraction to America. The Irish repulsion consists of whatever the Milesian Irish suffer in Ireland, such as the inferiorities of a conquered race subject to a foreign land-proprietary and a foreign established religion, together with a starvation-rate of wages, arising from excess of population in a country where the accumulation of capital is checked by political and social disorder. The American attraction consists, in some measure, of the entire religious equality which prevails in America, but far more of the high wages of labour and high profits of capital for which Anglo-Saxon America is so remarkable. The *Times* (of Thursday last) says: "The emigration began and has been mainly kept up by the failure of the potato." No, it began with the general peace of 1815, and has been going on ever since at a continually increasing rate: and the potato rot only caused it to take a great step in advance. The repulsion is of old date, but not so the present amount of attraction. As the *Times* says most truly, "Emigrations commonly begin in repulsion, and go on with attraction. The leaders of the column fly their country because they cannot stay in it; but their followers go off more cheerfully *because they hear a good report of the new country*, and because their friends are already settled in it." Just so; the present attraction is the past and present well-doing of the hundreds of thousands, nay millions, of poor Irish, who have gone to America since 1815,

[1] Extract from the London *Spectator*, XXIV (October 18, 1851), 997.

and of whom, just at present, a far greater number than ever before are enjoying high wages and profits in America, and are sending back to Ireland, not only detailed reports of their own prosperity, but money wherewith to assist their relatives in following their example. Certainly not less, perhaps considerably more, than 500,000 pounds was transmitted in this way from America to Ireland during the last twelvemonth. The Atlantic is "bridged over" for Irish paupers, or, at any rate, it will be soon, when the always increasing attractive power shall suffice for drawing off all who may wish to go. That these will ere long be the whole remnant of Celtic Irish, seems probable, when one reflects that the only serious check to Milesian emigration of late years has been the natural unwillingness of the Roman Catholic clergy to see their flocks diminished; and that Milesian emigration is starving the Milesian clergy in Ireland, whilst it is creating in America an ample provision for them. Bishops, priests, and people, let all go together, from their evil lot in Ireland to a happy home in the West; so be it, amen.

It has been taken for granted as a matter of course, that the vacuum created by emigration from Ireland would be filled up by emigration from England and Scotland; but a new element is growing into importance, which may probably derange this calculation. Emigration *from England and Scotland* to America has recently acquired a force and measure which raise the question, whether Ireland, however thoroughly divested of her Celtic population, will present attractions to a Saxon immigration from Great Britain equal to those which America affords. To a considerable extent, doubtless, and under any conceivable state of things as respects America, Ireland, losing her Roman Catholic Celts, would gain a new population of Protestant Saxons: and we may even reckon with confidence that her immigrant Saxon population would be as dense and their capital as large, in proportion to the field of employment for both, as were those of Great Britain: but these conclusions leave untouched the query, whether the whole British exodus—that is, the emigration of people and capital from England and Scotland, as well as from Ireland, to America—may not be such as to equalize profits and wages on both sides of the Atlantic, and therefore to have the same effects upon every part of these islands with regard to the density of wealth and population, as is produced upon the seaboard States of America by the emigration of capital and people to the interior States. May not North America as a whole become to Great Britain and Ireland what the American Far West is to the State of Massachusetts or New York? If it should, there is a chance, not to say a prospect, of social changes in this country, and in our own time, in comparison with which, we say with the *Times*, the greatest constitutional or dynastic revolutions may be deemed insignificant. For, let it be observed, our whole social system—our kinds and methods of production, our constitution, laws, customs, and even manners—are founded on the principle of sharp competition and constant dependence for the bulk of the people. Neither have we any slaves—still less, as the Americans have, between three and four millions, representing a productive power worth at market about five hundred million pounds sterling, and actually producing not far from the whole of the exports, which pay for the imports, of the United States. And further, if there occurred in this country the same scarcity of free labour for hire as is usual in America, we should not, in the whole case supposed, have the American resource of a vast immigration of Irish paupers to serve as our hewers of wood and drawers of water. This picture is ugly at first sight, almost terrible. On the other hand, old-country poverty would disappear; it would become a British, as it is now an American saying, that "victuals are no object"; the cradle of the great Anglo-Saxon race would be continually replenished to the utmost; and unless the providential course of human improvement were reversed, the whole process would be good no less for this country in particular than for mankind. But the attempt would be idle now, to fathom the depths of those profound changes which must result from making labour for hire as scarce and dear in this country as it is in America: so let us rather notice for a moment the circumstances which indicate that a time may be approaching when the whole subject must be investigated to the bottom.

These circumstances are all those which are giving a new and far more powerful impulse to emigration from the British Islands. The repulsion of low wages and low profits at home is an old cause; and the new-country attraction of high profits and high wages is as old as the time when Anglo-Saxon colonies had taken a firm root of prosperity and abundance. But until of late years the great mass of the people in this old country were ignorant of the peculiar state of prosperous new countries. New-country profits and wages existed, but, being unknown to the masses, were not attractive. The present force of British emigration is then immediately due to a new degree of intelligence amongst the common people of this country. The labours of Bell and Lancaster have a great deal to do with it. It is little suspected by our higher classes what a large amount of printed matter relating to America circulates among those classes which supply the stream of British emigration; and this influence is probably trifling when compared with that of private letters from America, addressed in countless numbers to a class which has only of late years learned to read. New facilities of locomotion and communication have reduced the distance between these islands and the American Far West to a tithe of what it used to be. In a word, the fertile basins of the St. Lawrence and the Mississippi, capable of holding hundreds of millions of people, are becoming part of one country with Great Britain and Ireland.

### 33. Stimulation of Emigration by American States

A. REPORT OF THE COMMISSIONER OF EMIGRATION FOR WISCONSIN[1]

Although I omitted no opportunity that presented itself to labor for the good of our State in New York itself, I yet directed my chief aim to the press here and in Europe, and in a long series of articles, presented Wisconsin in general; its advantages above other States; descriptions of particular localities; its commerce; the wealth of its mineral, timber, and agricultural districts; its climate, public institutions, political privileges, means of education, &c., before the eyes of all those, who for whatever cause, were determined to change their residence.

I also sent copies of the pamphlets, which in the meantime I had received, to the editors of a large number of newspapers in the United States, Germany, Ireland, England, Scotland, Norway, Sweden, Holland, and Switzerland, with the request to insert extracts therefrom in their respective journals.

The journals which I selected for the advertisement and correspondence are, especially, the *New York Tribune, Herald, Staats Zeitung, Irish American, Abend Zeitung, New York Democrat, Daily Wisconsin, Sentinel, Wisconsin Banner, Volksfreund, Niewsbode, Newarker Zeitung, Phoenix*, and *Anzeiger des Nordwestens*, and *Republicaner* in America, and the *Times, Tablet*, and *Tipperary Free Press*, in England and Ireland, in the *Leipziger Allgemeine Zeitung, Schwäbische Merkur, Casselsche Zeitung, Allgemeine Auswanderungs Zeitung*, in Rudolstadt, *Nürnberger Correspondent, Leipziger Zeitung, Bremer Auswanderungs Zeitung*, in Germany, and *Baseler Zeitung*, in Switzerland.

[1] Extract from *Second Annual Report (1853) of the State Commissioner of Emigration* (Herman Haertel) in Wisconsin, Appendix to *Senate Journal*, 1854, Document C, pp. 4–10.

. . . . The results thus accomplished exhibited themselves in a surprising degree in a very short time, in written and personal inquiries from nearly every State in the Union and from many parts of Europe and in the daily increasing number of inquiries at my office. . . . .

Over three thousand persons visited my office, during the same period, of whom nearly four hundred were from New York and vicinity, two or three hundred from other States and Wisconsin, and over two thousand came direct from Europe, many of whom again, of course, often represented one or more families. Besides these, many emigrants were spoken with on the arrival of the ships in port.

The visitors were two-thirds Germans, a small number Americans, and the remainder Irish, Norwegians, Swedes, English, Scotch, and Hollanders.

If it be true that the Irish emigration is nearly as extensive as the German, the reason why comparatively so few of them appeared at the office is, as Mr. Byrne, an Irishman by birth, and who had the most intercourse with them, can affirm, that the greater portion arrive with but limited means, and are therefore induced to seize upon the first work offered them for subsistence, which, indeed, is abundantly furnished by railroads and other important enterprises. Competition among employers is at present so great that, for example, the contractors upon the Illinois Central, and many other roads, have established agencies in New York, where not only are high wages offered to those seeking employment, but they are also transported, free of cost, or, at least, at much reduced rates of fare, to the place of their labor. The Irishman, also, is more inclined than the German to a residence in large cities. . . . .

I have received, mainly from Wisconsin, remittances of money, in sums of from $5 to $20, amounting to more than $3,000, with the request to pay them to relatives, children, sisters, brothers, and parents, who were expected, but had not sufficient means to complete their journey. . . . .

Of the descriptions of the State placed at my disposal I have made the most liberal use, and have circulated them not only among the emigrants on the arrival of the ships, but have sent them off by mail, especially to Europe. In this, the U.S. Consul at Bremen, and his Secretary (both from Wisconsin), afforded me the most cheerful aid. . . . .

From the month of July, a ship rarely entered the harbor with emigrants, some of whom were not already in possession of my pamphlets, or had read some of my notices and communications: often indeed, my address had been given them by emigrant societies or ship-owners, with the advice to follow my directions before all others. By living together during a long sea voyage, utter strangers often became strangely attached to each other, and thus it frequently happened that my station on the arrival of a ship was known to nearly all on board, when, at the departure from the foreign port, usually but a few in-dividuals had any knowledge of me, thereby often one-half met me with confidence, which was again the occasion that those who were yet un-decided about their destination in America, generally chose Wisconsin as their new fatherland.

The number of pamphlets distributed and sent abroad is nearly 30,000, of which one-half found their way to Europe. . . . .

My efforts to bring the State of Wisconsin, with its healthful climate, and its rich and boundless resources and advantages, to the notice of the inhabitants of Europe, by means of the press, and the result of those efforts cannot exhibit themselves at once, as every one knows who is partially acquainted with such affairs, but their effects will more evidently appear in the coming season of 1854, for such are the circumstances in Europe, that it often requires a year or more of preparation before the emigrant can leave his old home. . . . .

Every unprejudiced citizen and observer of our State must confess and acknowledge that the continued prosperity of its inhabitants is in a great degree dependent upon further accessions to its population from abroad. If they are large, the prosperity and power of Wisconsin will increase in an equal degree; if not large, they will suffer many re-verses. Whether he comes from other States of the Union, or from Europe, each individual contributes some thing to the general wealth and expansion, whether in physical strength, knowledge or capital. . . . .

Of late, nearly all European Governments have attempted to check the constantly increasing drain of population and capital from their dominions; and though they fail entirely to stop the stream, yet the measures they have adopted are not without effect. It is also too well known that on many sides the growing power of the United States is regarded with dissatisfaction, and begins to excite their serious ap-prehensions. But it is also known that every adopted citizen strength-ens this power and, therefore, recently these Governments have em-ployed every means in their power to divert the stream, the flow of which they cannot stay, in another direction, to such countries whose governments sympathize with their own.

Among others, Brazil, which has many millions of acres of yet unoccupied lands lying within its boundaries, has just discovered the importance and profit of immigration, and has not only passed a law granting to every immigrant the necessary land for a home without price, but the Government has appropriated $400,000 yearly to the furtherance of immigration. . . . .

### B.   REPORT OF THE WISCONSIN COMMITTEE ON IMMIGRATION, 1854[1]

The Select Committee to whom had been referred so much of the message of his Excellency the Governor, as relates to the subject of the Commissioner of Emigration, and also the report of said officer, have had the same under consideration, and beg leave to report . . . .

1. The operation of the Agency thus far, although in the incipiency, has been manifestly advantageous, as emigrants have been induced, through the instrumentality of the Commissioner, to locate in Wisconsin, bringing with them a large amount of capital, which together with the known frugality, industry, and economy which characterizes a great portion of our immigration, will add to our annual revenue more than the amount expended annually in keeping up in its activity and usefulness our Agency in New York.

2. The course adopted by the Commissioner, of writing and placing himself in communication with agents in the various shipping ports of Europe, will, in the opinion of your committee, result in the greatest advantage to the interest of our State. Many now in Europe upon the representations made by our Commissioner in such communications, are, doubtless, now preparing to avail themselves of the opportunity offered them through the Agency, of reaching our State, with the certainty of being met on their landing from ship board, by one whose duty it is to protect the interests of the emigrants and speed them, with as little delay and expense as possible, to find a home and a new fatherland within the limits of Wisconsin.

3. The statistical information which has been sent, through the Agency, to the several portions of Europe, will tend much to direct the attention of capitalists to the mineral and agricultural wealth, with which our State, in almost every locality, is teeming: and it is not unreasonable, to your committee, to suppose that a large amount of

[1] Extract from "Report of the Select Committee to whom had been referred so much of the message of his Excellency the Governor as relates to the subject of the Commissioner of Emigration," in Wisconsin, Appendix to *Senate Journal*, 1854, pp. 3–5.

capital will be brought or sent from Europe to Wisconsin, to assist in developing the resources of our State.

4. Good faith on the part of the State, should be kept with those who, by its accredited agents, have been induced to leave the place of their nativity and seek a home in this Western World. And your Committee, from the report of the Commissioner, are convinced that many emigrants will arrive during the ensuing year in New York, destined for Wisconsin, relying upon this State having there an Agent in whom they can place confidence, and from whom they may expect such necessary instructions as will enable them to be transported with as little delay as possible to the place of their destination. Many of our adopted fellow citizens have already transmitted to Europe, money, to enable their friends to reach Wisconsin, and have instructed them on arrival to apply to our Agent for information. Should the Agency be continued, the benefits arising from it will be made manifest during the coming year. Should it be discontinued, especially at this time, we may expect a great falling off of the immigration to this State, caused by the loss of confidence and distrust which will assuredly follow. . . . .

5. The demand for laborers is at present great, and every inducement should be offered, to secure for Wisconsin an increased supply of that respectable and most useful class of our population; and with proper exertions on the part of an active Agent, our State will soon be supplied with a sufficiency of resident laborers, to whom constant employment can be given in prosecuting the railroad enterprises which are now in hand and fast verging to completion. . . . .

### 34. The Work of a German Emigration Society[1]

The Texas experiment was a most interesting one; that of using associated capital for the transportation and settlement of emigrants on a large scale; in fact, the removal, in organized bodies, of the poor of an old country to the virgin soil of a new.

In the year 1842, among many schemes evolved in Germany by the social stir of the time, and patronized by certain princes, from motives of policy, was one of real promise. It was an association, of which Count Castel was the head, for the diminution of pauperism by the organized assistance and protection of emigrants. At this time, an-

---

[1] Extract from Frederick Law Olmsted, *A Journey through Texas; or, A Saddle-Trip on the Southwestern Frontier; with a Statistical Appendix* (New York, 1857), pp. 172-77. See *The Germans in Texas*, by G. G. Benjamin (Philadelphia, 1909), chap. iii, for an interesting account of the *Adelsverein*.

nexation being already almost a certainty, speculators, who represented the owners of large tracts of Texas land, appeared in Germany, with glowing accounts of their cheapness and richness. They succeeded in gaining the attention of this association, whose leaders were pleased with the isolated situation, as offering a more tangible and durable connection with their emigrants, and opening a new source of wealth and possible power. . . . .

The following year [1844] the association commenced active operations. It obtained, under the title of the Mainzer Adels Verein, a charter from the Duke of Nassau, who assumed the protectorate. It had the Prince of Leiningen as president; Count Castel as director; Prince Frederick of Prussia, the Duke of Coburg-Gotha, and some thirty other princes and nobles as associated members. A plan, inviting emigrants, was published, offering each adult, subscribing $120, a free passage and forty acres of land; a family, subscribing $240, a free passage and eighty acres. The association undertook to provide loghouses, stock, and tools at fair prices, and to construct public building and roads for the settlements.

Prince Solms, of Braunfels, was appointed General Commissioner and proceeded to Texas. Had he procured from the State Legislature a direct grant of land for the colony, as he might have done, all would have been well. But, most unfortunately, the association was induced, without sufficient examination, to buy a grant of the previous year. It was held by Fisher and Miller, and the tract was described by them as a second paradise. In reality, it lay in the heart of a savage country, hundreds of miles beyond the remotest settlement, between the Upper Colorado and the great desert plains, a region to this day almost uninhabited. This wretched mistake was the ruin of the whole enterprise. The association lost its money and its character, and carried many emigrants only to beggary and a miserable death.

In the course of the year, 180 subscribers were obtained, who landed with their families in the autumn upon the coast of Texas, and marched towards their promised lands, with Prince Solms at their head. Finding the whole country a wilderness, and being harassed by the attacks of Indians, on reaching the union of the Comal with the Guadalupe, they became disheartened, and there Prince Solms, following the good advice of a naturalist of the company, Mr. Lindheimer, encamped, and laid out the present town of Neu-Braunfels. This settlement, receiving aid from home, while it was needed, was a success.
. . . .

In the course of the next year, 1845, more than 2,000 families joined the association. The capital which had been sufficient for its first effort was totally inadequate to an undertaking of this magnitude. These poor people sailed from Germany, in the fall of this year, and were landed in the winter and early spring, on the flat coast of the Gulf, to the number of 5,200. Annexation had now taken place, and the war with Mexico was beginning. The country had been stripped of provisions, and of the means of transportation, by the army. Neither food nor shelter had been provided by the association. The consequences may be imagined. The detail is too horrible. The mass remained for months encamped in sand-holes, huts, or tents: the only food procurable was beef. The summer heats bred pestilence.

The world has hardly record of such suffering. Human nature could not endure it. Human beings became brutes. "Your child is dying." "What do I care?" Old parents were hurried into the ground before the breath of life had left them. The American who saw the stragglers, thought a new race of savages was come. Haggard and desperate, they roved inland by twos and threes, beyond all law or religion. Many of the survivors reached the German settlements; many settled as laborers in American towns. With some of them, Meusebach founded another town—Fredericksburg—higher up than Braunfels. He also explored the Fisher grant, and converted the surrounding Indians, from enemies, into good natured associates.

"It is but justice," says Mr. Kapp, "to throw the light of truth upon all this misery. The members of the association, although well-meaning, did not understand what they were about to do. They fancied that their *high protection*, alone, was sufficient to make all right. They had not the remotest idea of the toil and hardship of settling a new country. They permitted themselves to be humbugged by speculators and adventurers; they entered into ruinous bargains, and had not even funds enough to take the smallest number of those, whom they had induced to join them, to the place of settlement. When money was most wanted, they failed to send it, either from mistrust or neglect. To perform the obligations imposed by the agreement with Fisher, they induced the emigration to Texas by the most enchanting and exaggerated statements. The least that even the less sanguine ones expected, was to find parrots rocking on the boughs, and monkeys playing on the palm-trees."

This condemnation seems to fall justly.

Such was the unhappy beginning. But the wretchedness is already forgotten. Things soon mended. The soil, climate, and the other realities found, were genial and good, if not Elysian. Now, after seven years, I do not know a prettier picture of contented prosperity than we witnessed at Neu-Braunfels. A satisfied smile, in fact, beamed on almost every German face we saw in Texas.[1]

Of the general appearance of Neu-Braunfels I gave some notion in describing the route to San Antonio. We now took pains to obtain some definite facts with regard to its condition. The dwellings in general are small and humble in appearance, but weather-tight, and, generally, provided with galleries or verandahs, and with glazed casement windows. In the latter respect, they have the advantage over most houses we have seen in Texas, and, I have no doubt, the average comforts of life within are much greater than among the Anglo-Americans, generally, in the state.

The citizens are, however, nearly all men of very small capital. Of the original settlers scarcely any now remain, and their houses and lands are occupied by more recent emigrants. Those who have left have made enough money during their residence to enable them to buy farms or cattle ranches in the mountains, to which they have removed.

Half the men now residing in Neu-Braunfels and its vicinity, are probably agricultural laborers, or farmers, who themselves follow the plough. The majority of the latter do not, I think, own more than ten acres of land each.

## 35. "What Does North America Offer to the German Emigrant?"[2]

The motive common to all men for changing their homes is the hope of improving their condition. If something is annoying or oppressive to a man in one place and he cannot remove the untoward conditions, he is then inclined to betake himself to the place where he thinks he can remain undisturbed by such vexations. In Germany as

[1] [This account, Olmsted explains, is based on notes of oral statements that he made on the spot, and on the report of a lecture by Frederick Kapp upon the Germans in Texas in the *New York Tribune* of January 20, 1855.

C. von Meusebach succeeded Prince Solms as general commissioner of the Association. According to Olmsted, the first settlement was a success "in spite of the Prince, who appears to have been an amiable fool, aping, among the log-cabins, the nonsense of medieval courts. In the course of a year he was laughed out of the country" (p. 175)].

[2] Extract translated from Gottfried Menzel, *Die Vereinigten Staaten von Nordamerika mit besonderer Rücksicht auf deutsche Auswanderung dahin, nach eigener Anschauung beschrieben* (Berlin, 1853), pp. 342–53.

elsewhere, there are two things particularly which are disagreeable and burdensome to many of the inhabitants and from which they escape by emigrating to America.

In Germany as in most of the European states many people are dissatisfied with the state organization and institutions. They feel themselves hampered by the government, complain of lack of freedom, of too much government, and the like, and direct their gaze to the free states of the great North American Republic, as the land of desired freedom. . . . .

Germans who voluntarily exchanged their homes in Germany for new homes in North America to obtain greater freedom, especially those who have emigrated since the year 1848, always say in their accounts from America that they are entirely satisfied with American freedom, and sincerely pity all those who are not yet sharers in it. But through the newspapers of the day other opinions are heard. There are many things with which they are really dissatisfied. Some existing institutions they wish to remove and to replace with others, but they have not yet been able to change anything in these republican constitutions and democratic institutions. The Americans do not approve of these efforts at reformation and say, "These Germans wish to dictate everything, but do not wish to be dictated to themselves."

Much greater is the number of those who leave their fatherland on account of the poverty of its material resources and in order to better their condition in America. For many people industrial conditions in Germany are such that you cannot blame them for emigrating when they learn that in North America there are far greater productive natural resources and that work has a greater value than in Germany.

He who in Germany has to suffer from want and misery, or must expect these in the near future, finds that hope of better fortune overcomes his attachment to the *Vaterland*. He easily separates himself from his old home and wanders to a distant land believing that he will find life more favorable there.

That it is easier to make a living in America cannot be denied; but it is a matter of regret that those who could better their condition in this way frequently lack the means. Many people who take this risk find only their misfortune or ruin. The numbers of those who return to Germany from America prove that many are not successful there. When an emigrant ship is prepared to sail from the harbor of New York for Hamburg or Bremen, there are usually twenty or more people leaving the land of their disappointed hopes for the old home country after one or two years' bitter experiences. They have left, out of their fortunes, scarcely the necessary money for the return passage. Still others would follow them if they had the means for the trip or if they were not ashamed to return.

Therefore everyone who is thinking of emigrating to America should take care to determine whether or not he is fit for America. He should carefully weigh what he leaves here against what he may find there, lest he should be guilty of too great haste or light-mindedness and make a mistake that he may regret only too soon and bitterly. . . . . The emigrant must rely upon others and believe what they tell him about that country, either to give up his decision or to fulfil it. But most of them are guilty of credulity which may be regarded as the chief cause of the numerous emigrations.

A great many books about emigration to America have been written, and every year new ones appear. *Rathgeber, Führer, Wegweiser* for emigrants are the customary titles of these books. A book written against emigration, or one advising emigration only for the few, would have little charm and would find few purchasers. But as soon as a book appears which describes the land to which the emigrant would go as a land of paradise, then it is sold and read diligently, and thousands are moved in this way to become emigrants. Many a book on emigration very truly describes what is good and what is agreeable in America, but passes over in silence the disadvantages or disagreeable features of American life. Through this one-sided presentation of American conditions many are lured to emigrate. It is obvious that the countless speculators who every year gain many millions of emigrants will make a great effort to bring to the attention of the people many books through which the desire for emigration is awakened and increased. They are themselves completely indifferent to the fate of the emigrants, and if emigration turns out to be for their ruin they do not care. Again, many who read books on emigration see only what they like; and they overlook the disagreeable, which is moreover only painted in faint colors, and do not give it mature consideration. Thus they themselves help to make the work of deception easy and complete.

But the descriptions and the letters of the emigrants to their relatives and friends and acquaintances—are they not then true and reliable? This I deny. First, because no one who has emigrated will confess that he was disappointed, that he had not found there that on which he had counted with certainty and which he had so joyfully anticipated. He is very right in thinking that few in the old home will have sympathetic pity for him, and many only malicious joy and bitter ridicule. Even sympathy for misfortune brought on one's self is not agreeable. One does not wish to confess to those who advised against emigration that they were right in their forebodings and warnings, and that they had seen more clearly and correctly than he had.

Secondly, the immigrants wish, for many reasons, to have many of their relatives and countrymen follow them and settle near them. On the one hand, because of the neighborly society and support, the need of which many of them have bitterly experienced. On the other hand, one desires everywhere new arrivals of immigrants because they will buy land, and stock, and so on from those already settled, by which ready money, of which there is always need, comes into this part of the country and the value of the land and its produce increases. The following of relatives, especially if they are well off, is much desired by their predecessors whether circumstances are favorable or unfavorable.

Therefore, it is easy to understand that there are no complaints in the letters of the immigrants in spite of the causes of complaint that many a writer may have. Before my trip to America I received many letters from people living there, who described their condition as quite satisfactory, but when I had personally investigated their condition and when I expressed my surprise at their letters which had gone so far from reality, I received the answer, "Others ought to try their life too. In Germany there are more than enough people, while here there are too few."

### WHAT DOES NORTH AMERICA OFFER THAT IS GOOD?

This great country offers its inhabitants noteworthy advantages which may be summarized as follows:

1. Although the citizens of the United States are not, as is popularly supposed, free from taxes, yet the taxes on land and cattle which the farmer has to pay are not high, and artisans pay no taxes on their business.

2. The citizens are, during a certain age, under obligation to serve in the militia, but except in the case of war this is rarely asked of them except perhaps for suppression of a riot. For regular military service volunteers are always available, since they are well paid. The quartering of soldiers in time of peace is not allowed.

3. Complete freedom in the trades and professions, hunting and fishing is allowed to everyone. . . . .

4. There is no difference in rank. The terms "upper class" and

"lower class" have no significance. The public official has no advantage not shared by the farmer, the merchant, or the teamster.

5. North America, as a country with fertile land still partly unoccupied, a country thinly populated with flourishing trade and general freedom of trade, offers far greater and more abundant means of livelihood than Germany.

6. Labor there has a high, and cost of living a lower, value; therefore on the whole the people are far less oppressed by want and need and the tormenting anxiety for one's daily bread.

Against the advantages just enumerated . . . . the following disadvantages will not please those who are eager to emigrate.

The long and distant sea-voyage appears to many of them as the great hardship of emigration, and they think if only this were accomplished all would be well. Although this is accompanied by danger and much inconvenience, it is soon over. Seasickness is indeed painful for many, but it is not dangerous, and need not be feared since it is good for their health after the sea journey. Far more hazardous and more serious in their consequences are the following:

1. [The danger, after landing in America, of losing one's property through the deception and thievery of the runners.]

2. The unhealthy climate. . . . .

3. The German in America is a complete stranger. Everything is strange, the country, the climate, laws, and customs. One ought to realize what it means to be an alien in a far distant land. More than this, the German in America is despised as alien, and he must often hear the nickname "Dutchman," at least until he learns to speak English fluently. It is horrible what the German immigrants must endure from the Americans, Irish, and English. I was more than once a witness to the way German immigrants were forced by the American captain or pilot with terrible brutality, kicking, etc., to carry wood from the shore to the boat, although they had paid their full fare and had not been engaged for those duties. Only in the places where the Germans are in the majority does the newly arrived immigrant find, after all the hardships of the journey, an endurable existence. The Americans are accustomed to alter their behavior to him only after he has become Americanized. The rabble who also emigrated from Germany in former times have brought the German name into discredit.

4. The educational institutions are, in America, defective and expensive or they are completely lacking. Therefore parents can give their children the necessary education only through great sacrifices or, in case they are poor, the children must be allowed to run wild. . . . .

5. The majority of the Germans emigrating to America wish to seek their fortunes in agriculture. But the purchase of land has its dangers and difficulties. The price of the land is, in proportion to its productivity, not so low as is generally believed. To establish a farm on new and uncultivated land is for the newcomer an almost impossible task. The life of a North American farmer is not at all enviable as many think. Where labor is so dear and where agricultural products are so cheap, there no one can exist except the man who is able and willing to do all his own work and does not need to employ outside labor. . . . .

I have been approached since my return from North America by a large number of persons for information concerning conditions there and for advice concerning their projected plan of emigration. Either because of their personal qualifications or circumstances, hardly one-fourth of these people could be advised with confidence to undertake this important step. I found most of them unsuitable for emigration for the following more or less serious reasons:

1. *A weak constitution or shattered health.*—The emigrant to America needs a strong and healthy body.

2. *Advanced age.*—The man who is already over forty years of age, unless he has some sons who can help him with their labor, cannot count upon success and prosperity in America.

3. *Childlessness with somewhat advanced age.*—What will a married couple do when their capacity to labor disappears with the years? They could not earn enough when young to support them in later years. If they have a substantial property to bring over from Germany, then emigration would be a very unwise step for them, since for the man without employment living is much higher in America than in Europe, especially if one needs servants or cannot do without the comforts and luxuries of life.

4. *Lack of experience in the field of labor on the part of those who expect to establish their fortunes there through hard labor.*—The duties of the agriculturists, as well as the occupations of the artisan, involve heavy labor. Many harbor the delusion that they are already accustomed to the labor required there, or that they will easily learn it if they have worked a little here in this country. But he who has not from his youth up been performing continuously the most severe labor, so much the more will he lack, in America, where work is harder, the necessary strength and ability. He will certainly not be a competent and contented workingman. In America . . . . labor is much more severe and much more work is required for the higher wages he re-

ceives than is usual in Germany. Those who spent their youth in schools, offices, or in other sedentary work, play in America a very sad and pitiable rôle.

5. *A slow easy-going habit of living a life of ease and comfort.*—One may find in the great cities of North America all the comforts and conveniences which European cities offer, but in America they are only for the few—for the rich—and to this class German emigrants do not usually belong. Not many persons in America can command even the comforts of the ordinary citizen of Europe. Many people seek compensation in whiskey for their many privations and hardships and this is the way to certain ruin.

6. *Destitution.*—If the passage for a single emigrant costs only 50 thaler, at least as much again must be counted for the land journey here and in America. Unfortunately this amount is beyond the reach of those who would have the best chance of improving their condition in America. The artisan, even though he cannot carry on his business there independently but must work in great workshops and factories must often make yet a further land journey in order to find the most suitable place, and he needs, especially if he has a family, a not inconsiderable amount of money. Seldom is a place found in the vicinity of the port of arrival where places are not already filled with laborers. If the means of traveling are not available, he falls into difficulties and distress, is obliged to sell the effects he brought with him for a trifling sum, or considers himself fortunate if he finds a job anywhere at the lowest wage—a wage that will barely keep him and his family from hunger. Those who wish to move on to the land should not come to America without capital unless they are young, strong, and eager to work. It is necessary to earn the means to independence through service or through daily labor which is, to be sure, not easy, but is surer than to purchase immediately an independent position with money brought from Germany.

### 36. Advice to Immigrants: Another German View, 1855[1]

It is not our problem at the present time to compile a historical outline of emigration nor to discuss the reasons why it goes on at a steady rate. We intend merely to assist those who have decided to leave their

---

[1] Extract translated from Karl Büchele, *Land und Volk der Vereinigten Staaten von Nord Amerika. Zur Belehrung für Jedermann, vorzüglich für Auswanderer* (Stuttgart, 1855), pp. 403–410. Translation by Elsie P. Wolcott, graduate assistant, School of Social Service Administration.

old homes, to tear themselves away from relatives and friends, and to give up all their cherished customs and habits in order to seek their fortune in a strange country which has another language, other customs, institutions, and views of life. We wish to advise and instruct intending emigrants as to the most suitable way of carrying out their decision and to give them information that will enable them to save themselves from repentance and destruction. As compared with the increasing poverty in Europe, the uncertainty of political conditions, the increasing pressure of expenses, and the difficulty of earning a modest living even with great industry, the possibility of emigration to the United States exercises an extraordinary attraction. The ease with which land can be earned there, the absence of restrictions on commerce, trade, and traffic; low cost of living, political and religious freedom, absence of a standing army, and, at the same time, the undisputed internal as well as external peace—with such conditions one is quite willing to overlook the fact that many of these advantages are only apparent or are fully outweighed by evils intimately associated with the good points.

In Europe people still adhere too much to the picture of the American republic as it was conceived by its founders, whereas if they could only look back into this world they would be little pleased with the many new traits that have in the course of time mingled with the old. The increase in population, the progress and improvement in many phases of the prosperity of the nation, show in less glaring colors the weakening of moral elasticity and of the true Republican spirit, as well as the preponderance of the tradesman spirit. Today many still seek to locate the moral consciousness of America in the forests and prairies of the West, when they can no longer hide from themselves the decayed spots of the cities. . . . .

If prosaic North America has, so to speak, appeared to the European emigrant as the country in which the life of the golden age is reproduced, this has not been due to the impossibility of procuring more accurate knowledge of the true state of affairs, but has rather grown out of illusions to which people gradually became accustomed, so that in the end truth became the victim of misrepresentation. Who does not know people who are tired of Europe? Who has not, at some time or other, heard them express the idea that institutions on this side of the ocean have outlived their usefulness, and that the intellectual culture of man always proceeds westward. Inhabitants of European countries believed they had found in America a pledge of the reality of their ideals, and the flattered national vanity of the Americans regarded the conditions in their own country as the most praiseworthy in the world. In this way the two peoples played into each other's hands in the overestimation of America, although from different motives. When at last the day of reality arrived, people in Germany could not or would not renounce the illusions that they had themselves created.

Here, German immigrants of the educated class were accustomed to look at America from the sentimental point of view, while in the new home they suddenly saw her as she really was. In vain did many a one seek for America in America. If they did not find their expectations satisfied in the East, they followed the goal of their desires to the West. If, in the end, the farther they progressed, the Utopia which they desired was wafted out of sight and disappeared farther and farther into hazy distances, they finally complained that, on the other side, in their own country, no news of the real state of affairs was available. The same people who at the beginning of their erratic wanderings would not open their eyes to the truth about the country which they had finally reached, remarked in a naïve way, "All that may be true, but at home no one will believe you." Here in Europe, then, people do not believe true accounts, and over there in America, people complain that it was impossible to obtain information here.

There is a statement which we found confirmed in thousands of instances: "To cure anyone who is dissatisfied with the social and political conditions in his country, send him to America." Nowhere are idealistic dreams and fancies dispelled as fully and completely as under the disintegrating influence of the rudely materialistic Philistinism existing in America. As compared with the moral deterioration of Europe, the American, to be sure, possesses a certain strength, but from this one must not assume a general preponderance in strength. A very obvious narrowness of spirit is only too often coupled with a proud feeling of independence. People give the impression of haughtily looking down upon European culture, and, in worldly and spiritual things, allow the first adventurer and cheat to trick them. In trivial phrases they praise their liberty and independence, while at elections and in other public matters they follow the party leaders like children, and allow their representatives to impose upon them laws which often greatly encroach upon the personal rights of the individual. Direct taxes are not paid to the state, but local assessments, taxes, etc., are that much larger. People are spared the burdensome surveillance of police officials, but this supervision is exercised by the neighborhood itself which, with unbearable curiosity, looks in your windows. If neighbors see anything of which they do not approve, they express their condemnation, and your life is made unpleasant. People boast of religious freedom and do not mention that this freedom is curtailed by prejudice and fanaticism. . . . .

Conditions in America may be very different from those in Europe, but the differences are hardly as great as people here often imagine. Moreover, since America more or less assimilates all foreign elements, a new and definite Americanism might develop out of the magnificent process of transformation and amalgamation. . . . .

If, from the standpoint of the immigrant, we look more closely at the picture described above, it is true, to be sure, that America's political institutions are of a liberal character such as is unknown on this side. A certain degree of political education is common, and knowledge necessary for practical life is nowhere lacking. Industry, activity, and a certain degree of prosperity are to be found everywhere, and a definite "poorer class" in the European sense, in contrast to excessive riches, does not appear. However, the powerful position of America has given its inhabitants a conceit which is expressed not only in foreign relations, but toward everything foreign coming into the country, particularly in a ridiculous, often brutal disdain for foreign immigrants, although they primarily contribute to the growth of the country. . . . . The unbelievable arrogance of the American makes a painful impression upon the German immigrant, and the German's only defense is to rid himself as soon as possible of all the earmarks of German descent, and by transforming himself into a complete Yankee, to put an end to the insults from which he suffers. At best, he succeeds only in the course of time, but in the meantime rarely does he lend a helping hand to the countrymen coming after him, the so-called "greens," who are likely to have the same fate as he, and to help them rise. Unfortunately, he can find nothing more fitting to do than to mimic the Yankee in his repulsive arrogance toward them.

At the present time thousands emigrate who are not driven to such a step because of need or privation. . . . . Some people emigrate who are prompted only by a spirit of enterprise, a certain desire for change, or are, in general, dissatisfied with their personal circumstances. These people . . . . after successive disappointments, discouraging experiences, and hard losses, become convinced that what they have gained is a very slight recompense for what they have sacrificed. Shame and pride, however, may keep them from confessing this. Even those craftsmen or day laborers who, as they well say, left their country only to escape starvation, soon arrive at the conclusion that if at home they had made the untiring efforts and had exposed themselves to the same privations as were waiting for them in America, life in the old home would have been far less deplorable than it is now. . . . .

So far as the exceptional conditions of the present are concerned, they are, in spite of their temporary character, nevertheless of such a nature that for the immediate future all thoughts of emigration should be dispelled. As a result of the unhealthy eagerness of the majority quickly to become wealthier and wealthier, America has been the scene of fabulous speculation and panic. . . . . Thousands of workmen in the large cities of the East have been destitute, and the misery among immigrants in New York who were helplessly stranded on inhospitable shores increased to a deplorable degree, and the next few years will still be full of hardship and poverty for the working classes. For this reason many immigrants have returned to their own countries, and it is a fact that during the months of May to September, 1854, about 12,000 immigrants, or 6 per cent of the total number arriving there during this period, returned to Europe from New York. This fact is even more worthy of attention when one considers that for every 12,000 who really returned one must figure at least thirty to forty thousand others who would have followed if they had possessed the means. If the hostility toward immigrants which is at present so general and closes many opportunities for earning a livelihood which were formerly open to them is considered, then one understands that many of the new arrivals have had sufficient cause to repent very bitterly the step which they took when they left the fatherland.

### 37.   Difficulty of Regulating Emigration[1]

There is no way of directing emigration as long as there are countries in which uncontrolled emigration exists and is effective. English emigration furnishes an uncommonly instructive example of this. Canada, although not to the same extent as the United States, must nevertheless be regarded as a favorable country for the settlement of European immigration. One would think, moreover, that, to the English emigrant, settling in an English colony would appear an advantage outweighing the more magnificent development of the United

[1] Extract translated from Emil Lehmann, *Die Deutsche Auswanderung* (Berlin, 1861), pp. 99–101.

States. However, this is not the case. It is found in the yearly reports made to Parliament by the English Emigration Commission that, on the average, three times as many Englishmen emigrate to the United States as to the British colonies. In view of their antipathy against England, it is not surprising that the Irish almost exclusively turn to the United States. But that the majority of Englishmen with their strong patriotism should prefer settlement among a strange people, although it is of the same origin, to living in an English colony which, especially to Englishmen, offers splendid opportunities for happiness and prosperity, is decisive proof that, in the estimation of the man who has fully decided to emigrate, the prospect of greater economic prosperity and greater individual freedom outweighs every other consideration and is decisive in the choice of the country of immigration. Every German state would have quite similar experiences, if it were to try to direct German emigration to a definite country, no matter how advantageous the conditions.

Even more of a failure would be any attempt to stop the stream of emigration. Those who consider it possible to put into effect regulations for this purpose should be reminded that emigration was not discouraged by strict prohibitive laws passed repeatedly in the last and in the present century. Not even the edict of July 7, 1760, which threatened emigration with punishment or possibly death could stop the movement. Every attempt of this sort would be in vain because it could not be carried out. It would also be unwise because one could not render Germany a worse service than to hold back by force those who wish to leave the country. . . . . Police regulations, as they were recently proposed in the German diet, would, if it were at all thinkable that they could achieve their purpose of decreasing emigration, only result in embittering those who are dissatisfied with their economic and political position, and draw attention to a forcible remedy for conditions from which they wanted to escape. Emigration is best left to regulate itself, in destination as well as extent. If the amount of emigration were abnormal, there is only one remedy to reduce it to the proper proportions, that is, bettering conditions at home. Not to mention more extensive political improvements, and limiting one's self to that which can be carried out in the near future, let freedom of trade be granted where it does not exist, and make it possible for the peasant to become a landowner. Then a state like Mecklenburg, which has furnished the largest contingents to emigration because it is unable to offer its peasants any other life than one approaching serfdom, will find that it no longer needs to devote all its efforts to set a limit by force to a truly menacing withdrawal of its working forces.

## 38. Causes and Racial Character of European Emigration: A General View, 1815–60[1]

From 1792 to 1815 European emigration was insignificant. But peace returned, and with peace came again the need of expansion, of migration, of movement, which, with certain peoples, seems to be the result of material well-being and of prosperity. Moreover, the war had created tastes, habits, and conditions that were incompatible with the peaceful activities of the new era that had been inaugurated by the treaties of 1815. In addition to this, the colonial world had been enlarged during this period. . . . .

Thus stimulated by various special circumstances, emigration resumed its course in 1816. The movement was favored, as regards Germany, both by liberal modifications of the legislation relating to expatriation and also by a series of bad harvests (1816–18), which aggravated to an extraordinary degree the privations that twenty years of war had imposed on that country.

To these reasons for abandoning the native soil others were added later. Colonization societies were formed, stimulated by private interests or by the influence of religious or political considerations. These societies, of which the first traces are found between 1818 and 1820, very rapidly assumed considerable importance. . . . .

The disillusionments of 1830 and 1848 were complicated by the economic crises which always follow revolutions; . . . . the severe measures adopted in Germany against the socialists and communists and even against purely religious organizations such as the Separatists, the Mennonites, the Rappists, etc.; the increase in prices in 1846–47; the organization of numerous societies for assisting emigrants both in Europe and in America; the protective measures adopted directly by the countries of origin and of destination; the formation of powerful shipping companies which lowered the prices of transportation to the level of the most humble pocketbooks; the extraordinary prosperity of the United States, with the twofold attraction of this privileged country, the high level of wages and the low price of land; finally the gold discoveries; all these events, simultaneous or successive, have since made emigration a regular business, a normal and permanent institu-

[1] Extract translated from Alfred Legoyt, *L'émigration européenne; son impor tance, ses causes, ses effets* (Paris, 1861), pp. xx–xxxiv.

tion, which has taken its place among the most important economic and social phenomena of our time.

The people who have furnished, who are still furnishing at the present time, and will probably always continue to furnish the largest contingents of European expatriates are the peoples of Germanic origin, the Germans and the Anglo-Saxons. Among the Germans such social conditions as a bad organization of labor, excessive governmental regulations, particularly in the field of industry, the exclusive possession of property, at least in certain states, by a privileged class, help to develop this strange disposition to seek always a new fatherland. But in addition to these social conditions there exists also among the people beyond the Rhine an instinctive irresistible tendency, in some sort congenital, to extend themselves, to spread out, to carry their calm and persevering activity into the whole world.

They seem to obey unconsciously a superior and providential force which leads them wherever the work of civilization demands long continued efforts, prolonged sacrifices, an unusual exhibition of moral and physical force, the spirit of sacrifice and resignation. From these points of view the Germans are the leading pioneer settlers of the world, for they have in the highest degree this heroic confidence in the future, thanks to which one works with an indefatigable persistency for remote and uncertain rewards.

When the resource of transatlantic emigration was no longer open to them, they applied to their neighbors, with an incredible patience and tenacity, this power of penetration and absorption which drives them almost unconsciously to implant everywhere their deep-rooted nationality. . . . .

The Anglo-Saxon race has analogous qualities which may be explained by their common origin. But less flexible, less enduring, less disposed to accept, even provisionally, the domination of others, the Anglo-Saxon expands only in countries that belong to him or the countries that have belonged to him, where he still rules by customs, language, institutions, in fact by the Anglo-Saxon spirit and tradition.

In the emigration from the United Kingdom, the Irish element predominates. . . . . The Irish emigration is necessitous; the Irish emigrant accepts upon foreign soil any kind of work that is offered him. He is most usually employed upon public works (building of canals and of railroads) and in this capacity has rendered incalculable services in the United States. Outside of this type of work, the Irish emigrant seeks to establish himself in the cities where he finds useful

employment in various industries and, if necessary, in domestic serv-
ive. A hardworking race, but intemperate, ignorant, credulous, violent,
the Irish do not offer in their adopted country all guaranties of peace
and order that one might wish for.

The English-Scotch emigration is largely recruited from among
small farmers and small merchants and artisans. It owes its origin, in
large measure, to the results of the law of primogeniture, which, even
among the lower classes of society, leaves the younger sons to look
after their own future. However, these immigrants are not indigent.
It is rare indeed for parents not to come to the assistance of the children who are expatriating themselves, with gifts proportionate to their
means.

The English-Scotch emigrant is seldom upon foreign soil either an
agricultural or a day laborer and, less frequently still, a domestic. He
is either a farmer or a merchant  either on his own account or as a
salaried employee. He is also to be found as superintendent in great
industrial enterprises or as chief clerk in financial companies. The
English-Scotch workingmen are also found in large numbers in the
mines or in manufacturing industries similar to those common in England. Active, enterprising, hardworking, persevering, honest, incom-
parably more sober and temperate than the Irish, the English-Scotch
are welcomed everywhere and find employment without difficulty.

According to official information regarding European emigration
to the United States, France follows Germany and the United Kingdom in respect of the number of emigrants. But we fear that the
federal documents erroneously attribute to our country all the emigrants
embarked at our ports.

There is not much belief abroad, and especially in Germany, in
our adaptability as colonists. . . . .

But it must be recognized that the French rarely emigrate. The
fact is that among the various races of Europe there is none with a
greater regard for his native land than the French, with a more instinctive, more inviolable affection for his home, his village, and his
country. . . . . Only religious or political persecutions have led in
France to emigration on a scale of any importance. . . . .

After Germany and the British Isles, Switzerland furnishes in proportion to its population the largest contribution to European emigration. This contribution comes especially from the robust agricultural
laborers, who, because of the high price of land at home, have for a long
time been obliged to carry on their useful industry outside of their own

country. However, the rapid development of industry, by absorbing an ever increasing number of hands, has arrested, or at any rate percepti- bly diminished for some years past in Switzerland, a movement of expatriation which even at the old rate would have taken on very probably the character of a real depopulation. The Swiss emigrant, honest, industrious, economical, frugal, is welcomed abroad like the German.

The Scandinavian countries, in spite of satisfactory economic con- ditions, of political institutions worthy of a more advanced civilization, a civil law which, except as concerns property and liberty of conscience, appears to be satisfactory to the interests of all—have also begun to contribute to the great current of European emigration. Canada and the most northern sections of the United States receive with favor the Scandinavian farmers and fishers unless they go as recruits to the Mormon sect.

Belgium and Holland, though in large part of Germanic origin, have not the adventurous instincts of the mother race. They are satis- fied with their condition, living under an excellent government, not suffering from overpopulation, and are frequently instructed besides, by their paternal government, upon the dangers of distant colonization. They do not have, moreover, that vigorous spirit of initiative, that boldness of movement, the firm wish to go forward, that characterizes the Anglo-Saxons. Nor do they possess either the patience, the resigna- tion, the *vis durans* that Tacitus, even in his time, attributed to the Germans. The inhabitants of Belgium and Holland prefer the medioc- rity of their ancestral hearths to even a prosperous exile. . . . .

Italy is, after France and perhaps in the same degree, the land in which love of country has the deepest roots in the hearts of its in- habitants. The fact is that perhaps nowhere else has nature been so prodigal with its enchantments and seductions. Therefore, although Italy has been, since the fall of the Caesars, the object of European covetousness, the eternal battlefield of powerful neighbors, and the theater of the fiercest and most prolonged civil wars, her children have always refused to leave her. Save for some commercial colonies hastily thrown upon the shores of Asia by Genoa and Venice, history has not, in fact, recorded in Italy any important outward movement of popula- tion.

The two great empires, Russia and Austria, hold their populations closely bound to the soil. In Russia, emigration is simply prohibited; in Austria it is so surrounded with numerous difficulties and formalities as must inevitably check the desire to leave. The Germanic element constitutes only about one-fourth of the various agglomeration of diverse peoples who live under the scepter of the House of Habsburg, and the other races, situated far in the interior of the country, lacking even completed means of communication, and scarcely suspecting the existence of transatlantic regions are little tempted to give themselves up to expatriation, which always represents the formidable unknown.

### 39.  Causes of Swiss Emigration[1]

The attachment of the Swiss to their green mountains, their cool valleys, and their wooded lakes, as well as the great number of departures made in the hope of returning, indicate clearly that permanent emigration from Switzerland is reluctantly undertaken. Density of population there presses like an inevitable fatality. A density of 59 inhabitants per square kilometer has been reached (2,392,740 souls upon 40,378 square kilometers) and this proportion, which in other countries would be only a very moderate one, is high there, if not indeed excessive, in a country in which grazing lands and fields that are made impracticable for cultivation by their steepness or by their altitude cover so much area, in which long and cold snowy winters condemn a large part of the agricultural population to unemployment.

The potato blight and the bad harvests frequently aggravate the natural difficulties of existence, and the inborn industriousness of the people, although assisted by a great simplicity of habits, cannot everywhere triumph over poverty. "People emigrate from Switzerland today," said one of its citizens[2] in 1844, "neither for religious or political reasons, those two great and powerful causes of the emigrations of other centuries; an emigrant leaves the fatherland today in disgust because he cannot own there enough soil to live reasonably well, or at least in order not to die of hunger, and to live after some fashion." The events of the *Sonderbund* introduced temporarily the two causes that did not exist at the time when the above statement was made, but their effect was only passing while the economic cause still exists. There are many other causes in addition to the density of population and the

---

[1] Extract translated from Jules Duval, *Histoire de l'émigration européenne, asiatique et africaine au xix<sup>e</sup> siècle: Ses causes, ses caractères, ses effets* (Paris, 1862), pp. 145–49

[2] Huber-Saladin, *Discours prononcé devant la Société d'utilité publique fédérale, le 18 septembre, 1844.*

climatic severities which seem to increase the difficulties of subsistence.
. . . .

The causes of emigration peculiar to Switzerland have shown themselves most clearly in the canton of Glarus. "At the bottom of the
closed valleys," says the writer whom we have just quoted, "surrounded by the highest Alps, and the glaciers that separate the canton
of Glarus from the canton of Grisons, some communes faithful to the
pastoral manners of their fathers have maintained the traditions of the
Alpine life without taking part in the industrial activity of the lower
valley. Too careless perhaps of the future, living from day to day off
the communal lands and the small holdings they have inherited, and
some other minor sources of income, they have seen their population
increase to a point at which emigration alone can afford relief."

One of these communes, which numbers 1,200 inhabitants, possesses only 27,000 square *toises*[1] of cultivable, communal land divided into
250 communal rights. In another commune the population of 1,550
souls in 1817 has today (1844) 2,400, an average of 30 persons a year,
an increase always progressive, which is formidable even upon this
small scale, and indeed a most critical situation if one considers the
feeble resources of a valley which cannot be enlarged with the increase
in the number of its inhabitants. Here one sees a hundred families
without a handful of land, living by means of a communal right of
about 100 square *toises*. . . . .

Spinning has almost been given up, weaving no longer brings any
appreciable returns, wages have fallen, and the large factories which
might have employed some hands refuse to take on new employees; the
print-cloth industry, threatened by English competition and upon the
defensive, has become cautious and is not expanding.

In the face of such overwhelming distress, emigration has presented
itself to the minds of the inhabitants as the sole immediate remedy for
overpopulation. The communal councils have given notice of this
remedy to the cantonal council and have asked its assistance in a declaration marked by a simple and manly eloquence in which they refute
the criticisms which have been passed on their citizens. "We shall be
accused perhaps of inefficiency in the administration of our communal
property, it will be said that the inhabitants of Kleinthal are indifferent.
Doubtless there are some idle persons among us, for are they not found
everywhere? But ought not the lack of a certain kind of activity to be
excused among mountaineers accustomed always to the extreme sim-

[1] [An ancient long measure in France containing 6.395 feet in English measure.]

plicity of a pastoral life, separated from and, so to speak, forgotten by the rest of the world from which they have received no inspiration? When in spite of the most laborious efforts, people cannot secure a living for themselves, is it astonishing that discouragement, relaxation, and inertia spring up? We might point out that families who are the most hardworking and who unite all their efforts succeed in sustaining their existence only by enduring the greatest privations, and even so they succeed only so long as illness does not arrest their strength. If every individual in our commune, without exception, should employ himself in the most sustained exertions it would not follow that in the long run they could all exist."

The council of the commune asked, therefore, that the question of emigration should become a cantonal problem, that the government should purchase lands in America, in a section in which the climate was similar to that of. Switzerland, and that from among the possible or prospective emigrants, the necessary workers should be chosen in order that everything might be made ready to receive the families and that emigration should be regulated especially in the interest of the poorest. The state would advance all the expenses and would fix a method of reimbursing the cantonal treasury; finally, in agreement with the government of the United States, it would direct the progress and development of the colony, up to the time when it should be organized and admitted to the American federal union under the name of New Glarus, a name designed to preserve at least in the hearts of the expatriated children of Switzerland, the memory of the fatherland. A beginning has already been made in the execution of this plan: ten communes have purchased in Wisconsin 12,000 acres of land and have founded a New Glarus there.[1]

The adoption of this extreme remedy is prevented, in the greater part of the high valleys of Switzerland, only by the development of industries, the initial establishment of which is favored by the great

[1] [The later history of this colonizing experiment is interesting. The population of the town of New Glarus, Wisconsin, was 554 in 1920; 627 in 1910, 1,245 in 1900, and 1,180 in 1890. Founded in 1845, the agents sent out by the canton selected the present site on the Little Sugar River "because the rocky slopes of the valley suggested their Alpine home." The foundations of the colony were laid and the construction for settlers was begun by the advance agents before the emigrants left Switzerland. In April, 1845, approximately 200 colonists set out for America with a plan for the government of "New Glarus" drawn up by their cantonal council in Switzerland, providing for schools, a state church supported by tithes, etc. They remained for nearly half a century a prosperous but segregated community, an old-world village with the language, architecture, and customs of a Swiss village.]

number of waterfalls and the proximity of forests. Another preventive factor is the continual migration of the surplus inhabitants, who go down from the mountains into the plains where they find lands which require more labor and permit a less rugged life. This migration, which naturally is limited by the extent of lower valleys and the plain, is very noticeable in Valais, for example, and in all the districts which offer any space for intensive cultivation, for the clearing of land, and the increase of an agricultural or industrial population. . . . .

There comes finally a time when even the lowland has a larger population than it can support, and thoughts are then turned to the more distant horizons of foreign emigration.

The communes and the cantons recognize the necessity of emigration and assist it by their subventions. Some peasants depart with the price of their small inheritances, others trust themselves to societies or agents who smooth the way for them too often at the expense of their pocketbooks.

In the United States, and to this country most of them go, they find several Swiss centers already established. In Indiana, in the county of Switzerland, New Vevay was founded fifty years ago by emigrants from this commune. Their descendants are not numerous, but they have prospered and have retained the primitive characteristics of good Swiss citizens.

Other Swiss emigrants are distributed in compact groups in the states of the interior, some times isolated, but more frequently mingled with the Germans, in Michigan, Wisconsin, Iowa, Ohio, Indiana, Illinois, even Kentucky.

### 40. Emigration of Capital and Labor, 1865[1]

By the report of the Commissioners of Emigration, it appears that 184,700 emigrants reached [New York] City from Europe in the year 1864. In addition to these, thousands were landed at Boston and other points under the direction of Federal recruiting agents, who, as a matter of private speculation, sent over several shiploads, chiefly from Belgium and Germany. But the above figures do not fairly represent the influx of the foreign element into our midst. While the strife was pending and the issue still undetermined, the current of emigration slackened, and

[1] Two editorials from the *Commercial and Financial Chronicle*, published in the numbers of August 12, 1865, and November 25, 1865, Vol. I, pp. 199–200 and 675–76. For further discussion of the effect of the Civil War on immigration, see documents 32–35 in Section II.

its character was changed. It consisted principally of adventurers. But now the floodgates have been reopened and a more constant and healthier tide pours in. They come now with their wives and children in search of peaceful homes and fields of industry, and doubtless, in most cases, impelled by an instinctive appreciation of the stability and beneficence of our political system.

The masses of Europe, though perhaps ignorant of the questions involved in the late struggle, were nevertheless aware that the strength and vitality of the Republic was being tested, and in the triumph of the Federal arms they recognize a judgment in favor of republican institutions. The result of the war will, therefore, beyond a doubt, give impulse and vigor to the tide of emigration. It has already done so, as the emigrant returns for the past three months prove. The peasantry of the old world hear in the voice of peace an invitation to themselves to escape from their present ills, and seek new homes and new fortunes upon the soil of our redeemed republic.

After political security, there is nothing that the Republic needs so much as bone and sinew, for the development of its vast resources. We have established the supremacy of the principles of self-government so that they are not endangered by domestic treason or foreign envy; and now, having solved all problems and disposed of all doctrines and theories relative to the intention of our political system, we want flesh and blood, men, women, and children, to assist in fulfilling that intention.

To the emigrant there are now many and new inducements. The field for labor is now greatly enlarged. But first of all we would say to him, shake from your feet the dust of our great cities the moment you arrive, and without hesitation, without delay go westward or south- ward and invest what you have in broad acres of good land. There is no welcome for the emigrant in the great cities, and least of all in New York, unless, indeed, for such as are skilled artizans and practised mechanics; and even for them, unless they excell, the wilderness, re- claimed by axe and plow and the sweat of their brow, promises the earliest and surest competence and the largest share of independence, health, and comfort.

From the valley of the Mississippi to the Pacific Coast there is farm land for all who may come. Missouri, Minnesota, Montana, Arizona, Idaho, California, Oregon are Eldorados to any who have the will to work. The money squandered in searching for employment in the cities of the Atlantic slope would suffice to transport the emigrant and his family to the west, provided with the necessary implements of husbandry.

But it is not the great, growing, thriving west alone that now beckons to the working classes of the world. The abolition of slavery has put aside the barrier that turned away the tide of emigration from the south, and a new workshop is open to the masses of Europe who have the spirit and the energy to break from the profitless monotony of their present existence, and to seek a wider and more generous sphere of thought and action.

---

A gentleman now in business in London, but formerly a resident of this country, in a late letter to one of our leading citizens, which we have been permitted to read, presents in the following extract a good idea of the extent of the emigration from Europe to the United States which the next year promises:

Steamship lines hence to America are multiplying wonderfully, and I fully expect to witness next year the largest emigration from Europe to the United States ever known. Not only that, but the widespread publicity which, in every way and shape, is being given to the resources and attraction of our country, must be the means of directing the flow of capital thither in amounts hitherto unknown. The London *Times* during the war was our worst enemy; but now, as though anxious to atone for its past offenses, it is doing its best to write up our country and its interest, as will be seen, ere long, with wonderful effect. Letters from a well-known correspondent describing the Oil Regions of Pennsylvania and its wonderful scenes, its products and prosperity, are now attracting general attention, and will, I doubt not, greatly swell the tide of travel, as well as emigration, in that direction the ensuing year. It seems to me that the most sanguine of us must fail to realise the greatness and prosperity which are in store for the United States.

From every direction since the restoration of peace we have the same promise of increased emigration. The political changes in Europe within the last two years have tended to this result. The oppressive conditions imposed by the German powers upon Denmark, and the occupation of the two duchies of Schleswig and Holstein by Prussia and Austria, have already directed the attention of the inhabitants of those countries to the subject of removal. Whole districts contemplate coming to this country, bringing their property with them. Already have Swedish colonists in considerable numbers made their way into the interior of Virginia, and Danes are following in their wake. Large bodies of Germans are also on their way to upper Texas, and tracts of land have been purchased for the purposes of establishing settlements of Poles. It would seem as though a general exodus from Northern Europe to this country was in contemplation.

Nor could it take place at a more opportune period. We need both the labor and capital thus furnished, and we have greater inducements to offer the emigrant than ever before. The colonists will not come empty-handed. They generally possess little properties, the proceeds of which they will bring with them, aiding materially their own labor in developing the resources of their new homes. Thus the accession of half a million of emigrants from Europe to our population would make the addition of many millions to the capital of this country.

There are more inducements than formerly for such emigration. The events of the Civil War have served to exhibit our resources, and to acquaint the world with the advantages we possess. Its happy conclusion has also multiplied and diversified the branches of productive industry, so that every new-comer can find employment for his labor and capital with little delay or difficulty. The Western States abound with lands sufficient to give homesteads to the whole population of Europe, besides mines of coal and iron, lead and copper, zinc and other metals, only wanting capital and labor for their profitable working. The district lately in rebellion affords the most abundant opportunities for profitable investment for the purpose of agriculture, mining, and manufactures. . . . .

Already emigration companies have been formed to establish new settlements in eligible districts of the Southern States. One is in operation under the presidency of the Governor of Massachusetts; another has begun business with five millions of acres of land at its disposal for nominal prices, in different States and districts. Other similar associations will soon be organized to share in the advantages of the enterprise. Thus will not only the millions of emigrants from Europe be supplied with homes and employment for their capital, but adventurers now from our own free North will also repair thither to achieve fortune and position.

The different States of the Union are also competitors in the same field. Years ago Wisconsin and other Western States were in the practice of employing State Agents to visit Europe to induce emigration. Maryland this very year engaged in the same enterprise, sending an agent to Germany for colonists. Pamphlets describing the resources of the State, the fertility of the soil, the mildness and salubrity of the climate, were printed in German and widely circulated with gratifying success. In a few weeks shiploads of emigrants sailed directly for

Baltimore and have continued to arrive there ever since. The other States of the South afford greater inducements still, and hence colonists with large amounts of money are going thither.

**41. A Later View of Emigration from the United Kingdom, 1870[1]**

So long as there is inhabitable surface on the earth not yet occupied, it is probable we shall have emigration. This abstract thought, however, has very little to do with the actual facts of emigration as it now goes on. It is a great delusion for men to think that our emigrants are going away from us because there is no room for them in their native land. It is a still greater delusion to imagine that it is a relief to those who remain behind to be quit of those who go. . . . .

In 1815, the total emigration from the United Kingdom was 2,081 —in 1866, it had risen to 204,882. That is such an increase as may well arrest the attention of all who feel interested in their country. There were higher years than 1866; but these had to do with the gold fever. In 1852, for example, the number of emigrants rose to 368,764; but 87,881 of these went to Australia or New Zealand. It is to the steady flow of nearly 200,000 persons a year, as reached from the small beginning— 2,081 in 1815—that it is interesting to turn attention.

And yet it is far more interesting to consider the destination of these emigrants. The number from 1815 gives a grand total of 6,106,392 persons, and of these no less than 5,044,809 went to North America. Large as the Australian and New Zealand exodus has been, it reached only 929,181 in 1866; that is, it had not reached one million when the American had gone beyond six. It is important, too, to notice that by far the largest number of our emigrants to America go to the United States. In 1866 those to the "colonies" were 13,255, while to the States they reached the high number of 161,000. It is therefore very clear that it is with America we have specially to do in considering the bearings of this vast and growing emigration. The States of America *are not now a new country.* They begin to have all the characteristics of an old established nation, especially in their northern and eastern portions. New England is a well-peopled region of the world; and, to as great an extent as Old England, it may be regarded as a manufacturing country, and certainly not a land remaining to be occupied. An emigration from Britain to these States is not a going forth to subdue the wilds of the earth's surface, but to increase the population of large manufacturing centres.

[1] Extract from John Kirk, *Social Politics in Great Britain and Ireland* (London, 1870), pp. 112–19.

This leads us, however, to notice further, the nationality of the emigrants going from us. Up to 1847 the emigration was from Ireland in a very much larger proportion than from the rest of the empire. During the following eight years the flow from Ireland became comparatively low, though it still keeps up to a high rate. The emigration from Scotland was next in importance to that of Ireland, when the extent of our population is taken into account. England, with six times as many people as Scotland, sent but few emigrants till of late years. . . . . Now the chief stream of emigration is flowing from England. In the first or winter quarter of the year 1869 the emigration was 2,702 Scotch, 9,800 Irish, and 11,110 English. It need not be told any one who thinks and reads at all on the subject that it is now in England almost exclusively that we have excitement in connection with emigration. . . . .

What is the great relation in which these three kingdoms stand to each other and mankind? Ireland is agricultural and pastoral; so is Scotland to a great extent; England is the workshop for these and for the world. . . . . A pastoral people are the first to emigrate in the course of nature. An agricultural people are the next in order. From a land like this a manufacturing people would never emigrate if matters were right. The climate and mineral store of this country are such that no other country can at present compete with it in manufacturing power, if the natural course of things were followed. Even our shepherds have an immense advantage at home, and our farmers have a still greater advantage, but our manufacturers have so great facilities as can scarcely at present be equalled. It is, consequently, matter of extreme interest when we find that England is emigrating.

It introduces us to the mining, mechanical, and manufacturing character of our emigrants now. There are above 70,000 souls in the east end of London who must emigrate speedily or die. They are being shipped off as fast as charity and Government can transport them to North America. Above 25,000 of these are workmen more or less skilled in engineer and shipbuilding occupations. These are not shepherds nor are they ploughmen, nor will they ever be to any great extent one or the other. They are mechanics, and will be so, go where they may. In the vast hives of industry in Lancashire there are a greater number who must emigrate or die. These are getting off as fast as they possibly can to Massachusetts to find full occupation in cotton. Not one is either pastoral or agricultural, and few are likely ever to be either. Irishmen and Scotchmen can be anything, but not so Englishmen, and they will not need to be anything in the world but what they have been. Their skill is too valuable to be sent to the backwoods when abundance of rough hands are there already, and skilled men are needed to make a great country fit to manufacture for itself. Till within the last four years our emigrants were chiefly pastoral and agricultural, now they are chiefly mining, mechanical, and manufacturing. It is to this that we feel it of such importance to call attention. Our position as a nation depends, to a great extent, upon our usefulness to the world in a mechanical and manufacturing line. Commerce has its being in the fact that one nation is so situated that it excels in one thing, while another excels in another. It is in the exchange of produce that all trade lies, and such exchange clearly depends on the excelling we have mentioned. If this nation loses its excellence in manufacturing power, it loses its only possible share in the exchange of the world, and its commerce dies.

We must also look at the effect of emigration on the character of the population left behind. How do the Emigration Commissioners account for the vast deficiencies in the population of Ireland? More than two millions and a half of deficiency was double the emigration, but it was accounted for by the fact that the *young men and women* had gone off to such a degree that marriages and births had fallen off sufficiently to account for all. "The proportion of persons between the ages of twenty and thirty-five," in the ordinary settled course of society, is about 25 per cent—that proportion among emigrants is above 52 per cent. . . . . We dare not now send our criminals abroad, nor dare we send our paupers, nor should we be allowed to send any class unfit to support themselves. It is the best of our mechanical and manufacturing hands that are now going, and they are leaving the proportion of those who burden society largely increased. . . . .

Nothing can be more self-evident than that the wealth of a people depends on the largeness of the number who produce as compared with that of those who only consume. If by any means the producers are diminished while the consumers are increased in number, the prosperity of that community must be lowered. And yet this is the sure and certain effect of emigration, as it goes on from this country now.

## 42.   A Swedish Immigrant in His Old Home[1]

[In the winter of 1867] the legislature of Minnesota established a state bureau with the purpose of inducing immigrants to settle in the state,[2] and I was appointed by Gov. W. R. Marshall to be secretary of the board of emigration, with the governor and secretary o state as *ex officio* members. . . . . The St. Paul *Press* for March 14, 1867, contained the following concerning the new board:

The state board of emigration, composed of Gov. Marshall, Col. Rogers and Col. Mattson, was organized yesterday, and a general plan of operation agreed upon. We learn that the board concluded that, with the limited means at their disposal, it was not advisable to employ agents to work in Europe but to use every practicable effort to turn immigrants to Minnesota, after their arrival in this country. Efforts will be made to procure the publication of facts in regard to the state, in eastern and European journals; to make arrangements with railroads, more advantageous to emigrants than heretofore, and to afford them, through interpreters and otherwise, reliable information in regard to the best routes to the state from eastern parts. To give the emigrant a general idea of the characteristics of every locality in Minnesota, it is proposed to procure a map or chart of the state, showing its boundaries, streams, lakes, navigable rivers, timber and prairie sections, etc. . . . .

Our efforts, however, in behalf of Minnesota brought on a great deal of envy and ill-will from people in other states who were interested in seeing the Scandinavian emigration turned towards Kansas and other states, and this feeling went so far that a prominent newspaper writer in Kansas accused me of selling my countrymen to a life not much better than slavery in a land of ice, snow and perpetual winter, where, if the poor emigrant did not soon starve to death, he would surely perish with cold. . . . .

While laboring hard for immigration to Minnesota, my chief object was to get the emigrants away from the large cities and make them settle on the unoccupied lands in the northwest, where the climate was suitable to them, and where it was morally certain that every industrious man or family would acquire independence sooner and better than in the crowded cities of the east. I never attempted to induce anyone to immigrate, but tried to reach those only who had already made up their minds to do so, and the only people that I ever induced

[1] Extract from Hans Mattson, *Reminiscences: The Story of an Emigrant* (St. Paul, 1891), pp. 97–112, 296–98. Hans Mattson emigrated from Sweden in 1851 and became a colonel in the Union army during the Civil War and later held several public offices, including the office of secretary of state in Minnesota.

[2] [*General Laws of Minnesota*, 1867, chap. 28, "An Act to Promote Immigration." See also the following document, p. 167.]

to leave their mother country were a number of poor servants and tenants among my own or my parents' acquaintances for whom I myself paid partly or wholly the cost of the journey. . . . .

In December, 1868, . . . . I set out alone on my first visit to Sweden, after an absence of nearly eighteen years. The chief object of the journey was recreation and pleasure; the second object to make the resources of Minnesota better known among the farming and laboring classes, who had made up their minds to emigrate. . . . .

I decided to spend New Year's eve with one of my most intimate boyhood friends, Mr. Nils Bengston, in the little village of Skoglösa, where I was born. Some of the dearest friends of my parents and a number of my childhood acquaintances were present there, and on New Year's day we attended services together in the old church at Önnestad. My presence was expected, and the church was crowded with people who had been friends and neighbors of my parents, or school and playmates of myself. Even the pastor had chosen a text applicable to me: "I think of the bygone days, and of the time that is past." The solemn services made a deep impression on all of us. . . . .

At that time only a few Swedish emigrants had returned from America, and to see a man who had been eighteen years in America, and had been a colonel in the American army must have been a great curiosity, especially to the country people; for wherever it was known that I would pass, people flocked from their houses to the roads and streets in order to catch a glimpse of the returned traveler. So great was their curiosity that on New Year's eve the servant girls of Nils Bengston at Skoglösa, drew lots as to who should carry in our coffee, and thereby get a chance to take the first look at the American colonel. . . . .

Now followed a season of visits and entertainments in Christianstad and the neighboring country, which I shall ever hold in grateful remembrance. I was received with cordiality everywhere among the common people and the middle classes, while the aristocratic classes looked on with distant coldness, as they always do when a man of the people had succeeded in getting beyond what they would call his legitimate station, and is what we would call, in other words, a self-made man. My plain name and humble ancestry were in their eyes a fault that never could be forgiven. This did not trouble me, however, for I sought no favors, or even recognition from the great, but found plenty of delight in the cordial welcome of the middle classes. . . . .

There was quite a famine in some of the Swedish provinces that winter, and when the government asked the parliament for an appropriation of several millions for carrying on field maneuvers of the army during the coming season, the liberals made a strong opposition, preferring to use the money on some public improvement in the famished provinces. . . . .

Returning to Skåne I found myself besieged by people who wished to accompany me back to America in the spring. . . . . Time passed swiftly, and, as the crowds of intending emigrants were increasing daily, it was found that it would be impossible for one steamer to carry them all, so I went early in April to Helsingborg, where one shipload was started for Minnesota under the leadership of Capt. Lindberg, a veteran from the Anglo-Russian and the American war. A few weeks later I followed across the Atlantic with a party which numbered eight hundred people, and in due time returned to my home in my adopted country.

On the whole that first visit to Sweden was exceedingly pleasant, although there would occasionally come up disagreeable incidents whenever America was the subject of discussion. The laboring and middle classes already at that time had a pretty correct idea of America, and the fate that awaited emigrants there; but the ignorance, prejudice and hatred toward America and everything pertaining to it among the aristocracy, and especially the office holders, was as unpardonable as it was ridiculous. It was claimed by them that all was humbug in America, that it was the paradise of scoundrels, cheats and rascals, and that nothing good could possibly come out of it. They looked upon emigrants almost as criminals, and to contradict them was a sure means of incurring their personal enmity and even insult.

I remember a conversation at an evening party at Näsby between a learned doctor and myself. He started with a proposition that it was wrong to leave one's country, because God has placed us there, and, although the lot of the majority might be very hard, it was still their duty to remain to toil and pray, and even starve, if necessary, because we owed it to the country which had given us birth. . . . . My argument was of no avail; the doctor, otherwise a kind and humane man, would rather see his poor countrymen subsist on bread made partly out of bark, which hundreds of them actually did at that very time in one of the Swedish provinces, than have them go to America, where millions upon millions of acres of fertile lands only awaited the labor of their strong arms to yield an abundance, not only for themselves, but also for the poor millions of Europe. Hard as it is for the individual to change habits of long standing, it is still harder for nations and races to free themselves from prejudices centuries old, especially in a small country like Sweden, isolated from the great nations and thoroughfares of the world.[1]

Much has been said on the causes of immigration. These are numerous, but the chief cause I have found to be that the people of the old world are now being aroused to the fact that the social conditions of Europe, with its aristocracy and other inherited privileges, are not founded on just principles, but that the way to success ought to be equally open for all, and determined, not by privileges of birth, but by the inherent worth of man. And here in America is found a civilization which is, to a large extent, built on equality and the recognition of personal merit. This and the great natural resources of the country, the prospects for good wages which a new continent affords,

---

[1] [Hans Mattson made many later trips to Sweden after he entered the employment of the Northern Pacific Railroad Company. He gives an account in his *Reminiscences* (pp. 117–21) of his resignation of the office of secretary of state in Minnesota to accept the offer of the Northern Pacific, as follows]:

"During this year [1870] one of the greatest railroad enterprises in the world was commenced, namely, the building of the Northern Pacific, extending from Lake Superior to the Pacific coast, a distance of over two thousand miles. The celebrated financier Jay Cooke, of Philadelphia . . . . was at the head of the enterprise. The Northern Pacific Company had received a government grant of many millions of acres of land along the proposed railroad. . . . . One of the important financial questions with Jay Cooke was how to derive a revenue from the sale of lands, and how to get settlers and communities started along the line of the road. . . . .

"Late in the fall of 1870 I received a letter from Mr. Cooke, in Philadelphia, inviting me to come and spend a week with him and talk over the new Northwest. . . . . The result of my conference with him was my permanent engagement, at a salary more than twice as large as that I had from the state, to repair to Europe in the spring as agent of his enterprise, with headquarters in Sweden, my special duties being to make known in the northern countries of continental Europe the resources of the Northern Pacific, particularly the park region in Minnesota. I was also requested by Mr. Cooke to draw up a general plan on my return home for the disposal of the company's lands, which I did, and that plan was adopted for the guidance of its land and emigration officers and agents. . . . .

"Having been criticised by some of my countrymen, for resigning the office of secretary of state at that time, I owe them the following explanation: First: Personally, I was comparatively poor, and the salary which I received from the government . . . . was insufficient to support me and my family. . . . . Secondly: it was of greater importance to the public, and I could render better service to the state at this period of its early development, as agent for a great railroad company, which fact was fully recognized by our leading public men, and it was with their advice and at their earnest request, that I took the step."

and in many cases greater religious liberty, draws the people of Europe, at any rate from Sweden, to this country.

Sweden is a very good country, but more especially so for those who are fortunate enough to be born to title, honor or riches. To be sure, even there, instances are known of men from the ordinary walks of life making their way to wealth and prominence; but those are exceptions, possible only in cases of unusually great personal merit. Here, on the other hand, the reverse is the rule; the self-made man accomplishes most, as instanced by the history of our presidents, governors, financiers and other distinguished men. And this is quite natural, for the prospects and possibilities which a man sees before him in this country stimulate his ambition, and arouse his energies to surmount the greatest difficulties.

The new ideas now permeating society in Europe, and which will gradually transform it, have, to a great extent, originated in America, more particularly the idea of brotherhood, the sympathy with equals, the conviction that it is our duty to better the condition of our fellowmen, and not despise them, even if they are unfortunate. In this respect, as well as in many others, America exerts a great influence over Europe. To me the better situated classes of Swedes seem short-sighted in their hostility to emigration, for a man of broad views must admit that emigration has been beneficial to Sweden herself. It may not have benefited the higher classes directly, as they cannot hire servants and laborers as cheaply as formerly; but the people have benefited by it as a whole, their condition being now better than formerly, when competition between the laborers was greater.

America also exerts a great influence on the mental and moral development of the people of Sweden, although this may not be so apparent on the surface. The thousands and hundreds of thousands of letters written every year by Swedish-Americans to the people of the working classes of Sweden arouses the latter's ambition, and develop liberal, political, and religious ideas among them. No one can calculate the scope of this influence to say nothing of the eloquent language spoken by the millions of crowns which are annually sent home to poor relatives and friends, and which either lighten the burden of poverty or enable the recipients to prepare a brighter future for themselves in this country, and how many a poor, down-trodden fellow, who could expect nothing better than the poorhouse in his old age in Sweden has become an able and useful citizen in this country!

When the poor young laboring man or woman, who in Sweden has felt the oppression of poverty and looked forward to a life without hope, arrives in this country, the timid, bashful looks give way to hopefulness and self-reliance. . . . .

The tact and manner acquired within a short time by common laborers who looked thoughtless and careless while at home, are simply astonishing. A Swedish diplomat, who visited Minnesota and, among others, met one of his father's former farm laborers, who was now in good circumstances, in an official report to the government of Sweden expressed his astonishment at the change which the Swedish people had undergone in that respect.

It cannot be denied that many among the higher classes in Sweden feel very unfriendly toward the United States, and it was even not long ago a common saying among them, "America is the paradise of all rogues and rascals."

### 43. Efforts to Attract Immigrants to a Western State[1]

*Organization of the Board.*—The act of March 3d, 1871,[2] created a Board of five persons, two of whom were designated in said act by name; the Governor, Secretary of State and Treasurer of State constituting the other members *ex-officio*. It was made the duty of the said Board generally, "to adopt measures, which will insure the establishment of a thorough system of inducing immigration to the State."

Certain plans of carrying out this act were recommended, which we will give in detail:

*Correspondence in newspapers.*—One plan was to "engage suitable correspondents, publish or cause to be published, articles treating on and describing in a true light the developed and undeveloped resources of the State of Minnesota," etc. As far as desirable and effective this plan was adopted in our operations both in America and in Europe. Our agent in Germany, whose time expired in March last, caused to be inserted in a number of German papers ably written articles on our State. Our Commissioner of Immigration in New York has among his many successful enterprises for promoting immigration, also caused to be inserted advertisements calling the attention of the public to Minnesota and to the State Pamphlet and other publications on the subject, in some 600 newspapers in the New England and Middle

[1] Extract from *Report of the Minnesota Board of Immigration, 1871*, pp. 61–69.

[2] [*General Laws of Minnesota*, 1871, chap. 50. This law, which was also called "An Act to Promote Immigration," superseded the law of 1867 referred to in the preceding document, see p. 162.]

States. Hans Mattson, formerly Secretary of State, and the clerk of the State Board have for the same purpose issued a series of letters in the different Scandinavian newspapers in America, and as many hundred copies of these papers every week go to regular subscribers in Europe, said articles have also reached their destination abroad. The board found the promulgation of said semi-official articles the more useful, as the surrounding States through the Scandinavian press made strong efforts to turn the flood of Scandinavian immigration from Minnesota.

Emigration direct from England and Scotland has not been overlooked. Not only have there been many calls from there for information answered by letters and pamphlets, but the regular immigration pamphlet, by direction of the Board, has been republished in monthly installments in the columns of the *Free West*, an emigration paper of ability and extensive circulation published in London. By this means it has reached many thousands of additional readers. The immigration has been greater from the British Isles and less from Germany during the last two years (for obvious reasons) than during any one of several years.

*Distribution of pamphlets.*—The main work required may be divided into two branches: (1) Furnishing the necessary information as to the inducements and advantages offered by the State to all classes of desirable immigrants. (2) Aiding, protecting, and advising the immigrant on his way to our State.

The first part has been and is pursued to great effect by sending the State pamphlet to the very heart of the most remote emigrant districts in Northern Europe, in the English, German, Norwegian, and Swedish languages, and by addressing them, not by boxes sent to agents, but in every case to individuals, who contemplate leaving their fatherland. The most of them make up their minds as to their final destination before they leave. Letters and counsels from their friends and relations in America, will govern their movements, and as the State pamphlet is nothing but a condensed series of answered questions upon immigration, the people, as indicated by their thousands of applications, deem this or similar pamphlets the best medium for enlightening their transatlantic friends.

To this end an extra edition of 15,000 copies of the pamphlet prepared in 1870 by the commissioners of statistics was re-printed in English in the winter of 1871.

An edition of 5,000 copies translated into German, with some abbreviations and alterations, has been printed. Also 5,700 copies in

Norwegian, and 3,500 copies in Swedish; the two latter distributed in the countries of Norway, Sweden, Denmark and among the Scandinavians in the United States. An edition of 5,000 copies in English, especially for the Irish immigration, was also printed.

The editions printed in foreign languages contained, besides most of the information of the English pamphlet, many facts of value, especially to immigrants from Europe, which were not deemed necessary to those sent to citizens of the United States.

The throng of applications, for pamphlets, and of questions touching our State to be answered by letters, may be understood from the fact, that the immigration bureau received during the season from 50 to 150 letters per day, each of them containing more applications. Early in the season the Norwegian pamphlets—originally 5,000—were exhausted; so several thousand English pamphlets had to be sent Scandinavians in America, until a new issue could be procured for filling waiting applications to Norway and Denmark.

Thus altogether over 34,000 pamphlets have been printed, and mostly distributed in various tongues, and even this amount proved to be insufficient for the Scandinavian demand.

*Mode of distribution.*—The plan adopted in the distribution of the pamphlets was, as above stated, calculated to place them in the hands of the very persons seeking information in regard to Minnesota. In brief advertisements the Board stated that anyone wishing the pamphlet could have the same sent him free of postage by forwarding his address to the Secretary of State. This plan has worked still more admirably than in 1870, as the requisitions, partly direct from Europe and partly through friends in the United States, have amounted this season to several thousands. The high rates of postage on copies sent to foreign countries have greatly increased that item of our expenditures, but this may possibly be saved to a great extent in the future, if it should be found advisable to let the applicants themselves pay the postage to foreign countries.

*Maps.*—In all 23,800 copies of the pamphlet have been furnished with maps (English maps, 14,000; German, 4,000; Norwegian, 3,500; Swedish, 2,300). As most of the applications ask for pamphlets with maps, and as other States have adopted the plan of circulating their immigration documents with maps, the Board deemed it necessary to continue to provide the same. The maps last season were furnished at a considerable lower price than the preceding year.

*Agents and their work.*—The Board was also empowered to appoint agents for the purpose of aiding, protecting and advising the immigrant on his way to our State,[1] etc.

Local agents can do a great deal of good work in keeping runners from taking hold of new comers, in seeing the immigrants without unnecessary delay forwarded to their destination, and not the least in aiding the unfortunate and preventing imposition. On account of a deficiency from the foregoing year, which had to be covered by last year's appropriation, the Board did not feel at liberty to sustain more than one agency. The Board deemed it proper to establish as a rule, that its operations had to be limited and regulated in accordance with the fund appropriated. Consequently, it had to abstain from creating local agencies in Milwaukee, Chicago, and Quebec. The demand for these agencies had diminished from the fact, that the railroads during last season had procured experienced agents and guides, who performed their duties to the satisfaction of all parties, without expense to our State, and partly because the greater number of immigrants had taken notice of our timely warning in 1870: not to use the uncertain water routes, when railroad transportation was obtainable at reasonable prices.

The Milwaukee and St. Paul road deserves our thanks for having treated the immigrants liberally; the St. Paul and Pacific, and the Superior and Mississippi roads have erected more immigrant houses along their lines, thereby enabling immigrants to find shelter until they find their friends, or decide where to settle. The St. Paul and Pacific's agent, Mr. Christiansen, last season, as before, bestowed upon immigrants arriving at St. Paul all the kindness and care they are in need of in their often helpless condition after a journey of thousands of miles.

*Statistics of immigration.*—The whole number of immigrants for 1870 to our State is estimated at 35,000, namely: 22,000 direct from Europe, and the rest from the United States and Canada. Out of said 22,000, nearly 10,000 came from the Scandinavian countries.

As the Board during last summer had no agencies or reporters in the principal landing-places, it is of course impossible to give any accurate account concerning the actual number of foreign immigrants but from close observation of figures given in newspapers during the entire season, and judging from other sources of information, the immigration has certainly been as large this year as last. Attracted to

[1] [The act of 1871 also authorized the Board "to hire or lease houses at such places in this state as it may seem proper for the protection or keeping of poor and needy immigrants until they can reach their place of destination."]

lands available under the homestead laws, the majority of immigrants located on the surveyed and unsurveyed lands, especially in the Red River region and in the frontier counties farther South. The hardwood timber land belonging to the Lake Superior, and Mississippi R.R.Co. has also, to some extent, been settled. Northern Europe parts yearly with from 0.39 to 0.86 per cent of their population, nearly all of which emigrate to America. Of immigration last season from Northern Europe, Wisconsin received 3,000 Scandinavians; Minnesota 10,000. . . . .

The increasing correspondence and other pressing work connected with the duties of the Board—almost enough to make it a department of its own—necessitated the employ of a clerk acting under the direction of the Board.

His business has mainly been: (1) Receiving and filing some 9,000 letters and mailing pamphlets to at least 20,000 different applicants. Of this number about 3,500 are sent to Norway, 1,500 to London, and 300 to Denmark. About 4,000 copies were forwarded to Germany. (2) Answering letters in different languages upon immigration. (3) Assisting immigrants in cases of lost baggage and money. (4) Writing articles and answering attacks made on our State. (5) Translating the State pamphlet into the Norwegian language. . . . .

Of the value of an extensive immigration to the State, the Board has not had any good reason to change their views as expressed in their last annual report. Not only does our immigration add hundreds of thousands of dollars in property of all descriptions to the common wealth of the community, but it furnishes, from year to year, by far the greater numbers of those who supply the demand for hired laborers, as well as to replenish and multiply the artisans, mechanics and skilled laborers, upon whom we depend to build up and extend our manufacturing, mining and mechanical interests. Yet exceeding by far any of these interests is that resulting from bringing the cheap European labor in contact with our wild land. The national wealth has been by no other means so rapidly developed and accumulated as by bringing the cheap, and *there*, nearly valueless labor of the old world into direct contact with our equally cheap lands, which, *without that labor*, are of as little value to us, as is the surplus labor of the old world to it, without our lands.

From Northern Europe a man, only capable of earning a bare subsistence there, can be transported to, and set down upon, a homestead in Minnesota for from $50 to $75. He locates on land, which, in its raw condition is not worth over $1.25 per acre, and at the end of five years he has subsisted his family and by his labor has advanced his quarter-section of land to an average value of $1,000, an advance of 300 per cent on the capital with which the settler commenced. Persons residing in the older portions of the State and not on any of the thoroughfares leading to those sections, into which immigrants are flocking by the thousands, often fall into the error, that the State is receiving no immigration—that nothing is realized in exchange for the appropriation made for the promotion of immigration—in short, that the fund is *squandered*. Such objectors can easily be undeceived by taking a journey along our western frontier or sojourning for a time, from the first of May till the close of the season, on some one of the numerous routes of travel leading to those counties, into which the annual tide is flowing.

### 44.  Emigration as a Remedy for Economic Distress, 1870[1]

Mr. R. Torrens said, in undertaking to bring under notice of the House the efficacy of emigration as a remedy for the distress so widely prevailing, . . . . probably no one would be found to deny that the distress which they deplored would at once be alleviated if only it were possible to interpose Nova Scotia or New Zealand in the ocean space between Great Britain and Ireland, so that the labour and capital here in excess might pass over to fertile lands inviting cultivation. The competition in the market for each would be relieved—the Irish land famine would be appeased—and the previously impoverished, because inadequately employed, labourers would with their families become largely customers for the manufactured products of those whom they had left behind in the old locations. The beneficial agency of such a migration would therefore be two-fold—immediate in reducing competition for employment, and ultimate in increasing the amount of employment for those who remained. As this augmentation of acreage of these islands was impracticable, as the mountain could not move to Mahomed, Mahomed must move to the mountain. That was, for migration they must substitute emigration, and analogous, if not identical, results would be attained. He was aware that that had often been denied, and probably would again be denied, by those who pleaded that emigration drained the country of its strength, its best producers; since it was the young, the vigorous, the enterprising, who emigrated; leaving the aged, the feeble, the listless, to burden the rate-

[1] Extract from *Hansard's Parliamentary Debates*, Vol. CXCIX (3d series, 1870), cols. 1002–76.

payers of the country. To that he would venture to reply—first, that the emigration which went on spontaneously or with the aid of Colonial funds, and which could not be interrupted, was almost exclusively of that valued class; but the emigration which he was prepared to advocate for the relief and at the cost of the mother country, would be almost exclusively of middle-aged parents accompanied by their children. Secondly, that the young, the vigorous, and the enterprising were a strength only in the proportion in which the country afforded them employment. When they exceeded that limit they were not a strength but a danger and little less a burden than the aged and infirm. . . . . Large employers of labour need not be uneasy lest emigration be carried to such excess that upon a revival of trade they should find a scarcity of hands to avail of it. The ties of home and kindred were strong and not lightly broken. The reluctance to abandon an occupation in which skill and adroitness have been acquired by long practice, in exchange for one laborious and irksome, because unaccustomed, was also powerful, and would not be encountered except under pressure of circumstances amounting to something like necessity. Upon revival of trade, or any other cause supplying permanent employment at adequate wages, emigration would cease of its own accord. . . . . Voluntary efforts were being made, and in these the merchant princes of this city had, with the liberality which ever distinguished them, contributed large sums, to be expended under the auspices of the Emigration Aid Society, in furtherance of this great work of charity. . . . . But whilst voluntary efforts should be availed of and encouraged, it would be worse than folly to shut their eyes to the fact that the scope and magnitude of the work in this case requiring to be done was altogether beyond what could be accomplished by private benevolence. If anything effectual was to be done for the relief of the present distress, or for the permanent improvement of the condition of the working classes, it was not in hundreds, but in thousands that families must be transplanted; and for such work they must look elsewhere than to private resources and voluntary associations. It remained for consideration whether the funds required for this object might, with greater justice and expediency, be drawn from local rates, from the general taxation, or from both. . . . .

Mr. E. B. Eastwick said that . . . . even while he was speaking, it was a fact that hundreds of persons in this vast metropolis, and in the great towns throughout the country, were dying of a disease which the doctors called by various names, but which, in truth, was slow starvation, protracted by the doling out of an insufficient charity. Thousands of others were daily becoming demoralized by the want of employment, and by the operation of a law which blazoned abroad the necessities of those it relieved. He maintained therefore, that this question was one of the utmost urgency. He said, too, that its magnitude was not to be measured by the number of persons who left these shores under the present system of emigration, unaided as it was by Government. He knew that some persons were inclined to reason about it in that way, and to think that because the general amount of emigration from this kingdom had subsided more than one-third since the time of the Irish exodus, therefore there was no distress. But he would remind those persons that, while there had been a lull in the emigration movement in the ten years from 1858 to 1868, as compared with the preceding decade, there were now portentous symptoms of a corresponding rise. The number of English emigrants rose last year from 58,268, in 1868, to 90,416, the greatest number ever known, except in 1854. If any credence, then, was to be given to the emigration barometer, this was a clear proof of almost unparalleled distress. But, whatever the number, it was manifestly insufficient, for it left us with more than 1,000,000 of persons burdening the rates, and with at least another 1,000,000 who kept themselves above the necessity of asking relief only by the most desperate struggles. The provident societies had exhausted their resources in striving to keep the unemployed out of the workhouse. It was well known that the iron workers alone had paid away £300,000 in the last three years with this object. Besides this frightful burden, we were left with an ever-increasing pressure of population, which augmented at the rate of 250,000 a year. There was every reason, too, to believe that the severity of this pressure would be intensified in a ratio out of proportion to the annual numerical increase of population. He said this because, as had been clearly proved, while our agricultural population was diminishing, that of our towns was rapidly increasing, and an urban population was especially exposed to the calamities which were occasioned by the competition and vicissitudes of trade. It was also a fact that by the substitution of pasture land for arable the productive powers of the country were fast decreasing. However, even if the question were looked at simply with regard to the number and the destination of our emigrants under the present system, he said that it was one which demanded instant consideration. Now, what was the actual number of those who emigrated under the present system? Notwithstanding the Returns of the Emigration Commissioners, it was by no means easy to reply with precision to that question. . . . . For general purposes, however, and for the purpose of his argument, it would, perhaps, suffice to take the Return given by the Emigration Commissioners. The average number of emigrants, according to them, for the ten years from 1858 to 1868, had been 170,000; and deducting foreigners, 150,000. Of these, about 50,000 were Irish, who nearly all went to the United States, being assisted out by the remittances of friends in that country. It would seem at once impolitic and impracticable to disturb this arrangement; but it was within our power to determine the destination of the remaining 100,000. As an emigrant to our Colonies contributed more to our trade returns than one to the United States—in the case of Australia ten times as much—the destination of this stream of 100,000 emigrants could not surely be a matter of indifference. But the political aspect of the question was still more important. To build up our Colonies was to construct fortresses for ourselves in all parts of the world. . . . . Now, what were the objections to the Government lending its aid in this matter? The first objection with which he should be met, he supposed, was that the Colonies could not absorb a larger number of emigrants than that which had already reached them. He should be told, perhaps, that though the immigration into Canada from all quarters had been about 60,000 for the last few years, and 72,000 last year, not more than 10,000 emigrants, and last year 12,000, had remained there. It was said that the cup being full the rest overflowed into the United States. He admitted the facts, but not the inference. The truth was that thousands of emigrants went to the western provinces of the United States, by way of Quebec and Toronto, because that route was 500 miles shorter, and also more convenient, than the route by New York and Hamilton. These persons never had any intention of remaining in the Dominion, and it was unfair to represent them as overflowing. . . . .

But it was said that it would be inexpedient to stimulate emigration, because our best workmen would leave us. He could imagine no objection more futile than that. The experience of every day refuted it. All experience proved that emigration was not a matter of choice, but necessity. Englishmen loved their country too well to wish to change it. It was necessity alone that drove them to settle abroad. Would that that necessity did not exist, and that the discovery of some new productive forces, or of some new modes of employment, would render it possible for the population of this country to go on increasing, with an increasing means of subsistence! If the Government could make such a discovery there was an end of the emigration question; but, until the discovery was made, discussion like the present must go on. But, with reference to emigration not being a matter of choice, he had heard a curious proof of the tenacity with which Englishmen clung to their native country. There was great distress some years ago at Bradford, and an urgent application was made to the Emigration Commissioners to remove 5,000 of the population. The Commissioners then received large remittances, from the sale of Crown lands in the Colonies. They were able to meet the demand, and it was so urgent that they went down to meet it. They were astonished to find that out of the 5,000, not fifty were willing to go. . . . .

Mr. Monsell said that . . . . this was the first time for twenty-two years that this question had been raised in this House. The question occupied the mind of the country and of the House for many years anterior to the year 1847. It was taken up by the ablest men in the country. It had since remained dead, and disappeared from the minds of the Legislature. And why did it die? How was it that the question then passed from the minds of the nation? Because then it was seen what effect would be produced by leaving emigration to natural causes. Because a greater number of emigrants went forth from this country by voluntary efforts than the fondest advocates of State aid to emigration thought could be done through those means. . . . . The appointment of colonial agents in this country was due to an unfounded fear that our Emigration Commissioners, who had done their work so admirably, would select emigrants having regard rather to the persons we desired to get rid of than to the persons they desired to have. But the fact was that at present the Australian Legislatures showed no great desire to get emigrants at all. In South Australia, for example, one-third of the proceeds of the land revenue had been set apart for purposes of immigration, and £500,000 should be at present in the public treasury for that purpose; but a Bill had passed the House of Assembly three times, the object of which was to appropriate this money permanently to other purposes. In New South Wales a Bill was introduced last year for the purpose of promoting immigration, but it did not even reach a second reading. In Queensland the inducements offered by the State to emigrants were being diminished instead of being increased, while in Victoria—though he believed that there something more was now to be done for emigration—the only persons received were female servants and those who obtained passages by means of their friends in the Colony. In Canada, such was the fear of pauper emigration, that last Session special power was given to the Governor to prevent the reception of pauper emigrants, and heavy fines were imposed on all those who attempted to bring them. The influx of emigrants from Canada into the United States—of emigrants who went there from this country—must also be remembered. A very large proportion of the emigrants who left this country for Canada during the years 1866, 1867, and 1868 went on to the United States, after merely remaining in Canada for a short time, and he had been told by Lord Monck that during one year, when he was Governor General, 24,500 emigrants went from this country to Canada, almost all of whom went on to the United States. But with regard to emigration to Canada—for it was to that country they must look if any attempt were made to carry out the proposal which had been offered to the House—he must call the attention of his hon. Friend to the circumstances which happened in 1847 and 1848, and tested the comparative merits of free and of State-aid emigration. . . . . The Government of Lord Russell was willing to adopt a proposal similar to that which had just been made to the House by his hon. Friend. What was the result? What Sir Robert Peel expected to do by means of State-aided emigration was to send 35,000 persons per annum to the Colonies, and that they, by keeping up their relations with their families at home, should form a nucleus to which other persons would be attracted. What was effected by emigration free and unsupported by the State? Between 1847 and 1854, 2,077,317 emigrants went to North America at a cost of more than £8,000,000, of which sum not a shilling was contributed by the public treasury. It came all out of private resources. That gigantic work was done by the State leaving emigration alone. Did his hon. Friend imagine that sum would have been subscribed by persons who knew that they could get the State to aid them? Did his hon. Friend conceive that the poor Irish who went over to America and half starved themselves, or at all events denied themselves many comforts, for the purpose of saving money to pay for the emigration of their friends, would have contributed anything had they known that by dragging at the public coffers they would be able to procure the money? It was perfectly obvious that a choice between the two plans must be made. There could not be both State-aided and private emigration. Persons would never contribute money if they knew they could get it from the State, and therefore the House must face the fact that by adopting such a scheme as the one which had been proposed they would put an end to a source for promoting emigration far more prolific than any which could be substituted. . . . . There existed in Ireland an admirable and complete system of allowing Boards of Guardians to borrow money for emigration purposes. Yet, notwithstanding the gigantic emigration which has been going on, only £125,000 had thus been raised, by means of which 26,000 persons had been sent out, although in the same period nearly 3,000,000 had emigrated by the ordinary means. . . . . About £15,000,000 had been wrung from the pockets of the poor in paying for that emigration which had been carried out on so gigantic a scale. Would restitution be made to them? Would his hon. Friend propose to pay back the money which, if his principles were correct, the State ought to have paid? . . . . There were in that country many who were in sad distress, upon whom no ray of hope ever shone from the cradle to the grave, and he was sorry to believe that they exceeded in number those who were un-employed in London. They must have their share in any grant which Parliament might make, if it was so unwise as to make one, and those who have already paid for their own passages, would have an equitable claim to be recouped the money they had already paid. . . . .

Mr. Sinclair Aytoun said that . . . . it was said that it was in-jurious to the interests of this country to send away the best of our workmen, and that the Colonies would not have our worst; but it was evident that the best only could emigrate under the voluntary princi-ple, for they alone could find the necessary means, while under the present system the men who left our shores were, for the most part, young and unmarried. The Emigration Returns for 1865, 1866, and 1867 showed an excess of 42,000 men each year over the number of women who emigrated, so that now the tendency was to drain the country of its healthier and more vigorous blood and to leave behind those who could not work. Then, it was said that they could not send paupers to the Colonies. But, on the other hand, it must be remembered it was possible to relieve the labour market, although paupers were not sent, because it was obvious that if in a particular district there were 1,050 persons, and employment for no more than 1,000, and that, in consequence, fifty were on the parish, you could abolish pauperism by providing for the emigration of fifty of the workmen, and thus fur-nishing employment for the fifty paupers. . . . . If by giving a certain amount of assistance to emigration we could cause a portion of that emigration which went to the United States to flow into our own

Colonies we should be doing much to stimulate an increased consumption of our goods of home manufacture. . . . .

Mr. J. G. Talbot said that . . . . he had received a letter from the Rector of Woolwich, from which the House, perhaps, would allow him to read two short extracts. He had asked the rector to be kind enough to tell him what was the feeling in the parish on the subject of emigration, and the reply he received was in these words:

I have no difficulty in assuring you that the distress arising from want of employment is great in Woolwich and Plumstead. There are hundreds of men—artizans and labourers—who are at this moment in a sad state of poverty, many of them having been without any permanent employment since March, 1869, and in some instances for a longer period than that. I know many poor fellows who have been wandering about in unsuccessful search of work half over the country, leaving their wives and families in the meantime in great want, of course. As to the desire of numbers of these men and their families to emigrate to the Colonies, I need only to refer to a public meeting held at our Town Hall on the 7th of February, to consider and afford information on the subject of emigration. The subject was one of so much interest that the meeting was so crowded by working men that numbers were unable to obtain admission. I was obliged to tell them, much to their disappointment, that the British and Colonial Emigration Fund could only assist those to emigrate to Canada who could help themselves to the extent of £3 per statute adult. But it was arranged that the names of all those who were desirous of emigrating should be taken down, in the hope that some means might be found during the summer of obtaining a passage for them. Since the meeting there have been but two days—two Tuesdays—on which names have been received; but already we have on the list 566 statute adults, but of this number there are only sixteen men, making with their wives and families forty-nine statute adults, who can pay £3 per head. The rest, though most anxious to emigrate, have been so long out of work that they are utterly unable to help themselves at all, and of those few who have promised to find the money required I believe that nearly all have been able to obtain half from relatives and friends better off than themselves.

He had troubled the House with this extract, because he thought this was a matter for grave consideration by Government. . . . .

Sir James Lawrence said that . . . . he agreed that in encouraging emigration the greatest care ought to be taken that even those who were assisted to go out by private benevolence should be those only who were able to earn a livelihood in the Colonies. Reference had been made to what emigrants encountered when they reached the Colonies. Now, last year, the British and Colonial Emigration Society with which he was connected sent out some 4,000 emigrants. The Society had a list of those persons, giving the townships in which they settled and the employments in which they were engaged, and out of the whole 4,000 there were not 100 who did not almost immediately find remunerative occupation. He was surprised at one remark made by the Under Secretary for the Colonies, who, from his acquaintance with Ireland, must have known that the emigration from that country was not at the outset spontaneous or natural, but was largely supported from funds borrowed on the security of the poor-rates. From a Return which he had himself moved for, it would be found that a very great portion of the money at first spent on Irish emigration was supplied by the landlords from sums borrowed for the purpose. . . . .

Mr. A. Peel said that . . . . he could understand that, in the year 1847, when there were 2,000,000 of a starving Irish population on one side of the Atlantic, and 6,000,000 of acres in one district alone requiring strong arms to till them on the other, a strong appeal could be made in favor of State assistance to emigration. But was there in this country at the present moment such distress as had not existed here before, and as called for the interference of the Government to promote an extensive scheme of emigration? The amount of the distress was really the pivot on which the question turned. He would not enter into the larger question of political economy; but he might refer to what had been done on a limited scale under the Poor Law Board in the way of giving assistance to persons to emigrate. From 1834 to 1868, a sum of £147,000 had been spent by the parishes of this country, including those of the metropolis, in assisting persons to emigrate, the number so assisted being 25,000. He did not say that the restrictions imposed by law had not operated to prevent a greater outlay by parishes for that object. Strong pressure had been brought to bear on the Poor Law Board and the Government to induce them to withdraw some of these restrictions. . . . . A large number of gentlemen connected with the Colonies, colonial agents in the confidence of their respective Governments, had met his right hon. Friend the President of the Poor Law Board, and suggested that some modification should be made for the purpose of withdrawing the obstructions which stood in the way of the emigration of poor people. . . . . Those gentlemen having been consulted as to their views with respect to the emigration of the poor, they one and all expressed their determination to have nothing to do with pauper emigration. The assistance that the Poor-Law Guardians were empowered to give was not confined to the case of paupers. It could be given to poor persons who, through the vicissitudes of the seasons, or a temporary want of work, or any other such cause, would be reduced to a state of pauperism, but the colonial gentlemen said they had no confidence in the action of the Poor-Law Guardians in respect of emigration; they disapproved the choice which in many instances the Guardians had made, because, as they said, the persons who had been chosen were not persons able to battle with the difficulties of colonial life. . . . . It was a mistake to suppose that when emigrants went to the Colonies they found themselves in an El Dorado; but that was the prospect which in many instances had been held out to agricultural labourers. He had seen statements with reference to emigrants to the most favoured parts of the most favoured Colonies which did not justify the hope that, without the most careful selection, they would be able to discharge their duties properly or encounter the trials which they would have to undergo in their new homes. The British and Colonial Society and many other societies had sent out thousands and thousands to America, and he had been told that many of them complained of the hardships to which they had been subjected. He had asked a gentleman capable of giving him information on the subject whether colonial life was so hard as those persons represented it to be, and he was told it was not, but that many of the emigrants were shiftless, purposeless, aimless persons, whose lives in this country had been such as to give no promise of their success across the Atlantic. They were persons who objected to the amount of trial for which all emigrants should be prepared, and who wished to return and lead a life of idleness in England. He considered the view of the colonists a perfectly just one. They said—"We want, if we can get them, the flower of your population, the pick of your agricultural labourers, the first choice of your mechanics; but we do not want, and we cannot take, and we will not have, the refuse of your population." . . . .

Mr. Gladstone said . . . . the difficulties of the labouring classes have been keenly felt ever since the Peace of 1815; and since that time the minds both of intelligent speculators and of responsible statesmen have been directed to the discovery, if possible, of some systematic and extended emigration as the means of affording effectual relief to popular suffering. But the endeavour has never succeeded. It has never been found practicable to adopt the splendid speculation of wholesale emigration. And yet what periods have we passed through? We have passed through periods of distress certainly much more severe than the present in the sense of being more uniformly extended. . . . . Rely upon it that, if the question of public emigration had been the easy and simple matter which my hon. Friend supposes it to be, and some Gentlemen in the other parts of the House like him, we should not have passed through all these great and extraordinary crises without having brought into play the engine he now wishes us to make use of. You cannot expect that, while one portion of the people are sent out at the expense of the community, you will find another portion in the same circumstances ready to go out at their own expense. They will either stay at home, or demand—and they will be entitled to obtain—the same aid as you give to their friends. . . . . Whatever is done through public rates is suspected by the Colonies, and though the letter of the law does not restrict the action of the Guardians to paupers, you may depend upon it that you cannot induce your Colonies to receive persons whom you desire to send, or over whom they will not have effectual control. . . . . I would put this view to my hon. Friend. He said he would not send out paupers; on that point he was most distinct. But in the most impassioned portion of his speech he also said that, within earshot of the walls of this House, there were myriads of persons who did not know how to find means of subsistence for next week or the week after next, and who were looking anxiously to this House to find a remedy. . . . . How does my hon. Friend, with all his ingenuity, draw a line between the condition of those persons who know not, he says, where to find means of subsistence and those paupers whom the Colonies are unwilling to receive? It may be clear to his mind, but it will be very difficult to make it clear in public despatches, or in rigidly-worded documents, such as the Colonies will have a right to demand. Having overcome the difficulty of choice, the next question is as to destination. If our fellow-citizens have a right to come to us in their distress and to claim to be exported from this country in order that they may gain a means of livelihood which now they do not possess, I own it seems to me a most questionable exercise of power—aye, an exercise of power which it is impossible to defend—to say, "We recognize your destitution and our obligation to relieve it, but we insist upon your going to British Colonies." An enormous proportion of the former emigrants—three-fourths, I believe—proceeded to the United States. Of those who wish to go we may assume that the proportion would be about equal. It is not a way to make them love the British Empire to put them under this constraint, and to refuse them the relief which my hon. Friend says is necessary, except upon a condition which, if arbitrarily imposed, would be fraught with the most serious embarrassment. But here, after all, is the question. We are asked to recognize—I think for the first time—the principle that we are to send out not the class which is most destitute, for my hon. Friend repudiates the notion of sending out paupers; but that from a class above the paupers, another class of the population is to make selections, and to send these persons out to a foreign country. I should like to know where that is to stop? That is a door much easier to open than to shut. I do not hesitate to say that I think among the supporters of the Motion there is a large amount of mistake as to the desire to go abroad which is supposed to exist in the minds of the English people. My belief is that the English people desire to stay at home. Then you say, "These people are in want, and you are going to relieve their want by giving them the means of emigration." Now, I understood that at most of the meetings of the working classes . . . . to promote plans of State emigration, a considerable counter-current was visible. And it has been said with great force:

If you are going to pay to send us abroad, give us the money, and let us stay at home; a year or two ago there was abundant demand for labour, and we were all very well off. We love old England; we do not want to become Yankees, or in the phrase which is sometimes irreverently used of our Canadian fellow-subjects—"Bluenoses." We wish to stay at home; allow us to enjoy a little pension, and let us wait until the wheel of fortune turns round again; allow us to have a voice as to the manner in which we should begin to get contented, and instead of going away we shall be at home to support the law and the Throne as British citizens. . . . .

Now with regard to foreign Powers. I have said it would be difficult to limit this emigration to the Colonies, but in regard to foreign Powers I really know not how it is to be conducted. From one great foreign Power we have already very distinct intimations. When it was proposed to send some emigrants at the expense of the rates to the United States of America, we had distinct intimation from the agents of that Power that they would rather be excused from receiving them.

### 45. Effect of "Hard Times" on Emigration:[1] An American View

Our attention will naturally be first directed to the present falling off in immigration to the United States.

The tide from Europe reached its maximum height in 1854, when the arrivals were 427,833. Only once since, we believe, have they ex-

[1] Extract from a paper on "Immigration" read by Hamilton Andrews Hill, of the Boston Board of Trade, at the meeting of the National Conference of Charities and Correction, May, 1875, *Proceedings*, pp. 85–90.

ceeded 400,000 in any one calendar year; this was in 1873, when they were 422,545. In 1874 they declined to 260,814. This was less considerably than the immigration of any previous year since 1864, and less, by nearly forty per cent than that of 1873.[1]

The reason of this decline it will not be difficult to find. Mr. Kapp has tersely stated the rule which governs the movement of emigration to the United States: "Bad times in Europe regularly increase, and bad times in America invariably diminish, immigration." . . . . However serious the great failures of the autumn of 1873, and the general depression of trade throughout the country subsequently, have been felt to be by those at home, they have seemed much more serious when regarded from abroad, and especially by foreigners who know comparatively little of the resources and understand still less the recuperative powers of this young and vigorous country. Nor does the press of Europe at such times err on the side of underestimating financial and industrial difficulties in the United States. On the continent the ruling influence is directly opposed to emigration to any and all countries, and in Great Britain, it not unnaturally prefers and favors the British colonies. It can readily be understood, therefore, why many who may have been proposing, a year and a half ago, to cross the seas and settle among us, should have been induced, by what they have heard and read, either to postpone their emigration or to change their destination; and why many more, who, during the same period, may have been brought to consider emigration as a question personal to themselves and their families, should have left the United States out of the account. Perhaps, under all the circumstances, the wonder is that at such an unpropitious time, more than a quarter of a million of the people of Europe had the discernment and the courage to come hither in 1874 and cast in their lot with us.

There has not only been a check in the flow of the stream in this direction, but there has been a strong current setting from the United States towards the shores of Europe. The general dulness of trade in America, in connection with unprecedentedly low rates of railway and steamship fares, afforded an opportunity to our foreign born citizens, particularly to those engaged in mechanical and manufacturing industries, to return to their old homes for the purpose of visiting their friends, or of obtaining temporary employment, or for the two pur-

[1] The immigration to the United States during the first six months of 1875 was 106,825. The immigration during the fiscal year, ended June 30, 1875, was 227,498. which was less by 85,841, than that of the previous fiscal year.

poses combined. At one time last summer, owing to the severe competition among both the railway and the steamship companies, passengers were conveyed on through tickets from Chicago to Queenstown or Liverpool for seventeen dollars each, currency; and it is easy to see how strong the inducement to take a trip across the Atlantic must have been to those who, at the time, were out of employ, or could not obtain such wages as they desired. Instances there undoubtedly were of personal disappointment and loss among those who filled the steamship steerages between America and Europe last year; but we believe them to have been altogether exceptional, and that the large majority will return to us at no distant day. The number of those who landed from homeward bound steamers at Queenstown and Liverpool in 1874 is reported as 77,146 against about 38,000 in 1873. We have not been able to ascertain the number of passengers who landed at German ports, but we are informed that about 4,000 persons returned to Sweden during the year. It is probable not only that most of these people will return to the United States, but that they will bring with them, or influence the coming of, many others. It will appear, in due time, that they have been serving as most efficient promoters of emigration, in the countries to which they have gone, and the information they will impart in their personal contact with friends and acquaintances, and the encouragement which their appearance and experience will afford, will, no doubt, help to swell the numbers of immigrants to the United States for years to come.

This brings us to our second point, the probabilities with regard to the extent of immigration to this country in the future.

While we may confidently expect the circumstances on this side of the Atlantic, which have caused the present falling off in the arrivals on our shores, are temporary only and will cease to be operative before long, we may be sure, also, that the reasons which lead multitudes in Europe to decide upon changing their residence and allegiance, are, to say the least, becoming no less potential from year to year. Excepting in Ireland, emigration has caused no perceptible diminution in the population which crowds the countries of the old world; while many things conspire to render emigration desirable, if not indispensable, to an increasing number both of individuals and families.

Ireland has been our chief source of supply in the past, and during the last forty years has contributed to our population nearly three millions of her people. During the years 1847 to 1854 inclusive, the arrivals from Ireland averaged one hundred and fifty thousand per annum. In only one year since 1854 have they reached one hundred thousand; this was in 1867, when they were 108,857. Ireland still stands second in the tables, after Germany, which, since 1865, has been first. The exceptional circumstances and conditions which in past years increased Irish emigration to such large proportions do not now exist, and in the future it will be governed mainly by the same considerations which affect emigration in England and in Scotland.

Since 1869 the emigration of English to all parts of the world has been larger than that of Irish, and while the latter has hardly held its own from year to year, the former has been steadily increasing. In 1873 the English emigration outnumbered the Irish in the proportion of three to two, although, of course, it was far below the Irish when the respective populations are taken into account. In 1872, upwards of eighty thousand English arrived in the United States, and as soon as times improve with us we may expect a repetition of these numbers, and probably an advance upon them. . . . . The size of English families is such, as a rule, that except among the very rich adequate provision cannot be made for the younger children at home, and the increase in the cost of living seriously aggravates the difficulty.

Land is steadily increasing in value, and so much more capital is required now than formerly for its cultivation that, as the *Daily Telegraph* said, not long ago, it will soon have to be cultivated with a "silver plow." The position of the English farmer is a very trying one, between the landlord on the one hand, and the agricultural laborer on the other. In his relations with the former he has to deal with many perplexing questions connected with the granting and renewal of leases and the value of exhausted and unexhausted improvements, which, fortunately, we know nothing about in the United States; and he finds himself still more embarrassed by the demands of the laborer for more wages, backed as these are by union organizations. There can be little doubt that when the farmers of England, and especially the younger men among them and their sons, shall come to understand, as some of them are beginning to do, the advantages offered them by a settlement in this country, where there is plenty of land and free scope, where they can at once become their own landlords, and where they can buy a farm for what the rental for one year would be in England, or less, there will be such a movement hither from among this class as will take most of us by surprise, and from other classes also, for most Englishmen are fond of the land and take kindly to agricultural pursuits.

The settlers in the British colonies are English in about the proportion of two to three, but three-fourths of the total emigration from the United Kingdom is to the United States. Until 1873 the proportion of English going to the colonies as compared with other destinations had not varied much for several years; but during 1873 and 1874, by means of "assisted passages," "free grants," and other inducements offered in the interest of Canada, Australia and New Zealand, there has been a large increase in the number of emigrants to these countries, especially to that last named. The emigration to New Zealand alone, for 1874, is reported at about forty-two thousand, which is nearly three times as many as the departures for Australia and New Zealand combined in 1872. A large number of these people were agricultural laborers and their families. The preponderance of even English emigration, however, will continue to be in favor of the United States, not to name other reasons, because of the shortness of the voyage hither, as compared with Australia and New Zealand, and the superiority of the climate and the land, as compared with most of Canada.

Scotch emigration has taken a new start since 1868, and is now about twenty thousand a year. Of this number the United States receives rather more than one-half. Canada has succeeded in attracting a large share of these settlers, who, as agriculturists and horticulturists especially, are a most valuable acquisition to any country. It has been said of Scotchmen that "they are never so much at home as when they are abroad," and certainly there are no better emigrants than they, and none who more readily adapt themselves to new conditions and to a new country. In Scotland, also, as in England, the large capital now required for cultivating the soil, presses the alternative of emigration upon the attention of farmers and their sons. Professor Caird says that on a farm in the Lothians, rented at £1,000, while £25 was the outlay on foreign manures forty years ago, at the present day twice the rent would not be thought an extravagant expenditure on fertilizers and cattle food.

The emigration from Sweden and Norway has become important since 1866. Nearly the whole of it is attracted to this country, and as much pains have been taken of late to spread information about the United States in the North of Europe, and as the facilities for transportation hither are improving year by year, a large gain may be looked for from this source. Nothing could help this more than the return of the four thousand persons last year to whom reference has been made.

From Russia some important communities, Mennonites and others, have begun to transfer their homes to the United States. The arrivals in 1873 and 1874 (together about 11,000) were more than in all the previous years together, and are only the advanced guard of a great movement.

Germany has already sent us more than two and a half millions of people, and will, no doubt, continue to be our largest source of supply. The arrivals in 1873 were 133,141; in 1874, 56,927. The laws of the empire relating to military service and conscription, together with the prevailing fear of further continental wars, stimulate emigration from Germany more than all other considerations combined. The recent enactment of the Imperial Parliament which in the event of war, will render every able-bodied man in the empire, between the ages of eighteen and sixty, liable to do military duty, and which makes more stringent even than heretofore, all the regulations relating to military service, will influence thousands upon thousands to come to the United States, who; but for these laws and for the misgiving that occasion may come for their enforcement, would greatly prefer to remain in their native land. The German Government, which during the last few years, has bitterly opposed the emigration of its subjects, will, no doubt, seek to render it still more difficult for them to get away, but the effect of this opposition will probably be to make them only the more anxious and the more determined to leave.

## 46.   Emigration from Würtemberg, 1870–80[1]

During the nine years from 1871 to 1879, a total of 23,093 persons had exchanged their homes in this kingdom for new ones in the United States, but, what was more significant, 14,801 of that number had gone during the first three years of the nine, leaving only a scanty emigration of 8,292 persons during the remaining six. In other words, the average number of emigrants was from 1871 to 1873, 4,933.6 per annum, and from 1874 to 1879, 1,382 per annum, showing a decrease of nearly three-fourths from 1873 onward. . . . . Further and later statistics in relation to this important subject have been made public. It appears that during the summer of 1880 the ministry of the interior, having its attention called to an extraordinary increase in the number of persons leaving the kingdom, instituted a searching and thorough

---

[1] Extract from "Emigration from the Kingdom of Würtemberg, Report by Consul Catlin, of Stuttgart, on Its Cause, Character, and Extent, and the Laws by Which It Is Governed," in *United States Consular Reports*, II, No. 6 (April, 1881) 557–65.

inquiry into the matter. The results of this inquiry . . . . prove that the attention given the subject by the Würtemberg authorities is fully justified by facts. One noticeable feature is that the revised figures for 1879 show the emigration for that year to have been much greater than had been previously reported. . . . .

*A sudden increase in 1880.*—The official canvass above mentioned also embraced six months of the year 1880, and showed for that period an extraordinary increase, quite sufficient to arouse the authorities of a country which thus found itself the daily loser of able-bodied males, prolific mothers, and robust children of both sexes. It was found that between January 1 and June 30, 1880, emigration from the kingdom had suddenly increased threefold. . . . .

In the foregoing statement the term "emigrant" is used as applying to all those who have gone to lands outside of the German Empire with the intention of settling there permanently. Estimating the population of the kingdom in round numbers of 1,900,000 (the census of December 1, 1880, showed it to be 1,970,132), the emigration during the above fifteen months amounted to 3.6 per thousand for the entire period. But while the monthly average for the nine months of 1879 was 0.13, or at the rate of 1.5 persons from every thousand *per annum*, that of the six months of 1880 was 0.40, or at the rate of an annual emigration of 4.8 persons on every thousand of the population. This latter rate is largely in excess of the average emigration rate from the entire German Empire. At a rough estimate Würtemberg, while comprising only *one-twentysecond part* of the entire population of Germany, contributed last year *one-twelfth* of the German emigrants landed in the United States. The rate from all Germany during 1880 was 2.5 persons per thousand; from Würtemberg alone, as previously stated, 4.8 per thousand, as compared with 0.76 persons per thousand from all Germany, and 1.5 persons per thousand from Würtemberg during the preceding year, 1879.[1]

[1] [In discussing the general increase in emigration from Germany, an American commercial agent reported in 1880 as follows:]

"The emigration movement to the United States has assumed colossal proportions this year. According to the imperial statistical tables, 50,442 German emigrants have shipped for the different ports in the United States during the first six months of the year, 1880. There is hardly any doubt but the emigration to the United States will continue in about the same proportions for the next year, as there is no prospect that the conditions which underlie this large exodus from the fatherland will undergo any change in the near future. There are different factors which are at the bottom of this lately increased emigration, such as military compulsion, want of free movement,

*Comparative rate of increase and loss.*—Now, this comparatively large percentage of emigration from Würtemberg, as compared with the rest of Germany, is, unfortunately, not compensated for by any correspondingly more rapid increase of population than that prevailing elsewhere throughout the empire. Thus, during the last five years the annual excess of births over deaths in Würtemberg has averaged 25,500, or about $1\frac{1}{4}$ per cent of the entire population. If we estimate the excess of births over deaths annually in all Germany at 542,000 (as is shown by statistics for 1872–78), and the total population of the empire at 45,000,000 in round numbers, we have almost the same rate of increase, i.e., $1\frac{1}{5}$ per cent. In other words, Würtemberg, though slightly in advance of the rest of Germany in the relative proportion of births and deaths, yet shows no such excessive rate of increase as would be required to compensate for the greater proportional drain made upon her by emigration. . . . .

*Distribution of the loss by emigration.*—Inquiry has also been recently made by the Würtemberg authorities with a view to ascertaining from what section of the kingdom the emigrants who departed during the fifteen months covered by the report have principally been drawn. By this means it is discovered that the western sections, comprised in what are known as the Neckar and Black Forest regions, have furnished over three-fourths of the total number. Thus:

From the Neckar counties (northwest) there were 2,697 emigrants, or 0.46 per cent of the population; from the Black Forest counties (southwest) there were 2,559 emigrants, or 0.56 per cent of the population; from the Jaxt counties (northeast) there were 827 emigrants, or 0.21 per cent of the population; and from the Danube counties (southeast) there were 792 emigrants, or 0.17 per cent of the population.

I find no satisfactory means of accounting for this preponderance of emigration from the western sections of the kingdom, as similar

---

increased taxes, failures of crops, general depression of business, and ecclesiastical strifes; but the 'true inwardness' of, and the intrinsic motive power for, this extraordinary emigration is to be found in the simple fact that there is an instinctive trait in man to better his situation and that of his family, and as the greater part of the German people can, by their labor, acquire only the absolute necessaries of life without the prospective view of being able to lay aside some savings for 'rainy days,' they naturally cast their eyes to the country where *labor is well paid in proportion to the cost of living,* and this motive is the true solution of the question of emigration to the *United States"* (Extract from the annual report of Mr. Schoenle, commercial agent at Geestemunde, *United States Consular Reports,* II, No. 3 [January, 1881], 184.)

causes would seem to be in operation in both the west and the east. In point of comparison by localities, it is found that emigration is heaviest from the districts (including the environs) of Stuttgart, Cannstatt, Balingen, Tuttlingen, Schorndorf, Esslingen, Nürtingen, and Reutlingen.

*Age and sex.*—It is also of interest to consider the question of age and sex, as applying to the emigration of the fifteen months period referred to. Thus, of families there were 676, comprising in all 2,882 persons; of unmarried adults there were 1,682 males, 575 females—total, 2,257 persons; of minors not included above, 1,151 males, 585 females—total, 1,736 persons; making the aggregate of 6,875 persons.

*Avocations and callings.*—Not the least remarkable feature of this new tide of emigration is that it is almost entirely drawn from the rural population; that is, from among the tillers in the grain-fields and vineyards, and even, in many cases, from among the proprietors themselves. Stated in figures, the percentage is about as follows: farmers, 33.73 per cent; peasant laborers, 54.07 per cent; other callings, only 12.20 per cent.

It will thus be observed that 87.80 per cent of the adult emigration is made up of men and women whose manual labor has been devoted to agriculture, and whose absence will be sorely felt in the planting, raising, and harvesting of crops, not even now adequate to the necessities of the population of the kingdom.

*Views of a prominent official.*—I have recently been favored with an opportunity for a quite extended and, at the same time, informal conversation on this subject with a prominent official of the Würtemberg government. Allusion having been made to the recent remarkable increase in the number of those departing hence for America, the official replied that the question had indeed of late been occupying public attention, on account not so much of the actual loss in numbers occasioned thereby as the excellent quality of the material that is at present leaving this kingdom for the United States. . . . .

*Question.*—Of what class of people is the present emigration principally composed?

*Reply.*—Chiefly of tillers of the soil, hardy and robust men whose loss from the rural districts will be much more felt than would be the drawing off of a corresponding number of the population from the cities, which are comparatively overcrowded, and where the unemployed and criminal classes are generally found. As for the actual loss in population it is really no great subject for regret, for our rate of in-

crease is very rapid. The kingdom is quite thickly peopled, its productive capacities are taxed to the utmost for the support of its inhabitants, and a moderate emigration may therefore be considered
rather a relief than otherwise. But those who are emigrating are the
tillers in the fields and vineyards, men who are necessarily the largest
contributors to our agricultural welfare, and who have generally some
mechanical skill as well. They compose the element we can least
afford to lose.

*Question.*—Is there any reason for supposing that paupers and
criminals are sent from here to the United States as emigrants?

*Reply.*—None whatever; that is, in the case of persons known to
be such. It is of course impossible for the emigrant agents to make
thorough inquiry into the antecedents of every one of the many hundreds presenting themselves to be registered as intending to emigrate.
But there is no organized movement either on the part of local, county,
or town authorities, or of any philanthropic association, to send such
persons to the United States. A general belief and understanding exists here that even if sent thither they would not be permitted to land.

*Question.*—Are there any means by which the authorities here can,
if they so desire, arrest this tide of emigration?

*Reply.*—Practically none. Even the restrictions existing at the
German ports of embarkation, Hamburg and Bremen, are rendered
fruitless by the fact that any German, wishing to emigrate to America,
can easily avoid them by passing over into Belgium or Holland, and
taking steamer at Antwerp or Rotterdam. On the French frontier the
passport regulations are enforced with a somewhat greater show of
vigor, so that but few emigrants from Germany leave by way of Havre,
or other ports of France. Most of those leaving covertly go by way of
one or the other of the two non-German ports previously mentioned.

*Question.*—To what, in your opinion, may this sudden increase, or
rather revival, of emigration to the United States be attributed?

*Reply.*—Every season disastrous to agricultural interests gives an
impetus to emigration. The grape and grain crops have been poor for
three or four years now, causing much distress and want among the
lower classes and in the rural populations. These latter, hearing from
their friends in America of the, to them, fabulous rates of wages (two
or three dollars a day) paid there, and of the good crops and general
prosperity, naturally turn thither with longing eyes, and come to look
with discontent upon their lot here, where they see no chance of bettering themselves. Do what they will, few if any of them lay aside any

money here. The great evil in our rural districts is the tavern, where workingmen pass their evenings drinking beer instead of remaining at home with their wives and families. When their working hours are over they repair to the tavern; when Sunday comes they pass the entire day there. The result is they save nothing, and are no better off at the end of the year than they were at the beginning.

*Question.*—Is there no remedy for this prevalence of beer shops?

*Reply.*—Not so long as licenses to keep them are so easily obtained. Were only one or two allowed in each village, the evil would be to a great extent done away with, whereas now almost every other house is a beer saloon, and a laboring man finds it almost impossible, in passing along the street, to resist the temptation of dropping in at one or another of them before he reaches his home.

*Question.*—Are the peasantry here kept well informed of the condition of affairs in America by those who have previously emigrated thither?

*Reply.*—Perfectly. Every letter brings glowing accounts of high wages, good crops, and general welfare, and virtually says, "Come over and join us." It is easy to understand how ready a poor man with no prospects before him here is to listen to such an invitation.

*Question.*—Is the emigration proportionally large at present from the other parts of Germany?

*Reply.*—I can only speak with regard to Bavaria, from which kingdom the emigration is considerably less than from Würtemberg. As a general thing the Bavarians are not an emigrating people, and moreover their kingdom is not so densely populated as this. Formerly there was considerable Bavarian emigration to Hungary, principally to Transylvania; other parties of Bavarians emigrated to the Rhine Palatinate, but the present tide of departures from Würtemberg to America finds no parallel from the neighboring kingdom to the eastward. . . . .

*Illegal departures.*—One fact referred to in the conversation above cited is the departure of many young men who have not complied with the legal formalities. This is corroborated by statistical evidence showing that of the 6,875 persons who emigrated, from April 1, 1819, to June 30, 1880, only 1,308, or a little less than one-fourth, were formally released from their obligations to the Kingdom of Würtemberg; and of these 1,308, there were 1,280 who went to the United States. It is also noticeable that the proportion of those sailing from other than German ports—a route which suggests, at least, a covert departure—is very large. Thus there were 1,154 who left by way of Antwerp and

Liverpool; 1,404 by way of Antwerp direct; and 285 by way of Rotterdam, making an aggregate of 2,843 by non-German ports.

*The value of emigrants.*—It should be remembered, too, that the loss which the departure of these emigrants occasions to their native country is not to be computed merely by the lack of manual labor it causes in the agricultural regions. Were this the only evil, it might be looked upon as a temporary and remediable one. But when we come to consider that, according to the most eminent German statisticians, every member of society who has attained his fifteenth year, or a self-supporting age, represents in the money already spent on his support and education a sum equal to about $500, the question at once assumes a practical pecuniary interest, for at that rate of calculation Würtemberg has contributed during the year 1880 alone the snug sum of $4,500,000 toward the extinguishment of our national debt. But this estimate seems to me entirely too low. If, in the days of negro slavery, an average ignorant field-hand was valued at $500, how incalculably more valuable, in the pecuniary, moral, and intellectual scale, is the free white emigrant, with strong arms, an educated mind, and a spirit imbued with principles of freedom, who comes to our shores, bringing his all with him, to do battle with fortune.

The material wealth in the shape of money and personal effects brought over by emigrants averages, according to the commissioners of emigration reports, $112 per capita, and probably considerably more than that in the case of the excellent class of people now going from Würtemberg. One case has recently been reported to me of a family, consisting of ten members, who emigrated to the United States from the neighboring village of Falbach, taking with them 35,000 marks (or about $8,000) in money.

*The causes of emigration.*—Allusion has already been made to the failure of crops, and the discontent and misery resulting therefrom as the principal causes of emigration. The increase of demand for labor does not keep pace with the increase of the population. To this may be added the desire to avoid military service, although I am inclined to the belief that, in a majority of cases, this motive is only a secondary one. This belief is corroborated by the experience of former years, for it appears that during the year 1867–68 the apprehensions then expressed by many that the new Prussian military law would drive out the best material from the country, proved groundless. During that year, for instance, of 132 emigrants who left the town of Reutlingen, only 26 were liable for military duty. It is not the fear of military service, but a simple desire to better their condition that drives most young men to emigrate. The German country youth, seeing before him no future, no opportunity of being other than a peasant, and a hard-worked one at that, as his father and his grandfather were before him; hearing, moreover, from his companions, who have gone before him to the western Eldorado, glowing accounts of their success and prosperity, determines to follow their example. His dominant motive is a desire to better his condition. By the help of his friends, he scrapes together enough money to buy his passage ticket and land him on the wharf at New York or Philadelphia, with barely more than strong arms and a hopeful heart as guarantees of a successful manhood. But, on the eve of his departure, a specter confronts and claims him. It is a debt of military service which he owes his native land—a debt the payment of which will preclude for a term of years at least his contemplated departure. It is not to avoid this debt that he leaves, but its avoidance is simply incidental to the carrying out of his previously concerted plans. And so he quietly passes over into Holland or Belgium to take ship, Germany loses an able-bodied citizen, and the United States census report chronicles a gain of one.

It is probable that this emigration of young men would be much greater were some restraint put upon the liberty of marriage. Having, by marrying, given hostages to fortune, many a peasant young man finds himself anchored fast in his native village, compelled to remain there by sheer inability to find means to remove his wife and children across the Atlantic, or to provide for their support during his absence, should he go alone to pioneer the way. To early and improvident marriages, according to statisticians, may be attributed not only the evil just mentioned, but that unduly rapid increase of population which threatens to become, at no distant day, Germany's most difficult problem.

### 47. Review of German Emigration, 1881[1]

Emigration from the fatherland, principally to the United States, has assumed gigantic proportions in the course of this year. This unprecedented exodus is engaging the serious attention of the German economists, and especially that of the Imperial Chancellor. The former have been calculating the working value of the average emigrant, and state that the services of every working man leaving the country may be valued at $1,000; there can be but little doubt that every emigrant

[1] Extract from report by Consul Schoenle, in *United States Consular Reports*, IV, No. 14 (December, 1881), 625–26.

is worth that yearly amount to the United States. Computing the
wealth the United States acquire by the influx of population on this
basis, and estimating the number of emigrants to the United States
during the year of 1881 as having reached 600,000, the country would
have gained in that period $600,000,000.

As a matter of grave consideration, and in order to call urgent attention to the extraordinary drain on the young men population subject
to military duty, Prince Bismarck has lately submitted to the *Bundes-
rath* (federal council) a series of tables showing that during the year
1880 no less than 11,454 young men liable to military service have left
Germany for the United States, and, as in the course of this present
year the number of emigrants was unusually large, it seems not unlikely
that the army may be deprived of at least 20,000 young men.

In order to check this tide of emigration, the public posting of
placards from the emigration agents and foreign steamship companies
has been prohibited in Berlin, and a bill throwing all kinds of technical
difficulties in the way of emigration is likely to be introduced in the
next session of the Reichstag. In addition to this, the provincial authorities in Prussia have been ordered to inquire into, and report on, the
extent and causes of this alarming emigration.

The following table shows the progressive scale of emigration from
Germany for the last eight years:

| Year | Number |
|---|---|
| 1875, about | 30,000 |
| 1876, about | 29,000 |
| 1877, about | 23,000 |
| 1878, about | 25,000 |
| 1879, about | 34,000 |
| 1880, about | 110,000 |

The emigration fever has, to the amazement of the local authorities, spread to such regions during the present year as have hitherto
been free from it. This has been especially the case in the Rhenish
Westphalian coal, iron, and mining districts, to an extent which promises to prove a serious drain on the labor market of that locality. Exact
statistics of the movement from Rhineland and Westphalia are not
available, but it is calculated that at least 39,000 persons from those
two provinces have embarked within the summer season, and that the
coal mines in Westphalia alone have in all likelihood lost from 5,000 to
6,000 operatives by emigration during that period. It is of frequent
occurrence that the pioneers of the movement return as recruiting labor

agents amongst their companions, and there is every prospect that the exodus will be on a large scale in the coming year. The movement is by no means restricted to the ignorant, or destitute persons, for the average amount withdrawn by each family is estimated at from 2,000 to 3,000 marks.

That Germany, on account of the extraordinary increase of her population and her consequent overpopulation will have to give up from time to time to foreign countries a certain portion of her inhabitants, seems to be a settled conviction amongst her statisticians and economists. Emigration is considered a necessary consequence in the nature of events. But the principal object of the ruling powers here is to prevent the enormous waste of capital and labor consequent on emigration, to open up new markets for German manufactures, and to check the exodus to the United States, whose free institutions constitute so strong an attraction to Germans. The question of acquiring transatlantic territory for colonizing purposes is at present very elaborately discussed and ventilated through the press, in commercial circles, and in public meetings. It is proposed to organize settlements on a large scale in foreign territories, where Germans should remain dependent, to a certain degree, on the fatherland, and where the national spirit and customs should be upheld and cultivated, and German manufactures be consumed, and thus utilize the transatlantic brothers in the economical interests of the mother country. It is calculated that the colonists should mainly devote themselves to agriculture and send the products of their soil to the old country in exchange for German manufactures. The movement is undoubtedly gaining in extent rapidly amongst the people, and the chambers of commerce and boards of trade have submitted the feasibility and expediency of the colonial policy to Prince Bismarck in their respective annual reports. The Imperial Chancellor however, keeps, at present, aloof from the movement, and seems to regard it in a lofty way, but still with some inclination to favor and encourage it unofficially. He has not yet manifested any disposition to invest this matter with governmental authority, and it is hardly expected that he will do so in the near future. So far, the colonial policy is restricted to *private* enterprise, and is fostered and agitated by different societies, disseminated throughout the length and breadth of Germany. At the head of these organizations stands the Central Society for Commercial Geography, and Advancement of German Interests in Foreign Countries, having its field of operations in Berlin; next in importance is the West-German Branch Society for Colonization and

Export, which has its seat in Barmen. Besides these there have been organized, in furtherance of these colonial schemes, about a dozen other unions, in all parts of Germany, working very earnestly and harmoniously in promoting the movement by scattering gratuitous pamphlets over the country, by advocating it in public prints and by public speakers, and by striving to popularize it in every possible way. The southern part of Brazil and the Argentine Republic are proposed, as being favorable localities for the establishment of German colonies.

Whether these various colonization schemes will ultimately be shaped into a tangible plan of operation is yet a matter of mere speculation. But many German idealists dream that in times to come a great sister German empire will arise, wherein Germany could not only transfuse her overpopulation, but wherein, also, certain markets for her industrial products will be assured to the manufacturers of the fatherland.

WOLFGANG SCHOENLE, *Consul*

UNITED STATES CONSULATE
Barmen, October 28, 1881

# SECTION II

## ECONOMIC ASPECTS OF THE IMMIGRATION PROBLEM

# SECTION II

There are various ways of looking at the economic losses or gains resulting from emigration. There is the question of loss or gain to the individual emigrant, the question of loss or gain to the country of emigration, and the further question of loss or gain to the country of immigration. These losses or gains have not all been economic, either to the individuals or to the nations involved. There have been moral and spiritual, as well as economic, values to consider. But the economic aspects of the question were the determining factors in the policies of the nineteenth century. The attractions of the United States to the people of Europe were of many kinds: land, high wages, regular work, and political and religious liberty. But it has already been pointed out that, great as was the American tradition in political liberty and religious tolerance, it was the hope of economic freedom that lured the vast majority of immigrants across the sea.

To the European who was too poor even to pay his passage money, there was, in the Colonial period, and until well into the nineteenth century, the chance to pay his fare by work after his debarkation, as a redemptioner or indentured servant (Document 1). There were many abuses connected with the system, and public opinion gradually hardened toward it; but in the middle colonies, at least, large numbers of immigrants crossed the Atlantic and were provided for in this way.

When America became independent, the question of emigration was viewed in England in a new light. The sons who left her in voluntary exile were no longer going to develop her colonies, but to build up what might one day be a rival power. Immediately after the close of the Revolutionary War, a revival of emigration led to uneasiness in the "motherland" over the loss of population. The Americans were pictured as a "rustic and industrious people" living under simple rural conditions. It was reported that farmers and mechanics were needed. But the idlers were not wanted here, and they were warned that if they crossed the Atlantic they would be "disappointed, neglected, and perish." It was the members of the so-called "industrious classes" who emigrated; and it was charged that America, like an ungrateful child, having shaken off her connection with the mother country, was further "embowelling the nation of her most useful inhabitants" (Document 2). The British consul at Philadelphia sent home reports of the number of immigrant arrivals at the three ports in the Delaware. "We suffer a severe depopulation," he wrote in 1791, "and America derives vast benefit from it" (Document 3).

Again, after the Napoleonic Wars, fear was expressed in England over the "ruinous drain of the most useful part of the population of the United Kingdom." In America, immigration was looked upon as a means of increasing the wealth of the country. Even if the coast cities were crowded, there was still room in the interior—"a vast and almost exhaustless field for industry," and the economist estimated that the new arrivals created a home market to the value of what they consumed (Document 4).

The difficulties to be faced by the newcomers were numerous. Many arrived without means and were obliged to stop in the Eastern cities at least long enough to earn the money to go on to the new states and territories. Nor were the European immigrants always fitted for life on the prairie or in the wilderness. They were advised, after going West, to work for wages at first, to "hire out" to some farmer and learn the American method of farming while they were being paid for it. During this quasi-apprenticeship they were taught the work of the country—cutting timber, splitting fence rails, and other work with which they were not familiar. The failure of many Irish immigrants was early attributed to their disinclination or inability to reach the frontier. Too frequently they let slip the golden opportunity of securing land and a western home and crowded the city streets looking for work. As a last resort they sought employment on the turnpike roads for a dollar a day, out of which they paid for meat and drink, washing, and lodging (Document 5). Many of the immigrants who did go west went in colonies, like the English pioneers who founded the town of Albion on the Illinois prairie (Document 6).

Emigration to the United States was looked upon as the resource of the destitute. Those in England who were living upon the income of their property were told that they "ought by no means to entertain the idea of emigrating thither" (Document 7). The wealthy farmer was advised not to risk what he had; but the small farmer and farm laborer, and all sorts of "industrious laboring mechanics" were encouraged to hope for a betterment of their condition if they embarked on the great adventure of emigration. In his enthusiasm, the founder of the Albion colony wrote that emigration constituted for the farm laborers of England a wonderful change of destiny—"once poor laborers, their experience comprised within their parish bounds, or the limits of the farm on which they toiled for a bare subsistence," they themselves became farmers and owners of land in the New World. Not only that, but many of them also became "tradesmen and merchants on a large scale, commanding an amount of wealth they once never dreamed of possessing."

One class in England, those who were already paupers, living at the expense of the British taxpayers, had nothing to lose by emigration, and everything to gain. Since American laws at this time did not prohibit the landing of destitute persons,[1] the poor-law officials in England made various experiments, more or less extensive, with the emigration of those who were already a public charge. Some of these immigrant paupers were undoubtedly unsuccessful, and became in turn a charge upon the taxpayers of our American cities and states (Section IV), but others—and probably the vast majority—were paupers at home because they lacked opportunities that America could so plentifully supply, and they became useful hard-working citizens under the new conditions. The letters of the Watson family (Document 9) illustrate the gradual change from pauperism in the Old World to hopeful industry in the New.

With regard to the effect upon the country of emigration, the Parliamentary Committee on Emigration of 1826–27 (Document 10) saw possible benefits to the nation in the withdrawal of a surplus labor supply, and also in the domestic peace secured by the withdrawal of the unemployed.

The question how large an emigration would be necessary to improve wages at home was not easy to answer. One estimate placed the number at 100,000 for Ireland alone (Document 16). At any rate, by 1853 it was said that the great exodus of the famine period had been responsible for an increase in both wages and prices at home (Document 19).

The possible advantages of emigration to the mother country were set forth at length and with much vigor by Gibbon Wakefield in his *England and America* (Document 13). Wakefield argued that it should be the object of Great Britain to promote emigration—"to send forth continually all that portion of the constantly increasing labouring class for which there is no employment with good wages," in order to

[1] For material relating to the early immigration laws of the several states, see the preceding volume in this series, E. Abbott, *Immigration: Select Documents and Case Records*, Part II, Section I.

meet the labor needs of the United States and Canada. There were other advocates of an organized plan for promoting emigration to the British colonies, and in particular of directing the tide of emigration, in some measure at least, from the United States to Canada (Document 16). A proposal was made that a British emigration agent should be stationed at New York in order to give information about Canada to newly arrived immigrants as well as to those who had failed in the United States and who might be persuaded to try Canada instead of returning directly to Great Britain (Document 17).

It was, however, impossible to prevent emigrants sent out to Canada at public expense from crossing the border into "the States," and it was a difficult problem to find ways and means of making Canada as attractive to British emigrants as the United States, where employment could always be had on the construction of new canals and other public works (Document 11). As early as 1828 Mathew Carey of Philadelphia, estimated that 30,000 Irish laborers could secure immediate employment in the United States in construction work at "wages to which they could never, in the wildest range of their imagination, have dared to aspire to in their own country" (Document 12).

During the second quarter of the nineteenth century there were numerous travelers like Patrick Shirreff (Document 14) and the author of the *Practical Guide* (Document 18) who wrote careful accounts of the different parts of the United States, describing the opportunities for purchasing land, and methods of working one's way west. Shirreff reported that employment in agriculture was not easy to find along the Atlantic coast because the country was already thickly settled and there was a constant influx of immigrants without funds. The immigrant laborer was therefore advised to lose no time in pushing back into the western country, where wages were higher and land easy to obtain. The path to success in America was not, however, an easy one. "Energy of mind, steadiness of purpose, and persevering industry" were necessary; and trustworthy observers like Shirreff called attention to the ease with which the native Americans outstripped the immigrants, even when the latter were of the same stock and spoke the same language. Estimates of the cost of purchasing and stocking a farm showed clearly the reason why so many emigrants stayed in the Atlantic coast cities. They could not go west and begin farming until they had earned and saved the necessary money. Shirreff's estimate was $609 for an 80-acre farm even when the land could be bought for $1.25 an acre.

Similar advice was given to the Germans, who emigrated in colonies (Document 15) and were frequently commended as cultivators of the prairie soil in contrast to the Irish, who were reported to prefer the cities (Documents 15, 22, 23). Every German emigrant was warned that success in America could be achieved only through toil. "Let him remember," was the advice to the German peasant, "that he is going to settle amongst the most industrious people on earth," and that "nothing but personal exertion will ensure his ultimate success."

The increase in German emigration after 1848 led to the publication of a considerable body of German literature dealing with the emigration question—the kind of emigrants who might reasonably hope for success, the wages they might expect, the relative cost of living in the two countries, and the sections of the country best suited to them (Document 24). Educated immigrants were particularly warned of the difficulty of finding anything but menial work. Büchele warned such men that "the American axe is more difficult to wield than the pen; that the plow and the manure fork are very matter-of-fact and stupid tools"; and pointed out the dangers of an unhappy and discontented life in the New World even if economically successful (Document 25).

In this decade German economists and statisticians like Roscher and Wappäus began to regard very anxiously the loss of population through emigration (Documents 26, 27). Wappäus estimated that Germany lost annually not only 100,000 laborers, but also a capital of 100,000,000 thaler. The very rich, it was said, did not wish to emigrate, and the proletariat could not afford to. Therefore the emigrants belonged exclusively to a middle class, and their departure served to accentuate the contrast in Europe between great riches and great poverty. "The emigrating part of the nation," wrote Roscher, "may find itself benefited by emigration, but the great mass remaining behind may be poorer in capital and in men able to work and comparatively richer in the number of the poor" (Document 27).

Such benefits as were derived by the country of emigration fell almost exclusively to England. To the "workshop of the world," loss of population was compensated by an increase in the American demand for manufactured products and the profitable exchange of food and raw materials against these products. Germany, however, did not enjoy the benefits of this exchange, and Roscher complained bitterly of the losses suffered by the Fatherland through continuous emigration.

Later, however, in Great Britain questions were raised and doubts freely expressed as to whether emigration had produced in the United Kingdom a balance of losses or gains. The British Association for the Promotion of Social Science arranged a series of discussions of the effect of emigration on the country of origin. What would become of a country, it was asked, whose sons were leaving it in large and larger numbers? Could such a country hope to prosper when deprived of the labor of the young and hardy emigrants who were departing from its shores? On these questions the opinions of the economist are more important than those of the politician (Documents 37 and 38).

In the United States, the greatest of the immigrant-receiving countries, there was a general acceptance of the fact that what was Europe's loss was America's gain. The value of an increased population in a thinly settled country was accepted as a thing to be desired. It was pointed out that railway and highway contractors and all other employers of labor were largely dependent on the immigrant labor supply; and immigration was the foundation of the fortunes of real-estate dealers and of the shipowners of New York (Document 23).

There were, however, some dissenting voices. Fear that the immigrant invasion might adversely affect the rate of wages was discussed in the *North American Review* in 1852. Looking at the vast Irish immigration following the famine, the question whether the Irish invasion, "in conjunction with other causes," was likely to effect a general and great depression in the price of labor in the United States was seriously discussed (Document 20). It was even charged that foreign labor was being imported to lower wages or to keep wages from rising (Document 21), and the manufacturers who were advocating a high tariff on their products were said to believe in "the unlimited admission of workers without a sixpence of duty."

The "Native Americans" and the "Know-Nothings"[1] had some-

[1] For modern accounts of the Native American and Know-Nothing parties, see L. D. Scisco, *Political Nativism in New York State*, "Columbia University Studies," XIII (1901); L. F. Schmeckebier, *History of the Know-Nothing Party in Maryland*, "Johns Hopkins University Studies," XVII (1899); H. J. Desmond, *The Know-Nothing Party* (Washington, 1905); J. B. McMaster, "The Riotous Career of the Know-Nothings," *Forum*, XVII (1894), 524–36; Charles Stickney, *Know-Nothingism in Rhode Island* (in "Rhode Island Historical Society Studies in Colonial History," 1894, No. 1); G. H. Haynes, "Causes of Know-Nothing Success in Massachusetts," *American Historical Review*, III (October, 1897), 67–82; *ibid.*, "A Know-Nothing Legislature," *Annual Report of the American Historical Association for the Year 1896*, pp. 175–87; *ibid.*, "The Local History of Know-nothingism," *New England Magazine*, n.s. XV (1896–97), 82–96. And see also J. B. McMaster, *History of the People of the United States*, VII, 369–90; VIII, 77–87, 211–14, 227–30; and Edward Channing, *History of the United States*, VI, chap. v, 118–47.

thing to say about the economic consequences of immigration, and argued that, whatever the benefits might be from a long time point of view, the immediate result was an increase in the burden of pauperism and increased competition for American labor against workers with lower standards of living (Documents 28, 29). It was one of the "Know-Nothing" charges that immigration, if it were allowed to continue unchecked, would "sap the fountains of honest industry" and "bring the deserving to want." Less biased was the complaint made through the Association for the Improvement of the Condition of the Poor, that there was an oversupply of low-grade unskilled labor in New York City and that the immigrants who were destitute would not go west (Document 30).

The facts about the distribution of the foreign population were set forth accurately and in detail by the population census of 1860. The census returns showed some interesting differences in the distribution of the Irish and German immigrants so frequently commented on by native Americans and by European travelers. It seemed clear that the immigrant population had remained in relatively large numbers in the urban centers of the country and that only a small proportion of the immigrants were to be found in the purely farming regions, engaged in cultivating the earth, "the occupation which they had pursued in their native land and with which they were most familiar" (Document 31). Whether the immigrants remained in the urban centers from necessity rather than choice was rarely discussed. That the alien laborer was obliged to go first to the place where he could secure immediate and regular employment at good wages and that the industrial centers where labor was always needed were classified as urban centers was frequently overlooked.

A careful study of the Massachusetts statistics five years later showed that, so far as Massachusetts was concerned, it was clear that the labor of the immigrants was in demand whether they worked in the mills or went to the farms. But a review of the vital statistics of the state raised serious questions as to the relatively lower birth-rate among the American as compared with the foreign population, and as to whether or not a day could be foreseen when the foreign inhabitants would outnumber the Americans in that commonwealth (Document 32).

The Civil War created a new labor problem and a new attempt to evaluate the industrial contribution of the immigrant. To meet the labor shortage by encouraging immigration, the North American Land

and Emigration Company was organized.[1] Proposals to offer a bounty on immigrants was not approved by the congressional committee on agriculture, but various suggestions were made as to methods of promoting immigration (Document 33). But the close of the war and the demobilization of the armies changed the situation, and the common labor market was reported to be overstocked (Document 34). Skilled labor, however, remained in demand at good wages. The report of a distinguished economist, David A. Wells, who had been appointed special revenue commissioner of the United States, emphasized the scarcity of skilled labor in the industrial centers (Document 35).

Post-war labor conditions were reviewed in the *Financial and Commercial Chronicle* in the autumn of 1866. The tide of immigration, the *Chronicle* thought, had not yet reached its height, and with "millions of acres of virgin soil" still available in the West, and with improvements in transportation facilities both on sea and on land, rendering these lands more attractive "to the ill-paid sons of toil of the Old World," America would continue to increase its population at the expense of Europe (Document 36).

In America, General Francis Walker lent the weight of his authority as an economist and statistician to the theory that immigration had not been economically beneficial to the United States. This was due in part to the fact that the government had adopted a *laissez faire* policy instead of giving assistance and direction to the immigrants who arrived in such great numbers. The result was that the immigrants who might have been useful in the West were left to become a source of demoralization. General Walker, however, went further than this, and questioned whether the large supply of "cheap, untaught labor, derived from the misdirection of European peasants to mechanical pursuits," had even had a beneficial effect on production (Document 39).

But during the decade 1870–80, it was generally accepted that immigration had already made, and would continue to make, a great contribution to the economic life of the country. Estimates of the capital value of immigration were published, showing Europe's loss and America's gain, not only in labor but in capital. Nearly all the employees in American cotton, woolen, and worsted mills and in the foundries and rolling mills were of "recent foreign extraction." Most of the 30,000 miners in the Pennsylvania coal districts were English, Welsh, or Irish; the Germans were carrying on the clothing trades,

[1] For an account of this period, see E. Abbott, "Federal Immigration Policies, I," *The University Journal of Business*, II (March, 1924), 133–56.

and the heavy work on the railroads and canals had long been in the hands of the Irish (Document 42).

New aspects of the labor problem complicated the problem of post-war immigration (Document 43). "The sudden changes in trade and commercial centers, the growing facility of locomotion, the growth and importance of the unions" were all factors tending to make the problem of employment for immigrants more complicated. In Europe economic changes also affected the emigration movement. The industrial development of imperial Germany after 1870 (Document 44) probably tended to decrease the emigration of skilled labor by creating employment for it at home.

The French economist, Émile Levasseur, said, in reviewing the emigration of the nineteenth century, "There is no infallible system by which success can be absolutely guaranteed to all the members of the human race; yet that emigration is one of the best, there can be no question." It was, he thought, owing exclusively to its enormous alien population that the United States had been able to take rank with the great European powers (Document 45). There were, however, few who denied that American prosperity owed much to immigration. It was not difficult to set out on a grand scale the benefits that America owed to the millions of immigrants who had entered her ports and crossed her borders (Document 46).

# ECONOMIC ASPECTS OF THE IMMIGRATION PROBLEM

## 1. Methods of Meeting the Labor Shortage in America: Redemptioners and Indentured Servants[1]

### A. COMMENTS OF A SWEDISH TRAVELER, 1748[2]

The servants which are made use of in the English American colonies are either free persons, or slaves, and the former are again of two different sorts.

First, those who are quite free serve by the year; they are not only allowed to leave their service at the expiration of their year, but

[1] Among the poorer class of emigrants not only from Germany but from England, Ireland, and Scotland as well, there were many who had no money to pay for their passage and who earned their passage money after arrival in America by serving an apprenticeship for a term of years, chiefly in Pennsylvania, Maryland, and Virginia, as "indentured servants" (*Knechte*) or "redemptioners" (*Käuflinge*). The former entered into contracts of service in the old country which specified the number of years to be served; the latter were sold by the ship captain after arrival in Philadelphia or some other American port. The system was vigorously carried on during the eighteenth century and survived well into the nineteenth century. There is a considerable literature dealing with this subject. See e.g., the original narrative of *Gottlieb Mittelberger's Reise nach Pennsylvanien im Jahre 1750 und Rückreise nach Teutschland im Jahr 1754: Enthaltend nicht nur eine Beschreibung des Landes nach seinem gegenwärtigen Zustande, sondern auch eine ausführliche Nachricht von den unglückseligen und betrübten Umständen der meisten Teutschen, die in dieses Land gezogen sind und dahin ziehen*, Frankfurt und Leipzig 1756 (conveniently available in a translation by Carl T. Eben, Philadelphia, 1898); see also "Pastor Mühlenbergs Nachricht von merkwürdigen Exempeln aus seiner Amtsführung" (Sechstes Exempel) in *Hallesche Nachrichten* (neue Ausgabe), II, 459–61.

For further material dealing with this general subject, see Frank R. Diffenderffer, *The German Immigration into Pennsylvania through the Port of Philadelphia, 1700 to 1775*, Part II, "The Redemptioners"; Louis P. Hennighausen, "The Redemptioners and the German Society of Maryland," in *Second Annual Report of the Society for the History of the Germans in Maryland, with the Papers Read at Its Sessions, 1887–88;* Karl Frederick Geiser, *Redemptioners and Indentured Servants in the Colony and Commonwealth of Pennsylvania* (New Haven, 1901); James Curtis Ballagh, *White Servitude in the Colony of Virginia* ("Johns Hopkins University Studies in Historical and Political Science," Series XIII, Nos. 6–7); Eugene I. McCormac, *White Servitude in Maryland, 1634–1820* ("Johns Hopkins University Studies in Historical and Political Science," Series XXII, Nos. 3–4).

[2] Extract from Peter Kalm, *Travels into North America; Containing Its Natural History, and Circumstantial Account of Its Plantations and Agriculture in General,* translated from the Swedish by John R. Forster (2d ed. London, 1772) in John Pinkerton's *A General Collection of the Best and Most Interesting Voyages and Travels in All Parts of the World*, XIII, 499–500.

may leave it at any time when they do not agree with their masters. However, in that case they are in danger of losing their wages, which are very considerable. A man-servant who has some abilities, gets between sixteen and twenty pounds in Pennsylvania currency, but those in the country do not get so much. A servant-maid gets eight or ten pounds a year; these servants have their food besides their wages, but must buy their own clothes, and what they get of these, they must thank their master's goodness for.

Second, the second kind of free servants consist of such persons as annually come from Germany, England, and other countries, in order to settle here. These newcomers are very numerous every year: there are old and young ones, and of both sexes; some of them have fled from oppression, under which they supposed themselves to have laboured. Others have been driven from their country by persecution on account of religion; but most of them are poor, and have not money enough to pay their passage, which is between six and eight pounds sterling for each person; therefore they agree with the captain that they will suffer themselves to be sold for a few years, on their arrival. In that case the person who buys them, pays the freight for them; but frequently very old people come over, who cannot pay their passage, they therefore sell their children, so that they serve both for themselves and for their parents; there are likewise some who pay part of their passage, and they are sold only for a short time. From these circumstances it appears, that the price of the poor foreigners who come over to North America is not equal, and that some of them serve longer than others. When their time is expired, they get a new suit of clothes from their master, and some other things; he is likewise obliged to feed and clothe them during the years of their servitude. Many of the Germans who come hither, bring money enough with them to pay their passage, but rather suffer themselves to be sold, with a view that during their servitude they may get some knowledge of the language and quality of the country, and the like, that they may the better be able to consider what they shall do when they have got their liberty. Such servants are taken preferable to all others, because they are not so dear; for to buy a negroe or black slave requires too much money at once; and men and maids who get yearly wages, are likewise too dear; but this kind of servants may be got for half the money, and even for less; for they commonly pay fourteen pounds, Pennsylvania currency, for a person who is to serve four years, and so on in proportion. Their wages therefore are not above three pounds, Pennsylvania currency, per annum.

This kind of servants, the English call "servings." When a person has bought such a servant for a certain number of years, and has an intention to sell him again, he is at liberty to do so; but he is obliged, at the expiration of the term of the servitude, to provide the usual suit of clothes for the servant, unless he has made that part of the bargain with the purchaser. The English and Irish commonly sell themselves for four years, but the Germans frequently agree with the captain before they set out, to pay him a certain sum of money, for a certain number of persons. As soon as they arrive in America, they go about and try to get a man who will pay the passage for them; in return they give according to the circumstances, one or several of their children, to serve a certain number of years; at last they make their bargain with the highest bidder.

B.  COMMENTS OF AN ENGLISH TRAVELER, 1817[1]

A practice which has been often referred to in connection with this country, naturally excited my attention. It is that of individuals emigrating from Europe without money, and paying for their passage by binding themselves to the captain, who receives the produce of their labour for a certain number of years.

Seeing the following advertisement in the newspapers, put in by the captain and owners of the vessel referred to, I visited the ship, in company with a boot-maker of this city.

The Passengers on board the brig "Bubona," from Amsterdam, and who are willing to engage themselves for a limited time, to defray the expences of their passage, consist of persons of the following occupations, besides women and children, viz., 13 farmers, 2 bakers, 2 butchers, 8 weavers, 3 taylors, 1 gardener, 3 masons, 1 mill-sawyer, 1 white-smith, 2 shoe-makers, 3 cabinet-makers, 1 coal-burner, 1 barber, 1 carpenter, 1 stocking-weaver, 1 cooper, 1 wheelwright, 1 brewer, 1 locksmith. Apply on board of the "Bubona," opposite Callowhill-street, in the river Delaware, or to W. Odlin and Co., No. 38, South Wharves.

Oct. 2.

As we ascended the side of this hulk, a most revolting scene of want and misery presented itself. The eye involuntarily turned for some re-

[1] Extract from Henry Bradshaw Fearon, *Sketches of America* (2d ed.; London, 1818), pp. 148–51.

Fearon was charged both in England and America with presenting an unfair picture of life in this country. Sydney Smith said that he was "no lover of America and a little given to exaggerate his view of vices and prejudices"; and the *London Review* spoke of the "tone of ill-temper which this author usually manifests, in speaking of the American Character." See H. T. Tuckerman, *America and Her Commentators* (New York, 1864), p. 220.

lief from the horrible picture of human suffering, which this living sepulchre afforded. Mr. ——— enquired if there were any shoe-makers on board. The captain advanced; his appearance bespoke his office; he is an American, tall, determined, and with an eye that flashes with Algerine cruelty. He called in the Dutch language for shoe-makers, and never can I forget the scene which followed. The poor fellows came running up with unspeakable delight, no doubt anticipating a relief from their loathsome dungeon. Their clothes, if rags deserve that denomination, actually perfumed the air. Some were without shirts, others had this article of dress, but of a quality as coarse as the worst packing cloth. I enquired of several if they could speak English. They smiled, and gabbled, "No Engly, no Engly—one Engly talk ship." The deck was filthy. The cooking, washing, and necessary departments were close together. Such is the mercenary barbarity of the Americans who are engaged in this trade, that they crammed into one of those vessels 500 passengers, 80 of whom died on the passage. The price for women is about 70 dollars, men 80 dollars, boys 60 dollars. When they saw at our departure that we had not purchased, their countenances fell to that standard of stupid gloom which seemed to place them a link below rational beings. From my heart I execrated the European cause of their removal, which is thus daily compelling men to quit the land of their fathers, to become voluntary exiles in a foreign clime. . . . .

C.  REGISTRATION OF CONTRACTS OF IMMIGRANT "REDEMPTIONERS"[1]

WHEREAS, It has been found that German and Swiss emigrants, who for the discharge of the debt contracted for their passage to this country, are often obliged to subject themselves to temporary servitude, are frequently exposed to cruel and oppressive impositions by the masters of the vessels in which they arrive, and likewise by those to whom they become servants,

1. *Be it enacted, by the General Assembly of Maryland,* That the governor and council be, and they are hereby authorized, annually to appoint, in every port of entry in this state, some trustworthy person, skilled in the German and English languages, as register of all deeds

[1] Extract from "An Act relative to German and Swiss Redemptioners," passed February 16, 1818, *Laws of Maryland*, 1817, chap. 226.

Nearly thirty years earlier Pennsylvania had passed "An Act for establishing the office of a Register of all German passengers, who shall arrive at the port of Philadelphia, and of all indentures by which any of them shall be bound servants for their freight, and of the assignments of such servants in the City of Philadelphia" (April 8, 1785), *Laws of the Commonwealth of Pennsylvania, 1700–1782.* III, 78–80.

for the apprenticeship, or for the servitude of German or Swiss emigrants, arriving from foreign parts at such port or place.

2. *And be it enacted*, That it shall be the duty of said register, after he shall have taken an oath, to be administered by the clerk of the county court of the county wherein he shall reside, that he will faithfully execute the duties of his office, without prejudice, or partiality, to open an office, to draw up, as from time to time he may be required, and to see to the due and legal execution of the instrument of writing regulating the apprenticeship of every German or Swiss redemptioner, who shall after the passage of this law arrive within such port or place of this state, from beyond sea; and no indenture or writing relating to such apprenticeship shall be of any avail, unless the same be drawn up by said register, or be by him approved of.

3. *And be it enacted*, That it shall be the further duty of said register, immediately after the execution of any indenture relative to the apprenticeship of any such emigrant, to transmit the same to the clerk of the county court of the county where such emigrant shall arrive, there to be recorded, for which recording the said clerk shall be entitled to receive the fees usual for recording such writings, to be paid by the persons to whom such indenture shall be made; and the said register shall keep an accurate register or account of the name or names of every person indented or bound before him as aforesaid, their sex, age, time of apprenticeship or servitude, the country whence they came, to whom bound, and transmitted by said register as aforesaid for record.

4. *And be it enacted*, That no minor under the age of twenty-one years shall be indented before the said register, except by his or her parents, or next of kin; and in default of relatives, then by the direction of the orphans court of the county where such emigrant shall arrive.

5. *And be it enacted*, That every such indenture shall contain a covenant or stipulation by the master or mistress of any minor under the age of twenty-one years, to give to such minor, annually, at least two months schooling during his or her apprenticeship or servitude.

6. *And be it enacted*, That no emigrant shall in any case be bound to serve longer than four years, unless in case of male minors, under the age of seventeen years, and female minors under the age of fourteen years, who may be obliged to serve any period so that the males may be free at the age of twenty-one years, and the females at eighteen.

7. *And be it enacted*, That no German or Swiss emigrants arriving within any port, harbour, or place in this state, shall be detained on

board of the vessel in which he or she arrived, longer than thirty days after such arrival, and during this detention, such emigrants shall receive from the master, consignee, or owners of such vessel, good and sufficient provisions, without any increase in the period of apprenticeship or servitude, or any cost or charge on such emigrants.

8. *And be it enacted*, That if any emigrants shall be longer detained, or shall receive cruel or ill treatment from the master or officer on board of said vessel, or shall take sick, or be otherwise incapable of remaining on board, it shall be the duty of the register, after being informed of the complaint, to communicate the same to the judge of the county court of the county where such emigrant shall arrive, or to a judge of the Baltimore city court, if the emigrant shall arrive in the port of Baltimore, who on being satisfied of the correctness of the statement, may order and direct that such emigrant shall, with his property, be brought on shore at the expense of the owners of the vessel, until some one shall contract for a term of servitude with such emigrant, and if no purchaser shall appear within thirty days after such emigrant shall come on shore, that is, within sixty days after arrival, the master or owners of the vessel shall have no lien or claim on such emigrant, but the liability for the passage money, and other expenses, shall attach, like any other debt or contract, any contract, custom or usage, to the contrary notwithstanding.

9. *And be it enacted*, That no child or children shall in any case be answerable in any manner for the freight or passage money of their parents, dead or alive, nor shall parents be responsible for the freight or passage money of the deceased children, nor a husband for his deceased wife, nor a wife for her deceased husband, any custom, pretended contract, promise or agreement, made beyond sea, to the contrary notwithstanding.

10. *And be it enacted*, That all masters of vessels arriving . . . . shall in case of the death of any German or Swiss emigrant, within ten days after his, her, or their arrival, deliver to said register an accurate inventory, under oath, of all the property of such emigrant on board of such vessel, . . . . and that the said register shall dispose at public sale of the same, and apply the proceeds to the payment of the passage money due by such emigrant . . . . ; *Provided always*, that the passenger died before the expiration of one half of the duration of the voyage, no passage money shall be due, but the heirs of the deceased shall be entitled to the proceeds. . . . .

11. . . . . If the proceeds arising from the sale as aforesaid should remain in hand uncalled for during three years, . . . . in such case the proceeds, without interest, shall be paid over by the register to the treasurer of the German Society of Maryland, for the use of said society.

### D.  PUBLIC OPINION AND THE REDEMPTIONERS[1]

*To the honorable the Congress of the United States: The memorial of James Brown, a citizen of the State of Tennessee, and town of Nashville:*

Your memorialist humbly represents to your honorable body that he purchased in the city of Philadelphia, about the last of October, 1818, a number of German redemptioners; advanced a considerable sum of money in their behalf; and took their indentures for three years and five months, commencing when they should arrive at the place of their destination. Your memorialist, before indenturing of said servants, described to them the climate, and explained to them the kind of business which they would be required to follow. Your memorialist further represents to your honorable body that he informed said servants, and also suggested to some gentlemen in Philadelphia, that, if he did purchase said slaves, it was not with the prospect of great emolument to himself, but that he thought their residence in the State of Tennessee or Alabama would greatly ameliorate their condition, and, at the same time, their particular avocations would be of incalculable advantage in that section of country. With these laudable objects in view, your memorialist made the purchase, selecting vine-dressers and mechanics for the purpose above stated to your honorable body, and said servants urged with much solicitude your memorialist to make said advances for them; and your memorialist, in conformity with the agreement between himself and said servants, and at a very great expense, conveyed the said servants on their way to the place for which they had indented themselves as far as Marietta, in the State of Ohio, when, by the interposition, persuasion, and aid of Caleb Emmerson, . . . . with many others whose names are unknown to your memorialist, the said indented servants were induced to make their escape from out of the possession of your memorialist, and were conveyed away and secreted by the said persons, or some of them, before mentioned. Your memorialist applied to the proper authorities for the purpose of

[1] Extract from a memorial praying for a change of venue, communicated to the Senate, December 28, 1819, reprinted in *American State Papers*, Class X, "Miscellaneous," Vol. II, pp. 550–54.

reclaiming said servants, but all his efforts were defeated by the violent, oppressive, and illegal conduct of said persons, your memorialist being by the said persons unjustly arrested and imprisoned, together with the officer who had in his possession a precept authorizing the apprehension and arrest of said servants, the details of which transaction will more fully appear by the accompanying documents, to which your honorable body is particularly referred. Your memorialist would have sought redress by an appeal to the laws of his country at the time that this extraordinary proceeding took place, but was advised by counsel that there was no probability, under the present state of public feeling, that restitution would be made for the injury which your memorialist had sustained both in person and property; and your memorialist was further advised by several respectable citizens that, if he went into the country again for the purpose of arresting his servants, his life would be jeopardized. Application was made through his excellency Joseph McMinn, Governor of the State of Tennessee, on behalf of your memorialist, to the Governor of the State of Ohio; and he, in reply to the Governor of the State of Tennessee, in substance acknowledges the wrong and injury which your memorialist has sustained in that State, and regrets, in language equally just and proper, that such individuals should be permitted to disturb the public tranquility, and concludes by stating that he has been informed that justice had been rendered your memorialist: which is not the fact; for the six [servants] which he arrested by authority from the honorable Judge Bird were forcibly taken from him by the citizens of Cincinnati. . . . . And your memorialist represents to your honorable body that he has lost his servants entirely, and that he has no other redress than by suits at law; and your memorialist begs leave to state, furthermore, that such is the extent of the influence of the individuals, and such their activity in exerting that influence, and that such is the temper and feeling of the people generally, that your memorialist believes he would be unable in the State of Ohio to have justice done in the trial of his suits; and your memorialist is advised that there is no law which authorizes a change of venue from one State to another. Your memorialist therefore prays your honorable body to pass some general law authorizing such change of venue upon the case made out before the judge of the federal courts, or a special law to permit it in this particular case, so that your memorialist can have a trial in Virginia or Kentucky, or some adjacent State.

And your memorialist, as in duty bound, will ever pray, &c.

[*Signed*] JAMES BROWN

*State of Kentucky, Jefferson County, ss.*

Personally appeared before the subscriber, a justice of the peace in and for the said county, George Ross, who, being duly sworn according to law, doth depose and say: That he met with Mr. James Brown at Wheeling, Virginia, who had twenty-two German servants with him; that a boat was purchased at Wheeling, and we proceeded to Marietta, Ohio, with the Germans, where the boat was landed, and the Germans refused to go on board again; Mr. Brown then applied to Daniel H. Buell, Esq., a justice of the peace, for permission to carry his Germans out of the State of Ohio, who, upon satisfactory proof being adduced that service was due from the following enumerated persons to James Brown, granted him a certificate to remove John Gold, and Elizabeth Gold, his wife, Jacob Kopp, and Agatha Kopp, his wife, Joseph Geizer, and Caroline Geizer, John Beck, and Magdalena Beck, his wife, and Lorenz Beck, Johan Weirtzburger, and Maria Weirtzburger, his wife, John Hell, and Scolastico Hell, his wife, Anton Frytag, and Anna Maria Frytag, Christian Sherrer, Ferdinand Bengle, Jacob Fohr, Francez Anton Klohr, Carl Zimmerman, Sebastian Hog, and Johan Frederick Genevine. And this deponent further saith that he was present when the above-named servants personally appeared before Justice Buell, in the town of Marietta, Ohio, on the 30th day of November, 1818, and severally acknowledged that they had signed the several indentures produced before the said justice; that, through the interference of the citizens of Marietta, as this deponent believes, the Germans refused to go with Mr. Brown, and they absconded into the country, when a warrant was issued by Justice Booth, and the Germans were brought before him; and Caleb Emmerson and David Putnam, Esqs., appeared as their counsel, and after hearing, the said Justice Booth refused to grant Mr. Brown a certificate to remove his servants, although he admitted the evidence of the validity of the indenture. . . . . .

[*Signed*] GEORGE ROSS

Sworn and subscribed this 17th December, 1818

## 2.   Opportunities in England and America Compared[1]

The condition of society varies extremely in the provinces of America from that of England; and the emigrants will find themselves

---

[1] Extract from John King, *Thoughts on the Difficulties and Distresses in Which the Peace of 1783 Has Involved the People of England; on the Present Disposition of the English, Scots, and Irish, to Emigrate to America; and on the Hazard They Run (without Certain Precautions) of Rendering Their Condition More Deplorable.* Addressed to the Right Hon. Charles James Fox (5th ed.; London, 1783), pp. 31–40, 47–48.

egregiously deceived, in their expectations of ease and affluence: it is not a country matured and grown opulent by commerce; it is a new discovered land, occupied by ancient savages, and ravaged by late wars; for a century to come, it can require no more than mere labour on the soil; and it cannot suit the dainty sons of England, to cross the Atlantic for a scanty subsistence, earned by the sweat of their brows.

The government of America abounds with thoughtful and moderate men, inured to attentive industry, and to temperance; America has no kings, lords, and high-priests, whose devouring necessities might impel them to premature commercial adventures: in their present state of simplicity, the farmers are the people they want, and plain mechanics, for the works of necessity; their flourishing agriculture will yield a redundancy of heavy and rude superfluities, and the superabundant produce will teach the necessity of exportation; but all this will be done principally by her natives, and dreaming foreigners may be obliged to return to their own countries to exercise that dexterity and skill which was not wanted among a rustic and industrious people. . . . . The men who have applied to me to assist them in their departure, were persons who had formerly been employed in complicated branches of refined trade; persons who had suffered by imprudence and idleness; persons who sought to display their talents where they could neither be admired or understood; I speak from thorough knowledge and information, and I warn and apprize them, "that they are not wanted in America; and if they go there, they will be disappointed, neglected and perish."

The emissaries of America say differently. They are dispersed through England, Scotland, and Ireland, to inveigle our husbandmen and mechanics. . . . . After America, like an ungrateful child, has shaken off all connection with the Mother-Country, she is embowelling the nation of her most useful inhabitants. . . . .

I have seen letters from people in various parts of the kingdom, from Scotland, and from Ireland, which shew the almost general disposition to emigration—every one seems to have conversed with an American emissary, and to have been seduced by his insidious persuasions. . . . . A destructive war [has been] followed by a disadvantageous peace; and everyone fancies, that America will yield him the ease and plenty that is so abundantly and so confidently promised.

. . . . Depopulation is as certain a mark of political disease, as wasting is of those in the human body; the increase of numbers in a state, shews youth and vigour; when numbers do not diminish, we have an idea of manhood; and of age, when they decline; something should be done to prevent the fatal consequences of this rapid decline. Nothing consistent with liberty can be done to prevent emigration. . . . . Taxes have been deemed a stimulative to industry; but when they increase beyond due proportion, they become fatal, and an insurmountable obstacle to it; the wretched labourer, whose utmost industry will scarcely earn a moderate livelihood, can but ill afford the rigorous deductions which a hard government has imposed on him. While America offers ease and abundance, and England deprives her subjects of the means of subsistence, she must become depopulated. . . . . The late mismanagement in England must have occasioned extreme depopulation, though the influx from Scotland and Ireland has recruited it; but these supplies may now be diverted to the new hemisphere; the strangers who flock to England, in hopes of gaining a livelihood, are counterbalanced by those, who leave it with the same intention. . . . . If trade flourished and the labourer could live, he would not be seduced by the fascinating, though sometimes false colors held out by America; he would not desperately go to clear woods, drain marshes, or cultivate rank soils, in an unhealthy country, nor waste his days in golden delusive dreams of East-India voyages. England, the seat of wealth, of happiness, and of liberty, would still retain its superiority, and its grateful citizens would retain their attachment. . . . .

We may still hope for a mitigation of the public distress; and we shall then perceive, that it is not the barren solitary tracts of America that allure the people to emigration, but the calamities they endure at home, force them to search abroad for relief, though in their random wanderings they plunge into greater hardships.

### 3.  British Opinion of the Dangers of Emigration[1]

*January 3, 1790.*—I have been disappointed in obtaining an accurate list of passengers imported into Baltimore since the Peace; but I have assurances of being shortly furnished with it.

For two years after the war from 6 to 800 Irish passengers were imported annually; from the year 1785 to the year 1789 scarcely any arrived there; in the year 1789 there were about 240 Irish and about

---

[1] Extract from letters of Phineas Bond, British consul at Philadelphia, to the British foreign office in the *Annual Report of the American Historical Association, 1897*, pp. 455, 472–73, 488, 567–68. The first two letters are addressed to Lord Carmarthen, afterward Duke of Leeds, and the last two are addressed to Lord Grenville.

260 Palatines landed at Baltimore. Most of the Irish passengers paid their passage money; the Germans were chiefly indented servants.

New Castle, Wilmington and Philadelphia are the three ports in the Delaware into which passengers are imported; there are no other ports of the United States now engaged in this traffic.

Attempts will certainly be made, my Lord, to draw a large body of people from Ireland in the course of the next Summer; and I presume the attempts will succeed if difficulties be not immediately thrown in the way.

The paper I have the honor to enclose to your Grace affords a sad specimen of the brutal treatment of indented servants and would of itself, if generally promulgated, operate as the best means of discouraging a wretched race of people from leaving their homes. . . . .

*January 3, 1791.*—A plan is now under consideration, my Lord, for the disposal of vacant lands of the United States as an operation beneficial to the Finance of the country. This plan if carried into effect will lead to large speculations in lands which will be held forth for sale by the purchasers, and invite emigrants from Europe and elsewhere. Many private holders of great tracts of lands are already in Europe endeavoring to dispose of their property. There is abundant ground to excite a devout wish that persons would exercise great caution in making investments of this sort with a view of removing hither from Great Britain, Ireland, and other parts of Europe. Frauds of a most gross nature have already been practiced and new stratagems will be devised to seduce unwary purchasers. Moreover, my Lord, it should be observed that, except in the State of Pennsylvania no law exists to enable aliens to purchase and hold lands, and that the law of Pennsylvania is confined to a short term of years the greater part of which is expired. Certified copies of this act have been transmitted to England, which will probably be represented as a general regulation in force throughout the Union. In my letter of the first of November, I had the honor to inform your Grace, a society established here for the encouragement of Irish emigrants had interposed and prosecuted a master of a vessel in the passenger trade for the breach of an old law of Pennsylvania regulating that trade. The master of the vessel was a certain captain, Robert Coningham, master of the brigantine "Coningham" of London Derry. Upon the trial of the Indictment it appeared there was a scarcity of provisions so that the passengers were reduced to a short allowance for three weeks previous to their arrival, that there was little or no vinegar to keep the vessel clean, and it also came out that in the berths of four persons a passenger had stowed himself his wife and eight children who only drew the allowance of provisions for four people. The master was found guilty and fined £500 currency. In consideration however of his having remonstrated to his owners as to the inadequacy of his stores for the voyage, it is expected some reduction of the fine will take place.

This case will no doubt excite much murmur in the North of Ireland and perhaps may furnish the fittest season to interpose proper regulations applied to a trade in which very horrid practices too frequently prevail.

*September 10, 1791.*—The passenger trade from Great Britain and Ireland is a constant source of population and advantage to this country, manufacturers [factory operatives] are frequently introduced through this channel; besides, my Lord, we suffer a severe depopulation and America derives vast benefit from it. Already upwards of 4,500 passengers have arrived this season in the Delaware from Ireland alone—more are expected here, other vessels with passengers are destined for Maryland and S. Carolina. The trifling passage money paid from Ireland by the emigrants is from £3 to $3\frac{1}{2}$ guineas a head according to the part of the vessel they occupy; the price of the passage renders the profit of the voyage very precarious—a short passage puts money into the pockets of the merchants, but a tedious passage can be attended with little or no advantage, any obstructions therefore which may lessen the profit or increase the risque would effectually abolish this trade. These obstructions may grow out of regulations calculated to meet the convenience of the emigrants in their voyage and to correct the abuses committed in this traffic—a mode of reform I had the honor of suggesting to his Grace, the Duke of Leeds, in my letters of the 16th November, 1788.

*November 23, 1794.*—It would be an act of public utility as well as of private benefit to restrain these [land] sales under certain regulations of this sort, that as great frauds had been practiced it should be penal to offer foreign lands either at public or private sale unless the documents of the title were accompanied by a fit attestation that the lands were of a merchantable quality and as to intrinsic value bear a certain proportion to the price demanded for them.

There never was a period which required more constant attention to the execution of the laws[1] which prevent the enticing of artificers

[1] [The statutes 5 George I, c. 27 and 23 George II, c. 13 provided that any person who should "contract with, entice, persuade, or endeavor to persuade, solicit, or

to go into foreign countries, which impose forfeitures on artificers who shall go out of his majesties dominions to exercise or teach their trades to foreigners, and shall not return upon notice given them by persons authorized for that purpose. The penalties which are imposed upon persons contracting with or seducing artificers might be increased and extended to all handicraftsmen and labourers as well as individuals of every description.

The spirit of migration has gone forth, my Lord; it is assisted and encouraged not only by shipowners and shipmasters engaged in the passenger trade, but by societies formed here, to encourage emigrants, at the head of which are extensive landholders who by this adventitious increase of the population of this country effectually secure rapid and enormous fortunes.

This influx of emigrants from England into the United States naturally excites an alarm, that great quantities of money will be brought out of the kingdom and enforces the expediency of a most scrupulous attention to prevent the exportation of the current coin of the realm which appears to me, my Lord, to be a serious and increasing evil.

### 4. Immigration Following the Peace of 1815

#### A. JUNE 27, 1816[1]

[From a London newspaper.] The continued and increasing emigration from this country to America becomes every day more alarming. The immediate and earnest attention of government to this serious drain of the most useful part of the population of the united kingdom, to the growing privation of its best hands in arts and manufactures, and to the almost daily accumulating loss of the mechanical means of the country's prosperity, is imperiously directed.

It is stated that 1,600 men, women, and children had engaged passages in different vessels, at Newry, Dublin, and Belfast, to cross the Atlantic; and that emigration from Switzerland increased.

#### B. JULY 27, 1816[2]

The British and other newspapers teem with notices of the emigration of their people to the United States. The persons alluded to are

---

seduce" any workman or artificer in wool, mohair, cotton, silk, iron, steel, brass, or any other metal; or any clockmaker, watchmaker, or any other workman, in any other manufactures to go out of the kingdom into any foreign country was liable to be indicted, to forfeit 500£, and to suffer imprisonment for twelve months.]

[1] Reprinted in *Niles' Weekly Register*, X, 412.
[2] Extract from *Niles' Weekly Register*, X, 366

chiefly farmers and mechanics, to add to the labor, and in consequence increase the wealth of our country in peace, and hold the nerve to assist in defending it in war. We know that the Irish emigrants much aided to fill the ranks of the army during the war, and they fought gallantly for freedom, feeling that they had a share in the contest as their own. Several vessels with passengers from Ireland have arrived since our last, and nine more from Newry alone are immediately expected—they are British ships, one of them, of great burthen, had 350 engaged. An English paper of May 20, says: "Several farmers who lately occupied about 4,000 acres of land in Lincolnshire, have recently emigrated to America, after having sold all their live and dead stock. They were accompanied by the curate of the village." And a Genoa article of the 12th of the same month, tells us that "a great many Swiss from all the Protestant cantons are going soon to depart from Basle for America. Commerce and manufactures languish both at Basle and in the parts of Germany next the Rhine. As no German or Swiss manufactures are now permitted to enter France, many have almost wholly ceased to work. Last Thursday, many waggons with manufactures, both German and Swiss, having presented themselves at the French custom-house on the frontiers, to pay the duties, were ordered to return back, with the notification that, till further orders, no waggon with goods could enter France."

These are the sorts of men that we want. One Swiss is worth a hundred of the Cockney tape-sellers with which our cities have teemed.

### C.  AUGUST 10, 1816[1]

A ship has arrived at New York from France, with passengers, among whom is Mr. Lee, late consul at Bordeaux, and fifty-two artists and manufacturers of various descriptions, vine-dressers and husbandmen—232 other persons arrived at New York, in one day, from Hull, England, and Waterford, Ireland. Vessels are almost every day reaching some of our ports with passengers from England, Ireland, France, Germany, &c. The Swiss, heretofore spoken of, embarked in Holland, and sailed on the 11th of June. A Liverpool paper complains, that the spirit of emigration has reached "the metropolis and the heart of the United Kingdom"; and relates that a vessel has been seized in the Thames, for attempting to bring out 231 persons, instead of 174, all that she was entitled to carry, by the law allowing

[1] Extract from *Niles' Weekly Register*, X, 400.

one to every two tons. Many vessels are mentioned in England as being engaged to bring passengers to the United States.

### D. AUGUST 17, 1816[1]

We have not exactly added up the amount of the passengers from Europe, who have reached New York, Philadelphia, and Baltimore, for a week past; but believe we shall not be far from the truth when we estimate them at from 1,200 to 1,500 persons; of whom 410 are Swiss arrived at Philadelphia, via Holland—the rest are from Ireland, England, and France.

The current of emigration to the United States has been very strong for the last six months; but judging by what we see in the British and other foreign papers, we can consider it as hardly begun. The people are preparing, in many places, to leave their country by neighborhoods or parishes, as it were, and in the new world to possess and enjoy the friends of their youth, by settling together.

The proceeding has excited much alarm in England. The papers teem with paragraphs to check the hope of the people to benefit by the change; and government is loudly called upon to interfere to prevent this "ruinous drain of the most useful part of the population of the united kingdom." They note, in detail, the arrivals in New York with passengers, and on summing up the amount, which was only 229 for the week stated, they say, "These facts certainly are serious; coupled with the sentiments which are now prevalent in America with regard to England, and with respect to the avowed probability of another war, at no distant period, with this country, they cannot fail to awaken reflections of the most gloomy kind to all who wish for the peace and harmony of the world." . . . .

As a political economist, I am pleased that the current sets so strong this way. There is wealth and safety in it. We have no reason to fear an excess of labor for many years to come. Our cities are crowded and business is dull, but the interior presents a vast and almost exhaustless field for industry. Every man that arrives may be fairly considered as adding at least 300 dollars a year to the national wealth, while he also creates a home-market to the value of what he consumes; and increases the national safety by adding to the effective population of the republic. Let them come. Good and wholesome laws, with the avenues to wealth and independence opened to honest industry, will tame even Mr. Peel's "untameably ferocious" Irishmen; as

[1] *Ibid.*, pp. 401, 411.

well as suppress English mobs, crying out for employment and bread, without the use of the bayonet.

---

The spirit of emigration makes a great uproar in England. Cobbett says, "the hive is in commotion—the bees seem resolved no longer to support the drones and wasps." To check it many paragraphs appear like the following from the *Courier:* "Everything is very dull in America. So great is the stagnation of trade, that but very few of the merchant vessels are employed. Our countrymen who have emigrated, are in a most deplorable state; upwards of a thousand of them have applied to the British consul at New York to be sent home with passports as distressed British subjects."

### D.    AUGUST 24, 1816[1]

The sentiment of Washington is our sentiment. In his reply to a congratulatory address from the citizens of Baltimore, he observed that so long as this country continued sensible of the blessings, civil and religious, it had attained, so long would it continue to be the asylum of the oppressed from every land. We wish to the oppressed—the poor man seeking bread—peace and plenty, and health and happiness. "This be a main queer country," said a Yorkshireman who, with three well-grown sons and a large family of small children, was travelling from New York to Zanesville, to a gentleman who met him not far from Bedford, Pa. "It is a main queer country," said he—"for I have asked the laboring folks all along the road how many meals they eat in a day, and they all said three and sometimes four, if they wanted them. We have but two at home, and they are scanty enough, sir," continued he, in his broad dialect, which I know not how to express with English types. "Only think, sir," added he, "many of these people [the laborers] asked me to eat and drink with them—we can't do so in Yorkshire, sir, for we have not enough for ourselves." What a field for reflection is there in the facts here stated! What American would have thought of enquiring how many meals the working people eat in a day? But this was the first thing the poor Englishman thought of, and he had done it "all along the road," to be convinced of the truth of the matter. . . . .

The real number [of persons who have reached the United States from Europe] cannot be under 1,600 for the space of seven days! This will appear, indeed, astonishing, when to the common difficulties that interpose to prevent a man from leaving his country, is superadded the

[1] Extract from *Niles' Weekly Register*, X, 419, 431.

obstructions of government in so limiting the number of passengers to be brought out, as almost to forbid emigration to the laboring classes. The cost of bringing himself and family to the United States, under present arrangements, is a little fortune to the Irish peasant, which must be built up by years of industry, and extraordinary economy and good luck. Vessels that are now permitted to bring out only 70 or 80 passengers, used to carry from 250 to 350—hence the price of the passage is necessarily raised, and emigration is absolutely forbidden to those who with difficulty earn as much as keeps soul and body together at home. But, perhaps, the procedure does not operate to our disadvantage—it may give us a greater share of the bone and sinew—the middle class of the country. Indeed, it is a universal remark, that the quality of the emigrants who have lately reached us, is greatly improved and improving. Many of them are what are called "small farmers," some of them mechanics, and they generally appear to have a little money to begin the new world with.

### 5. How an Emigrant May Succeed in the United States[1]

I will now proceed to give some instructions to my own countrymen, who may hereafter emigrate, to the United States of America. I shall first take up the poor mechanic and the day labourer, next the farmer who may go there with money to purchase land, and next the merchant.

I will take the liberty, as an introduction, to point out some stumbling blocks that have been in the way of many emigrants to this country. We conceive the vessel coming to anchor, and the passengers preparing for going ashore. On setting their feet on land, they look about them, see fine houses, gardens, and orchards, the streets crowded with well-dressed people, every one pursuing his own business. Well, the question now is, where shall I go? I meet a person passing, and address myself to him, requesting him to inform me where I can have accommodations for some short time. He will point out a house which he thinks may answer my appearance, &c. I get my goods conveyed to this house. The landlord and his family receive me as a foreigner, and so long as I have cash will have a watchful eye over me, and treat me according to what money I spend with them. In the meantime, on the arrival of an Irish ship, a crowd of poor Irish, who have been in

[1] Extract from a letter written by Clements Burleigh, who lived for thirty years in the United States, published in the appendix to John Melish, *Travels through the United States of America in the Years 1806 and 1807, and 1809, 1810, and 1811* (London, 1818), pp. 620–25. Melish suggested that the letter would "be found useful to such persons as mean to emigrate."

that country for a number of years, are always fond of meeting their countrymen on landing, and of encouraging them to take a share of grog or porter, &c. The feelings of the open-hearted Irishman are alive to the invitation, and some days are spent in this way, in the company of men who are a disgrace to the country they came from, and who are utterly incapable to procure themselves work, much less the poor emigrant. I warn emigrants, therefore, to be upon their guard.

The plan therefore, which I would recommend, is that upon landing, as soon as convenient, they should divest themselves of any heavy luggage, such as chests or boxes; and in the meantime, if they are deficient of money to carry them to the inland parts of the country, stop some time, and if they can get work apply to it, and use what they earn with economy, and keep clear of all idle company, and also be particular in keeping clear of a certain description of their own countrymen. When they have acquired as much money as may help to bear their expenses, let them put their bundles on board one of the waggons, loaded with merchandize for the Western country. By being active and obliging to the carrier on the way, he will charge little or nothing on your arrival at Pittsburg, or Greensburg, or any other town in the western parts of Pennsylvania. You then take your property from aboard of the waggon, if it suits, and make inquiry for labour. The best plan would be to engage a year with some opulent farmer, for which period of service, you will receive $100, and during that time be found in meat, drink, washing, and lodging. This will be an apprenticeship that will teach you the work of the country, such as cutting timber, splitting fence rails, and other work that is not known in Ireland. Be temperate and frugal, and attend worship on Sundays with your employer's family. This will keep you clear of a nest of vipers, who would be urging you to go to tippling-houses with them, to drink whiskey, and talk about Ireland. At the expiration of the year, if your employer is pleased with your conduct, he will not be willing to part with you, and will enter into engagements with you, which is often done in the following way, viz., He will point out to you a certain number of fields to be cultivated, some to be under wheat, others in rye, Indian corn, oats, etc.; he will find horses, and farming utensils, and furnish boarding, washing, and lodging, during that year, and when the harvest is taken off the ground, he has two-thirds for his share, and you have one-third. Your share of wheat, rye, Indian corn or any other produce of the ground, which you have farmed in this way, you will always meet a ready market for. It is true, you must attend early and late to your work, and do it in a neat, farming-like manner. Pursuing this plan of industry a few years, you may save as much money as will purchase 150 acres of land in the state of Ohio, or the Indiana territory, or any other part of these new states. It is necessary to guard against imposition in the title, as titles are very uncertain in some places. . . . . This is pointing out to you the path that industrious men have pursued, who now live rich and independent. And I am confident, that in America, without the most close application to labour, and using frugality, land is not attained, by those who emigrate to that country destitute of funds. I am convinced almost to a certainty, that out of 20 emigrants from Ireland to the United States, 15 have not been able to procure one foot of land; but this is owing to their own bad management. In many instances they are often grossly deceived by false information, relative to that country, painting to them advantages that never existed, and when the poor disappointed emigrant lands on the American shore, he finds his golden views have taken flight. He spends his time in brooding over his misfortunes till his money is gone, and then he must work or starve; and in the cities, there is always a number of poor emigrants that will not go into the country. The streets are often crowded with them looking for work, so that it is very hard to obtain work for a stranger that is not known. The last resource is to engage to work upon the turnpike roads. Here the labourer will get one dollar per day, and must find himself meat, drink, washing, and lodging. Here he has for companions the most abandoned drunken wretches that are in exist- ence, and whose example he must follow, or be held in derision by them. The day's work is tasked, and if not accomplished, his wages are docked; this sort of labour, and that of working at furnaces and forges, employs a great number of Irishmen. I have known many hundreds of them who have wrought in this way for more than 30 years, who at this moment cannot put a good coat on their back, and now are old, infirm, and past labour. . . . .

My advice to mechanics is, to push back, and take residence in some of the inland towns; and as new counties are every year dividing off, and towns pitched upon to be the seat of justice for these counties, work for all kinds of mechanics is plenty, and money sufficient may soon be earned, to purchase a lot in one of these towns, where you may, in a short time, be enabled to build a house on your own property, and have no rent to pay. In these towns you will have an opportunity of educating your children, and putting them to trades at a proper time. But I am sorry to say, most of the tradesmen would suffer cold and hunger, even death itself, rather than go from New York and Philadelphia, into the country.

There is a number of young men who leave Ireland and go to America intending to be clerks or merchants. Of all classes of people, I can give these the least encouragement. We have ten people of this description, where we cannot get employment for one, particularly at this time, when all kinds of trade in the United States are at so low an ebb.

I will now take notice of the man who emigrates to America, and has money with him, and means to become a farmer. First, it is necessary to mention the price of land. East of the mountains, good land will not be bought under from 80 to 120 dollars per acre, where there are good improvements—other land may rate from 5 dollars to a higher amount, according to the quality of the land, and the improvements made thereon. Land at a lower rate than this, is not an object of purchase, as the soil is so thin and poor, that a living cannot be made on it, without manuring every other year with dung or plaster of Paris. West of the mountains in all the old settlements, land may be bought from 80 dollars per acre to 2 dollars. In the state of Ohio, and other new countries, very good land may be bought at two dollars per acre, but this land is in a state of nature, and far distant from any inhabitants. . . . .

The Americans, in general, are a brave and generous people, well informed, hospitable, and kind; it would be, therefore, the duty of emigrants when settled in that country, not to be the first to lend a hand in disturbing the peace of the country—it is the height of ingratitude, as they ought to consider that they have been received, and granted the rights of citizenship; it is their duty, therefore, to lend a hand to nothing that may be injurious to their adopted country. I hope Irish emigrants when they arrive will copy after some of the rules and instructions I have pointed out, which, if it should turn out to their advantage, as I hope it may, would truly be a great happiness and gratification to their countryman and friend.

### 6. English Pioneers in Illinois[1]

During the winter [1817–18] I was preparing and assisting others to prepare for a final emigration in the spring. . . . . I was constantly applied to in person and by letter for information and advice on the

[1] Extract from George Flower, *History of the English Settlement in Edwards County, Illinois, Founded in 1817 and 1818 by Morris Birkbeck and George Flower*

subject of emigration, by persons in every rank, but chiefly from those in moderate circumstances.

In describing western America, and the mode of living there, I found some difficulty in giving a truthful picture to the Englishman who had never been out of England. In speaking of a field, the only field he had ever seen was a plot of ground, from five to fifty acres in extent, surrounded by a ditch, a bank, and a live hawthorn fence; it has two or more well-made gates, that swing freely on their hinges, and clasp firmly when shut. The word field brings this picture to his eye. . . . .

The publication in England of our travels, my return, and personal communication with a host of individuals, had given a wide-spread knowledge of what we had done and what we intended to do. Our call had received a response from the farmers of England, the miners of Cornwall, the drovers of Wales, the mechanics of Scotland, the West-India planter, the inhabitants of the Channel Isles, and the "gentleman of no particular business" of the Emerald Isle. All were moving or preparing to move to join us in another hemisphere. The cockneys of London had decided on the reversal of their city habits, to breathe the fresh air of the prairies. Parties were moving, or preparing to move, in all directions. At one time, the movement appeared as if it would be national. Representatives from each locality, and descendants from every class that I have mentioned, are now living in the English Settlement of Edwards County, Illinois. The preparatory movements were completed. The first act of our drama here properly closes, and the history of the actual emigration, with the accidents and incidents of the journeyings by sea and land, now begins.

Early in March, 1818, the ship "Achilles" sailed from Bristol with the first party of emigrants destined for our settlement in Illinois. . . . .

Forty-four men and one married woman sailed in this ship. The men were chiefly farm laborers and mechanics from Surrey. . . . . Another party, of about equal number, composed of London mechanics, and tradesmen from various parts of England, formed another party that sailed in the same ship. . . . . [This] party landed safely at Philadelphia early in June. They made their way, some in wagons,

---

(Chicago Historical Society's Collection, Vol. I), pp. 92–96, 99–105, 110, 120–29, 165–66, 189–91, 287–90, 313–14, 350–53.

George Flower was the pioneer companion of Morris Birkbeck (see Document 10, p. 43) and had returned to England in 1817 to organize a party of emigrants, to secure money, and to make other preparations for founding the new settlement.

some on horseback, over the mountains to Pittsburgh, then descending the Ohio in flat-boats to Shawneetown, in August, proceeded without delay on foot, in wagons and on horseback, to Mr. Birkbeck's cabin on the Boltenhouse Prairie. . . . .

The next ship with emigrants for the prairies, which sailed from Liverpool in the following month of April, was chartered by myself for the party that came with me. My own immediate family and friends occupied the cabin; my domestic servants, and other emigrants going out to join us, filled the steerage; and my live-stock of cows, hogs, and sheep, of the choicest breeds of England, took up all the spare room on deck. . . . . We arrived without accident at New York, after a passage of fifty days, and but one week after the Bristol ship, that sailed a month before us. To remove all these people and their luggage, and the animals that I had brought, to our Settlement, nearly a thousand miles inland, was no small undertaking, at a time when there was neither turnpike nor railroad, and steam-boats few, and in the infancy of their management. Patience, toil, time, and money were all required and all were freely bestowed.

On reaching land, the ship's party was broken up, and smaller parties were formed of people of similar habits and tastes, clubbing together for mutual assistance on the way. Those of small means, proceeded on without loss of time. Those of more means, lingered a little in the cities, and with their new friends, before taking their departure for what was then the Far West. . . . .

In this manner, the various individuals and parties made the best way they could. Some of them were joined by individuals and families of English, that were lingering on the sea-board, without any specific reference to our Settlement; but seeing the emigration, and having read the publications, joined and went on. I think every accession from the East was English. . . . .

The various objects we had in view, for which I was sent to England, were all accomplished with singular success. My voyage across the Atlantic was of unusual speed. . . . . By a singular coincidence, my father had sold, a few days before my arrival in England, his dwelling and lands in Marden for £23,000, thus giving to himself, my mother, brothers, and sisters, an opportunity of returning with me in the spring, which they willingly embraced, to take up their abode in the prairies. . . . .

On entering the prairie, my large horses were covered with the tall prairie-grass, and laboriously dragged the heavy-laden vehicle. The cabin built for me was well sheltered by wood from the north and east, with an arm of the prairie lying south in a gently descending slope for a quarter of a mile; it was as pretty a situation as could be desired. The cabin could not boast of many comforts. With a clap-board roof, held on by weight-poles, and a rough puncheon floor, it had neither door nor window. Two door-ways were cut out, and the rough logs were scutched down inside. All the chips and ends of logs left by the backwoods builders lay strewed upon the floor. We were now face to face with the privations and difficulties of a first settlement in the wilderness. But greater than all other inconveniences was the want of water. There was no water nearer than the cabin in which the French family lived, a quarter of a mile off. . . . .

For a moment let us glance at the situation of these settlers, a thousand miles inland, at the heels of the retreating Indians. A forest from the Atlantic shore behind them, but thinly settled with small villages, far apart from each other. To the west, one vast uninhabited wilderness of prairie, interspersed with timber, extending two thousand miles to the Pacific Ocean. Excepting St. Louis, on the Mississippi, then a small place, and Kaskaskia, yet smaller, there were no inhabitants west of us. About the same time, one or two small American settlements were forming a few miles east of the Mississippi, as we were planting ourselves a few miles west of the Wabash. . . . .

There were no roads on land, no steam-boats on the waters. The road, so-called, leading to Vandalia (then composed of about a dozen log-houses), was made by one man on horseback following in the track of another, every rider making the way a little easier to find, until you came to some slush, or swampy place, where all trace was lost, and you got through as others had done, by guessing at the direction, often riding at hazard for miles until you stumbled on the track again. And of these blind traces there were but three or four in the southern half of the State. No roads were worked, no watercourses bridged. Before getting to Vandalia, there was a low piece of timbered bottom-land, wet and swampy, and often covered with water, through which every traveler had to make his way as he best could, often at the risk of his life. Such was the state of the country. No man could feel sure that he was within the limits of the State, but from knowing that he was west of the Wabash and east of the Mississippi. We had some difficulties, peculiar to ourselves, as a foreign people. The Americans, by pushing onward and onward for almost two generations, had a training in handling the axe and opening farms, and, from experience, bestowing their labor in the most appropriate manner, which we, from our in-experience, often did not. Fresh from an old country, teeming with the conveniences of civilized life, at once in a wilderness with all our inexperiences, our losses were large from misplaced labor. Many were discouraged, and some returned, but the mass of the settlers stayed, and, by gradual experience, corrected their first errors, thus overcoming difficulties which had well-nigh overcome them. The future success of the Settlement was obtained by individual toil and industry. Of the first inconveniences and sufferings, my family had its full share. . . . .

Emigrants kept coming in, some on foot, some on horseback, and some in wagons. Some sought employment, and took up with such labor as they could find. Others struck out and made small beginnings for themselves. Some, with feelings of petulance, went farther and fared worse; others dropped back into the towns and settlements in Indiana. At first, I had as much as I could do to build a few cabins for the workmen I then employed, and in erecting a large farmyard, a hundred feet square, enclosed by log-buildings, two stories high; also in building for my father's family a house of considerable size, and ap-pointed with somewhat more of comforts than is generally found in new settlements. I had as yet done nothing in erecting buildings for the public in general, as there had been no time. . . . .

The first double-cabin built, was designated for a tavern, and a single one for its stable. . . . . Another and second double and single cabin were occupied as dwelling and shop by a blacksmith. I had brought bellows, anvils, tools, and appliances for three or four black-smith-shops, from the City of Birmingham, England. There were three brothers that came with us, all excellent mechanics, and one of them, a blacksmith, was immediately installed, and went to work. There stood Albion,[1] no longer a myth, but a reality, a fixed fact. A log-tavern and a blacksmith-shop. Two germs of civilization were now planted—one of the useful arts, the other a necessary institution of present civilization. Any man could now get his horse shod and get drunk in Albion, privileges which were soon enjoyed, the latter especially. . . . .

From time to time little parties came in year after year, chiefly small tradesmen and farm-laborers. The latter, a most valuable class, came from all parts of England. The farmers brought with them their various experiences and tools, necessary to work the different soils. In this way a greater variety of workmen and tools are to be found in

[1] [The new settlement had been named "Albion."]

the English Settlement than perhaps in any one neighborhood in England.

Three brothers, Joseph, Thomas, and Kelsey Crackles, able-bodied farm-laborers, from Lincolnshire, came with a full experience in the cultivation of flat, wet land; and brought with them the light fly-tool for digging ditches and drains, by which a practised hand can do double the work that can be done by a heavy steel spade. They lived with me three years before going on farms of their own. Their experience has shown us that the flat, wet prairies, generally shunned, are the most valuable wheat lands we possess. . . . .

It is a noticeable fact that emigrants bound for the English Settlement in Illinois, landed at every port from the St. Lawrence to the Gulf of Mexico. This arises from the fact that the laborers and 'small farmers of England are very imperfectly acquainted with the geography of America. Indeed, among all classes in England there is a very inadequate idea of the extent of the United States. . . , . As various as their ports of debarkation, were the routes they took, and the modes of conveyance they adopted.

Some came in wagons and light carriages, overland; some on horseback; some in arks; some in skiffs; and some by steam-boat, by New Orleans. One Welshman landed at Charleston, S.C. "How did you get here?" I asked. "Oh," he innocently replied, "I just bought me a horse, sir, and inquired the way." It seems our Settlement was then known at the plantations in Carolina and in the mountains of Tennessee. The great variety found among our people, coming as they did from almost every county in the kingdom, in complexion, stature, and dialect, was in the early days of our Settlement very remarkable. . . . .

It will be seen that our position is not on any of the great highways of travel. We caught none of the floating population as they passed. Most of those who came set out expressly to come to us. . . . .

After [a temporary] check to emigration, . . . . the tide began to flow again. Individuals and families were frequently arriving, and occasionally a party of thirty and forty. A fresh cause induced this tide of emigration. It arose from the private correspondence of the first poor men who came. Having done well themselves, and by a few years of hard labor acquired more wealth than they ever expected to obtain, they wrote home to friend or relative an account of their success. These letters handed round in the remote villages of England, in which many of them lived, reached individuals in a class to whom information in book form was wholly inaccessible. Each letter had its scores of readers, and, passing from hand to hand, traversed its scores of miles. The writer, known at home as a poor man, earning perhaps a scanty subsistence by his daily labor, telling of the wages he received, his bountiful living, of his own farm and the number of his live-stock, produced a greater impression in the limited circle of its readers than a printed publication had the power of doing. His fellow-laborer who heard these accounts, and feeling that he was no better off than when his fellow-laborer left him for America, now exerted every nerve to come and do likewise. . . . . In this way we have given to Illinois a valuable population, men that are a great acquisition to the Country. It was observed that these emigrants who came in the second emigration, from five to ten years after the first settlement, complained more of the hardships of the country than those who came first. These would complain of a leaky roof, or a broken fence, and all such inconveniences. The first-comers had no cabins or fences to complain of; with them it was conquer or die. And thus emigrants came dropping in from year to year. . . . .

But it was the class of farm-laborers and small farmers, of whom I have before spoken, that furnished the bone and sinew of the Settlement. Well instructed in all agricultural labor, as plowmen, seedsmen, and drainers of land, habituated to follow these occupations with continuous industry, the result was certain success. Their course was a uniform progress and advance. Many of them without money, and some in debt for their passage, they at first hired out at the then usual price of fifty cents a day without board, and seventy-five cents for haytime and harvest. In two or three years they became tenants, or bought a piece of unimproved Congress-land at a dollar and a quarter an acre, and gradually made their own farms. Several of them, now the wealthiest farmers of the county, earned their first money on my farm at Park House. It is chiefly the labor of these men, extending over twenty, thirty, and even forty years, that has given to the Settlement the many fine farms to be seen around Albion. . . . .

The first years of our settlement, from 1818 to 1825, were spent by our settlers in putting up small houses (chiefly of logs), and shelter of the same sort for the work-horses and other domestic animals used in breaking up and fencing in the prairie for the first fields. In about three years [after 1818], a surplus of corn, pork, and beef was obtained, but no market. Before they could derive any benefit from the sale of their surplus produce, the farmers themselves had to quit their farms and open the channels of commerce, and convey their produce along until they found a market. At first there were no produce-buyers, and the first attempts at mercantile adventures were almost failures. In the rising towns, a few buyers began to appear, but with too small a capital to pay money, even at the low price produce then was. They generally bought on credit, to pay on their return from New Orleans. In this way, the farmers were at disadvantage; if the markets were good, the merchant made a handsome profit. If bad, they often had not enough to pay the farmer. Then the farmers began to build their own flat-boats, load them with the produce of their own growth, and navigate them by their own hands. They traded down the Mississippi to New Orleans, and often on the coast beyond. Thus were the channels of trade opened, and in this way was the chief trade of the country carried on for many years.

Afterward, partly from capital made in the place and foreign capital coming in, trade was established in a more regular way. The farmer is no longer called from his farm, but sells at home to the storekeepers and merchants, now found in all the small but growing towns, from ten to fifteen miles distant from each other, all over the country. They have now sufficient capital to pay for the produce on its delivery. In this way the trade established has continued, excepting in its increasing magnitude.

When considered, the enlarged sphere of action and change of destiny of these farm-laborers of England, now substantial farmers and merchants in our land is truly wonderful. Once poor laborers, their experience comprised within their parish bounds, or the limits of the farm on which they toiled for a bare subsistence; now farmers themselves in another hemisphere, boat-builders, annually taking adventurous trading-voyages of over a thousand miles, and many of them becoming tradesmen and merchants on a large scale, and commanding an amount of wealth they once never dreamed of possessing. And well they deserve their success. They have earned it by perseverance and hard labor, flinching at nothing. . . . .

A valuable experience was gained in the gradual taking up of land. Of course, the most inviting situations were first secured. The last land, left as refuse, was flat, wet prairie, that had not much thickness of hazle mould, so much sought after by the farmer. The surface wet, but aridly dry in summer, with a subsoil of whitish clay. The Americans said they could not get a living off such land. The English laborers, by a little judicious ditching, which made part of their fencing, found it to be the best soil for small grain and meadow in the country.
. . . .

Another favorable circumstance was the happy adaptation of the country to the settlers. Had our European settlers been placed in a heavy-timbered country, they would have desponded, despaired, and died. The cost of denuding a heavy-wooded district of its timber and preparing it for cultivation, is not less than twelve dollars an acre. What a source of national wealth this item is to a state like Illinois, with its thirty-six million acres of prairie land. Every individual, thus fortunately placed, is saved a generation of hard and unprofitable labor. This circumstance is not sufficiently appreciated by a pioneer settler.

One element of success may be traced to a happy proportion among the settlers of men of money, men of intelligence, and men of toil. A settlement all of needy laborers would have suffered much, and would probably have dispersed, . . . . as many others have done. It was the men of property that sustained the weight of the Settlement for the first five years, not only by its first supply of food and the building of its first houses, but in hiring the laborers as they came from the old country. This gave to the poor, but hard-working man, some knowledge of the ways of the country, while he was laying up a little store of money for his independent beginning. The sterling qualities found in the great bulk of the English laborers and little farmers, is another element of success. Their general sobriety, persevering industry, and habitual hard work, carried them through periods of long discouragements to final success. The first founders gave what they had of ability and money to the very last. All these circumstances working together have given that solid prosperity, which is characteristic of the English Settlement in Illinois.

### 7. Advice to Emigrants[1]

The torrent of emigration from Europe has for nearly forty years run in an unexampled manner towards the United States of North America. This infant and rising empire has received and nourished a part of the inhabitants of every country in the old world. The tide of emigration at present in a great measure has ceased to flow; but vast numbers yet fixing their longing eyes upon this "land of promise," have resolved at all hazards to go and reside in this transatlantic hemisphere. Before any persons determine to emigrate, they ought

[1] Extract from Isaac Holmes, *An Account of the United States of America, Derived from Actual Observation, during a Residence of Four Years in That Republic* (London, 1823), chap. vii, pp. 121–38.

seriously to reflect upon the measure. To leave country, friends, and relations, and fix their residence in a distant land, where the habits and the feelings of the people are so different, where there are none to rejoice in their prosperity, and where the voice of sympathy or condolence will not be heard in their afflictions, are circumstances which should be sufficient to cause every one duly to weigh the advantages or disadvantages of removal. When to this are added, the extremes of the climate of the United States, which are so disagreeable to Englishmen—the expense and trouble of a voyage across the Atlantic—and the risk of not succeeding in America: these, and many more reasons, demand a pause from all, before they take such an important step as to remove a family to this distant region.

Those who are in affluence in England, living upon the income or interest of their property, ought by no means to entertain the idea of emigrating thither. In the large cities of the United States, the expense of maintaining and educating a family will be little less than in Great Britain. Although there are no internal taxes to the general government, and the taxes to the state government will not exceed one-sixteenth of the rental of the dwelling; and although butcher's-meat, fish, vegetables, wine, spirituous liquors, &c. are cheaper than in England; yet house rent, fuel, servants' wages, and clothing, will nearly make up the difference. In the small towns and villages of that country, a family can be supported at one-third less expense than in the large cities; but a family residing in some villages in England, living in a careful and frugal manner, would be much more comfortable than they possibly could be in the United States, and the expense would not be much greater. That degree of freedom which the servants and lower orders assume in America, is really disagreeable to those who have not been accustomed to it. We may speak in favour of equality; but the fact is, that nearly all who advocate this doctrine "wish to reduce every one to the equality of themselves; but they by no means wish to raise those who are below or beneath them to their own level."

Another description of persons will find great difficulty in succeeding; these are, schoolmasters, clerks, attorneys, &c. Education being very easily attained in the Eastern New England States, there are always many Americans of these descriptions wanting employment.

Another class of individuals ought to be very cautious before they embark for the United States; these are weavers, cotton-spinners, and working manufacturers. The manufactures of America are yet in their infancy, and those workmen who can procure employment obtain good wages; but I have met with many, who, having travelled in vain from Massachusetts to Maryland, and from thence to the Western Country, in quest of employment, have expended what little they had saved in Britain, and have actually experienced great distress. Not having been accustomed to agricultural work, they were wholly unfit for it: unless this description of persons can obtain a certain or positive engagement, I would by no means advise them to emigrate.

The lower class of labourers will obtain employment during the harvest months; but in winter it will be difficult to find work. In New York, Philadelphia, and Baltimore, during the winter, the labourers are often reduced to great wretchedness: fuel is frequently enormously high; and those who have been in a country where the thermometer is sometimes several degrees below zero, or the freezing point, will be able to form an opinion of the sufferings of a family without fire, and with but little clothing.

Merchants, tradesmen, shopkeepers, and manufacturers, might probably succeed . . . . yet even in these departments there is a great risk for strangers, as they have to seek for connections, and to become acquainted with the mode of transacting business; and perhaps by the time they have acquired such knowledge, and obtained such connections, their resources are exhausted.

For the wealthy farmer, I do not believe that at present there are any inducements to emigrate, the price of all agricultural productions being so low. But the small farmer, who has resided near a town, who has a family, and has been accustomed to raise poultry and vegetables, and who understands well the management of milch cows, might succeed near any of the large cities in the United States; but such an one ought to take about five hundred pounds with him, to enable him to purchase and stock a small farm.

Industrious labouring mechanics, tailors, shoemakers, joiners, blacksmiths, &c. will find employment throughout the Union. I would, however, advise them, upon landing at the large sea-port towns or cities, not to remain there expending what little money they possess, but to leave immediately for some small town or village. If they land at New York, in the western part of that state, they are as likely to meet with employment as in any part of the United States. If they should arrive at New Orleans in November or December, they might remain there until June or July, and it is probable they will obtain work at high wages, about two dollars per day; and the females, by sewing or washing, may make nearly as much. Whoever goes thither should not remain there during the sickly months. By means of the numerous steamboats, they can go to a more healthy situation, and fix upon some place as a permanent settlement.

I have met with some mechanics, who have been much dissatisfied, and have deplored the circumstance of their quitting England; others, on the contrary, have expressed themselves in a different manner. One blacksmith, in a small town in one of the Eastern States, informed me, that by working only four hours in the day, he could maintain himself and family very comfortably. A tailor, in a town in New Jersey, with whom I had a conversation relative to his returning to England, spoke as follows: "I should indeed be foolish to think of returning. Here I can obtain work at a price at least one-third higher than in England; there it was with great difficulty I could get employment. Certainly, the climate and many other things are disagreeable, but that corroding anxiety of not knowing whether I could maintain myself, is removed; and this more than recompenses me for coming hither." This man had endured great distress in England; but in the United States, he, with five females, whom he kept at work (young ladies, as they are there called), had full employment.

In New York, on the contrary, I have met with some mechanics, who stated, that the high price of fuel and house-rent made their situation no better with the wages of one dollar and a half per day, than what it was in England. For two comfortable rooms, in the large cities or towns, the rent would be nearly fifteen pounds English money per annum. When good Liverpool coals are sold in the city of New York at thirteen dollars the chaldron, it is considered as cheap a fuel as can be there consumed. This will give a tolerably accurate idea of the expense of fuel in the larger cities.

Mr. Birkbeck,[1] in his letters from Illinois, has given a highly flattering description of the Western Country. He has published several statements, to prove the advantage of working a farm there. In these calculations he has valued Indian corn or maize, which is the chief product there, at five dollars the barrel: but what has been the price in 1821? not even one-half, and consequently all his calculations are of no account. Indian corn, and also wheat, sold at New Orleans in the spring of 1821, at the low price of 25 cents, or $12\frac{3}{4}d$. English [money], the Winchester bushel. . . . .

The man of education, likewise, will feel his situation uncomfortable, if he reside in a back settlement. There will be none with whom

[1] [For an extract from Birkbeck, see Section I, page 43.

to associate, and his remarks will often be laughed at. His only resource will be books; these are agreeable companions; and it is often delightful for a literary character to indulge, alone, in reading and meditation: but if there be none to whom he can communicate the knowledge he has acquired from books, and the speculations in which he has indulged, he will lose the zest or relish for scientific pursuits. . . . .

An emigrant cannot be too much on his guard before he involves his property by purchasing land. For one person who wishes to buy land in the United States, there are a thousand who are desirous to sell. In all the large sea-port cities, there are societies, whose object is to give information to emigrants: application may be made to one or more of these societies; but especially let the speculatist apply to some respectable individual for information. Let no one purchase any land without examining it; and, if possible, let him get the advice of some good practical farmer, who has long cultivated land in the neighbourhood of the spot he thinks of purchasing: the opinion of such an one would be of great benefit. I would also caution every person against purchasing a farm, unless it had a never-failing brook or stream of water in, or running through, the land: for in a country like the United States, where the dry weather in summer continues so long, it is of great importance to have a supply of water for the cattle, &c.

Birkbeck advises new comers to "head the tide of emigration," that is, to go far west to some of the new states. I by no means give that advice. There are many farms in the old-settled states, well situated, with good houses, barns, and a quantity of cleared land, which, although it may not be very productive in its present condition, with labour and manure might be easily restored: much less labour would also be required than to clear forest land, for which work Europeans are by no means calculated. The Yankees, or people from the Eastern States, will clear as much in one day as an European in three.

Some of the Americans are of a very roving disposition, moving from the Eastern States to the Ohio; there they purchase farms, and erect houses, and barns, clear a quantity of land, and plant peach and apple orchards. If a purchaser offers, they will dispose of this, and move to some other state, and do the same; and thus they will continue to move until they are obstructed by the shores of the Pacific Ocean. It is better for an European to give ten or fifteen dollars an acre for land, where there is a house and other buildings erected, and a quantity of cleared land, than to give half a dollar an acre for forest land, where he would have to erect a log-house, &c., to cut down trees, make fences, and encounter all other difficulties, which would require years of hard labour to overcome.

## 8. An Englishman in the Western Country, 1819[1]

INGLE'S REFUGE, BANKS OF OHIO, STATE OF INDIANA

25th December, 1819

*Once for all, from an inquiring Englishman in the United States to the Editor of the Stamford News*

SIR: To my esteemed friends and countrymen, living within the wide circuit of your paper, and expecting many long-promised epistles, say that the task is impracticable, and therefore justly abandoned. What they need, truth, is always difficult to attain; and a correct impression of things, made by weight of unwilling, or long-concealed evidence, examined and cross-examined, will, perhaps, be found in my journal, calculated to undeceive, disappoint, and, as usual, offend, nearly all those of whom, and for whom, I have written.

It is, I regret to say, too true, that the writings of emigrants, however respectable, present a partial or unfaithful portraiture; "shewing things as they should be, not as they are." Such authority, then, is questionable and deceptive. Each individual destined never to return, wants, and tempts, his friends to follow; the motive, perhaps, is innocent, or venial, but the consequences are evil and disastrous. . . . .

My inquiries have been, as promised, directed to one grand object; that of ascertaining, by first-rate means, the past and present condition, and future prospects, of British emigrants, and the consequent good or evil of emigration, in the hope of clearly defining and exposing its character, so that it may no longer remain a doubtful or desperate enterprize, a journey in the dark, alternately praised or blamed, but a cause, attaching to it certain consequences, which, for some persons to embrace, or shun, is become a visible, tangible, matter of duty.

To my countrymen disposed to emigrate, but who can, by increased exertion, keep their unequalled comforts and honour unimpaired, I would say, in a voice which should be heard from shore to shore, Stay where you are; for neither America, nor the world, have anything to offer you in exchange! But to those of decreasing means, and increasing families, uprooted, withering, and seeking a transplantation some-

---

[1] Extract from W. Faux, *Memorable Days in America: Being a Journal of a Tour to the United States, Principally Undertaken to Ascertain, by Positive Evidence, the Condition and Probable Prospects of British Emigrants* (London, 1823), pp. 328-31.

where, full of hard, dirty-handed industry, and with means sufficient for location here, I would say, Haste away; you have no other refuge from poverty, which, in England, is crime, punishable with neglect, and contempt everlasting! But, if you come, come one, and all of you, male and female, in your working jackets, with axes, ploughshares, and pruning-hooks in your hands, prepared long to suffer many privations, expecting to be your own servants, no man's masters; to find liberty and independence, anything but soft indulgence; and America, a land only of everlasting, well-rewarded labour. Thus, morally and physically qualified, the dark, lonely wilds and interminable forests, which now surround me, shall bow before you, yielding to your cultivation every common good thing, but not satisfaction, which is not of earthly growth! For you, even you escaped from prisons and pauperism, will, sometimes, "hang your harps on the willow, and weep," when you remember distant England. Very few emigrants, whatsoever may have been their disgusts and evils in the old country, or their successes in the new, can forget their "dear native land." The recollection is, indeed, an impediment to their prosperity; distance only enhances her value, and, as a much-loved, ungrateful mistress, her charms only are remembered and cherished. This seems an indestructible feeling; the incurable mania of the British exile.

I am now living on wild bucks and bears, mixed up, and barbarizing with men almost as wild as they; men systematically unprincipled, and in whom the moral sense seems to have no existence; this is the lot of all coming here. The climate is not good in any season, and though better here than east of the mountains, is yet unfriendly to industry everywhere. Summer, amidst breezy shades, champagne and brandy; and winter, with two down beds, one over and one under you, and a hiccory fire continually, are just tolerable! The autumn is pleasant enough, but too generally pestilential.

Having to commence in the morning, a journey of one thousand miles, on horseback, on my way to England, through the Cities of Washington and Charleston, and the worst roads and weather in the universe, the mercury being now three degrees below zero; riding, and not writing, presses on the attention of, Sir,

Your obedient servant,

W. FAUX

## 9. Letters from a Family of English Paupers Emigrated at Parish Expense[1]

SERIES I

SENECA, COUNTY OF ONTARIO, STATE OF NEW YORK

August 13, 1820

DEAR FATHER: We left Brunswick on the 8th last March. The severity of the winter determined me to take this step. We proceeded up the river St. John towards Quebec. On our way we encountered great difficulties, arising from the cold, and the country being almost an entire wilderness through which we passed. From Quebec we proceeded up the river St. Lawrence to Montreal; from thence to Kingston, and up the lake to Niagara, where we crossed over into the United States, and travelled east into the State of New York, 100 miles, to the English settlement (as it is here called), where I now live, but do not intend to remain here long; the land is all taken up, and too dear for a person in my circumstances to buy. The Ohio is my ultimate object; there land may be had in plenty for a dollar and a quarter, or 5s. 6d. sterling, per acre. I arrived here about the middle of June and have been for the principal part of the time since, in the employ of a Mr. Watson, an Englishman, from Northumberland, of whom I bought a cow, for which I paid him in work, besides supporting my family. An honest, industrious man can maintain his family better by three days' work here, than he can in England by six. . . . .

Your dutiful son,

JOHN WATSON

AURORA, DEARBORN COUNTY, INDIANA STATE

June 15, 1822

DEAR FATHER: . . . . Hearing a more favorable account of the State of Indiana, I once more started on a ramble, and, travelling across the State of New York, I came to O'Lean Point, on the Alleghany river; which river, a very rapid one, I came down in a flat boat to Pittsburg; here I staid two days, and, passing on, after being detained by head winds, and the waters being very low, landed at Aurora, situated at the mouth of Hogan Creek. Here I found myself a stranger, without friends, acquaintance, utensils of any kind, or money, having spent

---

[1] Extract from William Cobbett, *The Emigrant's Guide; in Ten Letters Addressed to the Tax-Payers of England* (new ed.; London, 1830), pp. 46–61.

our last dollar a day or two before; added to which, myself and all our family were caught by illness for six or eight weeks, without the power of doing anything. But no sooner was our situation known, than we had plenty of provisions brought to us, and, as our strength recovered, I obtained work at digging, &c. My wife took in sewing, and, by degrees, we have worked it to that I have 2 cows, 2 calves, 9 pigs, and one calf expected in August. James is now at school, and I intend to send two in the winter. I have joined with a farmer in cropping; that is, I received one-half of the produce, and had the team found me. I now am working for an English gentleman, named Harris, who is building in Aurora, and owns four quarter-sections up the creek. Much good land can be bought, not far distant, for one dollar and a quarter per acre, and improved land for not much more; indeed, so good is the prospect for a man who must live by industry, that I wish all my friends and acquaintances were here with me. I can safely say, I would not, nor would my Mary, return to England on any account whatever. We are now all in good health, and very desirous of hearing from you. . . . .

I remain yours,

JOHN WATSON

AURORA, DEARBORN COUNTY, INDIANA
April 26, 1823

DEAR FATHER: I now write with greater pleasure than I have ever yet done, as it is in answer to yours, dated February the 2nd, the only one I have received; the others, I suppose, must have gone to Canada, where you might think I was settled. It proved very gratifying to us to hear that you all enjoy such general good health, excepting father Vaughn and sister, who could not have been expected to remain long, having been ill so long. Though your letter was written by several persons, we cannot answer them separately, but must beg of you to read all to them. . . . . We would recommend all our acquaintances, who are tired of paying tithes and taxes, to come here, where tithes are unknown, and taxes hardly worth mentioning, compared to what they are with you. The only tax we have paid is one day's work on the road, and 50 cents, or 2s, 3d. for one yoke of oxen. You say England is in a very bad state, and farmers are got very low. We would say, let them come here; we were worth nothing when we landed at this place, and now we have one yoke of oxen, 1 cow, 9 hogs. . . . . Brother Stephen inquires if he could get employment; we answer, that any person desirous of obtaining a living may do it and that easily; if he comes, let him bring all the money he can, and what clothing he has; but not to spend any money in buying unnecessary things in England; here the money will pay him much better than there in land. . . . . Mary begs you will be particular in mentioning her relation in your next letter, which you must not be angry if we ask to be written closer, so as to contain more information, as the postage of letters is rather expensive; not that we grudge the money, but we think the sheet might be made to hold more. . . . .

Your ever dutiful and affectionate children,

JOHN AND MARY WATSON

AURORA, March 9, 1825

DEAR FATHER AND MOTHER: It is now two years since we heard from you, excepting in a letter from brother Stephen, saying you were all well. . . . . We should be very glad to hear from all our friends; we think they would do a great deal better here than in England; we cannot think what makes so many of them go back, for we would not come back again for Mr. Tidden Smith's farm and all he has got. The poor home-sick things! were it not for their poor children, we would not care if they went to bed without supper all their lives! As for brother Stephen, we should like to know if he has gone back too; for we expected him this last winter, but have been disappointed; we are rather uneasy at not receiving a letter before this; if you know anything about him, we should be glad if you would let us know. We are still farming, have got this season about 10 acres of very promising wheat, 7 acres of oats, 13 acres of corn, 1 acre for flax, between 1 and 2 acres for potatoes, and other garden stuff. We have got a horse, a yoke of oxen, a pair of young steers, a milch cow, and plenty of pigs and fowls. There are plenty of English people in and around our neighborhood: we rent land of an English woman. . . . .

From your affectionate son and daughter,

JOHN AND MARY WATSON

SERIES 2. FROM THE BROTHER OF THE PRECEDING

ALBANY, October 5, 1823

DEAR FATHER AND MOTHER: This comes with our kind love to you, and all brothers and sisters, and all friends, hoping to find you all in good health; for all our children have been ill . . . . and we are got to Albany safe. We was about 7 weeks on passage to New York. We stopped at New York a week, and then sailed to Albany, which is 165 miles; and we was seasick about 16 days; and I went up to Utica, which is 96 miles, and I could not find the country any better up there than at Albany; so I returned back to my family again. And a gentleman has took Jane, and he is to keep and clothe and send her to school; and Thomas, Mr. William Fisher has taken. And John Gardiner has found his brothers; and James Gardiner is moved from where he was at first; and we see Richard Cutney at New York, and he was very well, and he talked of coming to England again, and to send a particular account of what Thomas Rolfe said when he got back to England. But not to make yourselves any ways uneasy about us ne'er the more for his coming back; for if we can't get a living, here is a poor-house just the same as in England; and they will keep us till the spring, and then send us back to England; for there is thousands of Irish here. And if I can't support my family, I shall come back in the spring; for if a man can't support his family, they will send him back in the spring to England again; for I had not got half money enough to get up to my brother; so I wrote to him, and I have not had any answer as yet; but when I get an answer I will send to you again; and I can't give you any good account about coming as yet, for there is so many Irish keep coming every day, and they work so cheap, that it makes it bad for labouring people; and we live neighbours with James Fisher and Richard Fuller from Bodiam. And the ways of the people and the country is very different from what they are in England; and the land is not half so good; for when they clear land, as they call it, they chop the wood off about 2 feet from the ground, and then plough and sow between the stubs: and it is most the Indian corn in this part of the country. William is at work filling waggons with the stuff that comes out of the canal. I have $4 per week. A dollar is 3 shillings of New York State money. People work very hard here; for they work from sun-rising to sun-set; cattle the same. . . . .

Your dutiful son and daughter,

STEPHEN AND ELIZABETH WATSON

ALBANY, March 29, 1824

HONOURED FATHER AND MOTHER: We received your letter on the 23rd instant, and are happy to hear you are all in good health, as it leaves us. I have to inform you that I have had a good winter's work at sawing, and have no reason to complain of America. I don't wish to persuade any person to come to this country, but I am doing better here than I was in England. A man by industry can get a good living here. I was soon discouraged when I first came over; but now I am more used to the ways and customs of the people, I like it better. . . . . There are so many English people here that it seems much like home. We don't begrudge any one the pleasure we left behind us, for we are a good deal better off. The laws of this country are as good as in England. The poor are well taken care of; there is a large house in this place for the accommodation for the old and infirm that are not able to work. We can get our children educated better than we could at your place. The free school here is on the Lancastrian system; it has 400 scholars, both rich and poor, who pay according to their abilities; some pay one dollar a quarter, and some not more than a shilling sterling; the scholars are taught reading, writing, arithmetic, geography, &c. We remain,

Your dutiful children,<br>STEPHEN AND ELIZABETH WATSON

ALBANY, October 27, 1825

MY DEAR GRANDPARENTS: . . . . We hope you will write to us as soon as you get this letter, and send word whether uncle is coming or not. I was sorry to hear the parish said they would not send any more. Father has had a very good summer's work at sawing. He is now at work in the malt-house for this winter. We have got a very good house to live in, and well furnished; better than we had in England. . . . .

Your very affectionate granddaughter,<br>MARY JANE WATSON

### 10. Immigration of Skilled Workmen[1]

BLACKBURN, April 7, 1827

There is undoubtedly a very great tendency to emigrate, produced by the utter inability of the weaver to obtain adequate wages. They who are already barely able to sustain their families, and are almost starved, of course remain at home, because they have not the means of removing; but immense numbers who find that circumstances are rapidly hurrying them into that state, are now leaving this neighbourhood. I was told last week, that no fewer than fifty families had left

[1] Extract from a communication received by the Select Committee on Emigration from the United Kingdom, 1827. See *Minutes of Evidence*, pp. 301-2.

Blackburn in the preceding week, for the United States of America. The Committee will observe, that these are not paupers, but industrious families, who fly from the pauperism which stares them in the face. Consequently, although the abstraction of any given number of operatives, as it must diminish the number of hands that demand employment, does good, by tending to bring the demand and supply nearer to a level, it does not in the least diminish the present frightful burden of our poor's rates. The emigrants now go to the United States, because they there hope for employment as weavers. It would require some strong inducement to make them turn their thoughts to agriculture; and unless a sufficient motive to make them prefer settling in our own colonies is put before them by our government, the stream of emigration will run on (and must increase prodigiously) in the same channel. I last week saw a letter from a person in Philadelphia who left Blackburn last year, stating that for weaving a striped calico, he could earn from $4\frac{1}{2}$ to 6 dollars per week; in Blackburn, he would not earn much more than the same number of shillings. It is high time for His Majesty's government to take the subject of emigration into consideration, systematically, and as a part of the country's policy to be steadily pursued. Were proper channels opened, and adequate encouragement given to emigrate, the country would be repaid by the flourishing state of our colonies, and by their trade; and the system would go so far to prevent the accumulated misery occasioned by such convulsions as we have witnessed last year. Radicalism and disaffection would disappear gradually, if persons who cannot get an honest livelihood by their industry at home, had a certain prospect of independence and prosperity in our colonies. It cannot happen otherwise than that such persons continually (every 5 or 7 years, perhaps) thrown into involuntary idleness, half fed, and half clothed, will lay the blame on their rulers, and become discontented and seditious. . . . . At present our emigrants all flock to America, where they enrich a foreign state by their labour and mechanical skill, and imbibe there the opinions and feelings of the state, where they are adopted as citizens; they become *Americanis ipsis Americaniores*, nor do they retain much, if any, regard for that native country, which they quitted in distress and discontent. Thus does England's indifference to emigration operate mischievously to her interests, by swelling the number of her commercial enemies, and enabling them to establish a successful competition with her manufactures.

## 11. Economic Opportunities of the United States Compared with Canada[1]

*You said that the general opinion in Canada was, that after sixteen months' probation, as you termed it, the demand in the United States would carry the settlers there; what is the nature of the demand you there alluded to?*—I state the opinion as existing, I do not pretend to give reasons for it.

*What is the nature of the demand that you alluded to?*—Employment in working on the canals and other public works.

*Although labourers from England and Ireland may from time to time find advantageous employment immediately upon landing in the Canadas, without money or capital, and ultimately become prosperous settlers, must not that employment depend upon the demand existing at the moment for the services of such labourers; and if the supply of labour were too great, would not that employment be out of the question?*—There can be no doubt that for two or three years there will be great difficulty in finding employment for a very extensive voluntary emigration; by extensive voluntary emigration I mean from fifty to sixty thousand souls per annum; we know that the ordinary emigration, which has usually amounted to ten thousand souls, has found very little difficulty in placing itself, whether in the Canadas or in the United States is a matter of indifference, but it has found very little difficulty in placing itself. Latterly, it is true that on their first landing some little inconvenience has been experienced at Quebec, from the sick and destitute who formed a part of the emigration, and inconvenience has also been experienced during the winter season from a large portion of those who have found employment during the summer, being thrown out of work. . . . .

*You state that a person arriving [in Quebec] without any money at all, by getting work on the canals that were going on in the United States, afterwards found the means of settling himself?*—That is very frequently the case.

*You are understood to state that emigrants have arrived there in considerable numbers, and in consequence of a canal that was cutting in the United States, a number of those persons worked upon that canal till they got a sufficient sum of money to settle themselves either in the United States or in the Canadas?*—It has very frequently occurred that settlers have

---

[1] Extract from Great Britain, *Minutes of Evidence before Select Committee on Emigration from the United Kingdom, 1827*, pp. 120–22, testimony of W. B. Felton Esq.

collected sufficient capital to commence their operations, by the wages gained during one summer's good work on those canals; but it does not follow that their establishment was perfect; they were obliged to work out the next summer, and the next summer after that, to place their families in as independent a situation as they would be in if they had been furnished with twelve months' provision in the outset.

*If the English government should carry on any similar work in the Canadas, of course a considerable number of emigrants may also dispose of themselves by the wages of labour which they may obtain on such works?*—Unquestionably they might, and to much greater advantage than by gaining an equal sum of money in the United States, for this simple reason, that the habits of life acquired in the United States are not favourable to accumulation of money; a man who passes the whole summer at work upon the canals in the United States learns to live as an American, and he expends as much subsistence in the course of a week, in the support of himself individually, as would support the whole of his family; whereas if he never removes out of the Canadas into the United States, he retains the habits of frugality that he carried with him from Europe, and instead of eating three flesh meals a day, accompanied with tea and cream, and so on, he will be satisfied with a small quantity of meat and other inferior food sufficiently nourishing and wholesome for his purpose, but unaccompanied with the expensive comforts of an American meal; he will therefore be richer, thirty or forty per cent, at the end of the year than he would be if he had gone to the United States.

## 12.  "Reflections on the Subject of Emigration"[1]

### A

My object is two-fold—it is not merely to point out the description of persons to whom emigration to this country would be advantageous, but also to hold out a beacon to those to whom it would be unadvisable to remove hither. Many a man in comfortable circumstances in Europe, allured by golden dreams, has shipwrecked his fortunes by change of hemisphere.

[1] Extracts from Mathew Carey, *Miscellaneous Essays* (Philadelphia, 1830), pp. 120–21, 144, and 321–24. These two extracts are interesting as the reflections of an extremely successful Irish immigrant. The first extract is from "Reflections on the Subject of Emigration from Europe, with a View to a Settlement in the United States, Containing a Brief Sketch of the Moral and Political State of this Country," (May 25, 1826), and the second is from "Emigration from Ireland and Immigration into the United States" (1828).

While the United States have the capacity of maintaining hundreds of millions of inhabitants beyond their present numbers, . . . . Great Britain and Ireland, and many other parts of Europe, are groaning under a superabundant population, whose condition, in various countries, is gradually deteriorating, by the increasing competition for employment. It is not a very overstrained figure to say, that they are literally devouring each other. Is it not, therefore, highly desirable that such an understanding should prevail on the subject, as will enable one country to part with what it can so advantageously spare, and another to receive that of which it is in want, and which it can of course so advantageously receive? Not only would the condition of those emigrating, but of those who remained behind, be improved. Every hundred or thousand persons who emigrate from an overstocked country, increase the value of the labour, and improve the prospect of happiness, of those who remain. To produce this happy result is one of the objects of this publication.

Great Britain incurs great expense in promoting emigration from Ireland to the Cape of Good Hope and to Canada, in order to lessen the population of that ill-fated country. It would be a national benefit, therefore, to the British government, to open an asylum for distressed Irish in this country, and thus save it from the expense of their removal.

The superabundance of the unemployed population of Ireland arises from the ruinous policy of the government, and the extravagant drains of the national wealth by the absentees, being no less than $13,500,000 per annum. The same effect is produced in Great Britain by the wonderful improvement of machinery, which supersedes the labour of the working classes, reduces their wages in many cases to the minimum of the support of a mere existence; and in some, even below that wretched modicum, thus sinking a large proportion of them into the degraded state of paupers. . . . . [1]

There is scarcely any limit to the number of labourers, who are now and probably will be for twenty years to come, wanted in this country. The spirit of internal improvement, in canals, railroads, and turnpikes, is wide awake in every part of the union; and creates a great demand for that class, of which the number of native citizens bears no proportion to the demand. The Irish labourers are found uncommonly hardy and active, and for years have done a large portion of the work on

[1] [The essay contains newspaper extracts regarding unemployment and distress in England.]

canals and turnpikes. Their wages average about seventy-five cents per day, or four dollars and a half per week. Their board, which includes meat every day, and often twice a day, costs about two dollars, leaving a balance of about two dollars and a half, or 11s. 3d. sterling, which is far more than the whole of their earnings in their own country.

## B

The distressed situation of the Irish nation, particularly the working classes, from the redundance of population, and the want of adequate employment for them, even at the lowest possible rate to support existence, is well known, and has excited the sympathy of the humane and benevolent in this country.[1] Potatoes, one of the most abundant productions of the fruits of the earth, and perhaps the cheapest article of food, constitute three-fourths of the sustenance of nine-tenths of the labouring classes in Ireland. Thousands of them do not partake of animal food more than once a year.[2] A failure of the crop of potatoes produces famine—famine produces a species of pestilence—and this sometimes carries off its thousands and tens of thousands, who perish in the most deplorable state of destitution. One hundred and fifty thousand have been tenants of hospitals in one year.

On the other hand, the public works of the United States suffer great disadvantage from a deficiency of labourers, of whom 30,000 would be able to procure immediate employment in this country, and wages to which they could never, in the wildest range of their imagination, have dared to aspire in their own country.

There is, moreover, a great scarcity of hands for country labour, so many of the persons usually employed in that department being employed on canals and turnpikes. The harvest has suffered in various places in consequence of this scarcity.

This deficiency of labourers has greatly increased the rate of wages; a dollar, and a dollar and a half per day, with board, have been given to country labourers of late in this state. . . . .

I venture to propose a remedy, of easy application, and requiring only the co-operation of a few active individuals, and a very small sum of money.

[1] "The applicants for labour being so much above the demand, that they earn almost nothing, not even sixpence a day." (*British Report on Emigration* (1827), p. 111.)

[2] "The lower orders are in general very poor. Their usual food is potatoes and milk." (Mason's *Statistical Survey of Ireland*, II, 96.)

Let a suitable agent be appointed to proceed forthwith to Ireland, with an authenticated statement of the situation of this country—the unparalleled advantages it holds out to the labouring classes as to food and clothing—the wages of labour—the prices of provisions—together with all the other items of information necessary to make them perfectly acquainted with what they have to expect, so that they may not be discouraged by exaggerated difficulties or embarrassments—nor, on the other hand, be led to indulge in golden dreams, or to form extravagant expectations, likely to end in disappointment.

The emigrants from Ireland and from other countries may be divided into two great classes; those who are able to pay for their passage, and those whose poverty precludes them from this advantage.

For the former all that is necessary, in order to bring over thousands and tens of thousands annually, is to give them correct information, and to have associations in our sea-ports to direct them where to locate themselves in the interior, to prevent the waste of their slender means on their landing, and to guard them against becoming a prey to designing persons—a fate that has happened to too many of them heretofore.

The other class, unable to pay for their passage, will have to bind themselves for a term of time, adequate to compensate by their labour, for the expense of their passage, and the risk of sickness and of death. This subject requires great consideration.

Redemptioners, as they are called, have heretofore been greatly oppressed, and advantage been taken of their necessities. They have been bound for three and four years, and sometimes for five, which have appeared to them somewhat like an eternity. Their fetters bore hard on them, and they, accordingly, have frequently been discontented, sullen and dogged, and run away.

To avoid this result, and do impartial justice to both parties, it is proposed that the term of servitude be reduced to that point, which will afford a remuneration for the expense of passage, and the risk of sickness and death. Let us examine what is that point.

A steerage passage from Ireland is 12 dollars; provisions probably 15 dollars, say on the whole 27 dollars. Wages of labour on canals vary from 10 to 15 dollars per month, exclusive of board—say only 10. If, therefore, a canal contractor had the faithful service of an active redemptioner for three months, he would stand merely on the same ground as if he, for that period, hired a free labourer at the minimum of current wages. But as various contingencies may arise—among the rest, sickness, which would subject the contractor to expense and loss, I presume that the period of servitude might with propriety be fixed, for the present, at six months. This would save in wages, enough, beyond the passage money, to insure against every contingency. The period of service, too, would be so short, that there would be little temptation to, or danger of, elopement. . . . .

With regard to the immigrants it is delightful to reflect on the advantages this plan holds out to them. It will transport them from the extreme of poverty and wretchedness; from the most abject state of existence, to superabundance of food, good clothing, and the prospect—honesty, frugality, and industry presumed—of acquiring independence and wealth in due season! Those who may be the happy instruments of producing this result to 20, 25, or 30,000, persons per annum, will find it balm to their souls at the time when they shall be about to "shuffle off this mortal coil."

Numerous instances are to be found throughout this country, of Irish labourers on canals, who landed two or three years since in extreme poverty, and are now comfortably settled in small houses of their own.

### 13. Economic Advantages of Emigration to the Mother Country[1]

The word "colony" is used to express very different ideas. A conquered nation, among whom the victors do not settle, even a mere factory for trade, has commonly been termed a colony; as, for example, the English factories in India, and the actual dominion of the English in that country. Mere stations, also, for military or trading purposes, such as Malta or Heligoland, go by the name of colonies. In like manner the penal settlements, or distant jails of the English, are superintended by their colonial ministers, and were called colonies even when their whole population consisted of prisoners and keepers. Two societies more different than the people of India ruled by the servants of a London trading company, and the convicts of New South Wales, before Englishmen not criminals began to settle there, could not well be imagined. But the difference between the ideas often expressed by the term colony is matched by the caprice with which that term is used. The settlements of the Greeks in Sicily and Asia Minor, independent states from the beginning, have always been termed colonies; the English settlements in America were termed colonies, though in local matters they governed themselves from the beginning, so long as England monopolized their foreign trade and managed their external rela-

[1] Extract from Edward Gibbon Wakefield, *England and America: A Comparison of the Social and Political State of Both Nations* (New York, 1834), pp. 237–59.

tions; but from the time when England attempted to interfere with their domestic government, and happily lost both the monopoly of their foreign trade and the management of their foreign relations, they have not been reckoned as colonies. According to the loose way in which this term has been used, it is not dependence that constitutes a colony; nor is it the continual immigration of people from distant places, since in this respect the United States surpass all other countries. In order to express the idea of a society which continually receives bodies of people from distant places, and sends out bodies of people to settle permanently in new places, no distinctive term has yet been used. This, however, is the idea which will be expressed whenever the term colony is used here; the idea of a society at once immigrating and emigrating, such as the United States of America and the English settlements in Canada, South Africa, and Australia.

For the existence of a colony two things are indispensable; first, waste land, that is, land not yet the property of individuals, but liable to become so through the intervention of government; and secondly, the migration of people; the removal of people to settle in a new place. Further, it will be seen at once, that this migration must be of two kinds; first, the removal of people from an old to a new country; secondly, the removal of people from a settled part to a waste part of the colony. Colonization, then, signifies the removal of people from an old to a new country, and the settlement of people on the waste land of the new country. . . . .

Two very different societies may have a common interest in colonization, though with objects widely different in some respects. The English, for example, may have a deep interest in removing people to America for the sake of relief from excessive numbers; while the Americans, cursed with slavery, might gain incalculably by receiving numbers of people from England. . . . .

The objects of an old society in promoting colonization seem to be three; first, the extension of the market for disposing of their own surplus produce; secondly, relief from excessive numbers; thirdly, an enlargement of the field for employing capital. . . . . [Omitting a discussion of the first point, we pass on to the second—relief from excessive numbers.]

In modern times, no old country has ever obtained relief from excessive numbers by means of colonization. In no case has the number of emigrants been sufficient to diminish, even for a year, the ruinous competition of labourers for employment; much less to produce any lasting improvement in the condition of the bulk of the people. More than once, however, this has been the object, or has been called the object, of an old state in promoting colonization. Twice since their late war with the French, the English have sent out bodies of peoples to colonies under the rule of the English government, for the declared purpose of checking pauperism at home: first to the Dutch colony of South Africa, and next to the English colony of Upper Canada. On neither of these occasions was the object attained even in the slightest degree. Both these attempts were called experiments. This year, the English government is making, to use the expression of Lord Goderich, another "experiment" of the same kind, by providing the funds wherewith to convey to South Africa a number of destitute children; the prodigious number of twenty. Considering that the population of England is fourteen millions, this experiment may be justly called child's play. The previous experiment in South Africa, and the outlay of 60,000£ in taking English paupers to Upper Canada, at the suggestion of Mr. Wilmot Horton and the Emigration Committees of the House of Commons, were hardly less preposterous, if we are to believe that any benefit to the labouring class at home was seriously expected from them. To call experiments measures so futile, so obviously inadequate to the end in view, is an abuse of language, and one calculated to be mischievous; since, if these childish attempts had really been experiments, the signal failure of them would have been a fact tending to establish that colonization, with a view to relief from excessive numbers, must necessarily fail of its object. . . . .

Men who possess in a high degree the faculty of reason, but who, having made a religion for themselves, are often under the influence of

Those political économists who worship capital . . . . [say that the emigration question] deserves profound regard; but as employment for labour is in proportion to capital, as emigration would cost money and diminish capital, therefore it would diminish employment for labour, and do more harm than good. . . . . Those who object to emigration on the score of its expense deserve, on account of their reputation and authority, that their argument should be carefully examined. . . . .

Now upon what rests their assumption? It rests upon two other assumptions, one of which is true, the other false; first, that no labour is employed save by capital; secondly, that all capital employs labour. If it were true that every increase of capital necessarily gave employment to more labour; if it were true, as Professor McCulloch has said, that "there is plainly only one way of effectually improving the condition of the great majority of the community or of the labouring class, and that is *by increasing the ratio of capital to population,"* then it might be assumed that colonization would, on account of its expense, do more harm than good. But it is not true that all capital employs labour. To say so is to say that which a thousand facts prove to be untrue. Capital frequently increases without providing any more employment for labour. . . . .

During the last year (1832), it is supposed, about 125,000 people, men, women, and children, emigrated from Britain to the United States, Canada, and Australia. Of these a considerable number carried property with them, varying in amount from 500£ to a few pounds over the cost of passage. The passage of the whole of them must have cost, at the lowest estimate of 5£ for each person, not less than 625,000£. Supposing that they took with them a capital of 5£ each, upon the average, which seems a very low estimate, emigration from Britain carried off during the last year a capital of 1,250,000£. Does any one pretend that this abstraction of capital has diminished, to the extent of a single pair of hands, the amount of employment for labour in Britain? Might we not rather expect, if England had no corn-laws, that these 125,000 emigrants, employing their capital and labour in a wide and rich field, would create a new demand for the produce of capital and labour employed in Britain? Let these questions be answered carefully, and it will appear that much of the capital of such a country as England may be used in promoting emigration, without diminishing, to say the least, the amount of employment for domestic labour. Whether capital might be so used with profit to the owners of it; whether, by such a use of capital, effectual relief from excessive numbers might be obtained, are questions which belong rather to the means than to the ends of colonization. Here, my sole object is to show how groundless is the objection to emigration on the score of its expense; how futile is that a priori reasoning, by which some conclude that the cost of emigration would necessarily diminish, according to its amount, the amount of employment for labour at home. I have dwelt so long on this objection, not with a view to recommend emigration by means of an outlay of English capital (for I shall endeavor to show hereafter that it would be greatly for the advantage of colonies to provide a fund for the immigration of labour), but in order to remove a prejudice against colonization, on the ground of the mischievous loss of capital which it might occasion to the mother country; a prejudice which stops him who entertains it on the very threshold of this subject.

Supposing that, whether by means of English capital about, at all events, to fly off to foreign countries, or by means of a fund raised in the colonies, such an amount of labour should emigrate from England as considerably to diminish the proportion which, in England, labour bears to employment; then would the wages of labour be higher, then would the state of the bulk of the people be improved, then would relief be obtained from excessive numbers. This great end of colonization has never been so much as seriously contemplated by the ruling class in England. On the contrary, taught by certain economists to believe, that profits rise when wages fall, and fall when wages rise, that the prosperity of the capitalist is consistent only with the misery of the labourer, the late ruling class in England would have set their faces against any project of colonization which had seemed fit to raise wages. Late events have produced some change of feeling on this subject; and coming events, probably, will soon produce a greater change. . . . .

The new ruling class of England, those whom late events have made the great men of England, are placed in a situation which may render excess of numbers highly disagreeable to them. They may be glad to pay high wages for the security of their property; to prevent the devastation of England through the commotions arising from discontent in the bulk of the people. Even before the late change, while the fears of the great men were urging them to bring about that change, while fires were blazing and mobs exacting higher wages in the south of England, a dread of the political evils likely to come from excessive numbers, induced the English government to form a Board of Emigration, with the avowed purpose of improving the condition of the labouring class, by removing some of them to the colonies. A more foolish, or rather futile, effort by great men to remove what they felt as disagreeable, was, perhaps, never made; but the effort, feeble and puerile though it were, tends to point out that for a country, situated like England, in which the ruling and the subject orders are no longer separated by a middle class, and in which the subject order, composing the bulk of the people, are in a state of gloomy discontent arising from excessive numbers; that for such a country, one chief end of colonization is to prevent tumults, to keep the peace, to maintain order, to uphold confidence in the security of property, to hinder interruptions of the regular course of industry and trade, to avert the terrible evils which, in a country like England, could not but follow any serious political convulsion.

For England, another end of colonization, by means of relief from excessive numbers, would be relief from that portion of the poor's-rate which maintains workmen in total or partial idleness; an object in which the ruling order have an obvious interest.

For England, again, a very useful end of colonization would be to turn the tide of Irish emigration from England, to her colonies; not to mention that the owners of land in Ireland, most of them being foreigners by religion, might thus be taken out of the dilemma in which they are now placed; that of a choice between legally giving up a great part of their rental to the hungry people, and yielding to the people's violence the land which was taken by violence from their fathers.

Finally, comprised in relief from excessive numbers is the relief to many classes, not called labourers or capitalists, from that excessive competition for employment which renders them uneasy and dissatisfied. . . . .

The United States are still colonies, according to the sense in which the word is used here. They receive people from old states, and send out a much greater number of people to settle in new places. For promoting the immigration of capital and people, the motive of these states seems to be precisely opposite to that of an old country in promoting the emigration of capital and people. The old country wants an enlargement of its field for employing capital and labour; the colonies want more capital and labour for cultivating an unlimited field. By pouring capital and labour into England, you would augment the competition and uneasiness of capitalists, as well as the competition and misery of labourers; by pouring capital and labour into America, you would increase the wealth and greatness of that great colony. By pouring labour only into England, you would not increase the capital of that country, because the increase of labour would not find employment; but, as labour creates capital before capital employs labour, and as, in America, there is capital enough for the employment of more labour and room for the employment of more capital, therefore, by pouring labour only into America, you would provide more capital for the employment of still more labour. It follows, that colonies situated like the United States, colonies, that is, which already possess more capital than labour, have a greater interest in obtaining labour than in obtaining capital from old countries; just as a country situated like England has a greater interest in procuring relief from excessive numbers, than from the competition of capital with capital. As the main object of an old country in promoting emigration is to send forth continually all that portion of the constantly increasing labouring class for which there is not employment with good wages, so the main object of a colony in promoting the immigration of people is to obtain as much labour as can find employment with good wages. . . . .

In Canada, as in the United States, there is a want of free labour for works which require the combination of many hands and division of employments. The canals which the English government has lately formed in Canada could not have been finished, or perhaps begun, without a supply of labour from Ireland. The great Lake Erie canal, a work of which the public advantage, and the profit to the undertakers, was made manifest upon paper long before the work was begun, could not perhaps have been begun, most certainly could not have been finished, without a great supply of Irish labour. Capital from Amsterdam and London, and labour from Ireland, have lately been of infinite service to the United States. . . . . If the means by which the United States, Canada, and New South Wales obtain labour, should be taken away, no others being supplied, then must those colonies soon fall into the miserable state of other colonies which have never had any means of obtaining labour. In a word, from whatever point of view we look at this subject, it appears that the great want of colonies is labour, the original purchase money of all things.

### 14.    Opportunities for Immigrants in Agriculture[1]

Having travelled over only a small portion of the United States territory, lying between 37° and 45° north latitude, embracing the states of New England, Pennsylvania, New Jersey, New York, Ohio, Indiana, Illinois, and the territory of Michigan, my remarks shall be confined to this region. . . . .

The soil on the eastern side of the Alleghanies is generally of an inferior description, with exception of the lands on the banks of rivers. The cleared lands have been long cropped under the robbing system,[2]

---

[1] Extract from Patrick Shirreff, *A Tour through North America; together with a Comprehensive View of the Canadas and United States, as Adapted for Agricultural Emigration* (Edinburgh, 1835), pp. 392, 395–410, 416, 446–52.

[2] [The American method of agriculture was described as the "robbing" system. "The agriculture of a country is affected by local circumstances, and farming in Britain and in the remote parts of America may be considered the extremes of the art. In the one country the farmer aims to assist, and in the other to rob nature. When the results of capital and labour are low, compared with the hire of them, they are sparingly applied to the cultivation of the soil, in which case nature is oppressed and neglected, if I may be allowed to use such terms; and when they are high, compared with their hire, she is aided and caressed. Both systems are proper in the respective countries" (Shirreff, p. 341).]

and are far from being productive. The whole of the land that is worth occupying is owned by private individuals, although a great portion of it is covered with forest; and I was frequently told, that in all situations near a village, or which had ready access to water-carriage, forest land was more valuable than what had been cleared, fuel having become so dear of late years. Much of the land covered with wood is not worth cultivating, and should the forest be removed for fuel, it is likely to remain in pasturage or be suffered to produce trees again. The price of farms varies from £5 to £30 sterling per acre, according to quality of soil, buildings, and situation. Labour can at all times be had, and every description of produce finds a ready market. . . . . Market gardening is the most profitable department of farming, and the growing of grass ranks next.

Notwithstanding the good markets, command of labour, and low price of manure, the cultivation of grain in this part of the country is attended with little profit, which circumstance, joined to a grass crop being more lucrative, illustrates the parts nature and man perform in the production of farm produce which has been so often alluded to. And a Briton who has been accustomed to pay a high rent will be very apt to overlook, on first reaching America, many circumstances affecting the profits of farming.

Land which has been impoverished by a long succession of crops under the robbing system, will not yield much grain without a plentiful supply of manure, which the rate of labour may frequently prevent being applied without incurring loss. . . . . In grass husbandry, human labour is but little employed, nature being the chief agent of production, and hence it is remunerating. The difficulty of transporting certain kinds of grass produce from a distance, such as hay and fresh dairy produce, keeps up the price of these commodities, but the small quantity of labour bestowed on their production is the chief cause of their profitableness.

A man with capital may purchase a farm to the east of the Alleghany range, and occupy it with a prospect of having a good return for the capital invested, if he possess prudence and industry. He must not, however, lavish capital on fanciful improvements, or employ much labour on finical operations. Wages are so high that he will require to calculate the value of every day's labour, and render the closest personal superintendence, and perhaps also assistance. Unless this is done farming will be unprofitable, as a great many of the workmen are idle and unsteady. Farming cannot, however, be pursued on a large scale with a prospect of success, from the difficulty of superintending the operations and forming a proper division of labour with unskilful and untractable workmen. There is, however, an excellent field for prudent skill and industry near all towns. In short, science seems scarcely to have been thought of in American farming, and a cautious application of it in draining and other improvements, in particular situations, would be remunerative.

Land may be rented in many parts of the country on fair terms, more especially near towns. In such situations many British emigrants successfully pursue market gardening and dairy husbandry. Native Americans prefer occupying land of their own to paying rent for the use of a farm belonging to others.

The labouring emigrant does not readily find agricultural employment on the east coast, from the country being thickly settled, and the constant influx of emigrants without funds to support them. He should, therefore, lose no time in pushing back into the country, where wages are higher compared with the price of the necessaries of life and land, and where information necessary to a settler on cheap land, can alone be acquired.

The soil on the western side of the Alleghanies is generally much superior to the eastern, although it is to be found of all descriptions and degrees of fertility. It has not been very long cropped, and the natural composition of a great portion of it will, under any circumstances, render it productive of wheat and Indian corn. Almost all the land in the eastern part of this district is owned by private individuals, but much of it remains uncleared of forest. Towards the west the greater part of the land is held by the United States government, and costs $1.25 per acre. In every part of the country forest or improved land may be purchased, and the price is governed by local situation and other circumstances. Labour can generally be had, except in the extreme west. Farm produce is in constant demand, and prices are regulated by the markets of the towns on the east coast and New Orleans, to all of which there is access by rivers, canals, or railroads. Prices may, therefore, at all times be considered lower than the markets on the east by the expense of transport. Manures are very seldom used except in the neighbourhood of large towns, where the demand for vegetables and shortness of carriage render it worthy of the farmer's attention.

The money wages of labour may be stated to be nearly the same from the east to the extreme west, but any difference that exists is towards a rise in the west. In the same direction a decline in the price of produce takes place. Therefore, as the distance from the markets on the coast increases, the farmer pays a greater share of produce to the labourer, and must be remunerated either by the low price of land or its natural fertility. Labourers are of a more unsatisfactory description than in the east, land being so cheap that every prudent man is enabled to purchase a farm for himself in the course of a year or two, and it is only the imprudent who continue labourers. The character of the workmen renders labour dearer than is at first apparent.

The country to the west of the Alleghanies is of such extent, and gradually increasing in distance from the seaport towns which regulate the price of the land produce, that farms of equal quality of soil vary from 5s. 4d. to £12 sterling per acre. . . . .

An emigrant will not always find agricultural employment to the west of the Alleghanies from the low price of farm produce; but there is always a demand for labour in towns and villages, at high wages, and he need not remain idle if he is disposed to work. An industrious and sober man must rapidly accumulate wealth by working for hire, and many perhaps err by purchasing land instead of continuing to work under the direction of others. On leaving New York, a gardener, who was working at Haddington when I left Scotland, gave me ten pounds sterling, which he had saved since his arrival in America, to enable his wife and family to reach him. A young man, whom I had often employed at spade-work [in Scotland], at 1s. 6d. a day without board, was earning, by sawing stones at Cincinnati, 4s. 3d. a day with board.

A person cannot purchase and farm land to the east of the Alleghanies without possessing a considerable portion of capital; and to the west of the mountains land is not likely to be cultivated with profit without personal labour. The luxuries of life being prepared in the east, to meet an extensive demand, are cheaper than in the west by the expense of transport from one market to the other. It is the reverse with the necessaries of life; and the agricultural emigrant ought to be guided in his choice of residence on either side of the Alleghanies by his habits, finances, and wants. . . . .

The first settlers in this portion of the United States had to struggle with severe privations. Besides being engaged in warfare with the natives, they settled in insulated situations in the midst of a densely wooded surface, without experience as to the mode of rendering it fruitful, or possessing facilities of communication. They were unable to subsist by their labour, and many perished for want of food. But on every portion of cleared surface nature continued productive, and her exertions being aided by new skill and industry, wealth appeared in the progress of time. There being no rent, and scarcely a burden of any kind to pay, the inhabitants reaped the combined fruits of their own and nature's labour without division. Individuals had as much land as they chose to cultivate; and having every inducement to render it productive, they rewarded labour with liberal wages. The abundance of land induced labourers to turn landholders, and reward others with high wages, who likewise became landholders. Thus there was a constant progression in society, by the prudent and industrious labourers rising into wealth, and receding from the first point of settlement on becoming landholders. These movements continue up to the present time with the existing cause—abundance and cheapness of land, to which many of the peculiarities of the country and its inhabitants may be traced.

Good land being sold by the United States government at $1.25 per acre, people will not permanently hire themselves for a less reward than can be obtained by cultivating on their own account. When competition depresses wages, operatives commence farming, and wages rise. Thus the wages of labour are regulated by the profits of farming, and will continue to be so until all the good land is occupied. . . . .

The situation of an emigrant on reaching America must be very different from what it was at home. In the midst of a people whose manners and customs are in some measure new to him, he is an isolated being, without any one in whom he can confide for advice and assistance. If he cannot think for himself, and rely on his own resources in transacting business, he will be a helpless mortal, and in all probability become the prey of designing persons. It is the dependence of the inhabitants on each other in old countries which unfits so many of them to play their part in the newly settled portions of the United States, where each individual acts independently, and trusts to himself alone. Americans are, therefore, the most acute people in the world in the ordinary intercourse of life, and few foreigners need take up their abode in the country in hope of outstripping them. The most essential requisites in an emigrant are energy of mind, steadiness of purpose, and persevering industry. Without possessing these qualifications, no one need expect to mingle successfully in the bustle of life; although it is possible to exist as a farmer, without being so highly gifted. It is a wrong estimate of themselves which so often gives rise to disappointment and failure on the part of British emigrants. There is nothing in the soil or climate of America which can impart wisdom to the fool, energy to the imbecile, activity to the slothful, or determination to the irresolute. Examination of character should therefore form part of every emigrant's preparation, as his fate will perhaps altogether depend on it. It is folly for the idle and imaginative beings who float in British society to seek an Elysium in the United States, from whence they will again be speedily wafted to their native country. It is the industrious, prudent, and frugal people alone that can calculate on success. . . . .

The inhabitants of the States speak the same language as the English, which may be called the language of commerce. They are made acquainted with the improvements and discoveries of Britain a few months after they become known, and from the freedom of institutions, and energy of the people, greater effect can sometimes be given to them. On a general view of all the circumstances affecting the character and situation of the country and the people, it is scarcely possible to imagine a region promising such unchecked prosperity and future greatness. . . . .

There is perhaps no country in the world where a farmer can commence operations with so small an outlay of money, and so soon obtain a return, as in Illinois. This arises from the cheapness of land, and the facility with which it is cultivated, and will appear more evident from the following statement:

Suppose a settler with sufficient capital to purchase and stock a farm and maintain himself for six months. The farm to consist of two hundred acres, thirty-five of which being forest and the remainder prairie. If the purchase was made in spring, the expense might be thus stated:

| | |
|---|---:|
| Purchasing 200 acres of land at $1.25 | $250 |
| Fencing two fields of 40 acres with an eight-rail fence. | 80 |
| Ploughing by contract 80 acres, at $2 | 160 |
| Seed for 80 acres of Indian corn, 10 bushels at 15 cents | 1.50 |
| Cutting and harvesting stalks of Indian corn, and harvesting the crop, at $3 per acre | 240 |
| Seed for 80 acres of wheat, sown after Indian corn, 45 bushels at 45 cents | 20.25 |
| Harrowing wheat | 20 |
| Cows, 4, at $8; young cattle, 8, at $5; pig, $10 | 82 |
| Buildings and household furniture | 600 |
| Maintenance of family for six months, and purchasing s:eds of vegetables, potatoes, and poultry | 150.25 |
| Total | $1,604 |

With an expenditure of $1,604, or £340,17s. sterling, is obtained the dairy produce of 4 cows and the improvement of 8 cattle grazing on the prairie, and 3,200 bushels of Indian corn, besides vegetables and the improvement of a lot of pigs and poultry.

The attention of the settler and his family is supposed to be confined to the cultivation of vegetables, tending the cows and pigs, and planting and husking Indian corn.

In the spring of the second year, 80 acres additional would be fenced, ploughed, planted with Indian corn, and harvested at the same expense as the first year, $481.50; harvesting 80 acres of wheat at $3, $240; total, $721.50.

Supposing the Indian corn of the second year equal to the first crop, the wheat to yield 22½ bushels per acre, and cost 2½ bushels in thrashing—the farmer in eighteen months after settling would have expended $2,325.50, or £484, 4s. 6d. sterling. In the same time he would have reaped 6,400 bushels of Indian corn, and 1,600 bushels of wheat, and enjoyed abundance of vegetables, dairy produce, beef, pork, and poultry. With this produce and expenditure the farmer and his family do not perform any laborious work. It is presumed the farm would, with some ploughing to destroy weeds amongst the Indian corn, afterwards continue to yield yearly 3,200 bushels of Indian corn, and 1,800 bushels of wheat.

The data of the preceding statements[1] are unfavourable for industrious and frugal emigrants, being framed for a person disliking to work. . . . . The crops are estimated considerably lower than what I was told the land of Illinois generally yields; but from knowing how prone farmers are to speak of good crops, and conceal indifferent ones, I have made considerable deductions from the accounts received, with the view of avoiding exaggeration.

If an industrious man were to purchase the farm, and perform a considerable portion of the work himself, the result would be different. A saving might also be effected on the buildings and living to the extent of $250. If to this sum be added $150 for work performed personally above the other case, the same produce would be obtained with an outlay of £389 sterling. A person who would be content at first with cheap houses, little household furniture, and labour with his own hands,

---

[1] [The estimates for buildings and maintaining a family were taken by Shirreff from Adam Fergusson, *Practical Notes Made during a Second Visit to Canada in 1833* (Edinburgh, 1833), and were, as Shirreff himself said (p. 448), "too high for ordinary settlers."]

might reap the same produce with an outlay of £300 sterling. The expense of buildings and living until a crop is reaped, must in a great measure depend on the individual himself, and the nature of his family. . . . .

A person with little capital might commence farming on a smaller scale than has been taken for illustration; government selling lots of 80 acres. Supposing a farm of this extent, consisting of fifteen acres of forest, and the remainder prairie, the expense would stand thus:

| | |
|---|---|
| Purchasing 80 acres, at $1.25 | $100 |
| Fencing into two fields of 30 acres, and one of 5 acres for a garden | 80 |
| Ploughing by contract 35 acres, at $2 | 70 |
| Seed for 30 acres of Indian corn | .60 |
| Vegetable seeds and potatoes | 10 |
| A cow, $8; pigs and poultry, $4 | 12 |
| Assistance in harvesting corn | 20 |
| Seed for 30 acres of wheat | 15 |
| Harrowing wheat | 7.50 |
| Buildings and furniture | 150 |
| Household expenses | 40 |
| Ploughing 30 acres in spring at $2 | 60 |
| Two oxen for ploughing and harrowing | 14 |
| Assistance in harvesting wheat | 30 |
| Total | $609 |

With an expenditure of $609, or about £130 sterling, and the farmer's labour, 2,400 bushels of Indian corn and 675 bushels of wheat would be obtained, besides the produce of a cow, vegetables, pigs, and poultry for family use.

Notwithstanding the enormous quantity of produce exhibited by the preceding statements, high wages and low prices prevent much money being realized. By referring to the statement of the produce of an acre of land for two years, it will be seen the cost is $10.02, and Indian corn being estimated at 15 cents per bushel, and wheat at 45 cents, the produce amounts to $6 and $10.12½ for Indian corn and wheat respectively. . . . .

In a country where Nature is so bountiful and land so abundant and cheap, the wages of labour must necessarily be high. Accordingly, an ordinary mechanic obtains $1 per day, with board, including washing; and superior workmen, engineers, and millwrights, get from $2 to $3. Farm labourers are engaged at from $100 to $120 a year. Female house-servants obtain $1 in private families, and from $2 to $2.50 a week in hotels. As compared with the prices of produce and land, wages may be stated thus:

If an ordinary mechanic work five days in the week he will earn throughout the year, besides board, $260; or of Indian corn about 1,733 bushels; or of wheat about 580 bushels; or of beef about 13,000 lbs.; or of land about 200 acres.

An ordinary farm labourer will get during the year, besides his board, $100; or of Indian corn about 667 bushels; or of wheat about 222 bushels; or of beef about 5,000 lbs.; or of land about eighty acres; which is a sufficient extent of surface for any labouring man to possess.

Female house-servants in private families get in the year $52, which would purchase forty acres of land, and in hotels what would purchase eighty acres of land.

How very different is the situation of farm labourers in England, Scotland, and Ireland, compared with those in Illinois! Supposing the weekly wages of labourers to be 10s., 8s., and 3s. 6d., without board, in England, Scotland, and Ireland respectively, and they do not exceed these sums, the Englishman will earn during the year about seventy bushels of wheat, or of beef about 1,560 lbs.—the Scotchman about sixty-two bushels of wheat, or of beef about 1,400 lbs.—the Irishman about thirty bushels of wheat, or of beef about 750 lbs. But when the board of the workman, or simply what he himself would consume, is taken from these numbers, they will appear quite insignificant compared with the wages of Illinois.

An ordinary farm labourer in Illinois gets the value of eighty acres of land yearly: In Britain, when due allowance is made for the board of the labourer, he does not get one-tenth of an acre of good land. When wages are compared with land, the farm labourer of Illinois is about 800 times better rewarded than in Britain.

The wages of female servants, compared with the price of land, are also remarkable. . . . .

Illinois may justly be called "the poor man's country," if any part of the world deserves the title. The extraordinary reward which the labourer receives, and the bountifulness of Nature, are favourable to the poor, and no person who has health and strength, and leads an industrious and a virtuous life, can continue without the means of subsistence in Illinois. . . . .

The advantages of the country have only been made public of late years, and less seems to be known regarding it in the eastern portions of the United States and the Canadas than in Britain. Emigrants have, however, been streaming into Illinois for a year or two from the different parts of Europe and the eastern parts of America, and their number is likely to increase. I have frequently alluded to the anxiety of people in the eastern States and the Canadas to sell their lands. This desire proceeds from the advantages of a prairie country, in which many of the farmers in other portions of America obtain better farms than those which they formerly possessed, and at a twentieth part of the price at which they sell their original ones. There is consequently a class of comparatively wealthy settlers attracted to the West.

### 15. Advice to German Emigrants, 1837[1]

But the western territory of America is not wholly peopled by emigrants from the Atlantic states, a large number of the inhabitants being settlers from Switzerland and Germany. The Irish, though emigrating to the United States in large numbers, prefer generally a residence in a city, with such transient occupation as they may chance to find, to the quiet industry of the Germans, who are more particularly attached to the cultivation of the soil. The advantages of the German cultivators in the United States over all other competitors are, indeed, numerous; but most of them arise from the manner in which they emigrate, and settle in the various districts. Whoever has witnessed the parting of a caravan of Germans from their friends and relations, or their proceeding on the way until they reach the sea-port of their destination, will be convinced of their resolute determination to make America their home. . . . . They prefer the western states for their settlements, and being, in this manner, at once cut off from an uninterrupted correspondence with the country which gave them birth, soon learn to make themselves a home in America. They direct their undivided energies towards improving their estates, instead of lingering in a state of indecision with their eyes half turned towards their native land. The habit of remaining together, and settling whole townships or villages, serves to render their exile less painful, and enables them, if the phrase be permitted, to transfer a part of their own country to the vast solitudes of the new world. . . . .

They are less enterprising than the native Americans, especially the New Englanders, on which account they are often considered dull and inactive; but they yield to no part of the population of the

[1] Extract from Francis J. Grund, *The Americans in Their Moral, Social, and Political Relations* (London, 1837), II, 20–25, 54–61.

United States in unremitting labour and persevering industry. . . . .
The dwelling of a German farmer is generally humble; but his granary
and stables are of huge dimensions, and exhibit the provident husbandman. The improvement of his farm is with him a more urgent consideration than his own individual comfort. His cattle are the object
of much solicitude, and his labour is the more productive as it is
seconded by every member of his family. . . . .

Until recently, the emigrants from Germany were chiefly composed of agriculturists, with an occasional admixture of operatives;
but the late unfortunate struggle for liberty in Germany has, within
the last five or six years, caused the expatriation of a more intellectual
class; and, accordingly, settlements have been made in the valley of
the Mississippi and in the state of Illinois, by a body of Germans whose
education fitted them rather for the drawing-room and the closet than
for the hardships of cultivating the soil. Yet they have cheerfully embraced their new vocation; and physicians, lawyers, theological and
other students, who arrived about three years ago in the United States,
have become active husbandmen; though they were obliged to resign
the romantic idea of founding a "New Germany" in the western territory of the United States. . . . .

Europeans learn with astonishment the rapid progress of civilization and power in America; but all she has done to this moment is but
a feeble prelude to the gigantic part which she is destined to perform
in the universal drama of the world.

Already a most uncommon spectacle presents itself. Emigration to
America is no longer confined to those parts of Europe which are overpeopled (Würtemberg and Ireland); but communicates itself also to
the less populated parts of Germany and France. Large numbers of
the inhabitants of Old Bavaria and of the French province of Alsace
are annually wandering to the United States; and so inviting are the
letters of those who are already settled, to their friends and relations
in Europe, that some of the German governments have already been
obliged to make provisions to arrest by law the depopulation of their
country, and to enjoin the civil and military authorities to use their
utmost influence to prevent emigration in the future. Neither is it only
the lower and destitute classes who are daily embarking for the United
States. On the contrary, the obstacles thrown in their way are such
that only those who have property are able to receive their passports.
There is now a law in Würtemberg which obliges every subject, desirous
of emigrating to America, to deposit the sum of 300 florins (640 francs)

with the civil authorities of Stuttgart, which sum is only remitted to him at the sea-port of his embarkation. Thus every German emigrant, from that part of the country, must not only be able to provide for his journey to the sea-port, but must also have a sum of 640 francs to spare, which is sufficient to pay his passage, and leaves him on his arrival in America with sufficient funds to be able to proceed to the west. Much, indeed, has been said in America on the subject of foreign paupers; though it would be easy to prove, by the registers of emigration in Germany, that the emigrants from that country pay annually more than two hundred thousand dollars for their passage, independent of the money and goods which they carry to the United States. . . . .

Let no one go to America merely on speculation; but at once with the resolute determination of making it his home. Let him not expect to lead a life of comparative idleness; but, on the contrary, one of hard work and persevering industry, if he wishes to realize the fruits of his labour, and to become independent of the assistance of others. Let him remember that he is going to settle amongst the most industrious people on earth, whose constitution and government protect him, it is true, in the unmolested possession of property; but that he himself must be the principal artificer of his fortune; and that nothing but personal exertion will ensure his ultimate success. Let him come unencumbered with farming utensils, machines, &c., which will only increase the expenses of his journey, without being of any real use in practice. Most of them he will be able to buy, in the United States, not only cheaper and of better quality; but better adapted to the general use in the country. Many emigrants are in a habit of bringing ploughs, wagons, &c. to America, without reflecting, for one moment, that the expenses of transportation amount to more than their actual value; and that it is more than probable that these implements may prove entirely useless or unmanageable in a different soil or on a different road. Again, let them abstain from all mercantile speculations, of which they often know little or nothing, and which can never succeed unless they are thoroughly acquainted with the market. Let them remember, that once out of money they must sell their merchandize for what they will bring, not for what they are worth; that commerce requires capital and credit, and that without them they must necessarily become the tool of every trader and pedlar whom they meet on their way.

On their arrival in the United States let them not remain too long in the Atlantic cities. Every day they stay there without occupation is lost to their enterprise, and diminishes their funds. Let them rather begin humbly in the country, by working on farms, than become servants in the towns, or commence business immediately on their own account. If there are several members of a family, let only those remain in the cities who have learned a particular trade, or who may expect immediate employment; but it is far better for a whole family to move at once to the west, where they may find occupation much more suitable to their habits than they can hope to find on the sea-coast, where a too sudden transition from rural life to the refinement of the towns may prove destructive to their morals. Let them bear in mind, that in the cities, though individuals may prosper, they will hardly be able to raise themselves to an equality with the native inhabitants; whereas in the country, and especially on new land, they must, by persevering industry, become as respectable and powerful as the rest of their fellow-citizens. In the country they will enjoy an hundred indulgences of which they must necessarily be deprived in the cities. They will there be allowed to follow their own inclinations and habits, which they must never expect in a large city, in which they must necessarily conform to the manners and customs of the majority.

Let them, above all things, abstain from politics, before they have had time to study the institutions of the country, and to know the government under which they are going to live. A too hasty adoption of principles, before they have thoroughly weighed them, may be fatal to their own influence, and interfere with their prospects in life. It is the duty of every European settler to make himself acquainted with American laws and manners, in order to judge for himself to what party he is to lend his support. The Germans especially ought to show more zeal in acquiring the English language, without which it is impossible to understand the true meaning of a thousand things with which it is important they should be rendered familiar. The American papers contain infinitely more information than any of the German ones I have seen; which, with but few exceptions, contain nothing but mutilated extracts from the daily American press, in a language of which it is difficult to say whether it is less German or English.

I have said before, that in order to succeed in any one undertaking, but especially in farming, it is necessary that the proprietor should work himself, and not merely be an idle spectator or employer of the labour of others. I will now add, that without personal exertion on his part he will not only be unable to advance, but absolutely fail and be ruined. America, thanks to her institutions and the infinite resources of the soil, is not yet a country for a gentleman farmer; a circumstance which has been much regretted. . . . . An American prefers cultivating the smallest patch of his own to working on the largest farm of his neighbors, and rather emigrates further to the west than consents to become, in any manner or degree, dependent on his fellow-beings. The Germans who are found willing to hire themselves out on an estate are seldom content to serve for wages, but wish to be paid in land or produce, and become thus partners instead of servants to their employers.

## 16. Voluntary and State-aided Emigration Discussed[1]

Mr. William S. O'Brien said . . . . in advocating emigration, we seek to befriend, not only those who leave their country, but those also who remain; for, in proportion as the excess of labour, which at present prevails at home, is removed, will be the tendency of wages to rise, until they reach that standard below which they ought never to sink. It is difficult to calculate what number must be enabled to emigrate before any sensible effect can be produced upon wages; but I am inclined to believe, that the removal of about 100,000 labourers, with their families, from Ireland, would bring wages to the level of an average payment of 1s. per day throughout the year, in itself a very moderate pittance, but still a considerable advance upon the present remuneration of labour in Ireland. In addressing myself to those who are connected with Ireland, if there be any who are insensible to the considerations of humanity involved in this question, I would remind them that, from motives of self-interest alone, they ought to support the system of emigration, which is now proposed as a partial remedy for the distresses of the poor. In a very short time, the Irish Poor-Law will be in operation. The able-bodied, when unable to procure employment, will present themselves at the workhouses, and demand relief. Their claim, grounded upon undisputed destitution, will be irresistible; and, until the workhouse is full, they must be admitted. Compare, then, the average cost of maintaining a poor person in the workhouse, during even an inconsiderable period, with the expense necessary to enable him to remove to Canada, and it will be found that, even as a matter of economy, the balance greatly preponderates in favour of emigration. But whether a destitute labourer be sustained in the workhouse or not, this argument leads to the same result. If

[1] Extract from *Hansard's Parliamentary Debates*, Vol. LIV (3d series, 1840). cols. 839–40, 848–49, 854–55, 863–65, 885–91. For the earlier portion of this speech, see Section I, Doc. 24.

unemployed, his maintenance imposes a burthen upon the community; and, for the most part, upon that portion of the community which is least able to bear it. If, through the want of employment, 500,000 persons are, upon an average, supported, throughout the year, at the expense of others, the lowest amount at which their maintenance can be calculated is 1,500,000 £. per annum. Now, I am persuaded that half of this sum applied annually to emigration would, within a few years, almost wholly extinguish pauperism amongst the labouring population of Ireland. . . . .

The best proof I can give of the disposition which prevails amongst the population of the United Kingdom to emigrate is, to remind the House, that in one year (1832), above 100,000 persons emigrated from the United Kingdom; and, during the last fourteen years, not less than 790,398 persons have left this country in quest of a new home; of whom 348,117 have gone to the United States. Without mingling with the remark a single particle of jealousy towards the United States, I may observe, that the greater portion of this large band of emigrants would have directed their steps to our own colonies rather than to the United States, if due measures had been taken to direct them to the stream of British colonisation. We shall, probably, be told, in reference to this statement, that this immense amount of voluntary and unaided emigration clearly shows that it is unnecessary for the State to intervene with any assistance. The answer is obvious; those by whom emigration is most needed, are now unable to carry their labour to our colonies without the assistance of the State. . . . .

One of the measures recommended by the Committee of 1828 was, that parishes in England should be enabled to raise money, by way of poor rate, for the purpose of assisting the poor to emigrate. This suggestion has been carried into effect, a clause embodying this point having been inserted in the Poor-Law Amendment Act in 1834. It has been acted upon, to a limited extent. In 1836, as many as 4,600 persons were enabled to emigrate from different parishes in England to Canada, by the aid of the poor-rate. The beneficial operation of this act has, however, been much impaired by the absence of any organization, in Canada, for conducting the emigrants, on their arrival, to those parts of the colony in which there is an active demand for labour. It is not surprising that, when 20,000 or 30,000 labouring emigrants land at Quebec in the course of a few months, the surrounding district should be found unable to absorb so large a supply of labour; and though even a greater number would easily obtain employment if they were distributed through the more distant parts of those extensive regions, yet the influx into one sea-port of so great a number of persons unprovided with the means of going into the interior, and wanting the direction of adequate superintendence, often occasions great temporary suffering among the emigrants, and tends to create an unfounded impression at home with respect to the difficulties attending emigration to the Canadas. . . . .

There is one objection to the encouragement of emigration to British America at the expense of the State, which deserves to be considered, because it undoubtedly possesses some validity. This is the apprehension that the emigrants carried out at the public expense will pass over to the United States; so that the cost of their conveyance will fall upon Great Britain, whilst the benefit of their industry would be obtained by another nation. It seems to me that this danger has been overrated. If the number who have gone from our colonies to the United States had been as great as is supposed by some writers, the population of the Canadas could not have reached its present amount. Under a well-regulated system of emigration, there is little reason to apprehend that such removal would take place to any considerable extent. The climate of Canada is better than that of the United States, its soil as good, taxation is lighter, and the British emigrant enjoys, there, the advantages of living under those institutions to which he is accustomed and attached. If the same British capital which now finds investment in public works in the United States, were encouraged to seek employment in Canada, the remuneration of labour would be higher in our own colony than at the other side of the border; and if the emigrant labourer, instead of being thrown unaided and forlorn into the sea-ports of Lower Canada, from which he is frequently allured by misrepresentation into the United States, were conducted to those parts of British America where he would find certain and immediate employment, he would seldom be disposed to exchange the certain advantage thus secured to him for the chances of an adventure into the United States. Much might be done, also, to prevent such a result, by an improved administration of the land department of the colonies. There is abundant evidence to show that many persons who have gone out with the intention of settling in the Canadas, have been driven to the United States by the delay arising from the imperfection of surveys, and the difficulty of acquiring titles in the land department of our colonies. . . . .

Mr. Pyrme thought that the great evil which arose from emigration had been lost sight of, and it was this, that the persons who went out were the strong and adult part of the people. The country lost the most intelligent and industrious, and consequently the most productive part of the population. The expense of bringing up the labourer was borne in this country, and to induce him to emigrate when his labour became valuable, was like exporting a ready made machine. Such a proceeding might be necessary as a temporary remedy for a temporary superabundance of population, but such could not be proper to be adopted systematically.

Lord J. Russell said . . . . I will read to the House a statement of the number of emigrants who left this kingdom in 1839. In the year 1839, there left this country for the North American colonies, 12,658 persons; there left for the Cape of Good Hope, 227 persons; for Australia, 15,786 persons; and for the United States of America, 33,536 persons, making a total of 62,207 persons, of whom a great portion of those who emigrated to the Australian colonies, had a considerable amount of the expense of emigration defrayed either from the funds arising from the sale of land or the bounties, according to the system established in New South Wales, and a part had obtained assistance from the proprietors of land or others in this country. If, however, you will say that you intend to furnish means of emigration to all those who may wish to avail themselves of those means, you will not only do that which is inexpedient in itself, but you will by that means seriously injure the system of emigration which is now going on amongst persons who are actuated by a desire for emigration, and who take more care to secure their future interests, who will have a regard for their comforts, and who, it is supposed, will take care to secure the means of support when they arrive at their destination. Those are persons who are better qualified to embark on such a purpose, who have sufficient force to carry them through the difficulties that they may encounter, and who have sufficient strength of body and of mind to enable them to undertake a permanent settlement, not certainly in a foreign land, but in a distant land, and to endure all the hardships that they may undergo in the pursuit of their object. That is an emigration which will not be likely to entail misery on those who undertake it, for it will be undertaken by those who shall take some means to secure their future comforts. If, however, you say that you, the State, will undertake to send out all those who may feel inclined to go, you will only encourage an abandonment of those habits of caution and prudence which ought to influence men before they set out on such an undertaking. If, when they should arrive, they did not find themselves comfortably settled—if they were disappointed in the expectations which they had formed—if they were persons unfitted, from want of strength of body or mind, to succeed in the circumstances in which they should be placed, they might blame those who had sent them out. The Government ought to take only such a step as would not entail any such miseries.

## 17. Proposals for a Canadian Agent in New York[1]

CANADA HOUSE, ST. HELEN'S PLACE

11 November 1842

MY LORD:

Representations having been made to the Canada Company that it would be of great importance to the British American Colonies that a resident agent should be appointed by Her Majesty's Government at New York, whose whole time should be employed in communicating with, and affording information to, emigrants from Great Britain, great numbers of whom are always at that city, both on their way from this country, and on their return, and are unable to obtain authentic information there, of the advantages offered to settlers in the British provinces, I am requested by the Directors of the Canada Company to make this communication to your Lordship.

The advantages which have arisen from the establishment of Government agents in various parts of the British provinces, to whom emigrants may always resort for advice, without being exposed to the frauds and machinations of land-jobbers and others, have been generally admitted; and if any such protection is desirable in the British territories, it is surely more essentially necessary at New York, when it is considered how many British subjects arrive at that port, a large proportion of whom would proceed to the British provinces if they were correctly informed, upon proper authority, of the advantages to be had therein.

Circumstances have lately occurred, probably well known to your Lordship, which bear forcibly on this question. For some months past, the packet ships from New York have brought back to this country a considerable number of British emigrants, sometimes 200 or 300 in a

[1] Letters to and from Lord Stanley, colonial secretary, published in Great Britain, *Correspondence relative to Emigration; also Correspondence relative to the Sale of Colonial Lands in British North America* (Parliament, Sessional Papers, 1843, Vol. XXXIV, Paper No. 291).

ship, who, finding no employment in the United States, have, it may be supposed, in despair returned to the home they had already thought it better to abandon, and where, therefore, they can hardly hope for any improvement in their circumstances. To these persons, when at New York, the expense of a journey to the British provinces would have been trifling, compared with the charge of the voyage home; and I have every reason to suppose, from the accounts received from Canada regarding the emigration this season, from the observations in Sir Charles Bagot's speech on opening the session of the Legislature on the 8th September, and from the measures taken for proceeding with the public works in the province, that, if there had been an active British agent at New York, to whom these unfortunate people could have resorted for advice, they would, without hesitation, have proceeded to Canada, and been able to settle themselves advantageously there, instead of returning home at a useless expense.

It may, perhaps, be supposed that the British Consul at New York is the proper person to perform this duty, but it is stated to the Canada Company, that his other avocations make it impossible for him to attend to this business, which, if properly looked to, would be amply sufficient to occupy the undivided attention of any man.

The vast extent of emigration from this country to North America, which has been shown by the Parliamentary Returns for 1840 and 1841 to have amounted to 156,116 souls, whilst the number of emigrants to all other parts of the world was only 53,219, and the change which has taken place in the last few years, and particularly during the present, in the direction of the tide of emigration from the United States into Canada, makes the appointment of such an agent of peculiar importance at present in promoting the settlement of the British provinces.

Since the peace of 1815, and until within the last few years, the activity and apparent prosperity in the United States, which have arisen chiefly from the facility of borrowing British capital, and the employment afforded by its outlay in their public works, naturally induced numbers of emigrants from Great Britain to proceed to that country; many also to emigrate from the British provinces, and to proceed to the States through Canada as the cheapest route.

The management of affairs in the United States having proceeded upon speculative principles, chiefly dependent upon credit which has not been supported, the result is, that their public works remain unfinished, and this apparent prosperity is cut short. In the meantime the British provinces, especially Canada, whose soil and climate are as good or better than those of the United States, and whose geographical position and internal water communications are superior, have been making steady and safe progress, and little is necessary to secure for them a high degree of prosperity, and a vast addition to British power in North America.

These considerations render it very important to take advantage of the present moment in directing the tide of emigration to the British provinces. The appointment of an active agent at New York would greatly promote this object. His time and attention should be entirely occupied in this way; and he should be furnished with regular and frequent reports from the Government agents in the British provinces, stating the demand that exists for labourers, the expense and facility of travelling, the value of property, and all other information useful to settlers, either men possessed of capital or otherwise; so that, upon full and impartial authority, emigrants may be able to judge how best to establish themselves on the British territories without losing their time and money in search of information.

I have, &c.,

CHARLES FRANKS, *Governor*

DOWNING STREET, 26 Nov., 1842

SIR:

I am directed by Lord Stanley to acknowledge the receipt of your letter of the 11th instant, proposing that an active agent should be employed at New York by Her Majesty's Government to furnish information to emigrants on their arrival in that city, relative to the attractions offered to settlers by the British North American Provinces.

Lord Stanley has instructed me to acquaint you, in answer, that a full consideration of the proposal, in all its bearings, has induced him to think that the disadvantages outweigh the advantages to be anticipated from such an appointment, attended as it would be by a risk that an agent such as you contemplate would probably deem it his first duty actively to promote emigration from New York, without sufficiently adverting to the risk of over-stocking the market, an effect produced by a very small excess of supply in a country, where capital is not very abundant. In addition to which, in the case of Canada, there would arise the further difficulty, that if any large number of settlers were induced to remove from New York, it would very much increase the uncertainty as to the extent to which emigration from this country could safely be encouraged. Lord Stanley, therefore, thinks that it would not be advisable to establish such an agency at New York; at the same time, however, his Lordship considers it very desirable that the authorities in Canada should keep Her Majesty's Consul at New York periodically informed of the state of demand for labour in the province, the price of land, &c., in order that he may be able to communicate authentic information on those points to parties who may apply to him, and will bring the subject under the notice of the Governor-general.

I have, &c.,<br>G. W. Hope

### 18. Employment for Newly Arrived Immigrants[1]

On the emigrant landing in New York . . . . there will be very little likelihood of the stranger finding employment, the place being already crowded with mechanics, labourers, and loiterers. He must, then, shape his course westward, and embark on board a steam-boat, by the Hudson river, for Albany, a large commercial town, about 160 miles distant. The deck fare will be about five or six shillings, finding himself with provisions. Here may be some chance for work, by inquiring at the seed shops if he is a gardener or husbandman, or among the masters of his trade if a mechanic, etc. . . . .

If the emigrant has not yet realised his expectations, he can proceed to Rochester, the next town of commercial importance, where he will have a better prospect of success; in fact, the further he travels westward the greater will be his chance of meeting with employment. If unsuccessful at Rochester or the neighborhood, his best course will be towards Buffalo, also a large commercial town, which is rapidly increasing in buildings and commerce. . . . .

Independently of the large towns already named, the traveller will, in his journey from New York, pass through a number of towns and villages, at some of which he may meet with employment; and the masters of canal boats are frequently commissioned to communicate intelligence to strangers that will lead to it. The labouring man is recommended, in the first place, especially if his means should be limited, to

[1] Extract from *A Practical Guide for Emigrants to North America, including the United States, Lower and Upper Canada, and Newfoundland; with Full Information Respecting the Preparations Necessary for the Voyage, Instructions on Landing, Travelling Routes, Capabilities and Price of Land, Farming Operations, Price of Labour, and All Other Matters Requisite for the Emigrant to Become Acquainted with before Embarking.* By a Seven Years' Resident in North America [George Nettle] (London, 1850), pp. 23–31.

work for less than the ordinary wages, not only for the sake of an introduction, but he would be "going a-head," and at the same time improving his circumstances.

Some precaution is necessary as to the certainty of the real route
of the boats, and the information given to strangers. A most grievous
instance of this deception was witnessed some time ago at Cleveland,
and which had been practised, it was strongly suspected, by the master
of the boat. Some seventy or eighty Dutchmen or Germans had been
brought by the wrong route, and were landed on the wharf in the greatest distress and disappointment.

The emigrant's next course is west, by steam-boat, to Cleveland,
about 190 miles distant, in the eastern part of the State of Ohio, where,
or in the neighbourhood, he will most probably obtain the object of his
pursuit. The town is rapidly increasing in size and importance, in consequence of its vast imports·from the south-west by the Ohio Canal,
(300 miles long), and the trans-shipments to Buffalo, besides a great
western and eastern traffic. The soil in the neighbourhood is of excellent quality, producing abundance of peaches, melons, apples, cherries, currants, etc., though it is subject to blight by late frosts, owing
probably to its close proximity to Lake Erie. The inhabitants are kind
and respectable, the locality extremely pleasant, and the roads level
and in good order. . . . .

There still remains a very large field westward for the settler's travels and choice, to which thousands of the eastern Americans are drawing for new cheap land; and, indeed, great numbers of English settlers
are following their example. Should the emigrant be inclined to move
in that direction, he ought to avoid settling in Toledo, about 120 miles
distant; it is a very unhealthy locality, few persons visiting there without suffering, more or less, from the effects of the climate: it is, nevertheless, a place for making money by mechanics and traders who are
fortunate enough to retain their health.

Now, there are Detroit and St. Clair, nearly the same distance,
both healthy and thriving towns: there is, also, Milwaukee, a fast-
increasing town, about 740 miles from New York, and Chicago still
more so, to the prairies of which thousands of Yankees are flocking,
where land is less wooded and strong for all descriptions of crops, and
where agriculture, consequently, progresses upon a most amazing scale.
In short, the best land may there be had for little money, the one thing
needful being manual labour, which is in great requisition. . . . .

The settler would soon find a considerable improvement in his circumstances and prospects by hiring himself, particularly if he should happen to have two or three sons grown up and adapted for labour; and if he has a careful wife and a daughter or two willing to work, they may find profitable employment. The wife may earn at service from four to six shillings, and the daughters from two to five shillings per week each, including their board. It may be good policy for the whole family to go out to work for a while, and to put all their earnings into one common stock. In all their plans, this practice of earning and saving should be followed up as closely as practicable. It will be necessary, and, indeed, of the greatest importance, to be paid the full amount of wages every week, or to quit the employ at once; and it will be advisable, even when in work, to keep an eye around for some other situation, especially for improvement.

Wages are frequently paid, especially in towns, partly in cash and partly in "store pay," that is to say, in goods from the shop, or by an order for goods on some other person; if, however, they are for such articles as are really wanted, the payment may be considered as good as cash, with this difference, that the servant will be sure to pay high enough for his goods. In England, if a master does not pay his servant his weekly wages as it becomes due, an application to a magistrate has the effect of compelling him; but in the United States it is not so, as the defendant is allowed the means of such tedious procrastination in coming to a settlement as tires out the complainant, so much so that it is generally considered preferable to relinquish a just demand.

The wages of the Dutch and Germans at home being only about 2s. 6d. per week, out of which they have to provide themselves with food, which is necessarily of the poorest description, and who have lived under a rigid government, generally emigrate to America in companies, the "land of Goshen" to them when compared with their own homes, and soon get themselves into employment, by working at a lower rate of wages than the Yankees, which has caused a great reduction in the price of labour. One of this class, who had just arrived at Buffalo, and who was unable to speak a word of English, took a job of chopping firewood out of a Yankee's hands. They are very industrious people; they hoard up their money, get all their paper money converted into hard cash, and send their children about to the boarding-houses to beg the scraps of offal meat. They are utterly disliked by the labouring Yankees, and, indeed, by all except those who employ them; yet they are, notwithstanding, truly faithful and honest in their transactions.

In England the landed proprietor is generally considered to be a man of respectability and of some importance in society; from him and the farmer the labourer obtains his employment, and on whom he is dependant. It is, therefore, the natural desire of the labourer, as well as others in better circumstances, to become landed proprietors also. Now, no country on the face of the earth can afford such facilities for the accomplishment of this laudable object as the United States of America. The desire to possess himself of this important acquisition as soon as possible being, then, the emigrant's aim and ambition, he seeks for information, and soon meets with some one who was once in the same mind and circumstances as himself, but who is now desirous of selling at a great bargain! But the general emporiums for these negotiations are the land agents' offices, where there are hundreds of thousands of acres on sale, principally of "wild land," covered with trees, at a remote distance, which may be purchased at from four to seven shillings per acre. For that which is under cultivation, with a wooden dwelling, etc., a much higher price will be charged, according to its location and other circumstances. Either a man of capital seeking a landed investment, or a poor labourer (and there are fifty to one of the latter class), may gain some useful and much-needed information; as the nature and course of things will be found to be very different from those at home. Before entering into any landed speculation, the emigrant ought, by all means, to find employment of some description for at least a year. By this course he will effect two important and essential objects—he will put money into his pocket, and some practical knowledge into his head; for if he should go too precipitately into the possession of land, the chances are ten to one that he will have occasion to repent. He may have heard and read many plausible accounts; but, for a while, at least, he should pay no attention to them whatever. For want of this precaution, there are at this moment thousands who are "fixed," and who would willingly but cannot retract.

It is the practice of the Yankee farmers in the east to wear out their land without manuring, and when exhausted to sell it with the "improvements," as they are termed. They then go a thousand miles or more west, on new land, which may be purchased for about four or five shillings an acre, and which will bear very heavy crops for many years without manure. Hundreds of families may be seen journeying west for this purpose in their waggons, etc., at the end of every summer. The settler is, therefore, cautioned against purchasing "improved" lands; but if he has made up his mind to purchase, after having been long enough in the country to acquire sufficient knowledge, let him go west also, and as near to some new thriving town as possible.

Persons of property cannot be cautioned too seriously against going out hastily to purchase and improve land as a speculation, as hundreds of persons have, to their sorrow, been ruined by unadvised enterprises of this sort. As an instance, and for the sake of argument, it is only necessary to state that beef, pork, and mutton may be bought at $1\frac{1}{2}d$. per pound, indeed, sometimes for less, and that agricultural produce is equally cheap, whilst the labour to produce them is *double* the price of that in England; so that upon an honest and fair principle of reasoning, it would appear that it is better to pay high rents and taxes in this country than to emigrate. . . . .

It is very laudable and praiseworthy for young farmers to be anxious to be employed, and especially to have farms of their own to manage. In America there is a large scope for their enterprise; but they may rest assured that in America they must not expect to keep riding horses for their pleasure, as they do in England: they must be prepared to toil, labour, and sweat by the side of their workmen, late and early, or otherwise they had better remain at home and do the best they can.

### 19. Influence of Emigration upon Labour and Prices in England[1]

While much attention has been given to the supplies of gold as affecting prices, very little has been given to the influence of emigration and immigration. Remarkable, nevertheless, as this age is for the wonderful gold discoveries, it is no less so for an unexampled movement of population. The Irish exodus is only one in a chain of great operations; and if more apparent to us, because happening in our own neighbourhood, is not, therefore, the most important. If the Irish leave our shores, they flock to those of the United States, in company with large hordes of High Dutch and Scandinavians. This immigration into the States, and this draught upon Europe, embraces yearly two hundred and fifty thousand men, women, and children. Its operations will affect Europe and America; but it is more particularly in reference to this country [Great Britain] that it may be useful to consider it.

Taken in one point of view, the population of the British Isles consists of two classes—a Germanic or labouring population, and a Celtic, or low-conditioned population. This latter population, which for cen-

[1] Extract from an article by Hyde Clarke in *Bankers' Magazine*, XIII (London, 1853), 731–32.

turies had been driven into narrower spaces—further and further West —within the last years flowed back again from its Irish seats, and poured into the Eastern districts streams of immigrants to compete for the lower classes of rude employment, thereby keeping down wages here. The diminution of the area of the Celtic population in Wales, the Highlands, and Man, nevertheless, continued. Our cities, however, were crowded with Irish immigrants, generally in a low condition, herding by themselves, and not intermarrying with the population of English blood. It has been calculated, from the basis of the census returns, that the number of the Irish population settled in Britain, including those born there, and those born in Ireland, amounted to one million; and great fear was entertained at one time, from the existence and extension of such a distinct population.

The great famine in Ireland, the exodus, points out to us an epoch from which another state of affairs is to be dated. The Irish population has sensibly diminished in its own proper seat; the emigration of the Welsh and Highlanders is in progress; and the advance of the English population in the Welsh and Highland borders continues, while the Irish population in Britain is stationary, if indeed, it be not already largely diminishing.

The Celtic emigration has been accompanied by a large English emigration to Australia and America.

The economical results of these changes are already apparent. In Ireland, there is a marked rise in the rates of agricultural wages; and the surplus labour available for harvesting in Britain no longer exists. The rates of wages in Britain are necessarily rising.

There is, however, an independent cause for a continuous rise of prices and wages in Europe and India, which was pointed out some years ago, and which is now in operation—and that is the effect of railways. If the supplies of gold had not been so largely increased, this effect would have been shown, to some extent, in keeping down, or bringing still lower, the prices in the great centres of consumption; but one chief effect, which was always looked forward to with certainty, was, the rising of prices in the distant, and heretofore isolated markets. The period is approaching, when the prices of produce in London, and Caithness, and Connemara, will be virtually the same; and, likewise, when the prices in London, Stockholm, Warsaw, Moscow, Naples, and Paris, will be the same. The rates of wages for all rude labour, and, therefore, for the majority of the population, will follow prices. The operation of free trade in corn would, it was expected, produce this result, allowing for the difference of freights; but the operation of railways is so greatly to reduce the cost of carriage, that a virtual uniformity in the nominal rates of prices is to be looked forward to.

Thus we have three causes operating to produce a uniformity of prices in the tendency of a general rise in prices and wages, namely—railway transit, increased supplies of the precious metals, and movement of the population; and none of these can be looked upon as transitory, or otherwise than continuous. It is, however, with the movement of the population we now have to deal, in its progress as affecting England.

### 20.  Immigration and Wages[1]

. . . . The policy of American law favors the distribution of landed property, while the policy of English law favors its aggregation. We are safe, then, from the operation of one great cause of the monstrous inequality of wealth, which is the great plague-spot in the social condition of England and Ireland. But there is another tendency of a similar character—the gradual depreciation of wages—which may produce as lamentable consequences in the United States as in Great Britain, if a remedy be not applied in time. At present, our institutions are preserved, and general content exists among the people, because no class in the community finds itself doomed to irretrievable penury, and not one individual is without the well-grounded hope of improving his condition, and perhaps of rising even to the highest rank in the social scale. But let the rate of wages here be reduced to what English economists regard as their natural and necessary standard—that is, to a bare sufficiency for subsistence from day to day—and the class of laborers, who must always form the majority in any community, and who, with us, have also the control in politics, will not be satisfied without organic changes in the laws which will make a wreck at once of our political and social system. Our immunity thus far ought not to betray us into a blind confidence for the future. A few years have produced a marvellous alteration in our prospects, and the change has not been entirely for our advantage. The Atlantic has been bridged by steam, and the ties which connect us with Great Britain, and link our commercial and social well-being with hers, are strengthening every day. Ireland is depopulating itself upon our shores; and already the rate of increase from abroad is half as great as that of the natural growth of the population at home. The number of immigrants now annually landed in our sea-

[1] Extract from article by F. Bowen in *North American Review*, LXXIV (1852), 221–32.

ports, or brought to our inland frontier, exceeds 350,000 though, six years ago, it was little over one-third of that sum. Should this foreign influx continue to increase in so high a ratio, vast as our capacities are for employing labor, a few years must cause a marked diminution of the rate of wages. In one particular, this result is inevitable; we might as well try to dam up the Mississippi with bulrushes, as to stop this great westward migration of the nations. But we may enlarge the field of employment, and increase the number of the applications of industry, so that this immense influx shall not produce its full effect in depressing the price of labor.

The fatal year 1847, a year of terrible famine in Ireland, and of great distress in several other parts of Europe, first turned the tide of emigration with overwhelming force upon this country. . . . . .

The population of Ireland in 1841 was 8,175,124; the rate of increase for the ten years immediately preceding had been only five per cent. But during this period, the causes had already begun to operate which, in the succeeding decade, had so marked an effect in thinning the population. From 1820 to 1830, the rate of increase was fourteen per cent, which is the measure of the decennial growth of the population in England and Scotland. There is reason to believe that the Irish tend to multiply faster than the English and the Scotch; that is, that the births among them are proportionally more numerous. But we shall be safe in taking fourteen per cent as the natural measure of their increase in ten years, if their numbers were not diminished by famine or emigration. Adding this proportion to the Irish population in 1841, we have 9,319,641 for what their number would have been in 1851, if it had not been diminished by the two causes just mentioned. But the actual population of Ireland in 1851 was only 6,515,794; that is, 1,659,-330 less than it was ten years before, and nearly three millions less than what it should have been, if the natural law of increase had not been checked.

What has become of these three millions of human beings? The returns by the Commissioners of the total emigration from the United Kingdom for the ten years ending in March, 1851, show that only 1,741,476 emigrated during this period. This includes the drain from England and Scotland also; but it is probable that nearly as many Irish passed over into the sister island as would make up for the number of natives who left it to go abroad. And yet there remain over a million of the Irish to be accounted for—an immense loss of population to be attributed to famine and the diseases which are consequent upon extreme misery and want. And the drain still continues; a panic seems to have seized the population of Ireland, and they rush to the seaports to embark for any other portion of the earth, as if the whole island labored under a curse. . . . .

Of course, the depopulation is greatest in those portions of Ireland where the pressure of famine was most severe. In the north and east, Ulster and Leinster were comparatively prosperous; they did not suffer much more than the most destitute portions of England and Scotland in the year of famine; and in them, we find that the population has not diminished more than fifteen or sixteen per cent. But in the south and west, in Munster, where the destitution is great, and in Connaught, the sink of Irish misery and degradation, the rates are respectively twenty-three and twenty-eight per cent; that is, one-fourth of the people have perished or emigrated. Among the counties, Roscommon is that portion of Connaught which lies nearest to Dublin, a great port of embarkation, with which it is partly connected by a railroad, so that it has great facilities for emigration; and here, accordingly, we find the loss is greatest, amounting to thirty-one per cent. In other words, within ten years (in fact, within half that time, for the calamity first reached its crisis in 1846), nearly one-third of the population have perished by fever or starvation, or have emigrated. . . . .

We do not dwell upon these astounding facts merely because they afford a spectacle and a problem which may well claim the attention of the whole civilized world. They have a peculiar meaning and pertinency for us here in the United States; they must affect our future prosperity, whether for good or ill, far more even than that of Great Britain. It is to our shores, not to those of England and Scotland, that this great Irish exodus is directed. These exiles are coming to us, mostly in a state of utter destitution, bringing with them Irish habits, and Irish willingness to live in squalor upon the meanest pittance that will support life. Cheapness of provisions is not the attraction that brings them here; at this moment, all the common articles of provisions are as cheap in Ireland as in the Atlantic States of this Union; many of them are cheaper. Nor is it comparative freedom from taxation which they seek; for the annual amount of Irish taxes is only about ten shillings a head, which hardly exceeds the burden of government here in America But they come in quest of constant employment and higher wages. These are the tangible tokens of our prosperity, the causes of the general well-being of our people; and these have made the United States a harbor of refuge for the poor of the civilized world. If our superiority in these respects should be done away with, if employment should become difficult to be had, and the wages both of rude and skilled labor should fall to the English standard, not all the advantages of our popular form of government, or of the cheapness of land in the far West, would attract a tithe of the body of immigrants who now annually throng our shores.

We come, then, to a question which all must admit to be of transcendent importance. *Is this immense immigration, in conjunction with other causes, likely to effect a general and great depression in the price of labor in the United States?* Besides the natural rapid growth of our population, an annual addition to our numbers of over 300,000 immigrants, all of them, except an insignificant fraction, being of the poorest class, cannot but produce a marked effect of some kind, even if the field for the employment of industry here were widening under the most favorable circumstances. Two-thirds of the exiles are Irish, who have been accustomed to regard six shillings ($1.50) a week as liberal wages for the father of a family, even when they could get employment only for half of the time. If the agriculture and the manufactures of this country were in a flourishing condition, if their enlargement kept pace with the rapid increase of our native population, this great addition of such materials to our working power could hardly fail to depress the price of labor.

But they are not flourishing. An alteration of the tariff in 1846, which was virtually an abandonment of the protective principle, has parályzed the chief branches of manufactures, and has brought down the price of breadstuffs and other provisions to a point which gives the farmer no temptation to raise more of them than are necessary for home consumption. . . . .

Great Britain is now pouring upon us in a full tide the surplus both of her population and the products of her overtasked manufacturing industry. She is giving us more mouths to feed at the moment when she is taking away from us the means of feeding them in any other way than by forcing them into agricultural industry, and thus cheapening still further the agricultural products which alone she can receive from us in exchange. The ocean, which once separated us, steam has contracted to a span. For all purposes of free intercourse, we are now virtually two contiguous countries, separated by no mountain barriers, by no differences of race, language, or polity, by no fundamental dissimilarity of our political institutions, and governed by the same system of municipal law. We are rapidly becoming as much one people as the English and the Irish, or the English and the Scotch. To expect that, in two countries thus situated, without any special direction of public policy towards maintaining some barrier between them, the pressure of population, the profits of capital, and the wages of labor can long remain very unequal, would be as idle as to believe that, without the erection of a dam, water could be maintained at two different levels in the same pond. Throw down the little that remains of our protective system, and let the emigration from Great Britain and Ireland to our shores increase to half a million annually, and within the lifetime of the present generation, the laborer's hire in our Atlantic States will be as low as it is in England. Our manufactures would flourish then, as those of Great Britain flourish now; cheap labor is the only requisite for placing them upon the same level. It is not, then, for the sake of the capital now embarked in our manufacturing enterprises, that we would advocate a return to what has been well denominated "the American policy." But that the bulk of our laboring population should fall into that condition where they would be exposed to such evils as have visited the laboring classes of Great Britain and Ireland during the last ten years—that the necessary standard of wages, as the English economists call it, should be here, as well as there, the smallest sum which will give a mere subsistence—this, we should regard as the greatest calamity which the folly of men or the wrath of heaven could bring upon the land.

### 21.  Immigration Harmful to the American Laborer[1]

And what have I learned in the course of my travels and observations concerning the unlimited and unguarded admittance of foreigners into the country? What conclusion have I come to? That it is a glaring and grievous evil; an evil to the United States, and an evil to many of the emigrants themselves. Why? Because anybody, or everybody, may come without let or hindrance. The rogues and vagabonds from London, Paris, Amsterdam, Vienna, Naples, Hamburg, Berlin, Rome, Genoa, Leghorn, Geneva, &c., may come and do come. The outpouring of alms and work houses, and prisons and penitentiaries, may come and do come. Monarchies, oligarchies, and aristocracies may and do reduce the millions of the people to poverty and beggary, and compel the

[1] Extract from *Emigration, Emigrants, and Know-Nothings*, by a Foreigner (Philadelphia, 1854), pp. 30–36. The author of this book was an English emigrant who had been in the United States thirteen years and a naturalized citizen for seven years.

most valueless to seek for a shelter and a home in the United States of America, and they do so. And what are the consequences? The consequences are that about 400,000 souls, from Europe, chiefly Germans, Irish, and Dutch are annually arriving in this country and making it their permanent abode. That a vast number of these emigrants come without money, occupation, friends, or business; many, very many, have not the means of buying land, getting to it, stocking it, and waiting for first crops, and many others would not settle upon land if they could. That, go where you will in the United States, you find nearly all the dens of iniquity, taverns, grog-shops, beer houses, gambling places, and houses of ill fame and worse deeds, are kept by foreigners. That, at the various ports, the alms-houses and hospitals are, in the main, occupied by foreigners; and that numerous objects of poverty and destitution are to be seen crawling along the streets in every direction. That not a few become criminals, filling our prisons and putting the country to great expense.

This is a fearful catalogue of consequences, but they are by no means all. This unlimited and unrestricted admission of foreign emigrants is a serious injury to the native laboring population, socially, morally, religiously, and politically; socially, by overstocking the labor market and thus keeping wages down; morally and religiously, by unavoidable contact and intercourse; and politically, by consequence of want of employment and low wages, making them needy and dependent, whereby they become the easy prey or willing tools of designing and unprincipled politicians. And in this way the native population is deteriorated and made poor, needy, and subservient: and these realities produce want of self-respect, hopelessness, laxity in morals, recklessness, delinquencies, and crimes.

But there is another consequence which is deserving of notice, and it is this: Our manufacturers, ironmakers, machinists, miners, agriculturists, railway, canal, and other contractors, private families, hotel-keepers, and many others, have got into the way of expecting and seeking for cheap labor, through the supply of operatives, workmen, laborers, house-help, and various kinds of workers, kept up by the indiscriminate and unrestrained admission of emigrants. Indeed it is no secret that emigrants, or rather foreign workers, have become an article of importation; professedly for the purpose of providing for the deficiency of supply in the labor market, but in reality with the intention of obtaining efficient workers at lower wages.

I remember well in the early part of 1846, when our manufacturers and ironmakers, far and near, were struggling hard for the retention of the high protective tariff then in existence, and the profits on cotton spinning and manufacturing ranged from thirty to one hundred per cent, that hundreds of operatives were imported from England for the purpose of obtaining practised hands and to keep wages from rising. And I remember also that some years ago when there was an attempt to reduce the wages of ironmakers and machinists at Pittsburgh and elsewhere, and the men resisted, that importation was resorted to with considerable success; and that those importations, and others both before and since, were obtained in a great measure by partial, fallacious, and incorrect representations.

This last mentioned consequence has had, and probably will continue to have, a very unfair and deplorable effect upon the native laboring population; for it needs no proof to sustain the assertion, that but for these specific and large importations of cotton and woolen manufacturing operatives, machinists and ironworkers, the wages of the then located population must have risen, and the natives been made better off. It is worthy of mention and attention in this connexion, that master coal miners, master ironmakers, master machinists, master cotton and woollen manufacturers, &c., are to a man advocates for a very high tariff upon coal, iron, steel, machines, tools, and cotton and woollen goods; and for the unlimited admission of workers without a sixpence of duty; by which means the consumers of all those articles are made to pay exorbitant prices for their benefit (the benefit of the masters), while they can and do avail themselves of the free importation of labor in order to keep wages from rising or for the purpose of lowering them. This is certainly the protective system, but it is protecting the masters and not the workers; the strong against the weak; the high livers and little workers, against the low livers and hard workers. If any protective system is wanted, I am an advocate for a protective system which shall *prevent* pauper labor from coming into the country, and admitting all merchandise free, which by making it abundant and cheap would add to the comfort of the masses. . . . .

Then what ought to be done? I will say what I am convinced ought to be done, and what would be for the honor and welfare of the country at large; and that is, restrict by law the admission and importation of emigrants to within prudent limits. None should be permitted to land at any of our ports and remain in the country unless he, she, or they could show satisfactorily to the proper authorities (made and provided for that purpose) that they were engaged in trade, had a living occupation to go to, or were fully prepared to comply with the regulations which require them immediately to settle upon and cultivate permanently the public lands appropriated to that purpose.

We would have these public lands given in limited quantities, say from fifty and not exceeding one hundred acres, to emigrant settlers, according to the number of persons in a family and their power of improving and cultivating it. Plain and full instructions in pamphlet form should be prepared and given to every settler, whereby they would learn how to get to the lands at the least cost and in the most direct way, requiring them to go in companies and to own and occupy adjoining allotments, and recommending them to adopt a simple, reciprocal associative manner of labor and living. Nay, rather than we should continue emigration upon its present basis, through which we should go on producing paupers, delinquents, and criminals, and causing numbers of new comers to take up low and vile occupations, and for the much to be desired and wise purpose of raising up "A bold peasantry, their country's pride," we would even consent to defray the expense of conveying them to their new homes out of the national exchequer.

Such an alteration of the system, or rather such an introduction of a system, would soon become generally known throughout Europe, and would deter and prevent the vicious, the destitute, and the very ignorant from coming among us, and would in consequence stop the rapid increase of pauperism, degradation, and crime at our ports. On the other hand, it would encourage such foreigners as had laid up a little money, and were likely to prove industrious and respectable citizens, to come over and help us to become truly great, by intelligent industry, honesty, and frugality.

Among other regulations, under the new system, all owners and captains of vessels should be formally notified of the fact, and that they would be held liable to take all emigrants back, free from charge, and to maintain them whilst in port, whom they had brought out contrary to the emigration law.

But I expect this scheme or proposition will be objected to by many, who will say, "such restrictions would be inconsistent with our liberties and the spirit of true republicanism, would prevent hundreds and thousands of monarchially oppressed subjects from participating in the benefits to be derived from our free institutions and more equitable governments, and that without the present free and unlimited admission of emigrants we should be prevented from executing great public works as heretofore."

To these objections, I reply, that the unrestricted exercise of any liberty or privilege which is productive of so much evil as this is, ought to be restrained; not only for the sake of our national respectability and the well-being of our native population, but for the sake also of those unfortunate persons who having already filled our ports, cities, and towns, with the poor and the helpless, are, some of them, in worse positions than when at home and living under European governments. Moreover, it is evidently injudicious and impolitic for us to place it in the power of kings and aristocracies and their suborganizations, to send hither hundreds of thousands of their ignorant, superstitious, and least valuable subjects for us to educate, reform, and maintain. And as it respects the prosecution of great public works, I say, that a great number are got up without necessity, as matters of speculation, and go into forgetfulness, never having been intended for the public use, and never brought to maturity; I say that we have no occasion to do the work of five centuries in one, and whatever is done hastily and recklessly is sure to be done ill; and therefore we had better do less and do it well. But railroad, canal, and other companies might, upon showing that they could not obtain laborers and operatives, be permitted to import workers and become chargeable with their maintenance and traveling expenses on their arrival.

## 22.  An Irish View of the Emigrant's Opportunities

### A.  1854[1]

Now, look at the poor immigrant, who, on reaching the shores of the Republic, thanks heaven that he has "got to America," and then sits down quietly in some back lane or alley in New York or Philadelphia, and remains there to the last of his days, "a hewer of wood and drawer of water" to the rest of the community. He is not only a despised drudge himself, but his children are reared among evil influences; and as for the "social position" of himself and family—what is it? On the other hand, were he, on landing here, to proceed directly westward, to the broad green lands that lie there, clothed in flowers and sunshine, he would possess, in a few years, a pleasant country home, and be what he never can be in the lanes of the city; namely, an independent man, under obligation to no being but the God above him. His children will

---

[1] Extract from the *Citizen*, I (New York, Feb. 18, 1854), 105. See below, p. 625, note 1.

have no vicious examples daily before their eyes; but they will grow up in virtue, and be—as many sons of Irishmen are—among the noblest and most distinguished citizens of the Republic.

I am happy to state that a large proportion of immigrants do pursue the course here indicated. The great majority of Germans do, and a number of the Irish; but it is my earnest wish that they would all do it, and that the poor labourers now inhabiting the lanes and alleys of our Atlantic cities may bestir themselves, and go out to the beautiful lands of the far West as soon as possible, where they can all become respectable farmers if they have the will. . . . .

### B. 1855[1]

Westward Ho! The great mistake that emigrants, particularly Irish emigrants, make, on arriving in this country is, that they remain in New York, and other Atlantic cities, till they are ruined, instead of proceeding at once to the Western country, where a virgin soil, teeming with plenty, invites them to its bosom. Here, from the inadequate protection afforded them by the Commissioners of emigration, they become the easy prey of runners, boarding-house keepers and other swindlers; and, when their last cent is gone, they are thrown into the street, to beg or starve or steal, for employment there is none. Many, who in their native land were strangers to drunkenness and other vices, are here seduced by acts of the villains by whom they are surrounded, till they are steeped to their lips in infamy, their character is lost, their peace is gone, and the bright prospects, for which they encountered the perils of the ocean, have vanished like a vision. They sink into a pauper's grave. Had they continued their journey westward, without halting, many of them would be now enjoying the happiness of independence, "monarchs of all they surveyed, with none their right to dispute." Their children and their children's children would revel in the glories and the grandeur of nature, and a healthy progeny would transmit their names to latent posterity. Here, in the crowded cities of the seaboard, reeking with vice and crime, they are not only exposed to temptation, but they are jostling with the natives, and even with those who have reached these shores but a few years before them. Either their squalid misery is an eye-sore, and the Irish name is loathed for their sake; or they have strength and skill to work, and their labor, if they find employment, comes into competition with the labor which already exceeds the demand, and the result is to drive good men out of

[1] Extract from the *Citizen*, II (New York City, February 3, 1855), 73.

employment, or to reduce wages to starvation prices, on which human beings may vegetate and rot, but upon which it is impossible for them to live.

What then is the duty of the unemployed or badly paid emigrants residing in New York, Philadelphia and Boston? To start at once for the West.

In connexion with this important subject, we would advert to a letter published by a gentleman in Staten Island, containing the results of a circular he addressed, through the newspapers, to the farmers last Fall, for information respecting the demand for labor, the rates of wages, the cost of board, and the prospect of a poor man becoming the owner of an estate.

This gentleman, whose name is Olmsted, states that he received eighty-eight replies from various districts in nineteen states, and that out of these there were only nine who did not ask for more laborers, and seventy-three replies say that instances of workmen becoming proprietors are frequent. Eighty-six out of the eighty-eight represent the employees of both sexes as sitting at the same table with the employers, the women dressing quite as well as the farmers' daughters, and all of them sure to get well married whenever they please.

In some of the villages four-fifths of the owners of the land were laborers. One or two years' service is sufficient to earn enough to enable them to purchase 80 to 100 acres of Government land, erect a house upon it, set up farming on their own hook, and employ the next new comers.

Mr. Olmsted has compiled, from the letters he received, a table of wages. In Iowa, $240 are given, in Michigan, $230, in Illinois, $220, in Wisconsin from $100 to $150, in Connecticut, $180, the highest in Northern States. In New York, wages range from $85 to $100. In all cases these prices are in addition to board.

There are two million and a half of farmers in the United States, inviting the idle labor of our large cities. What hinders this labor from supplying the demand? In many cases no legitimate reason can be assigned—there is no excuse for emigrants with money in their pockets becoming loafers in New York. But there are other cases in which extreme poverty is an effectual barrier. What is the advice of common sense to these? Mr. Olmsted observes: "Common Sense seems to say, 'Give not soup, but railway-tickets, to your unemployed; distribute them with careful minuteness, and, in ten days, every willing man may be permanently provided for.'"

This is the way in which the Commissioners of Emigration ought to dispose of the funds raised by the tax on emigrants, instead of wasting them in keeping an army of able-bodied paupers and another army of officials on Ward's Island.[1] Let the poor but brave man who is too proud to enter such an asylum proceed even twenty miles into the country in any direction, and his labor will find a market. A farmer even in Madison County, New York, states that three hundred laborers could find employment all the year round in a single town, and more than 4,000 might easily obtain work in the whole county.

To the West, then, ye starving sons of toil—to the West! where there is food for all, employment for all, and where for all there are happy homes and altars free.

### 23. Advice to Emigrants[2]

. . . . Emigrants should leave the overcrowded cities on the sea coast as soon as possible and go up the country, and further the better, and, leaving the main lines of travel, where emigrants are in each other's way, scatter right and left, inquiring for work on any terms. The propensity of emigrants to remain about large cities, and especially those on the sea coast, is very much complained of by Americans, and with too much foundation. There they land at the rate of a thousand or more daily throughout the year; many of them loiter days, weeks, and months, wasting their money and idling away their precious time, quietly waiting for Providence to turn up something for them, until their last penny is spent, their trunks are retained by the lodging-house keepers to pay their bills, and they are turned out beggars on the streets. Meanwhile, a few hundred miles up the country throughout the spring and summer they are badly wanted, and might at such times, if common labourers, be earning 4s. 2d. sterling a day, boarding themselves, or if good harvesters, even as much as 8s. 4d. sterling, besides their board. They should not stickle for high wages at first, when their abilities are not known, but care more to learn during the first month how to earn high wages afterwards.

The American import duty on poor emigrants seeking to better their condition, ought to be abolished. What would be thought of the justice of levying an equal amount of poor's-rate from the poorest as

[1] [For the work of the Commissioners of Emigration, see the first volume in this series, E. Abbott, *Immigration: Select Documents and Case Records*, pp. 140, 172.]

[2] Extract from Vere Foster, *Work and Wages; or the Penny Emigrant's Guide to the United States and Canada* (London, 1855), pp. 10–12.

from the richest classes of society? Besides, the owners of city property in America are immensely benefited by this immigration. . . . .

Some of my readers may have been lately cautioned by those who wish to check emigration, against emigrating at all to America, on account of the distress in its overcrowded Eastern Cities this winter from overspeculation and bankruptcies as eighteen years ago, and universal short crops, and a partial stoppage of trade caused by the European war. . . . .

Other persons may have been cautioned against emigrating to America on account of the political prejudice which has been growing there of late against foreigners, and more especially against Irish Catholics, on account of a numerous faction who have nicknamed themselves Know-nothings, seemingly because, like upholders of slavery, they know nothing of true republican principles, since they profess in the same breath civil and religious liberty, and uncompromising hostility to Roman Catholics. Should immigration to the United States receive any material check, these people would soon be brought to their senses, since railway and highway contractors, builders, farmers, and other employers of labour, though the most arrantly bigoted know-nothings, can hardly get on without a supply of labourers, mechanics, and domestic servants, whose industry is the foundation of their fortunes, as well as of those of New York shipowners and owners of city property, &c.

They will therefore be interested in inviting as much as possible, instead of checking immigration to their shores, putting up with its few drawbacks for the sake of its great benefit. The know-nothing movement may be looked upon as a passing gust of popular bigotry, provoked by injudicious conduct on the part of many foreigners, showing its strength in the ballot box, but . . . . not interfering with the prospects of the working classes, and honourably opposed by much of the most respectable and popular press in America for instance, the *New York Times* and *Tribune*, which, with the *Herald*, have the largest circulation.

In conclusion, I am anxious to repeat that, in my opinion, the apprehension of a more general war in Europe, and consequently of more stoppage of trade and employment, and of increased taxation and distress in this country, which are already beginning to be felt, render it more especially desirable that the poorer classes of this country should emigrate now, for the sake of all who are dear to them, and whom they would wish to shield from future suffering. Emigration lotteries might,

I think, be instituted with great advantage, as a more effectual means of raising wages, and otherwise bettering the condition of the working classes, than strikes, or any probable parliamentary reform.

## 24. Advice to Germans Contemplating Emigration, 1853[1]

At present, among all the countries to which European immigrants are accustomed to go, the United States offers the best chance for a successful future for German emigrants, and, in some cases, even offers an opportunity for an improvement in their condition. There remains the further question, "To what part of the United States ought the emigrants to go?" And this question has been answered from time to time very differently because individual experiences, opinions, and interests have furnished the basis for, or modified, the opinion expressed.

The greatest stream of immigrants arriving from Europe (including Germans) spreads from New York to the western states and regions: Michigan, Wisconsin, Illinois, and Iowa. Americans from the East also emigrate to those states as well as to Texas, California, and Oregon. Through the emigration of these Americans in the West, room has been left for European immigrants in many a region of the eastern states where the land, through the American method of exhausting the soil, has become impoverished and has fallen in productivity as well as in price. By the German methods of fertilizing with manure the soil can easily be restored to productivity; and, because of the better means of communication and other advantages of the East, they are preferred by the Germans to the poor and desert regions of the West, where the settlers for the most part still have to struggle for years with the hard conditions of cultivating a virgin soil, with little apparent progress. The western parts of the states of New York, Pennsylvania, and Virginia seem to be the most suitable regions of the United States for the German system of agriculture. Along the Alleghany river in the western part of Pennsylvania the green meadows cut through by many brooks between wooded hills, the prosperous friendly towns, the numerous farms with granaries and with manure heaps on the fields vividly remind the immigrant or the traveler of Germany. The young but large state of Texas has become the emigrants' goal through the *Mainzer Verein zum Schutze deutscher Auswanderer*, which was founded in

[1] Extract translated from Gottfried Menzel, *Die Vereinigten Staaten von Nordamerika, mit besonderer Rücksicht auf deutsche Auswanderung dahin; nach eigener Anschauung beschrieben* (Berlin, 1853), pp. 354–60.

1844. Although this *Verein*[1] soon began to decay and was obviously destined for an inglorious end, it still deserves to be commended for having founded a place of colonization for German emigrants, which in spite of all unfavorable, or prejudiced, accounts and warnings attracts more and more Germans. To the northwest of San Antonio—New Braunfels and Austin, where the higher mountain region begins—there spreads out a very great region chiefly settled by Germans, which may be described as a very favorable district for immigrants because of its healthy situation, the price of the land, opportunities to market the products, and free opportunities to raise cattle on the prairies. But in the unhealthy southern and southeastern parts of Texas the Germans should not settle, however fertile the ground may be.

Toward California and Oregon the immigrants are chiefly adventurers and criminals.

*Observations for artisans desiring to emigrate.*—Skilled laborers command in North America rather good earnings; but not every German artisan can expect to make full use of his skill immediately. As regards this point one must note the following:

1. Many artisans emigrate to America because in the German home they could not compete with their trade associates and fell behind because their work did not meet the demand of the public or because they were lacking in physical strength or in skill or diligence or because they did not accomplish enough and therefore remained at a lower level of earnings.

Such artisans as these, who, in Germany, found themselves inferior to others, lack the very qualities most needed for real success in America, and they will find themselves over-seas in the same inferior position in relation to their working companions as in the old home. Such immigrants stay where they find positions in the workshops of the eastern states and are obliged to work for a lower wage and where their work is rated at the same low level as in Germany. . . . . Therefore when it is reported that such and such an artisan earns from one to two dollars in America, then these inferior workers ought to count on receiving one dollar only.

2. However, in considering the high American wages of one to two dollars a day, people, always leave out of consideration the fact that over there money, in proportion to other things, has a far lower value

[1] For an account of the *Mainzer Adelsverein*, see Document 34, Section I, pp. 133–36.

than in Germany. That is, a dollar in America does not purchase as much as the equivalent of the dollar (2 Fl. 4 Kreuzer) in Germany.

The habit of saving is not common in America, and the Germans lose it after they emigrate and adopt the less thrifty habits of the Americans. One spends a coin more easily there because it is soon earned easily again. In general the workingman's standard of living is higher; in food and clothing the artisan demands as much as the tradesmen.

Many things are much more expensive in America than in Germany. This is true, for example, of lodgings. It is necessary to pay in the small towns $5 to $6 a month for a wooden hut in which the wind often blows out the light on the table. In Germany one would hardly pay as many dimes for this, if one should be satisfied with such a lodging. Medical help, which is very often needed, and schooling for the children, are equally high in America in comparison with Germany.

Attention must also be called to the fact that public taxes are by no means unimportant. And to these regular taxes the exceptional taxes must be added. In the larger and smaller cities in the United States the immigrant Germans are at first shocked to find that many things are lacking which must be furnished at the expense of the inhabitants, public buildings, pavements, bridges, water-supply, and for these things the citizen must make considerable contributions. There must be added also contributions for church affairs. . . . .

If these and similar conditions are taken into account the high earnings of America shrink very considerably. The man who earns in Germany 30 Kreuzer every day and who can only count on one dollar in America does not gain any material advantage from emigration except that he gets better food there.

3. Many an immigrant artisan does not find over there a place where he can carry on his trade with success. He gets into a place where he finds no opportunity to practice his trade or where he is not needed or where his products can be bought better and cheaper in the stores. If weavers, belt-makers, stonemasons, etc., go to Texas or Wisconsin they will not earn anything by their trade. It is a very astonishing fact that many persons emigrate to America completely in ignorance of the condition of the trades over there. Thus I was asked in Albany by a recent immigrant, a German gamekeeper, if I did not know where he could get good employment as gamekeeper or forester, and he was highly astonished when I explained to him that in the whole union there was not a single gamekeeper or forester employed.

4. Many artisans cannot carry on their trades independently in America but must look for employment in the different large workshops or factories where all articles are produced by machinery cheaper and better than by hand. To this group among others belong: comb-makers, dyers, weavers, machinists, belt-makers, and distillers.

5. Those artisans who want to play the master in America but do not want to work themselves ought to understand that every other journeyman could be a master just as well as he and could handle his trade independently if he did not have to have considerable capital for it.

6. Without knowledge of the language and of American conditions it is difficult and dangerous for an immigrant to start a large business by himself. If he does not know the markets and the sources of raw materials but must rely on others he will always come out short in the speculative life of America. Enterprises founded by newly arrived immigrants always come to an early end with the loss of the capital invested. Every immigrant who has been an independent artisan and tradesman in Germany must be again an apprentice in America and he who thinks himself above serving a new apprenticeship will not succeed there.

7. The different trades vary in the opportunities and earnings they offer to immigrant German workmen in North America. Artisans in the following trades are most certain of finding a living and a wage of one to two dollars a day and sometimes more in exceptional circumstances, although not always immediately or in the ports of arrival: rifle-makers, blacksmiths, tinsmiths, locksmiths, watchmakers, wheel-rights, joiners, carpenters, tailors, barbers, saddlers, if they are at the same time harnessmakers, and liquor sellers, among whom there are many Germans who do not know how to make their living in any other way.

The following can count on earning nearly as much as the above, but only in the larger cities of the eastern states or their neighborhoods: confectioners, brewers, distillers, millers, dyers, soap-boilers, coopers, turners, masons, stonecutters, brickmakers, file-cutters, belt-makers, gardeners, tanners, papermakers, shoemakers, hatmakers, ropemakers, potters (who are seldom wanted). Miners and glassmakers must go out from Philadelphia to where the mines and glass works are. Persons employed in cotton-spinning and weaving, for which children are chiefly employed, earn little, and a great many have been laid off for some time because the cotton manufacture is in a state of depression.

The following have little chance of making a living: merchants, bakers, except in a German neighborhood, cloth-weavers, booksellers, printers, and bookbinders.

No work at all will be found by goldsmiths, glovemakers, linen-weavers, because their products are imported from Europe; and glazers because the panes which the carpenter uses are already cut in definite sizes in the factory; nailmakers, because nails of all kinds are made very cheaply with machines in factories; finally gamekeepers and forest wardens, because in America everyone hunts wherever there is any game. . . . .

People who desire to emigrate should take these remarks to heart and examine themselves earnestly to see if they are free from the many personal qualities and circumstances unfavorable for emigration lest they let themselves be blinded by foolish hopes and thoughtlessly decide on this important step. Let them refuse to gamble with their own welfare and the welfare of their families by making an experiment which they may soon repent very bitterly. Even those who possess the necessary personal qualities and who have trades adapted to American conditions will have to withstand many a danger and undergo many a trial before they reach the prosperous state to which they look forward. I found unsatisfied Germans in all trades in North America, the fewest among the women who go as maids. Everywhere women who are willing to engage as servants find a living and good treatment and work far easier than in Germany and, if they prove worthy, even an acceptable offer of marriage; even the American men like German girls with good morals for wives because they are more industrious than Americans and make fewer demands for service and luxuries.

### 25.  The Educated German in America[1]

It has been intimated before that those for whom in the native land things do not go according to their wishes and desires, only too often have the mistaken idea that mere landing at an American port is all that is necessary to make their fortune easily and quickly. For this reason many who, if they were wiser, would stay at home, start on their way to the New World. They believe that because one does not need money here, all other requirements for success can be fulfilled. That is a sad and serious mistake for which many, soon after their arrival, suffer in the hospital, in the poorhouse, and in the cemetery.

[1] Extract translated from Karl Büchele, *Land und Volk der Vereinigten Staaten von Nord Amerika. Zur Belehrung für Jedermann, vorzüglich für Auswanderer* (Stuttgart, 1855), pp. 476–81.

Even though a fortune is not always needed to found an independent existence in America, other capital is necessary: that of youth, health, physical vigor, and untiring endurance. Those who come with ragged and empty pockets but are equipped with these characteristics will certainly in the course of time become honorably independent. The farmer, first of all, and after him the manufacturer, mechanic, chemist, and technical man may find a carefree livelihood here. Those also who are without the strength or inclination to devote themselves to agriculture and think it more desirable to act as servants to the Yankees in the cities will get ahead easily and be able to put aside many a dollar. The American has too much pride and sense of independence to be forced by anything but the most pressing circumstances to undertake the rôle of servant. Therefore, we find all the most inferior positions in the American home occupied by Irish or German immigrants. Almost the whole contingent of American servants is supplied by European immigration; and, if fate at some time forces an American to such a state of dependence, he applies all his energies to escape from a situation which according to American ideas means degradation.

For many years rich sources of opportunity will be open to the working classes of Europe who, because of need, unemployment, and overpopulation turn to the New World; if they only fulfil the foregoing requirements, they will also overcome and forget the familiar memories of the mother country the easiest because of the material advantages of the adopted country. Making a livelihood is much more difficult for that class of immigrants which the political change in European conditions drove to the longed-for land of the future, of which they had dreamed. The position of the educated immigrant who is bound to the old country and his fate by all the ties of the heart, while only his intellect becomes familiar with the progressive movements of the New World, becomes all the more oppressive for him as his prospects become less bright day by day because of the enormous increase in educated immigrants. His field of endeavor becomes more and more limited, and it is not surprising that many a man becomes alienated from the goddess of liberty when he sees that she deserts her most ardent followers even in this country. If it is, in general, more difficult for the educated person than for the tradesman to make his living in a strange land where he always lives only as an exotic plant, these difficulties are even increased in a country where everything moves toward a positive goal and serves some real purpose.

The whole army of impractical German philosophers, journal-ists, and literary men has to become altogether degraded here or at least resort to the lowest, most unaccustomed work. Men who are by profession political agitators of the lowest class, lazy tramps, and rascals, find in America the most thankless field.

The man with capital who thinks he can enjoy idleness here will soon get rid of his good money as well as his illusions. The German philosopher who, on account of *Weltschmerz*, has here become a farmer, finds that the American axe is more difficult to wield than the pen, and that the plow and the manure-fork are very matter-of-fact and stupid tools. The German Romanticist is grieved because the speculating Yankee lacks all appreciation of the magic and fairy world of medieval poetry, and the German titled landowner in New Braunfels, Texas, is vexed because no one but he himself uses his title of "Herr von."

The man of higher social levels adapts himself to the new world with a difficulty out of proportion to that experienced by the man of the middle class, because in his case the exchange value is the opposite. At home he enjoyed the advantages of a certain exclusive position and profited by the poverty as well as the humility of the lower classes, in that it was easy for him to find obliging individuals who not only contributed to the comfort of his domestic life, but also to his economic prosperity. In America, where no one is submissive and nobody eager to serve, the educated man is without these advantages. He is forced to lend a hand himself or purchase assistance of others, and this hired service is much more expensive than at home. Again he finds that his aesthetic needs are meagerly satisfied and he misses many of the finer enjoyments of the life of fashionable society. The immigrant of good education who brings with him to America a love for art, science, and all that is beautiful, as a rule soon changes his passion and even loses the inclination to read books. Even the scholar becomes more practical here, but without feeling satisfied with the change. Among the so-called "Latin farmers,"[1] there are scholars who have altogether discarded their old likes and dislikes. They are just as matter-of-fact, and just as averse to reading as the Yankees, but at the same time have not become as practical and happy as they, because along with the other things, they could not rid themselves of old memories.

We would advise the educated man to emigrate only after a searching examination of his character and achievements. There are too many examples in the West of men of good breeding who even under quite

[1] [The educated German farmers in the West were sometimes called "Latin farmers."]

favorable economic conditions are very uncomfortable and, unable to decide to return, drag out a sad and dissatisfied existence.

The man for whom it is a great sacrifice to substitute for his previous habits of life a simple way of living; who cannot, if necessary, absolutely restrict himself to his family and his home; who cannot bring himself to value more highly republican institutions, political freedom, and personal independence and freedom from restraint than the satisfaction of aesthetic needs, the intimate contact with men of similar ambition and level of education, those manifold enjoyments of European capitals . . . . will never find happiness in America, and had best give up the idea of emigrating.

In general, one in advanced years should never voluntarily tear himself away from old customs, unless driven to do so by the pressure of circumstances. Satisfying activity and true contentment are rarely possible for an immigrant who is much past the twenties. In the first years of his life in America, the proletarian as well as the educated man, in the midst of a society whose language he does not understand, whose customs and character in part are sharply contrasted with those of the German, is overcome by a peculiarly oppressive sensation of strangeness which often becomes a painful feeling of homesickness. If the German, as a whole, has no patriotism, he is not without love for his more immediate home, and devotion to the place of his birth, which is natural for all men and is even deeper in uneducated individuals than in persons of the higher ranks of society.

As a rule, one is not even very grateful for the different advantages which, in the end, are offered by a strange country. Exchanges are never made without some discontent, even though everything should succeed in the beginning, the small enjoyments of the past for the richer gratifications of the new life. If one asks serious and dejected countrymen in America who have not completely overcome this process of reaction, what they miss under such apparently favorable conditions the usual answer is: "We do not know ourselves. We do not lack anything; we have bread, live unmolested, and are not kept in leading-strings by the police and officials, but we simply cannot become accustomed to things here." Years and often decades are necessary before time and habit are victorious, and the people learn to appreciate the value of their newly acquired possessions. Even then pictures of the old life in the native land usually appear in one's memory in a rosier light than they deserve. Only the very small minority of the stronger characters perhaps feel nothing of this process or do not allow it to be noticed. Some become fully conscious only in America of many a political chain under which they suffered at home. Then they scold and swear a good deal about German conditions, but many a low sigh is suppressed about one thing or another which in the end one still misses in the exchange.

The women, like all sociable natures, suffer most from unspeakable torments of homesickness. The man who throws himself into the new stream of activity and is seized with new passion for action gets rid of homesickness more quickly. The German woman in the city feels herself excluded from the circle of American women or, little attracted by their activities, hardly ever feels at home among them. In the country she is obliged, even under the most favorable circumstances, to stoop to do work which at home would fall to the most ordinary servant. She has also renounced all the charming enjoyments of a more elegant household, more intimate neighborliness, periodical local festivities and amusements, and finds herself banished in a solitude which is only enlivened by pictures of the past which seem all the more dazzling from a distance. Life in the New World is made bearable for German women only because of dutiful consideration for their families. Without number are the tears which they shed with aching hearts on the soil of America, which at last gives them in its bosom the peace which, while living, they were never able to find.

Whoever wants to adapt himself quickly in America and become altogether happy must come here as a child. There are, to be sure, some highly educated men in the West who find in the new freedom of America a substitute for all they have lost. Such men, however, are usually solaced in part in the more intimate family life, reading Goethe or playing the violin, when they are overcome by feelings of loneliness and sadness. Or they seek and find enjoyment in the life of nature as farmers, hunters, and fishermen. The number of such men, however, is not large, and among German immigrants only the life of youth is untroubled by any shadow of homesickness. . . . .

But how easily could thousands who have sought their fortune on the other side of the ocean have made their living at home, if they had wanted to suffer voluntarily the privations which they were forced to undergo over there. Whoever has associated with the lower- or middle-class German population of New York, probably still remembers meeting many a family which was crowded into a room or rather a corner of a cellar serving as living-room, sleeping-quarters, and even kitchen. A hollow was made in the wall, and there was a small earthen pot with a double bottom (for coal) and airholes, the only cooking utensil in which at noon the meager meal was prepared. He saw workshops with two windows, at one of which a clock repairer, at the second a shoemaker, plied his miserable trade, while in the background a barber took care of his business; beer houses consisting of two rooms in the basements where in the front room at a few tables, the small number of guests served with brandy or beer, in the adjoining back room, which was barely covered with plaster, man and wife and children slept and, besides, in a corner, behind a wooden partition, sublet some space to a boarder. Two-thirds of them would in the first years, oh, how gladly, have returned to the native land if they had only been able to obtain the means, and perhaps would have been much wiser and better off. Gradually their senses become dulled, and, with pitiful apathy, they put up with a fate which they are no longer able to change. However, instead of warning their countrymen at home, they feel a kind of spiteful satisfaction in watching them face a similar fate, which they perhaps even try to bring about as far as it is within their power.

### 26.  Emigration and Population Statistics, 1850–60[1]

The influence of emigration upon statistics of population has varied greatly in the different states of Europe. In most of the states of Western Europe in the last thirty years the number of emigrants has considerably exceeded the number of immigrants, and this has been particularly true of Great Britain, and especially of Ireland, of Switzerland and of the western and southwestern parts of Germany (Würtemberg, Baden, Grand Duchy of Hesse). At present, in all the German states, emigration is greater than immigration except in the districts of the free cities, where there is an increase in population coming from the outside. However, it is very significant that it has been proved that in Prussia in the last twelve years there has been a considerable excess of immigrants over emigrants. During the eighteen years from 1823 to 1840, Prussia increased its population by at least 700,000 persons, that is, an annual average increase of 0.3 per cent of the entire population, and this increase from the outside has been growing during the whole of this period. At present this situation has also changed very greatly in Prussia. . . . . The population of the German federated states at present (1856) amounts to approximately 44,000,000, and in 1846 it

[1] Extract translated from J. E. Wappäus, *Allgemeine Bevölkerungsstatistik* (Leipzig, 1859–61), Vol. I, 99–107.

was, at most, 42,000,000. The increase during this decade has been about 4.76 per cent, or on the average annually 200,000 persons. . . . .

On the other hand, German emigration in the year 1854 reached its highest point, the huge number of nearly 252,000 persons. It fell off in the following year to 81,698, and although it has since risen, going up to 98,573 in 1856, it has yet in these last years remained much below the level of 1854. Before 1846 German emigration, which first began to be considerable in the forties, had in no year reached the number 100,000. From Bremen there went, in the ten years from 1834 to 1843, only 64,-690 German emigrants to North America, and from 1846 to 1856 the annual average was a little more than 130,000. These figures, however, do not take into consideration the return immigration, which in the year 1854 was in the proportion of 1 to 32, and in 1855 1 to 11. After these years the annual loss by emigration equaled the large figure of two-fifths of the natural increase of the population of Germany. But for the whole period for which we have calculated the movement in the previously mentioned German states, this influence is reduced to very small proportions. In the other European states . . . . the effect of emigration upon the movement of population has been even slighter. The only exception is the United Kingdom of Great Britain and Ireland, where the population is extraordinarily influenced by emigration, especially in Ireland. . . . .

The movement of emigration has much greater influence upon the population of the country to which the emigrants go than upon the country which they leave. This is especially true of new countries where there are vast regions of fertile uncultivated land, and where the material development is encouraged by free political institutions. In such states an important and continuing increase of population may be seen. Probably the influence of immigration upon the population of the United States would have reached its maximum in these last months if emigration had not been given a new and strong impulse through newly created conditions. These were, especially, the increasing misery in Ireland, the revolutions in France and Germany in 1848, the increase of the territory of the United States through the annexations, especially of Texas and California, and the discovery of gold in California. Through the combined influence of all these factors in addition to the always strong influence of the masses of immigrants already settled in a new country upon friends and relatives in the old home, immigration reached unexpected heights . . . . and without doubt the next American census (1860) will show the very important influence of immigration upon population.

Such an increase of population from outside has never been shown in any other state. Of course, some British colonies, Canada, Australia, and New Zealand, in more recent times have shown greater population gains than the United States, but such cases need not be taken into account, since they are not independent states but only colonies, parts of larger states from which they receive the population overflow just as the population of the older states of the New World overflows to the other new territories.

If a regular and long-continued increase of population in a state is to be regarded as a sign of prosperity, this is even more the case if the increase is due to immigration. Immigration not only brings hands for labor but capital as well. On the other hand, immigration must bring with it certain disadvantages on the political side, but this influence is very different in the different states. Under the present circumstances, when the European emigrants go across the ocean, those European nations that have no colonies to receive the emigrants suffer the loss not only of labor but also of a substantial withdrawal of capital, for which they are not compensated by the flourishing condition of the over-seas territories. Thus, for example, those German states . . . . from which an annual tide of emigration flows to the United States and other countries over-seas, lose and have lost not only the people who leave, but also whatever they take with them to help them settle in the new country. Poor people whom the state would be glad to see emigrate very seldom are able to emigrate to the new countries because they have not the means. It is different in states like Great Britain, where large numbers of emigrants go to the British colonies. There the losses of the motherland are compensated in the prosperity of her colonies, and there the state can assist in the emigration of the indigent since their productive force goes to benefit the colony. This is not the case in Germany, where no compensation is received for the emigrants she loses. If you calculate on the basis of 100 thaler per head,[1] then, in the last ten years, counting the average annual emigration at 100,000 persons, Germany has lost 100,000,000 thaler capital. Somewhat different is the proportion if, as has been frequently the case in Germany, part of the emigration goes to the neighboring states to remain for a shorter or longer time. . . . . This is true especially of those persons who without means find positions as servants, especially sons and daughters of

[1] [A thaler was equal to three marks.]

cottagers and the younger sons and daughters of peasants. They take no capital away from the country; on the contrary they bring something back to the country because they very often return with their savings. Through this kind of emigration the country does not lose as much as through the emigration of families to the over-seas countries, from which, if they are well off, they seldom return.

Any gain to the country of emigration is, however, exceptional. On the whole, as has been said, the state to which immigration brings an increase of population has the advantage for its gains not only in labor force but in capital. But here again there are certain differences. If a European state already highly cultivated and densely populated increases its population by immigration, as was, for example, the case with Prussia, the greater number of immigrants are probably not entirely destitute adults, but are artisans, manufacturers, farmers, merchants, artists, and scientists and so on. No European state will admit entirely destitute people. Here, therefore, immigration brings still greater gains than in countries which attract the emigrants by their supplies of unoccupied and fertile land. To these latter the emigrants go for the most part in families consisting of laborers and persons who are not yet able to support themselves by their own labor, i.e., children and old people who must be supported by others. It must, therefore, be accepted that under present conditions Germany suffers certain economic losses because of over-seas emigration, yet on the other hand the theory that the increase in German emigration is threatening to the prosperity of Germany and will lead to the prevalence of great political, social, or industrial distress must be contradicted.

For if one takes into consideration the fact that emigration, especially emigration to America, has become very much easier in recent times since it has become a subject of commercial speculation, then the increase in emigration does not as a matter of fact seem to be so important. In no other country is the business of emigration so well organized as in Germany. It is well known that Bremen owes the recent flourishing growth of its shipping interests to the transportation of emigrants to North America. . . . . Bremen recognized the great importance of the transport of emigrants for its shipping and its trade.

The supremacy of Bremen having been established, great competition developed, especially after the American export trade to Germany had been attracted to Bremen through the cheap return freights of the emigrant ships. Emigration via Bremen, however, became constantly more elaborately organized, and could therefore still be lucrative in spite of a great reduction in the price of passage. For a long time the shipping agencies have contributed enormously to the increase of emigration, not only through making emigration easy but also through direct stimulation, partly by alluring public advertisements and partly by methods that were almost unlawful, and thus many people emigrate who if left to themselves would never have thought of such a step. Of these emigrants many a one later regrets bitterly in America that he ever left the Fatherland.

These agencies Bremen has gradually spread over all Germany to secure emigrants. In our country not only every small town, but many a village has been favored with such an agency.

It is a matter of regret that Hamburg, which for a long time kept itself free from the endeavor to base the rise of its shipping industry on the passenger traffic, recently has followed Bremen and appears even to attempt to surpass it especially in the transport via England, which for the most part lies in the hands of English speculators. It is obvious that as a result of this commercial speculation in German emigration, the English transport business inevitably increases.

### 27.  Emigration in Relation to Overpopulation in Germany[1]

The most common hope expressed in Germany with regard to emigration is that it will be a safe cure for the ills of overpopulation from which so many parts of our fatherland either actually suffer or at least think they suffer. I say "think they suffer" because the evil certainly, in a large part of Germany, is of a kind that could be overcome through the development of native industrial resources. . . . .

The hope must be abandoned that real overpopulation can be remedied merely by emigration.[2] The great majority of people always believe what they wish to believe, and especially in respect to this subject where speculation has run riot and there are so many basely selfish interests continually seeking to increase the emigration mania. But the exaggerated opinions and hopes which a whole people forms of the value of emigration are a great misfortune. The increase in population, taking human nature as it is, always has a tendency to go just as far as the means of subsistence, in the broadest sense of the word, will permit. This law of nature is as certain as the law of gravity. Every in-

---

[1] Extract translated from Wilhelm Roscher, *Kolonien, Kolonialpolitik und Auswanderung* (zweite verbesserte und stark vermehrte Auflage; Leipzig, 1856), pp. 344–62. Some of Roscher's footnotes have been omitted in this extract.

[2] Casual emigration is little more than bleeding at the nose for inflammation of the lungs.

crease in the food supply, whether it rests upon increased production or decreased needs, brings with it an increase in the number of inhabitants. Thus a generally supposed increase in emigration must have the same consequences that would follow an actual increase in this movement.

Emigration has at the present time become so immensely the fashion that millions of Germans believe not only that the immigrants themselves profit by it but also that those whom they leave behind will have room for a comfortable increase themselves. Undoubtedly because of this hope numerous marriages are contracted and more children are born than would otherwise have been the case. This can naturally, if our supposition was wrong, only make the existing overpopulation still worse if such extraordinary myths are believed as that of the five million Germans who for more than ten years have been living in the confines of the United States.

One might mention, for example, the principality of Osnabrück, where since 1841 a slight decrease of population occurred—about 45 persons to the square mile, and who may be for the most part ascribed to the rapidly increasing emigration (1841, 156,430 inhabitants; 1847, 154,509, on $42\frac{1}{2}$ square miles). In a still greater degree this may be seen in Ireland, where the population in 1841 was 8,175,000 persons, and in 1851 only 6,515,000—to be sure not merely the result of emigration but also of starvation and disease. Even the population of the whole United Kingdom may at the present time be less than seven years ago, as, for example, in 1852 the excess of births over deaths amounted to only 225,000. But one must realize that the decrease of population which emigration causes appears suddenly, while the increased birth-rate, which is caused by the larger possible food supply and hope of spreading out, appears only gradually. Already, however, in England marriages and births have increased since the great emigration. Thus there were annually in 1847–49, 138,000 deaths and 560,000 births; and in 1852, there were 158,000 deaths and 624,000 births; and in the first six months of 1853, there have been already 320,000 births. . . . .

Let no one think that men who are really useless at home could be of any use in the colonies. Oh no! The laborer is paid well over there, but much is expected of him in return. I could mention a great many statements of colonists in which they vigorously objected to the emigration of those who had been inmates of the English poor-houses. Those classes of people who are most eager to emigrate—the idle and restless who are eager for a change, fathers of families with too many children, tradesmen who have lost their means of livelihood by sudden changes in industry—it is especially difficult for those people to find an occupation on the other side of the ocean. For example, three government ships arrived in Australia some time ago, when there was a great demand for labor. One of the ships was filled with agricultural laborers from Sussex and Kent, the second with people from Gloucestershire who had formerly worked in factories, the third with Irish. How different was the ease with which these people found a means of livelihood in their new homes. The agricultural laborers were already being rapidly engaged, the second only tolerably well, but half the poor Irish could not find any work. During the first fourteen days after their arrival these immigrants who had nowhere to go were given free room and board in the barracks, after which time they were dismissed. A great part of these Irish thereupon became a charge upon public and private charity. What would have happened to those poor Silesian weavers[1] who even at home had been too weak for agriculture and felling trees. Most of the colonists refuse to accept emigrants who are more than forty years old. But now a young laborer who is mentally and physically vigorous can succeed everywhere in Europe; only the weak go to the ground in the general pressure of overpopulation. . . . .

The emigrating part of the nation may find itself benefited by emigration, but the great mass remaining behind may be poorer in capital and in men able to work and comparatively richer in the number of the poor. The immense contrast at home of great riches and great poverty and destitution may be accentuated by emigration because it is almost exclusively a small middle class that emigrates to the places where there is opportunity for agricultural pursuits. The very rich as a rule do not wish to emigrate, and the proletariat cannot afford to emigrate.

All these doubts could be laid aside if the emigrating part of the population remained closely connected economically with the part of the population remaining behind. For not only is "elbow room" created by emigration in the motherland, but there arises at the same time an increased demand for trade products and an increased supply of raw materials through which an absolute increase of wealth and trade is made possible. For, as Torrens has shown, there is no kind of trade so favorable for productivity and economic expansion as the exchange of food and raw materials against manufactured products.

England enjoys, as is known, these advantages to the highest de-

[1] The English have arranged for emigrating weavers to undertake the light work of sheep farming in Australia with good results.

gree. We Germans, however, with our emigration, unfortunately not at all. Our emigrants, whether they go to Canada or to the United States, to Russia or to Australia or to Algiers, are as a rule forever lost to the fatherland with all that they are and all that they take with them. They become the customers and the producers of foreign peoples and not infrequently of our rivals and enemies. M. H. Say shrewdly compares the German emigration of today to the annual sending out of an army of more than 100,000 men fully equipped, which, as soon as it steps over the frontier, disappears forever. Also it appears from the national point of view, that the condition of our emigrants gives cause for very little rejoicing. Most of them are not sufficiently well educated to be able to resist the onslaught of the Americans. The glorious literature of their old home exists for them no more. Almost the only national peculiarity to which they cling over there is the tendency to quarrel with one another. Therefore, in a few generations, after a soul-destroying period of transition, they become completely "de-Germanised." Also the Anglo-Americans with their hundred-fold more energetic interest in speculation, soon bring it about that all the better pieces of land lie in their hands. They then assume the rôle of landlords and officials while the poor Germans play the rôle of day laborers. How rarely do German names appear on the lists of those holding public offices, even in Ohio, while, for example, upon the New York "poor lists" the number of Germans is very significant. One has for this situation the contemptuous but characteristic name, *Völkerdünger* (refuse of the population).

Quite otherwise would the situation be if the stream of German emigration were guided to the neighboring lands lying east of us, to the fruitful and thinly peopled parts of Hungary, to the Polish provinces of Austria and Prussia, finally toward those parts of Turkey which in the future, if God wills it, shall form the heritage of Germany —Moldavia, Wallachia, Bulgaria, and the northern shore of Asia Minor. This is, as is known, an idea which Friedrich List vigorously advocated, and List's unquestioned genius was not at all theoretical but essentially practical. In this way there could arise by peaceable conquest a new Germany which would even surpass the old Germany in greatness, size of population, and wealth, and, at the same time would form the safest bulwark against any Russian danger, Pan-Slavism, etc. This land might be very easily developed for our exclusive use for economic purposes, as the Mississippi Valley and the Far West of the United States. . . . .

Under present conditions the German emigration must be regarded as a total loss to our agricultural industry and trade. As long as these conditions continue, our government authorities will do very wrong if, by carrying their welfare work for emigrants beyond what is necessary for safety of the emigrants, they seem to promote or encourage emigration.

### 28.  Occupations of Immigrants Viewed Unfavorably[1]

The statistics of the occupations of the inhabitants of the United States are very meagre and unsatisfactory. The census of 1850 fails, in this respect, in several important particulars. The number of persons, both male and female, pursuing the various trades and occupations is given, but the nativities are omitted.

To institute a comparison between the native and foreign population, to ascertain the relative proportion of each class pursuing any particular occupation, and to deduce from such a comparison the advantages and disadvantages of immigration to the various trades and professions, it is essentially necessary to have authentic statistics concerning the same. In these investigations, it has been, and will continue to be, the aim of the author to base the facts upon, or deduce them from, official and authentic data.

The only statistics in the census of 1850 in relation to this subject are in a table showing the occupation of passengers arriving in the years 1845, 1847, and 1852, from which, and from the annual report of the Secretary of State for 1854, is compiled the following table [Table I]:

TABLE I

| Occupation | 1845 | 1847 | 1852 | 1854 |
|---|---|---|---|---|
| Laborers................... | 18,656 | 37,571 | 82,571 | 82,420 |
| Servants................... | 1,659 | 3,198 | 948 | 3,310 |
| Not stated, or no occupation.. | 52,768 | 115,167 | 209,131 | 234,396 |

The occupations of laborers, servants, and "not stated," or no occupation, have been selected, because they comprise the whole number of immigrants who are brought in direct competition with American labor.

[1] Extract from Samuel C. Busey, *Immigration: Its Evils and Consequences* (New York, 1856), pp. 77–82, a volume belonging to the Know-Nothing literature of the period.

The following table [Table II] exhibits the number of each of these occupations, and the arrivals for the years stated:

TABLE II

| Year | Arrivals | Servants | Laborers | No Occupation |
|------|----------|----------|----------|---------------|
| 1845........ | 119,884 | 1,659 | 18,656 | 52,768 |
| 1847........ | 239,480 | 3,198 | 37,571 | 115,167 |
| 1852........ | 398,470 | 948 | 82,571 | 209,131 |
| 1854........ | 460,474 | 3,310 | 82,420 | 234,396 |

Half of the arrivals in these four years had no occupation, one-fifth were laborers, and only three-tenths were mechanics, farmers, and tradesmen. Seven-tenths of the arrivals in the years enumerated were laborers or had no occupation, and it is more than probable that seven-tenths of the whole number of arrivals or immigrants are laborers or have no occupation. The effect of this immense influx of the laboring "no-occupation" immigrants, will inevitably depreciate the value of American labor. The price of labor depends upon the demand and supply, and it is indisputably true that for the last few years the supply has increased in a greater ratio than the demand, and consequently the value has diminished, and a large accession has been made to the "no-occupation" class of population; or many, even among the native, who earn their livelihood by the "sweat of their brow," have been compelled to toil for barely sufficient to supply the actual necessaries of life. The meeting of foreigners which took place in the city of New York during the winter of 1855, which was addressed by Roedel, originated in the fact that in that great city the supply of labor was far greater than the demand.

This influx of labor from abroad, which is so antagonistic to the interests of the American laborer, is another circumstance which is likely to hasten that conflict of races which is daily threatened and from which so much danger is to be apprehended.

The following table, compiled from the census, exhibits the number of American laborers of the states enumerated as compared with the number of foreign laborers who arrived during the year 1854. The native laborers of the male sex only are given; and much the larger proportion of female laborers, both native and foreign, are enumerated under the heads of "servants" and "no occupation," therefore the comparisons instituted in the following table approach very nearly to absolute accuracy:

| State | Laborers |
| --- | --- |
| Maine | 21,000 |
| New Hampshire | 13,662 |
| Vermont | 21,993 |
| Massachusetts | 52,661 |
| New York | 174,867 |
| New Jersey | 36,361 |
| Pennsylvania | 148,967 |
| Maryland | 28,908 |
| Virginia | 46,989 |
| Ohio | 86,868 |
| North Carolina | 28,143 |
| Indiana | 28,165 |
| Illinois | 27,910 |

*Number of emigrant laborers who arrived in the year 1854, 82,420.*

The immigrant laborers of 1854 exceed the number of native laborers in each state, with but three exceptions (New York, Pennsylvania, and Ohio). And the aggregate immigrant laborers of 1852 and 1854 exceed the native in each of those three states. The whole number of male laborers (slaves not included) in the United States in 1850, as shown by the census, was 909,786; and the whole number of immigrant laborers for the years 1845, 1847, 1852, and 1854 was 221,218.

Add to the laboring population of any state the immigrant laborers of any one of the years since 1850, or of any one of the five immediately preceding that date, and then conjecture the effect upon the value of labor in such state. For instance, in 1850 the native male laborers of Maine numbered 21,000, each one of whom commanded a certain price, and it is to be presumed the supply was equal to the demand. Say each received one dollar per day, and the number of working days in a year was three hundred. This would give $300 per year per laborer, and the aggregate cost of American labor, in Maine, for the year 1850, would be $6,300,000. Add to the American laborers the immigrant laborers of 1854, the aggregate of the two classes will be 103,420. Labor is worth but $6,300,000 in Maine, which would yield an average yearly income of $69.91 to each of the laborers of both classes, or $23\frac{1}{3}$ cents per day. A similar calculation might be made in reference to the other states. In those states where the native laborers number less than in the state of Maine, the reduction would be much greater, and in those states where the native laborers exceed in number those of Maine, the reduction would not be so great. The instance cited is sufficient to demonstrate the practical effect of immigration upon the value of American labor. The calculation has been based upon the presumption that the *per diem* of the laborers remains the same, thus omitting entirely the effect of competition, the tendency of which is to depreciate the value of labor

In view of the consideration here presented, is not immigration an evil? To the capitalist it is not. It is the ally of the money power of the country, and this money power is being constantly exerted to depreciate the value of labor and of property in which it seeks investments, and the depreciation of the value of any description of property indirectly lessens the value of labor. The capitalists of this country are the allies of Great Britain, and the two in conjunction rule the money market of the world. American labor is the great antagonist to this money power, and it behooves the government of the United States to foster and nourish it, for it is the great bulwark of freedom, and the foster-mother of liberty. It is now being crippled by immigration, and by the same the money power is being made more potential. The augmentation of the money power will more closely unite America and England, and oppress the laboring classes, and especially the American laborers; because immigration both directly and indirectly contributes to this power, in the first instance, by creating a demand for capital and money, and secondly, by depreciating the value of American labor.

### 29. Immigration and Labor: A Know-Nothing View, 1856[1]

The question before us at the present moment is this: Can the American mechanic retain his rights and high social position against the competition of immigrant labor? "Coming events cast their shadows before." The view that I have given of this class is a view of the primitive, natural position of the mechanic, under the unadulterated workings of our system of government. It is a view of his position where all things and all men are in that state of social as well as moral and political equilibrium which is contemplated by our institutions. If that equilibrium is destroyed by any unnatural or uncontemplated antagonism between capital and labor—if the interests of capital become from any cause opposed to the interests of labor, it follows that the rewards of labor must be reduced, and although the intrinsic rights of the mechanic remain, his means of acquiring and assuming those rights are proportionately lessened.

Before the unequal competition of immigrant labor cast its shadow

[1] Extract from Thomas Richard Whitney, *A Defence of the American Policy as Opposed to the Encroachments of Foreign Influence* (New York, 1856), pp. 307–15.

over the industrial interests of our country, every American journey-man mechanic was enabled, by the force of his industry, to maintain a financial position equal to that of his social, moral, and political position. He was sure of employment, at wages adapted to the dignity of his franchise, to the necessities of the present, and the vicissitudes of the future. He could dwell in his own cottage, supply his family with comforts and luxuries, rear his children respectably, find time for his own mental improvement, and lay by a little of his earnings each week for a rainy day. Neatness and cleanliness pervaded his home, and the cheerful hearth was to him the ever-welcome refuge from toil. But with a superabundant immigration from Europe came a train of evils which are now rapidly developing themselves. Many an American mechanic still lives in the enjoyment of all his just privileges, but how great the proportion of those who, from want of employment, or reduced compensation, or both, have been alienated from their homes, their comforts, their ambitions! How vast the number of those who have been driven from their employments to make room for the under-bidding competition of the foreign labor! The American mechanic cannot live upon the pittance demanded by his European competitor. It is not his custom—it was not the custom of his fathers—it is degrading to his sense of self-respect.

I will relate two instances of the manner in which this disparaging competition is carried on.

A German cabinetmaker, who received work from storekeepers, occupied a spacious loft in Ann Street, in the city of New York. In that loft was his workshop and his dwelling. He employed three apprentices, all Germans, and with them was constantly occupied in manufacturing furniture. This man, under a plea of destitution, obtained all his winter fuel, with other necessaries, from the Alms-House department of the city!

The other case is that of a tailor, also a German, who obtained a constant supply of work from clothiers. He employed from eight to ten hands, all of whom boarded with him. This man kept his two children constantly employed *in begging for broken victuals from door to door, by which means his table was supplied with provisions!*

Here are the elements of competition which the American mechanic is called upon, by excessive immigration, to withstand—*imposture and pauperism!* The elements are too unequal. The odds are against him. He cannot contend with them. His moral sensibilities, his sense of self-respect, forbid it. The alternative presented is poverty or disgrace. He chooses the former, and quits his shop, in hopes that something will "turn up" to his advantage. He seeks in vain for employment at remunerating prices. It is not to be had. He must work at the prices of the foreign pauper, or remain idle. He turns to the country, but even there the same spectacle is presented. Foreigners are working the farms. The teeming earth, which has till now sent forth its abundance from beneath the hand of the hardy American farmer, struggles on in a succession of short crops, under the cheap system of European tillage.

In his pressing necessities, the discharged workman bethinks him of the public service. He determines, as a last resort, to obtain some subordinate public office, from the emoluments of which he may support his family with respectability. He has done good service to his party in times past, and he is sure it will not deny him an appointment. For the first time in his life he looks into the public departments, and applies for a situation. He finds every post occupied—occupied by foreigners. There is nothing left to him but submission or beggary. In the workshop, on the farm, and in the public offices, the aspect is the same. In every department he encounters the drudging and importunate foreigner.

To turn from the home of childhood and the associations of early life, and seek subsistence on the broad prairies of the far West—to build his house in the wilderness, and endure the hardships of a pioneer life, becomes his final recourse. But even there he finds the same competition. The foreign squatter has staked out the best portions of the public domain.

Thus the personal interests of the American mechanic are submerged, his rights neutralized, and his hopes thwarted by excessive immigration of the poor of Europe. . . . .

The respectable mechanics of our country . . . . have witnessed the gradual and ruinous absorption of their interests, their social position, and their political rights, through the channel of European pauper competition. The labor of years devoted to the acquirement of an honorable trade has been thrown away, because they could not compete with beggars and impostors. They have appealed in vain to their countrymen, to their employers, and their legislatures for relief, and, as a last resort—as the only means of self-preservation left to them, they have, like their fathers of old, resolved to take the matter into their own hands, and by a combination of action and interest maintain the rights and the dignity of their class. . . . . From these causes sprung the order of United American Mechanics.

The incipient meeting of this organization was held in the city of Philadelphia, Pa., on the evening of the 8th of July, 1845. At that meeting several trades were represented. The object of the meeting was stated by the President, to be the formation of a secret society for the protection of American Mechanics, and a committee was appointed to draft resolutions expressive to this object.

At a subsequent meeting, held July 15th, that committee reported the following:

That we form a society to be called "The American Mechanics' Union," whose object shall be:

1st. To assist each other in obtaining employment.

2d. To assist each other in business, by patronizing each other in preference to foreigners.

3d. To assist the unfortunate in obtaining employment suitable to their afflictions.

4th. To establish a cemetery for deceased members of the society.

5th. To establish a funeral fund.

6th. For the establishment of a fund for the relief of widows and orphans of deceased members.

This code, with the exception of the title, was adopted, and at the next meeting, held on the 22d of the same month, it was "resolved, that the title of the society be 'The United American Mechanics of the United States.'"

On this basis and with this title the society was formed, and an appropriate constitution subsequently adopted.

Whatever may appear to be partial in the 2d clause of this code, as related to foreigners, is justified, first by the exigency which suggested its adoption, and especially by the precedent which had already been set by foreigners themselves. Secret societies, composed entirely of foreigners, and having for their objects the patronage and support of their own countrymen in preference to Americans, existed at that time in almost every city of large population in the United States. . . . .

They must have discovered that the first great cause of the evils which called the order into existence were to be found in a system, of which the pauper competition from Europe was but the natural fruit. The existing laws of naturalization, by which the meanest serf of Europe could be converted into a voter in five years, offered great inducements to the home demagogue to encourage, or at least to wink at, that class of immigration. Were it not for the fact that these men can be used as political instruments by the wire-pullers of the once great parties, the voice of the whole country would long since have been raised against the admission of that class of immigrants, and the two parties, instead of encouraging it, would have vied with each other in the adoption of measures to prevent their admission. . . . .

The interests of the American mechanic lie in the adoption of measures that will check the tide, the overwhelming tide, of European immigration, or, at least, of that class of immigration which, while it imparts nothing to the genius of the country, saps the fountains of honest industry, and brings the deserving to want.

### 30. Immigrants in New York City[1]

#### A. 1852

The subject of occupation also claims attention, because of its direct bearing on the condition of the poor. In all our Atlantic cities, more than half the needy are Irish and German; but whether foreigners or natives, the men requiring aid are generally without mechanical skill, mostly mere day laborers, who have been accustomed only to the rudest and humblest employments. The women of the same class are like the men in these respects, with the additional disadvantage of finding less demand for their services, and less wages. It is true, moreover, of both, that they are generally too far advanced in life to acquire much profitable dexterity in those handicraft operations, which even in youth, when the habits are most pliant, require an apprenticeship of years. But little evidently can be done to increase the productiveness of this class of laborers; yet some have vainly imagined in respect to the women, that they could be so improved in the art of sewing and other appropriate female occupations, as to command for them employment and good wages. But were this practicable, as experience has proved it not to be, yet the promised result cannot be realized while there is so large a surplus of such labor in the market. All correct inductions from facts, would have demonstrated the fallacy of such an expectation, anterior to experiment.

The result of special inquiries directed to the occupations of the poor, show that of the foreigners relieved, more than three-fourths are common laborers, among the men, and washers, house-cleaners, sewers, &c., among the women, there being about an equal proportion of each. In other words, they are mostly persons who have been trained to no trade or regular employment, and having little skill in any, are forced

[1] Extract from *Annual Report of the New York Association for Improving the Condition of the Poor*, 1852, pp. 25–33; 1858, p. 36.

to accept of such as is offered. Hence, during the busy season, the men work about the wharves, or as diggers, hodmen, &c., and the women as rough washers, house-cleaners, coarse sewers, or in any other rude work they can find to do. Such occupations being, at best, irregular and pre-carious; and the women especially, being poorly qualified even for these, it is not surprising that they have but little work and small wages, or that they often need extraneous aid. But to such, relief is cheerfully given, when sobriety, activity, cleanliness, and proper in-struction and training of children can be induced, or where there are other satisfactory indications, that the attentions and assistance be-stowed will not be perverted, so as to weaken the incentives to virtuous industry.

But in this city, where there is so large a redundance of labor, even the possession of industrial skill affords no guaranty either for em-ployment or good wages. Here are probably more than twelve thou-sand seamstresses, whose dependence for a livelihood is on the needle in its various applications for the clothing trade; about two thousand cap-sewers, and several thousand shoe-binders, exclusive of numerous other thousands, who in different ways "ply the polished shaft" for support. Take the case of one of these females for an illustration. The prices paid usually range so low, that with steady work and long hours, the most expert sewer can make but a scanty living. This, as elsewhere shown, is in consequence of the rivalry of the employed among them-selves, and not the fault of the employer. Every person in every busi-ness has to compete with every other person in the same business; and no business man will blame himself or his neighbor, for laying in his goods at the lowest rates. This principle pervades all mercantile operations. The difficulty exists in the fact, that there are more la-borers of this class pressing on the market than the market can ab-sorb. . . . .

And as most of the swelling tide of the emigrants which is pouring into the United States, enter at the port of New York, upon this city devolves, in a peculiarly important sense, the duty of protecting itself, and so far as is practicable, the nation, against the influx of this ter-rible evil. Whatever advantages may generally result in the country from such accessions to the population, the disadvantages are mostly felt at the great point of debarkation. The worst part of the refuse class which is thus thrown upon our shores, here clan together and re-main in the city, nor can they be persuaded to leave it. These mostly consist of imbecile and thriftless parish paupers and dependents, the former inmates of poor-houses and even of prisons, who being unwilling or unable to gain an honest subsistence anywhere, have been sent here, in order to rid the country from which they come of their support, and who become a burden and a nuisance from the moment of their arrival. Many of them are afflicted with pestilential diseases, more or less developed, which, as they wander about in search of shelter, are disseminated through the city to the manifest detriment of public health, and to the destruction of life. During the past year, nearly 80,000 persons of this class, exclusive of those in the Almshouse and Emigration Hospital, were gratuitously attended and prescribed for by three of our City Dispensaries.

## B. 1858

The relief of our over-burdened city of its pauperism, by migrations to the country, is a very popular idea. An inspection of [our statistics] may suggest some of the practical difficulties in the way of so desirable a result. Who and what are the vagrants that swarm our streets, and the indigent that so heavily tax our public charities? The table shows that 73 per cent of a better class aided by this Association, were of foreign birth. Our actual pauperism consists mainly not only of immigrants, but of the accumulated refuse of about two and a half millions of that class, who have landed in New York, within the past ten years. Our city, operating like a sieve, lets through the enterprising and industrious, while it retains the indolent, the aged, and infirm, who can earn their subsistence nowhere, to become a burden, and often because of their vices, a nuisance to the community. Of those relieved by this Association the past year, one-third were laborers, mostly Irish, some few Germans, and others of a similar class. Of the remainder, 44 per cent were reported as washerwomen, chiefly Irish; 44 per cent sewing women, and the balance, about 12 per cent, principally natives and Germans, who were poor and needy, but being willing and anxious to earn their living, were not paupers.

Of a large number of Irish immigrants, it may be said, that they are but little disposed to change their thriftless habits with a change of country. Here, as in their own land, many of them evince too little force and energy to be the arbiters of their own destiny. They are prone to stay where another race furnishes them with food, clothing, and labor. There are very few mechanics among them, and one marked peculiarity, is their settled aversion to agriculture. Unlike immigrants of other nationalities, they have an utter distaste for felling forests, and turning up the prairies for themselves; hence, they are mostly found loitering in cities and villages, and on the lines of our public works. And this disrelish for migration into our new countries, especially to the "far west," appears to decide the impracticability of relieving our city of this class in this way; for if they will not go, where is the power to coerce them? It is not less certain, moreover, especially in respect to the *residuum* of immigration—the pauper class which so largely burdens our city—that if such were willing to go, they are unfit to be their own masters, or to be thrown on their own resources in a new country, or anywhere else. In respect to them therefore, it appears probable, that the means which might be expended for their migration into the interior, would mostly be thrown away. So pauperized in spirit and inefficient is the great mass in question, to say nothing of the ignorance, and physical and mental imbecility of many of them, that they cannot be made profitable laborers even in our Almshouses. And these things, be it observed, are predicated of single male paupers. The trouble and expense of sending such to some distant home where labor was wanted, if at all practicable, would be sufficiently difficult. How greatly then would be the difficulties and expense of the undertaking be increased, when most of them are encumbered with dependent wives and children!

### 31.  Distribution of Immigrants, 1860[1]

We now proceed to that portion of the census termed "the nativities." The resulting amount of foreign immigration at the end of ten years is here determined, with their several nationalities, and chosen States of residence. . . . .

Referring to the general tables for more detailed statistics, the following aggregates will first claim attention:

|  | Census of 1860 | Census of 1850 |
|---|---|---|
| Born in the United States | 23,301,403 | 17,737,578 |
| Born in foreign countries | 4,136,175 | 2,210,839 |
| Birthplace not stated | 51,883 | 39,154 |
| Total free population | 27,489,461 | 19,987,571 |

[1] Extract from *Population of the United States in 1860; Compiled from the Original Returns of the Eighth Census under the Direction of the Secretary of the Interior*, by Joseph G. Kennedy, Supt. of Census, Washington, D. C., 1864, pp. xxviii–xxxii. The material following the dividing line on p. 332 is taken from another volume of the Eighth Census, *Statistics of the United States (Including Mortality, Property, &c.) in 1860; Compiled from the Original Returns and Being the Final Exhibit of the Eighth Census* (Washington, D. C., 1866), pp. l–lviii.

Thus the free population has increased to nearly twenty-seven and a half millions, of which seven and a half millions has been the gain of the past ten years, a period of unexampled prosperity. It is due to the peaceful course of immigration and the natural increase of births, and not to acquisition of territory during the period. In the same ten years, the foreign population has nearly doubled, and now amounts to more than four millions of people, besides a few thousand included among those of unknown birthplace.

The different races and nations in the United States are represented as follows:

### NATIVITIES OF FOREIGN RESIDENTS

| Natives of: | Census of 1860 | Census of 1850 | Proportions in 1860 | Proportions in 1850 |
|---|---|---|---|---|
| Ireland | 1,611,304 | 961,719 | 38.94 | 43.51 |
| Germany | 1,301,136 | 573,225 | 31.45 | 25.94 |
| England | 431,692 | 278,675 | 10.44 | 12.61 |
| British America | 249,970 | 147,700 | 6.05 | 6.68 |
| France | 109,870 | 54,069 | 2.66 | 2.44 |
| Scotland | 108,518 | 70,550 | 2.63 | 3.19 |
| Switzerland | 53,327 | 13,358 | 1.29 | 0.60 |
| Wales | 45,763 | 29,868 | 1.11 | 1.34 |
| Norway | 43,995 | 12,678 | 1.07 | 0.57 |
| China | 35,565 | 758 | 0.86 | 0.03 |
| Holland | 28,281 | 9,848 | 0.68 | 0.45 |
| Mexico | 27,466 | 13,317 | 0.66 | 0.60 |
| Sweden | 18,625 | 3,559 | 0.45 | 0.15 |
| Italy | 10,518 | 3,645 | 0.26 | 0.17 |
| Other countries | 60,145 | 37,870 | 1.45 | 1.71 |
| Total foreign-born. | 4,136,175 | 2,210,839 | 100.00 | 100.00 |

During the past ten years, the increase of population coming from Great Britain and Ireland has been 858,267. From the German States, the decennial accession has been 716,416; yet, according to the last columns, the British element compared with the whole foreign population has diminished, while the German element has increased, relatively speaking. The migration has also received a new impulse from the north of Europe, Norway and Sweden, which were a part of ancient Scandinavia; also from Belgium and Switzerland. From France, it should be remarked that a large number are natives of the provinces of Alsace and Lorraine, who are really Germans by descent, and speak the German language, although they have been enumerated indiscriminately with the other natives of France. Of Russians and Poles speaking the Slavonic language, the migration has been inconsiderable in amount. . . . .

A general view of [the distribution of immigrants] is given in the following simple statements:

1. The largest number of foreigners reside in the following States in their order, to wit: New York, Pennsylvania, Ohio, Illinois, Wisconsin, Massachusetts. It will be observed that the total population also follows the same order, as regards the first four States, indicating a similarity of composition of native and foreign.   . . . .

2. Foreigners reside in the least numbers in North Carolina, Florida, Arkansas, Oregon, Mississippi, Delaware.

3. The greatest foreign increase, from 1850 to 1860, has been in New York, Illinois, Wisconsin, Pennsylvania, California, Ohio.

4. The least foreign increase, from 1850 to 1860, has been in Vermont, Florida, North Carolina, South Carolina, Arkansas.

5. The greatest number of English reside in the States of New York, Pennsylvania, Illinois, Ohio, Wisconsin, Michigan.

6. The least number of English reside in Florida, Arkansas, Oregon, North Carolina, South Carolina, Mississippi.

7. The greatest number of Irish reside in New York, Pennsylvania, Massachusetts, Illinois, Ohio, New Jersey.

8. The smallest number of Irish reside in Florida, North Carolina, Oregon, Arkansas, Texas, Kansas.

9. The greatest number of Germans reside in New York, Ohio, Pennsylvania, Illinois, Wisconsin, Missouri.

10. The least number of Germans reside in Vermont, Maine, New Hampshire, Florida, North Carolina, Rhode Island.

11. It will further be found that 3,582,999—that is, 86.60 per cent of the whole number of foreign-born—were inhabitants of the free States, and 553,176, or only 13.40 per cent, of the slave-holding States. In 1850 the corresponding percentages were 88.94 and 11.06, respectively, or as 8 to 1. In other words, for each white immigrant located in the slave-holding States, eight have settled in the free States. It may be noted the number of free colored and slaves in this country are almost precisely as 1 to 8, or in opposite ratio to that of the foreign white population, the total number being nearly equal, though the European class would be far more numerous were their descendants also included.

12. The decennial increase of the foreign population from 1850 to 1860 has been 87.1 per cent, being nearly a doubling of numbers; in some States more, and in others less. In round numbers, the State of New York has a million of foreign residents, which is a fourth part of all in the United States, and also a fourth of the total population of the

States; but, on an average of all the States, the number of foreigners is about one-eighth part of the whole population. . . . .

The following table shows, in the second column, the proportion

## PERCENTAGES OF THE NATIVE, THE ENGLISH, THE IRISH, AND THE GERMAN POPULATION IN EACH STATE AND TERRITORY IN 1860

| States and Territories | Total Native | Total Foreign | English | Irish | German |
|---|---|---|---|---|---|
| Alabama | 98.72 | 1.28 | 0.12 | 0.59 | 0.27 |
| Arkansas | 99.14 | 0.86 | 0.09 | 0.30 | 0.26 |
| California | 52.02 | 47.98 | 4.00 | 10.85 | 7.10 |
| Connecticut | 82.46 | 17.54 | 1.93 | 12.05 | 1.85 |
| Delaware | 91.82 | 8.18 | 1.41 | 5.41 | 1.13 |
| Florida | 97.64 | 2.36 | 0.23 | 0.60 | 0.34 |
| Georgia | 98.90 | 1.10 | 0.11 | 0.62 | 0.23 |
| Illinois | 81.03 | 18.97 | 2.44 | 5.12 | 7.65 |
| Indiana | 91.25 | 8.75 | 0.69 | 1.81 | 14.94 |
| Iowa | 84.29 | 15.71 | 1.71 | 4.16 | 5.71 |
| Kansas | 88.16 | 11.84 | 1.31 | 3.63 | 4.03 |
| Kentucky | 94.83 | 5.17 | 0.39 | 1.93 | 2.36 |
| Louisiana | 88.56 | 11.44 | 0.56 | 3.98 | 3.48 |
| Maine | 94.04 | 5.96 | 0.43 | 2.44 | 0.06 |
| Maryland | 82.72 | 11.28 | 0.62 | 3.62 | 6.39 |
| Massachusetts | 78.87 | 21.13 | 1.94 | 15.07 | 0.81 |
| Michigan | 80.09 | 19.91 | 3.44 | 4.01 | 5.18 |
| Minnesota | 66.22 | 33.78 | 1.99 | 7.37 | 10.59 |
| Mississippi | 98.92 | 1.08 | 0.11 | 0.49 | 0.25 |
| Missouri | 86.41 | 13.59 | 0.85 | 3.68 | 7.50 |
| New Hampshire | 93.58 | 6.42 | 0.70 | 3.91 | 0.13 |
| New Jersey | 81.73 | 18.27 | 2.36 | 9.23 | 5.93 |
| New York | 74.27 | 25.73 | 2.73 | 12.84 | 6.61 |
| North Carolina | 99.67 | 0.33 | 0.07 | 0.09 | 0.08 |
| Ohio | 85.97 | 14.03 | 1.40 | 3.28 | 7.19 |
| Oregon | 90.24 | 9.76 | 1.32 | 2.41 | 2.06 |
| Pennsylvania | 85.19 | 14.81 | 1.60 | 6.95 | 4.74 |
| Rhode Island | 78.58 | 21.42 | 3.64 | 14.48 | 0.47 |
| South Carolina | 98.58 | 1.42 | 0.11 | 0.70 | 0.38 |
| Tennessee | 98.09 | 1.91 | 0.18 | 1.12 | 0.35 |
| Texas | 92.81 | 7.19 | 0.28 | 0.58 | 3.40 |
| Vermont | 89.61 | 10.39 | 0.52 | 4.28 | 0.07 |
| Virginia | 97.81 | 2.19 | 0.26 | 1.03 | 0.66 |
| Wisconsin | 64.31 | 35.69 | 3.94 | 6.44 | 15.97 |
| District of Columbia | 83.37 | 16.63 | 1.37 | 9.66 | 4.33 |
| Territories | 83.89 | 16.11 | 4.45 | 2.31 | 1.86 |
| Total in United States | 86.85 | 13.15 | 1.37 | 5.12 | 4.14 |

of native-born, and in the third column the proportion of foreign-born; the sum of the two proportions representing an average population of 100 persons in each State. The corresponding proportions of English, Irish, and Germans, are given in the remaining columns.

From this summary it appears that the States having the largest percentage of foreign-born are California, Wisconsin, Minnesota, New York, Rhode Island, and Massachusetts. The States having the smallest percentage of foreigners are, similarly, North Carolina, Arkansas, Mississippi, Georgia, Alabama, South Carolina, in order, all of which are slave-holding States. In like manner the smallest percentage of English and Irish reside in the slave-holding States, without exception, and the largest in the free States, while the corresponding percentages of Germans refer mostly to the States before designated for the absolute number of emigrants.

. . . . The great mass of immigrants are well known to have changed their condition for the better, by immigration, and improved their prospects for the future; indeed, to many the advantages offered in the New World have proved of incalculable value. The swelling tide of immigration only concurs with other evidences of this. With such agreeable associations will be contemplated the largeness of the numbers who have here found wider and more inviting fields of enterprise.

---

Every nation and almost every principality of Europe, and also Asia, Africa, South America, Australia, the West Indies, and the islands of the Pacific Ocean, have, in past time, sent their natives to live in the United States, and they are still adding, in the same way, to the numbers of our people. These are distributed through all the land, and every State has the representatives of almost every nation abroad. Moreover, the natives of every State are found in each other State and in each Territory. The population, then, of the several States is composed of foreigners of many nations and of the natives of many States, brought together in various proportions. In the States, and especially in the old States, the natives constitute the great majority of the people. In the Territories the inhabitants are necessarily strangers, who were born in other States or in other countries. . . . .

From the first settlement of the country, the Old World has continually sent its people to dwell and leave their posterity in this country. But comparatively few came during the early part of this century. The records are very incomplete from 1800 to 1820, and there were probably few facts of this kind to record. Since 1819 the law has taken cognizance of the passengers arriving from abroad, and their numbers have been ascertained and published in official documents. From that time immigration has increased, and in the last twenty years it has increased rapidly and greatly. . . . .

In 1860 there were 4,136,175 natives of other countries living in the United States. Although the Teutonic and Celtic races, through Great Britain and Germany, and their descendants, constitute the main portion of the inhabitants of this country, yet the representatives of almost every civilized nation on the earth were here in 1860. Every nation in Europe, and every continent, had its children in every State, save that there was no Russian in New Hampshire, no Spaniard in Arkansas, no Belgian and no Austrian in Delaware, and no Würtemberger or Norwegian in Vermont. All other States held the sons or daughters of all other European nations within their borders. Even the natives of the principalities of Germany were thus diffused throughout our land. . . . .

### RURAL AND CIVIC RESIDENCE OF IMMIGRANTS AT HOME AND IN THE UNITED STATES

The distribution of the foreigners has an importance in connexion with the original residence and occupation of the great majority of those coming from some countries, and perhaps all the others. The emigration reports of Ireland, which are within reach, show that 84.5 per cent of the Irish male emigrants over fifteen years of age, and 92.1 per cent of those under fifteen, were farmers, farm laborers and servants, ploughmen, graziers, and herdsmen; and that of the females, 79.4 per cent of those over fifteen, and 88.3 per cent of those under fifteen, were farmers, farm laborers, and servants, and must, therefore, have been inhabitants of the country districts. Most of the other emigrants, 15.4 per cent of the males and 21.3 per cent of the females, were of such occupations as might have been carried on either in city or country. The flow of emigrants from Ireland was greatly increased from 1841 to 1851. In this period the population of the rural districts diminished 1,648,823, while the population of the civic districts increased 26,084. From 1851 to 1861 the decrease in the rural population was 849,160, and the increase in the civic population was 61,318 in the same period.

Previous to the enactment of the Irish "encumbered estates bill," many of the large estates were let and sub-let, and again distributed among tenants of smaller means, until they were divided into manifold small holdings of one to five acres, more or less, and on these were erected houses of the "fourth class," described in the government reports as "comprising all mud cabins, having only one room." After the passage of the bill above noted, many of these estates were sold and consolidated into single farms, the system of small tenantry so far broken up, and the tenants removed from those lands, and their humble dwellings destroyed.

In 1841 there were 491,278 of these fourth-class houses, single-roomed mud cabins, inhabited in Ireland. During the next ten years 355,689 of them were destroyed, and only 135,589 were left in 1851. In these ten years 8,415 houses of the third class, "a better description of cottage, still built of mud, but varying from two to four rooms, and windows," were erected, increasing the whole from 533,297 in 1841, to 541,712 in 1851; 54,574 houses of the second class, "a good farmhouse, or, in town, a house in a small street, having from five to nine rooms and windows," were built, increasing the whole from 264,318 in 1841, to 318,758 in 1851. In the same period 10,084 houses of the first class, "all of a better description than in the preceding classes," were added to the 40,080 in 1841, making the whole 50,164 in 1851.

Thus, in ten years, 355,689 houses of the worst class, the mud cabins of the poorest, were destroyed, and 73,073 houses of the better class were built. Of the 355,689 mud cabins thus destroyed, 2,026 were in the cities and 353,663 were in the rural districts. Probably some of the 355,689 families displaced from their one-roomed cabins went into some of the houses of the third and even the second class, but they would contain but a small proportion of those rendered houseless. The others must have sought homes elsewhere out of Ireland. They probably were the emigrants to the colonies and to the United States.

The British philanthropists often speak with satisfaction of the great blessing offered to their surplus and suffering population in the cheap lands in the new States and Territories of this country, inviting the willing laborer to possess and cultivate them almost without cost. It is supposed by many that these emigrants, who have suffered from the want of occupation in their native land, can here find comfortable homes in our western wilds, and opportunities of employment in the way they have been accustomed, and gain thereby a sure reward and plentiful means of subsistence in the new States and Territories of America.

According to the immigration reports, about 30 per cent of the foreign male passengers who landed on our shores were farmers, and about 42 per cent were laborers. No distinction is made as to nationality of these farmers and laborers, whether they were Irish, German, or of other nations. But as the proportion of the whole who were farmers and laborers approaches so near the proportion of the Irish emigrants who were engaged in the rural employments, it is safe to assume that a very large part of the continental Europeans who came to live in the United States had been accustomed to agricultural employments in the rural districts at home.

Many of these strangers at once seek the new regions of the West, where they were found by the census enumerators in 1860. But a large part of them remain in the old States, and engage, not in agricultural employments, with which they were familiar, but as laborers in commercial and manufacturing cities, towns, and villages.

The table[1] on the following page shows the relative distribution of the native and foreign population in the great cities and the remaining parts of the States to which these cities belong.

Thus it is seen that while the Irish immigrants constitute 23 per cent of the white population of the cities of New York, they constitute only 12 per cent of the population of the rest of the State of New York; and while they constitute 16 per cent of the population of Philadelphia, Alleghany, Pittsburgh, and Reading, they make only 4 per cent of the rest of Pennsylvania. The ratio in Baltimore is twice as great as in the rural districts of Maryland, three times as great in Boston, and in the other cities of Massachusetts twice as great, as in the country of that State, and more than four times as great in Chicago as in the agricultural regions of Illinois. Their proportion in St. Louis is ten to one among the farming counties of Missouri, and nearly five in Cincinnati to one in the other parts of Ohio.

The Germans show a similar preference of the city to the country in the selection of their places of occupation and residence, and a similar disproportion between city and country residents is found generally among the foreign citizens of the United States. This comparison is only of the great cities quoted in the tables, with all the residue of their respective States. If a further analysis could have been made, and all the smaller commercial and manufacturing cities and compact towns could be separated from the exclusively agricultural districts, probably it would show a still smaller proportion of the foreign population living in the purely farming regions and engaged in cultivating the earth, the occupation which they had pursued in their native land, and with which they were the most familiar.

[1] [The original table, which gives absolute numbers as well as percentages, has been condensed.]

PROPORTION OF NATIVES AND FOREIGNERS IN THE PRINCIPAL
CITIES AND RURAL DISTRICTS OF SEVERAL STATES TO
THE TOTAL FREE POPULATION

| PLACE | RATIO TO TOTAL FREE POPULATION | | |
| --- | --- | --- | --- |
| | Native | Foreign | Irish |
| *Maine:* | | | |
| Portland.................. | 84 | 15 | 10 |
| Rest of state............... | 94 | 5 | 2 |
| *New Hampshire:* | | | |
| Manchester................ | 72 | 27 | 19 |
| Rest of state............... | 94 | 5 | 2 |
| *Massachusetts:* | | | |
| Six cities.................. | 67 | 32 | 23 |
| Rest of state............... | 82 | 17 | 12 |
| *Rhode Island:* | | | |
| Providence................ | 74 | 25 | 19 |
| Rest of state............... | 79 | 20 | 1 |
| *Connecticut:* | | | |
| Two cities................. | 70 | 29 | 20 |
| Rest of state............... | 84 | 15 | 6 |
| *New York:* | | | |
| Seven cities............... | 55 | 44 | 23 |
| Rest of state............... | 83 | 16 | 12 |
| *Pennsylvania:* | | | |
| Four cities................ | 68 | 31 | 16 |
| Rest of state............... | 89 | 10 | 4 |
| *New Jersey:* | | | |
| Two cities................. | 61 | 38 | 18 |
| Rest of state............... | 84 | 15 | 7 |
| *Delaware:* | | | |
| Wilmington................ | 78 | 21 | 14 |
| Rest of state............... | 92 | 7 | 4 |
| *Maryland:* | | | |
| Baltimore................. | 71 | 28 | 8 |
| Rest of state............... | 92 | 7 | 2 |
| *District of Columbia:* | | | |
| Washington................ | 78 | 21 | 12 |
| Rest of state............... | 84 | 16 | 9 |
| *Virginia:* | | | |
| Richmond................. | 79 | 20 | 9 |
| Rest of state............... | 97 | 2 | 1 |
| *South Carolina:* | | | |
| Charleston................ | 73 | 26 | 13 |
| Rest of state............... | 98 | 1 | |
| *Georgia:* | | | |
| Savannah................. | 66 | 33 | 22 |
| Rest of state............... | 98 | 1 | |
| *Alabama:* | | | |
| Two cities......... ........ | 69 | 30 | 13 |
| Rest of state...... ......... | 99 | | |
| *Louisiana:* | | | |
| New Orleans............... | 55 | 44 | 16 |
| Rest of state............... | 92 | 7 | 1 |

PROPORTION OF NATIVES AND FOREIGNERS IN THE PRINCIPAL
CITIES AND RURAL DISTRICTS OF SEVERAL STATES TO
THE TOTAL FREE POPULATION—*Continued*

| PLACE | RATIO TO TOTAL FREE POPULATION | | |
|---|---|---|---|
| | Native | Foreign | Irish |
| *Tennessee:* | | | |
| Memphis................... | 62 | 37 | 22 |
| Rest of state............... | 98 | 1 | 1 |
| *Kentucky:* | | | |
| Louisville.................. | 62 | 37 | 10 |
| Rest of state............... | 95 | 4 | 1 |
| *Ohio:* | | | |
| Three cities................ | 55 | 44 | 11 |
| Rest of state............... | 88 | 11 | 2 |
| *Illinois:* | | | |
| Chicago.................... | 49 | 50 | 18 |
| Rest of state............... | 84 | 16 | 4 |
| *Michigan:* | | | |
| Detroit..................... | 51 | 48 | 13 |
| Rest of state............... | 81 | 18 | 4 |
| *Wisconsin:* | | | |
| Milwaukee.................. | 49 | 50 | 6 |
| Rest of state............... | 65 | 34 | 6 |
| *Missouri:* | | | |
| St. Louis................... | 38 | 61 | 18 |
| Rest of state............... | 92 | 7 | 1 |
| *California:* | | | |
| San Francisco.............. | 49 | 50 | 16 |
| Rest of state............... | 36 | 63 | 7 |

## 32. The Foreign Element in Massachusetts, 1866[1]

There are two modes by which the population of a community may
be increased: 1st, By an excess of Births over Deaths, or natural increase; and 2d, By the number emigrating into a place exceeding those
removing out of it, or increase by emigration. . . . .

The population of Massachusetts is reported at different periods as
follows: In 1765, 222,563; in 1790, 378,787; in 1800, 422,845; in 1810,
472,040; in 1820, 523,287; in 1830, 610,408; in 1840, 737,700; in 1850,
994,514; in 1860, 1,231,066. We here see that the increase for 30 years
—from 1790 to 1820—was comparatively small, averaging 11 per cent;
that, from 1820 to 1830, the population increased over 16 per cent;
from 1830 to 1840, over 20 per cent; from 1840 to 1850, 34 per cent;
and from 1850 to 1860, 24 per cent. . . . .

But in order to understand correctly the increase and the changes

[1] Extract from "Dr. Nathan Allen's Statement" in the *Third Annual Report
of the Board of State Charities of Massachusetts* (January, 1867), pp. 19, 23–31.

in our population, the history and number of those of a foreign origin must be carefully noted. The rapid increase of this class, and the changes consequent upon its future growth, afford themes which deserve the most grave consideration.

The Census at different periods returns this element as follows: 1830, 9,620; 1840, 34,818; 1850, 164,448; and 1860, 260,114. Here within 30 years, commencing with less than 10,000, we have an increase by immigration alone of over 250,000. It should be observed that this does not include the great number of children born in this State of foreign extraction. The first Registration Report that discriminated in the births as to parentage was that of 1850, returning 8,197 of this class, and 3,278 mixed or not stated. In 1860, the number had increased to 17,549, besides nearly 1,000 not stated. In 1850, the foreign births were only one-half as many as the American, but they continued to gain every year afterwards upon the American till 1860, when they obtained a majority. This year will ever constitute an important era in the history of Massachusetts when the foreign element, composing only about one-third part of the population of the State, produced more children than the American. Since 1860 they have gained every year upon the American, till in 1865 their births numbered almost 1,000 more than the American.

From 1850 to 1860, the Registration Reports make the foreign births 137,146, besides 18,598 not stated, a large portion of which undoubtedly were of foreign origin. Then the number of such births from 1830 to 1850 cannot be definitely stated, but, judging by the amount of foreign population at this period and its fruitfulness at other times, the number of births would certainly come up to 50,000 or more. Now what proportion of those of this character born from 1830 to 1860, might have been living when the Census of 1860 was taken, we cannot tell; all that can be determined upon the subject is only an approximation to the truth. It is estimated where the mortality is largest that only from two-fifths to one-half of all those born—including both the city and the country—live to reach adult life. After making allowance for this fact, and considering that by far the largest proportion of these births occurred in the years immediately preceding 1860, we think it perfectly safe to say that there must have been over 100,000 persons of this class included in the United States Census returned as native born in Massachusetts, or in other words as American. This fact would change materially the Census report. It would take at least 100,000 from the American portion—970,000—and add 100,000 to the

260,000 reported as born in foreign countries. This result makes at that time almost one-half of our population strictly of a foreign origin! It is expressly stated both in the United States and State censuses, that the returns are made upon the nativities of the population. Judging by these facts and figures it would seem that the foreign population is actually much larger in this State than has generally been considered.

If the localities and occupations of the foreign population are considered, it may aid in a better understanding of the whole subject. The Census of 1860 makes the following return [Table I]:

TABLE I

THE AMERICAN AND FOREIGN POPULATION OF MASSACHUSETTS, BY COUNTIES

| Counties | Total Population | American | Foreign | Percentage American | Percentage Foreign |
|---|---|---|---|---|---|
| Barnstable | 35,990 | 34,439 | 1,551 | 95.69 | 4.31 |
| Berkshire | 55,120 | 45,310 | 9,810 | 98.22 | 1.78 |
| Bristol | 93,794 | 77,101 | 16,693 | 82.21 | 17.79 |
| Dukes | 4,403 | 4,212 | 191 | 95.67 | 4.33 |
| Essex | 165,601 | 136,107 | 29,494 | 82.20 | 17.80 |
| Franklin | 31,434 | 29,104 | 2,330 | 92.59 | 7.41 |
| Hampden | 57,366 | 45,237 | 12,129 | 78.86 | 21.14 |
| Hampshire | 37,823 | 32,522 | 5,301 | 85.99 | 14.01 |
| Middlesex | 216,364 | 166,126 | 50,238 | 76.51 | 23.49 |
| Nantucket | 6,094 | 5,802 | 292 | 95.22 | 4.78 |
| Norfolk | 109,950 | 83,693 | 26,257 | 76.12 | 23.88 |
| Plymouth | 64,768 | 58,077 | 6,691 | 89.67 | 10.33 |
| Suffolk | 192,700 | 125,439 | 67,261 | 65.09 | 34.91 |
| Worcester | 159,659 | 127,783 | 31,876 | 80.04 | 19.96 |
| Total by census, 1860 | 1,231,066 | 970,952 | 260,114 | 78.88 | 21.12 |
| Add 100,000 for foreign-born in Massachusetts | | 870,952 | 360,114 | 70.75 | 29.25 |

It will be seen by this table that the foreign element is very unequally distributed in the State; for, while Suffolk, Norfolk, Middlesex, Hampden, and Worcester Counties are largely represented, Berkshire, Barnstable, Dukes, Nantucket, and Franklin have a small representation. But, in order to show the residences of the foreign population in a more definite form, we here give the number of the two classes in all the Cities of the Commonwealth, as taken from the State Census of 1855. The U.S. Census of 1860 does not contain this statement, and the State Census of 1865 is not yet available.

In examining the following table [it] should be borne in mind .... that this table, representing the foreign portion, does not include the children of foreigners born in this country, which are here reckoned in the American column, but should be taken out of this, and added to the foreign. Could this be done, especially according to the present population, it would bring the figures in the foreign column up almost to those in the American, if not in some instances, to exceed them.

TABLE II

SHOWING THE NATIVE AND THE FOREIGN POPULATION OF OUR CITIES

| Cities | Population 1855 | Native | Foreign | Percentage Native | Percentage Foreign |
|---|---|---|---|---|---|
| Boston.............. | 160,490 | 98,018 | 62,472 | 61.07 | 38.93 |
| Lowell.............. | 37,554 | 24,359 | 13,195 | 64.86 | 35.14 |
| Worcester........... | 22,286 | 16,609 | 5,677 | 74.52 | 25.48 |
| Charlestown........ | 21,700 | 16,530 | 5,168 | 76.13 | 23.87 |
| Salem.............. | 20,934 | 16,436 | 4,434 | 78.50 | 21.50 |
| Cambridge.......... | 20,473 | 13,903 | 6,544 | 67.90 | 32.10 |
| New Bedford........ | 20,389 | 18,500 | 1,889 | 90.73 | 9.27 |
| Roxbury............ | 18,469 | 11,282 | 7,187 | 61.08 | 38.92 |
| Lawrence........... | 16,114 | 9,384 | 6,730 | 58.23 | 41.77 |
| Lynn............... | 15,713 | 13,332 | 2,381 | 84.85 | 15.15 |
| Springfield.......... | 13,788 | 10,959 | 2,829 | 79.47 | 20.53 |
| Taunton............ | 13,750 | 10,271 | 3,479 | 74.69 | 25.31 |
| Newburyport........ | 13,357 | 10,844 | 2,513 | 81.18 | 18.82 |
| Fall River.......... | 12,680 | 7,900 | 4,780 | 62.30 | 37.70 |
| Chelsea............. | 10,151 | 7,340 | 2,811 | 72.30 | 27.70 |
| Average percentage... | .......... | .......... | .......... | 72.94 | 27.06 |

*Distribution and employment of the foreign population.*—But this class of people do not all live in the cities. They are found scattered in almost every town and neighborhood in the Commonwealth. The men came first to build railroads, to dig canals, cellars, and aid in laying the foundation of mills, dwellings and public buildings. Then came the women to act as servants and domestics in families, as well as to find useful employment in shops and mills. Then came parents, children, and whole families. To such an extent have they increased by immigration and birth that they now perform a very large portion of the domestic service in all our families; they constitute everywhere a majority of the hired laborers upon the farm; they are found extensively engaged in trade and mechanical pursuits, particularly in the shoe business, and compose by far the largest proportion of all the operatives in the mills.

Within a few years, they have become extensive owners of real estate. In the cities they have built or bought a very large number of small shops and cheap dwellings, and in the rural districts as well as in the farming towns throughout the State, they have purchased very extensively small lots of land, small places, and old farms partially run out; and (what is significant) they pay for whatever real estate they buy, and are scarcely ever known to sell any. In fact, it has come to such a pass, that they perform a very large proportion of the physical labor throughout the State, whether it be in the mill or in the shop, whether in the family or upon the farm. As far as muscular exercise is concerned, they constitute "the bone and sinew" of the land, and it would be very difficult, if not impossible to dispense with their services. Every year the Americans are becoming more and more dependent upon them for manual labor, both in doors and out-of-doors. Should the foreign population continue to increase as they have in the past twenty or thirty years, and the American portion remain stationary or decrease, a question of no ordinary interest arises, what will be the state of society thirty or fifty years hence in this Commonwealth? It may be well to examine the probabilities of some such changes. Here are figures from the Census at different periods:

|  | 1830 | 1840 | 1850 | 1860 |
|---|---|---|---|---|
| American | 600,788 | 702,882 | 830,066 | 970,952 |
| Foreign | 9,620 | 34,818 | 164,448 | 260,114 |

Should the same ratio of increase, from 1830 to 1860, as exhibited in this table, continue twenty or thirty years longer, a majority of the population in this State, within that time, will be composed of those of a foreign origin. But these figures do not fairly represent the two classes. Under the Census of 1860, of the 970,952, called American, more than 100,000 are the children of the foreign portion, reckoned American because born in this country.

*Comparative increase of natives and foreigners.*—From 1850 to 1866, the fifteen Registration Reports return 208,730 births of strictly foreign parentage, besides 22,376 not stated, a large portion of which must be foreign. All of these living when the census is taken, would be considered according to present usage, American; whereas they should be counted strictly under the foreign head. A careful analysis of the Census and Registration Reports presents the following facts:

The increase of population in the State has been confined principally to cities and towns where manufacturing, mechanical and commercial business is carried on. In the purely agricultural districts, there has been very little increase of population. Railroads have had a powerful influence in changing the population of the State from the hills and country towns to the valleys and plains. Wherever water-power, or steam-power has been introduced, or where trade and commerce has found advantages, there population has greatly increased. The eastern section of the State has increased far more than the middle or western districts. Population in manufacturing places has increased about five times more than in agricultural districts. It is found also, wherever there has been much or a rapid increase of population, it has been made up largely of a foreign element. Now if a line could be drawn exactly between the American and foreign population, as it respects this increase, it would throw much light upon the subject. According to the Census of 1860, it appears that two counties—Dukes and Nantucket—had actually decreased in population. There were eighty-six towns also which had diminished in population between 1850 and 1860. In a small part of these towns, this change is accounted for by the fact that some section of the place had, in the meantime, been set off to another town. The places in the State that have increased the least, or declined in population, are found to be settled generally with American stock.

A serious question here arises, Is there a natural increase in this class of the community? It is generally admitted that foreigners have a far greater number of children, for the same number of inhabitants, than the Americans. It is estimated by some physicians that the same number of married persons of the former have, on an average, three times as many children as an equal number of those of the latter. This gives the foreign element great power of increase of population—derived not so much from emigration as from the births, exceeding greatly the deaths. It is alleged that great numbers of Americans move out of the State, and that this accounts for their apparent decrease in population. It should be remembered also, that large numbers of the same class move every year into this State from other States. If we take, from the Census of 1860, the difference between the number of persons from Massachusetts living in other States, and those born in other States, residing in this State, the gain in this difference from 1850 to 1860, was less than 11,000. It is evident from this fact that the actual loss of population of purely American origin by emigration, is not very great, amounting to less than three thousand persons annually. In this three thousand persons, allowance is made for filling the places of those deceased natives of Massachusetts residing in other States, in excess of the number of persons deceased in this State, but natives of other States. This general statement deserves repetition—that is, that the strictly American population of Massachusetts is not diminished by emigration annually three thousand persons over and above the number of the same class moving from other States into this State. But the question of *natural* increase is far more important; for if the increase from this source is small or none at all, the loss of three thousand persons every year from the best portion of our population becomes a very serious matter.

It has been alleged that the births are not all reported. For many years after the Registration Laws went into force, it is well known that this was the fact, but of late years there are reasons to believe that pretty full returns are made. The United States Census for 1860 reports under one year of age in Massachusetts 31,312 persons. The Registration Report of the State returns for the same year 36,051 births, and 4,821 deaths of infants under one year of age, which leaves living 31,230, only eighty-two less than the Census. These separate results are obtained by two distinct agencies, and modes of collecting the statistics entirely different, so that there could be no collusion or repetition. We have not the same means to verify in other years. The Registration Report for 1864 gives 30,449 births, and 28,723 deaths; for 1865, 30,249 births, and 26,152 deaths; making only 1,726 births in 1864 more than the deaths, and 4,097 more in 1865. Now since the foreign population have two or three times as many children as the same number of married persons among the Americans—a fact well established—is it not very evident that the strictly American deaths exceed the births? In examining the Reports, it appears that the counties containing the least foreign population, return in 1864 and 1865, more deaths than births. Take the towns containing none or scarce any foreign population, where in 1864 and '65 not a single birth is reported (there are thirty-four such towns in the State), and the whole number of deaths in these towns for 1864 and '65 exceeds each year the births. On the other hand, an examination of those cities and towns containing a large foreign element, shows that the whole number of births there invariably exceeds the deaths.

There is a difficulty in discriminating in the Registration Reports between the deaths of Americans and of foreigners, since the deaths of all those of foreign origin born in this country are understood to be returned as Americans. This mode of reporting the deaths is unfortunate where it is desirable to ascertain the natural increase of population in the two classes separately. Still, very correct knowledge upon this subject can be obtained in any city by a careful examination of the books of the undertakers, the Superintendent of Burials, and of the City Clerk, together with the places of burial. In the cities of Lowell and Lawrence, where there is a very large foreign element, we have obtained from these sources the exact number of deaths, foreign and American, for 1864 and '65, and the number of deaths in the former city over the births were rising one hundred each year, and in Lawrence for the two years, they were over one hundred.

In a report upon the comparative view of the population of Boston in 1849 and '50, made to the city government, November, 1851, Dr. Jesse Chickering, after a most careful analysis of the births and deaths in Boston, states that "the most important fact derived from this view, is the result that the whole increase of population arising from the excess of births over deaths for these two years, has been among the foreign population." Since 1850 we think it will be very difficult to prove that there has been any natural increase of population in Boston with the strictly American population.

It may be said the force of the statistics from the Registration Reports of 1864 and '65, is very much impaired by the effects of the war. The births may have been somewhat diminished, and the deaths increased by such means, but then the foreign element would have been affected as well as the American, since it was largely represented in the war. But a similar state of things in reference to the increase of the two classes existed for years before the war, and there is abundant evidence to prove that for a long time there has been a relative decrease of births with the Americans. In the Colonial Census of 1765, taken one hundred years ago, when the main population was purely American, the total inhabitants were then 222,563, and the number under sixteen years of age returned as 102,489—almost one-half of the whole population. Now it is estimated that only about one-third of the whole population is under fifteen years of age. According to this estimate, a careful analysis of the natural proportion of the children to each class, will show that scarcely one-fifth of the Americans are at the present time under sixteen years of age. This makes a surprising difference in the relative number of children of the same people at the two periods, 1765 and 1865.

Again, many towns in the State have been settled over two hundred years, and their history will include from six to eight generations. The records of several of these towns have been carefully examined with respect to the relative number of children in each generation. It was found that the families comprising the first generation had on an average between eight and ten children; the next three generations averaged between seven and eight to each family; the fifth generation about five, and the sixth less than three to each family. What a change as to the size of the families since those olden times! Then large families were common—now the exception; then it was rare to find married persons having only one, two or three children; now it is very common! Then it was regarded a calamity for a married couple to have no children—now such calamities are found on every side of us—in fact, they are fashionable.

It is the uniform testimony of physicians who have been extensively engaged in the practice of medicine, twenty, thirty, forty, and fifty years in this State—and who have the best possible means of understanding this whole subject—that there has been gradually a very great falling off in the number of children among American families.

Two general remarks should here be made. (1) That this decrease of children is found to prevail in country towns and rural districts almost to the same extent as in the cities, which is contrary to the general impression. (2) From the bills of mortality it is an established fact that, on an average, only about three-fifths of all persons born, including the city and the country, ever live to reach adult life. It will be seen at once that, with this rate of mortality, if the deaths exceed every year the births, or are only slightly in excess, the children will not keep the original stock good in point of numbers. In view of these facts, several questions naturally arise: If the foreign population in Massachusetts continues to increase as it has, and the American portion remains stationary, or decreases, as the probabilities indicate, what will be the state of society here twenty-five, fifty, or a hundred years hence? How long will it be before the foreign portion will outnumber the American in our principal cities and towns, or constitute even a majority in the whole Commonwealth?

The cause why there should be such a difference in the number of children, between the American families now upon the stage, and those of the same stock, one, two, and three generations ago, is a subject of grave inquiry. Again, why should there be such a difference in this respect, between American families and those of the English, German, Scotch, and Irish of the present day? Is this difference owing to our higher civilization or to a more artificial mode of life and the unwholesome state of society?

### 33. An Official Report on the Encouragement of Immigration[1]

[The Committee] deem the encouragement of foreign immigration as of the highest importance, and have given the subject the consideration demanded by it. The rapid growth of our country arises from three causes, equally necessary: first, the extent of unoccupied soil, with a climate and fertility not surpassed in any portion of the world; second, a native population, free, hardy, industrious, improved by a mixture of the blood of all the European nations, engrafted on the Anglo-Saxon stock, and incited to great activity by institutions offering the highest honors and rewards to those who, by industry and merit, deserve them; and third, the addition to and absorption into our population of a large number annually of immigrants, whose labor adds to our annual production an amount increasing at a compound ratio, and not to be computed by numbers.

The advantages which have accrued heretofore from immigration can scarcely be computed. The labor of immigrants has contributed vastly to the value of our cities, towns, and villages, our railroads, our farms, our manufactures, and our productions. Comparatively few of the race now predominant on this continent can trace their American ancestry more than a century back. Though a seeming paradox, it nevertheless approaches historical truth, that we are all immigrants. In 1790 the population of the United States was less than four millions; in 1860 it was little less than thirty-one millions and a half, showing an increase of twenty-seven millions and a half in seventy years. . . . .

The advantages of foreign immigration, as between the United States and the people of European countries, are mutual and reciprocal. If our prairies and mineral lands offer inducements to the immigrant and promise him requital for the pangs of severed family ties and separation from the scenes of his early childhood, he, in his turn, contributes to the development of the resources of our country and adds to our material wealth. Such is the labor performed by the thrifty immigrant that he cannot enrich himself without contributing his full quota to the increase of the intrinsic greatness of the United States. This is equally true whether he work at mining, farming, or as a day laborer on one of our railroads.

The special wants for labor in this country at the present time are

[1] Extract from *Report from the Committee on Agriculture . . . . on the Enactment of Suitable Laws for the Encouragement and Protection of Foreign Immigrants Arriving within Jurisdiction of the United States, February 18, 1864* (United States Thirty-eighth Congress, first session, Senate Report No. 15), pp. 1–8.

very great. The war has depleted our workshops, and materially lessened our supply of labor in every department of industry and mechanism. In their noble response to the call of their country, our workmen in every branch of the useful arts have left vacancies which must be filled, or the material interest of the country must suffer. The immense amount of native labor occupied by the war calls for a large increase of foreign immigration to make up the deficiency at home. The demand for labor never was greater than at present, and the fields of usefulness were never so varied and promising.

The south, having torn down the fabric of its labor system by its own hands, will, when the war shall have ceased, present a wide field for voluntary white labor, and it must look to immigration for its supply.

The following may be mentioned as the special inducements to immigration:

1st. High price of labor and low price of food, compared with other countries.

2d. Our land policy, giving to every immigrant, after he shall have declared his intentions to become a citizen, a home and a farm, substantially as a free gift, charging him less for 160 acres in fee-simple than is paid as the annual rent of a single acre in England.

3d. The political rights conferred upon persons of foreign birth.

4th. Our system of free schools, melting in a common crucible all differences of religion, language, and race, and giving to the child of the day laborer and the son of the millionaire equal opportunities to excel in the pursuit and acquirement of knowledge. This is an advantage and a blessing which the poor man enjoys in no other country.

The mutual interest of the United States and the immigrant being established, the next inquiry is, what facilities have been extended by the United States to promote emigration? And when we come to examine this subject, we find that very little is done by the government to promote this most desirable end. The movement, so far, has been purely voluntary on the part of the immigrants, or induced by letters from their friends in this country advising them to join them here. No bounties are offered or pecuniary aid extended, and it is but recently that emigrants have been protected by passenger laws. . . . .

Your committee have considered the bill entitled "A bill to incorporate the North American Land and Emigration Company," but perceive this radical objection to a private corporation: Such a body will necessarily look to their own pecuniary interests, and in the effort to advance these will neglect or sacrifice the interests of the immigrants.

It has been proposed to offer a direct bounty to immigrants, or to pay their passage money. The objections to this system are conclusions, of which these are obvious: (1) The bounty must be paid to all immigrants, whether it was the inducement to immigrate or not; and though the bounty was small, it would involve an annual expenditure of millions. (2) Those who would be induced to immigrate would be only the idle, very poor, or vicious of foreign populations, while the thrifty would not be influenced by so trifling a consideration. (3) Foreign governments would unquestionably object to their populations being induced, by bounties, to immigrate, and might justly prevent the great depletion of labor that would result from it.

Your committee are of the opinion that the only aid to immigration the United States can now render would be: (1) To disseminate in Europe authentic information of the inducements to immigrate to this country. (2) To protect the immigrant from the impositions now so generally practiced upon him by immigrant runners and the like, and, (3) To facilitate his transportation from New York to the place of his destination, or to the place where his labor and skill would be most productive. These objects may be accomplished without great expenditure, and without changing the relation heretofore held by the United States to the emigrant.

### 34. Common Labor in New York, 1866[1]

The common labor market in the United States is at present completely overstocked. The increase of immigration which has taken place since the cessation of hostilities, the disbanding of a considerable portion of the army employed in suppressing the rebellion, and the large numbers that have, to my own knowledge, left Canada during the past season for the States, have, as might be expected, tended to render the supply of labor far in excess of the demand, in fact were it not for the new field of labor thrown open in the Southern States, a larger amount of destitution than is now apparent would be the inevitable result.

The causes above mentioned have served to produce an almost overwhelming mass of poverty and distress in the city of New York, and it is calculated that, in round numbers, about 50,000 persons, many

[1] Extract from Thomas D. Shipman, *Report on the State of the Labor Market, etc., in New York* (Appendix to the *Report of the Minister of Agriculture of the Province of Canada for the year 1865*, in Sessional Papers of the Province of Canada, Vol. XXVI [1866], No. 5), pp. 68, 74–75.

of whom are families of unemployed workmen and widows with dependent children, cannot subsist without aid from charitable societies.

In many of the large cities of the union a similar state of things is observable, and it is unnecessary to explain how much the newly arrived immigrant suffers from its effects.

The demand for labor at present in the Southern States is very large, and may be expected to increase considerably during the ensuing summer, and the opinion prevails amongst persons engaged in hiring labor, that a large proportion of this year's immigration (which, according to information I have received from authentic sources, is likely to reach 300,000), will be driven to seek employment in the unhealthy districts of the South.

I found in my visits to the different employment and registry offices (which abound in the city), that numbers of working men are almost daily leaving for the States of Virginia, Tennessee, Mississippi and Arkansas, and that it is a general desire of the plantation holders, to supplant, as far as practicable, black by white labor. Even the German Society of New York draws the attention of its countrymen, in glowing terms, to the many advantages offered by the Southern States, to all in search of employment, and asserts that the German settler is particularly sought for by the Southern Planter.

Large as is the number of the whites who have undoubtedly of late removed to the Southern States, it must be borne in mind that this movement bears no comparison with the exodus of the blacks.

The inducements at present offered are $15 a month by the year, including board, one acre of land for tillage, and all the cotton, the produce of his own labor, the immigrant can raise during the season over and above eight bales. (The produce of an ordinary black man is generally eleven bales.)

In some cases one-third of the crop is offered. Any person brought out at the expense of the employer will, in the event of his remaining one year in that person's employ, have half his passage money returned to him, and if two years the whole. I may, however, be permitted to assert that I do not think that the prospects of the immigrant in the South, as a general rule, are likely to be of a promising nature owing to these causes, viz., the present unsettled state of the country, the deficiency of capital, and the exorbitantly high rates of provisions, clothing, &c.; and I may also add that gentlemen of influence and experience in New York expressed their opinion to me that the climate in many districts would prove fatal to the white laborer.

With reference to the mechanics, the demand for them in New York and other large cities of the Union is considerable, and will continue to be so for some time to come.

Machinists, boiler-makers, workers in iron, piano-forte makers and goldsmiths are greatly in request, and the wages paid to these classes (on account of the difficulty of obtaining them in sufficient numbers) . . . . are uncommonly good.

I was informed by Mr. Farley, the Assistant Superintendent at Castle Garden, that they had no difficulty in procuring employment for any quantity of good servant girls, at remunerative wages, say from $7 to $10 per month.

It must be borne in mind that these amounts (as are also all others in the report), are in the United States currency, and that one dollar of United States currency is only equivalent to about 70 cents of gold. . . . .

The number and various nationalities of the Immigrants who landed at Castle Garden in 1865 were, I am informed, as follows:

| | |
|---|---:|
| English................................ | 27,184 |
| Irish.................................. | 75,046 |
| Scotch............................... | 4,012 |
| Germans.............................. | 82,894 |
| Swedes............................... | 2,512 |
| French............................... | 2,054 |
| Swiss................................. | 2,337 |
| Other countries...................... | 3,970 |
| Total.................. | 200,009 |

The preponderance of the Germans and Irish over every other nationality will excite attention. Much of the development of the natural resources of America during the last forty years, may be said to owe its origin to the energy and industry of the Irish and German settlers. These two races are vastly dissimilar in character. The German is quiet, persevering, frugal and cautious; he seldom commits himself by noisy demonstrations, and acts in his new home with becoming discretion.

The Irish is not less industrious than the German, but he lacks the frugality and caution of the latter, and his easily excited feelings and impulsive nature often lead him into difficulties with his neighbors. It is admitted on all hands that the Irishman ranks first in the industrial community, but it is, nevertheless, undeniable, that he is looked upon with anything but favor or friendship by the native American.

It would, perhaps, be superfluous to advance the reasons which induce the Irish to emigrate in such large numbers, inasmuch as they are too widely known to need comment.

There are two causes which produce the German emigration. The first, the severity with which the conscription law is enforced in Germany, and the second, the low standard of wages in that country.

There are many conflicting opinions as to which race thrives best in the United States, and it would, perhaps, be invidious to draw comparisons. I may state, however, that my experience goes to prove that, as agriculturists, the Scotch stand pre-eminent in the estimation of the American people.

I now proceed to give the destinations of this large body of immigrants:

|  | During Year 1865 |
|---|---|
| Arkansas | 4 |
| Alabama | 27 |
| Canada | 1,367 |
| California | 877 |
| Connecticut | 2,323 |
| Cuba | 50 |
| Delaware | 149 |
| District of Columbia | 1,229 |
| Illinois | 17,177 |
| Iowa | 3,400 |
| Indiana | 2,730 |
| Kentucky | 1,060 |
| Kansas | 388 |
| Louisiana | 266 |
| Massachusetts | 8,947 |
| Maryland | 1,888 |
| Maine | 413 |
| Michigan | 3,178 |
| Minnesota | 1,514 |
| Missouri | 5,016 |
| Mexico | 71 |
| Mississippi | 52 |
| New Hampshire | 202 |
| Nova Scotia | 45 |
| New Jersey | 5,395 |
| New York | 99,333 |
| Nebraska | 116 |
| North Carolina | 37 |
| New Brunswick | 50 |

|  | During Year 1865 |
|---|---|
| Oregon | 18 |
| Ohio | 10,314 |
| Pennsylvania | 22,276 |
| Rhode Island | 1,353 |
| South Carolina | 77 |
| South America | 34 |
| Texas | 41 |
| Tennessee | 393 |
| Vermont | 263 |
| Utah | 1,092 |
| Virginia | 560 |
| West Indies | 15 |
| Wisconsin | 6,127 |
| Unaccounted for | 439 |
| Total | 200,306 |

With reference to the excessive number remaining in the City of New York, viz., 99,333, I may remark that the greater proportion of these emigrants arrived immediately after the cessation of the war, when it was thought increased vitality would be given to every branch of trade.

### 35.  Scarcity of Skilled Labor in the United States[1]

The diversion from the industries of the northern States, consequent upon the war, is variously estimated at from five hundred thousand to seven hundred and fifty thousand men. It is not to be understood that these figures represent an absolute loss to the industry of the country, although such loss, from casualties and diseases incident to war, was undoubtedly very considerable; but the universal testimony of manufacturers is, that the operatives who entered the army from their establishments have not, as a general thing, returned to their old employments. . . . . Of this deficit, some have engaged in the cultivation of cotton, and in various other industrial pursuits of the south; a much larger percentage have sought new homes and new employments at the extreme west, or on the Pacific coast; while others, taking advantage of the capital made available to them through the payment of bounties and previous savings, have become principals rather than subordinates in business, or, in cases of persons of foreign birth, have returned to the countries of their nativities. . . . .

[1] Extract from *Report of Hon. D. A. Wells, Special Commissioner of the Revenue, December, 1866* (United States Thirty-ninth Congress, second session, Senate Ex. Doc. No. 2), pp. 21–23.

The continued rapid and disproportionate growth of nearly all large cities, as compared with the small increase of population in the rural districts, shows that speculation, and the profit obtainable by exchanging rather than by producing, offer greater inducements at present to many than the pursuits of their ordinary or former industries, and must be recognized as one of the causes which have contributed to a scarcity of skilled labor.

The opening up of many new employments to women, coupled with an increased prosperity of the agricultural classes, has also produced, in many sections of the country, an unusual scarcity of female operatives. This is particularly the case in the manufacturing districts of New England, and has not been remedied by a large advance in wages. The average rate of wages paid to adult female operatives in New England cotton mills is reported to be one dollar per day, while in cases of the more skilled operatives, earnings of from twenty to thirty, and even forty, dollars per month, exclusive of board, are reported. As an illustration of the independence of labor over capital in this department, it may be stated that, during the summer of 1866, the product of the cotton mills of New England was variously reduced from five to twenty-five per cent through the inability to obtain female operatives, even with the inducement of the highest rates of wages ever paid in this branch of manufacture. In one instance specifically reported to the commissioner (viz., the Amoskeag Manufacturing Company, New Hampshire), at least twenty-five per cent of the machinery stood still for a period of three months in 1866, for the sole reason of an inability to procure operatives.

Another result growing out of this great and competitive demand for labor is that the labor itself becomes unstable in its character; to meet which a not uncommon practice has prevailed in New England of offering ten per cent in addition to the ordinary rates of wages, conditioned on the continuance of the engagement for a certain definite period. It is, therefore, obvious that, how much soever this instability in the prices and in the supply of labor may be to the advantage of the operatives, it constitutes an almost insuperable obstacle to production at the minimum cost, and must, therefore, be reckoned as one of the disadvantages from which the foreign competitor of the American manufacturer is at present wholly exempt.

The volume of immigration now pouring into the country affords but little immediate relief to the acknowledged scarcity of skilled labor, inasmuch as the bulk of it is purely agricultural, and seeks a home and employment in the extreme west. Owing to this immigration, however, and to the circumstance that agricultural labor has been supplemented and relieved by machinery to a greater extent than almost any other department of production, the interests of agriculture have suffered much less than those of manufactures and commerce. This statement finds a striking illustration in the fact that during the period of the war, notwithstanding the great draught from the agricultural States to the army, the harvest, through the more extensive use of machinery, increased rather than diminished. Thus the State of Iowa, which, out of a population, in 1860, of 675,000, furnished to the army, from May, 1861, to the end of 1863, 52,240 men, nevertheless increased her number of acres of improved land from 3,445,000 in 1859, to 4,700,000 in 1862, and 4,900,000 in 1863; and her product of wheat from 8,795,000 bushels in 1862, to 14,592,000 in 1863. Again, in 1859 the amount of wheat raised in the State of Indiana was 15,219,000 bushels; while in 1863, notwithstanding the State, out of its population, in 1860, of 1,350,000, had furnished to the army more than 124,000 fighting men; the annual product of wheat exceeded 20,000,000 of bushels.

Another fact worthy of note in this connection is the change which recent high prices and the great demand for skilled labor have occasioned in the character of the workmen employed in the various mechanical establishments of the country. Formerly these operatives were almost exclusively of American birth; now a large proportion are of foreign birth; while the testimony as respects the comparative skill and constructive ability of the latter is almost invariably favorable. This result is certainly a gratifying one, inasmuch as it proves that the influences which surround the immigrant in the United States, even in her large cities, are of a character which on the whole tend to elevate him, and to induce him to leave the crowded walks of unskilled and less productive labor for those which are certain to increase much more rapidly the wealth, not only of the individual, but also of the state.[1] . . . .

[1] [At a later point in the report, when the question is raised whether or not a proposed increase of the tariff would "prove effective in relieving the industry and stimulating the industry of the country," it was said "that although there has been a large absolute advance in the prices of labor since 1862, yet the advance on the whole has been greater during the same time in the price of commodities; and that through the decrease in the purchasing power of wages thus occasioned, the American laborer has not been relatively benefited by his increase of wages, but is in reality in a worse condition than he was before the war."

The commissioner also maintained "that a continuance in the present condition

## 36. Immigration and the Labor Market[1]

It might have been very reasonably anticipated that the circumstances connected with the war would materially interfere with the course of emigration to the United States. Foreign opinion was against us, and every effort was used to weaken confidence in the stability of our Government and in the value of our institutions. The classes from which the emigrants chiefly come were specially warned by the press of foreign countries not to risk their fortunes among a people who could not govern themselves without civil war, and whose resources were being wasted by fraternal strife. It was argued that, should our Government survive the shock of war, the people of the United States would be taxed as heavily as those of the most severely-burthened nations of Europe, and that, consequently, America offered no inducements to the emigrant to forsake his fatherland.

For a period, there doubtless appeared to distant observers to be some force in these views, and they had their effect upon the volume of emigration. In 1861, the number of emigrants arriving at New York was only 68,311, and in 1862, 81,458; which is only 62 per cent of the average number of arrivals for the five preceding years. The very energy and harmony with which the war was prosecuted appeared, however, ultimately to command the respect of the masses of the European populations, and in 1863 the stemmed current broke forth with doubled volume. In that year 161,648 passengers were landed at Castle Garden; in 1864, 184,700; in 1865, the number reached 200,031. During the five years from 1861 to 1865 inclusive, 696,148 immigrants were landed at this port; while the aggregate for the five preceding years was only 605,356.

---

of things, so far from holding out any inducement to an emigration of skilled labor from other countries, in fact tends to repel such emigration. Investigations made under his direction indicate that skilled labor, taking the relative prices of commodities and of rents into consideration, is equally well or better paid in many departments of industry in Great Britain at the present time than in the United States. In some instances the evidence to this effect is conclusive."

Finally he said: "Further confirmation of this point is also to be found in the fact, that within a comparatively recent period skilled laborers in the manufacture of metals have visited the United States with a view of engaging in their special industries, but after investigation have returned, feeling convinced that the wages obtainable at home, though nominally less than in this country, were, taking all things into consideration, in reality equal, or greater."]

[1] Editorial from the *Commercial and Financial Chronicle*, III (September 1, 1866), pp. 260–61.

It thus appears that during the war period the rate of immigration increased fifteen per cent. This year, the arrivals have been unusually numerous. . . . . This enlarged influx is no doubt due to a certain extent to the disturbed condition of Ireland and the contest in Germany, to which countries we are chiefly indebted for the supply of foreign population. Thus the political misfortunes of other countries have contributed, to a material extent, to replace the population sacrificed during the late war.

There are obvious reasons why the high prices prevailing in this country should not have checked immigration. In the first place, prices are also high in the Old World; for the comparative scarcity of leading products which has contributed so largely to the advance here has had a similar effect there. And again, although prices have advanced largely in the United States, yet wages have also risen in proportion, so that it may perhaps be safely affirmed that, as a rule, the condition of the working man is as good now as it was before the war. The great scarcity of male labor, resulting from the losses in the war, has had a tendency to draw here an unusual number of emigrants. Employers of labor have, in some instances, combined for the purpose of importing hands which they were unable to procure among our own population. The efforts of the agents of these parties have naturally attracted attention to emigration to this country and to the inducements arising from an inadequate supply of labor, causing many to emigrate whom they did not directly engage. The promptness with which European population has flowed hither to fill the vacuum caused by the war is an illustration of the readiness with which the irregularities in the world's labor market are adjusted. It is in this very principle of self-regulation that we must confide for recovery from the effects of the loss of producing population during the last four years, and for such a re-inforcement of the ranks of labor as will restore the lost equilibrium between production and consumption, and assist to bring us back to the former range of values.

The severe panic in England and the reaction in trade in Germany, consequent upon the war, will have a tendency to induce emigration to the United States. In England the tendency is toward lower prices for labor, employers in some of the leading branches of manufacture having required their hands to work for reduced wages. Here, on the contrary, the several branches of labor have been, and in some cases are still, demanding an advance of pay. Last week a national convention of working men assembled at Baltimore, one of the chief objects of which was to secure a legal limitation of the daily term of labor to eight hours, which is equivalent to a very important advance in the price of labor. Movements of this character, especially when they occur immediately after an exhaustive war, from which the working classes might be expected to suffer severely, have a very direct tendency to draw foreign labor to this country.

The increased employment of steamers in the transportation of emigrants also facilitates emigration. The charges upon this class of vessels are now about equal to those of sailing vessels, and as the risks and inconveniences of a long and tedious voyage are obviated, an important objection to crossing the Atlantic is removed. In 1856, 126,459 emigrants arrived in sailing vessels, and only 5,111 in steamers; last year 116,579 arrived in steamers, and only 83,452 in sailing vessels— a fact which indicates the important change occurring in the transportation of emigrants. The constantly increasing intercourse between the United States and Europe, and the union of the two continents by the cable, will tend to make known more generally throughout the Old World the advantages to labor afforded by our virgin resources, and will, with other influences, help to promote a larger influx of European population than we have yet witnessed.

In view of these considerations, we are far from yielding to the supposition that the tide of emigration to the Western continent has yet reached its height. We have still millions of acres of virgin soil as fertile as any that has contributed to enrich the emigrant in times past; and, every year, the increase of transportation facilities is rendering these lands more attractive to the ill-paid sons of toil of the Old World. With our wonted rapid increase in population and wealth, the heavy public burthens, which now appear forbidding to the emigrant, will either be removed by the liquidation of our debt, or, if obtained, will bear with comparative lightness upon our vast resources. Should it prove, as some predict, that the emancipated negro will produce less than the negro in slavery, there will then be an opening for foreign laborers in many parts of the South.

## 37. Emigration from the Scottish Highlands[1]

[Various] influences . . . . were operative in inducing the Highlanders to emigrate.[2] . . . . Sheep-farming has led to an immense

[1] Extract from Thomas McLauchlan, "The Influence of Emigration on the Social Condition of the Highlands," *Transactions of the National Association for the Promotion of Social Science*, 1863, pp. 605–10.

[2] [The emigration of the Highland population commenced about the middle of

amount of emigration. In evidence of this it is only necessary to quote the case of the county of Sutherland, where the introduction of the system of sheep-farms has led almost to the peopling of Cape Breton, and a large portion of Prince Edward's Island. Nor could it well be otherwise, seeing that during the inclement portion of the year sheep require the shelter of the low grounds with their more nutritious pasture, and that in order to furnish them with this, the land must be cleared. Whole parishes in Sutherland have in this way been cleared of their population, who will now be found in large numbers cultivating the forests of America. Portions of Sutherland have become desert, while America is stocked in several parts with its people.

Poverty has driven many of the inhabitants of the Highlands to emigrate. Since the failure of the potato crop in 1846 this cause has operated with increased effect. The means of subsistence are diminished at home, and must be found elsewhere. Some of the emigrants from this cause find their way to the colonies, while a large number

---

the eighteenth century and continued so steadily that there were said to be perhaps as many Highlanders and descendants of Highlanders in North America as could be found in 1860 in their native country. "The causes which led to the removal of so large a body of the Highland people were very fully stated in a work published about the year 1805, by the then Earl of Selkirk, who was engaged at that time in securing settlers for an extensive territory of which he had become the owner in British North America. . . . . The suppression of the Rebellion in 1745–46 of the Highlanders in favour of Charles Edward, with the consequent legislation of the British Parliament, originated to a large extent this movement. Previous to that event the power of a Highland chief depended on the number of men he could raise. War of one kind or other was his occupation, and his success in it depended largely on the force which he had at his command. The changes introduced after 1745 led to an entirely different state of things. The clan system was virtually uprooted in the abolition of heritable jurisdictions, or the right possessed by chiefs of administering criminal law, and the whole of the Highlanders were brought under the same legal system with the rest of the empire. One great effect of this was that money and not men became the most valuable return which property could make, and as a necessary consequence, rents came to be looked after, in a way hitherto quite unusual. The process was slow but certain. Lands rose in money value. A price was laid upon them which, although now utterly inadequate, was then looked upon as exorbitant, and large bodies of the people, in fear of utter ruin, and altogether unused to such a state of things, began to seek their way to America. . . . . Between 1745 and the close of the century, the emigration from the Highlands, chiefly to what is now the United States, was very extensive, one of the colonies having been led by the famous Flora Macdonald, the guide and deliverer of Charles Edward. This colony was planted in North Carolina, and in the memory of men still living there were seven or eight congregations in which the Gaelic language was preached in the neighborhood of Fayetteville, in that State" (*ibid.*, p. 603).]

crowd into the towns, and add much to the existing mass of pauperism and distress there. The influence of this emigration upon the social state of the large cities of Scotland is very marked. It does not tell to the same extent as that from Ireland, but if proper statistics were obtained, the writer is convinced from his own observation in this city, that it tells much more extensively than is generally supposed.

A large amount of emigration arises from the spirit of enterprise existing among the Highland people. This most creditable cause has produced a very large portion of it in every part of the country. . . . .

All these causes together have contributed to furnish a large annual stream of emigration from the Scottish Highlands for the last hundred years—a fact amply evidenced by the mass of Gaelic-speaking settlers found scattered over the British colonies and the United States. Cape Breton, Prince Edward's Island, Nova Scotia, New Brunswick, and both the Canadas contain a large Gaelic population. Australia and New Zealand have recently attracted even a larger number than America, while, besides the older settlements in North Carolina, the mass of the population in Caledonia County, state of New York, are of Highland extraction; and there are large settlements in the state of Ohio, besides numerous families and individual settlers in other parts of the United States. Highland names are numerous among the generals of the United States armies on both sides in the present civil war.

The effects of this extensive emigration on the social condition of the Highland population is a question of deep interest. On the emigrants themselves there is little doubt that, generally, the effect has been to improve their circumstances. The writer of this paper has visited most of the Highland settlements in both the Canadas, and from personal observation he can testify that there is a large amount of physical comfort among the people, although one will hear the common remark among the settlers, that they have escaped the landlord to fall into the hands of the storekeeper, to whom they are very usually in debt, and who is by no means the less exacting of the two, or the less ready to have recourse to a process of eviction. At the same time, in judging of the happiness of a people, allowance must be made for moral as well as physical considerations. The Highlander is deeply attached to his native land, and it is doubtful whether he ever comes to cherish a real home feeling in that of his adoption. The writer has met in America with hundreds of cases, where the mind reverted with inexpressible longing towards the old country, with all its hardships, even amidst the physical abundance of a Canadian settlement, and where the circumstances that constrained the separation were deeply mourned. As has been well said, the twig torn from its place still continued to drop drops of blood. At the same time the physical comfort is a decided gain, although there are numerous cases where even this gain has not been made. There is much poverty in many of the Canadian settlements.

The influence of emigration on the social condition of the home population cannot be judged of from a mere cursory view. There are districts where it has relieved the population who remain, by leaving room for judicious management on the part of the landowners improving the condition of their tenantry, by furnishing them with suitable holdings. In the valleys of the Spey, the Findhorn, and the Nairn, the effect of this is very manifest. A declining population has led to a marked amelioration in the appearance of the country and in the condition of the people. In these extensive districts the lands are chiefly held by the native tenantry, but these have received at the hands of judicious and considerate landlords such treatment, as that they have risen rapidly with the general improvement of the country, and all parties have been gainers. In other portions of the country it has been the reverse. The home population has been sinking in spite of emigration, and is likely to sink, until it may be necessary for the Legislature to interfere to prevent the starvation of whole families. The effects of the removal of a large body of the people upon the remnant population, would thus seem to depend entirely upon the purpose to which their removal is turned by the owners of the soil. Where taken advantage of, so as to give the full benefit to the people left behind, the removal from certain districts of a portion of the people has served to promote the social welfare of the rest. . . . .

It has already been stated that in certain sections of the eastern Highlands emigration seems to have been instrumental in promoting the material interests of the general population; in the west Highlands, and more especially in the Islands, such does not seem to have been the case. This very year the cry of destitution in Skye has been loud as ever, and yet from no part of the Highlands has there been a more extensive emigration. From the very earliest period in the history of emigration down to this date, Skye has been largely drawn upon, and yet the body of the people in Skye were never more wretched than at this moment. Even Government at one time interposed to aid in the removal of the people from Skye, and yet with no permanently beneficial effect on the population of the island. This seems to have arisen from several causes. Thus, no attempt has been made to give the remaining population the benefit of the change. The lands of emigrating tenants are added to some existing sheep-run, and the small tenants whose holdings are altogether inadequate to their support, are left just as they were. Until the smaller farms are really made sufficient to support the families of the tenants, no real improvement can take place in their condition. Then, again, it is the most enterprising of the people who go. These have usually some little capital, they see their situation at home helpless, and they are glad to remove ere they are reduced to entire penury. The young also leave, seeing they have no openings at home for their industry. In this way, the youth and the capital being drained away, and the aged, the poor, and the spiritless being left behind, the consequences must be the general sinking of the condition of the population. This is perfectly manifest in many portions of the Hebrides. With these causes, bad seasons and the loss of the potato concur, and have, more especially of late, concurred in reducing the physical comforts of the people in Skye and others of the Western Isles. It is clear that their emigration has not tended to benefit the condition of the general population, and as things are at present managed, cannot by any possibility do so. Whether it might not be otherwise is an entirely different question.

## 38.  The Effects of Continuous Emigration upon Ireland[1]

. . . . About forty years ago Great Britain and Ireland and Germany sent forth annually about 20,000 emigrants; now the number has risen to about 500,000, and of these Germany contributes about 155,-000, Great Britain about 135,000, and Ireland the remainder.

Many causes have tended to increase this outward flow of the people in our own time. The spread of education has revealed to the masses the riches of other lands, and in the gold mines of California and Australia, the El Dorado of many an ancient dream is found to be a glorious reality. But other causes, besides the spread of education, have been at work. Increased facilities of communication, resulting from the enormous expansion of commerce under a system tending more and more towards free trade throughout the world, have virtually lessened the distance, greatly diminished the cost of passage, and

[1] Extract from John McKane, "What Are the Economic Results of the Continuous Emigration from Ireland," *Transactions of the National Association for the Promotion of Social Science*, 1867, pp. 577–84.

thereby removed the seemingly impassable barrier that blocked up the way to the distant goal. These are the general attractive forces acting upon the peoples of the old world, and leading them to America and Australia, and strong as they are in themselves, their influence has been increased in some countries by repellent forces, existing, in a greater or less degree, at home. Thus, in regard to Ireland it is only necessary to mention the terrible famine and the necessary changes that resulted from such a momentous incident. Other special causes have also been at work, to which I shall refer in the course of this paper.

Two great practical questions naturally arise from a consideration of the subject of emigration, and to these very different answers have been given. The first has reference to the prosperity of the emigrant himself; the second to that of the country he leaves behind. On the first there does not exist much difference of opinion. The simple fact that since 1847 the Irish emigrants to America have remitted upwards of £10,000,000 is conclusive as to the independence and prosperity that they have acquired. Instead of living a wretched life here, stagnating in hopeless poverty, and trembling on the verge of starvation, they have in their new homes earned high wages, and, in many cases, become the proprietors of rich and fertile farms. . . . .

But another, and to us more important, question remains behind. What has been the effect upon Ireland itself? What is to become of a country whose most industrious sons leave it in large numbers? Can it hope to prosper when deprived of their labor, and when, if the drain continue, it may appear to some that only the very young and the very old shall be left behind? This is a subject on which much difference of opinion has arisen. There are some who seem to go so far as to regard the diminution of the population as the great panacea for all the ills of a nation, the unfailing medicine for every weakness of the social system, and who are of opinion that when a sufficient number shall be drawn off, we may expect that those who remain will enjoy the greatest possible amount of prosperity. Others consider such a remedy as worse than the disease, and, believing that the main strength of a nation consists in its hardy sons, they regard any diminution of the population as a diminution of every source of material wealth and a withdrawal of the motive power from the great engine of national prosperity. I cannot agree with either of these extreme opinions. It is impossible to say at once whether a diminution of the population is an injury or an advantage to a country. In different circumstances it may be either the one or the other, and we cannot determine which of them it is until we consider the condition of the country, at the particular time, the amount of its accumulated wealth, the purposes to which that wealth is applied, the form of its industry, and the extent and productiveness of the soil in relation to the number of its inhabitants. When we are in possession of these data, and not till then, can we decide with any certainty whether emigration in a given case is an evil or a good. . . . .

A few years ago the universal cry was, that Ireland's miseries all spring from an excessive population, and that the country could only be saved by extensive emigration. The Government of the country was loudly called upon to assist in the work; but the sternest of all necessities, the absolute want of food, had a far greater power than any intervention of Government, and in less than a quarter of a century more than a quarter of her people had left the shores of Ireland and sought out for themselves new homes in distant lands. On the eve of the famine, the population of the island must have reached nearly eight millions and a half; it is now about five millions and a half; and even these figures fail to show the real change, as they do not show what the natural increase would have been. The tide of emigration which then set in still continues to flow, and now a fear is expressed that if this continues production must come to a standstill within the country, and as great anxiety is shown to find some means by which the people may be induced to stay at home, as was formerly shown to discover the means by which they might be encouraged to leave it. In this new phase of the public mind there is too great a proneness to forget the past. But if we seek to ascertain what was the condition of the vast population even previous to the famine years, we shall learn enough to make us hope that such a condition may never return again. Professor Ingram, speaking of those who deplore the emigration, says: "While intensely alive to the immediate material inconvenience and moral pain which the emigrants feel on leaving their homes, they forget the far worse miseries which lie but a little way behind us in our national history. They forget the terrible picture of chronic destitution given by the Commissioners of 1834, and repeated, without any alleviation of its gloomy tints, by the Devon Commission of 1845. They forget the 83 per cent of our rural population, who, in 1845, were found dwelling in wretched cabins unfit for human habitation." At that time the standard of comfort—if we can speak of a standard at all in such a case—was very low. The potato afforded a cheap means of subsistence, and the population increased until even enough of that food was scarcely obtainable by the lower classes. The great body of the people were barely able to earn the merest necessaries of life. The cottier farmers struggled so much for the small patches of land into which the country was divided, that they paid or promised, for its use or abuse, a price that left them almost as poor as the class beneath them. They never dreamt of reaping profit by farming. They lived from hand to mouth, and were content, if, in the struggle for life, they were able to gain the barest subsistence. Ignorance went hand in hand with destitution, for, as Mr. Mill observes, "Education is not compatible with extreme poverty." Those who, in happier circumstances, would have been scholars, were made labourers by poverty, and so the people, from generation to generation, became more numerous, more poor, and more ignorant, until the famine came and drove them beyond the ocean, or swept them into their unknown graves. Ireland was wholly unfitted to bear such a pressure as was put upon it by the failure of her chief crop. She had no unlimited extent of rich virgin soil on which to fall back, no extensive manufactures which might have given remunerative employment to those who were unable to support themselves by agriculture. When the potato crop failed all was lost. The pauper masses were uprooted from the soil to which they had clung with such unreasoning tenacity. They had no resource but the poor-house or emigration, and it is not a matter of regret that many of them chose the latter alternative. The ordeal was indeed a terrible one, but it has been attended with beneficial results. The inordinately excessive numbers at home have been reduced, and, for the working classes who remain, there is not only *constant* employment, but an *increased* rate of wages in consequence of the reduction.

With reference to this part of the subject, two different opinions seem to prevail, both as to the matter of fact, and as to the consequences that would result from it. Some hold that real wages have not increased, and that the advance is only nominal, being caused by a fall in the value of money, and the consequent rise of wages and everything else. They say that the labourer is not better off, for that, while he may get more for his labour, he requires to pay more for the articles on which his wages are spent. This is no doubt to some extent true; but if we reflect that employment is now *constant* instead of being, as it was before, only *casual*, and if we consider the proportionate rise of wages compared with the proportionate rise in the prices of commodities, we must come to the conclusion that the condition of the labourer is not only nominally, but really, bettered. In many parts of Ireland money wages have increased from 50 to 87 per cent, and the price of the necessaries of life has not increased in anything like the same ratio. But then it is said, If wages have risen, or if they continue to rise, how are farmers to be made thereby wealthier or more enterprising, how are manufactures to be created by increasing the difficulty of production? The extraordinary increase of communication between different parts of the world, which has made so large an emigration possible, is leading to the further result of a far more intense competition between the agricultural and manufacturing products of different countries. The very *rise* of wages then to which one party was looking as the great desideratum, is viewed by another, not as a help, but as a hindrance to the production of increased wealth. A very little thought is surely sufficient to solve this apparent difficulty. If there is any force in it, why did not the farmer and manufacturer make great gains when the wages were lower here than probably in any other civilised country? Simply because a people, trembling on the verge of starvation, and steeped in the ignorance which such poverty produces, have neither the heart, the hand, or the head to work. Their labour is inefficient, and, though it may yield but little to the worker, it costs much to the employer. In theory at least everyone can recognize the distinction between the rate of wages and the cost of labour, and a comparison of the work of an Irishman at home and of an Irishman abroad would furnish the best illustration of the distinction.

Besides, we must take into account that emigration has led to a better distribution of the soil of the country. In many instances the holdings were so small, and the rent so high previous to the famine, that the cultivators were little better off than the common labourers. The subdivision of farms was so great as not to afford continuous employment to the occupiers with the wretched knowledge of the method of farming which they possessed. In some parts, as in Ulster, where during the intervals of farm labour the members of the household were able to find profitable employment in domestic manufactures, the small plot of land was, to use their own phrase, "an accommodation." Of these manufactures the most important was hand-loom weaving, and much of the rent for many years was paid, not by the produce of the farm, but by the wages of the shuttle. The extensive introduction of steam power has now greatly reduced the wages of those still employed at the hand-loom. Most of this kind of weaving is at present done in factories by young persons, and the men, who formerly lived by combining hand-loom weaving and agriculture, have either been compelled to take larger farms and live by agriculture alone, or to seek employment in other quarters.

We may thus account in part for the circumstance that while in 1841 there were upwards of three hundred thousand holdings below five acres, in 1861 there were not one-third the number, and that the holdings between five and fifteen acres had considerably diminished, whilst those between fifteen and thirty had increased. There are some who view with alarm the increase in the number of very large holdings, but while I object as strongly as they do to the country being turned into "an immense grazing farm," it will not, I think, be denied that the greater number of the farms previous to the extensive emigration were so small as to be utterly incapable of supporting the cultivator and his family even in a moderate degree of comfort, and that while the change from very small to very large farms is to be deprecated, that from small to others of moderate size is accompanied with increased prosperity. And when we consider the effect of free trade on the farming interests of the country this conclusion will be strengthened. A writer in the *Economist*, I believe Professor Cairnes, says, "All the leading incidents of the industrial economy of Ireland as it stood in 1846 were identified with the maintenance of its tillage system, and of that system free trade sounded the inevitable doom, for free trade struck at the root of the large cereal cultivation which had previously existed." The necessity then arose for a different species of farming—for capitalist instead of cottier cultivation, and in one district of the country tillage was superseded and grazing was resorted to in consequence of the high price of cattle and live stock, while in another the profits made by the growing of flax consequent on the extension of the linen manufacture, and an improved system of rotation, still made tillage in this country an economic success. In both cases, however, farms larger than those which had previously existed became necessary, and more capital was required to cultivate them with advantage. The fact that there are still large sums left by farmers on deposit in the banks notwithstanding the very low rate of interest, shows that the capital so required was not wanting. From this change in the distribution of the soil of the country we may naturally expect a more skilful method of agriculture, and a consequent increase of returns to capital, capable of yielding not only higher wages to the labourer but higher profits to the farmer at the same time.

The effect of emigration on this country hitherto has thus been to improve the condition of its remaining inhabitants. The labourer is now constantly employed and better remunerated, and the farmer at the same time reaps a larger profit. Manufactures too in one part of the island have made rapid progress. The spinning mills and power-looms of Ulster are busy at work, and during the last few years new factories have been springing up on every side. But notwithstanding this improvement, emigration is still going on, and we are beginning to ask, might not our people be profitably employed at home?

It is true that one of the leading features of our age is the discovery and development of the resources of remote and hitherto unknown places, and there is really a great industrial enterprise in emigration, but the question is, might not this industrial enterprise be applied at home? Are there no natural advantages in Ireland which might be developed, and give employment and profitable employment for the people? When once the rate of wages in a country has reached a certain point which ensures to the labourer the necessaries and decencies of life, emigration ceases to be of such paramount importance, and no man could contemplate the expatriation of so many brave hearts and strong right arms with equanimity. The true remedy is to be found in the development of our commerical enterprise, of our mineral resources, of our manufacturing industry: "It is not blood-letting to relieve a plethora, but stimulants to restore the balance of a congested circulation, that are needed."

### 39. Occupations of Immigrants, 1870[1]

Viewed in respect of their industrial occupations, the foreigners among us may be divided as those who are where they are, because they are doing what they are doing; and those who are doing what they are doing, because they are where they are. In the former case, occupation has determined location; in the latter, location has determined occupation. In either case, the location being given, we have a clew to the occupation.

Respecting a foreigner at the West, the presumption is very decided that his chosen occupation, perhaps his hereditary occupation, has determined his location; but at the East the presumption is rather the other way. Here we find the peasants of Ireland and Germany engaged, painfully to themselves and often wastefully to their employers, in all sorts of mechanical operations to which they have no traditional or acquired aptitude; while, on the other hand, not a few of the skilled

[1] Extract from Francis A. Walker, "Our Foreign Population, II, What They Are Doing," *The Advance*, VIII (Chicago, December 10, 1874), 261–62.

mechanics and cunning artificers of Europe, finding here no demand for their labor in the very special direction in which alone they have been trained, or being excluded from competition by trades-union regulations, or being disadvantaged by their poverty, their strangeness, and their foreign speech, have settled down by the mere force of circumstance, to breaking stone for highways, to working on railroads, to menial service, or to day-labour in any capacity. They are found in our mills, earning a mean living by the side of utterly untaught and untrained laborers; or, they have joined their fortunes to those of some ward-ring of politicians, and have become its bullies and strikers—very much as they would have done had they found themselves, equally helpless and forlorn, in Rome, in the year 63 B.C.

In a word, no one can travel much in the East without seeing that with no small proportion of our vast foreign element, occupation is determined by a location that is accidental, or practically beyond the control of individuals; that these people are doing what they are doing, because they are where they are. And the reason for such a wholesale subjection of labor to its circumstances, is found in the miscellaneousness, the promiscuousness, and we may say the tumultuousness, of the immigration of the United States since the days of the Irish famine. Of all who have come to us in the past twenty-seven years, by far the greater part have come unprovided and uninstructed for the experience of their American life. Whether pushed fairly out of their own country by the pressure of population, or escaping from military conscription, or moved by restlessness and the spirit of adventure, or burning with the gold fever, or allured by the false reports of relatives and acquaintances on this side of the water; they have fallen on our shores, the migratory impulse exhausted, their money gone, with no definite purposes, with no special preparation, to become the victims of their place and circumstances, to seek such occupation as offers itself, to underbid native labor, to adapt themselves painfully to the conditions of our industry such as they have found them, or to join the rabble that troops after a Tweed, a Morrissey, a Hayes, and an O'Brien. A little direction and assistance from government would have sufficed to carry hundreds of thousands of those who have remained at the East, to their own misfortune and that of the communities on which they were thus thrown unprovided and uninstructed, to the far West, where, accustomed as they were to agricultural labor, and with nature so kindly and bounteous as to tolerate their early mistakes, and almost to make them free of their mere necessary subsistence, they would have added to the real strength and wealth of the Union, as well as have secured their own success and the happiness of their families. Many a wretched beer-guzzler hanging about the saloons of New York, Philadelphia, and Boston, many a desperate ballot-stuffer and shoulder-hitter, the scourge of our politics, would, had he once been carried through Castle Garden and dropped 500 miles beyond New York, have become a useful and prosperous citizen. . . . .

It is commonly believed that this supply of cheap, untaught labor, derived from the misdirection of European peasants to mechanical pursuits, has had a beneficial effect upon our production. Doubtless it has served to promote the growth of some early and coarse forms of industry; but doubtless, also, it has exerted an influence prejudicial to the development of the higher and finer manufactures. Contrary to current economical maxims, employers of labor are just as liable as common folks to the illusion that what brings a low price is therefore cheap, and also just as liable as common folks to accept a small present gain at the sacrifice of large future advantage; and this opportunity of securing low-priced labor, which has not only been offered every manufacturer at the East, but has fairly been thrust in his face, has generally proved a temptation too strong to be resisted. Not to dwell upon the consideration, the result has been to disparage our goods in the opinion of consumers, and to discourage skill and care and pains in American manufacturing industry.

Of those foreigners whose occupations have determined their location, the most notable instances are the Welsh and the Scandinavians.

Why should there be nearly four times as many Welsh in Pennsylvania as in New York? Why four times as many in Ohio as in Illinois? The reason is obvious. The Welsh are famous miners and iron-makers. Their labor has not been wasted. They have come out to this country under intelligent direction, and have gone straight to the place where they are wanted.

Quite as striking has been the self-direction of the Swedish and Norwegian immigrants. Four States, all west of Lake Michigan, contain 94 per cent of all the Norwegians in the country, and 66 per cent of the Swedes; while of the remaining fractions, by far the greater part is also found in other States and Territories, within the same meridians. These immigrants have gone straight across the country, a far greater journey than was required of the Welsh, and have set at once about their chosen occupation, agriculture, in their chosen homes, Illinois, Wisconsin, Iowa, and Minnesota, without loss of time, or injury to character by exposure, unemployed and unprovided, to the temptations of city life.

Although the Scotch have not in the same way emphasized their choice of locations, in which to pursue their chosen vocations, being, indeed, scattered somewhat widely, we have the strongest evidence that they have placed themselves to suit themselves (not merely been thrown ashore by a wave of immigration), in the fact that very few of the men of this country are employed as day-labourers.

### 40. "Capital Value of Immigration to the United States"[1]

It is a common mistake of statisticians and writers on political economy to limit their enquiries to the amount of means which immigrants bring with them, to ascertain the aggregate thereof, and to conclude that the few millions thus obtained are the only addition to the nation's wealth.

In 1856, the Commissioners of Emigration in New York examined every immigrant as to the amount of his means, and the average cash of each of the 142,342 new-comers of that year amounted to $68.08. The Commissioners afterward discontinued this examination, for the reason that, in spite of all their endeavors, they could not obtain correct answers on the part of the immigrants, who were suspicious of their motives.

Superintendent Kennedy, in his report of January 14, 1858, says:

The main object for enquiring of passengers the amount of cash means they possessed, was secured, when it was shown to the public that on the average they were in possession of a larger amount of such means than is held by the localized residents of any known community; and that, although a part of the immigration is among that class of persons who seek refuge on our shores and subsistence by labor, with little or no cash means, yet a large portion bring with them of that kind of property a sufficient quantity to sustain themselves, and to aid in the enrichment of the country. It was justly apprehended that a continuance of the investigation might lead to mischievous results, from their manifest inaccuracy. For, while the table of 1856 presents the average amount of cash means at $68.08 per head, subsequent but reliable information showed that the concealment of large amounts had been constantly and successfully practised; and that, had full admission been made of the funds in possession, the average would have been at least double the amount reported.

[1] Extract from Friedrich Kapp, *Immigration, and the Commissioners of Emigration of the State of New York* (New York, 1870), pp. 142–51. See the following document, p. 379, for some comments on the Kapp estimates.

I was myself at that time a witness of the unreliability of the statements of immigrants concerning their means. Being present when, in the summer of 1856, the passengers of a German ship were examined at Castle Garden, I observed an old farmer and his three adult sons, who, in answer to the enquiry of the Superintendent, opened their pocket-books, counted the contents of each, and hesitatingly declared it to be about $25. I interposed and explained to these people, who evidently apprehended that they would be taxed on account of their money, the reason of the interrogatories, whereupon the old farmer showed me a bill of exchange of $2,700 on a New York banker, and remarked that each of his sons had about the same amount with him. These men had been entered as having about $100 together, while in fact they ought to have been credited with about $11,000.

"German immigrants alone," says a report of the Commissioners of Emigration, December 15, 1854, on the subjects in dispute between the Commissioners of Emigration and the Almshouse Department of the city of New York, "have for the past three years, as estimated by the best German authorities, brought into the country annually an average of about eleven millions of dollars. A large amount of money in proportion to numbers is estimated to have been brought from Holland and other countries. The amount of money thus introduced into the country is incalculable."

These estimates are corroborated by statements which I happened to find among some German statistical tables. It appears from the statistical records of the grand duchy of Baden, that from 1840 to 1849 the ready cash which each emigrant carried with him amounted to 245 florins, or $98 gold. Again, of the Bavarian emigrants between 1845 and 1851, each was possessed of 233 florins, or $93.20 gold; between 1851 and 1857, each of 236 florins, or $94.40 gold; while the Brunswickers, who emigrated in 1853, had 136 thalers, or about $96 gold, each. The Würtembergers, in 1855, carried only $76 gold each with them; which sum in 1856 increased to $134 gold, in 1857 to $145 gold, and in 1858 even to $318 gold per head. Other official data concerning this I have not been able to obtain, but the instances just cited throw sufficient light on the subject.

The money, however, is not the only property which immigrants bring with them. In addition to it, they have a certain amount of wearing apparel, tools, watches, books, and jewelry. Assuming that their cash amounts to only $100 a head, I do not think I exaggerate in estimating their other property at $50, thus making $150 the total of the personal property of each immigrant. The total arrivals at New York for the year 1869 were 258,989 immigrants, and the amount added to the national wealth, through this port alone, in one year, did consequently not fall short of $38,848,350. Large as this sum appears, it is insignificant in comparison with the hundreds of millions which have been, and will be, produced yearly by the labor of immigrants. And here the question suggests itself: What is the economic value of each immigrant to the country of his adoption?

We are perfectly familiar with the estimates which, during the existence of slavery, were made of the value of negroes. A good field hand was considered to be worth $1,200 and over; a good cook was valued higher; and a seamstress or housekeeper was, in some cases, held at even $1,500 or $2,000. In order to obtain a proper idea of the importance of immigration to the United States, we must endeavor to capitalize, so to speak, the addition to the natural and intellectual resources of the country represented by each immigrant.

A prominent German statistician, Dr. Engel, of Berlin, Director of the Prussian Statistical Bureau, in an able treatise on the price of labor, distinguishes three periods in the economic life of each man: two unproductive, and one productive, period. The first comprise the raising and education of the individual, and continues until he reaches his fifteenth year. It is, of course, not only unproductive, but causes considerable outlay. The second, extending from the fifteenth to the sixty-fifth year, is the productive time of life. The third comprises the unproductive years of old age after sixty. Dr. Engel calls the first the juvenile, the second the labor, and the third the aged, period.

It is only during this productive period that man is able to subsist on the results of his own labor. In the juvenile period he is dependent on the assistance of others, and in the aged period he has to live upon the accumulated fruits of the productive years. Whether or not the child in its first period lives at the expense of his parents, there must be means for its maintenance and education, and as nature does not spontaneously furnish these means, and as they cannot be provided by others without danger of impoverishment if not replaced, they must be obtained by labor. This labor is performed during the productive period, in which the following three objects should be attained, viz., (1) The payment of the expenses incurred for the support and education of the child in the juvenile period. (2) The satisfaction of the daily wants, and the maintenance of the productive power of the individual. (3) The laying up of a surplus fund for his sustenance during the aged period. Thus, the cost of the bringing up and education of a man constitutes a specific value, which benefits that country which the adult individual makes the field of his physical and intellectual exertions. This value is represented by the outlay which is necessary to produce an ordinary laborer. An immigrant, therefore, is worth just as much to this country as it costs to produce a native-born laborer of the same average ability.

It is evident that the capital value which a grown-up, able-bodied immigrant represents is different according to his station in life and the civilization of the country whence he comes. The wants of a skilled and unskilled laborer from the same country differ widely. Those of the Englishman are different from those of the Irishman. The German must be measured by another standard than the Mexican or South American. Their mode of life, their economical habits and practical pursuits, have little in common; and hence the benefit to the country of their adoption varies according to their respective previous relations. It is certain, however, that each immigrant brings, independently of his personal property, a certain increase of wealth to this country, which increase is paid by the country from which he comes, and accordingly must be credited to it.

In order to arrive at the most accurate possible estimate of this addition of wealth, it is necessary to enquire into the cost of raising and educating, in this country, a man whose means of living are wholly derived from his physical labor. I shall not include in the following calculation the professional man, the scholar, the lawyer, the clergyman, the physician, the engineer, and others, who in the course of years, have likewise come here by thousands, and added to the productive wealth of the country in proportion to the greater cost of their education; but I shall confine myself to the class named, which forms the great majority of immigrants.

Dr. Engel computes the cost of raising a manual laborer in Germany at 40 thalers a year for the first five years of his life; at 50 thalers for the next five years; and at 60 thalers from the eleventh to the fifteenth year, thus arriving at an average of 50 thalers per year, or 750 thalers in all. From my knowledge of German life, I consider this estimate as correct as it can be; and, assuming that in this country subsistence costs about twice as much as in Germany, I do not think I shall be far from the truth in doubling Engel's estimates, and in assuming the expense of bringing up an American farmer or unskilled laborer for the first fifteen years of his life to average 100 thalers per year, or a total of 1,500 thalers, equal to about $1,500 currency. Following Dr. Engel's estimate, an American girl will be found to cost only about half of that, or $750, for the reason that she becomes useful to the household from an earlier age. Allowance must be made, it is true, for the fact that about one-fifth of the emigrants are less than fifteen years old; but this is fully balanced by the great preponderance of men over women, and by thousands who represent the highest order of skilled labor. Hence I feel safe in assuming the capital value of each male and female emigrant to be $1,500 and $750, respectively, for every person of either sex, making an average for both of $1,125. My friend, Mr. Charles Reemelin, one of the most prominent American political economists, confirmed these figures in a very able address made before the German Pioneer Association of Cincinnati, on May 26, 1869, in which he estimated the value of each immigrant who had come to that city to live at $1,500, and the total value of the fifty thousand emigrants who have taken up their residence there in the last forty years at seventy-five millions of dollars.

The number of emigrants who have arrived at the port of New York from May 5, 1847, to January 1, 1870, is no less than 4,297,980. Adding to the capital value of $1,125 represented by every emigrant, $150 per head for the average value of personal property brought, as I have shown, by each, we find that immigration increased the national wealth, in the stated period, by more than five billions of dollars, or more than twice as much as the present amount of the national debt. The total immigration into the United States being now at the rate of 300,000 souls per year, the country gains nearly four hundred millions of dollars annually, or more than one million per day.

My friend, Mr. Charles L. Brace, in a very able communication which, on November 3, 1869, he addressed to the New York daily *Tribune*, has taken exception to these statements and estimates, which were contained in a paper read by me before the American Social Science Association.

"Mr. Kapp," he says, "deserves high commendation for the ingenuity and industry he has shown in thus analyzing our emigration statistics, and proving the economical value of this current of population.

But, in the light of science, we are compelled to point out what seem to us omissions in these economical reasonings, which will somewhat modify the results. The capital value of an object is not determined merely by the cost of its production, but also by another element—*the demand for it.* Thus, if a hundred new sewing machines are produced, they are worth to the community not merely what they cost to make, but what the demand for them will bring. If there has been an overproduction of sewing machines, or they are of poor quality, their worth sinks, and their money value to the community may fall below the cost of manufacture. The same is true of all articles which are parts of the capital of a country. Their money value or price is conditioned by cost of production and the relation of demand to supply. It is true also of animals. A cow or a horse is worth not alone what it costs to produce it, but what the demand will bring. Some, from adventitious circumstances, will fall below the cost of production; some will rise above it. Many fine horses, which cost no more to raise than poor ones, are worth far more to the country, because the demand for them is greater, while many poor ones sink below their cost, because the demand is unreasonably small. So with human beings, if we look at them purely as instruments of production. An idiot costs as much, perhaps more, to raise as a lad of ordinary intelligence; but he is of no capital value. A farmer's boy, whose brain has worked intensely as he broke the sod, though costing no more in education than a dull clodhopper in the next house, finds himself at fifteen worth double the other in his market value, solely because the demand for his labor is greater. The wages or salary of men in the professions is not measured solely by the cost of their education, but by the price which their services will bring in the market; and this is determined mainly, though not entirely, by demand and supply.

When an emigrant lands in this country, his capital value is conditioned by these two elements, cost of production and demand. There are, probably, every year among the emigrants, a few thousand of poor, ignorant, and rather weakly women who become sewing-women in the great cities. These, on Mr. Kapp's estimate, should be worth $750 each. But, owing to the crowded state of the market for such instruments of production, and to their own ignorance, and the consequent small demand for each seamstress, those women are probably of scarcely any pecuniary value to the community, and are often a burden. On the very property of the Commissioners of Emigration there will be, this winter, some thousands of able-bodied men, who not only produce nothing, but are supported by the contributions to the Emigration Fund of their more industrious fellows. These certainly are not worth $1,125 capital to the nation. Then take the very considerable number of the four million emigrants who have been entirely non-producers, being either paupers, or criminals, or diseased, or who have, as neglected children, fallen into the hands of the public authorities, or whose labor, as destitute women, has not supported themselves. When these are all subtracted from the four millions, there will be a very considerable deduction from Mr. Kapp's enthusiastic estimates of the value of this golden tide.

We do not question, however, the general conclusion of the Commissioner's paper—the immense value of this current of labor to the production and development of the country. We would only diminish somewhat his numerical estimate of the pecuniary worth of each emigrant.

Articles which are in universal demand, such as gold and silver, depend for their value mainly on the cost of production. So universal is the demand here for ordinary male labor, that its value will not vary much from the expense of its production in this country. This cost Mr. Kapp has probably exaggerated in making it double that of Germany. It would be safe, however, reckoning from the expense of supporting a laborer's male child in Germany, to call the capital value of the most ordinary farmhand at least $1,000 or $1,100 in the United States.

This estimate alone would justify all the Commissioner's enthusiasm as to the pecuniary value of emigration.

It is a little less than was the old market value of the male slave, for the reason, probably, as Mr. Olmsted has shown, that the pecuniary value of slaves was somewhat speculative, based *on the expectation of profit* from the best cotton lands.

There is another method of obtaining "the capital value" of the male emigrant, which we throw out for the consideration of your readers interested in questions of political economy.

Each laborer is worth (pecuniarily) to the country the profits from his production over and above the expense of his support. His average cost to his employer is, say $20 per month and "keep," or about $400 per annum. It is believed that an ordinary profit on common labor upon a farm is from 15 to 18¾ per cent. This would leave the gain to the country from $60 to $75 annually. This, at seven per cent interest, would represent just about the capital value estimated above, or about $1,000 or $1,100 for an average male laborer.

So far Mr. Brace. I freely admit that the economical principles set forth by him are incontrovertible; but, on the other hand, I claim that actual experience has established the correctness of the position I have assumed. The basis for my statements and estimates is chiefly thus:

In a comparatively new country like the United States, with its immense area and the rapid development of its resources, the demand for labor is always greater than the supply. There are, it is true, some pursuits in which this is not the case. During the winter, too, in large cities, hundreds and thousands of emigrants are often unable to find suitable employment or an adequate reward for their labor; but this state does not continue for any length of time. Seamstresses who cannot find work in their line turn to other occupations, such as housemaids, nurses, etc. The character of the European workingwoman in this respect is just the reverse of that of the American. While the latter considers labor in a factory to be of a more elevated character, and would never descend to common housework, the former is content to exert herself in any decent sphere of labor.

But for argument's sake, let me admit that every year there are a few thousand poor, ignorant, and incapable men or women who become a burden to the community. What proportion does their number bear to the total immigration of a whole year? The New York Commissioners of Emigration have annually to support an average of about 2,000 sick and destitute in their institutions, and, besides, a few hundred criminals, who are confined at their cost in the city prisons; but all this does not amount to one per cent of the entire immigration. It must be borne in mind that the poorer emigrants remain in New York City, and that, consequently, it cannot be presumed that any large number of the others become a burden to the several States.

However, I will even go so far as to admit that the number of those who not only produce nothing, but are supported by the contributions of States or counties, reaches 5 per cent. Taking the number of immigrants in 1869 as a basis, this percentage would give between 12,000 and 13,000 non-producers. But even such a percentage would be more than counterbalanced by the large number of emigrants better educated than the ordinary laborers who form the basis of my computation.

An emigrant population contains a very small percentage of helpless and incapable individuals. Apart from the law which prohibits the landing of cripples, blind, deaf, and aged persons, it is self-evident that only the strong, the most courageous and enterprising natives of a country emigrate to a foreign land. The unequal representation of the several ages and sexes among emigrants is due to this fact. Out of the whole immigration to the United States from 1819 to 1860, more than 22 per cent were from one to fifteen years old; a little over 50 per cent were from fifteen to thirty years of age; more than 73 per cent were less than thirty years old; more than $46\frac{1}{2}$ per cent were from twenty to thirty-five; more than 60 per cent were from fifteen to thirty-five, and nearly 90 per cent less than forty years old. Moreover, the sexes approach equality only among children and youths. Of individuals under twenty years of age, about 18 per cent were males, and 17 per cent females, while the male immigrants from twenty-five to forty years of age were double the number of females of the same age.

Of the total immigration to the United States within the above-mentioned period (1819 to 1860), amounting to 5,459,421, the occupation of 2,978,599, including 2,074,633 females, is not stated, while

1,637,154 are put down as farmers and laborers, leaving 843,668 persons who were either mechanics or professional men. In the census tables for that period, we find 407,524 mechanics, 4,326 clergymen, 2,676 lawyers, 7,109 physicians, 2,016 engineers, 2,490 artists, 1,528 teachers, 3,120 manufacturers, 3,882 clerks, and 5,246 seamstresses and milliners, enumerated among the immigrants. This enumeration, incomplete as it is, shows that about 15 per cent of the immigration belongs to that class of population which produces more than the common laborer, and that therefore the 5 per cent, if so many, of helpless and unproductive emigrants are more than balanced by the percentage of higher mechanical and professional ability.

### 41.  An Official Estimate of the Value of an Immigrant[1]

In making an intelligent estimate of the addition to the material wealth of the country by immigration, several distinct conditions should be regarded. The character of the immigrants as industrious and law-abiding citizens, their nationalities, education, and previous condition, as well as their occupation and ages, are elements to be considered when determining their value.

As regards nationality, more than one-half of those who have thus far arrived in the United States are British, and come from the United Kingdom, or from the British possessions of North America. These speak our language, and a large part are acquainted with our laws and institutions, and are soon assimilated with, and absorbed into, our body-politic.

The German element comes next, and embraces nearly two-thirds of the remainder, being at once an industrious and an intelligent people, a large proportion settling in rural districts and developing the agricultural resources of the West and South, while the remainder, consisting largely of artisans and skilled workmen, find profitable employment in the cities and manufacturing towns.

The influx of Scandinavians, who have already made extensive settlements in the Northwestern States, constitutes a distinctive feature of the movement, and though but a few years since it received its first impetus, is already large and rapidly increasing. Industrious, economical, and temperate, their advent should be especially welcomed. . . . .

The Latin nations contribute very little to our population, and the

[1] Extract from Edward Young, *Special Report on Immigration; accompanying Information for Immigrants*, March 15, 1871 (United States Forty-second Congress, first session, House Ex. Doc. No. 1), pp. vi–x.

Slavic still less, while today, as from time immemorial, the different branches of the great Teutonic trunk are swarming forth from the most populous regions, to aid in the progress of civilization.

While a brief review of the ethnic derivation of the millions who have transferred their allegiance from the Old World to the New, exhibits a favorable result, other elements of their value to this country require consideration. The wide contrasts between skilled and unskilled labor, between industry and laziness, between economical habits and unthrift, indicates a marked variation in the capital value of the immigrant to the country. The unskilled laborers, who at once engage in subduing the forests, or cultivating the prairies, are of far more value to the country than those who remain in the large cities.

Deducting the women and children, who pursue no occupation, about 46 per cent of the whole immigration have been trained to various pursuits. Nearly half of these are skilled laborers and workmen who have acquired their trades under the rigorous system which prevails in the Old World, and come here to give us the benefit of their training and skill without repayment of the cost of such education. Nor are the farm laborers and servants destitute of the necessary training to fit them for their several duties, while those classed as common or unskilled laborers are well qualified to perform the labor required, especially in the construction of works of internal improvement. Nearly 10 per cent consist of merchants and traders, who doubtless bring with them considerable capital as well as mercantile experience, while the smaller number of professional men and artists, embracing architects, engineers, inventors, men of thorough training and a high order of talent, contribute to our widely extended community not only material, but artistic, aesthetic, intellectual, and moral wealth. . . . .

Recurring to the money value of an immigrant, it may be stated that the sum of $1,000 has usually been regarded as the average worth of each permanent addition to our population, an amount somewhat too large, but yet an approximation to the true value. Mr. Kapp,[1] one of the commissioners of emigration of the State of New York, who has given much consideration to the subject now under review, assumes the average value to be $1,125. . . . .

But the question, what is the average money value of an immigrant, is yet unanswered. To resolve it, other elements than those already mentioned must receive consideration. The immigrant must be

[1] [See the preceding document p. 374 for the Kapp estimates.]

regarded both as a producer and as a consumer. In treating the whole number of immigrants as producers, the non-producers must first be excluded. These consist of the very aged and the very young, and of those who are unable to labor, whether from sickness, physical inability, or mental condition, whether in or out of charitable or reformatory institutions, and of the criminal or vicious class, whether in or out of prison. In this category may also be included those whose occupations or pursuits tend to demoralize or injure society. The social statistics of the foreign-born population being imperfect, it will perhaps be possible to estimate the productiveness of the whole by taking the earnings of unskilled laborers; offsetting the increased productiveness and earnings of the skilled workmen against the unproductiveness of the classes above mentioned.

The wages of laborers and unskilled workmen throughout the country average very nearly $400 per year. Assuming that the families of these men consist of four persons, we have $100 as the amount which each individual produces, and to which also he is restricted in consumption. The estimated yearly expenditures of the family of a laborer, consisting of two adults and two small children (if any are larger it is probable that they earn something in addition), is as follows: For tea, coffee, sugar, and other foreign goods, which pay a duty of about 60 per cent to the Government, $60; flour, meat, and butter, about $150; rent, $50; fuel and light, $30; vegetables, $30; milk, eggs, &c., $20; leaving $60 for clothing, housekeeping goods, &c. As most of these expenditures are for articles of domestic product which pay a succession of profits not only to the retailer, wholesale dealer, and producer, but to the transporter, the sum of these net profits constitutes the aggregate amount which this family contributes to the wealth of the country. A careful computation gives $160, which sum is the measure alike of their production and consumption. As producers and consumers, then, each is worth to the country $40 per annum, which capitalized at five per cent, gives $800 as the average value of an immigrant.

As a large number, especially those from Northern Europe, engage at once in the cultivation of the soil on their own account, it is desirable to ascertain the increment to the wealth of the country consequent upon their industry. This appears in the form of productive fields reclaimed from the wilderness, buildings and fences erected, agricultural implements and stock accumulated, &c. In the absence of correct data, the sum of $160 by a family of four persons, or $40 each, is considered an approximate estimate of the yearly addition to the realized wealth of the country by such improvements. The figures of the census recently taken will doubtless show that an immense aggregate increase in the national wealth is due to this source alone. Being the result of voluntary industry and self-imposed economy, it is an increase which remains in the hands of the immigrants themselves, who thus contribute to the state that highest form of wealth, a sturdy, moral, intelligent, and independent yeomanry, the very balance-wheel of national machinery. Data will soon exist by which the average production will be tested. It is believed that the statistics of the census of 1870, when compiled, will exhibit the average value of real and personal estate in the Union at about $800 per capita, and the annual increase about 5 per cent, or $40. Now, while the property owned by the foreign-born population does not average $800, yet in productiveness, it is believed, they contribute their full share.

It should not be forgotten, however, that these immigrants bring with them some money, estimated at $100 by Mr. Kapp, and at $80 by Mr. Wells, but inasmuch as a careful investigation was made at Castle Garden, New York, which resulted in establishing $68 as the average sum brought by alien passengers, that amount is assumed as the correct one. As the greater part, if not the whole of this sum, is required to take the immigrant to his destination, and to support him until he becomes a producer, the amount of money which he brings with him is omitted in the foregoing estimate of his capital value. If his annual value to the country be capitalized at 6 per cent instead of 5, and the largest estimate of money brought with him ($100) included, it would aggregate less than $800, the amount already estimated as his capital value.

From the foregoing considerations, therefore, the sum of $800 seems to be the full average capital value of each immigrant. At this rate those who landed upon our shores during the year just closed, added upwards of $285,000,000 to our national wealth, while during the last half-century the increment from this source exceeds $6,243,880,800. It is impossible to make an intelligent estimate of the value to the country of those foreign-born citizens who brought their educated minds, their cultivated tastes, their skill in the arts, and their inventive genius. In almost every walk of life their influence has been felt. Alike in the fearful ordeal of war and in the pursuits of peace, in our legislative halls, and in the various learned professions, the adopted sons of America have attained eminence. Among the many who rendered timely aid to our country during the late war, it may seem invidious to mention a single name, except for the purpose of illustration. In the year 1839 there arrived at the port of New York, in the steamship "British Queen," which sailed from the port of London, a Swedish immigrant, better known as Captain John Ericsson. What was his value to the country, as estimated on the 9th day of March, 1862? Was it eight hundred, eight hundred thousand, or eight millions of dollars?

### 42.  Opportunities for Emigrants, 1870[1]

The steady influx of immigrants within the last twenty years has produced a marked effect on Americans in their choice of occupations, and has created a decided disinclination on their part to share in the rough toil of purely muscular labour in which the newly arrived foreigner is ready to engage.

The American system of common school education has elevated the moral standard of the native working man, and has disposed him to prefer those occupations in which the exercise of the brain is in greater demand than that of the elbow. His chief object of ambition is to attain the position of a master workman, or, in the parlance of the country, to become a "boss," or to obtain a situation of clerk in an office, or of assistant in a shop, and rather than engage in work which he may deem derogatory to his moral culture, he will follow the setting sun and settle on the public lands of the country which the National Government offers, at almost nominal prices, to any man who will cultivate them.

Nor are the labouring capacities of the nation likely to be perceptibly strained for want of hands so long as the tide of emigration flows to the shores of America, or so long as native ingenuity maintains its present high standard of merit in the invention of labour-saving machinery. . . . .

A love of change, and a constant pursuit of fresh fields of industry has taken possession of the mind of American operatives, and a spirit of restlessness is noted in the working community that has sensibly affected the former reputation it enjoyed for mechanical skill.

The system of apprenticeship, moreover, has almost entirely disap-

[1] Extract from "Report by Mr. Francis Clare Ford on the Condition of the Industrial Classes in the United States (Washington, December 31, 1869)," in Great Britain, Foreign Office, *Reports from Her Majesty's Diplomatic and Consular Agents abroad respecting the Condition of the Industrial Classes in Foreign Countries, 1870* (London, 1870), pp. 317–18.

peared, and Americans in general appear to begrudge the time necessary to make themselves thoroughly acquainted with the details of
a business, and even those who have learnt one are very rarely found
to follow it up.

The consequence has been that foreign is every day replacing
native skilled labour.

Indeed, the great number of foreign workmen employed in all the
branches of American industries is very remarkable.

Nearly all the hands at present in American cotton, woollen, and
worsted mills, and in the foundries and rolling-mills of the country,
are of recent foreign extraction.

Of the 30,000 miners engaged in the Pennsylvania coal districts,
but few will be found who are not English, Welsh, or Irish. The largest
proportion of manual work performed on railroads and canals falls to
the lot of Irishmen, and in the clothing trades established in the great
cities of the Union the German element preponderates, whilst the comparatively few Frenchmen in the country are met with in the barbers'
shops.

It is a common remark in the United States that foreign workmen
who come to this country seldom return to their native land with the
intention, at least, of permanently residing there; and the inference is
drawn that the prosperity of the artizan class in America is superior
to that abroad. To a certain extent this may be true, although it must
be admitted that, at the present time, the high cost of living, and the
fluctuating condition of the irredeemable currency of the country,
very seriously affect the interests of the working community. It is,
moreover, reasonable to suppose that a residence of a few years in the
United States, where the principle of "equality" is carried out to so
high a degree, will often unfit a man belonging to the artizan classes
for living in the old countries of Europe where the relative positions of
social life are so strictly defined and, as a rule, so vigorously enforced,
and where the accident of birth is held of such account.

Married and single men, be they of sober and active habits, will
find ample opportunities for improving their condition by emigrating
to this country, and the peculiar educational advantages to be derived
by the working classes in it cannot be overrated. Every man, woman,
and child, has the means at his door of acquiring, gratis, an excellent
course of instruction. . . . .

To no quarter of the globe can a man turn with so reasonable a
chance of finding work as to the United States of America; neverthe-

less, let no man unadvisedly undertake so grave a step as expatriation, or forego the enjoyment, if in possession of it, of steady employment in the Old World for any prospective advantages to be derived in the New. . . . .

The unusual activity existing in most of the manufacturing establishments of the country is greatly enhanced by the operation of the highly protective United States' Tariff, which has had the effect of artificially stimulating the fabrication of a variety of articles on which the American market is more or less dependent for its supply, and which are sold at exorbitant prices as compared with those which the similar class of goods would cost if they could be imported at reasonable duties into the country. The demand for skilled workmen is consequently great, and falls far short of the supply. In view, however, of the easy means of communication between Europe and the United States, foreign skilled workmen who may contemplate emigrating would do well to assure themselves previously as to the state of the particular trade in which they may desire to seek employment. . . . .

### OPENINGS FOR LABOUR

The American labour market undoubtedly presents abundant openings for the introduction of labour from abroad. Nevertheless, a prudent selection of time and location is indispensable. Thus, whilst artizans might confidently rely on obtaining constant work in the City of Philadelphia, they would find a glutted market in the City of Chicago, where, it is stated, there are today 10,000 persons out of employment.

The demand for, and supply of, mechanics and labourers in the State of Massachusetts is represented as being, at present, well balanced. It is exceedingly difficult, however, to obtain work there in the first instance.

Mr. Edwards, Her Majesty's Vice-Consul at New York, supplies the following information with regard to the condition of the labour market in the State of New York:

In a new country like the United States, with its vast uncultivated tracts of fertile land, and its immense and undeveloped mineral wealth, the demand for labour of all kinds must necessarily be very great. At no time has the supply exceeded the demand, and perhaps at no time has that demand been greater than at present. The demand for artizans of a certain class, such, for instance, as stone-cutters, is very great, and cases have occurred recently in which a large number of them belonging to this trade might have found employment at wages ranging from 15£ to 20£ a month, and when, even at these rates, but a very small portion of the requisite labour could be obtained. . . . .

Women household servants are always largely in demand, but in this, as in most cases, preference is given to all other nationalities before the Irish, and most of the orders for labour received in New York from other parts of the State, as well as from distant States, contain a provision that labourers of any other nationality will be preferred to those of Ireland.

The field for female domestic labour in the United States is unbounded, and the introduction of an orderly and respectful class of household servants would be a boon to the country at large. Except in those houses where negroes are employed, nearly every household is dependent, at present, for servants on the Irish, who emigrate to this country, and that the nature of their service is, with rare exceptions (to say the least of it), highly unsatisfactory, will be concurred in by any person who has resided in the United States.

It is a curious fact, in connection with the emigration of Irish, that although the majority come from agricultural districts of Ireland they settle down, as a rule, in the cities and towns of the United States. The contrary is the case in South America, where the majority of Irish are met with in the rural districts, particularly of the Argentine Republic. The cause, in the case of the United States, may be traced to the Roman Catholic clergy, who principally reside in the cities of the Union, and whose influence over the Irish population is very great.

Mr. Edwards reports:

The amount of unskilled labour supplied to railroad contractors and the like, has not exceeded more than 12 per cent of the demand of the country. Here, again, the very strongest prejudice exists against the Irishman, and, were it possible, contractors, as a rule, would not give them employment; but as labourers of no other nationality can be induced to work with them, and as the supply of this kind of labour is principally derived from that nation, contractors are constrained to engage them.

The supply, however, of agriculturists has, perhaps, been that in which the greatest continued deficiency has been met with, and this has been experienced in an extraordinary degree since the beginning of the present year. The class of agriculturists which is preferred by proprietors, whether as permanent settlers, or as permanent farm hands, is those having wives and families.

It is the opinion of well-informed persons that the Southern States of the Union present today the most promising field for emigrants and labourers. One of the effects of emancipation has been to impair, to a great extent, the value of negro labour, and to raise, in a corresponding degree, that of white men.

### 43. "The Rationale of Emigration"[1]

The emigration question, however, is not one which, in the present state of the labor market and trade, can be definitely and for all time settled; indeed, it is one which, with every new steamboat line between here and Europe, and every new railroad line between here and the West, will become more difficult of final settlement. In modern economy, there is nothing more noticeable than the rapid creation and depression of trade in particular spots, and the ease and rapidity with which a trade which finds itself depressed in one place reappears in another shortly afterwards in a prosperous condition and with the necessary attendant labor. Sometimes it is a war which is the cause of the phenomenon, as when the shipbuilding industry was driven out of this country during the Rebellion; sometimes it is a tariff; in another case, it might be the condition of the currency which caused a change. New England has changed within the last generation from an agricultural to a manufacturing country; already since the war manufactures are springing up in the South; shipbuilding is reviving in Maine. Every one of these changes as it occurs has an influence of some kind, now depressing, now elevating, on the labor market, and the effect has been not to render the emigration question simpler, but much harder than it was before. So long as a trade once established was likely to remain in a country or city a hundred years, the emigrant could very easily make long calculations. But now, if he emigrates on account of a depression in the particular trade which he follows, then years hence, perhaps, that very trade may be flourishing in the very place he left it depressed.

On the other hand, it is far more important for all but the most unskilled labor to remain steadily at the same occupation. Formerly, in this country, the theory and the practice both were that the European who came over here came ready to turn his hand to anything—saw wood, dig, be carpenter, blacksmith, mason, lawyer, or member of Congress, as opportunity might occur. But the increasingly minute subdivisions of employment are making it every year more and more dangerous for the emigrants to attempt this old-fashioned rôle. Therefore, the question is not so much, Is there not plenty of land in the

[1] Extract from an editorial by E. L. Godkin in the *Nation*, XIX (New York, August 20, 1874), 117–18.

United States, and a welcome for all? as it is, Can a particular individual find in the United States the particular work for which he is trained? And where, and when? . . . .

Again, the rise to power and influence of the unions makes the question more difficult. The trades-union is, as every one knows, a voluntary organization of a democratic character, which has a general jurisdiction over the particular labor-market related to a particular trade. It has a general fund, levies assessments, supports men during strikes, and exercises a general supervision over them. In the last resort, as in the case in hand, it advises and very likely furnishes the means of emigration. The result of all this is that the laborer learns more and more to rely on this organization, to be idle when it is idle, and to work when it works. Indeed, he subjects himself to great inconvenience, if not suffering, by remaining outside the union. Therefore, it is obvious that the question of emigration will now be considered with reference not so much to the happiness of the individual laborer as to the prosperity of the union to which he belongs; and in many cases when, if left to himself, he might very likely choose to emigrate, as he is not left to himself, he does not choose at all. In the agricultural laborers' strikes, the men seem in process of being driven out of the country against their will, though by accepting their employers' terms last year they might have stayed, because their enforced idleness has exhausted the funds of the union.

We do not by any means intend to say that the emigration question is not one which deserves study. It needs more than it has ever received. What we desire to point out is that the discussions usually carried on on this subject are illogical and futile, because based on insufficient or inapplicable evidence; that the question will not be settled by a comparison of certificates of national character given or refused to individual emigrants; nor will it be settled once for all at any time. The sudden changes in trade and commercial centres, the growing facility of locomotion, the growth and importance of the unions, all make the question much more complicated than formerly. We shall have no solution of the vague question, "Is America, or New Zealand, or Canada a good country for the emigrant?" But what the laborer might fairly expect, and what he ought to have, is information of a detailed and precise kind as to the condition of the market in particular trades and at particular times and places. Last winter, when Father Walsh was taking so gloomy a view of the future of the country, and when no sane man would have advised the emigration of a laborer in any trade to this city, negotiations were going on, and very seasonably so far as one party at least was concerned, between our Government and the Russian sect known as the Mennonites—a simple agricultural people who merely needed a quantity of unoccupied land—for the cession of a large tract in the West. The laborer who did not emigrate to New York, and the Mennonites who are now on their way, both understood the logic of emigration thoroughly. A great deal of stress is now laid by the newspapers on the fact that there is an apparent tide of re-emigration to Europe from the United States, and this is supposed to point to a cessation of emigration from the other side. But apart from the difficulty of obtaining any reliable statistics, it should be taken into consideration that the rush to this country must be expected to fall off after a commercial panic. At the same time that we hear of this re-emigration, we hear of the emigration from England of two large bodies of men, one from the agricultural, the other from the mining, districts.

### 44. Effect of the Industrial Development of Germany on Emigration[1]

The great tide of emigration ebbs and flows in a clearly defined movement consequent upon the economic situation in the original country, as compared with the prospects of success in the country to which emigration tends. It is the difference between economic well-being in Europe and that in the United States, being so much to the advantage of the latter, that has turned the stream of population hither, and not to younger communities where the conditions of success are now less favorable, though becoming more and more advantageous to the emigrant. . . . .

There is one phase of the question that may be dwelt upon . . . . the migration of skilled labor. The mobility of labor, whether skilled or unskilled, is a comparatively recent economic phenomenon, and has done much to modify the conditions of production, still more of competition whether local or national. The extended employment of machinery, which demands a lower or less intelligent grade of labor than was

---

[1] Extract from report by Worthington C. Ford (Bureau of Statistics, Department of State) on emigration and immigration covering a period of thirteen years, 1873–86, but transmitted February 9, 1887. The report is made up chiefly of replies from consular officers to questions regarding the extent and character of emigration from their consular districts, but the extract given is taken from Mr. Ford's report based on the consular replies (United States Forty-ninth Congress, second session, *H. of R. Ex. Doc. No. 157*, pp. 2–3, 31–32, 35–38.

needed when the processes required skill and judgment of the worker, has still more tended to equalize, and at the same time to intensify, the conditions of competition. By displacing labor, these forces tend to encourage and even force emigration. The demand for labor being temporarily lessened, a double result follows—labor readily passes from place to place and from country to country, and competes more sharply with itself.

The movement of population from European countries, and in this connection it may be stated that Europe alone supplies any real basis for study and comparison, has assumed vast proportions, more than half a million of souls annually leaving their own countries to seek homes in another. In 1884, a year that was not marked by an exceptional migration, the twelve leading nations of Europe gave 567,588 emigrants, the United Kingdom and Germany supplying nearly 70 per cent of the total. . . . .

Nearly two-thirds of this movement were directed towards the United States, and since 1874 nearly 5,000,000 of such immigrants have been received, constituting a total equal to about one-eleventh of the present population of the country. . . . .

This vast movement of population cannot be of uniform quality, for the advantages of migration and the opportunities are quite as accessible to the highest forms of skilled labor or to men of property, as to the masses of unskilled labor and the idlers who congregate in the great cities. The immigrants received from one nation may be far more desirable than those from another. . . . . There has of late been shown no little restiveness among workingmen, caused by the increasing difficulty of obtaining what they consider to be adequate wages, always tending downwards, it is claimed, by reason of the flood of "cheap labor" coming from Europe. It is no part of my intention to pass upon the justice of this complaint, or to show how the domestic laborer, himself usually of foreign origin, may be protected from foreign competition. . . . .

[Detailed tables of the occupational distribution of immigrants taken separately for each country] show the remarkable predominance of the United Kingdom and Germany in supplying the United States with skilled labor, and also the fact that the Germans represent those industries that depend upon hand labor or the requirements of everyday life, while the English supply the mechanical element. While Germany sends blacksmiths, butchers, carpenters, coopers, saddlers, shoemakers, and tailors, the United Kingdom supplies miners, engineers, iron and steel workers, mechanics and artisans, weavers and spinners. This distinction is clearly marked, and is certainly important.

Since 1879 a new factor has been introduced that may affect the emigration of skilled labor from the Continent of Europe to the United States, and nowhere is the influence to be stronger than in Germany. I refer to the active interference of the state with a view (1) to render the demand for labor more active by giving it a wider range of employment, by raising its standard of living by means of a more careful regard for its comfort, of a provision for sickness, accident, or old age; or (2) by so controlling or directing the stream of emigration that it may inure to the benefit of the mother country and not of other and foreign countries.

In Germany, in 1878, a system of inspection of mines, factories, etc., in the interest of the laborer was introduced, the duty of the inspectors, who are Government officials, being to see that shops, mills, factories, and mines be properly ventilated, that the machinery be placed so as not needlessly to endanger the safety of the employé, to guard against the employment of children in dangerous or overtaxing labor, and to protect generally the worker against oppression. . . . .

The thrift of the German laborer is proverbial, and the efforts of Government and of individuals have been of late chiefly directed to fostering this feature of his character. Banks, public and private, labor legislation, such as factory inspection, insurance of workingmen, and the like, have been the main instruments of raising the workingman as far as is possible outside of direct gifts or charitable offerings out of a state of dependence upon his daily labor for his daily bread. This has reacted upon his condition, and has given him that slight encouragement to remain at home, the lack of which formerly directed his attention to new fields of labor—as in America. The margin between want and sufficiency has been widened by ever so little, but no one is in a better position to take advantage of that little than is the German.

The consciousness that the Government is taking active interest in protecting the persons and rights of the laborer may without doubt be counted an important factor in leading the German to remain at home, and to hinder his seeking in other lands that greater prosperity which he could undoubtedly find. The recent report of the German factory inspectors gives a picture of the life of a factory operative that is far from favorable. The inspectors would have no interest in exaggerating the unfavorable aspects of a laborer's situation, and would be more apt to err on the other side. Yet the detailed statements give ample evidence of the urgent necessity for emigration as well as of the inability of the workingman to migrate without state or private assistance.

Of the German population, about 35.5 per cent is engaged in manufacturing industries, counting also the families of the earning persons. The effects of the rise of manufactures in Germany have been exerted chiefly on only about one-third of the total population. There remain more than 19,000,000, or 42.5 per cent, of the total population engaged in agriculture not immediately subject to these influences. The import duties upon grain have not resulted in higher prices to the farmer, and his situation is little better than it was in 1879, though a succession of fair harvests have in a measure repaired the losses incurred in the succession of bad years that followed 1873. The German farmer still constitutes the larger part of the emigration from Germany, and supplies the largest contingent of that class in the immigrants into this country.

The position of Germany is peculiar, in that it has a rapidly increasing population, that is continually crowding upon the limited areas, as yet unoccupied or uncultivated, and upon the opportunities for profitable employment. There is no outlet, such as the vast plains of Russia offer, to the increasing population of that country for colonizing from within—if I may use the term—a process that has prevailed in the United States. Prussia was long the "colony" of the other parts of Germany, the tide of migration flowing from the rural districts into towns, from towns into cities, and from the cities to the capital, wherever the highest returns were offered to labor. The advantages to be gained by a change of this sort are much reduced, the movement itself tending to equalize conditions. Yet the German population must increase and does increase. . . . .

The action of the state may also be exerted in directing the stream of emigration into certain channels where the supposed advantages will be greater to the directing state. The colonizing policy of Germany had for its object the founding of colonies, where room may be found for the surplus population, where the inhabitants will still be subject to the mother country, and where new markets will be found for German manufactures.[1]

[1] On this point Consul-General Raine wrote in 1885:

"The necessity for extending the dominion of Germany, in view of such steady excess of births over deaths, forced itself upon the statesmen of the Empire, and even if we place the number of emigrants on the average at 80,000, according to German statistics, or more (about 100,000 according to ours) per annum; such emi-

The foundation of colonies and the encouragement offered to emigrants are too recent measures to be as yet judged. The flow of emigration shows little change. . . . .

Without attempting to enter into a discussion as to what the real effects of Germany's protective policy has been, there is no doubt that the opportunities for the employment of labor has been greatly increased since 1879. For example, in 1879, 170,509 men were employed in mining black coal; in 1883 the number had increased to 207,577, though 503 works were in operation in 1879 as compared with 489 in 1883. So again 721 brown coal mines in 1879 engaged 24,150 miners; in 1883, 665 mines employed 26,824 men; in 1879, 19 copper mines contained 9,118 miners, and in 1883, 36 mines contained 14,326 miners. In 1879, 2,487 mineral works in operation gave employment to 275,711 miners, and in 1883, 2,567 works contained 334,137 miners, the increase in the number of works being about 3 per cent and in the men employed more than 21 per cent. So again in the furnaces and foundries the number of works increased from 227 to 270, or about 19 per cent, and the hands employed from 32,242 to 42,724, or about 33 per cent. The returns for other great industries, such as the textile and sugar industries, are not at hand, and while the metal industries, and more especially the iron and steel industries, have been greatly, almost abnormally stimulated, there can be little doubt that other industries would show a like movement, though on a more moderate scale.

It does not follow, however, that the absolute welfare of the laborer has been improved through an artificial creation of a greater demand for his skill. The continued fall of prices consequent upon an enormously increased production is a general feature of the present period, and Germany offers no exception to the rule. . . . .

This movement of prices has resulted in enforced economy, and it may be questioned whether the full effects of the increased demand for labor have not been felt, and not only must there ensue a more

---

gration does not balance by far the increase of births, 540,000 per annum; hardly 16 per cent of the increase are absorbed by emigration. It is but necessary to add that under such circumstances the colonial policy, so unexpectedly inaugurated, met with universal approval throughout Germany. A Berlin paper says:

" 'We Germans have long been colonizers on a large scale; but, unlike the English, French, Dutch, and Portuguese, we have always colonized lands belonging to other Governments, and not our own.' "

"Considering the annual growth of the nation, the question was then asked: 'Could not the Government acquire for them territories where they would continue to be under German jurisdiction and enjoy the fatherland's protection?' "

moderate extension of industry, but also a reduction of the number of workingmen, either by the shutting down of unprofitable works or by the substitution of machine for hand labor. This means that the increase in the number of laborers is no longer commensurate with the extension of industry; that the period of expansion is ending, and a period of contraction will in all probability follow. . . . .

So that while the economic policy of the Empire has probably tended to discourage the emigration of skilled labor by creating employment for it at home, such an artificial structure cannot remain intact. The sugar industry is an example of extreme inflation, and the iron industry is not far behind it. In default of foreign markets the home markets must be glutted, mills and works run on short time or shut down, and labor without employment. The strenuous endeavors of German manufacturers to cultivate a foreign trade, and in this they have had all possible favors from the Government, have been attended with a noteworthy success, and especially in Central and South America. But such new markets are gained at great cost and are not without their limits. It follows, therefore, that the task of finding an outlet for an over-stimulated production must be more and more difficult, and the time will come when the skilled labor of Germany, crowded out at home, must seek employment elsewhere, which means in United States.

### 45. The Effects of Emigration in Europe and America[1]

The modern period of colonization may be said to date from the treaties of 1815, and its successive stages are marked by important political events and by the development of industrial enterprise which have had so powerful an effect in modifying the commercial currents of the world. . . . .

The emigration of the present day is a far more important fact than the colonization of the past three centuries, and statistics show us how largely it has been influenced by the increased facility in means of communication. As an example of this let us take the case of the United Kingdom, where from the various ports of the Kingdom a constant stream of emigration—English, Scotch, and Irish—flows toward remote quarters of the globe. . . . .

For many years the United Kingdom has not only been a country from which immense supplies both of men and merchandise have been

[1] Extract from Émile Levasseur, "De l'émigration au XIXᵉ siècle," *L'Economiste français*, September 27 and October 4, 1884, translated in U.S. Bureau of Foreign Commerce, *Emigration and Immigration* (Washington, 1887), pp. 720–34.

drawn to provide for the wants of non-European countries, but it may be considered as the greatest emigration dépôt of the world. It has a dense population, which is rapidly increasing, and is therefore well able to withstand the drain of a considerable portion of her virile population; as regards her trade, shipping, and colonial possessions, her commercial relations are more extended than those of any other country.

Her dominions extend over an area of 13,000,000 square miles, and her sovereignty is exercised over 300,000,000 subjects; thus it must at once be apparent that England is well able to spare a considerable number of her working population, and her emigrants carry with them to their new homes their language, national customs, and spirit of social organization, thus benefiting to a very considerable extent the country in which they have decided to establish themselves. . . . .

Germany also, as well as England, has a population both numerous and prolific, though the stream of emigration flowed at first more slowly from its shores than was found to be the case in England, one reason for this phenomenon being that she had not the same facilities of communication with the New World. But with the development of steam navigation and the extension of the railway system this volume of emigration rapidly assumed gigantic dimensions, until at the present day we find the Germans overrunning the New World as of old the hordes of barbarians overwhelmed the Roman Empire.

The movement extends to the north and the east of Europe. Scandinavians, and particularly the Norwegians, familiar with the sea as the English, and as poor as the peasants in certain districts of Germany, Poles, Hungarians, and even Russians, whose emigration has been greatly augmented by the emancipation of the serfs, generally set out for America, which they look upon as an El Dorado. In Austria and Hungary the returns of emigration show a considerable increase during the last twenty years, and Holland, who sends her merchants and government officials to the East Indies, and Belgium, who, possessing no colonies of her own, yet is enabled to carry on through the port of Antwerp a very extensive maritime trade, also contribute their quota to swell the volume of European emigration, although the part taken by these two countries is not of any great importance, and as regards the latter the immigration into the country amply compensates for the migration from it.

France, which is a densely populated country, ought to count for far more than she does in this movement of European emigration; but the French as a race are not infected with the eagerness of change; in fact, there appears to be a rooted antipathy on their part to expatriation. On the question of emigration a Frenchman is apt to observe that he finds no inducement held out to him to leave his native country, as the conditions of life are most favorable to him there, and he is not disposed to leave his home and seek in foreign lands what is so easy to obtain in his own country. He does not object to an occasional migration from town to country, but he is altogether averse to settling in lands where the manners and customs are generally so entirely different to those to which he has always been accustomed, and where the language spoken is totally unknown to him. France may be considered as the country rather of immigration than of emigration, for two reasons, the first being that the birth-rate is exceedingly low, and the second that wealth is relatively abundant. . . . .

Those countries to which immigration has been mainly directed have been direct gainers by the movement of European immigration, for through it their lands, which were lying waste, and either sparsely populated or inhabited chiefly by savages who lived on the produce of the fisheries or the chase, have been brought under cultivation; they have supported a more numerous population, their mining industries have been developed, their rivers and streams rendered navigable, and railways constructed, thereby greatly facilitating commercial intercourse.

As a remarkable instance of the complete transformation which has been effected by immigration, we cannot do better than take the case of the United States. From 1820 to 1882 this country has benefited by immigration alone to the extent of 11,907,000 persons. . . . .

And the fact must not be overlooked that the great majority of immigrants into this country are composed of persons of a productive or marriageable age, and therefore the value of this immigration is not to be measured so much by its numbers generally as by the number of strong and healthy adults who are a direct addition to the producing and wealth-increasing elements of the country. . . . .

It may approximately be estimated that the number of representatives of European races, pure or mixed, at the present day living out of Europe exceeds 85,000,000. For the most part either they or their fathers were originally attracted by the prospect of gaining higher wages than they were receiving in their own country, or of receiving a free grant of land that they might cultivate and call their own; in a word, it may be said that they have yielded to the inducement held out of ameliorating their position, and of obtaining under more favorable conditions the means of subsistence. Events have shown that taking this emigration *en masse*, their anticipations have been more than realized, and the countries to which emigration has been mainly directed have vastly increased in wealth, this augmentation being indirectly due to the labor of the inhabitants of the country, and remaining to benefit them.

On leaving the mother country emigrants have been influenced in their choice of the land in which to establish themselves by affinities of climate, religion, race, and language, as well as by the natural resources of the country. . . . .

We are already acquainted with the general causes determining emigration, one of the principal being the difficulty of procuring the means of subsistence' in the mother country; but though this is undoubtedly a very important factor in determining the volume of emigration, it had not so powerful an effect in past years, and we are therefore forced to the conclusion that there are other and special influences which have been at work in inducing so enormous an exodus.

The most powerful of these influences is unquestionably liberty.

It is owing to liberty, both political and commercial, which has superseded the prohibitive régime of past ages, that the population of the United States rose from 3,936,000 in 1790, to 50,155,000 in 1880; that the population of Canada has been quadrupled, and that the inhabitants of the old Spanish colonies have increased from fourteen to about twenty-five millions.

The second in importance is the increased facility of communication, the extension of steam navigation, and the railway system having brought distant continents in closer proximity; railways have penetrated into the interior of countries previously but little known and almost unexplored, and at the present day the iron road often precedes the settler; transportation may be effected both rapidly and economically, and regions which had been to a great extent inaccessible, and of little or no value in the past, are now brought within the reach of all, and have become a source of wealth to the present generation.

A third cause which has also led to an increase of emigration is the existence of human currents, which are the natural sequence of the two first causes we have enumerated.

Emigration may be said to have induced emigration. The positions attained and the fortunes made by the first settlers fired the imagination of those who remained in the mother country, and operated powerfully in inducing many to leave it; and the relations maintained between the colonists and their friends at home also materially contributed to this end. . . . .

In Europe, however, this stream of emigration, by reason of the gigantic proportions it has sometimes assumed, has been looked upon very unfavorably by a certain class of politicians, and the exodus has frequently engaged the serious attention of the various governments for the following reasons: That it subjects the mother country to the pecuniary loss of supplying and educating their youth until the productive stage of life, when they take their departure with all these advantages for their new homes, and that the money taken away by these emigrants must be looked upon as the withdrawal of so much of the country's capital; that the youth and backbone of the country are being extensively withdrawn from the military services, and the numerical strength of their armies is by so much diminished, which will be seriously felt in the hour of danger; that the landed interests and manufacturers complain that this constant withdrawal of hands from the labor markets is causing a considerable advance in every description of wages, and the competition they have to encounter from foreign countries becomes every year more severe.

It must be admitted that a country is quite within her right to look very carefully into the question of the burdens imposed upon her, and is justified in expecting that each of her sons should bear his share in supporting them; and when a country is in a position to colonize her own foreign possessions it is much more to her advantage to do so than to supply other nations with her virile population. Experience, however, has shown in Russia and Germany that it is a difficult task to stem the current of emigration; and this brings us to the question as to whether it is wise or the reverse to restrict emigration, and on this point we would observe that a country which checks emigration attacks the liberty of the subject, as it cannot be justifiable to prevent those who are suffering from misery and want in their country leaving it for countries where the prospect of a brighter future is held out to them.

To be logical, a government which interposes to prohibit emigration should at least provide for the wants of those whom it retains at home, and it would seem that the only case in which a government is justified in prohibiting it is when the intending emigrant has not fulfilled his obligations of military service, and it is even then an open question whether the advantage which a country gains by emigration would not sufficiently compensate it for the loss to its military services.

Emigration, taken from an economical and a political point of view, is manifestly an advantage to the new country, whose wealth is greatly increased by the introduction of fresh labor and capital to develop its resources. It is an advantage to the country which the emigrant leaves, as it is a decided gainer if the stream of emigration is directed to its own colonies, and it is an advantage to the emigrants themselves, as they obtain for themselves and their families the necessaries of life with increased facilities and in greater abundance. They leave the mother country with the intention of improving their condition, and though some may fail, yet many succeed. There is no infallible system by which success can be absolutely guaranteed to all the members of the human race; yet that emigration is one of the best there can be no question, as is evidenced by the rapid development of wealth in those countries in which immigration is welcomed, and of which the population is chiefly composed of aliens. In the country of adoption the natural resources, through want of sufficient labor and capital, had hitherto remained undeveloped, and to the task of developing these resources the immigrant brought his capital and his skilled labor, and by the aid of these evolved the latent wealth, manifestly to the advantage of the country and himself. The interests, therefore, of the country of adoption and the immigrant are to a great extent identical, and this will account for the wonderful change that has been effected in America, Australia, and parts of Africa; and it is owing exclusively to its enormous alien population that the United States is at the present day in a position to take rank with the great European powers.

It is true that the mother country suffers a loss in the withdrawal of so many of her virile population that she has reared and educated to a producing age, but if the country to which they depart happens to be one of her own colonial possessions, she directly benefits by the deportation, and if the country for which they leave belongs to another power, it is benefited indirectly, for fresh colonization must of itself be productive of great good, inasmuch as its immediate effect is to give an impetus to her trade, owing to the establishment of new commercial centers and by reason of the introduction of its language, manners, and customs.

As an illustration of this we may refer to the case of Germany, which, although it has no colonial possessions of its own, yet exercises an immense moral influence over the United States; and England, again, whose merchants and traders are established in every quarter of the habitable globe, is in a better position than other powers to understand the trade demands of her numerous customers and to satisfy them.

We are clearly justified, then, in maintaining that emigration is rather beneficial than the reverse to the countries from which it is drawn, provided that the emigrants themselves remain united in the country of their adoption, and that they maintain the national traditions.

For the time being they certainly deprive the mother country of a portion of her productive forces, but the void is soon filled by the natural increase of her population, and there is a greater prospect of the interests of the mother country being materially advanced by reason of the introduction into a new country of its language, manners, and customs.

That emigration, which is one of the most national and historical facts, must not be restrained, admits of no argument. Through it the European race, whose commerce before the American war was confined to the border seas and to the Mediterranean, have now established themselves and their industries throughout the world, and it is through emigration that man has taken, and is taking every day, possession of the land, his natural domain. Through it the national wealth of the world is being developed, and distances are diminished not only by the facilities of communication, but by the community of ideas, and through the interests of a race which has done much to introduce civilization into the two temperate zones.

Regarded from a political point of view the question of emigration, so far as it affects the balance of power, is a most important one, and we must not lose sight of the fact that the world's equilibrium has been somewhat disturbed since the United States has become one of the great nations and a new center of civilization has been created in Australasia. It is safe to assume that the equilibrium will be still further disturbed, but it must at all times be productive of good results to the European race, which has driven back or exterminated the inferior races in the countries it has colonized, and has enrolled in its service negroes, Hindoos, and Chinese to aid in developing the resources of these countries.

To some extent there must always be a rivalry between European and American nations, and the claim to supremacy will be disputed by them. Those countries which are anxious not only to retain their rank among the great powers, but to preserve their trade and maintain and extend their moral and political influence, must take their part in this constant stream of the civilized race, and do so by the aid of colonization and emigration. Colonization is adapted to the possessions of the mother country conquered or annexed; but emigration may be extended to any country in the world, and it is well within the range of probability that in course of time the current of emigration will augment in proportion to the increased facilities of communication, and for many years to come there will be wanting neither men in Europe to emigrate nor land and natural wealth to require their labor in cultivating and developing.

As a free and unfettered commercial intercourse between two countries is advantageous to both, for by the exchange of their commodities the producer and the consumer are both benefited, so also must the unrestricted circulation of the human race be advantageous to all countries concerned.

Each country, therefore, being interested in this movement, it behooves the one to encourage, or at least to refrain from interposing obstacles or raising difficulties to impede the tide of emigration, and the other to place every facility in the way of the intending settler. In briefly summing up the advantages or drawbacks of this movement, it may be said that the emigration question, which is interesting alike to the philosopher and the statesmen, should not be confined to the narrow-minded calculations of the advantages it simply brings to the emigrant, but must be viewed in the more comprehensive and enlightened scope of the enormous benefits it confers upon the human race at large.

### 46.  Immigration and American Prosperity[1]

The year 1881 has witnessed the largest emigration to the United States ever known. The number of immigrants was, in the fiscal years ending June 30, 1879, 177,826; June 30, 1880, 457,257; June 30, 1881, 669,354.

It is evident that this influx of the laboring element must strengthen the industrial interests of this country, and that the money brought into the United States by immigrants must be, in the aggregate, a very large sum. . . . .

[1] Extract taken by permission from the *North American Review*, 134 (1882), 346–51, 361–67: "Why They Come," by Edward Self.

Immigration generally follows our periods of business prosperity, as will be seen by the following summary:

The alien arrivals were, in 1836, 76,242; in 1837, 79,340. The financial troubles of the latter year reduced immigration in 1838 to 38,914; renewed confidence is shown in 1839 by the arrival of 68,069; in 1840 the number reached 84,066.

The population of the United States in 1840 was 17,069,453; the number of immigrants that year was, therefore, almost one-half of one per cent of the population. In 1845 these arrivals increased to 114,371. The Irish famine in 1846–47, and the general uneasiness in Europe upon the eve of the revolutionary period of 1847–48, sufficiently account for the large accessions of the time, viz., in 1847, 234,968; 1848, 226,527; 1849, 297,024; 1850, 310,004.

In 1850, the population was 23,191,876, so that the alien arrivals that year equaled one and three-tenths per cent of the whole people. In 1851, the arrivals had increased to 379,466, declining in 1853 to 368,645. In October, 1853, Turkey, followed in March, 1854, by England and France, declared war against Russia. Emigration to the United States in that year attained the remarkably high total of 427,833, doubtless attributable to apprehensions of a general European convulsion.

The rapid diminution which followed may be accounted for by the improved condition of Ireland, consequent upon the enormous emigration from 1846 to 1854, the rush to the Australian gold fields, and the termination of the Russian war in 1856. The arrivals in 1855 were 200,877; in 1856, 200,036. In 1857, the immigrants numbered 246,945. In August, the Ohio Life and Trust Company failed; in October, the New York banks suspended specie payments, and the financial panic spread throughout this country and Europe; terrible losses of life and property by earthquakes, shipwrecks, and the Sepoy rebellion added to the commercial disasters. Emigration was checked at once, for men would rather bear the ills they have, than fly to others that they know not of. Accordingly, in 1858 the new-comers numbered 119,501; in 1859, 118,616; in 1860, 150,237.

The census returns of this year show that the population had increased to 31,443,321; the immigration of that year being nearly half of one per cent.

The outbreak of the War of the Rebellion, in the spring of 1861, naturally retarded immigration, which, in 1861, fell to 89,724; and in 1862 to 89,007. The necessities of the war, and the demand for labor, soon attracted increasing numbers from abroad; amounting in 1863 to 174,524; in 1864, 193,195; 1865, 247,453; and in 1866 to 318,491. The disbandment of the armies and their rapid absorption in the ranks of peaceful industry, was a discouragement to immigration; a falling-off in its volume is shown in 1867 by the arrival of only 293,601; followed in 1868 by the smaller number of 289,145. This diminution was only temporary, for the period of inflated values and speculation attracted foreigners in immense numbers. In 1869, the arrivals increased to 385,287; in 1870, they numbered 356,303.

At this time the population was 38,558,371. The immigration of 1870 was, consequently, a little less than one per cent.

The arrivals in 1871 numbered 346,938; in 1872, 437,750; in 1873, 422,545. The great reverses of 1873 were felt in Europe almost as much as in the United States. The effect is apparent in the returns of the succeeding years. In 1874, the immigrants numbered 260,814; in 1875, 191,231; in 1876, 157,440; in 1877, 130,503.

The general belief that "hard pan" had been reached in 1877, and the signs of returning prosperity, led to such a rapid increase as the country had never before seen. In 1878 the arrivals were 153,207; in 1879, 250,565; in 1880, 593,713.

In the census year 1880, the population numbered 50,155,783. The immigrants of that year exceeded 1 18/100 per cent of that number. . . . . The number of immigrants arrived in the year 1881 is 720,045.

The number received at Castle Garden was 441,043. These gave their destination as follows:

| | |
|---|---:|
| New York | 152,421 |
| New England | 22,146 |
| Pennsylvania and New Jersey | 57,925 |
| Southern states, including Missouri and District of Columbia | 25,385 |
| Northwestern states | 170,585 |
| Western states and territories, including Pacific slope | 10,603 |
| Other countries | 1,978 |
| | 441,043 |

It is not to be supposed that 152,000 immigrants intended to remain in the State of New York longer than necessary to determine their future course. But unquestionably many of the baser sort do remain in the great cities of this State, and swell the ranks of the vicious classes.

The chief gain from immigration is in the wheat-growing regions, which received more than one-third of the immigrants landed in New York.

Immigration to the South and the Southwest has fairly commenced, and the day would seem to be not very distant when the genial climate, abundant forests, diversity of crops, and comparatively cheap lands of that section will attract many more settlers than the bleak treeless regions of the Northwest. The old slave States possess natural advantages that commend them to settlers from Southern and Middle Europe. Some of them have already initiated measures to attract aliens, and the percentage of immigrants going southward is larger than ever before. But these States have not put forth such systematic efforts in this direction as are exhibited by the railroad lines having land grants to sell in the West.

The railway transportation for such an army is a considerable item. Westward-bound emigrant trains constitute a feature well known to travelers. The agent of the Erie line estimates the value of all emigrant inland tickets, sold in New York in 1881, at five million dollars certainly, and perhaps more.

When the dissatisfied laboring people of Europe decide to emigrate, the United States is naturally the first choice of the immense majority, by reason of its cheap lands, cheap ocean-passage, wide territory, and political and religious equality.

The emigration from Great Britain and Ireland to the United States greatly exceeds that to the British colonies, prosperous as they undoubtedly are.

During the existence of slavery, the cash value of an ordinary "field hand," unintelligent and descended from a barbarous ancestry, was five hundred dollars and upward. Each immigrant may safely be valued at double this amount, if we consider the commercial value of hereditary intelligence and the large proportion of skilled and professional men who are comprised in the immigration of each year. Assuming that each immigrant has, in his brain and muscle, a power equal to a capital of $1,000, we gained, in the year 1881 alone, something like $720,000,000, and a cash capital (at $85 per head) of over $61,000,000.

Surely the causes which lead to, or divert from, our shores such a perennial and prolific source of population and wealth are of interest to us and worth our attention. . . . .

An examination of the ages of the immigrants in the fiscal years [1879–1881] reveals the following facts:

Twenty per cent are under fifteen years of age, the males slightly preponderating. This youthful portion easily assimilates.

Seventy per cent are in the reproductive period of life, between fifteen and forty years of age, forty-six per cent being males, and twenty-four, females.

Ten per cent, only, exceed forty years; in the ratio of six males to four females. Not more than ten per cent come with habits rigidly formed, or political or social ideas permanently fixed; while probably less than five per cent of the entire accession have passed the period in which population is recruited.

The comparative youthfulness of those who seek asylum here seems to have been overlooked. It explains the rapid increase of our population, and the exceedingly rapid process of their assimilation. Were it in our power to choose the ages best adapted to our needs in respect to labor, growth of population, and social and political life, would a better selection be possible than that already provided by this promiscuous addition?

If the immigrants comprised old and young in the natural proportion, as found in settled communities, the gain to the United States, and corresponding loss to Europe, would be much less. After Ireland's losses by famine and emigration, the birth-rate became one in forty, against one in twenty-eight in England.

Aside from certain unruly elements in a few cities, and the re-enforcement of the Mormons, little or no complaint can be justly made of the multitudes who come.

Immigrants constitute a much larger percentage of the population in the Northwest than in the old States, yet public order and general integrity are no less assured there than on the Atlantic sea-board.

The population in 1880 was 50,155,783, about thirteen per cent (6,679,943) being foreign born. . . . .

The population in 1790 was 3,929,827. If the increase had been confined to the excess of births over deaths, the population in 1880 would not have been 15,000,000. Without immigration, the country would not have had 50,000,000 people for a hundred years to come (if we take the reported increase of 1850 as a criterion). Whence it appears that the population and consequent expansion of the settled area, the development of agriculture, manufactures, mining, and railways, as well as of domestic and foreign trade, have been anticipated more than three-quarters of a century by the quiet influx of Europeans. . . . .

European governments no longer send infirm paupers or criminals here, but local authorities occasionally do. When persons of this character are discovered, they are promptly sent back. . . . .

The conditions and motives which impelled the great influx of 1881 are as powerful now as they were twelve or twenty months ago; indeed the coming influx may be greater, for popular movements grow by accretion and are not quickly restrained by reasoning. This movement has been caused by deficient crops, old uneconomical methods, grinding poverty, overtaxation, military burdens, and social discontent; while, through all and over all, there rises that dreaded shade, American Competition; no longer a shade, but a tangible power, young, vigorous, growing. Has this new factor in the perplexities of Europe been offset by any advantageous changes? Has the price of labor advanced? Have taxes been reduced? Have new markets been opened to European producers, or have they adopted better methods? Have the events of the last few years really established a reign of "peace with honor"?

On the contrary, armies are being strengthened, fortifications improved, navies made more formidable. Von Moltke's famous remark, "Germany for the next fifty years must make constant exertions to consolidate her power and maintain her recent acquisitions," stands, a warning to European governments and people alike.

We infer, then, that the burden of taxation cannot be greatly lessened; that wages cannot be much increased; that the social and political condition of the lower classes, with some few exceptions, cannot be considerably improved; and, therefore, that they will seek abroad what they cannot get at home. . . . .

In ninety years, a feeble people of 3,900,000, occupying the country adjacent to the sea, has been transformed into one of the greatest nations of the world, having a population of 50,000,000, spanning a continent, and possessing untold wealth and boundless resources.

# SECTION III

# EARLY PROBLEMS OF ASSIMILATION

# SECTION III

INTRODUCTORY NOTE

Anxiety regarding the admission of immigrants in numbers too large to be assimilated by the population already here has given rise to public discussions and controversies in various periods of our history not only in the nineteenth century, but in the eighteenth century as well. On the economic side, in spite of occasional doubts immigration was accepted as necessary and desirable; but on the social side there were many reservations. Our ancestors were inevitably concerned about the safety of the social and political institutions which they had established. They were confident that these were the most perfect the world had ever seen, and they were suspicious and intolerant lest a flood of newly arrived immigrants should mar or destroy the character of the work that had been reared with so much labor and devotion.

This anxiety was expressed even during the Colonial period, for those who were immigrants themselves were suspicious of other immigrants who arrived at a slightly later date; and there were grave discussions as to whether the late arrivals could be assimilated or not. This was especially true in Pennsylvania, where so many of the later colonial immigrants were Germans, who spoke a strange language and tended to form isolated communities. Could these immigrants be so "assimilated" as to make a unified population? More than one colonial statesman answered this question in the negative. So great, however, was the need of an increase in population that even Franklin, with all his misgivings about the Germans, felt they should be encouraged to come in (Document 1).

An interesting analysis of the problem of assimilation was made at an early day by Crèvecoeur, in the *Letters of an American Farmer* (Document 2). The immigrants of all nationalities and of all countries soon found their loyalty transferred from the old home to the new. "Where bread is, there is my country" was, in the eighteenth century, as it was destined to be in the nineteenth and twentieth centuries, a phrase explaining the readiness with which citizenship was renounced and reacquired. Crèvecoeur called the Americans of the eighteenth century "a promiscuous breed"—"a mixture of English, Scotch, Irish, French, Dutch, German, and Swedes." Although the American was either a European or a descendant of a European, he had, in coming to America, been quickly influenced by a new mode of life, a new form of government, and a new social system; and he became, in America, a new man, acting upon new principles and forming new opinions.

But although this was true in the large, there were, of course, troublesome incidents that raised doubts and questions. When, in 1789, Benjamin Rush wrote his account of the Pennsylvania Germans, they were living in German "colonies," keeping their old domestic habits, using the German language, and supporting German churches and schools. So little progress did they make in the use of English and so large an element did they form of the population that it was even thought desirable to have some of the laws printed in German as well as in English. But Rush thought the Germans desirable citizens whether they assimilated or not, because they possessed "the republican virtues of industry and economy." Frugal and simple in their manner of living, they were immensely successful as farmers, and contributed greatly to the wealth of the state. "If it were possible," wrote Rush, "to determine the amount of all the property brought into Pennsylvania by the present German inhabitants of the state and their ancestors, and then compare it with the present amount of their property, the contrast would form such a monument of human industry and economy as has seldom been contemplated in any age or country" (Document 3).

There were many Americans, however, who cherished a growing fear of the difficulties of assimilating the new arrivals. Mathew Carey, in 1796, wrote a spirited reply to those who, after the Revolutionary War, began to complain that the subjects of monarchies would never mix with the citizens of a republic (Document 4). This reply, however, tended to emphasize the economic gains from immigration which would be lost if prejudice prevailed.

Later, when Timothy Dwight (Document 5) traveled through the city and state of New York, he found the immigrants from the different nations retaining the characteristics and habits of the countries from which they came. But he was impressed by the almost miraculous growth of the state. It was, he thought, true that mankind had never "seen so large a tract changed so suddenly from a wilderness into a well-inhabited and well-cultivated country as that which extends on the great Western road from the German Flats to the Genesee River." And whatever differences the immigrants from different nations might have, he foresaw a time when they would "be so entirely amalgamated with those from New England as to be undistinguishable."

The tenacity with which the German immigrants continued to use their language and their success in resisting Americanizing or Anglicizing influences is illustrated in the account given in 1829 by Brauns, the German traveler (Document 6), who had only scorn for the Germans who did not remain German. Other German travelers followed Brauns in expressing contempt for the Americanized German (Document 18).

Francis Lieber, however, who was emphatic in thinking it important to teach German to children, was clear that this ought to be only a second language, and that English should be taught at the same time. He was also emphatic in describing as chimerical the schemes for maintaining isolated German settlements.[1] "Living in an isolated state," wrote Lieber, "the current of civilization of the country in which they live does not reach them; and they are equally cut off from that of their mother country: mental stagnation is the consequence" (Document 7).

Difficulties in the way of the absorption or assimilation of immigrants increased with the increase in the number of new arrivals, but such criticisms and questions as were raised were largely confined to a few points, such as (1) the tendency of the new arrivals to settle or "clan" together in national groups, for the large numbers of immigrants arriving made it convenient for them to settle in "colonies," and this in turn made it easy for them to retain their old-country customs, habits, and mode of thinking; (2) the cherishing of old-country loyalties, which was regarded as incompatible with the duties and obligations of naturalized citizens; (3) the disposition of the Irish to vote as a unit; (4) the insistence of the Germans upon the use of their own language in their churches and schools; (5) the fear lest immigrants were coming in numbers too large proportionately to the natives to make assimilation possible. This last point was emphasized by a writer in the *North American Review*, who said, "Wide as the country may be, and urgent as is everywhere the demand for mechanical industry, the access of foreign population may yet be too rapid and indiscriminate for easy and healthful absorption into the community" (Document 8).

The growing antagonism to the Irish immigrant during the decade 1830–40 and the formation of the so-called "Native American Association" in 1837 were due in part to the aggressive self-consciousness and political activities of the large masses of Irish immigrants in the Eastern cities. Foreign nationalistic societies of all kinds were a great irritant. Even so harmless an organization as the Boston Hibernian

[1] Such as the plan for an independent German state, see *Americana Germanica*, Vol. I, No. 2, p. 62.

Lyceum aroused the wrath of the unreasonable "Nativists"[1] (Document 9).

A German traveler, Friedrich von Raumer, thought the Germans in America created fewer difficulties than the Irish. The blending of Irish with Germanic stock was, he thought "certainly very difficult" in America, as it has been in England. However, he noted that part of the American hostility to the Irish was due to "business jealousy and religious intolerance" (Document 10).

There were, on the side of the immigrant, many difficulties in the way of adjustment to the new conditions of American life (Document 11). With all their criticism of the foreigner, few of the native Americans did anything to promote assimilation by bringing the immigrant under American influences.

There were, from time to time, tolerant and sympathetic voices, like that of Edward Everett Hale, raised in behalf of the immigrant (Document 12). Dr. Hale urged "private action and public policy" to promote assimilation and absorption, but, as in other such cases, he failed to make any concrete or definite proposals.

The hostility of the "Know-Nothings" aroused great bitterness among the immigrants and tended to increase their isolation (Document 13). In particular, the orders given by the governors of Massachusetts and Connecticut to disband the foreign militia companies were fiercely resented (Document 14). Archbishop Spalding said, in his spirited reply to Know-Nothing attacks (Document 15), that the existence of the "foreign vote" was due to the political methods of the rival parties and politicians who found it convenient to organize and use the foreign voter for selfish purposes.

The formation of the Irish Emigrant Aid Society (Document 16) during the period of Know-Nothing activities increased the suspicion that the foreigners, particularly the Irish, were more loyal to the country they had left than to the country whose citizenship they had adopted. The court opinion in the Lumsden case (Document 17) is a careful statement of the attitude of thoughtful Americans toward Irish nationalism in the United States. Dismissing the defendants as not guilty of organizing a military movement in behalf of Irish freedom, the court called attention to the objections to the Irish-American secret societies and clubs. "I censure no Irishman," said the court, "for sympathizing with his native land and ardently desiring the restoration of the rights of its people; but with all candor and kindness,

[1] For earlier references to the Native American and Know-Nothing movements, see the preceding section, Note 1, p. 206.

I would suggest that these feelings ought not to be indulged at the hazard of the interests and peace of the country of his adoption. . . . . There can be no such thing as a divided national allegiance. The obligations of citizenship cannot exist in favor of different nationalities at the same time."

There was less criticism of the Germans than of the Irish, in spite of the fact that the Germans spoke a different language. The Irish maintained a closer contact with their old homes (Document 25). The "wrongs of Ireland" formed a bond of allegiance that kept not only the Irish immigrants of the first generation but their children and their children's children interested in Irish affairs and ready to make sacrifices for the great cause of Irish independence (Document 27).

The Germans, on the whole, were less aggressive in their national organizations. They had no traditional "grievance" as a bond of union. They were divided into different groups: Lutherans, Catholics, and "Freethinkers," and these groups were often unfriendly and even hostile to one another (Document 19).

The Know-Nothings directed their attack against the groups of German radicals or Social Democrats who were charged with believing not in the liberty of law but of "unrestrained license." The German dislike of the Puritan Sunday was also a cause of much ill-feeling, and the Know-Nothings made much of the reports that the Germans did not believe in the observance of the Sabbath (Document 21).

In some of the German settlements there was a tendency to mingle very little with the Americans. The most striking example of this isolation was, of course, the case of the Pennsylvania Germans, but there were many other German communities in the newer states in which German life and customs were tenaciously maintained. Olmsted was much interested in the German settlements in Texas. "A large proportion of the emigrants," he wrote, "have remained apart, in German communities. . . . . Others, by their scattered residence in isolated positions, are excluded from any other than individual life. Such as have settled in American neighborhoods or towns, feeling the awkwardness of newcomers, and ignorant of the language, have hitherto almost refrained from taking part in politics." On the great political issue of the day, however, German public opinion was sound and unified. The Germans were everywhere attached to the antislavery party, and were abolitionists even in Texas (Document 20). They voted for Lincoln, and they and their sons joined the armies of the Union (Document 24).

The publication of newspapers in the German language and the making of political speeches in German aroused hostile criticism, but they found a vigorous defender in Carl Schurz (Document 26). The older immigrants, he pointed out, did not learn English well enough to understand articles on political subjects in English newspapers. "The suppression of the German-American press would, therefore, be equivalent to the cultivation of political ignorance among a large and highly estimable class of citizens." Nor was their loyalty to America any less because they were not able to read or speak English. Even the Pennsylvania Dutch, who had clung to a foreign language for more than one generation were, he thought, as patriotic as any of those "whose patriotism is uncontaminated by the knowledge of any other language."

The difficulties in connection with "assimilation" were by no means all on the side of the immigrant, for the new arrivals encountered prejudice and met disappointments everywhere (Document 22). Godkin, writing in 1859, drew a most discouraging picture of the Irish in America. The great numbers of immigrants had made it so easy for them to settle together "in masses in the large towns." "The mass of Celts," wrote Godkin, "is now too large and unwieldy for American temperament to permeate it; and I despair of any change for the better until the supply of the raw material from the Old Country is so checked as to allow the supply we already possess to become scattered and the native element to work upon it more freely" (Document 23). Nearly a quarter of a century later a fair-minded Englishman, who wrote an interesting book on *The American Irish* (Document 28), found the Irish a new power in politics, but still forming a large proportion of the dwellers in the New York slums. Had the government directed the tide of immigration and assisted the arriving immigrants to go west, the difficulties and dangers of the concentration of large masses of immigrants in city slums would have been avoided.

# EARLY PROBLEMS OF ASSIMILATION

## 1. Colonial Misgivings[1]

I am perfectly of your mind, that measures of great temper are necessary with the Germans; and am not without apprehensions that, through their indiscretion, or ours, or both, great disorders may one day arise among us. Those who come hither are generally the most stupid of their own nation, and, as ignorance is often attended with credulity when knavery would mislead it, and with suspicion when honesty would set it right; and as few of the English understand the German language, and so cannot address them either from the press or the pulpit, it is almost impossible to remove any prejudices they may entertain. Their clergy have very little influence on the people, who seem to take a pleasure in abusing and discharging the minister on every trivial occasion. Not being used to liberty, they know not how to make a modest use of it. And as Kolben says of the young Hottentots, that they are not esteemed men until they have shown their manhood by *beating their mothers*, so these seem not to think themselves free, till they can feel their liberty in abusing and insulting their teachers. Thus they are under no restraint from ecclesiastical government; they behave, however, submissively enough at present to the civil government, which I wish they may continue to do, for I remember when they modestly declined intermeddling in our elections, but now they come in droves and carry all before them, except in one or two counties.

Few of their children in the country know English. They import many books from Germany; and of the six printing-houses in the province, two are entirely German, two half German half English, and but two entirely English. They have one German newspaper, and one half-German. Advertisements, intended to be general, are now printed in Dutch and English. The signs in our streets have inscriptions in both languages, and in some places only German. They begin of late to make all their bonds and other instruments in their own language which (though I think it ought not to be) are allowed good in our

[1] Extract from letter of Benjamin Franklin to Peter Collinson, May, 1753, from *Complete Works of Benjamin Franklin*, compiled and edited by John Bigelow (New York: G. P. Putnam's Sons, 1887–88), II, 296–99.

courts, where the German business so increases that there is continued need of interpreters; and I suppose in a few years they will also be necessary in the Assembly, to tell one half of our legislators what the other half say.

In short, unless the stream of their importation could be turned from this to other colonies, as you very judiciously propose, they will soon so outnumber us that all the advantages we have will, in my opinion, be not able to preserve our language, and even our government will become precarious. The French, who watch all advantages, are now themselves making a German settlement, back of us, in the Illinois country, and by means of these Germans they may in time come to an understanding with ours; and, indeed, in the last war, our Germans showed a general disposition, that seemed to bode us no good. For, when the English, who were not Quakers, alarmed by the danger arising from the defenceless state of our country, entered unanimously into an association, and within this government and the Lower Counties raised, armed, and disciplined near ten thousand men, the Germans, except a very few in proportion to their number, refused to engage in it, giving out, one amongst another, and even in print, that, if they were quiet, the French, should they take the country, would not molest them; at the same time abusing the Philadelphians for fitting out privateers against the enemy, and representing the trouble, hazard, and expense of defending the province, as a greater inconvenience than any that might be expected from a change of government. Yet I am not for refusing to admit them entirely into our colonies. All that seems to me necessary is, to distribute them more equally, mix them with the English, establish English schools where they are now too thick settled, and take some care to prevent the practice, lately fallen into by some of the shipowners, of sweeping the German gaols to make up the number of their passengers. I say I am not against the admission of Germans in general, for they have their virtues. Their industry and frugality are exemplary. They are excellent husbandmen, and contribute greatly to the improvement of a country.

## 2.  "What Is an American?" [1]

I wish I could be acquainted with the feelings and thoughts which must agitate the heart and present themselves to the mind of an enlight-

[1] Extract from J. Hector St. John de Crèvecoeur, *Letters from an American Farmer* (London, 1782), pp. 45–53, 58–63. For another extract from Crèvecoeur, see pp. 16–22.

ened Englishman when he first lands on this continent. He must greatly rejoice that he lived at a time to see this fair country discovered and settled; he must necessarily feel a share of national pride, when he views the chain of settlements which embellishes these extended shores. When he says to himself, this is the work of my countrymen, who, when convulsed by factions, afflicted by a variety of miseries and wants, restless and impatient, took refuge here. They brought along with them their national genius, to which they principally owe what liberty they enjoy, and what substance they possess. Here he sees the industry of his native country displayed in a new manner, and traces in their works the embryos of all the arts, sciences, and ingenuity which flourish in Europe. Here he beholds fair cities, substantial villages, extensive fields, an immense country filled with decent houses, good roads, orchards, meadows, and bridges, where an hundred years ago all was wild, woody, and uncultivated!

What a train of pleasing ideas this fair spectacle must suggest; it is a prospect which must inspire a good citizen with the most heartfelt pleasure. The difficulty consists in the manner of viewing so extensive a scene. He is arrived on a new continent; a modern society offers itself to his contemplation, different from what he had hitherto seen. It is not composed, as in Europe, of great lords who possess everything, and of a herd of people who have nothing. Here are no aristocratical families, no courts, no kings, no bishops, no ecclesiastical dominion, no invisible power giving to a few a very visible one; no great manufacturers employing thousands, no great refinements of luxury. The rich and the poor are not so far removed from each other as they are in Europe. Some few towns excepted, we are all tillers of the earth, from Nova Scotia to West Florida. We are a people of cultivators, scattered over an immense territory, communicating with each other by means of good roads and navigable rivers, united by the silken bands of mild government, all respecting the laws, without dreading their power, because they are equitable. We are all animated with the spirit of an industry which is unfettered and unrestrained, because each person works for himself. . . . .

We have no princes, for whom we toil, starve, and bleed: we are the most perfect society now existing in the world. Here man is free as he ought to be; nor is this pleasing equality so transitory as many others are. Many ages will not see the shores of our great lakes replenished with inland nations, nor the unknown bounds of North America entirely peopled. Who can tell how far it extends? Who can tell the millions of men whom it will feed and contain? for no European foot has as yet travelled half the extent of this mighty continent!

The next wish of this traveller will be to know whence came all these people? They are a mixture of English, Scotch, Irish, French, Dutch, Germans, and Swedes. From this promiscuous breed, that race now called Americans have arisen. The eastern provinces must indeed be excepted, as being the unmixed descendants of Englishmen. I have heard many wish that they had been more intermixed also: for my part, I am no wisher, and think it much better as it has happened. They exhibit a most conspicuous figure in this great and variegated picture; they too enter for a great share in the pleasing perspective displayed in these thirteen provinces. . . . .

In this great American asylum, the poor of Europe have by some means met together, and in consequence of various causes; to what purpose should they ask one another what countrymen they are? Alas, two thirds of them had no country. Can a wretch who wanders about, who works and starves, whose life is a continual scene of sore affliction or pinching penury; can that man call England or any other kingdom his country? A country that had no bread for him, whose fields procured him no harvest, who met with nothing but the frowns of the rich, the severity of the laws, with jails and punishments; who owned not a single foot of the extensive surface of this planet? No! urged by a variety of motives, here they came. Everything has tended to regenerate them; new laws, a new mode of living, a new social system; here they are become men; in Europe they were as so many useless plants, wanting vegetative mould, and refreshing showers; they withered, and were mowed down by want, hunger, and war; but now by the power of transplantation, like all other plants they have taken root and flourished! Formerly they were not numbered in any civil lists of their country, except in those of the poor; here they rank as citizens. By what invisible power has this surprising metamorphosis been performed? By that of the laws and that of their industry. The laws, the indulgent laws protect them as they arrive, stamping on them the symbol of adoption; they receive ample rewards for their labours; these accumulated rewards procure them lands; those lands confer on them the title of freeman, and to that title every benefit is affixed which men can possibly require. This is the great operation daily performed by our laws. . . . .

What attachment can a poor European emigrant have for a country where he had nothing? The knowledge of the language, the love of a few kindred as poor as himself, were the only cords that tied him: his country is now that which gives him land, bread, protection, and consequence: *Ubi panis ibi patria*, is the motto of all emigrants. What then is the American, this new man? He is either an European, or the descendant of an European, hence that strange mixture of blood, which you will find in no other country. I could point out to you a family whose grandfather was an Englishman, whose wife was Dutch, whose son married a French woman, and whose present four sons have now four wives of different nations. *He* is an American, who leaving behind him all his ancient prejudices and manners, receives new ones from the new mode of life he has embraced, the new government he obeys, and the new rank he holds. He becomes an American by being received in the broad lap of our great *Alma Mater*. Here individuals of all nations are melted into a new race of men, whose labours and posterity will one day cause great changes in the world. Americans are the western pilgrims, who are carrying along with them that great mass of arts, sciences, vigour, and industry which began long since in the east; they will finish the great circle. The Americans were once scattered all over Europe; here they are incorporated into one of the finest systems of population which has ever appeared, and which will hereafter become distinct by the power of the different climates they inhabit. The American ought therefore to love this country much better than that wherein either he or his forefathers were born. Here the rewards of his industry follow with equal steps the progress of his labour; his labour is founded on the basis of nature, self-interest; can it want a stronger allurement? Wives and children, who before in vain demanded of him a morsel of bread, now, fat and frolicksome, gladly help their father to clear those fields whence exuberant crops are to arise to feed and to clothe them all; without any part being claimed, either by a despotic prince, a rich abbot, or a mighty lord. Here religion demands but little of him; a small voluntary salary to the minister, and gratitude to God; can he refuse these? The American is a new man, who acts upon new principles; he must therefore entertain new ideas, and form new opinions. From involuntary idleness, servile dependence, penury, and useless labour, he has passed to toils of a very different nature, rewarded by ample subsistence. This is an American. . . . .

As I have endeavoured to shew you how Europeans become Americans; it may not be disagreeable to shew you likewise how the various Christian sects introduced, wear out, and how religious indifference becomes prevalent. When any considerable number of a particular sect happen to dwell contiguous to each other, they immediately erect a temple, and there worship the Divinity agreeably to their own peculiar ideas. Nobody disturbs them. If any new sect springs up in Europe, it may happen that many of its professors will come and settle in America. As they bring their zeal with them, they are at liberty to make proselytes if they can, and to build a meeting and to follow the dictates of their consciences; for neither the government nor any other power interferes. If they are peaceable subjects, and are industrious, what is it to their neighbours how and in what manner they think fit to address their prayers to the Supreme Being? But if the sectaries are not settled close together, if they are mixed with other denominatiohs, their zeal will cool for want of fuel, and will be extinguished in a little time. Then the Americans become as to religion, what they are as to country, allied to all. In them the name of Englishman, Frenchman, and European is lost, and in like manner, the strict modes of Christianity as practised in Europe are lost also. This effect will extend itself still farther hereafter, and though this may appear to you as a strange idea, yet it is a very true one. I shall be able perhaps hereafter to explain myself better, in the meanwhile, let the following example serve as my first justification.

Let us suppose you and I to be travelling; we observe that in this house, to the right, lives a Catholic, who prays to God as he has been taught, and believes in transubstantiation; he works and raises wheat, he has a large family of children, all hale and robust; his belief, his prayers offend nobody. About one mile farther on the same road, his next neighbour may be a good honest plodding German Lutheran, who addresses himself to the same God, the God of all, agreeably to the modes he has been educated in, and believes in consubstantiation; by so doing he scandalizes nobody; he also works in his fields, embellishes the earth, clears swamps, etc. What has the world to do with his Lutheran principles? He persecutes nobody, and nobody persecutes him, he visits his neighbours, and his neighbours visit him. Next to him lives a seceder, the most enthusiastic of all sectaries; his zeal is hot and fiery, but separated as he is from others of the same complexion, he has no congregation of his own to resort to, where he might cabal and mingle religious pride with worldly obstinacy. He likewise raises good crops, his house is handsomely painted, his orchard is one of the fairest in the neighborhood. How does it concern the welfare of the country, or of the province at large, what this man's religious sentiments are, or whether he has any at all? He is a good farmer, he is a sober, peaceable, good citizen: William Penn himself would not wish for more. This is the visible character, the invisible one is only guessed at, and is nobody's business. Next again lives a Low Dutchman, who implicitly believes the rules laid down by the synod of Dort. He conceives no other idea of a clergyman than that of an hired man; if he does his work well he will pay him the stipulated sum; if not he will dismiss him, and do without his sermons, and let his church be shut up for years. But notwithstanding this coarse idea, you will find his house and farm to be the neatest in all the country; and you will judge by his wagon and fat horses, that he thinks more of the affairs of this world than of those of the next. He is sober and laborious, therefore he is all he ought to be as to the affairs of this life; as for those of the next, he must trust to the great Creator. Each of these people instruct their children as well as they can, but these instructions are feeble compared to those which are given to the youth of the poorest class in Europe. Their children will therefore grow up less zealous and more indifferent in matters of religion than their parents. The foolish vanity or rather the fury of making proselytes, is unknown here; they have no time, the seasons call for all their attention, and thus in a few years, this mixed neighborhood will exhibit a strange religious medley, that will be neither pure Catholicism nor pure Calvinism. A very perceptible indifference even in the first generation, will become apparent; and it may happen that the daughter of the Catholic will marry the son of the seceder, and settle by themselves at a distance from their parents. What religious education will they give their children? A very imperfect one. If there happens to be in the neighbourhood any place of worship, we will suppose a Quaker's meeting; rather than not shew their fine clothes, they will go to it, and some of them may perhaps attach themselves to that society. Others will remain in a perfect state of indifference; the children of these zealous parents will not be able to tell what their religious principles are, and their grandchildren still less. The neighbourhood of a place of worship generally leads them to it, and the action of going thither, is the strongest evidence they can give of their attachment to any sect.

Thus all sects are mixed as well as all nations; thus religious indifference is imperceptibly disseminated from one end of the continent to the other; which is at present one of the strongest characteristics of the Americans. Where this will reach no one can tell, perhaps it may leave a vacuum fit to receive other systems. Persecution, religious pride, the love of contradiction, are the food of what the world commonly calls religion. These motives have ceased here: zeal in Europe is confined; here it evaporates in the great distance it has to travel; there it is a grain of powder inclosed, here it burns away in the open air, and consumes without effect.

### 3. The Pennsylvania Germans[1]

The State of Pennsylvania is so much indebted for her prosperity and reputation to the German part of her citizens, that a short account of their manners may, perhaps, be useful and agreeable to their fellow citizens in every part of the United States.

The aged Germans, and the ancestors of those who are young, migrated chiefly from the Palatinate; from Alsace, Swabia, Saxony, and Switzerland; but natives of every principality and dukedom of Germany are to be found in different parts of the state. They brought but little property with them. A few pieces of gold or silver coin, a chest filled with clothes, a bible, and a prayer or an hymn book constituted the whole stock of most of them. Many of them bound themselves, or one or more of their children, to masters after their arrival, for four, five, or seven years, in order to pay for their passages across the ocean. A clergyman always accompanied them when they came in large bodies. . . . .

The German farmers live frugally in their families, with respect to diet, furniture and apparel. They sell their most profitable grain, which is wheat; and eat that which is less profitable, but more nourishing, that is, rye or Indian corn. The profit to a farmer, from this single article of economy, is equal, in the course of a life time, to the price of a farm for one of his children. They eat sparingly of boiled animal food, with large quantities of vegetable, particularly salad, turnips, onions, and cabbage, the last of which they make into sour crout. They likewise use a large quantity of milk and cheese in their diet. Perhaps the Germans do not proportion the quantity of their animal food, to the degrees of their labour; hence it has been thought, by some people, that they decline in strength sooner than their English or Irish neighbors. . . . . The furniture of their house is plain and useful. They cover themselves in winter with light feather beds instead of blankets; in this contrivance there is both convenience, and economy, for the beds are warmer than blankets, and they are made by themselves. The apparel of the German farmers is usually home spun. . . . .

[1] Extract from Benjamin Rush, M.D., "An Account of the Manners of the German Inhabitants of Pennsylvania" (1789), in *Proceedings and Addresses of the Pennsylvania-German Society*, XIX, 40–47, 62–64, 78–81, 104–5, 110–19.

All the different sects among them are particularly attentive to the religious education of their children, and to the establishment and support of the Christian Religion. For this purpose they settle as much as possible together—and make the erection of a school house and a place of worship the first object of their care. They commit the education and instruction of their children in a peculiar manner to the ministers and officers of their churches. . . . .

The intercourse of the Germans with each other is kept up chiefly in their own language; most of their men, who visit the capital, and the trading or county towns of the state, speak the English language. A certain number of the laws of the state are now printed in German for the benefit of those of them who cannot read English. A large number of German newspapers are likewise circulated through the state, through which knowledge and intelligence have been conveyed, much to the advantage of the government. There is scarcely an instance of a German, of either sex, in Pennsylvania, that cannot read; but many of the wives and daughters of the German farmers cannot write. The present state of society among them renders their accomplishment of little consequence to their improvement or happiness.

If it were possible to determine the amount of all the property brought into Pennsylvania by the present German inhabitants of the state, and their ancestors, and then compare it with the present amount of their property, the contrast would form such a monument of human industry and economy as has seldom been contemplated in any age or country. . . . .

Citizens of the United States learn, from the account that has been given of the German inhabitants of Pennsylvania, to prize knowledge and industry in agriculture and manufacture, as the basis of domestic happiness and national prosperity.

Legislators of the United States, learn from the wealth and independence of the German inhabitants of Pennsylvania, to encourage by your example, and laws, the republican virtues of industry and economy. They are the only pillars which can support the present constitution of the United States.

Legislators of Pennsylvania, learn from the history of your German fellow citizens that you possess an inexhaustible treasure in the bosom of the state, in their manners and arts. Continue to patronize their newly established seminary of learning and spare no expense in supporting their public free-schools. The vices which follow the want of religious instruction, among the children of poor people, lay the foundation of most of the jails, and places of public punishment in the state. Do not contend with their prejudices in favour of their language. It will be the channel through which the knowledge and discoveries of one of the wisest nations in Europe, may be conveyed into our country. In proportion as they are instructed and enlightened in their own language, they will become acquainted with the language of the United States. Invite them to share in the power and offices of government; it will be the means of producing an union in principle and conduct between them, and those of their enlightened fellow citizens who are descended from other nations. Above all, cherish with peculiar tenderness, those sects among them who hold war to be unlawful. Relieve them from the oppression of absurd and unnecessary militia laws. Protect them as the repositories of a truth of the gospel, which has existed in every age of the church, and which must spread hereafter over every part of the world.

#### 4. "Thoughts on the Policy of Encouraging Migration"[1]

Amidst an exuberant variety of fanciful and new-fangled opinions, lately obtruded on the public, and defended with all the dexterity that casuistry can afford, there is none more absurd than that of those persons who decry and endeavour to prevent the migration of Europeans to America. A paragraphist, in one of the late papers, in support of such conduct, tells us that "water and oil may as easily be made to unite as the subjects of monarchies with the citizens of the republics of America." . . . .

This *sage* politician asks in a triumphant style, "How few of the men who have come among us since the peace, have assimilated to our manners and government?" With much more foundation and justice may it be demanded, how few are they who have not thus assimilated themselves? . . . . Had "the subjects of monarchies," who have given this genius so much uneasiness, been excluded from these shores, the aborigines would have possessed them to this day unmolested. . . . . Those Germans to whom Pennsylvania owes so much with respect to agriculture, improvements, industry, and opulence, were transplanted from the most despotic soils. Here they became meliorated, and have furnished some of the most active and zealous friends and supporters of America's independence. The same will hold equally true of those numerous swarms of Irishmen, who both before and during the arduous

---

[1] Extract from Mathew Carey, "Thoughts on the Policy of Encouraging Migration," in his *Miscellaneous Trifles in Prose* (Philadelphia, 1796), pp. 110–24.

struggle, came into this country.—Their valour and conduct were displayed by sea and land—and history will bear the most honourable testimony of their heroism.

What then becomes of the random assertions of this writer? What end can he propose to answer but to divide the people of this country, and create dissensions and ill blood between the old citizens, and those who are on every occasion spoken of with a kind of supercilious and impertinent obloquy and contempt as *new comers—new comers?* Are not the unhappy divisions between constitutionalists and republicans, enough to impede and prevent the welfare and happiness of the state? Must more distinctions and differences be created, in order to counteract the efforts of true patriots to promote the common good? . . . . Surely, then, he must be a most dangerous enemy to this country, who endeavours to excite jealousy and disunion here, from which so many evil consequences must naturally and inevitably arise. Let all such persons meet with the detestation and scorn they merit. Let the Americans, to use the words of this paragraphist, "give a preference to our old citizens," whenever their merit and abilities entitle them to it. But should the *new comer* be found to possess those qualities in a higher degree, let him not be exposed to neglect, abuse, or scurrility, merely because, actuated by a love of liberty, he has given this country a preference to his own, and abandoned his friends and relatives to coalesce with the inhabitants of America, who, as general Washington declares in his farewell address, "Have opened an asylum for the oppressed and distressed of all nations."

As this is a subject on which many well meaning persons have been led to form erroneous opinions, by the artful insinuations of designing men, it will be allowable to pursue it a little further. In Europe, the importance of preventing emigration is fully understood; and in most states no pains are spared to chain the inhabitants to the soil. To entice artists and manufacturers from Britain is a high crime and misdemeanor; and, according to Chambers, in the same country, artificers in iron, steel, brass, or other metal, or in wool, going out of the kingdom into any foreign country, without licence, are liable to be imprisoned three months, and fined any sum not exceeding one hundred pounds. And those who go abroad, and do not return on warning given by the British ambassadors, are disabled from holding lands by descent or de-devise, from receiving any legacy, &c., and are deemed aliens. It is the same in several other states of Europe. . . . . Sage policy requires America to hold out every possible encouragement to industrious persons to migrate here, with their acquirements, their property, and their families? What then shall we say of those who are incessantly heaping scurrility and abuse on them? The answer is obvious. They must be either ignorant, illiberal, and mean persons: or those who have some selfish or party purpose to answer by such a vile conduct.

### 5. The Population of New York, 1812[1]

The inhabitants of [New York] city are composed of the following classes, arranged according to their supposed numbers: (1) immigrants from New England; (2) the original inhabitants, partly Dutch, partly English; (3) immigrants from other parts of this State; a considerable proportion of them from Long Island; (4) immigrants from Ireland; (5) immigrants from New Jersey; (6) immigrants from Scotland; (7) immigrants from Germany; (8) immigrants from England; (9) immigrants from France; (10) immigrants from Holland; (11) Jews.

To these are to be added a few Swedes, Danes, Italians, Portuguese, Spaniards, and West-Indians.

The children born of immigrants are numerous.

Among so many sorts of persons, you will easily believe it must be difficult, if not impossible, to find a common character; since the various immigrants themselves, and to some extent their children, will retain the features derived from their origin and their education. . . . .

In every large city there will always be found a considerable number of persons who possess superior talents and information; and who, if not natives, are drawn to it by the peculiar encouragement which it holds out to their exertions. The field of effort is here more splendid, and the talents are more needed, honoured, and rewarded, than in smaller towns. New York has its share of persons sustaining this character; men really possessing superiou1 minds, and deserving high esteem. Together with these, there is not a small number, here as elsewhere, who arrogate this character to themselves, and some of whom occasionally acquire and lose it; men accounted great through the favourable influence of some accident, the attachment of some religious or political party during a fortunate breeze of popularity, or the lucky prevalence of some incidental sympathy, or the ardent pursuit of some favourite public object, in which they have happened to act with success. These meteors, though some of them shine for a period with considerable lustre, soon pass over the horizon, and are seen no more.

[1] Extract from Timothy Dwight, *Travels in New England and New York,* III (New Haven, 1822), 469–73, 529–34

The citizens at large are distinguished as to their intelligence in the manner alluded to above. To this place they have come with the advantages, and disadvantages, of education, found in their several native countries. Some of them are well informed, read, converse, and investigate. Others scarcely do either and not a small number are unable to read at all. Most of these are, however, Europeans.

The language spoken in this city is very various. When passing through the streets, you will hear English, French, Dutch, and German, and all the various brogues spoken by the numerous nations mentioned above, when imperfectly acquainted, as most of them are, with the English tongue. Those who are of English descent, speak the language with as much propriety as any other inhabitants of the Union. The well-educated descendants of the Dutch speak it substantially in the same manner. . . . .

The inhabitants of the State of New York, like those of the city, are derived from many countries. At least three-fifths of them are of New England origin; and the number of these is rapidly increasing. The next largest class consists of the descendants of the original Dutch planters. After these are the Scotch, Irish, German, English, and French Colonists, and their progeny. As I before observed, it is impossible to ascribe to these numerous classes a common character.

Those who have immigrated from New England retain extensively, and many of them absolutely, their original character. When considered *en masse*, they exhibit such varieties as would be naturally expected from the account which I have given concerning the early settlers of a forested country, connected with that of the New England people. They are ardent, enterprising, resolute, patient, active, industrious, and persevering. Many of them are sober, orderly, moral, and friends of learning and good government. Many of them are intelligent, ingenious, acute, versatile, ready when disappointed in one kind of business to slide into another, and fitted to conduct the second, or even a third, or fourth, with much the same facility and success, as if they had been bred to nothing else. . . . .

The mass of this population forms at the present time a most important accession to the State of New York; and is continually increasing, both in its numbers and value. Their energy is already felt in every part of the country. The efforts by which they have changed its vast forests into fruitful fields, and gardens, are unparalleled, perhaps, in the world. It is questionable whether mankind have ever seen so large a tract changed so suddenly from a wilderness into a well-inhabited and well-cultivated country as that which extends on the great Western road from the German Flats to the Genesee River. Nor is it probable that any such tract has assumed within so short a time an appearance equally beautiful. Before the year 1784, . . . . there was not a single spot, cultivated by civilized man, between the German Flats and Lake Erie; except a solitary farm near the falls of Niagara, known by the name of the Stedman farm. In the year 1810, this region contained 280,319 inhabitants; all planted in it within twenty-six years, and almost all within twenty-two. . . . .

The Irish Colonists in this State differ from each other, as they did in their native country. Those who are descended from the English and Scotch are better informed, and, therefore, of a superiour character. They are also generally habituated to a just sense of the importance of good order, and good government; are usually industrious, sober, and possessed of apprehensions, not incorrect, of the nature and value of religion. This is particularly true of those who are descended from the Scotch. It will be easily believed that persons of such a character must, of course, be extensively good subjects, and prosperous in their business. The Western and Southern Irish are, often, almost absolutely uneducated. This renders them liable to many impositions, and consequent misfortunes. They are also to an extensive degree hostile to the government under which they were born; and very naturally transfer some portion of that hostility to any other government under which they may live. So far as they know anything concerning religion, they are generally Papists. From the dissocial nature of Popery it can scarcely be supposed that here, more than elsewhere, they should view Protestants with complacency. From their extreme ignorance, their apprehensions concerning moral obligation must be essentially defective; and this defectiveness must be increased by the doctrines taught in the Romish church concerning absolution, indulgences, and other licentious tenets, easily comprehensible, even by men growing up in these unhappy circumstances. As they have been originally and only directed by others, it is hardly possible that they should direct themselves. With these things in view, it will follow, of course, that in very many instances they must be bad managers, poor, and vicious.

The evils, which I have specified, are not, however, derived from the native character of these people. From what I have read, and heard, and particularly from my own observation, I am persuaded that the native character of the Irish is inferiour to that of no other people. To me they appear not to be surpassed in native activity of mind, sprightliness, wit, good-nature, generosity, affection, and gratitude. Their peculiar defects and vices, I am persuaded, are owing to the want of education, or to a bad one. Give them the same advantages which are enjoyed by others, and they will stand upon a level with any of their neighbours.

The Scotch Colonists preserve, unaltered, the character which they brought with them. They are industrious, frugal, orderly, patient of hardship, persevering, attached to government, reverential to religion, generally moral, and often pious. At the same time they are frequently unwarrantably self-complacent, rigid in their dispositions, unbending in their opinions, sequestered, avaricious, ready to unchurch those who differ from them, and to say, "Doubtless we are the people." Most of them acquire property, and leave it to their children. As a body, they are better citizens than any other class of immigrants. Such as are well educated and liberally disposed are as agreeable neighbours and friends as are furnished by any nation; and such as give themselves up to vice, are as absolute profligates. The number of these is, however, very limited.

The Germans, who settled themselves in this State, were among the most ignorant inhabitants of their native country; and a great part of them have transmitted this unfortunate characteristic to their descendants. A small collection of these, at Germantown, in the South-Western corner of Columbia, have been mentioned to me by authority, which I cannot dispute, as a very worthy and respectable body of plain people, distinguished for their industry, good order, sound morals, and attachment to religion. Those on the Mohawk are, in many instances, of a different character.

The French Protestants who colonized New Rochelle have chiefly, if not wholly, become mere Americans; in no way distinguishable, except by their surnames, from the descendants of the English Colonists. It is a fact, deserving of notice, that a considerable number of these people have been persons of high respectability, and have been elevated to very honourable stations; and many others have acquired ample fortunes, and sustained very desirable characters in private life. A prophet might attribute their prosperity to a particular blessing of God, who on many occasions has been pleased to shower his favour upon the descendants of those who have been persecuted for their piety.

Of all these classes of Colonists it is to be observed, generally, that they will soon be so entirely amalgamated with those from New England as to be undistinguishable.

### 6. The "Anglicizing" of the Germans in America, 1829[1]

"Will the German language in America survive or die out?" In order to answer this question properly we must get in our minds an exact picture of the German settlements in America.

The German-Evangelical-Lutheran synods of Pennsylvania in 1823 numbered 74 ministers with 278 churches or parishes; and the remaining synods of this religious group were distributed as follows: synods of Ohio, 26 preachers; synods of Virginia and Maryland, 22 preachers; synods of New York, 20 preachers; synods of North Carolina, 19 preachers; synods of Tennessee, 10 preachers; or a total of 97 preachers. If we count for every minister of the synods just mentioned four parishes (many of them have ten, others only one or two), then 400 parishes have probably been formed in these states. Adding the parishes in Pennsylvania already mentioned, we have 678, or at the most 700 German Lutheran parishes founded in North America. To these should be added 400 parishes of the German Reformed church and 200 of the smaller sects: the Catholics, Baptists, Methodists, Moravian Brethren, "Harmonyites," etc. But since Anglo-mania has made great progress in these small parishes, we may accept it as certain that half of them have already been completely Anglicized, and therefore we can count that out of the 200 parishes of the smaller sects there are only 100 in which the German language is maintained for church services. On the whole, therefore, there may be said to be a total of 1,200 German parishes in America.

We must note further that the parishes above are not all so large as the German Lutheran Zions parish in Philadelphia, which numbered 3,000 or 4,000 souls; but in many of them, especially in the recently formed parishes in the new states where the membership is small, the proverb "Three make a college" may be said to apply. Frequently these little communities have no minister for the very good reason that they cannot afford one. In the German Reformed church there were something like 60 or 70 of these small parishes in 1824 in the states of Virginia, North Carolina, South Carolina, Tennessee, Kentucky, Indiana, Missouri, and Illinois; and in these same states there were between 130 and 140 parishes of the German Lutheran church.

---

[1] Translated from Dr. Ernst Ludwig Brauns, *Praktische Belehrungen und Rathschläge für Reisende und Auswanderer nach Amerika* (Braunschweig, 1829), pp. 210–21, 351–69. Extract from chap. xviii, *Wird die deutsche Sprache in Amerika bestehen oder untergehen?* and from chap. xxvi, *Die Englisirung der Deutschen in Amerika*.

Whether these small parishes later on form regular parishes with German ministers or become part of English parishes no one can tell, and it must be left to the future to decide. At the present time they can probably not properly be counted as German parishes at all. If we should subtract from the total number of 1,200 these 200 which practically exist only on paper and which count scarcely a thousand families, there would still remain a thousand German-speaking parishes in North America with about a million Germans not yet Anglicized, a not exaggerated estimate. . . . .

In the larger German country towns one finds generally two or three and often more German churches representing the various religions, the Lutheran, the Reformed, and the Catholic; in the smaller German country towns we usually find only one church. The religious communities of the Moravian Brotherhood, Bethlehem, Nazareth, Lititz, Gnadenhütten, etc., should especially be mentioned on account of their pure unmixed Upper-Saxon dialect. It is a striking fact that north of Reading the German language is purer than farther south and west in the districts near Lancaster and Harrisburg. . . . . In this district many ministers have established very well-selected German libraries, not only in the cities but frequently also in rural communities. Because of this and because of the regular communication of the Moravian Brothers with the original community in Herrnhut, they keep in touch with the progress of modern German literature, the result of which is the better education of many of the inhabitants of these German regions. In the vicinity of Hamburg on the Schuylkill, Kutztown (Coolstown), Allentown, Reading, and Lebanon and many others, one finds several thousand German families who understand or pronounce scarcely any English words, neither can they use English for purposes of communication. For this reason, the courts in those districts allow the witnesses to give testimony in German. From this lack of acquaintance of so many Germans with the English language, which has long been customary and which now still continues, the very praiseworthy custom has originated of having the laws of the Pennsylvania legislature annually translated into German. Several thousand copies of this German edition are sent to the German settlements of the state.

A second very important region where the German language is spoken begins in southwestern Pennsylvania on the banks of the Susquehanna . . . . and goes through the state of Màryland as far as the Potomac. South of the Potomac the German language is not heard

. . . . but in the north, where Virginia begins, the language is found with few interruptions as far as the sources of the lovely Shenandoah. Nor does it stop even there, but continues often in an uninterrupted chain to the German settlements in North Carolina and Tennessee. In this district should be mentioned Neumarkt (Newmarket), Winchester, Point-Pleasant, Culpepper, Martinsburg, Schäfersstadt (Shepherdstown) and several smaller places . . . . where the numerous German inhabitants have maintained the German language and have desired to hand it down to their descendants. In Maryland the German language is the chief language in the two very important and flourishing country towns, Fredericktown and Hagerstown and a very considerable number of smaller places. In the same way the German language prevails in the neighboring Pennsylvania cities, Chambersburg, Schiffensburg, Carlisle, Gettysburg, Hanover, and York. One may add the two last very prosperous and flourishing cities with many smaller places to the list of completely German cities. Very few Anglo-Americans were found in these places.

Beside those two large and very fertile German districts, there are several other districts which contain more than one hundred English square miles where the German language is spoken everywhere even though it does not prevail so exclusively as in the two districts already described. . . . .

In all the port cities and commercial towns from Boston to New Orleans there are German inhabitants and the German language is more or less spoken. In Philadelphia there live about nine thousand Germans whose forefathers built ten churches and chapels, in four of which the chief service is still conducted in the German language. This is also the case in several churches in Baltimore, and in New York. In New England the German language has been steadily maintained in daily life as well as in church services among the descendants of a German colony in Waldoborough (Waldenburg) in the state of Maine, and the same situation exists in British America, in several regions of Upper Canada and New Scotland.

The Swedish language has already completely disappeared, and the Dutch language has almost completely died out and has been mixed with other languages, especially English and German. Likewise the German language in the seaports, where luxury and ambition prevail more than in the country districts, will hardly survive another century without the arrival of new immigrants. This is illustrated by the case of the once purely German community in Charleston which has become completely Anglicized, and several other German communities in the two Carolinas which have similarly become Anglicized. On the other hand there is no reason to fear that the German language will die out in Pennsylvania, Ohio, Indiana, Illinois, Maryland, Virginia, and New York in the settlements where it now prevails. Altogether the German communities, both of the Lutheran and Reformed faith, which have become English, number less than fifty, while the communities that have remained German number one thousand.

The truth of the above statement will be more apparent if we realize that after Latin and Greek the German language is now most studied by the scientists and the really educated people in New England. Many German books by Storr, Jahns, Heeren, and several others have been translated into English in New England, and, since 1824, not a year has passed in which translations from the German have not appeared. At Harvard College, near Boston, Herr Karl Follen has, since 1828, held the position of professor of the German language and literature. Since 1815 there have been, every year, between twenty and thirty New Englanders in German universities studying philology or theology. As the professors in the southern states of the Union are for the most part of New England descent or formerly were educated there, so in those states German literature is zealously studied. Thus a chair of German language and literature has also been established in the university at Charlottesville, in Virginia, founded by Thomas Jefferson. . . . .

Thus we see the German language spreading out and becoming more firmly established in the North and South and in the central states as well. Already for more than a century the German language has been used in America, and we shall probably never see it disappear and give way to English, though many a pseudo-German minister and many a rich Anglo-maniac ardently wishes this to happen. We therefore see how false it is when a modern author says: "German is not at all taught in America, but the immigrant Germans very soon learn English, Spanish, and Portuguese, depending upon where they settle. . . . ."

With the beginning of the nineteenth century a new impulse, very dangerous to their welfare, suddenly began to take possession of the once quiet and peaceful German settlements in North America. Some Germans who had become rich thought that they were superior to their less wealthy associates, and their children began to be ashamed of the German language, and to regard it as the language of the rabble.

They demanded that in addition to German the English language should be introduced into the German churches, although there were already enough English churches everywhere. Experience had already taught that the two languages could not be united in one church, since in such cases German gradually disappeared. This desire for change therefore caused a violent upheaval in numerous communities which not infrequently ended with a division into two parties—the German and the Anglicized-German. The latter party was supported by the Irish and the Anglo-American allies, and when this party prevailed, the Germans were completely absorbed. . . . .

The desire for change applies only to the language. This party wants to banish the German language from the churches and wants to introduce English because their wives and their English-speaking children no longer understand German.

In reply, we say that if these people no longer understand German, it is the fault of the older generation; and we ask them why do not the German communities which have been a longer time in St. Petersburg and other parts of Russia introduce the Russian language into their churches, how do the German communities maintain their church services in German not only in Petersburg and even in Asiatic Russia, e.g., at Barnaul in Siberia, but also in Denmark, Sweden, London, Poland, Hungary, . . . . Constantinople, and even Smyrna? Why do even the Germans at the Cape of Good Hope, in Surinam (Dutch Guiana), Berbice (British Guiana) and other parts of the world much more remote than North America continue their church services in German?

Surely the Germans in North America are able to do what these other German communities have done to maintain the German language. And as for the Irish-Germans, who dislike everything German and who wish to attend an English church service, why do they not visit one of the numerous places where church services are held in English—places which are only too common in America in the cities and country districts? The answer is easily found. They want to take the churches which are richly endowed from the Germans who built them and they wish to reap the harvest which the Germans have sown. But these persuasive Irish-Germans whose watchword is *luxus et avaritia* say, "We have no wish to banish the German language from the German churches. We only wish to introduce the English language along with the German, which will satisfy both parties and establish peace at once. We shall be satisfied if only once a week or every other week there is a sermon in the afternoon in English." Now many short-sighted Germans think that this request is fair and justifiable and that generosity demands that the request be granted. But we declare this request to be presumptuous and Jesuitical as well as unfair. By such insidious means the Irish-Germans try to smuggle the English language into the German churches. But beware if once it gets a foothold! . . . .

The acceptance of English customs usually has very serious consequences for the Irish-Germans. Unlike the old German forefathers who sought to make their fortunes through industry and honesty, the modern Irish-German substitutes tricks, deceit, and intrigues for the old praiseworthy virtues, and wastes his time in coming and going with idle good-for-nothings. The inheritance that was left by the industrious and religious German elders is often wasted upon finery and elegant furniture and art by the young educated Anglicized "gentlemen and ladies" who are ashamed of their awkward forefathers. . . . .

If all the German preachers in America had been as zealous to maintain the German language as Dr. Justus Heinrich Christian Helmuth, who died in February, 1825, in Philadelphia, and who for more than fifty years was in charge in the Lutheran Zions community and the German Lutheran community in Lancaster, German would very probably now prevail in the central states of the Union. Helmuth's appeals to the Germans in America published in the *Evangelical Magazine* attempted in very fitting and persuasive words to move the Germans to take an interest in this important national subject and it is a matter of congratulation that he was not wholly unsuccessful. For since that time (1813) there has been an earnest attempt to revive the German schools that were so nearly extinguished, and noteworthy progress has been made in this important field. To these appeals and to the numerous German immigrants in this state, who numbered, between 1813 and 1829, more than 50,000 souls, we owe the fact that now so much enthusiasm for the German language has been awakened in Pennsylvania that when the last legislature met, a request was brought in to have the German language declared an official language of the state with the same rights as English. In spite of the fact that the educated Anglo-Americans favored this proposal, it failed at this time because of the Anglo-mania of those who were formerly Germans but who voted against it. But the number of those who voted to make German an official language was so great that they needed only one more vote to pass this measure. But people in Pennsylvania hope that this proposal will be renewed in the next legislature and will be victorious. . . . .

The present governor of Pennsylvania, who was formerly a German-Lutheran minister, and a very large number of educated German-Americans and Anglo-Americans who have been elected to the legislature are enthusiastic about this proposal. If this is carried in the next session, of which we are absolutely confident, then German will be established for all time in America, and the plot of the foolish and arrogant Irish-Germans will be completely destroyed forever.

### 7. A German Political Exile on the Problem of Assimilation[1]

At my landing on the wharf in New York, I found several groups of German emigrants, just arrived from Europe. Some of them looked pretty well dressed, and showed that they had come with sufficient means to proceed immediately to the west, and to settle there; others, who looked very poor, had first to go through the ordeal of a poor emigrant, who is obliged, for want of means, to tarry in or about a large city, where he is, of course, exposed to the miseries inherent to a residence in a populous, foreign place, without any means of independence, and often becomes a prey to swindlers, with numbers of whom, as you may well imagine, they meet among their own countrymen; worthless fellows who have arrived long before them, and know all the ways of robbing these poor and helpless creatures of their last farthing. I know it from many of my acquaintances in New York, who belong to a charitable society, one of the objects of which is to assist destitute emigrants, that one of the great dangers which await the latter in that city, is, their falling into the hands of certain boarding-house keepers of their own nation (of course only *certain* of these) who strip the poor families of every thing they had the good luck to be able to bring along with them; like wolf-dogs, they are the enemies of their own species. A German emigrant generally remains in a large city only as long as he cannot help it; his great and laudable desire is always to get a farm, and to own it. The Irish are, in this respect, very different; they prefer the cities, and wherever you meet with a populous place in the United States—I do not only speak of the Atlantic cities, but also of those in the interior, such as Albany, Utica, Cincinnati, Louisville—you are sure to find a great number of poor Irish in and about it. The German, as I said, pushes on; if he has not the means to proceed immediately to the west, and must take his temporary abode in a large place, it is only in order to save, as soon as he possibly can, the requisite sum

[1] Extract from Francis Lieber, *The Stranger in America* (London, 1835), I, 83-101; II, 40-45, 58-59. For an account of Lieber's emigration, see above, p. 54.

to carry him and his family to those parts of the Union where land is cheap and fertile. Here again he has not, perhaps, the means to purchase a few acres, though government sells public lands for the low price of one dollar and twenty-five cents per acre. If this is the case, he will first work for another farmer, never, however, losing sight of his main object, the having of a farm to himself. As soon as he has it, he loves it as a German trooper loves his horse;[1] it becomes his "all in all," so that he sometimes forgets the proper mental education of his offspring. Scotch emigrants, I imagine, generally arrive here provided with sufficient means to begin farming immediately. . . . .

You can judge from what I have said how valuable German emigrants are to our country, if they mingle with the Anglo-American race. . . . .

The Germans, as I said, form a most valuable addition to our population, when mingled with the great predominant race inhabiting the northern part of this continent. Whenever colonists settle among a different nation, in such numbers and so closely together that they may live on among themselves, without intermixture with the original inhabitants, a variety of inconveniences will necessarily arise. Living in an isolated state, the current of civilization of the country in which they live does not reach them; and they are equally cut off from that of their mother country: mental stagnation is the consequence. They remain a foreign element, an ill-joined part of the great machinery of which they still form, and needs must form, a part. . . . .

Those, therefore, who lately proposed to form a whole German state in our west, ought to weigh well their project before they set about it, if ever it should become possible to put this scheme into practice, which I seriously doubt. "Ossification," as the Germans call it, would be the unavoidable consequence. These colonists would be unable, though they might come by thousands and tens of thousands, to develop for themselves German literature, German language, German law, German science, German art; every thing would remain stationary at the point where it was when they brought it over from the mother country, and within less than fifty years our colony would degenerate into an antiquated, ill-adapted element of our great national system, with which, sooner or later, it must assimilate. . . . .

[1] The German farmer loves his farm sometimes to the disadvantage of his own family. In some parts of Pennsylvania, the love of the farm has degenerated, it might be said, into a kind of mania. You can find there barns as large as well-sized chapels, with glass windows and blinds; whilst in these very parts, little has been done for the *schooling* of the people. . . . .

Quite a different question it is whether German emigrants ought to preserve the knowledge of German language, and German education in general among them. By all means! Have schools in which both German and English are taught. Nothing is easier than to learn from infancy two languages at once, and few things are more important than the knowledge of two languages, especially if the one besides the native idiom is the German. . . . .

The Irish—in spite of what I have said above of their facility in assimilating with the Americans—clan more together than the emigrants of any other nation. They, in fact, openly retain their name, and often, in the very moment that they make use of the highest privileges of citizenship which any country can bestow, they do it under the banner of Irishmen. There is no election in any of the large cities without some previous calls upon the "true-born sons of Ireland," to vote so or so. On the election day itself banners are seen floating from the windows of taverns, some of which, you may be certain, are ornamented with mottos having reference to the Irish alone. They go farther, sometimes; they will bring forward their own candidate, if they feel strong enough. All this is, to speak guardedly, at least impolite towards the natives, who receive the foreigner with a degree of national hospitality unequalled by any other nation. Every career on the wide field of enterprise which is open to the natural citizens of this republic, is equally open to the naturalized. After the brief period of five years' residence, any alien may take the citizen's oath, and this done, he enjoys every privilege of which a free-born American can boast, an unstinted citizenship, with the single exception that he cannot become a president of the United States. The least that could be expected, in return for such a boon, it should be supposed, would be the frankest and most heartfelt union, in every thing, with the nation which so hospitably makes no difference between its own sons and the new comers. But the Irish are desirous of becoming Americans and yet remaining Irish, and this serving of two masters will not do. Whatever the inmost feelings of an emigrant toward his native country may be, and with every generous heart will be, as a citizen of America, he should be American and American only, or let him remain alien. As the latter, he is protected as much by the law of the land as is a citizen; there is no necessity whatever for his becoming naturalized. It is, therefore, with great concern, that a good citizen must observe that disturbances at elections are not unfrequently caused by those who do not enjoy their citizenship by birthright, sometimes by those who do not enjoy it at all.

What are the reasons that the Irish in this country can clan more together than the emigrants of any other nation? I believe they are three-fold. First, more Irish than people of other countries come to the United States, and, as I think I have observed in a previous letter, they have a predilection for large cities, so that they remain in greater numbers together. Secondly, the Irish feel that they have been wronged in their country; they have, in a degree, been driven from it; the feelings with which they look back to it are, therefore, of a more intense character than they would otherwise be; or, if this be not the case, they feel among themselves the strong tie of bearing one common wrong. Thirdly, they are encouraged to this clanship by party men; their Irish feelings are flattered and excited, in order to win them; they are called upon as Irish in order to gain their votes, which become, in some quarters of large cities, or, indeed in some whole counties, at times, very important, when, otherwise, the parties might be nearly balanced.

Let me throw in, here, the remark, though it be not quite in its place, that the common language of the English, Scotch, Irish, and Americans, causes the last, unconsciously to themselves, to consider emigrants of the three first nations, when settled among them, nearer akin than those of other countries. There are many Irish in congress, of whom it is hardly known that they are strangers by birth. I have been told a story, which I feel inclined to believe. A German offered himself for a professorship of one of the colleges in the middle states; he was unsuccessful in his application; and it was pretty generally understood that a native would be preferred; but a short time after, an Irish gentleman obtained the chair, certainly not on account of his superiority. This, however, is not always the course of things; for instance, in Cambridge, Massachusetts, there are two Germans who hold prominent professorships. But if you glance over the list of officers of the United States, you will find very many Irish; nor does any difficulty arise at the appointment of one of that people, while the contrary would, probably, be the case were a German, or a Frenchman by birth, to offer himself for a place, which easily might be filled by some one else. This, I think, is not quite fair; the Irish emigrants do by no means deserve more confidence, than those of other countries; and though the existence of a common language may naturally lead the Americans not to feel so strongly the difference between themselves and the Irish, they ought to be careful not to act upon this feeling. . . . .

[The Germans] are a valuable addition to our population, if they mix. But let truth prevail every where: twisting of facts, and stating or being silent according to convenience, is an unmanly thing—unworthy of a lover of his species, and a man who thinks he has expanded his views by travelling into other countries, and by studying history back into other ages. It is painful, indeed, for a German, that the descendants of his nation in this country, where they live closely together, have not only done less for the common education of their offspring than their neighbors, but have actually often frustrated the endeavours of the government to establish a system of general education. How a scion of a people, who have done more for education than any other on earth, comes thus to neglect one of the most sacred duties, would be inexplicable, were it not for the fact, on which I think I have touched on a former occasion, that it is difficult for a community, severed from the mother country, and separated from a surrounding population by the barrier of a different language, to prevent mental stagnation. There lies upon all well educated men, who enjoy the confidence of those hardy and well-meaning people, especially upon the German clergy in Pennsylvania, a duty, superior to which I can conceive of none in the whole sphere of their activity; namely, to enlighten the Germans of America with regard to this subject of all-absorbing importance.

## 8. Difficulties of Assimiliation, 1835[1]

For the most part then the emigrant arrives in our sea-ports, wholly destitute of property, and, under the name of a redemptioner, is often indented to labor in order to defray the expenses of his voyage. This, in his actual circumstances, is perhaps the most favorable lot which can befall him, for being thus supplied with immediate occupation, and placed in direct subordination to the habits, genius, and character of American society, he is provided with a species of national education, acquires a real as well as a legal citizenship, and in many instances obtains an interest in the rights of property as well as of persons. The residue, however, with whom our business at present principally lies, are such as have either expended their little property in the purchase of a passage, or have been sent out at the charge of the parish to which their support had become a burthen. Emigrants of this description find themselves in our principal cities, without personal resources or friends, and in many instances with very erroneous impressions of the nature of our political and municipal regulations. The inequalities of European law, by robbing labor of its just fruits, . . . . have probably deprived the individual of a just reliance upon his own

[1] Extract from "Immigration," by A. H. Everett, *North American Review*, XL (1835), 460–76.

resources, and prevented the acquisition of those habits of patient and unremitted application, which can scarcely be implanted with success, except in early life and by the animating expectation of a fair and certain profit on personal effort. Ignorant therefore from necessity, and idle through the absence of a wholesome stimulus, the emigrant's preconceptions of American freedom form generally the converse of his, who pronounced that "money was liberty," and in looking forward to his adopted country, the vision of wealth unattended by labor, and indulgence won without the inconvenience of toil, floats before an imagination which has unhappily confounded a land of equal rights with a land of voluptuous license. Even when the moral condition of the emigrant is more favorable, many circumstances occur to prevent his easy reception into the great mass of society which is floating around him. He is destined to feel the sharp encounter of many a prejudice which has sprung up, not altogether without reason, in a scene where the emigrant has so often avenged on individuals the unconcern and indifference with which his wants and sufferings have been regarded by the community. Whether therefore the human beings thus cast unfriended and unknown on a foreign shore, be left to loiter away their time in the obscure retreats of the cities, or marched off to the service of some public work, where they must still be insulated from all the friendly influences of the society into which they have been transplanted, much time must in either case intervene before they can be properly distributed through the country to furnish a supply of labor where it is needed, or to undergo that nationalizing process, which can only result from intimate and friendly contact in the walks of private business and domestic life. . . . .

Under such circumstances it cannot be a matter of surprise, if the emigrant, unfortunate alike in his previous disqualification and in his sudden investiture with new and untried privileges, be found sometimes disposed to add his weight to that portion of society which is most susceptible of partial impressions, and most exposed to violent and hurtful impulses. Bringing with him all the prejudices of his native land, and subjected to no moral quarantine at all adequate to their purgation, he is still, in his new locality, such both in character and opinion, as when he formed a part of the altogether differently constituted societies of Europe. . . . .

The effect which a promiscuous immigration may thus produce upon the political condition of the state is not without some illustration in the past experience of republicanism. Montesquieu, in tracing the causes of the decline of Roman liberty, arrives at the conclusion that the disastrous change was occasioned not more by the enlargement of the empire, than by the indiscriminate extension of the rights and immunities of citizenship. . . . .

We do not mean to deny that there are important differences in the circumstances under which this accession of suffrages took place in the Roman commonwealth, and those under which a similar accession annually occurs in the political census of the United States. Yet these differences must proceed upon one of three suppositions; either that stricter guards have been here annexed to the right of suffrage, or that the materials of which the immigration is composed are themselves of better quality, or that, being dispersed over a larger tract of country, and becoming immediately interested in the welfare of the community, they present a very different moral spectacle from the condensed, yet fluctuating and venal, population of Rome. If it appear, however, on examination, that in fact very feeble guards are opposed around the national ballot; that of the numbers who take refuge here from the oppressions of the Old World, many have been not only impoverished but demoralized by the arbitrary and capricious exactions of the governments under which they have lived; and that, so far from being speedily and systematically absorbed into the mass of the native population and dispersed through the country, they are allowed, by the neglect or indifference of the nation, to collect in masses and to settle upon particular points of the body politic, then we presume that the supposed differences will lose much of the practical importance which we might at first have attached to them.[1] At all events, no one will deny that wide as the country may be, and urgent as is everywhere the demand for mechanical industry, the access of foreign population may yet be too rapid and indiscriminate for easy and healthful absorption into the community under existing circumstances. A single glance at our large maritime cities will convince us that some such predicament has already occurred . . . . [and] we may be permitted to doubt whether as much attention has been given to this subject, either by individuals or legislatures, as it deserves; whether, in a word, some meas-

[1] [The writer of the article notes that, "there is undoubtedly some ground for the distinction which is there drawn between the conduct of an election at the North and at the South. We do not know how this can be accounted for," he says, "except by the accumulation of needy and uneducated emigrants in our principal sea-ports. We have ourselves heard an eminent citizen of Virginia express his satisfaction at the existence of negro slavery in that State, as tending to preserve it from the indiscriminate immigration of the lower class of Europeans."]

ures might not be usefully resorted to, in order to facilitate the transit of the emigrant from the sea-port to the interior, and to promote by other means his safe and speedy resolution into the political and social body of which he is to be thenceforward a constituent portion.

There are some considerations of an economical nature, connected with this subject, upon which it may be worth while to bestow a moment's attention. The almost unlimited demand for labor in America, occasioned by the extent of unoccupied land, and the comparative scarcity of that class of population which devotes itself to agricultural production, with a view only to the wages of such application, manifestly leads to the conclusion that nothing can be more beneficial to all parties than an unobstructed immigration of persons from the Old World, disposed and qualified to avail themselves of the advantages in the New. . . . . A spirit of restless speculation is destined, we apprehend, to be kept up for ages, not merely in the emigrant, but in the native American also, by the persuasion that beyond the great "father of waters," and yet farther and still farther onward, new settlements await the hand of enterprise, and court the acceptance of the most daring adventurers. . . . .

It would seem but natural that while this process is going on, by which the Eastern part of the continent is drained of a laborious population in order to supply the demands of the West, it should itself be supplied in turn by the regular course of emigration from Europe. Yet this, under existing circumstances, is by no means the case. The immigration to America, in reference to the countries from which it proceeds, and its ulterior destination, may be divided into three classes. Of these, it is remarked that the Irish are most inclined to linger about the cities by which they have been first received, and into the vices and follies of which they are most liable to be betrayed by the ardor of their temperament and the recklessness of their habits. The Germans, the Swiss, and other natives of the continent would seem to be inclined to seek a more remote settlement in the West, where they form detached associations, as at Vevay and Harmony, and while they subsist in a friendly connexion with the community, for a long time resist an entire integration with it. As far as our own observation extends, it is the Englishman chiefly who passes, by an easy transition, into the bosom of American society, and, repelled by no inaptitude or prejudice, readily adapts himself to the pursuits of American industry, securing, at the same time, his own permanent attachment to the country. In this distribution, we do not, of course, contend for any high degree of exactness. Individuals of every denomination may be found, we are aware, in each of the situations which we thus distinguish. Yet our distribution is sufficiently exact to enable the philanthropist to contemplate the emigrant under several existing conditions, and to lead, consequently, to the adoption of correspondent measures for his relief and disposal. The end to be attained would probably be to bring the first of the three classes above-mentioned, and perhaps the second, into the same intimate and beneficial relation to society at large which is borne by the latter.

The German carries with him for the most part, into the interior settlements of the country, the same patient and laborious habits which had distinguished him in his native land. A peaceable citizen and a judicious husbandman, the colonies which he founds, though strikingly characterized by national peculiarities, are yet, almost without exception, models of well ordered and productive industry. The Swiss, too, will be found not to have lost that characteristic application and perseverance which enabled him to clothe the most rugged cliffs of his native country with unaccustomed verdure, and to force its most churlish soil into a kindly subservience to his wants. . . . . All that can be desired with respect to such emigrants is that in free and intimate communication they may soon lay aside the shibboleth of a foreign language, and arrive at a just understanding and appreciation of the character and institutions of the republic. It is the Irishman, and all who, like the Irishman, have been destined to contend with the ceaseless and disorganizing exactions of provincial vassalage, that must still present the most anxious and perplexing subject of contemplation to the philanthropist and the statesman. We take our illustrations of this class of emigrants from authorities which will scarcely be disputed, none perhaps having so good a title to paint the effects of misgovernment as those who have been instrumental in producing them. We can scarcely suppose such artists willing to overcharge the picture.

That Ireland is overwhelmed with a beggarly and redundant population; that its millions are starving in the midst of plenty, and seem to live only to bring into the world millions as miserable and distracted as themselves, is matter of common observation, not only to all who have visited the country itself, but to all who have compared it with other states, even in the lowest stage of civilization, and under circumstances generally supposed the most adverse to human improvement. That its population is redundant as well as miserable to the very greatest degree is demonstrated, not merely by the immense tide of emigration which annually flows over the Atlantic, but the enormous multitudes who are daily transported across the channel to overwhelm the already overpeopled shores of Britain. . . . . Humboldt was the first who took notice of the extraordinary, and, but for his accuracy, almost incredible fact, that between the years 1801 and 1821 there was a difference of a million of souls between the increase of the population of Great Britain as demonstrated by a comparison of the births and the deaths, and the actual increase of its inhabitants; a difference which he justly considers as chiefly owing to the immense influx of Irish during that period. There is no instance on record of so great an inundation of inhabitants breaking into any country, barbarous or civilized, not even when the Goths and Vandals overwhelmed the Roman empire. . . . .[1]

Such is the estimate which is formed in Great Britain of the Irish character, and such the apprehensions entertained of the irruption of the wretched and starving population of that kingdom into the sister island. While our extracts furnish unequivocal evidence of the general destitution and misery of Ireland, the immediate cause of these, we may observe, is sufficiently explained by the want of industry, which is perhaps too justly imputed to the Irish peasantry as a national characteristic. It forms no part of our present purpose to ascend to higher sources, in order to account for the strange phenomenon which is presented to us in this wholesale destitution, demoralization, and obloquy of an entire people. It only concerns us to know, that whatever causes may have produced these disastrous effects, they are not likely to remain subjects of distant and indifferent speculation to the American statist. Such as the Irishman is on his native shores, such is he found to be when landed on the quays of New York, Boston, or Philadelphia. There is no charm in the middle passage to remove from his character the impress of recklessness and ignorance. The three pounds which bring him to America buy him no more exemption from the inevitable consequences of his own want of industry and subordination, than the sixpence which lands him on the wharfs of Liverpool or Glasgow. Nor is it the Irishman alone, although constituting much the larger portion of the class, of whom the same disinclination to labor and incapacity to avail himself of the advantages of a free and unexhausted country may be predicated. There are hundreds of refugees annually entering the United States, whom the same political influences, which operate in the case of Ireland, have reduced to the same state of disqualification for every pursuit of laborious and persevering industry. In the condition of such emigrants, something more is needed than the mere removal of those legal impediments, which had hitherto obstructed their acquisition of property and independence.

[1] *Blackwood's Magazine*, January, 1833.

The desire of possessing these advantages is not necessarily consequent on the restoration of the natural ability to procure them; we must contrive in some manner to instil a sense of their value, before the emigrant can be animated to a course of rigorous self-denial and strenuous exertion. It is necessary to implant in him a taste for many of the gratifications of life to which he has hitherto been a stranger, and to enlarge the scope of his purposes beyond the mere support of a reckless and precarious existence. Without this previous discipline, the increased facility of satisfying his animal wants, so far from supplying a stimulus to increased exertion, will be found to afford the strongest solicitation to renewed and indolent indulgence.

We wish certainly to speak upon this subject not merely with forbearance, as remembering that our own fathers were once also strangers in the land, but even with a sense of the deepest gratitude to those who from time to time confer upon our country the honor of affording a sanctuary to those to whom injurious laws have denied even a home. . . . . But if we are not deceived by testimony emanating from different and independent sources, a new species of emigration, without example in the history of nations, and not to be embraced in the ordinary reasoning upon the subject, has already commenced its gloomy procession to our shores. The poor-houses and parishes of England, no longer able to endure the weight of pauperism, which a system of poor-laws, whose policy and administration seem equally open to censure, conspiring with the evils of a crowded population and a preter-naturally stimulated industry, has thrown upon the country, design to transfer a part of this incumbrance to the charity of the United States. It is not sufficient that the *penal colonies* of Australia are open to her convicts, England it would seem, needs also that a species of *pauper colony* should be opened in America for her poor. Thus, while her own parishes guard with the keenest jealousy every avenue by which they may possibly become burthened with more than their proper and unavoidable share of the evil, and while the indigent and houseless Briton is scarcely permitted to pass the invisible line which separates Cornwall from Devonshire, or Durham from Yorkshire, it is held no wrong to transport the mendicant and vagabond by ship-loads across the Atlantic, and to abandon them, all helpless and aimless, on the territory of the young republic. That such things have been perpetrated, there can be no doubt, while more than one warning has lately reached us that the practice was growing into a system, distinctly meditated and embraced by more than one parish and county in England. While the inhabitants of Great Britain, therefore, are themselves exclaiming, as we have seen, against the incursions of the Irish, who, to say the least, are physically capable of labor, no compunction it appears is felt in shifting off a still more helpless and pernicious population on the hands of a younger people, still struggling with the difficulties and embarrassments of early settlement. . . . .

We are gratified at observing, that the American public is not altogether indifferent to this subject. The legislature of New York has already provided, that any master of a vessel arriving from a foreign country, who shall knowingly bring any convict as a passenger, or otherwise, into that State, shall be deemed guilty of a misdemeanor, and be subject to a fine not exceeding three hundred dollars, and to imprisonment for a term not exceeding one year. We cannot but think that such a law strongly recommends itself to the adoption of all our maritime States. . . . .

Having taken such measures to avert from this country the injurious operation of the British poor-laws, and to bar the oppressive influx of convicts and mendicants of every description, we should be in a situation to employ such measures as might suggest themselves for the relief of the immense body of destitute emigrants, to whom our ports and our hospitality would be still open. . . . .

With this view we should rely mainly upon the organized benevolence of individuals. It is, surely, no vain calculation to presume that in an age like the present, a very extensive and effective association might be formed for the purpose, not merely of relieving the immediate wants of the emigrant, but of enlightening him with respect to the choice of an ulterior destination, and of enabling him to reach that destination as soon as possible after his arrival in the country. We are aware that many laudable associations already exist for the first of these purposes, but we know of none, so extensively ramified and possessing such means of communication with the interior, as to qualify it for the competent discharge of the latter. Such a society, being national in its object, should be national also to the fullest extent in its structure and operations. From our principal cities it should spread its branches into every district and village of the country, so that on the arrival of an emigrant, it should not only be ready to take cognizance of his wants and capacity, but be prepared likewise to pronounce at what point of the confederation his services would be most acceptable, and where, consequently, he might be most speedily and effectually engrafted into the community. . . . .

We cannot forbear, however, to express our surprise that, amongst the benevolent enterprises of the age, the case of the destitute emigrant should have been comparatively overlooked. While, as a nation, we acknowledge the evils of ignorance, and practically endeavor by diffusive education to avert its disastrous effects from our national institutions, we regard with unaccountable indifference the condition of some thousands of persons, who, by the process of naturalization, may be said without violence of language to be annually born into the Republic, although it is a well-known fact that most of them require to be not merely endued with new principles, but divested of innumerable prejudices that disqualify them for the proper exercise of even the lowest of those offices, which must necessarily devolve on the private American citizen. It seems to be one of the most common practical errors of the age to follow up the acknowledgment of a right by a hasty and inconsiderate surrender of all the privileges which may accidentally appertain to it, forgetful that in transferring power to those who have long been its victims, and investing men with rights of the correspondent duties of which they have been kept in entire ignorance, we contravene a clearly established law of nature, which dictates that all great and momentous changes should be introduced not merely with caution, but with assiduous preparation.

## 9. A "Native American" View, 1835[1]

Few, out of the great cities, are aware what sophistry has of late been spread among the more ignorant class of foreigners, to induce them to clan together, and to assert what they are pleased to call their rights. The ridiculous claim to superior privileges over native citizens, which I have noticed, is a specimen. . . . . Already has the influence of bad councils led the deluded emigrant, particularly the Irish emigrant, to adopt such a course as to alienate from him the American people. Emigrants have been induced to prefer such arrogant claims, they have nurtured their foreign feelings and their foreign nationality to such a degree, and manifested such a determination to create and strengthen a separate and a foreign interest, that the American people can endure it no longer, and a direct hostile interest is now in array

[1] Extract from Samuel Finley Breese Morse, *Imminent Dangers to the Free Institutions of the United States through Foreign Immigration, and the Present State of the Naturalization Laws*. A series of numbers, originally published in the New York *Journal of Commerce* in 1835. By "An American." (New ed.; New York, 1854), pp. 23–29; Appendix, p. 30.

against them. This is an effect natural from such a cause; it is one long predicted in the hope of averting the evil. If evil is the consequence, the writer at least washes his hands of the guilt. The name and character of foreigner has, by this conduct of emigrants and their advocates, become odious, and the public voice is becoming louder and louder, and it will increase to unanimity, or at least so far as real American feeling pervades the hearts of Americans, until its language will be intelligible and audible even to those deaf ears, who now affect neither to hear, nor to heed it. . . . . It is that anomalous, nondescript . . . . thing, neither foreigner nor native, yet a moiety of each, now one, now the other, both or neither, as circumstances suit, against whom I war; a naturalized *foreigner*, not a naturalized citizen; a man who from Ireland, or France, or Germany, or other foreign lands, renounces his native country and adopts America, professes to become an American, and still, being received and sworn to be a citizen, talks (for example) of Ireland as "his home," as "his beloved country," resents anything said against the Irish as said against him, glories in being Irish, forms and cherishes an Irish interest, brings hither Irish local feuds, and forgets, in short, all his new obligations as an American, and retains both a name and a feeling and a practice in regard to his adopted country at war with propriety, with decency, with gratitude, and with true patriotism. I hold no parley with such contradictions as Irish fellow-citizens, French fellow-citizens, or German fellow-citizens. With as much consistency might we say *foreign natives*, or *hostile friends*. But the present is no time either for compliment or nice discrimination. When the country is invaded by an army, it is not the moment to indulge in pity towards the deluded soldiers of the various hostile corps, who act as they are commanded by their superior officers. It is then no time to make distinctions among the officers, lest we injure those who are voluntarily fighting against us, or who may be friends in the enemy's camp. The first thing is to bring the whole army to unconditional surrender, and when they have laid down their arms in a body, and acknowledged our sovereignty, then good fellowship, and courtesy, and pity will have leisure to indulge in discriminating friends from foes, and in showing to each their respective and appropriate sympathies.

We have now to resist the *momentous* evil that threatens us from *Foreign Conspiracy*. The Conspirators are in the *foreign importations*. Innocent and guilty are brought over together. We must of necessity suspect them all. That we are most seriously endangered, admits not of the slightest doubt; we are experiencing the natural reaction of European upon American principles, and it is infatuation, it is madness not to see it, not to guard against it. A subtle attack is making upon us by foreign powers. The proofs are as strong as the nature of the case allows. They have been adduced again and again, and they have not only been uncontradicted, but silently acquiesced in, and have acquired fresh confirmation by every day's observation. The arbitrary governments of Europe—those governments who keep the people in the most abject obedience at the point of the bayonet, with Austria at their head, have combined to attack us in every vulnerable point that the nation exposes to their assault. They are compelled by self-preservation to attempt our destruction—they must destroy democracy. It is with them a case of life and death, they must succeed or perish. If they do not overthrow American liberty, American liberty will overthrow their despotism. . . . . Will you despise the cry of danger? Well, be it so. Believe the foreign Jesuit rather than your own countrymen. Open wide your doors. Yes, throw down your walls. Invite, nay allure, your enemies. Enlarge your almshouses and your prisons; be not sparing of your money; complain not of the outrages in your streets, nor the burden of your taxes. You will be repaid in praises of your toleration and liberty. What though European despots have compelled you to the necessity of employing your lives in toiling and providing for their outcast poor, and have caused you to be vexed, and your habit outraged by the expatriated turbulence of their cities, instead of allowing you to rejoice in the prosperity, and happiness, and peaceful neighbourhood of your own well-provided, well-instructed children. . . . .

What were the circumstances of the country when laws so favourable to the foreigner were passed to induce him to emigrate and settle in this country? The answer is obvious. Our early history explains it. In our national infancy we needed the strength of *numbers*. Powerful nations, to whom we were accessible by fleets, and consequently also by armies, threatened us. Our land had been the theatre of contests between French, and English, and Spanish armies, for more than a century. Our numbers were so few and so scattered, that as a people we could not unite to repel aggression. The war of Independence, too, had wasted us. We wanted *numerical strength;* we felt our weakness in numbers. *Safety*, then, national *safety*, was the motive which urged us to use every effort to increase our population, and to induce a foreign emigration. Then foreigners seemed all-important, and the policy of alluring them hither, too palpable to be opposed successfully even by the remonstrances of Jefferson. We could be benefited by the emigrants, and we in return could bestow on them a gift beyond price, by simply making them citizens. Manifest as this advantage seemed in the increase of our numerical strength, Mr. Jefferson looked beyond the advantage of the moment, and saw the distant evil.[1] . . . . Now, if under the most favourable circumstances for the country, when it could most be benefited, when numbers were most urgently needed, Mr. Jefferson could discover the evil afar off, and protest against encouraging foreign immigration, how much more is the measure to be deprecated, when circumstances have so entirely changed, that instead of *adding strength* to the country, immigration *adds weakness,* weakness physical and moral! And what overwhelming force does Mr. Jefferson's reasoning acquire, by the vast change of circumstances which has taken place both in Europe and in this country, in our earlier and in our later condition. *Then* we were few, feeble, and scattered. *Now* we are numerous, strong, and concentrated. *Then* our accessions by immigration were real accessions of strength from the ranks of the learned and the good, from the enlightened mechanic and artisan, and intelligent husbandman. *Now* immigration is the accession of weakness, from the ignorant and the vicious, or the priest-ridden slaves of Ireland and Germany, or the outcast tenants of the poorhouses and prisons of Europe. And again: *Then* our beautiful system of government had not been unfolded to the world to the terror of tyrants; the rising brightness of American Democracy was not yet so far above the horizon as to wake their slumbering anxieties, or more than to gleam faintly, in hope, upon their enslaved subjects. *Then* emigration was natural, it was an attraction of affinities, it was an attraction of liberty to liberty. Emigrants were the proscribed for conscience's sake, and for opinion's sake, the real lovers of liberty, Europe's loss, and our gain. . . . . Now emigrants are selected for a service to their tyrants, and by their tyrants; not for their affinity to liberty, but for their mental servitude, and their docility in obeying the orders of their priests. They are transported in thousands, nay, in *hundreds of thousands,* to our shores, to our loss and Europe's gain. Again, I say, let . . . . the law of the land be so changed, that no foreigner who comes into the country after the law is passed shall ever be entitled to the right of suffrage. This is just ground; it is practicable ground; it is defensible ground, and it is safe and prudent ground; and I cannot better close than in the words of Mr. Jefferson: "The time to guard

[1] See extract from Jefferson, in Section V, p. 703.

against corruption and tyranny is before they shall have gotten hold
on us; it is better to keep the wolf out of the fold, than to trust to
drawing his teeth and talons after he has entered. . . . ."

. . . . What reason can be assigned, why they who profess to have
become Americans, should organize themselves into Foreign National
Societies all over the country; and under their foreign appellation, hold
correspondence with each other to promote their foreign interest? Can
any good reason be given why such *foreign associations* should be
allowed to exist in this country? The Irish have been thus organized
for many years. The objects of *one* of these Irish societies will serve
to illustrate the objects generally of all these associations in the midst
of us. "The Boston Hibernian Lyceum," says the *Catholic Diary* of
March 14, 1835, "organized about *two years ago*, is composed of Irish
young men, for the diffusion among each other—of what?—"of mutual
sympathy and mutual co-operation, in whatever may aid to qualify
them to meet and discharge their responsibilities as the representatives
of their native, as well as citizens of their adopted, country, as Irishmen
and Americans." Here we have an avowal directly of an organization
to promote a foreign interest in this country! . . . .

It is notorious that the excitement respecting the Roman Catholic
emigrant has existed scarcely a year. The exposure of foreign designs
through the Roman Catholic religion, and the discussions arising out
of it, all the riotous conduct of Catholics and others, and among other
things the public notices of these very *organizations*, have all occured
within the last year. But the organizations of the Catholics, and particularly of the Irish, are of many years standing. The Society at
Boston above quoted, and one of the most recent, was formed long
before any excitement on the subject "two years ago," says the *Catholic
Diary*. It was discovering these organizations, already formed on the
part of foreigners, that excited the jealousy and distrust on the part
of the American people.

### 10.  A German Traveler's Impressions[1]

Complaints have been made against the morals and character of
many of the immigrants; and a fear has arisen that they will convert
North America into a sort of Botany Bay. It is true that many
criminals, idlers, malcontents, and the like, seek here a place of refuge,

[1] Extract from Friedrich Ludwig George von Raumer, *America and the American
People*, translated from the German by William W. Turner (New York, 1846), pp.
146–50.

but their number is proportionately very small, and bitter experience or punishment forces them to begin a new life in the New World.

The United States proffer to immigrants the noblest moral and political education; and he who rejects it, who proudly considers himself above it, who trusts more to luck than to prudence and sagacity, who thinks to become rich without exertion, or perhaps to renovate and revolutionize mature America with superficial theories, will soon and rightly find himself deceived in his foolish anticipation.

On the whole the German settlers are highly commended as industrious, moral, persevering, and adverse to novelty and change. Hence they are useful as a restraining, tranquilizing counterpoise to the unquietness of other inhabitants. But unhappily there are exceptions to this rule also. One German traveler relates how he was deserted and cheated by some of his countrymen to whom he had shown kindness; and another mentions that a German clergyman in America said to him: "The German teachers here, like many of their countrymen, have acted like complete rogues. One ran away with a foster-daughter of mine; and another, a music teacher whom I had recommended, made off, after cheating a number of people and leaving many debts behind him, so that one is almost ashamed to speak German or to bear a German name."

While for my own part I heard no complaints against the Germans and nothing but praises of them, the reproaches cast upon the Irish were loud and frequent. The blending of this foreign stock with the Germanic, in America as in England, is certainly very difficult; still even those who dislike them cannot deny that on the whole they are industrious and contented, and in the second generation are scarcely to be distinguished from those of a different origin. Where, too, one considers what an immense leap it is from Irish bondage to American citizenship, one ought to hold them excusable, if in excess of joy at their newly acquired freedom they fall into a few errors and extravagances. It is complained that they suffer themselves to be led and dictated to by their priests; but it may be questioned whether this influence is more hurtful than that of many other demagogues.

Still more numerous than the rogueries of immigrants are the follies which they enact to their own hurt; as for instance when one goes to America to teach Sanscrit, and another to get for himself the situation of butler to a prince, and for his wife the care of the plate. . . . .

In recent times a party has been formed, chiefly in some of the seaport towns, which takes to itself the name of Native Americans. Their object is to throw difficulties in the way of immigration, and they wish to prevent naturalization until after a residence of twenty-five years; because, as they say, no immigrant can acquire the necessary knowledge in a shorter time, and a too early qualification of foreigners abridges and undermines the rights of native citizens.[1]

Even granting the truth of the loudly proclaimed and probably too well founded censure that these views and doctrines proceed mostly from business jealousy and religious intolerance (toward the Irish catholics), they still require a satisfactory investigation, and the movement might more properly be termed a European than a truly American one. When even in the dangerous times of the French Revolution, the Alien Law was rejected as imprudent, unjust, and un-American, how can it now be sought, in quieter times and on weaker grounds, not merely to revive it, but to render it more severe? In comparison with the immense number of native votes, those of the foreigners annually admitted to the rank of citizens are wholly insignificant and indecisive; besides which most of them are divided amongst the different political parties. Again, if some few venture to vote, as it is complained they do, before the expiration of the time prescribed, the fault lies, not in the perfectly clear and satisfactory laws, but in the fact that the natives and magistrates are afraid to apply the laws, or wink at abuses in order to bring the majority of votes on their side.[2] Let the natives bind and engage themselves to support these admirable laws; but let them not for that purpose surrender all the principles of American liberty, and in pretended patriotic songs (as in Philadelphia) proclaim fire and sword against foreigners, and then put their own exhortations into effect.

Time is not the only measure or the only source of a citizen's understanding and knowledge; many a newcomer stands at once on a par with the natives as regards these qualifications, and what he will not learn in five years he will probably never learn at all. Moreover it is not intended, or at least is not possible, that every American citizen should fully comprehend the most difficult questions of political science; confidence in the leading men of the country is always necessary. . . . .

[1] [A footnote referring to the early "passenger acts" is omitted as irrelevant at this point.

[2] [Von Raumer adds in an explanatory note, "Judge Elliot in Louisiana sold 1,700 false certificates of citizenship for $17,000; for which he was properly punished. It is asserted, however, that even in New York, out of 40,000 voters, only about a couple of hundred vote without having the right to do so."]

Some indeed, impelled by ignorance or passion, assert that one of the great American parties can suddenly convert and has converted whole masses of foreigners (contrary to the provisions of the law, and unnoticed or uncensured by their opponents) into citizens having the power to vote, and has thus gained the victory in the presidential contest; but such an absurdity is not deserving of a serious refutation. I will merely remind the reader that 40,000 newcomers per annum certainly bring with them a million of property, and their yearly labor is to be estimated at more than five times as much. And yet it is sought to turn away this importation, and send it to other countries.

Most of the governments of Europe, notwithstanding their tendency to govern too much, have made but very few regulations, and those for the most part absurd, with respect to emigration. Their only thought was to throw obstacles in its way—nay, it was regarded as a sort of crime, or else as an infectious disease; while it was rarely that anything was done or could be done to remove the causes that made the emigrants averse to a longer abode in their native land. *Where the threefold pressure of standing armies, enormous taxes, and ecclesiastical domination continues*, many, even where there is no excess of population, will seek to better their condition by emigration.

The spreading of the human race over the whole earth and the reducing of all the land to cultivation, is moreover a commendable object, designed by Providence itself, and to which governments should lend a suitable degree of assistance by causing accurate inquiries to be pursued in all directions, by disseminating information, and appointing honest men to protect the emigrants against error and fraud, etc.

## 11. Difficulties of Adjustment[1]

Among the special phenomena of our time, the *Emigration* which is going forward on so large a scale *from the old world into the new*, is one that well deserves a thorough consideration. . . . . One is involuntarily reminded by it of those migrations of whole tribes, which preceded the Etrurian and Grecian states, of the *Völkerwanderung* that helped to bring in the Middle Ages, of the crusades and their associated schemes of colonization, which broke the way for the Reformation and introduced into Europe a new view of the world. True, the emigration of our time may easily be distinguished from these kindred manifestations. It is not the act of any one people as such; it is not

[1] Extract from "The Immigration," by W. J. Mann, in *Mercersburg Review*, II (1850), 620–630.

the result of religious fanaticism; it carries in it no warlike tendency; it is for the most part the fruit of what may be styled best *family need:* only in *Ireland* perhaps might we refer it more suitably to a real *national* need. It springs prevailingly, either from the inviting picture of future prosperity which the fancy of the would-be emigrant sets in contrast with the harsh realities of his previous condition, or from vexation and disappointment, in not being able with the best will and . . . . the best judgment, to get forward rightly in previously existing relations. In the case of the *German* indeed (with which we are here more particularly concerned), there comes in besides, in very many instances, his peculiar tendency to go out into the wide world, a sort of *Heimweh nach dem All* —that same *cosmopolite* feeling, which is the occasion at once of the genial all-sided humanism, as well as of the political weakness, of the German fatherland. There is America open before him, a new world; and with the opportunity of making it the home of his family, he follows without difficulty its full adoption as his proper country. . . . .

Many may be ready to say indeed, What good is there that can be done? Who can exercise an influence on these immense crowds, now pouring themselves on the shores of the new world? We grant it is no small task. But this precisely forms the strongest requisition on every man to do his part, and such vigorous concert of effort could not fail to have a good effect. And it is not to be concealed, that every single man must himself undergo a distinct influence from so mighty an influx of foreign life into the United States; so that every inhabitant of the country is more or less concerned in it, whether he choose to lay the fact to heart or not. The complaint is often repeated, *that immigration is bringing the most important institutions of the land into danger.* This may proceed often, we know, from the most impure motives, from a narrow-minded selfishness mistaking even its own interest, from extreme political short-sightedness, or from a generally contracted and malignant nature; but still it carries with it a side also of deeply earnest and solemn significance, which is entitled to serious attention. All goes to settle the reception which the foreigners must meet, on the part of the community whose citizenship they come to share. On the whole, both the General Government and the separate States treat the immigration with every sort of encouragement; and from this it is reasonable to conclude, that those who represent the highest intelligence of the country, not only apprehend no injury to the nation from the enormous accession it is gaining to its population, but expect from it rather the most real advantage. . . . .

The numerical amount of the immigration must itself satisfy any one who considers it without prejudice, that aside from all other relations its mere mass alone forms a highly significant factor, notwithstanding the immense extent of territory over which it is spread. Several thousand came lately in only two days into a single town of the United States; and from the present condition of Europe, the new facilities that are offered for going abroad, and the political views also gaining ground more and more in the old world, it may be concluded, that if no special unforeseen events interpose a bar, the movement for a long time to come will increase rather than diminish. In three months, during the present year, as many as ninety-five thousand emigrants came into the harbour of New York. Great as the West of our continent is, if such numbers are to be taken as anything like a measure, it will not need centuries to cover it with as full a population beyond St. Louis as is found now in any part of the East. . . . .

And now—the surplus population of this old Europe supplies the mass of our immigration. The Irishman, who there learned to know and hate Protestantism as the great cause of his country's misery, comes here, and sees Romanism and Protestantism peacefully and with fully equal rights dwelling side by side. The French Socialist, on the wide field of the United States, may reduce his theory to practice, and so long as he is not against the law, the law is not against him, but on his side. The German Rationalist, whose heart resented in Germany the necessity of bringing his child to baptism, can here turn his back on Christianity, and the Church will look upon his open honest withdrawal as her real gain. But is not all this along with our circumstances generally a proof, that we have pushed the centrifugalism of our time to its farthest extreme, have clothed the individual with the rights of the absolute? We will not forget however, that this land of liberty has not had within it heretofore in full force the antagonisms, which are now making themselves more and more felt. The *Roman Catholic Church* is assuming every year a more commanding form; the state of Protestantism grows confused and helpless; the land of liberty is in a fair way to become the asylum and home of the *Jesuits*, expelled from despotic countries; here, where pious sentiment and the fear of God should sanctify law and usage and so uphold our freedom, *infidelity* rears its altars; here, where nothing should pass for right but actual righteousness, the *Red Republican* finds a retreat, whose bloodthirsty mind seeks to advance right by wrong, and peace with the wild spirit of revenge; under the protection of our laws, the Socialist and

Communist, who proclaims property to be theft and possession crime, may spread his doctrine in peace. Wonderful land, which for every poison offers an antidote, where every stone, under superior command, turns itself into bread and every curse into a blessing! Yet—perhaps we say too much, and believe too soon that we should first only hope and wish. May faith among us, and freedom and peace, never be endangered by foreign influence! . . . .

With this brief notice of the possible bearings of such vast immigration on our country, and the course of its history, showing that it brings with it certain dangers to be feared along with all its advantages, let us now take note on the other side of the *manifold seductions and snares, which the free new world offers to the bewildered strangers thus brought into its bosom.* If the immigration in their case often works badly for the individual at least, though a vast benefit for the whole, the reason lies to a great extent in this, that the new comers are thrown immediately into relations whose questionable operation it is not hard to understand. With all of us custom does much, that must otherwise be enforced by law and punishment. If we do much that is bad through custom, we do much that is good also out of custom, for which of course we deserve no thanks. The place where we have lived surrounds us with countless securities for our moral personality. Not only has the law there become usage, but usage has also grown into law. . . . . The control which one citizen in this way exercises over another, is of more account than any written law. With this goes the work of every man's calling, the blessing of which is mainly just that it calls him to diligence and work. Add the love of family, the dearest regard of the heart, and we have named the most powerful factors that go in regular civil life to hold the individual to the track of a true moral co-operation for the general good. But now take away at once all these restraints, tear the man completely out of this complex chain of motives—and into what danger is he not hurled! If he be without inward morality, he must fall a prey wholly to his passions; the last bands that held him are rent asunder; the last restraining considerations are gone; and then the depth into which he plunges will be in proportion as his new connections may prove to be without salutary force. . . . .

For by far the greatest number of emigrants, the sudden breaking up of their past relations of itself involves serious danger. It may be with them a deliverance from many oppressive restraints, but along with this goes the rupture of many a wholesome living moral check. Now begins however, from the point of quitting home, a still more dangerous period. This is the time strictly of *migration*. It comprehends with the most of our German emigrants a term of from three to six months. . . . .

More deplorable subjects than those into whose hands they generally fall at the stations and ports they pass through, are scarcely to be found in common prisons. In Germany itself indeed religious care has provided, in the large cities, at least some check on vice and temptation, and police regulations are put in force. But let any one go to a sea-port like Havre in France. There is to be found continually a set of men, who have been forced to quit Germany, and with the purpose of going to America or who can say by what other chance have got to this place, where they now seek to keep up their life by making themselves busy with the emigrants. In all our travels in different countries, we have never met with more miserable men, a class more destitute of morality, than these land sharks, who lie in wait for those that thus come by thousands from Germany, thrust themselves upon them as countrymen and friends . . . . detain their victims, plunder them, and abuse their inexperience in the most shameful way. . . . . The same dangers and temptations, however, repeat themselves to a great extent in the American sea-ports; and here also it is mainly again German idlers and drunkards, that suck out of the emigrant both his money and his morals, and turn his head especially by their godless talk before him of liberty and independence, deceiving him and filling him with the most false conceptions of the new land of promise, its customs and its rights. There is no doubt but that the subsequent course of life for very many emigrants has been determined in a great measure by the companions into whose hands they fell during the first three weeks of their life in the new world. . . . . Many a German man who had his trade in the old world, has come here, and not knowing at once how to continue it has thankfully hearkened to the advice of his officious friends, and set up forthwith a *beer-shop* or drinking grocery; by which he has neither become a useful citizen, nor led his family in a way of safety—nay, has been himself perhaps the first victim. How many hundred such beer houses, kept mostly by Germans, there are at this time in our cities! . . . . Every orderly German at the same time must suffer from it, in more than the reputation simply of his nation. Let any one only pass on Sundays by our German beer-shops. . . . . The taverns are full, but how is it with the churches? We have perhaps 30,000 Protestant Germans in Philadelphia alone. Of these not more than 3,000 at most ordinarily attend church on Sundays. But where are the rest? Who can be foolish enough to expect much good from this state of things, as regards domestic life, social position, or public influence? However we may dislike all extreme principles and one-sided views, and though we may find in the relations of the foreigners themselves much to account for such evils, and excuse what can bear excuse, the case is still one of real anxiety, that calls for the most vigorous and decisive remedies, and that should stir the heart especially of every capable German to sorrowful feeling, and engage him to the most earnest counteraction both in word and deed.

## 12.  A Plea for the Irish Immigrant[1]

In any other nation than ours, it would have seemed natural to ask first, what view the National Government took of this annual invasion of three or four hundred thousand souls; and to have begun by enumerating the inducements offered by it to emigrants, the information it extends to them; its oversight of their movement, and its care of their sick and ignorant.

It happens, however, that by an exaggeration of the let-alone system, really lamentable in its consequences, the National Government, having arranged even its naturalization laws with difficulty, has passed by, almost entirely, all other considerations in this matter.

There is an annual return made by the Department of State at Washington of the number of males and females who have arrived in the United States from different countries, in the year ending on the 30th of September. . . . . Defective as its plan, its execution has never come up even to that.

The Supreme Court of the United States, February 7, 1849, decided the emigration laws then existing, of the Northern States, to be unconstitutional. The Government thus forced on those states the roundabout way in which they now collect their emigration revenue.[2] . . . .

These two efforts of the National Government and the law regulating ships for passage are, with the partial exception of the old naturalization laws, the only notice it has taken of the fact that a world of

[1] Extract from Edward Everett Hale, *Letters on Irish Emigration* (Boston, 1852), pp. 47–58.

[2] [The so-called "commutation" system which was substituted for the head tax after the decision of the Supreme Court in the so-called "Passenger Cases" (1849), 48 U.S. 282. For extracts from the Supreme Court opinion in the series of so-called "Passenger Cases" and for an account of the commutation system, see E. Abbott, *Immigration: Select Documents and Case Records*, p. 151 and p. 168.]

emigrants is landing in America, whose numbers are now nearly 400,000 a year. They show the only provision it makes for their comfort on arrival, or for forwarding them to its distant Western lands, which they are to occupy and make valuable. . . . .

It is the interest of every section of the country to see that the National Government does take the whole care, and the humane care of newly arrived emigrants into its hands. . . . .

I have intentionally passed over to this point . . . . a suggestion of the great value of emigration . . . . the nature and the immensity of the gift which God has thus made to this nation.

As to its nature, there needs here to be said only this, that the Irish emigration, as we see it, the Celtic Exodus, as it has been called, seems as clearly to belong to the established, uninterrupted fortune of the Celtic race, as if it had been the immediate result of battle and bloody defeat. . . . . Defeats have driven them further and further westward, and have absorbed more and more of their race, either to enrich the battle-fields, or to serve as the slaves or as the wives of the conquerors, until the last two centuries have seen it pure only in its western fast-nesses. Through those centuries it has stood at bay on the headlands of western England and France, and, I suppose, Spain: it has had full inhabitancy, though not the government, of most of Ireland and northern Scotland. Those points of the world are . . . . the last rest-ing-places where a great gallant race has been driven in by its conquer-ors, before their last destructive attack upon it.

This last attack the conquerors have now made; not intentionally, but because they did not know how to resist their destiny; not as Cromwell destroyed the Irish at Drogheda . . . . but in the more destructive, though more kindly meant, invasion of modern systems of agriculture, manufactures, and commerce. The untaught and wretched Irish Celt, of the pure blood, could no more stand the compe-tition of the well-compacted English social system than could his progenitors or their kinsmen stand the close-knit discipline of Caesar's legions. In the effort to stand it, poor Ireland counts her millions of slain. They have died of deaths more terrible than battle, and the rest, conscious of their last defeat, have nothing left for it but to flee farther yet westward, and leave their old homes to this invasion which will not end.

But this westward faring [of the Celtic race] is now a plunge into the sea. And, at just the needed moment, Providence sends the needed means to relieve it. For, till times quite recent, till the large shipments, that is, of cotton eastward from this country, the large shipments of men and women westward would have been impossible at the cheap rates which, only, have made them any relief to Ireland. As it is they are the only relief after this last struggle of hers. The beaten Celts pass westward again. The American empty cotton ships are lying ready to pick up the defeated stragglers. But it is no longer an emigration in mass; this time it has no chief, like those of which Caesar tells us; it has no discipline; it is only a horde of discouraged, starved, beaten men and women. . . . .

The Irish emigration, then, is the dispersion, after its last defeat, of a great race of men, which, in one way or another, has been undergoing defeat for centuries. In the order of history it is our duty to receive the scattered fugitives, give them welcome, absorb them into our own society, and make of them what we can. This point of view suggests the whole spirit in which in these letters I speak of them. They are fugitives from defeat, or, without a metaphor, fugitives from slavery. Every Irishman who leaves Ireland for America seems to be as really driven thence, by the intentional or unintentional arrangements of stronger nations, as if he had made a stand in fight on the beach at Galway, and been driven by charged bayonets into the sea. We are, or ought to be, welcoming these last wrecks of so many centuries of retreat. And if I speak bitterly of the utter inattention in which our government leaves this duty, of the complete want of system of our State Legislature, and its complete recklessness of the fact that these undisciplined stragglers are taking refuge here, it will be because there is a shameless inconsistency in such indifference. Here in Massachusetts we writhe and struggle, really with one heart, lest we return one fugitive who can possibly be saved to Southern slavery; but when there come these fugitives from "Irish Bastilles," as they call them, we tax them first and neglect them afterwards, and provide by statute, and take care, in fact, to send back to Ireland at the public expense, poor creatures who are as entirely fugitives from a grinding slavery as if their flight had been north instead of west. . . . .

That inefficiency of the pure Celtic race furnishes the answer to the question: How much use are the Irish to us in America? The Native American answer is, "none at all." And the Native American policy is to keep them away.

A profound mistake, I believe, for the precise reason that, in the pure blood they are so inefficient as compared with the Saxon and other Germanic races which receive them, I am willing to adopt the Native

American point of view, and to speak with an *esprit du corps*, as one of the race invaded.

If this were a superior race, a race of superior ability coming in on us, we might well complain. If I were a Japanese, with Japanese *esprit du corps*, I should have every reason to keep up the Japanese policy, and exclude, as they do, all races superior in practical ability, from coming in. They would be sure to rise above me and mine and crush us down. Thus the free blacks in Baltimore, complain very naturally, of the emigration thither of the Germans. The Germans work better and cheaper than the blacks can, bring into competition the superior executive faculty of the white race, and the poor blacks, whose ability is in other directions, are crowded out, and have to go to the wall. Now if we Americans were likewise inferior in ability of such sorts to the Celts, we might complain too. But this is not true. We are here, well organized and well trained, masters of the soil, the very race before which they have yielded everywhere besides. It must be, that when they come in among us, they come to lift us up. As sure as water and oil each finds its level they will find theirs. So far as they are mere hand-workers they must sustain the head-workers, or those who have any element of intellectual ability. Their inferiority as a race compels them to go to the bottom; and the consequence is that we are, all of us, the higher lifted because they are here. . . . . .

It is clear enough, however, that there must, in any community, be manual labor. The soil is to be tilled and the roads built and repaired. If it has more than men enough for this, some can be released to higher duties. The number so released depends on the degree of its civilization. For in merely barbarous communities, the labor of a family only keeps that one family alive. Then there is no surplus for higher occupations. In civilized communities one hand-working family can produce much more than it will consume of the necessities of life. There are therefore, in proportion, laborers released for duties of a higher grade.

This is all simple and of course. If into the vessel of oil you pour water, the water floats the oil above itself on its surface. If into the civilized community made up of hand-workers, and workers in higher grades, you pour in an infusion of a population competent at first only to the simplest hand-work, they take the lowest place, and lift the others into higher places. They do the manual labor. They do it most cheaply, and so they leave those, whom they find, free to other and more agreeable walks of duty. Thus, practically, at this moment, our simplest drudgery of factory work and farm work comes into the hands of Irishmen. It does not follow that the natives who must otherwise have performed it do nothing or starve. They are simply pushed up, into foremen of factories, superintendents of farms, railway agents, machinists, inventors, teachers, artists, etc.; filling classes of society, some of which we could not else have had so well; some of which we could not have had at all.

I say they do not starve; for there is, as yet, no limit to the country's production; and by every laboring man who arrives, the danger of starvation becomes less and less. Nor is there any danger of a want of employment. Employment under our institutions, is not a fixed quantity, which cannot be enlarged. The more men there are, the more employment there is; in one walk or another.

Of course the rate of money wages paid does not affect the transaction; for the plethora of manual labor will keep down the price of the necessities of life, so that the money rates of wages may range as they choose. . . . .

In fact, by every spade blow which foreign hands have driven, by every child which foreign mothers in their own homes have reared to this country, is the country richer for the coming of the foreigner. By the worth of every spade blow, by the worth of every child would the country be poorer if it debarred them from this *privilege*, of doing its meanest work, and of taking its hardest fare, and yet, as that work is the only work absolutely necessary, the only work which we must have; as theirs is the only duty which we cannot do without, into *their* places would come those who are in more thoughtful duty yet. The whole organization of our society must descend: the whole fabric of our civilization be degraded. That would be the end of your quarantine, of your bars and bolts, of your successful restrictions. You would still have laborers on the railroad, and canal, and factory. Those you must have! You would have pressed into that service those fit for better things; and the restriction you have made is a surrender of so much civilization, so much wealth, so much refinement. You thought these men were ignorant ditchers and delvers. To your eye they were. But God, when he supplied them, was freeing other laborers for your higher and wider uses, to be your men of ingenuity and of trade, and of letters. And he punishes your unkindness, by such a change of the duties of your own people, that from the unknown regions of what might have been, you have kept artists and poets, and statesmen who were coming in upon you, of your own blood and land and lineage. You have chained them to the spade, and the barrow, and the pickaxe.

For if you will not let the foreigner stand upon your land even to hew your wood or to draw your water, you will chain down to that service the Burns, the Phaedrus, the Homer, who might have risen and triumphed among your own sons! . . . .

It is true, that to attain the full use of this gift [immigration], the emigrant must be cared for. In other words, the country must open its hand to receive the offering of Europe. . . . . The stranger cannot serve the country while he is a stranger. He must be a part of it. He must, for the purpose we seek, profit by the measure of its civilization. He must be directed by its intelligence. His children must grow up in its institutions. He must be, not in a clan in a city, surrounded by his own race. That is only to try a little longer the experiment which for centuries has failed. He must plunge, or be plunged, into his new home.

And, therefore, as I have intimated already, private action and public policy in this matter should unite to "stimulate the absorbents," that each little duct, the country through, may drink its share, of those drops which some do not taste at all, of the perpetual Westward flood, as it comes in.

There is no reason for despair about this. The process goes on to a much greater extent than is generally supposed. It is true we hear most of the clanned Irish in the large cities. This is of course. They are the only part of the emigration from whom we can hear much. But, from a hasty comparison of memoranda, I should say that there were not more than 120,000 of Irish birth in New York city, 30,000 in Boston, 30,000 in Philadelphia, 10,000 in Baltimore, 10,000 in Providence, 8,000 in Lowell.

Of Pittsburgh, Cincinnati, and St. Louis, I cannot speak; but I doubt if in any other place in America, there is a larger clan than the least of these.

The total of these, say 250,000, leaves nearly 2,000,000 Irish-born emigrants, who have been scattered up and down, in smaller localities, through the land.

So much has been done. Every consideration of humanity and policy demands that, by every means the process should be carried farther, out to the least subdivision possible.

Private men may do their duty to the emigration, by employing, training, teaching, and directing the emigrant; even to the point of making work on purpose to employ him. He, who takes the newest comer does most. . . . . She who teaches a servant girl to read does a great deal. The family which adopts an orphan of the foreign blood does more than its share. For, as I have said, the proportion as yet is but eight emigrants to every hundred natives.

The State should stop at once its effort to sweep them back. It cannot do it. It ought not to do it. It should welcome them; register them; send them at once to the labor-needing regions; care for them if sick; and end, by a system, all that mass of unsystematic statute which handles them as outcasts or Pariahs.

The Federal Government, having all the power, should use it; not growling in its manger, as it does, and only hindering those, upon whom, in its negligence, the duty falls.

And Nation, State, or man should feel that the Emigration is the greatest instead of the least element of our material prosperity; an element which should brace us to meet and handle any difficulties, real or fancied, which it may bring to our institutions of politics or of religion.

### 13.   Irish Attitude to Know-Nothingism[1]

Since the establishment of the *Citizen*, we have uniformly urged upon Irish citizens that they should not act together as Irishmen—should not isolate themselves from other American parties, should not place themselves in the hands of Irish priests, still less of Irish grog-sellers, to be disposed of as a political capital. We have made bold to propound the doctrine, that every Irish voter ought to vote upon his individual judgment about measures and men—not because the "Irish vote" goes this way or the other; that there ought, in short, to be no *Irish vote* at all; but that Irishmen in America should be so entirely absorbed into the American system as to be indifferently Democrats or Whigs, Hards, Softs, Silver-greys—anything except Garrisonian abolitionists.

But there is an element coming in, that alters the whole case. Here come a set of ignorant malignants, taking it upon them to represent the great nation, to maintain its honor and to guard its religion (the vagabonds!) and they say to their Irish fellow-citizens, "No, you shall never become wholly American—you are to be isolated for ever—you are unfit to enjoy the liberties, or to exercise the franchises of Americans —your religion is not to our taste—your brogue is unmusical to our ears."

Can there be any doubt as to how any Irish, or any German citizen,

[1] Extract from the *Citizen*, I (New York City, October 28, 1854), 681.

ought to treat these creatures? In this one case, at any rate, foreign-born men *are* isolated, though not by their own act. Whatever may be their political predilections, and however various on other points, here, at least, they must be one. No Irish voter, no German citizen, can, without abject disgrace, support—we do not say a No-Nothing candidate, but any candidate who courts or relies upon, or does not repudiate and spit upon, No-Nothing support.

Whosoever shall act otherwise at the approaching elections fawns upon the foot that spurns him, kisses the hand that would wrest the franchise from his children, and confesses that he and his are content to be helots and Pariahs in the free land of their adoption, as their strong tyrants made them Pariahs and helots in the land of their birth!

### 14. An Irish View of the Disbanding of Foreign Militia Companies[1]

"DISARMING OF CITIZENS—THE FIRST STEP TOWARDS
DESPOTISM," JANUARY 27, 1855

. . . . In the first place we must remark the fact which no doubt Governor Gardner knows well enough—that the separate military organizations, whether of Irish or of German citizens, although certainly an evil, are fully as much owing to the separate organizations of native Americans as to any disposition on the part of either Irish or Germans to isolate themselves. There are companies in New York which do not admit a foreign-born soldier, and doubtless in Boston too. These native Americans will not take the word of command from a foreign-born officer; so that if a naturalized citizen, no matter how educated and intelligent, were even admitted into these corps, he must be a full private. The plain consequence is that naturalized citizens desirous of bearing arms under the flag of their adopted country, if they will not submit to humiliation, *must* form corps of their own. We say this is an evil; but it is directly produced by the intolerance of the natives; yet the natives think themselves entitled to cry out in condemnation of it.

Since the *Citizen* was established, seeing that the existence of

[1] These two editorials by John Mitchel are taken from the *Citizen*, II (New York City, 1855), 56 and 632. The first one deals with the order given by Governor Gardner of Massachusetts, an early advocate of Americanization, ordering the disbanding of all militia companies whose members were born in other countries, that is, "companies composed of men of foreign birth." Governor Gardner called his order a step toward "Americanizing America." In the second editorial John Mitchel comments on a similar order by Governor Minor of Connecticut.

separate Irish, German, and Native American companies could not be helped, we have earnestly endeavored to impress upon the Irish soldier, what indeed we believe every Irish soldier feels without being tutored—that he bears arms solely for his adopted country, whose laws he is bound to obey, and whose flag and constitution he is to defend with his life. We have loudly condemned the anomaly and absurdity of what is called "the Irish vote" (another mischief invented and used by American politicians) and exhorted our countrymen *not* to vote in masses or in batches, as Irishmen, nor suffer electioneering intriguers to "make capital" of them by a few blarneying phrases. We have preached to them that here they are never to forget they are Americans, and exhorted them to be obedient to the laws, and to rely on the justice of their fellow-citizens and on the majesty of the constitution.

We repeat that advice still more earnestly *now*. Let no irritation at an insolent aggression tempt us to be false to the obligations we have taken upon us. In the difficulties that are approaching, let the Know-Nothings be still, as they are now, wholly in the wrong.

But what is of more importance still—submit to no brand of inferiority, no shadow of disparagement, at the hand of these natives. You are their equals by law; you are their equals every way. Disbandment of a military company is a direct imputation of *misconduct;* and we are happy to find that Colonel Butler of Lowell refuses to brook the outrage. He declines to transmit the order for disbandment to his captains, invites a Court Martial, and appeals to the law—for there is still an appeal to the law. And the Shields' Artillery of Boston have taken action in the case. If however the final decision be against them and against Col. Butler, and if the military companies of foreign birth are actually dismissed and disbanded, then for every musket given in to the State Armory, let three be purchased forthwith: let independent companies be formed, thrice as numerous as the disbanded corps—there are no Arms Acts here yet—and let every "foreigner" be drilled and trained, and have his arms always ready. For you may be very sure (having some experience in the matter) that those who begin by disarming you, mean to do you a mischief. . . . .

It is hardly to be conceived that the madness of faction and the insolence of race will proceed to such a length as to disarm independent companies, or private men. If they *do*, then the Constitution is at an end—the allegiance you have sworn to this Republic is annulled.

Would to God that thoughtful and just Americans would bethink themselves in time. They are strong: they far outnumber the foreign born: they are proud and flushed with national glory and prosperity; doubtless they *can* if they will, do great and grievous wrong to a race that has never wronged them; but seriously, earnestly we assure them, the naturalized citizens will not submit. This senseless feud must be reconciled; there must be peace; peace or else a war of extermination. We are here on American ground, either as citizens or as enemies.

"MORE DISBANDMENT OF CITIZEN SOLDIERS," OCTOBER 6, 1855

The Know-Nothing tyrant of Connecticut has imitated the example of his brother of Massachusetts. Minor, true to the proscriptive principles of the Order, has followed Gardner, and who will next follow both we know not; but of this we are certain, that American citizens, of Irish birth, ought to be prepared for the worst. By these arbitrary acts, the knaves and fanatics of New England are trampling on the Constitution of the United States, which knows no distinction as regards the militia of the country between the citizen of native and the citizen of foreign birth. Where this is to end, Heaven only knows; but the effect of it ought to be, to stimulate the Irish in America to greater exertions for the freedom of the land that bore them, in order that there they may enjoy in peace that liberty and independence, which, it seems, can only be secured to them by a continual warfare. The right to carry arms is equally the right of every citizen; and to strip a citizen of that right, without any other cause than the place of his birth, is an outrage upon American liberty, and upon the Federal Constitution, which guarantees to all immigrants who become citizens, the same rights, privileges, and immunities that belong to the native born. The following letter will show that some men in this free land only lack the power to be the most truculent despots that ever disgraced any country.

BRIDGEPORT, CONN., September 29, 1855

TO THE EDITOR OF THE CITIZEN:

I wish to announce to my fellow-countrymen, through the columns of the *Citizen*, that our Know-Nothing despot, Gov. Minor, has at length issued the order to disband the six Irish companies in this state. For this he had not the shadow of an excuse, they having at all times obeyed the laws in the smallest particular. In fact, you must think he was hard pushed when it took three Adjutant Generals to issue the order. The first, Hollister, was a whig; he refused, and was dismissed. The second, Hodge, who some say is a Know-Nothing, was then appointed, but he was too honest for such dirty work;

he saw some of the companies at their fall parade, and found there was nothing worthy of censure in their appearance or conduct; he likewise refused, and was dismissed. At length there was a proper person found, and our petty tyrant succeeded in pouring out the vials of his wrath on our devoted heads. I suppose, poor man, he is immensely inflated with the idea that he has saved Connecticut from having been carried on the points of our bayonets, and laid at the feet of his Holiness the Pope. . . . .

Yours truly,

EDWARD N. GOODWIN

The writer of the foregoing letter seeks our advice. We have no hesitation in giving it, and it is this. Keep up the organizations as independent companies, and just as if nothing occurred. Drill and parade more than ever. Purchase, as it is your right to do, arms which you can call your own. The men who seek to disarm you mean mischief. Baffle their base designs by purchasing weapons over which they can exercise no control. With these be ready at all times to defend your adopted or native country, as the occasion may arise; to defend perhaps or sell dearly your lives, as it was lately necessary for citizens of foreign birth to do at Louisville. Meantime, offer no physical resistance to the will of the despot. Await the decision of the courts in the case of the Massachusetts companies, and prosecute your own rights in the courts of Connecticut; in order that we may see how far the tribunals of justice will sanction the wanton acts of a faction who abuse their brief power in depriving peaceable citizens of their inalienable rights.

### 15.  "The Foreign Vote," A Reply to the Know Nothings[1]

But we are further told, that Catholics in this country stand aloof from their Protestant fellow-citizens, and form a virtually separate society, having neither feelings nor interests in common with others. . . . .

Catholics, especially those of foreign birth, vote together [we are told] and vote for a particular political party; the liberties of our country are therefore [said to be] endangered from this constantly augmenting foreign influence. This charge is groundless, both in its facts and in its inferences. . . . .

[1] Extract from Martin J. Spalding, *Miscellanea: Comprising Reviews, Lectures, and Essays, on Historical, Theological, and Miscellaneous Subjects* (Louisville, Ky.: 1855), pp. xlviii, lii–lviii.

The following candid and sensible remarks from the *Boston Post*, a political print of some standing, contains so much sound reasoning on this subject, based upon facts tending to show the glaring absurdity of the charge that "foreigners are taking the country," that we will be pardoned for republishing them entire:

It is said that we shall be overrun with foreigners; that they will rise upon native citizens and overpower them; that Catholicism will prevail and deprive America of its liberties. These assertions have been reiterated so often that thousands really fear such results. Take the former apprehension, and let facts, so far as they bear on the question of physical force, say how groundless that fear is. In the first place, for the whole time we have been a nation, it is a fact that no such attempt has been made; and if it ever should be made, such is the admirable working of our institutions, that the rule of a mob is utterly out of the question. Permanent success, even where the foreign population outweighs the native population, is an impossibility; for the whole force of the country would at once be invoked to suppress such a rule. In the next place, consider the utter folly, want of foresight, and suicidal policy of such an attempt, if it should ever be made. Of our now thirty millions of population one million[1] only are from Ireland; of the thirty-eight thousand churches that the census of 1850 shows as being in the country, the Catholic are set down at one thousand two hundred and twenty-one; and of the eighty-seven millions of church property, the Catholics have nine millions. Now, cannot this immense preponderance of Protestantism and of Americanism take care of itself? Is it not perfectly preposterous to suppose for a moment that the Irish Catholics will ever attempt to "rise," as the phrase is, with such an enormous disparity against them? It is due, it is but bare justice, to our foreign population to say, that not only has there been no attempt at rising, but their conduct—save only in cases when heated by liquor or otherwise excited—has been almost invariably that of peaceable citizens, submissive to the laws. They have a right to have such a certificate, as to the past, to stand in their favor; and when we consider their position among us, we believe there is no more danger of their "rising" than there is of the falling of the stars.

Much has been said and written of late years about the "foreign vote." Both parties, on the eve of elections, have been in the habit of courting "foreigners" who have thus, against their own choice and will, been singled out from the rest of the community and placed in a false and odious position by political demagogues for their own vile purposes. That they have been thus severed from their fellow-citizens, and insulted with the compliment of their influence as a separate body, has not been so much their fault, as it has been their misfortune. From

[1] The number is probably greater; but this does not affect the argument.

the successful party they have generally received—with a few honorable exceptions—little but coldness *after* the election; while from the party defeated, they have invariably received nothing but abuse and calumny. So they have been, without their own agency, placed between two fires, and have been caressed and outraged by turns. Any appeal made to them by politicians, in their character of religionists or foreigners, and not in that of American citizens, is manifestly an insult, whether so intended or not; and we trust that Catholics will always view such appeals in this light. Whenever it is question of state policy, they can have no interests different from those of their fellow-citizens. The laws which will be good for the latter, will be good for them; at least they can live under any system of equal legislation which will suit the Protestant majority, with whom they cheerfully share all the burdens of the country. . . . .

Never since the foundation of the republic has it been heard of that the Catholic bishops or clergy have taken an active part in conducting the proceedings of political conventions, or in fomenting political excitement, in the name of the religion of peace and love. They are not, and never have been, either abolitionists or free-soilers, ultraists or politico-religious alarmists. Nor have they ever ventured, either collectively or individually, to address huge remonstrances to Congress, threatening vengeance in the name of Almighty God, unless certain particular measures were passed or repealed! . . . .

Catholics of foreign birth are charged, in the same breath, with voting the democratic ticket, and with being the secret or open enemies of republican government! Is it then true, that a man cannot be a democrat without being a traitor to his country? If so, then have the destinies of this great republic been ruled, with very slight intermission, for nearly thirty years by an organized band of traitors, consisting of the vast majority of our population! . . . .

Those who are loudest in their denunciations of "foreigners" seem to forget what "foreigners" have done for the country. They have filled our army and navy; they have fought our battles; they have leveled our forests, peopled our vast unoccupied territory, and filled our cities with operatives and mechanics; they have dug our canals, built our turnpikes and railroads, and have thus promoted, more perhaps than any other class, the improvement of the country and the development of its vast resources; in a word, they have, in every way, largely contributed towards enhancing the wealth and increasing the prosperity of the Republic. Do they deserve nothing but bitter denunciation and unsparing invective for all these services? Are they to be branded as aliens and traitors, for having thus effectually labored to serve their adopted country?

But [we are told] they are foreigners in feeling and in interest, and they still prefer their own nationality to ours. We answer first, that if this their alleged feeling be excessive, and if it tend to diminish their love for the country of their adoption, it is certainly in so far reprehensible. But where is the evidence that this is the case? Has their lingering love for the country of their birth—with its glowing memories of early childhood and ripening manhood, of a mother's care and a sister's love—interfered in aught with their new class of duties as American citizens? Has it prevented their sharing cheerfully in the burdens, in the labors, and in the perils of the country? We believe not. Instead of their being unconcerned and indifferent, their chief fault, in the eyes of their enemies, lies precisely in the opposite—in their taking *too much* interest in the affairs of the Republic. We answer, in the second place, that this natural feeling of love for the country of their birth, growing as it does out of that cherished and honorable sentiment which we denominate patriotism, will, in the very nature of things, gradually diminish under the influence of new associations, until it will finally be absorbed into the one homogeneous nationality; and thus the evil—if it be an evil—will remedy itself. The only thing which can possibly keep it alive for any considerable time would be precisely the narrow and proscriptive policy adopted in regard to citizens of foreign birth by the Know Nothings and their sympathizers. The endeavor to stifle this feeling by clamor and violence will but increase its intensity.

We answer thirdly, that the influence of Catholicity tends strongly to break down all barriers of separate nationalities, and to bring about a brotherhood of citizens, in which the love of our common country and of one another would absorb every sectional feeling. Catholicity is of no nation, of no language, of no people; she knows no geographical bounds; she breaks down all the walls of separation between race and race, and she looks alike upon every people, and tribe, and caste. Her views are as enlarged as the territory which she inhabits; and this is as wide as the world. Jew and gentile, Greek and barbarian; Irish, German, French, English, and American, are all alike to her. In this country, to which people of so many nations have flocked for shelter against the evils they endured at home, we have a striking illustration of this truly Catholic spirit of the church. Germans, Irish, French, Italians,

Spaniards, Poles, Hungarians, Hollanders, Belgians, English, Scotch, and Welch; differing in language, in national customs, in prejudices—in everything human—are here brought together in the same church, professing the same faith, and worshiping like brothers at the same altars! The evident tendency of this principle is to level all sectional feelings and local prejudices, by enlarging the views of mankind, and thus to bring about harmony in society, based upon mutual forbearance and charity. . . . .

The character of the foreign immigration into this country has been undergoing a considerable change within the last few years; the German element now strongly predominates over the Irish, and perhaps the Protestant and infidel, over the Catholic. The disastrous issue of the revolutionary movements which convulsed all Europe in 1848–49, has thrown upon our shores masses of foreign political refugees, most of whom are infidels in religion, and red republicans, or destructionists of all social order, in politics. The greatest, and, in fact, the only real danger to the permanency of our republican institutions, is to be apprehended from this fast increasing class of foreigners, composed in general of men of desperate character and fortune—of outlaws from society, with the brand of infidelity upon their brow. Against the anarchical principles advocated by these men the Catholic church takes open ground; and she feels honored by their bitter hostility. It could not be otherwise. Her principles are eminently conservative in all questions of religion and of civil polity; theirs are radical and destructive in both. . . . .

If the lately organized secret political association warred against the pernicious principles maintained by such foreigners as these, we would not only have no cause to complain, but we would rather applaud their patriotic efforts in the cause of true freedom, and bid them Godspeed. But what is our astonishment to find that our boasted advocates of "American principles" instead of opposing, secretly or openly sympathize with these sworn enemies of all religion and of all social order, of God and man; as well as with the reckless and blood-stained Irish Orangemen! Say what you will, their efforts are directed almost solely against the Catholic element in the foreign immigration, and chiefly against the Irish Catholics. Their professions are belied by their acts, all of which point to Catholicity, as the victim whose ruin is to be accomplished, at all hazards, in this *free* and *republican* country. What else is indicated by the bloody riots gotten up by hired street brawlers against the Irish Catholics; what else by the wrecking and burning of Catholic churches? If the true policy of the country demands a revision or repeal of the naturalization laws, then bring about this result by fair, consistent, and honorable means; set about it in an open and manly manner, as men, as Americans, as Christians, not as cowards fearing the light of day, and skulking beneath the cover of darkness. If a new policy in regard to foreign immigrants is to be adopted, or if even the alien and sedition laws are to be re-enacted, let the country know your purpose in time, that all the true lovers of freedom may be prepared for the issue.

## 16. Irish Nationalism in the United States

### A[1]

FELLOW COUNTRYMEN:

The time has at length arrived for action. Every steamer that crosses the Atlantic, to our shores, brings intelligence of fresh disasters, distress, and difficulty to our old inveterate foe. Let us therefore unite in a bond of brotherhood to aid the cause of Liberty for Ireland.

The moment is propitious—the means are in our hands. Let us use them—use them with prudence, with caution; but with devoted energy and the determination of men, whose birthright is a heritage of vengeance—vengeance of seven centuries of wrong, of massacre, of spoliation, of rapine, of tyranny, deceit and treachery, unparalleled in the annals of the world's history.

Remember Limerick!—remember Skull and Skibberreen! And oh!

[1] Extract from "Address of the Massachusetts Irish Emigrant Aid Society to Irishmen in the United States," in the *Citizen*, II, (August 25, 1855), 536.

On August 14, 1855, in Boston a great state convention of Irishmen was held. Money was liberally subscribed, a platform was adopted, and this address was read and adopted.

The *New York Herald* said in commenting on this new organization:

". . . . These results are so evident to the most unreflecting mind, that on reading the programme of this association we could not help asking ourselves, if, under the cover of this visionary project, there did not lay concealed some practical scheme with objects having reference to the position of the Irish party in this country. What a powerful nucleus such an association would form for an organization intended to control our elections, and to neutralize the antagonistic influence of the Know-Nothing party? We do not say that such is the intention of its founders, but it is no great stretch of probabilities to suppose that, failing in its professed object, this new association may be easily diverted to mischievous interference in our home politics, and to the widening still further the breach which the agitation of such sectional interests has already made between the Irish and the native American parties. In any case we require to be on our guard."

remember the long, bitter years of exile, and think of that beautiful land, the home of your childhood and your affections; where repose the ashes of your fathers, and the martyrs of your race; and say, shall no effort be made to wrest the Island from the Robber Pirate who has so long held her in the grip of tyranny, depressed the energies of her people, and despoiled them of their inheritance?

It is for her exiled children to say, shall this cease, and Ireland be free, or shall the tyrant boast a perpetual tenant-right of the country.

The men in Ireland are ready, they wait only the assurance of our sympathy and aid, wisely taught by the experience of the past, they have ceased to bluster and brawl. The mind of the country is brooding over the vastness of the opportunity presented to it. It resembles the calm of a vast magazine, waiting but a spark of electricity to touch it, to burst forth in a terrible explosion. . . . .

We do not counsel you to form a fillibustering league, or raise an army of invasion, under the shadow of the stars and stripes, where we have found shelter and protection. We deprecate the violation of any law of the land in which we live. You will from time to time be advised of the course of action to pursue.

We now ask you to form in each city and town in the United States, a branch of the "Irish Emigrant Aid Society"; assemble in each locality at once; avoid all useless speeching; go to work; communicate with us; we will forward you charters and instructions to form "Auxiliary Aid Societies." Elect your own officers, appoint the most responsible man in your locality as Treasurer. Avoid all useless expense and parade. Work diligently and earnestly. Report to us the names of your subscribers and amount of money paid in. We, in turn, will report to the Supreme Directory, when elected, and then there will be unity of action; and we shall at all times know our strength and resources, and, when the moment of action comes, our leaders will not be working in doubt and darkness. . . . .

### B[1]

. . . . It is true that the character of the Association, its plan, and its principles, have all been grossly misrepresented by a large portion of the press, which, without sufficient inquiry, has thought proper to impute to it intentions altogether antagonistic to its honest and avowed

[1] Extract from manifesto of the supreme directory of the American Irish Emigrant Aid Society, "To the Friends of Ireland in America," in the *Citizen*, III (February 9, 1856), 89.

disposition. It is true that the Attorney General of the United States seems to have considered it his official duty to issue a letter of instructions to his subordinates in different quarters of the Union, contemplating a possible case when it might be necessary in his opinion, to restrain the organization in some act supposed to be violatory of the laws. And it is also true that certain well known citizens, presumed to be members of the Association, have been arrested—absurdly enough—at Cincinnati, and dragged before the United States Court sitting at that place, with the permission of the authorities of the government, at the instance and procurement of the British Consul there. But notwithstanding all this, it is now well understood that the Society, as presented in the Convention in New York, was composed, without exception, of respectable American citizens—either native born or naturalized; and that while every member present concurred in the opinion that it was the solemn duty of our government to avert, if within its power, so terrible a calamity as a state of war between Great Britain and this country, they unanimously adopted a series of resolutions, officially published at the time and presented as the Platform of the movement, and to which we again take leave to invite your most deliberate attention. The following are the resolutions to which we refer:

*Resolved*, That the first duty of all American citizens, whether native born or naturalized, of whatever political opinions, or of whatever nationalities, is to faithfully respect all their obligations of citizenship arising under the laws and constitution of our country.

*Resolved*, That neither the laws of nations nor the laws of the United States prevent any portion of the American people from meeting and combining to give weight to their opinions regarding the acts of a tyrant—to express their sympathy for the oppressed, whether an individual or a people—to encourage the down-trodden by a word of good cheer again to struggle for rights of which they may have been temporarily deprived by brute force, or to endeavor by combination, by facts, by arguments, and by action, so to shape the conduct of nations in certain contingencies as to induce this or any other when a lawful opportunity presents itself, to do some great act of moral historical justice.

*Resolved*, That the restoration to Ireland of that sovereignty which she has never willingly conceded; but against the desecration of which she has from time to time so constantly protested and her consequent relief from the worst government on the part of her vampire oppressor that the world ever saw, would be an act worthy of the noble character of American freedom, and under certain circumstances might be justified as well by the soundest national policy, as by the holiest sentiments of humanity. . . . .

### 17.   Loyalty of Immigrants to the Home Country[1]

The charge against the defendants is based upon Section 6 of the act of Congress of April 20, 1818 (3 vols., L. U.S. 447). It declares that:

If any person shall, within the territory or jurisdiction of the United States, begin or set on foot, or provide or prepare the means for, any military expedition or enterprise, to be carried on from thence against the territory or dominions of any foreign prince or state, or of any colony, district or people, with whom the United States are at peace, any person so offending, shall be deemed guilty of a high misdemeanor, and shall be fined not exceeding three thousand dollars, and imprisoned not more than three years.

In the progress of the argument, frequent references were made to the early executive and legislative history of the country, illustrative of its policy respecting the preservation of its relations with foreign powers with whom we were at peace. In the year 1794, during the second administration of Washington, the attention of Congress was earnestly called to this subject, by the arrogant interference with our national affairs of a diplomatic agent of the French government, threatening to disturb our amicable relations with Great Britain. As the result of this, the law of 1794 was enacted. After some intermediate legislation on this subject, the act of 1818 was passed, repealing all former laws, and embodying in it most of the provisions of the previous acts. Section 5 of the law of 1794 was transferred to, and became Section 6 of the act of 1818, before quoted. . . . .

No proposition can be clearer than that some definite act or acts, of which the mind can take cognizance, must be proved to sustain the charges against these defendants. Mere words, written or spoken, though indicative of the strongest desire and the most determined purpose to do the forbidden act, will not constitute the offense. It is true that proof of declarations of this nature, previously made, is admissible to explain or determine the character of acts, otherwise ambiguous or unintelligible; but for any other purpose they have no pertinency. . . . .

And in the first place, I will refer to the documentary or written and printed proofs before the court. These have been put in evidence by the prosecution, and it has been strenuously and forcibly insisted

---

[1] Extract from decision in case of *United States* v. *Samuel Lumsden et al.* (1856) (*Bond's Reports*, I, 9–27). In these proceedings against Samuel Lumsden and eleven others, all the defendants were natives of Ireland but naturalized citizens of the United States. The extracts from the decision explain the nature of the charge against them.

that they show the existence of societies and organizations among the Irish population of this country, the members of which are actuated by strong hostility to the government of Great Britain, and avow it as their purpose and desire to free their native land from British rule, and eventually to establish its independence. It is contended that in the furtherance of this design movements are in progress, with which these defendants are connected, which threaten to interrupt our peaceable relations with Great Britain, and which call loudly for the vigilant enforcement of the neutrality laws of the United States. . . . .

The first item of this documentary proof is the book containing the constitution and minutes of the proceedings of the Robert Emmet Club of Cincinnati, which is a branch of the Irish Emigrant Aid Association of Ohio. The defendants are all members of this club. It is a secret society, every member being required to take originally an oath —now a promise—whereby he pledges himself, in the presence of God, that he "will persevere in endeavoring to form a brotherhood of affection among Irishmen of every religious persuasion," and that he "will also persevere in his endeavors to uproot and overthrow English government in Ireland." Then follows an obligation to the effect that, under no circumstances, shall the member disclose the doings of the club, or inform on, or give evidence against, any one belonging to it, etc. It is also in evidence that the club have secret signs or passwords, by which the members are known to one another, and by which they obtain admission to any similar society elsewhere. In their constitution they avow, as one purpose of the organization, the subversion of the British power in Ireland. They also adopt the platform of the Massachusetts society, which has been in existence something more than a year. In that platform there are strong expressions of hostility to England, and of a desire to liberate Ireland from her power; and it avows a determination to pursue a course of action "perfectly consistent with our duty and obligations to America, but tending to ensure the success of the cause of liberty in our native land." One of the resolutions forming a part of this platform recommends a convention to be held in New York, "for the purpose of carrying out a united system of action throughout the Union and the colonies, and to adopt an address to our brethren in Ireland exhorting them to be of good cheer, for their friends in America are up and doing, and that they shall not be left alone in the struggle."

The Cincinnati club was organized on the 4th of September last, and at the time of the arrest of these defendants numbered seventy-three members. By the constitution, every member, upon his initiation, is required to pay one dollar, and afterward, twenty-five cents monthly.

A printed address, to "The Irishmen of the Buckeye State," dated the 27th of September last, issued in behalf of, and under the direction of, this club, has been read in evidence. It is unnecessary to make quotations from it. It is a glowing and fervent appeal to Irishmen to co-operate with the Emmet Club in the purpose of its organization, by the formation of similar clubs throughout the State. And the object of these is avowed to be the achievement of the liberty and independence of Ireland. It does not, however, propose or recommend any course in violation of the neutrality laws of the Union. It was evidently written under the influence of high excitement, and its style is somewhat prurient and hyperbolical; but it does not advise or advocate any military movement in behalf of Ireland. What is said about grasping the liberty of that country with "a strong and armed hand," is evidently a mere figure of speech, and has no reference to any practical military action. Or if such a purpose was in the mind of the writer, he has failed to indicate any time at which it is to be fulfilled, or any specific action by which it is to be effected.

The address and resolutions of the convention of the delegates of "the American-Irish Aid Society," held at New York on the 4th of December last, have also been read in evidence, and referred to in the argument. Samuel Lumsden, one of the defendants, was a member of that convention, as a delegate from the Cincinnati society, and acted as one of its vice-presidents. The defendants, Halpin and Kenefeck, were also present as delegates. I have looked over the published account of the doings of that convention; and whatever views may be entertained of the utility and propriety of such a meeting, nothing appears in the proceedings indicative of an unlawful purpose to invade Ireland. While there are some expressions warranting the inference of such a design, upon certain contingencies, an intention to violate the laws of the United States is explicitly disavowed. One of the resolutions declares "that the first duty of all American citizens, whether native born or naturalized, of whatever political opinions, or of whatever nationalities, is to faithfully respect all their obligations of citizenship, arising under the laws and constitution of our country."

But it is quite unnecessary to multiply references to these published documents. It is certain that, giving them a construction the most unfavorable to these defendants and to the objects and purposes of these associations of Irishmen, they do not establish the charge exhibited against them, nor fix upon them the guilt of any violation of the laws of the land. They prove no overt act of military movement or organization, looking to an invasion of Ireland, and bringing them within the provisions of the act of 1818. It is equally clear that neither the book containing the record of the constitution of the proceedings of the Emmet Club of Cincinnati, nor any of the papers offered in evidence, show a breach of any of the criminal laws of the United States. Whatever may be thought of the rightfulness or policy of secret societies or organizations, under our form of government, and the practice of enforcing the supposed obligations of their members by solemn appeals to Deity, whether in the form of oaths or promises, it is certain there is no legal prohibition of such acts. Neither is there any law, state or national, forbidding assemblies of the people for any lawful purpose, or restricting the right of a free expression of opinion, either by speaking or writing. . . . .

If the statements of these last-named witnesses are entitled to credence, the proof is clear that the club or association with which these defendants are connected, has not proposed or attempted any military movement, designed either presently or prospectively, for a descent on Ireland. The impracticability of an invasion of that country from the United States, while at peace with Great Britain, and the certainty that any such attempt would result in nothing but disaster to those engaged in it, affords a presumption, at least, that it was not seriously contemplated. And, if there existed in the minds of these defendants any ulterior purpose of such hostile demonstration against that country, it was to be carried out only upon the occurrence of a state of war, and would therefore involve no violation of law.

I have thus hastily noticed what seem to be the material parts of the evidence submitted to the court. Many facts have been developed by the testimony, which are not important, as applicable to the present inquiry. That inquiry is not whether these defendants harbor feelings of deep-rooted hostility to England, and a too ardent desire for the redress of the alleged wrongs of Ireland—not whether, as the result of the almost proverbial warmth and excitability of the Irish temperament, they have been imprudent, or indiscreet in words or actions—not whether their efforts to excite the zeal of their countrymen in the United States may or may not, in its results and developments, prove beneficial to the land of their birth—but whether, from the evidence, there is reasonable ground for the conclusion, that they are guilty of the specific charges against them, or of any other criminal violation of law. . . . .

I may be allowed further to remark, that while upon the evidence before me, and the law, which must govern my action, I have no hesitancy in adopting the conclusion that these defendants must be discharged, I am not insensible to the fact, that some of the developments made in the progress of this examination are of a character suited to attract public attention to them. These have been adverted to, and commented upon, by the counsel for the prosecution, with great impressiveness and force. I cannot concur with them in the position they urge, that the evidence shows there was the beginning of a military movement or organization, having an immediate reference to the invasion of Ireland, and bringing the defendants within the penalties and prohibitions of the statute. Whatever ulterior purposes they may have had in view, there is a lack of evidence to prove any overt act necessary to constitute the offense charged upon them. Yet, the views and suggestions of counsel, in reference to some of the aspects of this case, are certainly entitled to great consideration. It is true beyond a question, that strenuous and concerted efforts have been made in several of the States of the Union to organize the Irish population into clubs, the members of which are bound by a solemn oath or pledge not to reveal their proceedings, or under any circumstances to give evidence against those who are initiated. Already a national convention, consisting of delegates from these clubs, has been held in the city of New York. The avowed purpose of these movements, I am aware, is to produce unity and harmony of feeling among Irishmen, and prepare them for decisive action in the establishment of the independence of Ireland, in the event of a rupture of the present peaceful relations existing between this country and Great Britain. And doubtless, from a motive of this kind, many Irishmen, who, as adopted citizens of the United States, are loyal in feeling to our government and institutions, have given their sanction to, and aided in, these movements.

Would it not be well for such to pause, and seriously inquire, whether great mischief may not be concealed beneath this plausible assumption, and whether there may not be those who are laboring to produce excitement on this subject, who have less at heart the restoration of Ireland's liberties, than the promotion of their own interested views? Suppose it be true, as averred, that there is no intention to violate our neutrality laws, or compromit the peace of this country;

yet, is there not reason for the apprehension that these agitations will produce, as their results, hostile collisions between this country and Great Britain? Can it be otherwise, than that these constant and exciting appeals to the national animosities and religious prejudices of a portion of the Irish population of this country, are suited in their tendency, if not in their design, to involve us in the bloody conflicts of war?

I censure no Irishman for sympathizing with his native land, and ardently desiring the restoration of the rights of its people; but with all candor and kindness, I would suggest that these feelings ought not to be indulged at the hazard of the interests and peace of the country of his adoption. That country has freely conferred on all foreigners the rights of citizenship, and extends to them the guaranties of its constitutions and laws. In return for these privileges, may it not reasonably be insisted they shall in all respects be loyal to our government? There can be no such thing as a divided national allegiance. The obligations of citizenship cannot exist in favor of different nationalities at the same time. The foreigner who takes the oath of fidelity to our government necessarily renounces his allegiance to all others; and the obligation thereby incurred abides upon him so long as he remains within the limits of the country, and enjoys the protection of its laws. And it is an obligation that is paramount to all others, and demands of him who assumes it a course of conduct that shall be free from the suspicion of unfriendliness to the institutions and interests of the country, which he is solemnly pledged to defend.

In closing, I have only to remark, that it is in proof that several of these defendants have been long residents of this city, and occupy a highly respectable standing in the community. I should most reluctantly adopt the conclusion, that in the transactions in which they have been implicated, they were moved by any design to violate the laws of the country, or entertain any purpose inconsistent with their duty and obligation to it, as adopted citizens. I trust there will be no future developments, which will present the charge, from which they are now relieved by the decision of this court, in any different legal aspect from that which it now assumes. But, I may remind them, as already intimated, the order for their discharge from this complaint, will be no bar to its re-investigation, if, in the progress of events, such a course should be deemed necessary.

### 18.  A German Criticism of German-Americans[1]

The most numerous, after the Anglo-Americans, is the population of German extraction. . . . . It is most concentrated and relatively largest in numbers in Pennsylvania, Ohio, Indiana, Missouri, and Michigan, where it constitutes almost half of the population. But also in New York, New Jersey, Maryland, Virginia, Maine, Kentucky, Tennessee, Illinois, Iowa, and Wisconsin, the Germans are proportionately very numerous and in some parts make up more than one-third of the population. In California there are also more than 30,000 of them; a more considerable number lives in Louisiana. The German population would be even larger if their consciousness of nationality were stronger, and if so many did not gradually give up their language, and with it, their customs and peculiar characteristics. . . . . As the Yankee is preferably a woodcutter and lumberman who clears the forest; so the German in North America has always become and still is, by preference, a tiller of the soil and farmer. The country owes, in no small degree, its prosperity in agriculture to the example which the German set its citizens. He first bred cattle systematically; he introduced the culture of grapes and indigo; he first took up the culture of silkworms; and, from the beginning, distinguished himself in the crafts. He has shed his blood for the new world in the same measure, he has defended his new country as bravely against Indians and Europeans, as men of English and Irish descent. In cultivating the land, in lenient treatment of the natives and negroes, he has always surpassed them, and no matter what religion he professed, he never failed to give proof of practical Christianity. To be sure, that has become very different at the present time.

Whoever has become somewhat acquainted with the German life there will remember gratefully that he met many a noble personality who had retained the treasures of home life, righteousness, comfort, and a certain idealistic striving. However, these are always only exceptions, and, from ocean to ocean, it is sadly true that the Germans everywhere play a deplorable rôle, and in many respects deserve the contempt with which they are treated by the great majority of Americans.

We are not speaking here of the people of Pennsylvania, whose

[1] Extract translated from Karl Büchele, *Land und Volk der Vereinigten Staaten von Nord Amerika. Zur Belehrung für Jedermann, vorzüglich für Auswanderer* (Stuttgart, 1855), pp. 277–86. Translation by Elsie P. Wolcott, graduate assistant, School of Social Service Administration.

broken language still has a few thousand words reminding one of Germany. Their hard-headed farmer-conceit resists everywhere, in the most despicable manner, any education going beyond reading, writing, and the study of the Bible and catechism. The immigration of educated Germans of 1848 and 1849 has changed the state of affairs very little. One might even say that, since the best members of this immigration soon withdrew to themselves just as did the better people among former immigrants, and only the talkers and noisy ones remained as educators and guides of public opinion, they had a depressing, rather than an inspiring and improving, influence.

A national fault of the German is his love for the foreigner, and a submissiveness that follows him everywhere in life and history. The drunken and ragged Irishman, the irresponsible and dissolute Frenchman, the begging Italian, rank higher in the estimate of the American than the simple German immigrant. What is expressed as scornful disdain of the proletariat, develops into hate against the German of the ordinary type, from whom the American must still learn in many respects, for example, certain trades. Whenever the German submissiveness, and obstinate excessive modesty are contrasted with American independence; stupid, clumsy, German timidity with overbearing American self-confidence—whenever pitiable timidity is forced to give way to impudence—the fate of the German is sealed in spite of thoroughness and competence in his trade. He is incapable of behaving in a free and easy manner, crowds fearfully into a corner when the American proudly struts about. An understanding and application of the prevailing language are strange to him. He has to change his food and way of living, has to become accustomed to the trials of the climate and of vermin. The new life rushes in upon him with such tremendous force that after a formal farewell to this last possession—his plans and illusions—he humbly and patiently resigns himself to moral servitude under the Americans.

He even finds difficulty in adjusting himself to the daily routine of life. When he enters his boarding-house, his landlady looks at him with disdain, and children point their fingers at him. Between himself and the American there is, in a social way, no point of contact. Therefore in his need for companionship, he looks up his countrymen, if there are any in the neighborhood, devotes himself exclusively to them, and thereby becomes one-sided, stunted in growth, or clownish. However, if his countrymen are missing, he often unfortunately resorts to the negroes, and lowers himself even more in the estimation of the circle to which he belongs by treating the black men with a certain familiarity and good nature. . . . . The German especially incurs the dislike of the women by having nothing to do with the one-sided and hypocritical manner of celebrating Sunday in America, and, after hard work during the week, devoting this day to recreation. And so it may finally happen that in answer to the question, "Was he a white man?" one will hear, "No sir, he was a Dutchman." What an enormous amount of disdain lies in this scornful language! The German often believes that he is furthering his own interests by entering into partnership with an American, leaving him the management of affairs, buying and selling, and devoting himself solely to the physical labor. Unfortunately, however, only the American derives any benefits from such an association, while in case of a dissolution of the firm caused by a misunderstanding, the German usually loses everything and, ignorant of laws and chicanery, is forced to resign himself quietly to his fate and watch the American emerge richer from the association and, besides, honored with the name of a "smart fellow" by the community. If the German institutes a lawsuit he has an even more difficult time, and afterward he has to work for weeks and months to pay court and lawyers' fees.

Another even more precarious attempt to gain the respect of the community consists in seeking the hand of an American woman. Sometimes the German is granted the honor of being allowed to mix with Yankee blood, but later he is treated somewhat like a European parvenu who has married into an old, aristocratic family, and from then on is only the husband of his wife. He is obliged to let himself be branded as a criminal by aunts and cousins because he is a German, and suffer patiently all the tortures of nativism. His own children show him little respect and are sure to disown him when they are fourteen. He does not even dare to reprimand them for calling him "an old Dutchman" in his very presence. The children of such immigrant Germans are, therefore, also the worst "natives" and, as a rule, exhibit the very height of cruelty and worthlessness.

A second reason for the before-mentioned fact lies in the breaking up of the Germans into hundreds of little hostile factions, above all in the great division between the old immigrants, or "Grays," and the new arrivals, or "Greens."[1] The former, belonging mostly to the uneducated classes, came to the country, with the exception of a few

---

[1] [For an interesting account of these two German groups, see T. S. Baker, "America as the Political Utopia of Young Germany," in *Americana Germanica*, Vol. I, No. 2, p. 72.]

prompted by religious motives, only to better their material condition. They came at a time when conditions were, in almost every respect, more favorable to such aspirations than they are today, and so it was easy for them to reach their goal. When a man without education becomes rich quickly, he is generally called an upstart. The characteristics of such a man are, among others, especially disdain for everything which is not directly instrumental in making money, arrogance toward those whose capital consists only in intelligence and knowledge, and immeasurable self-elation in all other respects, based on the sight of boxes and coffers filled without trouble. If one summarizes these characteristics and adds to them the feeling of familiarity with conditions which, to the newcomer, are necessarily incomprehensible and uncomfortable, as well as the consciousness, based on reading of newspapers, of living in a free country and, therefore, as the proud simpleton thinks, of being privileged to play the brute toward everyone who has not yet American citizenship papers in his pocket, but especially toward the intellectually superior; if one summarizes all this, then one has a living picture of the "Gray."

As contrasted with him the "Green" appears, in estimable qualities, as an enthusiastic believer in aspiring to higher things, as a carrier of new ideas which he wants to put into practice. If he does not feel himself equal to this task and wants to associate with the quiet and simple people of the country, he at least brings with him a mind full of illusions which he has long harbored and fostered. What is then the relation of the "Gray" to the newly arrived countrymen? Decidedly hostile toward the ambitious, heartless toward the hopeful, traitorous and fraudulent toward the confiding, he will have nothing to do with new ideas which have no community of interest with the almighty dollar. . . . . These visionary people appear to him not only as deceived, but as deceivers, as good prey which he, with his knowledge of affairs, may make use of; as fools who must fare as he did when he landed here without a dollar in his pocket; but especially as a kind of plague against which he must defend himself, as competition with him threatens to arise from it. The result of this resistance on the part of the "Gray" is that the unwelcome "Green" gradually dries up, that the ambitious become weary, the hopeful despair of their goal, and that, if sometime a dam were built against the stream of immigration, or if it were directed into other channels, American Germanism would, in a few decades, present a "gray in gray," hopeless beyond all conception.

Adjusting one's self to the customs of the country as far as necessity demands is doubtless worthy of praise. However, it excites laughter and in individual cases even disgust, to see newly arrived Germans who have nothing better to do than to substitute for the customs and manners of their native land the manners of the Yankee even when this is not demanded, and when the old is not only more appropriate, but also more beautiful and noble than the mimicry of the new. Were the virtues of the Anglo-Americans taken as an example, there would naturally be no objection, but as a rule it is just the opposite which is imitated. Instead of allowing the really worthy characteristics which have, in many respects, left such a magnificent imprint upon life in the country, to serve as examples, people believe they must throw away honor and righteousness as though it were European trash. Instead of making their own the restless activity of the ruling race, they are much more likely to be concerned with learning the art of chewing tobacco, and instead of taking up the spirited impetus with which this race overcomes inferior things resisting them and seeks to grasp the higher on the leap, as it were, they cling to the motto of American Philistines "to save appearances," and timidly observe things which are at best only exterior trifles, often only ludicrous things. . . . . .

This is especially apparent in the attitude toward the language. If there were no other German than the senseless *mischmasch* which one hears in New York or Philadelphia in the lower ranks of German society, one could not blame anyone for discarding, with an easy conscience, this jargon for a decent English. But what should be said when not only the common man, but also the man who counts himself among the educated gives up unhesitatingly the language in which he was reared, and is even ashamed of it, disowns it, and exchanges it for an English which jars upon the ear. Of course to learn English is one of the first duties for the man who lives in America, but to declare it a nobler language, to make it the prevailing language in the household, and educate his children solely in it as is done by many respected Germans in New York, Philadelphia, and Cincinnati, is not only ridiculous, but almost disgraceful.

Another point of criticism is the unlimited indifference of the German whenever there is a question of the promotion of intellectual interests or of his own further education. The Anglo-American, on the other hand, as soon as he has worked himself up beyond supplying the first necessities, which is usually very soon, thinks of buying books and reading, although it is almost always with a view toward the material gains to be achieved by it, and often not showing the best choice. As a result, he generally acquires an average education, while the German, even when the means are not lacking, limits himself to the Bible, a few other religious writings, and the almanac. The more worldly-minded sometimes add half a dozen immoral novels or a newspaper. So-called "medical men," "lawyers," and "theologists," equip themselves with "ponies" and "cribs" adapted to their line and, besides, keep some illustrated magazine or similar publication for the family. Whatever is bought beyond this is considered interior decoration or is purchased for similar reasons, but not because of a desire for genuine learning and intellectual development. If some German-American booksellers have really made a success, they owe it more to their English publications, Anglo-American customers, and the sale of paper, stationery, and bookbinders' supplies, rather than to the sale of German scientific works, or else they made a good investment in some school- or prayer-book or collection of sermons.

If interest in literature is very small, one can speak even less of participation in any branch of art, except music, to which glee clubs ardently devote themselves. The theater in New York where more than 80,000 Germans are living is hardly comparable to the smallest municipal theater in Germany, and the one in Cincinnati even less. If German names are found among American painters, the bearers of these have long since become strangers to the language and ways of the people from whom they are descended, and if one of the transatlantic Germans has ever distinguished himself in any other phase of art, the encouragement to do this was certainly not extended by his countrymen. A noted student of the German tongue and nation has, so far as is known, not been born or reared, although three generations have passed since the first members of this nation landed in Philadelphia.

Finally, one must consider the lack of interest of the German-Americans in politics, and notice how they, with the exception of editors of newspapers and a few lawyers, have little respect for the rights which the "free country," of which they have tired of hearing, has given them. Even where they form a majority, the power is in the hands of the Yankees. One does not know whether one should become angry over this situation or rejoice in it as a punishment for disgraceful faithlessness. Were it conceivable that a capable personality should arouse the German citizens of the Union from their cowardice and unite them into a compact whole, then Pennsylvania and Ohio would from time to time have German governors and always a proportion of officials and representatives of the people in Washington would be one-eighth German, and the possibility that the United States would sometime elect a German as president would not be entirely out of the question, if circumstances were adroitly made use of. Directly, nothing would be won by this except honor, but thereby would be gained the advantage that the scorn with which the Yankee regards the "Dutch people," and which he only hides at election time,[1] would thus come to an end and be forced to give way to a genuine recognition of equality of rights. No money would be made thereby, and as the thinking of the majority of Germans would consider not the honor, but only the dollar, things will probably remain as they are; that means our German countrymen will continue to vegetate as those who are tolerated, and will act as miserable instruments of parties, while the Yankees represent the real life of the powerful body of states.

Only the aristocracy of German immigrants, such as the big business men of the principal cities, gain a higher position in the estimation of Americans. However, German business houses have here the most important connections and means; the German importers of silks and cloth are as such absolutely necessary to the American. The German commission merchants enjoy general recognition in all parts of America, because of their precaution and solidarity. As an American can never make the same connections with Germany as a German firm can, he is intelligent enough to make the best of things and, as a rule, grants the German business man the same rights as he possesses himself. Nevertheless, a German has never succeeded in becoming president of a bank in the larger cities of the East or South, just as government positions rarely have fallen to his share. As a reward for faithful services the Germans are taken care of by granting them subordinate positions. At most, they succeed in becoming consuls in places of third rank. The only senator whom the United States has had so far is a Mr. G. from Missouri, who by the way, was only three years old when he came to this country with his parents, and combines with other reactionary characteristics, American nativism. If three years ago "Judge" Körner, who came from Frankfurt-on-the-Main, was elected lieutenant-governor, it was quite evident from the rejoicing expressed

[1] At this time the American papers show their friendly side. All at once the German immigrants are called "most excellent colonists." Germany is the home of a nation of thinkers (*Denkernation*). After the election is ended the old names of contempt again come to the front.

by the German-language press that cases of this kind are as rare as white ravens. . . . .

Nevertheless, to throw a little light on the .dark shadows of this picture of the majority of Germans, one must not minimize the fact that especially as a result of larger immigration of educated, patriotic men from Germany, worthy attempts have been made here and there to strengthen and maintain the German nationality by increased cultivation of the language, by transplanting German literature and education, by greater political activity, and closer social contact. If we once assume the success of these attempts and believe at all in a mission which may be reserved in the future for the German immigration on the other side of the ocean, this mission might take the following form. Because of their steadiness, endurance, industry, and love for the soil which they cultivate, the Germans are far more suited than Americans for the cultivation and care of farm land. Wherever Germans settle as farmers, there is prosperity, just as with the arrival of nesting swallows. Many of them have already moved to the West, in order to transform, by their industry and persistence, the forests of Iowa and Minnesota beyond the Mississippi into smiling fields. While they now, by economy and temperate living, work themselves up to independence, they may still retain their truly German virtues—righteousness, industry, endurance—and thereby at the same time exercise a beneficial moral influence upon their surroundings, with which the German spirit soon becomes well acquainted.

In addition to this task of furthering the cultivation of the soil, a greater field of activity is open to German immigrants in their capacity of craftsmen, teachers, merchants, and doctors, and here one already meets many names of German origin which have gained recognition in smaller or larger circles. The Germans might be particularly qualified, given certain conditions, to contribute to the moral and intellectual development of the Union and to blend together, through intermingling with the American race, in a later generation, the love of comfort, idealism, and intellectual aspirations which nature has granted them as their inheritance, with the self-confidence, the craving for independence, and love of liberty of the American. The success of the future is, therefore, more to be expected in a mixing of both races than in a strict separation and divided effect. Only the person who has constructed a picture of American conditions from foolish illusions, rather than the man who knows them in reality, can dream of a separate New Germany in America. Because of the infinite inattention and carelessness which exists among the Germans from the moment of landing to the present day, the most active efforts of isolated individuals to awaken a common creative sense will come to nothing. Therefore a close combination of the two nationalities is better, but without allowing the German element to disappear completely in the strong, energetic American character, nor the practical, tough, Yankee spirit in the soft idealism of the German.

### 19.  The German Emigrant in America[1]

We believe that the condition of the great mass of emigrants is essentially improved by removal to America. They are, for the most part, farmers, mechanics, and laborers. The cheapness and fertility of our Western lands insure a good home to the tiller of the soil, and the high wages of the last two classes soon raise them above the destitution to which they are subjected in Germany. But the advantage to which all of them look is the hopeful career which is opened to their children in American life. . . . . These visions hover over the poor wanderers on their long and dreary voyage, and color every hardship with their bright and radiant hues. The German merchants who are found in our cities accumulate fortunes with rapidity. He who was the wealthiest man in America was born on the soil of Germany. German physicians of sterling worth receive the consideration which they merit, and the numerous quacks and impostors, who substitute unpronounceable names for solid attainments, reap a richer harvest than they ever dreamed of at home. Those alone really suffer who are too lazy or too proud to do the work for which they are suited. They complain that America offers no inducements to educated men; that it is too utilitarian for their aesthetic and speculative natures; that muscle and sinew may live, but genius must inevitably starve in our money-getting nation. . . . .

Let such men conform to our customs, and they will never lack patronage. . . . . In fact, the demand for men of high culture is unlimited. In science, the arts, the learned professions, everywhere, we have room. But he who has not the good sense to adapt himself to our social habits and our modes of thought must certainly fail. He really demands that we shall become Germanized in order that he may live. The merchants and mechanics have seen the folly of such an idea. They are fully Americanized in their business relations. They

[1] Extract from "German Emigration to America," by J. D. Angell, *North American Review*, LXXXII (1856), 263–68.

are divided by the same political and religious questions which divide us all into various parties. They are Whigs or Democrats, Pro-Slavery or Anti-Slavery, Lutherans or Calvinists, Deists or Atheists. They gathered under our banners in the battles of the Revolution, and they helped to plant them victoriously in the capital of Mexico. They are joined by the dearest of all earthly ties to our brothers and sisters, and their blood and ours flow together in the veins of thousands of fairhaired boys and girls. The lines which divided the races in the first generation are obliterated in the second, and the son of a poor emigrant from the Rhine surpasses in American enthusiasm the descendant of a signer of the Declaration of Independence.

It is painful to think that the measure of liberty which has proved so congenial to the industry and enterprise of the Germans, has also permitted the excessive development of some of the worst tendencies in their character. Errors which only germinated on the Continent, here bear the most poisonous fruit. License reaches the most daring recklessness and profanity. Vice swells into shameless crime. Democracy becomes lawlessness, and virtue but a name. The earnest and industrious mechanic of Nuremberg grows into the tumultuous haranguer and street-fighter of New York. The wayward boy of Stuttgart is the brawler and ruffian in Philadelphia. The free-thinker of Tübingen is here an editor, who regards none of the courtesies of our life, nor any of our most hallowed customs and beliefs. This is no exaggeration. Many a German is amazed and grieved at the great moral contrast between multitudes of immigrants and the quiet citizens of his ancient home. The cause is apparent. The tares are suffered to grow with the wheat. No hundred-handed police represses every budding vice. Even the reaction, which is natural after escape from governmental oppression, is not at all checked. Moreover, the wave of emigration always carries on its bosom many of the outcasts, who are bound by no ties to any place or institution. It is also well known that many of the workhouses and jails of Germany have cast their incorrigible and desperate inmates upon our shores. But the great cause of the apparent moral inferiority of many of our Germans to those in their native land is undoubtedly the unfounded liberty which is granted to all. Here thought becomes act; there it is locked in the breast. We fear that, if republican freedom were granted to Germany today, a part of her inhabitants would abandon themselves to a license which has never disgraced New York or Philadelphia.

There is a marked difference in the present condition of the emigrants who have come at different periods. Most of the descendants of those who arrived before 1815 are thoroughly Americanized, and are not to be distinguished in any respect from other American citizens. A class called the Pennsylvania Germans form a remarkable exception. Most of them reside in some of the eastern counties of the State from which they take their name. They preserve the old Frankish dress and customs. Time seems to have advanced a century without bearing them onward. They know little of the world. Their knowledge of Germany is limited to the vague idea that wine is cheaper and life merrier there than in America. Their strongest passions are love of beer and hatred of the Irish. It is difficult to decide whether German, Dutch, or English is the predominant element in their language. It is almost unintelligible to a German. They seem to be anchored in the past, unmoved by the rapid stream of American life which rushes by them on every side.

The emigrants who came between 1815 and 1845 were comparatively uneducated. Only few men of culture and influence were comprised in their ranks. But the diffusion of political intelligence and the longing for republican government prompted many men of liberal and enlightened views to remove to America even before the Revolution of 1848; and after the close of that tragi-comedy thousands were obliged to flee from their homes for safety. These were not alone the poor and helpless, but a large proportion of their number were possessed of moderate wealth, and of good education and talent. Among them were the most intellectual and accomplished of our German population. But among them were also too many of those turbulent and restless spirits, who are always evoked from obscurity by civil commotions. Representatives of every description of German society have been scattered by this last emigration throughout our large cities and the Western States. They are divided into classes that cherish the intensest hatred for one another. The republicans have a deadly hostility to the Roman Catholics, and many of them dislike the Lutherans almost as bitterly. They regard the established churches of Germany as the greatest enemies to civil liberty, and they stamp kingcraft and priest-craft with a common brand of infamy. The Germans are almost unanimously opposed to slavery, and to any prohibition of the sale of intoxicating liquors. As a class, they have always been attached to the Democratic party, though a respectable minority has ever been found in the opposite ranks. The great majority of the wealthy and educated are atheists or rationalists. They have the control of nearly half of the German newspapers in the land.

What will be the effect upon our institutions and character of the great influx of German immigrants, it is difficult to say. Our experience gives us almost unlimited confidence in our power to fuse heterogeneous elements into one harmonious whole. The Germans have thus far received our laws, our language, and most of our habits. They have been but slightly influenced by them. Our legislation cannot be materially moulded by their efforts. They have not the power to accomplish any great political undertaking. Besides, we confide in the sober sense of the thoughtful Germans. They see that conformity to the spirit and genius of our institutions is their highest duty and good. Their interests are identical with ours; therefore our language and customs are best suited to their needs. They may cherish the hallowed memories of their fatherland, they may study its sublime philosophy, they may enjoy its inimitable poesy, they may sing its thrilling songs, they may admire its learning and its arts, they may even speak its rich and expressive language, and still they may live in faithful allegiance to that Constitution which has so kindly sheltered them in their flight from tyranny, and in their struggles from poverty to opulence. They may labor for the maintenance of their genial life, but the idea of establishing a German republic within the limits of our country is exploded forever. Such are the views of their ablest journals and their experienced men.

But the irreligious influence of thousands of German infidels must be perceptibly felt by the children who come after them. They grow up as Americans, and it is sad to think of the heavy cloud which will rest on their hearts. That is a grave subject of meditation for the Christian patriot.

If the Germans in America will only be true to the higher and more generous impulses of their nature, if they will cultivate those tastes and perpetuate those customs which lend so many charms to social life in Germany, they may prove of essential advantage to the land which has ever extended to them the hand of friendship and hospitality. Already they are elevating our musical taste. If they will kindle within us an appreciating love of heaven-born Art, they will atone for many of the excesses by which they have awakened our solicitude. Well will it be, if we can unite to our resistless energy something of their unyielding and unfaltering patience. Well will it be, if we can temper our burning passion for the acquirement of wealth by something of that genial and refreshing spirit which stops in its hastiest flights after riches and honor to admire an image of the True and the Beautiful.

## 20.  The Germans in Texas[1]

### NUMBER AND POSITION OF THE GERMANS

There are estimated to be, at the commencement of 1857, 35,000 Germans in Texas, of whom about 25,000 are settled in the German and half-German counties of Western Texas.

The early emigration was of a somewhat humble and promiscuous description. While the great part was composed of peasants and mechanics, who had no other reproach than that of honest poverty, and a desire for improving their condition, there was a certain number, as among the early settlers of Virginia, who were suffered to escape justice at home on condition of becoming colonists; who were, in short, *sentenced* to Texas. But whatever of reckless energy was thus disposed of, seems to have found for itself a natural and harmless vent among the rough demands of frontier life.[2] The result, at least, favors an offer to every rogue of the chance to show himself the victim of circumstances; for it is certainly remarkable with what success the unpractical nation has joined issue with nature and the savages; and how here, where the comparison may every day be made, even Americans acknowledge the Germans their equals as pioneers.

After the events of 1848, the emigration became of a more valuable character, and included a large proportion of farmers and persons in moderate circumstances, who sought a hopeful future in the New World. With them came numbers of cultivated and high-minded men, some distinctly refugees, others simply compromised, in various degrees, by their democratic tendencies, who found themselves exposed to disagreeable surveillance, or to obstructions, through police management, in whatever honorable career they wished to enter, while others merely followed, from affection or curiosity, this current of their friends.

Few of this class have been able to bring with them any large amount of property; and, with the German tendency to invest in lands, they have chiefly lost the advantages belonging to even a limited capital-in-hand in a new country.

[1] Extract from Frederick Law Olmsted, *A Journey through Texas; or, A Saddle-Trip on the Southwestern Frontier* (New York, 1857), pp. 428-40.

[2] [Olmsted added the following explanatory note: "Our information on this point may be incorrect. At all events, the number of vagabonds was very small, as only cash subscribers were received by the association. Single men were required to be in possession of $120, married men of $240. This regulation excluded from Texas a pauper class, which has since furnished thousands of vigorous and valuable laborers to the northwestern States" (*Gesammelte Aktenstucke des Vereins*, p. 27). See also above, p. 133.]

I have described how wonderfully some of them are still able to sustain their intellectual life and retain their refined taste, and, more than all, with their antecedents, to be seemingly contented and happy, while under the necessity of supporting life in the most frugal manner by hard manual labor.

There is, as I have before intimated, something extremely striking in the temporary incongruities and bizarre contrasts of the backwoods life of these settlers. You are welcomed by a figure in blue flannel shirt and pendant beard, quoting Tacitus, having in one hand a long pipe, in the other a butcher's knife; Madonnas upon log-walls; coffee in tin cups upon Dresden saucers; barrels for seats; to hear a Beethoven's symphony on the grand piano; "My wife made these pantaloons, and my stockings grew in the field yonder"; a fowling-piece that cost $300, and a saddle that cost $5; a book-case half filled with classics, half with sweet potatoes.

But, as lands are subdued, and capital is amassed, these inconveniences will disappear, and pass into amusing traditions, while the sterling education and high-toned character of the fathers will be unconsciously transmitted to the social benefit of the coming generation. The virtues I have ascribed to them as a class are not, however, without the relief of faults, the most prominent among which are a free-thinking and a devotion to reason, carried, in their turn, to the verge of bigotry, and expanded to a certain rude license of manners and habits, consonant with their wild prairies, but hardly with the fitness of things, and, what in practical matters is even a worse error, an insane mutual jealousy, and petty personal bickering, that prevents all prolonged and effective cooperation—an old German ail, which the Atlantic has not sufficed to cleanse.

The poorer emigrants, who were able to purchase farms, have made the happiest progress, meeting a steady market for their productions, and a continuous appreciation in the value of their improved lands. The mechanics and laborers, after the first distress, found more work awaiting them than their hands could perform, and have constantly advanced to become themselves employers, offering their old wages to the new-comers of each successive emigration.

This is the source whence has been supplied the patient and well-directed muscle, which is the first demand of a new country, and which, had American, or even African arms been awaited, Western Texas must have long wanted.

In social and political relations, the Germans do not occupy the position to which their force and character should entitle them. They mingle little with the Americans, except for the necessary buying and selling. The manners and ideals of the Texans and of the Germans are hopelessly divergent, and the two races have made little acquaintance, observing one another apart with unfeigned curiosity, often tempered with mutual contempt. The Americans have the prestige of preoccupation, of accustomed dominance over Mexicans and slaves, of language, capital, political power, and vociferous assumption. The Germans, quiet, and engrossed in their own business, by nature law-abiding and patient, submit to be governed with little murmuring.

A large proportion of the emigrants have remained apart, in German communities, and have contented themselves with the novel opportunity of managing, after republican forms, their own little public affairs. Others, by their scattered residence in isolated positions, are excluded from any other than individual life. Such as have settled in American neighborhoods or towns, feeling the awkwardness of newcomers, and ignorant of the language, have hitherto almost refrained from taking part in politics.

The intelligent portion as early as possible make themselves citizens, and become voters; but until the recent agitation of the idea of restricting the privileges of persons of foreign birth, there has been, in fact, no topic of sufficient general interest to give rise to parties among them, or to force them, as is the result of this, into united action.

As to slavery, the mass living by themselves, where no slaves are seen and having no instinctive prejudice of color, feel simply the natural repugnance for a system of forced labor, universal in free society. Few of them concern themselves with the theoretical right or wrong of the institution, and while it does not interfere with their own liberty or progress, are careless of its existence.

But this mass is easily swayed by political management, and if brought to any direct vote, examining every question only in the light of personal interest, would move together against slave-owners as their natural enemies.

Among the Germans of the west we met not one slave-owner, and there are not probably thirty among them all who have purchased slaves.[1] . . . .

[1] A gentleman from San Antonio, from his business relations with Germans particularly well-informed in the matter, told me he knew, in all, of twelve German slave-proprietors in Texas. Ten of these have unwillingly bought housemaids to

The planter is by no means satisfied to find himself in the neighborhood of the German. He is not only by education uncongenial, as well as suspicious of danger to his property, already somewhat precariously near the frontier, but finds, in his turn, a direct competition of interests, which can be readily comprehended in figures.

The ordinary Texan wages for an able field-hand are $200. The German laborer hires at $150, and clothes and insures himself. The planter for one hand must have paid $1,000. The German with this sum can hire six hands. It is here the contact galls.

But actual collision is comparatively rare. The German shop-keepers and mechanics, in American towns, occupy, of necessity, an almost suspected position, and whatever their sentiments, they carefully avoid all open expression.[1] In the German settlements there is no direct occasion for thought on the subject. It is only where the population mixes in equal proportion—as in San Antonio—that ideas and interests clash, and bitter feelings are stirred.

The great body of Germans being devoted exclusively to their own material progress, there are, as might be expected, two rival influences at work among them. It is not to be believed that European democrats, who have suffered exile for their social theories would at once abandon them, and, by fraternizing with an aristocracy of slave proprietors, belie here every principle for which they had struggled at home. On the other hand, in every community a certain number of hangers-on are sure, from motives of petty selfishness, to attach themselves to any dominant party. The Americans have thus their allies among the Germans, who, with those who fear the agitation of any subject, but especially this, as detrimental or inopportune, form the party of eager subservience. In a slave state the opportunity does not often arise for any public expression of an opinion upon slavery, and for want of a practical question for discussion, neither of these divisions has been able to show any great activity, except of jealousy and acrimonious feeling. . . . .

The Germans, feeling their social influence too small upon the

---

relieve their wives, who were unable to find German servants; one gentleman owns four field-hands in Gillespie county; another about the same number in Washington county—both old Texans of '36.

[1] Not, however, from any motives of direct interest, as might be surmised, in business with planters. The empty cotton-wagons bring these their supplies from the coast direct, and they own their own slave-mechanics, avoiding Germans when possible.

public opinion of a community of which they constituted by intelligence and numbers, at least the equal half, undertook to assert themselves by some combined action. In May, 1854, advantage was taken of the concourse at their annual musical festival in San Antonio, to hold a simultaneous political convention. An extended "platform" was adopted and published, containing the condensed expression of their radical opinions. It had the disadvantage of proposing no particular action, but of being put forth as a simple manifesto of principles.

One of the resolutions discussed slavery, and declared it to be an evil which should be eventually removed.[1]

The novel attitude of the Germans was disagreeable to the Americans, and this resolution, meddling with the question of slave-property, particularly offensive. An excitement sprung up, which for a month or more was kept within the limits of conversation, but broke out into newspaper clamor and open threats of violence, when, by a series of articles from a German source, it was discovered that the Germans were not unanimous in their opinions.

In fact, the time was unpropitious for such a political demonstration. "Americanism" was just beginning to show its strength in the East, and to extend its lodges and its barbarizing prejudices into Texas. This independent movement on the part of foreigners, was a god-send to the new party. It gave it a tangible point of attack, and what with the cry of "foreign interference in politics," and "abolitionism in Texas," a universal howl from the American papers went up against the Germans.

The German newspaper had the brunt to bear. It had published and defended the resolution, and could not, like the convention, dissolve into silence. The editor, reading in the State Constitution the guarantee of his right to free speech, continued on his way, taking little notice of the outcry, answering only in earnest, such arguments as were worth the pains. He soon, however, found that some of his

---

[1] The following amendments were rejected:

"Slavery is according to our views a social evil, and possibly liable to conflict with white labor. But this institution comes too little home to Germans, and is too much connected with the interests of our American fellow-citizens, for us to feel ourselves urged to take, in this question, initiatory steps, or to act upon it politically.

"Negro-Slavery is an evil, perilous to the duration of the Union. Its abolition must be left to the individual States in which it exists. We German-speaking Texans, are not naturally in a position to initiate measures, but we wish the Federal Government's patronage of the same dispensed with."

subscribers were disposed to flinch. Two parties were evidently forming among them. At his suggestion, a general meeting of the stock-
holders was called, at which the course of the paper was sustained, but
as a measure of justice to the dissentients it was resolved to sell the
press, and allow the paper to stand upon its own merits. The editor
now became proprietor, and for a time was well supported. An English
department was added to this sheet, that Americans might read his
principles for themselves, not in garbled extracts and translations with
a purpose. This aroused again the fury of the American papers, which,
as time passed, had somewhat subsided. A determined effort was made
for the suppression of the sheet. Under threat of being denounced as
secret abolitionists, the American merchants were induced to withdraw
their advertisements. The publication was then carried on at a loss.
Friends began to waver, and to condemn the editor's course as "ultra,"
terminating one by one their subscriptions. The editor saw himself
becoming a victim to his allegiance to principles, but, for more than a
year, sustained with dignity his supposed right to free expression in
Texas. His resources at length exhausted, he surrendered to starvation, and became a second time an exile, the press falling into the hands
of the opposite party, who have established a journal whose first
principle is not to give offense to slaveholders.

During this singular struggle, threats of the application of Lynch
law were incessant on the part of the Americans. The American
journals even advocated it, the *State Times* of Austin going so far as to
indicate the mode of punishment, by drowning. The locality was
favorable, to the last degree, for this mode of disposing of opposition.
The respect for law is of the weakest, and the tribe of border-idlers,
always ready for an excitement, has its very headquarters in San
Antonio. In fact, the danger was imminent, and only averted by the
personal pluck of the editor, and the determination on the part of the
Germans, without regard to party, to resist force by force, and to stand
by their countryman, bullet for bullet, in a collision of races where the
laws were on their side.

The editor has since become a resident of Boston. He has some
amusing details of the various means brought to bear upon his obstinacy. While at work on his press one morning, he was interrupted by
a knock, which introduced a six-foot citizen of the region, holding in
his hand a heavy stick, and accompanied by a friend.

"Are you the editor of this German newspaper?" he asked.

"Yes, sir."

"You are an abolitionist, are you?"

"Yes, sir."

Then came a pause, after which the inquiry, "What do you mean by an abolitionist?"

The editor very briefly explained.

Another pause followed, after which the citizen announced that he would consult with his friend a moment outside. He shortly re-entered, saying:

"Well, sir, we've concluded that you are an abolitionist, and that such a scoundrel as you are ought to be thrashed out of the town."

"Very well, sir. Try it."

A third pause ensued, to terminate which, the editor opened the door, whereupon the individuals walked out. . . . .

I have been thus particular in describing the condition and attitude of the Germans, as the position in which fortune has placed them, in the very line of advance of slavery, is peculiar, and so far as it bears upon the questions of the continued extension of cotton limits, the capacity of whites for independent agriculture at the South, and the relative profit and vigor of free and slave labor, is of national interest.

The presence of this incongruous foreign element of Mexicans and Germans tends, as may be conceived, to hinder any rapid and extensive settlement of Western Texas by planters.

### 21.  Immigrant Organizations in Politics: A "Know Nothing" View[1]

To borrow the language of that bold and fearless champion of the American reformation (Hon. Wm. R. Smith), "The mass of foreigners who come to this country are incapable of appreciating the policies of our government, they do not sufficiently understand our institutions. Patriotism is natural in a native, but it must be cultivated in a foreigner. Their minds are filled with a vague and indefinite idea of liberty. It is not the liberty of law, but of unrestrained license. . . . ." Well, let us see if there is any truth in these suggestions. Here are the solemn resolutions of the German Social Democratic Association of Richmond, Virginia—an association existing in the centre of the "Old Dominion"—the home of the presidents:

*Reform in the laws of the general government, as well as in those of the states.*—We demand: (1) Universal suffrage. (2) The election of all officers

[1] Extract from Samuel C. Busey, *Immigration: Its Evils and Consequences* (New York, 1856), pp. 13–32.

by the people. (3) The abolition of the Presidency. (4) The abolition of Senates, so that the legislature shall consist of only one branch. (5) The right of the people to recall their representatives (cashier them) at their pleasure. (6) The right of the people to change the Constitution when they like. (7) All lawsuits to be conducted without expense. (8) A department of all the government to be set up for the purpose of protecting immigration. (9) A reduced term for acquiring citizenship.

*Reform in the foreign relations of the government.*—(1) Abolition of all neutrality. (2) Intervention in favor of every people struggling for liberty.

*Reform in what relates to religions.*—1) A more perfect development of the principle of personal freedom and liberty of conscience; consequently, (*a*) abolition of laws for the observance of the Sabbath; (*b*) abolition of prayers in Congress; (*c*) abolition of oath upon the Bible; (*d*) repeal of laws enacting a religious test before taking an office. (2) Taxation of church property. (3) A prohibition of incorporations of all church property in the name of ecclesiastics.

*Reform in the social condition.*—1) Abolition of land monopoly. (2) Ad valorem taxation of property. (3) Amelioration of the condition of the working class, (*a*) by lessening the time of work to eight hours for grown persons, and to five hours for children; (*b*) by incorporation of mechanics' associations and protective societies; (*c*) by granting a preference to mechanics before all other creditors; (*d*) by establishing an asylum for superannuated mechanics without means, at the public expense. (4) Education of poor children by the State. (5) Taking possession of the railroads by the State. (6) The promotion of education, (*a*) by the introduction of free schools, with the power enforcing the parents to send their children to school, and prohibition of all clerical influence; (*b*) by instruction in the German language; (*c*) by establishing a German University. (7) The supporting of the slave-emancipation exertions of Cassius M. Clay by Congressional laws. (8) Abolition of the Christian system of punishment, and introduction of the human amelioration system. (9) Abolition of capital punishment.

These are the "fundamental principles of reform of the Social Democratic Society of Germans," and are not confined to Virginia, but are ramified throughout the whole Union,[1] wherever the Germans go. . . . .

[1] [The author submitted "in proof" of this statement, the address and regulation of the American Revolutionary League adopted at the Revolutionary Congress, Philadelphia, January 29 to February 1, 1852. These documents are omitted here since they deal with affairs in Europe rather than domestic issues. The object of the League was said to be "the radical liberalization of the European continent," a cause which was said to demand "(1) agitation as well in Europe as in America; (2) accumulation of a revolutionary fund; (3) formation of armed organizations desirous of entering personally into the struggle and preparing for it by military exercise." The League was to be extended to "the principal towns of every state."]

And here is the platform of principles and purposes promulgated by the social German democracy of Louisville, Kentucky:

PLATFORM OF THE FREE GERMANS OF LOUISVILLE, ADOPTED
MARCH, 1854

1. *Slavery question.*—Notwithstanding that we consider slavery to be a political and moral cancer, that will, by and by, undermine all republicanism, we deem its sudden abolition neither possible nor advisable. But we, as republicans and men, demand that the further extension of slavery be not constantly urged, whilst not a single step is taken for its extermination. . . . . We further demand, that all and every one of the laws, indirectly transporting the principle and the influence of slavery in and upon free States, namely, the fugitive slave laws, shall be repealed, as demoralizing and degrading, and as contrary to human rights and to the Constitution. . . . .

2. *Religious questions.*—We consider the right of free expressions of religious conscience untouchable, as we do the right of free expressions of opinion in general. We therefore accord to the believer the same liberty to make known his convictions, as we do the unbeliever, as long as the rights of others are not violated thereby. But from this very principle of liberty of conscience, we are decidedly opposed to all compulsion, inflicted on dissenting persuasions by laws unconstitutionally restricting the liberty of expression. Religion is private matter; it has nothing to do with policy; hence it is despotism to compel citizens, by political means, to religious manifestations or omissions contrary to their private persuasions. We, therefore, hold the Sabbath laws, thanksgiving days, prayer in Congress and Legislature, the oath upon the Bible, the introduction of the Bible in the free schools, the exclusion of "Atheists" from legal acts, etc., as an open violation of human rights as well as of the Constitution, and demand their removal.

3. *Measure for the welfare of the people.*—As the foremost of such measures, we consider the free cession of public lands to all settlers; to occupy the natural soil, as exclusive property, this no individual has a right to do; it is, for the time, the common principal fund of that population which inhabits it, and anybody willing to cultivate it has an equal right to appropriate a share of the soil, as far as it is not disposed of, for purposes of common interest. It is high time the ruinous traffic with the public lands should be abolished, that the wasting of them by speculation should cease, and that the indigent people enter upon their rightful possession. . . . .

In the closest connection with the land reform question stands that of immigration, which, by its general importance, should be raised to the rank of a national affair, and for which a special office of colonization and immigration should be created as a particular department of the United States government. Such a board would have to provide for the various interests of immigrants, who are now helplessly exposed to so many sufferings, and wrongs, and abuses, from the place of embarkation in Europe, to the place of their settlement in America. North America is neglecting herself, when neglecting the immigration, for immigration is the mother of this republic.

The admission to citizenship must be rendered as easy as possible to the immigrants.

The welfare of a nation cannot be generally and permanently secured unless its laboring classes be made independent of the oppression of the capitalist. Labor has an incontestable claim to the value of its products. Where it is prevented, by the wants of the necessary capital, to secure this claim, it is, of course, referred to an alliance with capital of others. But if no just agreement can be obtained by this association with the capitalist, then the State, as the arbitrator of all contending interests, has to interfere.

This must either aid the associations of working men, by credit banks, or mediate between the claims of the laborer and the capitalist, by fixing a minimum of wages equalling the value of the labor, and a maximum of labor answering the demands of humanity. The time of labor shall not exceed ten hours per day.

In letting our State contracts, the preference shall be given, if it can be done without running a risk, to associations of workmen, rather than to single contractors. But when given to single contractors, the latter ought to give security for proper wages to the workmen employed by them.

In order to enjoy "life, liberty, and happiness," all, indiscriminately, must have the use of free schools, for all branches of education, in which, wherever a sufficient number of Germans live, a German teacher should be employed. . . . .

4. *Constitutional questions.*—Considering, as we do, the American Constitution as the best now in existence, we yet think it neither perfect nor unimprovable. In particular, we hold the following amendments and additions likewise acceptable for the State Constitution, as timely and proper means to check the prevailing corruption, to wit:

1. All elections, without any exception, should issue directly from the people.

2. Any eligible citizen of any State may be elected as member of Congress, by the citizens of any other State, and likewise may any eligible denizen of any county be elected by the citizens of any other county for a member of the State Legislature.

3. Any representative and officer may, at any time, be recalled by the majority of his constituents, and replaced by another.

5. *Free trade.*—We decidedly profess the principle of free trade. . . . .

6. *Foreign policy.*—The policy of neutrality must cease to be an article of our creed, and ought to be abandoned soon, as contrary to the interests of North America. The rights of American citizens, and immigrants having declared their intention to become citizens, must the more energetically be protected in foreign countries, since every American appears to monarchical

and despotical governments as a representative of revolution against despotism, and this republic ought to honor this point of view as the only one worthy and legitimate.

7. *Rights of women.*—The Declaration of Independence says that "All men are born equal, and endowed with inalienable rights, and to these, belong life, liberty, and the pursuit of happiness." We repeatedly adopt this principle, and are of the opinion that women, too, are among "all men."

8. *Rights of free persons.*—In the free States, the color of the skin cannot justify a difference of legal rights. There are not born two men of equal color, but still less, two men of unequal rights.

9. *Penal laws.*—It is our opinion, that all penal laws can only have the purpose of correction, but never the absurd purpose of expiation. We, therefore, consider the penalty of death, which excludes the possibility of correction, to be as irrational as barbarous.

All these demands are antagonistic to the fundamental principles and established usages of the government. The Bible is repudiated, the sanctity of an oath is rejected, the observance of the Sabbath is enumerated among the evils which these Germans seek to correct. The presidency is to be abolished, all powers are to be vested exclusively in the masses, and the Constitution must give way to the whims and caprices of the people. All the safeguards which protect the minority in the enjoyment of their rights and privileges are to be broken down, and every right, privilege, and immunity, all laws, the policy of the government, the institutions of the country, and its relations with other countries, are to be dependent upon the will of an uncontrollable and licentious majority; the government is to become "a heterogeneous, incoherent mass."[1]

These organizations have not stopped with a mere enumeration of their principles. They have boldly entered the political arena, asserted their right to share with us in legislation and with a zeal and determination worthy of a better cause, sought to engraft upon our institutions the "principles which they imbibed in early youth." The abjuration of their allegiance to the country of their birth has not divested them of their principles. The oath of allegiance to ours has not infused into them the spirit of our government. They have left home and kindred, severed associations, and cut asunder the ties of relationship, but the principles they "imbibed in youth" still cling to them. They have brought with them the "maxims of absolute monarchies," or exchanged them "for an unbounded licentiousness." Nor are the Germans the only class of foreigners who have organized for the purpose of concen-

[1] [See Jefferson, Section V, p. 703.]

trating their political power, and directing that power at the government. As early as 1814 the Irish were troublesome to our people and were not unfrequently denounced as such by the press of those days. . . . .

Forty years ago the Tammany Savage Society, composed of Irishmen, denounced President Madison for having recommended to Congress the repeal of the embargo laws. At that period there were not two hundred thousand immigrants in the country, yet they were organized into societies and into communities. . . . . The immigrants of 1814 were far superior to those of the present day. They came to seek an asylum in this land of constitutional liberty, and not to govern it; they came to enjoy the blessings of our laws and not to make laws; but even then so thoroughly had they imbibed the sympathies and feelings and principles of their respective races, that it was impossible to divest themselves of them. Since then the races have degenerated, and the immigrants of the present days are but the inferior specimens of these degenerate races. . . . .

In late years, immigration has greatly increased. Foreign organizations have become more numerous and formidable, and their attempts to obtain political power more frequent.

At a charter election, held in the city of New York, a few years ago, the following hand-bill was published by the Irish organization, and extensively circulated, to wit:

Irishmen to your posts, or you will lose America. By perseverance you may become its rulers. By negligence you will become its slaves. Your own country was lost by submitting to ambitious rulers. This beautiful country you gain by being firm and united. Vote the tickets Alexander Stewart, Alderman; Edward Flannigan, Assessor, both true Irishmen.

About the same time, at an election in the county of LaSalle, Illinois, a body of Irish immigrants, numbering about two thousand, brought forward and supported an Irishman for the office of sheriff, in opposition to an American of the same national politics, and of much longer residence in the country, and elected him, by upwards of one thousand majority.

In the town of Patterson, New Jersey, but a few years ago, an election was held, in which the foreigners elected thirty-three out of thirty-seven township officers.

Numerous instances could be cited where the leaders of political parties have been compelled to submit to the decision of the foreign population of their respective election districts, which of the candidates should be run by their party for an office; and the political history of our country, for a few years back, is full of instances, in which the foreign organizations have demanded of the candidates pledges. One of the most remarkable is that which occurred in the city of Baltimore, just previous to the election for members of Congress, in 1853. The German organization of this city addressed a series of questions to each of the candidates, and demanded of them written responses to the interrogatories. They were organized and determined to cast their votes *as a body of Germans*, for him who answered most satisfactorily. The following is the letter addressed to the Honorable Henry May, for whom they cast their votes, and the reader will perceive that the purpose, on the part of the Germans, was to preserve their organization as Germans, to retain their distinctive characteristics, and to force, by the power of their organization, an American candidate for office to yield to them:

BALTIMORE, June 23, 1853

DEAR SIR: At the third meeting of the German Citizens' Convention, being organized *to advise the German voting Community* of Baltimore how to cast their votes at the next election, it was unanimously resolved to authorize the Executive Committee to inquire of every gentleman having submitted the use of his name as a candidate for Congress, subject to a Democratic nomination:

1st. If he is convinced of the *justice and necessity of our organization?*

2d. If he openly pledges himself to represent us in Congress, according to the laws of equality and justice, without any preference to native-born American citizens. A written reply is requested.[1] By order of the President.

S. B. WENTZ, *Secretary*

. . . . The *Philadelphia Pennsylvanian,* of April 7th, 1856 (a Democratic paper), in speaking of the frequent attempts of foreigners to control the election of delegates to political conventions, says:

The two prominent causes which led to the organization of the Native party, and gave it great strength, were the placing of candidates in nomination, who possessed no one pre-requisite for office, and the indignation occasioned by the moving of large gangs of unnaturalized persons from poll to poll, to rob, by their votes, competent citizens of their rights. This latter evil, we regret to say, still exists. We have been informed, that it is the intention of a few depraved and worthless members of the Democratic party,

[1] [The reply of the candidate is omitted. One candidate who denounced the German convention was defeated. Two who replied commending the "justice and necessity" of German organizations were elected and later, according to Busey, opposed the bill to prohibit the shipment of foreign paupers.]

to practice this great outrage at some of the polls tonight. If such a great wrong be attempted, it should be resisted at every hazard. The Democratic party cannot be kept intact, if the legal voters attached to it are to have their votes rendered nugatory, by the introduction of fraudulent tickets into the ballot-boxes, voted by aliens. We should have honesty at our primary elections, and wherever an alien attempts to vote, he should be prosecuted on the charge of inciting to a breach of the peace. We hope that all good Democrats will resent the degradation that must attach to our party, if unnaturalized voters attempt to control our delegate elections.

Such authority as this cannot be doubted nor gainsayed. It comes from one who has been unremittingly a friend of the alien, and who is strenuously opposed to any further legislation upon the subject of naturalization.

The *Galveston Zeitung* of August 19th, 1855, the organ of the Germans of Texas, contains the following manifesto to the Germans of that State:

You have often observed that the continual clashing between natives and foreigners might easily come to a general eruption, which would result disastrously to the Germans, unless we consider in time the proverb that "He who desires peace should prepare for war."

The Cincinnati April scenes, and those at Columbus, have shown that the police in such cases are not fully sufficient for our guard, or suppression of the mob. In such cases, we must depend upon ourselves to defend our families and property, as is our duty and right. Without an organization this is impossible. In the moment of an attack it is too late to form such an organization; our duty is to organize beforehand. I therefore submit the following propositions:

1st. To form in every town where there is sufficient German population one or more guard companies who shall furnish their arms.

2d. The uniform must be everywhere the same, to preserve equality. The uniform is necessary to prevent confusion and to distinguish our friends.

3d. The arms must be everywhere the same, and we recommend as the best the arms of the Turners and revolvers.

4th. A member of any company shall be recognized as a member wherever there be such a company formed. All the companies in the United States must be in connection with one chief or leader.

5th. The decade system is the most commendable, i.e., every ten members to constitute one decade, and make one leader, who in case of necessity can call together his nine comrades. The leaders, then. elect their officers. Five decades would be enough for one company.

This is in direct contravention to the laws of the country, under whose protection they live. It is neither their duty nor their right to organize as Germans. They claim to be citizens of the United States, and as such are entitled to its protection. Their organization as a society or a community of Germans is inconsistent with the institutions of the country, and any effort to protect themselves, not from any armed body of natives, for none has dared to interrupt them in the enjoyment of either their social or political rights, but to protect themselves from the *influence* of the free, liberal, enlightened and republican institutions, by cutting off and preventing intercourse between themselves and the natives, is utterly subversive of these institutions.

Their association and free intermingling with the natives is disastrous to many of the habits, customs, and peculiarities, which they have brought with them from their fatherland, and which they desire to transmit to their children, and hence it is that these exclusive organizations are adhered to.

During the fall of 1855, at an election held at one of the interior towns of Texas, the Germans marched in a body to the polls. The Hon. Mr. Wilcox, formerly a member of the House of Representatives from Mississippi, gives the following account of the occurrence.

On the day of election here, the Germans paraded their flag (instead of the national) through the streets. They marched in procession through the city, chanting German national airs. The French singing the Marseillaise hymn. . . . . Yet, it is said, we have nothing to fear from German influence.

. . . . On Sunday, the 23d September, 1855, the German democrats of the city of New York, thus carrying out the principle in their German constitution of abrogating the Sabbath, assembled in general convention, composed of delegates from the several wards in the city, to take into consideration the welfare of the German organization, and to nominate candidates for the city and State offices, or to exact pledges from some of the candidates. . . . .

The convention then resolved to take speedy steps for the organization of committees in the various wards, so that the German vote might be thoroughly canvassed, and polled to its full strength. Various speeches were made, exhorting the Germans to unity, and encouraging them to assert their principles, and "dare maintain them." And on Sunday, 30th September, another German convention in the same city assembled for a similar purpose.

The German citizens of Galena, Illinois, held a meeting at the Courthouse in that city, during the month of January last, which was addressed by Mr. Stibolt, the editor of the *Vorwärts,* a German liberal paper; and after his address, the following, among other resolutions, were subscribed to by 157 persons of German birth:

*Resolved*, That we, as true democrats, for the present will preserve our independence of all political parties, and go only for principle.

*Resolved*, That slavery is a curse to our beloved republic, a stain for a free nation. . . . .

*Resolved*, That we will support only such candidates for state offices as are opposed to the Nebraska bill, and to Know-Nothingism.

. . . . When foreigners enjoying our hospitality as they do, assume to set up a standard of "Democracy" which proscribes a portion of their benefactors, it is high time that the birth-right qualification for office and voting should be established.

### 22. The Difficulties of the Irish in the New Anglo-American World[1]

. . . . It is, in fact, unquestionable, that the Irishman looks upon America as the refuge of his race, the home of his kindred, the heritage of his children and their children. The Atlantic is, to his mind, less a barrier of separation between land and land, than is St. George's Channel. The Shores of England are farther off, in his heart's geography, than those of New York or Massachusetts. Degrees of latitude are not taken into account, in the measurements of his enthusiasm. Ireland—old as she is, and fond as he is of calling her so—seems to him but a part and parcel of that great continent which it sounds, to his notions, unnatural to designate as the *new* world. He has no feeling towards America but that of love and loyalty. To live on her soil, to work for the public good, and die in the country's service, are genuine aspirations of the son of Erin, when he quits the place of his birth for that of his adoption. . . . .

And may it not here be asked, Is the man who thus comes into the country—a part of it by impulse, a patriot ready-made—a fit object of doubt and odium? and might it not be more generous, just, and politic to meet half-way his ingenuous views, to stretch out to him the hand of brotherhood, to join in the bond of fellowship which his heart has already ratified? Might not a fairer estimate of his character than that which generally prevails, and a higher trust in human nature itself, combine, and safely too, so as at once to invest him with the title he aspires to. . . . .

[1] Extract from Thomas Colley Grattan, *Civilized America* (London, 1859), II, 5-11, 28-30.

The expectations of the newcomer, romantic rather than reasonable, are too often cruelly checked in the first moments of his arrival. . . . . He speaks in the fulness of sincerity; but no voice responds in the same key. His uncouth air, his coarse raiment, his blunders, and his brogue are certainly unattractive or ludicrous, to those who consider him only as a machine for doing the rough work of the State, or as an object of political speculation. The Irishman soon sees the fact of his position, for he is sensitive and shrewd beyond most men; and it may be imagined how keen and how bitter is his annoyance. No man is sooner than an Irishman thrown back on his own feelings. The recoil is in proportion to the exuberance; and in the same degree in which they are originally warm and social, they become morose and gloomy when thus repelled. His natural gaiety overcomes this effect at times, or enables him to conceal what pains him so acutely. But the inward utterance of his disappointment is deeply echoed in his heart; and he is too prone to resent, or even avenge, a wrong done to his feelings, which, did it affect his interests alone, he would despise.

By a rapid transition, on finding himself slighted and despised, he assumes the offensive, becomes violent, throws himself into the open arms of faction; drinks, swears, joins in riots; and, fancying that the hostile outpourings, by which a "party" assails him, speak the sense of the nation at large, he withdraws his proffered sympathy; and, seeing that he is stigmatized as an alien—for he has learned the meaning of the word—he falls into the circle of his fellow-countrymen, becomes one of the mass of ignorance and intemperance which disgraces the Atlantic cities. . . . .

Yet, though baffled and disappointed, the ardent love of liberty rarely deserts the Irish heart, and it as rarely sinks into despair. Few of the exiles return to the old country. They, in a majority of cases, hold fast, and work their way. Nor do they cease to love America. But they love it now, not with the rapture of an abstract passion, but with a practical and business-like regard, as the birthplace of their children, and the field for the exercise of their own patient industry.

Thus, in the very best aspect of his fate, the immigrant drags on, for five long and weary years, in a probation of drudgery—which, to those who do not suffer it, seems a mere span—in a state of manifest inferiority to the citizen, who employs, makes a tool of, or, perhaps, bribes and buys him, for purposes of electioneering debasement. This cannot, certainly, increase the alien's self-esteem, or make him more fit for the exercise of a citizen's privileges. It must, indeed, add to his sense of degradation. Year after year he becomes, no doubt, more and more acquainted with the workings of party machinery. But those years do not teach him to love the country one whit more than he loved it on the day of his landing; and he has not that pride of conscious respectability and value, which leads the real freeman, however lowly his station, to take a wide and exalted view of public affairs. The longer the alien remains in this chrysalis state, may he not become the less suited for the enjoyment of the light and air, when he breaks his shell, expands his wings, and flies into his new political existence? Cramped, narrowed, and prejudiced, he is immersed in the low tricks of the intriguers, who have pounced upon and beguiled him; and more irritated and angry against those who, independent of strict party grounds, are adverse to him on those of birth alone. A deep-rooted sense of wrong, and a hatred to those who do it, are nourished in his heart and instilled into his children; and a large portion of the population is thus, for one generation at least, alienated from the rest, and driven, as it were, into a second exile from all the social advantages of citizenship. The theory of the naturalization laws of course is, that the five years shall be years of instruction for the duties of citizenship; but, in the actual want of such instruction, is not the effect of the delay too likely to be such as I have described? Yet, with all this, the Irishman can hardly be made a bad or a disloyal citizen, or prevented from embracing the first opportunity to serve the country, as is proved by the readiness with which he enlists in the naval or military force.

In thus stating impartially, and with a thorough knowledge of Irish character, the effects produced on great numbers of emigrants from that country, I am by no means making a reproach, on the score of feeling, or want of feeling, against those who are ignorant of the history of Ireland, who know the character of the people only through the medium of these very exiles, and who have had no means of scanning the hearts which beat under so coarse an exterior. Every candid Irishman who understands any portion of human nature beyond his own, will admit, that his over-ardent temperament is very likely to beget suspicion as to his sincerity, in those who do not partake of it in anything like the same degree; while his familiar, free-and-easy manners are little in accordance with the reserved and cautious habits of the majority of the American people. Taking things for granted is the curse of the generous-hearted, in all climes and at all times. No one suffers more from this too common mistake than the Irish immigrant, who, when he finds himself deceived in his sanguine estimate of men and things, makes no allowance for those who fall below his fancied standard, and who look askance or stand aloof from his companionship. But this is not altogether fair on his part. . . . .

It must be admitted that the Irish have to encounter considerable prejudices—no matter from what causes arising—in almost every section of the Union, though in different degrees. In some places they are openly and even violently expressed; in others, the feeling is slightly visible on the surface of common intercourse: but there is no observing Irishman, perhaps, who has not had, on some occasion or other, cause to notice the annoying fact. It must be remarked, that some of the different portions of the Union are much more congenial than others to the habits and feelings of Irishmen; and all seem to agree, that New England, taken on the whole, is the hardest soil for an Irishman to take root and flourish in. The settled habits of the people, the untainted English descent of the great majority, discrepancies of religious faith and forms, and a jealousy of foreign intermixture of any kind, all operate against those who would seek to engraft themselves on the Yankee stem, in the hope of a joint stock of interest or happiness. The bulk of Irish emigration to the Western States is comprised chiefly of agricultural labourers. Rigidly excluded in former times from improving by education his acknowledged quickness of intellect, the emigrant of this class has been hitherto fitted only for the performance of offices requiring mere muscular exertion. Without any of those incentives to improvement possessed by the educated man, the beings we now speak of were doomed to a hopeless state of social inferiority. Their incapacity to perform any work requiring the application of intellectual power marked them out as hewers of wood and drawers of water. The high wages and good living, in comparison to what they had been accustomed to in Europe, ought to have given them more comforts, and raised them in the moral scale. But the pernicious addiction to whiskey-drinking, common to those poor people, and the highly reprehensible habit of allowing it to them in large quantities, by the contractors for some of the public works, have, until lately, kept them in a state of mere brute enjoyment, so to call their degraded condition. This is the true source of every excess heretofore committed by Irishmen in America. Goaded by the stimulus of ardent spirits, their natural excitability of temperament knows no bounds. The memory of their ancient feuds in the old country revived by some chance word, they rush into conflict with their fellow-countrymen, or, in the words (scarcely exaggerated) of the song,

"Get drunk, meet their friend, and for love knock him down"

and present to the amazed, amused, but disgusted American spectators a scene unparalleled, except between tribes, in open warfare, of the savages on their borders.

These broils, happily of rare occurrence at present, tended much to lower the standard of the Irish character; but the improved deportment of those who have been long in the country, and the better description of emigrants who have of late years left Ireland, decrease every day the chances of such disgraceful outbreaks; while the certainty of comparative regeneration among the millions still in the old country, under the influence of temperance and liberal government, is a guarantee for the moral worth of those who may hereafter emigrate.

A deep and fatal error—the main cause of which has been already adverted to—among the immigrant Irish, is the energy with which they associate in clubs and societies, having laudable but mistaken views. The Motto, "Union is strength," is, in this case, a fallacy of the worst kind, and affords a parallel to that other Union at home, which hitherto produced little but weakness and discord. The more an Irishman abstracts himself from those associations exclusively Irish, the greater is his chance of amalgamation with Americans, among whom his destiny is cast, and in whose fraternity he is, after all, to look for the meed of his industrious career. It may be safely observed that those Irishmen who have thriven best in the United States are those who have taken an independent stand, and, separating themselves from all clannish connexions, have worked their way alone. Such a man was the late Mathew Carey, of Philadelphia, the record of whose life is, to his enterprizing fellow-countrymen, an example more valuable than a legacy, and to his own memory a monument more honourable than a marble statue.

## 23. Isolation of the Irish in America[1]

. . . . Smith O'Brien has been travelling through the country and devoting a good deal of attention *en passant* to the condition of his countrymen. I do not think he will find in it much that is very encouraging. The great mass of them have not, so far as I can see, very materially improved their condition, socially at least, by emigration. Physically, they are perhaps better off, though even in this respect their life in the large cities is pretty much what it is in London and

[1] Extract taken by permission from a journalist's letter, March 16, 1859, in *Life and Letters of Edwin Lawrence Godkin*, ed. by Rollo Ogden (New York: Macmillan, 1907), I, 181-84.

Dublin. They earn larger wages, but everything is dearer. The few that have a little capital and move West get on well. There is no prejudice against Irishmen as Irishmen which offers the least impediment to their prosperity, but the creed and mode of life and habits of the American public as they may be supposed to have descended from Cromwell's Ironsides. More incongruous elements it would be difficult to bring together than the jolly, reckless, good-natured, passionate, priest-ridden, whiskey-loving, thriftless Paddy, and the cold, shrewd, frugal, correct, meeting-going Yankee. There was a time when the Irish emigration was small, and purely American influence predominated in the country—when the Irishman, at least of the second, generation, lost most of the traces of his origin, and was absorbed into the American population. But that time has passed. The prodigious influx of Irish during the last twenty years has created a large Irish class, apart from the rest of the people, poor, ignorant, helpless, and degraded, contemned by the Americans, used as tools by politicians of all parties, doing all the hard work and menial duties of the country, and filling the jails and almshouses, almost to the exclusion of everybody else. Were the emigrants Protestants, I think the American church organization, which is immensely powerful, would be brought to bear on them. The religious public would feel itself responsible for their condition, and community of faith and strong religious sympathies would probably wipe out all traces of the old Puritan contempt for the "Irish papist." But, unhappily, to other divisions between the new-comers and the old inhabitants is added the crowning and damning one of difference of creed. The churches take but little interest in the half-barbarous stranger for whom the priest is waiting on the shore the moment he leaves the ship; and the speculative New Englander, who has been bred in a theological atmosphere, where intellect has been sharpened ever since he learnt to speak by controversy on "fixed fate, free will, foreknowledge," feels little brotherhood for poor Paddy, who never discussed a point of doctrine in his life. Fifty years ago, however, the Paddy would have been surrounded by a purely American society, and with his usual adaptability would soon have converted himself into a tolerable likeness of "a Descendant of the Pilgrims." Now this is no longer possible. As soon as he arrives he is lost in the crowd of his countrymen, who encompass him in such numbers that his glimpses of American manners, morals, and religion are few and faint.

The priests do all in their power to encourage this clannishness and keep their flocks apart from the American population. They refuse, as far as possible, to allow the Irish children to attend the common schools. Archbishop Hughes is vehemently opposed even to emigration to the West, because there the emigrants are scattered and isolated, and less able to resist the insidious advances of heresy. All the influence he possesses is exerted in keeping them together in masses in the large towns, where, though their life is miserable, their earnings precarious, and their dwellings squalid and unhealthy, their spiritual wants are more closely attended to. The result is that the line of demarcation between the English colonist and the "mere Irish" of the seventeenth century in Ireland was hardly more strongly marked than that which today separates the Irish American from the native American, political inequalities of course excepted. Emigration, instead, as is commonly supposed in England, of effacing all distinction, has traced it more deeply. The mass of Celts is now too large and unwieldy for American temperament to permeate it; and I despair of any change for the better, until the supply of the raw material from the old country is so checked as to allow the supply we already possess to become scattered and the native element to work upon it more freely.

### 24. "The Foreign Element in American Society"[1]

The foreign element in American society is a large and important one. True, we were all foreigners once; but there is a difference between the descendants of those who emigrated to America two hundred years ago and those who went there last year, or those whose parents were born in Europe.

Two countries have supplied America with the great mass of its recent immigrants—Ireland and Germany. An enthusiastic Irishman claims that not less than ten millions of the American people are of Irish birth or Irish descent. A careful estimate gives six millions of Germans. These calculations go back to the early settlement of the country. I judge that there are three or four millions of people of Irish blood, without counting more than three generations. And there are nearly or quite as many Germans of recent emigration, or children of Germans born upon the soil. There are portions of New York, and of nearly every large city, where the population is as thoroughly Irish as in Dublin or Cork. There are also large tracts of these cities crowded with Germans. The Germans have gone farther west, and scattered themselves more widely in the rural districts. There are large bodies

[1] Extract from Thomas L. Nichols, M.D., *Forty Years of American Life* (London, 1864), II, 68–80. Dr. Nichols was an American by birth, residing in London.

of Germans, for example, in Wisconsin, Missouri, and Texas. Crowds of emigrants land at New York, and go west by rail. Thousands also in past years have gone out in cotton ships to New Orleans, and ascended the Mississippi. There is a German quarter and an Irish quarter, as well as French and American quarters, in New Orleans. I found many of both races at Galveston, Texas. Nearly half of Cincinnati is German; and crossing a canal that divides the northern part of the city from the southern is popularly termed "going over the Rhine." It is much the same at Chicago and St. Louis. At Milwaukee, the Germans appeared to me to occupy nearly or quite a third of the city.

The Germans of recent immigration or birth in the United States are, I suppose, about equally divided in religion between Roman Catholics and Protestants, though a large portion of the latter class belong to the school of Rationalism, and can scarcely be said to have any religion. They are, to a great extent, ultra Red Republicans, and in America have also become what is called Black Republicans. They gave a large vote to Mr. Lincoln, and have also contributed a great many regiments of soldiers to the war, and several generals. . . . .

The Roman Catholic Germans are of a more conservative character, and mostly democrats.

The Irish population of the United States is Roman Catholic in about the same proportion as in Ireland. They are scattered over the Northern States, and to some extent in the larger commercial cities of the South. They have dug the canals, built the railways, and done the rough work of the cities of the North and West. They are settled in hundreds of cities and villages, on those great works of internal improvement, and wherever they have gone of course their priests have accompanied or followed them. They have had good wages, and are always liberal and open-handed, especially for anything connected with their religion. The result is that there are everywhere Catholic churches, convents, schools, and colleges.

The Irish in America have been a source of wealth and strength. One can hardly see how the heavy work of the country could have been done without them. They are not as prudent and thrifty as the Germans; but great numbers of them have accumulated property, and with wages at from four to ten shillings a day, and provisions one-half or one-third the price in this country, they could not fail to live and prosper.

The fact that whisky, of a very fiery and destructive quality, has been as cheap in proportion as corn and potatoes, has been against them. But their bishops and clergy have done much to keep them in habits of temperance. Politics, also, have been of little benefit to them. Doubtless it is very fine, five years after landing, to become a citizen of the great Republic, a voter at elections, and eligible to every office but that of president. Patrick loves excitement—he loves to be of consequence, and he loves a row. By a kind of instinct the Irish have attached themselves almost universally to the democratic party. They got the idea that it was the party of popular rights, the anti-aristocratic party, the liberal party. They at least knew their friends. The democrats always welcomed and guarded the rights of the foreigner. The Federal-Whig-Republican party always hated foreigners, and wished to restrict their rights of citizenship. A few years ago, the Irish, French, and Germans in America nearly all belonged to the Democratic party. A portion of the Germans have left it on account of their Abolition sympathies.

If Irishmen have been a great help to America in supplying the demand for rough and heavy work on canals, railways, etc., vast numbers of Irish girls have also found employment as servants in families. They are not in all respects the best, but they were the only ones to be had in sufficient numbers. And they have their virtues. They are reasonably honest, and almost invariably chaste. Their kindness and generosity to their relations also appeal to our best sympathies. Thousands—hundreds of thousands of poor Irish girls, working in American kitchens, have sent home the money to maintain their families, or enable them also to emigrate. Millions of dollars have been sent by poor servant-girls in America to the land of their birth.

The great hotels of American cities, some of which have accommodations for more than a thousand persons, are obliged to employ a large number of servants, in the kitchen, as waiters, and as chambermaids. . . . . The wages of men, with board, are from thirty-five to fifty pounds a year; those of girls, from twenty to forty pounds. Servant girls in families often have presents of clothing, so that they are able to save, or send "home," almost their entire wages. I have often been asked, when the month's wages were due, or those of several months had been allowed to accumulate, to get a bill of exchange on some branch of the Bank of Ireland, to enable some hard pressed father to pay his rent, or assist in bringing out a brother or sister to America.

When these helpful young ladies from the Emerald Isle have done their duty to their relations, they are free to indulge in their own tastes, which are apt, I must say, to be a little extravagant. I have been amused, on a Sunday morning, to see two Irish girls walk out of my basement door, dressed in rich *moire antique*, with everything to correspond, from elegant bonnets and parasols to gloves and gaiter-boots—an outfit that would not disgrace the neatest carriage in Hyde Park. These girls had been brought up in a floorless mud-cabin, covered with thatch, and gone to mass without shoes or stockings very likely, and now enjoyed all the more their unaccustomed luxuries. Who will blame them? They had better have saved their money, per-haps, but saving money is not, generally speaking, an Irish virtue.

There is another matter which may interest sanitary reformers. The great mass of the Irish people, of the class that emigrates to America, live in Ireland chiefly on potatoes, oatmeal, buttermilk—on a simple, and an almost entirely vegetable, diet. They have not the means, if they had the inclination, to drink much whisky, or use much tobacco. They land in America with clear, rosy complexions, bright eyes, good teeth, and good health generally. They are as strong as horses. They find themselves in a land of good wages, cheap provisions, cheap whisky, and tobacco. Flesh meat they have been accustomed to consider the luxury of the rich, and they go in for it accordingly. They eat meat three times a day, rudely cooked, and in large quanti-ties. Whisky, of an execrable quality, is plentiful and cheap; so is tobacco, and they drink, smoke, and chew abundantly. They grow sallow, dyspeptic, and lose health, strength, and spirits. They attribute it to the climate. Out of malarious regions, the climate has very little to do with it. It is the change in their habits of living—excessive eatings of flesh, and the whisky and tobacco—much more than change of climate that fills them with disease, and carries so many to an early grave.

There is one characteristic of the foreign population of the United States which deserves to be considered with reference to the future. There is a continuous influx of immigration, larger at some periods than at others, but always a stream of immense magnitude. Ireland, Germany, and Belgium pour out their surplus of poverty-stricken populations. These people, transplanted to a new soil, and surrounded with unwonted plenty, are wonderfully prolific. The Irish and Ger-mans in America increase with much greater rapidity than the Ameri-cans of an older stock. So remarkably is this the case, that there must, in a few years, be an Irish majority even in such old states as Massa-chusetts and Rhode Island. By a natural process and without counting on conversions, there must also be Roman Catholic majorities in several states. The nativist party, with its secret organization, was a futile effort to meet this danger, by attempting to extend the period during which foreigners must reside in the country before exercising the right of suffrage. It failed, because neither of the great parties could afford to lose the foreign vote. It is now too late for such constitutional changes. The foreign element is too strong and too conscious of its power.

Besides, distinctions of birth are essentially un-American. Why should the foreigners of yesterday proscribe the foreigners of today?

It should be noted that Englishmen, when, in rare cases, they become naturalized, usually vote with the once aristocratic party, and seldom if ever on the same side with the Irish. However, few Englishmen residing in America renounce their allegiance to their own government. They are patriotic John Bulls. They take British papers, frequent British beer-houses, drink British ale, and are proud and happy to call themselves "British residents."

When New York celebrates the Fourth of July with a military procession, there are German regiments, Irish regiments, a Scottish regiment, a French regiment, an Italian regiment, including Poles and Hungarians; but who ever saw even an English company marching under the stars and stripes? That phenomenon has yet to be witnessed.

Why Irishmen, Germans, Scotchmen, etc., are so much more assimilable than Englishmen, I cannot pretend to say. It may be that Englishmen, born in America, are different—are Americans. This is curiously true of Irishmen. In the second generation they are more American than the Americans. Germans have the difficulties of language to overcome, but the children of German parents, where they attend American schools, and mingle with American children, can hardly be induced to speak German at all, and if spoken to in that language are apt to answer in English. Germans learn enough English to trade with very rapidly; but you must not expect them to be able to converse on other subjects. They can neither understand you nor express themselves, except on matters of business.

Germans, Irish, Norwegians, and other foreigners of recent immigration and their children form from 30 to 50 per cent of the population of several of the northwestern states. From 10 to 20 per cent would be a large estimate of a similar population in the southern states, where the white population is English in a large proportion, and of a more remote European origin.

### 25.  The Immigrant's Obligations in the "Old Country"[1]

It is difficult to realise to the mind the magnitude of the pecuniary sacrifices made by the Irish in America, either to bring out their relatives to their adopted country, or to relieve the necessities and improve the circumstances of those who could not leave or who desired to remain in the old country. To say that they have thus disposed of a sum equal to twenty-four millions of British money, or, supposing there to have been no depreciation of the currency of the United States, one hundred and twenty millions of dollars scarcely conveys the true idea of the vastness of the amount of money sent within a quarter of a century by one branch of the same great family to the other. . . . . As a mere fact, more than £24,000,000 have been sent by the Irish to pay for passages and outfits and fares to distant places; to enable those "at home" to pay a high rent, perhaps in a time of scarcity; to support parents too old, or too feeble, or too prejudiced, to venture across the sea; or to secure the safety and education of brothers and sisters yet too young to brave the perils of a protracted voyage and a long journey in a strange country.

There is not a private banker, or passenger broker, or agent in any of the cities of the United States who could not tell of instances of the most extraordinary self-denial practised by the sons and daughters of the Irish race. The entries in their ledgers are prosaic enough—so many dollars sent, on such a day, by a young man or a young woman with an Irish name, to some person in Ireland of a similar name. . . . .

The great ambition of the Irish girl is to send "something" to her people as soon as possible after she has landed in America; and in innumerable instances the first tidings of her arrival in the New World are accompanied with a remittance, the fruits of her first earnings in her first place. Loving a bit of finery dearly, she will resolutely shut her eyes to the attractions of some enticing article of dress, to prove to the loved ones at home that she has not forgotten them; and she will risk the danger of insufficient clothing, or boots not proof against rain or snow, rather than diminish the amount of the little hoard to which she is weekly adding, and which she intends as a delightful surprise to parents who possibly did not altogether approve of her hazardous enterprise. To send money to her people, she will deny herself innocent enjoyments, womanly indulgences, and the gratifications of legitimate

---

[1] Extract from John Francis Maguire, *The Irish in America* (London, 1868), pp. 313–23, 331–32

vanity; and such is the generous and affectionate nature of these young girls, that they regard the sacrifices they make as the most ordinary matter in the world, for which they merit neither praise nor approval. To assist their relatives, whether parents, or brothers and sisters, is with them a matter of imperative duty, which they do not and cannot think of disobeying, and which, on the contrary, they delight in performing. And the money destined to that purpose is regarded as sacred, and must not be diverted to any object less worthy. . . . .

With all banks and offices through which money is sent to Ireland the months of December and March are the busiest portions of the years. The largest amount is then sent; then the offices are full of bustling, eager, indeed clamorous, applicants, and then are the clerks hard set in their attempts to satisfy the demands of the impatient senders, who are mostly females, and chiefly "girls in place." The great festivals of Christmas and Easter are specially dear to the Irish heart, being associated with the most sacred mysteries of the Christian religion, and likewise with those modest enjoyments with which the family, however humble or poor, seek to celebrate a season of spiritual rejoicing. Then there is joy in the church, which typifies in the decorations of her altars as in the robes of her ministers the gladness which should dwell in the heart of the Christian. Thus misery, and sorrow, and want, are not in accordance with the spirit of these solemn festivals, nor with the feelings which ought to prevail with those who believe in their teaching. Therefore, to enable the friends at home— the loved ones never forgotten by the Irish exile—to "keep" the Christmas or the Easter in a fitting manner—in reality, to afford them some little comforts at those grateful seasons of the Christian year— remittances are specially sent; and coming from the source which they do, these comforts, too often sadly needed, are the more prized by those to whom the means for procuring them are forwarded with touching remembrances, and fond prayers and blessings, grateful alike to piety and affection. There is something beautiful in these timely memorials of unabated love; they link still closer hearts which the ocean cannot divide.

What wonderful things have not these Irish girls done! Take a single example—and there is not a State in the Union in which the same does not occur: Resolving to do something to better the circumstances of her family, the young Irish girl leaves her home for America. There she goes into service, or engages in some kind of feminine employment. The object she has in view—the same for which she left her home and ventured to a strange country—protects her from all danger, especially to her character; that object, her dream by day and night, is the welfare of her family, whom she is determined, if possible, to again have with her as of old. From the first moment, she saves every cent she earns—that is, every cent she can spare from what is absolutely necessary to her decent appearance. She regards everything she has or can make as belonging to those to whom she has unconsciously devoted the flower of her youth, and for whom she is willing to sacrifice her woman's dearest hopes. To keep her place, or retain her employment, what will she not endure?—sneers at her nationality, mockery of her peculiarities, even ridicule of her faith, though the hot blood flushes her cheek with fierce indignation. At every hazard the place must be kept, the money earned, the deposit in the savings-bank increased; and though many a night is passed in tears and prayers, her face is calm, and her eye bright, and her voice cheerful. One by one, the brave girl brings the members of her family about her. . . . . Such is the humble Irish girl, who may be homely, who may be deficient in book knowledge, but whose heart is beyond gold in value.

There is no idea of repayment of the money thus expended. Once given, there is an end of it. This is not so with other nationalities. The Germans, a more prudent, are a less generous people than the Irish; and when money is expended in the bringing out of relatives, it is on the understanding that one day or other it will be refunded—that it will become a matter of account, to be arranged as soon as possible, or, at farthest, when convenient. . . . .

An Irish girl in Buffalo, who had been but four years in the country, had within that time paid for the passages of two brothers and two sisters, besides sending £40; and, when lately sending another remittance through the Irish Emigrant Society of New York, she said she "would not rest until she brought out her dear father and mother," which she hoped she would be able to do within the next six months.

In populous cities the women send home more money than the men; in small towns and rural districts the men are as constant in their remittances, and perhaps send larger sums. Great cities offer too many temptations to improvidence or to vice, while in small places and rural districts temptations are fewer, and the occasion for spending money recklessly less frequent; hence it is, that the man who, amidst the whirl and excitement of life in a great city, but occasionally sends $10 or $20 to the old people at home, sends frequent and liberal remittances when once he breathes the purer air of the country, and frees himself from the dangerous fascination of the drinking-saloon.

Whether the money is given as the price of the passage out, or in the form of a ticket paid for in America, and thus forwarded to Ireland, or is sent as a means of supplying some want or relieving a pressing necessity, practically there is no more thought of it by the donor. It not unfrequently happens that tickets are returned to the donors, the persons to whom they were sent having changed their minds, being unwilling or afraid to leave the old country for a new home. But the money—recouped through a friendly agent—is almost invariably sent back, with a remark somewhat in this form: "I intended it for you anyway, either in ticket or in money; and if you won't take it in ticket, why you must in money. It is yours, anyhow, and no one else is to have it."

A large amount is annually expended in the purchase of tickets at the American side; but this, large as it is, bears only a small proportion when compared with the enormous amount sent in the shape of assistance to relatives at home. For instance, there was sent last year (1866) by one firm in Lowell, $44,290; and of this amount $32,000 were for the material assistance of the friends at home, and but $12,000 in passage-tickets out. The total amount, though small in comparison to the vast sums sent from the great cities, is still not a little surprising, when it is considered that the Irish population, consisting for the most part of young persons working in mills and factories, is now about 15,000. . . . .

When a passage is paid for by an Irish emigrant to bring out a member of the family, it is the custom, when sending the ticket, to accompany it with a few pounds to defray incidental expenses.

As a rule, those who are newly come send more and make greater sacrifices to bring out their relatives, or to assist them at home, than those who have been longer in the country: the wants of the family in the old country are more vividly present to the mind of the recent emigrant, and perhaps the affections are warmer and stronger than in after years, when time and distance, and the cares or distractions of a new existence, have insensibly dulled the passionate longings of yore. But thousands—many, many thousands—of Irish girls have devoted, do devote, and will devote their lives, and sacrifice every woman's hope, to the holiest, because the most unselfish, of all affections—that of family and kindred.

"I would say, from my own experience, as agent and otherwise," remarked an agent in a New England state, "that emigration will never cease with Irish families as long as any portion of them remain at each side of the Atlantic, and as long as those at this side find means to send for those they left behind—or so long as the Irish nature remains what it is; and I must say I can't see much change in it as yet."

That the amount of money sent from America, including the British Provinces, to Ireland cannot be far from £24,000,000 I feel assured. The Commissioners of Emigration, in their Report of 1863, return the amount as £12,642,000. But they say it would not be unreasonable to estimate the amount, of which there are no returns, at *half as much again as that of which there are returns*. Taking this rather moderate estimate, the gross amount to the close of 1862 would reach £19,000,000. That at least a million a year has been sent since then must be assumed. For last year (1866) the Commissioners put down the amount at less than half a million. But I am aware that, for that year, one bank or society in New York—the Irish Emigrant Society—remitted over £100,000 to Ireland, and that some £130,000 was sent by agents in Boston whom I could name. Here, then, is more than half the entire amount of which the Commissioners have any official knowledge. In many cities I personally know bankers or agents who sent amounts varying from £20,000 to £30,000; and there is scarcely a place of any importance, or in which there is an Irish population, however inconsiderable, from which some contribution does not go to the Old Country, for one purpose or another. If, then, we add a million a year to the nineteen millions estimated by the Emigration Commissioners, we have, up to the 1st of January, 1868, the amazing sum of £24,000,000 sent by the Irish abroad to their relatives at home.[1] In the history of the world there is nothing to match this. It is a fact as glorious as stupendous, and may well stand against the sneers and calumnies of a century.

### 26. A German View of the Importance of the German Language and the German Press, 1869[2]

. . . . It may be in place here to say a word about a prejudice entertained by some well-meaning Americans, that the publication of newspapers, and perhaps even the making of political speeches in this re-

---

[1] Remittances from the Irish in Australia must be included in the gross result.

[2] Extract taken by permission from *Reminiscences of Carl Schurz* (New York: Doubleday, Page & Co., 1907–17), III, 257–62.

public in any other language than the English, is an undesirable, if not positively dangerous, practice. It is said that it prevents immigrants from learning the language of the country; that it fosters the cultivation of un-American principles, notions and habits, and that it thus stands in the way of the development of a sound American patriotism in those coming from foreign lands to make their home among us, and to take part in the working of our free institutions. I think I may say without undue assumption that from personal contact and large opportunities of observation, I have as much personal experience of the German-born population of the United States, its character, its aspirations, and its American patriotism, as any person now living; and this experience enables me to affirm that the prejudice against the German-American press is groundless. On the contrary, that press does the country a necessary and very important service. In the first place, it fills a real and very urgent want. That want will exist so long as there is a large number of German-born citizens in this republic. There will also be many among them, especially persons of mature years, who arrived on American soil without any knowledge of the English language, who may be able to acquire enough of it to serve them in their daily walk, but not enough to enable them to understand newspaper articles on political or similar subjects. Such persons must receive the necessary information about current events, questions to be considered and duties to be performed, from journals published in the language they understand, or they will not have it at all. The suppression of the German-American press would, therefore, be equivalent to the cultivation of political ignorance among a large and highly estimable class of citizens.

It is argued that the existence of the German newspaper is apt to render the German immigrant less sensible of the necessity of learning English. This is the case only to a very limited extent. A large majority of the German immigrants of mature age, being farmers or industrial laborers, do not acquire their knowledge of English in this country through regular linguistic instruction, or by reading books or newspapers, but from conversation or attempts at conversation with their neighbors who do not speak German, and that knowledge will, of necessity, remain very imperfect. Their acquaintance with the English language will always be, to a limited extent, of course, a speaking acquaintance, but not a reading acquaintance. It is not the existence of German newspapers that will keep them from reading English newspapers, but it is their inability to read English. German immigrants of education will read English newspapers, but many of them will read German newspapers too, because they find in them things of interest which the English papers do not give them. The young people, as a rule, learn English very quickly and in many instances turn to English journals for their daily reading. On the whole it may be said that the German newspapers rank with the English papers of the same class, according to their environment and their financial resources. Their tone throughout is clean and wholesome. The sensational "yellow" class is almost wholly unknown among them.

The charge that the existence of the German-American press promotes the use of the German language in this country and thus impedes the development of a healthy American patriotism among the population concerned, can be entertained only by those who do not know the German-Americans. I speak from a large personal experience when I say that their love of their new home and their devotion to this republic does not at all depend upon their knowledge of the English language. When not long after my first arrival on American soil I spent some time in the interior of Pennsylvania, I became acquainted there with farmers and inhabitants of little country towns, belonging to the class called "Pennsylvania Dutch," who, although their ancestors had come to this country generations ago, did not speak English but conversed only in their Pennsylvania Dutch dialect and read only newspapers published partly in German, partly in "Pennsylvania Dutch." They made upon me the impression of honest, law-abiding, thrifty, cheerful and eminently good-natured folk, appearing, as to the understanding of public affairs, perhaps a trifle more sluggish than their English-speaking neighbors—which may have been owing to their unfamiliarity with the language of the country—but intelligent and alert in the exercise of local self-government, and brimful of that sort of patriotism which swears by one's country and is ready to fight and die for it. In this respect their ignorance of the English language had not, within my experience, caused them to be inferior to any class of Americans who know only English, and whose patriotism is uncontaminated by the knowledge of any other language.

The same may be said of the inhabitants of German settlements of more recent date who have come with the *bona fide* intention to make this country their permanent home. Among them German may long remain the language of social and business intercourse, they may be slow in acquiring easy familiarity with the English tongue, but even if they have come here for the mere purpose of bettering their fortunes, they are as a rule not slow in appreciating the benefits conferred upon them by American conditions, and in conceiving an attachment to this republic which before long ripens into genuine devotion. Striking evidence of this was presented by the zeal and promptness with which, in all parts of the North, by the tens of thousands of young men of German birth flocked around the Union flag at the beginning of the Civil War, and by the patriotic ardor with which, even in the South, especially in Texas, German-born citizens at the peril, and not seldom the sacrifice of their fortunes and even of their lives, stood by the national cause in defiance of the terrorism which at that period was exercised by the secession fanaticism in that region. I have known German regiments in the Union Army in the ranks of which hardly an English word was heard, and these regiments did not consist of mere adventurers fond of fighting or serving merely for pay, but in the main of German-American citizens eager to serve their adopted country in its hour of need, whether they could read and speak English or not.

I have already mentioned that there are many foreign-born citizens among us whose American patriotism is in one respect finer than that of many a native. This republic being the land of their choice, they want to be and to remain proud of that choice, and to have that pride recognized as just. A man of that class is as sensitive of any reason for casting a slur upon the character of the Republic, as a bridegroom would feel and resent a shadow cast upon the fair fame of his bride. More than once I have heard one of my countrymen, when anything discreditable to the American nation had happened, exclaim with a pathetic accent of sincerest grief: "Ah, what will they think of this in the old country! I hope they will never hear of it." And such true patriotic sighs were uttered, and perhaps felt, not in English, but in German.

That the existence of the German press tells for the preservation in this country of the German language as a language of social and business intercourse is to a limited extent true. But what harm is there in this? While it is of great use to the older immigrants, it does not keep their children from learning English, even in settlements which are preponderatingly German, for such settlements are no longer isolated as the original German settlements in Pennsylvania were. But it does give the younger generation the advantage of knowing two languages. That kind of American patriotism which takes umbrage at an American citizen's knowledge of a foreign tongue besides the English—a sort of patriotism I have here and there met with—is certainly too narrow-minded, not to say too silly, to be seriously considered. No educated, nay, no sound-minded person, will deny, that the knowledge of more than one language tends to widen our mental horizon, to facilitate the acquisition of useful intelligence, and thus to broaden education.

But the preservation of the German language among us has done and is still doing this country a peculiar and very valuable service. It is said of the Englishman that he takes his pleasures and amusements seriously, even gravely. The native American also is somewhat inclined that way. He possesses little of the faculty of finding great enjoyment in small things and of thus making his daily life sunny and cheerful. The German possesses that faculty in a high degree. It manifests itself pre-eminently in the German love for music and especially in the cultivation of song. It may almost be said that one of the happiest and most amiable features of the German character is the German *Lied*. It constitutes one of the great charms of German social life. Its invasion of American soil, stimulating the love and cultivation of music and thus softening the rigors of American social life by popularizing a harmless and refining enjoyment, has been one of the special blessings the German immigration has brought with it. It seems to me very probable, if not certain, that the blessing of this influence would have been greatly curtailed had the German immigrants upon their arrival upon these shores permitted the German language to disappear from among them, for without the preservation of that language the German Glee Club and the German Musical Society would hardly have become soundly rooted in American soil.

## 27.  "The Irish-American"[1]

### I

Columbia the free is the land of my birth
And my paths have been all on American earth
But my blood is as Irish as any can be,
And my heart is with Erin afar o'er the sea.

### 2

My father, and mother, and friends all around,
Are daughters and sons of the sacred old ground;
They rambled its bright plains and mountains among,
And filled its fair valleys with laugh and with song.

[1] A poem by T. D. Sullivan, published in the *Irish-American Almanac* for 1875 (New York, 1874), pp. 30–31.

### 3

But I sing their sweet music; and often they own
It is true to old Ireland in style and in tone;
I dance their gay dances, and hear them with glee
Say each touch tells of Erin afar o'er the sea.

### 4

I have tufts of green shamrock in sods they brought o'er,
I have shells they picked up ere they stepped from the shore,
I have books that are treasures; the fondest I hold
Is *The Melodies* clasped and nigh covered with gold.

### 5

My pictures are pictures of scenes that are dear
For the beauties they are, or the glories they were,
And of good men and great men whose merits shall be
Long the pride of green Erin afar o'er the sea.

### 6

If I were in beautiful Dublin today,
To the spots I hold sacred I'd soon find my way,
For I know where O'Connell and Curran are laid,
And where loved Robert Emmet sleeps cold "in the shade."

### 7

And if I were in Wexford—how fondly I'd trace
Each field I have marked on my map of the place
Where the brave Ninety-Eight men poured hotly and free
Their blood for dear Erin afar o'er the sea.

### 8

Dear home of my fathers! I'd hold thee to blame
And my cheeks would at times take the crimson of shame,
Did thy sad tale not show, in each sorrow-stained line,
That the might of thy tyrant was greater than thine.

### 9

But her soldiers are many, abroad and at home,
Her ships on all oceans are ploughing the foam
And her wealth is untold—sure no equal was she
For my poor plundered Erin afar o'er the sea.

10

Yet they tell me that strife is not yet given o'er
That the gallant old Island will try it once more;
And will call, with her harp, when her flag is unfurled,
Her sons, and *their* sons, from the ends of the world.

11

If so, I've a rifle that's true to a hair
A brain that can plan and a hand that can dare;
And the summons will scarce have died out, when I'll be
Mid the green fields of Erin afar o'er the sea.

### 28.  Position of the Irish in America: An English View[1]

Since the final issue of the American war of Rebellion, the position
of the Irish in America has in every way changed. They have been
acknowledged as a power in politics, in religion, and society. They have
not increased in popularity as a section of the American population,
principally because they have always persisted, against their own
interests, in keeping up their distinctiveness of race and religion in a
manner antagonistic to the great mass of the American people. Their
bands, their societies, their newspapers, and their foreign politics, all
very well when unobtrusive, have from time immemorial been distaste-
ful to the undemonstrative and more Puritanic or native American.
But the Irish have grown great in numbers, and the shrewd Yankee
caucus-man has long since appreciated the big battalions of the Irish
at the ballot-boxes, and votes are facts in America often more potent
than even dollars.

But the subject of the Irish in America when discussed with an
American has evidently a sting in it. It is a subject the history of
which . . . . involves the conflicting tastes, passions, and prejudices
of the American community. The Irishman has long been taught to
look upon America as the refuge of his race, the home of his kindred.
His feelings towards her are those of love and loyalty. But when he
lands, his great expectations are sometimes checked. He often finds
himself slighted as a man, and his people despised as a race, and this
not by any means directly, but indirectly. Then he throws himself
with all the fervour of his race into party politics, determined to show
he is as good as the best. Five years' probation (sometimes less) in

[1] Extract from Philip H. Bagenal, *The American Irish and Their Influence on
Irish Politics* (London: K. Paul, Trench & Co., 1882), pp. 60–62, 69–75.

electioneering tactics makes him an able auxiliary at the poll, and soon the fierce zeal with which he enters political strife excites the jealousy and dislike of the native American. The most sober and tolerant cannot endure the boisterous patriotism of the newly-fledged citizens, nor feel at ease in seeing those who were a few years ago despised subjects of England acquire *per saltum* an equality of right with the offspring of home-born Republicans. It is this survival of Native-Americanism which makes the Irish question in America a delicate one from a political point of view. And when the fate of a Presidential election depends upon the votes of a single state, and that state is New York, the empire state of the Union, which is governed almost entirely by the Irish vote, we then see how bitter may be the thoughts of old-fashioned Americans when they find the election of a President virtually in the hands of a race whom for years they had looked upon as alien and inferior.

The more modern Americans, however, have accepted facts, and, with the well-known ingenuity of the race, have turned the Irish population to good advantage. They manipulate Irish nationality, flatter Irish pride, and "scoop" the Irish vote with the same aptness that they corner wheat in Chicago or "utilize the margin" on the New York Stock Exchange. But if the Americans are still jealous of the political power of the Irish race that is planted in their midst, there is also in some quarters a religious-born fear and distrust of the Catholic Church which has been built up by means of the Irish population to its present position of wealth and influence. . . . .[1]

The statistics of the Irish in New York city are worth examining closely, as through them we can best decipher their social and physical condition, and compare it with that of the Irish who have passed by the great city and settled upon land in the Western States. According to the census of 1876, the population of New York was 942,292, composed of 523,198, or 55.5 per cent, native Americans; 202,000, or 21.4 per cent, Irish; 151,000, or 16.1 per cent, Germans; and 32,000, or 3 per cent, English, Welsh, and Scotch. The balance comprised all other nationalities.

Of this population there are engaged at common drudgery of the

[1] [See the articles by James Anthony Froude, "Romanism and the Irish Race in the United States," *North American Review*, December, 1879, and January, 1880. Bagenal, in commenting on the Froude articles, said that he concurred with some of their conclusions, but not for the reasons given by Froude. Bagenal also quotes from Bishop Spalding's book *The Religious Mission of the Irish Race and Catholic Colonization* (New York, 1880).]

severest and worst-paid kind, 50 per cent of Irish; 20 per cent of Native Americans; 16 per cent of Germans; 14 per cent of English, etc.

At the best of times this class of toilers can barely live. A dull season, a severe winter, throws at least one-fourth of them out of employment. This one-fourth of 50 per cent of Irish have to seek their food from the 50 per cent who are not mere drudges, so that in hard times every four Irishmen have to support one pauper countryman. Under similar conditions twenty-one Germans have only one pauper countryman to support.

To prove that this degrading servitude and poverty is grinding the life and manhood out of the Irish New Yorker, and that a process of extinction is in active operation, we have only to consult the statistics of the city.

The deaths in New York City for the quarter ending March 31, 1877, were 5,986. Of these, 1,239 were Irish born, giving an annual death-rate of 24.50 per thousand; and 593 were of German birth, giving an annual death-rate for them of 15.7 per thousand. On arriving in this country the Irish are as healthy and as strong as the Germans; how is it that one improves and the other deteriorates? Here are 440 deaths of the Irish in one quarter, or 1,760 in the year, which might have been prevented by a more liberal diet and a toil less excessive.

The number of marriages tell better than anything else the prosperity of a people. For the year 1873, in New York only ten per thousand of the Irish indulged in matrimony, against forty-two per thousand of the Germans. This proves that the Germans are four times as prosperous as the Irish, or four times as reckless—which is not probable.

The poor food and excessive toil has also its bad effects on the American-born children of Irish parents. For the three months ending March 31, 1877, in New York, 1,218 children were born to Irish fathers, but in the same time there were 1,013 deaths, or 83 per cent of the births, of American children having Irish fathers. For the same time there were 2,407 births to German fathers. The deaths of American-born children having German fathers during the same time were 840, or about 35 per cent of the births. So that in New York we find the Irish dying faster than any others, less given to marriage than any others, and more given to hard work and fasting than any others.

As long as 50 per cent of the Irish are poorly paid and ill-fed drudges, so long will they be intemperate, for intemperance is often an effect of poverty as well as a cause. And in proportion as they are intemperate will they be disturbers of law and order. Their poverty will keep them from marrying, and, when combined with severe toil will bring them to an early grave.

I was not surprised at the statistics I have quoted when I visited the tenement houses in New York where the Irish population dwell.

The effect produced upon the mind by an inspection of these human rookeries is a vehement desire to pull down and raze to the ground the vast system which holds in bondage thousands and thousands of men, women, and children. These high brick houses tower up to heaven, each flat holding from five to ten families, and one building numbering frequently a population of six hundred souls. To their credit, be it said, the condition of the Irish is by no means the worst, but the atmosphere of the place is death, morally and physically. Crowded into one small room a whole family lives, a unit among a dozen other such families. Can such a place be called a house? Most assuredly not. There is a high rent to be paid—but no one dares in New York to say with Michael Davitt that such a rent is an "immoral tax." The street below is dirty and ill kept. In the basement is a beer saloon, where crime and want jostle each other, and curses fill the air. On the other side is an Italian tenement reeking with dirt and rags. Close by is a Chinese quarter, or a Polish-Jew colony. Everywhere the moral atmosphere is one of degradation and human demoralization. Gross sensuality prevails. The sense of shame, if ever known, is early stifled. Domestic morals are too often abandoned and simple manners are things of the past. There is no family life possible in such surroundings; no noble traditions can descend from father to son. The fireside is hired by the week, the inmate is a hireling, and his family are most probably chained as hirelings also in some great neighbouring factory or mill.

It is from these vast nurseries of poverty that the Irish in New York pour forth to attend the demonstrations of Mr. T. P. O'Connor, Mr. Healy, and Father Sheehy, and pay out their hard-earned dollars to keep up a political agitation thousands of miles away, in which they can never have actual hand or part, or derive any benefit whatever. How much better it would be for the *Irish World* to set on foot a gigantic fund for the transportation of some thousands of the tenement Irish to the West, than to lend its efforts towards transforming them into reckless Socialists and Communists, robbing them of their earnings, and filling their minds with dreams of the impossible.

Poor food and hard work have had terrible effects upon the American-born children of Irish parents, especially when the parents have succumbed to the one gigantic temptation of the country—drink. The general mortality of the foreign element is much greater than that of the native element of the American population; and of all the various foreign races the Irish fare worst. They show a marked liability to diseases of the "constitutional group," and a comparative exemption from the diseases of the "febrile group," especially the eruptive fevers and diseases of the digestive and nervous system. The diseases most common and most fatal are consumption, cancer, pneumonia, and diarrheal diseases; while an extraordinary liability to bronchitis and Bright's disease points to the prevalence of intemperate habits.

Thus live the descendants of the great Irish exodus of 1845–48. . . . . In those bygone days when the American-Irish nation began to grow on Yankee soil, had Government directed and assisted the tide of emigration, hundreds of thousands would have been carried out west. There, accustomed to agricultural pursuits, they would have become quiet and prosperous citizens, instead of firebrands and perpetuators of the animosity between England and Ireland. All other nations have directed themselves straight to the spot where their labour was most appreciated: the Welsh to the mining districts in Ohio; the Norwegians and Swedes to the four states west of Lake Michigan, where, with the Germans, they busy themselves in agriculture. But to their own loss and unhappiness, and more by their own misfortune than by their fault, the great bulk of the Irish have blocked up the channels of immigration at the entrances, and remain like the sand which lies at the bar of a river's mouth.[1]

[1] [The Irish settlements in the West were not overlooked by Bagenal, who after the account of the Irish in New York says, "Let us now see how the minority have succeeded in the far west, where tenement houses are unknown and life in a prairie cottage holds out prospects of health, wealth, and domestic contentment." In chapters vii and viii he gives an account of the work of the St. Paul Catholic Colonization Bureau and the Irish Catholic Colonization Association and the Irish-American Colonization Company. Bagenal himself went out to Minnesota and saw Bishop Ireland in order to give an authentic account of Irish life in the West.]

# SECTION IV

## PAUPERISM AND CRIME AND OTHER DOMESTIC IMMIGRATION PROBLEMS

Immigration on a large scale must inevitably bring social problems, more or less serious, to the country receiving the immigrants. There is involved not only the problem of the landing of undesirable immigrants, but there is also the possibility that the difficulties of adjustment may prove too great for the new arrivals, even when they are of the desirable classes, and may lead to physical, mental, or moral breakdown. There has been, in America, the further difficulty that the immigrants have constituted our unskilled labor supply, and, as workers on the lowest economic level, have suffered disproportionately from the hazards of industrial accident and disease, unemployment, and low wages. Added to this has been the further fact that the alien laborer has frequently been alone, without relatives or friends to help him during a period of distress, and he has therefore been more likely than the native-born laborer to become a public charge.

Complaints that immigration has increased the burdens of pauperism and crime have been numerous in every period of our history. The transportation of felons from the "mother country" was one of our earliest immigration problems and led to the first statutes relating to the admission of immigrants (Document 1). Pauper immigrants were also a source of complaint at an early day (Document 2), and the further problem of the danger to public health was likewise recognized in the Colonial period (Documents 3 and 4). The necessity for bringing the later arrivals up to the educational standard reached by the older immigrants and their children and, in particular, the need of schools for teaching English to German children existed in Colonial Pennsylvania (Document 5). So urgent were the problems arising from the presence of newly arrived immigrants suffering from ill-health and destitution that, before the close of the eighteenth century, various societies for assisting immigrants, such as "The Philadelphia Society for the Information and Assistance of Persons Emigrating from Foreign Countries" (Document 6) were organized in some of the port cities.

The documents in the earlier sections of this volume dealing with economic conditions and with the general causes of emigration describe the widespread conditions of misery and destitution in Europe from which the poor sought refuge in America. These documents, however, also show that many of these "pauper immigrants" about whom so much complaint was made on this side of the Atlantic (Documents 7, 8, 9, 11, and 13) became in an astonishingly short time useful and productive members of society. It has already been pointed out in the section dealing with economic conditions that those who were crowding into the poorhouses in Great Britain and Ireland were, in many, if not in most, cases, men who were able and willing to work and who demanded only an opportunity to work. It was said repeatedly that in America the most disagreeable, and in general the heaviest, work, such as the construction of turnpikes, canals, and railroads, was almost exclusively carried on by the despised foreigner. But, as is always the case with work at the lowest levels, and particularly at a time when there was no "protective legislation" on our statute books, the conditions of work were often very unfavorable to the development of economic independence or the physical or moral welfare of those engaged in it.

There was much feeling against the Irish laborers who, when they were unfairly treated by their employers, took the law into their own hands, as they had long been accustomed to do at home. Document 10, for example, shows how the Irish laborers were sometimes exploited, and how amply they were justified in feeling themselves wronged. Unfortunately, their method of righting their wrongs was to use violence and alienate public sympathy by concentrating public opinion upon the offenses they had committed instead of upon the wrongs they had suffered. Even before the great Irish famine there were data to justify the belief that our American "almshouses, prisons, dispensaries, and benevolent societies" were maintained largely for the benefit of immigrants. This situation was, of course, aggravated by the influx following the famine, and the report of the Joint Special Committee of the Massachusetts Legislature in 1848 (Document 14) shows how serious the condition was, both from the point of view of cost, which concerned the taxpayer, and of social demoralization, which was even more alarming. The fear (Document 16) that British poorhouses were being emptied and their inmates transported to the United States was, of course, an exaggerated one. But it was undeniable that, in statistical reports, the immigrant made a poor showing.

In Document 17, which contains an extract from a speech in the United States Senate, and Document 18, an extract from a House committee report of the following year, some of the data in the seventh census are set forth, showing how startling a case could be made against immigration on the basis of the contribution to crime and pauperism. At the dispensaries (Document 19), as well as the almshouses and the insane hospitals (Document 20), the recent immigrants were found in disproportionately large numbers, and their children filled the institutions for juvenile delinquents (Document 21). Election riots were another disorder attributed to the recent immigrants (Document 23). There were, of course, some persons of influence who viewed tolerantly the burdens of immigration (Document 22), but there were also many who saw with dismay growing problems of social disorganization.

Cholera epidemics directed attention to the wretched living conditions in the Irish settlements of Boston (Document 15) and in the "crowded shanties and tenant houses" where the immigrants swarmed in New York (Document 25). It was not surprising that, when accurate vital statistics became available, they showed a greater mortality to exist among the immigrant than among the native-born population (Document 32).

Social demoralization of another sort resulted from the early methods of naturalization and the temptations held out to the corrupt politician to exploit the foreign vote. Document 12 illustrates the naturalization scandals of 1838 by the cases of the Germans who were naturalized by fraudulent methods in New York City. The demand for a revision of the provisions of the law relating to naturalization (Document 24) became for a time an important political issue. After the war, the wholesale corruption of city government was charged to the speedy naturalization and the absorption into the electorate of so many uneducated European immigrants (Document 29). Naturalization was also used by Europeans as a means of evading responsibilities at home. Even a liberal paper like the New York *Nation* complained that naturalized citizens had returned to Europe to escape conscription and the payment of taxes. Naturalization papers were not infrequently secured so that the newly made citizen might return to his old home with American passports to avoid obligations to either country. There was much resentment and bitterness over these pseudo citizens (Document 28).

Complaints about criminality among the immigrant population, and charges that criminals were not only permitted, but assisted, to emigrate from European countries to the United States, continued after the Civil War (Documents 26, 27, 30, and 31) and culminated in the spectacular case of the "Molly Maguires" (Document 33).

During the decade 1870–80 the New York State Board of Charities complained persistently of the heavy burden of alien pauperism (Documents 34 and 35), and the *North American Review* presented in more popular form the statistics of a decade purporting to show the "Evils of Immigration" (Document 36).

# PAUPERISM AND CRIME AND OTHER DOMESTIC IMMIGRATION PROBLEMS

## 1. Attempted Exclusion of Convicts in Colonial Period[1]

### A. VIRGINIA[2]

April the 20th, 1670—The complaints of several of the council and others, gent. inhabitants in the counties of Yorke, Gloster, and Middlesex representing their apprehensions and fears, lest the honor of his majesty and the peace of this colony be too much hazarded and endangered by the great numbers of felons and other desperate villains sent hither from the several prisons in England, being this day read in council, we have, upon most serious and careful consideration of the same, thought fit to order and do hereby accordingly order, that for prevention and avoiding the danger which apparently threatens us, from the barbarous designs and felonious practices of such wicked villains, that it shall not be permitted to any person trading hither to bring in and land any *jail birds* or such others, who for notorious offenses have deserved to die in England, from and after the twentieth day of January next, upon pain of being forced to keep them on board, and carry them to some other country, where they may be better secured. And we have been the more induced to make this order, by the horror yet remaining among us, of the barbarous design of those villains in September, 1663, who attempted at once the subversion of our religion, laws, liberties, rights, and properties, the sad effect of which desperate conspiracy we had undoubtedly felt, had not God of his infinite mercy prevented it, by a timely and wonderful discovery of the same; nor hath it been a small motive to us to hinder and prohibit the importation of such dangerous and scandalous people, since thereby we apparently lose our reputation, whilst we are believed to be a place

[1] These colonial laws were, of course, in conflict with parliamentary legislation, which provided for the transporting of convicts to the American colonies. See e.g., 4 George I, c. 11, *English Statutes at Large*, XIII, 471. For an interesting discussion of this subject, see James D. Butler, "British Convicts Shipped to the American Colonies," *American Historical Review*, II (October, 1896), 12–33. For other documents dealing with this subject, see the first volume of this series, E. Abbott, *Immigration: Select Documents and Case Records*, Part II, Section I.

[2] Extract from the records of the general court, in *Hening's Statutes at Large, Being a Collection of All the Laws of Virginia*, II (1660–82), 509.

only fit to receive such base and lewd persons. It is therefore resolved that this order remain in force until his majesty shall signify his pleasure to the contrary, or that it is reversed by an order from his most honorable privy council, and that it be forthwith published that all persons concerned therein may take notice of it accordingly.[1]

### B.   MARYLAND[2]

Forasmuch as several masters of ships, merchants, sailors, and others have used and still do use to import into this province several notorious felons and malefactors which in several of his Majesty's courts have been convicted of crimes and felonies as aforesaid and afterward procured by masters of ships, merchants, sailors and others out of the common jails to import into this province and here to sell and dispose of such felons and malefactors as servants, to the great prejudice and grievance of the good people of this province, for the preventing whereof . . . . be it enacted . . . . at every office or place where ships and vessels are and shall be appointed to be entered and cleared, the clerk of such office or person appointed for the entry and clearing of ships and vessels shall administer an oath to every master of ship when he comes to enter that he shall declare whether any servant on board his ship be felons convicts as aforesaid and if it shall appear by his oath that they are such then the said officer shall take good security of the said master not to sell or suffer the same to be sold, given, or any otherways disposed of in this province but shall transport them and every of them out of this province before he or his ship depart out of this province or in his own ship when the same departs this province.

And it is further enacted by and with the advice and consent aforesaid that no master of a ship, merchant, sailor or any other person whatsoever shall presume to import into this province any such convicted felons or malefactors whatsoever to sell, give pay, or any otherways or in any other manner to dispose of either unto their own plantation (if any they have) or unto any inhabitant of this province whatsoever.

[1] [And see also entry of November 25, 1671: "Captain Bristow and Capt. Walker entered security in the sum of 1,000,000 lbs. of tobacco and cask, that Mr. Nevett shall send out the Newgate birds within 2 months according to a former order of this court."]

[2] Extract from "An Act against the Importation of Convicted Persons into This Province," *Archives of Maryland*, II, "Proceedings and Acts of the General Assembly of Maryland, April, 1666–June, 1676," p. 540, May-June, 1676.

And be it further enacted by the authority aforesaid that if any master of a ship, merchant, sailor or other person whatsoever from and after the first day of November next shall import and bring into this province any such convicted felons or malefactors and shall sell, give, pay, or any other ways dispose of unto any inhabitant of this province such felons or malefactors as aforesaid shall forfeit and pay for every such convicted felon or malefactor so imported, sold, given, paid, or any other ways disposed of unto any inhabitant of this province the sum of two thousand pounds of tobacco, the one half to the lord proprietary, the other half to the informer or him or them that shall sue for the same to be recovered by bill, plaint, or information in any court of record within this province wherein no essoin, wager, or protection in law to be allowed. This act to continue for three years or to the end of the next general assembly which shall first happen.

## C. PENNSYLVANIA[1]

*To the Honorable the Knights, Citizens, and Burgesses of Great Britain, in Parliament assembled:*

The petition of B.F., Agent for the Province of Pennsylvania, most humbly showeth:

That the transporting of felons from England to the plantations in America, is, and hath long been, a great grievance to the said plantations in general.

That the said felons, being landed in America, not only continue their evil practices to the annoyance to his Majesty's good subjects there, but contribute greatly to corrupt the morals of the servants and poorer people among whom they are mixed.

That many of the said felons escape from the servitude to which they were destined into other colonies, where their condition is not known, and, wandering at large from one populous town to another, commit many burglaries, robberies, and murders, to the great terror of the people, and occasioning heavy charges for apprehending and securing such felons, and bringing them to justice.

That your petitioner humbly conceives the easing one part of the British dominions of their felons by burthening another part with the same felons cannot increase the common happiness of his Majesty's

[1] Franklin's petition to the British Parliament against the transportation of felons to America (1767 or 1768). Extract from *Complete Works of Benjamin Franklin*, compiled and edited by John Bigelow (New York: G. P. Putnam's Sons, 1886–88), X, 120–21.

subjects, and that therefore the trouble and expense of transporting them is upon the whole altogether useless.

That your petitioner, nevertheless, observes with extreme concern in the votes of Friday last, that leave is given to bring in a bill for extending to Scotland, the act made in the fourth year of the reign of King George the First, whereby the aforesaid grievances are, as he understands, to be greatly increased by allowing Scotland also to transport its felons to America.

Your petitioner therefore humbly prays, in behalf of Pennsylvania, and the other plantations in America, that the House would take the premises into consideration, and in their great wisdom and goodness repeal all acts, and clauses of acts, for transporting of felons; or, if this may not at present be done, that they would at least reject the proposed bill for extending the said acts to Scotland; or, if it be thought fit to allow of such extension, that then the said extension may be carried further, and the plantations be also, by an equitable clause in the same bill, permitted to transport their felons to Scotland.

And your petitioner, as in duty bound, shall pray, etc.

## 2. Pauper and Convict Immigration: A Colonial Statute [1]

WHEREAS, Many persons trading into this government, have, for lucre and private gain, imported, sold, or disposed of, and daily do import passengers and servants into this government, who, by reason of age, impotence or indigence, have become a heavy burden and charge upon the inhabitants thereof; and likewise, do frequently import divers persons convicted of heinous crimes, who soon after their coming into this government, do often commit many felonies, robberies, thefts and burglaries, to the great hurt of his Majesty's subjects trading to and inhabiting the same. . . . .

SECTION 2. *Be it further enacted,* . . . . That all masters of vessels, merchants, or others, who shall import, land or bring into any port or place belonging to this government, at any time after the publication of this act, any person in the condition of a servant, or otherwise within the intent and meaning of this act, who hath been convicted of any murder, burglary, rape, sodomy, forgery, perjury, or any other felony, at any time before such importation or coming into this government, shall, before the said convicts be landed or put on shore, pay the

[1] Extract from "An Act Imposing a Duty on Persons Convicted of Heinous Crimes and to Prevent Poor and Impotent Persons Being Imported," 1740, *Laws of the State of Delaware, 1700–1797*, Vol. I, chap. lxvi, pp. 166–70.

sum of Five Pounds for every such convict so imported or otherwise brought in, the one moiety thereof to the Governor for the time being, for the support of government, and the other moiety to the Collector appointed by this act, or the informer; and further, shall become bound with good and sufficient security, to the Treasurer of the county, where such importation shall be made, for the time being, in the sum of Fifty Pounds, for the good behaviour of such convict person, for the space of one year next after his or her importation or coming into this government. . . . .

SEC. 4. *Therefore* to prevent such practices for the future, *Be it enacted*, . . . . That if any such convict as aforesaid, or servant, or passenger, being poor and impotent persons, shall be imported into the river Delaware, after the publication of this act, and shall be found within this government at any time within the space of twelve months, next after their being imported . . . . and if, upon examination, it shall appear . . . . that the said persons were shipped or took their passages for this government, then the Collector or Collectors, or Justice of the Peace . . . . shall demand and compel the persons, if convicts, immediately to comply with the directions of this act, by paying the duties hereby imposed on them, and giving the security directed in the case of convicts by this act; and shall . . . . send for the master or merchant of such vessel . . . . and if it shall appear that the said persons so apprehended, or any other persons, being convicts as aforesaid, were shipped and taken on board to be imported into this government . . . . the said master or merchant shall be . . . . held for the county where such examination is taken; and if, upon presentment or information, he or they shall be legally convicted of such fraudulent practice, he or they so offending shall forfeit the sum of Twenty Pounds for every person so by him or them brought in as aforesaid, . . . . without making such entry, and paying the duties, and giving the security required by this act, one-half to the Governor for the time being, and the other to the Collector or informer, and shall further pay the same duties, and give the same security for such convicts as aforesaid, as if such persons had been imported into this government, and report thereof made according to the direction of this act.

SEC. 5. And, *Be it further enacted*, . . . . That upon information given to any two Justices of the Peace within this government, that any old persons, infants, maimed, lunatick, or any vagabond or vagrant persons are imported, come or brought into this government, . . . . it shall and may be lawful for the said justices . . . . [to] compel said master, merchant, or other person who, imported any such infant, lunatick, aged, maimed, impotent or vagrant person or persons, to give sufficient security to carry and transport such infant, lunatick, maimed, aged, impotent or vagrant person or persons to the place or places from whence such person or persons were imported, or otherwise to indemnify the inhabitants of this government from any charge that may come or be brought upon them by such infant, lunatick, maimed, aged, impotent or vagrant person coming into or living within this government. . . . .

SEC. 7. And for the better discovery of such convicts, and poor and impotent, or idle or vagrant persons, who shall hereafter be imported into, and shall be likely to become chargeable to the inhabitants of this government, *Be it further enacted*, . . . . That all masters of vessels, merchants and others, who shall hereafter bring into any port or place belonging to this government, by land or water, any men or women passengers or servants, shall . . . . cause to be given, upon oath or affirmation, to the Collector of the said duties where such importation is made, a true and just account of all the names of the servants and passengers to be imported or brought in. . . . .

### 3. Demand for an Immigrant Hospital, 1741[1]

A. MESSAGE OF THE GOVERNOR TO THE ASSEMBLY

GENTLEMEN:

Several of the most substantial Germans now Inhabitants of this Province, have joined in a Petition to me, setting forth in Substance, That for want of a Convenient House for the reception of such of their Countrymen as, on their Arrival here, laboured under Disease Contracted in a long Voyage, they were obliged to continue on board the Ships which brought them, where they could not get either Attendance or Conveniences suitable to their Condition from whence many have lost their lives; And praying that I would recommend to the Assembly the Erecting of a proper Building at the publick Expence, not only to accomodate such as shall arrive hereafter under the same Circumstances, but to prevent the future Importation of Diseases into this City, which has more than once felt the fatal Effects of them.

[1] Extracts from the *Minutes of the Provincial Council of Pennsylvania*, IV (January 5–8, 1741) 507–8; 509–10; 510–11. For the respective attitudes of the governor, representing the proprietors, and members of the assembly representing the colonists, see Frank R. Diffenderffer, *The German Immigration into Pennsylvania through the Port of Philadelphia, 1700 to 1775.* Part II. chaps. vi–ix.

The numbers of People which I observed came into this Province from Ireland & Germany, pointed out to me the necessity of an Hospital or Pest-House, soon after my Arrival here; And in 1738 I recommended it to the Assembly of that year, who seemed so far from disapproving it that they gave me hopes of building one so soon as the Circumstances of the Province should admit. I very heartily wish for the sake of such familys, Inhabitants of this City, as suffered in the late Mortality by the Loss of some who were their Chief Support, and will therefore feel it for Years to come, and on Account of the Irish and German Strangers, that it had indeed been done so soon as the Circumstances of the Province did admit of it. But as it can profit nothing to bewail Evils past, I hope you will now make the proper Use of them by doing all in your Power to Prevent the like for the time to come.

I am not insensible that some look with jealous Eyes upon the yearly concourse of Germans to this Province, but the Parliament of Great Britain see it in a different Light, and have therefore given great Encouragement by a late Act to all such foreign Protestants as shall settle in his Majesty's Dominions; And indeed every Man who well Considers this Matter must allow that every industrious Labourer from Europe is a real addition to the wealth of this Province, and that the Labour of every foreigner in particular is almost so much clear Gain to our Mother Country.

I hope I need not take up more of your or my own Time to convince you that what is now again recommended is both for the interest of the Province and the Health of this City. Evils felt are the most convincing Arguments. I shall only add, that as Christians and indeed as Men, we are obliged to make a Charitable Provision for the sick Stranger, and not by Confining him to a Ship inhumanly expose him to fresh Miserys when he hopes that his Sufferings are soon to be mitigated. Nothing but the building an Hospital or Pest-House in a proper situation can, in my Opinion, be a suitable Charity or an Effectual security for the future, more especially as the Country people are grown so apprehensive of the Disease that they will not be persuaded to admit the infected into their Houses.

### B. REPLY OF THE ASSEMBLY

*May it Please the Governor:*

As great numbers of the People from Ireland & Germany are yearly imported into this Province, some of whom have been afflicted with

Malignant and Dangerous Distempers, it is Evident to Us that a convenient House to accommodate such as shall hereafter arrive under the like Circumstances, may be of great Use to them, and a means to prevent the spreading of infectious Distempers among Us, the Effects of which the City of Philadelphia has lately felt, altho' we think a due Execution of the Laws might in part have prevented them. How this failure happened, at whose Door it ought to lye, and the Means of preventing it for the future, we shall take another occasion to consider, and therefore waive further Notice of it here.

When the Governor was pleased to recommend the Building an Hospital or Pest-house to the Assembly in the Year 1738, it was thought too great an Undertaking for the Circumstances we were then in; and if it be Considered that the Province hath since been at great and unusual Expences, we think it may justly be said that the State of the Public Treasury neither at present nor at any time since the year 1738, hath been in a much better Condition for such an Undertaking than it was at that Time. Nevertheless, as it will not only be Charitable to Strangers who may hereafter come among us in the distressed Circumstances before mentioned, but also of benefit to the inhabitants of this Province, we are there determined to take this Matter into Consideration, and to direct a plan to be proposed and an Estimate made of the Money which would be requisite for the Building and yearly maintenance of such an Hospital, to be laid before Us at our next Sitting. In the mean Time, as it is a Matter of Considerable Importance, we may have the Opportunity of knowing more generally the Minds of our Constituents, and it will give such of them as shall think it fit an Opportunity of applying to Us touching the necessity of such a Building, and the Manner of doing it which may render it most useful & least burthensome to the Province; And on the whole we may the better be enabled to judge of the part it will become Us to act in the Affair.

Who they are that look with jealous Eyes on the Germans the Governor has not been pleased to inform Us, nor do we know; Nothing of the kind can be justly attributed to Us, or any preceding Assembly to our knowledge; On the Contrary, the Legislature of this Province, before the late Provision made in the Parliament of Great Britain, have generally, on application made to them, admitted the Germans to partake of the Privileges enjoyed by the King's natural born Subjects here, and as we look upon the protestant part of them in general to be Laborious, Industrious people, we shall cheerfully perform what may reasonably be expected from Us for the benefit of those already amongst Us, and such who may hereafter be imported.

### C. REPLY OF THE GOVERNOR

GENTLEMEN:

I am not a little pleased to find by your Message of Yesterday that you agree to the necessity of building a Pest-house for the reception of Sick strangers, and to prevent the Spreading of infectious Diseases they may happen to have Contracted in their Voyage hither, and I cannot allow myself to doubt of your taking speedy & proper Means for the Completion of so charitable a Work.

Whilst the German petitioners complain that many have lost their Lives by being confined to the ships, you express your Dissatisfaction that the Laws have not been Executed; that is, I suppose, that sick passengers were not confined to the Ships. A former Assembly, however, composed of many of the same Members with the present, after the very same Measures taken as to me, were pleased to tell me in their address "That they had a grateful sense of my Care in putting in Execution the Law for preventing sickly vessels coming into this Government." But all I say or do now must be wrong. The Resolutions of the last Assembly on this Matter sufficiently explain to me what is meant by "taking another occasion to consider at whose Door the late Sickness in Philadelphia ought to lie." I shall be glad to see your attempt to justify what was insinuated & assumed in those Resolves; Accusations & Complaints are no new things to me, but thanks to my Integrity they have been so far from doing me a prejudice that they have shown me to his Majesty & his Ministers in a light more advantageous than I could have otherwise expected; for this favor tho' not designed as such, Gentlemen, I thank you.

If I do not strictly adhere to form in imputing to you what was done by the two preceding Assemblys I hope you will excuse me, for as you are nine in ten of you the same Members, I know not yet how to separate your actions from your Persons.

I cannot but differ with you (which I am sorry is too often the Case) in the State of the Public Treasury since 1738, for the Public accounts in my Opinion shew that the Province has at no point of Time since been unable to Erect the proposed Building; you have, I confess, been at some unusual Expence, but I cannot call it great as you do, since £1,500 out of the £2,500 said to be Expended has been stopt out of my support. I know of no other call upon the Province since for an Unusual Expence. If you have generously and out of Compassion for the Sufferings of your fellow-subjects in Britain remitted £3,000 to your Agent for their Relief, I conclude you were well able to spare it, And that otherwise you would not have done it.

Either the Memorys of some of your Body who were Members in 1738, must have failed them very much, or their Sentiments of the Importance of foreigners are, for very Substantial Reasons, much altered; for, not to dwell upon a small Instance of the Assembly's Displeasure to me at that Time for saying a little too much of the Industry of the Germans, I refer you to your Minutes for the Assembly's address to the Proprietor in 1738, to convince you that what I said of their having been looked upon with Jealous Eyes by some, was not altogether without foundation. What follows may be found in that address.

And this House will, in a proper Time, readily join with the Governor in any Act that may be judged necessary, as well for protecting the property of the Proprietors and others from such unjust Intrusions for the future and for preservation of the peace of the Government, as for Guarding against the Dangers which may arise from the great and frequent Importation of foreigners.

GEO. THOMAS

January 8th, 1741

## 4. Sick Germans in Philadelphia, 1754[1]

### PETITION OF GERMANS IN PHILADELPHIA[2]

It is humbly requested that the Governor would please to take the present unhappy Situation of ye poor Germans dispersed thro' this City & the Neighbourhood under his Consideration.

Our Complaint is not so much of such as are called Sick Houses, that is Houses hired by the Merchants for the Reception of their Sick, tho' we have Reason to fear that there is not such sufficient Provision of Food, Cloathing & Fuel made for the sick, even in those Houses as their Weak Condition and the Severity of the Weather requires.

But our chief Complaint is on the behalf of such as the Importers don't look upon as under their Care, having as they term it, discharged themselves of them. These are People in Years, others with several small Children, & especially Widows with small Children, who not

---

[1] Extract from *Pennsylvania Archives* (1st. series), II, 217–18.

[2] Read in Council, December 21, 1754, by Richard Wistar.

being able to pay their Passages, nor fit to be bound out as Servants, the Merchants have discharged upon their own security, or after interchangeably binding them one for another, generally keeping their Chests which contains their Cloaths, Tools, &c., & often best bedding as a farther Security, Many of these are now dispersed as Lodgers in many Houses in Town, in the outskirts, & in the small Plantations near it, generally destitute of Necessaries, not only to restore them to Health, but even to keep them alive; such as are able go begging to the Terror & Danger of the Inhabitants, who from the smell of their Cloaths when brought near a Fire, & infectious Disorder which many of them are not free from, apprehend themselves in great Danger. And those who are not able to beg must inevitably Perish of Misery and Want, as is believed Scores if not Hundreds have already done this fall. It's therefore earnestly requested that the Governour would please to direct that a particular inquiry may be made in this melancholy Case.

### 5.   Charitable Schools for Immigrants[1]

For several years past, the small Number of reformed Protestant Ministers settled among the German Emigrants in Pennsylvania, finding the Harvest great, but the Labourers few, have been deeply affected with a true Christian Concern for the Welfare of their distressed Countrymen, and the Salvation of their precious Souls. In Consequence of this, they have, from Time to Time, in the most solemn and moving manner, entreated the Churches of Holland, to commiserate their unhappy Fellow-Christians, who mourn under the deepest Affliction, being settled in a remote Corner of the World, where the Light of the blessed Gospel has but lately reached, and where they are very much destitute of the Means of Knowledge and Salvation.

The Churches of Holland being accordingly moved with friendly Compassion, did, from Time to Time, contribute to the support of Religion in these remote Parts. But in the year 1751 a very moving Representation of their State having been made by a Person, whose unwearied Labors for the Benefit of his dear Countrymen have been for some years conspicuous, the States of Holland, and West Friesland,

---

[1] Extract from *A Brief History of the Rise and Progress of the Charitable Scheme Carrying on by a Society of Noblemen and Gentlemen in London, for the Relief and Instruction of Poor Germans, and Their Descendants, Settled in Pennsylvania, and the Adjacent British Colonies in North America* [By William Smith], Published by order of the Gentlemen appointed Trustees General for the management of the said Charitable scheme (Philadelphia, Printed by B. Franklin, 1755), pp. 3-17.

granted 2,000 Guilders per annum for 5 Years from that Time, to be applied towards the Instruction of the said Germans and their Children in Pennsylvania. A considerable Sum was also collected in the City of Amsterdam, and elsewhere; and upon a Motion made by the same zealous Person, the Rev. Mr. Thomson [a minister of one of the English churches in Amsterdam] was commissioned by the Synods of Holland and Classis of Amsterdam to solicit the friendly assistance of the Churches of England and Scotland.

When Mr. Thomson arrived in Great Britain, he found the readiest Encouragement among Persons of the first Rank, both in Church and State. It is the peculiar Glory of the British Government equally to consult the Happiness of all who live under it, however remote, wherever born, or of whatsoever Denomination. . . . . Considered in this Light, Mr. Thomson's Design could not fail to be encouraged in our Mother Country, since it was so evidently calculated to save a vast Multitude of Industrious People from the Gloom of Ignorance, and qualify them for the Enjoyment of all those noble Privileges, to which it is now their good Fortune to be admitted, in common with the happy Subjects of a free Protestant Government.

Mr. Thomson, having thus made his Business known in England and prepared the Way for Encouragement there, he, in the meantime, went down to Scotland and . . . . represented the Case to the General Assembly of the Church, then sitting at Edinburgh, upon which a national Collection was made, amounting to upwards of 1,200 pounds sterling. Such an Instance of Generosity is one out of many, to shew how ready that Church has always been to contribute towards the Advancement of Truth, Virtue and Freedom.

Mr. Thomson . . . . saw that it would be absolutely necessary to have some Persons in London, not only to manage the Monies already collected, but also to solicit and receive the Contributions of the Rich and Benevolent in England, where nothing had yet been collected, and where much might be hoped for. With this view, he begged a certain number of Noblemen and Gentlemen of the first Rank, to take the Management of the Design upon themselves.

This Proposal was readily agreed to by these noble and worthy Persons. They were truly concerned to find that there were any of their Fellow-Subjects, in any Part of the British Dominions, not fully provided with the Means of Knowledge and Salvation. They considered it as a matter of the greatest Importance to the Cause of Christianity in general, and the Protestant Interest in particular, not to neglect such a vast Body of useful People, situated in a dark and barren Region, with almost none to instruct them and their helpless Children, who are coming forward into the World in Multitudes. . . . .

The first thing the said Society did was to agree to a liberal Subscription among themselves; and, upon laying the Case before the King, his Majesty, like a true Father of his People, granted 1,000 Pounds towards it . . . . and the honorable Proprietories of this Province, willing to concur in every Design for the Ease and Welfare of their People generously engaged to give a considerable yearly Sum for promoting the most essential Part of the Undertaking. . . . . In the meantime the honorable Society have come to the following general Resolutions, with regard to the Management of the Whole:

I. To assist the People in the Encouragement of pious and industrious Protestant Ministers that are, or shall be, regularly ordained and settled among the said Germans, or their Descendants in America; beginning first in Pennsylvania, where the want of Ministers is greatest. . . . .

II. To establish some charitable Schools for the Pious Education of German Youth of all Denominations, as well as those English youth that may reside among them. . . . .

III. The said Honorable Society . . . . have devolved the general Management of the whole upon Us, under the names of Trustees General for the management of their Charity among the German Emigrants in North America. And as our Residence is in this Province where the chief Body is settled, and where we may acquaint ourselves with the Circumstances of the People, the generous Society hope that we cannot be imposed upon, or deceived, in the Direction or Application of their Excellent Charity.

IV. And lastly, the said honorable Society have, out of their true fatherly Care appointed the Rev. Mr. Schlatter[1] to act under our Direction as Visitor or Supervisor of the Schools, knowing that he has already taken incredible Pains in this whole Affair, and being acquainted with the People in all Parts of the Country can converse with them on the spot and bring us the best advices, from Time to Time concerning the measures fit to be taken. . . . .

As to the important Article of establishing Schools, the following general Plan is proposed, which may be from Time to Time improved and perfected:

[1] [See H. Harbaugh, *The Life of Rev. Michael Schlatter; with a Full Account of His Travels and Labors among the Germans in Pennsylvania, New Jersey, Maryland and Virginia* (Philadelphia, 1857), chap. viii, "Schlatter and the Charity Schools."

First, it is intended that every School to be opened upon this Charity, shall be equally for the Benefit of Protestant Youth of all Denominations, and therefore the education will be in such Things as are generally useful to advance industry and true Godliness. The Youth will be instructed in both the English and German Languages; likewise in writing, keeping of Common Accounts, Singing of Psalms, and the true Principles of the holy Protestant Religion, in the same Manner as the Fathers of these Germans were instructed, at the Schools in the Countries from which they came.

Secondly, as it may be of great Service to Religion and Industry, to have some Schools for Girls also we shall use our Endeavours with the honorable Society to have some few schoolmistresses encouraged to teach Reading and the Use of the Needle. . . . .

Thirdly, that all may be induced, in their early Youth, to seek the Knowledge and Love of God, in that manner which is most agreeable to their own Consciences, the Children of all Protestant Denominations, English and Dutch, shall be instructed in any Catechism of sound Doctrine which is approved of and used by their own Parents and Ministers. . . . .

Fourthly, for the Use of the Schools, the several Catechisms that are now taught to Children among the Calvinists, Lutherans and other Protestant Denominations will be printed in English and Dutch and distributed among the Poor, together with some Bibles and other good Books at the Expence of the Society. . . . .

With regard to the Number of Schools to be opened, that will depend partly on the encouragement given by the People themselves, and partly on the Increase of the Society's Funds. A considerable number of Places are proposed to fix schools in; but none are absolutely determined upon but New-Hanover, New-Providence, and Reading. These Places were first fixed upon, because People of all Persuasions, Lutherans, Calvinists, and other Protestants moved with a pious and fatherly concern for the illiterate state of their helpless children did, with a true Christian Harmony, present their Petitions, praying that their numerous Children of all Denominations in these Parts, might be made the Common Object of the intended Charity. And for this benevolent purpose they did farther agree to offer School houses in which their Children might be instructed together as dear Fellow-Christians redeemed by the same common Lord and Saviour, and travelling to the same heavenly Country, through this Valley of Tears, notwithstanding they may sometimes take Roads a little different in Points of smaller Moment.

. . . . And if the Petitioners shall recommend school masters, as was the case at New-Hanover, New-Providence, and Reading, such school masters will have the Preference; provided they are men of sufficient Probity and Knowledge, agreeable to all Parties and acquainted with both the English and Dutch Languages or willing to learn either of those Languages which they may not then be perfectly acquainted with.

These are essential qualifications; and unless the generous Society had made a Provision for teaching English as well as Dutch, it would not have answered their benevolent Design, which is to qualify the Germans for all the Advantages of *native English subjects*. But this could not have been done, without giving them an opportunity of learning English, by speaking of which they may expect to rise to Places of Profit and Honor in the Country. They will likewise be enabled to buy or sell to the greater Advantage in our Markets; to understand their own Causes in Courts of Justice where Pleadings are in English; to know what is doing in the Country round them; and, in a Word, to judge and act entirely for themselves, without being obliged to take Things upon the Word of others, whose Interests it may be to deceive and mislead them. . . . .

A Design for instructing a People and adorning the minds of their children with useful knowledge, can carry nothing in it but what is friendly to Liberty, and auspicious to all the most sacred Interests of Mankind. Were it otherwise, why are so many of the greatest and best Men, both of the British and German Nations engaged in the Undertaking? Why have they, as it were, stooped from their high Spheres and condescended to beg from House to House in order to promote it? Is not all this done with the glorious Intention of relieving you from the distressful ignorance that was like to fall upon you? . . . .

You shall know how to make the true Use of all your noble Privileges, and instead of mourning, in a dry and barren Land, where no Water is, you and your Posterity shall flourish, from age to age in all that is valuable in human Life. A barren Region shall be turned into a fruitful Country, and a thirsty Land into Pools of Water.

### 6. A Society for Assisting Emigrants, 1797[1]

The Philadelphia society for the information and assistance of Persons emigrating from Foreign countries, having become a Corporate Body, and desirous so excellent an Institution should become exten-

[1] An address to the public from the Emigration Society of Philadelphia. Reprinted in William Cobbett, *Porcupine's Works*, XII, 16–20.

sively useful, have resolved the following Address to be presented to the Public:

To relieve distress, and to lessen the ills of life, from whatever cause they may arise, is a conduct worthy of every virtuous and benevolent mind; but it is more or less praiseworthy, in proportion as the objects of our regard are destitute, or otherwise. If this be so, can any objects have a stronger claim upon public benevolence than those for whose benefit this Society was instituted, viz., distressed Emigrants from foreign countries, who, if there were no such institution, would probably sink, under their afflictions, into despair and death. Indeed, small as have been the means of this society, it has the happiness to believe, that it has preserved for future usefulness, the lives of several valuable individuals, who, from the complicated distress of poverty and sickness, without such assistance must have fallen under their accumulated weight.

Nor are such scenes uncommon amongst the thousands who, from various causes, emigrate to this country; for, if a foreigner, when he arrives in this city, be possessed of a small sum of money, if he do not get into immediate employ, the very high price of every necessary of life soon consumes it; especially if he happen to have a family, or fall sick, the latter of which is not improbable, from the change of climate and manner of living.

It was to prevent, or at least to alleviate as much as was in their power, these evils attendant on emigration, that a number of individuals instituted this society in August, 1794, and which has since been supported by an annual subscription of one dollar, together with a few but generous donations; and occasional charity sermons; and though it has not been enabled to do all the good which the members wished, from the want of adequate means, yet it appears from the report of the acting committee, "That it has given such information to sixty-seven emigrants, on their arrival, as to obtain for them almost immediate employment; that it has afforded pecuniary assistance to one hundred and twenty persons in actual distress, and, to many of them, advanced money to purchase working tools," etc., and from the report of the physician it appears, "That pecuniary and medical aid has been granted to between sixty and seventy sick and needy emigrants, many of whom laboured under infectious diseases, and who would most probably have been lost, but for the timely and unremitting attention which was given to them."

So much good having been effected by this yet infant society, what may it not be expected to accomplish, when it shall become more generally supported, as its friends doubt not it will, when the public shall be more fully apprized than it has yet been of its benevolent and beneficial tendency? For surely there are not many inhabitants of this country who, when they are told by a society which has made it a primary object to enquire into the subject, that there is much unalleviated distress amongst persons newly arrived here, arising from sickness and other causes, and for which there is no adequate public provision, who will withhold their support to an institution whose object is to comfort, advise and relieve this unfortunate class of our fellow men. This society, therefore, constantly make it their business to have advertisements delivered on board every vessel containing passengers, which comes to this port, immediately on its arrival, which advertisements invite all, who want assistance, to apply for it as therein directed, distress being the only recommendation to ensure to them all the good which this establishment has it in its power to afford.

The object of this institution being so purely benevolent, no other consideration should seem to be necessary to induce a general concurrence in its support. But it may be further asserted, with truth, to be closely connected with the public interests of the country, since the advantages resulting from emigration, in a national view, are great and obvious. Men of talents and industry coming here from every part of the world, add to the common stock of the talents and industry of the country, and are doubtless, therefore, a great acquisition, as by their means not only the arts and sciences are improved, but manual labour is multiplied, so that agriculture is promoted, and every national improvement is encouraged and effected.

If any thing more were necessary to shew the propriety (if not duty) of supporting this institution, the opinion entertained of it by the late President Washington might have some weight. He thus expresses himself in answer to an address presented to him by the society on the anniversary of his birthday, in 1796: "The principles of benevolence on which the society is founded, and which regulate its proceedings, entitle it to the approbation of all your fellow-citizens." If, then, this sentiment be true, the society trusts that this call for attention to the distressed emigrant stranger, will not be in vain.

By order of the Society,

HENRY ANDREW HEINS, *President*

Attest,

J. KENRICK, *Secretary*

Philadelphia, June 24, 1797

## 7. Destitution among Immigrants in New York[1]

The present sources of pauperism in the city of New York may reasonably be included under the following heads: (1) emigrations to the city from foreign countries; (2) emigrations from other counties and other states; (3) intemperance; (4) lawsuits in our criminal courts; (5) defects of the penitentiary system; (6) gambling houses; (7) want of cleanliness; (8) disregard of religious worship and religious institutions; (9) ignorance.

First, as to emigrations from foreign countries, the managers are compelled to speak of them in the language of astonishment and apprehension. This inlet of pauperism threatens us with the most overwhelming consequences. From various causes, the city of New York is doomed to be the landing-place of a great portion of the European population, who are daily flocking to our country for a place of permanent abode. This city is the greatest importing capital of the United States, and a position from which a departure into the interior is generally considered the most easy and practicable. On being possessed of a more extensive and active trade than any other commercial emporium in the union it naturally occurs to the minds of emigrants that we possess more means of employment. Our situation is peculiarly healthy, and no local objection, either physical or moral, exists to arrest the approach of foreigners. The present state of Europe contributes in a thousand ways to vast and unceasing emigration to the United States. A universal shock of commercial embarrassment has pervaded, and still pervades, the continent of Europe. The whole system of trade and exchange is affected; internal industry directed to new objects; nations are manufacturing for themselves, and abandoning the usual resorts; armies and navies are disbanded, and labor-saving machinery is daily lessening the necessity of manual industry. Hence an almost innumerable population beyond the ocean is cast out of employment, and this has the effect of increasing the usual want of employ. This country is the resort of vast numbers of these needy and wretched beings. Thousands are continually resting their hopes on the refuge which she offers, filled with the delusive visions of plenty and luxury. They seize the earliest opportunity to cross the Atlantic and land upon our shores. Many of them arrive here destitute of everything. When they do arrive, instead of seeking the interior, they

[1] Extract from the *Second Annual Report of the Managers of the Society for the Prevention of Pauperism in the City of New York, December 29, 1819, to Which Is Added an Appendix, on the Subject of Pauperism*, pp. 17–26.

cluster in our cities, or sojourn along our sea-board, depending on the incidents of time, charity, or depredation, for subsistence. On application by one of the managers to his honor the mayor, he states that from the first day of March, 1818, to the first day of November, 1819, there have been 35,560 passengers who have arrived in vessels at the city of New York, and been reported at his office; of these, 18,930 are foreigners.[1] How many others have crossed our frontier lines, and arrived by way of the Canadas,[2] or how many thousands have evaded our laws, which require a report of each person on landing, we cannot say; but the chief magistrate of this city has calculated that the number of eighteen thousand and upwards does not include more than two-thirds of the real number; and after making every reasonable deduction, this would give as an aggregate more than twenty-eight thousand who have arrived at this port in twenty months. What has been the destination of this immense accession of population, and where is it now? Many of these foreigners may have found employment; some may have passed into the interior; but thousands still remain among us. They are frequently found destitute in our streets; they seek employment at our doors; they are found in our alms-house, and in our hospitals; they are found at the bar of our criminal tribunals, in our bridewell, our penitentiary, and our state prison. And we lament to say, that they are too often led by want, by vice, and by habit, to form a phalanx of plunder and depredation, rendering our city more liable to the increase of crimes, and our houses of correction more crowded with convicts and felons. For years and generations will Europe continue to send forth her surplus population. The winds and the waves will still bring needy thousands to our sea-ports, and this city continue the general point of arrival. Over this subject can we longer slumber? Shall we behold a moral contagion spreading and expanding with the most inveterate ravages, amid the ranks of our growing population, without endeavoring to arrest its progress? Shall

[1] In 1794, the emigrants who arrived in the United States were estimated at 10,000 (Seybert's *Statistics*, p. 28) and in 1806, according to Mr. Blodget's *Statistical Manual*, there were but 4,000 in the whole United States. Mr. Seybert attributes the disparity to the impressment of England from passengers' ships, and other causes originating from the British government. In 1817, according to the work first referred to, the number of emigrants who arrived in this city was 7,634; in the whole United States, 22,240. Well may the increase excite apprehension and astonishment, when we look at the arrivals during the last few months at our own port.

[2] Within the space of five months during the last year, nearly 13,000 emigrants arrived at Quebec, in Lower Canada, from Europe.

this mass be suddenly identified with ourselves and our children, inculcating their habits and their principles, without an anxious effort on our part to stay the impending calamity? Why attempt to exclude the ravages of sickness and disease, and suffer the fatal ravages of moral desolation to stalk in triumph among us? At present the managers can suggest but three measures to be adopted on this subject.

1. An attempt to change and improve the existing laws, in relation to the reporting of foreigners to our municipal authorities.

2. An application to the legislature of the state by the municipal authority to aid in their removal, and finding them means of employment.

3. Such employment as can be furnished by the society.

In relation to the duty of foreigners to report themselves when they arrive in this city, the present legislative regulations are wretchedly defective. . . . .[1]

The evils here pointed out call for decided and prompt interposition. An accession of more than eighteen thousand foreigners, a considerable portion of whom may become paupers, is a subject of no ordinary moment. Perhaps it might be well to make some application to congress for a general regulation; but the managers believe it highly expedient that an application be made to the legislature of the state, for an alteration in the existing laws, affecting the landing of foreign passengers. As regards the reports to be made, and the bonds to be entered into, the mayor has given it as his opinion that a law ought to be passed, prohibiting vessels of every description from landing an alien passenger in this state, without having bonds duly executed, that he shall not become an object of public support for a certain period of time; and that not only the master of the vessel, but the owners and consignees of vessels and cargoes, shall be liable to penalties in case of a violation of the law, and the vessel herself be rendered liable to attachment and condemnation, by a very rigid and summary process; in addition to this, that every foreigner who lands in this city, or enters it in any way, and resides among us, shall be compelled to report himself to the mayor, under oath, and give an account of the means by which he entered the state, and that penalties be enacted against those who neglect this requisition. The managers contemplate an application to the legislature, for such judicious regulations as our public guardians may think proper to establish.

[1] [For material relating to the early laws regulating immigration, see Documents 1 and 2 of this section.]

But the city of New York has, in the opinion of the managers, other claims upon the constituted authority of our state than those which call for the change and reform of municipal regulation. The thousands of destitute foreigners now in this city must be supported. We cannot force them back upon the ocean: we cannot suffer them to starve at our own doors; we cannot drive them by force to the shades and fastnesses of the wilderness; these foreigners must live, whether they are paupers or not. And why should the city of New York be under obligations to feed and clothe, at her own expense, the foreign paupers who enter her harbor? Because we are contiguous to the ocean, and because it so happens that our only harbor and only emporium of foreign commerce is situated at the mouth of the Hudson, does it also imply that we, and we alone, should administer to the daily wants of the great numbers who pour in upon us in converging directions from every country of Europe? *They are not our paupers.* They come from the four quarters of the world, and are brought here by the four winds of heaven. New York is the resting place; and like another Constantinople in the days of the crusades, is liable to be devoured by swarms of people with whom she had no alliance, either local or moral, and who only make her a place of residence and convenience, until they find it their pleasure to seek the interior. Very often they live upon us through the winter season, and then when their labor becomes an object, pass into the interior country. Thus may one wave after another roll on, each increasing in volume and extent, until the most overwhelming consequences overtake our devoted metropolis. Where is this evil to stop, and who can compass its magnitude? An hundred thousand may land in a single year, and yet the single city of New York, at least during the inclement season of the year, be forced to shelter, clothe and sustain them. These paupers belong to the state and to the nation; and surely our law-givers must feel the appeals of reason and humanity, when we ask for some remedy for these evils. Is it not just, is it not reasonable, that the hand of public charity should be extended? . . . .

It would prove a great relief could means of employment for foreigners be found when they enter our city. Many thousands who arrive in this country from Europe have been servants or manufacturers, and do not understand the art of husbandry; yet many arrive in a destitute condition who have worked on the soil. A great many others are vigorous, healthy, and capable of learning the art of agriculture. Could some communication be opened with our great farmers and landholders in the interior, and ways and means be provided for the transportation of able-bodied foreigners into the interior, and labor be prepared for them, it appears to the managers, that beneficial consequences might flow from the expedient. Many, very many foreigners who are honest and industrious, and who, for want of employment, are liable to become paupers, would gladly depart into the country and labor upon the soil or in work-shops, could they thus obtain a bare living.[1] In this case our city would be somewhat relieved; the number on our criminal calendar diminished; and the emigrant, now on the brink of pauperism, or begging alms and receiving charitable aid, become useful to himself and to the community. Instead of bringing up his children in idleness, temptation and crime, he would see them amalgamate with the general mass of our population, deriving benefits from our school establishments, our moral institutions, and our habits of industry. The managers conceive that an attempt like the one here pointed out might result to much advantage; and in the meantime, that means of employment be opened, as far as possible, in the city and county of New York.

### 8. Importation of Paupers

#### A. APRIL 26, 1823[2]

New importation! A letter from England, dated Feb. 7, says: "I was down in the London docks, and there were twenty-six paupers going out in the ship "Hudson," to New York, sent by the parish of Eurbarst, near Battle, in Sussex, in carriers' wagons, who paid their passage and gave them money to start with when arrived in the United States; and other parishes must do the same or they will be eat up by them. Many parishes are in that state that the land is worth nothing to the landlord, and I see no remedy except sending the extra population somewhere."

This precious cargo has arrived safely, and will, no doubt, assist in creating a home market for some of our products, at the expense of the native industry of the country.

#### B. AUGUST 23, 1823[3]

*Emigration.*—Though many persons do not arrive in the United States direct from Europe, a large number, probably at the rate of

[1] Many foreigners of the above description are now usefully and profitably employed by the farmers of Vermont, along the shores of Lake Champlain. These emigrants came by way of the Canadas, and were in a poor and comfortless condition.

[2] Extract from *Niles' Weekly Register*, XXIV, 113–14.     [3] *Ibid.*, p. 393.

4 or 5,000 for the present year, have reached our country, by the way of Canada and New Brunswick. The greater part of these are Irish, miserably poor and destitute; assisted in obtaining their passages to America by charitable people at home, that they may live or starve, "as chance will have it," on the other side of the Atlantic.

### C. JULY 21, 1827[1]

Transportations! The *New York American* says: The captains of the two ships lately arrived from Europe with passengers, were brought up before the mayor on Saturday morning charged with having brought paupers into the city, sent out by the parishes. On investigation it appeared that one of them, from Liverpool, had a number whose passages were paid for by the parish. The captain, however, declared that he had no knowledge of it as the passages were taken by a broker, without his knowing who advanced the money. The penalty in such cases is very heavy and will no doubt be enforced. It would be well for ship owners to be particular that such frauds are not practised on them in future.

While the English are thus casting their refuse population on us, the Irish are playing the same game upon them. . . . . Mr. Leslie Foster, in the house of commons, in speaking of the investigation of the emigration committee, remarked that the whole of the witnesses examined by this committee from Ireland, differing as they did upon almost all other subjects, agreed upon the necessity of some plan being adopted to free that country from her surplus population. English gentlemen were more interested in this question than they were perhaps aware. He would not say that the conquest of England was in progress; but, certainly, the complete occupation of it by the Irish was silently going on. The steam boats between the two islands, were really so many bridges; and the number of low Irish in London was greater than the entire population of some of the capitals of Europe. A great portion of the unemployed, who had been drawn together in masses by the owners of estates, had been suddenly thrown upon the country, and were living, such as had them, upon their friends, or upon depredations, for which their miserable condition almost furnished an excuse.

### D. AUGUST 23, 1828[2]

*Paupers.*—A large number of English families have lately arrived in the United States, at the expense of their parishes, to relieve them-

---

[1] Extract from *Niles' Weekly Register*, XXXII, 344.     [2] *Ibid.*, XXXIV, 411.

selves of their paupers. We are much obliged to John Bull for his exportations! But there is room enough for the poor people and ourselves. However, if we are to receive and feed English paupers, we hope to be protected in the employment of them! John ought to take from us the surplus grain that they raise, or, at least, allow them to make their own clothing.

### 9. A Baltimore Protest against Foreign Pauperism, 1827–32[1]

*To the honorable, the general assembly of Maryland:*

The memorial of the mayor and city council of Baltimore, humbly represents, that the influx of foreign paupers into our city, had increased to such an extent, that this corporation applied to the general assembly for relief. No action having been had upon their application, in consequence, as we presume, of the lateness of the period at which it was made; we beg leave again, to call your attention to the subject.

The extent of the evil will readily be perceived, by reference to the annual reports made to the mayor and city council by those of our corporation officers, whose duties lead them to a full knowledge of our situation.

The health officer, who visits all vessels arriving at our port, reports the arrival of 1,429 foreigners in 1827, and remarks: "I have been grieved to see so many persons amongst the number brought here as passengers, so destitute of the means of support; as well as a number laboring under disabilities, both corporeal as well as mental. To the introduction of such without restraint, we may safely attribute, in some measure, the overwhelming state of our almshouse, and the multiplied calls on our charities." In 1828, the number arriving here was 1,843; in 1829, 1,581; in 1830, 4,100; in 1831, 4,381; in 1832, 7,946. These numbers do not, probably, include the whole, because, the health officer not being required to visit vessels arriving during the winter months, makes no report of passengers who reach this place

[1] Reprinted in *Niles' Weekly Register*, XLIII (February 9, 1833), 391. The editor of the *Register*, in commenting upon the memorial said: "The memorial of the mayor and city council to the legislature of Maryland, has reference to a subject of much, and increasing interest, to the people of Baltimore, and other cities and towns of the United States. These castings upon us of the paupers and vagabonds of Europe, must be checked. But it may be well to observe, *en passant*, that for saying in this paper what is now officially set forth by the mayor and city council (whose orthodoxy will not be disputed), certain 'most despicable' creatures were lately pleased in 'their vocation,' to denounce the editor as an enemy of foreigners! . . . ."

during that season.  In all his reports, since 1827, he has continued to call the attention of the mayor and city council to the destitute and diseased state of the emigrants, and mentions two cases (one of them extending to a whole vessel load) of paupers sent to this country at the expense of an European parish.

The annual reports of the trustees of the poor furnish a practical commentary upon the statements of the health officer.  We beg leave to refer you particularly to one made by that board in January, 1832, by which it appears, that of 1,610 persons admitted to the almshouse during the preceding year, 487 were foreigners—that 281 had not been six months in the city previous to their admission, and that, of this last number, 121 had not been here one week.

Our poor-rates are, thus, very much increased by the demands of foreign paupers.  This, though an evil of sufficient magnitude to require redress, is small, when compared with the annoyance we experience from a swarm of foreign beggars of both sexes, and all ages, who infest our streets, and who, we have every reason to believe, constitute the very refuse population of foreign cities.

As citizens of the United States, we glory in proclaiming our country an asylum for the oppressed of all nations, and are ready to extend the right hand of fellowship to every emigrant who is able and willing, by his own exertions, to support himself, but we do protest against the admission of those, who, in consequence of their infirmities or vices, are unable or unwilling to contribute to their own maintenance; and most respectfully request of the legislature, that they will take the case into consideration, and pass such laws on the subject as they, in their wisdom, may think just and proper. . . . .

### 10.  Irish Laborers Charged with Violence and Crime

#### A. BALTIMORE AND OHIO RAILROAD DISORDERS[1]

*July 16, 1831.*—On the 29th and 30th ult. it was known that a contractor on the 3rd division of the Baltimore and Ohio railroad, about 25 miles from the city, had absconded, leaving his laborers unpaid, and that they (as too often happens in Ireland, the country which, in general, they had recently left), had taken the law into their own hands, were wantonly destroying the property of the company, because their employer had wronged them! They were between 200 and 300 strong, and, with pick axes, hammers and sledges, made a

[1] Extract from *Niles' Weekly Register*, XL (1831), 338-39.

most furious attack on the rails, sills, &c. and whatever else they could destroy. The sheriff of the county, and his posse, was resisted by these ignorant or wicked men—and a requisition was made on Brig. Gen. George H. Steuart for a detachment of the volunteers under his command—and, though it rained very heavily, a sufficient number of patriotic soldiers started in the cars from the dépôt at about 10 o'clock in the night of the 30th of June, and reached the scene of violence before day-light next morning, fully prepared to put down such outrageous proceedings; but those who had resisted the civil officers so rudely and violently, suffered themselves to be arrested by the military, without opposition, or precipitately fled—and none of them were personally injured. In the afternoon, about 40 of those reported to be principals, were brought into Baltimore and lodged in jail, and 18 or 20, arrested by a detachment which remained behind for the purpose, were sent in and committed next day, and so the riot and ruin ended. The directors of the company have presented their thanks to Gen. Steuart and the officers and men of the detachment, for the promptness and energy, and moderation, with which they acted.

The prisoners, being brought before Judge Hanson on a subsequent day, were severally examined. But the judge discharged thirty-seven of them on their own recognizances, or without being bound to appear at all—having every wish, (in common with all the inhabitants of the city), to release those who had been led, or driven, into this monstrous outrage, by others—but the supposed leaders were remanded for trial, and will remain in prison till then.

In consequence of the flight of the contractor, the riots and arrest of the rioters, the wives and children of these laborers were in a very destitute condition. The railroad company immediately sent out liberal supplies of provisions under the charge of careful persons, and relieved them effectually.

We understand that the contractor was highly recommended, and that the agents of the company made every rightful effort to quiet the rioters, before even calling upon the sheriff to protect the road; and that there would have been no difficulty, but for the leadings of a few desperate men, who are now in a way to be taught, we trust, that there is law "in this land of liberty."

The company, surely, ought to be very cautious in the employment of contractors—but it is a delicate and difficult business to interfere between them and their laborers, over whom it is indispensable that they should have an entire control. And we understand that a large part of the money lost by these poor men, was rather caused by their suffering it to accumulate in the hands of the contractor, than on account of his inability, or unwillingness to make payment at the regular periods. We think that a plan might be easily contrived by which the company could be rendered responsible for all sums beyond the current weekly or monthly wages—whereby the working people would be secure in their earnings—and contractors, because of the smallness of the amount of money in their hands, have no sufficient inducement thus to prey upon the poor. But it is justice to add, that, with two or three exceptions, the contractors have faithfully performed their engagements—and are gentlemen of high respectability and great worth.

It is difficult to suppose persons so wrong-headed as to believe that such acts of violence could be tolerated and pass unpunished. The Irishman's heart generally is, and always would be, in the right place, but the oppression which he suffered at home has not yet ceased to have effect on his head, and, though his person has been transferred to America, it takes him some considerable time to shake off those prejudices and habits that belonged to and influenced him in the land of his birth,[1] trodden under foot by a conqueror, for centuries, and impoverished and abused for the glory of the oppressor, who to secure the dependence of Ireland, long discouraged, if not absolutely prohibited the establishment of numerous manufactures, and checked the education of the people, on the principle that, in some other places, makes it an offense to teach persons to read! Let us then pass over as easily as we can, the doings of the great majority of these men, and charge them to account of British domination—but the principals, who knew better, should severely be made to feel the just weight of the law.

[1] We have many and melancholy and disgraceful proofs of what is here stated, in the riotous contentions of natives of Ireland (though naturalized citizens of the United States!) about religious creeds—that which every genuine American regards with the utmost detestation; for he will not allow anyone to be violently questioned because of the faith which he professes if fulfilling those duties which every man owes to society. It was only the other day, at a celebration of the "Battle of the Boyne," by the Gideonites or Orangemen, at Philadelphia, by a procession and dinner, &c., that a regular fight with swords, clubs, brickbats, &c. took place between them and the "Catholic party," some of the peace-officers being knocked down, and a good many of the combatants strewed on the streets, nearly murdered. The mayor acted with great resolution and vigor; but there was a pelting of some houses with stones till the morning. Irishmen, in America, cannot be justified in that celebration which Englishmen contrived to keep the Irish in a state of hostility among themselves—nor can the other party be excused in violating the public peace on account of it Several persons were arrested, and of both parties, to answer for this outrage.

The damage done to the road is very extensive—and it will cost several thousand dollars to restore things to the condition in which they were.

### B. RIOTS ON THE BALTIMORE AND WASHINGTON RAILROAD[1]

*November 29, 1834.*—In the last *Register* we inserted some account of certain outrageous incidents that had happened on the Baltimore and Washington railroad, involving the cold murder of some of the deputy superintendents of construction. . . . .

No results of the examinations are yet published, but it is most probable, we fear, that the murderers will escape (though the gang consisted of about forty persons), because of an unholy league said to exist among the Irish laborers to conceal the crimes of one another, and support each other, right or wrong.

We annex the proceedings had on these bloody transactions in Anne Arundel county. They do not go ahead of the common feeling that prevails in this city and neighborhood—and we think that the resolutions adopted will be carried out! The public peace must not longer be violated with impunity and the law of nature be resorted to, in the absence of those means that are usually found sufficient for the preservation of the lives and property of unoffending persons. All must regret that the innocent should suffer with the guilty—but such infamous combinations must be broken up, and all taught that a land of liberty is also a land of law.

At a large and respectable meeting of inhabitants of Anne Arundel and Prince George's counties adjacent to the Baltimore and Washington railroad and held at Merrill's tavern on the 26th inst. . . . . the following preamble and resolutions were unanimously adopted:

WHEREAS, A portion of Anne Arundel and Prince George's counties, bordering on the Baltimore and Washington railroad has been the scene of successive riots, dangers and bloodshed since the commencement of said work down to the present time, and whereas, the recent scene of murders of the most wanton, diabolical, and atrocious character upon respectable and unoffending citizens, scarcely paralleled in the annals of our history, has given ample cause to our fellow citizens for alarm and apprehension for the safety of their lives, and whereas, while they suffer themselves to remain exposed to the deep-laid schemes of that population from which all these grievances emanate. And whereas, it is known to be confined exclusively to

---

[1] Extracts from *Niles' Weekly Register*, XLVII (1834–35), 196–97, 272–74, 356, 373. The extract under date December 20, 1834, is a reprint of a letter to the editor of the *Frederick Herald.*

that class of laborers which has generally been employed on the aforesaid work, and it having been established beyond all question, that the Irish laborers compose that class, and that they have formed secret associations, to which they are bound under the most awful and solemn oaths to keep each other's secrets, and under which association they are enabled to accomplish their hellish plots without being in danger of discovery. And whereas the good citizens of these counties have in vain set forth their grievances and remonstrances to the proper sources for the removal of the cause. And whereas, it is the right and bounden duty of our fellow citizens to defend themselves and their property against the hand of the ruffian, we the subscribers, citizens of the aforesaid counties, do unanimously agree to adopt the following resolutions:

*Resolved,* That we do consider and hold the present class of Irish laborers employed on the Baltimore and Washington railroad as a gang of ruffians and murderers, combined together under the most solemn ties to carry into effect such hellish designs as their passions or prejudices may prompt them to commit.

*Resolved,* That, inasmuch as by their plans of secret association, justice and the laws are deprived of their dues, it behooves our fellow citizens to adopt such measures as will tend to their quiet and safety.[1]

*December 20, 1834.*—Various causes have been assigned for the outrage; there is no doubt, that several motives operated in producing the catastrophe. Both of the victims were Irishmen, and had frequently been reproached as Orangemen. But it is probable that the immediate motive of the act, was in consequence of Mr. Watson having discharged many of the hands for their indolence and unruly behaviour, and having received the contract for the work in the district. These circumstances made him the special object of their vengeance. Mr. Watson had received many intimations of their design upon his life;

[1] [A letter addressed to the president of the railroad by the chairman of the meeting contained the following statement]:

"The residents of this section of the county are determined that in case the company do not adopt such measures as will in future secure them from being harrassed by these frequent riots on the road, that they will muster a sufficient force and drive every Irishman off the road from the Patapsco to the big Patuxent, at all hazards, and in this determination they are promised the cooperation and aid of other sections of our county.

"In making this communication, I assure you the people are actuated by no other motive than to put an end to these continued murders and riots, which, if they are permitted to go unpunished as heretofore, may in the end, lead those wretches to depredating still further on the surrounding neighborhood. If the ring leaders cannot be secured and punished, the whole force ought to be discharged and a new set employed. The work had better be delayed a short time than to be the scene of such frequent disgraceful outrages."

but, unfortunately disbelieved and disregarded all warnings. The laws have been violated in the persons of these unfortunate men, and it is hoped that public justice will not permit those miscreants to escape, and by ill-timed leniency encourage a second outrage.

*December 27, 1834.*—It has been stated in an eastern paper, that the late riots on the Baltimore and Washington railroad had their origin in the distribution of whiskey, by the contractors, to get more labor out of their men. This is not so—all such things are strictly forbidden. Whiskey is not allowed to be kept by any person employed on the road, nor used during working hours. The origin of these outrages lies much deeper than whiskey—they come from ignorance and prejudice, with superstitious adherences to unholy combinations, and accustomed resorts to force in their own land, to redress real or supposed wrongs—"taking the law into their own hands." And this will become absolutely necessary—to refuse employment to all such persons, unless purging themselves of such combinations, and then of separating them into small bodies, and placing other classes of laborers between them—the latter being sufficiently strong to command the peace, under direction of the civil authority. In one case, near Sykesville, some two or three years ago, when a mad mass of Irish laborers were breaking up the rails, the mob rolled back on a small body of Yankees presenting themselves, saying, pass not over our boundary (that of their contract), and it was not passed. The Yankees were provided with arms, and knew well the use of them; and so on the recent occasion—though ferociously threatened, a body of German laborers preserved the peace, being prepared and willing to defend it—their own subsistence and quiet employment depending upon it. But what a state of society is this—when murders, and arsons and other outrages escape the punishment that they so richly deserved?

*January 24, 1835.*—It will be recollected, that the military "swept" the Baltimore and Washington railroad of the Irish laborers who had been employed on certain parts of it, soon after the late horrible and bloody proceedings committed by some of them. These, to the amount of nearly 300 persons, were sent to the jail of Baltimore, and there personally examined; and all but nine persons, unless held as witnesses were discharged, and have scattered themselves, their return to the railroad being forbidden, as well by the company, as by the neighboring population, determined to drive them out of Anne Arundel county by force—if necessary to their expulsion. The offence charged being committed in the county just named, a special court was appointed to be held at Annapolis, for their trial, and one of them, named Murphy, has been found guilty of murder in the first degree—which awful verdict, it is believed, will fall upon several others; for this conviction will, probably, break a link of the combinations which, in certain cases, have screened others of this class from that justice which they richly deserved, for other murders on the railroads.

*January 31, 1835.*—Sentence of death has been pronounced on Owen Murphy (convicted of murder in the first degree), at Annapolis, for the murder of John Watson, on the Baltimore and Washington railroad; and Patrick Gallagher and Terrence Coil, found guilty of murder in the second degree, have been each sentenced to eighteen years hard labor in the Maryland penitentiary, including one year of solitary confinement. They are yet subject to trial for the murder of Mr. Mercer, and, with some others implicated, have moved their cases to Baltimore county court. They reached this city on Tuesday last, and were deposited in the jail.

Owen Murphy, it is said, is to be executed on the spot where the murder of Watson was committed.

## 11.  The Problem of Foreign Pauperism[1]

The alarming increase of this class of [foreign] poor in the country, especially within the last five years, has drawn public attention to the subject. In most parts of the eastern states there has been a diminution of native paupers and expenditure for their support, while the number of foreign poor has been constantly increasing.

As nearly as can be ascertained, the number of persons supported, for longer or shorter periods of time in the year 1834, in the almshouses of the four principal American Cities were as follows:

|  | Americans | Foreigners |
|---|---|---|
| New York | 1,893 | 2,093 |
| Philadelphia | 1,676 | 1,895 |
| Baltimore | 675 | 479 |
| Boston | 542 | 841 |
|  | 4,786 | 5,308 |

It is thus seen that Boston is more burdened by poor emigrants than any other Atlantic city, in proportion to population. In some of

[1] Extract from *Report of Artemas Simonds on Almshouses and Kindred Institutions in Several of the Northern and Middle States* (Boston Common Council Document No. 15, 1835), pp. 35–40.

the counties of New York bordering on the Canadian frontier, the evil is still greater. . . . .

The bulk of these foreigners are from Great Britain; in Philadelphia and Baltimore a small proportion are Germans.

It was unnecessary for the British "Poor Law Commissioners" of 1833 to recommend "that parishes be authorized to pay the passages of paupers out of the country." Such was already extensively the practice. Capt. John S. Davis, of Portsmouth, N.H., a respectable and intelligent ship master, states, that in May, 1829, he was in London, where he saw in the North American Hotel, two English gentlemen who stated, that they were the Wardens of a parish; that they had procured the passage to New York of about thirty of their parish paupers, had got them willing to go, clothed them, paid their passage money, and made them up a small purse. They further remarked, that this was the most economical disposition that they could make of their poor. At that time, says Capt. Davis, the exportation of parish paupers had become in England a well-known and regular business, and certain American vessels were called the "Workhouse line." It is an undoubted fact, that the ingress of foreign paupers into the United States has increased greatly since 1830, not so much by their introduction into United States sea ports direct, as by the way of the provinces, adjacent to New England and New York. The State laws requiring masters and owners to give bonds or pay commutation money for alien passengers, prevents, to some extent, the landing of paupers in the ports of the United States. But they impose no obstruction to the introduction of the late tenants of English workhouses from Canada by land.

The New York Almshouse Commissioners, in a report made to the City Council in September last, say:

The present law in relation to alien passengers, requires the master or consignees to give a bond of indemnity, to save the City harmless for two years; or it authorizes a commutation for such passengers instead of bond. The class of alien passengers, who have been arriving in New York for several years past, are not of so provident a character, taking them generally, as those which came to the country in previous years. In fact, there are cases constantly occurring, in which it is evident that the towns of Europe, and societies of individuals, pay the expense of sending to this country their paupers, and persons unable to get their living in any country.

Decrepit, and maimed, and lunatic persons, have been so transported and landed on our wharves; and from the wharves they come immediately under our charge. We do not see why the consignees should be released at the expiration of so short a term as two years. We think they should indemnify the City for at least four or five years, and that if the law was so altered, there would be a great saving to the City, by being relieved from supporting the poor of other countries, which the captains and owners of vessels are induced, by the money received from the Overseers of the Poor of other countries, to bring here.

In the cases we commute, the officers of the Board are very liable to be deceived; and not unfrequently, passengers, whom they have judged well and capable of getting a living one day, have, two or three days afterwards, been found to be entirely unable to do any thing for themselves. It is a practice we think should be followed with great caution; for it is believed that the number of operatives now arriving in our country, will find it difficult, in our cities at least, to procure employment, even were they both willing and able to work. For these reasons, we have advised the Mayor to commute for none at a less rate than $150 each.

After giving an account of affidavits taken in proof that parish officers, in England, ship paupers to this country, the Commissioners proceed:

The principle, or rather the want of it, which permits the British government or their parish officers to send their paupers here, will also lead them to send their culprits here, as the cheapest mode of getting rid of them. Some of these paupers arrive direct from England, Ireland, and Scotland; but many of them arrive at Quebec, and find their way down through the interior of the State. Now we apprehend that the subject is highly important, not only to New York, but to all our Atlantic Cities; and we know of no complete remedy for the evil, but some national or United States regulation on the subject.

It has been proposed by the City authorities of Baltimore, that the Atlantic Cities should memorialize Congress on this subject. . . . .

Complaints are everywhere made of the impositions practiced by foreign paupers and rogues who claim charity. While so many British poor crowd the Atlantic cities and the Canadian frontier, it does not appear that Canada is burdened by American poor. By the Annual Report of the Montreal General Hospital, an institution similar to the poorhouses in the United States, it appears that the inmates for the year ending May 1st, 1835, belonged: to Canada, 51; to England, 114; to Scotland, 54; to Ireland, 588; to United States, 5; to Germany, 7; total, 819.

## 12. "Naturalizing by the Job: A Case in the United States Circuit Court"[1]

We were not aware that the business of naturalizing was done by the job in this city, and that some foreigners actually carried on a business, till the case of Gosman, a German, came before the police. This Gosman, it appeared in court, had naturalized his hundreds of Germans, whom he undertook to make Americans of—by wholesale oaths before the marine court. His was a commission business in a new line of employ, for he received from eight to ten dollars from his countrymen for swearing them in, the fees of the court being but three and a half dollars. The character of the marine court of this city was proved by some of the witnesses to be a tribunal which would disgrace the adjudications of many a grog shop in the city. As a court of record it is a mere mockery of the name; and its acts of wholesale unexamining naturalizations seemed to be but of a piece of the perjury committed before it. We trust that the details of this trial will awaken attention to this court, which, as it is invested by the laws with the right of imparting citizenship, is one of the most important in the country, and particularly as it does a wholesale naturalization business for the whole United States.

The case was opened by Mr. Price on behalf of the prosecution, who called to the stand the clerk of the marine court, Mr. Barbiere, who testified that Gosman, the prisoner, subscribed and swore to an affidavit, setting forth that a countryman of his, named Frederick Altz, had been five years in the United States, but did not distinctly recollect whether Judge Scheiffelin was present at the time of administering the oath or not. It was also proved by several witnesses that Altz came here in 1832, that he was then over 40 years of age, had never been here before, and therefore that the statement sworn to by the prisoner of his residence of five years was totally false. A Mr. Wold swore that the prisoner "witnessed" him into a citizenship after having been in the country only four years, (although he was apprized by the applicant of that fact), for the sum of $10; and the district attorney offered to prove by a great many other witnesses, that the prisoner made a business of procuring the naturalization of aliens in this way. The testimony, however, was ruled out by the court. A German by

[1] From the *New York Daily Express*, March 3, 1838. Reprinted in United States Twenty-fifth Congress, second session, House Report No. 1040, pp. 113–16. For other references to Naturalization, see documents 24, 28, and 29 in this section and documents 5 and 15 in the succeeding section.

the name of Henry Otter was also called to prove that the prisoner
went with him to the marine court and procured his naturalization
upon the payment of eight or nine dollars, notwithstanding he had
been informed that he, Otter, had been in the country less than five
years. A Nicholas Everhard swore that Gosman followed no other
business for a living than hanging around the marine court and swearing in aliens for pay: that he was a shrewd fellow, and was one of the
principal agitators in the late difficulties with the Dutch reformed
church. Other testimony went to show that the prisoner could write
a good hand, and nothing being produced to show that he was ignorant
of the English language, it was fairly inferable that he understood perfectly what were the contents of the affidavits to which he subscribed
his name and made oath.

Mr. Bushnell, for the defence, contended that if his client had sinned
at all, it was through ignorance; that he had been led into error by the
loose and slovenly manner in which he had seen business of this nature
transacted in the marine court; and that the law in relation to naturalization was in itself defective, as he was prepared to argue to the satisfaction of the court. The learned gentleman then referred the court
to an ancient law applicable to the case—a law upon which all modern
laws have been based, and which emanated from a source that entitled
it to the highest credit. It was the law of Moses; and he quoted as
follows from the book of Numbers, chap. xv, verses 27, 28, 29, and 30:
"And if any soul sin through ignorance, then he shall bring a she-goat
of the first year for a sin offering. And the priest shall make an atonement for the soul that sinneth ignorantly, when he sinneth by ignorance before the Lord, to make an atonement for him; and it shall be
forgiven him," &c.

Witnesses were then brought forward, who testified that they were
present in the marine court when people had declared their intentions;
that the affidavits respecting the residence of applicants in this country
were never read or explained to them; that they were merely asked to
sign their names, and pay over to the clerk the fee of $3.50; that fre-
quently there was no judge present at the time of making oath; that
during the election last fall, politicians would bring in ten or a dozen
together, some with their foreign garments upon their backs, to get
naturalized; every thing was done in a hurry—a few questions were
asked—and individuals admitted to all the rights and privileges of
citizens, without duly examining into their qualifications. The answers
given by the witness, Benjamin Albert, to the district attorney, will

give the reader an idea of the intelligence of the "citizen-manufacturers" who usually officiate at the marine court to swear out naturalization papers for money.

Benjamin Albert, sworn. *Q.*—Have you ever been in the marine court when they were making citizens out of foreigners?

*A.*—Yaze, I vas.

*Q.*—Well, what did you see there?

*A.*—Vell I gome dare to be make zidizen myselifs, but dey not vould make me de zidizen vidout de vidness. But after dat I was vidness for oder mens.

*Q.*—You was, eh?

*A.*—Yaze. I sign my name for zome vidness.

*Q.*—Witness to what?

*A.*—Yaze. I vas vidness dat I vas de vidness.

*Q.*—Witness to what?

*A.*—Vell, I vas vidness to my frient.

*Q.*—Explain what sort of a witness you were?

*A.*—O yaze, I vas the zame ginde of vidness as I shall be now a vidness.

*Q.*—Well, tell us what you witnessed?

*A.*—Vell, I vitnessed a goot many dings.

*Q.*—Name the things you went to witness?

*A.*—Only to be vidness of vat I shall zee.

The counsel being unable to extract any other information from this witness he was desired to stand aside.

It was fully proved on the part of the defendant, that he was an honest, industrious, simple-hearted man; easily led away; and that he would at any time leave his business to do a good-natured act for a friend.

The court charged that it was not enough that false swearing had been proved, or even that an injury had been done by it to others; to constitute perjury it must be shown that the oath had been made in conformity with law. The proceedings upon which this oath had been taken, took place in reference to the naturalization law. This law was exceedingly liberal in its provisions, and is one that interests all classes of citizens; it had been amended and modified at different periods, and at present entitles any foreigner who has resided in the United States for five years to become a citizen, provided he declares his intention three years previous to taking out his naturalization papers. In 1804, an amendment had been made to the law, which provides that all persons arriving under age may become a citizen two years after he becomes of age, upon proof of his having resided three years in the country during his minority. The law as it now stands, places the foreigner, no matter from what country he comes, on an equality with a native-born youth of 16 years of age. In opening this broad privilege, as it was the policy of this country to encourage emigration, it was necessary for Congress to place some wholesale checks upon it. It therefore provided that all proceedings in relation to emigration should take place in a court of record, and that the examination into the qualifications of applicants should be made in open court, for the purpose of ascertaining whether the party is entitled to naturalization or not; and the court, before granting any such paper of naturalization, must be satisfied that the party so applying has been in the country five years. As no judicial proceeding can be recognized except by testimony or proof before the court, a court would act rashly by proceeding on any other evidence. The indictment upon which the accused was put upon his trial, alleges that he made an affidavit in open court, and in that oath he committed wilful perjury. The first count in the indictment charges that Frederick Altz, who had only been in the country four years, was sworn to by the prisoner as having resided here for at least five years; and, secondly, that he had resided here three years before he was twenty-one. In order to sustain the indictment the public prosecution must prove that the oath was false; was wilfully and knowingly false. As to the statement relative to the residence of Altz in the United States, that was clearly proved to be false by the testimony of a number of his countrymen. To prove the charge of perjury, it was necessary to show that the oath had been made wilfully. The ignorance of the prisoner of the language and proceedings of the court in this case, as testified to by several witnesses, made it fairly inferable that the party had not wilfully taken a false oath. The question was, did he know the residence of Altz to be less than five years; it was for the jury to determine from the evidence before them what was the prisoner's knowledge with respect to the fact he stated; if he had been trapped or deluded in this oath, it would not afford foundation of an indictment for perjury; something must be shown that he was acquainted with the matter of fact, and if he stated it differently, he swore false. As this oath had been taken in the shape of an affidavit, if it had not been read or explained and made known to the witness, it would be unjust to inculpate him. His honor, in allusion to the court where this proceeding had been made, took occasion to say that it did not become him to speak of the judicial acts of another tribunal, but that there had been some very extraordinary proceedings in the administration of the oath was very evident. It remained to be proved that the prisoner, when he was called up, was actually sworn, or that the party, if sworn, knew the nature of what he swore to, although the man of the most ordinary comprehension must have perfectly understood the nature of the affidavit. If the affidavit was administered, and the prisoner had really sworn to it, and it had been all false, it would not constitute perjury, unless sworn to in open court. The law of Congress intended that this process of naturalization should be an act of the court, and it must, therefore, appear unequivocally that it took place in a court of justice, before they could convict the prisoner. It was the duty of the officer who administers the oath, to be satisfied that the party understands what he is swearing to; and no magistrate can receive such a paper unless he is so satisfied.

It is perjury, also, when a party comes rashly and presumptuously forward, and swears to something he knows nothing about, although it should turn out that what he swore to was true.

The determining matter of this issue was, whether the oath had been administered; and if so, whether it was in open court, legally and solemnly sworn. Mr. Barbiere, the clerk of the marine court, had sworn that it was his usual practice to administer the oath in the presence of the court, but in this particular instance he could not say; although it was his invariable custom never to enter it upon record, unless sworn to in presence of one of the judges. If Mr. Barbiere's statement was to be relied upon, it was sufficient to establish this fact; but as the clerk did not distinctly recollect whether Judge Scheiffelin was present or not at the time of administering the oath, and as the testimony of various other witnesses respecting a great number of affidavits having been sworn to in the absence of the court, it went to shake Mr. Barbiere's recollection on this point. There should be no room for doubt that the judge was absent; and as the clerk had no right to administer an oath in the absence of the court, if this fact had been clearly made out, there could be no foundation for an allegation of perjury in this case.

Judge Betts concluded his charge by remarking that before the perjury could convict, they must be satisfied that the oath was administered in court; and if they had doubts that the court was in session at that time, and he admitted that there were doubts of that fact, they must acquit the prisoner of the charge of perjury.

The jury retired, and after an absence of two hours, returned with a verdict of guilty—recommending the prisoner to mercy.

### 13. Destitution among Immigrants[1]

. . . . The policy of our laws is to give the greatest possible liberty to the citizen consistent with the general good, and the most economical government; but in the application of this principle, great difficulty is always felt in the discharge of the civil obligations to the poor and the sick. In the early political history of this State this difficulty was apprehended and laws became necessary, which, in some degree, infringed upon personal liberty, that greater safety and happiness might inure to the great body of the people. Among the first of our statutes and the recommendation of our citizens, before and after we became one of the glorious thirteen free and independent States, were provisions to prevent the immigrant from becoming an evil or a charge upon the civil institutions of the country. This principle has ever been acted upon, but the liberal provisions of the law have been arrested in their good design, and made the instruments of evil to the citizen, and no benefit to him who left his native land for a better clime and a more liberal and free government.

The statute as now applicable to this subject, authorizes in its practical workings, the merchant or shipper to commute with and to receive from the passenger who seeks our shore a sum of money to satisfy the requirement of the law that he will not become a charge upon the government of the metropolis, and this amply indemnifies the merchant or shipper, from any liability he may be called upon to assume, and yet the difficulty of enforcing that liability and obtaining the payment for the city charge for food to the poor, medicine and attendance to the sick, the prison for the depraved, is often impossible and always difficult.

The bonding system, as it is called, has another evil. It holds out a premium for the defrauding of the immigrant, by requiring of him a larger sum for the indemnity of the merchant or shipper than he should pay, and enables the merchant or shipper to make gains, while the city is impoverished.

This has become so methodical that public economy demands a change of system, for the arrival of the great numbers of the poor, de-

[1] *Report of the Select Committee to Whom Was Referred the Memorial of the City of New York Relative to the Landing of Alien Passengers* (New York State Assembly Document No. 216, 1845), pp. 1–5.

graded, and dissolute of the old world has already overcharged the alms-houses, and hospitals, and penitentiary, in the city of New York.

By a report of the deputy-keeper of the penitentiary on Blackwell's Island, there were in December last, 1,419 inmates of the penitentiary and city prison; showing an increase of more than 400 from the preceding July, a period of only five months. Of this number, there were in the penitentiary:

| | |
|---|---:|
| Americans by birth | 333 |
| Natives of Ireland | 548 |
| Natives of England | 73 |
| Natives of Scotland | 20 |
| Natives of Wales | 4 |
| Natives of Canadas | 18 |
| Natives of Nova-Scotia | 4 |
| Natives of New-Brunswick | 2 |
| Subjects of Great Britain | 669 |
| Natives of Germany | 42 |
| Natives of France | 7 |
| Natives of Sweden | 3 |
| Natives of West-Indies | 7 |
| Natives of Spain | 4 |
| Natives of South America | 7 |
| Blacks | 126 |
| Total in penitentiary | 1,198 |

In city prison there are:

| | |
|---|---:|
| Native Americans | 39 |
| Natives of Ireland | 96 |
| Natives of England and Scotland | 26 |
| Subjects of Great Britain | 122 |
| Natives of Germany | 10 |
| Natives of Sweden | 12 |
| Natives of France | 2 |
| Blacks | 36 |
| Total in city prison | 221 |
| Total in penitentiary and city prison | 1,419 |

In the alms-house and its appendages, exclusive of the prisons there were at the same time two thousand nine hundred and thirty eight inmates; making the whole number of prisoners and paupers four thousand three hundred and fifty-seven, and showing an increase since July last of nearly one thousand! Besides this immense burthen upon the city treasury, the charity, in small sums, distributed to the "out-door poor," a class of poor people who make some exertions to support themselves, and who by a little timely aid, judiciously administered, are prevented from becoming wholly chargeable to the city, exceeds now, two thousand dollars a month.

The law in its benevolent design reaches another class more to be pitied, and yet in its effect upon the pecuniary interest of the city, is no less unworthy of our statute book. Many of the women, married and single, who are landed upon our shores, are far advanced in pregnancy and very frequently unprotected and destitute. These consequently have a double claim, and bring with them additional charges.

The whole number of children under the protection and support of the alms-house, appears to be 821. Of these, 602 are at the farm school, 457 are the children of foreign parents, and 145 Americans; more than three-fourths foreigners, and all a direct charge on the city treasury. The farm school includes only the children of three years of age and upwards. Of the 219 under the age at Bellevue, 185 are placed without the walls at nurse, and 34 remain within. Of the former, 137 are of foreign and 48 of native origin. Of the latter number, composed of the latest born infants, 32 are foreign and only two American, showing the ratio of the more recent births to be seventeen foreigners to one American. Of the whole number of children, 626 have foreign parentage, and 195 American, exhibiting the average of more than three foreigners to one native! and an alarming increase of the ratio of foreigners in the more recent births.

The expenses of the alms-house for the year ending January 1, 1845, exclusive of interest upon the very large outlay for grounds and buildings for alms-house purposes, was the enormous sum of $255,275.85.

The examination of one of the medical dispensaries of charity in the city presents other facts no less eloquent for reform. The attending physicians of the New York City Dispensary (and there are two other dispensaries in the city), report that during the year ending January 1, 1845, 16,746 patients have received at their hands advice and medicine; and that they were from the following countries, and in the following numbers:

|  | Males | Females | Total |
|---|---|---|---|
| United States | 2,556 | 2,490 | 5,046 |
| Ireland | 4,260 | 5,810 | 10,070 |
| England | 426 | 498 | 924 |
| Scotland | 106 | 41 | 147 |
| British North America | 24 | 97 | 121 |
| Germany | 142 | 124 | 266 |
| France | 59 | 14 | 73 |
| Other countries | 71 | 28 | 99 |
| Total | 7,644 | 9,102 | 16,746 |

Only 5,046 out of this enormous number, it will be seen, were Americans, and it is estimated that 4,000 of these were the children of foreigners, leaving, in fact, only one thousand (out of the seventeen thousand) natives, and these mostly blacks. No table has ever been presented that illustrates more fully from whence America derives her pauperism than this.

The truth is apparent, from these data, that our alms-houses, prisons, dispensaries and benevolent societies are kept up at an enormous expense, almost wholly for the benefit of foreign paupers and criminals; and consequently, from the present system of bonding passengers and the necessary ignorance of those who land among us, they become a charge upon the tax-paying and benevolent citizen.

The ignorance of our language often subjects the honest immigrant to imposition from the unprincipled mariner's agent or boarding-house keeper; and the wicked find, on their arrival, those who are willing to aid and abet them in their wickedness, and both contribute largely to deprave and injure, and oppress with taxation our citizens and expose us to everything unworthy of a free people. This system should be regulated, and the rights of those incapable of self-preservation be freed from violation, by sound and wholesome provisions of law, which the benevolent can admire, the good citizen approve and the immigrant be grateful for.

The committee apprehend that the evils complained of in the memorial of the common council of the city of New York may, in a great degree, be averted, and the immigrant at the same time essentially benefited by the enactment of the bill which the committee beg leave to introduce.

## 14. A Demand for the Control of Foreign Pauperism in Massachusetts[1]

The increase of foreign paupers in the state of Massachusetts, is a subject calculated to excite surprise and alarm the people. . . . . The fact, that there are actually seven thousand and thirty-five of these dependent persons in the Commonwealth, and that two thousand five hundred and one were brought here in the year 1847, who are now fed and clothed at the expense of the inhabitants of the state, and derive their daily support by a tax upon their industry, requires that the legislature should devise some mode of relieving them from a burden already onerous and grievous to be borne. And such is the present aspect of many parts of Europe, that a melancholy prospect of an increasing number of this class of unwelcome immigrants, is constantly anticipated.

So great has become the character and amount of foreign immigration to this country, that its influence on the social and political institutions of the United States is, in truth, becoming a matter of the deepest import and the gravest consideration. When we find, from a careful examination, that the increase of population by foreign immigration, is equal to the whole natural increase of the free white population of this country in 1840, the field for inquiry into the future influence this circumstance will have on the destiny of the nation, is large enough for profound philosophical investigation.

The number of alien immigrants, alone, is formidable, and is certainly a subject of just anxiety. In the commencement and earliest years of the government, those who came here were generally persons of education, of pecuniary means, industry and character. In coming, they added to the intelligence and wealth of the community; while, as producers, they assisted in developing the resources of the country. Those now pouring in upon us, in masses of thousands upon thousands, are wholly of another kind in morals and intellect, and, through ignorance and degradation from systematic oppression of bad rulers at home, neither add to the intelligence nor wealth of this comparatively new country. As a body, they are consumers, and not producers to an extent equaling their own physical wants.

[1] Extract from *Report of Joint Special Committee of the Legislature of Massachusetts Appointed to Consider the expediency of Altering and Amending the Laws relating to Alien Passengers and Paupers* (Massachusetts Senate Document No. 46, 1848). Various petitions were referred to this committee from citizens of Massachusetts asking changes in the state passenger act, which already contained provisions for an alien capitation tax and for the bonding of aliens likely to become a public charge.

Frequently it has been asserted that this is made the Botany Bay of all Europe, and its poor-house too—as though it were the moral cess-pool of the civilized world. The *North British Review*, in speaking of our immigrants, uses the following language: "instead of being the élite, they have generally been the refuse and off-scourings of the nations of Europe—needy adventurers and men who fled from justice, without character, without resources, without any wholesome influence to restrain them." This, indeed, is plain speaking; but it is from the lips of an Englishman. We are far from supposing that all immigrants are of this debased and unpromising description.

In the city of Boston, from 1841 to 1845, more than two-thirds of the state paupers were foreigners. Within the House of Industry, more than sixty-five per cent were from abroad. In the Lunatic Asylum, about fifty per cent, or one-half of the subjects, were from England and Ireland. Of those sent to the state prison at Charlestown, from Boston, from 1841 to 1845, twenty-two only belonged here, while fifty-four were foreigners. Within the same period, the whole number of state prisoners, who were natives, was 820, and those who were aliens, reached the number of 1657, being more than two to one.

Again: the annual cost of foreign pauperism in Boston, throwing out of the account the enormous increase of the past year, will not fall much below $50,000. If the receipts of foreign beggars could with propriety be added, another sum of startling amount is also drawn from the pockets of the charitable, to whom they get access through various pretexts.

Further: the cost of litigation in the courts of law, in Boston alone, and costs in criminal courts, for and on account of foreigners, must amount to very nearly $50,000 per annum, according to the representations of a gentleman of the bar, who has watched this remarkable state of things. In the police court, during a single day in the month of June last, there were sixteen cases, and the parties were not only all foreigners, but all Irishmen.

Under the accumulated and accumulating evils growing out of this state of things, petitions have been sent to the Legislature in past and the present session praying earnestly for relief; and the law-and-order-loving, the industrious tax-payers, on whom rests the weighty grievance of being compelled, against their pleasure, to support some foreign paupers, feel that they have a strong claim for immediate action in their behalf.

While we deplore the misfortunes, and sympathize with these

poor immigrants in the sufferings through which they have passed in the over-stocked and famine-stricken countries, from whence a majority of the helpless, ignorant, impoverished strangers come, it is the imperative duty of those who are selected to guard the public interest, and the domain inherited from our ancestors, to act with promptitude and decision in a matter of such immense importance to the health, happiness, and future prospects of the inhabitants of this Commonwealth.

By neglecting to interpose the arm of the law in the form of new legislation, according to the exigency of the case, before the swelling tide of the emigration to the United States, unprecedented in the history of the human race, becomes too formidable for remedy, the people will be discouraged. The thrifty, industrious producers, who cheerfully maintain the native-born poor, without a murmur too, from growing restless, will become obviously oppressed with the magnitude of the demand that must be made upon them for the support of a great multitude of strangers, of foreign origin, having no natural or legal claims upon us as a people. That they are daily on the increase in Massachusetts, to an extent that fills the minds of wise, far-seeing statesmen with apprehension, and arouses all orders of persons to the consideration of impending danger from that source, will not, it is believed, be called in question.

Happily, this is a subject in which all political parties can unite for mutual protection and for the preservation of their common rights and privileges; and the committee, therefore, consider it hardly necessary to dwell with that minuteness of detail, to show the progress of foreign pauperism in the United States, and particularly in Massachusetts, which they otherwise would, were not the public documents readily accessible to the members, and the facts of universal notoriety. Still, some statistical memoranda may not be inappropriate in this place, which have not heretofore been published. Suffice it, however, to remark, that, unless strong measures are adopted, and speedily too, the sums of money that will be required from the public treasury to maintain the foreign paupers already here, and the throngs that will have a permanent foot-hold on the soil of the state before the close of 1848, will be an intolerable source of perplexity; and in the end, if permitted to be perpetuated, our own, like the poor-law system of England, will prostrate the energies of the tax-payers, and involve the Commonwealth beyond the power of redemption, in that particular, by subsequent enactments.

A profound sense of danger from this prolific source, present anxiety and future forebodings, have led to various schemes for general amelioration, and special security against the augmentation of alien pauperism in our midst—which is manifested by the number of petitioners, and therefore demands a corresponding action on the part of the General Court.

It is admitted in the most open manner by transatlantic writers, corroborated by observation, that an effort is making in Great Britain to send her paupers out of the kingdom. They are so numerous, however, that the expectation of transporting the whole of them, will never be realized; still, however, enough of them have reached this country at various points, and threaded their way into the cities and large towns, to essentially embarrass the civil local authorities, and the cry comes up to the capitol for relief.

A remarkable feature in this heretofore unprecedented kind of emigration from Ireland, is the painful fact that those debilitated, half-starved human beings, brought in such masses as to produce an actual pestilence in the vessels that bear them over the Atlantic Ocean, when landed in the British colonies or provinces, where there are few or no permanent charitable institutions of any kind whatever, having in view the wants or necessities of paupers, speed their way as quickly as possible to the States, particularly New England, with a full expectation of being at once provided for, at the public charge, far better than they ever were in their father-land; and they are not disappointed in their calculations.

So many accounts have been circulated, on reliable authority, of the seductive means held out to the oppressed, needy peasantry of Ireland, of the advantages to be gained in going to America, the land of the free, where, in the old states of the confederacy, wealth and charitable institutions for the poor are on the amplest scale of munificence, that many who were comfortable are induced to force a sale of their small effects to purchase a passage. The hardships and privations of a long and often boisterous voyage, undertaken without reflection, with a scanty stock of food, and finding themselves wholly destitute of means on their arrival, together with underminings of health, death of friends, besides a host of other exhausting influences incident upon the buffetings of the ocean—and all other accompanying woes of their condition —unfit them for industrial efforts, on arrival, even were they all well disposed to labor.

In the agony of discouragement, many, who sustained themselves in their native country without parochial aid, are paupers in the truest sense of the word on touching the soil of Massachusetts. Those who have constitutions to withstand the force of disease are thrown upon us as helpless paupers, with little or no encouragement of ever changing their condition for the better. Thus they are an expense at once, and numbers like these are ever after destined to be a public charge to the end of their lives.

This picture of distress is no flight of the imagination, but a fact susceptible of positive demonstration. A member of the committee has had an experience of some years in the inspection of immigrant vessels, and can bear full testimony to all that is said on this painful topic. It is also true that it is a common circumstance for the afflicted immigrants to beg for food, the day of their arrival, of those officially visiting them from day to day, till they are disposed of at the quarters fitted up for their reception. Another circumstance should not be overlooked, in these general observations upon the destitution and wretchedness of these armies of foreign immigrants, viz., their ignorance, and total inability, even when in perfect health, to adapt themselves to the requirements of society here, without a long and tedious training, that operates against their progress in self-maintenance, even with those most disposed to exert themselves. Hence they cluster about cities, and rarely express a willingness to travel to the new settlements west, because there are none of those well-furnished, liberally-sustained institutions there, which are characteristic of Massachusetts, to which they cling with a tenacity commensurate with their moral debasement, want of self-respect, and abject and needy circumstances.

Assuming it as an established fact, that a profit accrues to those engaged in bringing them into Massachusetts, or they would assuredly abandon the traffic; and it also appearing from the class of vessels devoted to that express branch of maritime trade, it is increasing instead of diminishing, leaving wholly out of the question those owned in Europe, whose owners are enriching themselves by laying a sure foundation for permanently impoverishing our own citizens, it is both right, in law and equity, that they who reap the harvest should bear the whole expense that must naturally belong to a business so extensive, and no one else.

One of the committee has seen idiots, insane and blind immigrants, on board these vessels, direct from Liverpool and ports in Ireland. If a bond may have been legally executed to save the Commonwealth from any charge in the maintenance of such helpless individuals, they, from the nature of their position, must become the tenants of an alms-house, and may live to extreme old age. At the expiration of ten years, the specific life of the bond, they then become exclusively a charge upon the public treasury, ever after, because the bondsman is no further liable for them. . . . .

In the report laid before the senate in 1847, the number of alien paupers, stated to have received a complete or partial support in 1845, was 3,582, who cost the state $76,224, exclusive of the large amount paid for foreign lunatics. By deducting, says that paper, "$6,920 received for alien passengers, it leaves $69,304, being $10,314 more than the amount paid the legislature for the same year."

Further, continues the same instructive document, "in 1846, the number who received a like support was 4,411, and the amount which they cost the people (exclusive of expenses, as aforesaid), was $87,161; from which deduct $11,526 received from alien passengers, there will remain $75,635, being $8,891 more than was paid the legislature that year."

Of the alien paupers supported in 1845, 224 of them came into the state during the same year; and of those supported in 1846, 722 of them came into the state that year, which serves to show the progressive multiplication of such as may without impropriety be denominated imported paupers, to be alarmingly great.

During the year 1847, it appears from the public records that a few over 25,000 alien passengers arrived at Boston. The alien-commissioner says in a note, "Perhaps it might be well to state, that for about one month last year, a great number came over the Eastern Rail Road, that is, from St. Johns, via Portland." Of these, 441 actual paupers arrived in the city of Boston, and, with the exception of 32, entered the state before the month of July. It further appears, that the whole number of steerage alien passengers brought direct from Europe in British vessels in 1847, was 1,847, and in coastwise British vessels direct from the provinces, 7,072: all the remainder, 16,081, in vessels belonging to, or consigned to, American merchants. . . . .

In the Boston House of Industry, the past year, there were 2,434 paupers, and an average of 661 all the time, of whom only 70 were legitimately the city poor; yet 102 of the whole were state paupers, who received support through the entire year. Of the 2,434 who entered the institution, 1,396 were from Ireland, 48 from England, 14 from Scotland, 80 from the British provinces, 3 from France, 22 from Germany, and 35 from other foreign countries. This is indeed a discouraging statement, particularly when another fact is recorded, viz., that 651 of these foreign paupers came into Massachusetts in 1847.

Within the same period of twelve months, the overseers of the poor in Boston expended, for out-door assistance, $18,500, relieving, temporarily, 2,456 persons, 1,281 of whom were foreigners; 115, too, came into the state within the same year. From the opening of Deer Island Hospital, about the first of June, expressly and necessarily organized for the reception of alien passengers, as a precautionary measure to ward off a pestilence that would have been ruinous to the public health and business of the city, to Feb. 9th, 1848, 2,257 paupers were taken in and properly cared for, and still more are continually coming. Those conversant with this new source of profit to shipowners anticipate a far more active stream of immigration with the opening of spring.

By an examination of the doings of the overseers of Boston in the month of January, 1848, in the form of out-door relief, we find that they expended, for 1,174 foreigners, $2301.80. All other out-door assistance, rendered to our own native poor, who numbered but 148, was only $317.10, showing the amazing burden imposed on the citizens, for a class who may yet require very much more and long-continued aid, and who can never be reckoned among the producers or contributors to the public weal.

From Nov. 1st, 1847, to Feb. 4th, 1848, four months, there were admitted into the House of Industry at South Boston, 277 alien paupers and their children; whereas, only 88 native-born paupers, from all sources, entered there within that time, which demonstrates the vast predominance of foreign over paupers who are natives of the United States, and the increasing tendency to their uncontrolled majority in that useful and well-conducted charity.

On the 4th of February, says Mr. Simonds, a member of the legislature, who is officially connected with the House of Industry, the whole number of inmates was 615, about three-fourths being foreigners and the children of foreigners. Under date of Feb. 7th, of the present month, J. W. Ingraham, Esq., known for his incessant industry in the cause of common-school education, says that the number of scholars in the primary schools of Boston, on the last day of October, 1847, was 9,622, of whom those of foreign parentage was 4,045. "I have no doubt," continues that gentleman, "that the whole number is at least 50 per cent of the total number of children in the schools."

In the jails and houses of correction in Massachusetts, the number

of prisoners for the year ending Nov. 1, 1847, who were foreigners, was 1,605, and chargeable, to a certain extent, to the Commonwealth.
. . . .

The Trustees of the State Lunatic Hospital, in their fifteenth report, distributed but a few weeks since, use the following language, which is addressed directly to the legislature:

The increase of foreigners is an evil the more to be regretted, because there is reason to fear it may be still further an increase of incurables. The number of foreigners, mostly Irish, admitted the past year, is 60, being one-fourth of the whole number admitted, while the whole number of foreigners discharged, is 35, being only one-sixth of the whole number discharged. Their misery, their ignorance, and their jealousy, stand in the way of their improvement at the hospital.

Within the same cover, is the report of the physician, at page 32, which makes the following declarations:

The number of foreigners in the hospital was increased during the past year. This was to be expected from the greatly increased immigration to this Commonwealth. Several who had but recently arrived in this country have come to us. Only one, as far as we know, of all those who, since their arrival have had the ship-fever, that disease of filth and destitution, has been committed to our care: most of the foreigners are Irish. The want of forethought in them to save their earnings for the day of sickness; the indulgence of their appetites for stimulating drinks, which are too easily obtained among us; and their strong love for their native land, which is characteristic with them, are the fruitful causes of insanity among them. As a class, we are not so successful of our treatment of them, as with the native population of New England. It is difficult to obtain their confidence, for they seem jealous of our motives; and the embarrassment they are under from not clearly comprehending our language, is another obstacle in the way of their recovery.

To show, in connection with the foregoing survey, the machinery necessarily kept in motion in the city of Boston, alone, on account of this surprising and extraordinary influx of foreign paupers, it is proper to state that an office has been lately opened at the extremity of Long Wharf, for the sole purpose of a receiving room, to which the police convey those found in the streets sick, destitute, and wandering, without friends or a shelter to lay their weary heads, from whence they are afterwards removed in boats to Deer Island.

Notwithstanding the severity and hardship of the sea in the month of January last past, 657 immigrants came into port; and from one single vessel, 60 were sent to the Deer Island establishment, in a very sick and filthy condition, twenty-five having died on the passage.

It is assumed by a competent officer in the state treasury office, that the present annual expense of supporting alien lunatics, is $20,000. For several past years, the average cost has been $17,000; and with the acknowledged increase of population from immigration, five and twenty thousand dollars will very soon be required to meet this particular branch of expenditure. . . . .

Thus, a sad and depressing chart of the draughts the present immigration from Great Britain makes upon the industry of this Commonwealth is presented, aside from the moral influences exerted upon society in New England from this new and altogether singularly rapid increase of population from the most unenlightened and misgoverned parts of Europe. The committee therefore feel justified in this conclusion, viz., that the petitioners have made a reasonable request, in wishing to be relieved from further support of alien paupers, and in calling upon the legislature for the adoption of measures that shall effectually relieve the people of this Commonwealth from any further expenditures for that purpose. The actual cost to the Commonwealth, in the last financial year, for immigrant paupers, has not yet been ascertained. From 1838 to 1847, $555,426.80 was paid by the Commonwealth for the support of paupers, four-fifths, or $444,341.40, is believed to have been for aliens.

Between twelve and thirteen hundred citizens of Massachusetts have petitioned the legislature, thus early in the session, urgently beseeching that some special enactments may be passed, which shall hereafter prevent the expenditure of such large sums of money in a way that operates unfavorably upon the interests of the laboring and industrious citizens; for their experience convinces them that each succeeding year adds to the magnitude of the demands that will be made for this same discouraging object, unless there is a speedy and thorough revision of the whole scheme which has been the policy of the Commonwealth in regard to this engrossing question. If a single vessel freighted with emigrants from the United States, particularly those from the alms-houses of the sea-board—aliens by birth—were carried into any port in Great Britain, with a view to throwing them upon the community there for support, what would be the probable result? A sensation, unlike any ordinary mercantile transaction, would be manifested at once by the civil authorities, and if they could not be kept away by gentle means, we should be made to feel the indignation of an insulted government. Yet that very indignity is heaped upon Massachusetts from the beginning of a season to its termination; and instead of exhibiting a dignified resentment at such marked acts of injustice, we have quietly provided for the immediate necessities of increasing numbers, and voluntarily assumed the uncalled-for responsibility of wholly maintaining the lame, the halt, and the blind, to the termination of their lives, from whatever source they have been forced upon us by unprincipled statesmen, landlords, or poor-law commissioners, of the old world.

With these views of the justness of the claims of the petitioners, based as they are on statistical data that cannot be doubted—and feeling, too, that the evil has no tendency in itself to become less, but, from the very nature of the political condition of Europe, must be continually increasing in magnitude—the committee submit the accompanying bill.

### 15. Cholera in the Boston Slums, 1849[1]

. . . . . Personal habits seemed to be quite as important as locality, in determining an attack of the complaint. For the most part, the temperate, the moral, the well conditioned, escaped; whilst the imprudent, the vicious and the poorly fed, succumbed to its insidious influence.

The number of cases of Asiatic Cholera in the City cannot be given, as no account is known to have been taken of them; but, as all deaths are required to be reported at the Registrar's office before any permit for burial is granted, their number can be accurately ascertained. From his records, it appears that the first death from this disease occurred on the third of June, at No. 11 Hamilton Street, in the person of an Irishman, and the last on the thirtieth of September, at the Cholera Hospital, in that of an Irish woman from Wharf Street. The whole number of deaths between these dates was 611, of which 163 were Americans, and 79 Bostonians. The first patient at the Cholera Hospital was Rosanna Norris, an Irish woman, from Allen's Block, received June 29th; and from that time to November 15th, when the establishment was closed, the whole number of persons received were 262, of whom 166 died, and 96 recovered: 218 foreigners and 44 Americans.
. . . .

Before closing their report, your Committee deem it their duty to call the special attention of the Board of Health, and their successors in office, to the present unhealthy condition of many of the streets,

[1] Extract from Boston Committee of Internal Health, *Report of the Committee of Internal Health on the Asiatic Cholera* (Boston City Document No. 66, 1849) pp. 9–15.

in the lower parts of the City. They refer, particularly, to portions of the Neck and Harrison Avenue; to the South Cove, the territory bordering on the water, from South Boston upper Bridge to State Street, the neighborhood of Ann Street; a part of the Mill Pond lands, and certain tracts on the northerly side of Cambridge Street, near the river. In all these localities, there are many streets, courts, and lanes which are exceedingly contracted, ill ventilated, and dirty; without any proper grade and with no, or very insufficient, sewerage. . . . .

We would now refer to another subject which, in our view, also demands the attention and action of this Board. We allude to the very wretched, dirty and unhealthy condition of a great number of the dwelling houses, occupied by the Irish population, in Batterymarch, Broad, Wharf, Wells, Bread, Oliver, Hamilton, Atkinson, Curve, Brighton, Cove, Ann, and other streets. These houses, for the most part, are not occupied by a single family, or even by two or three families; but each room, from garret to cellar, is filled with a family consisting of several persons, and sometimes with two or more families. The consequence is an excessive population, wholly disproportionate to the space or the accommodation.

From the very necessities of the case, these residences soon become polluted with all manner of bad odors. In such a state of things there can be no cleanliness, privacy, or proper ventilation, and little comfort; and, with the ignorance, carelessness, and generally loose and dirty habits which prevail among the occupants, the necessary evils are greatly increased both in amount and intensity. In Broad Street and all the surrounding neighborhood, including Fort Hill and the adjacent streets, the situation of the Irish, in these respects, is particularly wretched. During their visits the last summer, your Committee were witnesses of scenes too painful to be forgotten, and yet too disgusting to be related here. It is sufficient to say, that this whole district is a perfect hive of human beings, without comforts and mostly without common necessaries; in many cases, huddled together like brutes, without regard to sex, or age, or sense of decency; grown men and women sleeping together in the same apartment, and sometimes wife and husband, brothers and sisters, in the same bed. Under such circumstances, self-respect, forethought, all high and noble virtues soon die out, and sullen indifference and despair, or disorder, intemperance and utter degradation reign supreme.

The houses above alluded to are also insufficiently provided with the necessary in and out of door conveniences, which are required in every dwelling place. The great mass of them, particularly in the region last referred to, have but one sink, opening into a contracted and ill constructed drain, or, as is frequently the case, into a passageway or street, and but one privy, usually a mass of pollution, for all the inhabitants, sometimes amounting to 100. Some of them have neither drain nor privy; and the tenants are obliged to supply their necessities as best they can. Many of them were originally designed for warehouses, and have been converted to their present uses as economically as possible; whilst others, which were once well fitted for the accommodation of a single family, have become wholly inadequate to meet the wants of the large numbers that now crowd into them. A great portion of those in Broad Street and Fort Hill are lofty buildings from three to six stories high, and contain from 40 to 100 inhabitants. The rent for each room ranges from one dollar to one dollar and a half; and is generally collected by a man who hires the whole building, or several buildings, and enforces prompt payment under the threat, always rigidly executed, of immediate ejection. . . . .

Your Committee have already, in a former communication, described to the Board the state of the cellars under the houses. . . . . These cellars are generally entirely beneath the surface of the ground, and, to most of them, the only entrance for light or air, is by the passage, or cellar doorway, leading down to them by steps from the sidewalk above. They are crowded with families, which lodge there and make them their sole place of abode. Besides a dwelling house, these places very generally serve the purposes of a grocery and vegetable shop; and, not unfrequently, a groggery and dancing hall are added. As might be expected, intemperance, lewdness, riot and all the evil spirits, to which poor humanity is at any time subject, enter in and dwell there. Few of the cellars have either drains or privies. Some of them are divided off into one or more rooms, into which hardly a ray of light, or breath of air passes, and where notwithstanding, families consisting of several persons reside. How the lamp of life, under such circumstances, holds out to burn, even for a day, is, perhaps, as great a wonder as that such a state of things should, in this community, be suffered to exist. That such residences become the permanent abode of fever, in some of its forms, is well known to the medical men who visit them; and, that they tend to shorten life, we may clearly infer from the statistical tables of Mr. Shattuck, who states that the average age of Irish life in Boston, does not exceed fourteen years. The number of cellars, used as dwelling houses, is, according to the return of the

City Marshal, 586; and the number of persons occupying varies from five to fifteen.

### 16.   Recommendations of Massachusetts Sanitary Commission[1]

We recommend that measures be adopted for preventing or mitigating the sanitary evils arising from foreign emigration.

This recommendation involves one of the most momentous, profound, and difficult social problems ever presented to us for solution. When carefully examined with its attendant circumstances, the view presented is startling and sickening. Every man in whose veins courses any Puritan blood, as he looks back upon the events of the past, or forward to the hopes of the future, is appalled and astounded. Public attention has been frequently called to this most important matter. We desire again to present the subject, with a special view to its sanitary relations. And we earnestly hope that the few facts which we shall now give, even if they come in the shape of figures and statistics, will arrest notice and careful consideration. In making an application of these facts and statements, it should be recollected that they are made concerning classes. There are individuals who are highly worthy. . . . .

We estimate the increase of the population of Boston, during [the last four years], at about 23,000; and that the whole of this increase was of foreigners. The American residents are believed to be no more numerous now than in 1845.[2]

Of 1,133 intentions of marriage entered by the City Registrar, in Boston, from July 12th, when the record commenced, to December 31, 1849, the foreigners were 621, or 55 per cent; and the Americans only 45 per cent! The actual marriages show a still greater proportion of foreigners.

Of 5,031 children born in Boston, in 1849, and returned to the Registrar's Office, 3,149, or 62 per cent, were the children of foreigners, and 38 per cent only of Americans.

[1] Extract from Massachusetts Sanitary Commission, *Report of a General Plan for the Promotion of Public and Personal Health, Devised, Prepared and Recommended by the Commissioners Appointed under a Resolve of the Legislature of Massachusetts relating to a Sanitary Survey of the State; Presented April 25, 1850* (Boston, 1850), pp. 200–206.

[2] While this sheet is passing through the press, the State Census of the City has been published; and it appears that the population is now 138,788—of whom 63,320, or 45.62 per cent, are foreigners. This proves the correctness of the above estimate, and shows a *decrease* of 1,879 Americans, and an *increase* of 26,031, or 13 per cent, of foreigners.

Boston has paid on the average, for the last four years, about $1,100,000 taxes; of this sum, $350,000 per annum is for the benefit of the public schools; and half of that sum, or $175,000, for the education of children of foreign parents, most of whom contribute little or nothing to the public expenses, in taxation or otherwise. And in many cases the admission of great numbers of these children excludes children of American parents.

The City Marshal of Boston estimated, in January, 1849, that there were 1,500 truant and vagabond children in the city, between the ages of 6 and 16 years, who, from neglect and bad habits, were unfit to enter the public schools; and of 1,066 whom he actually enumerated, 963, or 90.3 per cent, were foreigners, and 103, or 9.7 per cent, only were Americans!

The Boston Society for the Prevention of Pauperism, in their office for providing employment for females, have received, during the last five years, applications for employment from 15,697 females, of whom 14,044, or 90 per cent, were foreigners, and 10 per cent only were Americans. And at the male employment office, of 8,602 applicants, 5,034 or 58 per cent, were foreigners.

The whole number of persons relieved as paupers in the county of Suffolk, for the year 1849, was 7,728—of whom 4,549, or 58 per cent, were foreigners; and their proportion of the whole expense of $103,716, was over $60,000. The number of paupers in the whole State was 24,892—of whom 10,253, or 41 per cent, were foreigners, and their proportion of the whole expense of $441,675, was $182,311.

The number of foreign paupers was 7,413 in 1848, and only 2,765, in 1838; showing an increase in 10 years of 168 per cent. In the last 11 years, 42,928 foreigners have been assisted, at an expense, beside all money which has been received from them, of $737,564.

The city of Boston is this year building a large house at Deer Island for paupers, at an expense of $150,000; and an extensive jail, at an expense of $500,000 or $600,000; both of which are unnecessary for the native population! The existing public buildings would have been sufficient but for the great increase of foreigners.

Of 1,170 dramshops in Boston, in June, 1849, over 800, or 70 per cent, were kept by foreigners.

More than three fourths of all the arrests by the night watch and police in Boston, and nearly three fourths of all the commitments to the county jail, and of the cases before the police and municipal courts, were those of foreigners.

There have been committed to the house of correction in Boston, during the last five years, 3,737 persons—of whom 2,348, or 63 per cent, were foreigners, and 37 per cent Americans; and, in the last year, the proportion of foreigners was very much larger. And in the whole State, during last year, the commitments were 3,035—of which 1,770, or 58 per cent, were of foreigners. The increase of crime has been very great during the last eight years, but it has been almost entirely among the foreign population. Notwithstanding the increase of the native inhabitants, the number of commitments among them has not increased.

About one third of all the inmates of the State prison for the last twenty years have been foreigners. And the State has appropriated $100,000 this year for the erection of an additional building for the reception of prisoners, which would have been unnecessary were it not for the great increase of foreign criminals.

In the Boston Lunatic Hospital, 327 inmates were received, from the time it was opened, in 1839, to 1845, of whom 160, or 48.93 per cent, were foreigners.

For the nine years, 1837–1845 inclusive, the Boston Dispensary had under its care 21,908 cases; of these, 15,522, or 70.56 per cent, were those of foreigners and children of foreigners, and 1,876 only of Bostonians. And during the year ending September 30, 1849, it had 3,950 cases—of which 3,487, or 88 per cent, were those of foreigners, and 463, or 12 per cent, only were those of Americans.

At the Boston Almshouse establishment, on Deer Island, 4,816 persons were admitted, from the time it was opened, in 1847, to January 1, 1850, of whom 4,661, or 97 per cent, were foreigners; and 155, or 3 per cent, only were Americans. The number who were sick when admitted were 4,069, of whom 759 have died; 402 remained January 1, 1850, of whom 369 were foreigners, and 33 Americans.

In 1849 there died of cholera, in Boston, 707 persons, of whom 572, or 81 per cent, were foreigners; and 135, or 19 per cent, were Americans; 42 only were Bostonians.

In 1849, 5,079 persons died in Boston, of whom 2,982, or 58 per cent, were foreigners.

Similar facts might be multiplied; but if these will not command attention, it would be a work of supererogation to go farther.

As long ago as 1834, the commissioners for revising the poor laws of England, among other measures, "recommend that the vestries of each parish be empowered to order the payment, out of the rates raised for the relief of the poor, of the expenses of the emigration of any persons having settlements within their parish."[1] This recommendation was embodied in the 62d section of the Poor Law amendment act,[2] and there is no doubt, that, in very many instances, it has been carried into practical operation. Some poor houses have been emptied, and their inmates have been transported to America—to Massachusetts! The stream of emigration has continued to increase, and seems to gain a new accession of strength in every passing year. Massachusetts seems to have resolved itself into a vast public charitable association. Into her institutions are admitted the emigrant pregnant woman at her lying-in; the child to be nursed and educated; the pauper to be supported; the criminal to be punished and reformed; the insane to be restrained and cared for; the sick to be nursed and cured; the dead to be buried; the widow to be comforted; the orphan to be provided with a substitute for parental care; and here ten thousand offices of social and personal kindness and charity, not recognized by the public laws of the State, costing thousands upon thousands of dollars, are bestowed. The doors of these great institutions have been thrown wide open; the managers of the pauper-houses of the old world, and the mercenary ship-owners who ply their craft across the Atlantic and pour their freight freely in, each smile at the open-handed, but lax system of generosity which governs us, and rejoice at an opportunity to get rid of a burden, or make a good voyage. And a yet greater calamity attends this monstrous evil. Our own native inhabitants, who mingle with these recipients of their bounty, often become themselves contaminated with diseases, and sicken and die; and the physical and moral power of the living is depreciated, and the healthy, social and moral character we once enjoyed is liable to be forever lost. Pauperism, crime, disease and death, stare us in the face.

We will not attempt to suggest a remedy for this most pregnant anomaly. It requires to be more carefully studied, and more thoroughly surveyed than the present occasion allows. The State should pass suitable laws on the subject, and the general and local Board of Health should carefully observe these evils in all their sanitary bearings and relations. We would, however, suggest:

1. That emigration, especially of paupers, invalids, and criminals, should, by all proper means, be discouraged; and that misrepresenta-

---

[1] *Report of Royal Commission on Poor Laws, 1834*, p. 357.
[2] *First Report of Poor Law Commissioners*, p. 90.

tion and falsehood, to induce persons to embark in passenger-ships, should be discountenanced and counteracted.

2. That ship-owners and others should be held to strict accountability for all expenses of pauper emigrants, and that existing bonds for their support should be strictly enforced.

3. That a system be devised by which all emigrants, or those who introduce them, by water or by land, should be required to pay a sufficient sum to create a general sinking fund for the support of all who may require aid in the State, at least within five years after their arrival.

4. That such a description of each emigrant be registered as will afford the means of identification of any one, at any time, and in any place, within five or more years after arrival.

5. That encouragement be given to emigrants from places in this State, where there is little demand for labor, to other places; and that associations be formed among the emigrants for settling on the public lands of the United States.

6. That efforts be made, by all proper means, to elevate the sanitary and social condition of foreigners, and to promote among them habits of cleanliness and better modes of living.

7. That our system of social and personal charitable relief should be revised and remodeled, and that a general plan be devised which shall bring all the charities of the city, county and state, under one control, and thus prevent injudicious almsgiving and imposition.

8. That an establishment for paupers, including a farm and workshops, be formed in each county in the State, to which State paupers might be sent, and where they should be required to labor, as far as practicable, for their support.

### 17.  Immigration and Crime[1]

I presume, Mr. President, Senators are aware that a policy, which scarcely seeks concealment, prevails amongst several of the States of continental Europe, in virtue of which, convicted and unconvicted criminals and paupers are transported to the United States, at the expense, and by the direction of their Governments. This policy, which is as unjust as it is unfriendly, should be put to an end by legislation, if it cannot be accomplished by negotiation. Nations in amity

[1] Extract from the Speech of Hon. James Cooper in United States Senate, January 25, 1855, *Congressional Globe*, Thirty-third Congress, second session, pp. 389–91.

with us have no right to make of the United States a penal colony; yet they are becoming so, by the toleration with which our government has regarded the practice of sending hither paupers and felons. There is scarcely an emigrant ship which arrives in our ports that is not, to some extent, freighted with this kind of cargo. This has long been an evil; but latterly it has increased in magnitude, and to such an extent as to be justly regarded with alarm. But a month or two since, a single vessel landed in New York with one hundred and fifty paupers, and fifteen or sixteen convicts, wearing, as the badges of their conviction, chains upon their limbs. More recently another vessel, freighted with a similar cargo, was wrecked on Sable Island, from whence the passengers were carried to Halifax, and from Halifax were brought to New York, by the way of Boston. By an affidavit made by one of these passengers, it appears that they are natives of Switzerland, who, being unable to support themselves at home, were sent hither at the expense of the municipality to which they belonged. The following is the affidavit:

*City and County of New York, ss:*
We, the undersigned, being duly sworn, do depose and set out, that we and our families, whose number is correctly taken down opposite to our names, on the foot of this affidavit, are natives of Switzerland; that they were poor in their own country and could not support themselves there any longer; that therefore the mayor of their village has paid their passage money direct to New York, and that therefore their passage money has not been paid by these deponents; that they embarked at Antwerp on board the ship "Arcadia," which vessel was intended for New York, but wrecked at Sable Island; that they sailed from Boston on board the passenger steamboat "State of Maine," and arrived in the port of New York on board the said steamer on the 2d day of January, 1855; that they are now quite destitute and without any means for support, except from commissioners of emigration; and further they do not say.
[Here follow signatures.]
Sworn before me this tenth day of January, 1855,
EDWARD CASSERLY, *Commissioner of Deeds*

But it is not only thriftless paupers who are sent hither to add to the burden of our poor laws, and stand between native misfortune and the relief provided for it by charity. Felons, convicts, deep-dyed in crime, are sent to this country by their Governments. Lately, the Sardinian Government shipped to New York, on board a national vessel (the Degennes man-of-war), thirty-four convicted criminals.

Whether they have yet arrived, I am not able to say. But that they were shipped for the port of New York there is no doubt. The *Tribune* has the following paragraph in relation to the subject:

Information has been received here, from a private source worthy of the highest confidence, to the effect that the thirty-four persons in question are not mere political offenders, but are convicted criminals of the most dangerous description, taken from the prisons of that country.

It is a common practice in several of the States of continental Europe to auction off to the lowest bidder, to the person who will bring them hither cheapest, their paupers, and, in some instances, the inmates of their prisons and penitentiaries. Agents of the great passenger lines of packet ships are maintained in these States for the purpose of making arrangements with the municipal authorities of the various towns, for the removal of their paupers to Antwerp, Bremen, Havre, or other sea-port towns, with a view to their transportation to the United States. In England, or rather Ireland, a similar system is pursued; and Miss Dix, amiable, benevolent, and philanthropic, as she has proved herself to be, by a life of devotion to the interests of suffering and unfortunate humanity, writes to her friends in this country from Ireland, where she is now sojourning, in terms of indignation, excited by witnessing the practices of the English Government, in pouring upon our shores the polluted population of their hospitals, alms-houses, and prisons.

Mr. President, it is time that a stop should be put to these practices on the part of the Governments of Europe. If it cannot be effected by negotiation, surely we have the power to do it by legislation. The inherent right of every community to protect itself against the contagion of vice and crime, as well as of disease, will hardly be questioned. . . . . While our sea-ports and the gates of our cities and towns have been closed against the contagion of disease, they have been opened wide to admit the more fatal contagion which is flowing upon us, in the shape of pauperism and crime, from the prisons and lazar-houses of Europe. We dread fever and the plague, and endeavor to exclude them, while "the pestilence which walketh in darkness and blighteth at midday," has been suffered to enter without let or hindrance. It is time we should open our eyes and look the evil in the face; we should examine our prison and alms-house statistics, and provide a remedy, cost what it may. . . . .

But against emptying upon us the contents of hospitals, and houses of refuge, and prisons, we have nothing to object; we are tamely acquiescent, for fear that opposition might be construed into hostility to other classes of immigrant foreigners, whose vote may be esteemed necessary to the success of this party or that. Operated on by motives so unworthy and unmanly, American statesmen and legislators have stood by, with folded arms, and permitted the fairest heritage that Heaven has ever vouch-safed to a people to be overrun by the inmates of foreign prisons, and the corrupted and impoverished hordes of foreign capitals. I am willing that this country should continue to be the asylum of the oppressed of every land, that out of its abundance the virtuous needy should be fed as heretofore; that in its institutions, they should find protection for person and property. But, Mr. President, the time has come when the door of admission should be closed forever against all settled and legalized paupers, and all persons convicted or suspected of crime, who shall be sent hither through the agency of their respective Governments. . . . .

In the great cities of the Republic, in New York, Philadelphia, Boston, Baltimore, St. Louis, and New Orleans, the evils which have grown out of the admission of these classes of immigrants have become gigantic—frightful. Not only have the irresolute and timid become alarmed at the magnitude of the mischief which threatens the public peace and endangers the public morals, but firm-minded and far-sighted statesmen have likewise seen and appreciated the imminence of the danger, and the necessity of prompt and energetic measures to arrest it. The Mayor of the city of New York refers to the subject in a late message to the alderman and members of the common council, and has, also, addressed a communication on the same subject to the President of the United States. The following is an extract from his message:

It has long been the practice of many Governments on the continent of Europe, to get rid of convicts and paupers by sending them to this country, and most generally to this port. The increase of crime here can be traced to this cause rather than to defect in the criminal laws or their administration. An examination of the criminal and pauper records, shows conclusively that it is but a small proportion of these unfortunates who are natives of this country. One of the very heaviest burdens we bear is the support of these people, even when considering the direct cost; but when estimating the evil influences upon society, and the contaminating effect upon all who come within the range of their depraved minds, it becomes a matter exceedingly serious, and demanding immediate and complete eradication. I know of no subject of more importance; certainly we have the power to protect this city against the landing of so vile an addition to our population; the health, as well as the life and property of the people for whom you legislate, requires some action at your hands. I am confident the General Government will listen to any representations from you relating to it, and interpose its national authority in our behalf. On the 2nd instant, I made this grievance the subject of an official communication to the President of the United States.

By the extract from the message, which I have just now read, but a very few of the dangers and mischiefs to which the country is exposed from this class of immigrants have been adverted to. But it exhibits enough to lead to inquiry; and an inquiry into the poor and criminal statistics of the country is well calculated to startle the equanimity and alarm the apprehension of every Christian and patriot in the land. . . . .

But Congress, also, has a duty to perform in reference to this subject, by providing, as far as possible, against the admission into the country of those dangerous and desperate men who come here from foreign work-houses and prisons by the compulsory agency of the Governments to which they belong. If an adequate security against the future transportation of this class of men into the country cannot be provided by negotiation, it should be done by legislation. Congress has the power to make such regulations as will effectually close the door against the admission of this class of immigrants; and it will be recreant to one of its highest duties if it should fail to exercise it. Not only is the corruption of the public morals to be apprehended from the admission of these men, but the public peace and security are likewise endangered by it. The evil is not a new one, it is true; but it is frightfully on the increase. A number of years ago, during the period, I am informed, that General Samuel Smith was Mayor of the city of Baltimore, a ship-load of Hessian convicts, 260 in number, were brought into port, with manacles and fetters still remaining on their hands and feet. General Smith, having discovered the character of the passengers, detained the vessel at Fort McHenry until he could communicate with the Secretary of State, at Washington, on the subject, which he did. By the latter, however, he was informed that there was no remedy—there being no law to prevent their landing; and so the citizens of Baltimore were obliged to look on and see 260 convicts landed in their midst, and turned loose upon society. So desperate, too, was the character of these men, according to my informant, that they had to be brought over in chains, and were actually landed with their handcuffs and fetters upon them. . . . .

I shall pursue these statistics of pauperism no further, being compelled to turn to a calendar of crime absolutely sickening in its details. And I shall first call attention to the number of criminals who were convicted by the courts of several States in 1850. In Connecticut the whole number of convictions was 850; and of these, 545 were natives, and 305 foreigners. In Illinois the whole number convicted was 316; and of these 127 were natives, and 189 foreigners. In Maine the whole number convicted was 744; and of these 284 were natives, and 460 foreigners. In Massachusetts the whole number was 7,250; and of these 3,366 were natives, and 3,884 foreigners. In Missouri there were 908 convictions; and of these 242 were natives, and 666 foreigners. In New York the number of convictions was 10,279; and of these 3,962 were natives, and 6,317 foreigners. In Pennsylvania the number of convictions was 857; and of these 564 were natives and 293 foreigners. In Vermont the number convicted was 79, of whom 34 were natives, and 45 foreigners.

By a table published in the *Compendium of the Seventh Census*, giving the number of convicts in the prisons and penitentiaries of the several States, out of every 10,000 of the population, the proportion of natives and foreigners in that number is as follows:

In Maine, out of every ten thousand, is five foreigners to one native. In Kentucky, six to one; in Mississippi, ten to two; in New York, three to one; in Tennessee, fifteen to two; in Vermont, eight to one; in Alabama, fifty to one; in Georgia, six to one; in South Carolina, twenty-eight to one; in Indiana, four to one; and the average in all the States is a fraction less than six to one.

But it is in convictions for capital offenses that the proportion of foreign and native-born becomes startling. It is true, I have found no extended data from which to make the comparison. But out of 220 convictions, which took place, in about eighteen months, in seven States, viz., in New York, Pennsylvania, Missouri, Louisiana, New Jersey, Massachusetts, and Maryland, there were 138 of foreigners to 82 of natives. But our wonder at the magnitude of the proportion of foreigners to natives vanishes when we recollect that hundreds and thousands of convicts, from European work-houses and prisons are annually landed on our shores. Trained to crime at home, and sent hither only because their presence endangers the peace and security of society in the native country, these men arrive here, in many instances, direct from prison, and consequently destitute of means of support. To obtain it, they betake themselves to their old courses; and not only do they commit crimes themselves, but lead those with whom they become acquainted on their voyage, and who are equally needy, into their perpetration. These facts account, to some extent, for the enormous disproportion between the amount of crime perpetrated by the native and foreign-born. But it is not only the convicts who are sent hither and their pupils, who figure so large in the dark calendar of crime. The paupers, who are brought here by the compulsory agency of their Governments, being thriftless at home, become criminals here. Idleness is too often the parent of vice, as well as of want. At home in their own country, idleness begot want; and here, both together beget crime. Here, then, is another reason why the amount of crime committed by foreigners rises in such huge disproportion above the amount committed by natives. . . . .

I am aware that in European countries, especially, there are so many clogs to industry, so many burdens to be borne, and so much precariousness in the means of procuring a livelihood, that the honest and virtuous, as well as the idle and vicious, often fail in doing it. In those countries where every hour of the laborer's time is required to provide a scanty subsistence for himself and his family, a visitation of providence, afflicting him with disease, may render him destitute, and compel him to seek the aid of public charity, or see his family starve before his eyes. Here, where wages remunerate better, though disease and affliction should overtake the laborer, restoration to health may restore him to the possession of competence; but there, in the countries to which I have referred, if the laborer should get behindhand but for a month, or even a week, he becomes a slave, and his life a struggle with want. For desiring to free himself from the hardships of his condition, and find a happier home and plenty in a land of plenty, no one can find fault. To such our doors have been always open, and against them I trust, they will never be closed. Those who come to this country, fugitives from injustice and oppression, to cast in their lot and become one with us, will always find a welcome. It is not against the immigration into the country of such as these that objection is made. It is only against the admission of the turbulent, evil-doers, conspirators—not against thrones and throned oppression, but against society —that I object.

### 18.   Foreign Pauperism in 1850-55[1]

The census returns of 1850 show that the amount of public means expended during the preceding year, for the support of paupers, is

---

[1] Extract from *Foreign Criminals and Paupers. Report from the Committee on Foreign Affairs, August 16, 1856*, made by H. M. Fuller (United States Thirty-fourth Congress. first session, House Report No. 359), pp. 6-10.

$2,954,806, and the number of paupers supported during the same period, in whole or in part, was 134,972. They show further that, of the number thus supported, there were 68,538 of foreign birth, being over one-half of the whole number. Those of foreign birth then in the country numbered 2,244,625, and one out of every thirty-three of that number was, therefore, a pauper; while the native-born, including

TABLE I

| States | Native | Foreign | Total |
|--------|--------|---------|-------|
| Maine................................ | 4,553 | 950 | 5,503 |
| New Hampshire..................... | 2,853 | 747 | 3,600 |
| Vermont............................ | 2,043 | 1,611 | 3,654 |
| Massachusetts...................... | 6,530 | 9,247 | 15,777 |
| Rhode Island....................... | 1,115 | 1,445 | 2,560 |
| Connecticut........................ | 1,872 | 465 | 2,337 |
| New York.......................... | 19,275 | 40,580 | 59,855 |
| New Jersey........................ | 1,816 | 576 | 2,392 |
| Pennsylvania...................... | 5,898 | 5,653 | 11,551 |
| Delaware.......................... | 569 | 128 | 697 |
| Maryland.......................... | 2,591 | 1,903 | 4,494 |
| Virginia........................... | 4,933 | 185 | 5,118 |
| North Carolina..................... | 1,913 | 18 | 1,931 |
| South Carolina..................... | 1,313 | 329 | 1,642 |
| Georgia............................ | 978 | 58 | 1,036 |
| Florida............................ | 64 | 12 | 76 |
| Alabama........................... | 352 | 11 | 363 |
| Mississippi........................ | 248 | 12 | 260 |
| Louisiana.......................... | 133 | 290 | 423 |
| Texas.............................. | 7 | .......... | 7 |
| Arkansas.......................... | 97 | 8 | 105 |
| Tennessee......................... | 994 | 11 | 1,005 |
| Kentucky.......................... | 971 | 155 | 1,126 |
| Ohio............................... | 1,904 | 609 | 2,513 |
| Michigan.......................... | 649 | 541 | 1,190 |
| Indiana............................ | 860 | 322 | 1,182 |
| Illinois............................ | 386 | 411 | 797 |
| Missouri........................... | 1,248 | 1,729 | 2,977 |
| Iowa............................... | 100 | 35 | 135 |
| Wisconsin......................... | 169 | 497 | 666 |
| Aggregate...................... | 66,434 | 68,538 | 134,972 |

the free colored, and those whose birth was unknown, numbered 19,-979,563, of whom only one out of every three hundred was a charge on the public. Table I exhibits the number of foreign and native paupers, during the year preceding 1850. . . . .

The same census returns, from which the foregoing facts are collected, show the following condition of things in the poor-houses, in the States named, on the first of June, 1850: Massachusetts had at that time 3,712 persons in the poor-houses, not including the out-of-door paupers, who received public aid, of which number there were 989 foreigners, being over one-third of the whole number, of whom 803 were from Ireland, 13 from Germany, and 173 from other countries. Maryland had 988, of which number 243 were of foreign birth, being near one-fourth; of whom 128 were from Ireland, 88 from Germany, and 27 from other countries. Missouri had 276, of which number 151 were foreign born, being over one-half; of whom 77 were from Ireland, 43 from Germany, and 31 from other countries. A like disproportion of those of foreign birth existed in the other States, except in Virginia, North Carolina, and one or two other southern States.

Other statistics, of more recent date, but no less reliable, prove that this disproportion of the foreign born, on the public charge, still continues to exist, and is on the increase. The following facts, collated and derived from various authentic sources, present, if possible, a still more startling picture of the evils of foreign pauperism than do the census returns of 1850, startling as they must be to everyone who has not hitherto had his attention turned to the subject. . . . . According to the report [of the New York Commissioners of Emigration] for the year [1852], the number of immigrants arrived at New York was 300,992, and the number supported or pecuniarily assisted by the commission was 141,992! The reports of the commissioners for the years 1852, 1853, 1854, exhibit the following statistics:

|  | 1852 | 1853 | 1854 | Aggregate |
|---|---|---|---|---|
| Marine Hospital | 8,887 | 4,796 | 4,762 | 18,445 |
| Refuge and Hospital on Ward's Island | 15,182 | 14,365 | 15,950 | 45,497 |
| Lunatic Asylum | 355 | 362 | 260 | 977 |
| Total | 24,424 | 19,523 | 20,972 | 64,919 |
| Boarded and lodged temporarily in the city | 117,568 | 44,514 | 44,514 | 206,596 |
| Total cared for | 141,992 | 64,037 | 65,486 | 271,515 |

According to a report made to the New York legislature, by Mr. Hadley, secretary of state, the amount expended for the support and relief of the poor in that State, during the year 1855, was $1,379,950.50, and the number supported or relieved was as follows: county paupers, 84,934; town paupers, 18,412; total received and supported, 204,161; temporarily relieved, 159,092. The nativity of paupers is given as follows: natives, 80,324; foreign-born, 119,607; and of those relieved there were 94,127 of foreign birth. There remained in the poor-houses at the end of the year 11,997 paupers, of whom 5,773 were foreigners, being almost one-half.

The seventh annual report of the governors of the alms-houses, New York City, for the year 1855, exhibits a similar state of facts. The warden of the Bellevue Hospital, in his report to the governors, states the number of admissions during the year to have been 5,755, of which number but 856 were natives, and 4,899 were foreigners, being over 80 per cent of the whole number; of whom, 4,242 were from Ireland, 281 from Germany, 201 from England, 69 from Scotland, 23 from Canada, 16 from France, 61 from other countries, and 6 unknown. The warden of the alms-house, Blackwell's Island, reports the whole number of admitted, from 1st of January to 31st of December, 1855, inclusive, was 3,096, of which number 773 were natives, and 2,323 were foreigners, being three-fourths of the whole number admitted; of whom 1,949 were from Ireland, 148 from Germany, 121 from England, 38 from Scotland, and 67 from other countries. The report of the resident physician of the city Lunatic Asylum, states the admissions, during the year, to have been 371, of which number 78 were natives and 293 foreigners, being over two-thirds of the whole number; of whom 178 were from Ireland, 63 from Germany, 19 from England, and the remainder from other countries. Of 418 children admitted into the New York House of Refuge, during the year 1855, four-fifths are reported to have been of foreign parentage, and of these two-thirds were Irish. According to the New York newspapers, the number of patients to whom medical services and medicines were furnished gratuitously, by the various dispensaries in that city, during the month of March, 1856, were 7,928; of which number 3,414 were males, and 4,514 females; 2,925 Americans, and 5,003 foreigners, almost two-thirds of the whole number being foreigners. The number of patients attended during July, 1855, at the northern dispensary in New York city, was 996; of whom 630 were foreigners, 568 being Irish, 24 English, 15 Scotch, 12 Germans, and 11 from other countries. So of 1,945 patients at the Eye and Ear Infirmary of the same city, during the year 1848, there were 1,118 foreigners.

In Massachusetts there were relieved and maintained at the public expense, from 1837 to 1840, the aggregate number of 8,671 persons, of whom 6,104 were foreigners, being over two-thirds of the number. For the years 1850, 1851, 1852, and 1853, ending November 1, the whole number amounted to 107,776, of which 48,469 were foreigners, being not quite one-half, and of these over 40,000 were from England and Ireland. . . . .

The following is the aggregate of the monthly census taken of the inmates of the Blockley alms-house in Philadelphia, during the year 1855: Number of inmates 25,242, of which number 6,319 were Americans, 1,578 negroes, and 17,345 foreigners, being about 68 per cent of the whole number of inmates. The society for the relief of the poor, in Philadelphia, report that for the year ending March 31, 1855, there were received into their establishment 1,266 persons, of whom there were 816 foreigners, 182 of unknown birth, and 268 Americans; of the foreigners there were 605 Irish, 122 English, 41 German, 32 Scotch, 7 French, 3 Welsh, 2 Italian, 2 West Indians, 1 from Switzerland, and 1 from St. Helena.

In the Pennsylvania hospital for the insane, of 2,576 patients admitted, 635, being one-fourth of the number, were foreigners, of whom 346 were Irish, 118 English, 108 German, and the remainder from other countries. The following is a table of the admissions into the Pennsylvania hospital, at Philadelphia, for a period of twelve years last past, showing the nativities of the persons received.

| Years | United States | Ireland | Other Countries |
|---|---|---|---|
| 1842 | 438 | 300 | 86 |
| 1843 | 406 | 300 | 99 |
| 1844 | 474 | 348 | 116 |
| 1845 | 470 | 354 | 131 |
| 1846 | 479 | 447 | 147 |
| 1847 | 559 | 563 | 155 |
| 1848 | 627 | 702 | 217 |
| 1849 | 648 | 758 | 246 |
| 1850 | 760 | 812 | 243 |
| 1851 | 626 | 887 | 252 |
| 1852 | 607 | 783 | 256 |
| 1853 | 618 | 782 | 307 |
| 1854 | 579 | 902 | 350 |
| Total | 7,291 | 7,938 | 2,605 |

It thus appears that the aggregate number received was 17,834 in these twelve years, of which 10,543 were foreigners, being considerably over one-half of the whole number, and of which more than two-thirds were from Ireland. Of those admitted during the year 1854, there were, as above stated, 579 natives, 902 Irish, 350 from other countries, of whom 132 were German, 100 English, 38 Scotch, 13

French, 9 Welsh, 8 Swiss, 6 West Indians, 4 Danes, 3 from Italy and East Indies, each, 2 from New Foundland, Belgium, and at sea, each; and 1 from Hungary, Norway, Finland, Greece, Brazil, and Canada, each.

The number received into the Baltimore alms-house, during the year 1851, was 2,150, of which number about 900 were Irish and Germans; and of 2,358 admitted to the same institution in 1854, there were 1,397 foreigners, of whom 641 were German and 593 Irish. According to the report of the board of trustees, for the year 1855, the number of inmates during the year was 2,411, of which number 996 were natives, and 1,415 were foreigners, being a fraction less than fifty-nine per cent of the whole number of whom 646 were from Germany, 568 from Ireland, 78 from England, 32 from Scotland, and 21 from France. . . . .

So in Cincinnati, there were during the year 1848, about 3,000 persons admitted into the city hospital, of whom over two-thirds were foreigners; during the year 1854, the number admitted was 520, of whom 449 were foreigners; the number who received indoor relief was 1,599, of whom 1,307 were foreigners; and the total number of persons relieved at the institution during the same period, was 6,280, of whom 4,654 were foreigners. So at the Infirmary in the same city, the number admitted in 1854, was 660, of whom 505 were foreigners.

These are stubborn, undeniable facts, showing that a great and rapidly increasing public evil exists in our commercial cities, which demands a prompt and efficient remedy.

### 19. Destitute Foreigners at the New York Dispensary[1]

Dr. Elisha Harris being sworn, says: I reside at 102 Fourth Avenue, New York. I am attending physician at the New York Dispensary. At this institution, the destitute poor who apply receive gratuitous advice and treatment. The institution furnishes medical and surgical treatment. The number of patients per annum average over 40,000. We meet at the dispensary with a considerable number of recent emigrants during the spring and autumn. The proportion of such patients treated at this institution is about $33\frac{1}{3}$ per cent of all the patients treated; during the summer season less. In reference to the winter I have not kept an account. In the summer the average is from 16 to

---

[1] Extract from *Report of the Select Committee to Examine into the Condition, Business Accounts, and Management of the Trusts under the Charge of the Commissioners of Emigration* (New York State Assembly Document No. 34, 1852), pp. 97, 218–19.

20 per cent. In the winter it is more than in the summer. All my accounts have reference to those emigrants only who have been in the country less than four years. The annexed is a correct statement:

The nativity of the patients was as follows in 1850:

| | |
|---|---:|
| United States | 8,922 |
| Ireland | 28,875 |
| England, Scotland, and British possessions | 987 |
| Germany | 975 |
| Other countries | 234 |
| Colored persons | 842 |
| | 40,835 |

For several years previous to 1847 the number of patients applying at this Dispensary presented but little variation; from that time the increase was exceedingly rapid and progressive. It will be recollected that during this period, a combination of circumstances tended rapidly to augment the already vast tide of immigration which was pouring into this continent; while the famished and half-starved condition in which they arrived, owing to the scarcity of food in Europe, rendered them fit subjects for fevers and other epidemic diseases, which produced such terrible havoc among them. The number of alien arrivals at the port of New York in 1850 was 10,126 less than in 1849, and we might therefore confidently expect some diminution in the number of patients. This fact would not alone account for the entire discrepancy, which must undoubtedly be attributed to the prevalence of cholera and its kindred diseases during 1849. The past year has been remarkable for general healthfulness and freedom from epidemic diseases, while general commercial prosperity and the consequent certainty of employment have contributed in no small degree, to avert disease from that unfortunate class among whom our patients are found.

## 20. Insanity in Massachusetts among the Native and Foreign Born[1]

### FOREIGN ELEMENT

The results of this lunatic inquiry reveal the great number of foreigners among our insane; and this is the more remarkably seen in the public institutions appropriated to the guardianship and the care of those afflicted with this malady.

[1] Extract from *Report on Insanity and Idiocy in Massachusetts*, by the Massachusetts Commission on Lunacy (Boston, 1855), pp. 57–68.

The following table shows the numbers of the native and the foreign lunatics of the different classes. . . . .

### LUNATICS IN MASSACHUSETTS*

|  | Native | Foreign |
|---|---|---|
| Independent | 1,066 | 44 |
| Pauper | 941 | 581 |
| Both classes | 2,007 | 625 |
| At home | 1,227 | 57 |
| In hospitals, &c. | 780 | 568 |

\* The original table also gave the above facts for each county.

Here is a large number of foreign lunatics within the State, and in the hospitals and places of public custody; and these, unquestionably, bear a larger ratio to the same population of their own class than the native lunatics.

There are not the means of calculating the approximate number of the foreigners in Massachusetts as is obtained for the whole population of the State. If the same data, the census of 1840 and that of 1850, are assumed, 34,818 foreigners at the former and 164,448 at the latter period, and the calculations made, founded on the increase between these two periods, the result will indicate a number of people at the present time that will be extremely improbable and unworthy of belief.

But, taking the number of the foreigners ascertained to be here in 1850, adding to these the arrivals in the four subsequent years, according to the registers of the Commissioner of Alien Passengers, and making a deduction for those who passed beyond the State and who have died between 1850 and 1854, we have then the probable foreign population in Massachusetts of 230,000 in 1854. Subtracting these from the calculated number of the total population of Massachusetts in 1854, we have the native population of 894,676. Dividing these respectively by the ascertained numbers of the insane shows that the native insane were one in four hundred and forty-five of the total native population, and the foreign insane were one in three hundred and sixty-eight of the whole number of aliens in the State. There is, then, a larger proportion of the foreigners than of the natives who are lunatics.

It would seem from this, either that our foreign population are more prone to insanity, or their habits and trials, their experiences and privations, and the circumstances which surround them, and the climate of this country, are more unfavorable to their mental health than to that of the natives.

It is worth while to analyze this state of things, and see how far this excess of lunacy among the foreigners is due to any peculiarities in them, and how far any circumstances and conditions which are common both to them and to those who were born in the United States.

### FOREIGN POVERTY

The most observable fact among the foreign lunatics is, that they have a very great preponderance of paupers. . . . .

The following table shows this distribution of the alien lunatics, independent and pauper, in the several counties:

#### PECUNIARY CONDITION*

Independent.....................  44
Pauper........................  581

\* The original table also gave corresponding facts for each county separately, and also showed the types of insanity, prospect of recovery, and place of detention.

It is a noticeable fact, that most of the foreign lunatics, viz., 93 per cent, are paupers. It is also noticeable that only six per cent of these foreign pauper lunatics are supported by the towns and cities; while 94 per cent are State paupers. The State treasury, then, supports 87 per cent of all the foreign lunatics who are in Massachusetts.

The proportion of native insane who are dependent is much smaller, being fifty-seven per cent of all.

Among all the paupers, the natives, 13,454, who were relieved and supported in 1854, were as one in sixty-six of the whole native population; the foreign, 9,671, were as one in twenty-five of the whole foreign population.

These show that a much larger proportion of the aliens are dependent, or below the level of self-sustenance; and it is extremely probable that the proportion of those who barely support themselves when in health--that is, the poor--is much greater than even this. This is corroborated by the universal observation, that in most of the towns many, and in the eastern part of the State most, of the day laborers are Irish; and on the other hand, very few of the foreigners belong to the prosperous classes. Few of them have any capital; most are struggling with poverty and find some difficulty, and many find great difficulty in supplying their wants. It may be safely said, then, that most of the foreigners in Massachusetts are poor.

The greater liability of the poor and the struggling classes to become insane seems to be especially manifested among these strangers dwelling with us; and as a larger proportion of them are poor, they must, therefore, have a larger proportion of lunatics to their whole number than the Americans.

Besides these principles, which apply to the poor as a general law, there is good ground for supposing that the habits and condition and character of the Irish poor in this country operate more unfavorably upon their mental health, and hence produce a larger number of the insane in ratio of their numbers than is found among the native poor. Being in a strange land and among strange men and things, meeting with customs and surrounded by circumstances widely different from all their previous experience, ignorant of the precise state of affairs here, and wanting education and flexibility by which they could adapt themselves to their new and unwonted position, they necessarily form many impracticable purposes, and endeavor to accomplish them by unfitting means. Of course disappointment frequently follows their plans. Their lives are filled with doubt, and harrowing anxiety troubles them, and they are involved in frequent mental, and probably physical, suffering.

The Irish laborers have less sensibility and fewer wants to be gratified than the Americans, and yet they more commonly fail to supply them. They have also a greater irritability; they are more readily disturbed when they find themselves at variance with the circumstances about them, and less easily reconciled to difficulties they cannot overcome.

Unquestionably much of their insanity is due to their intemperance, to which the Irish seem to be peculiarly prone, and much to that exaltation which comes from increased prosperity.

Mr. Chadwick, the Secretary of the Poor Law Commission and of the Board of Health of England, in explanation of the apparent excess of lunacy among the Irish in the United States, attributes it to the sudden prosperity and means of indulgence which they find here beyond that which they left at home. He says: "If we were to take the poorest and the worst paid and the worst educated English, bred up in single-roomed hovels, with the pig for a companion, and suddenly give them three or four times the wages they had ever seen or dreamed of getting, and at the same time reduce the price of gin or whiskey and all stimulants to one-third the price which had formerly kept such physical excitements out of their reach, I should be very confident of finding a disproportionately large class of cases of lunacy amongst them."

There is no evidence that insanity is more prevalent in Ireland than in England or Scotland, or even in the United States among the natives. We are informed, by the best authority on these subjects in Great Britain, that they have a large Irish population in that island, who go there as they come here, to seek for labor in the lowest capacity. They congregate in the cities, and live in the most unhealthy districts, in narrow lanes and dense courts, in small and unventilated apartments, and even in the many cellars of Liverpool, Manchester, Glasgow, &c. They undergo great privations and suffering, and are much subject to fevers, dysentery, and other diseases incident to bad air and meagre sustenance; but there is no ground for suspicion that in that country they have more lunacy than the natives. . . . .

The foreign population are of comparatively recent introduction into this [state]; there were only 9,620 in 1830; 34,818 in 1840; and 164,448 in 1850; and probably 230,000 in 1854. Unless, therefore, there were some lunatics brought over from Europe, who, at most, were so extremely few that they can hardly be assumed as a part of the elements of this calculation, they would naturally have fewer of the old cases, and of course fewer of the incurables, than the natives.

Moreover, it is an undeniable fact that the foreigners, as a whole, have the best and the first advantage of our public institutions for the care or custody of the insane.

### FOREIGN LUNATICS IN HOSPITALS OF MASSACHUSETTS

Among the foreign lunatics, a little more than a third of the independent class are in any hospital; but almost the whole of the foreign paupers are in some public establishment for their restoration or protection: 71.9 per cent are in the curative hospitals, 17.7 per cent in the custodial receptacles and prisons, and 5.3 per cent in the State Almshouses, and most of those who are in the custodial institutions and State Almshouses have had a fair trial of the remedial measures of the public hospitals before they were sent to their present abodes.

Among the American lunatics, only 35.4 per cent of the independent class, and 42.7 per cent of the paupers, and 38.8 per cent of all were in these establishments, and only 35 per cent of the whole were in the curative hospitals. Of all the insane, 824 of the natives and only sixteen of the foreigners have never had the benefit of such an institution for the cure of their malady.

It is manifest, then, that the foreigners[1] have enjoyed and are now enjoying the blessings of our hospitals to a greater degree than has been allowed to our own children in proportion to their numbers.

This might be expected from the relation of the alien to the State, which is the provider of these institutions. Nearly the whole of the foreign lunatics, that is, 93 per cent, are paupers; and as but few of these have gained any local residence, they are mostly wards of the State. And if they are not originally paupers, but independent, or members of independent families, while in health, yet, as their friends cannot or will not provide for them when deranged, they are thrown at once upon the public treasury for support, and sent to the hospital as early as possible. In doing this, the friends incur no responsibility

[1] The following table was presented in the report, showing the "situation and nativity of foreign lunatics":]

| Present Situation | Where Born | | | | | | | | | | | | | |
|---|---|---|---|---|---|---|---|---|---|---|---|---|---|---|
| | Ireland | British Povinces | Great Britain | Germany | France | Spain | Holland | Italy | Sweden | Austria | Greece | Egypt | Unknown | Total |
| Worcester hospital.... | 110 | 3 | 13 | 4 | | | | 2 | 1 | | | | | 133 |
| Taunton hospital..... | 93 | | 5 | 8 | 1 | | | | | | | | | 107 |
| Boston hospital...... | 164 | 7 | 7 | 3 | | | | | | 1 | | | 2 | 184 |
| McLean hospital..... | 3 | 1 | 3 | 1 | | | | | | | | | | 8 |
| Ipswich receptacle.... | 26 | 2 | 6 | 3 | 4 | | 2 | | 1 | | | 1 | | 45 |
| Cambridge receptacle. | 42 | 1 | 3 | | | | | | | | 1 | | | 47 |
| Concord jail......... | | | | | | | | | | 1 | | | | 1 |
| Boston jail.......... | 1 | | | | | | | | | | | | | 1 |
| Boston house of correction.............. | 3 | | | | | | | | | | | | | 3 |
| Dedham house of correction........... | 1 | | | | | | | | | | | | | 1 |
| New Bedford house of correction........ | 3 | | | | | | | | | | | | | 3 |
| Bridgewater state almshouse........... | 8 | | | 1 | | | | | | | | | 5 | 14 |
| Monson state almshouse........... | | | 1 | 1 | | 1 | | | | | | | | 3 |
| Tewksbury state almshouse........... | 11 | | 2 | 1 | | | | | | | | | | 14 |
| At home—pauper.... | 21 | 2 | 5 | 1 | | | | | | | | | | 29 |
| At home—independent | 23 | 1 | 3 | | 1 | | | | | | | | | 28 |
| State prison........ | 2 | | | | | | | | | | | | | 2 |
| Brattleboro' hospital.. | 1 | | 1 | | | | | | | | | | | 2 |
| Totals......... | 512 | 17 | 49 | 23 | 6 | 1 | 2 | 2 | 3 | 1 | 1 | 1 | 7 | 625 |

of further burden. On the other hand, they are relieved of that which is already on them, for they are thereby saved from the expense of supporting the patient, and consequently expend less when he is in the hospital than when he is at home.

The Commonwealth owns the hospitals, and, of course, takes its wards at once to those houses which it has in possession; and if they cannot be restored, it still retains a part in these institutions, and provides for the transfer of the rest to the County Receptacles and the Houses of Correction, and recently to the State Almshouses, and in one or other of these places it still maintains them. There is, then, no hesitation, no room for doubt, on the part of the friends of a foreign pauper lunatic, in regard to removing him from home to the hospital, and no difficulty in his being received.

But the native lunatic is not so unhesitatingly and readily removed from his home to the public institution.

If he belongs to the independent class, there are the objections of both affection and economy. Many friends hesitate and doubt whether they will send a beloved relative away in the time of his sickness, when he seems to need their sympathy and care more than ever. Many of them cling to him, and are willing to make any sacrifice and try every domestic means and experiment before they can consent to part with him and consign him to the care of strangers.

Beside these, there are the motives of economy, which influence the friends in the choice of means of providing for those under their charge whose minds are diseased. The payment of the expenses of a patient in the hospital, in money, is a burden not easily borne by a large portion of our farmers, mechanics and professional men, although they may have sufficient income for sustenance and for the enjoyment of every comfort at their homes. These families, therefore, are induced to wait before they consent to assume this burden of boarding their lunatic member abroad, until the necessity of removal becomes too great to be resisted. But too often, as the returns show, these motives of affection or economy prevail effectually, and the patient is kept at home so long that his disease is suffered to become permanent and incurable.

The same motives of economy weigh with the municipal authorities in regard to the pauper lunatics under their charge. As they can keep them at their poorhouses at a less cost than at the hospitals, some are fearful of incurring the additional expense, and retain their patients, as long as possible, at their homes; some others never send them to a hospital; and in either case the disease becomes incurable.

Thus, while those who have the charge of the native lunatics, the friends and the overseers of the poor, are generally required to meet and overcome the obstacle of increase of expense in sending their patients to a proper place for cure or custody, and therefore find strong motives for delay or entire neglect of this measure, the friends of the foreigner find a relief of a burden and a dimunition of expense by adopting this measure and sending their patients to be cured.

The same economical reason that induces the friends and guardians of a foreign lunatic to provide the best means for the healing of his disease, or for his protection and comfort in the State hospitals, operates on the contrary to close them against the American, who is suffering from the same malady and has the same wants. So the State, while it offers a bounty to the foreign population and families for sending their lunatics to its hospitals, levies a tax upon the native population and families for doing the same.

We consequently find that, while 36 per cent of the American lunatics were sent to the Worcester Hospital within three months after their supposed attack, 70 per cent of the foreign lunatics were sent within the same period; and while 43 per cent of the natives were not sent until their disease had been established a year or more, only 11 per cent of the aliens were kept away as long.

In those protracted cases, where the best hospital measures are tried for the native patient and fail, and the disease becomes permanent, the resources or the courage of his friends and guardians are often exhausted; and, being unable or unwilling to bear the burden of maintaining him away from home or from the town poorhouse merely for the sake of custody, they take him back to their private dwellings or to the almshouses, where he remains, if possible, through the remainder of his days.

But the alien has no such home to fall back upon. His relations cannot receive him. Or if he be a pauper, he is not subject to the charge of the town, but to that of the State. He has, therefore, no poorhouses to return to, and must remain in the only places which the Commonwealth has provided for its wards—that is, the State hospitals, receptacles, &c.

Seeing, then, that the State necessarily makes the first use of its own dwellings, the public hospitals and receptacles, for its own wards, who are mostly foreign, and retains the incurables there permanently because it has no other home for them—seeing, also, that the independent and town pauper lunatic can be admitted only on condition of paying the cost, which keeps many out, and takes others away if they are not restored—the natural tendency is to fill the hospitals at Worcester,

Taunton, and Boston, and the receptacles of Middlesex and Essex with a great disproportion of foreign inmates, while their advantages are enjoyed in a comparatively small degree by the natives.

Thus, while our bountiful Commonwealth apparently provides hospitals liberally for its own people, and has, in terms, offered them to all within its borders who need them, the law and the custom, and the irresistible force of circumstances, have given these first to the children of another land. Whatever may have been the design and the theory, the practical operation of our system is, to give up our hospital accommodations for permanent residence without measure to almost the whole of the lunatic strangers, while these blessings are offered with a sparing economy to a little more than a third of our own children who are in a similar situation.

The propriety and expediency of this generous provision for the alien lunatics will not be questioned here, for not one of these thus provided for should be neglected. Indeed, it is the great honor of our Commonwealth that it has built—not monuments of glory—but these institutions for the relief of the suffering of even the humblest of the strangers that come among us. That which we have done in this way is well done; but then there is another duty superadded to this—many think it should take precedence—of providing for the cure and the protection of our own sons and daughters when bereft of reason, and of placing the means within the reach and the motives of those who stand to them as guardians in their illness, so that these may be practically enjoyed by them in as great a degree as they are by the aliens; for surely, "these ought we to have done, and not to leave the others undone."

### 21.  Immigration and "Juvenile Vagrancy"[1]

Juvenile vagrancy is another evil now exhibiting itself to a very alarming extent in all our large towns and cities, and an examination of the records of our juvenile delinquent institutions shows but too plainly from whence this painful increase comes. A few facts will make it apparent to the most doubting mind, and to the dullest comprehension. Let us examine them.

It is reported by the Massachusetts Reform School, that of 324 inmates in 1849, there were 66 of foreign birth, of whom 42 were Irish, and of the 258 native born, no less than 96 were of Irish parentage;

[1] Extract from *Foreign Criminals and Paupers. Report from the Committee on Foreign Affairs, August 16, 1856* (United States Thirty-fourth Congress first session, House Report No. 359), pp. 16–17.

and of 278 admitted into the New York house of refuge, in 1850, there were 25 foreign born, and 163 were of Irish parentage. During the year 1853, there were received 112 in the Rochester house of refuge, 73 of whom were of foreign birth, and of these 40 were Irish. Of 157 admitted into the house of refuge, in 1853, at Cincinnati, 107 were foreign born. Marshal Tukey, of Boston, made a report to the mayor of that city in 1849, respecting the number, character, social circumstances, &c., of the street children, in habits of vagrancy, wandering about and contracting idle habits, &c., from which it appears that the whole number of the class of children designated, between six and sixteen years of age, was 1,066, which were arranged as follows: of American parents 103, and of foreign parents, 963!

It has been stated in the public journals, that of 16,000 commitments for crimes in New York city, during 1852, at least one-fourth were minors, and that no less than 10,000 children are daily suffering all the evils of vagrancy in that city. In 1849 the chief of the police department of that city called attention to the increasing number of vagrant, idle, and vicious children of both sexes, growing up in ignorance and profligacy, and destined to a life of misery, shame, and crime, the number of whom were given upon authority and with an exactness which claims confidence. He stated that there were then 2,955 children of the class described, known to the police in eleven patrol districts, of whom two-thirds were females between eight and sixteen years of age. Most of the children, as was stated at the time, were of German or Irish parentage, the proportion of American-born being not more than one in five.

These facts present a melancholy picture of the evil influences that are operating upon a large portion of the rising generation of our country. A volume of well-attested cases might be cited to show the inevitable effects upon our free institutions from such a population. If it were one of the objects of our government to sow broad-cast the seeds of its own destruction, there could be no better nor more effective scheme devised, than to stultify itself on the subject, and adopt no means whereby the vast juvenile vagrant population, now so rapidly on the increase, may be rescued from its youthful career of immorality, vice and crime. The sources of this great moral evil may be almost wholly traced to the many vices of our foreign population, who afford no other examples to their children than habits of disorder, idleness, and uncleanliness, and degrading vices of all kinds, and who exercise no parental authority whatever over them. How can it be expected

that children, with no other examples to emulate, who are neither sent
to school nor church, nor put to work, will grow up otherwise than as
vicious idlers, with whom vagrancy is a confirmed habit, and thieving a
profession, long before they arrive at the age of manhood?

### NEGLECT OF EDUCATION

If it be true, and no rational mind will doubt it, as we are told by
Washington, in his farewell address, that "in proportion as the structure of a government gives force to public opinion, it is essential that
public opinion should be enlightened"; then we have another serious
cause of alarm in the deleterious influences the immense influx of vicious
foreigners must exercise upon our free institutions. Ignorance is the
parent of vice; and it is a lamentable fact, that a large portion of the
immigrant population are not only ignorant themselves, and wholly
incapable of communing with either the school book or the Bible, but,
what is yet words, permit their offspring to grow up in the same ignorance. Though our schools are open to all, it is nevertheless true that
thousands of the children of this class of our population do not attend
the schools, but grow up in ignorance, idleness, vagrancy, and vice. A
brief examination of the census statistics of 1850 will make this fact
apparent.

According to the returns in *Compendium of the Census*, there were,
in 1850, no less than 9,516,538 native whites, and 1,344,346 foreigners
in the country, who were over the age of twenty, of whom 962,898 were
not able to read and write. Of the number thus ignorant, 767,784 were
native whites, and 195,114 foreigners. These returns show a decided
difference between the native whites and the foreign born. One in
every twelve of the native white population, over twenty years, could
not read and write, while of the foreign, not one out of every seven
could do so. According to the same returns, there were, in 1850, in
this country, 4,792,576 native whites, and 313,681 foreign whites, who
were between five and fifteen years of age. Of the natives, 3,915,620
were at school, making a percentage of 80.81 of native whites at school,
while the percentage of those of foreign birth at school was 51.73. Here
we have an explanation from whence the increase of juvenile vagrancy
comes.

### 22. Immigrant Pauperism Viewed Tolerantly[1]

. . . . It cannot be denied that a state of things in a high degree

---

[1] Extracts from a speech on "Effects of Immigration," by Edward Everett,
April 18, 1852, in *Orations and Speeches* (Boston, 1892), III, 104–7.

novel has come rapidly over our beloved and time-honored city, changing very materially the character of its population. . . . .

You will all understand me to allude to the prodigious immigration
into the country which has taken place within the last few years, and
which now amounts to little less than half a million per annum; a phenomenon, I believe, unparalleled in the history of the world. Whether
this immigration is destined to go on increasing, as some suppose, or
has reached its term, and is likely henceforward to fall off, is a question to be settled by time and experience alone. It will, no doubt, however, continue for a long time to be very considerable. There is no
reason to think, that, while the greater part of us are on the stage,
there will not be an annual influx of large numbers of foreigners. . . . .
I use that word in no invidious sense; but . . . . acknowledge the
new-comers as brethren of the great human family.

Now, this prodigious immigration is, of course, not to be an idle
statistical fact. It has already produced, and will continue to produce,
important consequences, and, as usually happens in human things,
both for good and for evil. Of the latter description is the rapid increase
of that sort and degree of poverty which demands public and private
relief. I am aware that not a few immigrants are persons of substance,
and bring a good deal of property with them, which they invest in the
purchase and cultivation of land. Others bring health, strength, and
skill, and become valuable citizens in this way. But, of course, a number are persons of straitened means; many are flying from want.
What little they can scrape together is consumed in the expense of
removal from home, the cost of the outfit and passage, and their establishment here. There is no margin for accidents. If they miscarry
in their adventure; if, on getting here, they fail to meet the relatives
and friends who have encouraged them to come over; if they want the
energy required for a new country; if they want self-control to resist
the temptations of cheap indulgence; above all, if health fails them,
they drop at once into dependence. If they keep up the semblance of a
household, the main resource is too often the dismal basket which we
see going round the streets on the arms of the unhappy children, devoted, almost from the cradle, to this wretched industry; and, if this
resource fails, the almshouse is too often the only substitute. I suppose that it is in this way that the chief increase of pauperism, induced
by immigration, takes place.

I am aware that it is not the only way. An impression exists,
founded, I fear, in fact, but, I trust for the honor of humanity, some-

what exaggerated, that a practice prevails in some parts of Europe, especially in England and Ireland, of carrying on a transportation of what may be called professed pauperism at public expense. The alms-houses are emptied of their inmates, not excepting poor lunatics, who are thrown, without remorse, upon the United States. Such a practice I should regard as little better than highway robbery, or piracy upon the high seas; but I cannot think it exists to any considerable extent.

We must not infer its existence from the considerable number of paupers that are found in the train of immigration. Society in Europe consists of a gradation, of which, except from description, we know but little here, from heights of fortune almost fabulous, to depths of misery more profound than any of which we have much experience. The line is difficult to be drawn between the classes adjacent to each other. Whenever the population is in excess, and the able-bodied men cannot always find work, and the wages of labor for those who do are barely sufficient to keep body and soul together, by the side of the class which crowds the almshouse, there is a still more numerous class of kindred and friends that hardly keep out of it. Of those whom we call pauper immigrants, many, no doubt, have been helped to come to this country by relations and friends who stand a step above them in the social scale, who have found their way to America, and sent back their first earnings to help their weaker brethren to the land of promise. If some of these should relapse into the state of dependence here, to which they have been accustomed at home, we can hardly complain, that, in taking so much of the labor, skilled and unskilled, of the healthy, industrious, and serviceable portion of the community, we should have to take at the same time a share of its infirmity and want. With the stout and vigourous who are willing to work, who bring with them what we most want, strong hands to cultivate our boundless wastes of fertile land, and to aid us in the great constructions necessary for the development of the natural resources of the country, we must not murmur if there is also poured in upon us no inconsiderable amount of dependent and often helpless unthrift and poverty.

This is in the nature of human things, and is not to be complained of. The difficulty is that the increase of immigration has been so great and rapid, that, at first, the provisions to receive and dispose of it are inadequate. The old standing laws, which did very well for two hun-dred years, do not meet the new exigencies. The resources of public and private benevolence are heavily burdened; and when the best has been done, no very great impression seems to have been made on the mass of suffering. Too many mendicants swarm in our streets; and our hospitals, almshouses, and lunatic asylums are crowded with the misery of Europe.

These are, no doubt, unwelcome facts, and, if belonging to a state of things likely to be permanent, calculated at first to produce discouragement, and even alarm. I cannot deny that, at times, I have so regarded them; but upon the whole I think there is no ground for apprehension. We may be somewhat incommoded; but I do not believe the framework of society among us is going to be broken down, or seriously shaken. There is land enough in America for the inhabitants of all Europe, if they choose to come here; and the tide will no doubt continue to flow till the old world is relieved of its superabundant population, and the inducements to emigrate are outweighed by the restoration of a healthier state of things at home.

### 23. Election Riots

#### A. WILLIAMSBURGH[1]

The riot arose out of a collision between the deputy sheriffs, and some Irish voters, who, we are informed by the special reporter of the *Tribune*, were handled with indiscreet and unnecessary roughness by said deputies. A general fight ensued and fifteen or twenty persons, principally deputy sheriffs and firemen were injured—some of them fatally. No Irishman, it is said, was much hurt, though several pistol shots were fired. The firebells were rung, and terrible excitement prevailed through the city. It is stated in some of the papers that a number of Irishwomen were seen furnishing the men with clubs. The riot was eventually quelled, but William H. Harrison [one of the injured] died the next morning, which led to a renewal of the excitement. His funeral was attended by large numbers of firemen, the flags from the various engine houses were suspended half-mast, and the bells were tolled during the funeral procession.

At an early hour on Tuesday evening, rumors were afloat that a fearful riot would take place. About 11 o'clock a procession of men, numbering about five hundred, came marching four abreast through Fifth Street, three hundred of them from New York. At the corner of Grand and Fifth streets, they were met by Mayor Wall, who exhorted them to disperse. Mr. George H. Andrews, of the *Courier and Enquirer*, also addressed them, and quite a number left the ranks. Some twenty

[1] Extract from the *Citizen*, I (New York City, November 18, 1854), 732. The *Citizen* was an Irish weekly edited by John Mitchel and the "Young Ireland" group in New York.

special deputies then proceeded to the corner of Second and North Sixth streets, where the riot occurred, for the purpose of arresting some ten or twelve of the men charged with being engaged in the election riot. If assistance was required, they were to send up two rockets. The procession then proceeded down Fifth Street. In front of Alderman Linskey's house some twenty shots were fired in the air. They then moved down North Fifth Street to Second, where an Irishman was standing in the lot with a loaded musket and bayonet—he said he was on guard—when a number of pistols were fired, and·he ran away, leaving the pistol behind as booty. At the corner of Second and North Seventh streets, two more Irishmen were met with muskets; they were badly beaten, and the muskets were taken from them. The procession then marched up and down various streets, but met with no opposition —the houses all being closed and no persons in sight. A cry was then raised to "down with the church." Mr. George H. Andrews here addressed the crowd, advising them to retire. He was loudly cheered, and many heeded his advice. A firing was kept up throughout the line of march. In Second Street, between North Sixth and North Seventh streets, some persons fired from an alley way upon the procession, but without effect.

A young man named Bennett, narrowly escaped being shot, the bullet having been intended for an Irishman. It struck his left shoulder, but, having nearly spent its force, lodged in the coat sleeve without causing a wound.

About 12 o'clock, a party of about one hundred men made an attack upon St. Peter's and St. Paul's Catholic Church, in Second Street. They first tore down an iron cross over the gate entrance way, stoned the front windows, and broke in the panel of the door. The cross was borne away in triumph by the rioters to a public house called the Odeon. A cry was raised for straw and matches to fire the edifice. At this moment Mayor Wall, Sheriff Lott, and Mr. George H. Andrews, appeared, and prevailed upon the crowd to disperse.

About this time the Jefferson Blues, Capt. Riehl, and Captain John Gaus's company of troops, under Colonel Abel Smith, arrived at the City Park in Fourth Street, and were drawn up in front of the church to prevent further violence. Several Irishmen, mostly armed, came out of the church through the broken door. Colonel Abel Smith commanded them to lay down their arms, whereupon D. Brown attempted to draw a sword upon him, when he was immediately arrested by Officer Trinkam. The others who were armed were arrested by officers Hunt, Donevan, Miner, and Guischard, and taken to the first ward station house. Their names were: Thomas Smallfield, a bayonet; Jerry Dorcy, a pistol, powder, bullets, and a new dirk knife; Thomas Brown armed with a musket; John Murphy, a musket. They were discharged with a reprimand by the Mayor.

Alderman Smith was one of the persons who came out of the church. He was a trustee of the church, and came there to defend his property.

While the military were present—in consequence of a report that arms, ammunition and men were secreted in the church—it was thoroughly searched by a party of gentlemen, consisting of Mayor Wall, Sheriff Lott, Colonel Smith, Aldermen Willmarth, Baker, Sparke, Counsellor Dean, Mr. George H. Andrews, and the officiating clergyman. Neither men nor ammunition were found, notwithstanding the coal-bins were searched.

An Irishman, named McNally, was fired at by the rioters at the corner of First and North Third streets, and one ball took effect in the thigh, causing a wound about two inches deep.

### B.  RIOTS AT WASHINGTON[1]

In the Fourth ward [in the city of Washington], at about noon in the day, a disturbance took place, the commencement of which is variously stated—one version, that a citizen, having had his place in the line of voters temporarily filled, on resuming it was dragged from the line by a German named Schaffer, which led to an attack on the German, and then on the Irish who were present and in the neighborhood; another, that the German and a native citizen were playing a little roughly with each other, when an Irishman was also struck, who resented the blow, when the general mêlée commenced. There is a pretty general agreement, however, that after the beginning of the row the Irish were pursued, and beaten, and pelted with stones and brickbats, with very little resistance on their part; in some cases it being represented that Irish women were struck down while trying to draw off their children or trying to save their husbands or brothers. The conduct of the police is variously characterized, according to the

[1] From the *Washington Star*, reprinted in the *Citizen*, III (June 14, 1856), 375.
   The *Citizen* of June 21, 1856, also contains an account of an election riot at New Orleans where "at every voting place, inoffensive voters of foreign birth, because they were of foreign birth, were beaten, cut and shot from morning to night," if they were not timid enough to be frightened into voting for the Know-Nothings.

bias and partiality of the various persons who witnessed or were engaged in the fracas. It is represented that some shots were fired by the
officers, though not, we suppose, with very bad effects; as we understand that no one was killed or seriously wounded. We have been informed that after the disturbance took place it was with great difficulty
that foreign born voters could be got or induced to come to the poll;
and it is believed that a number of anti-Know-Nothing votes were lost
in the Fourth ward on this account. One individual (a Know-Nothing),
who figures prominently at the poll, is said to have spoken to some of
the anti-Know-Nothings substantially as follows: "We have let the
Irish vote all day up to this time; we will let no more of them vote;
and the peril be on them and on the native citizens who bring them
here, if they try to vote." Notwithstanding this threat, a single foreign born voter was now and then brought forward under the protection of some native anti-Know-Nothing citizens, and in this way a
few got their votes in.

### 24. The "Know Nothing" Demand for a Change in Naturalization Laws[1]

. . . . We are clearly of the opinion that unless some radical
change takes place in relation to the admission of foreigners to citizenship, they will work disastrous ruin to our institutions.

Men frequently rely too much upon the past, for the character
of the future, and in nothing may we be more deplorably deceived than
in a case like this. They tell us that these laws have worked well,
that it was a wise political measure, and that a judicious execution of
them will continue to work good. Here we raise an issue. I maintain
that laws may, and justly do, receive their complexion from the circumstances of the times in which they are framed; nay, that the condition of the people may not only have dictated the character of legislative enactments, but a change of those circumstances may as peremptorily demand a modification of those laws to suit their altered
condition, and sometimes a total abrogation of statutes when they
prove hostile to their interests. Now what were the circumstances
under which the Naturalization laws were formed? In regard to ourselves manifestly these—we were an infant nation, standing in need
of men, with an immense territory and a long line of unprotected coast,

---

[1] Extract from *The Sons of the Sires; A History of the Rise, Progress, and Destiny
of the American Party*, by an American (Phila., 1855), pp. 65–73. See above, p. 206,
n. 1.

and a powerful kingdom in a threatening attitude towards us. Our very existence was in peril, nothing was therefore more important to us than the rapid growth of our numerical strength. It was an object of paramount importance at the time, to have our lands occupied, our solitudes peopled, our roads opened, and our cities built. Such is not our condition now. There is at present no common danger whose external pressure can unite men of different nationalities in one body, to resist the encroachments of a terrible enemy. Much of our territory is peopled, our wide domain is rapidly filling up, our coasts are protected, our cities built, our roads and canals constructed, and we should now guard against the evils which do accompany the unparalleled influx of foreigners; so that they may not be prematurely invested with that power which in unskilful or designing hands might convert this asylum for the down-trodden of earth into a despotism of oppression.

But there has been another change wrought in our condition worthy of consideration. In the infancy of our national existence there was nothing to appeal to the ambition of strangers, nothing to kindle hopes of gain, nothing to inflame those powerful passions in human nature, the love of power and pleasure. Neither could a love of ease or indolence have any hope of gratification in a comparatively new country. Pickpockets would not promote their interests by coming where the pockets were all empty, and convicts were not then released and sent here to try their fortunes. The immigrants of those times were men who came with a view to enter the various pursuits of human industry. They came to seek a home for themselves and their children. And from men who felled the forest, turned up the virgin soil, built their cabins along the borders of civilized life, or entered some other laudable vocation, and thus contributed to the strength and wealth of the nation, no danger could be apprehended.

The vicious and the idle had no inducements to leave the old world to seek subsistence in the new. They would fare better in the old cities, or in the more populous countries of Europe, for there they might possibly live without toil, but here it was work or die. Those, therefore, who would fly to our shores then, were essentially different in their principles and character from the vast majority of those who now form that unbroken current which is pouring its millions upon our soil. They were men in whom the love of liberty was predominant, and whose souls throbbed with aspirations after freedom—men who fled from civil and religious oppression—men who either came for conscience sake, or in obedience to those noble impulses which inclined them to a nation of freemen. But the state of things is materially altered. Now while there are doubtless noble and excellent persons among those coming into our midst, a large proportion are unquestionably totally destitute of those elements of character, which our laws should require before adopting them as citizens. Some are idlers, who would subsist on the industry of others; others prove themselves the most infamous characters—adepts in all that is base, and proficient in villainy. Paupers sent over at the public expense, to be nourished in our almshouses or prisons. Criminals, who, instead of being transported to Botany Bay, are sent to America. It is a notorious fact that European governments have furnished passports and means to their refuse and pestilential population to emigrate to the United States. Recently a few of these were sent back from Boston, but thousands and tens of thousands remain. It was never the intention of the founders of our government to make citizens out of criminals or to invest such with the glorious, but in vile hands, dangerous right of suffrage, when they adopted our Naturalization laws.

Those enactments were adapted to the then existing state of things, to the nature of the times and the character of the men of that age, and while we readily grant that they were then wise, just, and patriotic; the times and the people for whose benefit they were intended, are so altered that there is no longer that adaption which existed at that period. We cannot be so unjust to the memory of those noble patriots as to entertain for a moment the idea, that if they were to legislate now upon the subject they would adopt the same provisions. No! it would be a libel on their wisdom, their patriotism, and their statesmanship, to maintain that, if living, they would leave these laws unaltered.

There are in all wisely constituted governments, some elementary principles which are permanent and admit of no change, while there are laws and regulations which are not immutable, but must undergo modifications to suit the necessities of the age, or the advanced condition of the nation. And while we regard the principles which make this land a home for the oppressed, as immutably fixed and perpetual elements in the charter of liberty, we resolutely maintain, that the laws relating to citizenship must in the very nature of things be subject to such reformations as the emergencies which do arise may dictate, as best suited to promote our prosperity and happiness. It is as clear as a sunbeam to a large majority of the people of this country, that the time has fully come when the safety, the peace and the perpetuity of this Union demand the change already indicated.

There are persons who object to a change in these statutes on the ground that it would be unjust and oppressive to the better class of immigrants, to exclude them for a long period from the rights of citizenship, because some of their number are in an unfit state for such privileges. To this objection, I reply that it is not oppressive or unjust to guard the rights and blessings of the whole even if such a measure would in some instances seem to aggrieve the individual. It is the duty of every member of this great commonwealth of freemen, whether fully invested or not with the prerogatives of a citizen, to sacrifice his personal good for the good of the public, if the case is such that one or the other must suffer.

If, therefore, the objection were founded in fact, the individual himself so aggrieved would by his complaint clearly establish his unfitness for the privilege for which he contends, because he is destitute of patriotism if he is unwilling to surrender what he conceives a personal benefit, for the greater advantage of the public. But the objection is destitute of truth. What claim has a foreigner upon our government? None whatever, except those of humanity or such as international law gives him. But who would have the presumption to maintain that the instincts of humanity make it the duty of government to invest him with all the immunities of citizenship, before the judgment of the nation should pronounce him qualified? The obligations which humanity imposes are more than met and discharged when we give him a place and a habitation, and extend over his person and his property the shield of our laws, that he may be secure in all his interests as a man. In many instances these men never enjoyed the right of suffrage in their native land, and hence there can be no sacrifice on their part if denied the privilege of voting for a longer term of years, because they never were in possession of the right anywhere, and therefore could not surrender it.

There are numerous other and weighty reasons which may be urged for a change in the laws relating to this subject. It may be successfully urged that persons reared on a foreign soil, frequently with little or no mental culture when they arrive here, cannot possibly possess the needful qualifications of citizenship after the few years' residence which is now the only condition. It is not unreasonable to maintain that even a residence of fifteen or more years is absolutely essential in most instances before a man can vote intelligently. Granted that a few are educated, yet their ideas of government have been formed under such adverse circumstances, that their opinions need to be recast before they could intelligently participate in public affairs. Others have no intellectual culture whatever, and have such occupations, tendencies, and impulses that they do none of their own thinking, nor are their votes governed by a conviction of the excellence of the men and measures they support. It is no disparagement to them to assume this fact: the same might be equally true of Americans in reversed circumstances. That our adopted population is guided by the will of others can be easily demonstrated, nay, we have ocular demonstration of it at every election. They move in a mass, they vote in the same way, think alike, and act alike, thus giving conclusive evidence that they are the pliant instruments of subtle politicians, or the obedient executioners of the will of their spiritual superiors. Where the priest uses no influence, which is rarely the case, they barter their votes to the highest bidder. The man who can present the most magnificent promises which he never intends to fulfil, or minister most abundantly to their appetites, he is their man. If I were disposed to record scenes which came under my observation where this foreign vote has been cast without intelligence or will on their part, I could multiply most shameful abuses of the right of suffrage.

A change in our Naturalization laws is absolutely demanded by considerations of our safety. It is an incontrovertible fact, that a large majority of these foreigners range themselves under the banner of socialism, of freethinkers, or Jesuits. All these classes are hostile to the interests of this land. Their principles are in conflict with those of a sound morality, and subversive of civil government. Their peculiarities and their designs will be more fully unfolded as we progress in this discussion; at present, I will only state that their numerical strength is such as to inspire the thoughtful with apprehensions for our safety. A writer from the West recently stated in a communication to a leading periodical, that in a certain city there are 60,000 Germans, and an equal number of Irish in a population of 200,000. These, though divided in their religious sentiments, manifest a singular unanimity in their hostility to all the leading interests of America. Suffer this influx of foreigners to continue for ten years, and clothe them as rapidly as they arrive on our shores with the right of suffrage, and no man may predict the result.

## 25. The Immigrant and the Tenement House Problem in New York[1]

### THE RAG-PICKING AND BONE-GATHERING TENANTS

The lowest of tenant-houses visited by the Committee in several lower wards, are the primary reconstructions or adaptations. In the 8th, 4th, 11th, 13th and other wards, there are many large buildings, or collections of houses, answering to this description. At No. 88 Sheriff street, a rambling row of wooden tenements, called "Rag-pickers' Paradise," was inspected by the Committee. The locality was infected for squares around by the effluvia of putrefying flesh, from numberless bone-boiling places, and bales of filthy rags stored in the cellars and sheds. "Rag-pickers' Paradise" is inhabited entirely by Germans, who dwell in small rooms, in almost fabulous gregariousness, surrounded by scores of dogs, and canopied by myriads of rags fluttering from lines crossing their filthy yards, where bones of dead animals and noisome collections of every kind were reeking with pestiferous smells. One establishment (which is devoted to the same purpose, situated on Third Street, and owned by a former member of our State Senate), contains more than fifty families. Though extreme squalor is apparent to a visitor, the Germans inhabiting these localities appear to be thrifty, and, in their way, comfortable. It is said that habits of economy and constant application to their wretched business enable nearly all, sooner or later, to accumulate sufficient funds to enable them to migrate to the west. We are told of a colony of 300 of these people, who occupied a single basement, living on offal and scraps, and who saved money enough to purchase a township on one of the western prairies. Nevertheless, their means of livelihood, degraded as it is, is likewise exceedingly precarious, especially in severe winters, when snow storms, covering the ground, hide the rags, shreds of paper, etc., on the sale of which they subsist. In such seasons, the children are sent out to sweep crossings or beg, and many of the most adroit practitioners on public charity are found among these urchins, who are generally marked by a precocity and cunning which render them, too often, adepts in vice at the tenderest ages.

The presence and customs of the bone-gathering tenants were made known to the Committee through other senses besides that of vision. In the yards, where ferocious-looking dogs greeted the visitors with threatening demonstrations, a number of bags of bones, just

[1] Extract from *Report of the Select Committee Appointed to Examine into the Condition of Tenant-Houses in New York and Brooklyn* (New York State Assembly Document No. 205 [1857]), pp. 20–22, 42–53.

brought thither from slaughter-houses, with decaying flesh clinging to them, saluted our nostrils with noxious effluvia. These bones were to be boiled on the premises, and their stench, mingled with the fetid exhalations from wet rags, was to be sent abroad over the neighborhood, thence to ascend and be carried by the wind, with all their deadly particles, to the chambers of sick people and the parlors of wealthy residents upon our avenues. On the wooden piazzas, and choking up the narrow entries, were bags and baskets of calves' heads, offensive with putrid portions of the jowls and bones in every stage of decomposition.

The class of tenants above mentioned, i.e., rag-picking and bone-gathering, have a sort of internal polity, by means of which they preserve an amicable understanding, though competing in the same miserable business. For the purposes of their daily life the city is districted or partitioned into streets and neighborhoods, certain individuals or families being allowed their distinct fields, over the boundaries of which they must not pass, to trespass on another's. The colonies sally out at daybreak with their baskets and pokers, disperse to their respective precincts, and pursue their work with more or less success throughout the day. On their return, the baskets, bags, and carts (for some aspire to the convenience of a dog-cart) are emptied into a common heap. Then, from the bones and scraps of meat, certain portions are selected wherewith to prepare soups and ragouts. The rags are separated from the bones and sorted, washed and dried; the bones, after everything that may serve for food has been scraped from them, are boiled, after which rags and bones are sold—the former to adjacent shopkeepers who live by the traffic, at about two cents per pound, and the latter for thirty cents per bushel.

When it is recollected that the process of washing filthy rags, collected from gutters, sinks, hospital yards, and every vile locality imaginable, is conducted in the single apartment used for cooking, eating, sleeping, and general living purposes, by the tenants (sometimes a dozen in one room) where, furthermore, bone-boiling, with its odors, is a constant concomitant; and where to these horrible practices are superadded the personal filth, stagnant water, fixed air, and confined, dark, and damp holes, all characteristic of the tenant-house system, such as witnessed by the Committee in every variety, it is no wonder that these unfortunate people are yearly decimated; it is not strange that the cholera and other epidemics have, as we are told, made frightful havoc among them in past years.

But we must pass over without description hundreds of dilapidated, dirty and densely populated old structures which the committee inspected in different wards and which come under the head of re-adapted, reconstructed, or altered buildings. In most of them the Irish are predominant, as occupants, though in some streets negroes are found swarming from cellar to garret of tottering tenant-houses. In this connection, it may be well to remark, that in some of the better class of houses built for tenantry, negroes have been preferred as occupants to Irish or German poor; the incentive of possessing comparatively decent quarters appearing to inspire the colored residents with more desire for personal cleanliness and regard for property than is impressed upon the whites of their own condition. . . . .

The Committee have witnessed, in their explorations, much calculated to shock the sensibilities and pain the heart. They have looked upon poverty in its nakedness, vice in its depravity. It is, then, no theoretical data which they bring to the support of such recommendations for legislative action, as they feel called upon to make. . . . . The measures introduced in this report are the result of patient investigation and singleness of object in seeking the surest curative means. We shall hasten to present them, pausing only to dwell upon a class of tenants constituting the primary strata of poverty in the city; that unfortunate class whose condition, combining ignorance and destitution with alienism from the habits of those around them, appeals to the pity of more favored citizens. These people are the immigrant tenants.

### IMMIGRANT TENANTS

That crime, in general, is on the increase in our community, is a melancholy fact, in spite of the prevalent taste for reading, the multiplication of means of education, and the continued efforts of christian philanthropy to improve the morals of the people. . . . . Intemperance, though accountant for much, is not the parent of all vice; destitution does not beget every variety of offence; ignorance cannot be charged as the author of such aggregate disorders; but it is likely that, in the combination of these impelling agencies, as allowed to gather strength and boldness, through municipal and popular neglect, may be discovered the foundation of a vast amount of sins against property, man and God. Where shall we look for the rankest development of this terrible combination, but in the hideous anomalies of civilization which are to be found in the tenant-house system? . . . .

How, then, if with the facilities provided for the introduction into our cities of the large and increasing foreign element, continually arriving at our seaports, there be established no adequate means of protecting the community against the disorderly constituents which it invariably comprises? How, if, instead, we place at its disposal districts, localities, neighborhoods and dwellings, especially, as it were, adapted to the habits and associations of the most degraded of foreign paupers, enabling them at once to renew their familiarity with squalor, misery and vicious practices? Is it thus, and with such incentives to the continuance and perpetuation of their customary filthiness and improvidence, that we are to render these immigrants good and useful citizens? Is it in this wise that, as civilized and christian men, we should be prepared to receive the promiscuous immigration pouring into our communities? Rather, should we not, by wise laws, foreseeing safeguards, and watchful social vigilance, so hedge in the hurtful element, that it shall at once quietly yield to improving influences, become accustomed to salutary checks, and ultimately thankful for the humane provisions which at once educate its ignorance and protect the community from its errors? Of a surety, we must, as a people, *act* upon this foreign element, or it will act upon us. Like the vast Atlantic, we must decompose and cleanse the impurities which rush into our midst, or like the inland lake, we shall receive their poison into our whole national system. American social virtue has deteriorated, and is constantly in danger of vitiation, through the operation of influences connected with the influx of foreigners, without corresponding precautions to counteract them. Not politically is this assertion made, nor with reference to the position of the immigrant population as voters, but solely in their relation to one another and to our native citizens, as members of the body social and moral.

The investigating Committee has carried its researches to doors and apartments of lodging-houses, into which the immigrant first sets his foot on landing upon these shores. Witnessing the disembarkation of shiploads, examining the ameliorating features of their reception, as instituted by the municipal authorities at Castle Garden, we have traced the after phases of immigrant residence and habits through the lodging-houses, where extortion is practiced, and in the tenant-houses, where a common level is reached. Whatever may be the estimate of individual means possessed by these people upon their arrival, however encouraging it may sound to hear that the average amount of cash in possession of immigrants is thirty or forty dollars per head, it is probable that the mass of them, settling in the city, are nearly, if not wholly, penniless. In fact, the impelling motive of their emigration is necessity. Driven by the pressure of poverty at home to make a spasmodic effort for the bettering of their condition, they scrape together, through personal exertion or the aid of friends, a sum sufficient to defray the expense of a passage to America, including actual necessaries of life during the voyage. They cannot, as a general rule, make provision for aught beyond the bare exigencies; consequently they become subjected to exposure, hardship, deprivation and sickness; and when these do not terminate in pestilence and death at sea, the poor creatures are cast upon our shores, worn with suffering, and destitute of means wherewith to begin life in a strange land.

What may be known of their immediate fate is revealed partially in the reports of our alms commissioners and pauper hospitals. Other data may be gleaned in the pest-breeding lodging houses, which fleece the immigrants of their last ragged scraps of clothing, in payment for a few weeks' beggarly fare. But the most important phases of immigrant misfortune must be sought in crowded shanties and tenant-houses, where newly arrived ship-loads are quartered upon already domiciled "cousins," to share their "bit and sup," until such time as "luck" may turn up, or the entire colony go to the poor-house, or be carried off by fever or smallpox.

Such, in a suggestive general view, is the condition of a great bulk of the foreigners daily landed at our wharves. What an American emigrant, finding himself in their situation, in a strange land, might attempt to do, cannot be known; he might conquer circumstances, or he might succumb to them. But these poor strangers, these immigrants, have none of the American element in them, whatever it may be; they are destitute, dispirited, sick, ignorant, abject. They demand immediate food, garb, shelter, and not only immediate but permanent means of obtaining these necessaries. But private charity doles its pittance, public almonry its degrading support, and labor, badly paid, fills up between. The male immigrant digs, while he can dig, the female nurses her squalid offspring, and ekes out a scant subsistence by the wash-tub. The sturdy young man, perhaps, may be able to start off on vigorous legs, to seek employment in the country; the young woman may find work as a domestic, if she be of more than ordinary intelligence, and can talk so as to be understood. But the men of families or feeble widows with three or four children, are forced to remain in the neighborhood of the landing-place, because absolutely unable to move away from it; and here they presently subside, and are lost to view in the great multitude, but still peopling the ranks of pauperism in lanes, alleys, and by-places of the city. They swarm in filthy localities, engendering disease, and enduring every species of suffering; they become known at "corner groceries," where they expend their few pennies, or pawn their miserable rags, for bread and vile liquor; and, finally, sinking by sure degrees deeper in the scale of human beings, they often become habitual sots, diseased and reckless, living precariously, considering themselves outcasts, and careless of any change in their condition. At this point they begin to operate, by example and precept, in forming the future character of their wretched offspring.' Here commence lessons in beggary, imposture, theft, and licentiousness, which the young misery-sharpened mind soon "sets in a note-book, learns and cons by rote," until the unhappy victims of their parents' misfortunes and errors, graduate in every kind of vice known in that curious school which trains them—the public street. Homes—in the better sense—they never know. . . . . .

The passage of the bill providing for a Board of Commissioners who shall, by their supervision of tenant-houses, have charge of the incipient pauperism of our city, will be attended with results affecting the self-interest of every tax-payer. State appropriations, municipal support, and private contributions, are now insufficient to provide for the host of paupers that appeals annually to our benevolence. But if this host be met on the threshold of its destitution, ere it becomes a public charge—if it can there be encouraged in industry and protected from extortion, tyranny and the temptation of vice, the effect must be to diminish the manufacture of adult and youthful paupers, and thereby save, ultimately, thousands and hundreds of thousands of dollars of public money, now expended in supporting beggary or punishing crime.

### 26.  Activities of a German Prisoners' Aid Society, 1860–80[1]

There has existed for many years in Würtemberg a charitable organization, known as the "Society for the Relief of Released Prisoners," with its headquarters in Stuttgart, and with branch committees in every one (but two or three) of the sixty-odd counties of the kingdom. The biennial report of this society for 1862–64 says:

We have applied 320 florins [$134.40] in support of the emigration of released convicts. In most cases these persons had been sentenced to serve for many years in the penitentiary, but, in consideration of their good

[1] Extract from *United States Consular Reports*, II, No. 8 (June, 1881), 895–98.

conduct, had been pardoned *on condition of emigrating.* We believe that we have furnished to one or the other of these persons, released from the penitentiary with better purposes of life, the possibility of an honest livelihood in a foreign country which they would have sought for in vain in their native land.

From the official records as published in the *Staats Anzeiger* of this city, it appears that from 1850 to 1865 about 7 per cent of the regular emigration was composed of paupers and released prisoners, shipped at the expense of the various townships, and of course through the medium of the regular emigration agencies. This evil might have gone on increasing to the present day when, with the present tide of emigration, it would have attained truly alarming proportions, had not a ministerial edict been suddenly launched against it. This edict, issued in June, 1875, was addressed to emigration agents and township authorities, and explicitly ordered that no persons who had been convicted of any one of a long category of crimes therein specified should be allowed to register as emigrants to the United States. With a view to determining what effect this edict had upon the operations of the society referred to, I have consulted its records from the year 1874 on, and find as follows:

TABLE I

The Amounts Expended by the Würtemberg "Society for the Relief of Released Prisoners," in Sending Ex-convicts as Emigrants to Foreign Lands.

| Year Ending | Amount Expended, Marks |
|---|---|
| June 30, 1875 | 1,549.71 |
| June 30, 1876 | 615.00 |
| June 30, 1877 | 100.00 |
| June 30, 1878 | 250.00 |
| June 30, 1879 | 50.00 |
| June 30, 1880 | 20.09 |

It will be observed that from the date of the promulgation of the ministerial edict (June 11, 1875), the outlays for shipping dangerous members of society to the United States have practically dwindled down to nothing.

Again, referring to the number of persons shipped, we find the numbers known in Table II (the reports in this case being biennial).

On the showing in Table II there were 43 ex-convicts who emigrated from Würtemberg to all foreign lands in the six years ending June 30, 1880, 25 of them having been aided to do so by the society referred to, and the 18 others going unaided. During the same period the total emigration from the kingdom amounted to 18,522 persons, showing a ratio of only 2.3 released prisoners to every thousand emigrants, but even this comparatively small percentage will, I think, disappear under the influence of the stringent laws enacted on this

TABLE II

NUMBER OF RELEASED CONVICTS EMIGRATED FROM
WÜRTEMBERG FROM JULY 1, 1874, TO JUNE 30, 1880

| HOW EMIGRATED | 1874–76 | | | 1876–78 | | | 1878–80 | | | TOTAL | | |
|---|---|---|---|---|---|---|---|---|---|---|---|---|
| | Men | Women | TOTAL | Men | Women | TOTAL | Men | Women | TOTAL | Men | Women | TOTAL |
| With aid from the Society.......... | 18 | .... | 18 | 4 | .... | 4 | 2 | 1 | 3 | 24 | 1 | 25 |
| Without aid from the Society.......... | 1 | 1 | 2 | 2 | 2 | 4 | 11 | 1 | 12 | 14 | 4 | 18 |
| Totals......... | 19 | 1 | 20 | 6 | 2 | 8 | 13 | 2 | 15 | 38 | 5 | 43 |

subject by the royal authorities. The emigration law of the kingdom is very explicit. It says:

No contracts for transportation shall be made with persons prohibited from emigrating by the laws of the place of destination. The same restriction holds good in the case of persons of whom the agent knows or must believe that they have no right to emigrate according to the laws of the country to which they belong (Article IX, Law of April 27, 1879).

And again:

Particular attention is called to the fact that only such persons can receive transportation as may, under existing laws, be permitted to land in the countries to which they are bound (Extract from instructions accompanying blank form of contract for transportation of emigrants).

In the biennial report of the "Würtemberg Society for the Relief of Released Prisoners" for the years 1878–80, the subject of the contribution of funds toward the emigration of ex-convicts, and of the laws bearing thereupon is quite fully discussed in a special article, a translation of which follows herewith:

DISCUSSION OF THE QUESTION OF THE CONTRIBUTION OF MEANS
TOWARD SECURING THE EMIGRATION OF EX-CONVICTS
TO THE UNITED STATES AND CANADA

In addition to our regular business, we have been engaged during the period embraced between July 1, 1878 and June 30, 1880, in considering the question of the emigration of released convicts, especially to the United

States of America. In the invitations issued to the branch societies February 9, 1879, to participate in the general convention of March 12, 1879, we had already, owing to frequent questions on this subject, called the attention of members to the edict of the royal department of the interior, No. 3813, dated June 11, 1875, addressed to district governments and the royal county authorities on the subject of emigration to the United States of North America, and published in the official organ of the department for the year, 1875, No. 14, page 169.

This edict begins as follows: "In an act promulgated by the President of the United States of America, on the 3d of March, 1875, as supplementary to the existing emigration laws, are to be found (in section V) the following stipulations, also having reference to German emigrants." . . . .

The edict continues in the third division, section V, as follows: "Those foreigners who have been sentenced for a penal offense (political offenses excepted), and those whose punishment has been remitted on condition of emigration, are strictly forbidden to emigrate to the United States." . . . .

Subsequently, repeated applications having been made to this society to pay either wholly or in part the traveling expenses of released convicts to America, particularly in the cases of young persons whose terms of imprisonment were for short periods, we deemed it desirable to obtain from some competent authority exact information as to the scope and meaning of the prohibition, in order, on the one hand, not to exclude prisoners released from punishment from the hope of being enabled to commence a new life under changed surroundings, and by means of emigration, to provide for themselves an honest living; and, on the other hand, to protect released prisoners desiring to emigrate against the consequences which the aforementioned supplementary act attaches to an infraction of the prohibition named; also, at the same time to insure the society against the reproach of promoting an unlawful emigration. . . . .

The Royal Prussian Government, in reply to inquiries addressed to it, has communicated the following results of investigations made in regard to an interpretation of the supplementary act to the emigration laws of the United States of America, of March 3, 1875, contained in the ministerial edict of June 11, 1875:

Decisions of American courts of justice, from which alone an authentic interpretation of the said act could be drawn, were not at that time (November, 1875) on record. American lawyers of repute have, however, expressed it as their undoubted opinion that the prohibition of March 3, 1875, contained in section 5, does not refer to all persons condemned on account of "felonious crimes other than political," but only to those who escape from punishment by emigrating, or to those released from punishment on condition of emigrating. The term "felonious crimes" includes all criminal acts punishable, under the common law or according to special legislation, with death or imprisonment, in state prison. . . . .

### 27.  Protest Against the Immigration of Foreign Criminals, March 19, 1866[1]

On motion of Mr. Sumner, the joint resolution (S. No. 45) protesting against pardons by foreign Governments of persons convicted of infamous offenses, on condition of emigrating to the United States, was considered as in Committee of the Whole. [In the resolution] the Congress of the United States protests against such acts as unfriendly and inconsistent with the comity of nations, and requests the President of the United States to cause a copy of this protest to be communicated to the representatives of the United States in foreign countries, with instructions to present it to the Governments where they are accredited respectively, and to insist that no such acts shall, under any circumstances, be repeated. The joint resolution was reported to the Senate without amendment.

Mr. Sumner.—Before the Senate vote on the resolution I will make a brief explanation. The preamble sets forth certain facts, to wit, that there is an official correspondence showing that the authorities of Basleland, in Switzerland, have recently undertaken to pardon a person convicted of murder on the condition that he would emigrate to America, meaning thereby the United States. That official correspondence has been printed and is now on your tables. There is also a further correspondence, which I have in my hand, which has been communicated to me by the Department of State since this resolution was reported from the committee, showing, I am sorry to say, that such acts have taken place under the Government of Great Britain; that especially has it been the habit in the island of Newfoundland to pardon persons convicted of infamous offenses on condition that they would come to the United States; and there are several very recent instances of pardons in the kingdom of Hanover in Germany. For instance, I have here a copy of two scraps from a German newspaper. One is from the *Luneberg Advertiser* of September 10, 1865, Luneberg being a town of the kingdom of Hanover: "Within the last few months our chief justice has pardoned three of the greatest criminals in the kingdom on condition they emigrate to the United States: Henry Gieske for theft, J. Sander for arson, and John Winter for robbery. The two former are already on their way to New York from Hamburg."

Then there is another scrap from the same newspaper, of the date of November 12, 1865: "The culprit Camman, who was condemned

[1] Extract from *Congressional Globe* Thirty-ninth Congress, first session, pp. 1492–93.

to death for highway robbery and murder, has had his punishment commuted to emigration to America."

Besides this, within a few days, since this joint resolution was reported, I have seen a gentleman who narrated to me an incident that occurred to him in one of the prisons of Baden-Baden during the last year. Visiting that prison he himself heard the jailer or an officer of the prison make a proposition to a criminal to the effect that he should be pardoned on the condition that he would emigrate to the United States.

The Committee on Foreign Relations had this subject under consideration, and they gave some attention to the point whether we could adopt any legislation to counteract this. If Senators will reflect on that they will find great difficulty in meeting it by legislation. For instance, suppose we should undertake to require passports or a system of surveillance of all persons who arrive from Europe, there you impose upon the innocent as well as the guilty a great deal of trouble. A system of passports has not been in use with us except during a very brief period of our recent war. It was thought that the case, perhaps, would hardly justify that.

Another proceeding, perhaps, might be to subject vessels to certain penalties, provided they should import such persons, if you could bring home to the master of the vessel any knowledge of the character of the persons. But there, again, Senators will see the difficulty of bringing home that knowledge. For the present, the committee thought that they would content themselves with the joint resolution which I have reported, which will put on record the sentiments of Congress on this subject, and will reinforce the action of the Executive. I understand that our representatives in different parts of the world have, wherever they have known of these offensive incidents, "earnestly entered their protest; but I desire, for one, that in entering that protest hereafter they should feel that they are supported by the solemn judgment of Congress on this question. . . . .

Mr. Grimes.—I should like to inquire of some of the Senators who seem to be so bitterly opposed to the passage of this measure what objection they have to it. I have not heard any. It is said to be beneath the dignity of this body to protest against what we all know has been going on for a great many years—the exportation to this country of criminals abroad. This is only a solitary instance that has been brought to our attention, and whether the Secretary of State has been doing his duty or not in protesting against it has nothing to do with what our duty is when our attention is once brought to the subject.

. . . . I am as conscious as I can be of a fact that is not within my own personal knowledge, that the exportation of criminals from Germany to this country has been going on for years. Last year I saw a gentleman, a citizen of my town, who visited his fatherland, and when he came back told me that he came in company with a detective, who brought several criminals to New York and turned them loose there. The Government of one of the little German principalities paid all the expenses of the transportation of those criminals and of the detective who brought them over in charge, and when they landed here gave them a certain sum of money with which to start, and probably within a short time they were within Sing Sing. . . . . There is no way but' for us to enter our protest against this kind of importation going on any longer.

### 28.  Misuse of Naturalization Privileges[1]

Americans who have contended for an absolute parity of rights between the native and the naturalized citizen, have often overlooked not only the principles of international law applicable to these questions, but the actual facts upon which the questions usually arise. Independently of the great number of foreigners who emigrate to the United States, in the hope of bettering the condition of themselves and their families by a permanent establishment in a new home, the recent political agitations of Europe have driven thousands of political refugees to seek temporary protection on American soil. In nine cases out of ten, these persons, as well as the multitudes of foreign fugitives from justice who infest our shores, go to the United States with no purpose of becoming American citizens, and many of both classes return to their native country on the first lull in political or judicial persecution, without ever having made even the preliminary declaration required by the naturalization laws. If, however, circumstances compel them to protract their stay in America, they commonly become naturalized, either because they despair of ever being able to repatriate themselves, or, more frequently still, in order that they may come back to Europe with a passport which will afford at least a partial protection against political persecution. I have personally known repeated instances where European political agitators have gone to the United States with the avowed purpose of acquiring a title to American protection and of returning to renew their operations as soon as they could obtain evidence of American citizenship. Not only such persons, but

[1] Extract from an article by G. P. Marsh in the *Nation*, III (N.Y., August 9 1866), 115–16.

many who have emigrated with the honest intention of becoming permanently domiciliated among us, are often called back by political changes, actual or prospective. If they find their party in the ascendant, they sink the American as long as is convenient and take office with their friends; but upon the first reverse, they whip out their American passports and claim exemption from all local jurisdiction.

Besides this, every commercial crisis in America sends back to Europe numbers of naturalized foreign speculators who have fled from American creditors, and who return to their native soil to commence business anew, with the privileges and immunities secured to them by an American passport; and our national credit has suffered severely from the disrepute thrown upon us by whitewashed bankrupts of this stamp. Within the last four or five years the number of returned emigrants has been vastly increased by the fear of taxation and conscription. Many thousands of naturalized Europeans have gathered up their property, and fled with their goods and their families to their fatherland; and I doubt whether it would be an exaggeration to say that one-half of the American "adopted citizens" now in Europe have left the United States, since 1860, to avoid the payment of taxes and liability to military duty. Very often these persons have come without passports, though provided with certificates of naturalization. When they are called upon for taxes, or for military service, they produce such papers as they have, and, in a great majority of cases, the local authorities, overawed by the seal of Mr. ——, or some other naturalization and passport broker, report them as foreigners, and they secure the desired exemption without any further proceedings. The number of persons who in this way escape taxation and military service on both sides of the Atlantic, and thus enjoy the protection of two governments without performing the duties of citizens of either, is vastly larger than those whose attention has not been specially drawn to the subject would imagine. There are in Europe thousands of naturalized American citizens who have never been enrolled among our national defenders, millions of property owned by these persons which have never paid a mill of taxes for the support of our Government. Besides all this, naturalized foreigners have been among the most active and efficient agents of the rebel cause in Europe. The ablest writer in England, in support of that cause, was an Americanized Swiss and a naturalized Italian. "Professor" Manatta is the author of a pamphlet on the Negro race, in which the religious and "scientific" arguments in favor of the perpetual slavery and degradation of the children of Ham are maintained with a zeal which has given great satisfaction to the Papal court and other sympathizers with the rebel cause at Rome.

I see no ground of justice or expediency upon which the United States should embroil themselves with European governments for the sake of "protecting" fugitives from taxation, from conscription, or from criminal justice; or, in fact, any other persons who do not become abiding members of our body politic, abiding elements of our national strength.

Great numbers of foreigners become naturalized without ever having acquired a legal residence, or fulfilled the conditions which confer State citizenship anywhere. They make a declaration in New York, float off to New Orleans, wander about in the West for a year or two, turn up gold-diggers, and obtain their certificate of naturalization in California, and then return to Europe, engage in commercial or political life under the protection of the American flag, without ever having contributed to the support of the American Government or performed any one duty of an American citizen, unless it be reckoned such to have cast a vote for the pro-slavery ticket in some town of which they were not freemen at the first election after they have obtained their certificate.

I am by no means disposed to deny or to undervalue the services which naturalized foreigners have rendered to our country in former and in recent periods, but I cannot shut my eyes to the notorious fact that a vast majority—certainly not less than three-quarters—of that class of our citizens have, from the organization of our Government to this hour, sustained the political interests of the South, slavery included, against the cause of the Union and of human liberty; and I do not hesitate to say that, but for the support which Southern policy has received from Irish and German-Catholic influence, slavery would long since have died a natural death, and we should have been spared the crimes and curses of the late rebellion. The naturalized American citizens who have swarmed over the continent of Europe during the war have been, with few exceptions, favorable to the success of the rebels, and it has not been easy to find an individual among them who has not been, if not an open enemy, at least a very lukewarm friend of the Federal Government.

It seems to me not unreasonable to demand from foreigners, of whose character and history nothing is usually known to those whose office it is to admit them to the right of citizenship, some guaranty before conferring upon them such large privileges. When Esau sold his birthright he got at least a mess of pottage in return from the brother to whom he surrendered it. Shall we bestow our birthright upon the stranger without asking even a small security against the abuse of that birthright?

It is now proposed, in many quarters, to impose an educational test as a qualification for the exercise of the elective franchise. Would it be too much to insist that the emigrant European, who asks admission as a citizen, should be able to read the certificate which testifies to his enrolment as a member of our political community? Would it be ungenerous to require him to show that he has fulfilled the conditions of State citizenship before he is recognized as a citizen of the United States? I do not know that the attainment of the moderate amount of knowledge which could well be demanded, or the possession of taxable property, would be an effectual security against the evils which we are suffering from the existence of a numerous class among us who have the largest measure of political rights and yet are attached to our commonwealth by no moral, no material interests; but I strongly suspect that the law breakers in the streets of New York in 1863, . . . . the servant girls who are contributing their wages to support the Fenian army, and the Fenian army itself, have been mainly persons who neither read letter-press nor pay assessments.

In my judgment, then, no foreign-born stranger should be admitted to the privileges of American citizenship without furnishing some evidence, some securities, analogous to those which nature herself provides in the case of the native. But if it be thought inexpedient to demand such from foreigners bona fide resident among us, let us, at least, not extend our aegis over those who, if they ever had moral claims upon us, have forfeited or voluntarily renounced them. Our ministers and consuls abroad ought to be instructed to recognize no man of alien birth as an American citizen, unless he produces a passport from the State Department; the State Department ought to be forbidden to issue such passports, except upon evidence of performance of military duty, if otherwise liable, during the preceding year of State citizenship and residence, the payment of taxes upon property, and the open possession of property sufficient to secure such payment during the contemplated absence; ministers should be empowered to renew passports from year to year, on satisfactory proof that the applicant is absent from the United States for temporary purposes only, and official evidence that he has paid taxes on all his taxable property for ten years preceding the application.

Such regulations as these would exclude from American protection no person who is morally or legally entitled to claim it; they would secure a considerable increase of our national revenue, and they would much reduce the number of vagabond adventurers who are disgracing our national character abroad by parading a nationality which they misrepresent, and of which they have no right to boast.

### 29. "The Government of Our Great Cities"[1]

The most interesting, most impressive, and most effective, because most picturesque, exposure of the abuses committed in the government of this city which has ever been made, is to be found in an article in the last number of the *North American Review*. . . . . It treats of something which concerns deeply not simply the inhabitants of New York, but of every other growing city in the Union, for every one of them is moving, some slowly, some quickly, but all surely, towards the pit of corruption and knavery in which this city is now wallowing. To talk of the government of New York as a scandal to republican institutions is a very mild way of characterizing it. It is literally a blot on our religion and on our civilization. The man who shuts his eyes to it, who pays his taxes year after year to the band of thieves in the City Hall, and who takes no further thought as to the use they make of them—who sees, without concern, the revenues of a kingdom used by a crew of bar-tenders and loafers for the plunder and demoralization of the poor, the robbery of the rich, and the corruption of the young, ought not to call himself a Christian or an American. And it must be remembered that the same causes are producing the same effects in every State in the Union in which commerce and manufactures are creating great aggregations of people. What is our shame and misfortune to-day will, if some remedy is not applied, be in a very few years the shame and misfortune of Boston, of Philadelphia, of New Haven, of Rochester, of Cincinnati, and San Francisco. The canker is at work everywhere. The purses of the rich cities are everywhere passing into the hands of the ignorant, the vicious, and the depraved, and are being used by them for the spread of political corruption, for the destruction of the popular faith in political purity, for the promotion of debauchery and idleness among young men of the poorer classes, for the destruction of our system of education. When knaves have reached such a point of audacity as to sell regularly the teacherships in our public schools in

---

[1] Extract from an article by E. L. Godkin in the *Nation*, III (N.Y., October 18, 1866), 312.

order to provide funds for their own carousals, it is almost time for us either to shut our churches up and confess ourselves canting humbugs, whose religion is but in words, and whose patriotism is but a sham, or to put an end to these abuses. There can be little question that the corporation of the city of New York is at this moment a greater stumbling-block in the path of democracy and freedom through the world than any single potentate, hierarchy, or body of aristocracy in existence.

We all know what the source of the evil is. In all our large towns a swarm of foreigners have alighted, ignorant, credulous, newly emancipated, brutalized by oppression, and bred in the habit of regarding the law as their enemy, the rich as their tyrants, and a longed-for but unattainable prey. They are welcomed for the sake of their labor, and are almost at once admitted to a share in the government. The form of government is one which notoriously presupposes considerable intelligence in the voters, or at least in the majority of the voters. When, thirty years ago, the changes were made in the law which committed this and other cities to the government of mere numbers, immigration was but a driblet. There was no difficulty whatever in absorbing all the European peasantry who came over. They were scattered amongst Americans, and, exposed at once to all the civilizing influences of our society and government, saw our institutions worked by trained and intelligent hands, and soon shared in the popular reverence for law; and it was an eminently wise change which shortened the term of probation necessary for admission to full citizenship. The long period which was at first prescribed would, at the rate at which immigrants have been arriving for the last twenty years, have speedily accumulated a large body of tax-payers and residents excluded from all share in making the laws they had to obey, which would have been a dangerous anomaly, the more particularly as the ground of exclusion would have been one which neither virtue nor talent nor industry could remove.

But it is now clear that a great mistake was committed when no test of intelligence or education was prescribed for the exercise of the suffrage. Foreigners now are no longer in the same relation with the American community which they were when they arrived at the rate of a few shiploads a year. They are not scattered through it, exposed at every turn to be acted on by its opinion, habits, and manners. They do not, in other words, become part of it, and are not absorbed by it. They form, on the contrary, large, compact communities of their own, perfectly impervious to American influences, in which no Americans are ever seen except on business errands, in which American opinions are never heard, American papers never read, and in which as little is known of the movements of American society as in Germany or Ireland—in which the prejudices, passions, habits, interest, and vices of the Old World retain all their sway—communities, in short, as distinctive, as essentially foreign, as the population of Dublin or Hamburg, and kept constantly recruited by fresh arrivals. The political significance of this may be inferred from the fact that out of the 129,000 voters in New York City, 77,000 or nearly two-thirds, are foreigners, and nearly all drawn from the most ignorant class of European society. This means, of course, that the government has been transferred to their hands without any restraint or condition except such as their consciences may impose.

And yet not to their hands either, but to the hands of knaves who use their ignorance as a stepping-stone to power and plunder. One of the results, and, perhaps, the worst, of this enormous addition of ignorant strangers to our voting population is that they have created a class of politicians formerly unknown, of which Fernando Wood and F. I. A. Boole may be considered as good specimens—keen, shrewd, cunning, unscrupulous Americans, determined to live on the public and ready to do anything that may be necessary for the purpose, who have thoroughly trained themselves to the art of cajoling the Irish—have learned all their foibles and prejudices, and pander to them with unequalled dexterity, and are utterly indifferent to public opinion. No such demagogues have appeared anywhere else in modern times—that is none gifted with so few of the arts or accomplishments which usually win popular devotion. Under their leadership the New York public has been for nearly twenty years a prey and a spoil to the vilest of the population. Enough money has been stolen from the city to have made it amongst the most beautiful of the modern world, the richest in works of art, in public buildings, in every convenience and every ornament that makes life either easier or more graceful. And what is worse than this, they have lessened the public horror of fraud by accustoming people to seeing it committed with impunity, and to the spectacle of notorious knaves and peculators occupying positions of trust and profit, sitting on charitable boards, occupying prominent pews in churches, and figuring in "good society," without any apparent loss of character. We believe there is no man who has carefully observed the tendencies of social opinion in New York during the last twenty years who has not perceived a rapidly growing indulgence for all forms of swindling, if perpetrated on a great scale.

### 30. "Immigration, Indigence, and Crime in New York"[1]

Foreign immigration for philanthropic considerations, and for its national advantages, has ever been advocated in these Reports. Industry is productive, and labor is here needed to develop the resources and wealth of our almost limitless country; for as these objects are promoted, commerce, manufactures, and the arts flourish, agriculture is encouraged and becomes remunerative and profitable. It is worthy of notice, that the most numerous class of immigrants are laborers; and the next in order are farmers, mechanics, merchants, and female servants. The enterprise and skill of some, and the industry of others, wherever they locate, not only increase the numerical strength, but augment the wealth and prosperity of the nation. In following the "Star of Empire" to this western hemisphere, who does not discern the guiding hand of Divine Providence in its bearing on their destiny, and on the country of their adoption? How largely this city is indebted to European emigration for its unparalleled growth, is indicated by the fact, that nearly one-half of the population are foreign born; while the addition of some five millions to our native increase, from the same source, satisfactorily accounts for the unprecedented progress of the nation in population, wealth, and power.

But immigration is not an unqualified blessing. It presents other less satisfactory aspects which should be well considered, especially in its bearing on the character and condition of our cities. In some there may be stronger counteracting and conservative forces than in others; but its deteriorating effects on morals, as observation and statistics show, are usually in the ratio of the foreign to the native population, in any given locality. In view of this principle, the exhibit in Table I of the proportion of foreigners to the native born in some of our leading cities, is not only interesting and suggestive, but it presents facts which are of great social and political importance. Though the figures may not in every instance correspond with the latest census, they are deemed sufficiently accurate for practical inference.

It will be observed that the western cities have not only the largest proportion of foreigners, but also an important advantage over eastern cities, in having a larger share of Germans, who are more intelligent, thrifty, and self-controlled than the Irish. In regard to the latter, New

[1] Extract from *Twenty-fourth Annual Report of the New York Association for the Improvement of the Condition of the Poor* (1867), pp. 36–45.

York and Boston have the pre-eminence, these two cities having more Irish than the other eleven named.

The City of New York has the largest number of foreigners, though not the largest ratio compared with the residue of the population; and while it is admitted that many of them become very desirable and estimable citizens, it must also be conceded that a large proportion in this and other of our eastern cities are, as respects intelligence and character, far inferior to the average of the native-born. Experience, moreover, has uniformly shown, that such immigrants as have pecuniary means, industry, and enterprise, mostly seek homes in the interior,

### TABLE I

|              | American | Foreign | Irish   | German  | Foreign Percentage |
|--------------|----------|---------|---------|---------|--------------------|
| Boston........ | 111,788  | 63,791  | 45,991  | 3,202   | 36                 |
| Providence..... | 36,559   | 12,576  | 9,534   | 343     | 25                 |
| New Haven..... | 27,134   | 10,645  | 7,391   | 1,842   | 28                 |
| Albany........ | 40,099   | 26,619  | 14,780  | 3,877   | 33                 |
| Buffalo........ | 42,636   | 37,684  | 9,279   | 18,233  | 45                 |
| New York...... | 409,469  | 383,717 | 203,740 | 119,984 | 49                 |
| Philadelphia.... | 373,914  | 169,430 | 95,548  | 43,643  | 31                 |
| Pittsburg....... | 39,054   | 27,071  | 12,261  | 9,762   | 41                 |
| Baltimore...... | 132,033  | 52,497  | 15,536  | 32,613  | 34                 |
| Cincinnati...... | 83,699   | 73,614  | 19,375  | 43,931  | 47                 |
| Chicago........ | 53,681   | 54,624  | 19,889  | 22,210  | 50                 |
| Milwaukee..... | 22,292   | 22,818  | 6,830   | 15,981  | 56                 |
| St. Louis....... | 61,390   | 96,086  | 29,926  | 50,510  | 60                 |

pressing onward to the north-west, and some, latterly, diverging to the Southern States, where they become valuable acquisitions, while the thriftless, the ignorant, and degraded, generally lodge, like driftwood, where they land, to fill our prisons, and burden our charities. As an indication of their lack of culture and low grade of civilization, official statistics show, that of the persons over twenty-one years of age in this city, who cannot read and write, there are about twenty foreigners to one native. In other words, while there are but 1,200 natives over twenty-one years of age who can neither read nor write, there are 40,580 of the foreign-born over that age who cannot read the English language. Is it, therefore, surprising that most of the social and political evils in the city, may be traced to the ignorance and debasement of our immigrant population?

It may be further remarked that the native-born, which comprise rather more than half the inhabitants, give about 23 per cent of our city indigence; the foreign-born, including those aided by the Commissioners of Emigration, amount to 77 per cent, which is nearly four imported paupers for one American. The statistics of crime exhibit results as marked and striking. Of the 68,873 persons arrested for offences against person and property, for the year ending October 31, 1865, 45,837 were foreigners; and of these 32,867 were Irish, and but 23,036, white and black, all told, were natives. Of the whole number arrested, 13,576 could neither read nor write. Nor should the fact be overlooked, that many of the native-born paupers and criminals are the offspring of foreigners, who were themselves paupers and criminals. Hence, much of our indigenous pauperism and crime is mediately traceable to foreign parentage, which, under our genial institutions, produces and perpetuates this noxious and parasitic growth of unproductive humanity.

### SOCIAL AND MORAL EFFECTS

Again, what class of our citizens most strenuously resist the moral restraints of the community, when irreconcilable with their own habits, and factiously combine to defeat the operation of the most benign laws, when they happen to oppose their own demoralizing indulgences, or supposed interests? Who among our population would give unrestricted and unregulated license to the ten thousand drinking places in the city, which are the chief receptacles of drunkenness, debauchery, villainy, and disease? Who is it that would annihilate the Sabbath—the very citadel of Christian institutions—the bulwark of private virtue, domestic happiness, national freedom, and prosperity—by converting it into a day of profligacy and dissipation? To these, and similar interrogations, which might be indefinitely multiplied, let facts respond, and there is but one answer.

All who are conversant with the social and moral condition of this city will admit, that there is now, in the lower strata of the population, a larger mass of ignorance, vice, and heathenism combined, than was ever before known in our history. Its chief source is familiar to us. It is the residuum or dregs of four millions of European immigrants, including paupers, felons, and convicts, that have landed at this port within the last twenty years. Uncultured as credulous, they brought with them the habits, prejudices, passions, and vices of the Old World. . . . .

### OFFICIAL DETERIORATION

It is not surprising, therefore, that such a state of social and political corruption should culminate in the memorable outbreaks of the foreign population, in the destructive and murderous four days' riots of July, 1863. One of its most extraordinary features was the utter absence of all conceivable apology for the uprising, and for the hideous atrocity of the insurgents which occasioned the sacrifice of 1,155 lives, at a cost to the city of nearly two millions of dollars. Its main causes were ignorance and depravity, goaded on to ferocity by political deceivers, disguised traitors, and cowards, to serve their own selfish ends. But, whatever the proximate excitements of the infuriated populace, it is evident that the latent elements of the diabolical outbreak had previously existed among the most brutal and debased of the foreign residents. Nor has the danger of a recurrence of those scenes passed away. The police authorities recently announced the discovery of organizations in progress, to resist by violence and bloodshed, if necessary, the execution and enforcement of the Excise and other laws that are obnoxious to certain classes of our foreign-born citizens. The conspirators, it appears, were only deterred from the attempt to carry their purpose into effect, by the warning, that the police authorities were fully prepared to suppress and to crush out all violent endeavors to resist the enforcement of the laws. But, is it not to be feared that insurrectionary fires are still smouldering, which only need vent to upturn the foundations of social order, and overwhelm society in anarchy and ruin?

### SEGREGATION OF IMMIGRANTS

But the subject presents other aspects not less important, which in this connection require grave consideration. The fact is obvious and indisputable, that the social relations of the foreign to the native population have, in late years, materially changed. They no longer, as formerly, melt away, or so blend with the native stocks as to become incorporated with it. So large are the aggregations of different foreign nationalities, that they no longer conform to our habits, opinions, and manners, but, on the contrary, create for themselves distinct communities, almost as impervious to American sentiments and influences, as are the inhabitants of Dublin or Hamburg. This principle or tendency of segregation extends to their private, social, and public life— which every new arrival augments in numbers and strength. They have their own theatres, recreations, amusements, military and national organizations; to a great extent their own schools, churches, and trade unions—their own newspapers and periodical literature. In further illustration of this tendency to sever themselves from everything American, we find that they have in this city seventy-three churches; they publish thirty-five newspapers and periodicals, in five different languages, and sustain several eleemosynary and philanthropic institutions, for the exclusive benefit of their own people. As these foreign masses, in short, have little intercourse with the native population, beyond the claims of business, and read few American papers, they are generally as ignorant of all that is peculiar to the institutions of the country, as if no such sources of information existed, or as if they still were subjects of a foreign power.

But these, it must be conceded, are natural results, and only such as should, in the sequence of things, have been expected. Such segregation, though neither desirable nor practicable in former years, latterly became a social necessity; and hence they have been formed according to the affinities of race, language, and religion. So heterogeneous, however, are these masses, that they cannot coalesce and harmonize with each other, much less with Americans. Even if the exodus from Europe should diminish or cease, as eventually it must from depletion, generations will elapse before they become thoroughly Americanized; and, until it does cease, the difficulty in our large cities of dealing wisely with the evils of a population so divided and constituted will continue to exist. . . . .

Let it not for a moment be imagined that the prominence which has been given to our foreign population is attributable to prejudice or unkindness. They have, on the contrary, been specially referred to for two reasons; first, because of their important relations to this Association and to the community; and second, to awaken a deeper social and moral interest in their welfare. The ignorance, debasement, and wretchedness of many of them, though fitted to repel intercourse and repress sympathy, should excite a more active and earnest concern in their behalf. They have been led hither by the guiding hand of Divine Providence for a beneficent end. They have been thrown upon our care, not to be neglected, scorned, and depressed, but to be lifted up to a better life. To the Christian benevolence of this city, and, in no inconsiderable degree, to the labors and influence of this Institution, God has intrusted this glorious stewardship. Though their character has been depicted with the fidelity which truth requires, yet toward no other class has the thoughtful solicitude of the Association been more deeply exercised than to them, for their benefit, and for the present and future advantage of the community.

The foreign-born, be it remembered, constitute about three-fourths of the recipients of this charity, and the attention and aid it gives are not grudgingly bestowed, provided they are attended with the desired results. They are, if not the majority, at least the controlling political element in the city. Every day they are increasing in numbers, and they know it. They are not circumstanced like the same classes in the Old World, and cannot be wisely or safely treated in the same way. Their best interests this Association would conscientiously promote. It believes, however, in no legislative encroachments on capital, nor in diminishing the hours of labor while the pay is increased; for all such class legislation and levelling endeavors will be generally disastrous, and ultimately work out their own defeat. The philosophy of the times, on the contrary, points not to legislative interference, nor yet to violence or to "strikes," but to the increased intelligence and enterprise of labor, to the power of organized industry to redress its own grievances, real or imaginary, and to "co-operative movements," perhaps, which severally recognizing the sanctity of property as well as the rights of labor, are essentially conservative as well as progressive, and will insure the largest recompense which the laws that govern labor admit. This being the course both of duty and safety, let no unkind opprobrium be cast upon the ignorant poor who need counsel and sympathy, nor yet upon the degraded that need pity and help; but rather may they be lifted up to the average level of intelligence and education. This is certainly the spirit of our impartial institutions, and the dictate of practical Christianity, which alike aim at man's highest physical, social, and moral good.

### 31.   Foreign Convicts in New York[1]

1. Letter from Mr. Bernard Casserly, the superintendent of Castle Garden Immigrant Landing Dépôt, to Mr. Hamilton Fish, the secretary of state, December 28, 1871:

OFFICE OF THE COMMISSIONERS OF EMIGRATION OF THE STATE OF NEW YORK
CASTLE GARDEN, NEW YORK, Dec. 28, 1871

Sir: I am instructed by the commissioners of emigration of the State of New York to submit for your consideration the enclosed affidavits concerning discharged convicts sent to this country from England on the ships "Hamilton Fish" and "Jas. Foster, Jr."

[1] Extracts from *Landing of Foreign Convicts on Our Shores* (United States Forty-third Congress, first session, House Executive Document No. 253), pp. 25–34.
The letters given are only a few of a long series transmitted to the House of Representatives by the Secretary of State (Hamilton Fish) in response to a resolution of May 9, 1874, requesting the President to communicate to the House "any correspondence between the State Department and other governments as to the

The commissioners have reason to believe that there have been landed here lately from these and other vessels a number of men of the same class, sent out under the same circumstances, whose affidavits, however, they have been unable to obtain.

I have, &c.,

BERNARD CASSERLY, *Superintendent*

*City and County of New York, ss:*

John Walker, John Butterworth, and Edward Maguire, being duly sworn, depose and say that they are emigrants, and arrived at this port by the ship "Hamilton Fish," from Liverpool, December 18, 1871; and that in October last they were discharged, John Walker from Brixton, and the other deponents from Portland prison, on tickets-of-leave, which tickets they received for good conduct during their imprisonment; that they had been each sentenced to seven years' penal servitude—Walker for theft, Butterworth for house-breaking, and Maguire for attempted robbery with violence —and that they were each rewarded on leaving prison with £6 sterling—a gratuity only given to prisoners whose conduct has been uniformly good; that these sums were not handed to deponents, but intrusted to James Foster, agent of the Manchester Discharged Prisoners' Aid Society, to be by him expended for deponents' benefit, and that said James Foster, with these moneys and other funds contributed by said society, purchased their tickets to New York, their outfits for the voyage, and supported two of them for two weeks in England; and that said James Foster told the deponents Walker and Butterworth that they would find at Castle Garden a letter addressed to the former, but that, having made inquiries at Castle Garden, they find that there is no such letter there.

And further the two deponents last named say that they are destitute and desire immediate employment.

JOHN WALKER
his
JOHN + BUTTERWORTH
mark
EDWARD MAGUIRE

Sworn to before me this 18th day of December, 1871,

H. D. GLYNN, *Commissioner of Deeds*

---

landing of foreign convicts on our shores, and what legislation, if any, in his judgment is necessary to prevent such outrages."

In his letter of transmittal, the Secretary of State writes that "the involuntary deportation to the United States by foreign officials of foreign convicts and of foreign paupers, idiots, insane persons, and others incapable of supporting themselves, has been frequently made the subject of official correspondence. Although the resolution of the House refers in terms only to the deportation of convicts, it is supposed that it will not be thought improper, in answering it, to transmit also correspondence relating to the other classes of involuntary emigrants. This objectionable practice has been the subject of official correspondence in previous administrations, as well as during the present administration" (p. 1).

2. Letter from the United States Consul-General at London to Mr. Hamilton Fish, secretary of state:

UNITED STATES CONSULATE-GENERAL
LONDON, February 8, 1873

SIR: I have the honor to report that I have this day received a communication from the consul at Dublin, dated the 7th of February instant, reciting that on the 7th a man, not an American citizen, and calling himself Bryan Fitzgerald, had applied at the consulate for assistance and advice under the following circumstances:

He stated that he was a convict of a prison in Dublin, when, on the 28th of July, 1870, he was sent to America, there being still two years and three months of his time to serve. He was released on condition that he went to the United States; and was sent to the Hancock copper mines in Michigan, and after some time returned to Ireland, where he was arrested, and on the 5th of February, 1872, was sent to prison as a returned ticket-of-leave man to complete his term. The time he had been in America was allowed him, and deducted from the two years and three months, but three months were added because he came back. He was released last week and is now free. He declared that he knew at least fifty ex-convicts in New York who had been released upon conditions similar to those by which he got out of jail.

His application to the consul was for assistance and advice in recovering money which he said he had earned while in prison, but which had been used against his will to pay his passage to America.

The consul concluded he could do nothing to assist the man, and so told him.

I have approved this decision of the consul, but desired him to investigate the matter further, to obtain the affidavit of Fitzgerald, and to ascertain whether his statement can be verified from any other source; and especially to satisfy himself as to the correctness of the assertion that others than himself have been released from British prisons on condition of going to the United States and remaining there. I cautioned the consul to proceed with due caution, so as to do nothing which could be fairly offensive to British authorities, and yet, at the same time, to ascertain the true state of the case.

I thought it possible that the minister of the United States at London might desire to take steps in the matter of his own motion, and have, therefore, communicated to him the statement of the consul at Dublin.

I am, &c.,

ADAM BADEAU, *Consul-General*

3. Letter from General Schenck, United States minister to Great Britain, to Lord Granville, British foreign secretary:

LEGATION OF THE UNITED STATES
LONDON, January 31, 1872

MY LORD: In the interview which I had the honor to have with your lordship on Wednesday last, I informed you of my having received a dispatch from Mr. Fish in relation to certain persons alleged to have been recently released from unexpired terms of imprisonment to which they had been sentenced for criminal offenses, and furnished with means by public authorities or prison aid societies in England to emigrate to New York. At the same time I expressed to your lordship, as I was instructed to do, my earnest remonstrance and protest against such deportation of convicted felons to the United States from any part of Her Majesty's dominion. You then asked me to communicate to you, for your better information and consideration, copies of the statements and affidavits accompanying the complaints on the subject made to my Government, and which, in the course of my explanation, I had read to you.

I now beg to inclose to your lordship copies of those papers. They consist of letters from the police department of the city of New York, and from the commissioners of emigration of the State of New York, to the Secretary of State of the United States, with the affidavits of four emigrants, discharged, respectively, John Walker from Brixton, John Butterworth and Edward Maguire from Portland Prison, and John Gordon from Kirkdale jail, near Liverpool—Walker having been convicted and sentenced for theft, Butterworth for house-breaking, Maguire for attempted robbery with violence, and Gordon for keeping a brothel.

Gordon's case appears to differ from the others in that he had served out the two years of imprisonment to which he was sentenced before he was aided by the agent of a society at Liverpool to reach the United States.

As I feel perfectly assured that Her Majesty's government would not willingly help, or give countenance to, any system of proceedings in this country designed to cast the depraved and degraded members of its population on the shores of the United States, I shall ask with confidence that your lordship will refer these cases to the proper department to be investigated, and with a view to preventing any persons or local authorities in Great Britain from a course of action which is in clear violation of the comity which should prevail between governments and people of friendly nations.

I have, &c.,

ROBT. C. SCHENCK

4. Letter from General Schenck, United States minister to Great Britain, to Mr. Hamilton Fish, secretary of state.

LEGATION OF THE UNITED STATES
LONDON, August 12, 1873

SIR: The deportation of convicts and paupers from Great Britain to the United States is a matter which has demanded my attention from time to time, and it has been for me already the subject of some correspondence with the Department.

The practice of sending to our shores, under any direct or official sanction of the British government, such disreputable or helpless additions to our population, does not now, I believe, exist. Still it is necessary to be watchful against any movement in that direction. It is a great temptation to people on this side of the Atlantic, in view of the free asylum and welcome we give so generally to emigrants, to resort to that easy method of relieving themselves of a portion of their public burdens. They find it a simple and comparatively inexpensive expedient for ridding European countries of criminals, who are to be either supported, if in prison, or guarded against, if at large, as well as of the miserably destitute who can only subsist as objects of charity. But while her Majesty's government may not be disposed to forget in this particular what is due to our country by the comity of nations, some of the local authorities in England and Ireland are not disinclined, if an opportunity occurs, to make of the United States a cheap place of banishment and settlement for the inmates of their jails and poor-houses.

In December, 1871, I first wrote to you on this subject, giving you full report of a protest I had made against a scheme entered into by a parish vestry at Liverpool for sending off certain pauper children to the United States; and I communicated at the same time some correspondence I had with Lord Granville about it. The result of that interference on my part, and of informal communication which it led to, was an abandonment, by the local authorities implicated, of that offensive undertaking.

Next in order came your dispatches, in relation to the cases of four persons who, it was alleged, had arrived at New York, released, before the expiration of their terms of sentence, from certain English prisons on condition of their going to the United States. In reply, I gave you a copy of my note to Lord Granville in regard to those cases, and a copy of his answer on the 16th of February, 1872, informing me that he had referred my communication to the secretary of state for the home department.

Afterward, on the 15th of March, 1872, I received another note from his lordship, communicating the report from the home department as to those particular convicts. It was explained that while it appeared that discharged prisoners desirous of emigrating to America were assisted in that object by certain prisoners' aid societies, yet no action was taken by Her Majesty's government, who have no power to prevent such persons from going wherever they please; and Her Majesty's government had no means of knowing whether the passage-money of those persons was supplied by their relatives in America, or by some charitable society. I inclose now herewith a copy of that last-mentioned note of Lord Granville. It was not satisfactory to me. I thought it did not sufficiently appear by the explanation given that those prisoners were not discharged before their terms of imprisonment expired or that their emigration was not made a condition of their release. However,

I concluded not to pursue that correspondence further at that time, but to reserve these objections for the future. I expected other occasions to occur.

In February last, you sent me for investigation the case of one Bryan Fitzgerald. This man was reported through the consul-general at London to have been released from jail at Dublin when he had yet two years and three months of his term of imprisonment to serve, on condition of his going to the United States, and it was averred that, having returned within that limit of time, he had been arrested and re-imprisoned for the remainder of his term of sentence. The statement was obtained from the man Fitzgerald himself. I took some pains to inquire after this man, to discover if his story could be verified, and had some correspondence with persons in Ireland in reference to him. As far as I could ascertain from unofficial sources his statement was substantially true.

But in the meantime my attention was attracted to another instance by a minute of the proceedings of the "North Dublin Union," published in a newspaper of that city on the 22d of May last. The publication was official. It appeared that a meeting was held on the 21st of May, attended and conducted by the guardians of the Union, and presided over by a public magistrate; and that it was voted to appropriate from a public fund the sum of £12, subject to the approval of the local government board, to provide an outfit and passage-ticket for a girl named Courtenay "an inmate of the Union workhouse," to enable her to accompany her mother who was at the time "a convict at Mountjoy prison," and was "about to leave for America." I immediately addressed a communication to Lord Granville in terms of strong remonstrance against any such procedure. I repeated the expression of my views in reference to the deportation of criminals and paupers from any part of Her Majesty's dominions to the United States; and I requested especially that a prompt investigation might be made of the circumstances attending the case of Fitzgerald, and this new action of the local authorities at Dublin, with a view to some decided measures being taken to prevent the recurrence of such wrong, or the continuation of a practice so hurtful and disturbing to the friendly relations between our two countries. I was fortunate in being able to enforce my views by a citation of language used recently by Lord Granville himself, when making a similar complaint against the government of France. . . . .

5. Extract from letter from General Schenck to Lord Granville, May 27, 1873:

I am sure that I shall need to use no argument to enforce the view taken by the Government of the United States in respect of such a mode of disposing of persons who are undergoing the penalty of their crimes, or who are unable to maintain themselves, and are liable to become a public charge. A very satisfactory and explicit statement of right in such cases is to be found in your lordship's note of the first of June last, addressed to Lord

Lyons, in reference to the banishment of communists from a neighboring country. I find that your lordship then emphatically, and certainly with great justice, declared that "Her Majesty's government cannot consent that England should be made a penal settlement for France"; and "cannot assent to the deportation to this country of the class of persons in question, whether they are provided or not with means of subsistence."

As between free nations the rule and the reason should certainly be stronger when applied, not to political offenders, but to persons convicted of crimes against municipal law, not to those accidentally impoverished, while, perhaps, not at all bereft of the ability to gain a livelihood by their labor, but to such as have before been, and are, the actual helpless inmates of workhouses and objects of public charity at home.

I have, &c.,

Robert C. Schenck

6. Extract from letter from the Irish Prisons Board to Mr. Burke (British home secretary) June 17, 1873:

With reference to Eliza Courtney's case, I beg to state that she was convicted of larceny in Dublin, in 1867, and, having been generally well-conducted, she became eligible for release on license under the rules, and, according to the uniform practice of the Irish convict-service, she was not released on condition of going to America, and would have been released at the same time had she chosen to remain in the United Kingdom. Having been informed that the license was granted, she stated she would proceed to the United States, as she had means to do so, and requested to be allowed to write to the guardians of the North Dublin Union to ask them if they would assist her to take with her her daughter, aged 17 years, an inmate of the union. I allowed her to do so, and it appears that the superintendent of the prison wrote herself for her. I beg to state distinctly that I have no power to pay for prisoners' passages to America, or to grant their release if they elect to proceed there. I cannot add to or diminish the gratuities they earn in the convict prisons, and on their discharge on license it is not within the power of the government to prevent their emigrating if they think fit to do so.

You are doubtless aware that the lower class in this country, if they compass sufficient means, very frequently leave for America. Many of the convicts have relatives in America, who write to them sending passage-tickets to enable them to join them on release, and at present there are cases where convicts have passage-warrants, but their release will not be granted until the regular periods at which they are entitled to it. The fact of a convict being on license does not prevent his leaving the United Kingdom any more than his license in no instance forces him to do so. I may add that, although every facility is given to convicts to memorialize Her Majesty's government for release, no memorials are considered by his excellency the lord lieutenant which appeal for remission of sentence on the ground that petitioners will leave the United Kingdom.

It should also be borne in mind that all convicts released on license before the expiration of their sentences earn such a remission by good conduct and industry, and are well able to earn their living honestly, and that the vast majority do so on release. None but really well-conducted convicts could earn a sufficient gratuity to enable them to leave the country, and so far from such persons being considered dangerous in this country, they readily obtain employment on their release.

I believe in the vast majority of cases they leave this country to avoid the evil companions and associations which in the first instance led them into crime, and their doing so voluntarily is a very strong proof of their reformation.

7. Extract from letter from Irish Local Government Board to Mr. Burke (British home secretary) June 26, 1873:

The circumstances connected with the emigration of Margaret Courtney (daughter of the convict Eliza Courtney), were these: The board of guardians of North Dublin Union had before them, at their meeting on the 21st of May last, a communication from the superintendent of Mount Joy convict-prison asking if the guardians would assist Margaret Courtney, an inmate of the work-house, to go to New York with her mother, and the guardians thereupon voted twelve pounds for the purpose, subject to the approval of the local government board; and the usual preliminary inquiries having been made as to health and other necessary particulars, and satisfactorily answered, the board gave their consent to the proposed expenditure.

The board are informed by Mr. Robinson, the inspector in charge of the Union, that Margaret Courtney is about eighteen years of age, and has been in and out of the work-house for several years, and that the master of the work-house informed him that she had been generally well-conducted, and had always borne a good moral character. She left the work-house for the purpose of emigrating with her mother on the 10th instant.

With reference to the objection expressed to paupers being sent into the territory of the United States, the board desire to observe that it very frequently occurs that persons who have emigrated to the United States send back passage-tickets or money to enable near relatives to join them; in some of these cases the relatives in question are inmates of work-houses in this country, in other cases they are not, but in each class of cases boards of guardians are in the habit of aiding in carrying out such arrangements by either providing an outfit or paying for the passage of younger members of the family for whom funds had not been sent, and thus preventing the separation of families.

The amount expended out of the poor-rates during the year ended the

25th March last, under the sanction of the local government board and the late poor-law commissioners, in emigration, was £1,564 14s. 8d., being less than the amount expended in any year since 1862; and with this sum 581 persons were assisted to emigrate to the colonies and the United States. . . . .

The board were not previously aware that there was any objection to the emigration of well-conducted persons to the United States under circumstances such as those above described, and they have reason to believe that the judicious exercise of the power of the board of guardians to grant aid in such cases has often been of much advantage to poor persons. So far, however, as relates to actual paupers, the practice of affording assistance might cease without inconvenience or hardship. Assistance to persons not paupers, to enable them to join relatives, would probably not be objected to.

### 32.   Mortality of Immigrants[1]

The following table [Table I] borrowed from General Walker's paper, shows in a clear light the differences which exist among the various foreign populations, compared among themselves, as regards

TABLE I

SHOWING THE PROPORTIONATE MORTALITY IN THE VARIOUS FOREIGN RACES
IN THE UNITED STATES IN 1870

| Foreign | Total Foreign | Irish | German | English and Welsh | Others |
|---|---|---|---|---|---|
| Population, U.S.A., 1870.................. | 100 | 33.3 | 30.3 | 11.2 | 25.2 |
| Decedents by all diseases................. | 100 | 41.0 | 28.2 | 10.8 | 20.0 |
| Decedents by consumption............... | 100 | 47.8 | 26.2 | 8.4 | 17.6 |
| Decedents by bronchitis.................. | 100 | 53.4 | 22.8 | 8.7 | 15.1 |
| Decedents by pneumonia.................. | 100 | 41.3 | 28.4 | 11.6 | 18.7 |
| Decedents by diarrhoeal diseases.......... | 100 | 38.4 | 27.1 | 11.8 | 22.7 |
| Decedents by small-pox................... | 100 | 20.3 | 44.1 | 3.6 | 32.0 |
| Decedents by scarlet fever and diphtheria... | 100 | 19.2 | 28.3 | 18.9 | 33.6 |
| Decedents by measles..................... | 100 | 17.5 | 24.0 | 12.3 | 46.2 |
| Decedents by cancer...................... | 100 | 41.2 | 30.7 | 11.7 | 16.4 |
| Decedents by Bright's disease............. | 100 | 57.6 | 21.3 | 11.0 | 10.1 |

mortality in general (deaths by all diseases), and as regards liability to death by various specified diseases.

In this table we find striking instances of national liability to particular diseases, and of national immunity from other diseases. . . . .

To sum up, it may be remarked that the diseases in liability to which the Irish considerably exceed their quota, and therefore tran-

[1] Extract from Boston Board of Health, *The Sanitary Condition of Boston: The Report of a Medical Commission, 1875*, pp. 63-78, 150-52.

scend the other foreign nationalities, present the following characteristics:

1st. They comprise those diseases which, in our community, are
at all times the most widely spread and the most fatal (namely,
bronchitis and pneumonia, consumption, and diarrhoeal diseases).

2d. They include constitutional diseases which are transmissible
by inheritance (consumption and cancer), showing in the Irish an
inborn predisposition to these diseases, which are thus imported by
them into our community.

3d. They include diseases which are strongly significant of defective hygiene, both public and private, and of a widely spread prevalence of habits destructive to health (diarrhoeal diseases, attributable
to "filth," Bright's disease of the kidneys, mainly dependent upon
alcoholism for its cause, etc.).

Now, when it is remembered that the Irish are the predominant
foreign race in Boston, when they number 22.7 per cent of the aggregate population, and 64.6 per cent of our foreign population, and that
Boston, of all the large cities of the United States, has the largest
proportion of Irish inhabitants, the significance and the importance
of these figures and facts will be recognized. . . . .

The foreign population of Boston, which, in 1870, was 35.12 per
cent of the total inhabitants, consists mainly of Irish, who numbered
64.6 per cent of all the foreigners in Boston. People from the British
American provinces (15.4), Germans (6.3), English (6.7), Scotch (2.0),
and other foreign nationalities (each falling short of 1.0 per cent), compose the remaining 35.4 per cent of our foreign population.

Now, the Irish so predominante as to exceed in number all the
other foreigners put together. We shall, therefore, direct the attention
of our readers principally to this element of our foreign population,
laying particular stress upon their national sanitary peculiarities in
our attempt to elucidate the kind and degree of influence which they
exert upon the sanitary condition of the city of Boston. . . . .

We find that in 1870, while their percentage to the total foreign
population was 64.6, their percentage of foreign deaths was 73.2; and
that during the last ten years (1865 to 1874) their contribution to foreign deaths was 72.5 per cent. So also, in 1865, the Irish, constituting
70.2 per cent of our foreign population, furnished 76.0 per cent of all
deaths that occurred among foreigners. It is therefore manifest that
the Irish in Boston, as throughout the United States, constantly exceed, to a considerable extent, their quota of deaths, which would be

the same as their contribution to population, did they not exceed the rest of our foreign inhabitants in mortality.

Consumption is the only specified disease respecting which the nativity of decedents is stated in the reports of the Registrar of the city. Let us see how the Irish fare among us as regards liability to this disease. In 1865, their percentage to foreign population being 70.2, the Irish numbered 77.9 per cent of all foreign-born decedents by consumption. In 1870 their contribution to population was 64.6 per cent, while to consumption occurring among foreigners it was 76.2 per cent. During ten years (1864 to 1873), among all foreign-born decedents by this disease, 75.1 per cent were Irish. These figures all testify to a marked liability to phthisis on the part of the Irish in Boston, as compared with the rest of our foreign population.[1]

All the foregoing comparisons between the native and foreign ingredients of our population, showing the superiority of the former over the latter as regards sanitary condition and bodily health, have been based upon vital statistics emanating from different communities of this country, in which the native and foreign races are living side by side under peculiar conditions. It may, perhaps, be objected to our deductions, that as our foreign population everywhere constitutes our poorest classes, poverty, with its attendant disadvantages, rather than nationality, is the real cause of the physical degradation, defective health, and excessive mortality which mark our foreign inhabitants, and especially the Irish, compared with the native stock. No doubt

[1] The same characteristics are observable among the Irish in New York, as the following quotation, referring to deaths by *phthisis pulmonalis*, will show: "With respect to nationality, we have to notice the same peculiarities to which we directed attention the previous year (see *First Annual Report of the Board of Health of New York*, p. 245), viz., the excessive death-rate among the Irish, as compared with the Germans." The following figures are also given: Irish population, 201,999; deaths by phthisis, 1,663. German population, 151,216; deaths by phthisis, 718. Total Irish mortality, 5,107. Percentage of deaths by phthisis on total mortality, 32.5. Total German mortality, 2,571. Percentage of deaths by phthisis on total mortality, 27.9. According to the last census throughout the whole United States, the percentage of deaths by consumption, upon total mortality for one year, was among the Irish 27.8, and among the Germans 22.2. (From the *Second Annual Report of the Board of Health*, New York [1872], p. 211.)

From these figures we learn that in New York, in 1871, there were among the Irish 8.24 deaths by consumption per 1,000 living, while among the Germans there were but 4.74 deaths by this disease per 1,000 living. These, be it remembered, are not true death-rates, the populations used being anomalous; but the figures can be fairly compared together, and exhibit the relative degrees of liability to phthisis among Germans and Irish.

can be entertained but that poverty, together with the ignorance and heedlessness which generally accompany poverty, is a most potent factor in the production of disease and undue mortality, among our foreign inhabitants; but in addition to these causes, . . . . we think that nationality exerts a most powerful influence, which, in the case of the Irish, is exceptionally marked.

Desiring to bring forward other proofs of the sanitary characteristics of this nationality in corroboration of the facts already adduced, we consulted the Reports of the Registrar General of Ireland. It soon became apparent, however, that no additional light could be obtained from that quarter, on account of the utterly untrustworthy character of Irish registration reports. Of the sanitary condition of the Irish at home we can learn little or nothing.

We know, however, that Liverpool, the most unhealthy of the great cities of England, owes much of its excessive disease and mortality to its large Irish population.

We then had recourse to the published "experience" of life assurance companies, and here obtained the conclusive proof that the national peculiarities which had appeared so striking in American health reports were not confined to Irish immigrants to this country, but prevailed with equal force in England, and presumably even in Ireland. A series of tables showing comparative expectation of life was published in 1843, by a well-known actuary. One of his tables exhibits the expectation of life of the Irish, from the age of twenty upwards, based upon the results of Irish experience. . . . .

The author says that "from the Irish experience it appears that, of that class of assurances, at some of the younger ages, the expectation of life is as much as six years less than that obtained from the combined English town and country experience." He also says that "the offices generally are getting very cautious of Irish lives." A committee of experienced actuaries states that "one of the most striking features exhibited in these tables is the great mortality that prevails among Irish lives."

The proofs of shortness of life and of excessive mortality contained in these figures, showing the Irish expectation of life, are certainly very striking, when we remember that one of the remarkable points in the comparisons of the expectations of life at different times, in different nations, and in various climates, is their great uniformity.

In support of our assertion that the native population of this community enjoys a remarkably satisfactory sanitary condition, admitting of comparison with the best standards elsewhere, we have been led to compare together the experiences of American and English life assurance companies. This comparison is all the more interesting that it affords almost the only means of eliminating from our vital statistics the influence of foreign mortality, inasmuch as life assurance in our community is, as we were assured by the president of one of our principal companies, limited almost exclusively to native lives. . . . .

The upshot of the testimony adduced from the experience of insurance companies in England and in this country, is to the effect that: (1) Among American assured lives (these being, as we have already said, almost exclusively native) the expectation of life is somewhat greater, and the rates of mortality are somewhat less, than among English assured lives. (2) Of the generality of American assured lives the mortality is least high in New England and the Middle States. (3) Among Irish assured lives the expectation of life is very considerably less than among the English and American lives.

Let us now briefly recapitulate the foregoing facts bearing upon nationality considered in relation to sanitary condition and mortality.

We have seen that our foreign population, though undoubtedly more prolific than the natives, still more surpasses the latter in mortality. This is seen to be true throughout the United States. In Boston the difference is exceptionally marked, inasmuch as the sanitary condition of our native population appears to be quite good, while our foreign population comprises large numbers of a nationality which is conclusively shown to be exceptionally liable at all ages to disease and death. These national characteristics, prevailing among an exotic population which, comprising foreigners and their offspring, constitutes 58.4 per cent of our total population, and thus outnumbers the native inhabitants, exert an influence which must be taken into account when any attempt is made to estimate our sanitary condition. A considerable portion of our yearly mortality is the result of morbid tendencies inherent in our foreign population, and imported by them into our midst, and which must, therefore, not be attributed to defects in the surrounding hygienic conditions. In another chapter an attempt will be made to discriminate between these two orders of causes; those, on the one hand, which are imputable to unhealthiness of population, and those, on the other hand, which are due to unwholesomeness of climate or of site, to defects of drainage, of ventilation, or of water supply, and other agencies preventable, such as usually come under the jurisdiction of health officers. Our object now is only to show the part played by our foreign population in the production of our yearly mortality.

The precise number of deaths which are imputable to the foreign element cannot be ascertained. The foreign contribution to mortality certainly cannot be measured by the number of deaths registered and classified each year, under the various headings indicative of foreign nativity or parentage; yet it has been conclusively shown, that, even by this defective estimation, the responsibility of the foreigners is very great, and out of all proportion to their numbers. But much of the mortality existing among the so-called "native" population of Boston is more or less remotely attributable to a foreign, or, more correctly speaking, to a Celtic source. By no scheme can we go back further than one generation in any attempt to separate the native from the foreign stock. Yet it is impossible to doubt but that many of the most potent causes of disease and death continue in operation through several generations among that part of our native population which is of comparatively recent foreign origin. Especially must this be the case among the Irish stock, which still so largely predominates among us. The hereditary character of certain constitutional diseases (consumption, cancer), which are rife among this race, the hereditary and educational transmission of mental peculiarities which go to make up the national type of character, together with various unwholesome habits and traditions in matters of hygiene, all conspire, among the American-born of Irish descent, to maintain in continuous action throughout the successive generations of naturalized foreigners (registered as natives) those potent causes of disease which are seen to be unmistakably active among the foreign-born of our population and among their offspring. . . . .

### INFANT MORTALITY

Ignorance and its products, heedlessness and criminal neglect, are the manifest origin of much disease and mortality among young children. Now ignorance, as statistically expressed in the form of illiteracy, is a condition which, in our community, prevails in its marked degrees almost exclusively among our foreign inhabitants. We therefore find that ignorance and foreign nationality go hand in hand in our community as causes of infantile diarrhoeal disease. In proof of the connection existing between these factors, we submit Table II, which follows and which exhibits facts derived from the national census of 1870 relating to nine States. These are arranged in the order of their increasing mortality by diarrhoeal diseases, and by cholera

infantum, while collateral columns show the proportions of foreign
inhabitants, of Irish inhabitants, and of illiteracy existing in the total
population of each State.

We see by these figures that, of the nine States compared, Massachusetts, with the highest death-rates by cholera infantum and diarrhoeal diseases, also has the largest proportion of Irish population, and,
except Rhode Island, the largest proportion of illiterate inhabitants.
Maine, on the other hand, heads the list in all these particulars. It is
impossible to escape the inference that these forms of mortality are intimately associated with the prevalence of mental deficiencies of exotic

TABLE II

| STATES | CHOLERA INFANTUM | | DIARRHOEAL DISEASES | | NATIONALITY | | ILLITERACY |
|---|---|---|---|---|---|---|---|
| | Death-Rate per 1,000 Living | Percentage to Deaths by All Causes | Death Rate per 1,000 Living | Percentage to Deaths by All Causes | Foreigners per 100 | Irish per 100 | Unable to Read, Aged 10 Years and Upwards, per 1,000 |
| Maine............. | 0.29 | 2.31 | 0.72 | 6.79 | 7.7 | 2.5 | 21.5 |
| Vermont............ | 0.32 | 2.92 | 0.92 | 8.47 | 14.2 | 4.2 | 45.9 |
| New Hampshire...... | 0.44 | 3.23 | 1.00 | 7.35 | 9.3 | 3.8 | 23.9 |
| Connecticut......... | 0.71 | 5.57 | 1.19 | 9.39 | 20.7 | 13.1 | 36.6 |
| Pennsylvania........ | 0.76 | 5.09 | 1.51 | 10.09 | 12.6 | 6.7 | 37.4 |
| New York.......... | 0.82 | 5.17 | 1.88 | 11.88 | 25.7 | 12.0 | 37.3 |
| New Jersey.......... | 0.86 | 7.39 | 1.47 | 12.60 | 20.8 | 9.5 | 40.8 |
| Rhode Island........ | 0.91 | 7.18 | 1.44 | 11.41 | 25.4 | 14.5 | 70.4 |
| Massachusetts....... | 1.16 | 6.51 | 1.93 | 10.81 | 24.2 | 14.8 | 51.4 |

origin, for which our community can hardly be held responsible. So
long as a large proportion of our inhabitants consists of ignorant foreigners, so long will the inevitable consequences of such ignorance as
characterizes them be apparent in our yearly records of mortality.

The lack of moral sense which so often accompanies ignorance is
the cause of much stupid, or wilful and even criminal neglect of the
most obvious duties involved in the care of infants. The heedless indifference with which the approach of alarming symptoms is viewed,
and the delay in seeking medical assistance, are undoubtedly the occasion of much avoidable mortality.

Poverty also tells severely upon infants, notwithstanding the limited number of their requirements, which comprise only food, pure air,
cleanliness, and clothing. When, by consequence of inability to gain a
subsistence, or from lack of thrift and intelligence, or by misspending
of wages on drink, the father cannot earn enough to maintain his fam-

ily, then the mother herself has to labor, and the exigencies of her work either take her altogether away from the care of her child, or prevent her from nursing it and attending to its wants when needful. Attempts are then made to replace or supplement the lack of mother's milk by cheap modes of artificial feeding, with such disastrous results as have been described. Intemperance enhances the poverty of the household by the waste of valuable resources which it entails, and thus impairs the vitality of the entire family. . . . .

## 33. The "Molly Maguires"[1]

Molly Maguire—a name identified with sad and terrible records of violence, of bloodshed, and murders in the anthracite coal regions of Pennsylvania, and recalling to memory tales of equal horror that have been borne across the ocean from the Emerald Isle. The murders committed in both localities have a striking resemblance in their inception, execution, and very frequently, in minute details, and yet, while we regard the one with a feeling of unmixed horror and repulsion,

[1] Extract taken by permission from F. P. Dewees, *The Molly Maguires: The Origin, Growth, and Character of the Organization* (Philadelphia: J. B. Lippincott and Company, 1877), pp. 9–24, 28–32, 36–45.

See also the court decision in the famous Molly Maguire cases, *Carroll et al.* v. *The Commonwealth* (1877), 84 Pennsylvania St. Rep. 107 and *Kehoe* v. *The Commonwealth* (1877), 85 Pennsylvania St. Rep. 127. See also the numerous reports of arguments of counsel in the different cases, e.g., *Report of the Case of The Commonwealth* v. *John Kehoe et al., Members of the Ancient Order of Hibernians, Commonly Known as "Molly Maguires,"* stenographically reported by R. A. West (Pottsville, 1876) and *The Great Mollie Maguire Trials in Carbon and Schuylkill Counties, Pennsylvania*, containing arguments of counsel in the case of *The Commonwealth* v. *James Carroll and Others* on trial for the murder of Benjamin F. Yost, chief of police at Tamaqua (Pottsville, 1876); and see also the article in a contemporary number of the *American Law Review*, XI (January, 1877), 233–60, "The 'Molly Maguire' Trials," by John T. Morse, Jr.

In addition to the volume by Dewees, from which the extract given above is taken, very full accounts of the activities of the "Mollies" will be found in James D. McCabe, *The History of the Great Riots . . . . together with a Full History of the Molly Maguires*, by Edward Winslow Martin (pseud.) (Philadelphia, 1877); Ernest W. Lucy, *The Molly Maguires of Pennsylvania, or Ireland in America; A True Narrative* (London, 1882); and for another view see George E. McNeill, *The Labor Movement* (1887), chap. x, "The Coal Miners," pp. 264–67.

For a historian's more recent account of the Molly Maguire organization, see James Ford Rhodes, *History of the United States*, Vol. VIII, "From Hayes to McKinley, 1877–96," chap. ii, pp. 52–87, and James Ford Rhodes, "The Molly Maguires in the Anthracite Region of Pennsylvania," *American Historical Review*, XV (April, 1910), 547–61.

the memory of the other is enveloped in a shroud of unhallowed romance. This difference of feeling is to a certain extent explainable. In the one case crime stands out unrelieved in its naked enormity, whilst in the other the feeling with which it is regarded is modified by the distance of the scene, the mellowing hand of time, and the magic pen of fiction. The tale of unprovoked and aimless murder in Ireland excites resentment and inspires horror; nevertheless, the peculiar position of the Irish peasant, his modes of thought, and certain characteristics of his race, compel a feeling of repulsive pity for the assassin. . . . .

[In Ireland] the political sufferer who met a felon's death was considered a martyr and a hero, whilst the "informer" was regarded with a feeling of utter detestation, as a traitor not only to the traditions of his race, to his country's honor and his country's future, but also to his family, his religion, and his God. When it is taken into consideration that they regarded their position as one of subjugation, the rulers of England as usurpers, the laws made without authority, and the lands held by illegal tenure, it may be regretted, but cannot be a matter of great wonder, that the detestation of an "informer," with which an ignorant, prejudiced, and romantic people were imbued, should extend to an informer of any kind. Such, unfortunately, has been the case: to *inform of a crime* had in many instances come to be considered *as great a wrong as the crime itself*, and to such an extent has this feeling developed that it has become a part of the Irish character, and is universal in its application, not only to acts *mala prohibita* but also to those *mala in se*.

Owing to this detestation of an informer, crimes without number have been perpetrated, not only in Ireland but also in this country, which have remained undetected and unwhipped of justice. Repeated murders have been committed in broad daylight before many witnesses, and the murderers have dwelt for years amidst those cognizant of the crime—despised, perhaps, but *unbetrayed*. It is not because the Irish people have not many good and true men and women among them, or that the majority are not well-disposed and law-abiding citizens; those who are in intimate communion with them know it to be the case that among no other people can there be found warmer friends, more generous impulses, more fervent piety. But they will also know and feel that even among many of the best of the race, among those whose character no man dare impugn or gainsay, whose lives are without blemish or reproach, is but thinly hidden the feeling of detestation against the Irishman as an "informer," who, cognizant of crime, seeks to bring the criminal to justice by due course of law.

By reason of this feeling the Molly Maguire has held "high carnival" in crime, both in Ireland and in the anthracite coal regions of Pennsylvania;[1] and this feeling must be thoroughly appreciated in order to understand how it is that a people of kindly, generous, and just impulses may in a civilized land keep the murderer and assassin among them, known, feared, and detested, and yet the crimes be concealed and the offenders allowed to defy the law and the authorities.

The Molly Maguire of Ireland stands in the birthplace of his ancestors. The history of his race and country, its wrongs, and his temptations, plead in extenuation of his offenses, and, while we detest his crimes, claim our pity for the criminal. But the Molly Maguire of the coal-fields of Pennsylvania can enter none of the pleas which may be urged in behalf of his prototype in Ireland. Upon this country he has no natural claim or natural right. The genius of our government guarantees constitutional freedom to the stranger and the alien as well as to the native-born citizen, and to the stranger and the aliens seeking to make this land their home the full rights of the native-born citizen are accorded. The enterprise of the people, combined with a sparseness of population, the vast expanse of territory, the varied climate, the magnitude of our resources, mineral and agricultural, the extended system of internal improvements and inland navigation, offer inducements to the workers of the world, whether capitalists, men of science, or laborers. It is true that incidentally "a refuge for

[1] [The author of the "Molly Maguire Trials," published in the *American Law Review* in January, 1877, in describing conditions in the coal fields, said:

"In 1875 these anthracite districts had become one vast Alsatia. From their dark and mysterious recesses there came forth to the outside world an appalling series of tales of murder, of arson, and of every description of violent crime. It seemed that no respectable man could be safe there, for it was from the respectable classes that the victims were by preference selected; nor could anyone tell from day to day whether he might not be marked for sure and sudden destruction. Only the members of one calling could feel any certainty as to their fate. These were the superintendents and "bosses" in the collieries; who could all rest assured that their days would not be long in the land. Everywhere and at all times they were attacked, beaten, and shot down, by day and by night; month after month and year after year, on the public highways and in their own homes, in solitary places and in the neighborhood of crowds, these doomed men continued to fall in frightful succession beneath the hands of assassins.

"The condition of things was like that which has occurred so often, at irregular intervals, in the melancholy history of Ireland. The shootings and the burnings of the Whiteboys and of the Ribbonmen were reproduced with terrible energy and

the suffering and oppressed of all nations" is offered; but this only from the fact that our form of government is liberal and our undeveloped resources present a field for labor; but the doors are opened as wide and the welcome accorded is as hearty to the stranger and the alien who has never suffered nor been oppressed. . . . .

But the privileges and advantages of our government and the country, though freely offered to the nations of the earth, are forced on none; the stranger may come and welcome, but if he does not choose to come, his right to stay away is fully accorded. The Irish peasant seeks this country of his own free will, and, being here, has the full rights of the native-born citizen. He is protected in his person; is encouraged to acquire property; his religion is respected; in choosing the rulers and making the laws of the land he has a potent voice. As a laborer, he has special privileges accorded by laws securing the payment of his wages before ordinary and common debts, and in the coal regions, through the medium of labor-unions and what may be termed the "unwritten law of the mines," he wields extraordinary power over the property of others. . . . .

The existence of a band of miscreants regularly organized for the commission of crime, extending throughout the anthracite coal-fields, had been suspected for twenty years past. Frequent and flagrant violations of laws, which, in the mode of execution and in the instruments employed, displayed organization, system, and a defined policy, induced this suspicion. The crime itself, in connection with

---

success upon this side of the Atlantic; and for a time it seemed that the disease was more incurable in its American, than it had been in its Irish, development. For the strong repressive force of an active and powerful dominant caste, and of military surveillance, were wanting in Pennsylvania. On the contrary . . . . the perpetrators of the outrages in this country were a political power as well as a social terror, and seemed not unlikely to obtain control of all that machinery and organization of justice which alone could be relied upon to control them. Otherwise, the parallel was complete. Amid the numerous class to which the criminals belonged, they were sure not only of shelter and protection, but of honor and distinction, in proportion to the heinousness of their villany. A system of signals aided their escape upon the few occasions when escape was thought to be worth while; a host of ready perjurers stood ready to prove an *alibi* in the improbable event of a capture and trial; while amid multitudes who were cognizant of various stages and circumstances of the guilty act, it was not often that a single one could be discovered to bear witness for the government. By a natural progression the state of affairs grew rapidly worse, until the whole district appeared to be upon the verge of a riotous outbreak, which would readily have become the chronic and normal condition of the neighborhood" (*American Law Review*, XI, 233–34).]

the mode of its execution, rendered inevitable the conclusion of a grievance, real or imaginary, to be redressed, a tribunal before which such grievance had been considered, the offender judged, and the penalty fixed, and an executive of some kind by whom persons were selected to carry into execution the decree determined upon.

In the years directly prior and subsequent to 1830, when the value of anthracite coal was fully recognized as fuel, an era of speculation in coal lands and coal mining, resembling in its main features the days of the gold fever of 1849 in California, and the later excitement in the oil regions of Pennsylvania, developed itself. . . . . The heterogeneous character of a population, native and foreign, suddenly thrown together under an unnatural business stimulus, produced a degree of lawlessness that would appear, from like results elsewhere, to be necessarily incident to such a condition of affairs. Violent altercations, sudden frays, contempts for authority or civilized usage, were frequent; but such violations of law were spasmodic, arising not from organized crime, but from the comparatively unorganized condition of a new population gathered from all points of the compass, acting under undue excitement and not yet settled into the calm routine of civilized life. The art of mining was considered, in those days, as being exclusively within the knowledge of foreigners, and, as a consequence, the foreign miner and laborer were soon in full force in the actual workings of the mines. The great majority of this class of workmen, who at that time, and since, have settled in the coal regions, have proven good and valuable citizens; but with them naturally came the outlaw and the desperado. To this last class is owing the reign of terror under which the coal region for years past has suffered.

After the first wild excitement had passed, when society had become more thoroughly organized, and coal mining had settled into a legitimate business—subject, however, to alternate periods of great reverses and unexampled prosperity—a peculiar distribution of population took place, which has not, perhaps, its parallel in any other portion of the United States.

Not only is the singular feature presented of nearly the whole population of the coal regions living in cities, towns, and small settlements, oftentimes called "patches," but the character and habits of the population in the several settlements differ widely from each other. . . . . Towns, such as Ashland, Shenandoah, Mahanoy City, Minersville, St. Clair, Hazelton, Pittston, Plymouth, and many others of large population, to a certain degree partake of the character of business and social centers, but the mining classes, being largely in the majority, regulate and control them. Besides these two classes of towns there are a great number of "patches," or settlements, whose population is entirely composed of miners and laborers and those whose business is either directly or indirectly connected with the mines. While the admixture of the foreign element pervades every part of the region, in the large cities and towns native-born citizens of the United States hold control, but at the colliery towns the power of the foreigner is absolute. In these last still further divisions are made, some being almost exclusively composed of Irishmen, with natives of Queens and other counties of Ireland, largely in the majority. In such towns not only have the manners, customs, and modes of thought of the Irish people been transplanted, but even the local prejudices incident to certain localities in that beautiful but, in many respects, unfortunate land. Coming here fresh from the contests with the land-lord and land-agent in Ireland, with no surrounding influences to teach them their error, they transfer a prejudice which has grown with their growth and strengthened with their strength to the coal operator and the boss, from whom they derive their subsistence, and under whose direction they work. Taught from infancy to believe that as against them capital is never used except as an instrument of oppres-sion, under the influence, sometimes, of real wrongs, but more fre-quently under a mistaken belief of an encroachment upon their rights, a spirit of resistance is aroused, which wicked and designing wretches have so used and controlled as to render the undetected commission of horrid crimes not only easy but, to a certain extent, sympathized with. That the above is no justification for such a state of affairs is true; nevertheless, it explains, or tends to explain, the possibility of its existence. . . . .

It has also been deemed necessary to explain how, by reason of the physical formation of the coal regions, the nature of coal mining and the method of carrying it on, settlements have sprung into existence not only composed of Irishmen, but representing also, to a great extent, localities in that country, each with its local ideas and preju-dices—Ireland itself, as it were, transported to the coal regions. It must not be understood that any imputation or reflection is intended against the character of the miners and laborers of the coal regions. Such laborers are composed in the main of foreigners—German, English, Scotch, Welsh, Poles, and Irish—and the assertion is made without fear of contradiction that in no large laboring community in the world can there be found better citizens or more abiding respect for law and others than among the majority of the coal miners of the anthracite regions. Nor is there any intention in any way to attack the Irish element or the Irish people. To do so would be in the face of the fact that Ireland is pre-eminently the land in which orators, poets, statesmen, and soldiers have claimed a birthplace or to which they trace their lineage. As a nation they are warm-hearted, generous, and impulsive to a fault; brave, romantic, and enthusiastic. Among no other people can be found examples of greater heroism or of more sublime self-sacrifice. . . . . It is from no mean or ignoble characteristic in the Irish people that has arisen the prejudice under the influence of which they class the witness who testifies as to the commission of crime in which he had no part with the "informer" who first instigates and then betrays. Nor is the impulse wholly bad which stands in behalf of the honor of old Ireland, of race and of religion, in earnest support of a criminal through good report and through evil report, in whose deeds they have no part, whose crimes they abhor, and whose professions of religion are felt to be a stigma and a disgrace. To despise meanness, to maintain confidence, to revere country, to cherish family and kindred, to uphold religion, are all virtues of the highest order, and yet the perversion of these virtues has rendered the existence of the "Molly Maguires" a possibility. The order is composed entirely of Irishmen and the sons of Irishmen, professing the Roman Catholic faith, and yet their crimes are regarded with intense horror by the body of the Irish people, and against the order the church has hurled its fiercest anathemas, denouncing its members as outlaws, and denying them Christian burial. That despite such sentiment of the people and such action on the part of the church the society should grow and flourish is to be accounted for, as before stated, in a romantic and perverted exercise of impulses founded on virtues.

The magnitude and length of the "strikes" in the coal region, combined with the influence of those "strikes," not only on business but also on domestic interests, throughout a very large section of the country, have drawn special attention to the "Laborers' and Miners' Union," and an impression has to some extent obtained that the "Labor Union," if not identical, is at least in earnest sympathy with the "Molly Maguires." The only color for such a charge exists in the fact that the great majority of the "Mollies" belong to the "Union," and that the counsels of such members were naturally for violent rather than peaceable redress, and, further, that most of the notorious outrages committed by "Mollies" were against capital, as represented in property or in the persons of superintendents and bosses. It is also true that decrees of the "Union" were enforced under the influence of a fear of violence against the disobedient, whether members of the "Union" or not—a fear strengthened by the marching of bodies of men from colliery to colliery, demanding an immediate stoppage of work, and the necessity that has arisen to call at different times upon the executive of the state for the military to preserve the peace and protect property. Nevertheless, the charge of sympathy or willing co-operation of the "Labor Union," as a body, with the "Mollies," is believed to be without foundation. . . . .

In consequence of large bodies of workingmen residing in distinct communities and at distant points, and between whose members existed a friendship in many instances formed beyond the ocean, but who had no acquaintance or intercourse with any coal operators, superintendents, or bosses other than their own, a system of enforcing dangerous or unlawful demands grew into being. For example, a demand for higher wages being made and refused, the parties so demanding would remain apparently acquiescent, either for the reason that no open conflict would be desired with the employer, or that a movement to enforce such demand did not receive the full sanction of the whole body of workmen, without whose active aid and co-operation it would be ineffectual. The next movement would be to write anonymous letters, delivered by a secret hand, or posted on the coal-breaker, or other building attached to the works, warning obnoxious parties, and generally containing threats of personal violence. Such letters or notices usually contained rude drawings of coffins and of pistols, and have attained wide-spread notoriety, both in this country and in Ireland, as "coffin notices." If these notices were disregarded, personal notice would be given, requiring a "strike," or whatever might have been determined upon, by strangers from a distant colliery, unknown to all not immediately engaged in the conspiracy. Upon those still refusing to obey, further notice was sometimes served, but at once the full force of social ostracism would be brought to bear upon them as enemies of the workingman, frequently followed by waylayings, abuse, and fearful beatings.

And here let it be remarked that it is a great error to assume that the evil deeds of the band of miscreants who have infested the coal regions have been altogether against persons and property representing capital. Their iron rule was felt by all, the high and the low alike, and many a poor laboring man has suffered untold hardships, his life rendered a curse from constant fear, or has met unexpected death at their hands in some unnoticed brawl.

The perpetrators of the outrages were generally disguised and unknown to the victim, and escape to the woods was easy. In those rare cases where a clue to the criminal was found or suspected, and the offender brought to the bar of justice, the ever convenient "alibi" was ready, and a verdict of "not guilty" was compelled. It can readily be understood how in such a condition of affairs the peaceable and well-disposed should succumb to the rule of the desperado and the ruffian, the more especially as the peculiar views relative to "informers" held by that large class of the laboring population represented by Irishmen rendered the detection of crime still more difficult.

Nor is it strange that crime, being a success, and going unwhipped of justice, should develop in strength, seek organization, and revel in the madness of Satanic power. A whisper of such organization spread abroad, and the names of "Buckshot"[1] and "Molly Maguire" became household words, inspiring far greater wonder and terror in the cot of the laborer than in the mansion of the wealthy or among the residents of the larger towns.

Under the influence of organization and of general prosperity, the "Mollies" increased in numbers and in power. Throughout the coal regions they completely controlled the organization known as the A.O.H., or Ancient Order of Hibernians, and, using that order as a cloak, endeavored to increase still further their numbers and their influence, on the pretext that the order is chartered by the legislature for legal and proper purposes as a benevolent association. The ambition of the leaders among them, many of whom deserted labor and the mines for the more congenial and influential positions of small tavern- and saloon-keepers, kept pace with their increased power. They sought not only to control the movements of the "Labor Union," to inspire the whole coal-mining interest with a fear of their displeasure, but also to have a potent voice in politics, township, county, state, and national. The most direct object of their ambition existed in the management of township affairs and the funds arising from road and school taxes. Lands having an immense salable value, as high as five hundred dollars, one thousand dollars, and even upwards, per acre, were under

---

[1] The "Buckshots" and "Mollies" are identical. The name first adopted in the coal region was that of "Buckshot." The organization can be traced back to 1854 or 1855 and even earlier.

their influence and control, as subjects of assessment and the collection of taxes. Possessed of but little taxable property themselves, these lands, especially in the way of the funds arising from road-taxes, were of immense importance in advancing the power and influence of the society. . . . .

It is doubtful whether the "Ribbon" society in Ireland, terrible as is its record, even in the days of its greatest strength, ever attained a moiety of the power and influence reached by the "Molly Maguires" of the anthracite coal-fields of Pennsylvania during the past fifteen years. This is perhaps owing to the fact that the Irish peasant in the land of his nativity, discontented and turbulent, for centuries has been held under subjection and control by the strong hand of England. Living on the same estate, and frequently in the same miserable cot, occupied by generations of his ancestors, poor and down-trodden, his means of intercourse with distant points were limited and rendered dangerous through the "spy" and "informer" in the constant employ of the authorities. Taught, however, the full value of combination through the various conspiracies instigated by the exiled House of Stuart, under the control and management of French emissaries, organizations more or less powerful were effected. Such organizations, however, although co-operating, bearing the same name, and having the same general object in view, never attained the same power of combination as that reached by the Molly Maguire in the comparatively limited area of the anthracite-fields, with its immense population and rapid means of transit from point to point.

Among the emigrants to this country, it must be borne in mind, an undue proportion of the discontented class of Irish peasants found their way.

In many instances those who had been lawless under the influence of bad association and dire necessity in Ireland, have by counter-influences in this land, developed into good and valuable citizens. But in too many cases a turbulent spirit of resistance to lawful authority, together with a morbid suspicion and fear of encroachments upon their rights and privileges, has developed itself into a wild and unreasoning cry for justice where no oppression was intended or offered, and has resulted in deeds of fearful crime, which have tended to sully the Irish name and thrown a stain—unjustly, it is contended and believed—on the Irish character. . . . .

The A.O.H., or Ancient Order of Hibernians, a society regularly incorporated under the laws of Pennsylvania as a beneficial association, and connecting itself with divisions of the order throughout the United States and Great Britain, has been controlled throughout the greater portion of the anthracite coal-fields of Pennsylvania for a few years past by the class of Irishmen known as the Molly Maguires. Through the medium of this order a thorough and complete organization of the worst classes throughout the coal region has been effected. The avowed object of the society as a beneficial association has been, so far as can be learned, entirely dropped, and in the heart of the most populous towns, before the eyes of the whole community, conventions have been held in which crimes have been planned, considered, and approved, and murder agreed to be awarded.

It was by means of this organization, through which unity of action was attainable, that a political influence was acquired that for a time seemed to render the Molly Maguire omnipotent for evil. That the society has existed in some form and under various names as far back as 1855, or perhaps before, there is little doubt, but prior to 1862 or 1863 it was confined to particular localities, and, although the instrument of much evil, had not reached the degree of arrogant confidence attained in after-years, and only now shaken by the terrible revelations in regard to its true objects and character.

The Ancient Order of Hibernians is a society having a large membership throughout the United States and Great Britain. It is said to contain among its active members men of high character and unblemished lives; and the avowed object of its formation is not only lawful but good. There is no conclusive evidence which connects the order outside of the coal region with criminal acts, in this country or in Great Britain, and it is but simple justice, until the contrary is shown, to believe that the name and charter of the association were taken possession of by the "Molly" outlaws in violation of the general principles of the order. . . . .

Whilst the "Molly Maguire" of the United States, in his inception of crime, in his method of notifying the intended victim, and in his mode of perpetration of outrage, bears a striking likeness to his prototypes, the "Ribbonman" and "Molly Maguire" of Ireland, it is believed that no other connection exists.

The Ribbon Society, whose deeds fill so large a space in the annals of crime in Ireland, was organized in maintenance of what were claimed to be the just and inalienable rights and privileges of the tenants relative to the landed estates. . . . .

As has been before remarked, no connection is known to exist between "Ribbonmen" and "Molly Maguires" of Ireland and the "Molly Maguires" of the coal region, without—and of that there is no present proof—such connection should be through the Ancient Order of Hibernians. The "Mollies" have often committed outrages here that resemble in the minutest details the crimes of their prototypes across the ocean, and this, too, without one single mitigating circumstance to relieve their horrid enormity. The "Molly Maguire" of the coal region comes into existence without cause, or pretense of a cause, in the past or present history of this country. Standing the equal before the law of any man or set of men in the land, his rights guarded, and even his prejudices respected, he becomes with fiendish malice and in cold blood an incendiary and assassin, a curse to the land that has welcomed him with open arms, and a blot, a stain, and a disgrace upon the character of his countrymen and the name of the land of his nativity.

### 34.   Alien Paupers in New York: 1868–73[1]

The large number of persons of foreign birth in the poorhouses, hospitals, and insane asylums of our State is a matter which gives rise to the suspicion that the State is bearing heavy burdens which belong in equity to various foreign countries. It certainly comes within the province of our Board to call attention to some facts which bear on this question. We accordingly give herewith a statement prepared by our secretary showing the nativity of the persons supported in the city and county poor-houses from 1868 to 1873 inclusive:

| Year | Native | Foreign | Total |
|---|---|---|---|
| 1868 . . . . . . . . . . . | 16,674 | 35,596 | 52,270 |
| 1869 . . . . . . . . . . . | 16,583 | 37,114 | 53,697 |
| 1870 . . . . . . . . . . . | 22,481 | 36,655 | 59,136 |
| 1871 . . . . . . . . . . . | 22,082 | 36,137 | 58,219 |
| 1872 . . . . . . . . . . . | 23,334 | 37,446 | 60,780 |
| 1873 . . . . . . . . . . . | 22,331 | 39,599 | 61,930 |

"The foregoing," the secretary remarks, "gives the nativity of those admitted to the poor-houses only. In 1868 and 1869 I attempted to learn the nativity of those temporarily relieved, but the returns were so imperfect that since then I have not tried to secure information upon this matter. It is probably a fact that of those temporarily relieved the proportion of foreign is greater than that of those receiving full support in the poor-houses."

[1] Extract from M. B. Anderson, "Alien Paupers," *Eighth Annual Report of the State Board of Charities of the State of New York* (1875), pp. 132–39.

By the census of 1870 it will be seen that the foreign-born inhabitants of New York were 1,138,353, or a trifle over one-third of the whole population of the State. But we find that of the paupers supported in poor-houses by taxation for the six years from 1868 to 1873 inclusive, sixty-four per cent, or about two-thirds are of foreign birth. This does not include the paupers supported by the Commissioners of Emigration on the proceeds of the "head-money" collected at Castle Garden. In view of these facts we can hardly escape the conclusion that a considerable number of these came to this country either as hereditary paupers, as insane persons, or in such a state of mental degradation as to sink at once into the pauper ranks. A large proportion of the emigrant paupers seem to remain in New York, while the more vigorous and prudent emigrants leave without delay for the western States.

It has been seen that the machinery of the Commission is entirely unable to reach those who are landed in other States or in Canada. From Canada especially there is an uninterrupted ingress of dependent persons into our State along the whole line of our northern border. Paupers and criminals consequently can enter without let or hindrance at every point except the port of New York.

### IS NEW YORK BOUND TO SUPPORT ALIEN PAUPERS?

Without making inquiries as to the mode in which they cross our border, or land at our ports, it may be well to inquire how far foreign governments assist their criminal and pauper population to migrate to our country, and also into the extent of their obligation to support their subjects now dependent on the State of New York for maintenance. Regarding those who have become naturalized citizens, there can be no question. These have repudiated their allegiance to the land of their birth, and have assumed the duties, and are entitled to the privileges, of American citizens. For all such we are, of course, bound to provide, if they become poor. But a very large portion of the foreign-born inmates of our poor-houses and insane asylums have never been naturalized, are still aliens. Upon whom then does the obligation to maintain such paupers rest? This is a somewhat complicated question, whether looked at in its legal aspect or in the light of public morality. If, however, there is reason to believe that convicts and paupers are transported to our country by foreign nations, as the readiest way of disposing of them, the matter becomes very much simplified. No nation has a right to transport its dependent and distressed population to another without that nation's consent; and no independent nation would assume such a burden thus thrust upon it. If the colonies of the British Empire in Australia, originally selected as places of punishment, have compelled the Imperial government to cease sending criminals to their shores, with far greater reason may we require from it the same exemption.

. . . . The people of the United States are always ready to receive an industrious and able-bodied emigrant, however poor he may be; but they are not willing to support that class of indolent and hereditary paupers which have been smuggled into our country by the connivance or direct agency of foreign nations.

Frequently complaints have been made of the number of paupers and dependent persons, who have been introduced into our country from various parts of Germany and Switzerland. It is quite difficult to reach direct proof of such transportation of paupers to our shores, but that considerable numbers have been sent here is almost universally believed; and the positive evidence upon which this general conviction rests, might be reached by a certain amount of time and labor. That convicts have been pardoned on condition that they should emigrate to the United States, is unfortunately only too evident. . . . .

### EVERY COUNTRY SHOULD CARE FOR ITS OWN POOR

. . . . How large a number of those alien paupers have come into our State by the assistance of their friends or benevolent associations, or municipalities, it is impossible for us to determine. That there are large numbers of such is clear. That it has been a systematic policy quietly and covertly pursued by various foreign countries to relieve themselves of danger and expense by assisting convicts and paupers to emigrate to our country, where they should be cared for at our expense, is unfortunately too clear. Many such persons have been detected and sent back by the vigilance of the Emigration Commission in New York. But that we have a considerable number of such persons now within our borders, seems beyond question. From no class of our citizens have such emphatic complaints been made of this condition of things, as from those who are of foreign birth. They come among us to be naturalized and earn their own living, and to become with us bearers of all public burdens. These abuses are more readily detected by such persons than by the native born citizens, and none will be more ready than they to give a sanction to any proper legislation calculated to remedy this serious evil. The State Pauper Law of 1873, authorized the State Board of Charities to send to the States to which they belong, all paupers who are found within our limits without a legal settlement. Under this law between three and four hundred have been sent out of the State during the past year. What is just and right between State and State in our Union, ought to be just and right between our own and a foreign nation. Should we not be justified in sending back to Europe to be cared for by their own people, these unnaturalized paupers and convicts, who have been surreptitiously introduced into our country and made a burden to the taxpayers of New York?

### 35. Further Complaints of the Burden of Alien Pauperism, 1880[1]

#### IMPORTATION OF BLIND, IDIOTIC, CRIPPLED, EPILEPTIC, LUNATIC, AND INFIRM PAUPERS

The observations and investigations of this Board have clearly established the conclusion that it has long been the practice of many of the cities and towns of different governments of Europe to send to this country their blind, idiotic, crippled, epileptic, lunatic, and other infirm paupers, incapable of supporting themselves, in order thereby to avoid the burden of their support. To this end, a steerage passage lands one of these helpless creatures upon our shores, and thus relieves the locality whence they were sent of twenty, thirty, and in many cases even more continuous years of their hospital treatment, nursing, and care. European countries find it much cheaper, therefore, to deport these classes of their dependents to America, than to provide support for them through life. The greater part of these, reaching this country by the seaports of the United States, land at New York, and, while some of them find their way into other States, most of them ultimately become life-long incurable dependents in the hospitals, insane asylums, and other public charities of this State. Moreover, large numbers of them come to this country by the way of Canadian or other British provincial ports, whence many of them drift, or are sent into this State to become permanent burdens upon its public charities.

To such an extent has this practice of sending confirmed helpless paupers to America increased, that it cannot be denied; indeed, little or no attempt at denial, or even concealment in the matter is made. These various classes of chronic dependent aliens come under the frequent observation of the members and officers of this Board in their

---

[1] *Thirteenth Annual Report of the State Board of Charities of the State of New York,* transmitted to the legislature February 5, 1880, pp. 41–43, 214–15, 221.

visits to our insane asylums, hospitals, poorhouses and other charitable institutions, and the fact of their fraudulent shipment to this country has been fully established. Within the past two years the evil has attained such proportions, that the Board has recently felt called upon to bring the subject to the attention of the Department of State at Washington, and to the representatives of this State in Congress. The matter has also been brought to the notice of the proper authorities of many of the other states, and has everywhere attracted marked attention.

And the extent to which this evil has now increased suggests also the need of protective legislation. Since the collection of head money on immigrants by our commissioners of emigration has been declared by the United States courts unconstitutional,[1] this exotic burden on the taxpayers of the State has become much more onerous, and has steadily increased. The classes referred to are in no wise the legitimate objects of our charity, and the state ought not to be burdened with their support; on the contrary, the task of supporting them should be thrown back upon the countries in which they originated. To this end every blind, idiotic, crippled, epileptic, lunatic, or other infirm foreign pauper, designedly thrust upon us, if in condition to encounter the return voyage, should immediately be sent back to the place whence he or she came. By a rigorous enforcement of this rule, it is believed that the evil complained of would be greatly reduced.

To accomplish this end fully, federal legislation will probably become necessary, and a bill to this effect has recently been introduced into Congress. Until appropriate legislation is had, if the State Legislature were to provide a small special fund to be used by this Board with power to send such helpless persons when found in our institutions of charity, to the countries from whence they were shipped, it would serve largely to protect the State and counties against these distressed classes, especially those reaching us by the way of Canadian and other British provincial ports, and greatly lessen the burdens referred to. The expense of maintaining a single one of these expatriated paupers in an asylum or poorhouse one year, would provide for the return to their homes of five of them. To return them would not only be humane and just, but an immediate economy. It would also save the State and counties future heavy annual expenditures in supporting them. . . . .

The execution of this law [the State Pauper law, 1873] has enabled

[1] [See the first volume in this series, E. Abbott, *Immigration: Select Documents and Case Records*, Part II, pp. 168-80.]

the Board to gain a more intimate knowledge of this class, and has revealed the fact that the State of New York is being burdened with large numbers of paupers, systematically forwarded from other States, especially from the State of Massachusetts. The geographical position of New York City, with her connecting lines of railroads and steamboats, also the fact of her being the principal port of entry for immigrants to this country, over which the same close scrutiny is not exercised as in the rural districts, renders her expenses from this source exceptionally heavy. These are the greater from the fact that the State of Massachusetts, the immigration into which from foreign countries by the way of New York City is large, holds this State responsible for persons landing at her port from foreign countries when becoming dependent in that State, sending such at once back into the State of New York. The magnitude of this evil led the Board to address a communication upon the subject to the State Board of Charities of Massachusetts on November 1, 1877, making complaint regarding the transfer of certain classes of persons by her public officials to New York State and protesting against the practice. . . . .

A person who, being an immigrant landing at the city of New York, proceeds directly to Massachusetts, and becomes a resident there, should, if reduced to pauperism, be cared for by Massachusetts, or be sent by Massachusetts to the country from which he came. The mere fact of his landing at New York creates no obligation for that State to support him when he becomes dependent. We recognize, of course, the binding force of the contract of our emigrant commissioners, arising from head money, to support him for five years. But even that contract lapses after that period expires. A very large proportion of the paupers which have been transferred by Massachusetts to this State, have had no claims whatever upon the New York emigrant commissioners.

### 36. "Evils Incident to Immigration"[1]

During the ten years ending June 30, 1882, we received 3,544,458 immigrants. . . . . About one-half of the immigrants are grouped under three occupation divisions—"professional," "skilled," and "miscellaneous," the remaining division being mainly women and children:

[1] Extract taken by permission from an article by Edward Self in the *North American Review*, CXXXVIII (1884), 79–88. In an earlier article the same writer had presented a collection of data bearing on the material benefits of immigration, see Doc. 46, Sec. II.

| | Profe.sional | Skilled | Miscellaneous | Not Stated and without Occupation; Mainly Women and Children |
|---|---|---|---|---|
| German............ | .6 | 11.5 | 29.4 | 58.3 |
| British............ | .9 | 17.8 | 29.8 | 51.4 |
| British-American ... | .3 | 11.9 | 36.6 | 51.0 |
| Irish.............. | .3 | 5.4 | 48.5 | 45.7 |
| Swedish........... | .1 | 6.8 | 47.2 | 45.7 |
| Chinese........... | .2 | | 96.0 | 3.8 |
| Norwegian......... | .3 | 9.8 | 38.9 | 50.9 |
| French............ | 3.8 | 18.3 | 34.7 | 43.0 |
| Occupation of the whole immigration of the decade | .6 | 11.1 | 38.7 | 49.5 |

The lowest ratios of skilled and professional are, in order, the Chinese, Irish, Swedish, and Norwegian, while the French, British, British-American, and German give higher ratios than the average. . . . .

The following table shows what proportion of these tradeless and poor people came from each country, and the percentage of the tradeless of each nativity compared with the entire immigration of that nativity:

| | Nationalities of 959,073 Laborers and Servants Arrived During the Decade Percentage | Composition of Aggregate Immigration (3,544,458) Percentage | Proportion of Laborers and Servants in the Immigration of Each Nationality Percentage |
|---|---|---|---|
| German........... | 15.6 | 26.9 | 15.6 |
| British............ | 12.8 | 15.8 | 22.0 |
| British-American ... | 8.7 | 14.6 | 16.2 |
| Irish.............. | 21.4 | 12.9 | 44.0 |
| Swedish........... | 8.2 | 5.8 | 38.0 |
| Chinese........... | 15.8 | 4.5 | 95.0 |
| Norwegian......... | 3.2 | 3.5 | 25.0 |
| French............ | 1.5 | 2.0 | 20.0 |
| All others......... | 12.5 | 13.6 | 24.7 |
| | 99.7 | 99.6 | |

. . . . To the solitary men and women without fixed principles, without means, and without a trade or an education, immigration is more likely to be a cause of moral injury than to those who come surrounded by domestic safeguards. Family life stimulates energy, moral restraint, a sense of responsibility and a longing for a home. . . . .

Children constituted nearly 21 per cent of the whole immigration. In the absence of any statistics of the married and single, the percent-

ages of children under fifteen years afford the only means of comparison
in regard to families in each national quota:

|  | Male | Female | Total |
|---|---|---|---|
| German | 13.3 | 12.3 | 25.6 |
| British | 11.3 | 10.9 | 22.2 |
| British-American | 8.8 | 9.0 | 17.8 |
| Irish | 7.2 | 7.7 | 14.9 |
| Swedish | 9.5 | 9.4 | 18.9 |
| Chinese | 7.2 | 0.3 | 7.5 |
| Norwegian | 11.2 | 10.0 | 21.2 |
| French | 6.8 | 7.1 | 13.9 |

Immigration by families distinguishes the Germans, British, and
Norwegians. Of these nationalities, the males of all ages numbered,
respectively, 59.4, 61.7, and 63.3 per cent of their several totals; the
Chinese, 98.1; the French, 64.1; and the Irish only 51 per cent—the
lowest percentage of males on the list. . . . . It will be observed that,
next to the Chinese, the ratio of children is smallest among the French
and Irish—a circumstance remarkable from the coincidence that the
population of France is stationary, if not actually declining, and Ireland has lost population steadily for a series of years.

Considering that the immense majority of immigrants are of limited means, some even suffering from poverty, the disposition to settle
in cities becomes important, because of the evil influences which
abound there. The following table gives the percentages of the foreign-
born from the countries named, living in our fifty principal cities at
the date of the Census of 1880, the cities in which they were most
numerous being arranged in order:

German . . . . . . . . . . . . 39.3 (New York, Chicago, Philadelphia, Brooklyn)
British . . . . . . . . . . . . . . 29.3 (New York, Philadelphia, Brooklyn, Chicago)
British-American . . . . . 18.6 (Boston, Chicago, Detroit, Lowell)
Irish . . . . . . . . . . . . . . . 45.8 (New York, Philadelphia, Brooklyn, Boston)
Swedish . . . . . . . . . . . . 17.0 (Chicago, New York, Minneapolis, Brooklyn)
Chinese . . . . . . . . . . . . 22.4 (San Francisco, New York, Chicago, Denver)
Norwegian . . . . . . . . . . 9.9 (Chicago, Minneapolis, Milwaukee, New York)
French . . . . . . . . . . . . . 39.0 (New York, New Orleans, San Francisco,
Philadelphia)

These exhibits reveal the following leading facts. The Germans are
somewhat superior to the average in their proportion of skilled and
professional; they bring the smallest proportion of mere laborers and
servants; the proportion of children is the largest. The marked pref-

erence for city life is, in some respects, objectionable; for the mere aggregation of numbers of one nationality perpetuates foreign and clannish associations. In this way the "German vote" and the "Irish vote" have been created—an anomaly in American politics.

The British, second only to the Germans in number, exceed them in the percentage of skilled and professional and also of laborers and servants, and rank next to them in the number of children, while a smaller proportion settle in cities.

The British-Americans are the third in point of numbers, and nearly the same as the Germans in the proportion of skilled and professional, and also of laborers and servants. Their percentage of children is less than either of the preceding, which is accounted for by the fact that so many young unmarried Canadians seek employment in New England.

In the fifty principal cities only 18.6 per cent of the British Americans are congregated, the majority of the remaining eighty-odd per cent are probably agricultural settlers, to whom most of the children belong. The British and the British-Americans in the decade under consideration were each numerically greater than the Irish. The former become so completely assimilated that their presence is scarcely perceived, and no one hears of nominating candidates to catch the British vote—in marked contrast with the Irish, who maintain social and political organizations based upon old national traditions or feuds. Of the Irish, it is to be remarked: (1) That the percentage of the skilled and professional is less than half the average: while these people constitute a trifle over one-eighth of the immigration, they furnished almost one-half of the poor and untrained laborers and servants. This lack of mental and mechanical discipline expected of skilled workmen suggests an almost certain irregularity of employment and small pay. Three-fourths of all the Irish males of fifteen years and upward are set down as laborers. (2) The breaking up of the family relation is indicated by the small number of children, and also by the large number of females who come seeking domestic employment. The females form a higher percentage (48.7) of the Irish than of any other immigration. (3) Nearly 46 per cent of this people in the United States reside in the fifty leading cities, the highest ratio on the list. This inclination to live in large towns exposes the unskilled and tradeless to the depredations of the unscrupulous, who easily prey upon their impulsive and improvident nature. Dense populations are always the scenes of crime; poverty and unfortunate impulses send the Irish into the densest of quarters. This fatal inclination to city life has much to do with the discreditable showing the race has made in the criminal records of the country.

The Swedish immigration, too, holds a low rank because of the paucity of the skilled and professional, and the correspondingly large proportion of laborers and servants. This immigration seems, however, to be more in families than the Irish- and British-American. Its distinctive character is agricultural, only 17 per cent being found in the cities named. . . . .

The Norwegians rank higher than the Swedes in respect to professional and skilled occupations, and bring a smaller proportion of laborers and servants. That this is a family immigration is obvious from the number of children, second only to the British; moreover, the Norwegians possess the pre-eminent advantage of having a smaller percentage in the cities (9.9) than any of the nationalities under review. . . . .

The breaking up of the homes and domestic life of multitudes of people; the adoption for a longer or shorter time of migratory habits; the difficulties which must be encountered in a strange land, perchance with a strange tongue; the fear of, and liability to, deception—all these experiences involve trials so formidable that it is not surprising that many succumb to temptation who would, under more favorable circumstances, have escaped contamination. Lives thus disordered cannot but tell unfavorably upon immigrants and their children; therefore it is to be expected that our criminals and persons dependent upon public charity will be largely of foreign birth, or, if native, of foreign parentage. Parents who, in their native villages in Europe, would have apprenticed their children to some honest trade, find it impracticable to do so here. The mere lack of apprenticeship does not always lead to crime; still, the connection between the two is very apparent. . . . .

The Catholic bishops, Ireland, of St. Paul, and Spalding, of Peoria, have shown in their colonization plans how business management and philanthropy can be united and applied to the settling of men and families in agricultural districts in the West—people who, left unaided, would have been likely to remain in the crowded cities of the East, subject to degrading influences. The labors of these prelates have not only built up waste places, but have saved many a man from destruction. If we continue to receive great numbers of poor immigrants for years to come, a way must be devised for helping them to help themselves. To let them alone is to increase the burden of criminality and wretchedness, as well as of public expense, for crime and want are always tax-gatherers. Apart from religious considerations, love of country calls for some plan of aiding and advising the poorer, unin-structed immigrants; otherwise, it is almost certain that their children will be led by surrounding evils into courses more or less doubtful, if not actually criminal. In the cities, observation justifies the opinion that the most dangerous class of young men, known as roughs, hoodlums, etc., is composed mainly of native-born sons of immigrants. Remem-bering that only 4 per cent of our prisoners "spring from healthy stock and favorable early influences"; and that "only 5 per cent or less be-longs to the well-to-do, educated classes"; and that the environment of immigrants, especially in the densely populated quarters of cities, is more likely to be positively demoralizing than anything else, we are prepared for the statement that a preponderance of our criminals are the children of foreigners. A few statements of nativities will prove this.

During the year ending June 30, 1882, 680 discharged convicts applied to the Prison Association of New York for aid. These appli-cants stated their nativities and those of their parents, as follows:

|  | Number of Convicts Born in the Several Countries | Number of Convicts Whose Parents Were Born in the Several Countries |
|---|---|---|
| United States (white) ......... | 431 | 133 |
| United States (colored)........ | 11 | 11 |
| Ireland...................... | 96 | 334 |
| Germany..................... | 48 | 80 |
| England..................... | 43 | 56 |
| Scotland.................... | 14 | 21 |
| All other countries........... | 37 | 45 |
|  | 680 | 680 |

The Massachusetts Reformatory Prison for Women gives the fol-lowing statement for the year ending September 30, 1881:

|  | Number of Prisoners Born in the Several Countries | Number of Prisoners Whose Parents Were Born in the Several Countries |
|---|---|---|
| United States................ | 94 | 33 |
| Ireland...................... | 53 | 108 |
| England..................... | 13 | 6 |
| British Provinces............. | 10 | 10 |
| Scotland.................... | 9 | 10 |
| Other countries.............. | 3 | 15 |
|  | 182 | 182 |

Down to December 31, 1880, 3,831 children had been committed to the State Reform School of Rhode Island:

| | Number of Children Born in the Several Countries | Number of Children Whose Parents Were Born in the Several Countries |
|---|---|---|
| United States (white) . . . . . . . . . | 3,018 | 1,280 |
| United States (colored) . . . . . . . | 360 | 360 |
| Ireland . . . . . . . . . . . . . . . . . . . . | 257 | 1,819 |
| England . . . . . . . . . . . . . . . . . . . | 119 | 200 |
| British-America . . . . . . . . . . . . . | 30 | . . . . . |
| Scotland . . . . . . . . . . . . . . . . . . | 18 | 45 |
| Germany . . . . . . . . . . . . . . . . . . | 10 | 69 |
| Other countries . . . . . . . . . . . . . | 19 | 58 |
| | 3,831 | 3,831 |

The State was obliged to support 1,640 children of native, and 2,191 of foreign, parentage, of whom 1,819 were of Irish parentage. The Rhode Island Workhouse and House of Correction had received, to December 31, 1882, 6,202 persons on commitment:

| | Number Born in the Several Countries | Number Whose Parents Were Born in the Several Countries |
|---|---|---|
| United States . . . . . . . . . . . . . . | 3,191 | 1,507 |
| Ireland . . . . . . . . . . . . . . . . . . . | 2,104 | 3,730 |
| England . . . . . . . . . . . . . . . . . . | 458 | 446 |
| British-America . . . . . . . . . . . . | 182 | 146 |
| Scotland . . . . . . . . . . . . . . . . . . | 170 | 177 |
| Germany . . . . . . . . . . . . . . . . . . | 30 | 38 |
| France . . . . . . . . . . . . . . . . . . . . | 11 | 17 |
| Other countries . . . . . . . . . . . . . | 56 | 141 |
| | 6,202 | 6,202 |

The native-born prisoners outnumber the others by 180; but only 1,507—less than one-quarter of the inmates—are the children of American-born parents. In Pennsylvania, 8,851 adults were admitted to the almshouses during the year ending September 30, 1881. Their nativities are given thus: American, 4,183; Irish, 2,494; German, 1,185; English, 404; Welsh, 124; Scotch, 99; other foreigners, 260; not stated, 102. We have yet to mention, but briefly, the saddest feature of immigration, viz., the growth of insanity. An official report of Dr. Kempster, superintendent of the Wisconsin Northern Hospital for the Insane, shows that, in addition to the ordinary causes which produce insanity, there exist among immigrant settlers "the depressing influences of homesickness and overwork and underfeeding—conditions always present in new countries settled largely by foreign-born persons." In consequence of this, that hospital receives "a larger percentage of cases of the depressed types of mental disease than are received into similar institutions in the countries from which the population of Wisconsin is largely drawn." To a certain extent the facts presented point unfavorably to at least one nationality; but it is impossible to arrive at a specific conclusion, because no clear and definite statistics are available from more than a mere minority of our public institutions. There should be a systematic uniformity in tabulating the records of penal, reformatory, and charitable institutions throughout the country. A condensation of the records of each year would reveal the growth or diminution of crime, pauperism, lunacy, etc., and also show to what extent each of the foreign immigrations swells the numbers of the criminal, dependent, and defective classes in the United States.

# SECTION V

# PUBLIC OPINION AND THE IMMIGRANT

# SECTION V

INTRODUCTORY NOTE

The documents that have already been given in the preceding sections throw light indirectly on the recurring changes in public opinion on this subject of immigration. In particular, the documents dealing with assimilation and domestic immigration problems (sections III and IV) reflect the judgment of citizens and groups of citizens in different sections of the country and at different periods of our history upon the effect of immigration upon American life and American institutions. The subject is so important, however, and the documentary material so abundant and so interesting, that it has seemed worth while to include what may be called a supplementary section bearing directly upon this subject.

It is probably true that there has not existed in any period of American history a unified public opinion on the subject of immigration. There have always been some groups of native-born citizens opposed to a liberal immigration policy while other native-born groups have been in favor of such a policy. Opposition to immigration has, however, been more organized, more vigorous, and more aggressive in certain periods of our history than in others. The first of these periods of hostility to immigrants preceded the Revolution, and various members[1] of the Pennsylvania Colonial Assembly adopted a critical attitude toward the German immigrants of that time (Document 1). Objection to the new arrivals was based partly on the fact that steerage conditions were so insanitary that the passengers were a danger to public health when they landed; but also on the further fact that the older settlers, who had become prosperous and were enjoying a high standard of comfort, looked upon the new arrivals as socially undesirable. "We have reason to believe," said their message to the Governor in 1755, "the importations of Germans have been for some time composed of a great mixture of the refuse of their people, and that the very jails have contributed to the supplies we are burthened with."

After the Revolutionary War, when large numbers of immigrants were again arriving, there were thoughtful statesmen, like Jefferson (Document 2), who questioned the political wisdom of a large increase in population from the monarchical governments of Europe. In general, however, the vast extent of unoccupied and undeveloped land

[1] See also above, Section III, Document 1.

and the commercial, agricultural, and industrial importance of immigration led people to take a generous attitude toward the subject (Documents 3 and 4).

The first serious anti-alien movement was during the period of the Alien and Sedition laws, at the close of the eighteenth century. The various opinions of the statesmen of that day are reflected in the congressional debate on the proposal to raise the naturalization fee to $20, a very large sum, of course, for an immigrant to pay in those days (Document 5). Although aggressive hostility died out with the political changes of the time, a considerable prejudice against aliens remained among certain sections of the population (Document 6).

The great exodus of emigrants from Europe following the peace of 1815 led to further discussions of the wisdom of the American policy of encouraging immigration, but the petition to Congress in behalf of Irish immigrants and the address of the Shamrock Society of New York in 1817 rest on an underlying confidence in the friendly attitude of public opinion toward the encouragement of immigration (Documents 7 and 8). In the year 1819, however, immigration appeared to be in excess of the immediate labor needs of the country, and there was some uneasiness lest the numbers of arrivals should be greater than could properly be provided for.

At the close of the first quarter of the nineteenth century there was a strong current of dissatisfaction with the growing importance of the foreign vote (Document 10), although immigrants were welcomed in the new settlements (Document 11). The next decade, 1830–40, saw the "nativist" movement[1] well developed. With the growing antagonism to the foreigner, there was a disposition to question the supposed advantages of immigration, even in the West (Document 12). And in the "Memorial of the Citizens of Sutton and Milbury," a congressional investigation was asked to determine whether "the vast influx of foreign immigration" was not likely to endanger the liberties of the United States (Document 13). The most convenient summary of the "nativist" principles will be found in the platform of the Native American party in 1845 (Document 16) and in the extract from a congressional speech of this period (Document 18). But there were also men who, although they avoided the extreme position of the nativists, yet felt a reasonable anxiety about the effects of immigration on so large a scale (Document 19).

[1] For references to histories of the Native American and Know-Nothing parties, see above, note 1, p. 206.

The immigrants, however, were not without their friends, even during the period of exaggerated nativism (Document 17). The report of the New York Legislative Committee on the question of land ownership by aliens shows how liberal was the attitude of men of generous views even when political excitement ran very high (Document 20). So wide was the range of public opinion during the period of Know-Nothing agitation that it is difficult to select a sufficient number of documents to picture it adequately. One phase of southern opinion is set forth in the speech of Garrett Davis, a "Henry Clay Whig," in the Kentucky Constitutional Convention, on his proposition "to impose further restrictions upon foreign immigrants" (Document 21). During the same period when the Know-Nothings were making dire prophecies of the results of the immigrant invasion, a sturdy western journalist maintained that "if we can give employment to all foreign emigrants at remunerating prices, their labor, added to our own, will produce results which, long before the close of the present century, will astonish the civilized world" (Document 22). "Let them come," said the West. "They will convert our waste lands into fruitful fields, vineyards, and gardens, construct works of public improvement, build up and establish manufactures, and open our rich mines of coal, of iron, of lead, and of copper."

The debate in Congress on the Homestead bill set forth more than one point of view. A Missouri congressman said, "The question is not whether we shall have foreigners in the United States, but what is the best disposition to be made of them." That is, should the immigrant be helped to live in the new states on the public lands instead of remaining in want in the seacoast cities of the older states (Document 23). In the same debate, a representative from Mississippi said, "Heaven made this mighty continent not only for our benefit alone, but for the use and benefit of all mankind. It is the gift of God, and we have no right to withhold it from his people." On the other hand, there was anxiety lest the public lands be too freely granted.

Edward Everett, in a famous oration delivered in 1853, acknowledged that "temporary inconveniences" were to be set off against the advantages of immigration, that asylums and almshouses were crowded with inmates born in Europe, and that "the value of our native labor may have been depressed by too sudden and extensive a supply from abroad." But, after saying that these evils had probably been exaggerated, he went further and preached the gospel of benevolence. Massachusetts and New York, he thought, "might do a worse thing with a portion of their surplus means than feed the hungry, clothe the naked, give a home to the stranger, and kindle the spark of reason in the mind of the poor foreign lunatic" (Document 24). A liberal minister also acknowledged the evils incident to immigration, but pointed to benefits far in excess of the evils, and counted as one of the compensations that immigration was strengthening the antislavery forces (Document 29). Documents 25 and 26 present extracts from typical Know-Nothing arguments of the period, and in Documents 27 and 28 will be found replies to the popular slogan, "America for the Americans." The statistical fallacies in the Know-Nothing arguments are set forth in Document 30. Extracts from southern newspapers show that the Democratic party was not hostile to the foreigner, and was ready to defend his rights (Documents 31 and 32). Nor did the movement disappear without arousing an interest in foreign countries. Europeans looked with concern at the American attitude to the foreigner (Documents 33 and 34). Finally, Document 35 contains an extract from one of the most famous of the Know-Nothing tracts, Thomas R. Whitney's *Defense of the American Policy.*

The New York Association for Improving the Condition of the Poor, in calling attention to the disproportionate number of foreign poor, nevertheless paid tribute to the importance of immigration as a great source of wealth and power. "The marvelous exodus from Europe," it was acknowledged, had brought with it "the wealth and skill and labor" which were needed in America, "as well as a vast amount of impotent and thriftless poverty." The report concluded that, as the gains of immigration could not be obtained without some losses, immigration should therefore be accepted as desirable, even with all its drawbacks (Document 37). On the eve of the Civil War New York was carrying a heavy burden of pauperism. She owed much to immigrants, but she also suffered much from the backwash of immigration which accumulated in her tenement districts.

During and after the war, public opinion regarding immigration changed radically, as the documents in the preceding sections have already indicated. Senator John Sherman's speech on the post-war bill "to encourage immigration" (Document 38) and the speeches of the arch-protectionist, Representative William D. Kelley, of Pennsylvania (Document 39), show some of the aspects of this new public opinion following the war. The point of view of the commercial interests is shown in the later proposal to encourage immigration by abolishing the head tax in New York (Document 40). On the other hand, at a meeting of the National Conference of Charities in 1881, the representatives of various public and private charitable agencies called attention to the heavy costs paid by Americans for supporting dependents from other countries (Document 41).

The extracts from the *Commercial and Financial Chronicle* and the *Nation* (Documents 42 and 43) give various points of view at a time when public opinion was becoming unified in favor of federal immigration legislation. The first federal immigration law was passed to prevent the evil effects of immigration from outweighing the good (Document 44). The duty of Congress was said to be threefold: "to protect the community from foreign paupers, lunatics, and criminals; to shield the worthy immigrants from the rapacity and corruption to which they were exposed; and at the same time to achieve these results without retarding or discouraging immigration."

# PUBLIC OPINION AND THE IMMIGRANT

## 1. Complaints of the Pennsylvania Colonial Assembly[1]

May 15, 1755

*May it please the Governor:*

Upon the Governor's Message of the Twelfth of December last recommending to Us a Revision of the Laws now in being relating to sickly Vessels and Passengers, and that we would make proper Provision for Preventing the ill Effects that might arise from such for the future, and as far as in our Power prevent the spreading of any infectious Disorders that might be introduced into this City and Province, We immediately prepared and sent up a bill which We presume would in a great Measure have answered that good Purpose, and at the same Time have left open to the fair Trader all the valuable Advantages which would accrue to the Province from such Importations.

The grievous Calamities we were then threatened with, the melancholy Spectacle of the Distress of so many of our Fellow Creatures perishing for Want of Change of Apparel, Room, and other Necessaries on board their Ships, and after being landed among Us the extreme Danger the Benevolent and the Charitable exposed them to in approaching those unhappy Sufferers, together with the Governor's own Recommendation, gave Us Reason to hope that he might be at Liberty and that his own Inclinations would have induced him to have passed such a Bill as might prevent the like for the future, but we are under the greatest concern to find Ourselves disappointed in those our reasonable Expectations. . . . . .

The German Importations were at first and for a considerable Time of such as were Families of Substance and industrious sober People, who constantly brought with them their Chests of Apparel and other Necessaries for so long a voyage. But these we apprehend have for some time past been shipped on board other Vessels in order to leave more Room for crowding their unhappy Passengers in greater Numbers, and to secure the Freights of such as might perish during the Voyage, which experience has convinced Us must be the Case of very many where such Numbers (as have been lately imported in each

---

[1] Extract from a message to the Governor from the Assembly, May 15, 1755, in *Minutes of the Provincial Council of Pennsylvania*, VI, 384–86.

Vessel) are crowded together without Change of Raiment or any other Means of keeping themselves sweet and clean. But this Provision the Governor has been pleased to throw out of our Bill; and yet we think it so essentially necessary that the Want of it must necessarily poison the Air those unhappy Passengers breathe on Shipboard, and spread it wherever they land to infect the Country which receives them, especially as the Governor has likewise altered the Provision We had made by the Advice of the Physicians for accommodating them with more Room and Air upon their Arrival here.[1]

We have reason to believe the Importations of Germans have been for some Time composed of a great Mixture of the Refuse of their People, and that the very Jails have contributed to the Supplies We are burthened with. But as there are many of more Substance and better Character, We thought it reasonable to hinder the Importer from obliging such as had no connections with one another to become jointly bound for their respective Freights or Passages; but the Governor has thought fit to alter this also in such a manner as to elude the good Purposes intended by the Act, by which means those who are of more Substance are involved in the Contracts and Debts of Others, and the Merchants secured at the Expence of the Country where they are necessitated and do become very frequently common Beggars from Door to Door, to the great Injury of the Inhabitants and the Increase and Propagation of the Distempers they have brought among us. Many who have indented themselves for the Payment of their Passages have frequently been afflicted with such secret and loathsome Diseases at the Time as have rendered them altogether unfit for the Services they had contracted to perform, for which we had provided a Remedy by the Bill; but the Governor has thought fit to strike it out and leave Us exposed to this grievous Imposition without a Remedy.

### 2. A Statesman's Calculations[2]

The present desire of America is to produce rapid population by as great importations of foreigners as possible. But is this founded in good policy? The advantage proposed is the multiplication of numbers. Now let us suppose (for example only) that, in this state, we

[1] [For material dealing with early steerage conditions, see the first volume of this series, E. Abbott, *Immigration: Select Documents and Case Records*, Part I, Section I.]

[2] Extract from "Notes on Virginia, 1782," in *The Works of Thomas Jefferson*, collected and edited by P. L. Ford (New York: G. P. Putnam's Sons, 1904), III, 486–89.

could double our numbers in one year by the importation of foreigners; and this is a greater accession than the most sanguine advocate for immigration has a right to expect. Then I say, beginning with a double stock, we shall attain any given degree of population only 27 years, and 3 months sooner than if we proceed on our single stock. If we propose four millions and a half as a competent population for this state, we should be $54\frac{1}{2}$ years attaining it, could we at once double our numbers; and $81\frac{3}{4}$ years, if we rely on natural propagation, as may be seen by the following table:

| Years | Proceeding on our present stock | Proceeding on a double stock |
|---|---|---|
| 1781 .................... | 567,614 | 1,135,228 |
| $1808\frac{1}{4}$ .................. | 1,135,228 | 2,270,456 |
| $1835\frac{1}{2}$ .................. | 2,270,456 | 4,540,912 |
| $1862\frac{3}{4}$ .................. | 4,540,912 | ......... |

In the first column are stated periods of $27\frac{1}{4}$ years; in the second are our numbers at each period, as they will be if we proceed on our actual stock; and in the third are what they would be, at the same periods, were we to set out from the double of our present stock. I have taken the term of four million and a half of inhabitants for example's sake only. Yet I am persuaded it is a greater number than the country spoken of, considering how much inarable land it contains, can clothe and feed without a material change in the quality of their diet. But are there no inconveniences to be thrown into the scale against the advantage expected from a multiplication of numbers by the importation of foreigners? It is for the happiness of those united in society to harmonize as much as possible in matters which they must of necessity transact together. Civil government being the sole object of forming societies, its administration must be conducted by common consent. Every species of government has its specific principles. Ours perhaps are more peculiar than those of any other in the universe. It is a composition of the freest principles of the English constitution, with others derived from natural right and natural reason. To these nothing can be more opposed than the maxims of absolute monarchies. Yet from such we are to expect the greatest number of emigrants. They will bring with them the principles of the governments they leave, imbibed in their early youth; or, if able to throw them off, it will be in exchange for an unbounded licentiousness, passing, as is usual, from one extreme to another. It would be a miracle were they to stop precisely at the point of temperate liberty. These principles, with their language, they will transmit to their children. In proportion to their numbers, they will share with us the legislation. They will infuse into it their spirit, warp and bias its directions, and render it a heterogeneous, incoherent, distracted mass. I may appeal to experience, during the present contest, for a verification of these conjectures. But, if they be not certain in event, are they not possible, are they not probable? Is it not safer to wait with patience 27 years and three months longer, for the attainment of any degree of population desired or expected? May not our government be more homogeneous, more peaceable, more durable? Suppose 20 millions of republican Americans thrown all of a sudden into France, what would be the condition of that kingdom? If it would be more turbulent, less happy, less strong, we may believe that the addition of half a million of foreigners to our present numbers would produce a similar effect here. If they come of themselves they are entitled to all the rights of citizenship; but I doubt the expediency of inviting them by extraordinary encouragements. I mean not that these doubts should be extended to the importation of useful artificers. The policy of that measure depends on very different considerations. Spare no expense in obtaining them. They will after a while go to the plough and the hoe; but, in the mean time, they will teach us something we do not know. It is not so in agriculture. The indifferent state of that among us does not proceed from a want of knowledge merely; it is from our having such quantities of land to waste as we please. In Europe the object is to make the most of their land, labor being abundant; here it is to make the most of our labor, land being abundant.

### 3. Immigration and the Needs of the New Nation[1]

How far emigration from other countries into this, ought to be encouraged, is a very important question.

It is clear, that the present situation of America, renders it necessary to promote the influx of people: and it is equally clear, that we have a right to restrain that influx, whenever it is found likely to prove hurtful to us.

Having obtained possession of a certain territory, any collection

[1] Extract from "An enquiry into the best means of encouraging emigration from abroad, consistently with the happiness and safety of the original citizens. Read before the society for political enquiries, at the house of Dr. Franklin, April 20 1787," in *The American Museum, or, Universal Magazine*, X (July–December, 1791) 114–16, 165–66.

of men have a right to exclude all others from settling in so much of that territory as is necessary for themselves. How much is necessary, ought, however, to be determined upon reasonable principles. A nation of hunters requires large tracts for their support; husbandmen less: merchants or manufacturers still less. . . . .

But though a body of people has no right to exclude others from settling in a territory which it cannot legally occupy; yet it will not be disputed, that it may wholly refuse or carefully qualify the admission into its own community.

In ceding the superfluous land to others, it yields to the original law, which alone supports its title to what it retains. In refusing admission to its own fellowship, it may consult another original principle, its own preservation.

When admission is to be granted, two objects are to be considered, (1) How the new citizens can best be rendered useful members of the community that adopts them. (2) How this can be effected, without endangering the happiness and safety of the original citizens. Subject to these two considerations the most effectual method of encouraging immigration is the third object of this enquiry.

The sooner the new citizens are fully incorporated, with the society to which they accede, the sooner they become useful members; they then grow attached to their new country: they consider themselves as part of it: they adopt the opinions and affections of their new brethren, and soon forget they have adopted them, and imagine they are natural.

But prudent men have considered, with some anxiety, the danger of admitting foreigners to an unlimited participation of the municipal rights of republics; and it has been apprehended, that if the mode of access was rendered too easy, foreign powers, to whom it was a sufficient object, might make use of that method, to interfere in the public measures; or that the new citizens, infected with ancient prejudices and attachments, might employ the privileges they had acquired, to the injury of the country that had adopted them.

I doubt whether there is much reason for either of these apprehensions. . . . .

Nor, if we consider the usual motives of emigration, need we fear much evil from the effects of predilections and attachments to the native country of the emigrant. The voluntary emigrant seldom looks back to the coast he has abandoned. Renouncing its connection and its name, he strives to transfer the whole of his former love for it, to the country he embraces. Driven away by the perception of evils, he cannot but wish to preserve the new clime from the same systems which rendered the old intolerable to him. Already acquainted with their pernicious tendency, he will more readily discover, and more anxiously pursue measures useful and salutary to his present country, than the native citizen, whose love of novelty may lead him into propositions, of which his inexperience prevents him from perceiving the danger. . . . .

With a most preposterous policy, the former masters of this country were accustomed to discharge their jails of the vilest part of their subjects, and to transmit ship loads of wretches, too worthless for the old world, to taint and corrupt the infancy of the new. If it would have been paternal to spare the advantages that might have been taken of our poverty and weakness—if it would have been politic to encourage the simplicity and industry which alone can raise colonies to opulence and strength—if it was absurd to inflict a residence in America, as a punishment upon some, while others were to be induced to remove there by describing it as a blessing, it will not be easy to distinguish these measures from the schemes of inhumanity or fatuity.

But colonies are obliged to accept many things of the mother country, which have little of the maternal character in them. Pennsylvania, swelling hourly with arrivals of honest, industrious Germans and others, wisely discouraged by a duty, what she dared not to openly prohibit. In some of the other provinces, labourers were perhaps more wanted; and, the present necessity subduing the sense of the general evil, the convicts were purchased for a term of years, and immediately became intitled to most of the civil rights of the freemen of the province. Some few became honest men.

It is not now likely that these states will be insulted with the transportation of this sort, directly ordered from any other sovereign power. A state may banish its criminals; but it cannot, consistently with the laws of nations, obtrude them on another. Yet, where there has been an opportunity of escape, after the commission of crimes, or where indiscriminate exile has been inflicted as the punishment, we are not exempt from the common hazard of unconsciously affording protection to undeserving objects, and admitting infamous names to be enrolled with the best and purest of our citizens.

Pennsylvania is the only state I recollect to have appeared sensible of this danger, the effects of which are so pernicious in a democratical form of government. A foreigner is required to be a good character, or he cannot acquire the rights of a natural born subject; though no definite evidence of his character is, however, pointed out; nor is it easy to settle a convenient mode of obtaining it.

### 4. "A Charity Sermon for Poor Emigrants," 1797[1]

Now all of you who now hear me, may be expected to have this sympathy for strangers, and emigrants, in some degree; since, if not yourselves, yet your fathers, or not very remote ancestors, were also strangers, and not in a distant country, as Egypt was with respect to the Israelites, but in this very country in which we are now met. We should, therefore, behave to one another, in this land in which we may all be said to be equally strangers, as brethren; brethren, not merely as partaking of the same human nature, but brethren in affliction, difficulty and trials. And therefore those who, by the favour of a kind providence, have surmounted their difficulties, and now find themselves at their ease, with something more than is necessary for the supply of their own wants, should remember those who are yet struggling with theirs, and *give* out of what they can well spare *to him that needeth.* . . . .

That, in some way or other, many poor emigrants are entitled to assistance, will appear to every person who shall consider their situation.

1. It may be depended upon that, in general, emigrants are of the more industrious class of people. For the enterprizing, as the emigrants in some degree must be, are chiefly of that character. The indolent, as well as the timid, stay at home, content to starve, rather than make any attempt, that shall appear in the least degree hazardous, to better their condition. The weak and the sickly, the aged and infirm, however willing, cannot leave their country, and the friends on whom they depend. It is therefore probable that, with a little seasonable assistance, the poor emigrant, being disposed to industry, will soon be in a condition to provide for himself, and even to reimburse his benefactor.

It may be said that persons must be very thoughtless and improvident, to leave their country, though ever so poor, without a

---

[1] Extract from Dr. Joseph Priestley (see Doc. 4, Section I), *The Case of Poor Emigrants Recommended, in a Discourse, Delivered at the University Hall in Philadelphia, Sunday, February 19, 1797* (Philadelphia, 1797), pp. 7–28.

This sermon was preached to raise money for the Philadelphia Society for the Information and Assistance of Persons Emigrating from Foreign Countries.

certainty of finding subsistence in another, and therefore that, on persons of so little foresight, money will be thrown away. This, no doubt, may be the case. But many, and we may well suppose, the greater part, of the necessitous and helpless persons, whose cause I am pleading, were only misinformed with respect to the country to which they have emigrated; and it is by no means easy, especially to persons in their low situation, to procure good information.

Those emigrants who had friends in this country will of course find employment with them, or assistance from them, and these are no objects of the present charity. But even some of these find their friends dead, or removed, or on some other account incapacitated to give them the assistance they had reason to expect. And many came without any friends at all, but with high expectations from such accounts as were given them of this country; as that they would meet with no difficulty, that if they were able and willing to labour, they could not fail to find employment, and that all labour would be abundantly rewarded. But many of these were manufacturers in their own country, and now find, to their great surprize, that their skill and industry are not wanted here, and can be of no service to them, and that there is no kind of labour, to which they have been accustomed, or to which they are equal, by which they can, at least can immediately, get a living.

Also many emigrants have suffered extremely during the voyage. They are landed in a sickly condition, or soon become sickly by the change of climate; so that for a long time they are unable to do anything at all, and they find expenses at inns and lodging houses much greater than they had any idea of; so that the little money they might bring with them is soon expended, and they are left wholly destitute. In this case, if they meet with no relief from the charitable and well disposed, they must inevitably perish. Whereas, with a little assistance and encouragement, which is often of more real use than money, they may soon recover their health, strength, and spirits; and with proper advice with respect to the disposal of themselves, they may, in a short time, become useful citizens.

For, I would observe, that the benefit of this institution is not confined to giving pecuniary assistance to emigrants. Advice how to dispose of themselves to the most advantage, directions to cheap places of accommodation, some care to see that they are not imposed upon, and especially directions where to find employment, are often of much more use to them than money. And the persons who give their attention to the business of this institution are particularly assiduous in this respect; and by this means contribute more to its real utility than those who only give money. Few persons, however, are qualified to serve the institution in this way. They can only give money. But this money, in the hands of persons who can give their time, and employ their knowledge of the country to this purpose, will be of unspeakably more use, than if it had been given by themselves as mere charity. For this, without putting the poor emigrant in the way of providing for himself, would soon be expended; and then he would be as destitute as ever. And if there was no public institution to which he could have recourse, conducted by persons qualified to give him the best advice, he would be reduced to the necessity of begging from door to door, and thereby become a nuisance, instead of a benefit, to society.

Hence then we see the use of a *public institution*, which being generally known, necessitous emigrants will of course be directed to it; and thus none of their time will be lost, or their money needlessly expended. But no institution of this kind can be supported without funds, as well as proper officers; and therefore this institution, the utility of which is so apparent, has a just claim to the benefactions of those who wish to employ what they can spare to the most advantage, for the service of their fellow creatures.

2. The present calamitous and oppressed state of Europe should more particularly draw the kind attention of the inhabitants of this country to the emigrants from that part of the world. Europe is not only overburdened with poor, but oppressed with servitude; so that the poor are not only unable to subsist by their labour, but lie under great restrictions with respect to civil and religious liberty. They are even, in a great measure, deprived of the satisfaction of expressing their feelings, of making complaints, or applying for redress of their grievances.

Many persons of better condition in those countries, especially in Great Britain and Ireland, unable to bear the encroachments that are continually making on their liberties, civil and religious, and despairing of doing any good by any exertions of theirs, are now coming hither, bringing with them very considerable capitals, by which this country is enriched. In consequence of the purchases that foreigners of various descriptions, and especially those of this class, who have the greatest confidence in this government, are making, the price of your lands is daily rising, and your labourers and artisans are getting higher wages. This circumstance adding much to the wealth of the country in general, you are better able, out of the emolument accruing to yourselves from European persecution, to assist those who are distressed in consequence of it. The poor emigrant, therefore, in fact, only asks of you some part of that which you have gained by his more opulent brethren. These more opulent emigrants will, no doubt, exert themselves in behalf of their distressed countrymen; but it is not reasonable that the whole of the burden should lie upon them. Many of them suffer considerably in their fortunes by the disadvantageous sale of their property in Europe, and the greater expense at which they are obliged to live here.

Let those, then, whose ancestors, if not themselves, were driven from Europe, by the same spirit of persecution which still prevails there, feel for those who are now in a similar situation; though it must be acknowledged, and with gratitude, that they now come with much better prospects. . . . .

But some distressed emigrants, you will say, are men who have fled from their creditors, perhaps from the justice of their country: Are these entitled to our assistance? I answer, that these cases cannot now be many, and it is not possible for us, at this distance, to distinguish them. Besides, the most vicious in one country, and especially a distant one, being separated from their former connexions, and entering into new ones, of a better cast, may become reformed and useful citizens. Our natures being the same, the greater advantage to which the best of us appear is owing chiefly to our education and connexions, for which we are indebted to a kind providence. Let us, then, show our gratitude to that providence which has favoured us, by our good will and liberality to those who, in this respect, as well as others, have been less favoured. Seasonable kindness may awaken the dormant seed of virtue, especially in a country like this, in which there are few temptations to vice. How many respectable, as well as opulent families in America, have arisen from the most indigent, and the most profligate in Europe. And this is so far from being the subject of reproach, that it is a just ground of praise.

## 5. Congressional Opinion, 1797[1]

Mr. Brooks did not think this sum [$20] excessive. He would not have the rights of citizenship made too common. He had no objection to the admitting of foreigners into this country; but there were foreigners came here, fugitives from justice, and others, who never would be of

[1] Extract from "Debate on the Proposal to Impose a Tax of $20 on Certificates of Naturalization," *Annals of Congress*, Fifth Congress (1797-99), I, 422-30.

any advantage to any country. These, for the small sum of twenty dollars, might become citizens; he would not have them admitted for less, as it would be necessary to have some security for the attachment of persons to the Government of this country; and such men as would be of advantage to the country would not think the sum too large.

Mr. Gallatin denied that the argument of the gentleman from New York would apply; and that a person's paying a sum of money would be no proof that he was well affected to the Government. A convict or a highwayman might possibly pay twenty dollars with greater ease than the worthiest man. . . . . A single man might in a short time save the money necessary to purchase his citizenship; but he knew a great number of persons, who came to this country with large families, very valuable emigrants, and upon whom we had more security for their good behaviour than upon single men, upon whom this tax would fall very heavy. . . . .

Nor did he conceive it would be perfectly safe to have one-fourth, if not one-third part of the inhabitants of a country living as foreigners in its bosom. These men, speaking the same language and having the same manners, after they had been in the country ten or fifteen years, would look upon the refusal to admit them to the common right of citizens, except upon the payment of twenty dollars, as unjust and oppressive. If so large a sum was charged, Mr. G. said, provision should be made in favor of the children of such fathers as should not themselves have been citizens. . . . .

Mr. Swanwick observed, that it had been urged in favor of this large sum that foreigners would not be obliged to become citizens, as they might get a living in the country without doing so. But was it not of advantage, he asked, that foreigners should become citizens, and not that a great part of the people of our country should be living amongst us without owing all allegiance to our Government? But it was said these emigrants might be highwaymen, or men of bad character; but did not the naturalization law require that every person applying to be made a citizen should produce two witnesses to speak of their moral character? And surely, after a residence of five years, and a guard of this kind, there could not be any reason for such arguments. It should seem, from what was said on this occasion, that twenty dollars was to be the price upon which we are willing to admit the worst characters to the privilege of citizenship.

But it was said, that if this tax were not laid, the rights of citizenship would become too common. This was a doctrine contrary to anything he had heard before on the subject. Since the year 1776, it had uniformly been the language of this country that we had in the Western world opened an asylum for emigrants from every country. This was our language: "Come and join us in the blessings we enjoy, in a country large and fertile, and under a Government founded upon the principles of liberty and justice." Were the inhabitants of this country all born in it? Certainly not—a great majority were foreigners; even in the Government itself there were many foreigners. And should they, because they came a little sooner, or had better fortune than others, say to their less fortunate brethren, "You shall not be admitted to the privilege of citizenship but on the payment of twenty dollars, though we received it without money and without price!" It was said, a man might soon earn twenty dollars to pay for this privilege; but supposing he could soon earn fifty dollars, he did not think that a good reason for laying this tax. . . . .

In a country like ours, he said, it was extremely impolitic to throw obstructions in the way of emigration. He was desirous that every attention should be paid to the moral character of emigrants before they were admitted as citizens, but he trusted they should not degrade the country in the eyes of foreign nations by putting so high a tax upon the privilege of citizenship. It would ill suit the high tone which had been held abroad of the liberty of this country; nor did he think their constituents would be well pleased with such a tax.

If they compared this tax with other parts of the bill, it would be found much heavier than any other. A lawyer was to pay ten dollars upon the entrance of his lucrative profession, whilst a poor foreigner was to pay twenty dollars to be admitted as a citizen. In doing this, gentlemen seemed desirous only of having rich emigrants as citizens, whilst the poor wanderer, flying from the hearth-tax of Ireland, or from the oppressions of other countries, who would be vastly useful in the cultivation of our land and in a very useful labor, would be in a great measure excluded from his rights in society. . . . .

He [Mr. Harper] did not agree with the gentleman last up on the propriety of inviting immigrations from all parts of the world. There was a moment of enthusiasm in this country, when this was thought to be right—when we were not satisfied with giving to immigrants every blessing which we had earned with our blood and treasure, but admitted them instantly to the rights of citizenship. An experience of ten or fifteen years, he said, had convinced us we were wrong. They had done something to prevent the evil in future; but he thought they should do more. He should be willing that no man should become a citizen of this country but by birth; he would have all foreigners freely admitted, and he would admit their children to have a right to citizenship. He believed this would be a proper polity for this and every other country. . . . .

Mr. Lyon was opposed to this amendment. It appeared to him injurious, cruel, and impolitic. It was injurious, because we had dealt out a different kind of language heretofore; we had told the world, that there was in this country a good spring of liberty, and invited all to come and drink of it. We had told them that the country was rich and fertile, and invited them to come and taste of our fruits; and he did not think it was right now to turn round to them and say, you shall not be admitted as citizens unless you pay twenty dollars. This looked like entering into a treaty offensive and defensive, with the Monarch of Britain, to prevent his subjects from leaving him and coming hither. He was almost led to suspect that the thing was introduced on the suggestion of a certain foreign Minister. . . . .

Mr. Sewall said, though he wished this country to be an asylum for men of every other who chose to come to it, yet he did not wish to see foreigners our governors; and, indeed, if they were admitted as voters at our elections, they in some degree became the governors of our country. He wished, therefore, that a longer residence should be necessary, before a foreigner should become a citizen. He liked this amendment, because it made it necessary for a man to have a little property before he could be admitted. . . . .

Mr. Thatcher said, gentlemen viewed only one side of the question; they constantly spoke of the twenty dollars, which they called an enormous sum; but they said nothing of the benefits which were to be received in return; they were to receive for that sum all the advantages which this country had obtained by much treasure and blood. He thought the doors of naturalization too wide. Too many foreigners emigrated hither; they were out of proportion to the natives; for he wished the American interest always to prevail over all foreign interest. He would much rather, therefore, that the certificate was forty dollars than twenty dollars.

Mr. J. Williams did not think this question was put upon its true ground. This bill was intended to raise funds towards paying off the national debt—the debt incurred while we were fighting for our liberty and independence; and shall those, said he, who come to partake of these advantages, pay nothing for it? If the country was not worth the tax imposed, foreigners would not come to it. If the tax were too high, it might be lowered; or, if too low, made higher. . . .

Mr. Otis . . . . agreed that the present amendment was merely a question of revenue, but the policy of a tax was always a fair object of discussion, and it was therefore proper to consider the indirect and remote effects of the present bill upon the naturalization of foreigners. He denied the expediency of affording too great a facility to their admission among us. In the infancy of the country it was necessary to encourage emigration, and foreigners of all countries had been wisely invited and allowed to settle in our country. To the industry of emigrants many parts of the country were indebted for the most valuable improvements in agriculture and the arts, and he knew foreigners who were an honor to the United States, who had aided in forming their constitutions, in fighting their battles, and who were not less meritorious citizens for not being born in the country. There were others in that House and other Legislatures who were entitled to the highest consideration and respect. He rejoiced in the advantages derived from persons of this description. They would not be affected by the present tax; but he was not anxious to give greater latitude to the laws of naturalization; on the contrary, he thought it wise to restrain that privilege. He did not believe it to be necessary to rely upon that source of population, but considered the native American germ to be amply sufficient for the production of such scions as were worth cultivation. He denied that the manners of Europe were the manners of this country. In that quarter of the world a revolution of manners, of the most formidable nature, threatened the subversion of all sound principle, of all social order; and a system of profligacy had swept off every vestige of whatever was most amiable and respectable in the eye of humanity. He trusted the case was different in this country. It was true that Virginia was indebted in a great measure for her prosperity to the industrious establishments formed by foreigners of various descriptions; but it should also be remembered that the foulest stain in the annals of that State was not to be imputed to natural-born citizens.

The amendment, he said, would not affect those men who had already lands in this country, nor the deserving part of those who might seek an asylum in it. Persons of that description would easily pay the tax; but it would tend to foreclose the mass of vicious and disorganizing characters who could not live peaceably at home, and who, after unfurling the standard of rebellion in their own countries, might come hither to revolutionize ours. . . . .

Mr. Baldwin was in favor of the smaller sum. He said this was a subject upon which it was always found difficult to legislate, as different parts of the country had very different ideas upon it. In the part of the country from which he came, the people would not approve of such a tax. He believed there were parts of the country which would not object to a tax of a thousand dollars upon this object, but it was not so in other parts. All the prosperity of some States depended upon emigration, and to lay a heavy tax of this kind, would be to do violence to their feelings. . . . .

Mr. Swanwick spoke at length on this subject, and dwelt particularly on the hardships which the poorer part of emigrants would experience in paying this tax, and if they did not pay it, they would be living in the country as foreigners, and not as citizens of a free country.

### 6. Prejudice against Aliens[1]

Throughout the States, I have remarked that there is a strong line of distinction drawn between citizens of native and of foreign birth; and, in some cases, where the latter have professed principles of republicanism in Europe (a sin which might, at least, one should suppose, be forgiven them in the United States of America), they are treated with scorn, as out-casts, who ought to have remained in their own country, and have submitted to whatever form of despotism it chose to exert over them. So deeply rooted, indeed, are these sentiments in the American mind, that they give some colour to, though they can hardly justify, the address which I find unanimously voted in the year 1809, at a meeting in New York of five hundred adopted citizens, from which the following are extracts:

At a respectable meeting, consisting of about five hundred Adopted Republican Citizens of the city of New York, held at Lyon's Hotel, Mott Street, Mr. Archibald Taylor being unanimously called to the chair, and Dr. Stephen Dempsey appointed secretary, the subjoined address was unanimously adopted, and ordered to be published:

*To the Adopted Republican Citizens of the City of New York*

FELLOW CITIZENS: A long train of disagreeable circumstances have called us together, and induced us to address you upon a subject which, for

[1] Extract from Henry Bradshaw Fearon, *Sketches of America* (2d ed.; London, 1818), pp. 348–52. See above, p 212, note 1.

years, we have acutely felt and deeply deplored. Some of you, groaning under oppression in your native land, have voluntarily emigrated from it, whilst others, more afflicted by despotism, and less favoured by propitious events, find yourselves in the condition of involuntary exile. All, however, have chosen, as a resting-place in the journey through life, this "asylum for the oppressed of all nations." Here, perhaps, mistaking the character of human nature, we pleasingly anticipated, from those who avow themselves the friends of freedom, exemption from that religious persecution and civil tyranny, whose inexorable reign had forced us from our native country. Alas! how greatly were we mistaken! how egregiously have we been disappointed! Our constitutions and governments are indeed free, but between these admirable institutions and ourselves a tyranny is intervened, much less tolerable than that from which we fled. We have made permanent settlements in the land of our forefathers; we admire and we are attached to our republican institutions; we have complied with the injunctions of the constitutions and the laws, and we will support them upon equal terms, with our lives and our fortunes. But how are we treated? What has been our reception? Has good faith been observed? Have the promises been performed? Are not we, who are citizens by all the solemnities and obligations of law, treated as aliens—stigmatized as foreigners? We complain not of the constitution and the laws; they are liberal in principle and benign in operation. They enjoin an abjuration of former allegiance; have we not with alacrity complied with the injunction? They require an oath of fidelity to the Union and to the States; devoted in spirit and in truth to both, we have eagerly taken it. What more is required? What more can be expected? The laws require no more. Shall an under-plot, a counter operation, individual jealousy, and pale-faced cabal, frowned upon by the very elements of the state, subvert the law—put it at defiance—trample it under foot? The law places upon the same undistinguishable level, the citizen of native and the citizen of foreign birth. Are we to be told, in this enlightened age, that the *law* is *not* to govern; that the essence of well-ordered society is *not* a government of laws, but a government of the worst passions? Go back then to a state of anarchy; tear out the bowels of society; revert to the rude condition of untutored nature, and let the strongest govern. We have never ceased to cherish and to inculcate those opinions which are most consonant to the civil and social state. We have remonstrated against distinctions, at once impolitic and unjust, between native and adopted citizens; but have not our remonstrances and efforts been in vain? No zeal, no exertions, no services, however disinterested, unremitted, or great, have been sufficient to shield us from an epithet which, while it poisons the social and impairs the enjoyment of political life, must ultimately terminate in the ruin of the republican party in this city. Alas! has our republic turned upon itself, and in the short period of a few years from the adoption of the constitution?

Resolved unanimously, that 500 copies of the above address and resolution be printed in hand-bills for the benefit of our fellow republican adopted citizens.

ARCHIBALD TAYLOR, *Chairman*

S. DEMPSEY, *Secretary*

### 7. Hints to Immigrants from an Immigrant Society[1]

That hospitality which, as Mr. Jefferson says, the savages of the wilderness extended to the first settlers arriving in this land, cannot be denied, by a free, civilized, and Christian people, to brethren emigrating from the countries of their common fathers; and the exercise of it is peculiarly agreeable to us, who have (some of us) been induced, by a similarity of fate and fortunes with your own, to quit the lands of our nativity, and seek freedom and happiness in America. . . . . We bid you welcome to a land of freedom; we applaud your resolution; we commend your judgment in asserting the right of expatriation; a right acknowledged and practised by people of all nations, from the earliest ages to the present time. . . . .

What is America? What sort of people may expect to succeed in it? The immortal Franklin has answered these questions. "America is the land of labour." But it is, emphatically, the best country on earth for those who will labour. By industry they can earn more wages here than elsewhere in the world. Our governments are frugal, they demand few taxes; so that the earnings of the poor man are left to enrich himself; they are nearly all his own.

Idlers are out of their element here, and the being who is technically called a man of rank in Europe, is despicable in America. He must become an useful member of society, or he will find no society; he will be shunned by all decent people. . . . .

It would be very prudent for newcomers, especially labourers or farmers, to go into the country without delay, and they will save both money and time by it, and avoid several inconveniences of a seaport town. By spending some time with an American farmer, in any capacity, they will learn the method of tillage, or working a plantation, peculiar to this country. No time can be more usefully employed than

---

[1] Extract from "Hints to Emigrants from Europe, Who Intend to Make a Permanent Residence in the United States of America; Pointing Out the Most Advantageous Places of Settlement, and Giving Directions for the Best Means of Preserving Health," by the Shamrock Society of New York, 1817. Reprinted in John Melish, *Travels through the United States of America* (London, 1818), pp. 625–39.

a year in this manner. In that space, any smart, stout man can learn how woodland may be cleared, how cleared land is managed; he will acquire some knowledge of crops and their succession, of usages and customs that ought to be known, and perhaps save something into the bargain. Many European emigrants who brought money with them have heretofore taken this wise course, and found it greatly to their advantage; for, at the end of the year, they knew what to do with it. They had learned the value of lands in old settlements and near the frontiers, the price of labour, cattle, and grain, and were ready to begin the work with ardour and confidence. Multitudes of poor people, from Ireland, Scotland, and Germany, have, by these means, together with industry and frugality, become wealthy farmers, or, as they are called in Europe, estated men, who, in their own countries, where all the lands are fully occupied, and the wages of labour low, could never have emerged from the condition wherein they were born. . . . .

In what part of this extensive country may an emigrant from the northern or western parts of Europe most advantageously settle? If he be undecided until his arrival, his choice will be agreeably perplexed or suspended by the different invitations offered by various sections of this empire. . . . . As the European is more patient of cold than of heat, he will be apt to prefer the middle and western, or northwestern states to the southern. There he will form connections with inhabitants whose manners most resemble his own. In some one of them we would advise him, after a proper examination, to pitch his tent, and fix his residence.

Farther to the south, where negro slaves are the only, or principal labourers, some white men think it.disreputable to follow the plow. Far be it from us to cast censure on our southern neighbours; yet, in choosing a settlement, we would have emigrants take slavery, with all other circumstances, into their consideration.

It is the opinion of some judicious men, that though persons newly arrived ought to go without loss of time into the country, yet it would not be prudent for them to retire all at once to the remote parts of the west; that they ought to stop nearer the sea-board, and learn a little of the mode of doing business. Perhaps this, in some instances, may be advisable; but we think that young men, whose habits are not fixed, cannot post too speedily to the fine regions beyond the Allegany. The labourer, however, will find great difference between them and Europe in every thing. The man who was accustomed to the spade, must now use the axe: he who used to dig ditches, will learn to maul rails and make fences. These are extremes that must be met; and the sooner, perhaps, the better. . . . .

As every emigrant does not mean to turn farmer, and our wish is to furnish useful hints to various classes, we will here, at the risk of repetition, state the ideas of a gentleman of much experience, respectability, and intelligence, concerning the pursuits of different persons.

Those who have acquired useful trades will, in general, find little difficulty, either in our large cities, or the towns and villages all over the country. There are vacancies for a large portion of them.

Clerks, shopkeepers, or attendants in stores, are seldom wanted; their occupation is an uncertain one; it requires some time, too, for such persons to acquire the mode of doing business with the same expertness as natives or long residents. . . . .

Before any other step towards forming a settlement, the stranger should take the proper measures for acquiring citizenship: and the advantages of this are important and obvious, independently of its conferring political privileges. Without it you will remain exempted, indeed, by mild laws, from wrong; but destitute of some valuable positive rights. The alien, in most of the states, is not entitled to hold any lands, can obtain no office under the state, nor participate in the shipping interests of the country.

It is fit the emigrant should be distinctly apprized (for it will conciliate his attachment and gratitude to the country of his adoption) that nowhere in the world is a well-conducted foreigner received into the bosom of the state with equal liberality and readiness as in America. When on the 4th of July, 1776, the Congress unanimously adopted a Declaration of Independence, and delivered their country from the dominion of the king of England, this was one of the complaints alleged against him: "he has endeavoured to prevent the population of these states; for that purpose obstructing the laws for naturalization of foreigners." The same liberal feeling has prevailed in the government of the United States, from that memorable day to this, with one exception—during the administration of President Adams. The stranger, however, is certainly exposed to incidents which may lead him to doubt the truth of this assertion. He may light upon an ignorant, a prejudiced, or illiberal wretch, who will manifest an ill will towards him because he is a foreigner, and perhaps revive British and royalist's taunts in a new form; but these, the scum of a country, are totally insignificant, compared with the mass of the people. The best men in

America have always been ready to welcome the valuable emigrant—the stranger of moral and industrious habits. . . . .

The source of every blessing, and itself the most valuable of all which America offers to the emigrants, is a degree of civil and political liberty, more ample and better secured in this republic, than any where in the whole world besides.

The principles of liberty which are embodied in our frame of government and in our laws, branch out likewise through every department of society, mould our manners, and determine the character even of our domestic relations. They have the effect of producing, generally, in the deportment of individuals, who know neither superiors nor inferiors, a certain degree of ease and dignity that is equally removed from servility and arrogance. It is one of the practical results of those principles that the poorer classes in this community are more civilized, more polite and friendly, though not so submissive, as persons of the same fortunes in Europe. They are also usually followed by impartial justice in the equal distribution of family property. Hence opulence is rarely seen to accumulate on one branch, while others languish in genteel beggary. As there is no where an aristocratic establishment, the amplitude of the community is never broken up into little compartments envious and contemptuous of each other. Every man's range of occupation is extended, while every state is held worthy of respect. Honest industry no where derogates, but the facility of providing for a family is every where enlarged.

Nothing is more worthy of regard than the contrast between the general demeanor of Europeans living here, and what is alleged of the same people, and others similar to them, whilst under the yoke of trans-atlantic governments. In New York city alone, there are supposed to be not less than 12,000 Irish, and the number of all other foreigners may probably be as many. The other great cities of the United States have an equal proportion, according to their population; and emigrants from the old world are settled, and in progress of settlement, every where throughout the Union; yet, here they are never accused of sedition or rebellion, or conspiracy against the government. They are never disarmed by a military force, and no magistrate trembles when they provide themselves with ammunition. They are, indeed, among the most strenuous supporters of the government; and it is evident that a country may exist in the utmost good order, peace, and prosperity, under such a system of law as they are willing to maintain with their lives. It is manifest, therefore, that if the laws were in Europe what they are here, Europe need not drive her children into exile. The same men who are called rebels there, are esteemed and tranquil citizens here, without having changed their nature or their sentiments. But here the law is made by the majority, for the good of the greater number; and for this reason, it is essentially equal and impartial. It prohibits nothing but what is in itself morally wrong. Hence, there are fewer laws, and fewer transgressions; but when a real transgression happens, an offended community is always prompt to support the law; for it then vindicates its own decision, and its own safety. It is often detested, because it seems to be the penalty of Providence, that inordinate power shall always corrupt the holder, and can never be possessed without being followed by such a train of evils, so much wretchedness to those who endure, and so much depravity in those who exercise it, that it is felt to be a forced state, and a perversion of nature.

### 8. Congress Petitioned by Irish Immigrants to Encourage Immigrants[1]

*To the Honorable the Senate and House of Representatives of the United States of America in Congress Assembled:*

The memorial of the New York Irish Emigrant Association respectfully showeth: That your memorialists, while they presume most respectfully to solicit your attention to the helpless and suffering condition of the numerous foreigners who, flying from a complicated mass of want and misery, daily seek an asylum in the bosom of the United States, are emboldened by the recollection that a liberal encouragement to the settlement of meritorious strangers has always characterized the Government and constituted authorities of the Union. The wise and brave founders of its independence held out to the oppressed and suffering of every nation the consoling assurance that in this country, at least, they should find a refuge and a home. The successors of these illustrious men have continued to redeem, in calmer and happier times, the pledge made to philosophy and benevolence amidst perilous scenes of distress and difficulty. From this humane and beneficent policy America has reaped a rich and happy harvest. She has added to the national resources the moral and physical strength to be derived from so many thousands and tens of thousands, who, actuated by attachment to her free Constitution,

[1] Extract from "The Memorial of the New York Irish Emigrant Association," December, 1817, in the *Annals of Congress*, Fifteenth Congress, first session (1817–18), I, 202–5.

have adopted the nation where liberty has made, and is making, her most glorious stand as the country of their choice.

Your memorialists, in addressing your honorable body, need not seek to enforce by argument the generally received maxim of political economy that the wealth and solidity of a nation consist in the number, the social comforts, and the productive industry of its people. In the dense and crowded States, and under the existing Governments of Europe, these sources of wealth and stability are not always found well combined. It frequently does not happen that the social comforts, or even the productive industry, are proportioned to the number of the people. In the extended territory and scattered population of the United States, however, and under their free and blessed institutions, it is an unquestionable and important truth, that every increase of inhabitants, when wisely and judiciously distributed and settled, adds to the social comforts and productive industry of the whole, and that the excess of population, which cannot be considered as giving stability to the various Governments of Europe, if suffered or encouraged to settle here, would incalculably increase our wealth and strength. But that accession is doubly valuable which also brings to the common fund, with a mass of laborious industry, unalterable attachment to the laws and constitution of the country. And, surely, to give a wise direction to that industry, and to secure by well-placed kindness that attachment, are among the noblest exercises of legislative authority.

Your memorialists beg leave respectfully to represent that at no period since the establishment of American independence have the people of Europe, particularly the laboring classes, discovered so great a disposition as at present to emigrate to the United States. But the people of Ireland, from the peculiar pressures under which that country has so long been placed, have flocked hither in the greatest number, and perhaps under the most trying and necessitous circumstances. They come, indeed, not to return and carry back the profits of casual speculations, but to dedicate to the land of their hopes their persons, their families, their posterity, their affections, their all.

It is, however, a truth, regretted by those who have the best means of observation, that, for want of guides to their steps, and congenial homes, where all their honest energies might be called at once into activity, and their hardy enterprise turned to their own advantage, as well as to the general good, they remain perplexed, undecided, and dismayed, by the novelty and difficulty of their situations. They have fled from want and oppression—they touch the soil of freedom and abundance; but the manna of the wilderness melts in their sight. Before they can taste the fruits of happy industry, the tempter too often presents to their lips the cup that turns man to brute, and the very energies which would have made the fields to blossom make the cities groan. Individual benevolence cannot reach this evil. Individuals may indeed solicit, but it belongs to the chosen guardians of the public weal to administer the cure. Nor is the misdirection or the destruction of the capabilities and industry of these emigrants to be regretted only on its own account. The story of their blasted hopes and fortunes is transmitted back, and retailed with malicious exaggeration. Others, possessing more abundant means and more prudent habits, who have been accustomed to look with longing eyes to this free country, and contrast its happiness with the present state of Europe, are discouraged and deterred by their sufferings and misfortunes; and thus a large current of active population and wealth, inclined to flow into and enrich the United States, is dammed up at the fountain-head. A serious consideration of these circumstances induce your memorialists to hope, and most earnestly but respectfully to request, on behalf of those whose interests they urge, that a portion of unsold lands may be set apart or granted to trustees for the purpose of being settled by emigrants from Ireland, on an extended term of credit. The conditions of this grant your memorialists wish to be such as may give to the settlers its entire benefit, and may exclude all private speculation in others. They also beg leave to suggest, after contemplating the various uncultivated tracts which invite the labor of man, that a situation adapted for a settlement of that description might be found among the lands lately purchased in the Illinois Territory.

Your memorialists are fully sensible that many of the most persuasive arguments in favor of their application must be addressed, and will not be addressed in vain, to the benevolence and sympathies of the Legislature; but they also confidently appeal to its wisdom and patriotism. The lands to which they have alluded being frontier and remote are neither likely to be speedily exposed to sale, to be rendered by cultivation subservient to the general prosperity, nor by settlement conducive to the general strength. The portion which might be granted on extended credit would probably be paid for almost as soon as if it had not been brought into the market before its regular turn. During that time, in which it would otherwise remain unproductive (and therefore unprofitable), thousands of families would have acquired opulence, would have benefited the country by its cultivation, by the establishing of schools, the opening of roads, and the other improvements of social and civilized life. They would form a nucleus round which a more abundant population would rapidly accumulate, and all the contiguous lands would be largely increased in value. The small loss which might appear to be sustained by the suspension of interest on the credit (if it should have any existence) will be abundantly compensated by the money and labor that must be almost immediately expended on works of general utility, which the convenience and necessities of the settlers will naturally induce them to accomplish. But who can calculate the physical or moral, or even the pecuniary advantages in time of war, of having such a strong and embattled frontier?

The Irish emigrant, cherished and protected by the Government of the United States, will find his attachment to their interest increase in proportion to the benefits he has received. He will love with enthusiasm the country that affords him the means of honorable and successful enterprise, and permits him to enjoy unmolested and undiminished the fruits of his honest industry. Ingratitude is not the vice of Irishmen. Fully appreciating his comparative comforts, and the source from whence they flow, he will himself cherish, and will inculcate in his children, an unalterable devotion to his adopted and their native country. Should hostilities approach her in that quarter, whether in the savage forms of the tomahawk and the scalping-knife, or with the deadlier weapon of civilized warfare, the Irish settlers, with their hardy sons, will promptly repel the invasion, drive back the war upon the enemy, and give to our extended frontier security and repose.

Your memorialists therefore humbly pray your honorable body to receive and listen favorably to their application. . . . .

### 9. "Too Many Immigrants"[1]

The tide of emigration still sets to the United States. Never before perhaps, except in the last year, did so many persons from Europe reach our shores to take up their abode with us, at this advanced state of the season, as are now arriving. We regret that it is so. Hundreds, perhaps we might say thousands of them, will be incumbrances on us during the ensuing winter; for many tens of thousands of our own people, accustomed to sustain themselves by their labor, will be out of employment, unless some extraordinary event shall take place.

[1] Extract from *Niles' Weekly Register*, XVII (September 18, 1819), 36.

We have always until just now greeted the stranger on his arrival here with pleasure. There was room enough for all that would come, and industry was a sure road to a comfortable living, if not to independence and wealth. We were glad of the addition which they made to our population, and of the impulse which they gave to the capacity of production, thus advancing our country to its weight of power and extent of resources which the patriot delights to anticipate, but which also every one desired to see realized. Now, however, our population in most of the maritime districts and in some parts of the interior also, seems too thick—there are too many mouths to consume what the hands can find business to do; and that hitherto sure refuge of the industrious foreign emigrant, the western country, is overstocked by the domestic emigration. Certainly, the present system cannot last long, and the time *must* come when home industry will be encouraged and protected, in all its branches. If this were the case, all would be busy, money would circulate freely, and happiness abound.

It appears that a good many persons who recently arrived from England, being disappointed in their prospects of employment, are on their return home. We have thought that some such were occasionally re-shipped, under sanction and perhaps at the cost of the British government, that they might check emigration. But this cannot be suspected now. The poor people are truly alarmed at the prostration of things presented to them, and will rather depend upon the resources they have been accustomed to, than suffer poverty in a land of strangers. Still those who have a little money, may certainly do better with it here than at home.

It is reported, that to relieve themselves of the support of their paupers, many such will be sent to the United States by the church-wardens, etc., of England! It will therefore become the state authorities to be careful to take the proper securities[1] of those who bring passengers, that they will not become chargeable on the public.

When we consider that the passengers arriving at many small ports are not reported at all, and the moral certainty that we have overlooked some who were reported even in the newspapers received at our office, it may be fairly presumed that the real number of those who arrive cannot be less than *four thousand*, for these two weeks; and from what we have learnt, it is also probable that 1,000 more may have

[1] [For material dealing with the regulations regarding the admission of aliens see the first volume of this series, E. Abbott, *Immigration: Select Documents and Case Records*, Part II.]

passed into our country from *Canada,* in the course of the last month. We observe that the Canadian papers are very zealous to prevent it— and hear of many proceeding to the western states.

TABLE SHOWING THE AMOUNT OF EMIGRANTS FROM EUROPE (AS REPORTED IN THE NEWSPAPERS) WHO REACHED THE UNITED STATES FOR TWO WEEKS, ENDING ON FRIDAY THE 3RD OF SEPT. 1819.*

| | | | |
|---|---|---|---|
| Liverpool | 813 | Londonderry | 55 |
| Halifax, St. Johns, etc. | 889 | Galway | 33 |
| Hull | 90 | Belfast | 279 |
| London | 237 | Waterford | 200 |
| Bristol | 100 | Cork | 163 |
| Weymouth | 119 | Limerick | 38 |
| Guernsey | 38 | Greenock | 60 |
| Havre (chiefly Eng.) | 174 | Amsterdam | 370 |
| Total | | | 3,658 |

*[The data for the separate weeks are given in the original but are omitted here.]

The returns for the last two weeks would probably have shown an amount of about 1,500 per week—568 arrived at Philadelphia in one day on Sunday last; many of whom were in one vessel from Antwerp.

The *New York Gazette* says:

We know a gentleman who has made a calculation, grounded upon the emigration of the present year, showing that in the course of five years, the number of emigrants to this country will amount to *half a million.* New York is calculated to receive one-sixth of the number, as it has done for the last year. The numerous emigrations, via the Canadas and Nova Scotia, are not taken into this calculation. This is a serious subject, and will naturally excite the attention of government.

This calculation, we apprehend, is much exaggerated. It must be recollected, that very few emigrants arrive before the month of May, and less after that of September. Admit that in the whole of these five months the rate should continue at 2,000 per week, the amount would be only 40,000 per annum. And this, we feel satisfied, is a greater number than ever arrived in the United States in any one year, even in or for the present, though the emigration has been so very heavy. But how it should "naturally excite the attention of government" we cannot tell, unless the *British* government is meant.

## 10. "The Spirit of Our Government as It Relates to Foreigners"[1]

No government was ever more benevolent or liberal to foreigners than that of the United States. It has holden out to them the greatest encouragements; nor has it disappointed their expectations. When arrived in this country, they have been fostered and cherished with the greatest care, and sympathy for their lonesome and exiled condition. They have been taken by the hand, not only by our citizens, but by the government itself. They have not only been aided in business, but have been made citizens, and honored with the public confidence, by appointments to offices under the government.

The object of our people and of the government itself, in this matter, has doubtless first been to promote emigrations from Europe. The first settlers in this country, while it was yet a mighty wilderness, considered themselves as in a kind of voluntary exile.

They seemed for a long time to want nothing so much as inhabitants. Even after they had grown so numerous as to feel no fear of the savages, still there was an almost boundless continent before them. They felt the want of people on all accounts; to clear off the woods; to cultivate the lands; to carry on the manual arts; to promote the liberal sciences; and, in short, for all the grand objects of peace and war.

To them, nothing was so desirable as the arrival of new settlers. They solicited emigrations, and received and caressed strangers from all nations with the utmost warmth and sincerity.

This disposition becoming habitual and universal, it descended from father to son, and lost nothing even by that revolution, which severed us from Great Britain, and made us an independent nation. When the present federal government was formed, it could not but savor of those notions of government, which were co-extensive with the Anglo-Americans, and had been coeval with their first settlement in this country. An immense country; few people; a territory, but the margin of which was as yet settled; universal liberty, both civil and religious; freedom of thought and speech; great sincerity of mind and simplicity of manners; respect for, and confidence in, strangers coming to live among us, were objects whose influence predominated in the minds of all classes, not excepting those, who formed our state constitutions.

[1] Extract from Samuel Whelpley, *A Compend of History from the Earliest Times; Comprehending a General View of the Present State of the World* (8th ed.; Boston, 1825), two volumes in one; II, 199–205.

To increase the population of our extensive territories, provision was made·for the encouragement of emigration. The warm benevolence of individuals prompted them to institute societies for the aid of emigrants, and legal provision was made, that, in a short time, and with little trouble, they might become our fellow-citizens, and partake of all the privileges and immunities of our country. Nor did our zeal to promote the cause of foreigners stop here. Several of them, in various parts, were promoted to offices of considerable trust and importance, and were allowed to share largely in the honors, powers, and emoluments of government.

The people of the United States, in their favor to foreigners, were prompted by purer motives than those of a selfish nature. Although they saw their interest in an increase of population, yet humanity itself, and that of the most generous and elevated nature, had much influence on this business. They wished their country might be an asylum for the poor and oppressed from all nations. It was their ambition to give strangers, who wanted a country and a home, so welcome a reception, and afford them such privileges as to efface from their memories the days of their affliction and distress, or to cause them to be remembered, only to heighten the contrast of their present good fortune and felicity. Many an unhappy exile can, with great propriety, say, *I was a stranger, and ye took me in.*

It is not unlikely, however, that the future historian will be compelled to say, that our government, in relation to foreigners, erred through excess of benevolence and urbanity. In general, the incentives to emigration were both needless and unsafe. From the natural progress of population, our increase was great, almost without a parallel. Far distant from the desolating wars of Europe, our fathers dwelt in the bosom of peace and plenty, and under the smiles of Providence had yearly accessions of strength, more to be relied on than mercenary armies, or any description of foreign emigrants.

The rapid increase of any nation, by means of an influx of foreigners, is dangerous to the repose of that nation; especially if the number of emigrants bears any considerable proportion to the old inhabitants. Even if that proportion is very small, the tendency of the thing is injurious, unless the newcomers are more civilized and more virtuous, and have at the same time, the same ideas and feeling about government. But if they are more vicious, they will corrupt; if less industrious, they will promote idleness; if they have different ideas of government, they will contend; if the same, they will intrigue and interfere.

The people brought up in the bosom of the British kingdoms, are essentially different from us, both in their views and feelings about government. Though they may use the same words that we use; though they express the same abhorrence of tyranny and oppression, yet liberty, considered as a creature of the mind, is with them a different thing, from what it is with us. It is no difficult matter to account for the licentious views of liberty, and the romantic ideas of the freedom of this country, entertained by the lower classes of Europeans. From their infancy, they have associated with government and law the idea of tyranny and injustice, and with liberty, a state of society as unrestrained, as a state of nature. When they come into this country, and find law and government of a sterner cast, than they had figured to themselves, they soon grow discontented and seek for a revolution.

The history of Rome furnishes a striking instance of the deplorable effects of an influx of strangers into a country. After the Romans had conquered Carthage, Greece, Asia, and Gaul, Italy presently was filled with enterprising emigrants from all quarters. Though they came, as it were, singly, and as humble suppliants, yet they in effect conquered their conquerors. They inundated all Italy. The majesty of the ancient Romans was obscured, overwhelmed, and utterly lost in an innumerable swarm of foreigners. The evil came on by slow and imperceptible degrees; but was at last irresistible and fatal. These were the persons generally employed in the civil wars. A multitude made up of such people is always fickle, inflammatory, outrageous, vindicative, and burning with ambition to level all distinctions.

It is not a common case that the most valuable members of society emigrate. . . . . Though many worthy characters are found in so great an emigration as has been to this country, yet, for the most part, they are poor, distressed, overwhelmed with calamities, discontented, oppressed by the tyranny of their government sometimes, but more commonly by their own vices or imprudence. . . . . .

As, in our form of government, the right of suffrage is among the most important of civil rights, it should be preserved inviolate; but it should be guarded with the severest caution. Foreigners, who arrive in this country, seldom come with an expectation of becoming legislators here. Their confidence in our government probably brought them hither, where they ought not to hope for more than complete security of life, liberty, and property. More than such security would, in the end, work injury to themselves. . . . . .

Every foreigner, soon after his arrival in our country, by a course neither circuitous, expensive, nor long, becomes a citizen in the fullest sense. He is one of the sovereign people of this country—is an elector, and eligible to many offices. He immediately becomes a politician—is profound in the science of government—is able to set all things right. From his cradle, his ideas of law and government have been closely associated with the most direful images of fear, terror and resentment; and he views liberty as some wild, enchanting mountain-nymph, roving through fields spread wide and adorned with flowers. With these views of law and liberty, he sets himself indefatigably at work, to mend the course of things. He declaims against oppression, flames with zeal for liberty, and seldom fails to be at the head or tail of innovation and reform, perhaps of insurrection.

It is worthy of remark, that emigrants from Europe are from a more advanced state of society, than is generally found in this country; or, at least, an older state. It thence happens that many of them, even of the lowest grade, have a certain knowledge of mankind, the necessary result of mingling with an immense mass of population. This knowledge, indeed, is chiefly made up of vanity and vice; but it helps them to great volubility of tongue, smartness of reply, and a seeming knowledge of things, which, handed out on all occasions, readily sets many people to staring at them as something extraordinary. For this very reason, many of them vulgarly pass for people of great information, especially in the circulating politics of the day. Of course they are pushed forward into offices of considerable responsibility.

The republic of Athens guarded the avenues to citizenship with great strictness. With them, foreigners could only become citizens in their great grandchildren. Their policy, in this respect, seemed not only safe, but necessary. Their state was so small that could foreigners have gained admittance, they would soon have outnumbered them. It is as dangerous to be outwitted, as outnumbered; and it would be the true policy of the United States to admit no foreigner ever to the right of suffrage. No person should hereafter become a citizen, but by being born within the United States.

Far be it that this rule should extend to the disfranchising of such as have by any means already obtained citizenship. Many of them came among us when their arrival was fortunate for us, and it should certainly prove so to them. Their presence gave countenance, and their assistance, strength. But those days are past; and a similar request will never return.

Let foreigners find in this country an asylum of rest, an escape from oppression. Here let them buy, and build, and plant; let them spread and flourish, pursuing interest and happiness in every mode of life which enterprise can suggest, or reason justify; but let them be exonerated from the toils of government. We do not need their hands to steady the ark. If we make good laws, they will share the benefit; if bad ones, the blame will not be theirs. Let their children, born among us, become citizens by birthright. . . . .

In spite of the most flattering hopes, considering the various means by which the number of citizens is daily and rapidly increased, it must be allowed to be possible, that the people of this country will grow far more corrupt. They certainly have the common inducements and temptations to that end. If ever the people of any country were corrupted by an influx of foreigners of different habits, manners, and customs, we are in danger.

### 11. Immigrants Welcomed in Western Pennsylvania[1]

*To All Those Who May Be Desirous of Emigrating to the Western Country:*

A number of the inhabitants of western Pennsylvania, many of them formerly from different parts of Europe, the New England states, the states of New York and New Jersey, and the eastern counties of this state, having taken into consideration the embarrassments and difficulties to which emigrants are too often exposed for want of proper advice and assistance, have formed themselves into an association, under the name of the "Western Pennsylvania Emigrant Society."

The object of the society is to furnish to emigrants all the information and assistance in its power, in procuring employment for them, locating them to the best advantage, according to their different situations, trades or occupations, in aiding them to make a judicious choice of the lands they may wish to purchase; in procuring these for them on the most advantageous terms; and in rendering them all such services in establishing themselves, that they may need. Believing that the inducements this country holds out to emigrants only require to be known, to be duly appreciated, the society have appointed a committee of correspondence, to make you acquainted with this portion of the United States and its advantages, natural and artificial, and to point out a few of the errors into which emigrants, particularly those from Europe, are liable to fall, on their arrival in this country.

The United States of America possess advantages which are not

[1] Extract from Hazard, *Register of Pennsylvania*, I (1828), 24–26.

to be found in Europe, nor in any other quarter of the globe. Enjoying an almost total exemption from taxation, the whole earnings of the inhabitants ensure to their own use, and every emigrant who settles here can by industry and economy not only provide amply for the wants and comforts of himself and family, but render himself independent, provided he is careful in the first instance in choosing a proper situation.

It is an error into which emigrants too frequently fall, to settle in the large cities on the coast, or in the thickly settled country in their vicinity, where property is high and competition great, instead of moving directly to the west, where an excess of lands, and a less abundant population create a greater demand for labour; and where in the course of a few years' industry, he may become the independent proprietor of property sufficient for the wants and comfort of himself and family. . . . .

Such are the inducements which this country presents to emigrants in general. To Irishmen it holds out an additional one, which must be dear to them on their arrival in a strange land.

This country is already in part settled by emigrants from Ireland, and the Irishman, on his arrival here, will find countrymen from every county of his native land, who with their characteristic hospitality, stand ready to welcome him, and to use their best endeavours to promote his views and secure his interests in this happy country.

To emigrants from other parts of Europe and the different sections of the United States, it may be remarked, that they too will meet with friends and acquaintances who will not be behind-hand in the offices of kindness and hospitality. The Germans in particular are informed that there is a large and respectable body of their countrymen already settled in this country, which is receiving almost daily accessions.

## 12. "Immigrants the Dupes of Demagogues"[1]

[This subject] is a delicate one, but of far too vital importance to the happiness of the American people to be passed over. *It is believed that the annual increase of foreign voters already exceeds that of the native Americans.* If this be true, it will not be long before the affairs of our country are managed by European subjects. A result more appalling

[1] Extract from "Emigration of Foreigners," *The Western Monthly Magazine* (edited by Joseph Reese Fry), V (Cincinnati, 1836), 743–48. The first part of this document up to heading "Emigration," is a preliminary comment by the editor of the magazine.

to every lover of his country cannot be imagined. Already the Congress of the United States has appointed a committee of investigation upon the subject. The people of New York, who are more directly and extensively in contact with the evil, have long regarded the influx of foreign paupers and convicts, who vote almost as soon as they set their foot upon our shores, as a national calamity of frightful and increasing magnitude. They have done what the whole country will soon be compelled in self-defense to do—formed an American party. In many parts of our country the elections are controlled by foreigners, and the native voters are thrust from the polls by those who know nothing of our institutions, who feel no attachment to our soil, but who have been surrounded, from childhood, with anti-American, European associations, which at best have left their political opinions, if they have any, so confused and licentious as to place them, even when honestly disposed, entirely at the mercy of those unprincipled demagogues, foreign and domestic, who abound in every village and hamlet of our country. This enormous mass of ignorant foreign mind and muscle, which is not animated by the American spirit, but which possesses such power over American affairs that we hardly dare lift up our feeble voice against it, is the soil whereon demagogues fatten; these demagogues themselves are in many instances aliens upon our soil, and in all cases enemies of our country. They know that the balance of electoral power is already in foreign hands, and it is in their interest to wield that balance to serve their own private purposes. For this purpose they lie to the honest German. They declaim to the mercurial and lawless Irishman. They prate of the rights of man to the revolutionary Frenchman, and of equality of property to the radical Englishman. They deny them the means of forming an independent opinion. They deny them the truth. They keep them in ignorance of our true policy, of our history, and even of our language. They withhold from them the right of examining any political opinion or assertion for themselves, and study to keep them excluded from all communica- tion with those who might enlighten them; with thousands of such bad men to act upon them, how could the poor aliens vote intelligently? Of what advantage to them is liberty to control the destinies of a people to whom they owe that liberty? How can they know better than we what governors and what laws we require? The present system of admitting recently imported aliens indiscriminately to the full electoral power and to equal privileges in all respects with the Ameri- can-born citizen, and that without inquiry or reservation, is about to be the corruption and downfall of our infant republic. Aliens ought here to have an asylum and even to hold property, but they ought never to vote if they arrive in the country after their habits are entirely formed. They can never become Americans—they can never know what Americans know, or feel as Americans feel. They will always be the dupes of demagogues. It is impossible to prevent it. It may truly be said that every demagogue is an enemy of his country. The demagogue is the only enemy we have cause to fear. We could shake off the united armies of the world from our shores. War, pestilence, famine, we could recover from by our natural energies. But the demagogue makes it his study to poison the very sources of our life. He attacks the most vital and essential defenses of our national existence. By this we mean that the business of his life consists in diffusing falsehood, prejudice, and ill blood among the simple yeomanry of the country. . . . .

Of the wickedness of deceiving the people for party ends we cannot speak too strongly. Base and ignoble as it is, it is at this moment the business and profession of thousands. Men of all parties are equally guilty of it, and the ignorance of the poor aliens who are the subjects of it makes it an easy task, requiring no talent whatever, unless a false heart and a traitor's tongue be a talent. Vast numbers of these alien voters can neither speak nor understand our language. Vast numbers of them are paupers gladly rejected by their native countries and thrown recklessly upon our shores. Not a few of them are convicts and refugees from justice, all these, without discrimination, are permitted to exercise the same portion of American sovereignty as the native-born citizen. Upon matters most deeply affecting the welfare of our country and requiring an accurate knowledge of our affairs, the question is frequently decided for us by their votes. Numerous cases have occurred, in New York and other places, when the honest and intelligent American has been bullied away from the polls by their riotous conduct, and foreign laborers collected in large numbers upon our public works have frequently put all authority at defiance by violent and bloody tumults, thus setting a most pernicious example to our own countrymen.

We do not deny that the alien should find an asylum in our country, but we deny that he ought to claim the right of regulating our affairs. We would not wish to deprive him of the right of holding property, or withhold from him the equal protection of our laws. We are willing he should enjoy every right but that of government. At least if it be necessary to throw our affairs into his hands, let him be prepared, by a long residence among us, to think and feel like an American. . . . .

## EMIGRATION

What are the advantages attendant upon encouragement of immigration? They are (1) an increase of population, (2) improvement in the arts and manufactures, (3) an increase of the capital and wealth of a country, by the introduction of laborers, and (4) it has been sometimes urged, an improvement in literature and science; though when we reflect how rare it is for men of science and literature to immigrate from old and wealthy countries, where these can be best appreciated and supported, I think we shall be inclined to give little weight to the fourth advantage. I propose to take up these different reasons for free immigration in their order, and weigh their advantages against the disadvantages, to see which preponderates.

First, then, free immigration serves to increase population; but in order to prove this advantageous, we must find (1) that we are in need of population; and (2) that this scheme introduces such a population as we want. Are we in need of population? Population is necessary first to defend a country, second to till the soil, and bring forth its resources. For the first purpose we are fully competent without the aid of foreigners; and for the second purpose it seems to me that the inhabitants of a country, if they are able to defend it, will be able likewise to bring forth its resources as fast as they can be needed; and any faster production would be rather an injury than benefit, as it would introduce surplus wealth, and with that wealth the minds of the people would be prepared to have the vices and immoralities of foreign and old countries, which these very immigrants would bring with them, grafted and fixed upon these characters, and we should thus exhibit a picture of a country which would be rotten, by means of contact with foreign decay, before it was ripe. Thus it seems to me that mere increase of population, beyond the natural increase of our own inhabitants, is no argument against restricting immigration. But supposing we were in need of inhabitants, would a system of free immigration give us such people as we wanted? Ignorance is the poison of a republic, and no citizens are really desirable save those who are well informed. Nothing but the strongest inducements could cause a man to leave the home of his childhood, and the country where are his friends and all that is dear and around whose scenes his fondest associations linger; and as long as he by any means could get bread there, he would not leave it, though superior advantages should be held out to him elsewhere. But if by idleness, or old age, or misconduct, poverty should seize upon him at home, it might break those ties of attachment to a country and he would be induced to seek a foreign land. But clearly these are not the people who are wanted; people of idle habits, infirm, and paupers.

There is also another class that would be induced to come. The lowest orders of the people who, from ignorance, poverty, and vice, have lost all particular regard for one country above another, who have, from education and association, been made to believe that those who are superior to them in fortune, or condition, were their natural enemies, against whom they must carry on an unceasing warfare of pilfering and pulling down,[1] such men as these in a republic are fire brands and arrows of death. Republics always tend strongly to radicalism—they always have their demagogues who excite the passions and prejudices of the ignorant, that they may be able to mislead them for their own advantage; and the great desideratum in a republic, its only safeguard, is to so educate the people as to enable them to avoid and reject the influence of these selfish partisans. What has been the character of immigrants for the last twenty years? From 1812 to 1821 inclusive, the number of immigrants to the United States from Ireland was 30,653; from England, 33,608; from Scotland, 4,727; and a large proportion are Irish, and since that time, this proportion has vastly increased. It is estimated that during the year 1830 there could not have been less than 25 or 30,000 Irish landed on the shores of the United States, and since that time, the number has constantly increased. The state of the elections in our large cities during the excitement of party, and the riots in various parts of the country of these poor ignorant creatures, speaks sufficiently loud and clear concerning their character, and shews that, unfit to govern themselves, they are unworthy of having any portion of the government of others intrusted to them.

The second great result claimed to be derived from free immigration is improvement in the arts and manufactures. This is undoubtedly true, and the only question is, Is it advantageous to a country?

Is not the manufacturing population of foreign lands worse than any other kind of population? And will not a people in the natural growth and development of their powers arrive soon enough, for their own advantage, at manufacturing and improvement in the arts, with-

[1] In making this classification, I of course wish to apply it as a general rule. There are individual exceptions of men who are induced to emigrate from the most honorable motives.

out encouraging this corrupt and corrupting mass of foreign immorality to come among them?

One man of bad moral character, no matter how ingenious he may be, will do more injury to a country than a thousand spinning jennies will do good. The state of the manufacturing population of Europe is such as to induce us to believe that the character of those who have been brought up in the midst of it must be bad—and yet these are the people who help to build up manufactures among us, and collect a mass of young and inexperienced people about them to receive bad influences and contamination.

Now if a manufacturing population is worse than any other, and if such is the character of those who serve to build up such a population among us, then the improvement in the arts and manufactures can certainly be no offset to these consequent deleterious influences.

The third great advantage is the increase of capital and wealth by the introduction of labor. Supposing, for the sake of argument, that, after deducting from the amount of labor performed and consequent capital introduced, the loss by pauperism and crime, there is a balance of real wealth and capital left to the country. Unless this wealth is well used, and unless the producers of it are otherwise good citizens, it can be of no service to a country; on the contrary it is a direct injury. Now it is clear to me that the majority of laborers and mechanics who emigrate to this country are not good citizens, and that their wealth is not well employed, and that for the reasons before mentioned.

### 13. Dangers of Immigration Suggested[1]

*To the Honorable the Senate and House of Representatives in Congress Assembled:*

GENTLEMEN: Considering the peculiar situation in which our country is now placed on account of the vast influx of foreign emigration; considering, too, the *character* of a very great majority of those who are landing upon our shores, settling in, and filling up, our States; and likewise the *bearing* which their increasing numbers and influence may have upon our Government; we, the undersigned petitioners, citizens of the United States, do humbly pray you to institute an *inquiry* which will afford a satisfactory solution to the following questions:

[1] *Memorial of 282 Citizens of Sutton and 325 Citizens of Milbury, in the State of Massachusetts, against Foreign Emigration, January 5, 1838* (United States Twenty-fifth Congress, second session, House Document No. 70).

1st. Whether there are not designs against the liberties of our country by means of this great influx of foreign emigration?

2d. Whether the *character* of many of the emigrants does not auger a vast increase of pauperism and of crime in our land?

3d. Whether there are not those now amongst us, who, by their oaths of allegiance to a foreign despotic Prince or Power, are solemnly bound to support his interests and accelerate his designs, so far as is practicable, notwithstanding their professed subjection to our laws and constitution to the contrary? And, if so, whether they have equal claims with dutiful subjects upon our Government, or are, in any measure, entitled to the confidence of our nation? And,

4th. Whether there is not a foreign *conspiracy* existing against the government of this great republic, and measures adopted, and plans now in operation, for its execution?

We earnestly and respectfully entreat you, honored gentlemen, to adopt measures that shall lead to a faithful investigation of the foregoing inquiries, and act as shall be for the benefit of our nation, the preservation of our laws, and the perpetuity of the independence of the United States of America.

So pray, as in duty bound, your humble petitioners.

### 14. A Sympathetic View of the Irish Immigrant[1]

Let us by no means join in the popular outcry against foreigners coming to our country, and partaking of its privileges. They will come, whether we will or no; and is it wise to meet them with inhospitality, and thus turn their hearts against us? Let us rather receive them as friends, and give them welcome to our country. Let us rather say, "The harvest before us is indeed great, and the laborers are few: come, go with us, and we will do thee good." Our hills, and valleys, and rivers, stretch from ocean to ocean, belting the entire continent of the New World; and over this rich and boundless domain, Providence has poured the atmosphere of liberty. Let these poor sufferers come and breathe it freely. Let our country be the asylum of the oppressed of all lands. Let those who come bent down with the weight of European tithes and taxation, here throw off the load, and stand erect in freedom. Let those who have dwelt in the chill shadows of the Castle of Ignorance, erected by kings, and fortified by priestcraft, come here, and be warmed by the free sunlight of knowledge. Let those whose

[1] An extract from Samuel Griswold Goodrich (Peter Parley), *Ireland and the Irish* (Boston, 1841), pp. 111–17. This article originally appeared in the *Token*.

limbs have been cramped by chains, those whose minds have been fettered by hereditary error, come here, and, seeing happiness, be permitted freely to pursue it.

Let us at least extend the hand of encouragement and sympathy to the Irish. Their story for centuries is but a record of sorrows and oppressions. They have been made to feel, not only how cruel, but how universal, are the miseries which follow a bad government; for government is as pervading in its influence as the air we breathe. In civilized society, we must eat and drink, and wear, and have shelter, and hold intercourse with our fellow-men; and government will come through bolted doors and grated windows, and reach us through these interests. The tyrant will come in and visit us at our homes, dimming the very light of our firesides. Not only do we feel his taxes, and find our industry cursed, but the minds of our children are perhaps injured —degraded or contaminated—by the vices which injustice and evil example, from high stations, inculcate upon society. And from these miseries there is no escape but death. No condition can shield a man from mischiefs so injurious and so pervading. As well might the air become contagious, and the springs and rivers be tainted, as bad government become established over a nation. Yet poor Ireland has been subject to such a condition for ages; and even if her children leave their native soil, they are obliged to carry with them the bitter memory of their country's wrongs. A people of quick and ardent sympathies, of a poetical and romantic love of country, they are, in exile ever looking back to the Emerald Isle, with mingled sorrow and sickness of heart. How heavy is the burden which such bosoms must bear as they wander over distant lands, in the bitter consciousness that their country is the desponding victim of oppression! Shall not those who come to our shores afflicted with such sorrows, find in the friends and sharers of freedom, both welcome and release? And let us beware of adding to their wrongs. Let us remember that there is other tyranny than that of chains and fetters—the invisible but cruel tyranny of opinion and prejudice. Let us beware how we exercise this towards the Irish; for it is wicked in itself, and doubly mischievous in its tendency. It injures both its subject and its object, and brings no counterbalancing good.

Let us be especially guarded against two sources of prejudice, to which we are peculiarly liable. In the first place, in our personal experience, we are familiar with the most ignorant and unfortunate of the Irish nation. We see, in servile employments, those who have been exposed to all the debasing influences that degrade mankind. Is it fair to draw from these a standard by which to judge the whole people? Let us rather ask ourselves where there is another nation, who have been so long trampled down by oppression; who have been born in poverty and nursed in adversity; who have inherited little from the past but sorrow, and can bequeath nothing to the future but hope— where is there a people so wronged, that has yet preserved so many virtues? How gallantly, indeed, do Irish wit, and cheerfulness, and hospitality, and patriotism, ride on the wreck of individual hopes, and sparkle through the very waves of adversity!

Let us beware of prejudice from another source. We read English books, papers, and pamphlets. We read them under the inspiring influence of Britain's great name. Say what we may of that country, the British empire is a mighty power, and her literature is even more potent than her armies and her navies. It is by this she casts a spell over the world, and binds the nations in moral fetters. We see in the English people nearly the same exclusive love of country that burned in the bosom of the ancient Roman. This spirit animates every offspring of the English press. It is this which leads them to vindicate the tyranny of the government in Ireland, by portraying the Irish as an untamable race, deaf to reason, and only to be ruled by the harsh inflictions of power. Let us, Americans, see that our minds are not driven from the moorings of justice, by this sinister current in which they are placed. Influenced by such considerations as these, let us by all fair means bring about a good understanding between the Irish emigrants and society. Let us deal gently with them, even with their errors; and thus we shall win their confidence; thus they may be persuaded to take counsel of the good, the wise, and the virtuous, and not throw themselves into the arms of those who flatter their vices and minister to their passions, but to use and abuse them.

Let this reasonable and just policy mark our conduct towards the grown-up Irish among us; and in regard to their children, let us individually and collectively use our best endeavors to bestow upon them the benefits of education. But let us remember that even an attempt to educate the Irish will fail, if it be not founded in a recognition of the elements of their national character, quick perception, a keen sense of justice, and ready resentment of wrong. If over these, prejudice, suspicion, and pride, have thrown their shadows, let us adapt the instruction we would offer to the light they can bear. In this way, a numerous people may be redeemed from misery to happiness, and rendered a blessing instead of a curse to our country. Let us deal thus with those Irish who have left their native land to find a dwelling among us; and in regard to the millions that remain at home, in the "green and weeping island," let us hope for the speedy dawn of a brighter and better day. A youthful queen now sways the sceptre of Britain; and what may not humanity hope from the generosity of *youth* and the heavenly charity of *woman?*

### 15. A Congressman's View of Naturalization, 1842[1]

Mr. Walker—It is true, the time for the naturalization of foreigners was afterwards very much elongated by the celebrated alien law. It was extended by that law to the period of fourteen years; and was afterwards reduced, step by step, by various enactments, until it was brought down to five years. I am for coming back to the period assigned by the first law. And why should we not? The number of aliens in this country, according to the census returns of 1830, was, at that time, 107,832. There was no call for a return of the number of aliens in the census of 1840; but if the number has increased in proportion to the tables of emigration, there will be 283,543. Now, I entirely object to having so large a number of aliens amongst the population of this country—particularly as I do not believe they desire to be aliens. They came here with the bona fide intention of becoming citizens—of making this their adopted country, in war and peace. The most, if not all of them, came here with the intention of entering upon and cultivating our soil, and developing the resources of the country; with the intention of making for themselves and families a permanent home, of amalgamating their interests with our interests, and of defending and sustaining our free institutions. Why, then, should they be debarred from the rights of citizenship? . . . .

Every steamboat that goes to the West is crowded with emigrants, who go there for the purpose of purchasing lands, and of placing their families there. The exclusion of these people from citizenship has been so severely felt, that two of the Western States have given them the

[1] Extract from the debate (August 4, 1842), on a bill to reduce the term of residence required by law for naturalization from five to two years. Mr. Walker (Robert J. Walker, of Mississippi) said he was merely reviving the original act which had had Washington's sanction. *Congressional Globe*, Twenty-seventh Congress, second session, p. 817.

For a convenient account of the early naturalization laws, see Frank George Franklin, *The Legislative History of Naturalization in the United States* (University of Chicago Press, 1906).

right to vote. This is an anomalous state of things; and it has been brought about by changing the state of the law from two to five years. There is no reason why they should not become citizens at the end of two years, as well as at the end of five.

The founders and the framers of the Government and the Constitution of the country thought with me, and I am desirous of restoring that state of the law which was established by them. But there is another consideration which makes it desirable that such a bill as this should be passed; and that is, in case of war you would have 300,000 aliens within the limits of your territory, and most of them residing along your Western frontier, who, if not naturalized, will undoubtedly be claimed by some foreign power. In case of war, it would be particularly proper that their number should be diminished; and this will be accomplished by the measure which I now propose.

I am rejoiced to see the immense numbers of foreigners that are landing upon the shores of our happy soil. I hold out to them the hand of welcome. Do we not see the efforts that are being made to divert emigration from this country to the British Provinces and to Australia? They are told that, by going to a British colony, they will at once be entitled to the privilege of citizenship; whereas, if they come here, they are subjected to a deprivation of those privileges for a period of five years. I wish to see them come, and become citizens; and populate our fertile and extensive regions in the West, that our institutions may be carried to the very shores of the Pacific.

Mr. Archer desired the honorable gentleman to be assured that . . . . he was totally adverse to the admission of foreigners, upon other terms than now existed, to a participation in the rights and privileges of citizenship. The reason which existed at the time of the formation of the Government for limiting the period of exclusion to two years only, did not apply in the present state of the country. The argument of the honorable gentleman in relation to the law which was passed at that period by our ancestors, was disproved by himself; for, according to his own showing, they very soon departed from it, and fixed fourteen years as the period of residence required before a foreigner could be naturalized, but finding that was too long, they came back to the intermediate term of five years, which he (Mr. A.) considered the proper, just, and reasonable time. The honorable gentleman had railed against his opposition to the introduction of this bill, as if he was desirous of repelling foreigners. He (Mr. A.) certainly did not desire that, upon their arrival in this country, they should at once be entitled to all the privileges of citizens; but he would not prevent them from acquiring property, and preparing themselves for the enjoyment of those political rights and privileges which belong to the citizens of this country. He did not believe that any good man ever entirely renounced his attachment to the soil upon which he was born. Would it, then, be proper, in any sense, to admit at once a large class of persons, having foreign attachments and feelings adverse to ours?

### 16. The "Native American" Declaration of Principles, 1845[1]

We, the Delegates elect to the first National Convention of the Native American body of the United States of America, assembled at Philadelphia, on the 4th of July, A.D. 1845, for the purpose of devising a plan of concerted political action in defence of American institutions against the encroachments of foreign influence, open or concealed, hereby solemnly, and before Almighty God, make known to our fellow citizens, our country, and the world, the following incontrovertible facts, and the course of conduct consequent thereon, to which, in duty to the cause of human rights and the claims of our beloved country, we mutually pledge our lives, our fortunes, and our sacred honour.

The danger of foreign influence, threatening the gradual destruction of our national institutions, failed not to arrest the attention of the Father of his Country, in the very dawn of American Liberty. Not only its direct agency in rendering the American system liable to the poisonous influence of European policy—a policy at war with the fundamental principles of the American Constitution—but also its still more fatal operation in aggravating the virulence of partisan warfare —has awakened deep alarm in the mind of every intelligent patriot, from the days of Washington to the present time.

The influx of a foreign population, permitted after little more than a nominal residence, to participate in the legislation of the country and the sacred right of suffrage, produced comparatively little evil during the earlier years of the Republic; for that influx was then limited by the considerable expenses of a transatlantic voyage, by the existence of many wholesome restraints upon the acquisition of political prerogatives, by the constant exhaustion of the European population in long and bloody continental wars, and by the slender inducements offered for emigration to a young and sparsely peopled country, con-

---

[1] Extract from *Address of the Delegates of the Native American National Convention, Assembled at Philadelphia, July 4th, 1845, to the Citizens of the United States,* pp. 2–9.

tending for existence with a boundless wilderness, inhabited by savage men. Evils which are only prospective rarely attract the notice of the masses, and until peculiar changes in the political condition of Europe, the increased facilities for transportation, and the madness of partisan legislation in removing all effective guards against the open prostitution of the right of citizenship had converted the slender current of naturalization into a torrent threatening to overwhelm the influence of the natives of the land, the far-seeing vision of the statesman, only, being fixed upon the distant, but steadily approaching, cloud.

But, since the barriers against the improper extension of the right of suffrage were bodily broken down, for a partisan purpose, by the Congress of 1825, the rapidly increasing numbers and unblushing insolence of the foreign population of the worst classes have caused the general agitation of the question, "How shall the institutions of the country be preserved from the blight of foreign influence, insanely legalized through the conflicts of domestic parties?" Associations under different names have been formed by our fellow citizens, in many States of this confederation, from Louisiana to Maine, all designed to check this imminent danger before it becomes irremediable, and, at length, a National Convention of the great American people, born upon the soil of Washington, has assembled to digest and announce a plan of operation, by which the grievances of an abused hospitality, and the consequent degradation of political morals, may be redressed, and the tottering columns of the temple of Republican Liberty secured upon the sure foundation of an enlightened nationality.

In calling for support upon every American who loves his country pre-eminently, and every adopted citizen of moral and intellectual worth who would secure, to his compatriots yet to come amongst us, the blessings of political protection, the safety of person and property, it is right that we should make known the grievances which we propose to redress, and the manner in which we shall endeavour to effect our object.

It is an incontrovertible truth that the civil institutions of the United States of America have been seriously affected, and that they now stand in imminent peril from the rapid and enormous increase of the body of residents of foreign birth, imbued with foreign feelings, and of an ignorant and immoral character, who receive, under the present lax and unreasonable laws of naturalization, the elective franchise and the right of eligibility to political office.

The whole body of foreign citizens, invited to our shores under a constitutional provision adapted to other times and other political conditions of the world, and of our country especially, has been endowed by American hospitality with gratuitous privileges unnecessary to the enjoyment of those inalienable rights of man—life, liberty, and the pursuit of happiness—privileges wisely reserved to the Natives of the soil by the governments of all other civilized nations. But, familiarized by habit with the exercise of these indulgences, and emboldened by increasing numbers, a vast majority of those who constitute this foreign body, now claim as an original right that which has been so incautiously granted as a favour—thus attempting to render inevitable the prospective action of laws adopted upon a principle of mere expediency, made variable at the will of Congress by the express terms of the Constitution, and heretofore repeatedly revised to meet the exigencies of the times.

In former years, this body was recruited chiefly from the victims of political oppression, or the active and intelligent mercantile adventurers of other lands; and it then constituted a slender representation of the best classes of the foreign population well fitted to add strength to the state, and capable of being readily educated in the peculiarly American science of political self-government. Moreover, while welcoming the stranger of every condition, laws then wisely demanded of every foreign aspirant for political rights a certificate of practical good citizenship. Such a class of aliens were followed by no foreign demagogues—they were courted by no domestic demagogues; they were purchased by no parties—they were debauched by no emissaries of kings. A wall of fire separated them from such a baneful influence, erected by their intelligence, their knowledge, their virtue and love of freedom. But for the last twenty years the road to civil preferment and participation in the legislative and executive government of the land has been laid broadly open, alike to the ignorant, the vicious and the criminal; and a large proportion of the foreign body of citizens and voters now constitutes a representation of the worst and most degraded of the European population—victims of social oppression or personal vices, utterly divested, by ignorance or crime, of the moral and intellectual requisites for political self-government.

Thus tempted by the suicidal policy of these United States, and favoured by the facilities resulting from the modern improvements of navigation, numerous societies and corporate bodies in foreign countries have found it economical to transport to our shores, at public and private expense, the feeble, the imbecile, the idle, and intractable, thus relieving themselves of the burdens resulting from the vices of the European social systems by availing themselves of the generous errors of our own.

The almshouses of Europe are emptied upon our coast, and this by our own invitation—not casually, or to a trivial extent, but systematically, and upon a constantly increasing scale. The Bedlams of the old world have contributed their share to the torrent of immigration, and the lives of our citizens have been attempted in the streets of our capital cities by mad-men, just liberated from European hospitals upon the express condition that they should be transported to America. By the orders of European governments, the punishment of crimes has been commuted for banishment to the land of the free; and criminals in iron have crossed the ocean to be cast loose upon society on their arrival upon our shores. The United States are rapidly becoming the lazar house and penal colony of Europe; nor can we reasonably censure such proceedings. They are legitimate consequences of our own unlimited benevolence; and it is of such material that we profess to manufacture free and enlightened citizens, by a process occupying five short years at most, but practically oftentimes embraced in a much shorter period of time.

The mass of foreign voters, formerly lost among the Natives of the soil, has increased from the ratio of 1 in 40 to that of 1 in 7! a like advance in fifteen years will leave the Native citizens a minority in their own land! Thirty years ago these strangers came by units and tens—now they swarm by thousands.[1] Formerly, most of them sought only for an honest livelihood and a provision for their families, and rarely meddled with the institutions, of which it was impossible they could comprehend the nature; now each newcomer seeks political preferment, and struggles to fasten on the public purse with an avidity, in strict proportion to his ignorance and unworthiness of public trust —having been sent for the purpose of obtaining political ascendancy in the government of the nation; having been sent to exalt their allies to power; having been sent to work a revolution from republican freedom to the divine rights of monarchs.

From these unhappy circumstances has arisen an *Imperium in Imperio*—a body uninformed and vicious—foreign in feeling, prejudice, and manner, yet armed with a vast and often a controlling influence over the policy of a nation, whose benevolence it abuses, and whose

[1] It is estimated that 300,000 will arrive within the present year.

kindness it habitually insults; a body as dangerous to the rights of the intelligent foreigner as to the prospect of its own immediate progeny, as it is threatening to the liberties of the country, and the hopes of rational freedom throughout the world; a body ever ready to complicate our foreign relations by embroiling us with the hereditary hates and feuds of other lands, and to disturb our domestic peace by its crude ideas, mistaking license for liberty, and the overthrow of individual rights for republican political equality; a body ever the ready tool of foreign and domestic demagogues, and steadily endeavouring by misrule to establish popular tyranny under a cloak of false democracy. Americans, false to their country, and led on to moral crime by the desire of dishonest gain, have scattered their agents over Europe, inducing the malcontent and the unthrifty to exchange a life of compulsory labour in foreign lands for relative comfort, to be maintained by the tax-paying industry of our overburdened and deeply indebted community. Not content with the usual and less objectionable licenses of trade, these fraudulent dealers habitually deceive a worthier class of victims, by false promises of employment, and assist in thronging the already crowded avenues of simple labour with a host of competitors, whose first acquaintance with American faith springs from a gross imposture, and whose first feeling on discovering the cheat is reasonable mistrust, if not implacable revenge. The importation of the physical necessities of life is burdened with imposts which many deem extravagant; but the importation of vice and idleness—of seditious citizens and factious rulers—is not only unrestricted by anything beyond a nominal tax, but is actually encouraged by a system which transforms the great patrimony of the nation, purchased by the blood of our fathers, into a source of bounty for the promotion of immigration.

Whenever an attempt is made to restrain this fatal evil, the native and adopted demagogues protest against an effort which threatens to deprive them of their most important tools; and such is the existing organization of our established political parties, that should either of them essay the reform of an abuse which both acknowledge to be fraught with ruin, that party sinks upon the instant into a minority, divested of control, and incapable of result.

From such causes has been derived a body, armed with political power, in a country of whose system it is ignorant, and for whose institutions it feels little interest, except for the purpose of personal advancement. . . . .

The body of adopted citizens, with foreign interests and prejudices, is annually advancing with rapid strides, in geometrical progression. Already it has acquired a control over our elections which cannot be entirely corrected, even by the wisest legislation, until the present generation shall be numbered with the past. Already it has notoriously swayed the course of national legislation, and invaded the purity of local justice. In a few years its unchecked progress would cause it to outnumber the native defenders of our rights, and would then inevitably dispossess our offspring, and its own, of the inheritance for which our fathers bled, or plunge this land of happiness and peace into the horrors of civil war.

The correction of these evils can never be effected by any combination governed by the tactics of other existing parties. If either of the old parties, as such, were to attempt an extension of the term of naturalization, it would be impossible for it to carry out the measure, because they would immediately be abandoned by the foreign voters. This great measure can be carried out only by an organization like our own, made up of those who have given up their former political preferences.

For these reasons, we recommend the immediate organization of the truly patriotic native citizens throughout the United States, for the purpose of resisting the progress of foreign influence in the conduct of American affairs, and the correction of such political abuses as have resulted from unguarded or partisan legislation on the subject of naturalization, so far as these abuses admit of remedy without encroachment upon the vested rights of foreigners who have been already legally adopted into the bosom of the nation.

### 17. An American Criticism of "Native Americans"[1]

The questions connected with emigration from Europe to America are interesting to both the old world and the new—are of importance to the present and future generations. They have more consequence than a charter or a state election; they involve the destinies of millions; they are connected with the progress of civilization, the rights of man, and providence of God!

I have examined this subject the more carefully, and speak upon it the more earnestly, because I have been to some extent, in former years, a partaker of the prejudices I have since learned to pity. A

[1] Extract from Thomas L. Nichols, *Lecture on Immigration and Right of Naturalization* (New York, 1845), pp. 3–4, 21, 24–32. See also above, Doc. 24, p. 517.

native of New England and a descendant of the puritans, I early imbibed, and to some extent promulgated, opinions of which reflection and experience have made me ashamed. . . . .

But while I would speak of the motives of men with charity, I claim the right to combat their opinions with earnestness. Believing that the principles and practices of Native Americanism are wrong in themselves, and are doing wrong to those who are the objects of their persecution, justice and humanity require that their fallacy should be exposed, and their iniquity condemned. It may be unfortunate that the cause of the oppressed and persecuted, in opinion if not in action, has not fallen into other hands; yet, let me trust that the truth, even in mine, will prove mighty, prevailing from its own inherent power!

The right of man to emigrate from one country to another, is one which belongs to him by his own constitution and by every principle of justice. It is one which no law can alter, and no authority destroy. "Life, liberty, and the pursuit of happiness" are set down, in our Declaration of Independence, as among the self-evident, unalienable rights of man. If I have a right to live, I have also a right to what will support existence—food, clothing, and shelter. If then the country in which I reside, from a superabundant population, or any other cause, does not afford me these, my right to go from it to some other is self-evident and unquestionable. The *right to live*, then, supposes the right of emigration. . . . .

I proceed, therefore, to show that the emigration of foreigners to this country is not only defensible on grounds of abstract justice— what we have no possible right to prevent, but that it has been in various ways highly beneficial to this country.

Emigration first peopled this hemisphere with civilized men. The first settlers of this continent had the same right to come here that belongs to the emigrant of yesterday—no better and no other. They came to improve their condition, to escape from oppression, to enjoy freedom—for the same, or similar, reasons as now prevail. And so far as they violated no private rights, so long as they obtained their lands by fair purchase, or took possession of those which were unclaimed and uncultivated, the highly respectable natives whom the first settlers found here had no right to make any objections. The peopling of this continent with civilized men, the cultivation of the earth, the various processes of productive labor, for the happiness of man, all tend to "the greatest good of the greatest number," and carry out the evident design of Nature or Providence in the formation of the earth and its inhabitants.

Emigration from various countries in Europe to America, producing a mixture of races, has had, and is still having, the most important influence upon the destinies of the human race. It is a principle, laid down by every physiologist, and proved by abundant observation, that man, like other animals, is improved and brought to its highest perfection by an intermingling of the blood and qualities of various races. That nations and families deteriorate from an opposite course has been observed in all ages. The great physiological reason why Americans are superior to other nations in freedom, intelligence, and enterprize, is because that they are the offspring of the greatest intermingling of races. The mingled blood of England has given her predominance over several nations of Europe in these very qualities, and a newer infusion, with favorable circumstances of climate, position, and institutions, has rendered Americans still superior. The Yankees of New England would never have shown those qualities for which they have been distinguished in war and peace throughout the world had there not been mingled with the puritan English, the calculating Scotch, the warm hearted Irish, the gay and chivalric French, the steady persevering Dutch, and the transcendental Germans, for all these nations contributed to make up the New England character, before the Revolution, and ever since to influence that of the whole American people.

It is not too much to assert that in the order of Providence this vast and fertile continent was reserved for this great destiny; to be the scene of this mingling of the finest European races, and consequently of the highest condition of human intelligence, freedom, and happiness; for I look upon this mixture of the blood and qualities of various nations, and its continual infusion, as absolutely requisite to the perfection of humanity. . . . . Continual emigration, and a constant mixing of the blood of different races, is highly conducive to physical and mental superiority.

This country has been continually benefited by the immense amount of capital brought hither by emigrants. There are very few who arrive upon our shores without some little store of wealth, the hoard of years of industry. Small as these means may be in each case, they amount to millions in the aggregate, and every dollar is so much added to the wealth of the country, to be reckoned at compound interest from the time of its arrival, nor are these sums like our

European loans, which we must pay back, both principal and interest. Within a few years, especially, and more or less at all periods, men of great wealth have been among the emigrants driven from Europe, by religious oppression or political revolutions. Vast sums have also fallen to emigrants and their descendants by inheritance, for every few days we read in the papers of some poor foreigner, or descendant of foreigners, as are we all, becoming the heir of a princely fortune, which in most cases, is added to the wealth of his adopted country. Besides this, capital naturally follows labor, and it flows upon this country in a constant current, by the laws of trade.

But it is not money alone that adds to the wealth of a country, but every day's productive labor is to be added to its accumulating capital. Every house built, every canal dug, every railroad graded, has added so much to the actual wealth of society; and who have built more houses, dug more canals, or graded more railroads, than the hardy Irishmen? I hardly know how our great national works could have been carried on without them—then; while every pair of sturdy arms has added to our national wealth, every hungry mouth has been a home market for our agriculture, and every broad shoulder has been clothed with our manufactures.

From the very nature of the case, America gets from Europe the most valuable of her population. Generally, those who come here are the very ones whom a sensible man would select. Those who are attached to monarchical and aristocratic institutions stay at home where they can enjoy them. Those who lack energy and enterprize can never make up their minds to leave their native land. It is the strong minded, the brave hearted, the free and self-respecting, the enterprizing and the intelligent, who break away from all the ties of country and of home, and brave the dangers of the ocean, in search of liberty and independence, for themselves and for their children, on a distant continent; and it is from this, among other causes, that the great mass of the people of this country are distinguished for the very qualities we should look for in emigrants. The same spirit which sent our fathers across the ocean impels us over the Alleghanies, to the valley of the Mississippi, and thence over the Rocky mountains into Oregon.

For what are we not indebted to foreign emigration, since we are all Europeans or their descendants? We cannot travel on one of our steamboats without remembering that Robert Fulton was the son of an Irishman. We cannot walk by St. Paul's churchyard without seeing the monuments which admiration and gratitude have erected to

Emmet, and Montgomery. Who of the thousands who every summer pass up and down our great thoroughfare, the North River, fails to catch at least a passing glimpse of the column erected to the memory of Kosciusko? I cannot forget that only last night a portion of our citizens celebrated with joyous festivities the birthday of the son of Irish emigrants, I mean the Hero of New Orleans!

Who speaks contemptuously of Alexander Hamilton as a foreigner, because he was born in one of the West India Islands? Who at this day will question the worth or patriotism of Albert Gallatin, because he first opened his eyes among the Alps of Switzerland—though, in fact, this was brought up and urged against him, when he was appointed special minister to Russia by James Madison. What New Yorker applies the epithet of "degraded foreigner" to the German immigrant, John Jacob Astor, a man who has spread his canvas on every sea, drawn to his adopted land the wealth of every clime, and given us, it may be, our best claim to vast territories!

Who would have banished the Frenchman, Stephen Girard, who, after accumulating vast wealth from foreign commerce, endowed with it magnificent institutions for education in his adopted land? So might I go on for hours, citing individual examples of benefits derived by this country from foreign immigration. . . . .

I have enumerated some of the advantages which such emigration has given to America. Let us now very carefully inquire, whether there is danger of any injury arising from these causes, at all proportionable to the palpable good.

"Our country is in danger," is the cry of Nativism. During my brief existence I have seen this country on the very verge of ruin a considerable number of times. It is always in the most imminent peril every four years; but, hitherto, the efforts of one party or the other have proved sufficient to rescue it, just in the latest gasp of its expiring agonies, and we have breathed more freely, when we have been assured that "the country's safe." Let us look steadily in the face of this new danger.

Are foreigners coming here to overturn our government? Those who came before the Revolution appear to have been generally favorable to Republican institutions. Those who have come here since have left friends, home, country, all that man naturally holds dearest, that they might live under a free government—they and their children. Is there common sense in the supposition that men would voluntarily set about destroying the very liberties they came so far to enjoy?

"But they lack intelligence," it is said. Are the immigrants of today less intelligent than those of fifty or a hundred years ago? Has Europe and the human race stood still all this time? . . . . The facts of men preferring this country to any other, of their desire to live under its institutions, of their migration hither, indicate to my mind anything but a lack of proper intelligence and enterprize. It has been charged against foreigners, by a portion of the whig press, that they generally vote with the democratic party. Allowing this to be so, I think that those who reflect upon the policy of the two parties, from the time of John Adams down to that of Mayor Harper, will scarcely bring this up as the proof of a lack of intelligence!

The truth is, a foreigner who emigrates to this country comes here saying, "Where Liberty dwells, there is my country." He sees our free institutions in the strong light of contrast. The sun seems brighter, because he has come out of darkness. What we know by hearsay only of the superiority of our institutions, he knows by actual observation and experience. Hence it is that America has had no truer patriots—freedom no more enthusiastic admirers—the cause of Liberty no more heroic defenders, than have been found among our adopted citizens. . . . .

But if naturalized citizens of foreign birth had the disposition, they have not the power, to endanger our liberties, on account of their comparatively small and decreasing numbers. There appears to be a most extraordinary misapprehension upon this subject. To read one of our "Native" papers one might suppose that our country was becoming overrun by foreigners, and that there was real danger of their having a majority of votes. . . . .

There is a point beyond which immigration cannot be carried. It must be limited by the capacity of the vessels employed in bringing passengers, while our entire population goes on increasing in geometrical progression, so that in one century from now, we shall have a population of one hundred and sixty millions, but a few hundred thousands of whom at the utmost can be citizens of foreign birth. Thus it may be seen that foreign immigration is of very little account, beyond a certain period, in the population of a country, and at all times is an insignificant item. . . . .

In the infancy of this country the firstborn native found himself among a whole colony of foreigners. Now, the foreigner finds himself surrounded by as great a disproportion of natives, and the native babe and newly landed foreigner have about the same amount, of either power or disposition, to endanger the country in which they have arrived; one, because he chose to come—the other because he could not help it.

I said the power or the disposition, for I have yet to learn that foreigners, whether German or Irish, English or French, are at all disposed to do an injury to the asylum which wisdom has prepared and valor won for the oppressed of all nations and religions. I appeal to the observation of every man in this community, whether the Germans and the Irish here, and throughout the country, are not as orderly, as industrious, as quiet, and in the habit of performing as well the common duties of citizens as the great mass of natives among us.

The worst thing that can be brought against any portion of our foreign population is that in many cases they are poor, and when they sink under labor and privation, they have no resources but the almshouse. Alas! shall the rich, for whom they have labored, the owners of the houses they have helped to build, refuse to treat them as kindly as they would their horses when incapable of further toil? Can they grudge them shelter from the storm, and a place where they may die in peace?

### 18. The "Native American" in Congress[1]

The proposition of the Native Americans [is] a plain one. If, in the time of Mr. Jefferson it was deemed necessary, in self-defence, to pass a five-year law[2]—when our western country was a wilderness— when educated and responsible men only came as emigrants—when only six or eight thousand annually landed at all the ports of the United States—and when they *melted* into the mass of American population, what ought to be the check now, in view of the change in the condition of our country—in view of the deteriorated character of the foreign population—in view of the fact that nearly two hundred thousand had landed *at the single port* of New York since the first day of March last, and that instead of amalgamating with the mass of the American population, they stand out as a distinct political organization, under the control of foreign leaders? Of these thousands of emigrants who annually flood our shores, how few are qualified to assume the functions of a republican voter, or discharge the duties of an American citizen in any of the political relations of life! In relation to their numbers,

[1] Extract from the speech of Mr. L. C. Levin, of Pennsylvania, in the House of Representatives, February 1, 1847, in *Congressional Globe*, Twenty-ninth Congress, second session (1846–47), Appendix, pp. 386–87.

[2] [That is, a requirement of five years' residence before naturalization.

they present a frightful array of power, especially when we cast a prospective glance into the future, and contemplate what they will be, if not arrested by timely legislation.

The quantity of this foreign material, imported for political manufacture, [said Mr. Levin] was not less alarming than its quality, and its quality caused the American to shudder when he reflected that such elements would be brought to bear to accomplish the overthrow of our inestimable institutions. Can the tenants of the poor-houses of Europe land on our shores with faculties so formed by nature, or so fashioned by education, as to become the conservative element of our free institutions, whose very basis demands intelligence, patriotism, and virtue in the voter? This question answered itself. No American was willing to rest the conservation of his freedom on such a foundation, were he not attached to one or the other of the two old parties of the day, who rely on it as a necessary means of political aggrandizement. And herein resides the evil of foreign immigration, and the evil of the foreign vote which both the old parties so devoutly court, as the only means by which they can vanquish each other. . . . .

The foreign vote in the United States now amounted to nearly half a million, and was fully competent to turn the scale from Whig to Democrat, or Democrat to Whig, at every annual election. Both the old parties seemed to feel that their very existence depended on the continuance of the supply: the Democrats having possession of it—the Whigs hoping to secure it; and hence neither seemed willing to choke up the fountain that nourished the upas tree of their power. . . . . Your naturalization laws are obsolete in principle—obsolete in object —obsolete in tendency and most destructive in practice. Their obvious and laudable design, when first passed, was to adopt a class of aliens as American citizens who were qualified by morals, manners, and education to aid in the expansion of our then wild country and the consolidation of our new and untried government. Wise in their generation, they have now become the political opprobrium of the nation. An enlightened policy conforming to existing circumstances appeals to us to wipe those antiquated laws from our statute books. Europe no longer drives her valuable and gifted sons, her useful and virtuous subjects from her domains by the persecutions of state policy, or the tortures of bigoted superstition.

A new era has broken upon Europe. Famine and liberality seem to go hand in hand. One plague now settles upon Europe, and that reaches only the lowest class of her population. The potato rot has spread famine among that class of her population, who, born to labor, languish in want and die in ignorance of their right to the morsel which would have saved them from an agonizing death. The policy of their governments now is, to burden us with this refuse mass of wretchedness, and rid themselves of those who populate their poor-houses. To feed these unhappy beings when they come among us, is a work of humanity. God forbid, while we have bread, we should refuse it to the cravings of hunger! But that is not the question. An American never disputes a point of charity, or benevolence. You may increase your poor-rates, according to the extent of your humane sympathies, and none will blame you for your effort to hush the cries of suffering humanity. But there stop. Feed them, clothe them, shelter them; but for the sake of humanity—for the sake of your country—for the sake of your children, do not endow them with the attribute of sovereignty, do not rally to the polls this living mass of moral putrescence and pitiable ignorance. This is the point at which to suspend the further operation of your naturalization laws, and protect your country against the political influence of the starved-out refugees of European poorhouses and almshouses—hundreds of whom, as the memorials from New York assert, perish on our wharves as they land, and thousands of whom are driven to crime to obtain the first morsel they eat among us.

Shall such men, sir, compete with free Americans in the exercise of the right of suffrage? Shall we taint our institutions by political fellowship with such as these, who in the hands of artful and designing demagogues are banded together, to give the casting vote for the rulers of the land, whether those rulers be honest or culpable—competent or incapable—patriots or traitors? No logic can refute the truth of this position as a general position, that in proportion as the constituency are debased, the Government will be corrupt, incapable, and unscrupulous, and our organic institutions in danger of dissolution from the disgust and want of faith excited by their infraction. A government certain of election will rush headlong into all party excesses, calculating on impunity in the vices or ignorance of the people to apply the political penalty to its violators. This combination of foreign voters devoted to the party which favors its political franchise, amounts to impunity for official folly and administrative crime.

### 19. Anxiety about Immigration: A Moderate View[1]

This country was settled by European immigrants, in the beginning of the seventeenth century; and from time to time additions have been made, for over two centuries. It would be difficult to trace the steps of these adventurers, and to show distinctly and specifically the localities of their abiding influence during most of this period. It is obvious, however, that it is owing to them and their descendants, united with the riches of the soil, that this country has become what it is.

It was natural that few restraints should be put upon the coming of those, whose circumstances induced them to seek a dwelling for themselves and their children in a country different from that of their birth. Those who had arrived welcomed others to join them in the wilderness; and local causes in Europe have always at times operated to induce its inhabitants to emigrate; and particularly has this last been the case since the establishment of the American government in 1789. From that date, liberal encouragement has been constantly given, in various ways, to those of other countries, to settle within our widely extended territory. After a few years' residence here, they have it in their power to become citizens and owners of real estate, and thus to be entitled to nearly all the privileges of those whose fathers achieved our national independence.

It was proper to have shown a liberal policy towards foreigners, to have sympathised with them in their wants and sufferings, and to a certain extent to have encouraged their settlement on our soil. It is proper that those who possess this abundance of soil and of natural resources, should be disposed to share it with others who are less favored by nature. But while such encouragement has been properly given, the question has presented itself to some, whether we have not given too great encouragement? These foreigners have been educated under influences very different from those in our country; and when mixed with our citizens, and forming an integral part of our population, are likely essentially to modify the social and political character of the mass of our people, and the character of our institutions and laws. . . . .

The British government has authorized the Poor Law Commissioners to aid poor persons in emigrating to the British colonies, and parishes and individuals have furnished means for the same object, so that large numbers have emigrated. The number to the respective

---

[1] Extract from Jesse Chickering, *Immigration into the United States* (Boston: Charles C. Little and James Brown, 1848), pp. 1–2, 52–65.

colonies has varied considerably, according to the distress in the United Kingdom, and according to the state of affairs in the colonies. In 1838 and 1839 the number was very small in the provinces in North America, in consequence of the political disturbance of 1838. Since 1841, the number to the Australian colonies and New Zealand has been very much reduced. The current is now strongly set towards the United States and the British colonies in North America.

During the last few years, since communication has been facilitated between the United States and Great Britain, large sums of money have been transmitted by immigrants in the United States and Canada, to enable their friends, particularly in Ireland, to emigrate to this country and to Canada.

Of late the subject of emigration has been introduced into the British Parliament. A motion was made and agreed to in the House of Lords, on the 4th of June, 1847, for the appointment of a select committee on the subject of Irish emigration. In the remarks which were made on the motion, a disposition was manifested favorable to the further encouragement of emigration to the colonies, particularly those in North America.[1]

On the continent of Europe there exists, we believe, no legal impediment to emigration. In France and in Germany the right is secured by law. From the latter country we have received a large number of immigrants, especially of late years. If we can depend upon the newspaper statements, in some instances whole villages have left, and in large bodies have made settlements in the United States, delighted with the possession of land which they can call their own, and stimulated in their frugal and industrious habits by the prospect of enjoying in peace and quietness the fruits of their labor.

A vast deal of anxiety, suffering, sickness, and death has been the lot of these emigrants, before they have planted themselves in this country in a manner to be considered in any way comfortably situated. Often it has happened that whole families have perished before arriving at the place of their destination; and generally we may suppose the chief advantage has accrued to their children, who either born in this new country or brought here when young, have not known the keen sensibility of being forever removed from the sight of fatherland, and have only come into the enjoyment of what their parents spent their lives in procuring for them.

But the sufferings attendant on immigration to America are be-

[1] See Wilmer's *European Mail*, June 19, 1847.

lieved to be now much less than they were in the early periods of its history. The facilities and the safety of navigating the ocean have been vastly increased since the first settlement of the country. This continent and the European have, by the rapidity, frequency and regularity of communication, been comparatively made one country. Now-a-days the European emigrants, as soon as they arrive at these shores, have stopping places filled with an abundance of the necessaries of life, and when want and sickness befall them, as is often the case, the charitable institutions are opened to soothe their sufferings, and often the hand of individual charity is extended to them in a manner to touch their hearts with emotions of gratitude. . . . .

The government of the United States has never taken any measures directly to encourage foreigners to immigrate to this country. The principle of equality runs through all our laws and institutions. The foreigner who comes here takes his chance of bettering his condition with the natives of the land. Some have succeeded, notwithstanding the disadvantages under which they have labored. If, after remaining here for a time, they signify a wish to make this their adopted country, and declare their allegiance, they are admitted to all the rights and privileges guaranteed to native citizens. . . . .

The people of the United States, considered as a whole, are composed of immigrants and their descendants from almost every country. The principal portion of them, however, derived their origin from the British nation, comprehending by this term the English, the Scotch, and the Irish. The English language is almost wholly used; the English manners, modified to be sure, predominate, and the spirit of English liberty and enterprise animates the energies of the whole people. English laws and institutions, adapted to the circumstances of the country, have been adopted here. Lord Durham very justly says, "the language, the laws, the character of the North American continent, are English; and every race but the English (I apply this to all who speak the English language), appears there in a condition of inferiority."[1] . . . .

Many of the early immigrants, unable to enjoy civil and religious liberty at home, were induced to immigrate to this country in hopes of enjoying it here. Many of them were poor and sought to better their conditions in the wilderness. . . . .

During the last twenty or twenty-five years, the number of immigrants from abroad has been much increased. At intervals before as

[1] See his *Report on the Affairs of British North America*, p. 105.

well as during this period, there have been seasons of great distress in England and in Europe, during which unusual numbers have emigrated. It has now become almost a habit among the dense and distressed population of Europe for large numbers of persons annually to emigrate. In Great Britain, individuals sometimes pay the passage money for the poor who are desirous of emigrating, and the governments authorize parish funds to be used for the same purpose. The question has been introduced into Parliament of making provision on a large scale for the emigration of the Irish population. The scarcity of provisions in Europe this year has very much increased the amount of emigration; and from all appearances the number will increase for some time to come.

The signs of distress to the poor in Great Britain, the coming winter, are appalling, and the inducements to emigrate from thence and from other parts of Europe will probably be as strong next year as this. We shall not be surprised to find that before long the British Parliament should conceive it to be a matter of prudence, no less than of necessity, to aid on a large scale emigration to their colonies; and we may expect that at least half of their emigrants to all countries will very soon find their way to the United States. It is said their poorhouses are crowded; and the expense of the transportation of paupers to America is probably not greater than that of their support for a single year; and when they are once landed in America, they will cease to be a pecuniary burden upon their native country. The indications also are equally strong in favor of a large emigration from Germany to America the coming year.

There will have come to the United States this year (1847) nearly 300,000 foreigners. Most of them arrive at the great ports of entry, as New York, Philadelphia, Boston, etc. Many of them are poor and sick, and humanity forbids our leaving them to perish without affording them some relief. Already their support has become an important item of expense in many of our large cities. The state of New York seems alarmed at the numerous hordes of foreigners who enter there. She has appointed Commissioners of Emigration to attend to the wants and necessities of these foreigners. These commissioners deserve the greatest praise for their faithfulness in the discharge of extremely arduous duties. According to their late report, 101,546 foreign passengers arrived at the port of New York alone, from May 6th to September 30th, inclusive, a period of less than five months. During this time, 6,761 were admitted to the hospitals and alms-houses under the authority of these commissioners. All but 443 arrived during the time. . . . .

We have thus arrived at a period in the history of foreign immigration, when the number of foreigners coming here, one-half of whom may be considered adults, nearly equals the whole natural increase of the white population of the United States. Such a mass of population annually diffused among these states must, as they mingle with the people generally, or as they concentrate in cities, or settle in large numbers in particular localities, have most important effects on the condition and character of the people. . . . .

The attention of Congress has been frequently directed to the subject of the naturalization of foreigners; but the conditions of voting, in which resides their direct political power, are determined by each state for itself. In most or all of the states naturalization is a prerequisite to voting; but, owing to the carelessness and fraud in obtaining naturalization papers, the looseness of the state laws and the connivance of partizans, it cannot be denied, as it has been proved by abundant testimony, that great frauds have been committed, and many individuals have been admitted to the polls, in times of strong party excitement, who were not entitled to the privilege by a fair construction of the existing laws of the United States or of individual states. . . . .

Is it not obvious that a few only of the foreigners who come here have any attachment to our institutions? and do not most of them in the fruition, find our liberty a different thing from the picture in their imaginations before crossing the Atlantic? In their disappointment, are they faultless? and are they as industrious as they should be to improve our institutions? or, in their zeal, is not their first step too often to tear them down?

The majority, however, of those who come here, know nothing of a rational or regulated liberty, nor consider the safeguards necessary to preserve it. The liberty in their minds is a licentiousness which has no respect for the rights of others. They come here smarting under injustice and oppression; to check by salutary restraints seems to them oppression; and to hate oppression and oppressive rulers is the only step they, in their ignorance, have thus far taken towards a rational liberty. By our laws they are admitted to political privileges upon easier terms than we admit our own sons—privileges, which, in almost every state, are denied to a man on account of color, though his father or grandfather was the friend and companion-in-arms of Washington. Is it that our privileges are too good for us—too good to be preserved? It is that in our ecstasy we would, like children, part with our birthright, and, after it is gone, weep for the loss that is irreparable? When they receive employment, and are well fed, are not they the first to insist on higher wages, in the cant language, to *strike?*

There may be some few exceptions. There may be those whose enlightened and liberal minds appreciate our institutions, and feel the value of their blessings—who forbear taking any undue part in the political affairs of our country? . . . .

But is the country truly benefited by this great foreign immigration? Have the people been made wiser or better or happier? It has been said that without these foreigners our railroads and canals could not have been constructed. These improvements, it is true, may have been made a year or two earlier (and in many of the states it would have been better if we had hurried less) in consequence of so many foreigners being in the country, whom we were obliged to employ in some way or other, or support them without labor. The progress of the internal improvements, a year or two in advance of what they would have been without this foreign labor, will be a very poor compensation, if offset by the corruption of manners, the forfeiture of freedom, and the transfer of power to those who know not how to use it wisely. There are other things of value in this world besides merely physical aggrandizement.

These foreigners come here to benefit themselves, not from any love of us or of our country.

### 20. A Liberal View of the Relation of the Alien to American Life[1]

[Mr. Benedict reported] that the committee are not unaware that, in legislating on the subject of aliens, many old habits of thought, as well as some modern prejudices, are in the way of free and unembarrassed action. Sprung, as a people, from nations who hold it as a cardinal principle of organized society, that allegiance cannot be changed or divested, and that devotion to the land of one's birth and

[1] *Report of Select Committee on Allowing Resident Aliens to Hold Real Estate* (New York Assembly Document No. 168 [1848]), pp. 1–5.

Mr. E. C. Benedict, from the select committee to which was referred "An act to amend an act entitled an act to enable aliens to hold and convey real estate, and for other purposes," and also "An act to extend for five years the second section of the act entitled an act to enable resident aliens to hold and convey real estate," with instructions to inquire into the expediency of allowing resident aliens to hold real estate in the same manner as citizens, made the report.

to its institutions, is the first and the last duty of citizen and subject, it is not to be wondered at that there should still be found, in the minds of some persons, traces of old fashioned fears, that aliens born under institutions with which we can never sympathize, would be dangerous to our peace if introduced into our midst, without being marked by exclusion from certain privileges and enjoyments, which are the common right of all who are born on the soil.

Such persons seem to the committee entirely to overlook the principle of our institutions, or to deny or disregard that too-often forgotten axiom of political science that nations can best prosper only as the details of their social and political relations are arranged in harmonious and easy sympathy with the spirit of their institutions and the fundamental feelings of their people.

The principle of our institutions in this regard is that of entire freedom and equality of self-reliance. Our ancestors, loyal colonists of European nations, founded our institutions in direct violation of the organic political principles of that proud old world, from which they sprung. In place of the divine right of kings, they built upon the glorious right of rebellion as a corner stone. Accustomed to privileged classes, a titled aristocracy, primogeniture, and feudal inequalities they considered it a self-evident truth that all men were born free and equal, and were alike the source and the subjects of political power. Taught from childhood that allegiance is unchangeable, indivisible and perpetual, and that foreigner is but another name for enemy, they held the whole doctrine in derision, threw open their gates and invited men of every nation to join us. Fighting for home, religion, and liberty, aliens ministered at our altars, and led our armies. Their eloquence and steady zeal encouraged the timid and gave new vigor to the brave, and their names echoed to the voice of our victories.

It was this confident self-reliance, that justified the wise and prophetic fathers of the republic in making no barriers to our ports and no gates to our cities. They placed no sentinels on our borders and no armed police in our streets, and established no government espionage. All men were permitted to come and go, everywhere, and at all times, without permission or hindrance, and without being asked for any passport or certificate or record of birth, or age, or profession, or destination.

The old common law doctrine which considered aliens as without heritable blood, incapable of taking or transmitting land by descent or by purchase, and as dangerous to the community, remained in many of the States, but without any real practical effect. A memorable attempt was made to give new life to that principle, and to transfer something of its spirit to the national government—where of course it should live or have no life. The effort was successful, and the alien and sedition law, the natural and vigorous offspring of the old prejudice, was placed on the statute book. It is not necessary to allude to the sudden destruction, which like a whirlwind, buried the law and its authors in a never-to-be forgotten ruin. For about half a century the subject was not again agitated, except that from time to time the States removed one restriction after another, and the common law rule was everywhere modified and meliorated, and in several of the new States, by a wise forecast, was entirely swept away. Aliens brought with them labor, and skill, science and capital, to supply our greatest want, and, uniting with our citizens, the light of civilization, and cultivation, and freedom were let into the wilderness of national territory on our borders. Millions of acres of the public lands were sold, and their proceeds poured into the general coffers, and all the sources of national wealth and strength—agriculture, commerce, and manufactures—were greatly multiplied.

What can there be to fear from allowing a few aliens to have the same right to enjoy the land, as they have to enjoy the sunshine, the air, and the water? How can land affect their principles or their morals injuriously? While every one of us is a part of the sovereign power, there is little to fear from treason, privy conspiracy or rebellion suggested or promoted by aliens. While we are all subject only to equal laws of our own making, where can aliens find arguments to induce us to take a foreign yoke? Such influences surely do not spring out of the ground. No one has thought of forbidding them to acquire all other kinds of property, the most easily transmissible, and convertible, and removable with silence and secrecy and rapidity. We invite them to invest their money in the stocks of our manufacturing, banking and railroad corporations, in ships, in merchandize, in naval stores and munitions of war. They may buy what they please, inherit and own what they please, except a farm to cultivate, a home to live in, a shop or a factory to work in, and a store to buy and sell in, everything, but that which will give them the strongest, permanent interest in the stability of our government, and the good order and peace of society.

In this State, this absurd idea has become but a shadow of what it was. Every alien that has asked for the privilege has been permitted to hold land, and general laws, of very liberal character, have been passed from time to time, always, however, making aliens the subject of some distinctive restrictions. Quite recently, it is true, the old prejudice was manifested in an attempt to arouse the people to a sense of danger from the presence and influence of persons not born on the soil. Honest and intelligent men took up this one idea, and excluding the light from all quarters but one, saw it as through a microscope, in proportions so magnified, that it filled the whole field of their vision. An excitement was raised, and those who partook of its spirit and motion, and went on with its currents, predicted with the confidence of inspiration, that its rising wave was to flow over the whole land and wash out all our political stains in the waters of Native Americanism. After a moment's reflection, it was gone!—furnishing as signal an instance as the alien and sedition laws, of the triumph of the sober feeling of our people and the healthy restorative power of the spirit of our institutions.

It has indeed been said that aliens should be required, before holding land, to take steps to be naturalized.

To all those foreigners, who in good faith desire to assume the political rights and duties of American citizens, we wisely offer a cordial welcome, and every facility for investing themselves with all the rights and privileges of our republican brotherhood. We act on the principle, that although they may not be as thoroughly American as those who are born on the soil, still they are sure to be much more so, with the rights, duties, and privileges of citizens voluntarily assumed, than they can be as the dissatisfied, partially proscribed, and merely tolerated inhabitants, whom we mark with disabilities, and look upon with suspicion. But who can desire that we should seek to bribe or compel any to be naturalized, who do not desire to do so—to take upon their consciences unwilling oaths, and solemnly renounce the country which, though they have left it, still in spite of themselves, they cannot cease to love. There are many, and those not the least worthy and conscientious, who would not disturb the country that gives them hospitality and a better home, nor seek, in the remotest degree, to interfere with its good order, and who rejoice unfeignedly, that their children and their children's children, to the latest posterity, like ourselves descended from aliens, will be as faithfully attached to our free institutions as we are, and who would not on any inducement forswear the country of their birth, nor renounce the allegiance which they had sworn to keep. All experience and observation has shown that there are no truer American citizens than the children of those who came among us as aliens.

## 21. Opinion in the South[1]

But why am I opposed to the encouragement of foreign immigration into our country, and disposed to apply any proper checks to it? Why do I propose to suspend to the foreigner, for twenty-one years after he shall have signified formally his intention to become a citizen of the United States, the right of suffrage, the birthright of no man but one native-born? It is because the mighty tides of immigration, each succeeding one increasing in volume, bring to us not only different languages, opinions, customs, and principles, but hostile races, religions, and interests, and the traditionary prejudices of generations with a large amount of the turbulence, disorganizing theories, pauperism, and demoralization of Europe in her redundant population thrown upon us. This multiform and dangerous evil exists and will continue, for "the cry is, Still they come!" Large numbers in a short time, a few months or weeks, after getting into the country, and very many before they have remained the full time of probation, fall into the hands of demagogues and unscrupulous managers of elections, and by the commission of perjury and other crimes are made to usurp against law a portion of the political sovereignty of the country. They are ignorant of our institutions and the principles upon which they are founded; of the great interests of the country, and the questions of policy which divide our people; of the candidates for office, and their capacities, views, fitness, and former course of life. Instead of being qualified to aid in the great and difficult business of upholding the most complicated structure of government that ever had existence, and of successfully administering it for the good and happiness of the people and its own perpetuation, they constitute an uninformed, unreasoning, and, to a great extent, immoral power, wielded almost universally by desperate and profligate men who by this agency become enabled to carry into success their own bold, mercenary, and pernicious purposes; and to defeat those which the wise and the good devise for the benefit of the country and the preservation of constitu-

[1] Extract from *Speeches of Hon. Garrett Davis, upon His Proposition to Impose Further Restrictions upon Foreign Immigrants: Delivered in the Convention to Revise the Constitution of Kentucky, December 15th and 17th, 1849* (Frankfort, Kentucky, 1855), pp. 7–11, 30–32.

tional liberty. We cannot, with any safety, continue to admit with such lavish liberality those ever coming and ever increasing masses of immigrants into full political partnership and share with them the sovereignty of government. We are taught this truth no less by nature and reason than by fact and experience. . . . . The most of those European immigrants, having been born and having lived in the ignorance and degradation of despotisms, without mental or moral culture, with but a vague consciousness of human rights, and no knowledge whatever of the principles of popular constitutional government, their interference in the political administration of our affairs, even when honestly intended, would be about as successful as that of the Indian in the arts and business of civilized private life; and when misdirected, as it would generally be, by bad and designing men, could be productive only of mischief, and from their numbers, of mighty mischief. The system inevitably and in the end will fatally depreciate, degrade, and demoralize the power which governs and rules our destinies.

I freely acknowledge that among such masses of immigrants there are men of noble intellect, of high cultivation, and of great moral worth; men every way adequate to the difficult task of free, popular, and constitutional government. But the number is lamentably small. There can be no contradistinction between them and the incompetent and vicious; and their admission would give no proper compensation, no adequate security against the latter if they, too, were allowed to share political sovereignty. The country could be governed just as wisely and as well by the native-born citizens alone, by which this baleful infusion would be wholly excluded. . . . .

I will present some statements and tables of immigration and population, the most recent and the most authentic that I have been enabled to command from the limited sources of information within my reach. Though by no means full and entirely satisfactory, this examination has convinced me that the great body of the people, and indeed of intelligent men, have no information or belief approximating the truth of the fearful and growing numbers of immigrants, of their general destitution and pauperism, of their ignorance and demoralization, and of the vices and crimes of very many of them, and of the enormous frauds which, through them, are perpetrated upon the elective franchise. . . . .

In 1790 the whole population of the United States was 3,172,464. The rate of increase ascertained by the latest and most reliable calculations, upon the principle of compound increase, is about 2.39

per cent per annum, by which the population would be doubled in
somewhat more than twenty-nine years. Make an estimate by this
rule upon twenty-nine years, and in 1840 there was a white population
of 11,104,659. But the census returns show a white population of
14,189,218 in 1840; so that there were then in the United States upward of four millions of persons, immigrants and their progeny. During
the decennial period indicated by each of the named years following,
I present the aggregate number of immigrants: 1800, 160,305; 1810,
229,755; 1820, 321,064; 1830, 494,491; 1840, 862,040. Since 1840, the
rate and aggregate of increase has been greatly beyond any prior
period. These numbers here given I presume are made up from the
custom-house returns; for the latter years I have no doubt they are.
I have been able to get the custom-house returns for two years only
since 1840; that of 1846, showing 158,648, and that of 1847, an increase
on the former year of about 47 per cent, and an aggregate of 239,256.
No returns are made by any ships under twenty tons, and from some
cause, none from the ports of New Jersey. It is well known that a
great many vessels neglect to make any returns, and also that most of
the immigrants who land at Halifax and Quebec come through the
British provinces into the United States. The great number of timber
ships which sail annually from England to Quebec afford large and
cheap facilities to the immigrants by that voyage, and great numbers
annually come by it. It is estimated that one-fourth of the immigrants
to the United States are either through the British provinces or through
our ports and not reported; and the actual white population reported
upon each general return of the census, above the combined aggregate
natural increase and custom-house numbers, shows this estimate to be
under the truth. I have, however, made some prospective estimates
upon the supposition that 20 per cent of the annual immigrants through
all channels were not comprehended in the custom-house returns.
Upon these principles I estimate the total white population of the
United States in 1850 to be the rise of 21,000,000, of which upward of
5,000,000 will be foreigners by birth, being about one-fourth. Thirty-
five years ago only one in forty of our population was estimated to be
of foreign birth. In 1843, one in five, and this disproportion is rapidly
decreasing. . . . . I have seen a statement that the immigrants from
the port of Bremen for the past year exceeded 56,000; and of something like the same number from Liverpool, that four-fifths of them
were Germans. The same rate of increase would bring immigrants to
the country, in 1851, 1,340,669; in 1852, 1,970, 783; in 1853, 2,897,051;

and in 1854, 4,258,664. So that it becomes obvious that this rate of increase cannot continue through many years. Nevertheless the increase will be steady, great, and continuous, and I believe may be safely assumed at more than 1,000,000 yearly for the decennial period between 1850 and 1860. Upon this hypothesis I assume the total population of the United States in 1860 will be 36,606,178, of which, allowing for their decrease by death, about 14,000,000 will be foreigners by birth; and the slaves being then about 4,000,000, added to the foreigners, will make nearly one-half of the aggregate population of the United States. The census returns of 1870 will unquestionably exhibit the native white population to be less than the foreigners and the slaves united, a state of fact which must fill every patriotic and sober mind with grave reflection.

This view of the subject is powerfully corroborated by a glance at the state of things in Europe. The aggregate population of that continent in 1807 was 183,000,000. Some years since it was reported to be 260,000,000, and now it is reasonably but little short of 283,000,000; showing an increase within a period of about forty years of 100,000,000. The area of Europe is but little more than that of the United States, and from its higher northern positions and greater proportion of sterile lands, has a less natural capability of sustaining population. All her western, southern, and middle states labor under one of the heaviest afflictions of nations—they have a redundant population. The German states have upward of 70,000,000, and Ireland 8,000,000; all Germany being not larger than three of our largest states, and Ireland being about the size of Kentucky. Daniel O'Connell, in 1843, reported 2,385,000 of the Irish people in a state of destitution. The annual increase of population in Germany and Ireland is in the aggregate near 2,000,000; and in all Europe it is near 7,000,000. Large masses of these people, in many countries, not only want the comforts of life, but its subsistence, its necessaries, and are literally starving. England, many of the German powers, Switzerland, and other governments, have put into operation extensive and well-arranged systems of emigrating and transporting to America their excess of population, and particularly the refuse, the pauper, the demoralized, and the criminal. Very many who come are stout and industrious, and go to labor steadily and thriftily. They send their friends in the old country true and glowing accounts of ours, and with it the means which they have garnered here to bring, too, those friends. Thus, immigration itself increases its means, and constantly adds to its swelling tides. Suppose some mighty convulsion of nature should loosen Europe, the smaller country, from her ocean-deep foundations, and drift her to our coast, would we be ready to take her teeming myriads to our fraternal embrace and give them equally our political sovereignty? If we did, in a few fleeting years where would be the noble Anglo-American race, where their priceless heritage of liberty, where their free constitution, where the best and brightest hopes of man? All would have perished! It is true all Europe is not coming to the United States, but much, too much of it, is; and a dangerous disproportion of the most ignorant and worst of it, without bringing us any territory for them; enough, if they go on increasing and to increase, and are to share with us our power, to bring about such a deplorable result. The question is, Shall they come and take possession of our country and our government, and rule us, or will we, who have the right, rule them and ourselves? I go openly, manfully, and perserveringly for the latter rule, and if it cannot be successfully asserted in all the United States, I am for taking measures to maintain it in Kentucky, and while we can. Now is the time—prevention is easier than cure.

The governments of Europe know better than we do that they have a great excess of population. They feel more intensely its great and manifold evils, and for years they have been devising and applying correctives, which have all been mainly resolved into one—to drain off into America their surplus, and especially their destitute, demoralized, and vicious population. By doing so, they not only make more room and comfort for the residue, but they think—and with some truth— that they provide for their own security, and do something to avert explosions which might hurl kings from their thrones. . . . . .

We have, Mr. President, a country of vast extent, with a great variety of climate, soil, production, industry, and pursuit. Competing interests and sectional questions are a natural and fruitful source of jealousies, discords, and factions. We have about four millions of slaves, and the slaveholding and free states are nearly equally divided in number, but the population of the latter greatly preponderating, and every portion of it deeply imbued with inflexible hostility to slavery as an institution. Even now conflict of opinion and passion of the two great sections of the Union upon the subject of slavery is threatening to rend this Union, and change confederated states and one people into hostile and warring powers. Cession has recently given to us considerable numbers of the Spanish race, and a greatly increasing immigration is constantly pouring in upon us the hordes of Europe, with their hereditary national animosities, their discordant races, languages, and religious faiths, their ignorance and their pauperism, mixed up with a large amount of idleness, moral degradation, and crime; and all this "heterogeneous, discordant, distracted mass," to use Mr. Jefferson's language,[1] "sharing with us the legislation" and the entire political sovereignty. . . . .

Washington and Jefferson and their associates, though among the wisest and most far-seeing of mankind, could not but descry in the future many formidable difficulties and dangers, and thus be premonished to provide against them in fashioning our institutions. If they had foreseen the vast, the appalling increase of immigration upon us at the present, there can be no reasonable doubt that laws to naturalize the foreigners and to give up to them the country, its liberties, its destiny, would not have been authorized by the constitution. The danger, though great, is not wholly without remedy. We can do something if we do it quickly. The German and Slavonic races are combining in the state of New York to elect candidates of their own blood to Congress. This is the beginning of the conflict of races on a large scale, and it must, in the nature of things, continue and increase. It must be universal and severe in all the field of labor, between the native and the stranger, and from the myriads of foreign laborers coming to us, if it does not become a contest for bread and subsistence, wages will at least be brought down so low as to hold our native laborers and their families in hopeless poverty. They cannot adopt the habits of life and live upon the stinted meager supplies to which the foreigner will restrict himself, and which is bounteous plenty to what he has been accustomed in the old country. Already these results are taking place in many of the mechanic arts. Duty, patriotism, and wisdom all require us to protect the labor, and to keep up to a fair scale the wages of our native-born people as far as by laws and measures of public policy it can be done. The foreigner, too, is the natural foe of the slavery of our state. He is opposed to it by all his past associations, and when he comes to our state he sees 200,000 laborers of a totally different race to himself excluding him measurably from employment and wages. He hears a measure agitated to send these 200,-000 competitors away. Their exodus will make room for him, his kindred and race, and create such a demand for labor, as he will reason it, to give him high wages. He goes naturally for the measure, and becomes an emancipationist. While the slave is with us, the foreigner will

[1] See above, Doc. 2 p. 703.

not crowd us, which will postpone to a long day the affliction of nations, an excess of population; the slaves away, the great tide of immigration will set in upon us, and precipitate upon our happy land this, the chief misery of most of the countries of Europe. Look at the myriads who are perpetually pouring into the northwestern states from the German hives—making large and exclusive settlements for themselves, which in a few years will number their thousands and tens of thousands, living in isolation; speaking a strange language, having alien manners, habits, opinions, and religious faiths, and a total ignorance of our political institutions; all handed down with German phlegm and inflexibility to their children through generations. In less than fifty years, northern Illinois, parts of Ohio, and Michigan, Wisconsin, Iowa, and Minnesota will be literally possessed by them; they will number millions and millions, and they will be essentially a distinct people, a nation within a nation, a new Germany. We can't keep these people wholly out, and ought not if we could; but we are getting more than our share of them. I wish they would turn their direction to South America, quite as good a portion of the world as our share of the hemisphere. They could there aid in bringing up the slothful and degenerate Spanish race; here their deplorable office is to pull us down. Our proud boast is that the Anglo-Saxon race is the first among all the world of man, and that we are a shoot from this noble stock; but how long will we be as things are progressing? In a few years, as a distinctive race, the Anglo-Americans will be as much lost to the world and its future history as the lost tribes of Israel. But let us avert such a fate; let us postpone it at least. Let us withdraw from the newcomers the premium of political sovereignty. These strangers have neither the right nor the competency to govern the native-born people, nor ought they to be allowed the power to misgovern them. It is our right and our duty to govern ourselves, and them too when they come among us; and it is best for all parties that it should be so, and this difficult and important work can be better performed without their taking part in it, even when their intentions are good; but, misdirected and perverted by designing and wicked men, it is fatal infatuation to allow it. This truly foreign power nestled in the bosom of our country may, in its arch and crooked policy, occasionally act with one or another of the parties that spring up inherent in this republic. But it has its own paramount ends to circumvent; and when it seems to ally itself to any party, it is only a ruse; and the true motive is the belief that it helps on to the consummation of those ends. With every civil right and liberty secured to the immigrant, and a full share of political sovereignty to be the heritage of his children, if he is not satisfied to come and remain with us, let him go to other lands.

Mr. President, no well-informed and observant man can look abroad over this widespread and blessed country without feeling deep anxiety for the future. Some elements of discord and disunion are even now in fearful action. Spread out to such a vast extent, filling up almost in geometrical progression with communities and colonies from many lands, various as Europe in personal and national characteristics, in opinions, in manners and customs, in tongues and religious faiths, in the traditions of the past, and the objects and the hopes of the future, the United States can, no more than Europe, become one homogeneous mass—one peaceful, united, harmonizing, all self-adhering people. When the country shall begin to teem with people, these jarring elements being brought into proximity, their repellant and explosive properties will begin to act with greater intensity; and then, if not before, will come the war of geographical sections, the war of races, and the most relentless of all wars, of hostile religions. This mournful catastrophe will have been greatly hastened by our immense expansion and our proclamation to all mankind to become a part of us.

### 22. A Western Forecast of the Results of Emigration[1]

Urged by necessity, induced by the prospect of improving their condition, and encouraged by the rich and privileged classes, we may reasonably expect that the emigration to this country will be augmented to an amount that will materially affect our own condition. The movement is gradually assuming a more systematic organization, and from present indications the number of passengers destined to our shores will, for years to come, be equal to the means provided for their transportation and subsistence on the voyage. And it is not extravagant to suppose that the time is near when the numbers annually arriving will exceed 500,000, or that they may even amount to 1,000-000, provided the nations of Europe should remain in peace during the next ten years.

It is not in the nature of things that so large an influx of foreigners can take place without producing important changes, as well in our commercial relations with other countries, as in our own public and private economy. . . . .

[1] Extract from "Emigration from Europe to America," the *Western Journal*, VI (St. Louis, 1851), 213–17.

It seems to be the general impression in this country that a large influx of foreign population will tend to reduce the price of labor to the European standard; but we are persuaded that instead of reducing the price, or, at least, the rewards of labor here, it will tend to raise the rewards, and perhaps the nominal money price in Europe to the American standard.

Owing to the abundance and cheapness of lands in the West, it is in the power of every able bodied and industrious man to become the owner of a homestead; and whatever may have been his condition before, he is then no longer a hireling; and it is a well established fact, at least in this country, that where lands are cheap the price of labor is always so high as to leave but little profit to the farmer who employs it. In rural districts, therefore, instead of depressing, emigration will tend to enhance the price of labor, provided the demand for agricultural products should keep pace with their increase. Many causes will operate to augment this demand. The emigrants of one year necessarily increase the demand for the products of the year immediately preceding: and from this cause alone the prices of bread and provisions always rule high in districts which are rapidly filling up with new comers. Besides, a large proportion of the emigrants are mechanics and artizans, who, locating in cities and towns, must be fed from the country; and if we take into consideration the numbers which will probably be employed in mining, on works of public improvement, and in the many new branches of industry which will be introduced by themselves or others by whom they will be employed, we shall find many reasons in support of the opinion that foreign emigration will not depress the prices of labor below the average rates heretofore obtained by the citizens of this country.

This is the first, and to us the most interesting point to be considered in connection with the subject of foreign emigration. For if we can give employment to all foreign emigrants at remunerating prices, their labor, added to our own, will produce results which, long before the close of the present century, will astonish the civilized world. Hitherto our population has doubled in about twenty-four years; but with the annual addition of 500,000 emigrants, it will increase 100 per cent in about fifteen years. Our tonnage, employed in commerce, has doubled in about sixteen years, and has increased about seventy-five per cent during the eight years ending June 30, 1850. It is now supposed to be equal in amount to that of Great Britain. Judging from the present aspect of the civilized world, we may calculate our population in 1865 at 46,000,000, and our civil marine, including steamboats employed on our rivers, at 10,000,000 tons. These estimates may be regarded as extravagant by some of our readers, more especially by our British patrons, as the latter will be reluctant to admit that the scepter of commerce is destined so soon to depart from those by whom it has been swayed so long over land and sea.

In this mighty tide of emigration now flowing to our shores, we recognize the progress of a great commercial revolution, especially in this country. It is bringing the consumers of our surplus breadstuffs and provisions nearer to the producers, and the manufacturers nearer to the raw material, by which all parties must be greatly benefited; but none so much, perhaps, as the American agriculturist. For, by the purchase and consumption of British goods, he assists the manufacturer to pay the British farmer a profit on his produce, after adding to its cost, land rent, tithes, poor rates, and other burthens imposed by an expensive government. By transferring the manufacturers and operatives to this country, these profits will inure, at least in part, to our own farmers and landholders, who now contribute to the support of foreign governments, minister to the extravagance of the rich, and assist in maintaining the poor of other nations. . . . .

The machinery and capital of Europe will, in due time, follow the operatives across the Atlantic; and when located here, the commercial revolution, to which allusion has been made, will be complete. We shall then, and not until then, have escaped from the provincial relation, which we have so long occupied towards Great Britain. It is true that our political relations as colonists were severed by the revolution, but we have, nevertheless, through the medium of our commercial relations, contributed largely to the support of the government and people of the mother country, and we must continue to do so, until our short-sighted policy shall be overruled by natural laws. The operation of these laws, however, is gradually becoming more apparent in the direction of our public and private economy, as we extend the area of our settlements, and increase in numbers. . . . .

The poor flock to our shores to escape from a state of penury, which cannot be relieved by toil in their own native land. The man of enterprise comes, to avail himself of the advantages afforded by a wider and more varied field for the exercise of his industry and talents; and the oppressed of every land, thirsting for deliverance from the paralyzing effects of unjust institutions, come to enjoy the blessings of a government which secures life, liberty, and the pursuit of happiness to all its constituents. Let them come. They will convert our waste lands into fruitful fields, vineyards, and gardens; construct works of public improvement; build up and establish manufactures; and open our rich mines of coal, of iron, of lead, and of copper. And more than all, they will be the means of augmenting our commerce, and aiding us in extending the influence of our political, social, and religious institutions throughout the earth. . . . .

The principal portion of the emigrants who reach our shores will finally locate in the valley of the Mississippi; and their numbers in some of the newer States will in all probability exceed the native born citizens. Reared under institutions widely differing from our own; many of them ignorant of the science of all governments; and all strangers to the practical operations of republican institutions, unceasing vigilance will be required on our part to guard against innovations and prevent the formation of parties, representing the interests and sentiments of those born in other lands.

To prevent such a result, we must give more encouragement to the cause of education, be more circumspect in the selection of our legislators, and by a liberal, yet firm and upright course of policy, secure the confidence and affections of our foreign population.

The considerations inducing the people of other lands to emigrate to our shores constitute the strongest guaranty on their part that they will cheerfully conform to the laws and social usages of this, their adopted country, and zealously co-operate in carrying out all necessary measures, calculated to promote the advancement of our national glory. This much we have a right to expect: it is all we claim at their hands.

Thus united in the great cause of civilization, and acting in concert, the influence of our political and social institutions shall gain strength from increase of numbers, until the principles of despotism which have enthralled the masses of the old world, shall be eradicated, and the condition of all nations improved by our example.

### 23. The Immigrant and the Public Lands, 1852[1]

Mr. Cyrus L. Dunham, of Indiana: Another of the objections urged to this bill is, that it grants land to foreigners; but I think it is sufficient-

[1] Extracts from debate on the Homestead Bill in the House of Representatives, April, 1852, *Congressional Globe*, Thirty-second Congress, first session, Appendix, pp. 409–10, 438, 481, 511–12, 519–20, 584.

ly restrictive in this respect, for its benefits are guardedly limited to those only who shall be in the country at the time of its passage; and even they are required to become naturalized, as a condition precedent to their availing themselves of the benefits of the measure.

But I must confess that if the proposition be true, that labor properly applied increases wealth, and is an advantage to the country, and that this land unemployed yields nothing to increase that wealth, I cannot see how it should be injurious to us, that the honest, industrious, and hard-working German should come here and settle upon a quarter section of this unemployed land, and make that which is now worthless, valuable and productive—that which is a wilderness, to blossom as the rose. I cannot see how the nation has lost anything by it. I cannot see how humanity has lost anything by it. I know something of the German and Irish who come to settle upon our soil. There is not a better, a more industrious, nor a more loyal population anywhere. They may come here with a little exuberance of republicanism, if you please, just as they have escaped from the shackles of tyranny, which have fettered their spirits and restrained their energies; but give them land to cultivate, and labor will soon sober down their judgments, and teach them the important lesson that that only is true liberty which is regulated by law.

But suppose gentlemen differ with me, and consider that this immigration of foreigners is an evil? Yet evil or no evil, its increased momentum every year is a fixed fact, and cannot be prevented. We cannot, if we would, adopt the Chinese policy of national isolation. No one, at this day, will think of preventing the oppressed victims of the tyranny of the Old World from seeking an asylum upon our shores. No one can be so selfish as to desire to prevent others from partaking of these blessings of liberty which have been showered upon us with so bountiful a hand, and, especially, when their enjoyment cannot diminish our own. So long, then, as your country maintains its superiority, so long as your institutions are worth enjoying—in short, so long as your liberties remain, this immigration will continue. It were better, then, to cease to inveigh against it, and endeavor to make it useful; to consider how we shall diminish its evils and augment its benefits. You can in no way so well accomplish this as by holding out such inducements as shall prevent these people from congregating in your towns and cities, as shall take them out upon your soil, where their labor can be profitably employed, and where, at the same time, they can obtain a permanent interest in that soil. There is something in the nature of man which makes him cling to that spot of earth he can call his own, and to the government that protects him in its enjoyment.

From whence came we? Your fathers and mine were of those very foreigners who heretofore came to this country, whose glory and prosperity you have so much at heart. Did they ruin it when they came? No, sir; our liberties, as you all know, and as our history will demonstrate, were won by emigrants, or the immediate descendants of emigrants. With no example before them, they established this Government, and its institutions; and shall we, at this day, fear to trust a similar people, who have fled from the same oppressions of the Old World to enjoy the liberties of the New—when, too, they have these institutions and their glorious results before them, as also the example of the millions who have been born beneath them, and who understand and have enjoyed them? Let us not, sir, by a narrow policy, in effect say, that the countries from whence sprung the progenitors of the Washingtons, Jeffersons, Lafayettes, Montgomeries, and De Kalbs, have exhausted "the breed of noble bloods"; and that henceforth nothing distinguished by talent, or exalted in patriotism, can spring from the countries of our own ancestors.

I cannot, Mr. Chairman, abide the narrowminded, cold-hearted policy that wraps itself in the cloak of its own selfishness, and says, It is well with me, let others take care of themselves. Nor can I appreciate this vaunting philanthropy, which talks of going forth to right the wrongs of other lands, yet would refuse a home to the oppressed in our own; would refuse to allow them to occupy what we cannot use or enjoy; and, especially, when by doing so they add to our wealth and greatness, and help us to bear our burden. I repeat, the wealth and prosperity of the Republic is produced by the application of the labor of such honest, industrious men to the material upon every side of us unemployed. If we take too much of your population from the old States, supply yourselves from those daily seeking homes upon our shores; and, in doing this, we shall be accomplishing the great mission for which we were sent—to relieve mankind, and restore to them liberty and happiness. I believe, Mr. Chairman, I am, perhaps, an enthusiast upon this subject, that we were placed here for wise and glorious purposes—to restore poor, downtrodden humanity to its long-lost dignity; to overthrow despots, and shed abroad the genial influence of freedom; to break the bonds of the oppressed, and bid the captive go free; to liberate, to elevate, and restore—not by going abroad sword in hand, conquering and to conquer, as did Mahomet—but our destiny is to be accomplished by peaceful means, by the sword of the spirit, by the genius of our institutions. . . . .

Willard P. Hall, of Missouri: But [it is said] foreigners will settle the public lands. Be it so. There was a time when every white man in this country was a foreigner. It is from such a stock that we have sprung. And I presume foreigners are just as worthy now as they were when the United States were first colonized. Two centuries have not been without their effect, in improving the mental and physical condition of the people of Europe. During that time they have learnt something of the rights of man, and something of the principles of free government. I am not afraid that their settlement in the United States will injure either our morals or our politics. But, aside from this, the people of Europe will migrate to this country. Every year our immigration is becoming more and more numerous. And no man supposes that this Government will undertake to prevent it. The question, then, is not whether we shall have foreigners in the United States, but what is the best disposition to be made of them. Now, I have no doubt but that it is much better for us in every point of view, that our foreign population should live in the new States as independent farmers, than in the old States in dependent want. At present the European immigrants crowd our large cities. That is not the situation most favorable to the study of the character of our institutions, nor best calculated to impress a stranger with the extent of our privileges. But if, by a system of legislation at once just and beneficial to our citizens generally, we can induce the foreign immigrant to make his home in the West, we secure his attachment and fidelity to our institutions. As soon as he finds himself in possession of a home of his own, and occupying a position that makes him a free man—free from the control, direction, and oppression of a superior, he will and must feel proud of American citizenship. He becomes identified with us in hopes, in interest, and feeling. He realizes the fact that our prosperity is his prosperity, and his study will be to discharge all the duties of a good and faithful citizen; and he will be bound, through good report and through evil report, to the cause of the country. The poor immigrant who remains in an old State, and is there subject to numberless annoyances and oppressions which men of his condition but too often experience, may, possibly, entertain but little concern for us or our Government, but the poor immigrant who, escaping from the pauperism and distress of Europe, is given a homestead in a new State, and is thus secured in an abundance for himself and family, must feel his heart swell with gratitude for the nation which has done so much to promote his welfare, and must labor for its success and perpetuity. . . . .

Mr. Richard I. Bowie, of Maryland: It may be recollected, Mr. Chairman, by those who did me the honor to listen to my introductory remarks, that I considered the tendency of this bill—its effects as a precedent—as one of the greatest objections to it. I repeat, that though this bill may not contain provisions which will *now* admit all future emigrants from Europe, yet, let it become a law, and it becomes a wedge by which our public domain will be forced open to them. . . . .

Mr. Chairman, can anything be more dangerous than the infusion of an undue proportion of a dissimilar people among our own? Can anything, in other words, be more dangerous at this period, than the infusion of an undue proportion of foreign sentiment, foreign habit, and foreign influence, into the American mind? Our census now shows us that almost every fourth, at least every fifth, man in this country is an European, or the descendant of an European, since 1790. Reflect, sir! See the large influence, social, moral, and political, which they are daily acquiring. Consider the increase of 1,500,000 within the last ten years, and, if newspaper accounts are to be credited, the increase of nearly a quarter of a million within the last nine months. What effect must these have upon the theory and action of this Government? upon our foreign and domestic policy? upon intervention at home and abroad? Is there no danger of European ascendancy in American councils? Ours is a Government which lives and acts by public opinion. . . . .

A. G. Brown, of Mississippi: The fear has been expressed that the passage of this bill will encourage an influx of foreigners, and, that instead of 500,000 per annum, we shall have 1,000,000 of emigrants to our shores. I do not think so. All come now that can get here. They come for freedom, and not for land. But suppose this prediction should prove true, I shall not be appalled. Let them come; yes, sir, let them come. They are of the same great family with ourselves. Heaven made this mighty continent, not for our benefit alone, but for the use and benefit of all mankind. Let them come to it freely. It is the gift of God, and we have no right to withhold it from his people.

What is the objection to an increase of our foreign population? I have heard but one that is worthy of consideration; and that is, that they congregate about our towns, oftentimes become unruly, and too frequently swell the calendars of crime. This bill strikes down this objection at a single blow. It encourages these people to abandon the purlieus of your towns and cities; to give up vagrancy and crime, and become the owners, occupants, and independent cultivators of the soil. Does any man object to the Irish or German emigrant who cultivates the soil with his own hands? Is he not as orderly, as quiet, and as law-abiding a citizen as your native sons? And do not the products of his labor go as far towards an increase of your national wealth? For one, I am willing to receive all who come to us from abroad, if they come to cultivate the soil.

Heaven has bounded our Republic with two mighty oceans, thus placing a barrier deep and wide between us and the despots of the old world. I would not impiously defy the protection of Providence by crossing this barrier to attack despotism in its stronghold; but upon every breeze that sweeps the Atlantic I would send a message to the oppressed millions of Europe, bidding them come—come to an asylum on these shores, prepared by the Almighty, and defended by his chosen people.

It is said again, that this is a scheme of the Jesuits to extend the Catholic religion in our country, and to cripple or put down the Protestant faith. I was raised a Protestant believer, and I hope to die a professor of the Protestant religion. But it is no part of my Protestant faith to fear the Catholics. I am no more afraid that the Catholics will upset the Protestant church, than I am that the subjects of crowned heads in Europe will overturn democracy in America. To the Catholic, as well as to the Protestant emigrant, I extend a hearty greeting, and a cordial welcome. If he cultivates the soil, he will most likely be a Democrat; and whether he worships in a Catholic or a Protestant church, he will make us a good citizen.

I have heard it said, the effect of this bill, if it becomes a law, will be to encourage foreign emigration, and that as most of these come to us with strong anti-slavery prejudices, we of the South are but nerving the arm of an enemy when we advocate its passage. If slavery is to be defended by excluding those from abroad who have prejudices against it, its doom is fixed, and the sooner the fiat for its extinction goes forth the better. I place my defense of this institution on the high ground of moral, social, religious, and political propriety, and if I cannot defend it on this ground I will not defend it at all.
. . . .

Mr. Fayette McMullin, of Virginia: Those gentlemen representing manufacturing interests dislike the idea of seeing this bill pass. Why?

They fear that the laborers—the manufacturing hands—will leave the manufacturing districts and go to the West, and that, in consequence of the diminution of laborers, the wages of labor will advance among them. This, they fear, will be the effect of the emigration of the laborer from the North and East to the West. Sir, I say let these men go to the West; and the emigration invited from abroad will fill their places—the foreigners will take their positions in the manufacturing districts at the North. Oh! some gentlemen have a holy horror of foreigners; some gentlemen in this country object to foreigners coming amongst us. I think that objection comes with a very bad grace from any man that is a descendant of a foreigner. And is there any man in this House, or in this country, who is not the descendant of a foreigner? When our Pilgrim Fathers first landed at Jamestown, were not they foreigners? And why did the gentleman from Maryland (Mr. Bowie) the other day get up here and undertake to abuse foreigners? Are there not in this House and in this country many gentlemen who have an aversion to the immigration of the Irish and Dutch? I was entertained by the gentleman from Mississippi (Mr. Brown) who addressed the House so ably and eloquently upon this question. He presents himself as the son of a land squatter. If it were proper to speak of myself, personally, I could show to the House that, although I am not the son of a squatter, yet I am the grandson of an Irishman and a Dutchman. My grandparents on both sides were Dutch and Irish. I feel mortified and disgusted at this aversion to the emigration of foreigners.

Mr. Chairman, I say to these gentlemen, be not alarmed. Let the foreigners avail themselves of homes in the land of freedom—let them come amongst us. Go back and examine the sentiments of Patrick Henry. What were his views? "Fetter not commerce. Invite foreigners to your country; let them fell the forests, and cultivate the soil." Mr. Chairman, I say let them come. I fear not the ecclesiastical influence of Catholics. I believe too firmly in the truth of the Protestant Christian theology, to fear any injury to our institutions by the influx of Catholics. I say let them come. Why do you wish them to remain in their own country, tied down by the most tyrannical laws upon earth—the mere dupes and serfs of the aristocrats of the Old World? Ah! if I were disposed to raise a political question—which by-the-by, I am not disposed to do—I could account for the dislike of certain gentlemen to the immigration of Dutch and Irish to this country; there is rather too much democracy amongst them; they are the most democratic of all the foreigners that come to our shores. Yes, sir, I say let them come. They will make you good citizens. They are good soldiers, and peaceable, quiet, orderly citizens.

But pass this bill, and what else will you do? You will rid your cities, New York, Philadelphia, Baltimore, and all the large cities of the Union, of their surplus population—a population weighing like an incubus upon those cities. Let them go to the West and settle upon those lands, where they may acquire a competency for themselves and for their families. . . . .

V. E. Howard, of Texas: But this bill will stimulate to emigration thousands in Europe who cannot reach the land in the West after they arrive in our Atlantic cities. They are coming fast enough at best, quite as rapidly as we can provide for them and educate them to our system of government. Eight thousand recently landed in New York in a single week. I have seen it stated that there are 15,000,000 in France, of a population of 35,000,000, in absolute want, or obtaining a difficult and precarious subsistence, which is constantly liable to terminate in actual destitution. The proportion is nearly as large in other European countries. They have no hope for the future, for themselves and children, but in emigration. The property-holders in those countries, for their own safety, are contributing largely to send them to this continent. They will come fast enough without any artificial stimulants from the legislation of Congress. . . . .

It is a great mistake to suppose that you will materially better the condition of the man in the old States, or the Atlantic cities, by giving him 160 acres of land in the far West. The difficulty with him is not that of procuring the land, but to emigrate himself and family to the country where it is, and to obtain the means of cultivating it. Without this the grant is useless to the poor man. The gift, to make it efficient, should be followed up by a further donation to enable the beneficiary to stock and cultivate it. It would be a far greater boon to all our citizens, of native and foreign origin, to furnish them for a few dollars, a rapid means of reaching the land States in the West; and this, in my opinion, may be accomplished by exercising the legitimate powers of the Government, and without drawing upon the Treasury, or diminishing the value of the public domain as a source of revenue. And the truth should not be forgotten, that the man who is upon the public lands and does not procure means to purchase, will never have industry and thrift sufficient to keep his farm, if you give it to him. Once in a new country, his labor readily commands a rate of compensation which will in a short time enable him to become a landholder. I have observed with astonishment the magical influence of this change of residence, in the case of the German emigrant in Texas. The first year of his emigration, without being able to speak the English language, he contrives to save enough from his earning, to purchase a tract of land ample for a moderate farm. The next year there appears upon it a neat cabin, and a moderate-sized, well-cultivated field, and about the house a few head of stock. In half a dozen years he has purchased some adjoining tract of land, enlarged his building and his fields, has numerous herds upon the prairies, and is a man of substantial wealth. He is a useful member of society. If he brought with him ideas of socialism, which is often the case, he has by this time abandoned them, as unfit for a new country, where wealth is within the reach of any man who is not ashamed of honest toil. Indeed, your German is a true practical philosopher. His sentimentality never stands in the way of his thrift. As soon as he has obtained and stocked his farm, he begins to lay by some cash for the purchase of a few negroes. I welcome the German emigrant. He is industrious, frugal, intelligent, conservative, and attached to republican government. The German does not require, or need this gratuity from Government. He is naturally a pioneer, and relies with confidence and success upon his own industry and perseverance. There are very few foreigners of other nations, who could be made agriculturalists by donations of lands. Neither can I see any necessity for this system of largesses.

## 24. A Sympathetic View of Immigration[1]

. . . . Within [our] vast domain there are millions of acres of fertile land, to be purchased at moderate prices, according to its position and its state of improvement, and there are hundreds of millions of acres in a state of nature, and gradually selling at the government price of a dollar and a quarter per acre.

It is this which most strikes the European imagination. . . . . Generally speaking, the mass of the inhabitants of Europe regard the ability to hold and occupy a considerable landed property as the summit of human fortune. The suggestion that there is a country beyond the ocean, where fertile land is to be purchased, in any quantity, at a dollar and a quarter per acre, and that dollar and a quarter to be earned in many parts of the country by the labor of a single day, strikes them as the tales of Aladdin's lamp or Ali Baba's cave would strike us, if we

[1] Extract from Edward Everett, "Discovery of America," June 1, 1853, *Orations and Speeches*, III (Boston: Little, Brown, 1892), pp. 213–16, 220–23.

thought they were true. They forget the costs and sacrifices of leaving home, the ocean to be traversed, the weary pilgrimage in the land of strangers after their arrival. They see nothing with the mind's eye but the "*land* of promise"; they reflect upon nothing but the fact, that there is a region on the earth's surface where a few days' unskilled labor will purchase the fee-simple of an ample farm.

Such an attraction would be irresistible under any circumstances to the population of an old country, where, as I have just said, the land is all appropriated, and to be purchased, in any considerable quantity, only at prices which put its acquisition beyond the thought of the masses. But this is but half the tale. It must not be forgotten that in this ancient and venerable Europe, . . . . a considerable part of the population, even in the most prosperous regions, pass their lives in a state but one remove from starvation, poorly fed, poorly clothed, poorly housed, without education, without political privileges, without moral culture. . . . .

Most of the governments are arbitrary, the taxes are oppressive, the exactions of military service onerous in the extreme. Add to all this the harassing insecurity of property and life. For sixty or seventy years the continent has been one wide theatre of scarcely intermitted convulsion. Every country in it has been involved in war; there is scarcely one that has not passed through a revolution. . . . . Terrified by the recent experience or the traditions of these miseries, thousands immigrate to the land of promise, flying before, not merely the presence, but the "rumor of war." . . . .

Ever and anon some sharp specific catastrophe gives an intense activity to immigration. . . . . Beyond everything else which has been witnessed in modern times, the famine which prevailed a few years since in Ireland, gave a terrific impulse to immigration. Not less, probably, than one million of her inhabitants left her shores within five years. The population of this island, as highly favored in the gifts of nature as any spot on the face of the earth, has actually diminished more than one million eight hundred thousand since the famine year; the only example, perhaps, in history, of a similar result in a country not visited by foreign war or civil convulsion. The population ought, in the course of nature, to have increased within ten years by at least that amount; and in point of fact, between 1840 and 1850, our own population increased by more than six millions.

This prodigious increase of the population of the United States is partly owing to the immigration from foreign countries, which has taken place under the influence of the causes, general and specific, to which I have alluded. Of late years, from three to four hundred thousand immigrants are registered at the several custom-houses, as arriving in this country in the course of a year. It is probable that a third as many more enter by the Canadian frontier. Not much less than two millions of immigrants are supposed to have entered the United States in the last ten years; and it is calculated that there are living at the present day in the United States five millions of persons, foreigners who have immigrated since 1790, and their descendants. . . . .

[The] "Celtic Exodus," as it has been aptly called, is to all the parties immediately connected with it one of the most important events of the day. To the emigrants themselves it may be regarded as a passing from death to life. It will benefit Ireland by reducing a surplus population, and restoring a sounder and juster relation of capital and labor. It will benefit the laboring classes in England, where wages have been kept down to the starvation-point by the struggle between the native population and the inhabitants of the sister island for that employment and food, of which there is not enough for both. This benefit will extend from England to ourselves, and will lessen the pressure of that competition which our labor is obliged to sustain, with the ill-paid labor of Europe. In addition to all this, the constant influx into America of stout and efficient hands supplies the greatest want in a new country, which is that of labor, gives value to land, and facilitates the execution of every species of private enterprise and public work.

I am not insensible to the temporary inconveniences which are to be set off against these advantages, on both sides of the water. Much suffering attends the emigrant there, on his passage, and after his arrival. It is possible that the value of our native labor may have been depressed by too sudden and extensive a supply from abroad; and it is certain that our asylums and almshouses are crowded with foreign inmates, and that the resources of public and private benevolence have been heavily drawn upon. These are considerable evils, but they have perhaps been exaggerated.

It must be remembered, in the first place, that the immigration daily pouring in from Europe is by no means a pauper immigration. On the contrary it is already regarded with apprehension abroad, as occasioning a great abstraction of capital. How the case may be in Great Britain and Ireland, I have seen no precise statement; but it is asserted on apparently good grounds, that the consumption and abstraction of capital caused by immigration from Germany amounts annually to twenty millions of rix-dollars, or fifteen millions of our currency.

No doubt, foreign immigration is attended with an influx of foreign pauperism. . . . . It is said, that, owing to some defect in our [Massachusetts] system or its administration, we support more than our share of needy foreigners. They are sent in upon us from other States. New York, as the greatest seaport, must be exposed also to more than her proportionate share of the burden. However the evil arises, it may no doubt be mitigated by judicious legislation; and in the meantime Massachusetts and New York might do a worse thing with a portion of their surplus means than feed the hungry, clothe the naked, give a home to the stranger, and kindle the spark of reason in the mind of the poor foreign lunatic, even though that lunatic may have been (as I am ashamed, for the credit of humanity, to say has happened) set on shore in the night from a coasting-vessel, and found in the morning in the fields, half dead with cold, and hunger, and fright.

But you say, "They are foreigners." Well, do we owe no duties to foreigners? What was the founder of Virginia, when a poor Indian girl threw herself between him and the war-club of her father, and saved his life at the risk of her own? What were the Pilgrim Fathers, when the friendly savage, if we must call him so, met them with his little vocabulary of kindness, learned among the fishermen on the Grand Bank, "Welcome, Englishmen"? "They are foreigners." And suppose they are? Was not the country all but ready, a year or two ago, to plunge into a conflict with the military despotisms of the east of Europe, in order to redress the wrongs of the oppressed races who feed their flocks on the slopes of the Carpathians, and pasture their herds upon the tributaries of the Danube, and do we talk of the hardship of relieving destitute foreigners, whom the hand of God has guided across the ocean and conducted to our doors?

Must we learn a lesson of benevolence from the ancient heathen? Let us then learn it. The whole theatre at Rome stood up and shouted their sympathetic applause, when the actor in one of Terence's plays exclaimed "I am a man; nothing that is human is foreign to me."

I am not indifferent to the increase of the public burdens: but the time has been when I have felt a little proud of the vast sums paid in the United States for the relief of the poor immigrants from Europe. It is an annual sum, I have no doubt, equal to the interest on the foreign debt of the States which have repudiated their obligations. When I was in London a few years ago, I received a letter from one of the interior counties of England, telling me that they had in their house of correction an American seaman (or a person who pretended to be) who from their account seemed to be both pauper and rogue. They were desirous of being rid of him, and kindly offered to place him at my disposal. Although he did not bid fair to be a very valuable acquisition, I wrote back that he might be sent to London, where, if he was a sailor, he could be shipped by the American Consul to the United States, if not, to be disposed of in some other way. I ventured to add the suggestion, that if her Majesty's Minister at Washington were applied to in a similar way by the overseers of the poor and wardens of the prisons in the United States, he would be pretty busily occupied. But I really felt pleased, at a time when my own little State of Massachusetts was assisting from ten to twelve thousand destitute British subjects annually, to be able to relieve the British empire, on which the sun never sets, of the only American pauper quartered upon it.

### 25. The Position of the "American Party"[1]

The American Party is denounced as fostering hostility to foreigners. This assertion is often presented under such colorings and with such statements of facts as, when examined, are not facts, that an air of plausibility is thrown over the portraiture drawn by the disordered fancy of its opposers. But where is the evidence that the new party is enkindling and fostering hostile feelings against foreigners? O, it is palpable, because they will not allow them to hold office—you proscribe them for their religion, because you would exclude Catholics from official trusts. With such premises, we are not surprised at their conclusions, for the former are as barren of intelligence, as the latter are destitute of logic. Could you conceive of a more indefensible and absurd assumption, than that I am hostile to a citizen and prejudice others against him, because I do not conceive him qualified to legislate or rule, and therefore would not consent to his elevation to an official position? There could not be a more stupid assertion. Upon the same ground, it must then be maintained, that whoever is not possessed of the needful qualifications to make or administer law, and therefore not placed in a responsible office, becomes an object of distrust and hate on the part of those who withold from him their suffrages. So that, if you regard an Irishman or German a useful citizen, because he

[1] Extract from *The Sons of the Sires; A History of the Rise, Progress, and Destiny of the American Party*. By an American (Philadelphia, 1855), pp. 115-18, 173-74.

has strength to dig canals and construct railroads; or because this one is a mechanic, and that one a farmer or merchant, and contributes to the general good by pursuing that vocation for which he is fitted; but if you do not nominate and elect him to some office, you are fostering hostile feelings against him—and all other classes under like circumstances?

Palpably absurd as such a mode of argumentation must appear to a man of good sense, it is all that can be alleged in support of the assertion that the American Party engenders and nurses malevolent feelings against foreigners. The members of this association are fully satisfied that however useful many foreigners are in the various departments of human industry, they are totally unfit to occupy official stations. . . . . But if we keep in view the education of these men, the peculiar influences which were active in maturing their character, and unavoidable predilections which the form of government under which they grew up produced in their minds, and the evidences found in each and every one of them that their distinctive nationalities are interwoven with the very texture of their being—we will assure ourselves of the wisdom of the policy, which aims to exercise that precaution in the choice of rulers necessary to avert the evils of a maladministration of the government. So far from being actuated by feelings of hostility towards foreigners, it can be demonstrated to the satisfaction of all whose minds are open to conviction, that whatever of apparent illiberality there may seem to be in this creed, it is after all the soundest and most liberal policy towards them. It is because we love them and the interests of our country, that we would give them no higher political position than citizenship, and that only after they are duly prepared. As such, they can be happy and useful, unless they are victims of unholy ambition; and if those fires are burning within them, they offer the most irrefragable proof of their own unfitness for an office of trust.

Those in our midst of foreign nativity, must agree with us as to the wisdom of this position, when they calmly look at the peculiar circumstances of our nation. The immense influx of foreigners has something alarming in its aspect. We grant that many come with the best intentions, but could the nation confide in their loyalty, should an emergency arise to endanger our liberties? However high our estimate of the immigrant population may be in general, it is notorious that a large number are of very questionable reputation, and others are tarnished with the deepest crimes. How are they to be distinguished? Or will those who had become obnoxious to the laws of their native land, be wise and just administrators of law here? To whatever extent the sympathies of others for aliens might carry them in the way of granting favors, we cannot hazard such a perilous experiment.

To exalt them to office would only tend to strengthen that inbred disposition to keep up their distinct nationalities, and thus retard the fusion of those antagonistic elements which agitate the social body, into one truly American character. Let them be contented with the tens and hundreds of thousands of native-born who fill the various occupations of life, and who never aspire to official stations. Let our foreigners first learn to obey, before they would rule. Let them teach their children that obedience and love due to the government that protects their persons and property. What then is the hostility fostered against aliens by the new order? It has no existence save in the heated brains of those who court that influence for vile political purposes. It is a cry raised by those who have long since been accustomed to barter for the foreign element. . . . .

[Foreigners in the United States] have carried themselves altogether too loftily, and have essayed to discourse of American habits and institutions, in a manner totally unbecoming in men who profess warm attachment to our form of government. Having scarcely touched upon American soil, they set themselves up for our teachers, and freely discuss all questions pertaining to the social state, while they understand them as little as would an imported Hottentot. It is positively insufferable to witness such arrogance and presumption. They have abused American generosity, and repaid their hospitality by gross insults or by officious meddlings in our elections. Having always been the victims of oppression, they understand not the just limits of liberty, and run to that other extreme, where they want nothing but the power to become the worst of oppressors. When we recount the officious interference of foreigners in our political affairs—their bearing at the polls—their dictation—their threats if their demands are not complied with by our rulers, we are really amazed at the measure of forbearance exercised towards them.

## 26. "America for Americans"[1]

Well, why not? Is there another country under the sun, that does not belong to its own native-born people? Is there another country

[1] From the *New York Mirror*, reprinted in *The Wide-Awake Gift: A Know-Nothing Token for 1855*, edited by "One of 'Em" (New York, 1855), pp. 40–43.

where the alien by birth, and often by openly boasted sympathy, is permitted to fill the most responsible offices, and preside over the most sacred trusts of the land? Is there another country that would place its secret archives and its diplomacy with foreign states, in other than native hands—with tried and trusty native hearts to back them? Is there another country that would even permit the foreigner to become a citizen, shielded by its laws and its flag, on terms such as we exact, leaving the political franchise out of sight? More than all else, is there a country, other than ours, that would acknowledge as a citizen, a patriot, a republican, or a safe man, one who stood bound by a religious oath or obligation, in political conflict with, and which he deemed temporarily higher than, the Constitution and Civil Government of that country—to which he also professes to swear fealty?

America for the Americans, we say. And why not? Didn't they plant it, and battle for it through bloody revolution—and haven't they developed it, as only Americans could, into a nation of a century and yet mightier than the oldest empire on earth? Why shouldn't they shape and rule the destinies of their own land—the land of their birth, their love, their altars, and their graves; the land red and rich with the blood and ashes, and hallowed by the memories of their fathers? Why not rule their own, particularly when the alien betrays the trust that should never have been given him, and the liberties of the land are thereby imperilled?

Lacks the American numbers, that he may not rule by the right of majority, to which is constitutionally given the political sovereignty of this land? Did he not, at the last numbering of the people, count seventeen and a half millions, native to the soil, against less than two and a half millions of actually foreign-born, and those born of foreigners coming among us for the last three-quarters of a century? Has he not tried the mixed rule, with a tolerance unexampled, until it has plagued him worse than the lice and locust plagued the Egyptian? Has he not shared the trust of office and council, until foreign-born pauperism, vice and crime, stain the whole land—until a sheltered alien fraction have become rampant in their ingratitude and insolence? Has he not suffered burdens of tax, and reproach, and shame, by his ill-bestowed division of political power?

America for the Americans! That is the watchword that should ring through the length and breadth of the land, from the lips of the whole people. America for the Americans—to shape and to govern; to make great, and to keep great, strong and free, from home foes and foreign demagogues and hierarchs. In the hour of Revolutionary peril, Washington said, "Put none but Americans on guard to-night." At a later time, Jefferson wished "an ocean of fire rolled between the Old World and the New." To their children, the American people, the fathers and builders of the Republic, bequeathed it. "Eternal vigilance is the price of liberty!"—let the American be vigilant that the alien seize not his birth-right.

America for the Americans! Shelter and welcome let them give to the emigrant and the exile, and make them citizens in so far as civil privileges are concerned. But let it be looked to that paupers and criminals are no longer shipped on us by foreign states. Let it be looked to that foreign nationalities in our midst are rooted out; that foreign regiments and battalions are disarmed; that the public laws and schools of the country are printed and taught in the language of the land; that no more charters for foreign titled or foreign charactered associations —benevolent, social or other—are granted by our Legislatures; that all National and State support given to Education, have not the shadow of sectarianism about it. There is work for Americans to do. They have slept on guard—if, indeed, they have been on guard—and the enemy have grown strong and riotous in their midst.

America for the Americans! We have had enough of "Young Irelands," "Young Germanys," and "Young Italys." We have had enough of insolent alien threat to suppress our "Puritan Sabbath," and amend our Constitution. We have been a patient camel, and borne foreign burden even to the back-breaking pound. But the time is come to right the wrong; the occasion is ripe for reform in whatever we have failed. The politico-religious foe is fully discovered; he must be squarely met, and put down. We want in this free land none of this political dictation. . . . . Our feeling is earnest, not bitter. The matters of which we have written are great and grave ones, and we shall not be silent until we have aided in wholly securing *America for the Americans!*

### 27. "Who Are Americans?"[1]

What is America, and who are Americans? . . . . Accordingly as you answer will the phrase appear very wise or very foolish. If you are determined to consider America as nothing more than the two or three million square miles of dirt included between the Granite Hills and the Pacific, and Americans as those men exclusively whose bodies

[1] Extract from *Putnam's Monthly; A Magazine of American Literature, Science, and Art,* V (May, 1855), 533-40.

happened to be fashioned from it, we fear that you have not penetrated to the real beauty and significance of the terms. The soul of a muck-worm may very naturally be contented with identifying itself with the mould from which it is bred, and into which it will soon be resolved, but the soul of a man, unless we are hugely misinformed, claims a loftier origin and looks forward to a nobler destiny.

America, in our sense of the word, embraces a complex idea. It means, not simply the soil with its coal, cotton, and corn, but the nationality by which that soil is occupied, and the political system in which such occupants are organized. . . . .

America is the democratic republic—not the government of the people by a despot, nor by an oligarchy, nor by any class such as the red-haired part of the inhabitants, or the blue-eyed part; nor yet a government for any other end than the good of the entire nation—but the democratic republic, pure and simple. This is the political organism which individualizes us, or separates us as a living unity from all the rest of the world. All this, of course, would be too elementary to be recounted in any mature discussion, if recent events had not made it necessary to an adequate answer of our second question—who, then, are Americans? Who constitute the people in whose hands the destinies of America are to be deposited?

The fashionable answer in these times is "the natives of this continent, to be sure!" But let us ask again, in that case, whether our old friends Uncas and Chingachgook, and Kag-ne-ga-bow-wow, whether Walk-in-the-water, and Talking-snake, and Big-yellow-thunder, are to be considered Americans par excellence? Alas, no! for they, poor fellows! are all trudging towards the setting sun, and soon their red and dusky figures will have faded in the darker shadows of the night! Is it, then, the second generation of natives—they who are driving them away—who compose exclusively the American family? You say yes; but we say no! Because, if America be as we have shown, more than the soil of America, we do not see how a mere cloddy derivation from it entitles one to the name of American. . . . .

The real American, then, is he . . . . who, abandoning every other country and forswearing every other allegiance, gives his mind and heart to the grand constituent ideas of the Republic—to the impulses and ends in which and by which alone it subsists. If he have arrived at years of discretion—if he produces evidence of a capacity to understand the relations he undertakes—if he has resided in the atmosphere of freedom long enough to catch its genuine spirit—then is he an American, in the true and best sense of the term.

Or, if not an American, pray what is he? An Englishman, a German, an Irishman he can no longer be; he has cast off the slough of his old political relations forever; he has asserted his sacred right of expatriation (which the United States was the first of nations to sanction) or been expatriated by his too ardent love of the cause which the United States represents; and he can never return to the ancient fold. It would spurn him more incontinently than powder spurns the fire. He must become, then, either a wanderer and a nondescript on the face of the earth, or be received into our generous republican arms. It is our habit to say that we know of no race or creed, but the race of man and the creed of democracy, and if he appeals to us, as a man and a democrat, there is no alternative in the premises. We must either deny his claims altogether—deny that he is a son of God and our brother—or else we must incorporate him, in due season, into the household. It is not enough that we offer him shelter from the rain— not enough that we mend his looped and windowed raggedness—not enough that we replenish his wasted midriff with bacon and hominy, and open to his palsied hands an opportunity to toil. These are commendable charities, but they are such charities as any one, not himself a brute, would willingly extend to a horse found astray on the common. Shall we do no more for our fellows? Have we discharged our whole duty, as men to men, when we have avouched the sympathies we would freely render to a cat? Do we, in truth, recognize their claims at all, when we refuse to confess that higher nature in them whereby alone they are men, and not stocks or animals? More than that: do we not, by refusing to confess a man's manhood, in reality heap him with the heaviest injury it is in our power to inflict, and wound him with the bitterest insult his spirit can receive?

We can easily conceive the justness with which an alien, escaping to our shores from the oppressions of his own country, or voluntarily abandoning it for the sake of a better life, might reply to those who receive him hospitably, but deny him political association: "For your good will, I thank you; for the privilege of toiling against the grim inclemencies of my outcast and natural condition, which you offer, I thank you; for the safeguard of your noble public laws, I thank you; but the blessed God having made me a man, as well as you—when you refuse me, like the semi-barbarians of Sparta, all civil life; when, with Jewish exclusiveness, you thrust me out of the holy temple, as a mere proselyte of the gate—your intended kindnesses scum over with malignity, and the genial wine cup you proffer brims with wormwood and gall."

We are well aware of the kind of outcry with which such reasoning is usually met. We know in what a variety of tones, from the vulgar growl of the pot-house pugilist to the minatory shriek of the polemic, frenzied with fear of the Scarlet Lady, it is proclaimed that all foreign infusions into our life are venomous, and ought to be vehemently resisted. Nor do we mean to deny the right of every community to protect itself from hurt, even to the forcible extrusion, if necessary, of the ingredients which threaten its damage. But that necessity must be most distinctly proved. The case must be one so clear as to leave no doubt of it, as an absolute case of self-defense. Now, there is no such overruling necessity with us, as to compel either the exclusion, or the extrusion, of our alien residents. . . . .

It will be replied to what we have hitherto urged, that our argument proceeds upon an assumption that aliens are to be totally excluded from political life; whereas nobody proposes such a thing, but only a longer preparatory residence.

We rejoin, that the persons and parties who are now agitating the general question, because they propose the exclusion of adopted citizens from office, do, in effect, propose a total political disqualification of foreigners. All their invectives, all their speeches, all their secret assemblages, have this end and no other. They agree to ostracise politically every man who is not born on our soil; they conspire not to nominate to any preferment, not to vote for, any candidate who is born abroad; and these agreements and conspiracies are a present disfranchisement, so far as they are effective, of every adopted citizen, and a future anathema of every alien. Whether the aim be accomplished by public opinion, by secret conclave, or by law, the consequences are the same; and the general objections we have alleged, to the division of society into castes, apply with equal force.

We rejoin again—in respect to the distinction made between a total exclusion of foreigners, and a change in the naturalization laws—that it is a distinction which really amounts to nothing. For, firstly, if the probation be extended to a long period, say twenty-one years, as some recommend, it would be equivalent to a total exclusion; and, secondly, if a shorter period, say ten years, be adopted, the change would be unimportant, because no valid objection against the present term of five years would thereby be obviated. . . . .

In fact, the entire logic of the Nativists is vitiated by its indis-criminating character. Because a large number of the Irish, and a considerable number of the Germans, have been reduced, by the long years of abuse which they have suffered at home, to an inferior man-hood, it is argued that all the rest of the Germans and the Irish, and all the Swiss, English, French, Scotch, Swedes, and Italians must be made to suffer for it: but what a grievous error! The poor exiles and refugees, many of them, are no doubt sufficiently debased—some, even, excessively insolent, too—but among them are others who are not so; among them are thousands upon thousands of men, of hardy virtues and clear intelligence, whose industry contributes vastly to the wealth, as their integrity does to the good order, of our society. Laboring like slaves for us, they have built our cities and railroads; piercing the western wilds, they have caused them to blossom into gardens; taking part in our commerce and manufactures, they have helped to carry the triumphs of our arts to the remotest corners of the globe. . . . .

The adopted citizen, no doubt, preserves a keen remembrance of his native land; but "lives there on earth a soul so dead" as not to sympathize in that feeling? Let us ask you, oh patriotic Weissnicht, all fresh as you are from the vociferations of the lodge, whether you do at heart think the less of a man because he cannot wholly forget the play-place of his infancy, the friends and companions of his boy-hood, the old cabin in which he was reared, and the grave in which the bones of his honored mother repose? Have you never seen two long-separated friends, from the old world, meet again in the new, and clasp each other in a warm embrace, while their conversation blossomed up, from a vein of common memory, in "Sweet household talk, and phrases of the hearth," and did you not love them the more, in that their eyes grew liquid with the dear old themes? Or is there, in the whole circle of your large and respectable private acquaintance, a single Scotchman to whom you refuse your hand because his affections melt under the "Auld Lang Syne" of Burns, or because his sides shake like a falling house when "Halloween" or "Tam O'Shanter" is read? Can you blame even the poor Frenchman if his eyes light up into a kind of deathless glow when the "Marseillaise," twisted from some wandering hurdy-gurdy, has yet power to recall the glorious days in which his fathers and brothers danced for liberty's sake, and with gay audacity, towards the guillotine? We venture to say for you, No! and we believe, if the truth were told, that often, on the lonely western plains, you have dreamed over again with the German his sweet dream of the resurrection and unity of the Fatherland? We have ourselves seen you, at the St. George dinners, oh Weissnicht, swell with a very evident pride when some flagrant Englishman, recounting, not the battles which his ancestors for ten centuries had won on every field of Europe, but the better trophies gained by Shakespeare, Milton, Bacon, or Cromwell, told you that a little of that same blood coursed in your veins! The blood itself, as it tingled through your body and suffused your cheeks, confessed the fact, if your words did not! How, then, can you, who gaze at Bunker Hill with tears in your eyes, and fling up your hat of a Fourth of July with a jerk that almost dislocates the shoulder, retire to your secret conclave, and chalk it up behind the door, against the foreigner, that he has a lingering love for his native country? Why, he ought to be despised if he had not, if he could forget his heritages of old renown, for it is this traditional tenderness, these genial memories of the immortal words and deeds and places, that constitute his patronymic glories, which show that he has a human heart still under his jacket, and is all the more likely, on account of it, to become a worthy American. Do not you delude yourself, however, into the shallow belief that the aliens, because of these sentimental attachments, will be led into the love of their native governments, which having plundered them and their class for years, at last expelled them to our shores. . . . . Now, these are experiences that are apt to make republicans of men, and to fill them with other feelings than those of overweening attachment to oppressors!

But this is a slight digression, and we return to the main current to our argument, to say—what we esteem quite fatal to all schemes for excommunicating foreigners, or even greatly extending their minority —that the best way, on the whole, for making them good citizens, is to make them citizens. The evils of making them a class by themselves we have already alluded to, and we now speak, on the other hand, of the benefits which must accrue to them and to us from their absorption into the general life of the community. It is universally conceded by the liberal writers on government and society that the signal and beneficent advantage of republican institutions (by which we mean an organized series of local self-governments) is that their practical influences are so strongly educational. They train their subjects constantly into an increasing capacity for their enjoyment. . . . .

At the same time, the lists of preferment being open to them, they cultivate the virtues and talents which will secure the confidence of their neighbors. Every motive of ambition and honor is addressed to them, to improve their condition, and to perfect their endowments; while a consciousness of their connection with the State imparts a sense of personal worth and dignity. In practice, of course, some show themselves insensible to these considerations, but a majority do not. The consequence is that the commonalty of the republic are vastly superior to the same classes abroad. Compare the farmers of our prairies to the boors of the Russian steppes, or to the peasants of the French valleys! Or compare the great body of the working men in England with those of the United States! Now, the American is not of a better nature than the European—for he is often of the same stock —nor is there any charm in our soil and climate unknown to the soil and climate of the other hemisphere; but there is a difference in institutions. Institutions, with us, are made for men, and not men for the institutions. It is the jury, the ballot-box, the free public assemblage, the local committee, the legislative assembly, the place of trust, and as a result of these, the school and the newspaper, which give such a spur to our activities, and endow us with such political competence. The actual responsibilities of civil life are our support and nutriment, and the wings wherewith we fly.

If, consequently, you desire the foreigner to grow into a good citizen, you must subject him to the influences by which good citizens are made. Train him as you are yourselves trained, under the effective tutelage of the regular routine and responsibility of politics. He will never learn to swim by being kept out of the water, any more than a slave can become a freeman in slavery. He gets used to independence by the practice of it, as the child gets used to walking by walking. It is exercise alone which brings out and improves all sorts of fitnesses— social as well as physical—and the living of any life alone teaches us how it is to be best lived. Nor will any one work for an end in which he and his have no part. They only act for the community who are of the community. Outsiders are always riders. They stand or sit aloof. They have no special call to promote the internal thrift and order, which may get on as it can, for all them. But incorporate them into it, and it is as dear as the apple of their eye.

### 28. "Know-Nothingism" Contrary to the American Tradition[1]

As a doctrine, . . . . what does Know-Nothingism propose? The political disability of vast numbers of men, on the ground of race or

[1] Extract from "Secret Societies—The Know-Nothings," by Parke Godwin *Putnam's Monthly*, V (January, 1855), 95–97.

religion. Can anything be more intolerant, narrow, or bigoted? Did the old priestly or warlike tyrannies, which man has been writhing under these centuries back, lend themselves to a meaner dominion than this would assert for our young Republic? The fetid and defunct dynasties which have become a loathsome remembrance to men, which were terrible fungi in their day, and a reproach for ever, grew from roots like these it is now proposed to plant in our soil. We that have made it our song ever since we were born, that here humanity had at last found a home, that here all the antiquated distinctions of race, nationality, sect, and caste, were merged in the single distinction of manhood—that here man was to be finally recognized as man, and not as Jew or Gentile, as Christian or Mohammedan, as Protestant or Catholic—we, who have made the world ring with self-glorifications of the asylum of the oppressed of all creeds and nations, of the city of refuge to all the weary exiles of freedom, "whom earth's proud lords, in rage or fear, drive from their wasted homes," we are now asked to erect political barriers, to deal out political excommunication as narrow, as mean, as selfish, and as unwarrantable as ever debased the elder governments.

That a preparatory residence and discipline should be required of foreigners, before their incorporation into the State, is reasonable; the extent and nature of such social quarantine may also be conceded to be a question for discussion; but the total exclusion of aliens from citizenship for the future is so monstrous a meanness that one is loath to entertain the conception. It is such an utter and unequivocal surrender of nearly every peculiarity of our institutions, that it would not merely lay all the new comers under ban, but denationalize ourselves! The cry is, "America for Americans," and we agree to it heartily, but what is America, and who are Americans? "He is not a Jew," saith the apostle, "who is one outwardly," and America, in the same sense, is not a certain measurable area of territory, nor the American every miserable biped that happens to be born upon it. America is the cognomen of a nation of men, and not of a collection of arable acres; and Americans are not simply the individual Indians, negroes, and whites who first saw light between Passamaquoddy and Pensacola but all who are Americans inwardly—who are built up on the American idea, who live in the true sentiment of democracy, whose political "circumcision is of the heart, in the spirit and not in the letter, and whose praise is not of men but of God." These are the true Americans, wherever they chanced to be born—whether Turk, Russian, Milesian, or Choctaw, and are infinitely to be preferred to the unthinking and virulent natives whose Americanism sinks no deeper than their skins, and had no existence before their flabby little bodies were first swaddled. America to the Americans, surely—not to the spurious, skin-deep, apparitional Americans, but to the real men worthy of the name!

We are apt to suppose, in projecting these exclusions, that the persons shut out are the only persons seriously affected by them, but that is a woeful mistake. He that commits injustice, he that perpetrates meanness, suffers from it as badly as he that is the direct victim. Curses, like young chickens, says the familiar old proverb, always come home to roost. Debar the half-million of emigrants who annually reach our shores from the elective franchise, and what would be the effect? Why, the growth, in the very midst of the community, of a vast disfranchised class—of an immense body of political lepers- -of men having an existence apart from their fellow-men, not identified with them, not incorporated with society; and consequently tempted on all sides to conspire against it, to prey upon it, and to keep it in disorder. Coming here ignorant, vicious, unruly, aliens would remain ignorant, vicious, and unruly; for they would have few of the strong motives which they now have to become orderly and estimable citizens. They would remain outside of those educational influences which are the glory as well as salvation of free institutions, the jury, the ballot, the legislative assembly, etc., and which render it so important to us to extend those influences to all who are members of our societies. We have already, in the midst of us, one class of outcasts, in the poor and degraded free blacks, and that, we should think, sufficient to appease anybody's malignity, without striving to raise up another from the Germans, the Irish, or any other nation.

It is scarcely possible, however, to believe that the Know-Nothings contemplate such an extreme error as the entire exclusion of future aliens from political life. It must be a calumny of their enemies, or a product of suspicion aggravated by fear. At any rate, we are certain that the late political *tourbillons* which have sent such swift consternation and dismay into the hearts of the old political foxes have not been caused by any affinity for such a project. We have too much respect for our fellow-citizens to suppose it; but we ascribe these extraordinary movements to other sources. They are a result of a double reaction— firstly, against the excessive cultivation of foreigners by the demagogues, and secondly, against the miserable folly and corruption of the old political parties.

It cannot be denied that, for some years now, both whigs and democrats have prostrated themselves before the alien voters, in a servile and disgraceful way. Holding the balance of power, as the latter did, between the two parties, there was no end to the concessions, the flummeries, and the substantial *douceurs*, too, by which they were courted. Honors and offices were heaped upon them with a profusion which recalled the début of some popular actress, and the showers of bouquets which greeted her from her adoring friends. It was better to be an Irishman, or a German than a native American; a "Mac" or "O'" to one's name was the handle which lifted him to fortune—and an unpronounceable German patronymic was a passport to all kinds of political favor. No ticket was a complete ticket which did not contain a sop, in the shape of a candidate to the Irish interest or the German interest, and the suppleness with which senators and governors bent themselves in that direction set new lessons in the art of fawning —gave new formulas for the preparation of adroit lies. Is it a wonder, then, that the Americans themselves, shoved so wholly into the sha-dow, should get a little tired of the game? More especially, when the same influences which introduced the foreigners into political office, were likewise introducing them into so many private places of emolu-ment and trust? Not at all! But the foreigners were not to blame for it, at least, for nothing beyond a little natural presumption occasioned by their good luck. The dastardly and unprincipled demagogues, who wheedled them into excesses, are the offenders who should bear the brunt of the punishment. Let all those, too, who hereafter appeal to the citizens under any other name than Americans, come in for a share, and then we shall have "America for the Americans," in the truest and best sense of the phrase.

### 29. "National Hospitality"[1]

[It has become apparent that] the questions arising out of the great influx of foreign population to our land, are of sufficient moral, social and religious consequence to demand the most careful investigation, and the utmost candor in discussion. . . . . We must look at them in the light of the past; in the light of those general laws which have ever moulded and controlled the social and political forms and movements of our race. We must look at them as matters, whose decision is to affect the future more than the present; the countless millions of our posterity, more than ourselves; and the entire civilization of the world,

[1] Extract from Rev. W. H. Lord, *A Tract for the Times: National Hospitality* (Montpelier, 1855), pp. 5, 21-44.

more than the interests of any party, religious sect or national government. . . . .

That the character of the emigrants, as a whole, has somewhat depreciated with the increase of their number is susceptible of easy proof. Formerly the emigration from the old countries was confined to that class which possessed both substance and intelligence, and were well fitted, after a suitable interval, to become useful and valuable citizens. But as the flood has increased in size, it has brought much of the dregs of European society, and its stream has been foul with the sediment and drift of the old world. Multitudes have been brought to the land, whose expatriation has been assisted by the selfish generosity of their various governments—those who "left their country for their country's good," and have but little claim upon our charity or hospitality. They are of a class most fitly designated by Carlyle as the "devil's regiments of the line," for whom he would neither build "model prisons," nor enclose them in the loving embrace of a sentimental philanthropy. Thus at the same time that this tide has been draining Europe of her peasantry and artizans, it has drawn in also, by the helping hand of foreign states, far too many criminals and paupers. These, like heavy and decaying substances, are for the most part stranded in the large cities where they land. . . . . In the two cities of New York and Boston, with a foreign population of 200,081, there were convicted of criminal offenses, in the year 1850, not far from 8,000 persons of foreign birth, while in all the north-western States, comprising aliens to the number of nearly 800,000, there were but 768 commitments of foreigners. The ratio of pauperism was nearly the same. If we compare the statistics of Massachusetts and New York with those of Ohio and Wisconsin, there will be found a like result. Massachusetts, with a foreign population of 141,850, on June 1, 1850, held within her alms-houses 4,059 natives and 1,490 aliens; and within her prisons, at the same date, 653 native-born and 583 foreigners. New York fed in her poor-houses, on that day, 5,755 of the children of her soil, and 7,075 of her 582,625 strangers; and in her jails and modern prisons 649 natives and 639 foreigners. At the same time Ohio, with an army of 200,722 aliens, supported at the public expense 1,254 native and 419 foreign paupers, and 102 native and 31 foreign criminals; while Wisconsin, with 87,117 foreigners, had from among them in her alms-houses, 166, and in her prisons, 35.[1]

These facts, while they certainly reveal fearful sources of imminent

[1] De Bow. *Compendium of the Census of 1850.*

danger, do yet indicate some ground of encouragement. They show that while the ratio per cent. of crime and pauperism is largely, almost incredibly, against the alien in the eastern cities, it is yet nearly equal between the native and foreign population of the western states. It is of some advantage to the whole country that the disease is *localized;* and if the bad municipal administrations of the seaports shall be re-formed, as now seems most probable, even this deadly evil may be greatly reduced. It is to be deeply lamented that the European emigration leaves such a fearful impress upon the large cities of our Atlantic States, and yet a calm looker-on must trace much of the evil, even in these places, to the sharp practices, impositions and temptations to which the newly landed emigrant is subject from American cupidity and mismanagement; and to the preceding corruptions and contacts and debasing influences of the ocean voyage. . . . .

Doubtless Europe has found it cheaper to send her beggars and convicts here, than to support them at home: still it is not because of a few thousands of this sort, who have been colonized by national appropriations, or swept along with the grand current of emigration, that we should deny the rights of hospitality to the millions of honest artizans and laborers; of the best industrial and mechanical forces the world has ever possessed; of our plowmen and vine-dressers; of our architects and teachers; of our manufacturers and machinists; of the finest materials of armies, whose loss England and Germany now bitterly mourn, and can never compensate; whose gain by us has given such unexampled development to western production and pros-perity; has covered our hills and plains with the vine and corn, and stimulated every form of ingenious and productive labor. . . . .

To the high character of the large part of the English and German emigration there is the most ample testimony. Very few paupers arrive from England, though there are occasional cargoes forwarded by the governments of Baden, Bavaria, Hesse, Würtemberg and Switzerland. But these bear an insignificant proportion to the whole. . . . . "It may be admitted as a fact that out of twenty German emigrants, nineteen take out with them the means to establish themselves in the inland States." They are, it is true, unlike us in many things; unlike us in their personal habits; in their untidiness and uncleanliness; in their low moral notions; in their want of versatility; as, also, in their patient assiduity and skill; in their concentration of energy, and in their reverence for authority and age. But yet they have many of the best elements of the Saxon race, and have exhibited ever in their religious, social, and civil relations—as history uniformly attests—a disdain of ecclesiastical superstition; a hatred of priestly domination; a strong dull common sense, proof against the assaults of fanaticism; an active instinct for personal freedom, secure possessions, and legislative power. . . . .

Yet while the principles on which our institutions are founded, . . . . require us to open our gates, and nail them back to the walls, . . . . there are yet limits to our national hospitality. . . . . There is no principle of charity that requires man to love his neighbor better than himself; no law of courtesy that can compel a nation to open its arms to the transported convicts of other powers, or to the expatriated ex-tenants of jails and dungeons. . . . . This heritage of our fathers is never to be made a penal colony. And as heartily as we would welcome the honest and industrious—however poor and ignoble—laborers of the old world, so heartily would we return its corrupt and outlawed inhabitants. Cheerfully as we should open our gates to its wandering artizans and ingenious workmen, so sternly should we close them on the outcast and abandoned. Discrimination is also to be made between poverty and crime, and between pauperism and poverty. Poverty implies neither intellectual nor moral nor physical debasement. Crime and pauperism involve each of them, to a greater or less extent. Hence, it is a duty we owe to ourselves, to the best portion of the emigration from Europe; to the virtue of coming ages, to re-ship to their native lands the exported convicts and paupers of foreign countries. A few such transshipments would induce the nations of Europe to solve their own problems of this sort. . . . .

But there are certain other aspects of this foreign question that should not be overlooked. The dangers to the integrity of the State are seriously urged upon our attention. It is said in objection to the kindly reception of a foreign population, that there is no room for them here; that it is unwise to open our territory to their occupancy. It is more than hinted that they crowd too closely upon our native residents; that they fill the places which belong to our own citizens; and that we must have "America for the Americans." A little reflection and analysis will refute all such objections. It is a palpable fact, that while the supply of laborers from the old world is so great, yet the demand for them has increased in a still greater ratio. The papers in all the agricultural states have been filled with calls for labor. Letters from every part of the country have been addressed to the overcrowded population of the cities. While the poor have been starving in the Atlantic ports, it has been impossible to find laborers at any price to cultivate the West. One Wisconsin journal calls for 10,000 laborers to be employed at the most remunerative wages. . . . . There is no reason to fear that the country will be made worse by any addition of healthy laborers, while there is work for them to do, and heads to direct them. Our native population dislikes to work; but is shrewd and intelligent, and is abundantly able to direct the foreign element. . . . .

No necessity of economy compels us to inhospitality; and the consciousness that we do not hold an equitable title to by far the larger part of our territory; that it has nearly all been wrung from the reluctance of the aboriginal inhabitants, either by conquest or fraud; should not add to our indisposition to open to the starving of other lands the blessing of this.

It is asserted that the political evils attending the foreign immigration are constant and stupendous, and consequently require the restrictive influence of law. That these evils are numerous and great, no one would be willing to deny; and yet it is not impossible to exaggerate and mistake them. The right of suffrage is one not to be trifled away or committed to unworthy hands. . . . . Yet it should be, on this account, most zealously guarded; and proper limitations to this right might exclude from its exercise as many natives as foreigners. And we imagine that the worst evils arising from the increase of an alien population are to be found in the corrupt truckling of the leading political parties to what they are wont to designate the foreign vote. The pleasant courtesies of native politicians have intoxicated the credulous alien; and the rival bids for his suffrage have invested him with an inflated consequence. For this great damning political sin, of cherishing and nursing a foreign vote, and consolidating the suffrages of the naturalized aliens, these parties are now suffering dismemberment and overthrow. Their retribution is just; and we have no more sympathy to waste over their destruction, than praise to bestow upon the means by which it is accomplished. But a reflecting man must need apprehend a greater consolidation of the foreign interest than ever before. The true policy was to divide and not to unite this vote. If it should ally itself with the *disjecta membra* of the old parties, it may present a new and more dangerous front than we have ever beheld. . . . .

It may be borne in mind also, as showing the small political influence that can be exerted by the aliens, that while they comprise one-sixth of the whole population, their vote is but one-twelfth; and doubtless four-fifths of that vote is cast by those whose hearts are enlisted in the prosperity of American institutions and principles. . . . . There is, it is to be feared, but little difference between the American and the foreigner who can be bought; or between the purchased voter and his native buyer. For all the political danger to be apprehended, we see not, therefore, with the exceptions already named, why aliens should be struck off the roll of national hospitality. . . . .

The real political evil of the immigration arises from the criminals and refugees of other countries; steeped in solid ignorance and vicious debasement; whom the governments of Europe have been engaged in transporting, at public charges, to our shores; and from that other class of noted and unnoted, restless, uneasy and furious revolutionists, who have exchanged the necessary rigor of military law, or discipline of penal colonies, for a liberty of speech and action, which degenerates in their cases, to reckless licentiousness. It is this class who seek to inflame the foreign desperadoes against the native citizens; who get up processions in cities; establish red-republican orders, which seek to dictate terms of administration to municipal authorities; are feasted by partizan leaders and legislatures; and carry on their hostile proceedings against other States under cover of our flag, that calls for exclusion and restriction. It is for their benefit that we would have a thorough revision of our emigration and naturalization laws; a revision that should teach them to preserve the modesty that belongs to guests, and the courtesy that is due to their hosts. . . . .

The moral and religious evils of foreign immigration are palpable to all eyes. The intemperance, vice, and immorality, the desecration of the Sabbath, the blasphemy and infidelity that attend its course, are neither to be palliated nor denied. They demand as correctives, not only the strong hand of legislative enactments, but also the most assiduous moral and religious instruction and rebuke. And were we not amply provided with resisting and antagonist forces, there might be some apprehension as to the result. . . . .

. . . . We should open . . . . the vast, rich and productive country stretching from sea to sea, and almost wholly lying waste, which the bounty of Providence has conferred on us. Freely we have received, and freely we should give.

It will, however, be instructive to notice the various compensating features of the foreign element. It would be difficult to compute the stimulating effect of this army of laborers on our productive industry, and on our national capital and resources. They have created more wealth than if all the kings and aristocracy of Europe had been driven to seek a refuge in this land. Beside bringing with them an amount equal to several millions annually, they add to our productive capital an incredible sum. Estimating the average productive value of the emigration at $500 per head—which is the computed value of the southern slaves—and there has been added to our active and producing capital in the last fourteen years, the vast amount of $1,430,167,500, or at the rate of $102,127,500 per annum. The results of their industrial labors can be reckoned only by hundreds of millions every year. They, chiefly, have created that wealth by which the United States are able to import $159,643,612 more than ten years since; and in that period have raised the exports $119,252,204, and increased the customs from 18 millions in 1842 to 59 millions in 1853. They have augmented, in the same period, the net value of agricultural and manufactured products—the value over the cost—75 millions.

These facts are sufficient to show the immense industrial energies which attend the course of the immigration to this country. Doubtless statistics also, if they were accessible, would disclose a similar beneficial effect upon the mechanical and manufacturing interests, though these have drawn—except in some of their higher departments—more upon our native population; while the vast field of agricultural and internal improvement has been thrown wide open to the foreign laborer. America would not have had her canals, her railroads, and the whole internal net work of commerce—most potent to excite and stimulate every industrial interest—had it not been for foreign aid. Without this, to this day, the journey from the Atlantic to the Mississippi might have taken two weeks, and the ungathered corn and wheat of the prairies might have still fatted the roving herds of the West. Without this, who would have done the hard work that was required in order to develop the resources of our new and boundless domain? Where would have been the bone and sinew and muscle to have levelled the mountains and filled up the valleys and subverted the soil of our land? These questions need only to be suggested in order to show how effectually this stream of foreign emigration has subserved the advancement and material glory of this country. . . . .

There are, also, high social and political benefits from this foreign influx, that compensate in a great degree for its evils. The progress of civilization keeps pace with the mixture of races. It is no small advantage to a people to combine two or three distinct types of national character, when they can unite harmoniously and peaceably. A people of which all its individual members are referable to a single type, is, among the nations, what a celibate is among individuals. Its life is unproductive and monotonous. . . . . The colossal greatness of England is the resultant of Danish, Norman and Saxon blood; and who shall say that the Anglo-Saxon type of American character, combining with German solidity and Celtic vivacity, may not achieve a far more splendid destiny than has been attained by any former nation; and that this destiny has not its elements in the blending and reaction of its primitive types. As other nations have become homogeneous, they have relapsed into lethargy. Hence a national hospitality, which is to result in the vast advantage of both parties, should never be declined or reluctantly granted. The inconveniences and evils of the transition and absorbing process are not to be weighed with the permanent benefits which will flow to national character from the union of these several types of humanity. . . . .

Still another political advantage of foreign emigration is, that it is gradually affecting the balance of power in the Union. In 1800, the entire population of the slave states was 48 per cent of the whole, and their representation in Congress was 45 per cent. In 1830, they had 45 per cent of the former, and 41 of the latter; and in 1850, but 41 per cent of the population, and 39 per cent of the representation.[1] It requires no prophet to foresee that the same disturbing causes will continue so long as the peasants and mechanics of Europe can find cheap homes, high wages and an improved moral and social position in the new world as easily as they have done. It requires no prophet to foretell the gradual investment of slavery by a cordon of free labor, and the ultimate diminution of the political power of the slave states to comparative insignificance. These results of the perpetuation of a policy of national hospitality to the honest emigrants of the continent, are as sure as the issues of any natural principle or law of Providence. . . . .

It is clearly then for our national advantage to welcome, with the utmost cordiality, to our territory and to our institutions, the whole

[1] [Mr. Lord quoted here the following statement made by Ex-governor Smith of Virginia: "The North has 55 more Representatives than the South already. The natural increase of the South is ⅓ greater than the North, because there are greater checks in population there; but the artificial element of foreignism brings 500,000 who settle annually in the free States with instincts against Slavery, making 50 Representatives in 10 years to swell the opposition to the South. To stop this enormous disproportion what is our policy? What is the frightful prospect before us? . . . . Our highest duty to the South is to discourage immigration. I deprecate it as a great calamity."]

industrial portion of the European emigration. With the exception of its transported criminals, and its exiled paupers, and its uneasy, discontented refugees; it is for our highest interest to extend the most generous and undiscriminating hospitality to these foreign races.

### 30. Immigrants Welcomed[1]

It will be seen at once that we have plenty of land yet unoccupied, and there is no danger as yet of crowding one another. Eight persons to a square mile give us a really sparse population. The case in Europe is considerably different. There, the smallest degree of density is to be found in the kingdom of Sweden and Norway, where the population numbers 4,645,007, and where there are but 15.83 inhabitants to a square mile. The largest degree is to be found in Belgium, with a population of 4,426,202, and a density of 388.60 to a square mile. Eight countries in Europe, namely, Austria, France, Great Britain and Ireland, Prussia, Belgium, Denmark, Holland, and Switzerland, have an average density of 207 inhabitants to a square mile. It is not surprising that, while we have so much land, which it is utterly impossible for us to use or occupy, the crowded population of Europe should annually send off immense numbers to find a home in the western world, where there is so much room for them, and such ample accommodations. We are glad that they come. We would welcome them and give them on our soil a free and happy home. We deprecate, to the utmost, that dog-in-the-manger policy which would attempt to prevent their using what we ourselves do not want, and cannot improve.

While we are on this branch of our subject, let us see to what extent this foreign element is mingled into our population. In the whole country, out of a white population of 19,553,068 in 1850, there were but 2,240,581 foreign born persons. The number may have increased to about 3,000,000 by the present time of writing. This is a ratio of about 9 per cent of the aggregate population. This population was divided in 1850 into 1,239,464 males, and 1,001,117 females. Such is the extent. It seems to us not a very formidable array of numbers.

Whatever danger there is to be apprehended from the mixture of foreigners with the native population, it certainly does not arise from the number of foreigners. For that is comparatively small. Does it come from the number of votes which they are able to throw, in a

[1] Extract from an article on "The Moral of Statistics," by A. Woodbury, in the *New Englander*, XIII (1855), pp. 189-91.

hotly contested election? By the tables presented in a speech delivered
by Hon. N. P. Banks, of Massachusetts, during the late session of
Congress, we find that, at the last presidential election, out of a canvass
of 1,931,024 votes in fourteen states, giving a majority of the electoral
vote, the foreign vote numbered just 258,548, or in a proportion of one
to seven and a fraction. In these states there was then a foreign
population of 1,763,497. The proportion of the number of voters to
the population is nearly the same with the proportion of foreign voters
to the whole number of votes cast. In these fourteen states it is found
that of the whole foreign population 856,480 were Irish born, who were
mostly Catholics. Of the remainder, nearly 1,000,000, a large proportion must be Protestants, or at least not Catholics. Assuming that
seven is the ratio, we have for the sum total, in these states, of Irish
voters, Catholic and Protestant, 122,354. We are very apt to hear of
"millions of foreigners," and of "a half-million of Catholic voters,
ignorant, superstitious, and semi-civilized, controlling our elections,"
and the like. We suggest that a little caution on this score, and a
stricter adherence to facts, in such a discussion as the nation happens
now to be engaged in, would by no means be amiss. We do not see a
great deal of danger in the number of foreign voters. We apprehend
that there is more to be feared from native demagogues.

That there is danger of some sort arising from a large number of
foreigners in a republic like ours, when they come as foreigners and
continue foreigners, there can be no doubt. We should be the very last
to deny it. But it does not depend so much upon the fact that, in the
Providence of God, they were born in another country, as upon the
fact of their character. We think there are thousands of native
Americans, voters too, who are exercising an influence dangerous and
detrimental to the best interests of the nation. If those persons, who
are borne to our shores from the old world, are disposed to retain their
old national characteristics, and refuse to blend themselves with our
ways of thought and life; if they come as monarchists, as tools of
despotism, as those who would attempt a subversion of our government and our institutions, and abuse the liberty which we give them,
if they reject the means we offer them of becoming republicans, there
can be no question of the exceeding peril to which we are this very hour
exposed. If such be the case, no very large number would be required,
provided there were sufficient shrewdness and tact among them. We
have evidence enough to satisfy the most skeptical, of the power which
a few resolute and determined men can exercise, in the success of the

slaveholders of the country, 347,525 in all, in forcing their policy upon the national legislation. But there is as yet very insufficient evidence of an intention among our "adopted citizens" to make any such attempt upon the country's liberties. The greatest part are those who have learned to look upon America as the field where their enterprise and industry will give them better returns than in the countries they leave. Many of them have a downright and settled hatred of oppression in the form in which it presents itself at home. They are really republican at heart, and come here to learn more of republicanism. So that a vast majority of them readily and easily become Americanized, and have a national pride in being Americans, so far as they can be, and glory in having American-born children. It is true that some are ignorant and semi-civilized. Yet they do not compare very unfavorably in this respect with some portions of our country, whose influence on the national character is unquestionably injurious, and just now controls the national government.

### 31. "The Humbug of the Know-Nothings"[1]

The present canvass has been prodigiously fruitful in all sorts of roorbacks, humbugs, misrepresentations and even downright falsehoods. . . . .

When a Democratic editor or newspaper points to the identity of the Know Nothing and the old Federal parties, as far as their common hostility to foreign immigration is concerned, he is invariably told that, although the objections to immigration fifty years ago were absurd, yet that the causes which made immigration desirable have ceased, the land has inhabitants enough, and that we should keep the domain for our children. Without stopping to point out, for the fiftieth time, that the repeal of the naturalizations laws will in no manner diminish or affect immigration, let us see whether our landed estate is already filling up too rapidly.

The census of 1850 furnishes us with the following facts, which effectually demonstrate the absurdity of this argument of the Know Nothings:

Area of the United States, 3,306,865 of square miles, or 2,116,383,-600 acres. Number of acres in farms, 293,560,614; number of acres improved, 113,032,614; number of acres unimproved, 180,528,000; total in farms, as above, 293,560,614.

[1] Extract from an article in the *Richmond Examiner*, May 1, 1855, by Henry A. Wise. reprinted in James P. Hambleton, *A Biographical Sketch of Henry A. Wise* (Richmond, Virginia, 1856), pp. 321-24.

It has therefore required, from this official statement, 320 years to bring 113,032,614 acres under cultivation, and we have yet left the small number of *two billions three millions* of unimproved lands. We are therefore certainly not in imminent peril of our dense population covering our limited possessions two or three layers deep, and the excess slipping off into the Atlantic and the Pacific oceans. The absurdity of this humbug of Know Nothingism might be rendered still more glaring by a calculation, demonstrating how greatly the two billions of unimproved acres, might be made to add to our national wealth, by cultivation and population; but the good sense of our readers will render such an argument unnecessary.

The second humbug maintains that immigration has increased the pauperism of this country, and that New York and the New England States are taxed to support the paupers of Europe. The simple fact that immigration profitably employs a large portion of the marine of the free States, renders their railroads and canals valuable, and enriches thousands who, in the shape of boarding-house keepers, agents, runners, and store-keepers, prey upon the immigrants after their long sea voyages, would be a sufficient refutation of this assertion. But there is still more conclusive evidence. The German emigrants alone bring into this country annually, it has been estimated, 11,000,-000 of dollars in gold and silver. The commissioners of emigration for the State of New York so state. But the enemies of immigration, pinned to the wall by this fact, say the Irish paupers, not the Dutch, are the rascals who are devouring the substance of New York and New England.

Here, again, stubborn and unquestionable facts nail the falsehood to the counter. . . . .

The president of the Irish Emigration Society . . . . proves that a tax laid upon the immigrants more than pays all their expenses, that there is now on hand a surplus of 64,000 dollars, and that there has been paid to the charitable institutions of the State of New York, for their disinterested care and support of the "pauper Irishmen," the sum of 93,500 dollars.

This then is a truthful picture of Irish pauperism, and New York philanthropy. . . . .

The third roorback and humbug of the Know Nothings, is "that the influx of foreigners depreciates the price of labor." This is the rankest and most transparent nonsense which we have yet heard, even from the order which has inaugurated misrepresentation as one of their cardinal virtues. The price of labor is, like everything else that can be bought or hired, regulated by the demand for it. If immigration did not open new resources by bringing immense tracts of land under cultivation, by opening roads for the exchange of commodities between the various portions of the country, and by an increased home consumption, it would necessarily come to pass, that a constant influx of foreign mechanics and laborers would soon glut the market and depreciate the price of labor.

But the fact is, that the wages of labor have increased more rapidly, during the last seven years, than they have ever done, and yet, during the last seven years, immigration has also more rapidly increased than at any subsequent period of our history as a nation.

## 32. A Democratic Reply to the Know-Nothings[1]

Not to arrest immigration by absolute prohibition, but to suffer foreigners to come hither and then to deny them the privileges of citizenship, is so foolish and fatal a policy that it is difficult to understand how any man of ordinary intelligence, can assent to it. A repeal of the laws of naturalization will not sensibly diminish the flow of immigration. By so harsh and illiberal a policy, we may repel some of the prouder, brighter and more aspiring spirits, who might seek freedom and distinction in this country; but as the vast mass of immigrants come here only in quest of peace and bread, they would not be driven away by exclusion from office or the polls. The tide would continue to flow with undiminished impetuosity; but the character of the immigration would be sadly deteriorated. And the effect of the Know-Nothing policy would be such, that in a few years the community would be divided into two distinct and antagonistic classes of privileged patricians and disfranchised plebeians. The native would be haughty and overbearing, from a sense of personal consequence and the distinction of caste. The foreign-born population, detached and dissociated from the community; exasperated by consciousness of wrong and degradation; bound by no interest to the state; driven into compact array by the blows of oppression and animated by exclusive sympathies and hopes, would be indeed an alien people in a foreign country; and instead of being, as they now are, an element of wealth in peace and of strength in war, they would become a source of distraction, disease, confusion

[1] Extract from an article in the *Richmond Enquirer* on "Immigration—Position of the Democratic Party," reprinted in the *Citizen*, II (New York, May 5, 1855), 283.

and inconceivable calamity. If, therefore, our foreign population be a pest, let us not strengthen them for evil, while we inflame their passions and exasperate revolt. The true policy is either to mitigate the evil, or else eradicate it by some sweeping and efficient remedy. Rather than pursue the insane policy of Know-Nothingism, it would be better by arbitrary enactment to expel our foreign-born fellow-citizens from the country, and to prohibit further immigration.

But the Democratic party denies that the foreign population is a pest. Without regard to the accidental abuses of immigration or naturalization, we contend that our foreign-born fellow-citizens have contributed incalculably to the power and glory of the country—that they have imparted a prodigious impulse to the development of its resources and to its progress in wealth and refinement. On the other hand, they have done nothing to retard the growth or to dishonor the name of America. Why, then, the proposition to proscribe and degrade them? Is it from the apprehension that they would ultimately subvert the liberties of the country. To this suggestion the Democratic party responds, "Sufficient unto the day is the evil thereof." When our foreign-born fellow-citizens manifest a disposition to overthrow the government and destroy the country, it will be time enough to fetter them with disabilities and to treat them as traitors. Meanwhile we maintain that any tendency to excessive immigration will be corrected by the irresistible laws of nature, or rather by the kind care of Providence. So long as the tide of immigration flows hither, it shows that the country is in want of labor—and when that is not the case, the current will turn without an artificial impulse, and run in another direction. The law of supply and demand, which is, in political economy, what the principle of gravitation is in the physical universe, will correct the evils of immigration. Indeed, we may already perceive that the tide of immigration is ebbing, and beginning to flow in the contrary direction.

### 33. A German View of the Know-Nothing Movement[1]

Enmity toward immigrants, religious hatred, professional envy, and the passion for oppression have cast off their masks and are appearing openly under the title "Know-Nothingism." They have already raised their banners in many states. Their main principles are: Those who are not born in this country can never hold an office or become

[1] Extract translated from Karl Büchele, *Land und Volk der Vereinigten Staaten von Nord Amerika. Zur Belehrung für Jedermann, vorzüglich für Auswanderer* (Stuttgart, 1855), pp. 411-13.

citizens. Catholics shall not be allowed to take any oath, because they will always remain enemies of the United States. Those who use strong drink, such as wine, beer, and whisky shall be declared incapacitated. Those who seek recreation or drink intoxicating liquor on Sunday are condemned.

German-American papers go on to say that, at the same time, these natives have an inner respect for European intellect which can expose their deficiencies and represent their ideas as lacking in truth. To be sure, they are conscious of the fact that European culture presents a strong contrast to the beaten path which they themselves follow mechanically. . . . . Members of this group have already proposed in Congress that only those immigrants from Europe who are able to pay $250 when entering the United States should be admitted. In state legislatures more far-reaching proposals are made, and it has already been advocated in some ports that every ship carrying poor people sent out by their communities should be immediately sent back. The same intolerance is shown in religious matters. Preachers who paint the Catholic church in darkest colors are hired to talk on the street, and the minds of people are stirred up to such an extent that it will soon be impossible to prevent bloody clashes in the large cities. . . . . It is, at least, certain that if the question of slavery does not frustrate the plans of the "Know-Nothings," little will prevent them from carrying out their plans. The place of refuge to which thousands of Europeans still look hopefully will remain closed to them or cease to give them shelter, and the star-covered banner of the Union will temporarily sink into the darkest night.

Only recently has the creed of the "Know-Nothings" been published in full. Without justifying the abuse of German-American newspapers to the degree indicated above, it deals neither with the domestic form of government, justice, nor the more narrow administration, the system of education, taxes, and tariffs. It does not mention the question of slavery or Cuba, and is silent on the position of the Republic in relation to foreign powers, peoples, and ideas. The origin and purpose of the organization, which is secret, must be found within special, narrow limits. It is the American antagonism against foreigners in general and especially against the Irish, against the influence of the Catholics and their participation in the political life of the Union. The organization wants to prevent the immigrant element, which it estimates at half a million annually, from being favored and used for party purposes to the same extent as heretofore. Above all, it has set itself the task of frustrating the attempt of the Roman hierarchy which wants to secure for itself a definite influence over the politics of the country to the detriment of the Protestant faith. The latter tendency had long been pointed out by different American newspapers as endangering the liberty and constitution of the country. It is well known that the Irish everywhere flocked with success around the Catholic Archbishop Hughes of New York, and that for them was formed their own press combination which has grown to large proportions. Not a little of this national uneasiness has been contributed by Brownson's *Quarterly Review*, published in New York, which is regarded as the official organ of the archbishop, and at one time summarized its political and religious views on the domination of the world in the following fashion: "The past has shown the difference between the worldly and the spiritual and even the combination of the two as external government, but we must go a step farther and show that all power is uniform in origin and principle, and that in a deeper, inner sense, the alleged independence of temporal power is nothing but atheism."

In the popular, fantastic conceptions of the future of America prevalent among immigrants and European writers, an important part is played by a notion which is not justified by actual experience; namely, that the rude materialism which now dominates American life, although it demoralizes and weakens man, will at some time descend from its throne and hand over its scepter to higher spiritual and moral development. That sounds very well, but when and how will this happen? No answer to this question can be found at present. . . . . If, however, in the near future, culture penetrates into those parts of the country where the log cabin now stands, it will be a culture like that of New York and Boston, judging from past experience. As the cities of the East develop, luxury and poverty only become greater and the increase in boats, houses, people, machines, railroads, trade, and industry in general, now thriving rapidly, is only a quantitative measure of progress. "America could be the real country of men," say certain newspapers, "if slavery, crudeness, and narrowmindedness did not prevent it from being the true country of man."

### 34. An Irish View of "Know-Nothingism"[1]

. . . . We have at all times been averse to the course taken by those who fled from Ireland, within the last six years, without taking

---

[1] Extract from the *Dundalk Democrat*, reprinted in the *Citizen*, II (New York, July 14, 1855), p. 438.

time to consider maturely the prospects before them, and the dangers
and difficulties they would meet with in a strange land. They rushed
headlong from their native country, instead of battling for land and
life, and flung themselves amongst a people who are proverbial for
their love of gain, and who welcomed the Irish, not because they
sympathized with their sufferings, but because they required them to
build their railroads, dig their canals, clear their forests, till their
fields, and work in their factories.

We are told now that Jonathan has got more of the Irish than he
requires, and lest the Celt should become his master, that he desires
to oppress him as the Egyptians oppressed the Israelites in Egypt.
A storm of Know-Nothing persecution rages against the Irish and their
religion in America, the object of which is to deprive them of many of
their civil rights, and if possible make it penal to profess their faith
openly.

We cannot believe that this persecution will continue very long.
We believe that the good sense of the country will again return, and
that the bastard policy of the Know-Nothings will speedily die out.
But while censuring the outrageous conduct of the Know-Nothings, let
us be impartial and just. Has this persecution been unprovoked? Have
all the Irish conducted themselves, as citizens of the Great Republic,
in that sober, orderly, and prudent manner becoming a persecuted
people who fled from the lash of tyrants and found a home and a refuge
in America?

We fear that some of them have been a noisy, turbulent, and
intolerant class, who did no credit to the character of their native
country, and were of little benefit to the land of their adoption. We
fear, too, that some of the ultra Catholic journals went far beyond
the bounds of prudence in writing on religious subjects.

We do not make these remarks to palliate the conduct of the native
despots, who assign and malign the Irish. We merely allude to the
matter for the purpose of stating that the conduct of some of the
Irish emigrants is not what it ought to be, and to counsel them to give
up their intemperate habits, their rows, their faction fights, and act
in such a manner as to earn the respect of their bitterest enemies.

If they do this they will at once disarm the Know-Nothings, and
bring to their aid every good citizen in the United States, those glorious
spirits who subscribe to the tolerant views of Washington, Jefferson,
and the other illustrious fathers of the Republic. But if by their follies
they disgrace themselves, can it be wondered at if the Americans

declare that such a people are unworthy to share with them the freedom and blessings guaranteed by the constitution of their country?

What, we ask, would the Irish people say, if two millions of Russians, Prussians, or Greeks should come amongst them, and by their conduct set us all by the ears, commence rows in our streets, faction fights on our railways; and in their journals assail our creed, and evince little willingness to respect our best institutions? Would not the native population begin to think it right to exclude them from public offices, and declare them dangerous foes to the country?

We still consider the United States a better home for the Irish emigrant than any colony belonging to despotic England. . . . . The Irish Catholics can maintain the freedom of their faith in the States, if they only act prudently, and warn their newspaper writers to be less intolerant on religious topics. What good can they effect for the faith by calling Protestants hard names? No man ever made a convert by such means as that; on the contrary, it is by showing themselves good Christians, full of charity, benevolence, and kindness to their neighbors, that they will prove the superiority of their religion, and attract persons differing from them to inquire into its dogmas, and in the end submit to its teaching.

These are our views. . . . . We have no doubt that many of the Irish in America are not faultless, and that they are not what they ought to be. Let those turbulent characters reform themselves and persecution will soon die a natural death. The good sense of the American people will revolt against it; and remembering how the Irish bled in the struggle for independence, Jonathan will clasp them to his breast, and both united will make the Republic of the West the enemy of slavery and depotism, the refuge of the persecuted, and "the home of the brave, and the land of the free."

### 35. "European Immigration—the Grecian Horse of the American Republic"[1]

The American people, those born and reared on American soil, have but one opinion as to the general principles which embody our institutions, or, in other words, our system of government. They differ only in measures of immediate or local policy. Out of that difference, political parties arise, and at our elections we determine, by the expressed wish of a majority of the people, what measure, or what course

[1] Extract from Thomas Richard Whitney, *A Defence of the American Policy as Opposed to the Encroachments of Foreign Influence* (New York, 1856), pp. 161-85.

of local policy, shall be adopted; but whatever it is, it is sure to be in conformity with the general principles of our government. The intelligence, the fidelity, the *home sentiment* of our countrymen are a sufficient guarantee of such a result. But what guarantee have we, where the votes of those bred under our institutions are overborne or neutralized by the votes of those who regard our system as not sufficiently democratic; or those who deem it too puritanical in its respect for the Sabbath; or those who declare that no government can be perfect unless it is subordinate to "the Church"? What guarantee have our sister States of the West, within whose fruitful borders the tide of European emigration is pouring like a living flood; what guarantee have they that their too liberal constitutions and laws will not melt like wax, before the consuming heat of imported opinions, and through the manipulation of foreign voters, be remodelled and made to assume new aspects, repulsive to rational liberty, subversive of religion, and hostile to the true interests of the State? None whatever. The chances are in favor of some such result, or at least, that the American residents of those States will be made to endure severe mortification growing out of this cause. They will find that they have encouraged a clannish sentiment among their foreign population, directly hostile to those of American birth and sentiment, and political demagogues are not wanting who will seize upon this very hostility and employ it to the detriment of the best interests of the State.

. . . . The distinguishing features of our form of government, as adapted to the happiness and prosperity of its individual citizens—the diversity of climate and the physical resources of the United States— have conspired to pour upon our shores a vast and still increasing tide of people, fleeing from the oppressions, restraints, and the burdens of life, engendered in the overgrown communities of the Old World. The loftiest intelligence and the meanest intellect—the man of wealth, and the starving millions—the statesman, the philosopher, the idiot, the criminal, and the insane, have been alike attracted from the scenes of their nativities, and, in one common flood, have cast their destinies and their opinions, their worth and their mendicity, their morals and their vices, their superstitions, their traditions, and their prejudices, upon the social bosom of America.

To believe that a mass so crude and incongruous, so remote from the spirit, the ideas, and the customs of America, can be made to harmonize readily with the new element into which it is cast, is, to say the least, *unnatural*. . . . . Where the new element, thus thrown into a community, is trivial and unimportant, and the surroundings of old habits and customs are few, the mind of the possessor is more easily reached and moulded to the new associations. A single savage may be readily civilized; a whole tribe, never. So it is with the immigrant. A few individuals, scattered here and there throughout a whole people of opposite notions and customs, will yield, in the absence of pervading reminiscences of their past habits, readily and easily to the notions and customs which surround them. But if, on the contrary, those individuals are thrown together, where the opportunities of an interchange of old thoughts, old memories, and old associations are uninterrupted, the *home* sentiment will wrestle with the new influence; a clannish spirit will grow up among them, and the recollections of the past will cluster tenaciously, and almost holily, about their hearts.

This is the condition of the immigrants from Europe, residing, and still pouring into the United States, and so palpable and pervading has the foreign element become, that its deleterious effects upon our welfare, as a nation, is no longer a problem. European immigration is unquestionably the "Grecian horse" of the American Republic. . . . . From September 30, 1843, to September 30, 1844, the number of passengers [immigrants] was but 84,764; and . . . . from December 31, 1853, to December 31, 1854, the number of passengers amounted to the enormous sum of 460,474! of whom only 32,641 were citizens of the United States. This vast immigration does not include the thousands who silently enter upon our territory by crossing the northern frontier from the Canadas. Those, if it were possible to enumerate them, would doubtless swell the aggregate to nearly all or quite half a million!

The immigrant aliens thus cast promiscuously upon our soil may be divided into four distinct classes, thus:

1st. Men of business, capital, and respectability, who take little or no interest in politics.

2d. Red republicans, agrarians, and infidels, a restive, radical, discontented people, at war with all government.

3d. Papists: men who will obey their priests *first*, and the law of the land *afterward*.

4th. Paupers: men, women, and children, who are sent to us by the municipalities of Europe, to be supported at our expense. The great proportion of this class may be included, also, in class No. 3.

The first of these classes is comparatively far from numerous. They come to America to make fortunes, with the intention, generally, of returning and enjoying their wealth at home. . . . . This class of immigrants is always desirable. It adds to the mercantile wealth and character of the country; it gives an impetus to commerce and finance, and without tampering with the public policy of the nation, enhances its power, and contributes to its general prosperity. It is a circumstance worthy of note, that this class of immigrants, the most qualified to perform, in a rational manner, the duties of citizens, and the most interested in our public policy, is the last to avail itself of the prerogatives of the citizen. The United States can well afford to spare the occasional fortunes borne back to Europe by these visitors, as a *quid pro quo* for the practical services which they render while on our soil.

The second class differs from the first in many important essentials. They are generally working-men and tradesmen, respectable in their sphere, and possessing the physical elements of usefulness. So far, they are, to a limited extent, desirable residents. . . . .

But it is the immediate *political* and moral aspects of this class of immigrants to which I purpose, mainly, now to call the reader's attention. They are mostly from France and the German principalities, to which we may add a few from Italy, and a very few of the most illiterate from England; and although embodying distinct theories, they are found sufficiently in harmony in their general political ideas to warrant their classification as a unit. They are the malcontents of the Old World, who hate monarchy, not because it is monarchy, but because it is restraint. They are such men as stood by the side of Robespierre, and aided him in pouring out the best, as well as some of the worst, blood of France; . . . . These are your red Republicans! red with the blood of the innocent! Men who would gladly abolish both law and Gospel at a single swoop! Such men clamor for "universal suffrage," "free farms," and "intervention in European affairs." They demand the abolition of all laws regulating the Sabbath, they forget their oath of allegiance to the United States, and call themselves "European democrats." . . . .

Viewing this subject philosophically or practically, we find that these men realize in the country of their refuge more liberty than they are capable of "enjoying and employing rationally." Bred to a hatred of their own home government, they have acquired an almost instinctive hostility to all government. Taught by sad experience to regard the rulers of their native land as tyrants, they do not realize the possibility of a government of equal and liberal laws. Never having seen liberty, they know not what it is, and with the first taste of its sweets, all restraints, civil and religious, become alike irksome to them. They soon begin to regard all laws as oppressive, whether they emanate from the edict of a despot, or the openly declared will of a free people. Thus, having nothing to lose, and, as they think, everything to gain, by agitation, they thirst eternally for change, fondly believing that the time is at hand when they can ride indolently into power or wealth, by the effect of the suffrage, or mount to them on the blood-red waves of revolution! . . . . To the fourth class of immigrants, viz., "Paupers," we may appropriately add Felons, because it is proven to a demonstration that both paupers and felons have been systematically sent from European governments and municipalities to the United States, in order to rid themselves of the support of the one and the villainies of the other. Within a short period, several nests of convicted felons have been actually intercepted on their way into the port of New York. . . . . This infamous system is carried on under the name and prestige of "immigration," and thus our hospitality is abused, and the moral atmosphere of society contaminated. The extent to which this species of imposture has been carried on is beyond the reach of estimate. Probably the most accurate data on which an opinion can be based is the enormous disproportion of European criminals in the United States, as compared with those of American birth; a majority of all the capital crimes, the felonies, larcenies, and misdemeanors being committed by foreigners, whereas the foreign population of the country is only about *one-seventh* of the whole. . . . .

By the return of the Warden of the New York city prison, for the year 1850, I find the total number of commitments made during the year as 21,299, of whom 5,777 were natives, and 15,522 foreigners. Nearly three foreigners to one American are thus placed on the record of crime.

It is needless to enter upon further details in proof of the magnitude of this class of immigration; the records of our courts; the prisons of the several States; nay, even the gallows itself, stand forth, a grim, but incontestible witness of the fact, that to immigration alone we are indebted for the vast excess of crime which so often startles the moral sense of our communities, and casts a stain upon our national reputation. And yet, through our liberal system of naturalization, these same criminals, if they can manage to avoid conviction of crime long enough, become citizens and *voters* in five years after their arrival on our soil!

The magnitude of pauper immigration is readily measured at the overflowing eleemosynary institutions of the country, and especially those established for their special benefit. . . . .

With these facts before us, I feel justified in classifying "paupers" as one of the great subdivisions of immigration at the present day. They are fairly entitled to that dignity, and it should be a question —a prominent question—with the American people, whether this class of immigrants ought to be encouraged or tolerated. They are not merely useless, they are worse than useless—they are a moral sore on the body politic, a disease, both moral and physical, a leprosy, a contamination—and the American authorities and people are made to be their servants, their physicians, their nurses, their hewers of wood and drawers of water!

The plea, that the commutation tax paid by immigration supports this aggregation of moral filth in our community, is paltry, if not meanly mercenary. It is as much as to say, "If Europe is willing to pay us for doing her dirty work, we are willing to do it for her"; and for the sake of a few officials, who grow fat and lusty by their speculations on this capital of infamy, the people consent to suffer it. It is a system of low, miserable fawning to the political influence of the foreign element in our midst, and it needs reforming at the hands of an honest but confiding community.

European immigration to the United States will be found, on a clear and impartial view, to have been attended with its advantages and its disadvantages—the latter greatly preponding. It has afforded us limited advantages in commerce—it has supplied us with servants and laborers, and it has added to the numerical power of the nation. But it has also brought upon us a train of evils not easily eradicated.

### 36. Conclusions of a Federal Investigating Committee, 1856[1]

The subject referred to the committee is one of grave importance, as affecting not only the fiscal affairs of the nation, but the morals, habits, and character of the people, and the safety of our institutions. . . . . A nation of freemen, no matter how great or powerful, cannot long continue as such without religion and morality, industry and frugality; for these are indispensable supports of popular government. Crime and pauperism are the bane of a republic, and they cannot be too carefully considered, nor too stringently guarded

---

[1] Extract from Report from the Committee on Foreign Affairs, on *Foreign Criminals and Paupers*, United States Thirty-fourth Congress, First Session H. or R. Report No. 359, August 16, 1856, pp. 1–4, 26–29.

against, if those in authority would be true to the trust reposed in them by their fellow-citizens. That these evils have, of late years, grown far beyond the ratio of the increase of our population, and have alarmed the considerate and reflecting portion of all classes of the American people, is an admitted fact. That this increase is traceable to the immense influx of foreigners within the last ten years past, no one who examines the subject can deny. Thousands have come hither within that period to fill our streets as beggars or to become the inmates of our alms-houses, and other charitable institutions. Undesirable as such a population may be, we are yet afflicted with one of a still worse character, derived from the same source. Our country has been converted into a sort of penal colony, to which foreign governments ship their criminals. It is not only the thriftless poor who come hither, spending their last cent in crossing the Atlantic to add to the burden of our poor-laws, and to stand between native misfortune and the relief provided for it by charity, but inmates of the prisons of Europe are sent hither by their governments to prey upon society and to contaminate our people with their vices. Of the truth of this, there is ample proof. The evil complained of, and asked to be remedied, exists in a most fearful reality; and such powers as are conferred upon the government by the Constitution to protect and guard the people against it, should be promptly employed in their behalf. Already the fountains of public morality have been corrupted and the public safety compromised. Our commercial cities have become filled with these foreign felons, deep dyed in crime, who themselves constituting a powerful class, are not only constantly engaged in committing crimes, but conspiring against the public peace. They are the stuff that mobs are made of in those cities, who invade the sanctity and purity of the ballot-box, and destroy the freedom of the elective franchise.

That a large part of the foreign-born population resides in the cities and towns may readily be perceived by examining Table I, showing the number of inhabitants, native and foreign, of the cities therein named.

It will thus be seen that almost one-third of the entire population in the country reside in the twenty cities named in the foregoing table, while they contain but about the fifteenth part of the native population of the United States. It will be seen, also, that of the foreign population of the New England States, there were in the cities of Boston, Providence, Portland, and New Haven, no less than 63,555, being over 20 per cent of the whole number in these States. In the cities of New York

Philadelphia, Newark, and Albany, there were 386,345, being 38 per cent of the foreign population of the three middle States of New York, Pennsylvania, and New Jersey. In Cincinnati, Chicago, Detroit, and Milwaukee, there were 92,932, being 17 per cent of their number in the western and northwestern States, comprising Ohio, Indiana, Illinois, Michigan, Wisconsin, and Iowa. In the cities of St. Louis and Louisville, there were 50,858, being 43 per cent of the number in the southwestern States of Kentucky, Missouri, Tennessee, Mississippi,

TABLE I

| Free States | Native | Foreign | Slave States | Native | Foreign |
|---|---|---|---|---|---|
| New York | 277,752 | 235,733 | Baltimore | 130,491 | 35,492 |
| Philadelphia | 286,346 | 121,699 | New Orleans | 50,470 | 48,601 |
| Boston | 88,948 | 46,677 | St. Louis | 36,529 | 38,397 |
| Cincinnati | 60,558 | 54,541 | Washington | 33,530 | 4,282 |
| Albany | 31,162 | 16,591 | Louisville | 25,079 | 12,461 |
| Providence | 31,755 | 9,669 | Charleston | 17,809 | 4,643 |
| Chicago | 13,693 | 15,682 | Richmond | 15,441 | 2,102 |
| Newark | 26,561 | 12,322 | Mobile | 9,565 | 4,086 |
| Detroit | 11,055 | 9,927 | | | |
| Portland | 17,265 | 3,512 | | | |
| New Haven | 16,641 | 3,697 | | | |
| Milwaukee | 7,181 | 12,782 | | | |
| Total | 868,917 | 542,832 | Total | 318,914 | 150,064 |

Aggregate of free States................. 1,411,749
Aggregate of slave States................ 468,978

Aggregate population.................... 1,880,727
Native............................... 1,187,831
Foreign.............................. 692,896

and Arkansas. In the cities of Baltimore, Richmond, Charleston, Mobile, and New Orleans, there were 94,924, being 54 per cent of those in the South Atlantic States of Delaware, Maryland, Virginia, North Carolina, South Carolina, Georgia, Alabama, Florida, and Louisiana. . . . .

These facts clearly show that a very large portion of the immigrant population is in the cities and towns, and though we are without statistics on the subject, we may fairly draw the inference that the major part of the worthless portion of it may be found in the cities and towns. It is there where the outcasts, mendicants, and convicts, disgorged from the jails and workhouses of Europe, are mostly exercising their corrupting influence upon public morals, and oppressing the honest and virtuous citizen with heavy taxation. Need it then be wondered at that both national and State interference are now demanded? The evil has become oppressive, and hence it is that sentiments like the following, taken from the last annual report of the governors of the New York city almshouses, are now uttered in official documents in all parts of the country.

There are points of expenditure which are forced upon the department that ought to be obviated. Every effort is being made to prevent it in future, and obtain redress for the past.

The board need not remind you that they refer to the unjust imposition upon the citizens of New York, by the large number of vagrants, prisoners, and lunatics, as well as the out-door poor, who are thrown upon them through the inability of the commissioners of emigration to support those who are thrown upon the public charity during the first five years of their residence here. The sum already expended is $60,000, without including any previous time when no account was rendered. This evil still exists, and unless some action is had to remedy it, the burden will reach far beyond the present claims made for their support.

There is no good reason why the city should not be protected against this unjust use of its charities, by national or State interference in its behalf, or an increase of the fund of the commissioners of emigration, by an addition to the present passenger tax. . . . .

### STATE MEASURES OF REFORM

The only deductions fairly to be drawn . . . . in regard to the immigration of foreign paupers and criminals are plainly and unmistakably these:

First, That it is the chief source of intemperance, and the main cause of the alarming increase of that great public evil in our country.

Second, That it has filled our commercial cities with a foreign convict and pauper population, the material of which mobs are made, to such an extent as to endanger the public peace and the public morals, and to be generally regarded as a frightful evil.

Third, That it is a fruitful source of pauperism, and the chief cause of its fearful increase within the last few years.

Fourth, That it is a prolific source of crime, and that to it the enormous increase of crime may almost wholly be attributed.

Fifth, That it has brought upon the country a large juvenile vagrant population, now growing up to prey upon society, which is fearfully on the increase, and almost entirely of foreign origin.

Sixth, That it is the source of ignorance, the mother of crime, filling our country with a people whose vicious propensities predominate over both the moral and intellectual faculties, and who, urged on by ungoverned appetites and passions, with fancied or superstitious objects in view, constitute a population from which the country has nothing to expect but evil to its free institutions.

Seventh, That it has brought into the country a large body of men who are inimical to our free institutions and our social organization, and who are devoted to dogmas and creeds, which experience as well as all past history have shown to be not only incompatible with republican institutions, or a well-regulated constitutional liberty, but antagonistic to the welfare and happiness of mankind; and which, if carried out here, would make this country a pandemonium on earth.

Eighth, That it has flooded our country with irreligion, immorality, and licentiousness, and is the source from whence infidelity comes. State legislation can reach many of these evils, and it behooves the State legislatures to institute the necessary measures of reform on the subject. Among those which commend themselves as most likely to be effective are:

*a*) The adoption of a State policy which will discountenance the *esprit du corps* now so studiously cultivated among foreigners in our large cities, which is calculated, if not designed, to keep them foreigners in feelings, sentiments, and habits, though they enjoy the benefits of our institutions and owe allegiance to our laws. Let their separate and distinctive civil and military organizations, wherever they exist, be frowned down, and a policy be pursued which will break up and destroy those foreign organizations, and oblige those belonging to them to identify themselves with the country of their adoption, and to be naught else than what they ought to be—Americans, and only Americans.

*b*) The rigid enforcement of all license laws authorizing the sale of liquor, promptly punishing those who violate them, and the adoption of a provision in all those laws, like that passed by the recent legislature of Pennsylvania, prohibiting a license to be granted for the sale of liquor to any other than a citizen of the United States. Experience demonstrates that most of the grog shops in cities are kept by unnaturalized foreigners, who will thus be excluded from pursuing a business fraught with misery and crime.

*c*) The adoption of measures, as far as practicable, to indemnify the State in case those landed upon its shores shall become paupers, and to compel those maintained by the public to earn their support, if possessed of sufficient health and strength to do so, and thus present to them the alternative of honest industry or starvation. A rigid enforcement of such a policy would soon rid the public of the body of mendicants who, too indolent to work, though abundantly able to do so, now crowd our thoroughfares and fill our poor-houses.

*d*) The more prompt conviction and more certain punishment of all offenders, and the abandonment of that mistaken zeal of philanthropy which now steps in so often between the outraged laws and their violators.

*e*) The establishment of institutions so as to take charge and provide for all that class of juveniles known as delinquents or vagrants. Though our common schools are in a more advanced state than those in any other part of the world, our reformatory efforts to save neglected and forsaken children have not kept pace with our progress of common school education, and hence our country is now cursed with so large a juvenile population growing up in vice and crime. . . . . Not only have we been remiss in establishing and maintaining a sufficient number of these juvenile reformatory institutions, but, good as our common schools are, much too is yet required of us in regard to them. Thousands of children, especially those of foreigners, do not enjoy their benefits, though open to them. . . . .

*f*) Lastly, and most important of all at the present juncture, is the adoption and enforcement of a truly American policy on all subjects— one which will tend to cultivate and develop an undying attachment to our country, its history, and its institutions, and to inspire a profound veneration and respect for the examples of our patriotic revolutionary ancestors. . . . . Is it not then of the first and highest importance, now that the land is flooded with foreign infidels, who, taught at home to repudiate everything to be revered in human institutions, have already here raised the black standard of atheism, and declared a war of extermination against the faith which supported our ancestors in establishing the republic, and the hope which animates us for the future—is it not, in view of all this, the sacred duty of all Americans who love their country, and mean to perpetuate its institutions, to imitate the illustrious example of their sires, and to insist upon having their children taught in our schools the lessons of wisdom to be found only in the Bible, and thus have that Holy Book as one of the textbooks of our public schools?

### 37. Immigrants in New York City[1]

. . . . According to the last published census, that of 1855, the nativities of our city inhabitants were as follows: from England,

[1] Extract from the *Seventeenth Annual Report of the New York Association for Improving the Condition of the Poor* (1860), p. 47.

Scotland, and Wales, 32,135; from Germany, 95,986; from Ireland, 175,775; from all other countries, 22,287; total population of foreign birth, 326,183; nativities of the United States, 303,731; total population of the city, 629,914.

It thus appears, that the number of the foreign-born at the foregoing date—and the ratios have not, probably, since changed—exceeded the native more than seven per cent.

As there are considerable fluctuations in the amount of relief, it might not be safe to assume that any one year would fairly represent the average. To guard, therefore, against any misstatements drawn from insufficient data, the average of the six preceding years has been taken, that is, from 1854 to 1860, and the subjoined is the result. Of those relieved, there were: natives of the United States 6,424, or $14\frac{2}{10}$ per cent; natives of Ireland, 31,002, or 69 per cent; natives of England and Scotland, 2,012, or $4\frac{5}{10}$ per cent; natives of Germany, 4,872, or $10\frac{8}{10}$ per cent; natives of France and all other countries, 640, or $1\frac{5}{10}$ per cent; total, 44,950.

The number of persons thus relieved amounts to about $7\frac{2}{10}$ per cent of the population—while more than eight-tenths, or 86 per cent, are of foreign birth. The aggregate of the entire indigence in the city would show a larger percentage of native poor; but the above is a correct induction from official documents, and does not invalidate the statements in previous annual reports, relative to the proportion of the native to the foreign poor. . . . .[1]

The most striking fact is the great disparity between the number of the native and immigrant poor. This disparity, though probably

[1] [The following explanatory comment is also given:

"It is proper to remark, that the 44,950 persons relieved, strictly refer to those who received in-door or out-door aid in money or fuel from the almshouse department. A large majority of them, of course, are only occasionally, not permanently assisted, but being the recipients of public alms, are properly included in the indigence of the city. Almshouse relief, however, embraces but comparatively a small part of the city poor. There are the city Dispensaries, for example, with their more than one hundred thousand patients annually—the Quarantine and Emigration establishments, that assist some fifty thousand more. Several other public institutions of expanded scope whose benefits are mainly gratuitous, to say nothing of our numerous voluntary charitable organizations for specific objects which are almsgiving societies, nor of this Association, which of itself relieves numerically a greater number than the almshouses, and none of which should be overlooked, in estimating the aggregate indigence of the city. But such is not the present design; the object being rather to show the characteristics of our city poor as respects its nationality, on the basis of the almshouse report."]

without a parallel in our own country, and certainly with none in the Old World, admits of a ready explanation. Of what other great city is it true, that more than half of its population have been transplanted from countries beyond the ocean, three thousand miles off? And of this can we justly complain? It is only a consummation of the time-honored policy of our government, which has strongly encouraged emigration both on humanitary and economical grounds. To the oppressed and suffering of all nations our country has ever offered an asylum, while our boundless tracts of fertile soil invite cultivators. We need labor. The modern Macedonian cry is, "Come and help us." Every honest, industrious man who comes to the country, whether poor or rich, is an addition to its strength and wealth. Unique, there-fore, as is the fact under consideration, it is not less owing to our national policy, than to the peculiar position of our city as the gate-way, or grand *entrepôt*, of the marvellous exodus from Europe, which has brought with it, not only the wealth, and skill, and labor which we want, but also a vast amount of impotent and thriftless poverty we do not want. But as the one cannot be obtained without the other, should we not be content to accept the one with all its drawbacks, for the sake of the other? For while the burden of this poverty falls most heavily on New York, it is obviously attended in a commercial or pecuniary view, by counterbalancing advantages.

Recurring again to the statistics of public relief, the exhibited ratios of the indigent, according to their nativity, suggests a few remarks. The almshouse returns show, that about 86 per cent of the persons relieved by it are of foreign birth, of which 69 per cent were Irish, and about 10 per cent Germans, or nearly seven Irish to one German. As the Irish population, however, is nearly twice that of the German, the actual ratio is about three and a half Irish to one German, and five Irish to one American.

The excess of poverty and of crime also, among the Irish, as com-pared with the natives of other countries, is a curious fact, worthy the study of the political economist and ethnologist. But with the philoso-phy of different races, as Celtic or Teutonic, this Report has less to do, than with their traits of character as integral parts of our popula-tion. Some reference to the peculiarities of each may tend to explain the causes which give to the Irish so unenviable a prominence, both on the poor list and the criminal calendar.

Probably a far larger percentage of the Irish in question, than of other nationalities, are indebted to the earnings and remittances of friends who preceded them to this country, for the means of migration. Many, consequently, arrive here extremely poor, without sufficient money to establish them in eligible employments, or to transport them from the seaboard into the interior. Hence, they lodge like drift-wood where they land, and burden our city. Poverty, however, would not prove a serious bar to their advancement, provided they possessed those qualifications on which success in life so obviously depends. For here the elements of prosperity pre-eminently abound. The poor immigrant amongst us can find a cheap home, gratuitous education for his children, plenty of work and fair wages; if he is sick, there are hospitals and dispensaries to cure him; if friendless, those who are willing and able to advise him; so that there is really nothing in the way of his thrift and social elevation, excepting his own incompetence, ignorance, or perverseness. But, unfortunately, they are mostly rude, uninstructed laborers of the lowest grade, who have but little knowledge of work beyond what has been derived from farming their impoverished potato patch, which has given them a decided distaste for agriculture, to which they were pertinaciously attached in their own country. Hence, they are seldom found felling the forests, or turning up the virgin prairie on their own account, or, indeed, their own masters anywhere; but generally on the line of our public works, in villages, and especially in the worst portions of our large cities, where they compete with the negroes between whom and themselves there is an inveterate dislike, for the most degrading employments. With many good qualities and excellent traits of character, they are excitable and impulsive—have little thrift, economy, or forecast, and are often addicted to intemperance. It is not surprising, therefore, that so many soon find themselves at the foot of the social ladder—or that their wives are often deserted, their children neglected, and themselves and families beyond any other class of our population in the way of becoming subjects of the almshouse or penitentiary. And when the conditions of social advancement are so flagrantly violated, it were a sad error to expect a better issue.

The Germans supply the next most considerable part of our immigrant population and ratio of pauperism. Of them it may be said, that they are the opposite of the Irish, being generally a self-reliant, sober, frugal, thrifty people. Some few paupers have been sent here by the governments of Bavaria, Baden, Hesse, Würtemberg, and Switzerland; but these bear a small proportion to the whole number. They often move in families, sometimes by villages, accompanied by their minister and doctor, bringing with them ample means to establish themselves in the country of their adoption. Very many have been trained to agriculture, and find congenial homes in the fertile regions of the West. According to Hamburg statistics, however, the proportion of mechanics and tradesmen migrating in different years, varies from 48 to 71 per cent. Those of the latter class settle in our large towns, where they almost monopolize certain branches of trade and industry. They can work for less wages than Americans, and live where an Irishman would starve. As they limit their wants to their necessities, and rarely spend all they earn, they generally become prosperous, money-making citizens. All, it is true, are not equally energetic or successful. Labor may be overstocked and poorly paid, as often happens in our city; and some being overtaken by misfortune, be brought to indigence. But these are only such exceptions as should be expected among the large masses of foreigners shipped to our shores; and notwithstanding these drawbacks it must be conceded, that if education, industry, artistic skill, and sober, saving, accumulating habits, are valuable and desirable, the Germans constitute the best portion of our immigrant population.

But there are more practical aspects of the subject, identified with the ultimate and general good, which may be summarily noticed. It may be remarked:

That while immigrants continue to pour in upon us like the ocean tides, there will always be some who, either from physical or moral causes, perhaps both, are unable to support themselves; and it is not probable that any international regulations against the importation of paupers will entirely prevent it. This is one prolific source of our pauperism. Another is, the exceeding large ratio of immigrants, who, through predisposition, improvidence, intemperance, and other vices, become poor and dependent. If to these a third class is added, viz., the sick, the decrepit, the infirm and aged, who are incapable of labor—we have the bulk of those who so enormously swell the pauperism of the city.

Nor are these statements affected by the legislative enactments for the care of indigent immigrants, through the Commissioners of Emigration. For that provision being limited to five years from the time of their arrival, after the lapse of such period, there are constant and numerous accessions from among them to the permanently dependent poor, who become a public charge.

### 38. Federal Encouragement of Immigration[1]

The bill provides for the appointment, by and with the advice and consent of the Senate, of an officer to be styled the Commissioner of Immigration. . . . . To encourage, facilitate, and protect foreign immigration to and within the United States, the Commissioner is to collect from public documents and other authentic sources full and accurate information in regard to the soil, climate, mineral resources, and agricultural products, rates of wages and prices of labor in different portions of the United States, and also the means of communication, and the wants of agricultural, manufacturing, and other industrial interests of the United States, and to disseminate such information throughout Europe in a concise and popular form, from time to time, in such manner as will best conduce to the accomplishment of the objects contemplated. The information thus collected is to be printed in different languages. . . . . The Commissioner is to correspond with the various consuls at European ports, and the consuls are to aid the Commissioner in disseminating the information; and where, in the opinion of the Secretary of State, it is practicable, the consuls are to transmit a full manifest of the emigrants on board of vessels bound from the ports to which they are accredited to any port of the United States. The Commissioner, for the purpose of disseminating the information, may employ such newspapers, publishers, agencies, or transportation companies as he may deem advisable, the aggregate annual expense of which shall not exceed $10,000.

There is also to be established at the port of New York an office to be known as the United States Emigrant Office, and, . . . . a superintendent of immigration is to be appointed. . . . . The superintendent, under the direction of the Commissioner of Immigration, is to make contracts with the different railroad and transportation companies of the United States for transportation tickets to be furnished to the immigrants, and to be paid by them, and under rules prescribed by the Commissioner to protect the immigrants from imposition and fraud, and to furnish them such information and facilities as will enable them to proceed in the cheapest and most expeditious manner to the place of their destination, or, where this is undetermined by the

[1] Extract from the speech of John Sherman, senator from Ohio, introducing the bill to encourage immigration, March 21, 1864, *Congressional Globe*, Thirty-eighth Congress, first session, p. 865. For an account of this act, see "Federal Immigration Policies," 1864–1924, I, *The University Journal of Business*, II (March, 1924), 133.

immigrant, to the place where his labor will be most profitable. The superintendent of immigration is to perform such other duties as may be prescribed by the Commissioner of Immigration; but the duties imposed on him are not to be held to affect the powers and duties of the commissioners of emigration of the State of New York. The superintendent is to see that the provisions of the act, commonly known as the passenger act, are strictly complied with, and all breaches thereof punished according to law. . . . .

This bill has been very carefully considered by the Committee on Agriculture, and the subject has been maturely examined. We had a great variety of projects before us. We deemed the object a very important one, and after full consideration we came to the conclusion that this was all the Government could do, and that this would be important to aid immigration and to protect immigrants from fraud. Nearly all of the western States have appointed agents to encourage immigration. The controversies growing out of the clashing interests of different States are creating trouble and embarrassment in the city of New York, and this is increased by the competition of runners on board of vessels, and by the transportation companies. . . . .

It is found that many persons who desire to come to this country cannot rely upon information which is furnished to them by interested parties, and that some of the most intelligent among them are often deceived and misled. If an official document prepared from official sources could be furnished them, giving them accurate information as to the needs of labor in this country, there is no doubt it would encourage a great deal of immigration. In the western States labor is absolutely demanded; common laborers are receiving a very high price; and if it should be clearly shown to any intelligent person in Europe that it was his interest to come to America, because the prices as compared with each other are decidedly in favor of the laborer in this country, there would be a great increase in the number of immigrants.

I think while this would involve very little expense—the sum cannot exceed $50,000 a year under the limitations of the act—it might increase the immigration into this country within a year probably to the extent of 100,000 able-bodied persons, and within a short time might still more increase immigration. That is the testimony of our consuls, and of intelligent persons from different countries. . . . .

### 39. "Free Trade in Men"[1]

#### A.    PROTECTION TO AMERICAN LABOR

Vast as is our indebtedness, strangers will come and cast their lot with us and liquidate it if we so legislate as "to set at work all the poor" of the United States "with the growth of our own lands." They will bring with them arts and industries and implements with which we are not familiar; will open new quarries, mines, and ore banks; will build new furnaces, forges, mills, and workshops; will revive wasted lands and open new fields, and by creating a home market will enable the farmer to practice skilful and remunerative husbandry, and will create American commerce by enabling our merchants to supply ships with assorted cargoes of American goods.

Sir, the pressing want of our country is men. We need not sigh for additional territory. We need go to no foreign nation for any product of agriculture. Abundant as are our ascertained stores of gold, silver, coal, iron, copper, zinc, lead, cinnabar, kaolin, petroleum, and the infinite number of substances man has utilized, the extent of our mineral wealth is unmeasured and unimagined. And our ocean-bound coasts, the immense inland seas that bound us on the north, the land-locked Gulf that laves our southern shores, and our grand rivers, impel us to commercial enterprise, and proclaim the one great want of our country to be men. Labor alone can make these unparalleled resources available; and when, by securing to industry its just reward, we shall develop and attract hither from other lands a supply of labor that will make the march of our conquest over the elements of our wealth steadily progressive, our debt, though expressed by the numerals required to tell it now, will shrink into comparative insignificance, and the powers which by treachery and disregard of international law during the last four years would have destroyed us, will assume relatively Lilliputian proportions. . . . .

##### DOMESTIC COMMERCE IS MORE PROFITABLE THAN FOREIGN

Commerce is the traffic in, or transfer of, commodities. It should reward two capitals or industries—those of the producer of each commodity; and where trade is reciprocal, and really free, each man selling

[1] These extracts are taken from two different speeches on "Protection" by William D. Kelley, of Pennsylvania, in the House of Representatives. The first extract is from a speech delivered January 31, 1866, *Congressional Globe*, Thirty-ninth Congress, first session (1865–66), pp. 550, 560–62. The second extract is from a speech delivered March 25, 1870, Appendix to the *Congressional Globe*, Forty-first Congress, second session (1869–70), pp. 210–14.

or buying because he wishes to do so, it does reward both. It is, therefore, apparent, that if we consume American fabrics, as well as home-
grown food, these two profits, and a third (two of which now accrue to
foreigners, one absolutely and the other in great part) would remain
in the country. These are the profits on the production of raw material, on its manufacture, and on its too often double transportation.
But trade between a country in which capital is abundant, and the
machinery of which, having paid for itself in profits already realized,
is cheap, as is the case in England, and a new, or in these respects
poor, country, as is ours, is never reciprocal; for the party with capital
and machinery fixes the terms on which it both buys and sells.

In addition to keeping both profits on our commerce at home and
doing our own carrying, the diversification of our industry will insure
markets for all our products, and render the destruction of any one of
the leading interests of the country by a foreign commercial power an
impossibility. By securing the home market to our industry, and giving
security to the investment of capital in furnaces, forges, mills, railroads,
factories, foundries, and workshops, we can steadily enlarge the tide
of immigration. Men will flow into all parts of our country—some to
find remunerative employment at labor in which they are skilled;
some, finding that land, mineral wealth, water-power, and commercial
advantages are open to all in an eminent degree, will come in pursuit
of enterprises of moment, and each new settlement, and each new
branch of industry established, around which thousands of people may
settle, will be a new market for the general products of our skill and
industry: so that we shall not only become independent of Great
Britain in so far as not to depend on her for that which is essential
to our comfort or welfare, but independent in having a population
whose productions will be so diverse that though the seas that roll
around us were, as Jefferson once wished them, "seas of fire," our commercial, manufacturing, and agricultural employments could go on
undisturbed by what was happening in other lands. . . . .

### WHAT CONGRESS SHOULD DO

I may, however, remark that I am opposed to prohibitions or
prohibitory duties, but will gladly unite in imposing on foreign manufactured commodities such discriminating duties as will defend our
industries from overwhelming assaults at the hands of the selfish
capitalists who see that Britain's power depends on Britain's manufacturing supremacy, and are ever ready to expend a portion of their

surplus capital in the overthrow of the rising industries of other nations. Judicious legislation on this subject will, by inviting hither her skilled workmen and sturdy yeomen, so strengthen us and enfeeble England that she will not make railways and other improvements for military purposes in Canada, for she will see that, when Canada shall be made the base of military operations against the United States, her American dominions will pass promptly into our possession. . . . .

### WE ARE STILL IN COLONIAL BONDAGE TO ENGLAND

The western farmer and railroad man say, "Let me buy iron and steel cheap; it is my right to buy where I can buy for least money"; and their Representative, complying with their wishes, refuses to put an adequate duty upon iron and steel. May it not be pertinent to remind these gentlemen that the manufacturers of the iron and steel they import live in houses built of British timber and British stone, and furnished with British furniture; that they are taught, so far as they are educated, by English teachers; attended in sickness by English doctors; clothed and shod by English artisans; and that their wages are expended in confirming British supremacy by augmenting British industry and British commerce; that they are fed with wheat gathered on the banks of the Nile and the Baltic, or wherever England can buy it cheapest; and that General Jackson's assertion, that to transfer six hundred thousand men from agricultural to manufacturing employments would give us a greater market for our agricultural products than all Europe now supplies, is as true now as it was when first uttered—but that, if we import the men to make the iron and steel we will need for 1866, 1867, and 1868, the implements with which they will dig the limestone and ore, and mine the coal, will be of American production; the food they will eat will be grown on American soil; the timber of the houses they will occupy will be cut from American forests; the stones with which it will mingle will be quarried from American quarries; and the tailor, shoemaker, and hatter, the teacher, preacher, and doctor, and all others whose services they will require, and whose presence will augment the population of the village, the town, or the city will be Americans, and depend for their supplies on American labor. . . . .

### PROTECTION CHEAPENS GOODS

Consistent with the experience of other nations has been our own. Under the tariffs of 1824 and 1828 the prices of all those commodities in the production of which our people engaged to any extent fell rapidly. When the tariff of 1842 went into effect our country was flooded with British hardware of every variety, from a tenpenny nail to a circular saw, and from table cutlery to butt hinges, thumb latches, etc. But when 1847 came round, four years of adequate protection had so stimulated the skill and ingenuity of Americans, and had brought from Great Britain so many skilled workmen, that our own market, at least, was ours for an infinite variety of ironware, and we have held it in many departments of the business from that day to this, no nation having been able to undersell us in our own streets. If, sir, we are now paying too high for iron and steel-ware, we are but suffering the penalty of our folly. Had we continued the protection afforded by the tariff of 1842, or modified it from time to time as branches of business and the condition of the market required, by transferring the duties that had defended and advanced a branch of industry to articles needing greater protection, we would now be producing an adequate supply of cheap iron for our own use, and competing with France and England in the markets of Mexico and Central and South America.

By excluding from our markets one third of the annual export of railroad and bar iron from England we will bring hither the men who make it. Why should we, with the capacity established in five years— for when the war began, and furnished its incidental protection, the manufacture of steel was unknown in our country—why should we, who in five years have created facilities for manufacturing about fifty thousand tons of steel per annum, buy from England one-half of her entire export of unwrought steel?

B.  PROTECTION STIMULATES IMMIGRATION[1]

Sir, I want to show gentlemen from the West what effect the tariff has on immigration. I have before me the tariffs from the organization of the Government down to the present time, given in *ad valorem* percentages, and a statement of the number of immigrants that arrived in each year, from 1856 to 1869 inclusive. By comparing them I find that whenever our duties have been high the volume of immigration has increased. This seems to be a fixed law. . . . .

I find by these tables that in the nine years from 1856 to 1864, inclusive, we received 1,403,497 immigrants; and in the four years of the protective tariff, of which so many gentlemen from the West whose States are not overcrowded complain, we have received 1,514,816, or

[1] The extract from the second speech, in which the same subject was discussed in 1870, begins at this point

over 111,000 more in the four years of protection than in the nine preceding years of free trade and low tariff. But I had better let the statement speak for itself.[1]

The following is a revised and the most accurate attainable statement of the course of alien immigration into the United States since and including the year 1856:

| | |
|---|---:|
| 1856 | 200,436 |
| 1857 | 251,306 |
| 1858 | 123,126 |
| 1859 | 121,282 |
| 1860 | 153,640 |
| 1861 | 91,920 |
| 1862 | 91,987 |
| 1863 | 176,282 |
| 1864 | 193,418 |
| 1865 | 248,120 |
| 1866 | 318,554 |
| 1867 | 298,358 |
| 1868 | 297,215 |
| 1869 | 352,569 |

Total in fourteen years 2,918,213

Total from July 1, 1865, to June 30, 1869, five years, 1,514,816.

In 1856 the rate of duty on the aggregate of our imports was 20.3, and the number of immigrants were 200,436; in 1859 the rate of duties had been reduced to 14.6, and the number of immigrants fell to 121,282. In 1861, by the Acts of March 2, August 5, and December 24, the rate of duties was further reduced to 11.2. This broke the camel's back. So many men were thrown out of employment and wages sunk so low that none but agriculturists could come to us with any prospect of improving their condition, and immigration sunk to a point lower than it had been since the ever-to-be-remembered free-trade crisis of 1837–40. In 1861 but 91,920 immigrants arrived, and the depression continued through 1862, during which the number of immigrants was but 91,987. By the Act of July 14, 1862, the duties were raised, so that in 1863 they were up to 23.7, and the immigration nearly equaled that of the two preceding years, having gone up 176,282. By the several Acts of 1864, 1865, and 1866, the duties were increased so that the duties on the importations of 1866 averaged 40.2 per cent, and immigration went up to 318,554. Last year, when the West was further oppressed

[1] [The statistics which follow are from Mr. David A. Wells.]

by the increase of duties on wool and copper, they averaged 41.2, and the number of immigrants went up to 352,569; and the commissioners of immigration assure us that this year the number will exceed 400,000.

It is thus historically demonstrated that precisely as we make our duties protective of high wages for labor, do we bring skilled workmen from Germany, Belgium, France, and England to work in our mines, forges, furnaces, rolling-mills, cotton and woolen factories, and create a home market for the grain of Iowa, Illinois, and other States, whose farmers complain that they have no market for their crops. . . . .

### SKILLED WORKMEN THE MOST VALUABLE COMMODITY WE CAN IMPORT

Mr. Schenck.—We have free trade in men.

Mr. Kelley.—The chairman of the Committee of Ways and Means suggests in this connection that we have free trade in men. Yes, men are on the free list. They cost us not even freight. Yet how they swell the revenues and help to pay the debt of the country! They are raised from helpless infancy, through tender childhood, and trained to skilled labor in youth in other lands, and in manhood, allured by higher wages and freer institutions, they come to us and are welcomed to citizenship. In this way we have maintained a balance of trade that has enabled us to resist without bankruptcy the ordinary commercial balance that has been so heavily against us. We promote free trade in men, and it is the only free trade I am prepared to promote. . . . .

### TIN AND NICKEL

The present law puts a duty of 15 per cent on tin in pigs or bars. We produce no tin, though I believe they have recently discovered a bed of ore in California, and it is thought to exist in Missouri. I hope it does, and that it may soon be developed. We cannot make tin plates by reason of the duties on block tin and palm-oil. This bill of the committee proposes to put palm-oil, an African product, and block tin on the free list; so that we may begin the manufacture of sheet tin, for which we export annually $8,000,000 in gold.

While we have no well-ascertained deposits of tin ore, the country abounds in deposits of nickel. Missouri, Kentucky, Virginia, Pennsylvania, New Jersey, and Connecticut have large deposits of it: yet when the law of 1861 was passed its manufacture had not been attempted; and a duty of 15 per cent, the same as that on block tin, was put on nickel. Our bill proposes to enable the men of Missouri to work the vast deposits of mine La Motte; the men of Kentucky to work the large deposits in that State, and the people of Connecticut to establish nickel works, in the immediate vicinity of their great factories of Britannia and other white-metal wares by putting the same rate of duty on nickel that we have on copper, zinc, lead, iron, and other metals.

### THE EFFECT OF PROTECTING NICKEL

Now let me show you what will be the effect of this measure. I hold in my hand a letter from Evans & Askin, the great nickel manufacturers of England. They tell us how they will punish us if we increase the tariff on nickel; and I hope you will join me in invoking their punishment. But let them speak for themselves, as they do in this letter. It reads thus:

BIRMINGHAM
March 18, 1868

DEAR SIR:

Although it is now some time since we had the pleasure of corresponding, we hear from time to time of the progress you are making in the nickel trade in America, and we trust you find the business a remunerative and successful one.

We hear that attempts are being made to influence Congress to increase largely the import duties on refined nickel, and although perhaps we might at first regret that the duties should be raised, we are not quite sure it would not ultimately be to our advantage; for, if the duties are so raised as to render the import of nickel almost prohibitory, we shall at once adopt measures to send out one of the junior members of our firm and erect a nickel refinery in the States. In fact, from the large quantities of nickel and cobalt ores offered to us by mine La Motte, the Haley Smelting Company, and several others, we are almost disposed to do so at once, as we think it might answer our purpose better than forwarding the refined article from this country. We are not, of course, selfish enough to wish a monopoly of the nickel trade in America, but we hope and intend to have a share of it, either by shipment to, or refining in, the States.

Should we decide upon erecting works in your country may we reckon on any supply of ore from your mine, in addition to other sources?

We are, dear sir, yours faithfully,

EVANS & ASKIN

Let them come on with their skilled nickel-makers; let them bring their capital by millions; let them, if they can, bring 100,000 people to consume the grain of Missouri; and we will give them all welcome. By increasing the duty on nickel from 15 to 40 per cent, mine La Motte will thus become a great manufacturing center, and there will be a new market, not dependent on long lines of railroad or ocean transportation for the grain and wool of the valley of the Mississippi.

Now, Mr. Chairman, in conclusion, I plead with the gentlemen of the committee to forget their sectional feelings, to put aside party strife, to remember that the glory and the power of their country depend on the prosperity, intelligence, and aspiring hopes of the laboring people and their children. I beg them, as I know they all love their country, to stand by her industries, and to aid the poor and oppressed laborers of other lands to escape from a diet of "rye and potatoes" to a land of free schools and liberal wages, in which the daily fare of the family will be of wheat, mutton, beef, or pork, with the vegetables and the fruits of all the States of our broad, and then assuredly prosperous, country.

### 40. A Business Man's Views of "Our Duties to Immigrants," 1875[1]

It remains for us to speak of our duties to immigration and to the immigrant. It need hardly be said that the general government should encourage such immigration as has been referred to, in every practicable way. Not that it is called upon to send its agents to the Old World to make the people there dissatisfied with the institutions and conditions under which they have been born and trained, and to urge their coming across the sea to us. These people are finding out for themselves, in a natural and spontaneous way, the advantages to be gained by emigration, and they receive all the special information they desire from our consuls, from the representatives of the great railroad companies which have lands to sell, and from the steamship companies which are competing among themselves for their conveyance to the New World. Nor need we offer assisted passages or any pecuniary inducement to those who, without them, cannot emigrate at all. We will extend every opportunity, on their arrival, to those who may land upon our shores absolutely poor, and will point them to the encouraging example of hundreds of thousands of the same condition who have preceded them, and who, by industry and Providence, have marvellously changed their circumstances for the better; but we can afford to let the majority of this class go to the colonies, where they are needed more than by us, leaving those to come here who bring something with them with which to make their own start in life.

[1] Extract from a paper on "Immigration," read by Hamilton Andrews Hill, of Boston, at the meeting of the National Conference of Charities and Correction, May, 1875, *Proceedings*, pp. 92–96.

The duty of the general government in this matter, as we conceive, is to protect the immigrant by suitable enactments in his passages across the sea; to welcome him on his arrival, with the promise, after the lapse of a proper interval, of full and equal citizenship; and to secure him in the enjoyment of all his newly acquired rights, by treaty with the power from whose sovereignty and protection he has separated himself; and this threefold duty the government has already sought in good faith to perform.

Both the United States and Great Britain have endeavored by stringent legislation to regulate the steerage passenger traffic on the Atlantic, and with a good degree of success.[1] Of all classes of travellers, none, probably, are protected in their lives and persons by such thorough precautions, as emigrants. . . . . In the vessels of the great steamship lines which navigate the Atlantic, the wants of the steerage passengers are, upon the whole, well cared for, and there seems to be an honest desire on the part of the companies to do all that, under the circumstances, can be done for their comfort. Still, for every reason, this traffic should be closely watched, and it is most desirable that the laws which regulate it should be uniform on both sides of the Atlantic. . . . .

When the passenger has been landed and has passed through the custom house with his effects, the direct responsibility of the general government with regard to his movements, terminates and ceases; and it would be most undesirable, as, indeed, it would be found most impracticable, to seek to extend it further; the several States and the several municipalities under whose jurisdiction immigrants come, after the custom house officer has done with them, are abundantly able to protect them; and they may safely be trusted to frame such local legislation in the interest of this traffic, as will attract to each, and enable each to hold its proper share of it. All things considered, Castle Garden is open to but little criticism, while the arrangements at Boston and Baltimore are unexceptionable. We would take occasion, however, to protest against the imposition of the head money or capitation tax at the port of New York. Massachusetts, in the interest of her commerce, and as a matter of principle, has abolished this tax. She does not wish to support any of her hospitals, asylums, or other charities, at the expense of the immigrant, or to levy upon him, in any form, a

[1] [Accounts of steerage conditions at this time will be found in an earlier volume of this series. See *Immigration: Select Documents and Case Records*, pp. 3–53.]

toll for the privilege of crossing her domain on his way to the West. It is said, to be sure, that the steamship company, and not the immigrant, pays this tax; but there can be no question that every outlay incurred by a steamship company in bringing immigrants to this country and in landing them here, is and must be taken into the account beforehand in determining the rate of passage; and as competition increases and the margin of profit is continually diminishing, every particular expenditure, large or small, must be carefully scrutinized and allowed for. It is by no means clear that the capitation tax is a constitutional one;[1] its collection, certainly, is unworthy of any of the great commonwealths on the seaboard; and it is opposed to the interests of the country at large.

Nothing more liberal can be asked for than our naturalization laws as they now stand. The treaties also, into which our government has entered with various European powers, by which the absolute American citizenship of those who transfer their allegiance to the United States is recognized and confirmed, are satisfactory. We hope, however, that the government will hesitate before giving its consent to the limitation of these treaties in any of their existing provisions. It is said, for example, that German parents, anxious to save their sons from involuntary military service, send them to America, where they remain long enough to become American citizens, and are then recalled to Germany to take up their permanent abode there. There are such instances, undoubtedly, but they are exceptional, and no law or treaty can be found to meet every exceptional case that may arise under it. It is the duty and privilege of the United States to throw wide open the portals of its citizenship, and to welcome all who come hither, without seeking to inquire into the particular motives of self-interest which prompt each instance of immigration. Neither can our government undertake to deal with the considerations which lead naturalized citizens to return, for a longer or shorter period, to their native country. It is not its fault if these motives, in the one case or the other, are thought to conflict with the supposed necessities of nations, which, for their own purposes, maintain immense military organizations, and which enact stringent military laws under which their people grow restive. It must protect everywhere those who have

[1] [This tax was later declared unconstitutional in *Henderson et al* v. *Mayor of New York et al* (1875), 92 U.S. 259. Extracts from this decision and other documents bearing on this subject will be found in the earlier volume of this series, *Immigration: Select Documents and Case Records*, pp. 139, 147, 151, 168.]

sworn allegiance to it, leaving them free to go and come at their pleasure. No citizens of the United States, native or naturalized, are more warmly attached to their country than those of German birth: still, various circumstances may and do require many of them to return to, and for a time to remain in, the fatherland, and there should be no difficulty, whether of treaty stipulation or of any other nature, in the way of their doing so.

The unwillingness of the countries from which we are drawing population to part with that which in such volume flows toward us, may fairly be taken as measuring for us the importance of this immigration to the national prosperity. Sir Walter Scott makes one of his characters, in *Peveril of the Peak*, say: "The land has shaken from her lap, as a drunkard flings from him his treasures, so much that is precious in the eyes of God and his children." This is not the estimate now put by the nations of Europe on either individual emigrants or emigrating classes. Even Great Britain, overcrowded as she is, looks wistfully after the tens of thousands of her vigorous and enterprising children who, year by year, are leaving their island home, and, at the least, she would retain their services and their fealty under her flag in the various colonies, the younger sisters of the United States, which still cling to their old mother. We have seen what the feeling of Germany is. The Swiss government regards with as little favor as any of its neighbors the disposition of its people to become citizens of the Great Republic. Russia, for special reasons, is just now permitting the emigration of certain communities outside the Greek Communion, but we believe a limit has been fixed to the time during which this movement will be permitted.

It is more than probable that, for all these nations, there are compensations that more than make up to them for what they are losing numerically by emigration; but whatever this may be, it becomes us to be no less closely observant than they of the perpetual tendency of population to migrate from the Old World to the New; and we ought to make it manifest to the immigrant on his arrival among us, that his coming here is as much an occasion of gratification to us as his departure from his native land is a cause of dissatisfaction to those he is leaving behind him.[1]

[1] [In the discussion that followed Mr. Hill's paper, Mr. Letchworth, of the New York State Board of Charities, said: "Without attempting to enter into any discussion upon the able paper which has just been presented, I desire to express a single thought in reference to it. Embodied in the views elaborated by Mr. Hill there is a broad philanthropic sentiment so acceptable to our American ideas, that

### 41. Views of State Charitable Officials[1]

Dr. Rogers, of New York [superintendent, Queen's County Insane Asylum]:—It will be remembered that I presented this matter at Cleveland last year. It is a subject of vast magnitude, of deep Christian charity. . . . . We feel that we, in New York, are burdened unjustly. I do not propose to detail any of the grievances which New York feels in this matter, but to take it in its broad scope of Christian charity. . . . . The arrival of these immigrants on our shores opens a door through which they enter the school of crime. Statistics show this; they fill our prisons, our jails, our asylums, our poorhouses. In this case, as in so many others, the old adage is true, "An ounce of prevention is worth a pound of cure." Let us, as a Christian nation, place ourselves at the door of entrance, and enable them to become (what they intended to be when they left their fatherland) good citizens.

Dr. Luther, of Pennsylvania [secretary, board of state charities]:— As a member of this Committee I desire to say that, while I subscribe

without care, we might, perhaps, under our immigration system, be led to overlook the necessity of enforcing certain necessary measures of State policy, and in consequence not only retard the prosperity of that class of emigrants who come to our shores impelled by motives of industry and hopes of respectable citizenship; but, at the same time, plant among us seeds of social corruption which must with the lapse of time bear most baneful fruit. My personal observation in various poorhouses in the State of New York leads me to believe, that the number of unnaturalized foreign paupers is greater than is generally supposed, and I am convinced that at the present time an organized system exists in other countries for shipping hopelessly dependent persons to this country. The very latest case that came under my notice was that of a sickly lad in a county poor-house, who had been about forty days in this country, and who had been shipped without any home destination. He had been sent away from his native province after becoming blind in consequence of an injury, and immediately after it had become evident that he must be a public charge for life. The exportation of dependents and criminals to this country is a grievous evil, and should not be lost sight of. If the "head-money" tax, as it is called, has a tendency to diminish it, then it should rather be increased and made more generally applicable than set aside altogether. If upon principles of universal philanthropy we should receive with open arms all that come to us, should we not at least exact some slight tribute from the emigrant class as a whole, to bear a proportion of the burden of the infirmities they bring with them?"]

[1] Extract from Debate on the Report of the Committee on Immigration, in *Proceedings of the Eighth Annual National Conference of Charities and Correction* (Boston, 1881), pp. 218–27. The report of the committee "reached the conclusion that, owing to the large number of immigrants now arriving in this country, urgent necessity existed for Federal action to regulate immigration, supervise and protect immigrants, and to guard against the shipment to this country of criminals, and of lunatic, idiotic, crippled, and other infirm alien paupers."

freely to the importance of some legislative provision to protect ourselves against the introduction of life dependents, and the criminal
class from foreign countries, yet, in view of the difficulties by which the
question is surrounded, without offering any objection to the proposed
action of this Conference, I must take the liberty of suggesting extreme
caution. In the first place, in Pennsylvania we do not suffer so much
as the seaport States, though since the extension of our railroad lines
to New York harbor, and the establishment of our new steamship
lines, we do have this class of undesirable immigrants. They go through
the State westward, and we find them in our poorhouses, and in other
charitable institutions. But we cannot help observing that the tendency of things in this country is opposed to restriction. By the changes
in our constitution of civil government, by the changes in all our
charitable institutions, in all the organic forms of government, restrictions of every description have been removed. Our charities are to be
dispensed without reference to creed, color, or nationality, all over
this broad land. And even in our private institutions, by the acts of
incorporation, the managing boards have to pledge themselves that
the admission shall be free to all. The character of immigration has
changed. Instead of males only, entire families come over now, and
they must bring their infirm and disabled with them. Then, from the
very large extent to which immigration has grown, the casualties
incident to great movements of population must occur, and consequently, in providing for them, we may be providing for the mere
accidents of life. . . . .

Mr. Elmore, of Wisconsin [president of state board of charities]:—
The particular objection we have in our section to this immigration
arrangement is that they foist upon us constitutional paupers, born
or made so. We gladly admit the reputable poor, but the paupers, the
vicious, the vagabond, we don't want here at all. We have too many
of them now. Go through our poorhouses, jails, hospitals, and insane
asylums, and you will find the majority of the paupers there are immigrants, foreigners, many of whom have recently come to this country.
In the county where I live a good many immigrants are coming this
year, and some of them are of the class that I mention, very undesirable; a Danish insane man, for instance, who came here insane, with
the family, and was taken to the hospital before he was a week in
this country. We feel this burden very much. Certainly we can devise
some plan by which foreign nations shall not foist upon us whole
families of paupers and criminals.

Judge Robinson, of Illinois [president of board of state charities]:—So far as the Illinois Board of Charities is concerned, we feel that some legislation on this subject is absolutely necessary to prevent this evil which has been spoken of. But that legislation shall be uniform, and in order to be uniform it must be by Congress. This is an evil which is perhaps more felt in Massachusetts and New York than in Illinois, but it pervades the entire country; and the people of the West are beginning to feel this more and more every day. As immigration continues to increase, this evil will increase in the West. I understand that there are organizations in Europe whose duty it is to ship these paupers and criminals to this country, not to better their condition, but to avoid the expense of there maintaining them. These organizations do this, and not only this, but families there send defective members of their families here for that purpose. . . . .

Mr. Barbour, of Michigan [president of Detroit Association of Charities]:—It should not be overlooked that the evil is not confined to immigration from Europe. The border States have suffered considerably by immigration from Canada. You heard from Buffalo yesterday and you can hear the same fact all along the line of the border States. During the last two years we have found frequent cause to complain in Detroit, because insane persons and paupers have been sent to us by the towns in the interior of Canada for temporary relief. Paupers have come over to receive the benefits of outdoor relief where that is given in cities. We found two years ago in Detroit about thirty families who had come over from Canada, to remain during the winter, in order to receive public instruction, and from the poor fund such allowances as they could obtain. . . . .

Rev. Cooley, of Cleveland:—It occurs to me to be a very important thing, if true, that something like every twenty-fifth person of the men, women, and children of this republic belong to the class of immigrants of which we are now talking. Now we must understand that, without going back very far, we shall find ourselves among this number. We shall find that our fathers or our grandfathers came over the same path that these people come. And while it is true, as I have occasion to know, that among them is a large class of the poor that need help, it is also true that we have a large class of strong able-bodied men among the immigrants. If you will come to Cleveland, into our workshops and into our machine shops and our manufacturing establishments and rolling mills, I can point out, by the score and the hundred, men that are an absolute necessity to the carrying on of our industries, who all came during the past two years from the old country. You will find them in all the workshops. If you go into our best houses, into the homes of those men who are living in affluence and wealth, you will find that the domestics in all the departments of the house came largely from the old country. Now when you consider this important fact, that we have so many who are adding to the wealth of our country, ought we not to "hasten slowly" when speaking against the immigration movement, or throwing any obstacle in the way of its progress? You say the pauper comes. That is true. So the pauper is born in our own land also. How can we help others coming? They come by the score and the hundred, and they are born here of pauper parents, and how can we help that? Here is something that demands a broad charity, a charity which must be extended to the unfortunate who are foreign-born as well as to the unfortunate home-born. I do not, in saying this, mean that I object to enacting stringent laws to prevent the landing of paupers, the imbecile, and the lame, and the blind, and the criminal, who may be imported into our country; but I do say that charity knows no nationality; that rivers and mountains make no boundaries in the broad domain of charity. In immigration, the strong man comes, and soon becomes self-supporting, and able to support others; and if we have the poor and the unfortunate, somebody else has not got them. I once asked a pious Methodist brother how he felt when a poor preacher was sent to his church. "Well," said he, "we think nobody else has got him on their hands," and so we must think of these paupers. . . . .

Mr. Moore, of Boston, rose to ask if it were not possible for Congress, in the legislation on this question of immigration, to legislate so as to reach a certain class of individuals who come to this country and become citizens for the purpose, apparently, of turning round and bombarding the home government, and depending upon the forces of the United States to defend them from the consequences. He referred especially to the reports of missiles and infernal machines prepared for blowing up public buildings in England. . . . .

Mr. Sanborn [of Massachusetts]:—There was a time when New York and the other seaboard States received the first shock of the immigration, and also the first benefit of it. They certainly received, and have been receiving for many years, the evil which results from this immigration. But as immigration is now managed, the Western States are almost equally exposed, not only to those benefits, but to these evils; and I think by the time Congress has its attention turned to this subject that our friends from Illinois and Michigan, and even from Colorado, will be ready to represent that they are suffering as well as we. We do not wish to restrict immigration; it is the life-blood of this country. No American in his senses wishes to restrict immigration in the least. But what has restricted immigration in the past more than any other single influence, is the fact that the immigration itself was so mixed, so lacking in supervision in some respects, that it was unsafe for immigrants in many cases to make the voyage and establish themselves in different parts of this country. The hardships of women and children and feeble persons, and of persons without the knowledge of our language, and with some money in their possession, made immigration unsafe; and if we had not had a system of supervision in New York and the other seaboard States, we should have seen our immigration materially fall off in consequence of the risks to which the immigrants were exposed.

Now if any one wishes to promote immigration to this country, the very first step he should take is to see that this immigration is properly supervised; that there is not one pickpocket in every hundred immigrants; that the immigrants shall be properly protected on their passage, and after their arrival. I understand that one great reason why immigration is now so immense is that the parties interested—the railroad companies and persons who have land for sale—have made, at their own expense and with a great deal of prudence and foresight, those provisions for the protection of the immigrants which for years to come must be made by somebody. These railroad companies and land agents carry these passengers over thousands of miles in this country, as well as thousands of miles in their ocean passage, and bring them through to the place where they want to settle. Now that is a supervision of immigration which has been secured at private expense, reaching, in part, the same result that public supervision would secure.

### 42. Importance of the Increase in Immigration[1]

#### A

The steady increase in the number of persons who annually reach these shores from Germany with the fixed purpose of finding in this country a permanent home, is a marked and suggestive feature of these

[1] These two editorials are taken from the *Commercial and Financial Chronicle*, XXXIII (December 31, 1881), 732–33, and XXXV (August 19, 1882), 201–2.

times. There is no evidence that the early future will witness any diminution. On the contrary, we learn from Berlin that the emigration in 1882 promises to be more colossal than that in 1881. No fewer than fourteen thousand tickets have already been taken for transportation by vessels leaving Bremen for America in the spring; and it is asserted that the emigration from Hamburg will be on a scale of equal magnitude.

For the year ending June 30, 1881, the total immigration into the United States was 669,431. Of these, 210,485 were Germans, almost one-third of the whole. For the five months ending November 30, 1881, the total number of immigrants was 291,318, of whom 100,479 were Germans, showing that about the same proportion still rules.

These figures are especially suggestive, when we are told that in the coming year they are to be greatly increased. There can be no doubt that there is something radically wrong with the state of things in their own country when so many Germans are abandoning it and seeking homes in the New World. It is not without good reason that they leave their home and kindred.

No one will deny that Prince Bismarck accomplished a great work when he secured the unity of Germany. But neither will anyone deny that that unity was purchased at a tremendous price. In one sense it was an undoubted gain to the German people. It broke down many useless barriers. It gave them bulk, strength, and importance before the world. In her former condition, Germany was divided and weak; now she is one of the most important and powerful of the nations of the earth. All this must be admitted.

But there is reason to fear that the German people have lost in real comfort all and more than all that they have gained in importance. They have become a great military nation. The spirit and the enterprise of the people are given to and consumed by the army. The best years of the best lives of the youth of Germany are spent in barracks—years which, if given to business pursuits, would add greatly to the wealth of the nation. The maintenance of the army necessarily involves tremendous expense. To raise the needed revenue the people have been taxed accordingly. In the dread of military service, and in the difficulty and cost of living, we have two of the principal causes of this German exodus.

To us this immigration is of course an increase of our wealth-producing power. Among our naturalized citizens we have none more useful than the Germans. Seldom, if ever, do they arrive on these shores empty-handed. They bring money in their purses and strength in their arms. They are law-abiding, industrious, saving. They already form an important element in the community. They take kindly to our institutions, assimilate readily; and, without ceasing to be Germans, they soon become devoted and enthusiastic Americans. The children of German parents have already become the backbone of some of our Western States. In those regions there is still room enough and to spare. There are mines to be developed, forests to be cleared, broad acres to be cultivated, towns and cities to be built; and we know of no fitter class for the work to be done than the hale and hearty German immigrants. We have no fear that they will come in too large numbers, even if the two hundred thousand should swell to half a million.

### B

An important factor in the present and prospective development of the United States is the immigration movement. Every immigrant that lands on our shores adds to the wealth-producing capacity of the nation. More than that, he infuses new life and energy into every branch of business, trade, and industry. Both consumption and production are increased by his presence. In the very act of coming and traveling to reach his destination, he adds not immaterially to the immediate prosperity and success of certain lines of business. Not only do the ocean steamers engaged in the work get very large returns in carrying passengers of this description, but in forwarding them to the places chosen by the immigrants as their future homes the railroad companies also derive great benefit and their passenger traffic is greatly swelled.

All the trunk lines from New York (where the bulk of the movement enters) find this immigrant traffic of growing importance, and actively compete for it. The Central, the Erie, and the Pennsylvania, all share in it, though not in equal degree; and in the case of the Grand Trunk of Canada the increase in passenger business (to be attributed in part, no doubt, to immigrant traffic) has for some months been sufficient to offset the loss on freight. Western and Northwestern lines, however, appear to be especially favored in this particular, as is natural considering that so many of the immigrants arriving here wend their way to the great Northwest, the South and Southwest being still comparatively neglected. The Northern Pacific, the Chicago & Northwestern, the Milwaukee & St. Paul, the Minneapolis & Manitoba, and other roads in the same section, do a very large and lucrative traffic in this class of passenger business. Thus, even as a factor in increasing the business of public carriers this immigration movement assumes great importance, and cannot be overlooked.

But it is in its bearing upon the future that the movement derives its chief and greatest significance. The class of immigrants now reaching our shores is composed largely of thrifty, industrious, and able-bodied persons. There are some indigent, lazy, and worthless characters, like the Russian refugees, but in the main the immigrants form a very desirable addition to our population. Now, with such an in-pouring of labor as the last two years have witnessed, it cannot but be that we are greatly enlarging the basis of our industrial fabric and widening and extending very materially the limits of all departments of business. Yet the full effects of this beneficent stream of immigrants upon our internal commerce are not felt or seen at once. It takes time. The immigrant, for instance, who takes to farming, probably does not make any very great progress on his farm during the first year of his arrival. He is a stranger to the land, the mode of conducting agriculture is in many respects different from that in vogue in his own country, and the capabilities of the soil, together with its adaptation for special crops, are unknown to him. In the second year he will do better than in the first, but it is not until the third or fourth year, doubtless, that he attains full results. It follows, therefore, that in the present immigration movement we are laying the foundations for great activity in the immediate future, and probably paving the way for business expansion on a greater scale than ever before.

These immigrants not only produce largely, and thus add to our exportable surplus, but, having wants which they cannot supply themselves, create a demand for outside supplies, which acts and reacts upon all industries, and is felt in every department of business. Thus it is that the Eastern manufacturer finds the call upon him for his wares and goods growing more urgent all the time, thus the consumption of coal keeps on expanding notwithstanding the check to new railroad enterprises, and thus there is a more active and larger interchange of all commodities. And it is in this connection that the figures of immigration for the late fiscal year, issued by the Bureau of Statistics, impress one as being of more than ordinary significance. From these it appears that during the twenty-four months ended July 1, 1882, no less than 1,458,434 immigrants came to this country. In view of what has been said above, it will not be difficult to appreciate the importance of this infusion of new life into our industrial system; but it should be borne in mind that this vast body of immigrants has scarcely as yet had time to get fairly started at work. The full measure of their power and influence upon our industries still remains to be revealed. There is no previous movement of similar size with which to compare it. The total for the last two years is greater than the aggregate for the six years ended with July 1, 1880, and the total for the last three years (1,915,-691) is but slightly below the aggregate (2,033,584) for the full eight years immediately preceding. This makes it evident that in any estimate as to our industrial development in the near future this influx of labor, with its attendant bearings upon trade, must receive a prominent place.

### 43. Current Opinion, 1882–83[1]

The unprecedentedly heavy stream of immigration that poured into the country last year—over 430,000 arrivals in eleven months—seems to alarm timid citizens with serious apprehensions as to whether this mass of humanity, consisting of people wholly unacquainted with American life, can be safely absorbed by the body politic. It is true, the number of newcomers seems very large, almost sufficient to form three new states out of territory hitherto uninhabited, were the immigrants all to settle down together. But the effect produced by the sudden accession of a foreign element to our people depends in a great measure upon the proportion it bears to the general population, and its distribution among the different parts of the country. From this point of view it appears that the heavy immigration of 1881 will not put our institutions under as severe a strain as they have been put before. We have now a population of over fifty millions, and the number of immigrants for the whole year will be about 440,000. In 1854 the population of the United States was about twenty-five millions, and the number of immigrants in that year was 319,223, a number more than two-thirds as large as that of the present time, while the aggregate population of the country was only half of what it now is. It is also reported that the majority of the immigrants who arrived last year were of an uncommonly good class, people of working habits and generally of some means. More than one-third of them were Germans, mostly belonging to the agricultural classes, who proverbially make good citizens and are easily assimilated. Immigrants from Great Britain, mostly Irishmen, come next, forming something less than

[1] These editorials dealing with the various aspects of the immigration problem at the close of the old period, in 1882–83, are taken by permission from the New York *Nation*, XXXIV (January 5, 1882), pp. 1–2; *ibid.* (April 27, 1882), 348; XXXVI (June 28, 1883), 540; XXXVII (July 12, 1883), 22; *ibid.* (August 9, 1883), 106–7.

one-third of the aggregate, a valuable addition to our working forces. Norway, Sweden, and Denmark furnish the next largest contingent, about one-eighth of the whole, and the rest is divided among other nationalities. The bulk of the immigration is going to the West. It is a fact worthy of note that the Northwestern States, which receive among their people the largest proportionate number of foreign immigrants, rank among the most orderly of American communities.

---

A petition has been presented to the House from Milwaukee asking for the prohibition of the Irish immigration by a bill framed on the same lines as the Chinese Bill. The objections to the Irish immigration seem to be very similar in character to those urged against that of the Chinese, with this additional one, that the Irish owe allegiance to a foreign Pope. In fact, there appears to be no race of immigrants in the country which does not think that it would be far better if all the other foreigners were kept out of it, and some even go so far as to think that America would be much improved by the exclusion of the natives. If ever the passion for exclusion gets so strong that the wishes of each race will have to be gratified, the country will be left uninhabited, because all will have to "go." There is no race here whose presence the other races admit to be wholly useful or improving, or in no sense an unavoidable calamity. The "ignorant foreigner" is somewhat serviceable to the native, as furnishing somebody to blame for all the crime and corruption, but the other foreigners get no good out of him, and think he lowers wages, and does not live nicely enough. But in practice all seem to get on amazingly well together, make plenty of money, and contrive to be happy and comfortable.

---

The consternation displayed by the Commissioners of Emigration over the landing of the "assisted immigrants" at Castle Garden, if it comes from their fear that a lax enforcement of the emigration laws will get them into trouble, is natural enough; but the idea spread by them that the British Government has concocted a cunning scheme of flooding this country with its own paupers does not seem borne out by the facts. Exactly how many paupers and tramps there may be in the British Isles we do not know, but there must be a good many thousands, and it is difficult to conceive a more dastardly outrage than an attempt on the part of a friendly government, in a time of profound peace, to deposit this pauper population on our shores. Considering

what we have done in the past, and are all the time doing, in the way
of relieving England of her surplus able-bodied population, how warmly
we have welcomed it on landing, and how we have always called for
more, it would be an act of peculiar baseness and ingratitude quietly
to ship over here all her tramps, cripples, beggars, and paupers.
Fortunately, there is no reason to think that she is doing anything of
the kind. In the first place, the vessels now landing immigrants are
not bringing any large number even of "assisted emigrants." There
do not appear to be a dozen well-ascertained cases of pauperism in the
whole list. Some of the Commissioners seem to be laboring under the
delusion that "assistance" in these cases is a test of pauperism, because
the assistance is furnished by a government. The English government
is now undertaking to do for a surplus agricultural population, which
has not food enough to live upon, exactly what is usually done in
individual cases by private means. Of course, among the people it
assists in this way, in the present condition of Ireland, there will be
more real paupers than is customary among the emigrants, and these
ought to be, and, we trust, will be, weeded out; but the idea gravely
suggested of sending back all the "assisted" emigrants as paupers is a
monstrous proposition.

---

The Collector in Boston has made an examination of the "assisted"
Irish emigrants arriving in that port, owing to a note of alarm sounded
by the Board of Health in that city, and reports that they are "fully
up to the average standard of immigrants," and finds nothing to complain of in them. The truth is that the whole clamor about these assisted emigrants reflects but little credit on the Americans who have taken
part in it. It was got up by the Irish agitators in this city as an enterprise in which they would be likely to gain some of the American
sympathy which they have forfeited or repelled by their brutal
indulgence for the policy of assassination. They thought that Americans would be pretty sure to join them in an uproar about paupers
which would help to embarrass the British government, even at the
cost of compelling hundreds of their unfortunate countrymen to recross
the Atlantic when on the very threshold of a new life. But there never
has been any good foundation for it. The agitators doubtless well know
that probably three-fifths of the 2,000,000 of Irish now in the United
States came out as "assisted emigrants"; that is, their passage was
paid wholly or in part by landlords anxious to get rid of them, or by
remittances from friends in this country. The proportion of them who

have come with the help of relatives who have preceded them is probably very large indeed, although no statistics on the subject are attainable. If no Irish emigrants had come over except those who could pay their way out of their own pockets, there would probably not be half as many in the country as there are. Nor does the fact that his passage money comes wholly or in part from the government instead of from his old friends in any degree lower an assisted emigrant's value to this country, or increase the probability of his becoming a burden to the taxpayers. It simply shows that the times have been worse in Ireland than usual—so bad as to compel the government to come to the aid of the local authorities in relieving distress. That his passage has been paid by the British Treasury raises no presumption whatever against the Irish laborer's capacity to support himself. It simply indicates that he could not at home have found the means of earning his passage even had he desired it.

Some features in the "assisted emigrant" discussion have bordered on the amusing. To read certain articles upon the subject, one might suppose that the United States was a country strictly reserved for small capitalists, and that only people of means, holding a letter of credit on a responsible banker, were allowed to land at Castle Garden. The truth is, however, that the reason why the vast majority of emigrants come here, and have always come, is that they are very poor, and, in a majority of cases, have just been able to scrape enough money together to pay their passage. The emigrants who come here with capital looking for investments are very few in number. The mass have nothing to dispose of but their labor. What heightens the ludicrousness of the recent denunciations of the Irish emigrant's poverty is that we have for one hundred years been announcing to the world that this was the place for "the pauper labor of Europe" to come, and that the only conditions of welcome and success were good health and willingness to work. Of course, it is against a man that he has been relieved from the poor-rates, or has lived in the poor-house. But it would be monstrous to convert this into absolute and ineffaceable disqualification for emigration to the United States. There are paupers and paupers in all countries. The pauper we do not want and ought to send back is the man who will not work, and who habitually quarters himself on the rates to avoid work. A pauper who has become a pauper owing to the wretched condition of his country—that is, owing to the absence of all demand for his labor—is not *ipso facto* an undesirable addition to the population of a country in which the demand for labor is unlimited. And this is really the condition of the great bulk of the able-bodied poor in Ireland. No employer of labor has ever, we believe, in any part of Ireland, found any difficulty in getting laborers.

---

The end of the pauper immigration "scare" has probably been reached. The official report of the Commissioners to the Treasury Department instead of proving any baleful intent on the part of the British government to unload their paupers upon our shores, shows that extraordinary care had been taken to have only those persons sent here who would be certain not to become a public burden. Out of the hundreds and even thousands who have come, only a few families were returned as paupers, and the British officials had no reason to suspect that the promises of homes for these, which had been sent in letters from this side, were less genuine than in other cases. The wonder is that so few mistakes were made.

### 44. Federal Control Recommended[1]

The unprecedented prosperity of the American republic brilliantly illustrates the advantages to the country of immigration in the past. Its importance in the development of our vast unoccupied domain, in recruiting our industries, and its bearing upon American civilization and American institutions in the future, cannot be overestimated.

With the establishment of the Pacific railways and the opening of unoccupied sections in the South, Southwest, and West, the tide of immigration will continue to increase.

The state of Texas alone, six times the size of the state of New York, would, if as thickly populated as Massachusetts, contain a population of fifty millions.

The great benefit of encouraging and protecting immigration inures not to the Atlantic States, not to New York only, but mainly to the western and southern states; but, while encouraging immigration, we must guard against spoliation upon the immigrant, and the landing of paupers, destitutes, and criminals upon our soil.

It is impossible fully to appreciate the value of immigration to this country without recalling to some extent the number of immigrants who have served to swell our population, and the skill, energy, and genius which they have added to the body politic.

[1] Extract from Levi P. Morton, *Immigration: Its National Character and Importance to the Industries and Prosperity of the Country*. Speech delivered in the House of Representatives, April 22, 1880, on House Bill 2408, to regulate immigration (Washington, 1880), pp. 6–14.

Authorities differ as to the wealth which immigration has brought to our shores. Mr. Edward Young, chief of the Bureau of Statistics, in his report dated March 17, 1871, estimates the increase from this source for the fifty years preceding to be more than $6,243,880,800, and for 1870, at $285,000,000. But even this is based upon an estimate of the mere physical, uncultivated powers of the immigrant.

How shall we determine the measure of value to our country and its institutions of the rare intellects, the skilled artisans, and the creative geniuses who have poured in upon us from foreign lands? In all the walks of public and private life, they have appeared and left their impress—in the avenues of commerce, in the workshop, and in the delicate functions of government.

What estimates can be placed upon the value to the country of that skilled artisan and creative genius, Captain John Ericsson, the inventor of the Monitor, the Swedish emigrant who landed in New York in 1839—of the value of that almost invisible object, the creation of his brain, which, under the command of that heroic sailor, Captain (now Admiral) Worden, proved on March 9, 1862, such a glorious bulwark to American commerce and American ports?

Mr. Chairman, what estimate can we place upon the value to the country of the millions of Irishmen and Germans to whom we largely owe the existence of the great arteries of commerce extending from the Atlantic to the Pacific, and the results of that industry and skill which have so largely contributed to the wealth and prosperity of the country?

From 1776 to 1820 about 250,000 immigrants landed in this country. From 1820 to 1875 about 8,000,000 arrived, and of these, 6,000,000 entered the country at the port of New York. . . . .

The arrivals in 1879 were nearly sixty thousand in excess of the previous year, and more than any year since 1874.

On the nineteenth of the present month, 2,392 immigrants arrived at Castle Garden, and 2,916 on the twelfth.

The arrivals on these two days alone exceed the total population of Chicago forty years ago. . . . .

The time has now arrived, however, when the magnitude of the subject and the inability of the states longer to establish regulations, makes interference by Congress a duty which cannot be evaded. It can no longer be safely left to take care of itself.

The condition of Europe today is such as to render it reasonably certain that, with the new era of prosperity upon which this country has entered, the number of immigrants will continue to increase largely. It remains for the national government to do its part, alike for its own protection and that of the immigrant.

Immigration has not flourished without attendant evils. At a comparatively early date some of the states passed laws to meet and counteract them. It was soon perceived that, on the one hand, there were foisted upon our communities numbers of paupers, lunatics, and criminals, and, on the other hand, there grew up in our ports of immigration a class of men that preyed upon the poor and ignorant, crippling and oftentimes so completely stripping them as to make them charges upon the public bounty. These evils grew to such an alarming extent and filled the public with such abhorrence, that the legislature of New York was prevailed upon to investigate the subject, and to devise for these evils a more comprehensive remedy.

The efforts of philanthropic and public-spirited citizens of New York finally resulted in the establishment of an institution, which, for the motives of those who inspired it, the character of those who managed it, and the helplessness of those who came within its fostering care, stood among the most benign and efficient in our land. I refer to the Board of Commissioners of Emigration of New York. Through the exertions of Thurlow Weed, Archbishop Hughes, Moses H. Grinnell, Charles O'Conor, Robert B. Minturn, and other eminent citizens of New York, the passage of a bill to organize this board was secured in 1847. . . . .

After nearly thirty years the powers of this board were paralyzed by the decision of the supreme court to which I have referred,[1] and the whole subject was by that tribunal recommended to the consideration and control of Congress. The court does not, it is true, declare that the board is unconstitutional or illegal; but it does declare that the exacting of bonds from masters, owners, or consignees of vessels to indemnify the state, as provided by her laws, is unconstitutional.

Mr. Chairman, the duty of Congress in this matter is threefold: To protect the community from foreign paupers, lunatics, and criminals; to shield the worthy immigrants from the rapacity and corruption to which they are exposed; and at the same time to achieve these results without retarding or discouraging immigration.

Now, this bill has all these objects in view, and it contemplates effecting them by the appropriation of a general fund in lieu of the old and unconstitutional "head-money," which really came out of the

[1] See note 1, p. 845.

immigrants, although ostensibly paid by the steamship companies. There is no mode since the supreme-court decision, except by federal law, by which to guard immigrants against those who would prey upon them, and protect our people from the refuse of foreign prisons and poorhouses. . . . .

In view of these facts, legislation such as this bill provides becomes imperative. It would secure to the government more exact statistics of immigration and would enable it to invoke the aid of foreign states and the services of its own ministers and consuls in promoting such immigration. But there are other and more urgent ends to be accomplished by the bill. If immigration to these shores is to be encouraged, there must be some legal method of protecting ourselves from the influx of the most degraded and burdensome classes of foreign populations. If, on the other hand, the immigration of those who will advance our prosperity is to continue and increase, there must be such legal provisions as will protect the inexperienced stranger who lands for the first time upon our shores from becoming the prey of every harpy who may choose to take advantage of his ignorance and helplessness.

I will repeat, Mr. Chairman, that the protection of the immigrant from the rapacity of extortioners and thieves is demanded as a duty of the government, if it is to continue to foster immigration. It is demanded by a common humanity. The states are virtually denied the power to protect the immigrant, and that power is declared to rest with Congress.

Our present national disregard of the interests of those who seek a home in our land is a discredit to humanity and to the honor of the nation.

INDEX

# INDEX

Abolitionists, German immigrants as, 413; *see also* Slavery

Adopted citizens, 133, 632, 645, 796, 797, 812; *see also* Citizenship, Naturalization

Adopted Republican Citizens of New York, 716

*Advance* (Chicago), 367

Advantages: of America, 22, 332, 403, 732; to England of emigration, 203, 256; to United States of immigration, 346, 558, 651, 698, 751, 752, 753, 787, 824, 859; *see also* Benefits, Value of immigration

Adventurers, 13, 14, 24, 25, 31, 81, 156, 158, 302, 368, 585, 746, 758

Advertising emigration, 3, 13, 167, 169, 314

Advice to immigrants, 238, 299, 709; to German immigrants, 136, 142, 271, 301

Agents, emigration, 3, 13, 14, 15, 24, 26, 90, 91, 122, 155, 196, 219, 356, 522, 525, 748; British colonial, 176, 180, 279; British government, 89, 104, 112, 204, 255; Canadian, 279; federal, 155; German government, 192; railroad, 165, 170; state, 133, 158, 167, 169, 835

Ages of immigrants, 161, 404

Agriculture: American methods of, 141, 262, 301, 854; European system of, 262, 323, 705; German system of, 301; in Ireland, 365, 366; opportunities for immigrants in, 29, 204, 228, 262, 306. *See also* Farms and farming

Agricultural: districts, distribution of immigrants in, 335; industry, state of, in United States, 291; laborers, demand for, 254, 298, 316, 385, emigration of, 72, 150, 187, 191, 224, immigrants as, 72, 327, 340, 353, 368, in United Kingdom, 94, 101, 106, 186, wages of, 57, 94, 95; people, emigration of, 160, 161; population, British, 174

Agriculturists, Germans as, 271, 272, 274, 785; *see also* Farmers

Albany, 248

Albion, 202, 234

Alien and sedition laws, 454, 475, 698, 742, 765

Allen, Nathan, 337

Almshouses: Europe, 292; New York City, immigrants in, 327, 573, 581, 609, 761, 827; United States, immigrants in, 540, 560, 566, 572, 693, 699, 825. *See also* Workhouses

Alsace, 272, 329

"America for Americans," 700, 791, 800, 801, 802, 805

American Democracy, 451

*American Historical Association Annual Report*, 220

American institutions, 754, 757, 758, 762, 764, 767, 777, 778, 779, 799, 801, 807, 819; danger of foreign influence upon, 449, 744, 828. *See also* American principles of government

*American Law Review*, 673

*American Museum*, 705

American party, 628, 734, 789; *see also* Know-Nothings

American policy, 292, 734, 829

American principles of government, 450, 474, 631, 673, 704, 738, 757, 768, 781, 794, 819; *see also* American institutions

American principles of liberty, 580, 721, 739, 744, 754, 762, 778

American Revolutionary League, 503

American social institutions and conditions, 38, 42, 165, 288, 777

*American State Papers*, 216

*Americana Germanica*, 56

"Americanism," 145, 500

Americanization, 467, 812

Americanized Germans, 411, 492, 493

Americanizing foreign masses, difficulty of, 655

Americanizing influences, 411, 412

Americans, 18, 19, 242, 252, 264, 271, 275, 301, 305, 306, 448, 449, 463, 467, 498, 751; attitude of, toward foreigners, 350, 485, 486, 490, 700, *see also* Hostility, Prejudice; character of, 145, 230, 266, 267, 303, 421, 485, 637, 799; a mixed breed, 409; as pioneers, 233